D1083963

FREDERICK BARBAROSSA

JOHN B. FREED

YALE UNIVERSITY PRESS
NEW HAVEN AND LONDON

For information about this and other Yale University Press publications, please contact:

U.S. Office: sales.press@yale.edu yalebooks.com
Europe Office: sales@yaleup.co.uk yalebooks.co.uk

Typeset in Adobe Caslon Pro by IDSUK (DataConnection) Ltd
Printed in Great Britain by Gomer Press, Llandysul, Ceredigion, Wales

Library of Congress Cataloging-in-Publication Data

Names: Freed, John B., author.
Title: Frederick Barbarossa : the prince and the myth / John B. Freed.
Description: New Haven : Yale University Press, 2016.
LCCN 2016001788 | ISBN 9780300122763 (cl : alk. paper)
LCSH: Frederick I, Holy Roman Emperor, approximately 1123-1190. | Holy Roman Empire—History—Frederick I, 1152-1190. | Germany—Kings and rulers—Biography.
Classification: LCC DD149 .F737 2016 | DDC 943/.024092—dc23
LC record available at http://lccn.loc.gov/2016001788

A catalogue record for this book is available from the British Library.

10 9 8 7 6 5 4 3 2 1

In memoriam dilectae coniugis meae

Susan Anderson Freed

CONTENTS

ACKNOWLEDGMENTS

I HAD NOT THOUGHT ABOUT writing a biography of Frederick Barbarossa until Heather McCallum, an acquisitions editor at Yale University Press, approached me, unexpectedly, in 2005. I was flattered but hesitant. I had been trained in the 1960s as a social historian and had never studied Frederick; I had just started working on the official history of Illinois State University at the request of the president; and I had long planned to write a monograph about Count Sigiboto IV of Falkenstein. I decided that I could hardly turn Yale down. Besides, my knowledge of Sigiboto, an almost exact contemporary of Frederick, might prove useful. However, I could not begin my research about Barbarossa until I had completed my history of the University in January 2008. Throughout this book's long gestation period, Heather encouraged me to persevere. I leave it to the reader to judge whether she was right to do so.

It soon became clear to me that it would be impossible to write, as Yale initially wished, a short biography of Frederick that could be assigned to a college class without totally distorting the historical record, because of the ambiguities in the primary sources and the extensive, often contradictory secondary literature. The major problem was how to make Frederick comprehensible to readers, including many professional medievalists, who know little about the history or geography of twelfth-century Germany and Italy. I am deeply indebted to readers who critiqued successive drafts of the manuscript. The first were my colleagues, Katrin Paehler, an expert on modern Germany, who pointed out that the material now in the Epilogue did not belong in the Introduction, and my successor Kathryn Jaspers, who was far too kind in her assessment. Rachael Lonsdale, an editor at

Yale, provided gentle but firm guidance as to how a later draft could be reorganized and shortened. I am especially grateful to Professor Jonathan R. Lyon of the University of Chicago, whom I have known since he was a graduate student at Notre Dame and whose influence is readily apparent in my account of Frederick's familial relations. Jon read with extreme care what proved to be the penultimate draft and pointed out numerous places where my narrative could be tightened and the chapters reorganized. Finally, there is Richard Mason, my very meticulous copyeditor. Richard rewrote some of my overly Germanic sentences, did his level best to clarify the bewildering cast of characters—many of whom are named Frederick, Henry, Conrad, or Otto—and caught many slips in the footnotes and bibliography. If the manuscript is still too dense in places, I alone am to blame.

The staff of the inter-library loan department in the Milner Library at Illinois State were extremely helpful in procuring materials that were unavailable on campus, at the University of Illinois or other public universities in the state, or online. Faith Ten Haken in the History Department printed the numerous drafts of the manuscript and helped me with other clerical details. I wish to thank, in particular, Sebastian Schuster of the Kreisheimatmuseum in Bad Frankenhausen/Kyffhäuser for locating the photograph of the interior of the Kyffhäuser Monument during the Nazi period. Besides providing guidance with the manuscript, Rachael Lonsdale intervened when I encountered difficulties in procuring the illustrations and she answered all sorts of technical questions. Martin Brown at Yale University Press did an excellent job of turning my rough genealogical and cartographic sketches into genealogies and maps. Candida Brazil and Melissa Bond oversaw the production process. I am very grateful to all of them.

The reader is advised to consult the bibliography because, for reasons of space, I did not always include complete citations in the footnotes, for example, when a book was published in a series or when an article was reprinted in a collection of articles. My general rule was to employ in most instances the current name of a place, 'Bratislava' rather than 'Pressburg', unless there is a preferred English form, for example, 'Vienna' instead of 'Wien', or the usage is anachronistic—the Byzantine emperor did not live in Istanbul.

My wife, who wrote computer science textbooks and knitting books, which have been translated into many languages, urged me to accept Heather's offer. To inspire me, Susan bought a reddish golden retriever whom she named Frederick Barkarossa. Freddie has been my constant companion since 2008, as I researched and then wrote about his namesake. I regret that Susan did not live long enough to read the manuscript. It is only fitting that this biography is dedicated to her memory.

John B. Freed, March 2016

ILLUSTRATIONS

Plates

Maps

Genealogies

Genealogy 1. The Staufer Lineage.

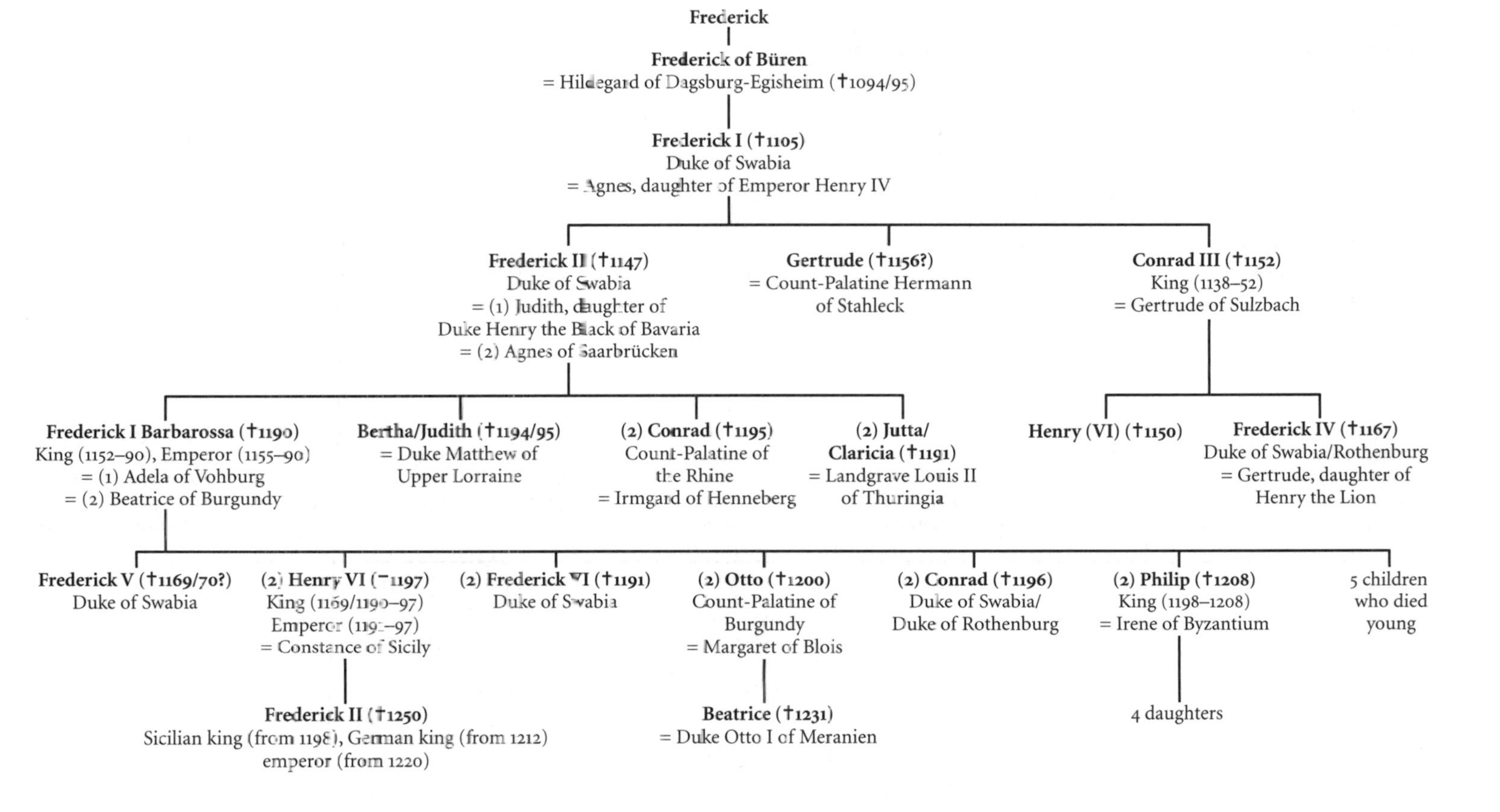

Genealogy 2. The Babenberg Lineage.

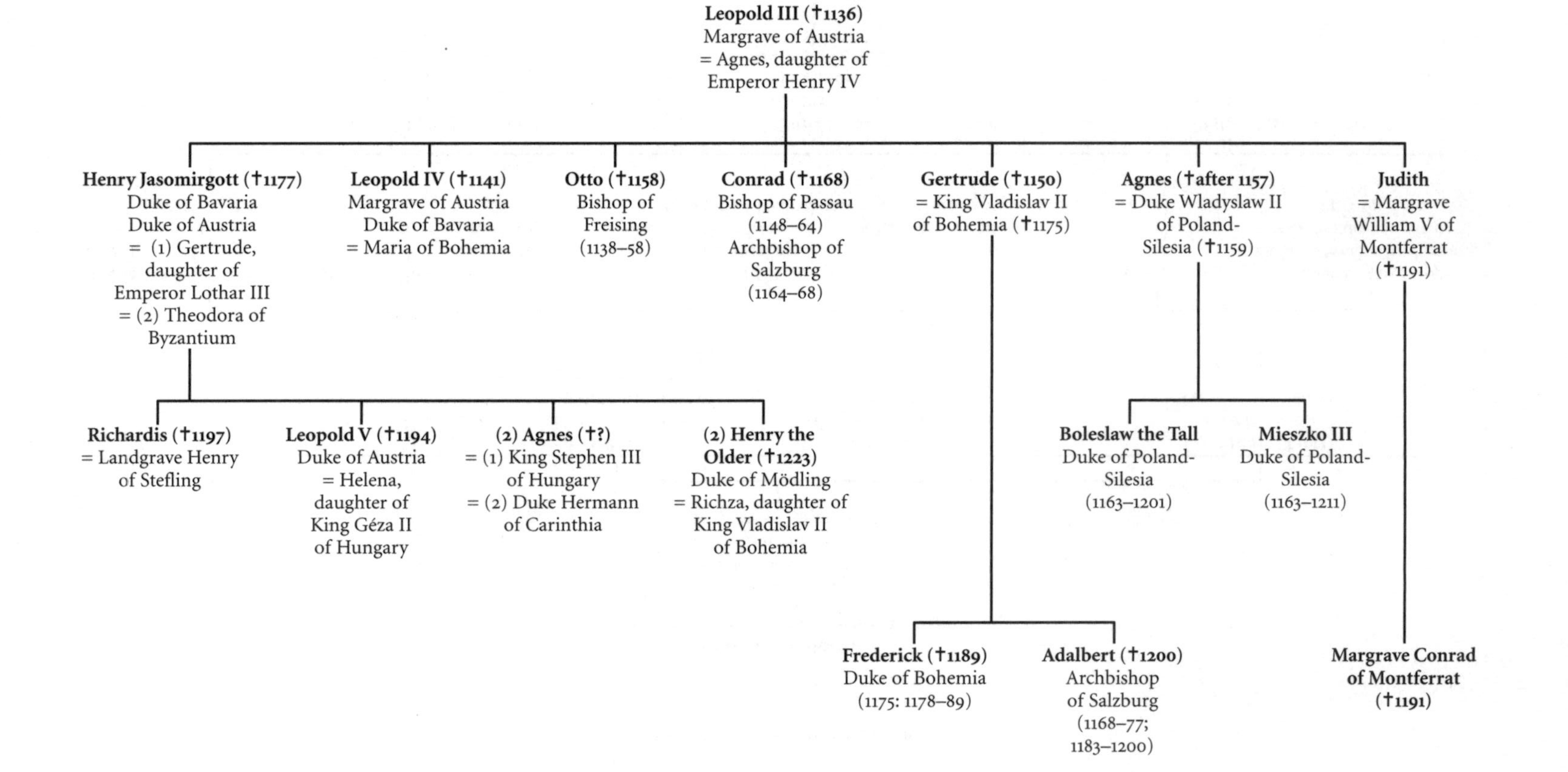

Genealogy 3. The Welf Lineage.

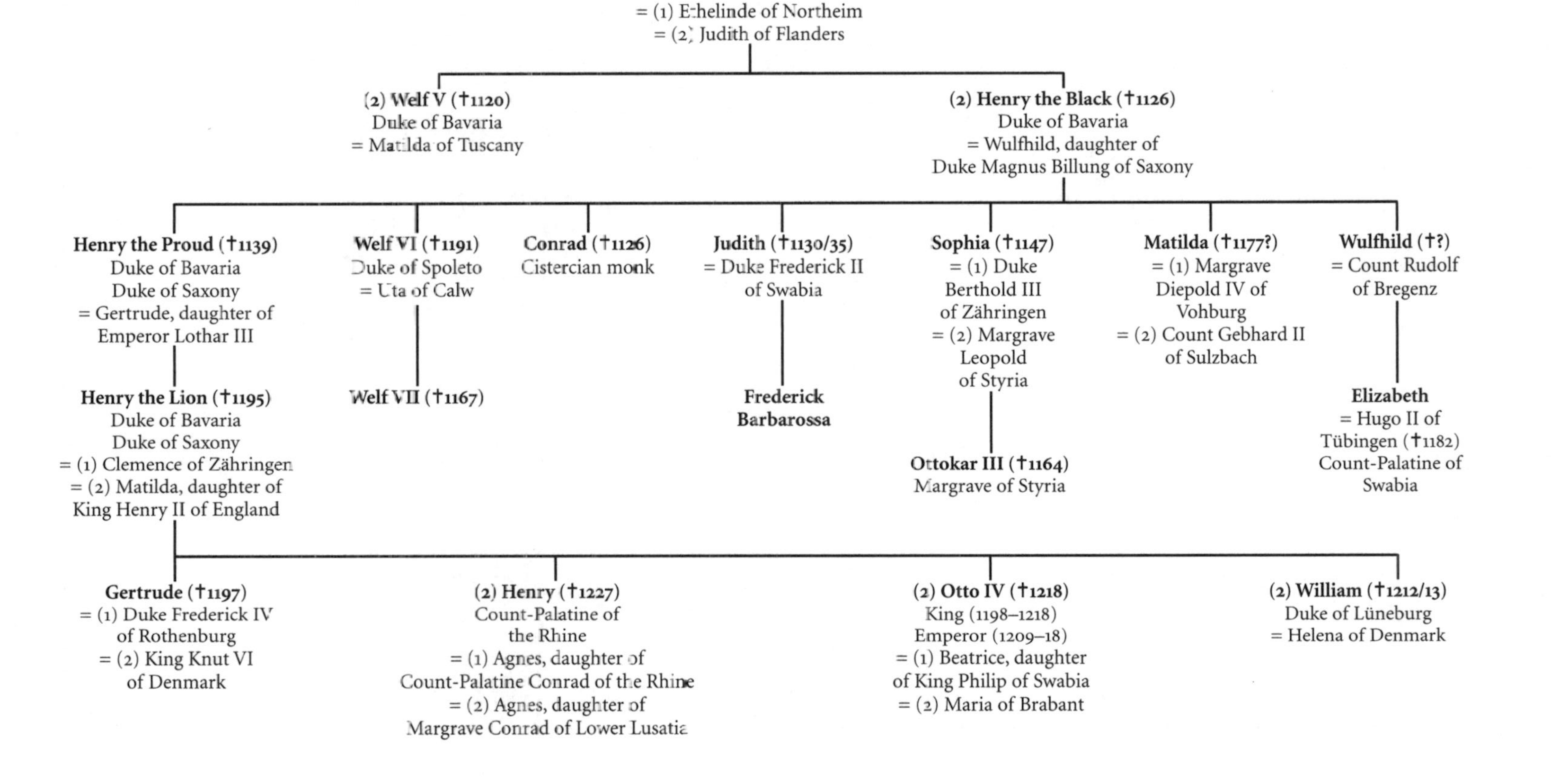

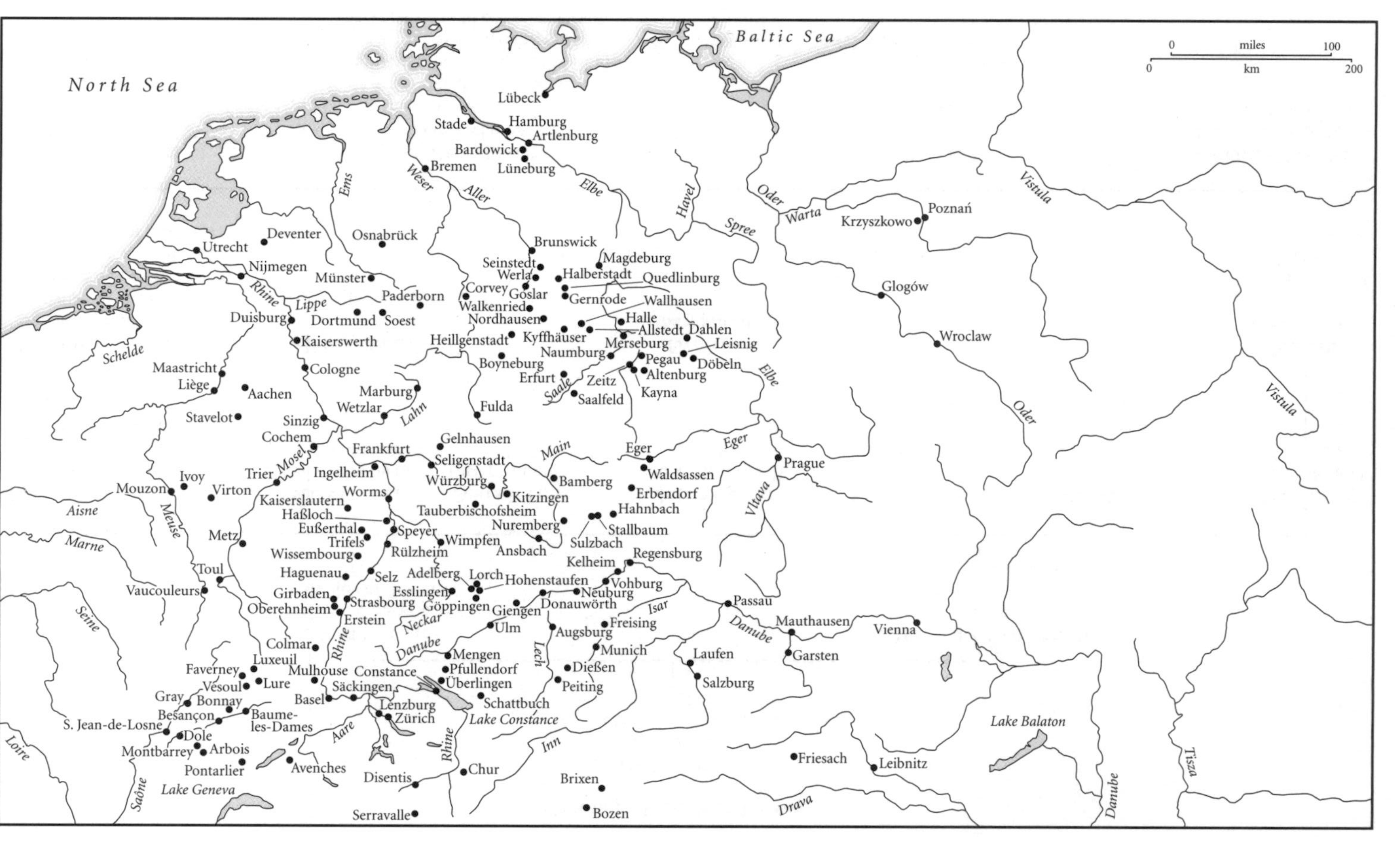

Map 1. Germany in the Twelfth Century.

INTRODUCTION

On 22 June 1941, Germany launched Operation Barbarossa. Hitler decided personally to name the Nazi attack on the Soviet Union after Emperor Frederick Barbarossa (b. 1122, r. 1152–90).[1] However, historians had portrayed Frederick as the embodiment of German manhood and as one of the nation's greatest monarchs long before the Führer's rise to power in 1933.[2] In 1923, for example, Dietrich Schäfer had written in a general history of the Middle Ages:

> Insofar as our nation recalls its mediaeval history, the figure of Frederick Barbarossa stands in the foreground of its memory . . . Frederick's perfect Teutonic frame contained an equally sublime soul. His knightly valor adorned his majesty not less than this valor ennobled him. He was a man of rare spiritual sensitivity, worthy in every way of his position. An understanding of power, something necessary to every ruler, was possessed by him to the highest degree . . . When all is said and done, Frederick, along with Otto the Great, was the greatest ruler our nation had in the Middle Ages.[3]

Paul Kirn anticipated Hitler's linkage of Frederick with German aggression in eastern Europe during a lecture he delivered in February 1941 on the services that the Staufer emperors had performed for the Reich. The lecture was published later that year in Germany's foremost historical journal. Kirn conceded that the Staufer's "foreign policy" had been directed primarily at Italy, but they had prepared the way for permanent acquisitions in the "German East." Barbarossa's victorious Polish campaigns in 1157 and 1172 had been the first step in the Germanization of Silesia, now once again, ironically, thanks to Hitler, part of Poland.[4] Hermann Heimpel associated Frederick with Emperor Wilhelm I (r. 1871–88) and Hitler in a festive address—"Emperor Frederick Barbarossa and the Turning-Point of the Staufer Epoch"—that he gave on 30 January 1942, the Day of National Resurgence, at the University of Strasbourg in Alsace. This was to celebrate both the proclamation of the Second German Reich on 18 January 1871 and the ninth anniversary of the Nazi assumption of power.[5] Hitler's choice of the name, Operation Barbarossa, was the culmination of the nationalistic appropriation of Frederick.

The twelfth-century monarch must be separated from the mythical figure who slept inside the Kyffhäuser mountain in Thuringia until Germany was united in 1871. Even Frederick's familiar epithet, *Barbarossa*, Red Beard, is a later invention that was first used by the Florentines only in 1298 to differentiate the emperor from his grandson, Frederick II (b. 1194, reigned in Germany, 1212–50), and was never employed in medieval Germany. Since red hair was associated in the Middle Ages with malice and a hot temper, the nickname may not have been intended as a compliment. Besides, Frederick was a blond.[6] The real Frederick was an illiterate, courageous, often violent and cruel prince and a man with enormous stamina, ready to avenge every slight to his honor. But he was also an astute ruler who managed to maintain an uneasy peace among his squabbling princely peers until in 1180 they forced him to proceed against his cousin, Henry the Lion (c. 1134–95). Modern German nationalists distorted Frederick's historical image as part of their nation-building project. However, his uncle and biographer, Bishop Otto of Freising, and Otto's secretary and continuer Rahewin, provided the raw material and the framework not only for such an interpretation of Frederick's reign and the Staufer period in general, but also for construing the course of German history as a succession of declines and revivals. Despite Leopold von Ranke's famous dictum "wie es eigentlich gewesen ist" ("as it really was"), in many instances we will never know with complete certainty what Frederick actually did; and we will have to be content with multiple possible narratives and explanations for many of the events in his reign, such as his confrontation with the future Pope Alexander III at Besançon in 1157 or his estrangement from Henry.

It is impossible to write a biography of Frederick that probes his feelings or the evolution of his thinking. The type of information—personal letters, diaries, and memoirs—available to biographers of men and women in more recent centuries does not exist; moreover, the illiterate Frederick cannot be separated from the learned clerics who recounted his deeds and drafted, in his name, charters and letters whose content he may not have known.

Accordingly, the "real" Frederick remains largely hidden behind the public persona. However, it is possible to see Frederick as a man of his own time, place, and social status, and not as the medieval precursor of Wilhelm I, let alone Hitler.

A Twelfth-Century German Prince

My Frederick is first and foremost a twelfth-century German prince.[7] He was an accidental king. The selection of his paternal uncle Conrad III (b. 1093, r. 1138–52) as the anti-king in 1127, two years after Frederick's father, Duke Frederick II of Swabia (b. 1090; duke 1105–47), had failed to procure the crown, indicates that the Staufer did not expect that the duke or his young son would ever sit on the throne. Frederick's dependence on translators throughout his life is decisive proof of Barbarossa's exclusion from the succession, since royal heirs, unlike even powerful nobles, were taught to speak and read Latin—his contemporaries, Louis VII of France (r. 1137–80) and Henry II of England (r. 1154–89), and Frederick's five surviving sons, were literate.[8] It was only after the sudden death, in 1150, of his cousin Henry (VI), Conrad III's older son and designated successor, that Frederick, by then in his late twenties, became a possible candidate for the diadem.[9] Since it was unprecedented for even a minor son of a regnant king to be bypassed, the hasty election on 4 March 1152 of Frederick rather than Conrad's younger son, Duke Frederick IV of Swabia (b. 1145; duke 1152–67), has all the earmarks of a coup d'état. Frederick rewarded his supporters, most notably his maternal Welf relatives, his uncle Welf VI (c. 1115–91) and his cousin Henry the Lion, and surrendered Swabia to Frederick IV. Frederick had obtained the crown, but he lacked a strong territorial base in Germany until Frederick IV died in 1167.

Another oddity of Frederick's position in 1152 was that he was a man with many kinsmen but with few immediate male relatives, in an era when kinship was the most important societal bond. His closest male blood relation was his much younger half-brother Conrad (1136/40–1195), who became the count-palatine of the Rhine in 1156. Frederick's first known legitimate child, the sickly Frederick V (d. 1169/70), was born only in 1164, when Barbarossa was already forty-one. Without a major territorial or dynastic stake of his own, Frederick was for more than a decade the fairly impartial arbiter of the princes' disputes. Their periodic assemblies were essentially the gatherings of an extended family. His reliance upon the consent and judgment of the princes, the tenants-in-chief of the crown, and his personal prestige, rather than upon formal institutions of government to rule his kingdom, has been described as "consensual lordship."[10] In another strange quirk, his cousins, Henry the Lion, Frederick IV, and Welf VII, were likewise childless and without siblings in 1152. The peace that prevailed in Germany after Frederick's accession, and which Bishop Otto of Freising hailed in 1158 in his account of his nephew's deeds, was due in no small measure to the peculiar circumstance that the most powerful men in the realm lacked a strong familial motive for territorial aggrandizement.[11]

In June 1156, and in the hope of fathering a son, Frederick married Beatrice (c. 1144–84), the young heiress to the county of Burgundy (the later Franche-Comté). Her lands provided ready access both to his own domains in Alsace and to the passes in the western Alps that led to Italy. To compensate for his loss of Swabia, Frederick was determined to reassert imperial rights in Italy, which had lapsed during the Investiture Conflict (1075–1122) and during the reigns of his two immediate predecessors, Lothar III (1125–37) and Conrad III. It is anachronistic to judge that decision in nineteenth-century nationalistic terms—until the eighteenth century, rulers routinely acquired territories situated anywhere on the map of Europe, without consideration of their ethnic composition—or to depict Frederick as oblivious to the differences between the advanced urban economy of northern Italy and the backward agrarian society of Germany. Princes who promoted land clearance and founded markets and towns were fully aware of the profits and power that could be gained from furthering the economic development of their territories.[12] The issue was rather who would benefit from the communes' wealth. Since Frederick did not possess sufficient military forces of his own to control Lombardy, and since the princes were not legally obligated to assist him after he procured the imperial crown in June 1155, he had to rely, increasingly, on men supplied by the Italian cities and magnates and on mercenaries from the Low Countries. He thus became entangled in the rivalries among the communes and could not be, as in Germany, an impartial judge. Imperial rule in the Po valley was oppressive and Frederick's treatment of the inhabitants of Tortona, Spoleto, Crema, and Milan was barbaric.

The curia perceived, understandably, the assertion of imperial authority in northern Italy as a potential threat to the freedom it had gained during the Investiture Conflict—earlier emperors had routinely intervened in papal affairs—and imperial and papal rights were in dispute in central Italy and in Rome itself. After a divided papal election on 7 September 1159, Frederick recognized as the rightful pope Victor IV (1159–64), the minority candidate, rather than Alexander III (1159–81), who as the papal legate at Besançon in 1157 had greatly offended Frederick; and Barbarossa found himself increasingly isolated during the ensuing eighteen-year schism (1159–77). Frederick's claim as Roman emperor to be the ruler of the entire Italian peninsula challenged both the new Norman kingdom in southern Italy and Byzantium, which had not renounced its territorial aspirations in Apulia and along the Adriatic. Not surprisingly, the popes, the kings of Sicily, and the Greek emperor backed the communes' resistance. These political considerations were coupled with unresolved theoretical concerns: the proper relationship between the royal and sacerdotal powers, the right of the king of the Romans to assert imperial prerogatives prior to his coronation by the pope, and the claims of both the western and eastern emperors to Rome's imperial legacy. Learned clerics pondered these issues in histories, theological treatises, the expository introductions to charters, poems, and *The Play of Antichrist*, written around 1160; but the question remains how much such formulations and speculations were indicative of Frederick's own thinking, if he thought about them at all.[13]

The striking thing is how long Frederick clung to failed policies, most notably his stubborn refusal to recognize Alexander III as pope, and how often he behaved in an emotional rather than a rational way, as in his humiliation and destruction of Milan in 1162. In such situations he acted more like the hero of an Icelandic saga concerned with the vindication of his honor than a calculating politician in the mode of Bismarck.[14] It was the German bishops who finally forced Frederick at Venice in 1177, in a public personal humiliation, to acknowledge Alexander at the first international peace conference in European history, and to recognize that he did not have the authority as emperor to decide a disputed papal election.[15] He might claim to be the ruler of a holy empire, but the monarchy had been desacralized.

The most important shift in course occurred after the imperial army succumbed to dysentery in 1167, immediately following Frederick's seemingly triumphant installation of his anti-pope, Paschal III, in Rome. The deaths of the emperor's cousins, Frederick IV and Welf VII, and other nobles permitted him for the first time since 1152 to exercise power directly in Swabia and so to accept in 1183, albeit reluctantly, the autonomy of the Lombard communes. At the same time, after 1164 Frederick needed to provide his growing number of sons with positions commensurate with their birth. His dynastic aspirations clashed with the similar ambitions of the other princes, in particular those of Henry the Lion, who became a father in the 1170s, and may have been a factor in the cousins' estrangement. However, it was the Saxon princes, long resentful and fearful of Henry's almost viceregal position, who compelled Frederick to deprive Henry of the duchies of Saxony and Bavaria. The downfall of Henry, from which Frederick gained little, was not a sign of the emperor's strength, as historians long thought, but of his weakness. Since the princes no longer trusted in Frederick's impartiality, they absented themselves from his court; and his own itinerary was increasingly confined to southern Germany, where the Staufer's domains were situated. By the 1180s Frederick's kingship resembled more that of Rudolf of Habsburg (r. 1273–91)—a monarch chiefly concerned with the advancement of his own dynasty—than his own at his accession in 1152.[16] If Frederick had died at home, he would be remembered as a ruler whose reign had ended with bitter defeats in Italy and a diminution of his authority in Germany. His death in 1190 on the Third Crusade redeemed the reputation of the former persecutor of the Church and laid the basis for his association with a resurgent Germany—but drowning while bathing was not a heroic end.[17]

Bishop Otto of Freising and Rahewin

German nationalists were able to distort Barbarossa's life, indeed the whole course of German history, because Otto of Freising (b. 1112; bishop 1138–58) may have served his nephew too well in *The Deeds of Frederick Barbarossa*, the chief source on the first eight years of his reign. Otto presented Frederick as the instigator of a new age of peace after decades of turmoil, and Wilhelm I and Hitler, the creators of the Second Empire and the Third Reich respectively, could be depicted in turn as following his example in 1871 and 1933.

Otto was the much younger half-brother of Frederick's father, Duke Frederick II of Swabia. As the fifth son of Margrave Leopold III of Austria (r. 1095–1136), Otto was intended from birth for an ecclesiastical career. He studied in Paris and joined the Cistercians. When his other Staufer half-brother Conrad became king in 1138, Otto was quickly appointed bishop of Freising—today an outer suburb of Munich; and he became entangled in the efforts of his older Staufer and Babenberg brothers to wrest the duchy of Bavaria from the Welfs, the family of Frederick's mother Judith.[18]

In the middle of the fighting, Otto wrote his masterpiece, a pessimistic, theological exposition of the history of the world from creation until 1146, alternatively known as the *Chronicle* or *The History of the Two Cities*. A period of harmony between the royal/imperial and priestly powers had followed the conversion of Rome, the fourth and last world empire, to Christianity. The imperial dignity had been transferred in due course to the Greeks, then the Franks, and after 911 to the Germans, the rulers of the eastern Frankish kingdom (6.17). According to Otto's calculations, Conrad III was "the ninety-third [emperor] in line from Augustus" (7.22) and Frederick thus the ninety-fourth.[19] Pope Gregory VII's unprecedented excommunication in 1075 of the Staufer and Babenberg brothers' common maternal grandfather, Emperor Henry IV (r. 1056–1106), had shattered the unity (6.35) and started the seventh and last age in the history of mankind, a period of incessant crises that preceded the coming of the Antichrist, the topic of the eighth and final book in the *Chronicle*.[20]

In 1156 Frederick requested that his uncle send him a copy, and Otto complied some time after 24 March 1157. Otto declared in his dedicatory letter that knowledge of "what was done in olden times by kings and emperors" would be highly advantageous to Frederick, because it would teach him to live in fear of God and would assure him of a long reign. Frederick replied in his letter of thanks for receipt of the book that "[a]fter the sweat of war we ardently desire from time to time to delight ourselves therein and to be instructed in the virtues by the magnificent achievements of the emperors."[21] The *Chronicle* was, in fact, in Frederick's baggage, because he or at least members of his entourage consulted it in August 1167 in order to ascertain the location of the relics of the Apostle Bartholomew; they cited the relevant passage in the charter confirming a Roman church's possession of those relics.[22]

By the time Otto sent the *Chronicle* to Frederick, he was contemplating writing Frederick's biography. Otto indicated that he would be delighted to undertake the task if the emperor wished his exploits "to be remembered by posterity" and if he would "arrange the main topics with the aid of the secretaries of Your Highness and transmit them to me," that is, prepare a list of his notable achievements. In return, Otto asked only for his nephew's help if the church of Freising required it. The basic interpretive theme was already in Otto's mind. He declared: "you, most glorious Prince, are indeed, The Peace Maker, and are rightly so called, since you have changed the night of mist and rain into the delightful splendor of morning calm by preserving for each man what is his, and have restored lovable peace to the world." He restated that idea in the prologue to the first book of the *Deeds*: "For, after the turbulence of the past, not only has an unprecedented brightness of peace dawned again, but the authority of the Roman empire prevails so greatly by reason of the virtues of our most victorious prince that the people living under his jurisdiction rest in humble quiet, and whatever barbarian or Greek dwells outside his bounds is overawed by the weight of his authority and trembles."[23] Perhaps the meaning of Frederick's name, "rich in peace," inspired the theme of the king as peacemaker.

Otto conceded that he had altered his assessment of the current state of human affairs since completing the *Chronicle* a decade earlier. Indeed, he had hesitated even to send the book to his nephew because, he admitted: "I wrote this history in bitterness of spirit, led thereto by the turbulence of that unsettled time which preceded your reign, and therefore I did not merely give events in their chronological order, but rather wove together, in the manner of a tragedy, their sadder aspects, and so ended with a picture of unhappiness each and every division of the books even down to the seventh and the eighth."[24] There have been several attempts to explain the difference in tone between the *Chronicle* and the *Deeds*.[25] The most likely explanation is that while Otto's understanding of the overall course of redemptive history remained the same, he no longer perceived the Investiture Conflict as a fundamental caesura in human affairs, but simply as the troubled period when the Staufer replaced the Salians, just as the Carolingians had succeeded the Merovingians and had been followed in turn by the Ottonians. Frederick, who in 1155 had just been crowned in Rome, had restored the harmony between the pope and the emperor that had been shattered by Henry IV's excommunication in 1075.[26]

Otto had resumed work on the *Chronicle* during the temporary peace that had accompanied the preaching of the Second Crusade in 1147, but had desisted, he speculated, in the unconscious hope that a "most vigorous prince" would establish permanent peace.[27] He seems to have taken the material he had prepared for this continuation, most notably a truncated account of the Second Crusade and an irrelevant discussion of theological disputes, and placed them in the first book of the *Deeds*. Otto added a history of the Staufer prior to Barbarossa's accession in 1152, most of which had not been in the *Chronicle*, to fit his new interpretation that the Staufer were the rightful successors of the Salians, though Otto viewed them as members of a single dynasty, "the Henrys of Waiblingen" (2.2). Frederick's father the duke of Swabia is the center of attention in these chapters, though he nearly disappears from the narrative after Conrad's accession in 1138. Very little of the first book, covering the more than thirty years prior to Frederick's election, is about its ostensible hero. For example, Otto does not indicate when and where Frederick was born and says nothing about his childhood.

Book Two of the *Deeds*, which begins with Frederick's election as king on 4 March 1152 (2.1), adheres closely to the synopsis of his achievements that the emperor had compiled at his uncle's request. All of Frederick's actions are successes or are construed as such. Only three chapters contain material that is not directly related to the information Frederick had supplied, and these deal with a subject that was of particular concern to Otto: the reconciliation of his brother Henry Jasomirgott (r. 1141–77; "Yes, so help me God"), the duke of Bavaria and margrave of Austria, with the Welfs (2.7, 2.9, and 2.11). Otto's omissions, for example, the dissolution of Frederick's first marriage to Adela of Vohburg in 1153 or his treaty with the papacy in 1153, are thus, in all likelihood, topics that the emperor did not want to be mentioned. Frederick left it to Otto's "brilliant intellectual powers" to "exalt what is insignificant and write much from slight materials." It is impossible to tell how much Frederick contributed personally to the list of his accomplishments, but it is probably as close as anything we have to his own words and thoughts.[28]

Along with the *Chronicle*, Otto also sent an almost obsequious letter to Rainald of Dassel (c. 1120–67), Frederick's most famous chancellor. Otto prayed that Rainald would not be "an unfavorable but a kindly interpreter." Besides rendering the text from Latin into German for Frederick, Otto specifically asked that Rainald exercise care in handling those passages where Otto appeared to be critical of Frederick's "predecessors or ancestors," because it was "the art of the historian . . . to clear away and to avoid [certain things] and others to select and arrange properly; for it avoids lies and selects the truth."[29] Otto reiterated in the *Deeds* that it was the task of Frederick's clerical interpreters to differentiate between those sections that were intended for the emperor's ears and those that were meant for their eyes alone (1.70); but this raises the question how familiar Frederick was with anything that was written in his name. In any case, it was never Otto's intention to write a positivist, annals-like history of Frederick's reign. He selected those facts that fit his eschatological exegesis of history.[30]

Otto ended the second book of the *Deeds* with the final settlement, in September 1156, of the fight between the Welfs and Babenbergs for control of Bavaria. "Thereafter," he concluded, "from that day to the present time, so great a felicity of peace smiled upon the entire transalpine empire that Frederick may rightly be called not only Emperor and Augustus, but also Father of the Country" (2.55–56). Otto's assessment of his nephew's reign, written only six years after Frederick's accession, was exceedingly premature given that he would rule for another thirty-two years. Perhaps, if Otto had been forced to deal with Frederick's defeats, later Germans might have been more conscious of the limitations of power. On his way to the Cistercian general chapter, Otto died on 22 September 1158 at the abbey of Morimond in Burgundy, where he had been the abbot, and was buried there.

Otto's chaplain Rahewin (c. 1120–70/77), to whom the bishop had dictated the text of the *Chronicle* and who had delivered the finished work to Frederick in the spring of 1157,[31] had been with Otto in Morimond. In early November 1158 Rahewin brought the news of his master's death to Frederick in northern Italy and sought official authorization to continue the emperor's biography, as Otto had charged him to do.[32] Rahewin came from the opposite end of the social spectrum to his master. Rahewin's family of origin is unknown, but his name suggests that he belonged to one of the interrelated families of Freising episcopal ministerials who employed the name *Rahewin*. The ministerials, who will be mentioned frequently in this biography, were members of an estate unique to the medieval kingdom of Germany. They were legally serfs, but they were gradually ascending into the ranks of the lower nobility through their service as knights, court officeholders, and princely administrators.[33] In all probability Rahewin, who was first identified in 1147 as Otto's chaplain and secretary, had been educated in the cathedral school in Freising and had benefitted from Otto's informal instruction. He was rewarded with a prebend in the cathedral chapter.[34] Rahewin did not have Otto's personal contact with the emperor, and he addressed Frederick directly only once in the two books he added to the biography (4.86). Rahewin, who remained at court only until the late spring of 1159, compensated for his lack of access to Frederick by inserting into his text numerous documents he received from various prelates. His chief source was the proto-notary, Henry of Würzburg, the head of the chancery's secretariat; and the terminal dates of Rahewin's portion of the *Deeds*, August 1157 to February 1160, coincide with Henry's presence at court.[35] The chief problem in using Rahewin as a source is that roughly a quarter of his text, excluding the inserted documents, is a pastiche of quotations and paraphrases from biblical and classical texts rather than, say, an eyewitness account of a battle or siege.[36]

Rahewin ended his narrative in February 1160 with the Council of Pavia that recognized Frederick's anti-pope, Victor IV, as the rightful pontiff and with the disbanding of Frederick's army (4.84–85). He sent both Otto's text and his own longer addition, which he had finished by June at the latest, to Ulrich of Dürrmenz, the imperial chancellor (1159–62), and Henry of Würzburg, for emendation and correction. They could be responsible for the fairly significant textual differences between those manuscripts derived from the official copy that may have been deposited in the royal palace in Haguenau in Alsace but does not survive, and those manuscripts based on the unemended copy Rahewin retained in Freising.[37] Rahewin's facile explanation as to why he ended his account with the Council of Pavia was that he did not wish to exceed the number of the Gospels (4.84), even though that biblical precedent had not prevented Otto from dividing the

Chronicle into eight books. Rahewin may have stopped writing the *Deeds* because his chief source of information, the proto-notary, left on a diplomatic mission to Constantinople in February 1160.[38] However, Rahewin may also have found it increasingly difficult to continue working on a laudatory biography of Frederick in the ecclesiastical province of Salzburg, the center of opposition to the emperor in Germany during the schism; and he devoted himself thereafter to his duties as the scholastic in the cathedral chapter.[39]

Otto's contrasting views about the course of human affairs in the *Chronicle* and *Deeds* provided until well after World War II the basic interpretive framework not only for Barbarossa's reign but also for the entire Staufer epoch (1138–1256). Frederick's reign was, from this perspective, a moment of national revival after the collapse of the monarchy during the Investiture Conflict and the failed kingships of his immediate predecessors, Lothar III and Conrad III. Their most important modern biographer, Wilhelm Bernhardi, writing during Bismarck's battle with the Catholic Church, depicted Lothar as an overly pious, too compliant tool of the Church, who lacked any dynastic claim to the throne and who never asserted effective control over Germany as a whole.[40] Bernhardi's assessment of Conrad was even more devastating. Every one of the king's major undertakings had ended in failure. Conrad had left the Reich in a forlorn condition because he was from the very start of his reign trapped in the "nets" of the Roman Church, and he had heeded too much the advice of Rome's chief agent in Germany, Abbot Wibald of Stavelot (b. 1098; abbot 1130–58).[41] In fact, Wibald remained until his death one of Frederick's most influential advisers. In contrast to these negative portrayals, Henry Simonsfeld, the author of the most scholarly biography of Frederick ever written (1908), which was published in the same series as Bernhardi's books, declared in the first sentence that "a new period in German history commenced and a new revival of the Roman-German empire began" with Frederick's election. Frederick was "the most German of all of the German emperors of the past"—Simonsfeld conceded that this designation might not be totally correct, presumably because no ruler before 1871 bore the official title of German emperor.[42] Otto offered the scholarly proof for seeing 1152, like 1871 and 1933, as a new beginning in German history after a period of national decline.

Otto was the source of another interpretive paradigm. To justify the unprecedented exclusion of Conrad's son, Duke Frederick IV of Swabia, from the throne, Otto explained that the princes elected Frederick I because as the son of a Staufer father and a Welf mother he united in his own person two families whose enmities had "often disturbed the peace of the state" (2.2). Their repeated confrontations between 1125 and 1218 formed the main storyline of high-medieval German history. Bernhardi declared in 1879, for example: "this hatred dominated for a century the history of the German Reich. It tore the Volk into parties . . . through it the Roman Church . . . gained the opportunity to extinguish the power of the monarchy. The hatred between Staufer and Welfs, in the final analysis, destroyed the magnificence of the German Reich."[43] Since the Welf king of Hanover sided with Austria against Prussia in 1866, the Welf opposition to the Staufer still resonated politically in the nineteenth century. In reality, the Staufer and Welfs did not conceive of themselves in the twelfth century as members of tightly knit agnatic lineages, because every man, except for brothers, had different sets of paternal and maternal relatives. Frederick was personally closer to his maternal uncle Welf VI and cousin Henry the Lion than to his father, his paternal Staufer uncle, Conrad III, Conrad's son Frederick IV, and his own younger half-brother, also called Conrad.[44]

Above all, Otto laid the foundation for the transformation of Frederick into a heroic, almost mythic figure. Although the bishop was writing only five or six years after Frederick's accession, long before any final judgment could be made of his long reign, Otto called his nephew the "most famous of the Augusti," whose virtues could be superimposed "upon those of your predecessors like a precious stone upon gold." The emperor possessed the four cardinal, pre-Christian virtues: he was "temperate in prosperity, brave in adversity, just in judgment, and prudent and shrewd in courts of law . . ." These traits had been granted to him "by God for the general advantage of the whole world."[45] Otto may have intended to write an admonitory mirror of princes rather than a panegyric, but the nuances could easily be overlooked by historians caught up in the Wilhelmine nationalistic frenzy.

Other Sources about Frederick

There is no single narrative source comparable to the *Deeds* for the remaining thirty years of Frederick's reign, though the following authors utilized it in constructing their own works. Between 1181 and 1184 the poet Gunther, who may have been identical with the Alsatian Cistercian monk Gunther of Pairis (the tutor of Frederick's children), wrote an epic about Barbarossa's battles in Italy, the *Ligurinus* (Milan, Frederick's main opponent, is in Liguria), which he gave to the imperial family in 1187. Although it was written after Frederick's defeats in Italy, it does not deal with events following 1160.[46] Godfrey of Viterbo, a long-time member of the chancery, wrote the so-called verse *Gesta Friderici* (*Deeds of Frederick*) as part of his larger compendium of world history.[47] Provost Frederick of St. Thomas in Strasbourg, who served as Frederick and Henry VI's chaplain after 1182, and as their emissary to the pope on the eve of the Third Crusade, utilized Otto's (but not Rahewin's) section of the *Deeds* in writing the so-called *Marbach Annals*. Otto of St. Blasien continued the *Chronicle* and *Deeds* until 1209.[48]

Several authors provided eyewitness accounts of Frederick's Italian campaigns in the 1150s and 1160s. The annals of the Bohemian canon, Vincent of Prague, who assisted Bishop Daniel of Prague (1147–67) in implementing imperial control in Italy, offer a German perspective. Italians, on both sides of the communal divide in Frederick's wars against the Lombards, wrote chronicles. In 1161 Otto Morena, a burgher and consul of Lodi, who had already served Lothar III as a judge and envoy, started a history of his pro-imperial, native city's conflict with its neighbor Milan. His son Acerbus Morena, who served as a judge at Frederick's court, continued the chronicle until 1164. Otto Morena resumed work on the chronicle after Acerbus' death outside Rome in 1167. In contrast to the Morenas, an anonymous Milanese author, who was hostile to Frederick, wrote about the emperor's conquest and oppression of Milan.[49] An unnamed poet, probably from the pro-imperial city of Bergamo, composed *The Song of the Deeds of the Emperor Frederick in Lombardy*. The extant text ends with Frederick's defeat at Carcano on 9 August 1160, but may have concluded originally with Milan's second capitulation in 1162.[50] The Swabian Premonstratensian chronicler Provost Burchard of Ursberg, writing in 1229/30, utilized a lost work by an otherwise unknown, pro-imperial author, John of Cremona. Burchard relied on the *History of the Welfs* (*Historia Welforum*), an account of Frederick's maternal ancestors and relatives, for his information on events in Germany during the emperor's reign.[51]

Less information is available on Frederick's actions after 1160 in Germany than in Italy. Numerous German chroniclers recorded specific incidents and rumors that had come to their attention, but none of them produced a master narrative of the later decades of his reign. Three works should be singled out for special mention: *The Cologne Royal Chronicle* of Abbot Nicholas of Siegburg; Arnold of Lübeck's pro-Welf *Chronicle of the Slavs*, which is a major source on Frederick's confrontation with Henry the Lion in 1180–81; and Gilbert of Mons' *Chronicle of Hainaut*.[52] The regional focus is apparent in the titles of these works.

Since we are far better informed, thanks to Otto of Freising and Rahewin, about the first eight than the last thirty years of Frederick's reign, all modern biographies, including mine, are skewed in the same fashion. For example, Peter Munz devoted 219 of the 399 pages—not counting the bibliography and index—in his 1969 biography of Frederick to the period up to and including the Council of Pavia in February 1160.

Serious scholarship about Frederick was hindered for a long time by the absence of a critical edition of all his charters and letters, which were scattered in archives throughout Europe. It was necessary to locate the documents and to distinguish between authentic, partially falsified, and forged charters. This task was made even more difficult because the majority of the charters do not survive as originals but as later copies in cartularies. Paul Scheffer-Boichorst began preliminary work on this project in the 1880s. After his death in 1902, the Institute for Austrian Historical Investigation (Institut für Österreichische Geschichtsforschung) at the University of Vienna began preparing critical editions of the charters of Lothar III, Conrad III, and Frederick; but political and economic conditions in Austria were hardly conducive to such a venture for much of the period after 1914. The relatively small volume on Lothar III and his wife Richenza—135 items—appeared in 1927. The Monumenta announced in 1931 that there were no further obstacles to publishing the charters of Conrad III—except, it turned out, for a complete lack of money—and that volume with 309 items finally saw the light of day in 1969. Serious work on Barbarossa's documents commenced only in 1956 with the appointment of Heinrich Appelt as the editor-in-chief; the five massive volumes, containing 1,259 charters, letters, and mandates, were finally published between 1975 and 1990.[53] These documents are only a small fraction of the total number that must have been produced during Frederick's reign, and their distribution, both chronologically and geographically, is determined by the accidents of survival rather than the intensity of his activities in a given time and place. The surviving documentation thus both illuminates and distorts Frederick's actions.

Several letter collections, which include some letters that were sent in Frederick's name, supplement Appelt's edition of his charters. The most important of these is that of Abbot Wibald of Stavelot (Stablo in Flemish and German) and Corvey, who was Conrad III's chief adviser and who continued to serve Frederick. Only the material from the years 1147 to 1154 and 1156/57 survives from Wibald's collection and so reinforces the emphasis in the extant historical record on the early years of Frederick's reign.[54] Two other important letter collections were preserved in the Benedictine monasteries of Admont in Styria and Tegernsee in Bavaria. The Admont collection is a major source on the schism, while the Tegernsee collection includes material on the diplomacy that preceded the Peace of Venice in 1177, when Frederick finally recognized Alexander III as the rightful pope.[55] The material in all three collections indicates that Frederick and his entourage made much more extensive use of written communications than the extant correspondence would suggest, and that if more of it had survived, Staufer Germany might not appear to be quite so backward, in comparison with Angevin England or Norman Sicily, in its mechanisms of governance. Finally, Ferdinand Opll's *Regesta Imperii* (1980–2011) is an invaluable tool for writing Frederick's biography. Opll summarized and listed in chronological order all references to Frederick in charters, letters, and chronicles, evaluated their trustworthiness, and cited the printed editions and relevant secondary literature about each item.[56] The publication of Frederick's charters and the *Regesta Imperii* has transformed the study of his reign.

Historiography

In spite of Frederick's importance for medieval and modern history and the countless monographs and articles about him, he has not been especially well served until recently by scholars, who have found the task of writing a full-scale biography daunting. Because of the centrality of the medieval empire for the German nation-building project, German historians wrote detailed, often day-by-day, biographies of the individual rulers in the *Yearbooks of German History* (*Jahrbücher der Deutschen Geschichte*), in which all the narrative and documentary evidence was related and evaluated in accordance with the highest standards of nineteenth-century source criticism. While Bernhardi's biographies of Lothar III and Conrad III had appeared already in 1879 and 1883 respectively, the first volume for the admittedly much longer reign of Frederick was published only in 1908. This was because Simonsfeld, who had been commissioned to write the book in the 1880s, kept waiting in vain for the publication of Frederick's charters and the relevant volumes on him in the *Regesta Imperii*, and had finally decided to proceed. The 784-page book, a monument to positivist historical scholarship, in which the footnotes often overwhelm the text, ends with Otto of Freising's death in September 1158.[57] Simonsfeld died in 1913 and the remaining volumes were never finished. Thus his work also reinforced the focus on the first years of Barbarossa's reign.

For a century after Simonsfeld's death the volumes on Frederick in Wilhelm von Giesebrecht's monumental *Geschichte der Deutschen Kaiserzeit* (*History of the German Imperial Epoch*; 1855–88), which had originally been intended for a lay audience, became by default the standard scholarly work on Frederick; but this, too, was jinxed. The publication of the first two volumes in the 1850s had triggered a scholarly debate on whether the medieval Empire had been beneficial for Germany's development as a nation; but by the time Giesebrecht wrote during the Second Reich about Barbarossa, the dispute had been resolved in favor of Germany's imperial destiny. Volume 5, which continued the story of Frederick's reign until 1181, appeared in two parts in 1880 and 1888. Typically, the first part carried the subtitle, *New Rise of the Empire under Frederick I.* However, Giesebrecht died in 1889. His student Bernhard von Simson (whose father had presented Wilhelm in 1870 with the petition of the Reichstag that he accept the imperial crown, and who subsequently published in 1912 the critical edition of the *Deeds of Frederick Barbarossa*) finished the book and added the footnotes for the entire reign in the sixth volume, which appeared in 1895.[58] Thus until nearly the end of the twentieth century, scholars, even in Germany, had to rely for a general overview of Frederick's reign on a semi-popular history.

English-speaking readers' knowledge of Frederick was long limited to general histories of medieval Germany, most notably Geoffrey Barraclough's *The Origins of Modern Germany* (1946). This was an attempt, based on prewar German scholarship, to explain the disastrous course of German history.[59] The nearly simultaneous publication in English, in 1969–70, of two biographies of Frederick was not much of an improvement. Marcel Pacaut's book, *Frederick Barbarossa*, was an abridged version of the French edition, in which the explanatory background information was deleted. Pacaut, an expert on Frederick's contemporaries, Alexander III and Louis VII of France, did "not pretend" that the biography was "a minute and painstaking analysis of the archives"; rather it was, in his words, "an unashamed work of populari-sation [sic] and has no pretensions other than to interest the educated reader in the most stirring pages of German and Italian history in the Middle Ages."[60] Peter Munz's *Frederick Barbarossa: A Study in Medieval Politics* has been until now the standard introduction to Frederick's reign for anglo-phone readers. Munz, a German émigré educated in New Zealand and at Cambridge, was not trained as a medievalist.[61] He had a considerable command of the secondary literature and the sources that were readily avail-able in the 1960s, but he favored interpretations that have not been generally accepted. He argued, for example, in his best-known formulation, that Frederick pursued a geopolitical scheme, "The Great Design," which entailed the creation of "a fairly centralized state, which would have been . . . bureau-cratically administered," in the contiguous regions of Swabia, Burgundy, and Lombardy. Munz overlooked that Barbarossa's cousin, Frederick IV, whom the author does not even mention, was the duke of Swabia until 1167.[62]

The publication of Frederick's charters, starting in 1975, and of preparatory articles and monographs by scholars who worked on the edition, as well as the postwar abandonment of the extreme German nationalism of the Kyffhäuser legend, have transformed the study of twelfth-century German history. It was possible, for example, to reconstruct Frederick's itinerary and, by implication, to identify those regions where he asserted his lordship more intensely, or to analyze the changing composition of the imperial court both during these peregrinations and over the course of the reign. Examinations of the charters revealed changes in the ruler's title and imperial nomenclature, and who was responsible for their introduction into the chancery's practices. New light has been shed on Frederick's assertion, in Italy, of his regalian rights, that is, the prerogatives of the king and the revenues that were derived from those rights, which precipitated the bitter resistance of the communes. Scrutiny of the *arengae*, the general, seemingly formulaic statements about the grantor and the reasons for the charter's issuance, revealed shifts in policy. The problem is, of course, ascertaining how much Frederick was personally responsible for and aware of the formulations in charters that were ostensibly issued in his name.

This intense focus on Frederick's charters has led in the last quarter-century to the publication of several biographies. Ferdinand Opll, the director of the Vienna municipal archives, is the foremost living authority on Frederick. Besides compiling the volumes on the emperor in the *Regesta Imperii*, he is the author of major monographs on Frederick's itinerary and Staufer urban policy.[63] Opll was the obvious person to write in 1990 the first substantive German biography of Barbarossa since the appearance of the Giesebrecht–Simson history a century earlier. Like that book, Opll's short biography was intended for an educated lay audience. Since Opll assumed that his readers would have some prior knowledge of German history, the biography is divided into two parts: Frederick's life and deeds and structural connections.[64]

A couple of decades later two other experts, Johannes Laudage and Knut Görich, incorporated the most recent scholarship into their biographies with nearly identical titles that appeared almost simultaneously. Laudage was killed in an accident in 2008 without writing the section on the 1170s. There is a bibliography but no footnotes. His views on what happened in the 1170s can be ascertained in part from his earlier monograph about Frederick's relations with Alexander III. Görich presented in a biographical format the thesis he had put forth in his 2000 second dissertation (*Habilitationsschrift*): honor, understood not as some internalized moral imperative but as a nobleman's concern for his reputation and social standing, was the driving force behind Frederick's actions. The emperor was not a medieval precursor of Bismarck with a plan for creating a German state but a man who responded immediately and often violently to any slight, real or imagined, to his dignity. Görich pointed out that as long as scholars focused on Frederick's alleged political program and use of power, there was little incentive to write the emperor's biography.[65] I have tried to integrate Görich's insight into the centrality of honor in Frederick's thinking in a bibliography that situates him in a world of familial politics and the exercise of brute power.[66]

The panegyric chronicle of Peter of Eboli, dedicated around 1196 to the emperor's successor Henry VI (r. 1190–97), includes the following verses about Frederick's death: "Already he sees the goal of his wishes [the Holy Land];/ there he migrates in joy to Christ." In the accompanying illustration an angel hands the emperor's soul, dressed like a baby in swaddling clothes, into the outstretched hand of God (Fig. 1). Seemingly undercutting this image of salvation, Frederick is depicted plunging from his horse into the water, like a representation of the fall of Pride or of Pharaoh drowning in the Red Sea. The emperor's crown already lies at the bottom of the stream. This jarring depiction and its ambivalent assessment of Frederick's reign were soon covered up with a layer of paint that was not removed until the beginning of the twentieth century.[67] The time is long overdue to uncover the prince beneath the myth.

CHAPTER ONE

"TWO RENOWNED FAMILIES"

The Staufer

TO EXPLAIN THE UNANIMOUS choice of Frederick Barbarossa as king, Otto of Freising wrote:

> There have been hitherto in the Roman world, within the borders of Gaul and Germany, two renowned families ("due . . . famose familie"): one that of the Henrys of Waiblingen, the other that of the Welfs of Altdorf. The one was wont to produce emperors, the other great dukes. These families, eager for glory as is usually the case with great men, were frequently envious of each other and often disturbed the peace of the state. But by the will of God (as men believe), providing for the peace of his people in time to come, it came about that Duke Frederick [II], the father of this Frederick, who was a descendant of one of the two families (that is, of the family of the kings), took to wife a member of the other, namely, the daughter of Henry [the Black], duke of the Bavarians, and by her became the father of the Frederick who rules at the present time. The princes, therefore, considering . . . that being a member of both families, he might—like a cornerstone—link these two separate walls, decided to select him as head of the realm (*Deeds* 2.2).

In this famous passage Otto linked his nephew to the Salian dynasty (1024–1125), the family of Frederick's paternal grandmother Agnes, the daughter of Emperor Henry IV and the sister of Henry V. If Frederick listened attentively to the reading of Otto's *Chronicle*, he would have learned that as one of the "Henrys of Waiblingen" he was descended from a daughter of Otto the Great (r. 936–73), "from the ancient and glorious stock of the

Carolingians," the family of Charlemagne, and from the Frankish king, Clovis I (r. 481–511). On one occasion, Frederick referred in a charter to Charlemagne as his forefather.[1] Otto's statement is the *locus classicus* for the long-dominant interpretive paradigm that Staufer–Welf enmity is the central theme of high-medieval German history. It is also a proof text for the thesis that the German nobility was organized by the twelfth century in agnatic lineages. Such dynasties allegedly emphasized their paternal ancestry and employed leading names like "Frederick," which recurred in each generation. The dynasties were identified with a particular property like Waiblingen, the center of their lordship like Altdorf, a castle like Stauf, or even, uniquely in the case of the Welfs, with a distinctive leading name.[2] It is striking that Otto employed the word *family* for such lineages, because *familia* in normal usage referred to the dependent members of a household who were subject to the authority of the paterfamilias, a meaning that survives in English in the term "the Devil's *familiars*."

In reality, maternal relatives continued in the twelfth century to be as important, if not more so, than paternal kinsmen; and the bond between a man and his maternal uncle was often especially close. In the 1160s, for example, Frederick sided in the Tübingen Feud with his maternal uncle Welf VI and his cousin Welf VII against his paternal cousin, Duke Frederick IV of Swabia. Which relatives or ancestors a king or noble favored or highlighted depended upon the political context or the significance of the inheritance, just as Elizabeth II as queen of England emphasizes that she is a descendant of Alfred the Great and William the Conqueror rather than of Charlemagne or Frederick Barbarossa.[3] Frederick was chosen as king precisely because he was, unlike Frederick IV, just as much a Welf as a Staufer. In large measure the lineages were the imaginary constructs of learned clerics and monks like Otto. He identified his nephew as one of the Henrys of Waiblingen; Frederick never styled himself so in any of his charters. Although Otto as Agnes' son was just as much a "Salian" as his Staufer half-brothers, he traced his own paternal ancestry with considerable hesitation in the *Chronicle* to a Count Adalbert, who had resided in Bamberg and who was executed in 906 (6.15). Otto is thus the source of the name *Babenberg* for the margraves and later dukes who ruled Austria for 270 years (976–1246), but there is no scholarly consensus whether the Babenbergs were really, and in what sense, the descendants of Count Adalbert.[4]

Frederick's paternal "Staufer" ancestry was, in fact, irrelevant to the emperor and his contemporaries. It was the royal Salian line of his grandmother that counted. Notaries referred only once in Barbarossa's charters to Duke Frederick I of Swabia (r. 1079–1105), without identifying him as the emperor's grandfather,[5] while specifically calling Henry IV Barbarossa's great-grandfather.[6] Otto never mentioned his mother's first husband in the *Chronicle* but indicated in the *Deeds*, in connection with Duke Frederick's marriage to Agnes in 1079 and his enfeoffment with Swabia, that Frederick "traced his descent from the most noble counts of Swabia," whom he did not name (1.8). Abbot Wibald of Stavelot included in his letter collection the only contemporary Staufer genealogy, which he had prepared to prove that Barbarossa's marriage to his first wife, Adela of Vohburg, was consanguineous. Wibald wrote:

> The children of the same father and mother were: Frederick begat Frederick of Büren. Frederick of Büren begat Duke Frederick [I], who built Stauf. Duke Frederick of Stauf begat by a daughter of King Henry [IV] Duke Frederick [II]. Duke Frederick begat King Frederick.
>
> Bertha begat Bezelin of Villingen. Bezelin of Villingen begat Berthold with the Beard [Duke Berthold I of Carinthia]. Berthold with the Beard begat Liutgard. Liutgard begat Margrave Diepold [III of Cham-Vohburg]. Margrave Diepold begat Adela.[7]

Since there is no other extant reference to a Frederick of Büren, genealogists have sought in Swabia for a pair of "most noble counts" named Frederick, who could have been the father and grandfather of the first Staufer duke. The first two Fredericks in Wibald's genealogy are most commonly identified as the count-palatine of Swabia, Frederick, and Count Frederick, who appeared together as witnesses in 1053 and who resided in northern Swabia. (Duke Frederick I's brother Louis also served as the count-palatine.) *Büren* is a common place name, but it is usually identified as Wäschenbeuern, which is situated between the Staufer's dynastic monastery of Lorch in the Rems valley, a tributary of the Neckar, and the castle of Stauf, just to the south. These three places are located north of Ulm on the Danube.[8]

Frederick of Büren married Hildegard of Dagsburg-Egisheim (d. 1094/95), a niece of the great papal reformer, Leo IX (r. 1049–54). Such a distinguished match suggests that Frederick of Büren was a man of some importance. Sometime between 1087 and 1094, Duke Frederick I and his brothers—Bishop Otto of Strasbourg, the only "Staufer" to hold high ecclesiastical office, and Conrad—visited the Benedictine abbey of St. Foy in Conques, located on the pilgrimage route to Santiago de Compostela in Spain. They were so impressed that they, their mother, and their other siblings in 1094 conferred on St. Foy a church, dedicated to the saint, which they had built in Sélestat in Alsace. It was the only monastery in the Empire that was affiliated with this French abbey. Hildegard was buried there, and Duke Frederick I subsequently specified that the Staufer who was the duke of Swabia should serve as its advocate. Barbarossa confirmed these arrangements in 1153, and after he defeated Milan in 1162 he gave St. Foy in Sélestat a stained-glass window to commemorate his victory, according to an inscription recorded by a sixteenth-century Alsatian humanist.[9] It is striking how little Barbarossa, seemingly, knew or cared about his Staufer ancestry, perhaps because he did not wish to be reminded of the first Staufer duke's comparatively humble origins.

The Staufer's irregular contacts with their dynastic monastery at Lorch are indicative of how vaguely defined was their identity as Staufer. Families often converted a castle into a monastery—Klosterneuburg, where Otto of Freising began his clerical career, means quite literally "Monastery New Castle"—that was intended to serve as the lineage's necropolis. The monks remembered their benefactors in prayer and often promoted their earthly reputation by writing dynastic histories. The oldest family member in each generation often served as the abbey's advocate (*Vogt*) or protector. Such advocacies and the indirect control that they offered over the abbey's resources were a major component in the development of noble territorial lordships. The complex of graves and the annual liturgical commemorations of the deceased reinforced the sense of family unity over the generations.[10]

In 1136 Pope Innocent II accepted the donation to the papacy of the Benedictine monastery that Duke Frederick I of the Swabians and Franks, his wife Agnes, and their sons the future Duke Frederick II and King Conrad III, had allegedly founded on their allodial property at Lorch. Three years later Conrad, now king, appointed as the advocate his brother Frederick, whom the abbot and monks had freely chosen, and determined that the senior member of the lineage was to be elected thereafter as the advocate. It was probably in conjunction with these events that Conrad transferred his father's remains to the abbey.[11] Barbarossa confirmed his uncle's arrangements in 1154, but stipulated that the monks were to select as the advocate the eldest among the descendants of the lineage of King Conrad and Duke Frederick II. In this instance, Barbarossa clearly considered his paternal cousin, Duke Frederick IV (King Conrad's son), and his own half-brother Conrad, who headed the list of witnesses, as belonging to his own agnatic lineage.[12]

Yet Lorch never served as the Staufer's common burial site. Besides Duke Frederick I, the other family members who rested there, or may have, were: Barbarossa's mother Judith; his cousin King Henry (VI) (d. 1150);

two of Barbarossa's sons, Rainald and William, who died in infancy; their sister Beatrice (d. 1174); Barbarossa's son Duke Conrad of Swabia (r. 1191–96); and Barbarossa's daughter-in-law, the Byzantine princess Irene/Maria (d. 1208), who had been the wife of King Philip of Swabia. The Salian princess, Agnes (wife of Duke Frederick I), lies in her second husband's foundation outside Vienna, Klosterneuburg. Duke Frederick II and his second wife were buried in the Benedictine abbey of St. Walbourg near Haguenau; Judith's heart is there, too. Conrad III's queen, Gertrude of Sulzbach (d. 1146), and his younger son Duke Frederick IV (d. 1167), were interred in the Cistercian abbey of Ebrach in Franconia. Although Conrad wished to be placed next to his father's grave in Lorch, his body lies in the cathedral of Bamberg. Barbarossa's half-brother, Conrad, the count-palatine of the Rhine (d. 1195), and his wives chose Schönau, a Cistercian house outside Heidelberg, for their entombment. Frederick's wife, Beatrice of Burgundy, and daughter Agnes were laid to rest in 1184 alongside the Salians in the cathedral of Speyer; and it is likely that Barbarossa would have chosen Speyer as his burial site, as a thirteenth-century chronicle implies, if he had died in Germany. The selection of Speyer rather than Lorch as the imperial family's final resting place underscores Frederick's identification with his royal rather than his ducal Staufer ancestors.[13]

The designation of the lineage as the Staufer is, in fact, a convenient scholarly convention, but it is anachronistic since key members of the lineage, including Barbarossa, were never called as such. (The name of the castle is *Stoph* or *Stauf*, the lineage is the *Staufer*, and the hill on which the destroyed castle stood is the *Hohenstaufen*.)[14] Wibald, in his genealogy, indicated that Frederick of *Stophe* built *Stophen*, but since Otto merely said that Frederick I established his residence in the castle of *Stoyphe* (*Deeds* 1.8), perhaps in connection with the foundation of the monastery of Lorch, it is not certain that the duke commissioned the building. He may simply have moved into an existing structure.[15] Odo of Deuil related in his eyewitness account of the Second Crusade how he approached King Louis VII in mid-November 1147, after Conrad III's army had been routed, and told Louis that, in violation of the rights of St. Denis, Conrad held one tower of the castle of *Estufin* and Duke Frederick III (Barbarossa) the other. The latter was also in "the exclusive possession of Esslingen," which is located west of Stauf. The French king entreated Conrad, first privately, then publicly, to return both to St. Denis; but Conrad refused. Whatever the truth of this tale—would Louis have really importuned his despondent guest in such an undiplomatic way?—Odo's story indicates that Conrad and Barbarossa had joint custody of Stauf as well as Lorch and the monk thought that the castle had been constructed on land belonging to St. Denis, the burial church of the French kings outside Paris.[16] After his accession Barbarossa stayed in Stauf, as far as is known, only once, in 1181.[17] In addition to Duke Frederick I, Frederick II and Barbarossa's cousin Frederick IV were occasionally given the toponymic surname *Stauf*; but Conrad III, Barbarossa, and his half-brother never were. Around 1215 a chronicler referred to the "emperors of Stauf," but Emperor Frederick II was in 1247 the first member of the lineage to speak, in an isolated reference, about "a Staufer house" ("domus Stoffensis").[18] To overstate the case, his grandfather Frederick Barbarossa was not a Staufer.

If anything, the high-medieval designation for the lineage was *Waiblingen*, the source of the name *Ghibelline* in the thirteenth century for the pro-imperial party in Italy—the pro-papal party was the *Guelphs*, or Welfs. Writing around 1230, Burchard of Ursberg stated, correctly or not, that Barbarossa "prided himself that he descended from the royal lineage of the Waiblingens, who, as is known, sprang in a two-fold way from two royal houses, namely, the Merovingians . . . and the Carolingians . . ."[19] Why Otto associated his nephew with Waiblingen in the first place is less clear. Henry IV had given Waiblingen, which had been the site of a Carolingian palace and which was situated on the Rems downstream from Lorch, to the bishopric of Speyer in 1080; and the place was never mentioned again. Later medieval historians offered fanciful explanations for the designation. For example, Burchard, who specifically quoted Otto's account of the Salians' ancestry, added that the Merovingians had originated in Waiblingen. As proof, Burchard pointed out that Clodius (c. 392–448), the purported progenitor of the Merovingians, had erected, outside Waiblingen, a monument over the grave of his wife that was supposedly still standing in 1230.[20] Modern scholars can only speculate, as Burchard did, why Otto connected his mother's family with Waiblingen.

Otto's account of Henry IV's bestowal of both his daughter Agnes, who was at most seven, and the duchy of Swabia on the obscure Duke Frederick I at Easter 1079 reads, one historian has said, like a chivalric romance. The bishop even concocted a speech in which Henry quoted Ovid. Duke Frederick had distinguished himself, so Otto related, as a wise adviser and courageous warrior in the king's service; and because of the great danger the Reich faced, Henry assigned to Frederick the task of combating vassals who had broken their oaths of fealty to the king. Seemingly, no one remembered eighty years later the specific reasons for Henry's actions.[21]

The geopolitical rationale for Frederick's selection as duke of Swabia is quite clear. Henry had been temporarily reconciled in January 1077 at

Canossa with Pope Gregory VII. But in March the king's diehard princely opponents had elected as their new king the duke of Swabia, Rudolf of Rheinfelden, Henry's former brother-in-law. In retaliation, Henry deprived Rudolf and the two other hostile south German dukes, Berthold I of Zähringen and Welf IV, of their respective duchies, Carinthia and Bavaria. The king chose Duke Frederick I as Rudolf's successor because of the strategic location of the Staufer lordship in northern Swabia. The lordship was on the road that led from Saxony, the major center of opposition to Henry IV, through Franconia, via Ulm, to the Zähringer and Welf strongholds in southern Swabia. Frederick I's appointment thus split the opposition. In June 1079 Rudolf's supporters elected his son Berthold of Rheinfelden as the rival duke of Swabia. After the latter's death in 1090, his partisans chose as the new duke in 1092 his son-in-law, Berthold II of Zähringen.

The long conflict over the duchy of Swabia was settled in 1098 with a de facto division of the stem duchy of Swabia into three smaller territorial duchies: the Staufer north of the Danube, the Zähringer on both sides of the Black Forest and south of the upper Rhine, and the Welfs north of Lake Constance. Berthold II abandoned his claim to Swabia but retained his ducal title. To finalize the reconciliation, Henry IV gave Berthold in 1098 Zürich, the most important royal and ducal stronghold in Swabia. Zürich linked the Zähringer holdings in southwestern Germany with the lands between the Jura mountains and Aare river (in what is now northwestern Switzerland), which Berthold had just inherited from the Rheinfelder. Henry IV had already restored Bavaria to Welf IV in 1096. In effect, Duke Frederick I's power was limited to the small portion of the old duchy of Swabia situated north of the Danube.[22] This was the duchy that Barbarossa ruled in 1152.

The Zähringer rather than the Welfs were the Staufer's chief opponents in the twelfth century. They derived their name, which they first employed in 1100, from the castle of Zähringen, located within the modern city of Freiburg im Breisgau in the later grand duchy of Baden, which the descendants of Berthold II's brother governed until 1918. While the Welfs intermarried with both the Staufer and the Zähringer, the only known genealogical connection between the Staufer and Zähringer is Barbarossa's and Adela of Vohburg's common descent from Wibald's unnamed couple. Indeed, Wibald's genealogy may have an anti-Zähringer slant to it. Wibald identified Frederick I as a duke but omitted the title in the case of Berthold I (Berthold with the Beard). The intended implication may have been that Adela was not a suitable wife for Barbarossa, who was of royal ancestry. Moreover, Otto disparaged the Zähringer in the *Deeds* as being dukes in name only, since they lacked a duchy and denied that they had ever possessed the duchy of Carinthia from which they derived their ducal rank (1.9). Wibald and Otto's tendentious treatments of the Zähringer testify to the bitterness of their rivalry with the Staufer.[23]

In short, while Frederick is remembered today as the greatest of the Staufer monarchs, he seemingly knew little about his paternal ancestry and/or was ashamed of his grandfather's relatively modest origins—and he was never identified in his lifetime as a Staufer.

Duke Frederick II

Frederick II and Conrad III were, respectively, fifteen and thirteen when their father, Duke Frederick I, died in 1105 and their mother Agnes married Margrave Leopold III of Austria. Technically, the new duke, Frederick II, was of age; but he was young enough not to be forced to choose sides between his grandfather, Henry IV, and his maternal uncle Henry V, who had just rebelled against his father. Otto of Freising, who was more than twenty years younger than Frederick II and who grew up in Austria and lived in France, would have had little contact with his older half-brother until they met at Conrad III's court after 1138. According to Otto, Frederick II "was in all things like his father. He was so faithful a [vassal] to his sovereign and so helpful a friend to his uncle [Henry V] that by his valor he supported the tottering honor of the realm, fighting manfully against its foes until the members that were at variance with their head by seeking their sovereign's favor returned again to his affection."[24]

Otto's depiction of Frederick II as Henry V's chief lieutenant requires some qualification. Frederick II served at least thirty times as an intercessor or a witness in Henry's charters, whereas Conrad III did so on just three occasions. However, the count-palatine of the Rhine, Godfrey of Calw, and Count Berengar I of Sulzbach, the father of Conrad III's queen, made, respectively, fifty-eight and thirty-three appearances as witnesses. The young duke appeared at court only once before Henry V left Germany in 1110 for his imperial coronation. However, Frederick II's name headed the list of men who guaranteed on 4 February 1111, prior to the coronation in April, that the king would observe the terms of the tentative agreement that he had reached with Pope Paschal II. According to this, Henry surrendered his right to invest bishops, while the pope agreed to the return of all the regalian rights, such as the right to mint money or levy tolls, which the Church had obtained from the crown since the time of Charlemagne. The other guarantors were identified by their titles or offices, but Frederick II was listed simply as the son of the king's sister. His kinship with the king was the basis for his preeminence. Until Henry V returned to Italy in 1116 to claim the inheritance of Margravine Matilda of Tuscany, Frederick witnessed more imperial charters than anyone except the count-palatine, Godfrey. On his departure the emperor left his nephews and Godfrey in charge in Germany.[25]

During Henry V's absence in Italy, Frederick II fought Henry's former chancellor, Archbishop Adalbert I of Mainz (1109–37), who along with Duke Lothar of Saxony was the leader of the princely opposition to the king. It was the beginning of Frederick's confrontations with Adalbert. Otto declared that Frederick "gradually subjected to his will the entire stretch of country from Basel to Mainz [the upper Rhine valley], where the principal strength of the realm is known to be." He built so many castles that it was said of him, according to Otto, "Duke Frederick always hauls a fortress with him at the tail of his horse." Oddly, archaeologists have not been able to verify Otto's statement.[26]

However, Frederick II did develop Haguenau, where his son may have been born in 1122 and which became one of Barbarossa's favorite residences, and the adjoining Holy Forest as the center of his northern Alsatian lordship. The duke built a castle at Haguenau, probably in 1114/15, and by 1125 a settlement ("villa") had formed around the castle—Barbarossa was quite explicit in 1164 that his father had established the "villa" during the reign of Henry V (he died in 1125). In 1143 Conrad III announced that his brother, Frederick II, whom he styled on this occasion as the duke of the Swabians and Alsatians, had arranged for the growing community to become a separate parish. Barbarossa granted Haguenau its first municipal charter in 1164, though some of the provisions—which are unclear—dated back to his father. The charter dealt with such things as the citizens' legal status, rights of inheritance, the cutting of timber in the Holy Forest for building and heating, the penalties for various crimes, the market, and the burghers' freedom from tolls throughout the Empire. Barbarossa was represented in the city by a judge, who presided at the court, and a subordinate *Schultheiss* (bailiff), who exercised police functions, especially in regard to the sale of food. While the emperor appointed these magistrates without any formal involvement of the burghers, an association of citizens assisted these officials in the discharge of their duties.

The final provision in Barbarossa's charter indicates that the imperial marshal was responsible for arranging, without detriment to the inhabitants, for the emperor's maintenance when he visited the "villa." He had been in Haguenau in 1158, and he stayed there at least eight more times after 1164, perhaps so he could hunt in the Holy Forest. Between 1158 and the mid-1170s the ducal castle was converted into a royal palace. On his last visit in April 1189, just before he left on the Third Crusade, Frederick conferred on the Premonstratensians a hospital that he had built and endowed in Haguenau.[27]

The Salians and the counts of Lützelbourg (east of Sarrebourg in Lorraine), as well as the Staufer, had rights in the Holy Forest. Duke Frederick II and Count Peter of Lützelbourg were identified as the co-heirs and founders of the Benedictine abbey of St. Walbourg, located north of Haguenau in the Holy Forest. To benefit the soul of his brother who had been interred in the abbey, Conrad III conferred on the monks in 1151 market rights in a village they owned. In 1159 Barbarossa, likewise concerned for his father's eternal well-being, took under his protection the monastery that his ancestors had founded and endowed, confirmed their donations, and granted the monks the right to elect their abbot freely in accordance with the Benedictine Rule. He retained the advocacy for himself and stipulated that after his death it was to belong to that member of his lineage who obtained Haguenau.[28]

Two Cistercian houses situated in the Holy Forest also came under Staufer control: the abbey of Neubourg, which was founded around 1131/33 by Reinhold, the last count of Lützelbourg, and the nunnery of Königsbrück. In 1156 Barbarossa took Neubourg, which, he said, his father and Reinhold had established, under his protection—and the tutelage of all members of his lineage who would succeed him, whether emperors, kings, dukes, or counts. (In 1156 Barbarossa was childless.) The emperor issued in 1158 a similar charter declaring that the abbey belonged to him by hereditary right. However, he specified that imperial ministerials and serfs required his permission to make donations to it, that the monks could pasture their animals, except sheep, in the forest, and that they could procure firewood there but needed the permission of his bailiff to obtain lumber for building.[29] Frederick thus continued his father's policy of developing Haguenau as the center of the Staufer domains in northern Alsace. Abbeys, along with the castle-palace complex and the nascent city, were the major components in realizing that objective. If Frederick considered any place to be "home," it was Haguenau.

Contrary to Otto's assertion that Duke Frederick II, as Henry V's paladin, forced the recalcitrant princes to submit to his uncle, it was the war-weary princes, including the duke, who compelled the emperor to make peace with the pope. Reports that members of the opposing princely parties planned to meet in Würzburg caused Henry to return to Germany from

Italy in the second half of 1118. The princes agreed at Würzburg on 29 September 1121 to negotiate a settlement between the pope and emperor that would preserve imperial rights. For his part, Frederick II was distancing himself from his uncle, because he witnessed only two of the eleven extant charters that the emperor issued between his return and the Concordat of Worms that ended the Investiture Conflict on 23 September 1122.[30]

The emperor and the three cardinals who represented Pope Calixtus II during the negotiations exchanged brief charters in a bilateral agreement. This has been known since 1693 as the Concordat of Worms, and its interpretation became a source of contention during Barbarossa's reign. Henry V relinquished his right to invest bishops and abbots with a ring and crosier, and granted all the churches located in either the kingdom of Germany or the Empire the right to hold free canonical elections and consecrations. The emperor acted "with the consent and counsel of the princes" whose names were affixed to his charter; Frederick II was listed second among the nine lay subscribers. In return, the pope conceded that all bishops and abbots, who pertained to the German kingdom (*Teutonicum regnum*), were to be elected in the royal presence but without simony or violence. In a disputed election, the emperor could approve and assist the candidate whom he deemed to have the better case, with the advice or judgment of the metropolitan and the bishops of the archiepiscopal province in which the church was located. The emperor could bestow on the bishop or abbot-elect the "regalia" by means of a scepter—the *regalia* were not defined but the term came to mean all the secular rights and properties that the prelates held from the crown—and the recipient was to perform, in return, all the unspecified duties he owed the monarch. In Italy and Burgundy, the new bishop or abbot, except those directly subject to the Roman Church, was to procure the "regalia" within six months of his election.[31]

Although both charters avoided specific feudal terminology, the Concordat feudalized the relationship between the monarch and those bishops and abbots who were his immediate vassals. It came to be understood that in Germany, unlike Italy and Burgundy, the elect had to swear an oath of fealty and render homage to the monarch before his consecration. There was some question whether a consecrated bishop was required to pay homage to a new monarch, because the hands of a ruler, as a layman, were always stained with blood. Lothar may have foregone the bishops' homage in 1125, but Conrad demanded it in 1138, and Otto explicitly stated that in 1152, after Frederick's coronation at Aachen, "all the princes" were bound to him "by oaths of fealty and homage" (2.3). The Concordat was thus the origin of the estate of the ecclesiastical princes. They comprised nearly all the German bishops and those abbots and abbesses who held their secular rights of governance and possessions directly from the crown.

Constitutionally, the Concordat was significant for at least two other reasons. First, while the princes had always advised rulers, after 1122 the princes expected to be consulted and to participate in the making of key decisions. Barbarossa's major actions took the form of princely judgments. In effect, the monarch and the realm were no longer identical; the ruler and the princes together constituted the Reich. Second, the Concordat distinguished for the first time legally between the German kingdom, or *regnum*, which Pope Calixtus specifically identified as such, and the Empire, or *imperium* as a whole. (The distinction is lost in the German word *Reich*.)[32]

Frederick II continued to act independently of his uncle during the last years of Henry V's reign. For example, in 1124 the duke sided against the emperor and with the burghers of Worms, who sought the return of their long-exiled bishop. It is unclear when Frederick II, who was only three or four years younger than Henry, came to see himself and was seen by others as his uncle's probable successor. Henry had married Matilda, the daughter of King Henry I of England, in 1114, when she was at most twelve; but the marriage remained childless. (Henry V had fathered an illegitimate daughter, and Matilda subsequently became the mother of King Henry II of England, his father being Geoffrey of Anjou. Henry V and Matilda were each thus potentially fertile.) As early as the autumn of 1111, when Henry V became seriously ill, Archbishop Adalbert of Mainz appears to have viewed Frederick II as the likely heir. On his deathbed in Utrecht on 23 May 1125, the dying monarch conferred the Salians' allods, that is, their own family holdings, on his nephew and entrusted Matilda, but not the imperial insignia, to Frederick's care. Henry thus named his oldest nephew as the chief heir of his private fortune, but did not designate him as his successor. For his part, after 1118 the duke may have deliberately joined the other princes to distance himself from his unloved uncle and so promote his own candidacy for the crown. Perhaps for that very reason Frederick was perceived, according to a later account of the royal election of 1125, as overly ambitious, as being guilty, in the classical Latin meaning of the word *ambitio*, of an excessive desire to please.[33]

Around 1120, in the middle of the negotiations that led to the 1122 settlement, Frederick II married Barbarossa's mother Judith. She was the daughter of Duke Henry the Black of Bavaria, whose name headed the list of the lay subscribers to the Concordat, and the granddaughter of Welf IV. About the same time her sister Sophia married Duke Berthold III of Zähringen, the son of another of Frederick I's opponents. These marriages strengthened the uneasy peace among the three rival Swabian dynasties and furthered the general princely reconciliation that preceded the resolution of the Investiture Conflict at Worms.[34]

The Welfs

The Welfs were and are Germany's most aristocratic family, the only lineage that can trace its ancestry, allegedly, in an unbroken succession back to the Carolingian period. Their first appearance in European history was spectacular. In 819 Judith, daughter of the eponymous Count Welf, became the second wife of Emperor Louis the Pious; and in 827 her stepson, the East Frankish king Louis the German, married her younger sister Emma. Already in the eleventh century the distinctive leading name was Latinized as *catulus*, the English *whelp* or cub, from which it was deduced that the notorious Catiline, who had conspired against the Roman Republic, had been the Welfs' distant ancestor. The Welf kings of Burgundy (888–1032), none of whom was named Welf, descended from the sisters' brother Count Conrad the Elder. The south German Welfs forgot most of this history because it was irrelevant to their position in Swabia. It is impossible to establish with any certainty the affiliation between the ninth-century "Welfs" and their later progeny.

The Swabian Welfs emerge from obscurity with Rudolf (d. 992), who established a church at Altdorf, north of Lake Constance, where, until 1126, he and his descendants, including Barbarossa's maternal grandparents, were buried. The family was known in the twelfth century, accordingly, as the Altdorfer rather than as the Welfs. (Otto identified them as the Welfs of Altdorf.) Rudolf's son Welf II (d. 1030) built the castle of Ravensburg above Altdorf and married Imiza of Luxembourg, a niece of Emperor Henry II's wife, Kunigunde. Emperor Henry III granted the duchy of Carinthia to Welf III (d. 1055) in 1047. He was the first Swabian Welf to attain ducal rank. In 1053 Welf III moved the convent in Altdorf, which was known thereafter as Weingarten, to the top of a nearby hill; and the childless duke left all his property to Weingarten. Imiza prevented the implementation of her son's wishes. Instead she summoned her grandson Welf IV to claim his maternal inheritance; he was the son of her daughter Kuniza (Kunigunde) and the Italian margrave Albert Azzo II, whose lordship was centered on Este, southwest of Padua. To counter the claims of Altdorf/Weingarten to the Welf inheritance, Imiza moved the nuns of Altdorf to Altomünster and transferred the monks of Altomünster to Weingarten.[35]

Welf IV (d. 1101), a staunch supporter of the papal party and the grandfather of Barbarossa's mother Judith, was the progenitor of the so-called "younger" Welfs who were descended in the female line from the "older" Welfs. In 1070 Henry IV appointed Welf IV duke of Bavaria, because of his extensive holdings in southeastern Swabia and western Bavaria and his Italian connections. Shortly thereafter he married Judith, the daughter of Count Baldwin IV of Flanders (d. 1035) and widow of Earl Tostig of Northumbria (d. 1066), brother of the last Anglo-Saxon king of England, Harold. The duke's marriage is indicative of the Welfs' international standing. The counts of Flanders descended from yet another Judith, the daughter of the first Judith's son, Emperor Charles the Bald.

The name of Barbarossa's mother Judith thus resonated in Welf history. Otto said that Barbarossa's sister, his only full sibling, who married Duke Matthew of Upper Lorraine (1139–76), was named Judith (1.47); but in Matthew's charters she was called Bertha (d. 1194/95), the name of Duke Frederick II's maternal grandmother (the wife of Henry IV). Either Barbarossa's sister had two different names or Otto got his niece's name wrong. Barbarossa had three daughters, all of whom died young. The eldest was named Beatrice after her mother and the youngest Agnes; the unnamed middle daughter, who was engaged in 1184 to Richard the Lionheart, might have been called Judith.[36] In any case, the later Staufer avoided the name Judith just as they did not use Welf, even though they were the chief heirs of the south German Welfs. However, the Saxon Welfs, the descendants of Barbarossa's other maternal uncle Henry the Proud, also abandoned the names Judith and Welf.

In 1089 Welf IV arranged the "marriage" of his seventeen-year-old son Welf V (r. 1101–20) to Margravine Matilda of Tuscany (d. 1115), the mainstay of the papal party in Italy; she was forty-three. The groom testified later that he had not consummated the marriage, and the couple separated in 1095, never to meet again, but did not divorce. The lineage continued with Welf V's younger brother, Duke Henry the Black of Bavaria (r. 1120–26), who before 1100 married Wulfhild (d. 1126), daughter of Duke Magnus of Saxony (r. 1072–1106) and the Hungarian princess Sophia. Through his maternal grandmother Wulfhild, Barbarossa was thus also related to the most prominent Saxon noble families and the Hungarian royal house.[37] Compared to the Welfs, the Staufer were upstarts. Otto of Freising had good reason to say as little as possible, even if perhaps he knew more, about Duke Frederick I's paternal ancestry.

However, Barbarossa referred to his Welf ancestry in only one charter. On 1 March 1181, in the midst of his confrontation with his maternal cousin Henry the Lion, he confirmed the properties which the dukes of Bavaria, from whom he descended, had conferred on the Benedictine abbey of Kremsmünster in the modern province of Upper Austria. Frederick singled out donations the monks had received from his great-grandfather, Welf IV, and his maternal uncle, Henry the Proud. Perhaps he hoped by doing so to conciliate his cousin's remaining supporters in Bavaria.[38]

Although Otto perceived Duke Frederick II's marriage to Judith as providential, neither he nor any other source indicated when or where their son Frederick (Barbarossa) was born. However, Abbot Wibald of Stavelot informed Pope Eugenius III in March 1152 that the new German king was not quite thirty. The date of Frederick's birth has now been placed, on the basis of circumstantial evidence, in mid-December 1122. I would hazard the guess that his birthplace was Haguenau because of its importance for his father Frederick II and for Barbarossa in his later years.[39] The choice of Otto of Cappenberg as the infant's godfather sealed the peace that had been made at Worms between the Church and the Henrys of Waiblingen.

CHAPTER TWO

BAPTISMAL HOPES

Frederick's Godfather: Otto of Cappenberg

IN 1161 AND 1187 Frederick confirmed the liberties and possessions of Cappenberg. This was the oldest Premonstratensian abbey in Germany, founded by his most beloved kinsmen, Count Godfrey II of Cappenberg (c. 1097–1127) and his younger brother Otto, the third provost of Cappenberg (1156–71). The emperor referred to Otto in the 1187 charter as his godfather.[1] Frederick gave Otto, probably after his imperial coronation on 18 June 1155, a silver bowl 24.4 centimeters in diameter and 4.4 centimeters in height (Fig. 2). The rim and the depiction of Frederick's baptism engraved at the center of the bowl, along with the inscription surrounding the scene, are gilded. The scene shows a child, identified as Emperor Frederick, immersed as far as his chest in a baptismal font. An unnamed bishop, standing to the right of the font and assisted by a deacon, places his right hand in blessing on the child's head and holds the infant's left upper arm with his own left hand. To the left of the font, a bearded layman, labeled Otto, grasps Frederick's right upper arm with both his hands in order to lift the infant from the font. Two unidentified lay people—only a kerchief-like head covering is visible on the third figure—stand behind Otto. They are presumably the infant's parents, Duke Frederick II and Judith.

Two inscriptions encircle the scene. The outer one reads: "Frederick, Caesar and Augustus [emperor and increaser of the realm], conferred these gifts on his godfather Otto; the latter consecrated them to God." The inner inscription commands: "You, whom the water cleanses from the outside, be mindful of the inner man; so that you will become what you are not, wash and cleanse what you are." Otto almost certainly added the outer inscription. This unique bowl had no known liturgical function in the twelfth-century ritual of immersion and is not depicted in the baptismal scene, so it is unlikely that Frederick was returning to Otto an object that his godfather had originally conferred on him. The best guess is that it may have been intended for use as a basin for the ritual washing of hands prior to the Mass, so reminding the canons who used it of the close personal bonds that had linked their founders to the emperor. In 1171 Otto bequeathed to the abbey the bowl and the so-called Cappenberg Head (Fig. 3), a bust of the emperor that Frederick had also given to his godfather, as well as a chalice that Otto had received from the bishop of Troyes and a jeweled cross.[2]

Baptism forged a bond between the sponsor and the child, which could be activated in later life. Abbot Hugh of Cluny interceded, famously, with Gregory VII on behalf of his godson, Henry IV, at Canossa in January 1077 and procured the reluctant forgiveness of the excommunicated emperor. However, since the sponsor or the child often died before the infant reached maturity, the immediate relationship between the child's spiritual and carnal fathers was often the more significant one. Co-paternity, like a marriage alliance, was a way to seal an agreement between the two men. For example, in 1297 Archbishop Conrad IV of Salzburg and Duke Albrecht of Austria ended a lengthy war by having the archbishop lift the duke's unnamed daughter from the font. The chronicler commented that the peace would have lasted for a thousand years if they had lived that long. Nevertheless, we rarely hear about baptismal sponsorship in twelfth-century Germany.[3]

Otto of Cappenberg's sponsorship of the infant Frederick at his baptism in 1122 or early 1123 is the spectacular exception. Clearly, the provost, the duke, and the emperor attached great importance to their spiritual as well as their carnal kinship. The Cappenberg brothers and Duke Frederick II were third cousins—the maternal grandmother of the counts' mother was the sister of Adelaide of Turin, the maternal grandmother of Barbarossa's grandmother Agnes.[4] While kinship was undoubtedly a factor in Otto's selection as Barbarossa's godfather, the boy's parents had other relatives who were at least as important as the counts and to whom Frederick II and Judith were more closely related. There must have been, thus, another reason for the choice of Otto.

The Cappenbergs were in 1122 the central figures in a sensational conversion story that had astounded the highest ranks of imperial society. The brothers Godfrey and Otto had joined Duke Lothar of Saxony in February 1121 in reinstating the exiled bishop of Münster, Dietrich II of

Winzenburg, an opponent of Henry V, in his episcopal see. In fighting the imperial forces, the brothers had been primarily responsible for the burning of Münster and its cathedral, and the remorseful Godfrey subsequently decided to abandon the world. He persuaded his less enthusiastic brother Otto and his own even more reluctant wife, Jutta of Arnsberg, to follow his example. In October or November 1121 Godfrey met in Cologne with St. Norbert of Xanten, who had just established the abbey of Prémontré near Laon, the mother house of the Premonstratensian Order. The brothers' patrimony subsequently served as the endowment not only of Cappenberg but also of three other Premonstratensian houses. Bishop Dietrich sought to obtain the castle of Cappenberg, which was strategically situated just outside Münster, for his territorial lordship; but he was forced instead, against his will, to consecrate the new house on 15 August 1122.

However, Godfrey's chief opponent was his father-in-law, Count Frederick of Arnsberg. He had hoped that the combination of Jutta's inheritance with the Cappenberg domains would form the basis of a powerful lordship in southern Westphalia, and he was especially furious that her dowry would be diverted to religious purposes. When Count Frederick attacked Cappenberg, Norbert of Xanten and Godfrey opened the gates and, expecting to die, confessed their sins. In the end, the irate count decided to use judicial means to stop his son-in-law's renunciation of his lands. It was only after Frederick's death in 1124 that Godfrey and Otto formally joined the new order.

Duke Frederick II came to the defense of his kinsmen. At an imperial court held in Utrecht in May 1122, the duke pretended not to recognize Count Frederick. In his presence the duke extolled the Cappenbergs, who had conferred their entire patrimony on God and had been harassed by Frederick of Arnsberg, whom the duke called "the son of the Devil." Publicly shamed, the count was forced to leave the court. At Worms, probably on 23 September, the day the Concordat was ratified, Emperor Henry V, at Norbert's intercession, forgave the Cappenbergs their offenses, presumably their role in the destruction of Münster, confirmed the donation of their patrimony to Norbert, and took the abbey of Cappenberg under imperial protection. According to Godfrey's vita, the emperor received with great joy the shabbily dressed and unkempt Godfrey, who had arrived without an appropriate knightly entourage.[5]

The Cappenbergs conferred nearly all of their possessions on the Premonstratensians, except for two Swabian castles and the numerous ministerials and the approximately 2,000 hides that were attached to the fortresses. (Theoretically, a hide was the amount of land that a peasant household could farm.) They sold the castles for 500 marks to Duke Frederick II, who was identified in this context as Godfrey and Otto's kinsman. According to Godfrey's vita written in the mid-twelfth century, in lieu of 100 marks the duke gave the counts some relics of the Apostle John, who became the abbey's patron saint. Otto, whom the vita described as especially devoted to the Evangelist, subsequently placed the relics "in a gilded head." This was presumably the Cappenberg Head, because the inscription on the neck of the bust says that it contains "the hair of John."

In his 1171 will Otto also bequeathed to the canons of Cappenberg "a gold cross that I am accustomed to call [the cross] of St. John." He indicated that the cross was ornamented with jewels and that a small gold chain was attached to the cross. Otto entrusted the cross, bowl, head, and chalice to his successors and the canons with the same confidence, he said, as the dying Savior had committed His mother to the care of the Beloved Disciple. According to a seventeenth-century historian of the abbey, who may have had access to now lost records, Judith's mother Wulfhild had obtained the cross from her cousin, Empress Irene, wife of the Byzantine Emperor Alexius I (1081–1118) and grandmother of Barbarossa's imperial rival Manuel I. (Wulfhild and Irene were granddaughters of King Béla I of Hungary.) The cross had been part of Judith's dowry, and her husband Duke Frederick II had worn it around his neck as a talisman in battle because it brought him victory. The relics of St. John that the Cappenbergs obtained from Frederick II were thus some of the Evangelist's hairs that had been encased in the Byzantine cross. The author of Godfrey's twelfth-century vita added that the duke would have preferred to pay the 100 marks than to part with the relics of St. John. For their part, the counts, according to the later historian, esteemed the cross more than the money. They handed the money over to St. Norbert, who used it to obtain papal confirmation of his new order in 1126.[6]

Godfrey's vita does not indicate when the duke gave the Cappenbergs the 400 marks and the relics of St. John in exchange for the two castles. A likely moment is at young Frederick's baptism, because his mother Judith's consent would presumably have been required to alienate the relics that had been part of her dowry. Since the relics were a permanent reminder of the spiritual bond between the Staufer and the Cappenbergs and between Otto and his godson, it made sense to place them inside the Cappenberg Head, created in Frederick's likeness, after Otto turned the bust into a reliquary.

Frederick's baptism in late 1122 or early 1123 sealed the reconciliation between the opposing parties in the Investiture Conflict. By selecting

Otto, who had fought against Henry V, as the co-father of his firstborn son, Duke Frederick, who had been distancing himself since 1118 from his uncle, signaled his own sympathies for the most radical ecclesiastical reform currents. These were epitomized by the Cappenbergs' sensational renunciation of their earthly possessions, and the duke procured the intercessory prayers of a converted holy man for his infant son. The obvious question is why Otto rather than Godfrey became Frederick's godfather. Godfrey, who had appeared at the imperial court in Worms in disheveled clothes, who cleaned, according to his vita, the latrines at Cappenberg, and who was dismayed by the pomp and tumult of Norbert's new life as the archbishop of Magdeburg (1126–34), was probably unwilling to become entangled again in worldly affairs. Otto, the reluctant convert who retained his personal property as the provost of Cappenberg, was more accommodating.[7]

Staufer Patronage of the Premonstratensians

We do not know what role, if any, Otto of Cappenberg played in the spiritual nurture of his godson; but the Staufer, starting with Barbarossa's father and uncle, continued to support the Premonstratensians. At the request of Duke Frederick II of Swabia and Alsace, in 1144 his brother Conrad III re-established the abandoned house of secular canonesses at Münsterdreisen, located west of Worms in the Palatinate, and charged the Premonstratensians of Arnstein with its restoration. In 1163 Barbarossa asserted that his father, the founder of Münsterdreisen, had freed the abbey from the jurisdiction and abuses of its sub-advocates and had retained the advocacy solely for himself and his heirs. After the emperor's death, the advocacy was to pertain to the nearest person in his bloodline.[8] Duke Frederick and his son were advocates of Lorch. With their approval Conrad also authorized in 1144 two servile dependants of that monastery to establish a convent of Premonstratensian nuns on their own lands at Lochgarten (today Louisgarde, northeast of Bad Mergentheim, in Baden-Württemberg). When the sub-advocate of Lochgarten resigned the office in 1155, Barbarossa assumed the advocacy himself.[9]

Shortly after his accession as king in 1152, Frederick freed the Premonstratensians in his realm from the payment of all tolls on both land and water.[10] On 25 May 1181, during his only documented stay in the castle of Stauf, Barbarossa announced that his ministerial Folknand of Stauf, presumably the burgrave of the castle, had established the nearby monastery of Adelberg and that he had conferred it on the Holy See.

The lord of Stauf, that is, the member of the imperial lineage who was the duke of Swabia, was to be the house's advocate in the future. Pope Alexander III indicated on 22 July that his "most dear son" Frederick had introduced the Premonstratensian Rule in Adelberg. Both the emperor and his son Duke Frederick VI gave assistance to Adelberg, the latter on 25 April 1189, on the eve of his departure with his father on the Third Crusade. According to a late fifteenth-century history of Adelberg, Barbarossa and his sons Henry VI, Frederick, and Philip had been present at the church's consecration in 1188.[11] Altogether, the Staufer obtained the advocacy of thirty-nine Premonstratensian houses located throughout the Empire. In return, the German Premonstratensians, unlike the Cistercians, adhered to Frederick's anti-pope during the Alexandrine schism.[12] The Staufer and Frederick in particular, perhaps because of their familial and spiritual ties to the Cappenbergs, clearly promoted the Premonstratensians' expansion in Germany.

However, it is difficult to distinguish—if such a distinction can even be made—between measures like the assumption of the advocacy of an abbey, which served the dynasty's territorial interests, and Frederick's personal religious predilections. Only rarely does a possible personal note sound in his promotion of the canons. In 1164 Barbarossa took the Welf foundation of Weissenau, located near Ravensburg, under imperial protection and specified that the advocacy pertained only to the emperor. He did so for the benefit of his soul and for the salvation of his dearest wife Beatrice and their firstborn son Frederick V. Since the infant prince was a sickly child who died a few years later, Barbarossa may have trusted in the special efficacy of the canons' intercessory prayers.[13] Besides the hospital in Haguenau which Frederick gave the Premonstratensians before leaving for the Holy Land in 1189, he also established, according to his grandson Emperor Frederick II, a Premonstratensian hospital in Kaiserslautern. Barbarossa conferred the parochial rights in both towns, including in the upper and lower chapels of the palace in Kaiserslautern, on the hospitals.[14] Otto of Cappenberg should probably be credited for the Staufer's ongoing association with the Premonstratensians.

The Cappenberg Head

According to Godfrey's vita, Otto of Cappenberg placed the relics of St. John he had acquired from Duke Frederick into a gilded head ("in capite . . . deaurato"), the other even more extraordinary gift he had received from his imperial godson. (The inscription on the bowl refers to gifts in the plural.) There is little scholarly consensus about what the Cappenberg Head, a unicum, represents, let alone why it was made and given to Otto. The bronze head and its base are 31.4 centimeters high and weigh 4,605 grams. Otto himself described it in his 1171 bequest to Cappenberg as "a *silver* head fashioned in the likeness of the emperor" ("caput argenteum, ad Imperatoris formatum effigiem"). (Some scholars have speculated that Cappenberg had two heads, a silver one, and the gilded one that survives.) It is widely considered to be a portrait bust of Frederick, and as such it appears on the covers or dust jackets of Frederick's biographies. It is not known whether the entire bust or just the flesh parts, in contrast with the golden hair, were originally silver-plated. In the nineteenth century the whole figure was (re)gilded, and dark enamel replaced the niellated eyes that had semi-precious stones for pupils. The restored piece has been called "a gold gaping idol."[15]

The hair is tightly curled. A fillet, 1.25 centimeters wide, is set into the hair and tied in a bow at the back of the head. A silver or gold band, perhaps adorned with semi-precious jewels or laurel or oak leaves, may once have been attached to the fillet—the holes for affixing such an object survive. The model for the headdress may have been an antique cameo of Emperor Augustus, who wears a laurel wreath tied in the same fashion, which was set around 1000 into the Lothar Cross in Aachen (Fig. 4). The patron and/or artist may have been trying to replicate the iconographic representation of an ancient Roman emperor, specifically, the first Christian ruler Constantine, because curly hair was an imperial attribute. Like the head of the fragmentary statue of Constantine in Rome, the eyes in the bust, especially when seen in profile, seem to look upward to the source of the monarch's authority. The reliquary head of Pope Alexander I (107–16), which is notable for its classical features and which Wibald of Stavelot commissioned in 1145, may have inspired such a classicizing representation of the emperor (Fig. 5).[16]

Two bands, which may represent two borders of the same garment, perhaps the emperor's purple mantle, or the borders of two separate overlapping items of apparel, encircle the neck with a large bow on the upper band beneath the mustachioed and bearded mouth. The inscription on the upper band reads: "What is preserved here comes from the hair of John." The lower one requests: "Hear, St. John, those who beseech you in prayer." The inscriptions were almost certainly Otto's addition after he turned the bust into a reliquary.[17]

The prominent German medievalist Herbert Grundmann compared the figure with the descriptions of Barbarossa's features by Rahewin and by the judge of Lodi, Acerbus Morena, both of whom had seen the emperor in person. Grundmann concluded that the bust was a reasonable likeness. Rahewin offered the following description of Frederick's physiognomy:

> His hair is golden, curling a little above his forehead. His ears are scarcely covered by the hair above them, as the barber (out of respect for the empire) keeps the hair on his head and cheeks short by constantly cutting it. His eyes are sharp and piercing, his nose well formed, his beard reddish, his lips delicate and not distended by too long a mouth. His whole face is bright and cheerful. His teeth are even and snow white in color. The skin of his throat and neck (which is rather plump but not fat) is milk-white and often suffused with the ruddy glow of youth . . . (4.86).

The problem is that Rahewin's description is largely taken from Apollinaris Sidonius' depiction of the fifth-century Visigothic king Theodoric II, and to a lesser extent from Einhard's *Life of Charlemagne*. Grundmann contended that Rahewin selected those passages that matched Frederick's features. Acerbus Morena was briefer: "his fair countenance was rosy in color, his hair nearly blond and curly; his face was bright, and he always appeared as if he wished to smile; his teeth were white, his hands very beautiful, his mouth graceful . . ."[18]

Scholars today are skeptical about the bust's verisimilitude. For example, Peter Cornelius Claussen says: "The carefully curled little beard, the huge eyebrows, and the small mouth hardly appear natural, but could as exterior characteristics bear some resemblance to the emperor's actual features. But they appear to the modern viewer as ludicrously exaggerated."[19] The head was probably thus not intended to be a realistic portrait in our sense but to represent the type of an emperor—that is, Otto of Cappenberg meant that it was made in "the likeness of *an* emperor" rather than "*the* emperor" (Latin does not employ the definite or indefinite article)—but some effort may have been made to give it Frederick's own features. After all, the figure is bearded, not clean shaven. However, Frederick may have grown a beard precisely because it was an imperial attribute—Rahewin noted that the barber kept Frederick's hair and beard carefully trimmed "out of respect for the empire."[20] In short, both Rahewin and the goldsmith had their own preconceived ideas as to what an emperor looked like.

The pedestal on which the head is mounted is even more problematic. Four dragon heads serve as the feet of an eight-sided structure. (The base of Pope Alexander's reliquary head also rests on such feet.) Four alternating round and square towers stand at the junctures of the sides between the feet at the other four corners. There are three battlements on each side, twenty-four in all. Three angels stand inside the structure above each of the dragon heads and seem to hold on their bent backs, burdened with the heavens like Atlas, a second bronze ring on which the head rests. A now-lost fourth angel presumably once stood behind the neck. (The base plate of the ring actually rests on a "lantern," which is open on all four sides, at the center of the lower level.) The ring, too, was once adorned with sixteen crenulations, one above each angel and three between each pair of angels.

The octagonal lower level is often considered to be a representation of the New Jerusalem, which St. John described in Revelation 21:10–27 as a four-sided cubical city with twelve gates, an angel at each gate. While an octagon is not a square, an eight-sided structure was the common way to depict the Heavenly City: for example, the church of St. Mary's in Aachen and the imperial crown are octagons. (An inscription on the eight-sided chandelier Frederick gave St. Mary's after Charlemagne's canonization in 1165 states that it is a representation of the New Jerusalem.) The octagon was itself composed of the two squares formed by the angels and by the towers. (The imperial crown likewise has two squares: the four plaques with images and the alternating four jeweled plaques.) The placement of the angels above the dragons may be an allusion to the Archangel Michael and his angels. In Revelation 12 the angels cast out the great red dragon that threatened the woman and her child who was destined to rule all nations. The lantern may be the throne of God at the center of the Heavenly City, which is surrounded by the heavenly hosts represented by the angels.

Otto continued in smaller letters on the pedestal the inscription he had engraved on the neck bands. He wrote on the battlements of the bronze ring: "O, Seer of the Apocalypse, receive graciously this gift given to you." On the ring itself, he implored: "And, benevolent one, hasten to aid the donor Otto who beseeches you."[21] Otto's name, which alone is niellated, is placed conspicuously at the back of the bust. The omission of any verbal reference to Frederick is one of the perplexing features of the ensemble.

The head is slightly elliptical and fits, quite noticeably, only awkwardly into the ring. It has been proposed, therefore, that Otto commissioned the pedestal or at least the upper level when he converted the head into a reliquary; but two prongs that were cast at the same time as the head fit into openings in the base plate of the ring. Since no provision was made to attach the head to the octagon, it is unlikely that the ring is a later addition. The most convincing argument against the later creation of the base, the ring in particular, is that Otto did not leave adequate space on the ring for the inscription. Presumably, the goldsmith would have done so if Otto had commissioned the pedestal after he decided to convert the bust into a reliquary.[22] However, if the head and the pedestal were intended from the start to be a single piece, it is hard to explain why the two parts fit together so poorly.

The apparently presumptuous placement of a living emperor, upheld by angels, above the New Jerusalem poses considerable explanatory problems. The most widely accepted interpretation of the ensemble is that the bust and pedestal are a three-dimensional representation of the image that appears on Frederick's seals. The front of the golden bull that was prepared in conjunction with his imperial coronation in 1155 depicts him as the ruler of Rome (Fig. 6). He wears a crown with pendicles (strips of cloth with jewels attached to them), holds an orb with a cross on top in his left hand and a scepter topped with a lily, a Trinitarian symbol, in his right hand, and is surrounded by the walls of the city of Rome. The inscription reads: "Frederick by the Grace of God Emperor Augustus of the Romans." More significantly, on the obverse, the Colosseum, a symbol of the Eternal City, towers above the walls (Fig. 7). The inscription reads: "Rome, Head of the World, Holds the Reins to the Entire Globe" (ROMA · CAPVT · MVNDI · REGIT · ORBIS · FRENA · ROTVNDI). The angels elevate Frederick into the sacral sphere.[23] Caroline Horch, who has studied the bust most recently, has proposed that while the octagon is the New Jerusalem, the ring is Rome, and that the angels mediate between the earthly and heavenly spheres.[24] If she is right, I find it odd that Rome was placed above Jerusalem.

The Cappenberg Head thus depicts the emperor, the ruler of Rome, in this reading, as obtaining his authority directly from God. This view was stated explicitly, as we will see, in the announcement of his election that Frederick sent to Pope Eugenius III in 1152; in Frederick's use of imperial epitaphs prior to his coronation in Rome; and, most famously of all, in his response in 1157 to Cardinal Roland's apparent insinuation at Besançon that the emperor received the Empire in fief from the pope. The earthly and heavenly spheres, Rome and the New Jerusalem, represented in the present age by the emperor and pope respectively, are in harmony. In short, Frederick is the ruler of the fourth and last world empire, the second Constantine, who had restored the unity that had existed, according to Otto of Freising, between Constantine's conversion in 312 and the Investiture Conflict. Frederick thus delayed the coming of the Antichrist, whose totem, the dragon of the Apocalypse, lies temporarily subdued beneath him. The most likely moment for the commissioning of the bust would have been during the euphoria that followed the imperial coronation on 18 June 1155, when

Otto of Freising could declare that Frederick and Pope Adrian IV had discussed "[b]oth ecclesiastical and secular matters ... as though a single state had been created from two princely courts ..." (2.28).

Since there are understandable doubts that the illiterate emperor could have conceived of such an intellectually sophisticated object on his own, it has been proposed that learned clerics in his entourage gave the bust to their master, in an act of homage, after the coronation, and that the bewildered emperor could think only of conveying the unprecedented and perhaps even unwelcome present to his godfather. The equally perplexed Otto turned it into the only analogous object he knew, a reliquary head.[25] However, Frederick was not the only layman who commissioned a representation of himself as a memorial. In 1165/66, before leaving on the emperor's ill-fated, fourth Italian campaign, Count Sigiboto IV of Falkenstein had a sketch of himself, his wife, and their two sons placed at the front of the family archive he prepared for the use of the boys' guardian in his absence. The inscription on Sigiboto's portrait reads: "Sons, bid your father farewell and speak respectfully to your mother. Dear one who reads this, we beseech you, remember us. All may do this, but especially you, dearest son."[26] Remembrance meant, above all, prayers, an obligation especially incumbent upon a godfather.

Frederick probably entrusted the task of designing suitable gifts for his godfather to Abbot Wibald of Stavelot. In 1145 Wibald had commissioned the reliquary bust of Pope Alexander that may have served as a model for the head, initiated the chancery's use of imperial epithets for the king prior to his coronation as emperor, and drafted the announcement of Frederick's election. The emperor had also charged Wibald immediately after his election with the procurement of his royal seal and golden bull, that is, the presumptive two-dimensional model for the head, and subsequently ordered the abbot in 1156 to obtain a seal for his second wife, Beatrice of Burgundy. Moreover, Wibald had corresponded in 1148 with a goldsmith. Finally, the abbot had probably been a student, in Liège, of Abbot Rupert of Deutz, who had been the first exegete to interpret the Apocalypse in the context of redemptive history; and Wibald would have had ample opportunities to discuss with Otto of Freising the bishop's exposition of the course of salvific history. The abbot was thus in close personal contact with Frederick, was familiar with the beliefs that were given a visual representation in the Cappenberg Head, and had worked previously with a goldsmith who could turn such ideas into a physical object.

If Wibald was responsible for the design of the Cappenberg Head, then it must have been commissioned prior to the abbot's death, 19 July 1158.

While Frederick could have sent the bowl and bust to Otto at any time between June 1155 and Otto's death in 1171 or could have given them to his godfather when he paid an undocumented visit to the court, the most likely time for bestowing the presents was after Frederick's return to Germany in September 1155 from his imperial coronation. As it happens, the emperor's only known stay in Münster was at Easter, on 15 April 1156, immediately after the death of Otto's predecessor on 30 March.[27] Perhaps Frederick even persuaded the canons on this occasion to select his godfather, the co-founder of the abbey, as their new provost. Presumably, they would not have needed much prompting.

If the Cappenberg Head was really intended to show the restoration of harmonious relations between the priesthood and the kingship, then it was an especially appropriate gift for Otto of Cappenberg, who had been selected as Frederick's godfather to symbolize the reconciliation, at Worms, between the two highest earthly authorities. The hopes of both parties in 1122 had seemingly been fulfilled by Frederick's imperial coronation in 1155. While the head had not been designed to serve as a reliquary, it made sense to place the relics of St. John, which may have been exchanged for the two castles at Frederick's baptism, into the bust as a reminder of the ongoing relationship between Otto and his godson. When the provost converted the bust into a reliquary, he may have gilded the silver head, because while it would have been hubristic for an emperor to commission a gold statue of himself, it was an appropriate finish for the reliquary that housed the precious relics of the Beloved Disciple and the abbey's patron saint.

If the bust was supposed to be a reminder of Otto's duty to pray for his godson, it is odd that St. John was asked to intercede for Otto rather than Frederick. Moreover, there is no evidence that the canons ever remembered Frederick's anniversary. To resolve this conundrum, Horch proposed that it was the canons who after Otto's death added the inscription on the ring asking John to aid Otto, and who placed Otto's niellated name in a prominent place at the back of the neck. She pointed out that while the inscriptions on the neck address John in the plural, the ones on the ring appeal to him in the singular as the "Seer of the Apocalypse"; whereas Otto in his charters, will, seals, and on the neckband referred to the saint as John, the Evangelist, the Apostle, or the Beloved Disciple, but not as the writer of Revelation. In doing so, the canons obscured until the late nineteenth century the Cappenberg Head's association with Frederick.[28]

Otto of Freising ended the seventh book of the *Chronicle* with an account of the "various orders of holy men by reason of whose sanctity . . . the wickedness of the world is still endured by a most merciful judge" (7.34).

Surely, Godfrey of Cappenberg and even the reluctant convert Otto, who had renounced their earthly rank and all their worldly possessions to endow the first German Premonstratensian abbeys, were numbered among the saints who had delayed the coming of the Antichrist. They had thus prepared the way for Frederick's accession and the restoration of the harmony between papacy and empire prior to the Investiture Conflict. Until 1150, few people could have imagined that Otto of Cappenberg's troublesome godson would one day be emperor.

CHAPTER THREE

A FORTUNATE YOUTH

Childhood

THE FIFTEEN-YEAR-OLD Frederick appears for the first time in the documentary record in April 1138, when he and his father witnessed in Mainz a charter for his uncle Conrad III, who had been elected king on 7 March.[1] Frederick said nothing in the list of his accomplishments that he sent his uncle about his life prior to his own accession to the throne at twenty-nine, and Otto of Freising was reticent about filling in the gap. We can only speculate how the conflict between the Staufer and Welfs during Frederick's childhood and youth might have affected him, and what his behavior in later life may reveal about his experiences during these formative years.

Frederick grew up during the nadir of the Staufer's fortunes between the death of Henry V in 1125 and Conrad's election. After the anti-king Rudolf of Rheinfelden agreed at his election in March 1077 that his son would not have an automatic right to succeed him, the elective principle had gradually prevailed over hereditary succession in the choice of the German king.[2] Indeed, Otto asserted in regard to Frederick's election in 1152 that "this is the very apex of the law of the Roman empire, namely, that kings are chosen not by lineal descent but through election by the princes . . ." (2.1). However, royal blood remained a factor in the decision.[3] Otto may have stressed the elective nature of the German monarchy in beginning his account of Frederick's election in the *Deeds* precisely because he needed to justify the unprecedented exclusion of a king's son, his other Staufer nephew, Duke Frederick IV of Swabia, from the succession.[4]

There is no indication that Duke Frederick II formally claimed the royal crown in 1125 on the basis of his kinship with Henry V. As the late emperor's oldest nephew, however, the duke probably considered himself the most suitable candidate when the princes assembled in Mainz on 24 August. There were three other possible contenders: Duke Lothar of Saxony; Duke Frederick's stepfather, Margrave Leopold III of Austria; and Count Charles the Good of Flanders.[5] As propriety demanded, Lothar and Leopold humbly demurred. However, Frederick refused to commit himself when Archbishop Adalbert of Mainz asked whether, for the honor of the Church and the Reich and to assure in perpetuity the principle of a free election, he was prepared to do the same; an affirmative answer would have automatically excluded Duke Frederick, while a negative response would have shown his unseemly arrogance and ambition. Princely opinion quickly turned against him. Otto explained in the *Deeds* that Adalbert, whose territorial ambitions clashed with those of the Staufer along the middle Rhine, had not forgotten "the reverses he had endured at the hands of Duke Frederick" and had acted "more out of regard for his own interests than for the common weal" (1.17). The decisive moment came when Duke Henry the Black of Bavaria assented to Lothar's selection, and he was unanimously elected as emperor on 30 August. Henry probably abandoned his son-in-law, Duke Frederick, because Lothar had promised to engage his only daughter and heir, the ten-year-old Gertrude, to Frederick's brother-in-law, Henry the Proud, who was seventeen in 1125. Since Henry the Black's wife Wulfhild had inherited Lüneburg in Saxony, the marriage offered the Welfs an opportunity to expand their holdings in that duchy.[6] Frederick rejected Lothar's offer of a 200-mark money fief on 1 or 2 September, but he did pay homage to the new king.[7]

Otto declared in the *Chronicle* that Lothar "humiliated" Frederick and his brother Conrad, who were "afflicted for the sins and transgressions of their fathers" (7.17), that is, for Henry IV and Henry V's mistreatment of the Church during the Investiture Conflict. The Salian allods which Henry V had bequeathed to Frederick on his deathbed quickly became the cause of conflict. The problem was distinguishing between the Salians' dynastic properties and crown lands—just as it would be difficult today to differentiate between Elizabeth II's possessions as the hereditary head of state and as Elizabeth Windsor. In response to Lothar's formal inquiry, the princes ruled in Regensburg in November 1125 that lands that had been confiscated or exchanged for crown properties were not dynastic holdings but pertained to the royal fisc. At the Christmas court held in Strasbourg, Frederick was outlawed for seizing after Henry V's death many castles and other properties that belonged to the Reich.[8] The result was a decade-long civil war.

Both sides sought to control Speyer with its Salian tombs to legitimize their claims. In the spring of 1128, the Staufer brothers Conrad and Frederick were able to seize the city, expel the bishop and install a garrison, as, Otto said, the "inhabitants had received them with due respect because of their loyalty to the emperors who were buried there and because they were descended from the same stock." Lothar, assisted by Archbishop Adalbert, besieged Speyer from August to November 1128 but lifted the siege after many prominent inhabitants swore allegiance to him and provided hostages. After the townspeople violated their oaths, Lothar renewed the siege on 15 July 1129 and summoned his son-in-law Henry the Proud, who arrived with more than 600 knights and set up his camp on the opposite bank of the Rhine. Frederick attacked one night but was repulsed. Henry pursued his brother-in-law as far as Markgröningen, north of Stuttgart, on the road that led from Speyer, via Stauf, to Ulm, and captured rich booty and most of Frederick's horses. Frederick had sent his wife Judith to Speyer to rally the burghers during the siege. The starving population surrendered on 28 December. Lothar released Judith after showering her with gifts befitting her rank. The king then expelled the Staufer from Alsace and circa 1131 established landgraviates in Upper and Lower Alsace and in the area around Speyer.[9] We would dearly like to know whether Barbarossa, who would have celebrated his seventh birthday in December 1129, was with his mother in Speyer and witnessed his uncle's siege of his own sister—and whether that experience explains why Frederick became, in Werner Hechberger's words, the "born mediator" among his feuding kinsmen.[10]

Judith died some time after her departure from Speyer, almost certainly before her son turned ten.[11] Since she was interred at Lorch rather than at St. Walbourg, outside Haguenau, where Frederick II was subsequently buried, the family probably resided in Stauf after its expulsion from Alsace. The duke married, perhaps in 1131 or 1132, in a dramatic change in policy, Agnes of Saarbrücken, the niece of his old enemy, Archbishop Adalbert. Lothar's establishment of the landgraviates in Alsace and in the area around Speyer threatened the interests of the counts of Saarbrücken as well as the Staufer; and the creation of the landgraviate of Thüringia, also in 1131, was contrary to Mainz's territorial interests around Erfurt. Conrad III subsequently consolidated the family alliance by securing the archbishopric of Mainz after Adalbert's death in 1137 for Agnes' brother, Archbishop Adalbert II (1138–41)—and at Frederick II's urging, as Otto explicitly stated. On his deathbed in 1147, Frederick committed Agnes and "her little son," Conrad, to Barbarossa's charge.[12] Barbarossa never mentioned

Agnes in one of his charters, but, since he never referred to Judith by name either, we can draw no conclusions about his relations with his stepmother from the silence.

Conrad III had been on a pilgrimage to the Holy Land at the time of the 1125 election, and he returned home during the summer of 1127. After Lothar failed that summer to take Nuremberg from the Staufer and they repulsed Henry the Proud's invasion of Swabia, Duke Frederick and the Staufer's Frankish and Swabian adherents proclaimed Conrad king, at Rothenburg, on 18 December 1127. There is no indication that any bishop participated in the proceedings or that Conrad was crowned in Germany. At Christmas the bishops who had joined Lothar in Würzburg excommunicated the Staufer brothers. In the spring of 1128 Conrad crossed the Alps to claim the lands of Countess Matilda of Tuscany, as Henry V had done in 1116; and the archbishop of Milan crowned Conrad at Monza, outside Milan, on 29 June 1128. After losing most of his men, Conrad returned to Germany, probably in 1131; but he had replaced his older brother as the head of the lineage.[13]

The selection of Conrad rather than Frederick II for the role of anti-king is puzzling. Later sources indicated that Frederick was one-eyed, but no contemporary source mentioned this disability as disqualifying him in 1125. Unless he was blinded afterwards, this alleged handicap should be ruled out as the reason for his exclusion two years later. Other possible explanations for the choice of Conrad are that Frederick had paid homage to Lothar in Mainz, whereas the absent Conrad could not be accused of breaking his oath of fealty; the brothers were responding to the perception that Frederick had been overly ambitious in 1125; and/or that Conrad as a younger son was temperamentally more inclined to embark on such a risky adventure.[14]

The fighting in Germany turned against the Staufer in the early 1130s, and in October 1134 the barefoot Frederick appeared at the royal court in Fulda and requested that his kinswoman, Empress Richenza, intercede on his behalf with her husband. (Both Frederick and the empress were descended by different marriages from Empress Gisela, the wife of Conrad II.)[15] At her instigation the papal legate absolved the excommunicate duke. Frederick swore to serve Lothar faithfully and, with the advice and aid of the princes, to seek at the next court his restoration to the emperor's grace. At Bamberg, on 18 March 1135, Frederick prostrated himself, after some hesitation, at Lothar's feet, and with the help of the princes and at the intercession of St. Bernard of Clairvaux he was restored to favor. The duke promised to join Lothar's second Italian campaign. Conrad, too, submitted to Lothar in a similar fashion at Mühlhausen in Thüringia in September 1135. Otto's withering comment about Conrad's abandonment of his royal pretensions was that his brother had "recovered his senses." The brothers retained some of the Salian allods but did not gain their main objectives, Nuremberg and Speyer.[16]

Frederick II did not accompany Lothar to Italy, and he did not appear at the emperor's court after his submission at Bamberg. In contrast, Conrad distinguished himself in Italy as Lothar's standard-bearer. Helmold of Bosau, writing thirty years later, even declared that Conrad became Lothar's best friend.[17] On his return trip to Germany, Lothar died on 4 December 1137, after entrusting Henry the Proud with the imperial insignia in the expectation that his son-in-law, the duke of Bavaria and Saxony, would be his successor; but Henry's power and pride made him unacceptable to many of the princes and Pope Innocent II. The imperial election was scheduled to occur in Mainz on 22 May 1138, but a handful of princes and the papal legate chose Conrad instead of Henry at Koblenz on 7 March. Most of the other princes, notably the Saxons under the leadership of the Empress Dowager, Richenza, accepted Conrad as their king in Bamberg on 22 and 23 May, in spite of the irregularity of his election, because they feared the power of the absent Henry and because they had been impressed by Conrad's conduct during Lothar's Italian campaign.[18]

Conrad's displacement of his older brother as the dominant figure in the Staufer lineage may explain Barbarossa's illiteracy, because only an heir presumptive to the throne or a boy destined for an ecclesiastical career, but not a great German magnate, was taught to read Latin.[19] According to John of Salisbury, either Conrad or Frederick, all of whose sons were literate, is alleged to have told Louis VII of France that an illiterate king was a crowned ass.[20] Wibald of Stavelot assured Pope Eugenius III, however, that the newly elected Frederick Barbarossa "spoke brilliantly in the vernacular idiom of his tongue."[21] Barbarossa relied throughout his life on interpreters, and not just to translate the historical writings of his uncle Otto of Freising. In 1157 Rainald of Dassel translated or mistranslated at Besançon Adrian IV's letter for the benefit of Frederick and the other lay magnates. Patriarch Ulrich II of Aquileia rendered into German for Frederick the sermon which Pope Alexander III delivered in Latin on 25 July 1177 in St. Mark's, Venice.[22] In 1162 Castellanus, "the imperial notary of the sacred palace," had identified himself in a witness list as the "interpreter of the lord emperor."[23] Nevertheless, Frederick acquired some facility in oral Latin, and he may have become more proficient, out of necessity, during the course of his reign. Rahewin adapted Einhard's statement, that Charlemagne was fluent in Frankish and Latin but could understand Greek better than he could speak it, to Frederick's command of Latin (4.86). The family archive that Frederick's almost exact contemporary, Count Sigiboto IV of Falkenstein, commissioned may provide a hint about the extent of Barbarossa's familiarity with Latin. The most unusual and personal entries are the inscription on the family portrait, addressed to the count's young sons, and the secret letter in which Sigiboto ordered the murder of an enemy. Their tortured Latinity may well convey Sigiboto's own voice and may provide by extension an insight into Frederick's own linguistic abilities. The really noteworthy thing is that for forty years Sigiboto was the driving force behind the compilation of the archive.[24] Frederick had no formal education, but like Sigiboto he may have learned to appreciate the value of written communications and records.

Besides his uncle's *Chronicle*, the only books Frederick is known to have requested were a missal and, in a separate volume, a lectionary containing Gospel and Epistle readings which he asked Abbot Rupert of Tegernsee to copy, since he had heard that there were outstanding scribes in that Benedictine abbey.[25] There was a library in the palace at Haguenau that contained law books, historical works including probably the dedication copies of Otto's *Chronicle* and *Deeds*, treatises on the liberal arts, classical poets, Aristotle, and the ancient medical authorities, Hippocrates and Galen; but this collection may have been assembled, at least partially, by Barbarossa's son and successor Henry VI.[26] We do not know how much Frederick was personally involved in making such requests for books or in creating the library.

Otto indicated that his nephew had been "trained, as is customary, in military sports" (1.26). Rahewin added that the emperor was "a lover of warfare, but only that peace may be secured thereby" and that "his camp display[ed] the panoply of Mars rather than of Venus" (4.86). Boys often spent time at the courts of other lords to acquire such knightly skills and to become familiar with chivalric etiquette. For example, the "noblest men" of Bavaria and Swabia entrusted Frederick's great-uncle Welf V with the education of their sons; and Count Baldwin V of Hainaut sent his son Baldwin VI in 1189 to Frederick's son Henry VI, so that his heir could "learn the German language and the customs of the court."[27] Frederick completed his own knightly instruction in 1142 at his uncle Conrad's court. There he became friends with Sven, the son of King Erik Emune of Denmark. Sven was Frederick's own age and was installed by him in 1152, in a disputed succession, as King Sven III (r. 1152–57).[28] We do not know whether Frederick received his initial military training at home or elsewhere, but the most likely teachers, Emperor Lothar and Frederick's Welf uncles, were out of the question.

Frederick showed throughout his life great personal courage in combat. Otto said that in the battle that ended with the capture of Spoleto on 27 July 1155, one month into Frederick's imperial reign, "none fought more energetically than the prince, no one, not even a common knight, was quicker to take up arms, no professional soldier was more ready than he to undergo dangers" (2.35). Lest it be thought that the bishop flattered his hero, the hostile Cardinal Boso depicted Frederick, then fifty-four, in the midst of the battle of Legnano on 29 May 1176: "At the first onslaught, the standard-bearer of Frederick fell to the ground transfixed by a lance and the corpse remained under the feet of the horses. The Emperor himself, appearing in full armour among the others, easily noticeable because of his gleaming arms, was strongly assailed by the Lombards. He fell from the saddle and straightway was lost sight of."[29] He had been an apt pupil.

Closely connected to knightly combat was its leisure counterpart, hunting. Rahewin wrote about his sovereign: "If he engages in the chase, he is second to none in training, judging, and making use of horses, dogs, and falcons and other such birds. In hunting he himself strings the bow, takes the arrows, sets and shoots them. You choose what he is to hit, he hits what you have chosen." Next to the palace Frederick built, early in his reign at Kaiserslautern in the Palatinate, was "a fish pond like a lake, supporting all kinds of fish and game birds, to feast the eyes as well as the taste. It also has adjacent to it a park that affords pasture to a large herd of deer and wild goats" (4.86). When Frederick enfeoffed Arnold of Dorstadt in 1167 with the castle of Annone in northwestern Italy, he required Arnold, in memory of the grant, to give him each year "a good falcon."[30] Frederick had undoubtedly acquired his skills as a hunter and his love of the chase during his childhood and adolescence. He was a typical nobleman.

His personal piety was also conventional for a twelfth-century German noble. He had been associated since childhood with the Premonstratensians. Rahewin portrayed Frederick as a pious ruler, which is all the more noteworthy because he was becoming deeply embroiled in a fight with the papacy as Rahewin penned his words in the late 1150s. Borrowing from Apollinaris Sidonius' description of a fifth-century Visigothic king, Rahewin indicated that Frederick went daily, before dawn, either alone or with only a small entourage, to a church or to a Mass conducted by his own chaplains. A madman attacked Frederick at dawn, in fact, as he was leaving his tent outside Lodi to say his daily prayers in the presence of the saints' relics. Rahewin added, parenthetically, in a dig at the Lombards, that the emperor's devotion was a model and example, for the Italians, of the honor and respect that were due to bishops and clerics. Frederick showed such reverence for the divine office, according to Rahewin, that he was silent during every hour that Psalms were sung; and no one dared at such times to approach him with secular business. After his prayers and the Mass had ended and he had kissed the Gospels, Frederick devoted the rest of each morning to the governance of his realm. Like Charlemagne, Frederick distributed, usually with his own hands, alms to the poor and faithfully conferred a tithe of his income on churches and monasteries. Rahewin singled out Frederick's extraordinary generosity in restoring the palaces and churches at Monza and Lodi, "and in other places and cities that the entire empire will enjoy forever the munificence and memory of so great an emperor."[31] Acerbus Morena limited himself to the generic observations that Frederick feared God and distributed alms.[32]

Frederick's gifts to individual churches have left few traces in the extant sources. According to Rahewin, Frederick, before leaving in 1158 for his second campaign in Italy, spent time in Kaiserslautern putting his personal affairs in order. He "summoned religious and saintly men" and, as if they were "divine oracles," bestowed with their advice lavish gifts on various unidentified churches (3.15a). His donations of liturgical vessels and/or cash were recorded in the necrologies of the cathedrals of Bamberg, Speyer, and Geneva, and of the monastery of Weingarten. For example, Speyer, where his second wife Beatrice was buried in 1184, received £500 and Weingarten, the Welfs' dynastic monastery, a chalice and twenty-five marks. Bamberg, the recipient of a dozen donations, none of which is recorded in an extant charter, remembered Frederick as a "lover of churches."[33] A few months after his accession in 1152, Barbarossa gave a castle to Speyer to benefit the souls of his father and mother and his royal and imperial predecessors. This gift may be a hint that he always intended to be interred beside his Salian ancestors in the crypt of Speyer Cathedral.[34] In 1182 he joined the prayer fraternity of the Benedictine abbey of St. Ulrich and Afra in Augsburg. Frederick and three of his sons attended on 6 April 1187 the dedication of the new abbatial church; and the emperor and three bishops transferred the relics of St. Ulrich to their new resting place. On this occasion he gave the monks three farms. In return they were to remember him with vigils, Masses, and prayers on the three ember days before Christmas and after his demise on the anniversary of his death. The monks were also to celebrate the anniversary of his late wife.[35] The emperor indicated in charters for the Hospitalers that he had seen with his own eyes in Jerusalem, during the Second Crusade (1147–49), the works of mercy they performed for the poor, strangers, pilgrims, and the sick.[36] These words may not be simply rhetorical formulations of the chancery, because Frederick did establish hospitals in Haguenau, Kaiserslautern, Altenburg, and Reichardsroth, north of Rothenburg, on the road from the Main river to the Danube. Beatrice, too, endowed a hospital for sick women in Burgundy in 1173; and in 1176 Frederick purchased for £300 some properties that he gave to the Knights of St. John in Lombardy for the benefit of his own soul and the souls of his ancestors, wife, and sons.[37]

As his patronage of these hospitals shows, Frederick was receptive to the new religious currents of the twelfth century. Thanks to his parents, he had been associated since birth with the Premonstratensians; and he went on two crusades. Hildegard of Bingen exhorted Frederick after his election in 1152 to rule justly and not to heed evil advisers, and sent him at least three other admonitory letters, none of which can be dated precisely. In a letter to Hildegard, Frederick indicated that he had invited her to his court in Ingelheim, that the things she had predicted had come true, and that he would deal fairly with the unspecified matter she had brought to his attention. In spite of her opposition to Frederick's policies during the schism, Hildegard sought and procured from him in 1163 a charter of protection for Mount St. Rupert near Bingen.[38]

Above all, the revered Bishop Hartmann of Brixen (Bressanone) (1140–64), "a man then preeminent among the bishops of Germany for his sanctity and the austerity of his life," was Frederick's "special adviser and faithful confidant for his soul's welfare." Rahewin, who as Otto of Freising's secretary knew his master's episcopal colleague personally, singled Hartmann out among the "religious and saintly men" whose advice the emperor sought at Kaiserslautern in 1158. Frederick "reverently submitted his private affairs to the counsels of this pious prelate, thereby acting the part of a devout and most Christian prince, in order that, when about to go to war, he might fortify his soul with spiritual weapons before arming his body, preparing himself with heavenly instruction before himself giving military instruction to the soldiers setting forth to battle" (3.15a).

Hartmann's vita, written around 1200 in Brixen in the hopes of procuring his canonization, depicted his relations with Frederick in similar terms. Although Frederick was lacking, according to the author, in other ways, he was accustomed to honor clerics and monks; and he was not ashamed, as a token of his humility, to kiss the feet of priests after they said Mass. Above all, Frederick esteemed, with filial devotion, Hartmann, whom he exempted from all the payments and impositions other bishops owed and to whom he deferred in all matters. The emperor confessed his sins humbly to his spiritual father and sought his intercessory prayers.[39]

Hartmann, who as dean had introduced the strict Augustinian Rule into the cathedral chapter of Salzburg, promoted the expansion of the Augustinian canons in the Austro-Bavarian area, both before and after his election as bishop. The canons became the major opponents, in Germany, of Frederick's ecclesiastical policies during the schism; but at least two of their houses, Klosterneuburg and Seckau, remembered Frederick in their prayers. Although Hartmann refused to attend in February 1160 the Council of Pavia, where Frederick engineered the recognition of his antipope, Victor IV, Hartmann remained in contact with Frederick after his excommunication. According to his vita, Hartmann consecrated a portable altar for the emperor; and he witnessed in 1163 Frederick's charter for Hildegard of Bingen's nuns. In the spring of 1164, Frederick even charged Hartmann with settling a dispute between his Babenberg uncles, Bishop Conrad of Passau and Duke Henry Jasomirgott of Austria.[40]

Frederick was thus linked personally to two men who were at the center of the spiritual renewal of the German Church in the twelfth century: Otto of Cappenberg and Hartmann of Brixen. Frederick's attraction to the new religious orders that emphasized pastoral ministry and care of the needy, rather than to the traditional contemplative Benedictines, may have been a legacy of his childhood.

The Son of the Duke

Otto of Freising concluded in the *Deeds* his account of Frederick's feud, in 1146, with Duke Conrad of Zähringen with these words: "These and other exploits as arduous he performed even in the years of youth, to the amazement of many, so that not inappropriately it might be said of him, in the words of the Gospel [Luke 1:66]: 'What manner of child shall this be?'" (1.27). The bishop chose to be silent about the disastrous outcome of the Second Crusade, but he could not "shroud in silence the good fortune of our present Emperor Frederick which from his youth to this day has never turned on him a completely clouded face," because he and his uncle Welf VI, who had pitched their tents on a hillside, apart from the rest of the army in the valley, were alone spared from the flood that destroyed the German camp at Choirobacchoi, outside Constantinople, on 8 September 1147 (1.47). Otto also explained that the princes had elected his nephew after they had considered "the achievements and valor of the youth ('juvenis') . . ." (2.2). Finally, in November 1158, after Frederick had spoken at the court in Roncaglia in Italy, the attendees "marveled and were amazed," according to Rahewin, "that one who was not a scholar and who was little more than a youth had displayed the gift of so great wisdom and eloquence in his speech" (4.5). Frederick was then a month shy of his thirty-sixth birthday!

In an oft-cited article Georges Duby argued that youth (*juventus*) was a distinct phase in the lives of young aristocrats in twelfth-century northwestern France. *Juvenes* referred to individuals who were no longer boys or adolescents (*pueri*, *adolescentes*) undergoing military training, but who had been dubbed knights. This stage of life extended from the late teens until a man married and established his own household or even until he became a father. With few resources of their own and resentful of paternal authority, the future lord and his companions wandered about and engaged in mayhem. The repeated rebellions of the sons of the Plantagenet King Henry II of England against their father may be an extreme example, but relations between fathers and sons were often strained because the average generational span was about thirty years—thirty-two years in the case of Duke Frederick II and his son.[41]

In accordance with Duby's model, Otto stressed that Frederick Barbarossa had been knighted in his father's lifetime. "Now Frederick, the son of the most redoubtable Duke Frederick, had grown to manhood and had already buckled on the belt of military service, a man destined to be the nobler heir of a noble father. Accordingly, not concealing the virtue of his good inheritance, and trained, as is customary, in military sports, he at length girded himself for the serious business of a soldier's career *while his father was still alive and in full possession of his land* [italics added]" (1.26). However, unlike the Plantagenets, the only explicit hint of trouble in the *Deeds* in Frederick's relations with his father occurred in the winter of 1146–47, when he joined Conrad, against his father's wishes, in taking the cross and embarking on the Second Crusade; but Duke Frederick II blamed his brother rather than his son for Frederick's decision (1.41). Frederick, identified simply as the son of Duke Frederick, witnessed in his father's company ten royal charters between April 1138, when he makes his first appearance in the documentary record, and May 1145. Frederick thus dutifully accompanied his father on the latter's visits to his brother's court and acquired in this fashion the practical political knowledge and personal contacts he needed for his later role in life as a powerful prince. Frederick provided his considerably younger half-brother Conrad, whom the duke had entrusted on his deathbed to Frederick's care (1.41), with similar tutelage.[42]

After his election in 1138, Conrad III's decision to deprive Henry the Proud of the duchies of Bavaria and Saxony reignited the Staufer–Welf feud, but not in the sense of a clash between two monolithic agnatic lineages. Rather, each member of both dynasties had different territorial aspirations and, except for full brothers, different sets of kinsmen to whom they were attached. Thus, Frederick, who may have resented Conrad's preferment at his father's expense, supported his maternal uncle, Welf VI, against Conrad. The latter relied on his younger Babenberg half-brothers and on the relatives of his wife, Gertrude of Sulzbach (d. 1146), whose fortunes the king advanced.[43] As Tobias Weller has noted, Conrad III, who was far more of an authority figure than Barbarossa's own father, probably viewed Frederick as a "shifty fellow, an unreliable customer."[44]

Although Henry the Proud had surrendered the imperial insignia to Conrad, the princes outlawed him at Würzburg in mid-July 1138 and deprived him of the duchy of Saxony. Without consulting the Saxon princes, Conrad conferred Saxony on Albrecht the Bear, who, like his cousin Henry the Proud, was a grandson of Duke Magnus of Saxony and thus also had a hereditary claim to the duchy. The result was a civil war in Saxony, in which Henry gradually gained the upper hand. The two sides were negotiating when Henry died unexpectedly on 20 October 1139. Albrecht the Bear reasserted his claim to Saxony, but Empress Richenza (d. 10 June 1141) and her daughter Gertrude procured the duchy for the son of Gertrude and Henry the Proud, Henry the Lion, who was at most six in 1139.[45]

In the meantime, Conrad had also deprived Henry the Proud, at the Christmas court in Goslar in 1138, of Bavaria, and had conferred that duchy in March or April 1139 on his Babenberg half-brother Leopold IV, who had succeeded his father as margrave of Austria in 1136. Leopold's death on 18 October 1141 opened the way for a temporary resolution of the conflict. At Frankfurt in May 1142 Albrecht formally resigned his claim to Saxony and was reconciled with his Saxon opponents. During fourteen days of festivities Gertrude married Conrad's half-brother Henry Jasomirgott, who had succeeded Leopold as margrave of Austria. After Henry the Lion, heeding his mother's counsel, renounced his right to Bavaria, Conrad granted the duchy to Henry Jasomirgott, probably in January 1143. Gertrude's death in childbirth on 18 April removed the familial basis for the settlement.[46]

Otto said nothing about Frederick's actions in the early 1140s, when he was in his late teens; but he presumably fought alongside his father against the Welfs. However, according to the *Cologne Royal Chronicle*, Frederick joined Welf VI after Henry the Lion renounced his rights to Bavaria in 1142 and Welf claimed the duchy.[47] Welf invaded and devastated southwestern Bavaria in 1143 before returning to Swabia. The furious Henry Jasomirgott gathered a large army, despoiled various Bavarian churches, and even destroyed the fortifications of Otto's own see, Freising, because some of its inhabitants were, allegedly, supporters of Welf VI. The latter prepared to counterattack but retreated at the news that Conrad III was approaching. The king and his half-brother besieged the castle of Count Conrad II of Dachau, who had sided with Welf. After laying waste the surrounding countryside, they burned Dachau, northwest of Munich, in May 1143.[48]

Since Frederick's backing of Welf VI was, seemingly, so contrary to later notions of agnatic dynastic solidarity, let alone to modern conceptions of loyalty to king and country, German scholars long ascribed their hero's behavior in this incident to youthful indiscretion or his outrage at Conrad's unjust treatment of the Welfs and preference for the Babenbergs, or even denied the truth of the report in the *Cologne Royal Chronicle* altogether. However, Frederick's support of his maternal uncle becomes explicable if one realizes that he was acting neither as a Staufer nor as the future king but as a German prince who felt that the king, by enfeoffing Henry Jasomirgott with Bavaria, had violated Welf VI's inheritance rights as a collateral relative. (The right of a brother to inherit a fief was in dispute.) Beyond that, Frederick was more closely related to Welf VI than to Henry Jasomirgott, who was only the half-brother of Duke Frederick II.[49] Finally, there was often a strong emotional bond between a maternal uncle and his nephew—Charlemagne's love of Roland in *The Song of Roland* is the classic twelfth-century literary example—because a maternal uncle was likely to be considerably closer in age than a paternal uncle to his nephew and could thus serve as a role model, and a maternal uncle could not profit from his nephew's death if he became the boy's guardian.[50] Welf was only six or seven years older than Frederick, whereas Conrad III was his senior by twenty-nine years. Frederick's attachment to Welf was on display during the Second Crusade when they camped together.

There is documentary evidence that Frederick's relations with his father and Conrad III were tense in the mid-1140s. When the king charged the Premonstratensians in 1144 with the restoration of Münsterdreisen, he admonished his nephew, "Count Frederick," at his father's insistence, not to interfere with the return of the properties that Margravine Beatrice of Tuscany and her daughter Matilda had conferred on the defunct house of secular canonesses.[51]

Frederick did not witness a charter between May 1145 and 4 January 1147, when he appeared for the first time on his own during his father's final illness.[52] Since Frederick II continued to witness charters until August 1146,[53] Barbarossa appears to have absented himself from Conrad's court for a year and a half.

Otto hinted discreetly in two half-told stories, whose details must have been so well known to his readers that he could not ignore them completely, that Frederick's conduct in the mid-1140s displeased his father and especially Conrad. After Frederick had been knighted, "he denounced as his enemy," Otto related, "a certain noble named Henry of Wolfratshausen and invaded Bavaria with a large army." The Bavarian counts and nobles assembled outside Wolfratshausen, south of Munich, as if they were engaged in a tournament; and Frederick attacked them in 1146. After a long and valiant fight, the Bavarians withdrew into the castle; but the "noble count," Conrad II of Dachau, lingered outside and was captured. "The youth," taking his captive with him, returned home victorious. Many men advised Frederick to extort a large ransom, but out of his innate nobility Frederick released Conrad, who had fought valiantly. Otto added in an aside that Conrad subsequently became the duke of Croatia and Dalmatia (1.26). (He was identified for the first time in this fashion in June or July 1152, within months of Frederick's election as king, and died in Bergamo in 1158 during Frederick's second Italian campaign.)[54] Otto offered no explanation for Frederick's hatred of Henry of Wolfratshausen, and the bishop quickly shifted the focus of his account from his nephew's feud with Henry to an example of Frederick's magnanimity. The unmentioned fact in the narrative was that Count Henry II of Wolfratshausen was the first cousin of Conrad III's queen, Gertrude of Sulzbach (Henry's father was her maternal uncle); and if we are to believe a tale told in Tegernsee, Frederick's dislike of Henry continued after his accession.[55]

Otto's other story was an account of Frederick's feud with a traditional Staufer enemy, Duke Conrad of Zähringen. After his attack on Henry of Wolfratshausen, Frederick defied Conrad and in 1146 captured Zürich, where he stationed a garrison. Then, joined by unnamed Bavarian nobles—Conrad of Dachau and Otto V of Wittelsbach?—Barbarossa advanced, encountering no resistance, as far as the castle of Zähringen. Shortly thereafter, he took a castle that had hitherto been judged impregnable, in all probability the nearby castle of Freiburg im Breisgau. Conrad of Zähringen was forced to go to Duke Frederick II and Conrad III as a suppliant and to sue for peace, but Otto did not indicate how the feud was settled. For example, what concessions did Conrad of Zähringen have to make to Frederick to regain Zürich? Could the king have pressured his nephew to return Conrad of Zähringen's castles, without extracting anything in return, as part of the peacemaking preparations for the Second Crusade; that is, was Frederick really victorious?[56] I believe that the king may have arranged Frederick's marriage to Adela of Vohburg, which Otto consigned to oblivion in the *Deeds*, to seal the peace between his troublesome nephew and Conrad of Zähringen and the queen's relatives.

As late as 2 March 1147, Frederick was still called "the younger duke"; and he witnessed three more charters on his own later that month. On his father's death, he succeeded him as Duke Frederick III on 4 or 6 April.[57]

The sources are completely silent about how Frederick satisfied his sexual desires, though it is hard to believe that a robust knight remained chaste until he married. Unlike Henry I or Henry II of England, Henry the Lion, let alone Barbarossa's grandson Emperor Frederick II, there is no hard evidence that Barbarossa engaged in premarital sex or extramarital affairs or fathered a child out of wedlock. The total absence of such reports is all the more surprising because Frederick's opportunities to satisfy his urges within marriage were limited until he was well into his thirties. However, circumstantial evidence suggests that the Carthusian lay brother, Dietrich of Silve-Bénite, whom Frederick employed for more than twenty years in diplomatic negotiations with Pope Alexander III and Milan, may have been his son. The choice of a member of this austere order of cloistered monks for such a role was highly unusual, but the words of the emperor's son would have carried extra weight in secret discussions. Since Frederick sent Dietrich on his first diplomatic mission in 1167/68, he must have been born, if he was Frederick's son, at the very latest in the mid-1140s.[58]

The news of the fall of Edessa to the Muslims in December 1144 triggered the calling of the Second Crusade, which began in 1147. St. Bernard of Clairvaux arrived in imperial territory in October 1146 to win Conrad III for the undertaking and to stop the unauthorized preaching of a renegade Cistercian monk Radulf, who was stirring up violence against the Jews in the Rhineland. While delivering sermons in the diocese of Constance, basically the duchy of Swabia, Bernard won over Welf VI, perhaps at a meeting around 12 December in Constance. Since Welf's brother Conrad (d. 1126) had been a Cistercian, Bernard may have expected a favorable reception from Welf VI.[59] The news of Welf's decision probably reached Conrad III at Speyer, where he was celebrating Christmas. In a private meeting on 27 December, Bernard persuaded Conrad, who had previously undertaken a pilgrimage to the Holy Land and had been mulling over his plans for several weeks, to go as well. After a fiery sermon the next day in the cathedral, Bernard signed Conrad with the cross. Other princes and nobles, most notably Frederick, followed the king's example.[60]

As part of the preparations for the crusade, Conrad procured in Frankfurt in March 1147 the election of his ten-year-old son as King Henry (VI). He was crowned in Aachen on 30 March (even though he never actually succeeded to the throne). At this assembly Henry the Lion demanded the return of Bavaria, which had been unjustly taken, he claimed, from his father Henry the Proud; but Conrad persuaded Henry the Lion to defer his suit until the crusaders returned.[61]

Just before the army left Regensburg for the Holy Land at the end of May, Frederick was the first witness when Welf VI conferred two farms on the Benedictines of Wessobrunn, south of Augsburg.[62] The five other named witnesses of Welf's donation are a striking group: Count Ulrich IV of Lenzburg, northwest of Zürich; Count Werner of Baden, north of Zürich; Count Poppo of Giech, near Bamberg; Count Rudolf of Pfullendorf, north of Lake Constance; and Adelgoz of Schwabeck, the advocate of the see of Augsburg. Poppo died on the crusade, but Frederick made his brother, Berthold III of Andechs, margrave of Istria. The other four witnesses were after 1152 among Frederick's most loyal supporters. According to Acerbus Morena, Rudolf belonged to the inner circle of Frederick's advisers; and the Staufer inherited the domains of all four lineages.[63] Had they participated in Frederick's earlier adventures? Except for Poppo, the location of their lordships made them natural allies in Frederick's attack on Conrad of Zähringen; and they joined, presumably, the combined military retinue of Frederick and Welf VI on the Second Crusade. The companions of Frederick's youth were his lifelong friends.

Frederick's friendship with Otto V of Wittelsbach (d. 1183), the count-palatine of Bavaria, may date likewise to the 1140s. Otto of Freising characterized the count-palatine's father, Otto III, the advocate of the church of Freising, as an oppressor of the Church; and after Otto V insulted Otto of Freising while he was saying Mass, Conrad III outlawed Otto III and in June 1151 besieged the Wittelsbach castle of Kelheim on the Danube, upstream from Regensburg, forcing the Bavarian count-palatine to hand over one of his sons as a hostage. Yet, Otto V became Frederick's most trusted lay lieutenant and in 1180 the duke of Bavaria. Kinship helps to explain why Frederick, who was distantly related through his maternal grandmother Wulfhild to Otto V, was on better terms than Conrad III or Otto of Freising with the Wittelsbachs.[64]

Only the dying Duke Frederick II objected to his son's decision to set out for the Holy Land. According to Otto, the duke was furious that his brother had permitted "the first-born and only son of his most noble first wife," whom "he had made the heir of his entire land" and to whom he "had committed . . . [the] charge [of] his second wife with her little son [the future Rhenish count-palatine, Conrad]—to accept the cross." St. Bernard visited the duke, "blessed him, and prayed for him. But unable to endure the pain of his grief, he died not many days later" (1.41). The duke's wrath must have been great and well known enough to warrant inclusion in Otto's laudatory account of Frederick's deeds. Certainly, leaving on a crusade seven weeks after his accession as duke without an heir of his own was not the wisest thing to do.

Perhaps to assuage his father's anger, Frederick married.

Adela of Vohburg

Several chroniclers recorded that in the cathedral of Constance on 4 March 1153, exactly a year after Frederick's election as king, two papal legates and Bishop Hermann of Constance annulled his marriage to Adela of Vohburg.[65] No contemporary source mentioned when, where, and why they had married. Otto of Freising, who no doubt knew, was especially discreet. To explain why Frederick sent envoys to Constantinople in September 1153, the bishop wrote in his only oblique reference to Adela: "Now the king, because he had been separated from his wife by legates of the apostolic see not long before, on the ground of consanguinity, was negotiating for another marriage" (2.11). On 11 April 1154, Frederick confirmed the donation of various properties to a Cistercian monastery in the diocese of Halberstadt. He indicated in passing that his unnamed former wife (the only time she is mentioned in his charters) and her brother Berthold (identified in the charter only as Berthold) had consented to the gift of a meadow.[66] Clearly, Frederick and Adela's marriage and divorce were touchy subjects, and Otto and the chancery deemed it wise to omit her name. Since Frederick left for two years on the crusade immediately after their marriage and since he initiated divorce proceedings shortly after he became king, they had lived together as husband and wife for at most three years.

Adela was Frederick's social equal. Her paternal grandmother Liutgard was the daughter of Duke Berthold I of "Zähringen." Adela's mother Adelaide (d. 1127) was the daughter of Duke Wladyslaw I of Poland, a Piast, and Judith, the daughter of Emperor Henry III (see the Table of Consanguinity). Adela's father, Margrave Diepold III of Cham and Vohburg, had for several decades been a major player in imperial politics. He and Berengar I of Sulzbach, the father of Conrad III's queen, had been in 1104/05 the Bavarian instigators of Henry V's rebellion against his

Genealogy 4. Table of Consanguinity.
Frederick Barbarossa and Adela of Vohburg.

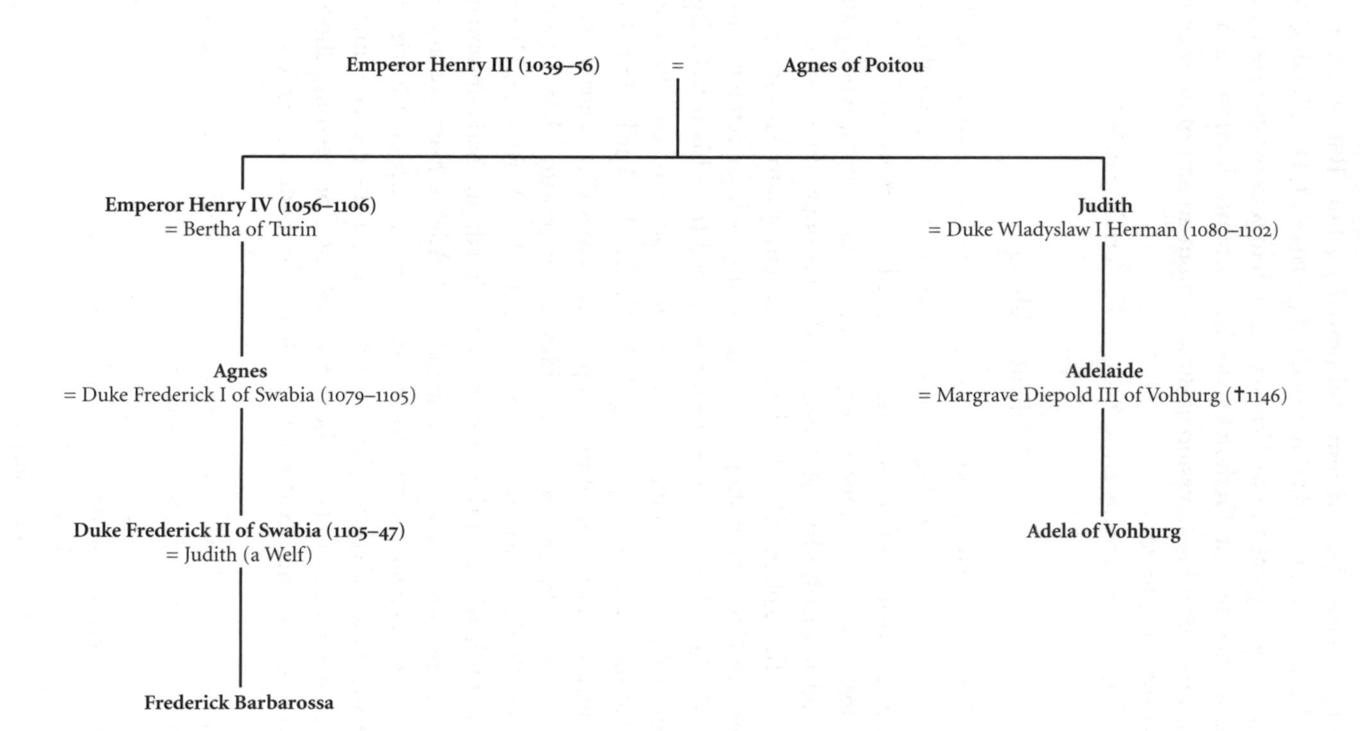

father; but Berengar was subsequently more influential than Diepold. While Berengar witnessed thirty-three of Henry V's approximately 130 extant charters, Diepold was present only fourteen times; but, significantly, on twelve of these occasions he appeared together with Berengar. Diepold initially supported the Staufer brothers after Lothar's election, but in 1128 he was reconciled with the king and married, as his second wife, a cousin of Empress Richenza. At the same time his son, Diepold IV (d. before 1136), married Frederick's Welf aunt Mathilda (who subsequently became the wife of Gebhard II of Sulzbach). Prior to his death on 8 April 1146, Diepold III had witnessed nine of Conrad III's charters. Adela was therefore a perfectly acceptable bride for a duke's son.[67]

Still, the choice of Adela as Frederick's wife was problematic. Cham and Vohburg are situated in the Bavarian Nordmark, the mark north of the Danube that bordered on Bohemia, where the Sulzbachs were the other leading magnate family. Adela's younger half-brother, Berthold II, and her nephew, Diepold V, did not succeed Diepold III as the margrave(s); Conrad III's brother-in-law, Count Gebhard II of Sulzbach, did. Some scholars have proposed that Conrad was angry that Diepold III had opposed, on account of his familial ties to the Piasts, the king's Polish policy and that Conrad had punished the Vohburgs by seizing the Nordmark as an escheated fief. Since it is inexplicable why Frederick would have become the husband of a woman who came from a disgraced and politically disempowered family, Jürgen Dendorfer has suggested, more plausibly, that Gebhard was simply serving as the guardian of Diepold's minor heirs, one of whom was his stepson. In any case, Berthold had been restored to his father's position by 1154 at the latest.[68]

Even more perplexing is the report in the fourteenth-century chronicle from the Cistercian monastery of Waldsassen that Frederick had received as Adela's dowry the Egerland (*regio Egere*), a heavily forested area around Eger, now Cheb, at the extreme western point of the Czech Republic.[69] (Waldsassen, which means forest inhabitants, is situated southwest of Cheb, on the German side of the modern border.) Since Frederick, "the younger duke," was the only important lay witness on 2 March 1147 when Conrad placed Waldsassen, founded by the late "most illustrious Margrave Diepold," under royal protection,[70] it is likely that Frederick was married by this date to Adela. The problem is that the Egerland was by 1154, at the latest, in the possession of Duke Frederick IV of Swabia, and that Barbarossa did not acquire the Egerland until after the death of Conrad's son in 1167. It is thus possible that the report in the much later Waldsassen chronicle is erroneous and that Conrad had claimed the Egerland as an escheated fief.

But that explanation raises again the questions why the king treated Diepold's heirs so harshly and why Frederick would have married Adela under these circumstances.[71] If the Egerland was, in fact, Adela's dowry, Frederick could have exchanged the area, whose acquisition allowed Conrad to continue his policy of expansion eastward from Nuremberg and Bamberg,[72] for Staufer domains closer to Frederick's own holding; or Frederick could have sold the Egerland to finance his participation, over his father's objections, in the Second Crusade. The latter alternative would explain why Duke Frederick II was so angry with his brother for abetting his son in taking the cross. In any case Frederick obtained, presumably, as part or all of Adela's dowry, Diepold's possessions around Giengen northeast of Ulm, in the Staufer's Swabian duchy.[73]

There is another angle to consider. Since Diepold III was the first cousin of Conrad of Zähringen, whom Frederick had attacked in 1146, and since Diepold was closely associated with the queen's Sulzbach relatives, with whom Frederick had been at odds,[74] Conrad III may have arranged the marriage of his troublesome nephew to Adela for two overriding reasons: to ensure that the kingdom was at peace before he left on the Second Crusade, and to establish a familial tie between Frederick and Henry (VI)'s maternal relatives. Marriage was, in fact, one of the most potent and frequently utilized weapons in Conrad's (or any ruler's) arsenal. Shortly after Conrad's accession, Barbarossa's only full sister Bertha/Judith (d. 1194/95) married Duke Matthew of Upper Lorraine (r. 1139–76). This marital connection was important not only because Lorraine bordered on the Staufer domains in Alsace but also because Matthew's father, Duke Simon I (r. 1115/16–39), was Lothar's half-brother. The Saxon emperor in 1131 had made his loyal adherent, Count Louis the Leaper, the landgrave of Thuringia. Around 1150 his son, Landgrave Louis II, became the husband of Barbarossa's younger half-sister, Jutta/Claricia (d. 1191). Both marriages bound previously hostile dynasties to the Staufer. Since Conrad had no other marriageable female relatives, he turned for marital partners to the sisters of his wife Gertrude of Sulzbach. In 1139 Conrad arranged the marriage of Liutgard of Sulzbach to the new duke of Lower Lorraine, Godfrey II. The union recognized the claims to the duchy of the house of Louvain rather than its rivals, the Limburgs. Most spectacularly of all, the queen's sister, Bertha (d. 1160), renamed Eirene in Constantinople, became in 1146 the wife of the Byzantine emperor, Manuel I Komnenos (r. 1143–80). Since the daughter of a count was not high-born enough for the *basileus*, Conrad adopted Bertha as his own daughter.[75] In the context of Conrad's marital diplomacy, the engagement or marriage of the king's nephew, just before he succeeded his father as duke of Swabia, must have involved greater political calculations than simply Conrad's acquisition of the Egerland.

The total silence in contemporary sources about Frederick and Adela's marriage suggests that Conrad's plans quickly went awry. Relations between the king and his brother-in-law, Gebhard II of Sulzbach, deteriorated rapidly after Queen Gertrude's death on 14 April 1146. Writing to his son from Jerusalem in mid-April 1148, the king approved the terms of Henry (VI)'s reconciliation with his maternal uncle Gebhard. They had agreed that the young king would retain unidentified castles, ministerials, and allods until his father's return. Conceivably, Gebhard and Henry (VI) had argued about which Sulzbach properties were part of the queen's dowry that her sons had inherited.[76] In addition, as Henry (VI)'s maternal uncle, Gebhard may have tried to assert unwanted control over his young nephew. In any case, Gebhard, identified as the margrave of Sulzbach, appeared at the royal court for the last time in Conrad's reign at the assembly the king held in Regensburg on 1 June 1149, immediately after his return from the Holy Land. Neither Gebhard, even though he was married to a sister of Frederick's mother and was thus Frederick's uncle by marriage, nor Gebhard's Wolfratshausen maternal uncle, Bishop Henry of Regensburg, was a major figure at Barbarossa's court. Frederick repudiated Adela along with Gertrude of Sulzbach's other relatives and friends.[77]

No source indicates that Adela attended Frederick's coronation in Aachen on 9 March 1152, or that she was crowned as queen. It is worth noting that while Wibald of Stavelot procured a seal for Beatrice of Burgundy, Frederick's second wife, immediately after their marriage in 1156, he did not obtain one for Adela, as far as we know, when he commissioned Barbarossa's seal in March 1152.[78] The couple may have separated even before Frederick's accession.

The official reason for the annulment was, as Otto of Freising indicated, consanguinity. Wibald of Stavelot attached the table of consanguinity, which showed how the great-grandparents of Duke Frederick I of Swabia and of Duke Berthold I of "Zähringen," Adela's great-grandfather, had been siblings, to the preliminary draft of the Treaty of Constance in his letter collection.[79] For this reason scholars assumed until recently it was this genealogical connection, a 6:5 affiliation, that was the grounds for the annulment of the marriage at Constance in 1153. Technically, this tie was within the canonically prohibited seventh degree of kinship, but Pope Eugenius III had denied an annulment in 1149 to the French king Louis VII and Eleanor of Aquitaine, who were more closely related (5:5); and no one objected to Frederick's subsequent marriage to Beatrice of Burgundy, even though they, too, were connected in the same degree as Frederick and Adela (6:5). However, Frederick and Adela's common descent from Henry III and Agnes of Poitou, the grandparents of Frederick's grandmother, Agnes, and of Adela's mother, a 4:3 tie, clearly fell within the prohibited degree. It is hard to believe that this fact was not well known when the couple married, an indication of how much importance everyone attached to the union if they chose to overlook such an obvious impediment. The fortuitous discovery of the consanguinity immediately after Frederick's accession to the throne—Wibald's table may have been additional evidence to bolster the case for an annulment—was obviously a legal pretext for obtaining a divorce that was desired for other reasons.[80]

There has been considerable speculation about what those reason(s) might have been. There is little merit in modern scholarly arguments that Adela, who descended like Frederick from the Salians, was somehow a good enough match for a duke but not for a king or that the couple were still childless in 1152—after all, they had lived together as husband and wife for at most three years and both subsequently had children with other spouses. Later chroniclers accused Adela of fornication and numerous adulteries.[81] It is possible that Otto of Freising covered up this embarrassing fact—the image of Frederick as a cuckold was hardly very flattering—and that men writing decades later were no longer under the same restraint to remain silent. Adela's subsequent marriage to a Welf ministerial, an incredible misalliance, has been adduced as evidence, if not for her wantonness, at least for her lack of a sense of social propriety.[82] How plausible is it, however, that if Adela really was an adulteress she would have remained free to remarry and that the Vohburgs would not have imprisoned her in a convent to avoid further scandals? In any case, adultery was not grounds for divorce and the innocent party was not permitted to remarry.[83] The most likely reason for the divorce was that Frederick wanted to disentangle himself from the Sulzbach connection that had been imposed upon him by his uncle and to make a more politically and territorially advantageous match after he ascended the throne. Perhaps Frederick also found Adela personally and sexually repulsive, as Philip Augustus did Ingeborg of Denmark.[84]

Still, there is something strange about Adela's fate. She was not the only noble wife who was repudiated in the mid-twelfth century, ostensibly on the grounds of consanguinity: Louis VII separated from Eleanor of Aquitaine in 1152 and Henry the Lion divorced Clemence of Zähringen in 1162. Unlike Adela, these women made perfectly acceptable second marriages: Eleanor became the queen of England as Henry II's wife and Clemence married Count Humbert III of Maurienne-Savoy (d. 1189). Moreover, in the case of a divorce a woman regained her dowry and inheritance, as Eleanor did. *The Saxon Mirror*, Eike von Repgow's codification of Saxon law around 1220, stipulated, for example: "If a woman is lawfully divorced from her husband . . . [t]he property she brought into the marriage shall be returned to her possession, or that portion of her husband's property that had been promised her when they first came together."[85] If the Egerland was really Adela's dowry, why was it not returned to her and the Vohburgs, who never quite recovered from Adela's disgrace?[86] Was there something else about Adela's marriage to and divorce from Frederick Barbarossa that we may never know?

The Second Crusade

We know far more about the French than the German forces in the Second Crusade, because Otto of Freising, an eyewitness, wanted "to write not a tragedy but a joyous history" and left the sad task to others (1.47), most notably, it turned out, Louis VII's chaplain Odo of Deuil. Consequently, we have only fragmentary information about Frederick's experiences on crusade, some of it supplied by Odo.

There were repeated clashes between the crusaders and the local population and the Greeks as the German army marched towards Constantinople. Frederick was involved in one nasty incident. Greek soldiers in August 1147 robbed and killed a sick German crusader who was recuperating in a monastery outside Adrianople. On Conrad's orders Frederick went back to the monastery and burned it, executed the perpetrators, and sought the return of the stolen money. Only the intervention of the Greek commander Prosuch prevented a further escalation of the conflict. On 8 September a German army was destroyed during a flash flood, in which only Welf VI and his nephew were spared because they had camped together on a hillside, away from the rest of the army in the valley.[87]

Conrad arrived outside Constantinople after 9 September 1147, but did not enter the city and for reasons of protocol the two monarchs—Conrad and Manuel I—did not meet. The German forces crossed the Bosporus at the end of the month and reached Nicaea (now Iznik). The bulk of the army under Conrad's command left Nicaea on 15 October and set out on a diagonal course across Anatolia in the direction of Iconium (now Konya) via Dorylaeum (now Sarhüyük), located at the edge of the Anatolian plateau and in the no man's land between the Greeks and Turks. Otto of Freising led a smaller contingent, composed largely of non-combatant pilgrims, on the much longer but supposedly safer coastal route, where they were ambushed. The king grossly underestimated how long the passage across Anatolia would take and overestimated the availability of supplies. Mounted Turkish archers, employing hit-and-run tactics, constantly harassed the army; and on 26 October, Conrad called a council of the princes. Odo of Deuil summarized their dilemma thus: "They had to advance or retreat, but hunger and the enemy and the unknown mountain labyrinth kept them from advancing; and hunger and fear of dishonor kept them from retreating. . . . Certainly they would prefer a glorious death to a base life, but if baseness stains both alternatives it is better to be saved basely by prompt action than to die basely, though without reproach." They decided to return to Nicaea. On the way back, the rearguard was annihilated and Conrad was wounded. The king sent Frederick to Louis VII to inform him of the disaster, to invite him to a meeting, and to ask for his help.[88]

The two monarchs met for the first time near Nicaea and decided to continue on together. At Esseron, on the coastal road between Nicaea and Smyrna (now Izmir), Conrad and Frederick allegedly rejected sometime after 11 November Odo's entreaty, relayed by Louis, that the Staufer return Stauf and Esslingen to St. Denis. Conrad celebrated Christmas at Ephesus (now Efes), where he became ill; he was visited by the Byzantine emperor Manuel and his wife Eirene, Conrad's adopted daughter. Louis went on alone, while Manuel and Eirene transported the sick Conrad and his entourage, including presumably Frederick, by ship to Constantinople for treatment. They remained at the imperial court until 7 March 1148, when they left on Byzantine vessels for the Holy Land. Before their departure, Manuel supplied Conrad with money to raise a new army; and they agreed to a joint attack, upon Conrad's return, on King Roger II of Sicily. Conrad along with the chancellor, the bishop of Basel, Frederick, Henry Jasomirgott, and Welf VI, arrived in Acre the week before Easter (11 April) and visited Jerusalem after Easter. It was on this occasion that Frederick was so impressed by the charitable activities of the Hospitalers. The leaders of Germany, France, and the Holy Land met at Palmarea near Acre on 24 June and decided to attack Damascus. The participants included Conrad, Otto of Freising, Frederick, Henry Jasomirgott, Welf VI, Louis VII, King Baldwin III of Jerusalem, and his mother Queen Melisende. The brief siege of Damascus lasted from 24 to 28 July. Frederick, according to Gilbert of Mons, writing five decades later, "is said to have prevailed in arms before all others in front of Damascus." On 8 September, Conrad sailed from Acre for the Byzantine Empire.[89]

Henry Jasomirgott married Manuel's niece Theodora on Conrad's return to Constantinople; their union sealed the Babenberg-Byzantine anti-Hungarian alliance.[90] Before Frederick departed for home, he and Conrad, in the so-called Treaty of Thessalonica, confirmed with an oath the agreement the king had reached with Manuel in the winter of 1148 to launch a joint attack on King Roger II of Sicily. Conrad sent Frederick "ahead to inquire into, or rather to strengthen, the condition of the empire." Traveling via Bulgaria and Hungary, Frederick arrived in Germany in April 1149; he hanged several of his ministerials who had disturbed the peace in his absence. After spending some additional time in Greece to recuperate, Conrad sailed along the Dalmatian coast and entered imperial territory in Pola (now Pula, Croatia) at the southern tip of Istria. He reached Regensburg, where from 29 May to 1 June he held a well-attended assembly. Frederick and his uncle met for the first time after the Second Crusade in Frankfurt on 21 August.[91]

Frederick learned from the debacle of the Second Crusade the need for careful preparation. While only five months elapsed between Conrad's taking of the cross in Speyer (28 December 1146) and his departure from Regensburg (end of May 1147), Frederick spent nearly a year making diplomatic and logistical arrangements before leaving in 1189 on his meticulously planned expedition, namely the Third Crusade.

Conrad III's Legacy

The Second Crusade brought to a head the problems that would confront Frederick on his accession in 1152: the return of Bavaria to Henry the Lion; the intertwined relations with Byzantium, the Normans in Sicily, the papacy, Hungary, and the Roman commune; and the imperial prerogatives of the German king prior to his coronation in Rome. For the most part, Frederick continued his uncle's policies, except that he relied on the Welfs rather than the Babenbergs and Sulzbachs. Eventually, this meant a break, too, with Manuel I, who was linked to Conrad via his marriage to the king's adopted daughter Bertha/Eirene of Sulzbach and the marriage of Manuel's niece Theodora to Henry Jasomirgott. More fundamentally, while both the western and eastern empires opposed Norman control of southern Italy and Sicily, Frederick ultimately concluded that the Normans were preferable to a re-establishment of the Greeks in Apulia. The reversal of alliances culminated in the 1186 marriage of Frederick's son, Henry VI, to Roger of Sicily's posthumous daughter, Constance.[92]

As the emperor of the Romans, the king of Germany claimed lordship over the entire Italian peninsula, while the Greek monarchs had not abandoned hope of regaining Byzantium's lost southern Italian possessions. At Thessalonica in early 1149, Manuel reminded Conrad that he had previously promised that *Italia* would be Eirene's dowry. *Italia* almost certainly did not mean the entire Italian peninsula but merely Byzantium's former southern Italian possessions that the Normans had conquered—Constantinople had lost Bari, its last foothold in Italy, in 1071. By the autumn of 1149 rumors had reached Rome that Conrad and Manuel had formed an alliance that was detrimental to the papacy, which opposed the re-establishment of a Greek presence in Italy. Wibald of Stavelot managed to assuage Pope Eugenius III's fears, it has been proposed, by devising a scheme for a dowry exchange: Eirene's dowry would be returned to the western empire as the dowry of the Byzantine princess who would marry Conrad's son, Henry (VI). However, the young king's Byzantine marriage had probably already been arranged, prior to the pope's objections, during Conrad's second stay in the Byzantine Empire; but the idea of a dowry exchange cannot be dismissed out of hand, because Conrad sought a Greek bride for himself after his son's death and because Frederick, who had been a sworn party to the Treaty of Thessalonica, also sought the same after his divorce. Conrad's illness after his return to Germany and his conflict with Welf VI prevented a German campaign against Roger, but Frederick assured Manuel in 1153 that, in accordance with his uncle's deathbed wishes of the year before, he would remain true to the alliance.[93] The whole scheme was fundamentally unrealistic because neither empire gained if it expended its resources to install the other in southern Italy in place of the Normans.

Besides their divergent territorial interests, the claim of both monarchs to be the successors of the Caesars was a source of tension. For example, in Conrad's letter of 12 February 1142 to Manuel's father, John II Komnenos (r. 1118–43), whom he addressed as the emperor at Constantinople, Conrad had defined their relations in filial terms: "As our ancestors, namely, the emperors of the Romans established friendship, honor, and glory with your predecessors, namely, the realm and the people of the Greeks, so do I establish it . . . There is no race, kingdom or people that knows not that your New Rome is called and shall always be called the daughter of the Roman republic." Conrad styled himself in this letter as "august emperor of the Romans" ("Romanorum imperator augustus"), whereas John II, who referred to himself as "born to the purple, exalted, valiant, Comnenus and emperor of the Romans," addressed Conrad only as king.[94] Since Conrad was the first German king since Otto the Great in 962 never to be crowned emperor, his use of the imperial title implied that he, like the *basileus*, derived his imperial authority independently of the pope, the position Frederick was to assert in 1157 at Besançon.

The use of a particular title for the monarch or designation for the Reich thus involved more than concerns about protocol but it also raised questions about the relationship between imperial and papal authority. Until the Investiture Conflict the East Frankish kings had usually been identified in their charters simply as king (*rex*) without any ethnic modifier. The Salian kings occasionally referred to themselves as *King of the Romans* (*Romanorum rex*), but this title became the standard designation for the German king only between 1106 and 1111, that is, in the period between Henry V's accession and imperial coronation. The title indicated that the king was the emperor-designate and was a response to Pope Gregory VII's styling of Henry IV, starting in 1074, as *rex Teutonicorum*, nomenclature that had placed the king of the Germans on the same level as the other monarchs of Europe. Both Innocent II and the anti-pope, Anacletus II, addressed Lothar as *Romanorum rex* after the double papal election of 1130, and thereafter this became standard papal usage for the German king before he was crowned in Rome. Henry IV employed the term *regnum Teutonicum*, the German kingdom, only once, in a letter to Pope Paschal II in 1105, in which he differentiated between the German and Italian kingdoms; but the terminology became official only in the Concordat of Worms, which distinguished between the monarch's right to participate in the selection and investiture of bishops in the two realms. The Latin terms *regnum* and *imperium*, like the German *Reich*, could refer to both the German kingdom and the empire, to both as territorial entities, or to the monarch's regal or imperial authority, whether in a personal or a transpersonal sense.[95]

A notary added in 1129 the imperial epithet *augustus* (majestic, august, venerable, worthy of respect) to *Romanorum rex* in the only extant charter that Conrad issued as an anti-king, but since the document was drafted by the recipient, the terminology may not reflect chancery usage. Conrad was identified as the *Romanorum rex augustus* in several charters written immediately after his accession, but Wibald of Stavelot drafted in 1144 the first charter that emanated from the royal chancery and that styled the king in this fashion. In March 1147 Wibald expanded Conrad's title further by adding *semper* (ever / always), thus *Romanorum rex et semper augustus*, in the letters in which the king informed Eugenius III of his son's election as king, his reasons for taking the cross, and Wibald's election as abbot of Corvey. The intention may have been to differentiate between Conrad and Henry (VI)'s status as kings—this had not been a problem in previous elections of a son as king in his father's lifetime, because the father was already the emperor. The expanded title was employed initially only in correspondence with the pope and Manuel I, and in charters for Italian recipients, as a way to signal the king's future imperial dignity.

Barbarossa was styled either *augustus* or *semper augustus* in 66 of the 110 charters he issued before his imperial coronation in June 1155. Thereafter, *semper augustus* was added to the imperial title, but it took several decades for this usage to become the norm, and it was subsequently (mis)translated in the German version of the title as "at all times an increaser of the realm." Neither Eugenius III nor Adrian IV used either imperial epithet in addressing Conrad or Frederick as *Romanorum rex*. While Frederick's anti-popes added these epithets to his imperial title, it became standard papal chancery practice only under Alexander III's successor, Lucius III (r. 1181–85); but the papacy continued to deny the imperial epithets to the *Romanorum rex*.[96] Titular distinctions were thus indicative of different conceptions of the nature of royal authority.

Conrad was identified for the first time as "Romanorum imperator augustus" in his letter of 12 February 1142 to John II Komnenos. The purpose of this title was to indicate that the two monarchs were, at the very least, equals. The royal chaplain Albert, who drafted the letter, had been sent previously on an embassy to Constantinople and was thus familiar with Byzantine protocol. While Conrad's chancery employed the imperial title only in its correspondence with the *basileus*, royal legates also referred to Conrad as emperor in the privileges they issued on their own.[97]

Conrad's claim to imperial rank antedated, in fact, his diplomatic negotiations with Byzantium. We customarily identify him as the third East Frankish king—the first two were Conrad I (r. 911–18), who had never been emperor, and Conrad II (r. 1024–39)—but he called himself from his accession in his charters Conrad II, that is, the second emperor. In doing this, the chancery was following the precedent set by his predecessor Lothar III, who could be the third Lothar only by counting as his predecessors Charlemagne's grandson, Lothar I (r. 840–55), and King Lothar of Italy (r. 948–50). Until Lothar III's election, notaries had distinguished between the monarch's regnal numbers as king and as emperor.[98] Thus both Lothar and Conrad, like Frederick, believed that they exercised imperial rights from the moment of their election as king of the Romans. Frederick's subsequent claims at Besançon in 1157 were thus not unprecedented.

News of the German–Greek alliance prompted Roger II of Sicily to reactivate his alliance with Welf VI and King Géza II of Hungary—who was at odds with his Babenberg neighbors in Austria—against the two empires. According to the *Historia Welforum*, both Roger and Géza, fearful of Conrad's intentions, had supplied Welf VI in the 1140s with large sums of money—Roger had allegedly given Welf an annual pension of 1,000 marks—and Welf had reciprocated with raids in Bavaria, Swabia, and along the Rhine to divert Conrad from an attack on Hungary or Sicily.[99] No source indicates what role, if any, Frederick had played in these events. On the Second Crusade, Conrad had treated Welf VI, according to both Conrad himself and the *Historia Welforum*, as his comrade-in-arms and had given him a share of the gifts the German king had received from Manuel I. Illness, real or feigned, had prevented Welf from participating in the attack on Damascus; and he had sailed for Sicily. Roger had welcomed the duke with great pomp and had persuaded him with lavish gifts to rebel against Conrad on his return to Germany.[100]

While Welf VI was passing secretly through Rome on his homeward journey in the winter of 1148–49, the senators, the grandiloquent name for Rome's communal magistrates, arrested several members of his retinue and discovered that they were carrying letters from Roger. They were addressed to Frederick, Henry the Lion, Conrad of Zähringen and his son Berthold IV, and they urged them to join Welf's revolt. The letters thus almost certainly never reached their intended recipients, but the significant point is that Roger thought, after speaking to Welf VI, that both of the duke's nephews might follow their uncle's example and rebel against Conrad. At the same time Roger was also negotiating with Pope Eugenius III about a possible truce and about supplying him with troops to suppress the Roman commune. Louis VII, who blamed Manuel for the ignominious outcome of the crusade, joined the coalition in August 1149 as he was traveling through Roger's kingdom.[101]

Instead of joining the conspiracy, Frederick played the role of mediator between his paternal and maternal uncles, namely Conrad III and Welf VI. Upon his return to Germany in 1149, Welf invaded the lands of Conrad's sons Henry and Frederick and built fortifications in their domains. When Welf attacked the Staufer castle of Flochberg, situated between Nördlingen and Bopfingen, north of the Danube in Swabia, Henry (VI) rushed there and on 8 February 1150 defeated him. There were few, if any, casualties; and the young king captured 300 of Welf's knights, though Welf himself escaped. Wibald of Stavelot urged Conrad to utilize Welf's defeat to attack his weakened opponent, but the princes, conveniently citing the prohibition against fighting in Lent and perhaps fearing an intervention by Henry the Lion, indicated their preference for a judicial resolution of the conflict. With Frederick serving as an intermediary, Welf agreed, perhaps on 24 September at a princely assembly held at Langenau, near Ulm, to forego in the future any hostile actions against Conrad. In return, the king released the duke's knights and assigned to Welf income from the royal domain along with the village or manor at Mertingen, south of Donauwörth, which controlled access to the Staufer possessions in northern Swabia. On 7 January 1152 for the first and last time Welf witnessed, along with Frederick, one of Conrad's charters.[102]

Henry the Lion's demand that the duchy of Bavaria be restored to him, which he had first voiced at Frankfurt in March 1147, remained unresolved. He began styling himself in 1150 duke of Bavaria and Saxony and ignored repeated summonses to the royal court to settle his claims in accordance with feudal law. Conrad's attempt in December 1151 to capture by surprise Brunswick, the center of Henry's Saxon holdings, while the duke was preoccupied with fighting Henry Jasomirgott in Swabia, was foiled by the Lion's sudden return.[103] Arriving at a permanent settlement with his Welf relatives, to whom he was more closely related than to his father's Austrian half-brother, was thus Frederick's most urgent task upon his accession as king in 1152; but the decision to favor the Welfs, at the expense of the Babenbergs, also had implications for imperial relations with Byzantium, Hungary, and the Normans.[104]

The Crown of the Holy Roman Empire

On 17 September 1151, at Würzburg, the princes formally swore to accompany Conrad to Rome for his imperial coronation and then to attack the Norman kingdom. The date of departure was fixed at 8 September 1152.[105] In conjunction with this decision, Conrad may have commissioned the octagonal crown of the Holy Roman Empire, which is now in the imperial treasury in Vienna (Fig. 8). The crown itself is dated most frequently as a work of the second half of the tenth century, which was made perhaps for Otto the Great's imperial coronation in 962; but in that case the arch and cross on top must be later additions by Conrad II (1024–39), because it is inscribed: CHVONRADUS DEI GRATIA ROMANORV(M) IMPERATOR AUG(VSTUS).[106] The octagon has four jeweled, inscribed enamel plaques that depict David, Solomon, Christ as the Pantocrator, flanked by cherubim, and the prophet Isaiah with King Hezekiah. However, the inscriptions on the plaques have been dated for paleographical reasons as no earlier than the second half of the eleventh century. More importantly, the biblical verses that appear on the David, Solomon, and Pantocrator plaques were first cited in royal charters only in the late eleventh and twelfth centuries. It has been proposed, therefore, that the crown was made in preparation for Conrad's imperial coronation.[107]

Two other facts should be taken into consideration. First, in the letter he sent in 1142 to the Byzantine emperor Conrad was styled "Conradus dei gratia Romanorum imperator augustus" ("Conrad by the grace of God august emperor of the Romans"), the same title that appears on the crown.[108] More significantly, the selection of the otherwise odd text from Isaiah 38:5 on the Hezekiah plaque makes the most sense if Conrad commissioned the crown (Fig. 9). The king became seriously ill during the Second Crusade, and tertian malaria hindered him, as he explained to Eugenius III, Manuel, and Eirene, from carrying out his responsibilities from the end of August 1149 until April 1150.[109] Hezekiah, likewise, was at the point of death; and he implored God to heal him with fervent prayers and bitter tears. God then sent Isaiah to Hezekiah with the words: "I have heard your prayer, I have seen your tears; behold, I will add fifteen years to your life." The inscription on the plaque reads: "ECCE ADICIA(M) SUP(ER) DIES TVOS XV ANNOS" ("Behold, I will add fifteen years to your days").[110] If the crown was made in preparation for Conrad's coronation in Rome, it was Frederick who would be the first monarch crowned with it.

CHAPTER FOUR

KING OF THE ROMANS

An Unprecedented Choice

UNLIKE THE ELECTIONS OF Lothar and Conrad in 1125 and 1138, the princes, traveling by horse and boat in winter, moved with striking rapidity to assemble and then to elect and crown Frederick Barbarossa as their new king. Conrad III died in Bamberg on 15 February 1152; the princes chose Frederick in Frankfurt on 4 March; and he was crowned king of the Romans in Aachen on 9 March. Frederick merely indicated in the list of his accomplishments that he sent to his uncle Otto of Freising for inclusion in the *Deeds* that "[a]fter we were anointed at Aachen and received the crown of the German realm, we held a general assembly at Merseburg [in Saxony] on Whitsunday [May 18]."

Otto of Freising, an eyewitness, is the chief source on his nephew's election and coronation. According to the bishop, Conrad III became ill, but continued on his journey to Bamberg to hold a court. He died there on 15 February after he had entrusted the royal insignia and his son, likewise named Frederick, to his nephew. "For, being a wise man, he cherished little hope that his son, who was still a small child, would be raised to the rank of king. Therefore he judged it more advantageous both for his family and for the state if his successor were rather to be his brother's son, by reason of the many famous proofs of his virtue." Conrad's retainers wished to inter him at Lorch, the Staufer's dynastic monastery; but the clergy of Bamberg prevailed in their desire to lay him to rest next to the tomb of their recently canonized founder, Emperor Henry II (*Deeds* 1.70 and 2.1).

Amazingly, Otto explained, "it was possible to bring together the entire company of the princes . . . in the town of Frankfurt, from the immense extent of the transalpine realm (as well as certain barons from Italy) by . . . [March 4]."

The leading princes consulted with each other and chose Duke Frederick of the Swabians, who had been "sought by all." Otto pointed out in an aside that election by the princes rather than hereditary succession was the distinctive feature of the Roman Empire. As far as we know, Frederick issued no charter in Frankfurt, so we can only infer who participated in his election. The decision had been unanimous, according to Otto, because the princes were impressed by Frederick's achievements and valor and because as the scion of the "two renowned families," who had "often disturbed the peace of the state," the electors hoped he might end the strife. In spite of Conrad's deathbed recommendation of Frederick, Otto felt compelled to add that the princes had preferred Barbarossa to Conrad's young son "not because of dislike for King Conrad, but . . . in the interest of a universal advantage . . ." (2.1–2).

After Frederick had received the princes' oaths of fealty and homage, he dismissed most of the attendees and "with a few men whom he considered suitable" embarked on 6 March from Frankfurt and sailed down the Main and Rhine as far as Sinzig, north of Koblenz. From there, they galloped to Aachen. In three days the royal party had covered by horse and ship a distance of approximately two hundred miles. The next day, the third Sunday before Easter, *Laetare Jerusalem* (Rejoice, Jerusalem—*Laetare* Sunday in mid-Lent is a joyful occasion that celebrates Israel's return from Babylon), the bishops escorted Frederick from the palace to Charlemagne's chapel, St. Mary's. With everyone's approbation, Archbishop Arnold II of Cologne, Conrad III's long-time chancellor, assisted by the other bishops, crowned Frederick and seated him "on the throne of the realm of the Franks" that Charlemagne had placed there. (It is still there.) Otto added that many people "marveled that in so short a space of time not only had so great a throng of princes and of nobles of the kingdom flocked together, but that some also had arrived from western Gaul, whither the report of this event was supposed not yet to have arrived" (2.3).

Between 9 and 14 March, Frederick issued in Aachen four extant charters. Presumably, the most influential men who attended the coronation were the witnesses. As Otto indicated, there was a large contingent from "western Gaul": the rival claimants to the duchy of Lower Lorraine, Count Godfrey III of Louvain and Count Henry II of Limburg, and his brother Gerhard; Count Henry the Blind of Namur; Bishop Henry II of Liège; Wibald of Stavelot; and Conrad of Dalhem, who hailed from northeast of Liège. The bishops who assisted Archbishop Arnold at the coronation were Archbishop-Elect Hillin of Trier, Otto of Freising, Frederick of Münster, Ortlieb of Basel, Hermann of Constance, and Eberhard II of Bamberg. The other lay magnates were Frederick's kinsmen: Welf VI, identified as

Welf of Ravensburg; Henry the Lion; Duke Matthew of Upper Lorraine, Frederick's brother-in-law; and his mother Judith's cousin, Albrecht the Bear, who was already called the margrave of Brandenburg, even though he did not gain firm control of the mark until 1157. Henry Jasomirgott was conspicuous by his absence. A striking addition to this list of attendees is the Franconian nobleman Markwart II of Grumbach, who frequently attested Barbarossa's charters and whose like-named son subsequently served as Frederick's *podestà* or governor in Milan.[1] The south German bishops and magnates were presumably the "suitable" men who had accompanied Frederick from Frankfurt to Aachen.

Otto's account is too neat. Later chroniclers reported that Conrad had tried to procure his son Frederick's election, but got the boy's name wrong, or that Duke Frederick (Barbarossa) had obtained the crown by trickery and force. Most famously, Gilbert of Mons, writing in the 1190s, related that the princes could not agree on a candidate and committed the decision to four powerful princes, one of whom was Duke Frederick. He secretly promised each of the others, whom Gilbert did not name, that he would choose them if they entrusted the election to him. Frederick then selected himself because he was of royal blood and most suited to rule. No one dared to oppose his deception because Frederick had arrived in Frankfurt with 3,000 knights. To eliminate any further resistance, he hastened to Speyer to be crowned. Most scholars have given little credence to Gilbert's flagrantly erroneous report, but such tales indicate that the selection of Conrad's nephew rather than his son puzzled later chroniclers and that Otto did not tell the whole story.[2]

The exclusion of a king's son, even a minor, was unprecedented. At the time of their elections, Otto II had been five, Otto III three, Henry III nine, Henry IV three, Conrad (III) thirteen, Henry (VI) ten, and Frederick's own son Henry VI four. Indeed, Frederick of Rothenburg was the only son of a French or German king during the Early or High Middle Ages whose claims to his father's throne were rejected in favor of another candidate. The difference was that their elections had occurred in the lifetime of their father.[3] Otto of Freising was clearly defensive about the rejection of his other Staufer nephew. That is why he stressed Conrad's recommendation of Barbarossa, the elective nature of the German monarchy, and the utility of Frederick's election.

We can only speculate why Conrad had not tried, seemingly, to secure his son Frederick's election. Perhaps the continuing conflict with Henry the Lion over the duchy of Bavaria had made such an action politically unfeasible. However, Otto insisted, in spite of Conrad's failed attack on

Brunswick and a disputed episcopal election in Utrecht, that he was ready to obtain the imperial crown, because "everything had been set in good order in Gaul and Germany" (1.67–70). Surely, arranging for his son's succession prior to his own departure for Rome would have been part of Conrad's preparations. The sticking-point may have been the problem of choosing a regent, during the king's absence and in the eventuality of his death, when the queen mother was dead. Archbishop Henry I of Mainz had served as regent and as Henry (VI)'s guardian during the Second Crusade, but Pope Eugenius III had excommunicated the archbishop in 1148 for his failure to attend the Council of Reims, and relations between the archbishop and Conrad III had deteriorated after 1150.[4] Frederick of Rothenburg's maternal uncle, Gebhard II of Sulzbach, had overreached himself after Conrad's departure in 1147 and was absent from the court after the king's return from the Holy Land. That left Frederick, the boy's closest agnatic relative, as the most likely alternative. Conrad, perhaps mindful of Henry IV's tumultuous minority and what sometimes happened to orphaned boys with powerful kinsmen who would profit from their ward's demise, may have decided on his deathbed, as Otto put it diplomatically, that it was more advantageous for both private and public reasons that his nephew succeed him (1.70). According to the *Cologne Royal Chronicle*, Conrad "urged Frederick to speak to the princes about procuring the kingdom for himself."[5]

For his part, Frederick Barbarossa insisted in 1153 in a letter to the Byzantine emperor Manuel I Komnenos, drafted by Wibald, that his uncle had formally designated him as his successor; but Frederick said nothing about his election by the princes. No doubt he needed to allay the suspicions of Empress Eirene, Conrad's sister-in-law and adopted daughter, as to why her nephew/brother had not succeeded his father.[6] However, Wibald ascribed no such role to Conrad in the proceedings in the official and private letters he wrote to Eugenius notifying the pope about Frederick's accession. Both of these letters stressed that the new king had been the unanimous choice of the princes.[7] If nothing else, the account of Frederick's elevation to the throne was tailored to the specific audience.[8]

How unanimous the princes' choice really was depends on the definition of unanimity. The formal election in Frankfurt was almost certainly unanimous because dissenters absented themselves from such proceedings. There is a later report that Archbishop Henry of Mainz, whom Pope Eugenius deposed in 1153 at Frederick's request, had tried to block Barbarossa's election;[9] and Henry Jasomirgott may not have attended the assembly because he sensed that his nephew's election would occur at his expense.

There are some clues about how the princes reached their decision. Aware of Conrad III's precarious health, presumably they discussed the succession at their periodic assemblies after Henry (VI)'s death in 1150. During the first two weeks of January 1152 a group of princes who were the major beneficiaries of Barbarossa's accession accompanied the king from Basel to Constance and then to Freiburg im Breisgau. Besides Frederick, they included his half-brother Conrad, who witnessed on this occasion his first royal charter; Welf VI in his only appearance in one of Conrad III's charters; Conrad of Zähringen, who died suddenly on 8 January, and his son Berthold IV; and the Zähringer's agnatic kinsmen, Margrave Hermann III of Baden and his son Hermann IV. Every adult Staufer, Welf, and Zähringer, except Henry the Lion, was present. The latter may subsequently have met on 1 February with Frederick and Welf VI in Memmingen.[10]

Wibald of Stavelot notified Pope Eugenius shortly after Frederick's coronation that he and Archbishop Arnold II of Cologne, who were returning from their legation to the pope to arrange Conrad's imperial coronation, had learned on 17 February in Speyer about Conrad III's death two days earlier—an indication of how quickly the news of the king's death spread. (It is 114 miles from Bamberg to Speyer.) Wibald had been invited to various gatherings to report on his embassy to the pope. The chief princes had exchanged envoys and letters and had arranged to meet in Frankfurt, seventeen days after Conrad's death. Although only a few men had been expected to attend at such short notice, a great multitude of princes and nobles had assembled.[11]

Four days after the king's death, on 19 February, Frederick himself met with Bishops Gebhard of Würzburg and Eberhard II of Bamberg, at an unidentified location along the Main, to discuss the reform and unification of the realm.[12] Sometime in the seventeen-day interval before Frederick's election the following individuals had joined him, probably in Mainz, in witnessing a charter: Archbishops Henry of Mainz and Arnold II of Cologne; Bishops Gebhard of Würzburg and Gunther of Speyer; the count-palatine of the Rhine, Hermann of Stahleck, who was the husband of Frederick's paternal aunt Gertrude; and, most significantly, Henry the Lion.[13] The terms of Frederick's accession were presumably worked out at these meetings.

The most striking thing about Frederick's election and coronation is the rapidity with which they occurred. Even Gilbert of Mons stressed, in his otherwise erroneous report, Frederick's haste to be crowned. In fact, no king was elevated to the throne so quickly after the death of his predecessor in the entire history of the East Frankish-German kingdom between 911 and 1254.[14] Barbarossa may have acceded to the cathedral canons' request that Conrad III be buried in Bamberg rather than Lorch, because he did not wish to waste time accompanying the body to a monastery situated 155 miles from Bamberg and so give his cousin's followers a chance to act. It has been proposed that Conrad, in preparation for procuring the imperial crown in Rome, had already summoned the princes to elect his son Frederick in Frankfurt, the same place where Henry (VI) had been chosen in 1147 (Frankfurt had not previously been the site of an election). Moreover, Conrad may even have arranged for his son's coronation in Aachen on *Laetere Jerusalem*, the same Sunday in the liturgical year on which he and Henry (VI) had been crowned. Such a prior summons to elect Frederick of Rothenburg would explain why so many princes and notables were able to gather at short notice in Frankfurt and Aachen. Conceivably, Frederick Barbarossa had already discussed with the Welfs and the Zähringer in the first two weeks of January and at Memmingen on 1 February the possibility of elevating him to the throne at the planned assembly in Frankfurt in place of his cousin; Conrad's knowledge of such plans would explain his deathbed recommendation of his nephew as a way to protect his young son from harm. Or the opponents of the Babenbergs and Sulzbachs took advantage of the changed circumstances after Conrad's death to secure Frederick's election.[15]

The major weakness in this hypothesis about the intended election of Frederick of Rothenburg is that, unlike the elections of Lothar, Conrad, and Henry (VI), no papal legate was present in either Frankfurt or Aachen. If Conrad had summoned the princes to Frankfurt to elect his son in preparation for his imperial coronation, it would have made sense to invite papal representation as well. A cardinal or two could easily have accompanied Wibald of Stavelot and Archbishop Arnold of Cologne on their return from their Roman embassy in February 1152. Perhaps Conrad had called the princes to Frankfurt to plan the transalpine expedition—this would explain the presence of the unidentified Italian barons—and to Aachen to deal with the disputed episcopal election in Utrecht. Whatever really happened, Frederick moved with astonishing speed and with considerable diplomatic finesse to ensure his accession. His elevation to the throne has all the earmarks of a coup d'état.

Political Theater

Otto of Freising indicated that two other events, laden with symbolism, occurred in St. Mary's on the day of the coronation at Aachen. The same bishops who had anointed Frederick as king also ordained the bishop-elect of Münster, who just happened to be named Frederick. Otto drew the obvious moral. "So it was believed that the Highest King and Priest was actually participating in the present rejoicing: and this was the sign, that in one church one day beheld the anointing of the two persons who alone are sacramentally anointed according to the ordinance of the New and of the Old Testament, and are rightly called the anointed of Christ the Lord" (2.3).

The ordination of a bishop who was also named Frederick, rich in peace, may have been a fortunate coincidence; but the second event was clearly choreographed in advance. While the crown was being placed on Frederick's head, one of his ministerials who had lost Barbarossa's favor on account of his grave offenses prostrated himself at the king's feet in the hope of regaining the sovereign's grace on so happy a day. "But Frederick maintained his previous severity and remained unmoved and thus gave to all of us," Otto said, "no small proof of his firmness, declaring that it was not from hatred but out of regard for justice that this man had been excluded from his patronage." Everyone admired "that pride could not dissuade the young man (already, as it were, in possession of an old man's judgment) from virtuous firmness to the fault of laxity." Otto concluded: "Neither the intercession of the princes, nor the favor of smiling fortune, nor the present joy of so great a festival could help that poor wretch. He departed from the inexorable prince unheard" (2.3). It is inconceivable that a man who was legally a serf and had incurred the king's displeasure would have dared, on his own volition, to disrupt the coronation in such a manner.

The episode sounds suspiciously like a series of incidents that had occurred at the coronation of Conrad II in 1024. As Conrad was approaching the cathedral of Mainz for his consecration, he was accosted by three petitioners: a tenant farmer, an orphan, and a widow. The princes urged the king to hurry on, but Conrad "responded like a vicar of Christ" that it was his duty not to delay justice. Then a man who had been wrongly exiled appealed to Conrad for help, and the king took the man by his arm to the throne and commended his case to one of the princes for resolution. Conrad's biographer Wipo added: "The zeal for mercy was more abundant in the King than the desire for consecration." In his coronation sermon Archbishop Aribo of Mainz urged Conrad to forgive everyone who had offended him, in particular a noble named Otto, because God had on that day changed Conrad "into another man" and made him "a sharer of His will." Only so could Conrad hope to obtain forgiveness for his own transgressions. Weeping, Conrad had pardoned everyone.[16] The contrast between Frederick's "severity" and Conrad's "laxity" is striking.

It is possible that such playlets were part of every coronation ceremony or that a cleric who was familiar with Wipo's text—the finger of suspicion points to Otto of Freising, who used him as a source[17]—suggested to Frederick the staging of the ministerial's appeal; but what was the message of this piece of political theater? The emphasis in the twelfth century on the king's justice rather than his mercy was a response to the desacralization of the institution of monarchy during the Investiture Conflict, and Wipo and Otto's coronation accounts are a striking illustration of the change in ideology. The crown, which may have been prepared for Conrad III's imperial coronation and which had just been placed on Frederick's head, emphasized the king's role as a minister of justice. The inscription on the David plaque, taken from Psalm 98:4 (99:4 in the King James Bible), reads: "The honor of the king loves a just judgment" ("HONOR REGIS JUDICIV(M) DILIGIT").[18] Frederick was certainly merciless in his treatment of such rebellious cities as Tortona, Spoleto, Milan, and Mainz. However, a coronation was an odd venue for the Lord's anointed—the servant of the Savior who had forgiven His enemies on the cross and who had linked divine with human forgiveness in the Lord's Prayer—to display implacable justice. Each member of the princely audience at St. Mary's may have interpreted the scene differently, but the real message may have been that Frederick intended to administer justice impartially—he would not be swayed by princely importuning. He thus differentiated himself from Lothar III, who, Otto noted, had "humiliated" and "persecuted" the Staufer brothers after his election.[19] No doubt, the Welfs felt the same way about Conrad III's treatment of Henry the Proud and Welf VI. The performance in St. Mary's was programmatic.[20]

After the coronation Frederick withdrew to the private quarters of the palace and summoned the next day the most experienced and important of the princes to consult with them about the state of the realm. They decided, according to Otto, to dispatch Archbishop-Elect Hillin of Trier and Bishop Eberhard II of Bamberg across the Alps to notify the pope, the city of Rome, and all of Italy of Frederick's accession to the throne. Wibald informed Pope Eugenius that the bishops, led by Archbishop Arnold of Cologne, had urged Frederick to undertake his uncle's planned expedition to Rome; Wibald also hinted, in exoneration of Frederick, that the king had heeded the perhaps naive arguments of the lay princes that he first address the internal problems of the Reich and that it was more seemly for him to go in response to a papal invitation than on his own initiative.[21]

The princes subsequently blocked, in June, Frederick's proposed attack on Hungary. Otto professed not to know the reason for the princes' opposition: "But being for certain obscure reasons unable to secure the assent of the princes in this matter, and thus being powerless to put his plans into effect, he postponed them until a more opportune time." The princes, in particular Welf VI, who had been an ally of the Hungarian king Géza II, may have wanted Frederick to resolve the Bavarian question first and to reconsider Conrad's anti-Hungarian, pro-Babenberg policy and not do the bidding of Otto's brother, Henry Jasomirgott, who had fought Géza unsuccessfully in the 1140s. These incidents offer a rare glimpse into the behind-the-scenes, decision-making process and Frederick's dependence upon the princes' consent.[22]

Frederick headed from Aachen to Utrecht in the modern Netherlands to punish its clergy and people for contumacy. After the death of Bishop Hartbert of Utrecht on 11 November 1150, the clergy with the consent of the nobility had elected Provost Hermann of St. Gereon's in Cologne; but some of the ministerials had forced other clerics to select Frederick, the underage son of Count Adolf of Berg. Conrad had invested Hermann with the regalia, but Frederick's backers had procured a postponement of the final decision and had expelled Hermann from the city. Conrad had tried to resolve the dispute informally, but when that failed, he had initiated formal proceedings. The Berg party had refused to appear at the king's court because, in a clear violation of the Concordat of Worms that authorized the king to decide such disputed episcopal elections, Frederick's supporters had appealed to the pope. Conflict with the Wittelsbachs in Bavaria had prevented Conrad from punishing immediately the treason of the people of Utrecht, but Conrad had obtained at Liège in July 1151 general recognition of Hermann and papal confirmation of his decision. On his arrival in Utrecht, Frederick imposed a fine upon the inhabitants for their offenses against his uncle and confirmed Hermann's selection as bishop. Frederick's action was a clear signal that he intended to enforce the crown's rights over the German Church and to punish any such infringements of royal authority. He celebrated his first Easter as king on 30 March in Cologne.[23] Between Conrad's death on the first Friday after Ash Wednesday and Easter Sunday, Barbarossa had secured the crown for himself and displayed his determination to be a strong ruler.

Notifying Eugenius III

Wibald drafted, at the bishops' insistence, in consultation with Bishop Eberhard II of Bamberg and the proto-notary Henry of Würzburg, Frederick's letter notifying Pope Eugenius of his accession and authorizing his envoys to negotiate with the pope. It was a task of some delicacy, especially if Eugenius had expected news of the election of Frederick of Rothenburg, because the election had occurred without papal participation. Much has been made of the fact that Frederick, unlike Lothar and Conrad III, did not request papal confirmation of his election; but Conrad, in another letter written by Wibald, had not asked Eugenius in 1147 to confirm the election of Henry (VI).[24] Repeating in part the words of the coronation oath, Frederick promised to protect the Roman Church and the clergy, to ensure that widows, orphans, and all peoples entrusted to his care dwelled in peace, and to restore the Roman Empire to its former excellence in accordance with the teaching of Pope Gelasius I (492–96) that "this world is chiefly ruled by two [powers], namely, the sacred authority of the priesthood and the royal power . . ." Pope Gregory VII had rejected during the Investiture Conflict the Gelasian formula, which had originally been intended to protect the Church from imperial interference, because it treated the spiritual and temporal authorities as equals; but imperial propagandists had employed it to stress the emperor's autonomy or even superiority over the pope.[25] However, Eugenius had quoted Gelasius' words in his letter of 27 January 1152 to the archbishops, bishops, counts, and barons of Germany, urging them to aid Conrad's pending Italian campaign. Since the papal exhortation survives in Wibald's letter collection and since he probably brought the letter with him on his return from Rome in February, the abbot had almost certainly borrowed the formula from the pope to express Frederick's commitment to cooperation with the papacy on the basis of equality.[26] The letter closed with Frederick's promise to honor his predecessor's agreements with the Holy See and to treat the pope's enemies as his own.[27]

Wibald sent along with the envoys his own letter to the pope, in which he described, as has already been indicated, how he had learned, in Speyer, of Conrad's death, Frederick's election and coronation, and the princes' decision not to leave immediately for Italy. Frederick, who was not quite thirty, was endowed, the abbot wrote to Eugenius, with a sharp mind, and was always ready to give advice. The new king was fortunate in war, eager for fame, an abhorrer of injustice, affable, generous, and a skilled speaker of his native German. Wibald ended the letter with the counsel that the pope "announce (*declarare*) that Frederick was the king and the defender of the Roman Church" and that Eugenius enjoin Frederick and "the princes to do all that was advantageous for the honor of the Catholic Church and the well-being of the Christian people." In short, Wibald recommended that the pope recognize Frederick's election and that the pontiff remind

Frederick and the princes of their obligations toward the Church, which they had been reluctant to fulfill in Aachen.[28]

John of Salisbury later wrote in 1160 that he had been in Rome when the imperial embassy arrived and that Frederick's "audacious scheme" to "reshape the governance of the whole globe" had caused consternation at the curia. John's unreliable memories were shaped by the outbreak of the schism in 1159, but Eugenius was probably surprised by the news of Frederick's unexpected election. Wibald's private letter was designed to allay the pontifical misgivings. The pope's reply indicates that he made his own enquiries.[29]

Upon their return from their embassy, at the assembly held in Regensburg on 29 June 1152 the envoys delivered to Frederick the papal response of 17 May. Eugenius indicated he had heard the news of Frederick's unanimous election with great joy because he had already received good reports about the king from Cardinal Octavian, the future anti-pope Victor IV; the cardinal had been in Germany from the autumn of 1151 until the spring of 1152 and had probably met Frederick during his stay. The pope assured Frederick of his favorable disposition toward him and of his willingness to crown him as emperor, reminded him of his uncle's promises to the Roman Church and the words of the coronation oath, and informed him that a legate would soon be dispatched to Germany. Eugenius did not explicitly confirm Frederick's election, but the wording anticipated Pope Innocent III's assertion in the 1202 decretal *Venerabilem*, enunciated during the disputed succession to the throne after Henry VI's death, that the pope was under no obligation to crown as emperor the candidate elected by the princes.[30] The underlying tension in imperial-papal relations was on display in Eugenius' response.

Wibald, who had drafted by himself Conrad's correspondence with the papacy, grumbled that he had been forced to consult with Bishop Eberhard of Bamberg in writing the letter to Eugenius. The abbot's displeasure was long interpreted as a sign of his diminished influence after Frederick's election,[31] but it made sense to include Eberhard in the preparation of the announcement that the bishop delivered to the pope. In reality, until his death in 1158 Wibald continued to perform numerous services for Frederick: he procured the seals of Frederick and his wife Beatrice, the king's golden bull, and possibly the Cappenberg Head; he prepared a table of consanguinity providing additional evidence that Frederick was related within the prohibited degrees to Adela; and he went on two embassies to Constantinople on Frederick's behalf.[32] In the very first charter that Frederick granted, the new king confirmed on the day of his coronation Stavelot's privileges and he acknowledged the services Wibald had performed for Conrad and in securing the crown for Frederick—admittedly the vain but insecure Wibald had written the charter himself and had been quick to submit it to Frederick.[33] If there was any decline in Wibald's influence, it was because he was the overridden proponent of a harsh policy toward the Welfs,[34] not because he advocated good relations with the papacy on the basis of the Gelasian formula. Except for his reliance on the Welfs rather than the Babenbergs and Sulzbachs, in 1152 Frederick did not abandon Conrad's overall policies or replace his uncle's clerical advisers.

The Election of Archbishop Wichmann of Magdeburg

Although Pope Eugenius indicated in his letter of 17 May 1152 to Frederick that he would soon send a legate to the king, the papal envoys did not arrive in Germany until March 1153. The pope may have delayed sending a legate to signal his displeasure at the selection of Bishop Wichmann as archbishop of Magdeburg (1152/54–92). The previous incumbent, Archbishop Frederick, had died in January 1152, and the majority of the cathedral canons had elected their provost, Gerhard. A minority had chosen the dean. According to Otto of Freising, the two parties approached the king while he was staying in Saxony. Frederick expended considerable effort in trying to reconcile them, but when that failed, he persuaded the dean and his adherents to choose the aforementioned Bishop Wichmann of Naumburg-Zeitz (1149–52/54). Otto described him as "a man still young but of noble blood." Since the powerful Margrave Conrad I of Meissen was Wichmann's maternal uncle, Frederick may have wanted to show his favor to the margrave's family, the Wettins. Frederick granted Wichmann the regalia on 18 May at the Whitsunday assembly in Merseburg, with which Frederick ended his own account of his accession.

Otto justified Wichmann's selection by invoking the Concordat of Worms: "it was granted by the Church that when bishops died, if there happened to be a division in the choice of a successor, it should be the prerogative of the prince to appoint as bishop whomsoever he might please, with the advice of his chief men; and that no bishop-elect should receive consecration before having obtained the regalia from the prince's hand through the scepter." The Concordat did allow the emperor to intervene in disputed elections in Germany and, with the advice of the candidates' metropolitan and his suffragans, to select the better candidate; but in this instance an archiepiscopal see rather than a bishopric was at stake and

Frederick was rejecting both nominees (provost and dean) and replacing them with his own choice. Perhaps to counter these weaknesses in Wichmann's case, three archbishops and eight bishops, including Eberhard of Bamberg and Otto of Freising, wrote on Wichmann's behalf to Eugenius.

The real sticking point was the transfer of a bishop, in violation of canon law, to another diocese. Provost Gerhard hurried to Rome and accused Wichmann of usurpation. Eugenius could easily have granted Wichmann a dispensation, but in an irate letter to the German bishops, dated 17 August 1152, the pope refused. He accused them of seeking the favor of an earthly ruler rather than God. A transfer could be authorized only "with proof of evident advantage and necessity" and if the clergy and people were far more united than was true in Magdeburg. The pope ordered the bishops to desist and to persuade Frederick to do the same, and to "relinquish to the church of Magdeburg—as also to the other churches of the realm entrusted to him by God—the free privilege of choosing whomsoever it wishes, in accordance with God's will, and sustain that same election thereafter by his favor, as is seemly for royal majesty." In short, Eugenius desired an abrogation of the Concordat, which had permitted episcopal elections to occur in the royal presence with the king making "suggestions."

The dispute was resolved only after Anastasius IV (1153–54) succeeded Eugenius as pope. Frederick sent Wichmann to Rome in April 1154 to receive the pallium, the symbol of his archiepiscopal authority, even though the king had heard, as Otto reported, that some individuals in Rome were unalterably opposed to Wichmann's preferment. According to a later hostile source, Anastasius, who doubted the legality of Wichmann's election, placed the pallium on the altar of St. Peter's and told Wichmann to pick it up if he considered his election valid. When he hesitated, a Magdeburg cathedral canon and an archiepiscopal vassal did so and died, in a divine judgment, while they were still in Rome. Otto concluded his account of the Wichmann affair by observing that since the archbishop's receipt of the pallium, "the authority of the prince has very greatly increased in the administration not only of secular but also of ecclesiastical affairs." Frederick himself commented in the list of his accomplishments: "Then we transferred Wichmann, bishop of Zeitz, to the archbishopric of Magdeburg; and although many disputes and controversies between us and the Roman Church resulted from this, yet finally the apostolic authority confirmed our laudable act." Eugenius' attempt to abrogate the Concordat had been foiled. Wichmann's suitability for the episcopate seems never to have been an issue, and he became one of the major churchmen of the second half of the twelfth century.[35]

While Frederick, with the backing of the German episcopate, had in securing Wichmann's election exceeded the prerogatives granted to him by the Concordat, he rarely intervened so directly in the internal affairs of the Church. The emperor ordered the clergy to hold a new election in only three other disputed cases, and most elections, unlike Wichmann's, did not occur in the royal presence. Frederick was primarily concerned about installing his candidates in the six German archiepiscopal sees, particularly in Mainz and Cologne. Altogether, royal influence can be discerned in the filling of eleven of the nineteen archiepiscopal vacancies that occurred during Barbarossa's reign. He generally allowed the cathedral canons, sometimes along with the nobles and/or the ministerials of the diocese, to select the bishops in the other thirty-eight sees in the German kingdom—the thirty-five suffragans of the six metropolitans plus the bishops of Basel, Cambrai, and Trent. Direct involvement by the crown can be detected or suspected in only eighteen of the ninety-four elections that took place in these bishoprics while Frederick was king. He relied, instead, on his right to confer the regalia prior to the bishop-elect's consecration to ensure that the canons and the lay electors would select prelates acceptable to him. As had been true in the Wichmann affair, most of the bishops backed Frederick, even in confrontations with the papacy.[36]

Henry the Lion's Vice-Regency

The princes who had elected Frederick expected to be rewarded for their support. As we have already seen, on the day of his coronation the king confirmed Stavelot's privileges. Bishop Eberhard II of Bamberg—whose insistence that Conrad be interred in his city rather than in Lorch had allowed Frederick to hasten to Frankfurt before the adherents of his paternal cousin Frederick of Rothenburg could act—also did not leave Aachen empty-handed. On 12 March, three days after his coronation, Frederick conferred the allegedly impoverished and spiritually decayed imperial abbey of Niederaltaich in the diocese of Passau on Eberhard and his church. Bamberg acquired the advocacy of the Benedictine monastery, the right to invest the abbot, and the house's ministerials, serfs, and all its other appurtenances. The yearly payments the abbey had made to the imperial fisc were to belong to the bishop, but the bishop was to assume the obligations the abbey had owed the Reich and was to be responsible for alleviating its poverty.[37] However, Frederick's chief challenge was to fulfill the expectations of his lay supporters and potential adversaries: Henry the Lion, the king's maternal uncle Welf VI, and Berthold IV of Zähringen. He assigned to each of them, at least potentially, a vice-regal position on the peripheries of the Empire.

Duke Henry exercised little power per se as duke of Saxony. The ancestors of Henry and Frederick's common grandmother Wulfhild had been dukes in Saxony rather than dukes of Saxony. Henry shared power in the duchy with other clerical and lay lords who possessed their own extensive allods and royal fiefs and recognized no intermediary between themselves and the king. Unlike the duke of Bavaria, his Saxon counterpart lacked the authority to command the lords' attendance at his court or on his campaigns and exercised no superior ducal jurisdiction over the counts. Legally, the duke's only basis of superiority was his right, in the king's name, to preserve the peace. Besides his own counties, Henry's power rested on his extensive allodial holdings, centered around Brunswick and Lüneburg and garrisoned by a large ministerialage, and, even more importantly, on his approximately fifty advocacies of churches and monasteries.[38] Henry was in almost constant conflict with his clerical and lay peers.

The trouble had started when Duke Henry or more likely his guardians seized in 1144 the county of Stade at the mouth of the Elbe river from the future Archbishop Hartwig of Bremen (1148–68), who had inherited Stade from his brother and who became Henry's implacable enemy.[39] In 1148 Henry and his advisers set out, over Hartwig's opposition, to establish under Henry's control an ecclesiastical structure north and east of the lower Elbe, a region inhabited by pagan Slavs within the metropolitan province of Bremen.[40] Frederick granted Henry in 1154 the right to found bishoprics and churches beyond the Elbe and to endow them, as he deemed fit, with property that belonged to the imperial domain. The king authorized Henry and his successors to invest the missionary bishops of Oldenburg, Mecklenburg, and Ratzeburg, a right that was specifically identified in the charter as a royal prerogative, as if the prelates were receiving the regalia from the king's own hand. Barbarossa also permitted the duke to establish additional bishoprics in neighboring, not yet Christianized, lands. After receiving this privilege, Henry re-established the vacant see of Ratzeburg and endowed it with 300 hides, that is, around 13,500 acres. In 1160 he transferred the see of Mecklenburg to Schwerin, and Oldenburg to the newly founded Baltic commercial entrepôt of Lübeck, which Henry had just forced Count Adolf II of Holstein to surrender to him. These ecclesiastical measures were part of the duke's larger endeavor in the 1160s to create a strong territorial lordship in the Slavic lands beyond the Elbe.[41] Frederick, who had enforced the crown's rights in the disputed elections in Utrecht and Magdeburg, was prepared to forego those same prerogatives in his cousin's colonial domains.

Frederick had to be more cautious in settling the rival claims of Henry the Lion and another of Frederick's supporters and kinsmen, his mother's cousin Albrecht the Bear, to the domains of Count Bernard of Plötzkau and Count Hermann II of Winzenburg, who had recently died without heirs. Frederick was unable to resolve the conflict at Merseburg in May 1152, but at Würzburg on 13 October he assigned Plötzkau to Albrecht and the more important Winzenburg lordship to Henry. In doing so, the king rewarded both men and maintained the uneasy balance of power between the Ascanian and Welf heirs of the Billung dukes of Saxony, who had died out in the male line in 1106; but Albrecht was another of Henry's determined enemies.[42]

Finally, Frederick enfeoffed Henry in 1152 with the imperial advocacy over Goslar and its lucrative silver mines. However, the palace complex in Goslar, which Barbarossa visited frequently, remained under direct royal control. The king reclaimed the advocacy in 1167/68, and Henry's demand that Frederick return it was one cause of the cousins' estrangement in the 1170s.[43]

Henry the Lion thus assumed, thanks to his cousin, a vice-regal position in Saxony; and he was actively engaged in imperial politics until 1174. Between 1152 and 1162 the duke witnessed 40 percent of Frederick's charters—and 60 percent of the German ones—more than any other prince during this time period; and he still attested 20 percent of the charters between 1162 and 1174, when he was preoccupied with establishing his lordship beyond the Elbe while Frederick was in Italy.[44] However, Henry's preeminence aroused from the start the other princes' resentment. Helmold of Bosau reported that after the duke's departure in October 1154 on Frederick's first Italian campaign, Archbishop Hartwig seized Stade and then hurried to a conspiratorial meeting in the Bohemian Forest that had been summoned by unnamed Saxon and Bavarian princes. The other likely attendees at the gathering were: Archbishop Wichmann of Magdeburg; the bishops of Halberstadt, Meissen, Merseburg, Brandenburg, and Naumburg; Albrecht the Bear and his sons; Margrave Conrad I of Meissen and his sons; Duke Vladislav II of Bohemia; and Vladislav's brother-in-law, Henry Jasomirgott. This meeting between Henry's Saxon opponents and the Babenberg party was potentially a threat to Frederick as well as his cousin.[45] Frederick backed Henry because he needed his cousin's knights for his Italian campaigns, but "at its heart, Henry the Lion's ducal power was," as Joachim Ehlers put it, "a political concession by the emperor."[46] Henry's fatal miscalculation was that he forgot that fact.

Returning Bavaria to Henry, as the duke demanded, was a political rather than a legal decision. A son, unlike a daughter or a collateral relative like a brother, had a de jure right to inherit his father's fief; but Henry's hereditary claim to Bavaria had to be balanced against the constitutional principle, which had been invoked, allegedly, against Henry the Proud, that a vassal could not hold two duchies simultaneously,[47] and against the Lion's earlier renunciation, as a minor on his mother's advice, of Bavaria. Moreover, there was no legal basis for depriving Henry Jasomirgott of the duchy, for he had served his half-brother Conrad III faithfully.

On 18 May 1152 Frederick witnessed a charter in which his cousin Henry the Lion styled himself as the duke of Bavaria and Saxony;[48] but the king's presence did not constitute official recognition of Henry's claims. The Austrian margrave attended Frederick's court for the first time in Regensburg in June. He could not be removed, thus, for failure to pay homage to the new king; and the chancery identified Henry Jasomirgott as the duke of Bavaria. Frederick, "very anxious," according to Otto, "to end without bloodshed . . . [the] dispute over the duchy of Bavaria between his own relatives," summoned the pair to appear in October in Würzburg so the strife could be settled "by judicial decree or by his counsel," that is, either by a formal judgment of the royal court or in a settlement mediated by the king. Henry Jasomirgott ignored the summons and subsequent ones, but appeared, along with his rival, at the Whitsunday court in Worms in June 1153. Both men, identified, respectively, as the dukes of Bavaria and Saxony, witnessed on this occasion several charters. The case remained unresolved because Henry Jasomirgott claimed he had not been properly summoned. The dukes' ongoing dispute made it impossible for Frederick, at an assembly held in Regensburg in September, to make peace in Bavaria. The Christmas court in Speyer was a replay of the Whitsunday assembly, with Henry Jasomirgott again asserting that he had not been called in due legal form.[49]

Frederick, pressed by his cousin's insistent demands that his paternal inheritance be restored to him, finally had enough of his uncle's nearly two years of prevarication. More importantly, as Otto indicated, the king was on the verge of departing for Italy and needed Henry the Lion's military manpower for the expedition. Barbarossa summoned both men—Otto said in writing—to appear in Goslar in June 1154. Once again, Henry Jasomirgott, no doubt fully aware what the decision would be, absented himself and the princes ruled in the Lion's favor; but he could not be formally enfeoffed with Bavaria until his Austrian rival renounced his rights.[50]

The striking aspect of these protracted proceedings is Frederick's patience in dealing with his stubborn uncle. He did not charge Henry Jasomirgott with contumacy for ignoring several summonses, though the

Austrian manipulated the system by appearing occasionally and then citing procedural irregularities. Frederick exhibited great restraint not only because the margrave was his uncle. The Babenberger had been too weak to defend Bavaria on his own against the Welfs, but he was a powerful magnate who could not be antagonized needlessly. More importantly, Frederick could not afford to be perceived by the other princes as being unfair to one of their peers, especially because the grounds for depriving Henry Jasomirgott of Bavaria were legally dubious. Finally, Jasomirgott was a man with powerful relatives. Besides his two episcopal brothers, Otto of Freising and Conrad of Passau, the margrave had two influential brothers-in-law whose help Frederick desired: Duke Vladislav II of Bohemia and Margrave William V of Montferrat, the most powerful nobleman in northern Italy. Both subsequently provided Frederick, their wives' nephew, with valuable aid during his Italian campaigns. To avoid publicly rejecting as unsatisfactory Frederick's offers of compensation for abandoning his claims to Bavaria, Henry Jasomirgott asserted, for his part, that there had been procedural irregularities in his summonses to the royal court and so preserved both his own and the king's honor. Finding an acceptable compensation for his paternal uncle's loss of Bavaria was, thus, the most important unfinished piece of business that awaited Frederick upon his return from Italy in 1155.[51]

Welf VI and the Matildine Lands

According to the *History of the Welfs*, at an unspecified date after Conrad III's death Frederick enfeoffed his maternal uncle Welf VI with the margraviate of Tuscany, the duchy of Spoleto, the principality of Sardinia, and the domains of Countess Matilda. The notaries who drafted Barbarossa's charters identified Welf VI at Frederick's coronation in March 1152 as Welf of Ravensburg (the center of his Swabian lordship); as Duke Welf on 20 April; as Lord Welf, the maternal uncle of the lord king, on 8 May; again as Duke Welf on 9 May; and, finally, in an original charter dated the end of June or the beginning of July 1152, as Welf, duke of Spoleto, margrave of Tuscany, and prince of Sardinia. Welf's enfeoffment must thus have occurred by early summer. These titles were a formal recognition of Welf's ducal rank and—what he really wanted—his exemption as a duke from the jurisdiction of the dukes of Swabia and Bavaria, where his German lands were situated. However, neither Spoleto nor Sardinia was under Frederick's actual control. In essence, he gave his uncle a blank check to make what he could of his new Italian dignities.[52]

The Matildine Lands, the "terra Matildica," have been variously described as the "apple of discord" and the "snakepit" that bedeviled imperial-papal relations in the twelfth century, and that have confounded scholars ever since.[53] In 1102 Countess Matilda of Tuscany (1046–1115) declared that she had conferred on the Roman Church at the prompting of Pope Gregory VII, probably between 1074 and 1080, all the property she had inherited or might yet acquire, both in Italy and north of the Alps. She had requested, she said, that the pope have a charter drafted to this effect; but this written record of her donation had never been made public, and she had seemingly never actually granted her domains to the pope. Fearing that her gift would be forgotten or would be called into doubt, she was repeating the conveyance of her allods to the Holy See, which was to take immediate possession of them. The lands in question were situated not in Tuscany, but in Lorraine and, more importantly, north of the Apennines in the counties of Reggio, Modena, Mantua, Cremona, Bologna, Ferrara, and Verona, that is, in large part, south of the Po river, along the Via Emilia. However, Matilda continued to alienate her domains after 1102 as if she was still in complete control of them; and she met with Emperor Henry V, after fighting him and his father (Henry IV) for decades, on 6 May 1111, as he was returning to Germany after his imperial coronation, and made a "firm compact" with him. It is unlikely that she designated her distant kinsman as her heir on this occasion, as scholars long thought; but the emperor was able without difficulty to take possession of the Matildine Lands after her death on his second expedition to Italy. Inexplicably, the papacy never presented Matilda's original 1102 charter to imperial negotiators, including Frederick's representatives in Venice in 1177, as proof of its ownership of the contested properties; and the record of her conveyance survives only in late twelfth-century copies. While, in all likelihood, she did give her lands to Rome, neither the popes nor the emperors ever really profited from her beneficence. Matilda had dispersed through pious donations many of her properties prior to her death, while the communes and local nobles had seized most of the rest.[54]

After his election as the anti-king, Conrad III went to Italy in 1128 to take possession of the Matildine Lands as part of his Salian allodial inheritance. Innocent II countered this Staufer claim by investing Lothar III in 1133, after his imperial coronation, with the allod that Countess Matilda had conferred on St. Peter. Although the allod was supposed to revert to the Roman Church on Lothar's death, Innocent allowed Henry the Proud and Lothar's daughter Gertrude to retain the domains until their demise.[55] Yet, in an 1140 donation to the Benedictines of St. Blasien in the Black Forest,

Welf VI, who had not previously been called a duke, styled himself "duke of Spoleto, margrave of Tuscany, prince of Sardinia and lord of all the domains of Countess Matilda." He continued to call himself a duke for the next twelve years, but without any territorial designation. Since Innocent II's grant of the Matildine Lands had been limited explicitly to Henry the Proud and his wife, and since Gertrude was still alive in 1140, it is hard to see how Welf could have derived any rights to the disputed domains from their enfeoffment by the pope. It has been proposed, therefore, that Matilda had named Welf V as her heir when she "married" him in 1089 and that Welf VI claimed the lands in turn as the nephew of Welf V.[56] Whatever the truth, Frederick recognized in 1152 his uncle's titular usurpations and Italian territorial aspirations.

There may have been a strategic reason for Frederick's enfeoffment of his uncle with his Italian possessions. Welf VI's paternal grandfather, Welf IV, who had left Italy in 1055 to claim his mother's south German lands, was the son of Margrave Albert Azzo II of Este. Welf IV's younger half-brothers had retained the castle of Este, which is located southwest of Padua. Este is approximately halfway between Verona, the southern terminus of the road over the Brenner Pass, which was under Welf control, and Ferrara, which was part of the Matildine complex of territories. Este is also due east of the route that connects Verona, via Mantua, to Modena on the Via Emilia, all of which were part of Matilda's inheritance. The combined Welf–Este–Matildine–Tuscan lands thus secured the road that led from Germany to Rome. For their part, the Welfs asserted, presumably with Frederick's blessing, their rights to Este. While Frederick was encamped near Verona after crossing the Alps in October 1154, Henry the Lion claimed certain properties, including Este, which belonged to the margraves of Este. The margraves paid Henry 400 marks, and he enfeoffed them with the disputed domains. Welf VI repeated the investiture in January 1160 during Barbarossa's siege of Crema.[57] If Frederick hoped that his uncle would re-establish imperial authority in northern and central Italy, he was disappointed. It was Frederick who recouped in the winter of 1158–59 the alienated revenues from the Matildine Lands and returned them to his uncle.[58]

Frederick also exempted his one-time captive, Count Conrad II of Dachau, from the jurisdiction of the duke of Bavaria by making him, like Welf VI, a titular duke. Conrad, an agnatic kinsman of the Wittelsbachs, was identified for the first time in a royal charter at the end of June or the beginning of July 1152 as the "dux Meranus." (Otto called Conrad the duke of Croatia and Dalmatia; *Meranus* referred to the coastal area along the eastern Adriatic.) No source tells what services Conrad performed for

Frederick to warrant such preferment, but there is one possible clue. Conrad was in Bamberg in February, just before Conrad III's death. The count may well have played a crucial role in Frederick's elevation to the throne.[59]

The Zähringer and Burgundy

In light of Frederick's youthful attack in 1146 on Conrad of Zähringen, the king's relations with Duke Berthold IV of Zähringen, who had succeeded his father as the rector of Burgundy in January 1152, were a trickier matter. The kingdom of Burgundy, which stretched from Basel to Marseilles, had been added to the Reich after the death of the last Welf king, Rudolf III, in 1032; but the Salians had exercised virtually no authority in their new realm. In 1127 Count William the Child of Burgundy had been murdered in his sleep. Rainald III (d. 1148), a member of a cadet line of the comital house and, it should be noted, the father of Frederick's second wife Beatrice, had gained control of the county-palatine of Burgundy, the later Franche-Comté, the area around Besançon, located between the Saône river to the west and the Jura mountains to the east. Conrad of Zähringen, who had inherited the possessions of the anti-king Rudolf of Rheinfelden in the Aare valley, east of the Jura in northwestern Switzerland, had rather dubiously claimed William the Child's lands on the basis that he was his maternal uncle. To gain Conrad's support against the Staufer, Lothar III had conferred on him in 1127 "the principality of Burgundy," a vice-regal position; but the only concrete benefit Conrad had derived from this grant was a small portion of William's lands.

Berthold, who along with Frederick had witnessed Conrad III's charters in January 1152, had not accompanied Frederick to Aachen in March for his coronation, presumably because he was preoccupied with putting the affairs of the Zähringer in order after his father's death. Berthold and the new king met before 1 June to clarify their respective, largely theoretical rights in Burgundy. Frederick agreed to join the duke in the invasion and subjugation of the lands (*terrae*) of Burgundy and Provence and promised, with the counsel of the princes who would accompany them on the campaign, to confer both on Berthold. As long as the king remained in the kingdom, the lordship and governance (*dominatio et ordinatio*) of the two lands would pertain to him. After his departure, Berthold would assume power (*potestas*) in the lands and the governance of the kingdom; but Frederick retained the right to invest the archbishops and bishops who were directly subject to the crown. However, Berthold was authorized to confer the regalia on bishops whom Count William IV of Mâcon (d. 1155), the younger brother of the deceased Rainald III, or other princes had previously invested. Count William would be compelled, with the advice or by the judgment of the princes, to account for the Burgundian Palatinate he held on behalf of his niece Beatrice. Berthold obligated himself to supply Frederick with 1,000 heavily armed knights on the Burgundian campaign, which was to commence within the year, and to bring with him on the planned royal expedition to Italy 500 knights and fifty crossbowmen. There is no indication that this oral agreement, which spelled out the terms of Berthold's Burgundian rectorship without specifically designating him as the rector and which survives only as a summary in Wibald's copybook, was ever turned into a written treaty; but it is plausible that Wibald, who had previously drafted Conrad III's charters for Burgundian recipients, was the Burgundian expert in Frederick's entourage who had worked out the details of the convention.[60]

The agreement was never implemented. Frederick and Berthold were together in Colmar in Alsace on 30 January 1153; but the duke did not accompany the king to Mulhouse on 4 February and then on 15 February to Besançon, where Frederick, without an army, met Count William of Mâcon. By 4 March the king was back in Constance, where his divorce from Adela was finalized.[61] There are two possible explanations, not mutually exclusive, for this abrupt change in policy. The princes, believing perhaps that Frederick's imperial coronation took priority over asserting royal authority in Burgundy, may have blocked the Burgundian campaign just as they had refused in June 1152 to embark on the invasion of Hungary. Second, the soon-to-be-single Frederick may have seen Beatrice as a possible bride. It is worth noting that Frederick was from at least 25 December 1152 until 10 January 1153 in Trier and Metz, with his brother-in-law, Duke Matthew of Upper Lorraine, who was also Beatrice's maternal uncle.[62] Matthew—and Frederick's sister Bertha/Judith?—may have persuaded him to consider a Burgundian marriage, and he could have met Beatrice for the first time in Besançon in February. Territorially, such a connection made sense because it is easy to travel via the Belfort Gap, which separates the Vosges from the Jura, between Frederick's domains in Alsace and Besançon. Since Beatrice was still a minor in 1153 and since Frederick pursued later that year the possibility of a Byzantine match, marriage to Beatrice was at best one possible marital alternative after Frederick's divorce, but perhaps just enough of a possibility to forego an attack on Beatrice's uncle, Count William.

There is no indication that Berthold was upset by the non-fulfillment of his agreement with Frederick. He was present at the Whitsunday court in

Worms in June 1153, when Frederick confirmed the privileges of various Burgundian magnates. Berthold was identified in these charters as the duke of Carinthia, the office his great-grandfather had held before the Investiture Conflict, as the duke of Zähringen, and even the duke of the Breisgau in southwestern Germany, where Zähringen was situated; but not, significantly, as the duke or rector of Burgundy.[63] The notaries were clearly uncertain about the territorial basis for Berthold's ducal dignity.

In the months after his accession to the throne, Frederick recognized the territorial ambitions of Henry the Lion, Welf VI, and Berthold of Zähringen, and installed them in vice-regal positions on the borders of the German kingdom. He left it to them to restore the Roman Empire to its former excellence, as he put it in his election announcement to Eugenius III, in the Slavic territories beyond the Elbe, in northern and central Italy, and in Burgundy. Only Henry took advantage of the opportunity. It is impossible to tell whether their advancement was a consciously devised policy by a medieval geo-politician or simply the reward for their support in the weeks after Conrad III's death.

Three years later, on 13 January 1155, while staying near Turin on his first Italian expedition, Frederick issued a charter for a Burgundian magnate, Count Guigues V of Grenoble. Except for Welf VI, who did not accompany Frederick to Italy, most of the witnesses were the men instrumental in procuring the throne for him. The following individuals had also attended the king's coronation: Henry the Lion, Wibald, Archbishop Hillin of Trier, and Bishops Eberhard of Bamberg, Hermann of Constance, and Ortlieb of Basel. The only episcopal witness who had not been in Aachen was Patriarch Pilgrim I of Aquileia in northeastern Italy. The other witnesses were: Berthold IV of Zähringen and his kinsman, Margrave Hermann III of Baden, who had met with Frederick in January 1152; Frederick's uncle by marriage, William V of Montferrat; the king's first cousins, Duke Boleslaw of Poland-Silesia and Margrave Ottokar III of Styria; and Count Ulrich IV of Lenzburg, who had accompanied Frederick on the Second Crusade.[64] Frederick owed his crown to a group of men who had decided, for whatever reasons, that he was preferable to his cousin Frederick of Rothenburg.

Duke Frederick IV of Swabia

However, Frederick could not ignore completely the rights of his young Staufer cousin and the son of Conrad III, namely Duke Frederick IV of Swabia. Otto of Freising merely said that on his deathbed Conrad had entrusted his young son to the care of his nephew. But Burchard of Ursberg, writing around 1230, added that the dying monarch had stipulated that his son was to obtain the duchy of Swabia when he attained his majority. It is impossible to tell whether Conrad really issued such a directive or whether this was simply Burchard's retrospective explanation of what had in fact occurred. (Burchard reported, wrongly, in the same passage that Conrad was buried in Lorch.)[65]

Although children did not normally witness charters, Frederick of Rothenburg, the duke of Swabia and Alsace, attested two of his cousin's decisions at the royal court held in Worms in June 1153. Frederick of Rothenburg was called in one charter, drafted by Wibald—who had elevated his deceased lord to imperial rank in his correspondence with Emperor Manuel I Komnenos—the son of Emperor Conrad, and in the other, as he was elsewhere, the son of King Conrad. Even more unusually in a hierarchical society, where placement in a witness list was often determined by legal status, rank, time in office, and age, Frederick of Rothenburg, presumably in recognition of his royal blood, was listed ahead of his older fellow dukes: Henry Jasomirgott, Henry the Lion, and Berthold IV. When Barbarossa ruled in 1154 that the advocates of Lorch were to be chosen from both branches of the Staufer dynasty, the descendants of King Conrad and Duke Frederick II, the first two witnesses were Frederick (of Rothenburg), the son of King Conrad, and young Conrad, who was identified as the king's brother. Seemingly, being the son of a king took precedence over a fraternal bond. However, in a charter of 17 January 1154, Duke Frederick of Swabia was listed after Duke Welf of Spoleto and Duke Matthew of Upper Lorraine.[66]

As the similar case of Berthold IV indicates, the scribes who drafted royal charters, not all of whom even worked in the chancery, had considerable leeway in how they styled individuals and ordered them. The following example illustrates how inexplicable the listings can be. On 4 July 1157 Frederick returned to his Babenberg uncle, Conrad of Passau, a property in Swabia which the bishop had exchanged with Conrad III for properties in the diocese of Passau. The ducal witnesses appeared in the following order: Duke Vladislav of Bohemia and his brother Theobald, Duke Henry of Austria, and Duke Frederick, the son of King Conrad (without any territorial or ethnic identifier). The next day the same scribe recorded, in a charter that also survives as an original, that the emperor had taken under his protection the Augustinian collegiate church of Neustift, located outside Brixen in the Tyrol, in the presence of Duke Frederick of the Swabians, the son of King Conrad; Duke Henry of Austria; Duke Welf of Spoleto; Duke

Ladislas of Poland; and Duke Vladislav of Bohemia.[67] It is impossible to ascertain from such divergent listings a particular man's standing at court or why he witnessed one charter and not another.

However, several titular designations do give pause for thought about the status of Conrad III's son. The same notary who drafted the charters of 4 and 5 July had on 16 March placed Frederick of Rothenburg, identified simply as the son of King Conrad, among the counts. An 1156 charter of Bishop Burchard I of Strasbourg was dated as occurring during the reign of "King Frederick, the duke of Alsace." (In 1156 Frederick should have been called emperor.) Barbarossa styled himself on 2 February 1157 emperor and duke of the Swabians. (Unfortunately, this charter survives only in two nineteenth-century copies of an 1192 transumpt of Frederick's charter.) Finally, in October 1156 the emperor confirmed that his cousin, "Duke Frederick of Stauf," had renounced his rights to half the children of a cross-marriage between Staufer and Würzburg ministerials. (One of the marks of the ministerials' servile status was that their children were divided between the respective lords of their parents.)[68]

We can conclude, with due caution, from this evidence that shortly after his accession in March 1152 Barbarossa formally assigned Alsace and Swabia to Frederick of Rothenburg but retained actual control of the duchies as his cousin's guardian. The king soon regained direct possession of Alsace; at least Conrad's son was not called the duke of Alsace after June 1153. Barbarossa may have employed in 1157, as Frederick of Rothenburg's guardian, the title duke of the Swabians, just as Count Gebhard II of Sulzbach may have adopted the title of margrave as the guardian of Adela of Vohburg's nephew and half-brother. The emperor may have hoped, eventually, to reduce his cousin to the status of a titular duke comparable to the Zähringer—hence the designation of Conrad's son as Duke Frederick of Stauf—and to regain Swabia, permanently, for himself. The frequent public appearances of a minor at court and, unusually, in the witness lists of charters, may have been designed to allay suspicions about the fate of a king's son who had been bypassed for the crown.

According to Rahewin, Frederick of Rothenburg was girded with a sword and knighted at the insistence and in the presence of Byzantine envoys, that is, publicly declared of age, at the assembly held in Würzburg in September 1157. Empress Eirene, the boy's maternal aunt and Conrad III's adopted daughter, who had sent "many magnificent gifts" to her nephew/brother, had charged the ambassadors not to return until this had taken place. Her husband Emperor Manuel, "on account of the good will and friendship of long standing he had enjoyed with King Conrad," had "heartily supported her." The empress and her brother, Count Gebhard II of Sulzbach, may thus have blocked any attempt by Frederick to prolong his cousin's minority or to deprive him of Swabia. This counterstroke to his plans left Barbarossa with no other alternative than to try to establish his own territorial lordship in Lombardy. It is worth noting that when Frederick confirmed in 1156 his ward's agreement with Würzburg, he did not call him "dilectus" ("beloved"), as he often did kinsmen on such occasions. Relations between the cousins remained ambiguous, at times strained, in the following years.[69]

The Peace Ordinance (*Landfriede*) of 1152

Otto of Freising hailed Frederick, the scion of two warring lineages, as the bringer of unprecedented peace to the Empire. At the end of June or the beginning of August 1152, in preparation for his journey to Rome to be crowned emperor, Frederick issued in Ulm at his first Swabian court as king a *Landfriede*, or peace ordinance, addressed to all the "bishops, dukes, counts, margraves, [and] rectors" in the German kingdom. He was proclaiming, by his royal authority, the long-sought peace so that both divine and human laws would remain in force, that churches and clerics would be protected from all attacks, and that every person's rights would be preserved. The clauses of the ordinance offer an insight into the administration of justice, the governance of the realm, and economic and social conditions in Germany at the beginning of Frederick's reign.

The murder of anyone during a period of peace was, according to the *Landfriede*, a capital offense unless the perpetrator could prove in a trial by combat that he had acted out of self-defense; but the accused was not permitted to prove his innocence by these means if it was clear to everyone that he had acted out of his own volition (article 1). If the culprit fled, his heirs could inherit his allods if they swore never to aid him (2). Other provisions dealt with persons who injured or beat another man, with theft, and with the conduct of the hue and cry (3, 4, 5, 7, and 18). If a cleric violated the peace or harbored a criminal and was convicted of these offenses at the episcopal court, he was to pay £10 to the count in whose jurisdiction the crime had occurred, in addition to any canonical sentence the bishop imposed. If the cleric remained disobedient, he was to be deprived of his benefice and treated as an outlaw (6). Several provisions dealt with the resolution of disputes about the ownership of fiefs (8, 9, and 17).

If a peasant accused a knight of violating the peace, the knight was required to swear that he had acted out of necessity and to have four knights as witnesses to the oath. In the reverse instance, the peasant, too, was to swear that he had acted out of necessity; but he had the choice of proving his innocence through a divine or human tribunal, that is, an ordeal or an earthly court, or, in a third alternative, to clear himself through the testimony of seven suitable witnesses chosen by the judge. If a knight accused another knight of violating the peace or of another capital offense, the defendant could clear himself through combat, but only if he could prove that he and his kinsmen were of knightly ancestry (10).

As the last stipulation indicates, Frederick and the members of the court who compiled the *Landfriede* were concerned with delineating the boundary between knights and peasants. This was a matter of considerable concern because the ministerials, who were rising to increasing prominence in German society—Wibald, for example, was a ministerial—were knights who were legally serfs. Thus the ordinance directed that if a peasant was apprehended carrying weapons, specifically, a lance or a sword, the judge in whose jurisdiction the offense had occurred was either to confiscate the weapons or to receive a fine of twenty shillings (12). A knight, too, was to appear at the count's palace or court bearing arms only if he had been commanded to do so (15). Ministerials of any lord who were engaged in a feud were to be judged, in accordance with law and justice, by the count or by the judge of the district where the fight had occurred (19). A merchant traveling on business was permitted to carry a sword tied to his saddle or kept in his cart so he could defend himself against bandits, but he was not to harm innocent people (13).

The remaining articles of the *Landfriede* dealt, broadly conceived, with the regulation of economic activities. Every year, after the birthday of the Virgin (8 September), each count was to assemble seven men of good reputation who were to determine, in consideration of the weather and the size of the harvest, the price at which grain was to be sold in each district during the following year. Anyone who sold grain at a higher price was classified as a peace-breaker and was to pay the count a fine of £20 for each bushel he had sold above the specified price (11). (This stipulation appears to have been prompted by a poor harvest and famine in Swabia in 1151.) No one was to use nets, snares, or any other such devices to trap any animals except bears, wild boars, or wolves (14). Finally, the last article allowed anyone traveling through the countryside to pasture his horse along the road and to take from the forest the wood he needed for his own use (20).[70]

Unlike Henry IV's proclamation of the Truce of God in 1103, which merely prohibited acts of violence against particular categories of people, including the Jews, Frederick expected his subjects to resolve their grievances by judicial means rather than by resorting to a feud. However, he had no way of enforcing the peace ordinance, except in the domains that were directly under his control, or to check on its implementation in the rest of the kingdom. All he could really do was mediate or adjudicate disputes between the princes with the advice and consent of their peers, or hang the ministerials who had disturbed the peace in his own duchy during his absence on the Second Crusade. The *Landfriede* was not an enforceable legislative act but a communal definition of the peace and justice the king had sworn to uphold, and it is noteworthy that Frederick did not include the peace ordinance among his most significant deeds.[71]

The reality was that the counts had ceased to be removable royal officials who presided at public courts and settled conflicts among free men. Rather, they were the hereditary lords of non-contiguous complexes of allods, fiefs obtained from the king and other lords, advocacies over churches, castles, and armed retinues of vassals and ministerials. Their comital titles, like those of the titular dukes, were derived from an office that had once been bestowed on one of their ancestors or that they had simply adopted on their own and that were associated with the castle or castles from which they asserted their lordship. (For example, Sigiboto IV of Falkenstein also called himself the count of Neuburg, Hartmannsberg, and Hernstein to differentiate between his various Bavarian and Lower Austrian lordships.) The responsibility for punishing most criminal offenses or resolving property disputes, outside the royal domain or the king's own dynastic holdings, belonged to the magnates, including the new-style counts, to whom Frederick's mandate was addressed, and to their judges. The rulers of these territorial lordships, not the king, maintained the peace—such as it was—in most of Germany, and profited from the proceeds of justice.[72] How kingship functioned in the absence of even a rudimentary bureaucracy is the topic of the next chapter.

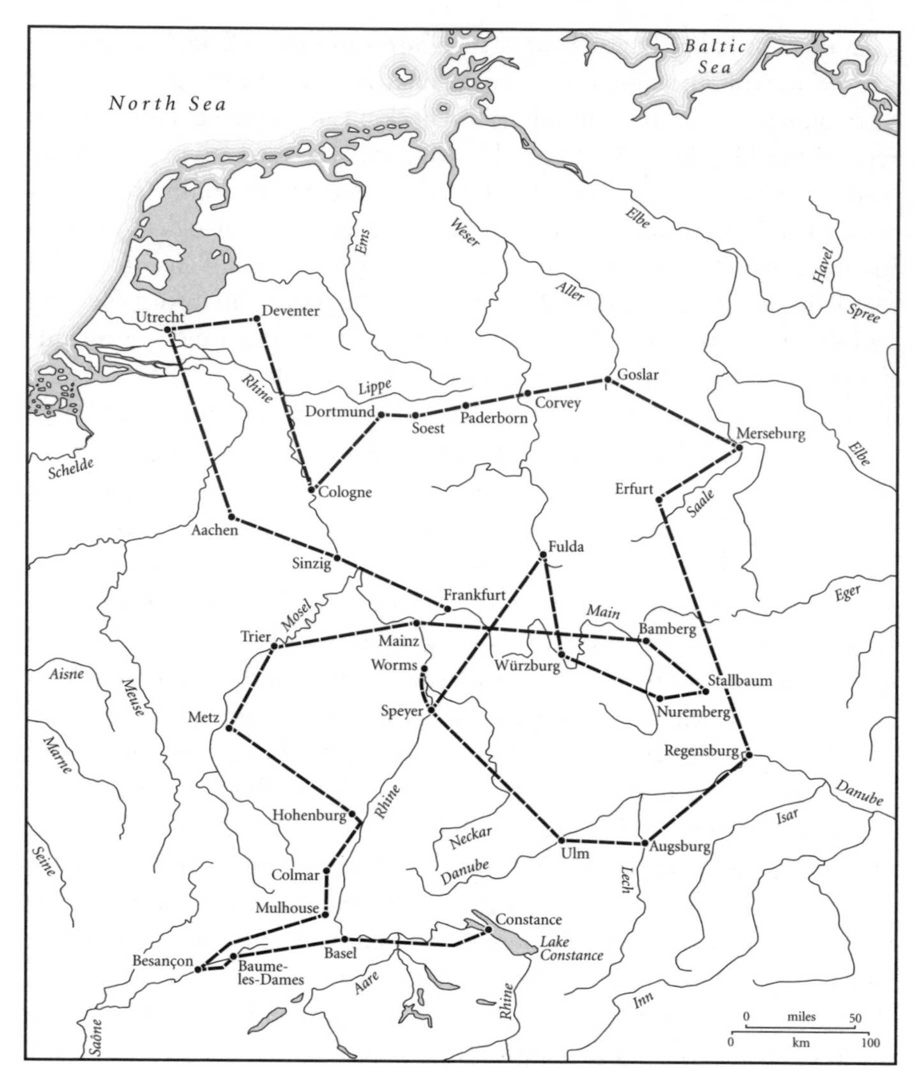

Map 2. Frederick's Itinerary, 4 March 1152–4 March 1153.

CHAPTER FIVE

ITINERANT KINGSHIP

A Mobile Monarchy

FREDERICK SPENT HIS REIGN in the saddle. His governance of his vast realm was intensely personal. The places he visited and the people who attended him are good gauges of the extent of his authority and of his changing relations with the princes during the course of his reign. Royal clerks made greater use of written communications than is commonly supposed. Yet, ultimately, in the absence of any permanent institutions of government except for the chancery, his rule depended upon the loyalty of the magnates who exercised power at the local level and their willingness to provide him with aid and counsel.

The Empire in the twelfth century covered an area of approximately 310,000 to 345,000 square miles (Alaska and Texas cover, respectively, 580,833 and 262,017 square miles). Between Frederick's election in March 1152 and his departure on the Third Crusade in May 1189, the outer limits of his travels were Lübeck on the Baltic, Albano, south of Rome, Mouzon on the Meuse, and Krzyszkowo near Poznań in western Poland.[1] It is approximately 560 miles, as the crow flies, from the Baltic coast in Holstein to the central ridge of the Alps, and about 500 miles from the upper Meuse to Lusatia, the region between the upper Elbe and the Oder. It took a bit more than a month for a traveler to reach Vienna from Lübeck. A courier on horseback could cover nearly 60 miles a day on flat terrain and up to 30 miles in the mountains. A papal embassy hastened in twenty-three days from Rome to Goslar. A king with a large entourage moved more slowly, around 12 to 18 miles a day.[2]

During the first year of his reign, when it was essential that Frederick meet as many magnates as possible and receive their homage in the traditional ride-about of a newly crowned king, he journeyed as follows (see Map 2): from Frankfurt (4 March 1152) he traveled to Sinzig on the Rhine, then Aachen (9 March), Utrecht, Deventer on the Ijssel in the Netherlands, Cologne (Easter, 30 March); across central Germany via Dortmund, Soest, Paderborn, Corvey (Wibald's abbey), Goslar, to Merseburg on the Saale river (Whitsunday, 18 May); southwestwards to Erfurt; south to Regensburg on the northernmost point of the Danube (29 June), then on to Augsburg on the Lech, Ulm on the Danube in Swabia (25 July); northwest to Speyer on the Rhine (19 August); downstream to Worms (24 August); back to Speyer (25 August); northeast to the Benedictine abbey of Fulda; south to Würzburg (13 October); east to Nuremberg, around 1 November at Stallbaum, then to Bamberg, down the Main to Mainz, from there to Trier on the Mosel (Christmas); in the new year, he was in Metz (10 January 1153) and in Hohenburg on the 27th, and then, as we have already seen, Colmar and Mulhouse in Alsace, Besançon in Burgundy (15 February); and finally, rounding out his first year as king, he arrived, via Baume-les-Dames and Basel, in Constance (4 March 1153). Frederick, who made similar circumventions for nearly four decades whenever he was north of the Alps, who undertook six expeditions to Italy and went on two crusades, must have been a man of enormous physical stamina.[3]

There was nothing unusual about Frederick's peregrinations. For centuries before and after him, medieval monarchs traveled to hunt at a favorite lodge, to worship at a shrine, and, above all, to see and to be seen. However, unlike, say, Charlemagne, who spent his last winters in Aachen, Frederick had no fixed winter quarters in Germany; and unlike the Norman kings of England and Sicily whose officials were beginning to stay at such fixed sites as Winchester, Westminster, Rouen, and Palermo, no German city assumed like Paris the function of the chief royal residence. Although Frederick referred in 1166 to Aachen as the "head of all cities," it was too peripheral to develop into a proto-capital city even though the German kings were crowned there until 1531. Frederick's promotion of land clearance and urbanization in the Wetterau, the forested area north of the lower Main, might have made the more centrally situated chief city in the region, Frankfurt, where royal elections were regularly held after 1208, a more natural location for a capital; but unlike Paris, Frankfurt was not an episcopal see, and the Wetterau, where the Staufer shared power with the archbishops of Mainz, was hardly comparable to the rich Île de France, where the Capetians had long cultivated extensive royal estates.[4] Frederick and his clerical advisers utilized written communications, were familiar with such administrative innovations as inquests, and set up a rudimentary administrative structure in

Lombardy; but except for the royal and Staufer domains he was content in Germany to rely, as the peace ordinance of 1152 shows, on his princely kinsmen to maintain order and administer justice. The key point is that such personal government worked for him. Unlike his predecessors and his counterparts in England, France, and Sicily, Frederick never had to deal with a rebellion against his authority in Germany. In 1180–81 his cousin Henry the Lion was fighting fellow princes, not so Frederick.

Frederick's travels in Germany were concentrated between the Rhine, Main, and Danube. Indeed, Otto of Freising described the stretch of the Rhine from Basel to Mainz as the region where "the principal strength of the realm" was located. Elsewhere he called the Rhine valley, which was "rich in grain and wine and affords [an] abundance of hunting and fishing," one of the "three most renowned" areas of Europe that could "maintain the sovereigns for a very long time when they remain in the transalpine regions."[5] The total number of Frederick's known stays in episcopal sees in the royal heartland south of the Main are: Worms (eighteen visits), Würzburg (seventeen), Regensburg (sixteen), Augsburg (ten), Speyer (ten), Strasbourg (ten), Constance (eight), Bamberg (seven), Basel (five), and Mainz (five). Even in this region, however, he never visited Eichstätt or Freising, which are still insignificant places. Altogether, more than a third of Frederick's known stops in Germany were in episcopal sees. The king had his own palace in some of these cities, shared with the bishop the ownership of the palace in other sees, or stayed in the episcopal residence. (It is impossible to define exactly what was meant by a palace [*palatium*], except that it was a substantial building utilized for important business and manifested the lord's power. The word should not conjure up the image of a medieval version of Buckingham Palace.) Two other regions Barbarossa visited with some frequency were southern Saxony and Thuringia (Altenburg six times, Erfurt eleven, Goslar eleven, and Merseburg six) and the lower Rhine (Aachen seven times and Cologne eight); but he never set foot in the latter region after 1174 and he rarely traveled north of the Main and Mosel after 1180.[6]

Specific political situations compelled Frederick to visit outlying places. For example, he went to Utrecht in 1152 to punish the diocese for its defiance of Conrad III the previous year in the disputed episcopal election; he traveled to Friesach, Carinthia, and Leibnitz, Styria, in 1170 in connection with Salzburg's election of his cousin Archbishop Adalbert II, a supporter of Pope Alexander III; and he journeyed in 1181 to Lübeck, his only sojourn on the Baltic, to force Henry the Lion to submit. Personal factors may sometimes have been involved. For instance, Frederick may have spent Christmas in Trier in 1152 because his sister Bertha/Judith, his only full sibling, was the duchess of Upper Lorraine (he was in Trier on only two other occasions); and he did not visit Bamberg again after the death of Bishop Eberhard II in 1172. Instead, he went three times to nearby Eger, which he had acquired after the death of his cousin Frederick of Rothenburg in 1167, and to Nuremberg (six out of twelve stays were after 1170).

In fact, as his reign progressed Frederick increasingly frequented royal palaces like Eger and Nuremberg, many of which developed into imperial cities and became the preferred stops for his successors. Rahewin indicated that Frederick restored the Carolingian palaces at Nijmegen in the Netherlands and Ingelheim, west of Mainz, and built a palace at Kaiserslautern (4.86). Barbarossa was in Nijmegen four times (never after 1174) and only once in Ingelheim (1163), but seven times in Kaiserslautern (five after 1170) and nine times in Haguenau (six after the palace was completed in 1174/78). A similar tendency for Frederick to prefer palaces he built himself to Carolingian foundations can be seen in the case of the Carolingian palace in Frankfurt, where he stayed ten times but never after 1174, and Gelnhausen, east of Frankfurt in the Wetterau, which Frederick commissioned and which he visited on seven occasions after 1170. Altogether, more than a quarter of Frederick's known stays were in such palace complexes. There is no indication he spent much time in his castles or at least conducted any public business that left a written record. He was in Trifels, south of Kaiserslautern in the Palatinate, three times, but only once in the palace-castle complex of Tilleda-Kyffhäuser (1174) and in Stauf itself (1181). He rarely imposed on the hospitality of the lay princes and magnates, though Otto mentioned that Frederick celebrated Whitsunday in 1156 in an unidentified castle of the count-palatine of Bavaria, Otto V of Wittelsbach (2.47). If he did visit the princes, such stays left few traces because the court did not adjudicate disputes on such occasions.[7]

When Barbarossa could not find suitable accommodation on his journeys in a castle, monastery, or royal or episcopal manor, he slept in a tent. In 1157 Henry II of England sent Frederick a tent, which Rahewin described as "very large in extent and of the finest quality. If you ask its size, it could not be raised except by machinery and a special sort of instrument and props; if you ask its quality, I should imagine that neither in material nor in workmanship will it ever be surpassed by any equipment of this kind." Rahewin related that while Frederick was camped at Lodi in June 1159, a madman tried to kill him when he left his tent at daybreak to say his prayers.[8]

Frederick was accompanied on his travels by his closest confidants, several royal chaplains and notaries, a sizeable armed retinue, and a large number of servants. We have no firm evidence for the size of the German kings' perambulatory court between the tenth and thirteenth centuries, but an educated guess is that it numbered over a thousand people.[9] Since Frankish times four court officers—the marshal, steward, butler, and chamberlain—had been responsible for the management of the king's household. The count-palatine of the Rhine, the duke of Saxony, the margrave of Brandenburg, and the king of Bohemia held, at least by 1220 and probably already at the Whitsunday court in Mainz in 1184, the ceremonial, hereditary offices of, respectively, arch-steward, arch-marshal, arch-chamberlain, and arch-butler; but increasingly influential imperial ministerials, who were likewise beginning to make their position hereditary, did the actual work and had after 1177 the king's ear. The chamberlain was in charge originally of the royal bedroom and the treasure that was kept there, but eventually he took over the running of the royal household. The steward saw to the provisioning of the royal table and the butler supervised the supply of wine. Most important of all, the marshal, who had originally taken care of the horses (the word meant "horse servant"), arranged for the monarch's accommodation on his travels. For example, Frederick indicated in his 1164 charter for the town of Haguenau that the imperial marshal and ministerial, Henry of Kalden-Pappenheim, was responsible for making the necessary arrangements during his stays there. By the reign of Frederick's son, the marshal was leading troops in battle because Henry VI, unlike his father, was not a fighter.[10]

Assemblies

It is sometimes difficult to distinguish between the routine stays of Frederick's court (*curia*), which dealt with local business, and larger assemblies where major decisions were made and whose super-regional influence might be indicated in the sources by the adjectives "general," "universal," or "renowned." Scholars have tried to differentiate between the two types of gathering in specific instances based on the number and the identity of the participants, the nature of the business the court handled, and the place and date in the liturgical calendar where and when a court met; but the application of these criteria is often subjective.

Nevertheless, during Frederick's reign 156 such major assemblies have been identified in Germany, seven in Burgundy, and seventeen in Italy. The most German gatherings, forty-one, occurred during the first eight years of his rule, but there were thirty-six in the 1160s, forty in the 1170s, and thirty-nine in the 1180s, or roughly about four a year. Preferred meeting times were Christmas, Easter, and Whitsunday, the Virgin's Ascension (18 August) and Birth (8 September), or major saints' days like those of Saints Peter and

Paul (29 June) and St. Martin of Tours (11 November). Late spring or summer meetings when travel was easier were preferred—hence the popularity of Whitsunday in late May or early June. The *Saxon Mirror* (*Sachsenspiegel*), the codification of Saxon law compiled by Eike von Repgow around 1220, specified that such assemblies could be held in five locations in Saxony: the imperial palaces in Grone, Werla, Wallhausen, Allstedt, and Merseburg (the one in Werla had been transferred, Eike said, to Goslar). Frederick held seven such assemblies in Goslar, four in Merseburg, one each in Wallhausen and Werla, and none in Allstedt or Grone. The preferred sites for such major imperial gatherings in Germany during his reign were: Worms (thirteen times), Regensburg (twelve), Würzburg (twelve), Nuremberg (ten), Ulm (nine), and seven each in Bamberg, Constance, and Frankfurt. More than a third of Frederick's assemblies were held in Franconia, the German heartland—Bamberg, Frankfurt, Gelnhausen, Mainz, Nuremberg, Speyer, Worms, and Würzburg. During the 1150s the assemblies were fairly evenly distributed throughout the German realm, though none was ever held in the extreme northern portion of the kingdom; but by the 1180s most met in Franconia and Swabia, and increasingly in imperial palaces rather than episcopal sees.[11]

The Reich, comprised of the emperor and the princes, constituted itself most visibly at such imperial assemblies. According to Eike von Repgow, writing roughly thirty years after Frederick's death, a king summoned such a court by a decree and proclaimed it "to the princes with his official letter and seal six weeks before it [was] to take place." The princes were required to attend wherever the king resided in the German realm. The fine for non-attendance by a prince was the equivalent of £100 and £10 for everyone else. Otto of Freising provided the same scale of fines but in a different context. Hartwig II of Regensburg had been elected bishop in 1155 while Frederick was still in Italy and had enfeoffed his own vassals before the absent monarch had invested him with the regalia. Hartwig pleaded that he was not aware he had violated the customary procedure, but he and all those whom he had enfeoffed were fined. Otto added that any prince who incurred the sovereign's anger was fined £100 and everyone else—nobles, freemen, or ministerials—owed £10. While anyone who disobeyed a royal summons to appear at court presumably incurred the king's wrath, there is no evidence that such a law was routinely enforced.[12] Several such written summonses survive. Frederick commanded Wibald, for example, to appear in 1152 at the *curia generalis* in Würzburg on 13 October (St. Michael the Archangel), in Cologne in 1153 on 1 November (All Saints'), and in 1157 in Nijmegen on the third Sunday after Easter (21 April); and he ordered

Abbot Rupert of Tegernsee in 1157 to be present for an assembly in Regensburg on 13 October.[13]

The most famous description of such a gathering is Gilbert of Mons' account of the Whitsunday court in 1184 in Mainz, where Emperor Frederick's two oldest sons, King Henry VI and Duke Frederick VI of Swabia, were knighted. Allegedly, 70,000 men, excluding the clerks and individuals of lesser rank, attended. Each of the princes was accompanied by a vast retinue of knights: for example, the duke of Bohemia brought 2,000 knights; the archbishop of Mainz and Frederick's brother, 1,000 each; and the duke of Austria, 500.[14] Gilbert's figures are undoubtedly greatly exaggerated, and the Mainz court was, in every sense, an exceptional assembly. Still, we have to assume that the princes, for reasons of prestige, arrived with sizeable retinues and with considerable pomp. According to Balderich, the biographer of Archbishop Albero of Trier, two dukes, eight counts, two eminent scholars whom Albero took on his own boat, and "such a multitude of clerics and knights that everyone who saw them expressed admiration," accompanied Albero in 1149 from Trier to Conrad III's court in Frankfurt. It took forty transport ships, in addition to "swift warships, cargo vessels, and cooking galleys," to convey the archiepiscopal party to the court.[15]

The arrival of a prince could be the occasion for an elaborate reception of the newcomer. When Archbishop Arnold of Mainz, who had imposed the interdict on the ministerials and burghers of his archiepiscopal see, approached Frederick's camp during the siege of Crema in November 1159, the princes went out a mile to greet him, kissed him, and escorted him to the emperor who was seated on his throne. A herald announced Arnold's arrival, and Frederick honored the archbishop by rising and then permitting him to sit at his side while the other princes stood. The emperor thus simultaneously demonstrated his preeminence while singling out one of the princes for a special honor. After Arnold presented his complaint against the people of Mainz, who were resisting his attempt to tax them to finance his participation in Frederick's second Italian campaign, the princes competed for the honor of accommodating the prelate. Arnold opted to stay with Frederick's brother Conrad, because "he was closer to the court and more familiar to him."[16]

The seating arrangements at such imperial courts were crucial markers of princely and ecclesiastical status. Archbishop Philip of Cologne deliberately picked a fight with Abbot Conrad of Fulda at the Whitsunday court at Mainz in 1184. The archbishop wished to demonstrate that the impoverished abbey's claims to precedence were a hollow pretense, because it could not supply the emperor with the same material and military resources as Cologne. The 1,700 knights whom Philip brought to Mainz far exceeded Fulda's 500—Arnold of Lübeck even placed the size of the archbishop's entourage at 4,064 men. When Frederick arrived at the cathedral for Mass on Whitsunday, Abbot Conrad complained that Philip had deprived him of his ancient right, bestowed by previous monarchs, to sit on the emperor's left side at courts held in Mainz. The emperor asked Philip not to disturb the joyous occasion and to allow the abbot to retain his customary place. The archbishop declared that he was willing to accede to Barbarossa's request but sought permission to return to his quarters. As he prepared to leave, Frederick's brother, the count-palatine, declared that as the archbishop's vassal he was obliged to follow his lord. The duke of Brabant, the count of Nassau, and many other lords said the same thing. Landgrave Louis III of Thuringia announced that as a vassal of Fulda he would stand by the abbot. To prevent further conflict Emperor Frederick's son, the young king, Henry VI, jumped up, embraced Philip, and begged him not to turn the celebration of his knighting into a cause for sorrow. Frederick joined his son in entreating Philip to stay. The archbishop reminded the emperor of all the services he had performed for him, both in Lombardy and in taking Brunswick from Henry the Lion, and how, despite pangs of conscience, he had supported Frederick during the schism. The abbot would not have dared to make such complaints against him, Philip asserted, if Conrad had not been certain that the emperor wanted to humiliate Philip; and he would remain only if he kept his traditional seat. Frederick offered to clear himself of Philip's suspicions with an oath, but the archbishop said that the emperor's word was sufficient for him. The quarrel ended when Abbot Conrad was forced, at Frederick's command, to take a lesser place.[17]

The monarch displayed his preeminence by wearing his crown at assemblies on major feast days. For example, at his first court in Saxony at Merseburg on Whitsunday 1152, which was considering a disputed succession to the Danish throne, Frederick recognized his old friend from knight school as King Sven III and crowned him. Sven, "wearing the crown," according to Otto, "bore the sword of the king who marched in state wearing his crown." The ceremony demonstrated that Sven was "bound . . . [to Frederick] by fealty and homage" (2.5).

Scholars have expended considerable effort examining the witness lists of charters to identify the monarch's confidants and to ascertain how the composition of the assemblies changed during Frederick's reign, in the full realization that such attestations can provide at best only an incomplete picture of the court's structure. We do not know the notaries' criteria for selecting and ordering witnesses by rank, though the less important witnesses were more likely than the princes to have a direct interest in the particular transaction they attested. As we have already seen, different men, listed in a different order, witnessed on 4 and 5 July 1157 two charters drafted by the same notary. In any case, more men were present at an assembly than served as witnesses. Sometimes we know about the presence of a particular individual who does not appear in a charter, because he is mentioned in another source. For instance, we know that Count Ekbert III of Formbach-Pitten accompanied Frederick on his second Italian campaign, because Rahewin recorded Ekbert's heroic but needless death outside Milan in 1158. Similarly, Count Sigiboto IV of Falkenstein probably commissioned his unique family archive in preparation for his departure on Barbarossa's fourth Italian expedition, but there is no charter evidence for his participation in that campaign. Finally, to assess a particular individual's relationship to the king, it is necessary to take into account not only the number of his attestations but also how far from home he accompanied the monarch on his journeys—the farther the witness traveled from his home region, the more likely that he was a member of the king's entourage—and whether he was there of his own volition or, like the two dukes and eight counts who accompanied Archbishop Albero of Trier to Frankfurt in 1149, as a member of another prince's retinue. Conversely, magnates like Wibald or Archbishop Christian of Mainz were often absent from the court because they were away on royal business. Altogether, around 2,000 men witnessed one or more of Frederick's charters.[18]

Most princes ventured beyond their own region only on matters of great personal concern, and Frederick was as likely to visit them as they were to come to him. Princes on the western fringes of the Empire rarely crossed the Rhine, while the Main was an informal boundary for lay princes from northern and southern Germany. Bishops were more likely than their lay colleagues to travel a greater distance to see the king; about a third of them appeared at court each year during the 1150s. Wibald of Stavelot and Markwart of Fulda were the only abbots of monasteries directly subject to the crown who visited the king at least once a year during the same time period. No abbot matched their record subsequently, and there is no evidence that an abbot of a third of these imperial monasteries was at court even once during Frederick's reign. As the gift of the impoverished abbey of Niederaltaich to Bamberg immediately after Frederick's coronation indicates, the old Benedictine houses had become spiritually passé and no longer had the resources to provide the king with military manpower and with hospitality. Frederick visited them mainly for religious purposes—for example, three of his eight visits to Fulda, the most prestigious house, were to celebrate the feast of St. Boniface, the apostle to the Germans—and he rarely made an effort to ease the monasteries' economic distress. Wibald was, in fact, the last Benedictine abbot to play a major role in imperial affairs.[19]

Personal factors were also, seemingly, in play in a magnate's decision to come to court on a regular basis. While most Swabian counts witnessed four to eight charters, normally within Swabia, Count Rudolf of Pfullendorf-Lindau, who had accompanied Frederick on the Second Crusade, did so forty-one times, on twenty-seven occasions outside the duchy. Rudolf was one of the thirteen members of Barbarossa's inner circle whom Acerbus Morena singled out for individual portraits in his chronicle—some of the others were his wife the Empress Beatrice, Frederick of Rothenburg, Henry the Lion, and Rainald of Dassel. Before 1167 Duke Matthew of Upper Lorraine witnessed 16 percent of his brother-in-law's German charters; his son and Frederick's nephew, Simon II made only one known visit to his uncle's court between 1176 and 1190. Margrave Hermann III of Baden served as a witness twenty-eight times, but his son Hermann IV did so on only three occasions between 1160 and 1190. Bishop Hermann of Verden, who participated in Barbarossa's second, third, and fourth Italian campaigns, was, according to Acerbus Morena, another one of the emperor's intimates. Hermann's successors did not show a comparable engagement in imperial affairs.

Until the late 1160s the quarterly or so assemblies of the princes were essentially gatherings of an extended family, in which Frederick, the linchpin who alone was related to all of them, presided over the adjudication of their differences. His Staufer kinsmen were: his half-brother Conrad, who in 1156 succeeded the husband of Frederick's Aunt Gertrude as the count-palatine of the Rhine; his cousin, Duke Frederick IV of Swabia; and his brothers-in-law, Duke Matthew of Upper Lorraine and Landgrave Louis II of Thuringia. His Babenberg relations were: Henry Jasomirgott; Bishops Otto of Freising and Conrad of Passau; and the husbands of their sisters, Agnes, Gertrude, and Ita/Jutta, namely Duke Wladyslaw the Exile of Poland, Duke/King Vladislav II of Bohemia, and Margrave William V of Montferrat. The Welf contingent consisted of Henry the Lion, Welf VI, Frederick's cousin, Margrave Ottokar III of Styria, and the cousin of Frederick's mother Judith, Albrecht the Bear, the margrave of Brandenburg. Between them, Frederick's kinsmen were the nominal lords of most of the German kingdom: Alsace, Austria, Bavaria, Bohemia, Brandenburg, eastern Franconia, the Palatinate, Saxony, Styria, Swabia, Thuringia, and Upper Lorraine.

Princely participation declined noticeably, as we will see, after Frederick's defeat in Italy in 1167 and the birth of his sons. For example, less than a tenth of the German bishops bothered to attend Frederick's court at least once a year during the last decade of his reign. Approximately half of all the known visits by lay princes to the court in the 1180s were by Barbarossa's closest relatives: his sons; half-brother; cousin, Duke Leopold V of Austria; and nephew, Landgrave Louis III of Thuringia.[20] The change in the composition of his court mirrors Frederick's loss of his good fortune and his retreat to south of the Main.

The *Tafelgüterverzeichnis* (The List of Mensal Manors)

The princes, like Albero of Trier with his "cargo vessels and cooking galleys," brought their own provisions to court. Wibald complained to the chancellor in 1150 that he had spent not a little amount at the court in Frankfurt in August 1149, 20 marks on a diplomatic mission to an exiled southern Italian count, and 40 marks accompanying Conrad III for nearly twenty weeks after he had been summoned to the Christmas court at Bamberg in 1149.[21]

For his part, Frederick entertained the magnates at banquets, presumably in a style that befitted royal largesse, and was responsible, like the princes, for the maintenance of his own retinue. The so-called *Tafelgüterverzeichnis*, "the register of manors that pertain to the table of the king of the Romans" and the provisions they supplied the royal household, has been called, with considerable justification, "the most disputed source in German economic history."[22] This list of the king's income from manors in Saxony, Rhenish Franconia, including Lorraine, Bavaria, and Lombardy, was entered between 1165 and 1174 into a codex of St. Mary's, the coronation church in Aachen. The register appears to have been a summary of an earlier response, in all probability immediately after Frederick's accession, to an enquiry, perhaps by the chancellor, Arnold of Selenhofen, who was the provost of St. Mary's, about the resources at the king's disposal. An 1152/53 date for the list would explain the designation of the monarch as king of the Romans rather than as emperor, the absence of Swabia from the register (Frederick was presumably familiar with conditions in his own duchy), and the uncertainty about the royal income in Lombardy until the unknown author went there—perhaps he was the notary Heribert, who became in 1159 the provost of Aachen and in 1163 the archbishop of Besançon. It is thus not clear whether the term, "the king's table (*mensa*)," which was borrowed from the ecclesiastical custom of distinguishing between a bishop or abbot's income and his community's revenue, was part of the original response or was added as a heading by the scribe who entered the list in the codex.[23]

The register lists twenty manors in Saxony, only fifteen of which can be identified with complete certainty; twenty-one in Rhenish Franconia and Lorraine, twenty of which pose no problem (this suggests that the compiler was most familiar with this region); and twelve in Bavaria, only five of which can be located with any confidence. Only fifteen of the fifty-three manors were also the sites of royal palaces—for example, Aachen, Goslar, Frankfurt, and Nuremberg—and thus likely stopping places on the royal itinerary. We have no knowledge that any monarch in the eleventh or twelfth centuries stayed in twenty of the other locations. The compiler included the number of *servitia* that the king procured in each duchy. A royal *servitium*, a unit for calculating the renders a manor owed, was defined in Saxony as thirty large hogs, three cows, five suckling pigs, fifty chickens, fifty eggs, ninety cheeses, ten geese, 5 *Fuder* of beer (a *Fuder* was 800 to 1,800 liters depending on the locality), 5 pounds of pepper, 10 pounds of wax, presumably for illumination, and an unspecified amount of wine from wherever there was a cellar in Saxony. Merseburg, a favorite destination on the royal itinerary, owed forty *servitia*. Altogether, the Saxon manors supplied "as many *servitia* as there are days in the year plus 40 more," that is, 405 *servitia*. One possible explanation for this rather strange accounting method is that the compiler's oral source simply said, with a rhetorical flourish, that there was more than a year's supply of provisions in Saxony and that the number was more symbolic than real. The Franconian-Lotharingian-Bavarian *servitia* were larger than the Saxon ones: forty rather than thirty large hogs, seven rather than five suckling pigs, five rather than three cows, 500 rather than fifty eggs (a scribal mistake in the case of Saxony?), and 4 large *Fuder* of wine rather than beer. Altogether, the Franconian-Lotharingian manors owed eighty-five *servitia* and the Bavarian estates provided, according to the compiler, twenty-six *servitia*, but thirty-two if the numbers owed by the individual manors are added up. (The numbers in Count Sigiboto's manorial register [*Urbar*], the oldest such accounting from a lay estate in Germany, do not tally either. The use of Roman numerals may have caused such problems with addition.) Altogether, the king received from these German estates at least 516 *servitia* and a total of 1,770 cows, 16,590 hogs, 2,802 suckling pigs, 5,160 geese, 28,500 chickens, 75,750 eggs, 46,440 cheeses, 5,160 pounds of wax, 2,580 pounds of pepper, 2,025 *Fuder* of beer, and at least 444 *Fuder* of wine.[24]

What, if anything, does the *Tafelgüterverzeichnis* tell us about the provisioning of Frederick's itinerant court? There are striking omissions: most obviously grain or bread, vegetables, say cabbages, and fodder for the horses, but also fish, an essential item for fast days, salt, and honey, the medieval sweetener. Count Sigiboto also received relatively little grain from his estates, and one possible explanation for the exclusion is that the other renders were fixed amounts, whereas the payments of grain, in a share-cropping system, were a percentage of the harvest. Were the provisions transported from the manors the king did not visit to his halting places, and what happened to the renders when the king was absent, say, in Italy, and did not require them for his own use? Finally, the total amounts seem large, assuming that the figures really represent the yearly income from the royal estates in much of Germany, but not if the provisions had to feed 1,000 active adult men for a year—each man would have received only one egg every five days. Besides, far less food was available on the middle Rhine and in Bavaria, where the king spent far more of his time, than in Saxony. In short, the royal estates supplied, at best, only a small portion of the provisions the court required.[25]

The real issue is, however, the nature of the German economy in the mid-twelfth century and, by implication, how alien the vibrant commercial society of northern Italy, the most advanced in Europe, was for Frederick and his fellow princes. We know nothing about how the royal domain was administered in the twelfth century, but Count Sigiboto of Falkenstein's manorial register, which he started in 1165/66, may provide a clue. The count had divided his lands into four offices and was converting portions of his demesne into rent-paying holdings and many of the renders into cash. This was especially true in the Lower Austrian lordship of Hernstein, outside Vienna, which was a considerable distance from his Bavarian domains. Its annual income was variously given as £12 220d, £13 30d, and £16 6s. By 1190 Sigiboto was receiving £33½ 12d from sixty-three vineyards in that lordship. Perhaps most intriguing of all in this context, Sigiboto was selling hides from his Bavarian lands in Italy and using the proceeds to purchase olive oil, which was a substitute for butter during Lent. It is thus hard to imagine that large quantities of foodstuffs were shipped great distances to feed the imperial court or that renders that were not needed during Frederick's absence were not sold. At the very least, Frederick's bailiffs were able to purchase, seemingly without difficulty, 2,580 pounds of pepper in markets located throughout the realm. Germany was not Italy, but its economy by the second half of the twelfth century was no longer archaic or autarchic.[26]

The chief burden for provisioning the court fell on the imperial churches, especially the bishoprics where Frederick repeatedly stayed. The economically hard-pressed imperial abbeys were increasingly being relieved of this duty and other services to the crown or they forged charters to this end. In 1137 Stavelot's yearly obligation to provide for the king's court was limited by Lothar III to 20 marks in cash or kind if the king came to Aachen or 30 marks if he visited Stavelot itself or one of its manors. Conrad III freed Benediktbeuern in 1143 from all the services it owed the Reich, and in 1147 he remitted, in exchange for three manors, the £100 in royal services that Lorsch had performed annually for the crown. Impoverished Niederaltaich, which could no longer fulfill its obligations, lost its status in 1152 as an imperial monastery.[27]

In 1155, during his third stay in the city since his accession, Frederick granted his loyal supporter Bishop Hermann of Constance the special exemption that neither he nor any of his successors would visit the city or demand hospitality there unless summoned by the bishop or for the sake of prayer or, in a major loophole, out of the necessity of the monarch's journey. There were fewer royal visits to Constance after 1155, especially in comparison to Worms or Würzburg; but Barbarossa was back in 1162, 1179, 1181, 1183, and 1187. Archbishop Conrad of Mainz asserted that all the revenue of his see between the death of his predecessor, Archbishop Christian, on 23 August 1183, and the new harvest in 1184, had been expended in service of the crown—except for 45 shillings in Mainz and £7 in Thuringia. No doubt, some of that money had been spent at the great Whitsunday court of 1184.[28] Episcopal resistance to such financial demands by the crown may have been a factor in the shift in the royal itinerary during the 1180s from the episcopal sees to the royal palaces and the cities that were forming around them.

The Governance of the Realm

Thanks to Otto and Wibald, we know that the princes withdrew to Frederick's chambers the morning after his coronation, 10 March 1152, and decided not to go to Italy until the pope invited him; but we have few such clues about how royal government actually worked behind the facade of public unanimity. As the 1152 *Landfriede* indicates, the magnates, not the king, were responsible for the apprehension and punishment of criminals and for adjudicating property and other disputes in their own territories. For example, Count Sigiboto of Falkenstein obtained in 1168 a ruling from the count-palatine of Bavaria, Otto V of Wittelsbach, that the *Hantgemal*, or allod of liberty, which proved that his lineage was of free ancestry and which he shared with two other seemingly unrelated dynasties, belonged to the senior member of his own lineage. (Some scholars believe that Waiblingen was the *Hantgemal* of the Salians and Staufer.) In 1182/83, at the court of Duke Otto I of Bavaria, Sigiboto, his wife Hildegard of Mödling, and their sons laid claim to the castle of Mödling and its appurtenances, which had belonged to her parents.[29] Sigiboto, unlike a contemporary English baron, did not pursue either claim at a royal court.

Frederick reaffirmed near the end of his reign, in December 1187, after receiving an enquiry from Count Baldwin V of Hainaut, that jurisdiction in cases involving the seizure and unjust possession of property belonged to the local magnates. The "imperial princes and other faithful men" determined that after the lord had received a complaint, he was to impanel from among the neighborhood men, i.e., jurors, who, duly sworn, were to ascertain the truth. If the property had been usurped, it was to be restored to its rightful owner, who was to be reimbursed his costs; and the offender was to pay a fine of £10 "to the lord of the county."[30] In England, the plaintiff would have procured a writ of novel disseizin from the king.

Unlike his English peers, Count Sigiboto was not directly bound to Frederick by any feudal tie until the last year of his reign. Sigiboto was in 1166 the vassal of three dukes, two counts-palatine, two margraves, seven counts, an archbishop, four bishops, and an abbot, but not the emperor. It was only after Frederick obtained upon the death of Gebhard II of Sulzbach on 28 October 1188 the fiefs which Gebhard had previously held from the church of Bamberg that Sigiboto became the emperor's vassal. Sigiboto hastened to Sulzbach in January 1189 and was sub-enfeoffed with the Bamberg fiefs, but he received no charter to that effect. The count merely recorded among his transactions that Emperor Frederick had granted him, in a heated room that had belonged to Gebhard, the fief he had held from the deceased count in the presence of "bishops and princes and friends," several of whom were named as witnesses. Sigiboto's enfeoffment shortly before Barbarossa's departure on the Third Crusade is one of only two documented occasions on which the two men ever met.[31] Sigiboto's mediated status was typical of many counts, especially in Bavaria, who owed their primary allegiance to their prince.

Yet, the judgment of a princely court could on occasion be appealed to the emperor. In 1188 the knight Robert of Beaurain complained to Count Baldwin V of Hainaut that the count's vassal and cousin, Gérard of Saint-Aubert, had falsely asserted that Robert was his serf. The comital court ruled against Robert and turned him over to Gérard, who placed him in chains. Gérard released Robert after he had, "as a man of servile status," pledged his fidelity to his lord. Robert promptly violated his oath and went to the emperor's court. With no one to counter his assertions, he procured from Henry VI, who was acting on his father's behalf, letters revoking the sentence. In accordance with this written mandate, the earlier verdict was overturned at Mons, even though Gérard had not been summoned and was not present. We do not know, in the absence of any administrative records, whether such appeals were exceptional or the norm.[32]

Like the papacy or Henry II of England, the imperial court could ascertain the specific facts of a case by delegating its agents to conduct an inquest and to report their findings in writing to the court. The day after his coronation, Frederick confirmed, at the request of Abbot Hugh of Saint-Rémi in Reims, who had come to Aachen, all of his abbey's possessions in the Reich—in particular a property pertaining to the manor of Meerssen, northeast of Maastricht in the Netherlands, which Duke Godfrey III of Brabant-Louvain had returned to the abbey only after Conrad III had admonished the duke. Frederick then sent the dean of Aachen, a bailiff, and his marshal to investigate the abbot's complaint that the advocate, Goswin II of Heinsberg, was infringing upon Saint-Rémi's rights in Meerssen. They issued a written report, based on the sworn testimony of the men of the manor, about the renders the manor owed and the division of the income from the three annual manorial courts between the king, advocate, and abbot. The report was incorporated into Frederick's charter.[33]

Frederick could also delegate some of his responsibilities for maintaining the peace and settling disputes. Wibald complained to Frederick in July 1152 that the abbot's vassals, Folkwin and Widukind of Schwalenberg, had in his absence attacked the town of Höxter, which belonged to Corvey. They had devastated it for three days, causing £900 in damages, extorting £253 from prominent captives, and destroying Höxter's fortifications. Frederick assured Wibald, the monks, and the burghers in writing that he would avenge their injury; and he ordered Henry the Lion to see that justice was done.[34] On the march to Rome for his imperial coronation in 1155, Frederick requested that his brother-in-law, Landgrave Louis II of Thuringia, look after the interests of Burgrave Henry of Altenburg, who had accompanied Frederick to Italy, and protect the properties that Henry had assigned in his absence to the royal chamberlain. In the spring of 1157 the emperor instructed Bishop Frederick of Münster to determine whether an individual called Maurinus was indeed, as Wibald claimed, a Corvey ministerial. Between Ash Wednesday, 25 February 1159, and Easter, 12 April, Frederick absented himself from his army during his second Italian expedition and left Bishop Eberhard II of Bamberg "to hear those who came and had business to transact, and to decide their cases after careful investigation."[35] It would be interesting to know how many cases involving non-princely plaintiffs reached the king's court, especially in Germany, and whether Frederick normally assigned their settlement to a trusted bishop like Eberhard or sat in judgment himself.

The settlement of a specific case could lead to a general enunciation of the law. Archbishop Frederick I of Cologne (1100–31) had alienated so many of the properties belonging to his see that Conrad III's chancellor, Arnold of Wied, had been reluctant to accept his election as archbishop. Conrad had procured a princely judgment that none of the properties pertaining to the archiepiscopal endowment could be enfeoffed or otherwise alienated. Barbarossa had already confirmed this judgment for Archbishop Arnold II at Dortmund in April 1152. At the solemn assembly in Worms on 14 June 1153, Count Godfrey of Arnsburg and the nobleman Markwart II of Grumbach testified in the presence of Frederick and the princes that Conrad had made such a ruling—there was, seemingly, no written record of Conrad's earlier decision. Duke Henry Jasomirgott of Bavaria, in the name of the assembled princes, then announced the court's sentence and affirmed the general principle that a bishop could not alienate such mensal properties and, if he did, his successor was not obliged to honor his predecessor's enfeoffments or pledges of property. Frederick confirmed the decision, and the charter was issued in his name.[36]

Essentially the same legal principle was upheld on 22 September 1184, in a ruling at an assembly held in Milan that was attended by both German and Italian princes. Bishop Roger of Cambrai complained that he was being harassed by merchants on account of the debts incurred by his predecessor, Bishop Alard. Archbishop Conrad of Mainz pronounced with the concurrence of all the princes that no ecclesiastical prince was liable for the debts of his predecessor unless the emperor and the cathedral chapter had consented to the loan, and that ecclesiastical properties could be sold or pledged only with the emperor's permission. Since Alard had not sought such imperial authorization, Frederick ruled that Roger was not liable.[37]

Frederick's royal interest in these two cases stemmed from the need to preserve the bishoprics' financial viability so they could provide the crown with hospitality and military service. Without a centrally maintained record of prior judgments, the court had to handle each case from scratch.

Most decisions took the form of such princely judgments. The proceedings themselves were oral. The princes and other knowledgeable and respected men who were at the court answered a legal question and applied their finding to the specific case. The sentence, like Conrad III's about the inalienability of episcopal mensal properties, was not necessarily committed to writing. The chancery or a scribe working for the successful plaintiff produced a written record only if the victorious party requested from the king a privilege confirming its rights or a mandate ordering the addressees to implement the decision or to desist from their prior actions. Since there was no prescribed format for recording such judgments, the scribes had considerable discretion in selecting and presenting the facts of the case. The court's judgments were *Weistümer*, that is, declarations of existing laws or customs, and not enactments of new laws.[38]

Although three charters issued by Conrad III and Frederick for the archbishops of Vienne and Arles referred to information contained "in the archives of our Empire," the mobile chancery maintained no archive that could be consulted in reaching a decision. The archives in these three instances were those of the churches of Vienne and Arles, which were considered to be imperial archives because the two archiepiscopal sees were directly subject to the Empire.[39] The chancery thus relied on documentation supplied by the interested parties, and therefore the opportunities to finagle the truth were almost limitless.

If we had additional letter collections like Wibald's or other family archives like Sigiboto's, or if the imperial court had maintained a register of its transactions, we might have a better grasp of how frequently the emperor heard appeals from princely courts, ordered an inquest, commanded a prince in writing to perform a specific task; or how often he sent a widely disseminated circular, as the chancery did after the confrontation with the papal legates at Besançon or after the decimation of the imperial army in August 1167. While Frederick and his advisers were familiar with such "modern" administrative techniques as an inquest and employed writing to make their wishes known, most communication between the emperor and princes was oral and the assemblies were the place where they normally interacted. Much of the communication, like the playlet with the ministerial at the coronation, was symbolic; and the king and princes enunciated general principles rather than passing enforceable laws. Unlike Angevin England, there were no royal judges to punish malefactors or to hear suits at county courts. Indeed, while Frederick was represented by legates in Italy, he made no provision for the governance of Germany during his extended visits south of the Alps. Royal government was ultimately personal. As Karl Leyser put it, Frederick was "accustomed for his authority to radiate from his own person. He did not try to institutionalise [sic] this authority, at least not in Germany; it sufficed as it was."[40]

The Chancery

The chancery, whose personnel overlapped with those of the royal chapel, was the only permanent institution of royal government. Under Lothar III and his arch-chancellor, Archbishop Adalbert I of Mainz, there had been a complete break with the traditions of the Salian chancery and its personnel; but under Conrad the chancery had reverted to the practices of Henry V's reign. The chanceries of the three kingdoms (Germany, Italy, Burgundy) were merged into one, but each realm retained its own arch-chancellor: the archbishop of Mainz for Germany and the archbishop of Cologne for Italy. In 1157 Frederick recognized the archbishop of Vienne as the Burgundian arch-chancellor on the basis of an allegedly ancient but lapsed claim to the dignity. The arch-chancellorships were honorary offices. The arch-chancellor was responsible for the so-called recognition clause in the charters, written in the first person, in which he verified that the contents of charters issued in the kingdom under his jurisdiction were in accord with the ruler's wishes; but frequently the chancellor or even the proto-notary wrote the recognition clause on behalf of the absent arch-chancellor.[41]

Frederick inherited the personnel of his uncle's chancery, including Conrad's last chancellor, Arnold of Selenhofen. While the chancellor could be involved with the preparation of charters, he was not the head, in our sense, of a government office. Rather, he was a prince of the Empire and the politically experienced and highly educated adviser to the monarch. The chancellor might be sent on important missions and he was responsible, most famously in the case of Rainald of Dassel at Besançon, for the translation and explication of crucial correspondence. When Arnold became the archbishop of Mainz in 1153, there was some uncertainty about filling the office. After a vacancy of nearly half a year, Zeizolf, the provost of the cathedral of Speyer, briefly assumed the position; but the office was again unfilled for nearly two years until Frederick's most famous—or infamous—chancellor, Rainald of Dassel, was named for the first time in that capacity on 10 May 1156. Altogether, Frederick had nine chancellors: Arnold, Zeizolf, Rainald, Ulrich of Dürrmenz, Christian of Buch, Philip of Heinsberg, Henry, Godfrey of Spitzenberg-Helfenstein, and John. Several of them were of noble or even, like Rainald, comital origin, though Arnold was of ministerial ancestry. As was the case with Thomas Becket, the chancellorship was a stepping stone to high ecclesiastical office. Five chancellors became archbishops (Arnold, Rainald, Christian, Philip, and John), two became bishops (Ulrich and Godfrey), and Zeizolf and Henry probably died too soon to be elevated to the episcopate.[42]

In the absence of the chancellor or during a vacancy, the proto-notary assumed his responsibilities. The proto-notaries possessed considerable legal expertise and were given the title of master in recognition of their learning. They did not concern themselves with the routine business of the chancery but might be called upon to draft crucial correspondence. For example, Wibald wrote the letter notifying Pope Eugenius III of Frederick's election in consultation with Bishop Eberhard of Bamberg and the first known proto-notary, the Würzburg cathedral canon Henry. The proto-notaries were often sent on diplomatic missions by themselves or joined higher-ranking envoys. The office originated during the Second Crusade when Conrad's long-time chancellor, Arnold of Wied, accompanied the king to the Holy Land; and Henry became the adviser of the young king, Henry (VI), and handled his correspondence. Wibald was the first to style Henry, in an isolated instance in 1150, as the *protonotarius*; and "proto-notary" became the standard designation after 1157 for the de facto head of the royal secretariat. Henry of Würzburg was one of Rahewin's main sources, and Rahewin asked Henry to correct the *Deeds* because he was intimately acquainted with the inner workings of the court. Henry remained in Frederick's service until the late 1160s. His successor, Master Wortwin (1172–80), who had previously worked for the bishops of Würzburg, was a member of the imperial delegations that negotiated the end of the schism with Pope Alexander III. The third proto-notary and chaplain, Rudolf (1182–87), served as the adviser of Frederick's son, Henry VI, and was rewarded for his efforts with the bishopric of Verden. The last of the emperor's proto-notaries, Master Henry, who was first identified as such on 10 April 1189 and who eventually became the bishop of Worms, was exclusively in the young king's service.[43]

Most of the charters were drafted by the largely anonymous members of the royal chapel, mainly Germans with some Italians and Burgundians, who were provided with prebends in various cathedral chapters and collegiate churches, but who, unlike their predecessors in the late Ottonian and Salian periods, rarely advanced to the episcopate. The provost of St. Mary's in Aachen served as the head of the chapel. Not all the chaplains doubled, however, as notaries. The scribes received little professional training in the practices of the chancery, so that the notaries had considerable leeway in drafting charters and letters. Modern scholars have been able to identify at least twenty-four men who worked for the chancery during Frederick's reign, on the basis not only of their hands in the case of original documents but also of their vocabulary, orthography, nomenclature, legal expertise, and citation of sources. Nevertheless, in spite of the freedom the notaries had in drafting the charters, the documents, especially the *arengae*, which articulated the general reasons for the issuance of the diplomas, conveyed the ruler's desired public image. The number of notaries who were employed by the chancery at any given moment varied. The high point appears to have been in 1163, during the third Italian campaign, when five notaries drafted documents; at other times only one man did so. In further instances, the recipients presented the chancery with an already drafted privilege to be approved and sealed. Of the 454 original documents in the edition of Frederick's charters, 314 were written by chancery personnel and 140 by outsiders.[44] The chancery was still very much an ad hoc institution during Frederick's reign.

The best known of Frederick's notaries was the historian Godfrey of Viterbo (c. 1125–after 1191), who has been identified as the notary Arnold II. C. (Diplomatists identify scribes by the chancellor under whom they first served—in this case Arnold of Selenhofen.) There is considerable debate about Godfrey's reliability as a source and how close he was personally to Frederick and Henry VI. Godfrey, who may have been of German ancestry, was born around 1125 in Viterbo in central Italy, and was sent by Lothar to the cathedral school in Bamberg. After a stint at the papal curia, he became one of Conrad III's chaplains and drafted his first charter for Frederick six weeks into his reign, on 20 April 1152. Godfrey provided this description of his forty years in royal service:

> As a chaplain I was occupied every day around the clock in the mass and all the hours, at table, in negotiations, in the drafting of letters, in the daily arrangement of new lodgings, in looking after the livelihood for myself and my people, in carrying out very important missions: twice to Sicily, three times to the Provence, once to Spain, several times to France, and forty times from Germany to Rome and back.[45]

Godfrey was rewarded for his services with prebends in the cathedral chapters of Lucca and Pisa, and possibly also in Speyer, Mainz, and St. Bartholomew's in Frankfurt, where a Godfrey was the provost. According to a charter Godfrey of Viterbo may have drafted himself, at Donauwörth in 1169 Frederick enfeoffed his beloved vassals, "Master Godfrey of Viterbo, chaplain of the sacred palace," and his brother and nephew—on account of their lengthy service and great devotion—with the palazzo they had built, in Frederick's honor, at their own expense on their allod in Viterbo. The emperor promised to reimburse them for their expenditures. He freed them from the jurisdiction of the consuls and people of Viterbo and all other ecclesiastical and secular authorities. They and their heirs were to be subject only to the emperor. Barbarossa reserved for himself the use of the palazzo when he was in Viterbo. Princes who were in Italy on an imperial legation could also stay there.[46] Godfrey's historical writing was hardly representative. Whether his career as a chaplain and notary in the emperor's service was typical is beyond our knowledge.

Likewise, we do not know how involved Frederick himself was in the day-to-day actions of the chancery. Was he kept informed of the contents of charters that were routinely issued in his name or only of major pieces of correspondence, say, a letter addressed to the pope? Since the Carolingian period a ruler's personal contribution to signing charters was limited to the completion of the royal monogram with the so-called "executive stroke," but Frederick no longer personally added the stroke.[47] As Frederick's relations with Adrian IV deteriorated, in 1159 he ordered his notaries to place his name before the pope's and to address the pontiff in the singular. Rahewin explained: "This custom of writing, though commonly used in antiquity, is supposed to have been changed by the moderns out of a certain reverence and respect for the persons addressed. For the emperor said that either the pope ought to observe the custom of his predecessors in writing to an imperial personage, or he himself should in his letters follow the style of the emperors of old" (4.21). If the emperor really issued such a directive on the basis of his own knowledge, it indicates that he was quite familiar with chancery protocol—but did he?[48]

Godfrey of Viterbo, identified as the king's chaplain, witnessed only two documents; but they were among the most crucial of Frederick's reign: the Treaty of Constance of 1153, which laid out the terms for Frederick's imperial coronation and which became a major source of contention between him and Pope Adrian; and Frederick's confirmation of the treaty to the pope in January 1155.[49] Only the princes who had elevated Frederick to the kingship accompanied him on the expedition to Rome, the *Romzug*, to obtain the crown; and he was thus dependent on the support of his Italian allies, most notably Margrave William V of Montferrat and Pavia, who embroiled him in the internecine quarrels of the communes and their striving for autonomy and hegemony. Frederick's system of personal rule based on familial ties was of little use in this alien urban world a monarch had not visited since 1137.

CHAPTER SIX

THE *ROMZUG*

The Roman Commune

THE PRINCES HAD DECIDED the morning after Frederick's coronation, 10 March 1152, not to undertake Conrad's planned Italian expedition to obtain the imperial crown, the *Romzug*, until Pope Eugenius invited Frederick to come. The pope had not yet sent a legate to Germany, as he had promised in his letter of 17 May 1152, acknowledging Frederick's election. At the court held in Würzburg on 13 October the princes determined nevertheless to undertake the expedition to Italy within the next two years, after hearing, Otto of Freising wrote, the piteous entreaties of the Apulian exiles. They may also have learned more about conditions in imperial Italy, in particular the dangerous further radicalization of the Roman commune, from Count Guido of Biandrate, who was also in Würzburg.[1]

Inspired by the example of the Lombard communes, in 1143 the Romans had seized the Capitol, the seat of the prefect, the pope's chief official in the city, and had established a council of townspeople to which they had given the ancient title of "the senate." The burghers had replaced the prefect in 1144 with their own chief executive, whom they called "the patrician" and who became the actual ruler of the city. According to Otto, "the Roman people . . . forced all the great and noble citizens to subject themselves to the patrician and, having destroyed not only the fortified towers of certain illustrious laymen but also the homes of cardinals and of the clergy, carried off an enormous amount of booty." Eugenius, who had been elected pope on 15 February 1145, was unable to reassert effective papal control; and he spent most of his time outside Rome. In late 1145 or early 1146 the evangelical reformer Arnold of Brescia had arrived in the city. He taught, according to Otto, "that neither clerics that owned property, nor bishops

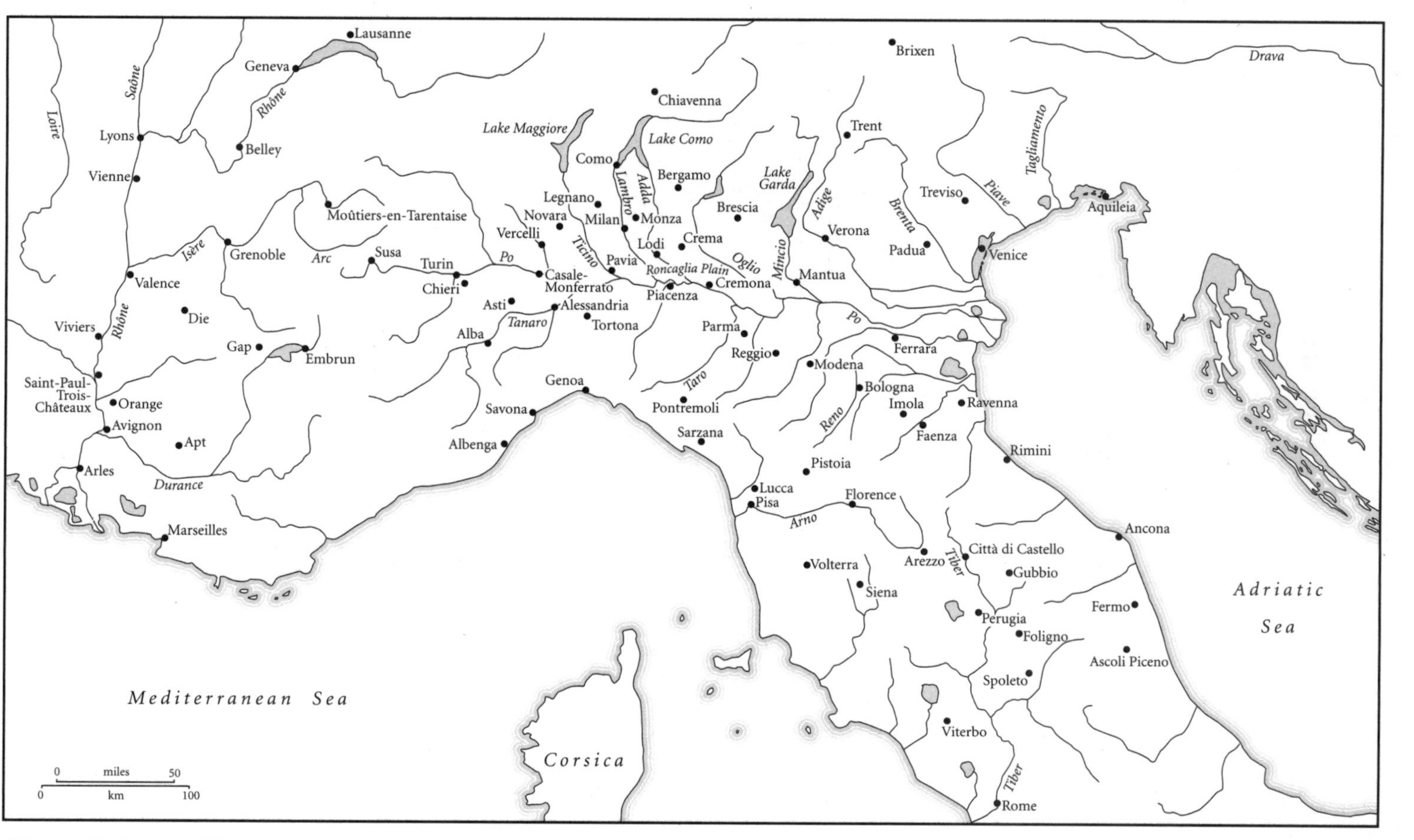

Map 3. Italy in the Twelfth Century.

that had regalia, nor monks with possessions could in any wise be saved. All these things belong to the prince, and should be bestowed of his beneficence for the use of the laity alone." Arnold thus provided a religious justification for the Romans' secular militancy.[2]

As part of his effort to counter the Byzantine alliance with Conrad, in 1149 Roger of Sicily had supplied Eugenius with troops to fight the Romans. The "senate and Roman people"—the first documented use of that ancient formula in centuries[3]—had responded, probably in early summer, by writing a letter to Conrad, whom they rebuked in deferential language, for ignoring their previous appeals. As the king's loyal subjects, they had reinstated the senate "to exalt and increase the Roman kingdom and empire," and, echoing the Staufer message of imperial renewal, "to restore it to that state in which it was at the time of Constantine and Justinian, who held the whole world in their hands by the might of the senate and of the Roman people . . ." Out of their loyalty to Conrad, they had already taken measures against those who had challenged his authority: the Roman nobles, the "Sicilian," and the pope. They had also reminded Conrad of the "great ills" the curia had caused his predecessors. The Romans were enduring the assaults of the king's enemies who were trying to prevent them from placing "the imperial crown upon the royal head as is fitting." They had invited Conrad to come quickly and to take up permanent residence in Rome, "which is the head of the world and by removing every obstacle of the clergy, to exercise dominion over all Italy and the German realm more freely and better than practically all your predecessors." Needless to say, Conrad, and later Frederick, rejected this assertion of popular sovereignty and any notion that the emperor derived his authority from the Romans; but both Otto and Wibald considered the letter important or bizarre enough to preserve it. In the end, Eugenius had been unwilling to ally with Roger against Conrad. The pope had returned to Rome in November 1149 after the Romans had renewed their oath of fealty and had surrendered to him the papal regalia and income, and he had recognized in turn the existence of the senate.[4]

At the end of 1149 "a certain retainer of the senate, the most faithful of the servants of the king," had written to Conrad, "the most illustrious and magnificent lord of the world." The author claimed to have labored in the senate and elsewhere for the exaltation of Conrad's realm and thus dared to advise the king to come to Rome without delay, to mediate between the pope and the senate, and to take the commune under his protection. Henceforth, as had been the case from the time of Gregory the Great to Gregory VII, the popes were to be installed in their office only at Conrad's command. The writer concluded that "neither wars nor murders should be caused in the world by priests. For it is not permitted to them to bear both the sword and the chalice but rather to preach and to confirm their preaching with good works and never to instigate wars and contention in the world." The anonymous "retainer of the senate" was thus an adherent of Arnold of Brescia, if not the reformer himself.[5]

Conrad did not totally ignore these Roman overtures. After the princes had consented at Würzburg on 17 September 1151 to the king's expedition to Rome, he had dispatched Archbishop-Elect Arnold of Cologne, Wibald, and the imperial notary Henry of Würzburg to the Romans as well as to Pope Eugenius to make the necessary arrangements. Conrad had thanked the Romans for the letters they had sent him after his return from the Second Crusade, in which they had expressed both their devotion to his person and their zeal for the reformation of the Empire. There was no reference in Conrad's letter to any role by the citizens in the selection of the emperor, to Rome as the capital of the Reich, or to the senate; but by addressing "all the Roman people, both small and great," as well as the prefect of the city, consuls, and captains, that is, the Roman nobles, Conrad was acknowledging the right of the Roman burghers to share in the governance of their city, subject to his and the pope's authority. The envoys appear to have come to a verbal understanding with Eugenius about his and the emperor's respective rights in the Eternal City, because the pope referred to Rome as the "royal city" in his summons to the German princes on 27 January 1152 to participate in the expedition; and on 17 May he had expressed to Frederick the hope that he would keep the promises his uncle had made to the pope and the Roman Church. Unlike the Treaty of Constance, fourteen months later, there is no indication that Conrad had agreed to the suppression of the commune or to any curtailment of his own right to negotiate with the Romans.[6]

Eugenius' stay in Rome had lasted only until the spring of 1150. He was once again at odds with Roger because the latter had crowned his son William as king of Sicily at Easter 1151 without bothering to obtain the consent of his nominal papal feudal overlord.[7] Eugenius thus needed Frederick's aid in 1152 when dealing with both the commune and Roger of Sicily.

Frederick's election announcement in the spring of 1152, which had been addressed, like Conrad's earlier message, to the city of Rome as well as the pope, prompted a rejoinder by Wezel, who was, judging by his name, a German follower of Arnold living in Rome. The tone is strikingly different from the earlier deferential language and is indicative of the radicalization, in the interim, of the communal movement or at least of some Romans. Wezel began with a calculated insult. He addressed Frederick not as king or emperor but as *clarissimus*, "most renowned," a late-antique designation for a senator. The salutation was a monumental political blunder because the Romans, who were dependent on the curia for their livelihood and who lacked the financial resources of the northern Italian communes, could hardly afford to alienate the king. Wezel congratulated Frederick on his election as king by his own people, but not as king of the Romans, let alone emperor. He then rebuked Frederick for heeding the advice of clerics and monks, who conflated divine and human teachings, and for notifying the pope of his election. The king had not sought the advice of Rome, "the sacrosanct city, the lady of the world, the creator and mother of all emperors," nor had he asked, "like a son his mother," the city, through whom princes alone ruled as emperors, to confirm his election. Rome, not the Church, was his true mother. Until now, Frederick's predecessors had been summoned to Rome by "heretics and apostate clerics and false monks," who had brought the Church and the world into disarray. In a series of biblical citations, Wezel pointed out that St. Peter, whose vicar the popes claimed to be, had warned against pontiffs who squandered the wealth of the world in riotous living. He then launched into an attack on the Donation of Constantine, according to which the imperial insignia had been conferred in simoniacal fashion on Pope Sylvester I (314–35). The Donation had been exposed in Rome as a lie and a heretical fable. Even day laborers and prostitutes could refute the arguments of the most learned men about its validity.

In a climactic insult Wezel commanded Frederick "to pay attention to what I say." An emperor needed to be learned in the law. Wezel quoted the same passage from Justinian's *Institutes* that had appeared in the election announcement, about how "it was fitting for the imperial majesty to be adorned not only with weapons but also to be defended with laws." He then cited the *lex regia*, the royal law, according to which all the rights and powers of the Roman people had been transferred to the Roman emperor, and he asked the rhetorical question: "What law, what reason prohibits the senate and people from electing an emperor?" (In spite of the Roman commune's republican rhetoric, Wezel could not conceive of a polity without a monarch.) He advised Frederick to send to Rome as soon as possible an embassy consisting of Count Rudolf of Pfullendorf, Count Ulrich IV of Lenzburg, and other suitable men, such as the otherwise unknown Eberhard of Bodman, as well as men who were learned in the law. Wezel concluded with the ominous admonition: "And take care that nothing novel occurs there that is aimed against you."[8] Since Wezel's letter seems to have reached Frederick in the summer or early autumn of 1152, it is quite possible that it contributed to the princes' decision at Würzburg on 13 October to go to Rome. It indicates, in any case, that it was widely known that Counts Rudolf and Ulrich, Frederick's companions on the Second Crusade, were his confidants.[9]

The princes may also have been informed at Würzburg about the alarming contents of the letter the pope had sent to Wibald on 20 September. A "rustic mob" of about two thousand men, under Arnold's leadership, had gathered and had determined, the pope wrote, to elect on 1 November a hundred senators and two consuls, "one of whom they want to call emperor." This radical plan to select in Frederick's place an emperor who derived his authority from the Romans may have been the substance of Wezel's admonition to Frederick to "take care that nothing novel occurs that is aimed against you." Eugenius forestalled the election by distributing "favors and money" among the Romans, and they welcomed him back "with the greatest honor" on 9 December 1152, in time to receive the envoys who were dispatched to Rome after the court at Würzburg.[10]

The Treaty of Constance

The size and composition of the imperial embassy testify to the significance Frederick and the princes attached to the negotiations with the pope in December 1152 and/or January 1153. The imperial representatives were: Bishops Anselm of Havelberg and Hermann of Constance; Count Ulrich IV of Lenzburg; and the Italian counts Guido Guerra III and Guido of Biandrate. Anselm, who had engaged in theological disputations in Constantinople while on a diplomatic mission for Lothar III and had written a treatise about these debates for Eugenius, was the Byzantine expert at the imperial court.[11] Hermann, who had attended Frederick's coronation in Aachen, had traveled in the fall of 1150 on Conrad III's behalf to Pisa and to meet the pope, presumably in conjunction with Conrad's planned coronation and invasion of the Norman kingdom.[12] The choice of Ulrich may have been a calculated response to Wezel's letter. There is no evidence that Guido Guerra, like Guido of Biandrate, had been in Würzburg in October 1152; but since Frederick sent him in 1155 to negotiate with the Apulian rebels,[13] it is possible that Guido Guerra had accompanied the Apulian exiles to Würzburg. Seven cardinals and a Cistercian abbot, Bruno of Chiaravalle, represented Eugenius in the negotiations. The cardinals included the future Pope Alexander III and his successor Lucius III; the later anti-popes, Victor IV and Paschal III; and the two legates who met with Frederick in Constance in March 1153.[14] Many of the leading players in the following years were thus intimately familiar with the provisions of the Treaty of Constance.

Eugenius, along with the cardinals, promised in Rome, on the strength of his apostolic authority and in the presence of the king's envoys, to observe the terms of the agreement. In return, an imperial ministerial was to swear on the king's soul that Frederick would do the same, and the king himself was to pledge his good faith by his own hand in the hands of a legate. (The oath "*in anima regis*" indicated that the agreement was to remain in effect after the monarch's death.) Both parties were bound to abide, without fraud or evil intent, by its terms, which could be changed only with the free and mutual consent of both parties. It was this exchange of oaths that validated the treaty. The text itself was merely a written summary of the oral agreement that had been reached and sworn. It is thus conceivable that the seemingly vague details in the text had been worked out by the negotiators and were known to both sides.[15]

The preliminary draft of the treaty that the envoys brought back with them from Rome survives only in Wibald's letter collection.[16] Two significant changes were made at Constance, presumably on the abbot's recommendation, in the final version that was inserted into the letter that Frederick sent to Eugenius on 23 March 1153, ratifying the accord. Frederick's title was changed in the inserted text from *king* to *emperor* to indicate that only the ruler of the western empire was the successor of the Caesars—the Byzantine monarch was demoted to the status of "king of the Greeks," and the pope committed himself "to the maintenance, increase, and expansion of the honor of the empire [*honor imperii*]," rather than the kingdom (*regnum*), to make clear that his obligation to aid Frederick continued after the imperial coronation. All the other references to the king and kingdom remained the same.[17]

Frederick's letter of 23 March to Eugenius is a curious hybrid document. He styled himself, to the pope no less, as "august emperor of the Romans," and as "most invincible emperor of the Romans" in the line where the royal monograph was drawn. Unusually, the pope as well as the emperor was said in the salutation to rule by the grace of God ("dei gratia"). The implication was that both owed their high offices solely to God and that Frederick was already the emperor.[18] More conventionally, Frederick expressed in the *arenga* his desire for perpetual peace and concord between the kingship and priesthood, who were bound to each other by indissoluble love. However, the conclusion of the letter has the format of a royal privilege, including a witness list and a recognition clause, in which the chancellor confirmed that the text was in accord with the king's wishes. The witnesses included, not unexpectedly, Bishops Anselm and Hermann and Ulrich of Lenzburg, but also Wibald, Welf VI, Hermann III of Baden, Count Werner of Lenzburg-Baden, another of Frederick's companions on the Second Crusade, and the royal chaplain, Godfrey of Viterbo, who had served at the papal curia before he joined the royal chancery and who had probably drafted the text of the treaty.[19] The last witness was the imperial ministerial and chamberlain Anselm, who had presumably sworn the required oath on the king's behalf.[20]

In the first article of the treaty, Frederick pledged "not to make a truce or peace with the Romans nor with Roger of Sicily [he was not given a title] without the free consent or will of the Roman Church and the Lord Pope Eugenius and his successors who wished to hold to the tenor of the said agreement with King Frederick," that is, a future pope but not Frederick could terminate the agreement. There was no similar explicit restriction on the pope's freedom to settle with the Roman commune and the Normans. Moreover, Frederick agreed "to labor with the strength of his kingdom to subject the Romans to the lord pope and to the Roman Church *sicut (melius) unquam fuerunt a centum annis retro.*"

Much of the scholarly debate as to whether the treaty favored Frederick or the pope hinges on the translation of this obscure Latin clause. Peter Rassow, who argued in 1940 that the treaty had not been a diplomatic defeat for Frederick, as had been believed until then, translated the clause "as they [the Romans] were a hundred years ago"—that is, during the reign of Henry III, who had been the patrician or protector of the pope and had chosen four successive pontiffs. In this reading of the text, the treaty established a papal–imperial condominium over the city with the emperor as the dominant partner. More recently, Jürgen Petersohn maintained that the time clause referred to the one-hundred-year statute of limitations Justinian had granted the Roman Church to regain its alienated rights. Thus, the correct translation of Frederick's concession, especially after the word *melius* was inserted in the version Frederick confirmed for Adrian IV in 1155 and the vague *they* was replaced with the more explicit *city*, is: "as the city was ever best subjected during the preceding one-hundred years," that is, when the pope exercised the most authority.[21]

Wezel's rants about the Donation of Constantine suggest that the papacy was basing its lordship over the city of Rome on that forgery, in which Constantine had allegedly conferred on Pope Sylvester, in Article 17, "the city of Rome and all the provinces, districts and cities of Italy or of the western regions." The papacy may also have invoked the Donation in the case of Sicily, because John of Salisbury, who spent considerable time at the curia between 1148 and 1152, reported that Eugenius objected to Roger's coronation of his son William in 1151, "since it was common knowledge that all Sicily belongs to the patrimony of the papacy." By agreeing not to make peace with the Romans or Roger without the pope's consent, Frederick, unlike his uncle who had retained the right to negotiate with the Romans, was tacitly recognizing the pope's sole dominion in the Eternal City and the papal claims of suzerainty over the Norman kingdom.[22]

In the second article, Frederick committed himself "as the devoted and special advocate of the Holy Roman Church to preserve and defend, as he was able, the honor of the papacy (*honor papatus*) and the regalia of St. Peter, which it now had, against all men." In addition, he would aid the Church, as he was able, to regain the regalia, that is, the rights of governance and possessions, it had lost, and would defend them. (The obligation to defend the regalia was omitted when the treaty was renewed in 1155.) This passage is usually considered to be a near verbatim repetition of the words in Lothar's coronation oath of 1133, but the clause, "as the devoted and special advocate of the Holy Roman Church against all men as he was able," does not appear in the earlier oath. In fact, the Treaty of Constance was the first time that the curia described the emperor as the advocate rather than as the defender or patron of the Roman Church. Unlike Germany, where the advocacies of churches were a key instrument in the creation of territorial lordships, the papacy conceived of the emperor's advocacy as an office that the monarch was to exercise at the pope's directive. Frederick's commitment could thus be interpreted as the obligation of a vassal to aid his feudal lord. The papal negotiators may in this way have quietly inserted into the Treaty of Constance a feudal interpretation of the imperial coronation and so prepared the legal grounds for the papal assertion at Besançon that the Empire was a papal fief.[23]

But which specific rights of governance and possessions in Rome and the Patrimony did Frederick obligate himself to protect and recuperate, and were the regalia papal allods or fiefs which the pope held from the Empire? This, too, was left unsaid. Moreover, what exactly was meant by the *honor papatus*? Rassow, who defined *honor* in narrow legal and juridical terms, conceded that the pope could use the second article to justify his claim to feudal lordship over the Norman kingdom—*honor* was a synonym for fief.[24] Or did the negotiators have something else in mind?

Both Frederick and Eugenius agreed, in a repudiation of Conrad's territorial concessions at Thessalonica, not to concede any lands in Italy to the "king of the Greeks." If Manuel I did invade the peninsula, each would labor, respectively, in accordance with the strength of Frederick's realm or of St. Peter, to expel him. Since Conrad may have tried to extricate himself from his commitment to provide his adopted daughter Eirene with a dowry in Italy by having his son marry a Byzantine princess, who would receive Eirene's dowry as her portion, or by marrying a Greek princess himself, Frederick was not so much breaking with Conrad's earlier policy as concurring with his attempt to circumvent the Treaty of Thessalonica. For his part, Eugenius may have agreed during the negotiations to the dissolution of Frederick's marriage to Adela so that he, too, would be free to seek a Greek bride. The papal legates and Bishop Hermann annulled the marriage at Constance.

Frederick subsequently sent Anselm of Havelberg, one of the imperial negotiators, and the Apulian exile Count Alexander of Gravina to Constantinople in September 1153. Their mission was to arrange the king's marriage to a Greek princess and plan a joint attack on Roger of Sicily. They carried letters from Frederick and Wibald announcing Frederick's election as king and his continuing commitment to his uncle's alliance with Manuel. The monarch responded favorably to these overtures, and Byzantine envoys accompanied Anselm back to Germany in January 1154. Anselm returned later that year to Constantinople to continue the negotiations. The basic problem was that it was impossible to gain Manuel's adherence to an anti-Norman alliance without conceding territory to him along the Adriatic and in Apulia.[25]

For his part Eugenius promised in the treaty that "he would honor Frederick as a most dear son of St. Peter and would crown him as emperor, without difficulty and opposition, as much as it was in him, when the king came for the fullness of his crown, and would help him, in accordance with the duty of the papal office, to maintain, increase, and expand the honor of his realm [*regnum* in the preliminary draft, *imperium* in the final version]." The pope was repeating here, in essence, his response to Frederick's election announcement and reiterating more explicitly that the receipt of the crown was the final step in the election of the emperor. This formulation left unanswered the questions whether the king of the Romans could exercise the power of the imperial office before his coronation—after all, Frederick called himself in the treaty "emperor of the Romans"—and whether the pope could deny him the crown. However, Frederick's designation as the pope's "most dear son" implied that he was the pope's subordinate and made it less important whether he exercised his imperial office from the day of his election or only after his coronation.[26]

The real conundrum is what the negotiators meant by the *honor imperii*, the honor of the Empire—a phrase that appears numerous times in Frederick's charters and that has become central to the interpretation of his reign—and its pendant, *honor papatus*. Rassow, who sought to prove that Frederick had not made one-sided concessions to the papacy, argued that *honor* meant in this context the Empire's political and juridical assertions of sovereignty: specifically, the Reich's claims to dominion in southern Italy and to the Matildine Lands, and to the regalian rights in Lombardy and Provence, which the papacy thus implicitly recognized in the treaty.[27] While the notaries who drafted imperial charters used *honor imperii* to refer to the trans-personal dignity and rights of the Reich, *honor*, both in Latin and English, has a wide range of meanings, including *fief*, *office*, *respect*, *fame*, *dignity*, *reputation*, and *esteem*. For a medieval nobleman like Frederick and his peers, it meant above all a man's public standing that demanded the avenging of any slight. The private and "public" dimensions of honor were inseparable for a monarch. Unpunished injustice injured both. After all, the inscription on the David plaque on the crown that Conrad may have commissioned declared: "The honor of the king loves a just judgment." Beyond that, there was a numinous quality to the medieval concept of honor that linked it to the Shekinah glory, the earthly manifestation of God's presence at Sinai.[28] In short, the emperor and pope committed themselves in the treaty to respect the sacral dignity of each other's office as well as their specific rights.

Finally, "if any persons dared, presumptuously, to trample under foot or to overturn the jurisdiction and honor of the realm (*regnum*)," the pope, out of love for the royal dignity, was to warn them, by canonical means, to satisfy the king and, if that failed, to excommunicate them. We can only speculate at whom in particular this provision was aimed: violators of the peace Frederick had proclaimed the preceding summer at Ulm, potential princely opponents in Germany during his absence in Italy, Roger of Sicily, the northern Italian communes that had usurped the regalian rights formerly exercised by their episcopal lords, or all of them?[29] Since there is no indication that Conrad, who had been crowned, after all, as the antiking by the archbishop of Milan, was at odds with the Lombards, it is not very likely that they were the unnamed specific targets of this provision. It may simply have been a generic commitment.

Three months later, at Worms on 7 June 1153, the legates deposed, at Frederick's prompting, four bishops: Archbishop Henry of Mainz, "a man often reproved for weakening his Church," according to Otto of Freising, "but never improved," who may have opposed Frederick's election; Burchard of Eichstätt, whom Otto described as "weighted down by years," but who also happened to be linked to Archbishop Henry; Bernard of Hildesheim, who was unable, allegedly, to carry out his priestly duties; and the blind Henry I of Minden.[30] This purging of the German episcopate, which enabled Frederick to replace the deposed prelates with men more to his liking, may have been negotiated in Rome as well. The papacy thus made significant one-time concessions to Frederick in Germany that were not included in the written text of the Treaty of Constance and that partially balanced Frederick's long-term concessions in Italy.

Although Rassow tried to prove that Frederick and Eugenius had concluded a bilateral agreement between equals, the best evidence that the treaty was a diplomatic defeat for the Empire is that neither Frederick nor Otto mentioned it in 1157 among the king's accomplishments. The real question is why Frederick's experienced negotiators agreed to such unfavorable terms. The answer may be that Frederick's position in Germany was not as secure as Otto presented it—during his absence in Italy, Henry the Lion's Saxon opponents met, as we saw, with the Babenberg party—and that Frederick needed to be consecrated by the pope as quickly as possible to legitimize his accession to the throne. The appeal of the Apulian exiles at Würzburg for assistance may have been a convenient pretext to set the date for the *Romzug*.

Lodi's Appeal at Constance

Otto of Freising ignored another event that occurred at Constance, according to Otto Morena (whom Lothar III had appointed as a judge). Morena began his account of Frederick's deeds in Lombardy with the arrival in Constance in March 1153 of two of Morena's fellow townspeople from Lodi. Albernardus Alamanus and Master Homobonus—a merchant and a jurist?—had come at the request of Bishop Hermann to do the bishop service. They did not know that Frederick had summoned an assembly to meet there—Otto Morena insisted that Albernardus had personally vouched for this. When they saw how many people, rich and poor, appealed to the king and the princes for justice and obtained it, they decided to bring the case of Lodi to his attention. Old Lodi was situated southeast of Milan on the Lambro, a river that leads from Lake Como to the Po between Piacenza to the west and Cremona to the east. The city was thus in a position to block Milan's access to the Po and ultimately Genoa. Albernardus and Homobonus went to a church, took two large crosses which they bore on their shoulders, and threw themselves with great sorrow at

Frederick's feet. The princes, who had never seen the like, were astonished. Normally, men of lesser rank required an influential intermediary to obtain access to the king and to arrange matters in advance, because the king's honor would be impugned if he could not give a favorable response to a petitioner. By assuming the guise of Christ carrying His cross, the Lodiese had to be received. (Carrying crosses was a customary Italian practice in making an appeal for justice or mercy.)

Albernardus, who spoke German—*Alamanus* means German—recounted the tribulations the Milanese had inflicted on Lodi. After the Milanese had destroyed the city in 1111, they had forced the exiles to swear never to live at the site again. The Lodiese had established a new market in a nearby settlement, but Milan had forced them to move it to an open field where no one lived. Albernardus and Homobonus entreated the king and the princes to order Milan to allow the Lodiese to re-establish the market at the customary site—the right to hold a market was a regalian right. Frederick, with the concurrence of all the princes, instructed his chancellor Arnold of Selenhofen to write such a mandate to Milan and he sent an envoy, Sicher, to deliver the directive. If Frederick acted without giving Milan a chance to respond to these charges, he was violating customary legal procedures and casting doubts on his own impartiality in adjudicating disputes among the Lombards.

When Albernardus and Homobonus returned home and told the consuls and the council of the wise men of Lodi what they had done, the communal leaders were terrified of Milan's possible response. They rebuked the two men and commanded them under the threat of death to tell no one. Sicher arrived in Lodi a few days later. The consuls implored him not to deliver Frederick's letter, but Sicher, although he was sympathetic to their predicament, carried out his mission. The Milanese consuls threw the royal mandate on the ground and trampled it and the seal to pieces. Their act, the medieval equivalent of burning the flag, was a gross insult to Frederick's honor, because the seal was the visible symbol of the king's authority. Then, in an additional affront to Frederick, the Milanese attacked Sicher; he was forced to flee and hide until he could escape that night. When the Lodiese learned from Sicher what had occurred, they scattered in all directions in fear of Milan's retribution. Sicher hastened back to Frederick and, prostrate at his feet, demanded vengeance. The king and the princes were livid and determined, Otto Morena said, to invade Lombardy immediately with a large army.

In the interim, the Lodiese had secretly sent Frederick a bowl of fine gold via Margrave William V of Montferrat, who had promised to aid them. Frederick took the Lodiese, joyfully, under his protection. Cremona and Pavia also offered Frederick gifts and complained about Milan and its treatment of Lodi, thus turning him, according to Otto Morena, into Milan's enemy. For their part, the Milanese tried to regain the king's grace by sending him a gold bowl filled with coins; but a public insult to the king's honor could not be assuaged with money, and he spurned their gift.

Lodi's appeal was the beginning of the long war in which Frederick "captured and destroyed," according to Otto Morena, some cities and restored others "to their former state through his most holy goodness and piety to the honor of the whole Empire . . ." Whether events occurred quite as Otto Morena recounted them is another matter.[31]

Lombardy

Frederick left Augsburg in early October 1154 and, like most of his predecessors, crossed the Alps via the Brenner Pass (4,494 feet). After stops in Brixen (Bressanone) and Trent, south of the pass, he camped near Lake Garda in the territory of Verona on 22 October. There the king sought the advice of the princes, according to Otto of Freising, because he feared that the army had angered God. Unable to find sufficient provisions in the barren mountains, the hungry men "had violated certain holy places." The king ordered "a collection to be taken from the entire army," and he conferred a considerable amount of money on the bishops of Brixen and Trent to reimburse the monasteries and churches along the route that had suffered losses from the soldiers' plundering. Frederick used the Brenner Pass on at least three of his five other Italian campaigns. (He opted to use the Mont Cenis Pass, 6,831 feet, between Savoy and western Lombardy on his fifth expedition in 1174, and may have gone directly from Swabia to Milan via the eastern Swiss passes in 1184—Lukmanier, 6,283 feet; Splügen, 6,946 feet; and Septimer, 7,579 feet.) Frederick returned to Germany via the Brenner only in 1155.

Vincent of Prague recounted that the Bohemian contingent on Frederick's second crossing of the Brenner in 1158 encountered similar logistical problems. The Bohemians had procured a large number of cattle and other supplies in Regensburg before heading toward the Brenner—these purchases showed considerable foresight since cattle were scarce in the Alpine foreland. The men suffered from a lack of food and drink, because the mountain population fled at the approach of the army—no doubt their farms had been plundered along with the holy places in 1154. When the Bohemians finally reached the area around Bozen (Bolzano), south of the Brenner, at the confluence of the Isarco (Eisack) and Adige rivers, they were able to obtain large quantities of wine, which refreshed and revived them. King Vladislav sent his agents ahead to Brixen and Trent to give surety for the Bohemians' good conduct and to arrange for the establishment of markets to supply the necessary provisions.

The cause of these logistical problems was that there was no city or even a market town in the twelfth century between Augsburg and Brixen, a distance of about 155 miles. Innsbruck, north of the Brenner, began to develop only after 1180, and even Bozen, for all of its vineyards, could not accommodate several thousand very hungry men. Basically, soldiers had to carry their provisions with them over the mountains, but a two-wheeled cart, pulled by oxen, was able to travel only about 9 miles a day and further retarded the movement of an army. Most goods were carried across the Alps, therefore, on pack animals. It was impossible to transport sufficient fodder on mountain paths to feed several thousand horses. The horses had to graze along the way, and it is no accident that, except for the second expedition that left in June, all of Frederick's other campaigns departed from Germany in September or October, when pasturage would have been most plentiful. In spite of these logistical difficulties, German rulers preferred the Brenner because it is the lowest of the important Alpine passes and its use required the traversal of only a single pass.[32] Crossing the Alps with an army, even under optimal conditions in the summer or early autumn, was a formidable undertaking.

Frederick informed his uncle Otto that he had taken only 1,800 knights with him to Italy. It has been estimated that the emperors between the tenth and thirteenth centuries normally had between 6,000 and 8,000 knights at their disposal during their Italian campaigns. Frederick himself allegedly commanded 15,000 knights in 1158 during the siege of Milan, though that figure included Italians, as well as an additional uncountable number of squires, foot soldiers, and camp followers. If the latter are included, then Frederick's army on the *Romzug* might have numbered between 5,400 and 7,200 men.[33] There is another way to determine the relative size of Frederick's forces on his campaigns. A total of twenty ecclesiastical princes, dukes, landgraves, margraves, counts-palatine, and twelve counts and lesser lords, many of them the men who had elected him, are known from the witness lists and other sources to have accompanied Frederick on the *Romzug*. In contrast, the imperial entourage in 1158 included forty-nine princes and twenty counts and lesser lords.[34] The small size of Frederick's army in 1154–55 is all the more surprising because Berthold IV of Zähringen alone had promised to supply him with 500 knights and fifty archers. But Berthold may have felt he was no longer bound by that commitment because Frederick had not undertaken the Burgundian campaign. Without adequate forces of his own, Frederick was dependent during the *Romzug* and his subsequent expeditions on the military support of his Italian noble and communal allies, like William of Montferrat and Pavia; but this meant that he was inevitably embroiled in their quarrels and could not be an impartial arbiter of the Lombards' disputes.[35] Frederick's forces were inadequate in 1154 either because he had grossly underestimated the number of men he needed to assert imperial authority in Italy and/or because his support in Germany was tenuous. In fact, Otto admitted that Frederick set out from Augsburg in October 1154 in spite of "no little murmuring" among the princes about his treatment of his uncle Henry Jasomirgott (2.11).

Frederick's predecessors had rarely set foot in Italy. The Ottonians had spent a total of nearly seventeen years in the peninsula between 951, when Otto the Great obtained the Italian crown, and the death of Otto III in 1002; but the German presence had diminished in the 150 years preceding Frederick's accession in 1152. Henry II, the Salians, Lothar III, and Conrad III, who never went to Italy as king, had been in Italy for only a combined total of twenty-two years.[36] Otto observed that the Lombards had become wealthy and powerful precisely because their princes had remained north of the Alps (2.13). Frederick, who eventually spent thirteen years of a thirty-eight-year reign in Italy, broke with this tradition of absentee kingship.

Frederick stayed most of his time during his six Italian sojourns in Lombardy. Of his 291 known Italian stopping places, 168 were located in Lombardy, twenty-one in Venetia, fifty-four in Emilia-Romagna, twenty-four in Tuscany, twenty in the duchy of Spoleto and the marks in east-central Italy, and only four in Rome or Latium. His preferred quarters were episcopal sees, though it is important to remember that most Italian cities, unlike German ones, were bishoprics. The kaleidoscopic shifts in communal alliances dictated where he resided. Frederick visited most frequently his chief urban allies, Pavia and Lodi, thirty and seventeen times respectively. He was in Turin on at least seven occasions; in Ravenna six times; in Bologna, Cremona, Milan, and Parma on five sojourns each; and in Piacenza on four visits. Altogether, he stayed 139 times in forty-five different bishoprics. He also spent time in more than 140 Italian castles, villages, and manors; for example, he was twice each in Crema, Marengo, Monza, Susa, and Viterbo. As was true in Germany, he rarely visited a monastery. The exception was monastery-palace complexes, like St. Zeno's in Verona, which were situated outside the walls of an episcopal see.[37]

Otto, who did not accompany his nephew to Italy but had been there at least twice in the 1140s,[38] included a famous description of Italy in the *Deeds*, whose substance he may have shared with Frederick before his departure. The Lombards followed the example of their Roman ancestors, Otto explained, in the governance of their cities. They were ruled by consuls, who were selected, usually annually, from the ranks of the great nobles, their vassals, and the commoners. The cities had subjected most of the surrounding countryside, the *contado*, and the nobles who dwelled there, to their authority. However, the Lombards had retained "traces of their barbaric imperfection, because while boasting that they live in accordance with law, they are not obedient to the laws. For they scarcely if ever respect the prince to whom they should display the voluntary deference of obedience or willingly perform that which they have sworn by the integrity of their laws, unless they sense his authority in the power of his great army" (2.13).

Since the Empire had been transferred from the Greeks to the Franks, it was customary, Otto said, for kings to send ahead of them to Italy experienced members of their household to collect from the cities and towns certain payments which they owed the royal treasury and which the inhabitants called the *fodrum*. The *fodrum* during the Ottonian and Salian periods had been the functional equivalent of the German *servitium regis*, the obligation to supply the itinerant royal household with provisions, and was distinct from the duty to quarter the king and from the tax to support the army. It had been converted by the twelfth century from the delivery of provisions into a cash payment. Contrary to what Otto said and the practice in Germany, all individuals or entities that were directly subject to the king—bishops, imperial abbeys, and nobles as well as the communes—were required to pay the *fodrum*, which was levied throughout imperial Italy, including in the Patrimony. Pope Adrian IV and the communes subsequently sought to limit the obligation to the *Romzug*, whereas Frederick tried to turn the *fodrum* into a tax that was due during all his stays in Italy and that was conflated, in those areas directly under imperial control, with the annual *fodrum* which the inhabitants of the *contado* owed to their episcopal, communal, or noble lord. Otto added that many cities, towns, and castles refused to pay all or part of the *fodrum*, so that when Frederick arrived at these places, he razed them as a warning to others.[39]

Moreover, Otto ascribed to the king rights in Italy, presumably on the basis of the Frankish conquest of the peninsula, which far exceeded his prerogatives in Germany. Otto asserted: "When the prince enters Italy all dignities and magistracies must be vacated and everything administered by his nod, in accordance with legal decrees and the judgment of those versed in law." The king's authority was so great that, according to the Italian judges, Otto reported, it was just for the monarch to requisition "as much as he needs from all that the land customarily produces that is essential for his use and may be of advantage to the army, only excepting [the oxen necessary for plowing] and the seed devoted to the cultivation of the soil."[40] It is inconceivable that any German prince, including Frederick as the duke of Swabia or Otto himself, would have tolerated such infringements of his lordship; but it is less clear whether Frederick and his advisers arrived in Italy with such notions of his prerogatives or whether such claims were a response to the resistance that Frederick encountered on his progress through Lombardy.

In 1157 Frederick himself provided his uncle with this retrospective summary of what happened when he set out, as he had in Germany after his coronation, to receive the homage of his Lombard subjects and to settle their disputes: "Because this land [Lombardy], on account of the prolonged absences of the emperors, had initiated rebellion, we were wroth and destroyed almost all its strongholds by the just and righteous anger not of our knights (*milites*) but of the lower ranks (*servientes*)."[41] Frederick's statement was an admission that he had left behind him a swathe of destruction and that he had not always been able to maintain proper military discipline.

Frederick did not head directly to Rome after crossing the Brenner Pass to suppress the commune, to receive the imperial crown, and then to attack the Normans, as the terms of the Treaty of Constance would seem to have demanded. Instead, he headed westward across the northern Italian plain on a royal ride-about. From Verona, he went via Brescia, Bergamo, and Cremona, to Lodi. Lodi's reception of Frederick when he arrived in its territory on 28 November 1154 belies Otto Morena's account of Frederick's tacit alliance with Lodi. The citizens, who had assembled in Piacentino, the site of the market that had been the subject of the Lodiese complaint at Constance, manfully resisted, according to Morena, the Germans' attempt to take the settlement. Fearful of the Germans, some of them fled initially with their wives, children and moveable property to another settlement, others went to Milan, but most hastened to either Cremona or Piacenza. They then returned to Old Lodi, because Frederick had set up his tent in Piacentino. He sent one of his chaplains to them and demanded they swear an oath of allegiance to him. The Lodiese responded that they could not do so without Milan's permission. When the Milanese consuls gave their consent after much deliberation, the Lodiese, who had perhaps feared

Milanese reprisals, joyfully complied.[42] Lodi hardly received Frederick as its liberator.

Between 30 November and 6 December, Frederick held an assembly on the plain of Roncaglia in the Po valley near Piacenza, which was attended "by the princes, consuls, and elders of almost all the cities." It was customary on the *Romzug*, Otto said, "for the kings of the Franks (who are also called kings of the Germans)" to muster their troops there. A shield was suspended from a wooden beam, and a herald summoned the king's vassals "to stand watch over the prince the ensuing night." The princes in turn called their men and confiscated the fiefs of anyone who had stayed home without permission. Frederick enforced this custom and seized the fiefs not only of "some laymen but also the regalia of certain bishops, namely, Hartwig of Bremen and Ulrich of Halberstadt." Otto added that this penalty affected Hartwig and Ulrich personally but not their churches, which had been granted the regalia in perpetuity. Since only two German archbishops and seven bishops are known to have accompanied Frederick to Italy, the very selective enforcement of the penalty for non-attendance strongly suggests that Barbarossa targeted Hartwig and Ulrich as part of his accommodation of his cousin Henry the Lion, by depriving two of the duke's most determined opponents of their material resources.[43]

It has long been assumed that the German bishops bore the brunt of the crown's military demands, especially during Frederick's reign; and in the twelfth century the German prelates acquired a reputation for their warlike demeanor. The ratio between the size of the retinues of the lay and ecclesiastical princes at Venice in 1177 and at Mainz in 1184—assuming the men were all able-bodied knights—was roughly 1:4.5 and 1:2.5 respectively. Except for Frederick's second invasion of Poland in 1172, more ecclesiastical than lay princes accompanied Frederick on each of his campaigns.[44] However, such figures are deceptive, because there were forty-four German bishops who were tenants-in-chief of the crown but only eighteen lay princes before 1180 in the same category. If one takes this disparity in numbers into consideration, then the bishops comprised 70 percent of the estate of princes and 67 percent of the princely participants in Frederick's wars. As was the case with the lay princes, some bishops, most notably the archbishops of Mainz and Cologne and the bishops of Worms and Würzburg, were more engaged in military affairs than others. With the notable exceptions of Rainald of Dassel and Christian of Buch, most bishops did not fight personally.[45]

On 5 December 1154, while he was still at Roncaglia, Frederick renewed, at the request of the Italian bishops and princes, Lothar III's 1136 constitution that had forbidden the selling or mortgaging of all or part of a fief without the permission of the vassal's lord; and, unlike his predecessor, Frederick made the prohibition retroactive. To stop a seller of a fief from concealing the transaction by means of a fraudulent investiture of the buyer, the court ruled that the fief would escheat to the seller's lord and that the notary who had drafted the legal instruments would lose his hand as well as his office. In addition, vassals in both Germany and Italy were to be deprived of their fiefs if they did not heed their lords' summons to participate in the *Romzug*.[46] Since there is no evidence that the German princes, as the king's tenants-in-chief, had been legally required before 1154 to provide him with such military service, the extension of this Italian legal practice to Germany was another step, like the Concordat of Worms, in defining the monarch's relations with the princes in feudal terms.[47]

In a tacit admission that it was impossible to prevent the commercialization of fief-holding, four years later another assembly at Roncaglia ruled that anyone who had purchased in good faith a fief that had been illegally alienated could sue the seller for the return of the purchase price. What was left unsaid was that the buyer retained the fief if the seller could not refund the money. In addition, vassals in both Italy and Germany were now required to participate, when summoned, in all imperial campaigns, not just in the *Romzug*. In lieu of their personal service, they could either send a suitable substitute or pay half the annual income of the fief, basically scutage or shield money as it was called in England. The penalty for noncompliance was loss of the fief. Frederick was trying to ensure that in future he would not have to fight with insufficient forces.[48] Judging by the princes' failure to participate in Frederick's later campaigns and by *The Saxon Mirror*, which was written around 1220, the princes' formal obligation to accompany the king to Italy continued to be limited to the *Romzug*.[49] Ultimately, accompanying the king to Rome for his coronation or on any campaign was not just, or even primarily, a legal obligation, but a matter of princely status and honor in a society suffused with a warrior ethos, and a way to earn fame and the emperor's favor. Serving the king secured both tangible and intangible rewards. To procure men, Frederick had to appeal to both desires.[50]

Genoese ambassadors, no doubt eager to secure Frederick's goodwill, gave him, at the 1154 assembly in Roncaglia, lions, ostriches, parrots and other gifts they had obtained when they captured, Otto said, Almeria and Lisbon (correctly Tortosa rather than Lisbon) during the Second Crusade. The bishop of Asti and Margrave William V of Montferrat, "practically the only one of the barons of Italy who could escape from the authority of the cities," according to his brother-in-law Otto of Freising, complained respectively about the insolence of the people of Asti and Chieri.[51] Both cities were destroyed a few weeks later by Frederick and Margrave William of Montferrat. It is possible that William had already conveyed his complaints to the king at Würzburg in October 1152, via his sister's husband, Count Guido of Biandrate, and when he had allegedly sent or delivered in person Lodi's gold bowl to Frederick.

Otto, who said nothing about what had transpired at Constance in March 1153, began his account of Frederick's confrontation with Milan at Roncaglia. The consuls of Como and Lodi made, he said, "a mournful lament over the arrogance of the people of Milan" in the presence of two Milanese consuls, Oberto de Orto and Gerardo Negri. Otto did not indicate how his nephew responded to these accusations. Instead, he related that Frederick, who was planning to visit the upper reaches of the Po valley, asked the two consuls to guide him through Milanese territory and to make suitable arrangements for his encampments. Oberto, who was the author of the first recension of the *Libri feudorum*, the compilation of Lombard feudal law, and who was described by an eyewitness as Frederick's chief legal adviser at Roncaglia in 1154, probably drafted Frederick's first law about fiefs. It is hard to reconcile Oberto's services with any notion of a fundamental antagonism between Frederick and Milan going back to Milan's destruction of his seal the previous year.[52]

Otto Morena conceded that at Roncaglia Milan had in fact allied with Frederick, but under false pretenses the judge hastened to add, and had promised the king 4,000 marks—more than 900 kilograms of silver. Frederick admitted as much. He wrote to his uncle Otto in 1157 that the "proud and cunning people of Milan" had sworn falsely and promised him "much money, that by our grant they might exercise lordship over Como and Lodi." Neither their entreaties nor their money could persuade him, he insisted, to do so. Frederick may have protested too much. If anything, the king appears to have been pursuing at Roncaglia a policy of resolving disputes in Lombardy so that he would be free to proceed to Rome without fear of conflict breaking out in his rear. The Milanese Anonymous, who shortly after 1177 wrote his history of Frederick's oppression of Lombardy, reported that Frederick had ordered both the Milanese and Pavians at Roncaglia to desist from their feud and to surrender to him the prisoners they had captured in the previous summer's fighting as hostages for their future good conduct. With the benefit of hindsight, the Milanese Anonymous accused Frederick of intending from the start to subject the Lombards to his authority and of cunningly realizing that this could be done best by backing the weaker Pavia against the stronger Milan; but there is no reason to ascribe such motives to Frederick in 1154.[53]

In reality, Frederick's relations with Milan soured only after the two consuls led his army astray, he thought deliberately in 1157, and the Milanese refused his command to rebuild Como and Lodi. It is quite possible that Frederick initially intended to go from Roncaglia, southeast of Milan, to Monza ten miles northeast of Milan, to be crowned king of Italy, as Conrad had been in 1128 and as the author of the poetical version of his *Deeds* said Frederick wished. Certainly, it would have been odd if he had not visited on his progression Milan, the most important city in Lombardy. Pro-imperial and pro-Milanese chroniclers differ on how the commune received Frederick and his forces but agree on the king's violent response to Milan's perceived affront. According to Otto of Freising, the Milanese consuls led Frederick through a "wasteland." The army was unable to procure provisions, and Frederick, further exasperated by the torrential rain, Milan's refusal to rebuild the two cities of Como and Lodi, and its attempt to bribe him, dismissed the two consuls. Otto Morena indicated that the royal forces, which were unable to find fodder for their horses, got as far as Landriano, which is located west of Lodi and where they spent three days (7–9 December 1154). The Milanese Anonymous told a very different story. Frederick released at Landriano the Pavian hostages he had received at Roncaglia, but he had the Milanese captives tied to the tails of horses and dragged through the muck. Some managed to escape and fled, whereas others purchased their freedom. The bakers and other purveyors who had kept the army supplied were robbed and sent packing. Since it would have made little sense for Milan to antagonize deliberately an imperial army in its immediate vicinity rather than to hasten the Germans on their way as quickly as possible, the most plausible explanation is that the city did make an effort to provision the royal forces; however, the supplies were inadequate, perhaps because the countryside had been devastated by the previous fighting between Milan and Pavia. Frederick consequently lashed out at the perceived Milanese treachery.[54]

Both pro- and anti-imperial sources agree on what happened next. The Milanese had stationed 500 knights in the town and castle of Rosate, 10 miles southwest of Milan. Frederick ordered the garrison, including the women and children, to leave; and they did. The royal forces plundered the provisions in Rosate and then burned it. Some of the king's knights advanced to the gates of Milan and wounded or captured many Milanese. In spite of these provocations, the Milanese showed remarkable forbearance and tried to avoid a complete break with the king. According to Otto of Freising's report, to assuage Frederick's anger the Milanese ordered the destruction of the house belonging to one of the consuls, Gerardo Negri, who was blamed for misdirecting the imperial army; but this act of expiation failed to achieve its goal, apparently, because Frederick had not been personally involved in determining either the consul's punishment or its execution. In spite of the grief and anger of the Milanese, the hostile Otto Morena conceded that they bore their losses with extraordinary equanimity in public. A few days later, while Frederick was staying at Biandrate, they also offered to pay him the promised 4,000 marks. The king called them a bunch of evil, conniving deceivers, expelled them from his court, and demanded, in an escalation of the conflict, that Milan fulfill unconditionally his demand concerning the restoration of Como and Lodi.[55]

Otto of Freising made no effort to disguise the fact that Frederick's next measures favored Pavia, Novara, and Count Guido of Biandrate. On 15 December 1154 Frederick's army crossed the Ticino, the tributary of the Po, west of Milan, and destroyed two wooden bridges that Milan had built to attack Novara, which had recognized Guido's lordship, and Pavia. Assisted by forces from these two cities, just before Christmas the king destroyed castles at Momo, Galliate, and Trecate, located north and east of Novara, which, according to Otto, Milan had built to subject the people of Novara to its control. Frederick told his uncle in 1157 that he had celebrated Christmas filled with great joy at the destruction of these Milanese strongholds.[56] He may also have imposed upon Milan at the end of 1154 a preliminary sentence of outlawry.[57] Perhaps the greatest insult to Frederick's honor was that he lacked the forces to do anything more substantive against Milan.

Frederick headed west, via Vercelli, to Turin, where he crossed the Po, and reached Chieri, south of Turin. The inhabitants of Chieri, who had presumably been outlawed at Roncaglia on the insistence of Margrave William, fled at Frederick's approach; and he spent several days there consuming its abundant supplies before destroying its fortifications and burning the town. Asti suffered a similar fate at the hands of Margrave William on 1 February 1155.[58] Before leaving Asti, Frederick issued an ordinance to maintain peace among his men. He required everyone, of high rank or low, to swear not to carry a sword in the camp's confines. Violators would lose a hand or even their head. Otto commented, perhaps somewhat sanctimoniously: "After this order—as wise as it was necessary—had been laid down, the thoughtless violence of youthful spirits was calmed" (2.19). Frederick may have learned on the *Romzug* the need to procure adequate supplies for his men and to maintain discipline among them.

The Siege and Destruction of Tortona

The culmination of Frederick's increasingly confrontational progress through Lombardy was the more than two-month-long siege and destruction of Tortona (13 February–20 April 1155), which is situated southwest of Pavia on the road that linked Milan to Genoa. Once again, there are diametrically opposed pro-imperial sources, Otto of Freising and Otto Morena, and pro-Milanese ones, namely, a cleric of Tortona who provided an eyewitness account of his city's destruction and the Milanese Anonymous, who may have used the cleric's narrative as a source. Their common subtext is the inadequacy of Frederick's forces, which made it difficult for him to capture even a minor, admittedly extremely well-fortified, city, and which made the king dependent upon his Italian allies, Pavia and William of Montferrat. Where the sources differ most significantly is about the circumstances surrounding Tortona's surrender and destruction.

The Tortona cleric insisted that Bishop Otbert of Tortona and the consuls had welcomed Frederick's envoys prior to his arrival in Italy, had sworn obedience to the king, and paid the *fodrum*. They had reluctantly complied with Frederick's demand at Roncaglia that they surrender the Pavians whom they had captured, but they had refused to pay him an exorbitant amount of money because the payment would have ruined them. According to Otto Morena, the Tortonians had ignored Frederick's summons to respond to Pavia's charges at his court because they deemed the king to be biased against them and, more probably, because they trusted in Milan's power. Otto of Freising indicated that Pavia considered Tortona a more dangerous enemy than Milan because of the threat Tortona posed to Pavia's territory south of the Po, and that Frederick proscribed Tortona because it was Milan's ally.[59]

Frederick moved from Asti to Bosco, southwest of Tortona, and on 7 February he sent ahead his teenage brother Conrad, Duke Berthold IV of Zähringen, and his standard-bearer, Otto V of Wittelsbach, to reconnoiter. The Tortona cleric indicated that they also launched a surprise attack on Tortona that was repulsed. The siege began on 13 February.

Tortona is situated at the foot of the Apennines. The citadel, which overlooked the plain of the Po valley, was on top of a mountain with nearly precipitous sides and was defended by massive walls and towers, one of which, the *Rubea* or Red, was said to have been built by Tarquin the Proud, the last king of Rome. Only one side of the citadel was even remotely scalable. Pavia's militia and Margrave William reinforced the imperial forces that besieged Tortona. The Milanese—around 100 knights and 200 archers under the leadership of their consuls—and the men of Margrave Obizzo Malaspina, who served as the overall commander of the garrison, were ensconced in the citadel. (Obizzo's presence in Tortona shows that members of the Italian high aristocracy were not fundamentally opposed to the communes but that their allegiances, like those of the cities, shifted as their interests dictated. By June 1157 Obizzo was fighting alongside William of Montferrat and Pavia against Milan.)[60]

Henry the Lion and the Pavians stormed and burned the lower city on 17 February, while the inhabitants retreated during the night to the citadel. Frederick wrote to his uncle Otto in 1157 that nightfall and a severe storm had prevented the imperial forces from also taking the citadel that day. Frederick built siege engines and bombarded the fortress. An attempt to undermine the *Rubea* was thwarted by the garrison. A groom set an example of personal courage by climbing, in a hail of spears and stones thrown down by the defenders, the wall in front of the tower. Frederick wished to honor the groom by making him a knight, but the man did not wish to ascend beyond his station, so the king gave him more material rewards. Members of the garrison sallied forth repeatedly, and Frederick hanged those who were captured. These sallies were directed at a spring that was the defenders' only source of water. Frederick made it non potable by commanding it to be filled with the corpses of men and beasts and then by having burning torches of sulfur and pitch cast into it. In the end, it was thirst that forced Tortona's capitulation.[61]

Frederick granted Tortona a truce from Maundy Thursday to Easter Monday (24–28 March). On Good Friday a procession of Tortona's clerics and monks, dressed not in penitential garb but in their ecclesiastical vestments, and carrying crosses, censers, and other liturgical vessels, approached the king's tent. Frederick refused to receive men who had lost his grace but sent bishops and educated men to ascertain the purpose of the clerics' visit. Otto of Freising, who, it should be stressed, was not there, included their lengthy response in his narrative. The clerics' speech cannot be dismissed simply as the bishop's invention, because the unnamed Tortona cleric, who may well have been part of the delegation, also reported that the clerics sought to speak with the king but were denied access to him. The major difference is that in Otto's version the clerics pleaded only on their own behalf. They were innocent, peaceful bystanders who had been trapped in a rebellious city. In contrast, the Tortona cleric, who wrote immediately after the event, indicated, more plausibly, that the clergy had come at the behest of the townspeople and had interceded on their behalf.

The intriguing feature of Otto's narrative consists of the words that a personified Tortona addressed to Pavia and Frederick. The king was punishing Milan on account of its destruction of Como, but Pavia was guilty of worse crimes. Tortona had allied with Milan out of fear of Pavia after the latter had through trickery destroyed the imperial town of Lomello, situated between Tortona and Pavia. Pavia had reduced the margrave of Lomello, "the most renowned among the nobles of Italy," to its client. Instead of Pavia paying taxes to the margrave, the count-palatine of Italy was paying tribute to Pavia. The margrave's subordination demeaned Frederick and the Reich. How could Frederick punish "the excesses of all the other cities of Italy," Tortona asked, if his chief judge fought under the banner of the worst offender, Pavia? Justice demanded that Pavia be held to account first. Tortona's supposed words may have been a veiled avuncular warning that partisanship threatened to turn Frederick's divine mandate to restore peace and justice in Italy into tyranny, but how likely is it that the king would have grasped Otto's meaning if his interpreters even bothered to read and translate the speech for him? Otto, in an unpersuasive attempt to soften the image of Frederick's severity, said that Frederick was inclined to show the clerics mercy, but to avoid the appearance of weakness he ordered that they return to the citadel.[62]

Otto may have dictated these words out of embarrassment at the circumstances surrounding Tortona's capitulation. According to him, the city was compelled by thirst to surrender. Frederick, whose mildness and mercy Otto hailed, allowed the wretched inhabitants to depart in safety before permitting the city to be demolished and burned, a just punishment for its rebellion. Otto Morena added that the men and women were allowed to take only what they could carry. Then the forces of the king and of Henry the Lion together with the Pavians entered the citadel, and, after plundering it thoroughly, burned and destroyed it to its foundation walls. After Frederick's departure, the Pavians remained another eight days in Tortona to complete the work of demolition.

The Milanese Anonymous indicated that Tortona surrendered on 18 April after the Cistercian abbot Bruno of Chiaravalle had mediated a settlement. (Bruno had been a member of the papal delegation in Rome that had negotiated the terms of the Treaty of Constance, so he was already known to some members of Frederick's court.) Frederick had promised to spare the city from destruction. Some of the inhabitants had left with what they could carry, but others had remained in the cathedral. Nevertheless, Frederick entered the city and destroyed it completely because the Pavians had bribed him. Abbot Bruno, overcome by pain and grief, is said to have died three days later.[63]

The Tortona cleric also ascribed to Abbot Bruno a mediating role. When Frederick realized that he could not capture Tortona by force, he decided to resort to guile. He pretended that he was prepared to negotiate, but the discussions were long fruitless until Bruno and other prominent members of the court succeeded in arranging the terms for the city's submission. The mediators promised in the king's name that the burghers' persons and property would be spared if they gave the city into the king's power. The contents of the churches and other sacred places were to remain inviolable, and the city's fortifications were to stay intact so it could defend itself. However, "the glory and honor of the king and of the holy Empire" required a formal, staged ceremony of submission. Accordingly, at three in the afternoon of Monday, 18 April, Margrave Obizzo Malaspina, the consuls of Milan, and the townspeople of Tortona—in all probability barefoot and in penitential garb as custom demanded on such occasions—appeared before the king and threw themselves at his feet. Frederick met them with a friendly countenance and received them in his grace, but at six o'clock he ordered them to be dispersed among the princes and placed under guard. The following morning the Germans and others stormed into the city and destroyed everything. The Pavians remained in Tortona until Friday of the following week to complete the destruction of the city and did not spare even the graves in the churches.[64]

It is impossible to tell with certainty what really happened. Deceit could be a virtue in the conduct of military operations, but it was less honorable, and in the long run counterproductive, for a king to break his word. Could Otto of Freising have known the truth and drawn an implied parallel between what happened at Lomello—the Pavians had captured the inhabitants of Lomello after inviting them to feigned peace negotiations—and what really occurred at Tortona? Or was the whole sorry incident indicative of Frederick's weakness? Since he lacked the manpower and siege engines to capture even a relatively insignificant city like Tortona by himself, was he powerless to control the actions of his allies even when he had given assurances that he would spare Tortona? The bitter irony was that the dispersed inhabitants of Tortona, aided by Milan, reoccupied the city on 1 May and quickly rebuilt it. Milan was stronger than ever. The only thing the siege of Tortona had accomplished, as Otto hinted, was to delay further Frederick's march to Rome; and a papal embassy urged him, in fact, after the fall of Tortona to come quickly. If Frederick ever really intended to attack the Norman kingdom—and the events at Tortona reveal how ill-prepared he was for such an invasion—arriving in the summer heat in southern Italy made any such scheme foolhardy.[65] Frederick himself, on his march to

Rome, wrote to his brother-in-law, Landgrave Louis II of Thuringia, that he had successfully completed all his tasks in Lombardy.[66]

The Pavians invited Frederick to their city to celebrate with a triumph his victory over Tortona, and he was crowned as king on 24 April 1155 in the church of St. Michael in Pavia. Gunther offered in the *Ligurinus* a poetical description of Frederick's entry into Pavia, which, admittedly, echoes the accounts of Christ's reception in Jerusalem on Palm Sunday. He was greeted by the bishop and clergy dressed in their liturgical vestments and by the knights on magnificently caparisoned horses. The festively clad people lined the streets that were hung with tapestries and covered with colored blankets and threw their garments before the approaching horses. Gunther's description cannot have been totally fanciful, because there are other succinct references to Frederick or his wife Beatrice's jubilant reception in other cities.[67]

The *Authentica Habita*

From Pavia, Frederick made his way, via Piacenza, toward the vicinity of Bologna, where he spent Whitsunday (15 May). He crossed the Apennines into Tuscany and instructed the Pisans to outfit ships to fight Roger of Sicily's son, King William I. At least officially, Frederick had not abandoned his commitment to attacking the Norman kingdom. At the end of May he invested Anselm of Havelberg with his new dignity, after Anselm had returned from Constantinople without a Greek bride for Frederick and had just been elected by the clergy and people of Ravenna as their archbishop. Many fortified places and princes in Lombardy, Romagna, and Tuscany submitted, according to Otto Morena, to Frederick as he made his way southward. The Lombard chroniclers were uninterested in what occurred outside Lombardy.[68]

Frederick's journey from Pavia to Rome was not quite so uneventful. The anonymous, pro-imperial Lombard poet, who wrote in the 1160s a verse version of Frederick's *Deeds*, reported that Frederick camped for several days along the Reno river, outside Bologna, so his men could get some rest. The population streamed out of the city bearing gifts for the king and abundant provisions for his men. It would be wonderful to know whether this idyllic scene is merely poetic license or was the kind of reception the king normally received from a pro-imperial city. The teachers of law and their students also approached Frederick, and he enquired about why they had chosen to live in Bologna and how the townspeople treated them. One of the doctors of law responded that Bologna was a very pleasant place and that they were treated extremely well, except that the individual students and teachers were liable for the debts of their fellow countrymen. After Frederick consulted with the princes, he issued a law that placed the students and professors under his protection at their place of study and on their journeys to and from that site, and that absolved them from any liability for their compatriots' obligations. These verses are a nearly verbatim summary of a privilege, the *Authentica Habita*, which Frederick granted the Bolognese teachers and students of law. The king directed that his law be inserted in Justinian's codification of Roman law after the title that freed a son from liability for his father's debts or the converse, a situation that was deemed to be analogous to the students' liability for the debts of others.[69]

This meeting with the Bolognese teachers of law was, almost certainly, Frederick's first encounter with the four doctors of law—Bulgarus, Martin, James, and Hugh—who probably drafted the privilege and subsequently formulated the laws that Frederick issued at Roncaglia in 1158. Such contacts between a monarch and experts in Roman law were not new. For example, Frederick's great-uncle, Henry V, had already utilized during his second stay in Italy the legal expertise of Irnerius, the founder of the legal school in Bologna and the doctors' own teacher.[70] The peculiar name of Frederick's privilege is derived from its inclusion in Justinian's Code. The last part of the Code consisted of the *Novels*, laws that were issued after the publication of the Code. *Authentics* were extracts from the *Novels* or subsequent imperial enactments, like Frederick's privilege, that were inserted into the Code. *Habita* was the first word in the portion of Frederick's privilege that was included in the Code; hence the new title became known as the *Authentica Habita*. Stripped in the Code of its specific Bolognese origins, Frederick's privilege became the generic legal basis for the development of academic freedom at medieval universities because of the privileged jurisdiction it bestowed upon all students.[71]

Of more immediate interest was the statement in May 1155, a month before Frederick's imperial coronation, that the knowledge of "divine and sacred laws" illuminated the world and taught subjects "to obey God and us, His servant." Even more significantly, Frederick did not hesitate, as Justinian's still uncrowned imperial successor, to command that his own privilege be added to the Code. The professors who drafted the *Habita* were asserting implicitly, in other words, that the emperor-elect obtained his power directly from God and that he exercised his imperial authority from the day of his election rather than from his coronation by the pope. Wibald had already staked out the same ideological position in the election announcement. Frederick did not need his future chancellor, Rainald of

Dassel, to instruct him in the origins and nature of his imperial authority.[72] The problem is that we do not know how familiar Frederick was with the contents of letters and charters that were written in his name.

Frederick's Meeting with Pope Adrian IV at Sutri

While Frederick and Otto simply ignored the Treaty of Constance in their accounts of the king's *Deeds*, they deliberately distorted what occurred when Frederick met Pope Adrian IV at Sutri, outside Rome, on 8 or 9 June 1155—the sources disagree about the precise date. Frederick wrote in the list of his accomplishments: "Then we advanced directly through Lombardy, Romagna, and Tuscany and reached Sutri. There the lord pope, with the entire Roman Church, met us joyfully, paternally offered us holy consecration, and complained to us of the injuries he had suffered at the hands of the Roman populace."[73] Otto embellished Frederick's stark statement: "Now on his way to the City [Rome] the king encamped near Viterbo [Sutri is southwest of Viterbo]. Thither came the Roman pope, Hadrian, with his cardinals, and was received with the honor due to his office. He was given a deferential hearing as he uttered bitter complaints against his people" (2.28). We would never guess from their words that there had been a major confrontation at Sutri.

Cardinal Boso, the chamberlain of the Roman Church, gave a very different version of these events in his *Life of Pope Adrian*. After Frederick's destruction of Tortona, the pope was alarmed by his rapid advance toward Rome and sent a delegation of cardinals to the "king of the Germans." Frederick welcomed them at San Quirico, south of Siena. He acceded to the pope's request that Arnold of Brescia, who had provided religious inspiration for the anti-papal communal movement in Rome and whom Frederick had apprehended, be turned over to the legates. Frederick was unwilling, however, to respond to the other papal demands until the embassy he had sent earlier to the pope to discuss the coronation had returned. The imperial envoys, Archbishop Arnold II of Cologne and Anselm of Havelberg, the new archbishop and exarch of Ravenna, had assured Pope Adrian of the king's good intentions; but the pope, suspicious of Frederick's purposes, refused to reply until the cardinals had come back from their mission to the king. The paths of the two embassies crossed and they decided to go together to Frederick, who was by then in Viterbo. In the presence of the entire court, an unnamed noble knight swore, on his and the king's souls, that the king would respect the honor of Adrian and the cardinals, cause them no harm, and would abide by the provisions of the Treaty of Constance. The pope agreed to crown the king, and a mutually satisfactory day and place were selected for their first meeting.

Frederick had established his camp at Campo Grassano, three miles east of Sutri, and on 8 June he dispatched a delegation of princes, with a large crowd of clerics and laymen, who with great joy escorted Adrian to the king's tent. When the king failed to perform, however, the customary squire's service, that is, strictly speaking, to lead the pope's horse by the bridle, the cardinals were terrified and hastened back to Civita Castellana. The perplexed pope, left alone, dismounted and seated himself on a folding stool. Frederick prostrated himself at Adrian's feet and kissed them, but the pope refused to grant Frederick the kiss of peace until he had performed the customary and due honors his predecessors, out of reverence for the Apostles Peter and Paul, had shown earlier popes. The king replied that he was not required to do so.

The following day, 9 June, was filled with discussions. The older princes, especially those who had been present when Lothar III had met with Innocent II in Liège in 1131, testified that it was indeed customary for the king to perform the squire's service. The curia cited as proof "old documents." It has been proposed that these were excerpts from the Donation of Constantine contained in a collection of canons, according to which the first Christian emperor had allegedly conducted Pope Sylvester I's horse; but there is no way to know for sure. The princes decreed, with the concurrence of the whole royal court, that the king, out of reverence for the Blessed Apostles, should perform for Pope Adrian the squire's office. Frederick moved his camp into the territory of Nepi, near Lake Monterosi, closer to Rome. In accordance with the princes' decision, on 10 June the king rode out a short distance from his tent, dismounted, and walked, as far as a stone could be thrown, towards the pope, who was approaching by another route. In sight of the army, Frederick joyfully led the pope's horse and held the stirrup, the so-called marshal's service, with all his might as the pope dismounted. Then, at last, the pope bestowed on the king the kiss of peace.[74]

Strictly speaking, there is no contradiction between Otto's statement that Frederick had received Adrian "with the honor due to his office" and Boso's account of their second meeting; but one could hardly guess from Otto's narrative what had really transpired. Since Otto must have learned the truth after Frederick's return to Germany, he must have omitted the story of the aborted meeting because it did not fit into his overall theme of harmony between the kingship and priesthood.

But is Boso's account completely reliable? Boso may very well have been present at Sutri in 1155, but he wrote a decade later, at the height of the schism, and he refreshed his own memory by using a description of the incident contained in the now lost papal register for Adrian's pontificate. Boso rejected the proposition that the king of the Romans exercised his imperial authority from his election as king by designating Frederick as the "king of the Germans," and Boso cast Cardinal Octavian, "breathing of sedition and schism," as he supposedly sought to disrupt the negotiations at Viterbo, in his future role as the anti-pope, Victor IV. Cardinal Albinus, who in the 1190s wrote a handbook on papal ceremonies, and the papal chamberlain Cencius Savelli in his 1192 register of the payments due to the papal treasury, also used independently of each other Adrian's lost register when describing the events at Sutri. Their accounts are similar to Boso's, except for one crucial point: Frederick did not refuse to lead the pope's horse but performed the ceremony incorrectly in the estimation of Adrian and the cardinals. Since Boso wrote a quarter of a century earlier than Albinus and Cencius and witnessed the incident, scholars have generally preferred Boso's version of the event.

However, Albinus and Cencius were not the only authors who indicated that the problem was not whether Frederick performed the ceremony on 8 June but how he did it. Helmold of Bosau, who obtained his information from his ordinary, Bishop Gerold of Oldenburg, who had been at the imperial and papal courts in 1155, related that Frederick hurried to meet the pope when he arrived at the camp, held the stirrup when Adrian dismounted, and then escorted the pope by the hand into his tent.

Bishop Eberhard II of Bamberg then formally welcomed the pope in the name of the king and the princes. The bishop pointed out Frederick's suitability for the imperial office, because he had shown his reverence for the Roman Church by doing for Adrian all that tradition demanded and had demonstrated his personal humility by holding the stirrup. The pope responded that Frederick had in fact scorned St. Peter by holding the left rather than the right stirrup. When the pope's words were translated, the king replied, modestly, that he had acted out of ignorance, not malice, because this was the first time he had ever held anyone's stirrup. Adrian countered that if Frederick had neglected, out of ignorance, to do little things properly, how could one rely upon him to do more important things correctly. The king, rather annoyed, said that he wished to know whether he was required to perform the service out of courtesy or as a legal obligation. If it was a courtesy, the pope had no reason to complain because Frederick had acted out of his own free will. If it was a legal obligation, then what was the difference between the left and the right stirrup as long as the prince bowed, humbly, at the feet of the supreme pontiff? A lengthy argument ensued, and they parted without exchanging the kiss of peace. The princes feared that the dispute might jeopardize the imperial coronation, and they persuaded Frederick, with much effort, to call the pope back to the camp. Frederick welcomed Adrian with the correct service. Everyone rejoiced, but the pope then demanded that the imperial army conquer Apulia from William I of Sicily before he crowned Frederick. The princes answered that they lacked the necessary forces to do so. Finally, God, to whom even those "who carry the world" bow, forced the pope to yield and concord was restored. Helmold's independent account, which depicts Adrian as petulantly picking a fight about a technicality, confirms that the meeting between pope and king had to be restaged because of a disagreement about how the emperor-elect was to receive the pope.[75]

If things did not go as smoothly at Sutri as Frederick and Otto claimed, the question is why they went so terribly wrong. There was nothing unusual about a monarch leading the pope's horse by the bridle. There were Carolingian precedents, and Lothar III had performed the service for Innocent II in Liège in 1131. Holding the stirrup was a more recent innovation, but Frederick's great-uncle, the anti-king, Conrad (III), had done so for Urban II at Cremona in 1095, though it is not absolutely certain that Lothar had shown the pope the same honor at Liège. Frederick subsequently performed both acts for his anti-pope, Victor IV, at Pavia in 1160, and for Alexander III at Venice in 1177. Nor did he hesitate to kiss Pope Adrian's feet, according to Boso, at their first meeting, surely a gesture as demeaning as holding the bridle or a stirrup. So why did Frederick suddenly object to a customary ceremony and risk the cancellation of his coronation a few days later?

The traditional answer is that Frederick perceived the holding of the pope's stirrup, unlike leading the pope's horse by the bridle, as the act of a vassal,[76] but no contemporary account of the ceremony interpreted it as a feudal gesture.[77] Since it was against Frederick's interest to endanger his coronation, the key to the puzzle may be the question Helmold had Frederick pose: was holding the stirrup voluntary or mandatory; that is, how could the emperor show appropriate deference to Adrian as the successor of St. Peter without slighting his own honor. If the gesture was a voluntary act, then the pope could not demand its performance and had to receive the courtesy, in return, with appropriate humility to preserve the equality between the two actors.[78] The problem is that Frederick raised this question only after the reception ceremony was bungled. Roman Deutinger proposed, therefore, that there was a misunderstanding about the correct protocol for a meeting between the two highest authorities in Christendom and that the replay on 10 June shows what went wrong with the first staging. Frederick had not gone out to meet the pope but had waited for him at the tent. He should have walked the distance of a stone's throw rather than ridden to welcome the pope, and he should have demonstrated more enthusiasm and love in performing the services. Even Helmold's inexplicable statement about holding the left rather than the right stirrup makes sense if Frederick thought that he was to hold the left stirrup because the pope dismounted (as is customary when riding a horse) on the left side—rather than, conceivably, holding the strap of the right stirrup to counterbalance the pope's weight as he pushed down on the left stirrup. The meeting at Sutri had been hastily arranged, Deutinger thought, before all the details could be worked out; and Adrian and the cardinals had overreacted to Frederick's failures of protocol because they were frightened by his conduct in Lombardy, most notably at Tortona, as Boso said, and perhaps also because they remembered what had happened when Henry V had met Paschal II in 1111. Historians have misunderstood, Deutinger said, a misunderstanding.[79] As Frederick's relations with Adrian deteriorated after his coronation, the confrontation at Sutri came to be seen by the papacy as a major step on the road to the schism. Perhaps Frederick and Otto did not yet grasp in 1157 the significance of the dustup at Sutri.

The Imperial Coronation

"[A]fter the supreme rulers of the world had been united amid their retinue [at Sutri]," Otto wrote, "they advanced together for several days, and pleasant converse was exchanged as between a spiritual father and his son. Both ecclesiastical and secular matters were discussed, as though a single state had been created from two princely courts." The first victim of the new concord was Arnold of Brescia, whom Frederick's envoys had agreed to turn over to the pope. The papal prefect tried and hanged Arnold. The corpse was burned and the ashes thrown into the Tiber "lest," Otto explained, "his body be held in veneration by the mad populace." The sources do not indicate where this occurred—almost certainly outside Rome—and disagree about whether it happened before or after Frederick's coronation on 18 June. Arnold's execution was an explicit recognition of the pope's exclusive jurisdiction in Rome, as the Treaty of Constance had stipulated.[80]

When Frederick and Adrian reached the outskirts of Rome, the Romans sent a delegation of learned men to meet the king and demanded, according to Frederick's own account, "a very large sum of money in return for their loyalty and submission, and also three sworn guarantees." The oaths entailed, undoubtedly, the emperor-elect's traditional confirmation of the city's privileges as he made his way from his camp on Monte Mario to St. Peter's; and the payments were the monetary gifts that the monarchs gave to the Romans who participated in the coronation ceremony. However, entering into such an arrangement would have been a de facto recognition of the Roman commune and thus a violation of the Treaty of Constance, so Frederick rejected the Romans' demands.[81]

Otto embellished his nephew's sparse statement with a speech by Rome, "the City that is the kindly mistress of the world—the City of which, by God's aid, you shall soon be prince, emperor, and lord," and with Frederick's indignant reply. Both speeches were the absent Otto's learned invention—Frederick would not have quoted Cicero's first oration against Catiline, and Rome's words echo the thoughts in Wezel's letter to Frederick after his election. There is no indication, for example, in Frederick's own summary of the Romans' demands that they had claimed in June 1155 the right to bestow the imperial crown on the emperor. The speeches thus say more about Otto's own views of the place of the Empire and Rome in the history of the world than Frederick's own thinking, though Otto may have conveyed his thoughts to his nephew. Since the Treaty of Constance had been consigned to oblivion by 1157–58, when Otto dictated his narrative to Rahewin, he had to provide an alternative explanation for his nephew's refusal to accede to the Romans' request that he confirm their privileges. Frederick's insistence in his response to the Romans that he was the ruler of Rome by right of conquest hardly fits the political situation in June 1155, when he was anxious not to antagonize the pope who was on the verge of crowning him; but a restatement of the basis for "German" lordship in Rome made sense after Adrian made peace with William I of Sicily at Benevento in 1156, in violation, the imperial court believed, of the terms of the Treaty of Constance, and Frederick considered himself released from his commitment not to negotiate with the Romans.[82]

Rome rejoiced that the king had come in peace, as he ought, to visit his people, who had long awaited his coming "to shake off," as Arnold of Brescia or Wezel might have said, "the unseemly yoke of the clergy." Frederick sought authority over the world; she gladly granted him the crown. Through "the wisdom of the senatorial dignity and the valor of the equestrian order," Rome had "extended her empire to the ends of the earth." On account of her sins, Rome had lost the senate, the "noble token of our antiquity"; but it and the equestrian order had been reinstated so "that by the decree of the one and the arms of the other" the City's "ancient splendor" might "return to the Roman Empire and to your person." Frederick had been a "stranger" and a "newcomer from ... beyond the Alps"; she had made him a citizen and a prince and had given him what was rightfully hers. In return, Rome expected, as was customary, the confirmation and observance of the "good customs and ancient laws" granted her by his predecessors; the payment of £5,000 to the officials who would acclaim Frederick on the Capitol as emperor; and his commitment to defend the Republic even at the cost of shedding his own blood. He was to guarantee these promises with privileges and with an oath sworn by his own hand. The pope played no role in the selection or installation of the emperor in Otto's imagined communal conception of imperial authority.

Frederick, infuriated by the Romans' insolence, interrupted what Otto described as a typical example of lengthy and ornate Italian oratory (of his own invention), and "with modest bearing and charm of expression ... replied without preparation but not unprepared." The king conceded that ancient Rome had once been renowned for its virtue, but she had "experienced the vicissitudes of time." Her strength had been transferred first to Constantinople—Otto was putting the theory of the transference of the Empire into his nephew's mouth—and then to the Franks and Germans, designations the bishop employed interchangeably. Charlemagne and Otto the Great had wrested the City and Italy from the Greeks and the Lombards and had added it to the Frankish realm. Frederick owed his imperial dignity to them and not to Rome—and by implication not to the pope either. (Frederick's alleged statement, at this point, that he had not received the city in fief ["beneficio"] from anyone, may in fact be a repudiation of the pope's supposed statement at Besançon in 1157 that he had enfeoffed Frederick with the imperial crown.) The Germans now possessed Rome's ancient glory, the senate, the equestrian order, the consuls, the Empire, and her former virtue. (Frederick—or, better said, Otto—did not mean that assertion to be literally true, though Otto probably equated the senate with the princes and the equestrian order with the knights. Rather, the essence of German "Roman-ness" was Germany's inheritance of Rome's virtues, most notably her balanced constitution, which was the mean, in Otto's political theorizing, between the extremes of Italian anarchy and Hungarian royal absolutism.) As for Rome's demands that Frederick swear to observe its laws and to defend the Republic, he did not require an oath to do what was just; and no oath could compel him to do what was unjust. He had already demonstrated his commitment, in the case of Denmark, where he had installed Sven as king in 1152, to the restoration of the Empire's frontiers. Frederick rejected the demand for £5,000 as disgraceful because an emperor bestowed his favors freely to those who had served him well.[83]

Since Frederick refused to purchase the imperial crown and anticipated treachery from the populace, he consulted with Adrian and the cardinals on how to proceed. The pope told Frederick, according to Otto, that the best way to deal with the treachery of the Roman rabble was to resort to a stratagem of his own. Heeding the pope's advice, the greater and better part of Frederick's army, almost a thousand knights, was sent during the night of 17 to 18 June, a Saturday, under the guidance of Cardinal Octavian, a member of a powerful Roman noble family and the future anti-pope, Victor IV, to occupy the Leonine City, the portion of Rome around St. Peter's on the right bank of the Tiber. They entered through a small gate near St. Peter's and occupied the basilica at dawn. Shortly afterwards, the pope, accompanied by the cardinals and clergy, preceded Frederick to the church and awaited him on the steps. Frederick, fully armed, left his camp on Monte Mario, located on the Tiber two miles north of the city, and entered the Leonine City through the Golden Gate. Some of his men remained outside the walls to guard the bridge across the Tiber that led from the Castel S. Angelo to the heart of the city on the opposite bank, so the Roman population could not disrupt the ceremony.

On the steps of St. Peter's, Frederick removed his armor, put on his coronation robes, and entered the church of S. Maria in Turri, situated on the steps to the basilica, where Adrian awaited him before the altar. Frederick bent his knee and publicly swore the coronation oath that had been incorporated into both the announcement of his election and the Treaty of Constance as well as the oath that the unnamed knight had already sworn on the king's behalf before his first meeting with Adrian at Sutri. The pope, followed by the king and his entourage, then proceeded to the main altar in St. Peter's. At the silver gate, the cardinal bishop of Albano said the first prayer, seeking divine illumination for the monarch. In the middle of the church, the cardinal bishop of Porto requested divine protection for Frederick, his army, and his rule. Frederick then prostrated himself before the tomb of the Princes of the Apostles while listening to the litany; and the cardinal-bishop of Ostia anointed Frederick's right arm and neck and beseeched God that the emperor, out of fear of the Lord, exercise his office with justice. After celebrating a Mass in honor of the Virgin because it was a Saturday, the pope conferred the sword and scepter on Frederick and placed the crown on his head. In his final words of blessing, Adrian prayed that Frederick would so love justice and would so live his life that he would attain the crown of eternal life. Otto concluded: "All who were present acclaimed him with great joy, and glorified God for so glorious a deed."[84]

Frederick, wearing the crown, left St. Peter's and rode on a caparisoned horse, through the same gate he had entered the Leonine City, to the camp that had been established on the field adjoining the wall, the former site of Nero's Garden. Everyone else walked. Adrian stayed in the palace next to the basilica. In the meantime, the Roman people and senate had assembled on the Capitol and learned about the coronation, which had occurred without their consent and, to deceive them and contrary to custom, had taken place on a Saturday rather than a Sunday. Furious at having been tricked in this way, they stormed across the bridge at the Castel S. Angelo and reached St. Peter's. There they killed at least two of Frederick's grooms and robbed some of the cardinals.

The imperial forces, "exhausted by the excessive exertion and by the heat," Frederick later wrote his uncle, were refreshing themselves with food and drink when they learned of the attack. Afraid that the Romans were assaulting the pope and the cardinals, the emperor ordered his men to arm themselves. The fighting extended from the Castel S. Angelo to the fish market in Trastevere, downstream from the Vatican—some of the Romans may have crossed the Tiber there as well—and lasted until nightfall. Almost a thousand Romans were killed or drowned in the river, about six hundred were captured, and the remainder fled. Incredibly, if we are to believe Otto, only one of Frederick's men was killed and another captured. The bishop added that the unhealthy climate and extreme heat were a far greater threat to the Germans than their enemies' weapons. Other sources, but not Frederick or Otto, ascribed the victory to Henry the Lion; and Cardinal Boso indicated that Adrian interceded on behalf of the Roman captives, procured their release, and turned them over to his prefect Peter. Otto could not resist a concluding rhetorical flourish that inflamed the hearts of pre-war German nationalists. As they were slaughtering the Romans, the Germans were "seeming to say: 'Take now, O Rome, Teutonic iron instead of Arabian gold. This is the price which your prince offers you for your crown. Thus do the Franks purchase empire. These are the gifts given you by our prince, these, the oaths sworn to you.'"

The victorious but exhausted imperial army spent the night in the camp outside the Leonine City. Since he could not procure supplies from the hostile Romans, Frederick, accompanied by Adrian and the cardinals, led his hungry men the next day, 19 June, to higher ground.[85]

Perhaps nothing better illustrates the inadequacies of Frederick's forces on his first Italian expedition and the poor prior planning than this Roman debacle. His army had to enter the Leonine City through stealth; the coronation occurred shortly after daybreak on a Saturday rather than on a

Sunday to thwart a Roman attempt to prevent it; the celebration ended in a bloodbath; Frederick and Adrian had to leave Rome quickly the next day, because there were not sufficient provisions to feed the men; and the commune had not been suppressed. Some triumph!

Frederick informed his uncle Otto in 1157 that he reached Albano in the Campania, south of the Tiber (the farthest he ever got in Italy), after he had brought under his control all the fortified places in the vicinity of Rome. It is possible, in fact, to follow in a bit more detail what the new emperor did after he left Rome on 19 June. He did not go south, initially, but upstream on the west bank of the Tiber past Monte Soratte, about 28 miles north of Rome. He forded the river there and visited Farfa, which received him in its prayer fraternity. It had been an imperial abbey in the Ottonian-Salian period, but by the 1120s it had come under papal protection, and Pope Adrian had stressed in an earlier letter to Frederick that it pertained to the Apostolic See. By taking Farfa under imperial protection, the emperor was reasserting the monastery's status as an imperial house. He headed south from Farfa to the lush valley of the Aniene, a tributary of the Tiber on the east bank, just north of Rome, where he gave his army a chance to rest.

The citizens of nearby Tivoli, located east-northeast of Rome at the spot where the Aniene descends from the Apennines, submitted to Frederick's lordship by giving him the keys to the city and swearing an oath of fealty. However, Adrian requested that Tivoli, which had previously sworn an oath of fealty to him, be restored to papal lordship. Accordingly, on 29 June Frederick notified the citizens that he had returned Tivoli, saving all imperial rights, to the pope and that he was releasing them, except for the obligations they owed the crown, from their prior oath of fealty to him. That same day, the Feast of Saints Peter and Paul, Adrian celebrated Mass, while Frederick, in a symbolic display of papal–imperial harmony, wore his crown. During the Mass, the pope, in accordance with the Augustinian theory of a just war, absolved all those who had shed blood during the combat with the Romans, Otto explained, because any soldier who fought for his own prince, and in this instance for the Church as well, was "not a murderer but an avenger." Beneath this apparent imperial–papal concord was, as the cases of Farfa and Tivoli show, the unresolved issue of the respective rights of the emperor and the pope in the Patrimony of St. Peter.[86]

Frederick continued his encirclement of Rome. On 1 July he was on the banks of the Tiber, near Monte Soratte, and on 7 July in the territory of Tusculum, southwest of Tivoli and 12 miles southeast of Rome. Otto stated that the army halted between Rome and Tusculum, presumably, as Frederick put it, at Albano. The imperial forces could have embarked from there, Otto insisted, on the restoration of joint papal–imperial rule in Rome; but the noxious vapors that rose from the swamps during the dog days of summer sickened the men—*malaria* means bad air—and Frederick decided, reluctantly, to move his camp to the mountains so they could recover. (Otto clearly did not think in 1157/58 that his nephew was bound to restore the pope's exclusive authority in Rome.) Adrian and Frederick parted at Tivoli, where Otto said his nephew turned over the Roman prisoners to the pope. The army spent several days recuperating in the Apennines along the Nera, a tributary of the Tiber. Frederick had begun his march northward.[87]

The March Northward

During his encampment along the Nera, Frederick demanded the payment of the *fodrum* from the neighboring cities, fortified places, and towns. The citizens of Spoleto, 30 miles southeast of Perugia in central Italy, were liable for £800 and angered the emperor by defrauding him of part of the payment and by paying the rest in counterfeit coin. Even worse, they had imprisoned Count Guido Guerra, whom Otto described as "one of the wealthiest of all the nobles of Tuscany" and who had represented Frederick in the negotiations in Rome that had resulted in the Treaty of Constance. Frederick had sent Guido, along with Prince Robert of Capua, Count Andrew of Rupecanina, and other Apulian exiles, to the Campania and Apulia to regain the cities, castles, and other possessions they had lost to the Normans and to stir up a rebellion against the new king, William I. On his return from that mission, Guido had been captured in Spoleto, which was ignoring Frederick's command that it release Guido. Spoleto's defiance of his express orders angered Frederick more, Otto claimed, than its deceit in the payment of the *fodrum*.

On 27 July Frederick attacked the city, and the inhabitants, instead of relying on their strong walls that were surmounted by nearly one hundred towers, counterattacked in the open. According to Otto, his nephew said: "This seems like a game of boys, not a conflict of men"; and no one fought more energetically and risked greater danger in the six-hour battle than the emperor himself. The men of Spoleto were forced to give way, and the imperial forces pursued them into the city. Spoleto was plundered, but before all the useful items could be seized, someone set it on fire. The survivors saved only their lives—Otto Morena said only after they had paid Frederick a lot of money. The imperial army spent the night there, but the stench from the burned corpses forced Frederick to move the camp a short distance from Spoleto the next day. They stayed at that site for two days until the army had collected all the spoils salvaged from the city's destruction.[88]

Frederick continued his trek from Spoleto northeastward to Ancona on the Adriatic Sea. The failure of his interconnected Norman and Byzantine policies became apparent there. His dilemma was how to obtain Manuel I's support against the Normans and a Byzantine bride without making any territorial concessions to the Greeks in southern Italy. At Ancona Frederick met the Greek envoys, Michael Palaiologos and John Doukas, who may have accompanied Anselm of Havelberg when he had returned to Italy in the spring without a Greek bride, and who now brought the emperor many valuable presents. At the same time the Norman exiles who had accompanied Count Guido Guerra to southern Italy reported that they had regained their lost possessions and that the local feudatories in the Campania and Apulia were awaiting Frederick's arrival to rebel against King William. Frederick wrote to Otto that the Greek envoys offered him an "enormous sum of money to induce us to go into Apulia and undertake by our mighty power the destruction of William, the enemy of both empires."

Frederick was eager to accept the offer, but he was unable to persuade the princes, who cited "the debilitating effects of the burning heat and the unwholesome air" and the number of men who had been wounded and killed. However, Otto of St. Blasien, writing at the beginning of the thirteenth century, indicated that Archbishop Arnold II of Cologne and Bishop Hermann of Constance had favored such a campaign. So there may have been the same division between the ecclesiastical and lay princes that had blocked the immediate execution of Conrad III's planned *Romzug* in 1152. Frederick accepted the princes' decision, according to his uncle, "not without bitterness of heart"; but was Otto's statement merely a face-saving device to cover up Frederick's failure to honor another of his commitments to the pope? Could he really have seriously contemplated an invasion of the Norman kingdom in the heat of August with a small exhausted army, and with a hostile Milan and a defiant Roman commune in his rear? Frederick dispatched Wibald, as the princes advised, to Constantinople to pursue Manuel's offer of the hand of his niece. In a lighter moment, Frederick relaxed at Ancona by swimming with Otto of Wittelsbach in the Adriatic.[89]

The imperial forces disbanded in Ancona. Patriarch Pilgrim of Aquileia, Bishop Eberhard of Bamberg, Count Berthold III of Andechs, Duke Henry of Carinthia, and Margrave Ottokar III of Styria chose to sail up the Adriatic to Venice and to return to Germany, presumably, via the Val Canale in Carinthia. Others crossed the Alps via the Great St. Bernhard or the Mont Cenis Pass. Frederick and his remaining forces headed via Ravenna toward the Brenner Pass.[90]

As for Palaiologos and Doukas, according to Otto before they left Ancona they "had surreptitiously secured" letters sealed with Frederick's seal that "falsely declared that regions along the [Adriatic] seacoast had been granted them by the prince [Frederick]." The two envoys succeeded in subjecting all of Apulia to their authority by displaying Frederick's supposed mandate and by a liberal distribution of gold. Palaiologos even managed to capture Bari and its citadel. The Norman exiles aided the Byzantines; and many of the inhabitants of southern Italy, long oppressed by Roger of Sicily and his son William I, joined the revolt. William, who was gravely ill during the autumn of 1155, remained in Palermo; and the rumor spread that he had died. It was not until the late spring of 1156 that William was sufficiently recovered to suppress the revolt, and he won a decisive victory over the Greeks and the rebels at Brindisi on 28 May.[91]

Frederick's incriminating letters were a political and diplomatic embarrassment. Had he, in fact, in a flagrant violation of the Treaty of Constance, surrendered to the Greeks the cities along the southern Adriatic coast of Italy, or at least commanded the local population to support the Greeks against William? If he had, it would explain why the matrimonial negotiations with Constantinople were not dead in 1155–56. When his duplicity was exposed, did Frederick, aided by his uncle Otto, spread the story that the letters had been purloined? Or had the Byzantine envoys obtained from some chancery notary, say, through bribery, a sealed piece of parchment that they used for their own purposes? We cannot know for sure what happened, but Frederick's failure to suppress the Roman commune and to attack the Norman kingdom, coupled, perhaps, with his conveyance of Apulia to the Byzantines, convinced Pope Adrian and Cardinal Roland that Frederick had violated the Treaty of Constance. They concluded that an alliance with the victorious William, the Treaty of Benevento of June 1156, in which the Norman king acknowledged his status as a papal vassal, was preferable to an accommodation with an emperor who had asserted too loudly his prerogatives in his dealings with the Lombards and the pope.[92]

The Outlawing of Milan

Frederick announced near Verona in early September 1155 that he had granted Milan's mint to Cremona. He explained in the charter of conveyance that it behooved imperial excellence to punish with just severity the contumacious and to reward with kindness the humble and those devoted to the Roman Empire. Milan had been deprived of his grace on account of its monstrous crimes and because it had unjustly destroyed the cities of Como and Lodi and prevented their reconstruction. Since the Milanese had repeatedly scorned his summonses to respond to the charges that had been levied against them, Frederick had, in accordance with a princely judgment, placed them under the imperial ban, probably already in December 1154. He had continued to show the Milanese clemency in the hope that they would return to their senses, but their evil grew greater daily, and they had abused his patience to the utmost.

Accordingly, the emperor had procured from the princes of both Italy and Germany and the entire assembly a sentence that deprived Milan of its mint, tolls, and all its jurisdictional rights, secular authority, and regalia. He was awarding Milan's mint to Cremona because it was preeminent among the cities of Italy in its loyalty and the military service it had rendered his predecessors and him—an assertion that required a considerable rewriting of history. At the same time Frederick notified the consuls and inhabitants of Mantua, Brescia, and Bergamo, both magnates and commoners, of these actions and ordered them to prohibit the circulation of Milanese coins in their territories and to treat the issues of the Milan mint as counterfeits. He also commanded them, as befitted men who had sworn oaths of fealty to him, to deny the Milanese assistance and transit through their territories to the detriment of Pavia, Cremona, and Novara, but rather to aid Milan's opponents. Oddly, no chronicler indicated when and where these legal measures were taken against Milan, but the execution of the princes' sentence was tantamount to a declaration of war against Milan.[93]

The awarding of Milan's mint to Cremona continued Conrad III's policy on the establishment of new mints in Italy. At the beginning of Conrad's reign, mints with super-regional circulations, like those in Pavia, Verona, Lucca, and Venice, dominated the economic life of the peninsula. For example, the issues of the old imperial mint in Pavia circulated more widely than any other coin in northern and even central Italy, including in Genoa, even though the silver content of the Pavian coins, to Genoa's detriment, was only a fifth of what it had been a century earlier. In December 1138 Conrad had granted Genoa the right, therefore, to strike for the first time its own coins; and around 1150 the king seems to have bestowed the same authority on Pisa. On his way from Ancona to Verona, Frederick confirmed Pisa's right to mint its own coins, whose weight and form were left to the city to determine. He authorized the circulation of the Pisan coins throughout Italy. He did so, the charter stated, in recognition of Pisa's celebrated achievements, most notably, its conquest of the Balearic Islands, which the city had placed under the lordship of his great-uncle Henry V, and its feats of arms against the tyrant, Roger of Sicily. The new mint in Cremona thus continued Conrad's policy of replacing super-regional issues with multiple territorial ones that better suited the growing needs of Italy's burgeoning commercial economy and, not incidentally, rewarded pro-imperial communes.[94] Such measures indicate that Conrad and Frederick, or at least their advisers, were attuned to economic developments in Italy.

Conflict with Verona

Frederick's passage through Veronese territory on his way to the Brenner Pass was a fitting coda to his Italian campaign. Otto of Freising and Otto Morena differ on what occurred, in part because the latter seems to have conflated two separate incidents: the fighting that accompanied Frederick's crossing of the Adige river north of Verona, and the subsequent ambush of the imperial forces in the gorge of the Adige.

It was customary when the emperors came or left Italy via the Brenner, Otto of Freising said, that they crossed the Adige above Verona, so that troops could not pass through the city and plunder it. The Veronese had built, he related, a flimsy pontoon bridge of boats "that one might rather have termed it a mousetrap than a bridge." They had also gathered large piles of logs upstream that were to be floated downstream in such a way that the bridge would be destroyed after the first detachment of the imperial army had crossed the river. The Veronese would then have been able, presumably, to attack and annihilate the separated halves of the army. This plan went awry because all of Frederick's forces succeeded—"perilously indeed yet without a casualty"—to cross the Adige. Instead, it was those Veronese forces that had followed the imperial army across the river who were isolated by the bridge's destruction and were soon slain as traitors. The army camped out that night near the city (2.39).

According to Otto Morena, the fully armed Veronese left the city in order to block the emperor's march; but the imperial forces counterattacked. Frederick pursued the fleeing citizens and captured around 1,000 men. He ordered the noses and lips of more than 200 Veronese to be cut off and had more than 200 others hanged. The remaining prisoners were led to his camp and put in irons. The burghers who had stayed in the city were so terrified that they made an agreement with the emperor and paid him a large sum to procure the release of the surviving captives.

Otto of Freising did not explain why Verona planned a surprise attack on his nephew instead of speeding him back to Germany as quickly as possible, but Otto Morena provided the all-purpose explanation that Milan had bribed Verona to impede Frederick's progress. However, shortly before his transit through Veronese territory, Frederick had commanded the rectors of Verona to respect the rights of their bishop, whom he took under imperial protection. Specifically, the emperor prohibited the city from summoning the men who resided in the episcopal lordship to its court, to tax them, or to muster them for an imperial campaign without the bishop's consent; that is, Frederick was trying to prevent the incorporation of the bishop's own domains into Verona's *contado*. This anti-communal mandate may have been the real reason for the city's hostility.[95]

Otto of Freising fleshed out the details in Frederick's own, oft-told succinct account of the army's derring-do passage through the gorge of the Adige, north of Verona: "Now how they [the Veronese] laid a trap for us on the precipitous slope of a certain mountain, and how they were slaughtered by us and twelve of them were hanged, you have heard."

At the southern entrance into the gorge, the waters of the Adige rushed so close to the mountainside that it was possible to enter the gorge only on a narrow path on the eastern side of the river. After the main body of the imperial forces had passed into the gorge, "a band of brigands," under the leadership of "Alberic, a noble knight of Verona," occupied the narrows and stationed itself on a large boulder above the northern exit from the gorge, trapping the imperial army in the defile. Frederick sent two illustrious Veronese knights, Garzabanus and Isaac, who had accompanied him to Rome, to persuade their fellow citizens to desist—clearly the "brigands" were more than they pretended to be. The robbers would not listen to the knights and other envoys, but drove them off with stones and demanded, as the price for permitting the army's passage, the horse and armor of every knight and a large sum of money from Frederick. A prince, Frederick made plain, did not pay tribute, but his options were limited. The river was unfordable at that site, the robbers had destroyed a bridge over the gorge, and the Veronese were barring his return to Verona. As a diversion, Frederick ordered that the camp be set up for the night in the gorge, while a way was found to scale the brigands' perch.

The emperor ordered everyone to arm themselves and consulted with Garzabanus and Isaac about possible stratagems. They pointed to a crag that overhung the pass and the boulder. A picked force of 200 men, under the leadership of the imperial standard-bearer, Otto V of Wittelsbach, made its way, undetected, to the overhang. To reach the top, they scrambled up on each other's backs and shoulders and then made a ladder of their spears. When they reached the summit, Otto unfurled the standard, which was the signal for the main force of the army to attack from below, while Otto's soldiers assailed the robbers from above. Most of the band, allegedly around 500 men, fell to their deaths. One man hid in a crevice and escaped, but the twelve remaining survivors, most of whom were knights, were captured and sentenced to hang. One of the twelve appealed to Frederick for mercy because he was a Frenchman and not a Lombard, a poor but free knight, who had been tricked into joining the band in hopes of repairing his estate. Frederick pardoned him on condition that he put the noose around the neck of each of his former companions. Otto of Freising's account, no doubt based on his nephew's oft-repeated tale, emphasized Frederick's tactical skills and, in the case of the French knight, the tempering of justice with the mercy that had been so clearly lacking on previous occasions.[96]

Frederick's forces camped that night in the territory of Trent, where he issued on 7 September a charter for the church of Liège in recognition of the outstanding services that its bishop, Henry II, had performed on the Italian expedition. From Trent, Frederick made his way back to Augsburg, from where he had departed almost a year earlier.

Otto commented that the terror his nephew's deeds inspired in the Italians could be seen in the Veronese embassy that arrived at the imperial court held in Regensburg in the middle of October 1155. It consisted of Bishop Theobald and the knights Garzabanus and Isaac, who had pointed out to Frederick the possibility of sneaking up on the overhang above the brigands. Theobald insisted that he had been reluctant to undertake the mission until he had been assured that the Veronese truly believed in their hearts what they professed with their lips, because it was inconceivable that his flock would ask their shepherd to lie on their behalf. They were utterly devoted to Frederick as their lord and emperor. The brigands, whom he had punished in a fitting way, had not been citizens of Verona; and the townspeople grieved that Frederick suspected them of complicity in the robbers' deeds. Whoever had spread such insinuations was a slanderer and a liar. Nevertheless, the city proffered its apologies; and if Frederick did not believe Theobald's arguments, it was ready to submit to a judgment by the princes. After consulting with the latter, the emperor restored Verona to his favor because it paid him a large sum of money and swore to supply him with as many soldiers as it could muster in the forthcoming campaign against Milan. Verona's payment is a good sign that Frederick and the princes did not believe the city's professions of innocence.[97]

The decision to fight Milan had thus been taken either before Frederick left Italy on this his first expedition there, when he deprived the city of its regalia, or soon after his return to Germany. Milan rather than the Norman kingdom became the chief target of the second campaign (1158) after Frederick learned, sometime in June 1156, that William of Sicily had succeeded in expelling the Greeks from Apulia. Although Frederick called the first campaign a "splendid victory" in his letter to his uncle, and Otto himself said that "the toilsome journey" had been brought to a successful conclusion, it was in fact neither victory nor success. Frederick had been unable to punish Milan, suppress the Roman commune, attack the Normans, or prevent the Byzantines from occupying Apulia. No wonder Otto omitted the Treaty of Constance from his account of his nephew's deeds. The emperor left behind, as Otto conceded, only the "terror the memory of his deeds inspired in the Italians": the destruction of Chieri, Asti, Tortona, and Spoleto; the bloodbath in Rome on the day of his coronation; the battle outside Verona and the terrible retribution; and the perilous passage through the gorge of the Adige. It was a "splendid victory" for an army of only 1,800 knights, if we are to believe Frederick's numbers; but why had he undertaken the *Romzug* with a totally inadequate force? Had his clerical and lay advisers, who were familiar with Italian conditions, completely misjudged the situation, or did Frederick have far less support in Germany than Otto intended to convey by celebrating his nephew as a unifier? After all, the princes had refused to embark on Conrad's planned *Romzug*, had stopped the expedition against Hungary, and never agreed to the planned reassertion of imperial authority in Burgundy. The magnates who did go with Frederick to Italy were the same men who had played a prominent role in his acquisition of the crown. The emperor learned from the failures of his first expedition. He assembled a far larger army for his second campaign, imposed rigorous discipline on his troops, and took steps to supply them with adequate provisions. However, before he could leave once again, in June 1158, for Italy and its tempting wealth, and the opportunity to establish a lordship under his direct control to replace the domains he had surrendered to his cousin Frederick IV of Swabia, the emperor needed to restore order in Germany, and to marry.

CHAPTER SEVEN

NEW ARRANGEMENTS

Carrying Dogs

Upon his return to Germany in September 1155, Frederick found the kingdom in disarray. "In fact," Otto of Freising admitted, "during the time that the prince was in Italy, practically the entire transalpine realm felt the absence of its head, being torn by uprisings and thrown into confusion by fire and sword and open warfare" (2.43). If Barbarossa was going to punish Milan for its defiance, let alone bring Lombardy under his direct control and invade the Norman kingdom, he required an army considerably larger than the 1,800 knights he had taken with him to Italy in 1154. To procure the necessary manpower, Frederick needed to restore order in Germany and to conciliate his uncle Henry Jasomirgott and Vladislav of Bohemia, who had met in his absence with the Saxon enemies of his cousin Henry the Lion. The emperor also needed to provide for his brother and his cousin Frederick IV of Swabia, who had attained their majority and were potential claimants to the throne, and to marry again to ensure the continuity of his branch of the Staufer dynasty. These new arrangements would remain in place until the annihilation of Frederick's army in 1167 gave him the opportunity to become more personally involved in German affairs.

After leaving Augsburg, Frederick headed at the beginning of October 1155 toward Regensburg, the chief residence of the Bavarian dukes. He met with his uncle Henry outside the city and tried in vain to persuade him to accept the award of Bavaria to Henry the Lion. Vladislav, Albrecht the Bear, Hermann of Stahleck, the count-palatine of the Rhine, and other unnamed "great men" then served as intermediaries between the two Henrys at negotiations that were held in an unspecified place near the

Bohemian border. Otto himself, as a Bavarian bishop, Frederick's uncle, and Henry Jasomirgott's brother, played a special role as a mediator; but the enmity between the rival Henrys was so great that they parted from each other without exchanging a word. Otto said nothing about the substance of these negotiations but commented about this unofficial princely gathering that the "splendor" of Frederick's exploits in Italy aroused "so great a fear" among "those who stayed behind" that they came voluntarily to the meeting and that "everyone endeavored by obedience to secure the favor of his [Frederick's] friendship." Perhaps it is reading too much into Otto's words, but the inference is that there had been less support for Frederick's *Romzug*—maybe even for his election as king—than the bishop's triumphal narrative suggests, and that the recalcitrant felt a need to get into the emperor's good graces upon his return from Italy. No wonder Frederick had taken only 1,800 knights with him.

At the subsequent court in Regensburg on 13 October, Frederick conferred on his cousin "the lands and the seat of his fathers." The Bavarian magnates also paid homage and swore oaths of fealty to Henry the Lion, and the citizens of Regensburg bound themselves to their new duke not only by an oath but also by giving Henry unspecified sureties, presumably hostages, so "that they might have no chance of wavering" in their allegiance. However, Frederick could not formally enfeoff his cousin with the duchy until his uncle had renounced his right to Bavaria. Since Frederick did not wish to antagonize the other princes by depriving one of them of his fief without due cause, he had no other choice but to placate his uncle. Jasomirgott could afford to be stubborn.[1]

At the same assembly Archbishop Arnold of Mainz and Hermann of Stahleck accused each other of disturbing the peace. According to Otto, "these two princes, so much the more effective in committing injuries as they were the most powerful, had stained almost the whole Rhineland and especially the renowned territory of the city of Mainz by pillage, bloodshed, and burning" (2.44–45). The cause of their conflict was Arnold's attempt to regain archiepiscopal lands and rights that his predecessors had alienated. These efforts aroused the opposition of the count-palatine, whose own territorial interests along the middle Rhine were threatened by Arnold's measures. Hermann, supported by his stepbrother Count Henry of Katzenelnbogen, several other Rhenish counts, and Arnold's own ministerials, had invaded the archbishop's domains. According to a letter Arnold wrote to Wibald in the spring of 1155, Hermann had destroyed the archbishop's castles, devastated his manors, plundered consecrated cemeteries, churches, and monasteries, despoiled reliquaries, and abducted the inhabitants. The archbishop had requested that Wibald, who was with Frederick in Italy, intervene on his behalf with the king, because Hermann had falsely claimed that he was acting on Frederick's orders. Arnold's ministerial ancestry may have intensified the nobles' dislike of the archbishop. (He was the first German primate to be legally of servile status.) In addition, Arnold's harsh rule was alienating the townspeople of Mainz—he is alleged to have called the citizens a stiff-necked people and averred that they needed, as Rehoboam had said after the death of his father Solomon, a tyrant to chastise them with whips and scorpions.

Frederick postponed a decision until the Christmas court at Worms in 1155. A princely tribunal convicted both men and their accomplices of terrorizing the "land by pillaging and burning." In one of the most baffling passages in his chronicle, Otto explained that an ancient custom, which had acquired the status of a law among the Franks and Swabians, determined that before a noble, ministerial, or peasant was executed, he was required to carry "from one county into the next . . . [a] token of his shame": respectively, in accordance with the culprit's estate, a dog, a saddle, or the wheel of a plow. Frederick spared Arnold this humiliation—a cleric usually carried a book as the symbol of his status—out of respect for his advanced age, dignity, and episcopal rank. However, the count-palatine—"a great prince of the realm," Otto noted—and ten counts who had been Hermann's accomplices had to carry dogs "the distance of a German mile." The message of this strange scene, like the playlet staged at Frederick's coronation in Aachen, was that the emperor administered justice impartially. In this instance, his uncle—admittedly, a kinsman by marriage rather than by blood—served as the admonitory example. The kingdom learned the lesson. Otto concluded: "When this stern judgment was promulgated throughout the breadth of the transalpine empire, so great a terror came upon all that everyone desired rather to keep the peace than to promote the confusion of warfare."

Arnold's clerical biographer omitted any suggestion that the archbishop had been sentenced to a penalty similar to Hermann's and presented the count-palatine's humiliation as an act of penance to regain the archbishop's grace. The excommunicate Hermann, barefoot and dressed in sackcloth and ashes, had carried the dog around his neck through the assembled throng "in the middle of the rawest time of the winter." The other culprits—nobles, ministerials, and peasants— had followed him, each bearing the emblem of his estate and shame. Afterwards, the archbishop exchanged the kiss of peace with his former enemies.

Otto and the hagiographer's accounts are irreconcilable. Either both the count-palatine and the archbishop were sentenced to be publicly shamed in a secular ritual for disturbing the peace or Hermann performed a sacramental act of penance to gain Arnold's forgiveness. Otto's version of events is more trustworthy; the *Annals* of the nearby Benedictine abbey of Disibodenberg named not only five of the ten counts who shared in Hermann's punishment but also two counts who, out of respect for the archbishop's dignity, had been excused from doing the same on Arnold's behalf. However, there is nothing in Otto's description of the ritual that indicates it was intended to be the prologue to an execution. For example, the culprits were not required to wear, say, an unsheathed sword around their necks to indicate that their lives were at the emperor's mercy.[2]

Nevertheless, the hagiographer's narrative indicates that this bizarre ritual, which he said was called in the vernacular *harnescharre* (*Harmschar*), that is, suffering or pain, served not only as a punishment but could also be part of a ceremony of reconciliation. Carrying a snarling, biting, and defecating dog—accounts of other stagings of the ritual emphasized these features—was certainly humiliating if not harmful; but a dog was also associated with the nobility because it was a hunting companion and, more importantly, because a dog's chief attribute was, according to the bestiaries, its loyalty. Both Arnold and Hermann had been disloyal because their feud had disturbed the peace during Frederick's absence. In addition, the count-palatine had broken his oath of fealty to the archbishop, and, even worse, according to Arnold's letter to Wibald, Hermann had falsely incriminated the emperor in his misdeeds. The two men needed to be reconciled with each other as well as with Frederick, and Hermann, in particular, had to atone for the injuries his lies had caused to Frederick's honor. Carrying dogs was a symbolic way to demonstrate the miscreants' remorse and submission to the emperor, and both princes were quickly restored to his favor. Less than six months later, Hermann witnessed an imperial charter on the occasion of Frederick's marriage to Beatrice of Burgundy; and three days before Hermann died on 20 September 1156, he made his final appearance among the witnesses of the *Privilegium minus*. Arnold together with some of his erstwhile comital opponents witnessed another of Frederick's charters on 6 April 1157.[3]

The emperor did not forgive as readily malefactors of lesser rank. After Frederick had dealt with Arnold and Hermann at Worms, he traveled extensively, Otto reported, and energetically destroyed the castles, fortifications, and hiding places of several "robbers." He executed some of them; the others were tortured on the rack. The owners of castles were hardly ordinary highwaymen. The best guess is that the Rhenish culprits were lesser nobles or ministerials who had participated in the princely feud or who had taken advantage of the chaos to engage in rapine of their own. Unlike Frederick's kinsmen, such men did not merit special consideration. Otto regretted that the continuing strife between the two Henrys prevented a similar pacification of Bavaria.[4]

The *Privilegium minus*

Frederick celebrated Whitsunday, 3 June 1156, upstream from Regensburg at a castle, probably Kelheim, which belonged to Otto V of Wittelsbach. The emperor's stay with the count-palatine of Bavaria on a major feast day rather than in an episcopal see, as was customary, is another sign that the two swimming companions were close personally. In all likelihood, they discussed the impasse over the duchy of Bavaria. Two days later, on 5 June, near Regensburg Frederick met with Henry Jasomirgott and persuaded him to settle his differences with Henry the Lion. The terms of the agreement were kept secret. Otto of Freising commented: "The prince prized this [accord] more highly than the successes of all his other undertakings: the fact that, without the shedding of blood, he was able to bring to friendly relations princes of the realm so mighty and so closely related to him." Frederick married Beatrice the following week in Würzburg, and he summoned the princes to assemble in Regensburg on 8 September. On the appointed day, in a display of respect for the margrave, the princes accompanied the emperor to his uncle's encampment nearly two miles outside Regensburg. This gesture spared Henry Jasomirgott the humiliation of appearing as a suppliant at the assembly and of renouncing his rights to Bavaria in the chief ducal residence. The terms were publicly announced on this occasion.

Otto, an eyewitness, feigned ignorance of the precise terms of an accord that was of the utmost personal interest to him as a Bavarian bishop and a Babenberg. Perhaps he was merely being cautious because he did not have a copy of the *Privilegium minus* at his disposal when he wrote, but some of the obfuscation may have been deliberate. As far as Otto could recall, his brother Henry Jasomirgott had resigned the duchy of Bavaria by surrendering seven banners to his nephew—the pendants that were attached to lances were symbols of a lay prince's enfeoffment with his chief fiefs. (Since the Concordat of Worms the monarch had invested an ecclesiastical prince with a scepter.) Frederick gave the banners to Henry the Lion, who returned two of them to him. These two flags represented the Eastern Mark (*marchia orientalis*) and the counties—three of them, Otto thought—that had pertained to the mark of old. The privilege referred, both more vaguely and more specifically, to the mark and the fiefs that Margrave Leopold—either Henry's father, Leopold III, or brother, Leopold IV—had held from the duchy of Bavaria. Otto and the notary who drafted the privilege about the resolution of the dispute may have been vague because no one knew for certain how far Bavarian ducal authority extended eastward into the modern province of Upper Austria and precisely which territories had been added to the mark the Babenbergs had received in 976. In accordance with a princely judgment, Frederick elevated the combined mark and the counties to a duchy and enfeoffed both his uncle and his wife Theodora with the two banners. Frederick stipulated that none of his successors was to alter the terms of the settlement. He was following the precedent that had been set in 1098 when the duchy of Swabia had been awarded to the Staufer family and a new duchy, composed of the Zähringer's own lands and Zürich, had been created for the latter. The new Babenberg duchy, in terms of the actual power of its duke, was the equal of Bavaria; and the separation of Austria from Bavaria significantly reduced the threat posed by Henry the Lion's investiture with two duchies.[5]

Most of the south German princes and Bavarian magnates witnessed the ending of the protracted dispute over the duchy of Bavaria. Count Gebhard II of Sulzbach, Conrad III's disgraced brother-in-law, and Margrave Diepold V of Vohburg, the nephew of Frederick's first wife Adela, were also in Regensburg and were included, presumably, in the general reconciliation. The proclamation of a year-long Truce of God in Bavaria formalized the peace.[6]

The *Privilegium minus*, which is dated 17 September and spelled out the terms of the settlement, has been the subject of generations of scholarly controversy because of its constitutional significance as well as the diplomatic problems the text poses. It is called the Lesser Privilege to distinguish it from the *Privilegium maius*, a blatant forgery by the Habsburg duke of Austria, Rudolf IV (r. 1358–65). Frederick's concessions to his uncle Henry Jasomirgott were incorporated into the Greater Privilege, Barbarossa's golden bull was removed from the Lesser Privilege and attached to Rudolf's concoction, and the original 1156 document was destroyed. The latter survives in its entirety only in a sloppy thirteenth-century copy. Scholars have debated whether it, too, is a forgery or whether individual clauses, most notably the highly unusual *libertas affectandi* (freedom to choose) clause, which authorized the ducal couple to select as their successor whomever they wished if they were childless, were later interpolations. The consensus today is that the text of Frederick's privilege was not falsified in the thirteenth century. The concessions Frederick made to his uncle addressed Henry and Theodora's immediate dynastic concerns in 1156 and were the price Frederick paid to procure his uncle's renunciation of the duchy of Bavaria.[7]

Frederick presented the settlement in the *Privilegium minus* as an exchange of properties between the two Henrys, which required, as such, he said, no written record because possession was itself sufficient proof. Nevertheless, he was intervening with his imperial authority to remove any doubts. He announced that the court held in Regensburg to celebrate the Virgin's birth had resolved the lengthy dispute "between his most beloved paternal uncle and his most dear cousin," with the assistance of Him "from whom peace is sent from Heaven to men" and "in the presence of many God-fearing and right-believing princes." The duke of Austria ("dux Austrie") had resigned to Frederick the duchy of Bavaria, which he had immediately conferred on the duke of Saxony, who had surrendered in turn the march of Austria (*marchia Austrie*) with all its rights and fiefs. Frederick did not mention the exchange of banners, but it is striking that while Otto referred to his family's ancestral lands as the *marchia orientalis*, a designation that could also refer, say, to the Saxon eastern mark, the notary chose to employ the word *Austria*; this name had been employed for the first time only in 1147 in a possibly falsified charter that Conrad III had issued for Klosterneuburg, the Babenberg dynastic foundation where Frederick's grandmother Agnes was interred. The purpose of the new terminology was, apparently, to give the Babenberg mark/duchy a feminine name comparable to those of other German polities like *Bawaria* or *Saxonia* and may have been another way to show that the new duchy was the equal of Bavaria. *Austria* immediately became the standard designation for *Österreich* in Latin and ultimately in English as well.[8]

However, to ensure that "in this act the honor and reputation of his most dear uncle would not appear to have been diminished in any way," Vladislav, the "illustrious" duke of Bohemia, with the advice, consent, and approval of all the princes, had ruled that the mark of Austria should be elevated into a duchy and granted in fief to Henry Jasomirgott and his "most celebrated wife," Manuel I's niece Theodora. In addition to this unprecedented joint enfeoffment of a couple, they and their children, male or female without distinction, were to possess the duchy by hereditary right from the Reich in accordance with a law that was to be perpetually valid. If Henry and Theodora were childless, they would have the right to bestow the duchy on whomever they wished.

Women like Frederick's grandmother Agnes customarily inherited allods and in practice fiefs, too; but an imperial principality was another matter. Henry Jasomirgott's first wife Gertrude had inherited Saxony from her father Emperor Lothar, but technically it had been her husband, Henry the Proud, and then her son, Henry the Lion, who had been enfeoffed with the duchy. The formal recognition of female succession was thus a major milestone in the transformation of the principalities from offices into hereditary dynastic holdings. Theodora's exalted birth, which the privilege acknowledged, was no doubt a factor in her enfeoffment; but by September 1156 the Byzantine alliance was dead and that was precisely her possible dilemma. At that moment the couple's only child was their five-year-old daughter Agnes. If Theodora was widowed, she would have found herself in an alien land, no doubt with an extensive widow's dower in the duchy, but without any powerful kinsmen to protect her and her child. To safeguard them, Henry Jasomirgott insisted upon the joint enfeoffment, the recognition of Agnes' inheritance rights, and the couple's right, especially if Theodora was a widow, to select their successor. Frederick had probably agreed to those concessions on 5 June.[9]

The only services the duke owed the Empire were attendance, when summoned, at courts the emperor held in Bavaria, and participation in military campaigns in realms and provinces that bordered on Austria. The new duchy was, thus, to retain the mark's traditional role as an anti-Hungarian bastion. In spite of these provisions, Henry Jasomirgott accompanied his nephew to Italy in 1158 on his second expedition; and Henry's son, Leopold V, attended the peace negotiations in Venice in 1177 and the great court in Mainz in 1184. Involvement in such undertakings was an expensive burden, but it was also, the privilege notwithstanding, a matter of princely prestige and a way to retain the monarch's favor.[10]

Only one clause dealt with the internal governance of the duchy. Frederick stipulated that "no person, whether of high or low estate, was to presume to exercise any jurisdiction within the dominion of the same duchy without the consent and permission of the duke." In essence, Frederick was confirming the extensive rights his uncle already possessed in Austria as a margrave, originally the commander of a threatened border region, without specifying the precise components of that authority as Frederick did when he conferred the regalia on Italian recipients or as he did in 1168 when he granted Bishop Herold of Würzburg ducal rights in eastern Franconia in the so-called "Golden Liberty" (*Goldene Freiheit*). On the latter occasion, Frederick defined the "jurisdictional superiority" (*omnis jurisdictio*), which the bishops of Würzburg had received from Charlemagne and his successors, as "the full power to exercise justice throughout the bishopric and duchy of Würzburg, and in all counties situated in that bishopric and duchy, in regard to robbery and arson, allods and fiefs, and vassals, with the right to impose capital punishment." The Würzburg privilege combined a lord's feudal jurisdiction over his vassals with the responsibility to enforce the peace ordinances. In the *Privilegium minus* Frederick granted his uncle, in other words, in delegation from the Reich, criminal jurisdiction in the duchy and specified, implicitly, that both Austrian counts and Bavarian nobles and churches with holdings within the duchy required the duke's approval to establish and maintain their own courts. It was the task of Henry Jasomirgott and his successors, just as it was Henry the Lion's north of the Elbe, to turn that authorization into reality, for example, by systematically acquiring the advocacies of all the churches in the duchy or of the lands held by non-Austrian bishoprics and monasteries within the duchy. Ironically, Frederick was forced at the assembly held in Regensburg in January 1158 to reconcile his Babenberg uncles, because Otto was resisting the efforts of his brother Henry to seize lands in the duchy that belonged to the church of Freising.[11]

In effect, Frederick recognized in the *Privilegium minus*, which defined for the first time in writing the relationship between the crown and a lay prince, the transformation of Germany into a confederation of territorial principalities, whose rulers, the vassals-in-chief, the lay princes as well as the bishops and the abbots of imperial abbeys, held their lordships in fief from the king. In fact, the duchies were called *fiefs* (*beneficia*) for the first time in the *Privilegium minus*.[12] Pope Adrian may have caused such an uproar at Besançon in 1157, when he employed the same word in reference to the crown, because the emperor and the lay princes were reconceptualizing their own relations in feudal terms. The resolution of the conflict between the two Henrys was Frederick's greatest diplomatic triumph, and Otto hailed the agreement as the dawn of a new age of peace (2.46).

The Founding of Munich

On 14 June 1158 in Augsburg, just before Frederick's departure for Italy on his second campaign, he was forced to settle another dispute. This one was between "his most noble blood relative," Henry the Lion, and another of the Babenbergs, in this case "his most dear paternal uncle," Otto of Freising, about their respective rights in Munich, which appears for the first time in the historical record on this occasion. It was long thought that Frederick favored Henry in this seemingly one-sided award, because he needed his cousin's soldiers more than his uncle's quill. However, Barbarossa may have been applying an earlier princely judgment about the usurpation of regalian rights.

The burghers and merchants of Würzburg had complained to Frederick in October 1155 about the new tolls that were being imposed on traffic on the Main between Bamberg and Mainz. Hermann of Stahleck had summoned, in the name of the princes, all the collectors of tolls to the Christmas court in Worms to present the imperial or royal privileges that authorized them to levy such imposts. When they failed to appear, Frederick had abolished all but three of the tolls.[13] He subsequently demanded, at Roncaglia in 1158, that the Italian magnates and communes provide written proof for their exercise of a wide range of regalian rights. His controversial Italian policy for recouping the crown's alienated rights was thus devised and first applied in Germany.

In the case of Munich both Henry the Lion and Otto of Freising may have acted without authorization. At Otto's request, in 1140 Conrad III had prohibited everyone, except the bishop, from minting coins or establishing a new market in the diocese of Freising and had permitted his brother Otto to hold an annual fair there. By 1158 Otto possessed a mint, a market, and a bridge over the Isar river, a tributary of the Danube, at Föhring, which is situated today within the city limits of Munich. At some unspecified date Henry the Lion had likewise erected a bridge over the Isar, just over three miles upstream from Föhring, and had set up a market in what is now the heart of the old city on land that belonged to the eponymous but unidentified monks after whom Munich (*München*; *Mönche*) is named. Both men were seeking to profit at the crossing of the Isar from the lucrative trade in salt which was being shipped westward from the saline in Bad Reichenhall, southwest of Salzburg. Frederick indicated in a privilege he granted in 1180 to Otto's successor, Bishop Albert I, that at some unspecified date Henry had destroyed the bridge and market at Föhring. For the past three centuries scholars have assumed that this act of violence triggered the dispute in 1158, but, if it did, Frederick would have been rewarding his cousin, uncharacteristically, for a gross violation of the peace. Freimut Scholz has proposed, therefore, that Henry's misdeed occurred later and that while he was clearly infringing on Freising's prerogatives, Otto, too, may have been exercising unauthorized rights at Föhring.

The Augsburg assembly ruled that Otto had to abandon the market, mint, and toll at Föhring. In compensation, Henry was directed to give the bishop one-third of the income from the mint in Munich and from the tolls on salt and all other commodities that were being transported in either direction. The bishop was to assign, in turn, one-third of the income from the mint in Freising to the duke on condition that Henry sub-enfeoff that share, as was already the case, to a person whom the bishop selected.

Frederick thus awarded two-thirds of the profits from the new settlement in Munich to the duke, but Otto did not leave Augsburg empty-handed. Frederick may also have rescinded, as part of the deal, his earlier order that Otto accompany him to Italy on the second campaign. Scholz has hypothesized that Henry subsequently destroyed the bridge and market at Föhring, perhaps in the 1170s, because Bishop Albert had not honored the 1158 agreement.

There is another intriguing angle to the story of the founding of Munich. The layout of the city, including the shape and location of the market, resembles the ground plan of the town of Höxter, which belonged to the abbey of Corvey and which is situated where the Hellweg road crosses the Weser. In their placement of Munich's five city gates, the surveyors employed the same measurement, 33.3 centimeters, as had been used at Corvey. As it happens, Henry the Lion was the advocate of Corvey; and Frederick had ordered Henry in 1152, at the request of Wibald, who was also the abbot of Corvey, to protect Höxter. Since Wibald had some architectural expertise, it is possible that Henry had consulted the abbot in planning the new settlement and even that Frederick was somehow involved. In any case, in resolving the dispute, the emperor successfully balanced the competing interests of his kinsmen without alienating either one and asserted the principle that not even his relatives could exercise regalian rights without permission.[14]

Polish Succession Disputes

Frederick's reconciliation with Henry Jasomirgott led to the resumption of Conrad III's failed attempt to reinstate the exiled Polish grand duke, Wladyslaw II, whose wife Agnes was Henry's sister and Frederick's aunt, and, coincidentally, an agreement to procure Polish troops for the forthcoming second Italian campaign. After the death of Duke Boleslaw III in 1138, Poland had been divided between his eldest son Wladyslaw, who had obtained Silesia as his hereditary duchy and the province of Cracow and suzerainty over Pomerania in his capacity as grand duke, and Boleslaw's younger half-brothers. Conrad had enfeoffed Wladyslaw with Poland on 14 April 1146. Shortly thereafter, Wladyslaw's brothers had defeated him; and he had fled to Conrad's court. The king had launched a military expedition against Poland in the summer of 1146, but he had turned around at the Oder after Wladyslaw's brothers, who were backed by Archbishop Frederick of Magdeburg, Albrecht the Bear, and Margrave Conrad of Meissen, promised Conrad their allegiance.

In 1157 Frederick assembled an imperial army in Halle on the Saale river in southeastern Saxony. He rejected the terms a Polish embassy brought on behalf of Boleslaw IV, who in 1146 had replaced his older half-brother Wladyslaw as grand duke; and Frederick began the Polish campaign on 4 August. The ostensible reason for the attack was the repeated refusals of Boleslaw IV and his brother Casimir to restore Wladyslaw to his former rank. Yet Rahewin, who relied almost exclusively on Frederick's own account of the war contained in a letter to Abbot Wibald, listed as a secondary cause the Polish dukes' failure to swear an oath of fealty to Frederick and to pay the annual tribute of 500 marks they owed him as their feudal suzerain. The latter was probably the real motive for the invasion, because Frederick informed Wibald that God had exalted the Roman Empire "with so great glory and honor" that Poland was again "under the yoke of our rule."

Nature and human artifice, Frederick wrote to Wibald, made the Polish territory west of the Oder nearly impenetrable; and the Poles tried to stop the imperial army by blocking the road with large piles of timber at narrow places. Nevertheless, the army reached the Oder at Głogów (German, Glogau), north of Wrocław (Breslau). Duke Vladislav II of Bohemia, who had been married to another of Frederick's Babenberg's aunts, joined the emperor there; and the Bohemians took the lead in crossing the Oder on 22 August. Although Boleslaw had succeeded in assembling a considerable army that included Russians, Prussians, Pomeranians, and possibly Hungarians, the frightened Poles retreated. They laid waste to their own lands and burned key fortifications, including Głogów and Bytom (Beuthen), downstream from Głogów, and so made it difficult for the German-Bohemian forces to procure provisions. The pursuing imperial forces ravaged with fire and the sword the dioceses of Wrocław and Poznań (Posen) in western Poland.

Boleslaw initiated negotiations with Frederick, both in person and via the princes, particularly through Vladislav, who guaranteed the Polish duke's safety; but the emperor insisted that the duke had to atone for his presumptuous conduct. Boleslaw appeared, in the customary ritual of submission and reconciliation, as a penitent before Frederick in September at Krzyszkowo near Poznań (the farthest east Frederick went in northern Europe). The duke was barefoot and carried an unsheathed sword in front of him to indicate the punishment he merited for his offenses. He prostrated himself at Barbarossa's feet and the princes interceded on his behalf. Boleslaw was restored to the emperor's grace on the following terms. He swore that he had not scorned the Empire by exiling Wladyslaw. He promised to give the emperor 2,000 marks of gold, the princes 1,000, and the empress 20, as well as 200 marks of silver to the members of the imperial court, in compensation for his failure to heed Frederick's summons and to swear the required oath of fealty for his domains. Boleslaw pledged that he would participate with 300 men in Frederick's second Italian campaign. Finally, he agreed to attend the Christmas assembly in Magdeburg and to respond there, in accordance with the sentence of the Poles and Bohemians, to the accusations of his exiled brother. After Boleslaw swore fealty to the emperor and handed over his brother Casimir and other nobles as hostages for his observance of the agreed-upon terms, Frederick returned to Germany in triumph. Boleslaw did not come to Magdeburg or send envoys empowered to act on his behalf, and he did not honor his commitment to fight in Italy. In short, Frederick had been tricked to leave Poland and had not succeeded in restoring his uncle as grand duke.[15]

At an assembly held in Nuremberg in August 1163, Boleslaw made peace with Frederick and agreed to the restitution of Silesia to the sons of his deceased brother Wladyslaw: Boleslaw the Tall and Mieszko III. After the brothers quarreled with Boleslaw IV about certain castles in Silesia that belonged to the latter as grand duke, Frederick, energetically assisted by King Vladislav of Bohemia and their nephew, Landgrave Louis III of Thuringia, undertook in August and September 1172 a second Polish campaign, with a large army composed of Bavarians, Swabians, Franks, and Saxons. Boleslaw IV met the emperor at the border and agreed to return to Wladyslaw's sons the parts of Silesia he had occupied, to renew Poland's tributary relationship with the Empire, and to pay the 8,000 marks in tribute for which he had been in arrears since 1146. Frederick's Polish cousins subsequently divided Silesia between them, and the Silesian branch of the Piast dynasty ruled parts of the duchy until the eighteenth century.[16] Although no less an authority than Leopold von Ranke, the founder of the academic study of history, hailed Frederick's 1157 Polish expedition as his most important and enduring achievement because it prepared the way for the Germanization of Silesia,[17] both Polish campaigns were just as much a Bohemian-Polish as a German-Polish confrontation; and the motivation was dynastic rather than nationalistic: the restoration of the husband and then the sons of Frederick's Babenberg aunt Agnes, who was also Vladislav's sister-in-law.

Vladislav II of Bohemia

Initially, Vladislav II's relations with Frederick had been strained. Although he had been summoned to attend Frederick's court in Merseburg in May

1152, the Bohemian duke refused, according to the Czech canon and chronicler Vincent of Prague, "to obey such a new creature," a turn of phrase that hints at the depth of the opposition in the Babenberg camp to Frederick's election. Nevertheless, Vladislav did send Bishop Daniel of Prague to represent him. Oldřich (Ulrich), the exiled son of Vladislav's predecessor, Soběslav I (r. 1125–40), also came to Merseburg and offered Frederick a large sum of money to confer the duchy on him. Frederick agreed—his repeated susceptibility to monetary inducements is striking—but Daniel persuaded Oldřich to renounce his claims to the duchy and to accept instead the Bohemian castle of Hradec Králové (Königsgrätz) with its appurtenances as a fief. However, Oldřich's continued presence at the imperial court after 1152 as a potential pretender to the Bohemian ducal throne put pressure on Vladislav to reach an agreement with Frederick.

They met near the Bohemian border in October 1155 during the failed attempt to reconcile Henry Jasomirgott and Henry the Lion. Subsequently, Vladislav accepted the emperor's invitation to attend his wedding to Beatrice of Burgundy in Würzburg in June 1156. The emperor concocted on this occasion a scheme, Vincent related, with Bishop Daniel and with Vladislav's chancellor, Provost Gervasius of Vyšehrad. If the duke promised to assist Frederick, in person and preferably with his own forces, in the planned siege of Milan, the emperor would adorn him with a royal diadem (*diadema*) and, to enhance the duke's honor, would return to him the castle of Bautzen situated north of the modern Czech–German border. Vladislav accepted the offer, and Daniel and Gervasius were, Vincent added, the only Bohemians who knew about this secret understanding. Vladislav's reconciliation with Frederick manifested itself in his pronouncement of the formal sentence that ended in September 1156 the Babenberg–Welf dispute over the duchy of Bavaria and a year later during the emperor's first Polish campaign.[18]

On 11 January 1158, at the imperial court in Regensburg, "what had been done secretly was publicly revealed," as Vincent phrased it; and Frederick, in the presence of all his princes, placed a diadem on Vladislav's head as a reward for his service and so turned the duke into a king. Rahewin, plagiarizing in part Sallust, described Vladislav as "a man of great talents, distinguished for his physical strength and courage, great in counsel and action," who had displayed "his exceptional valor" most recently in the Polish expedition and who was loved by all. Accordingly, the emperor and princes elevated Vladislav to the kingship; and "after he received a privilege about the use of the diadem and other royal insignia," he returned happily to Bohemia and prepared to go to Italy as a king, "together with the emperor, in regal splendor." Vincent indicated that Vladislav's homecoming was not quite so friendly. The Bohemian nobles were angry that he had committed them to the Italian campaign and were placated only when Vladislav agreed to assume the costs. They were even more incensed that he had altered the Bohemian constitution without consulting them. The nobles' displeasure explains why Vladislav's immediate successors did not use the regal title that Frederick had bestowed upon the Bohemian rulers in perpetuity.[19]

On 18 January, several days after Vladislav's elevation to the kingship, Frederick granted him "a privilege about the use of the diadem and other royal insignia," as Rahewin phrased it. Although the original charter survives, it poses a number of interpretive problems: for example, the only insignia the diploma mentions is Vladislav's headband (*circulus*). Frederick conceded in perpetuity to Vladislav and all his successors, in recognition of the duke's service and devotion and the achievements of all the Bohemians, the right to wear the circlet that had been bestowed "through the kindness ("beneficio") of imperial excellence" on the duke's grandfather, Vratislav, and Vladislav's other ducal ancestors as a sign of their preeminence among the dukes. (Curiously, the notary employed the same word, *beneficium*, whose translation had caused an uproar fewer than three months earlier at Besançon, when Pope Adrian had used it in reference to Frederick's crown and appeared to suggest that the Empire was a papal fief. Was the imperial chancery also playing with the double meaning of the word?) Vratislav was, in fact, the only previous Bohemian duke who had been honored in this fashion—Henry IV had granted him a crown in 1085—and, contrary to Frederick's normal modus operandi and Rahewin's account, there is no indication in the charter that the emperor had consulted with the princes. The failure of both Vladislav and Frederick to seek, seemingly, such consent from their magnates supports Vincent's contention that the two rulers had cut a secret deal in Würzburg in 1156.

Frederick stipulated that the duke was permitted to wear his circlet on the same occasions as Frederick wore "his crown (*corona*) and diadem of glory": Christmas, Easter, and Whitsunday, and the feast days of Bohemia's patron saints, Václav (Wenceslaus) and Adalbert of Prague. Vincent, Rahewin, and the notary were clearly trying to distinguish, in their choice of words, between Frederick's imperial crown (*corona*) and the headband (*diadema* and *circulus*) that adorned the brow of a subordinate monarch. Frederick specified that only Bishop Daniel of Prague and Bishop John III of Olomouc or their successors possessed the right to crown the Bohemian monarchs. If one of the bishoprics was vacant, each prelate was fully authorized to act on their own.

The biggest oddity is, however, that Frederick referred throughout the charter to Vladislav as a duke and not as a king. It has been suggested that he or the notary did so because Vladislav had not yet been crowned by a bishop, but Frederick displayed no hesitation in styling himself as emperor in the Treaty of Constance before his coronation by the pope. Moreover, there is no evidence that a Bohemian bishop ever crowned Vladislav, and the imperial chancery called him a king as early as 10 July 1158. The best explanation why the notary retained Vladislav's ducal title in January 1158 was that the chancery wished to indicate that Bohemia's relationship with the Empire had not been altered by Vladislav's new dignity. The crown was a reward for Vladislav's past and future services, not the symbol of an independent kingdom. Within the framework of the imperial constitution, the Bohemian ruler remained a duke, albeit the preeminent one. It is equally true that no effort was made in the privilege, unlike in the *Privilegium minus*, to define even minimally the nature of Bohemia's connection to the Reich. Vladislav kept his side of the bargain. The Bohemians crossed the Alps with Frederick in 1158.[20]

Conrad, the Count-Palatine of the Rhine

The death on 20 September 1156 of Frederick's uncle by marriage, Hermann of Stahleck, enabled Frederick to provide for his half-brother in a way commensurate with his high birth. In a charter of 18 December 1155, Conrad was already identified as the count-palatine of the Rhine; but that document poses so many diplomatic problems, including Conrad's title, that it is best to resist the tempting conclusion that he had been designated as the successor of the childless Hermann in the latter's lifetime. Conrad appeared for the first time as the count-palatine in the witness list of a charter in October 1156.[21]

Frederick's personal relations with his only brother are elusive. Since their father Duke Frederick II had entrusted his "little son" to the care of his older half-brother Barbarossa in 1147, and since young Conrad witnessed his first charter, in his brother Frederick's company, only in January 1152, perhaps at the age of fourteen, it is an educated guess that he was approximately fifteen years younger than the king and that the brothers had spent little time together during Conrad's childhood. Conrad participated in Frederick's first Italian campaign, and Otto thought it worth mentioning that Frederick sent him, along with Berthold IV of Zähringen and Otto V of Wittelsbach, to reconnoiter Tortona. Until 1156 Conrad was identified in the witness lists simply as Frederick's brother and sometimes also as a duke, but without any ethnic or territorial designation. The ducal title was merely an honorific bestowed upon a duke's son, and the chancery ceased to use the title after Conrad's enfeoffment with the Palatinate. Acerbus Morena described him as "compact in body, of medium build with blond hair, capable, rather modest, and not very talkative." Maybe Conrad was simply overshadowed by his older brother, but he was probably a man of limited abilities.[22]

Conrad crossed the Brenner Pass with his brother in June 1158, and Otto Morena recounted Conrad's heroic deeds during the siege of Crema that lasted from July 1159 to January 1160. He remained in Italy after Frederick dismissed most of the army in late February 1160. Yet Conrad cannot have stayed long because he did not witness any of his brother's precisely datable charters between 15 February 1160 and 3 June 1161, and because he returned to Italy along with the other German princes in the spring of 1161.[23]

Conrad had paid little attention hitherto to the Palatinate, but during the year or so he spent in Germany, he revived his predecessors' territorial ambitions and quickly learned that his older brother would not tolerate any actions that threatened his own prerogatives or the peace in his absence. Indeed, the count-palatine may have been at a disadvantage in his clashes with rival princes, because Frederick did not want his brother's actions to be construed as the implementation of his own wishes.[24]

Frederick put Conrad in his place when in 1161 he chose a new archbishop of Mainz. The ministerials and townspeople of Mainz had murdered their hated archbishop, Arnold, on 24 June 1160. Since the archiepiscopal territories in the Rhine valley separated the Palatinate's holdings north of Mainz from Conrad's share of the Salian inheritance south of the city, he had a considerable interest in the filling of a see that had once been occupied by his Saarbrücken great-uncle and maternal uncle, Adalbert I and Adalbert II. Conrad and his brother-in-law Landgrave Louis II of Thuringia, Mainz's territorial rival in Hesse and Thuringia, installed Christian of Buch, the provost of the cathedral chapter of Merseburg, as the new archbishop on 29 October 1160. However, the clergy of Mainz had already elected Rudolf of Zähringen, the brother of Duke Berthold IV. Frederick rejected both candidates at a council held in Lodi in June 1161, and the Mainz clerics who were present then chose at his direction Conrad of Wittelsbach. The emperor had nothing in principle against Christian, whom he soon made his chancellor and subsequently archbishop of Mainz in 1165; but Conrad of Wittelsbach's selection spared Frederick from having to choose between the candidates of rival princes while also allowing him to reward Conrad of Wittelsbach's brother, the Bavarian count-palatine, Otto V. More important, the choice was a clear signal to Frederick's own brother that he did not occupy a vice-regal position in the Rhineland and that archiepiscopal elections were to occur in the royal presence, a prerogative the clergy and ministerials of Mainz had affirmed at Frederick's insistence in 1157.[25]

During his brief stay in Germany in 1160–61, Conrad, as the advocate of the church of Trier, supported the opponents of Archbishop Hillin of Trier, even though Hillin had been a member of Frederick's inner entourage since his election. The count-palatine allied with, among others, his maternal uncle, Count Simon of Saarbrücken, and the townspeople and ministerials of Trier, who were seeking to free the archiepiscopal seat from Hillin's rule. The conflict embroiled the entire archiepiscopal territory, basically the Mosel valley.

Hillin complained to Frederick, who regarded the establishment of an Italian-style commune in Germany as intolerable; and he settled the dispute on 1 September 1161, at Landriano, near Lodi, after both princes had returned to Italy. The conflict forced Frederick to decide, as he put it in the charter that announced the terms of the settlement, between two "most intimately friendly and most dear" princes "to whom he was bound by ties of familiarity and kinship." "The convention of peace and concord" was another diplomatic masterpiece. Frederick avoided discussing the causes of the conflict, particularly his brother's role in fomenting the conspiracy in Trier after the emperor had expressly forbidden the city's strivings for autonomy. Conrad was forced, humiliatingly enough, to command the burghers, in writing, to desist and not to claim they were acting in his name; but he was also allowed to pretend that he had not been personally involved. Instead of punishing his brother, Frederick recognized the customary jurisdiction that both the archbishop and the count-palatine as the advocate exercised in Trier. The carefully devised agreement preserved the honor of both princes, but the long-term impact was the withdrawal of the Palatinate from the Mosel valley. Conrad's fraternal ties were thus not a great asset in advancing his own territorial ambitions.[26]

Conrad's marriage at an unknown date to Irmgard, daughter of Count Berthold of Henneberg, made sense in the context of Rhenish regional politics—Conrad obtained through his wife the advocacy of the imperial abbey of Lorsch;[27] but as the emperor's brother, he might have been expected to marry the daughter of one of the great princely German lineages or even, like Henry the Lion in 1168, a foreign princess. Perhaps the explanation for Conrad's "downward" match is that Frederick did not wish his brother to be seen as a possible heir to the throne and to gain powerful in-laws within or outside the kingdom. Even after the birth of Frederick's first son (Frederick V) in 1164, a considerably older paternal uncle was a potential threat to a child's well-being—as the cases of King John of England to Arthur of Brittany or Richard III to Edward V show, both princes having been murdered in mysterious circumstances.

There is one possible clue that Frederick may have been thinking along these lines. A Benedictine monk in the monastery of Affligem, northwest of Brussels, reported that during the siege of Milan in 1160 Frederick swore that he would remain there until he took the city. Moreover, if he died in the interim, his paternal cousin Frederick of Rothenburg and, in the case of the latter's demise, his maternal cousin Henry the Lion, should succeed him as *imperator*. The monk, though writing considerably after the event, was generally a well-informed and reliable source; but there is no other evidence that Frederick made such a recommendation about the succession to the throne. Thus it has been questioned whether the report is even true—the recommendation would not have been legally binding in any case—or whether the monk was employing *imperator* in its original sense as "general" rather than as "emperor." If the monk meant "general," it would explain why Frederick did not recommend that the absent Conrad take charge at Milan; but why would Barbarossa have preferred the younger and less experienced Frederick of Rothenburg to Henry the Lion as the commander of the imperial forces? If the childless Frederick was, in fact, trying to arrange for an orderly succession to the crown in the event of his death, Conrad's exclusion from consideration would say a great deal about the personal relationship between the brothers and, possibly, about Frederick's assessment of Conrad's abilities or the potential danger he posed. Still, Frederick's Staufer cousin was a far greater possible threat than Conrad.[28]

The rival territorial aspirations of the Palatinate and the archbishopric of Cologne in the Rhine valley, north of Koblenz, and, possibly as well, Conrad's resentment of Rainald of Dassel's predominant influence in Frederick's counsels, strained the brothers' relations in the 1160s. It has been proposed that Rainald, as the archbishop-elect of Cologne, antagonized Conrad on 7 August 1161, when he thwarted, intentionally or not, peace negotiations between Milan and Frederick, which had been arranged by Conrad, Duke Theobald of Bohemia, and Landgrave Louis II of Thuringia; but since Conrad, unlike the angry Theobald and Louis, fought in the ensuing battle and remained with Frederick in Italy until the end of the second expedition in August 1162,[29] it is probably best not to attach too much significance in Conrad's case to the events of 7 August 1161. However, Conrad did not follow Frederick to his abortive meeting with King Louis VII on the Saône in early September 1162; and he did not appear again at the imperial court until 18 April 1163. He remained there, seemingly, until 3 August 1163, when he witnessed Frederick's charter for the Premonstratensian abbey of Münsterdreisen, which had been founded by their father—Conrad could hardly absent himself on such an occasion. Conrad's next certain visit to the court was almost two years later, at the Whitsunday assembly in Würzburg in 1165.[30] As the emperor's brother, Conrad would almost certainly have been asked to witness a charter if he had been present.

During his prolonged absence from the court, Conrad became embroiled in 1164 in a feud with Rainald about the castle of Rheineck, downstream from Andernach and Koblenz on the left bank of the Rhine. The *Cologne Royal Chronicle*, the chief source on the feud, reported, cryptically, that Frederick spoke, briefly and rather harshly, with Rainald about Conrad at the assembly that was held in Bamberg on 18 November 1164, but that the archbishop-elect had managed to assuage the emperor's anger. Conrad had presumably complained to his brother about Rainald, and Frederick may have been angry at both men for disturbing the peace. According to a late fourteenth-century Cologne source, Landgrave Louis and Frederick of Rothenburg joined in the attack on Cologne. It is thus possible that Frederick's brother, brother-in-law, and cousin felt that Rainald had taken the place among the emperor's counselors that rightfully belonged to them as his kinsmen. Yet at the Whitsunday court in May 1165, Conrad and Louis were two of the four lay princes who were specifically identified as endorsing Rainald's policy of never acknowledging Alexander III as the rightful pope. Their stance is hardly compatible with some fundamental antagonism between them and Rainald, the architect of Frederick's anti-papal policy. In any case, the Rheineck feud ended with the Palatinate's complete defeat; and Frederick sealed Cologne's victory by conferring on Rainald in St. Peter's on 1 August 1167 the imperial manor located at Andernach with all its appurtenances, including the mint, toll, and the right to administer justice.[31]

Still, there is evidence that Conrad's relations with his older brother were troubled in the mid-1160s. The author of the *Annals* of the Dutch Benedictine abbey of Egmond, which were written, admittedly, after 1215, reported, in a garbled account of the Rheineck feud, that Conrad in his fool-hardiness insulted the emperor, empress, and their sons so outrageously—in 1164 the couple had only an infant son—that Frederick so humbled his brother that he hardly equaled in power an imperial ministerial. The continuer of Otto of Freising's *Deeds* noted that in 1167 Conrad traveled to Italy "to regain the imperial favor which he had some time before foolishly forfeited, but returned without success."[32] The birth of Frederick's sons—the true kernel in the Egmond *Annals*—ended Conrad's position as Frederick's possible spare heir and may explain the brothers' estrangement in the mid-1160s. Nevertheless, after 1167, Conrad witnessed 10 percent of Frederick's German charters—down from the 28 percent he had attested between 1156 and 1167—but most princes frequented the court less often after 1167.[33] Frederick's relations with his "most dear brother" were correct but not close.

The Tübingen Feud

Barbarossa's relations with his Staufer cousin, Frederick of Rothenburg, were even more ambiguous. Frederick had been pressured by his cousin's aunt and "sister," the Byzantine Empress Eirene, to knight Frederick of Rothenburg, that is, to declare him of age, at the assembly in Würzburg in September 1157, and to allow him to assume personal control of the duchy of Swabia. In the years immediately after his knighting, the younger man was identified in the witness lists of original charters as either the duke of Swabia or as Duke Frederick of Swabia, the son of King Conrad.[34] If the account in the *Annals* of Affligem is a true report of the arrangements Barbarossa made in 1160 about the succession in the event of his death without a son, then Frederick of Rothenburg as the son of the preceding king was considered to be the most likely heir to the throne.

The young duke was a member of the contingent that accompanied Frederick across the Brenner Pass in June 1158. Barbarossa put his brother and cousin in charge of the Swabians at the first siege of Milan in August 1158, and the Milanese decided to attack them, Rahewin reported, "either because they were fewer in number than the other detachments and their leaders younger, or because, being separated from the chief strength of the army, they could not obtain aid." The young princes were caught while sleeping, and Vladislav and the Bohemians had to come to their rescue.[35] The duke's lack of experience makes it highly unlikely that the emperor would have recommended two years later, in 1160, that Frederick of Rothenburg should assume overall command of the imperial forces during the second siege; but the repeated references to the duke as the son of a king suggest that he may have been viewed as the heir presumptive to the crown until the emperor became a father for the first time in 1164.

In contrast to Rahewin, Acerbus Morena provided a very positive description of "Duke Frederick of Rothenburg, the son of King Conrad, the paternal uncle of Emperor Frederick." He was "large, strong for his age, eager to prove his ability, well proportioned, solidly built, compact, pale complexioned, handsome and finely formed, cheerful, agreeable, and with thick almost white hair." The anonymous continuer of the Morenas' chronicle—possibly Otto Morena himself—described the son of the late king, when he was twenty-one or -two, as "a handsome man, and very vigorous, wise, and ingenious."[36] In short, the duke was an adolescent and youth who might have become, if he had lived longer, a magnet for opponents of the emperor. Revealingly, the notaries never employed any epitaphs like *beloved* in the charters drafted during the duke's lifetime to honor Barbarossa's cousin as they did the emperor's other kinsmen.

The ambiguity in the relationship between the two Fredericks was most apparent during the Tübingen Feud. In the early 1160s Hugo II of Tübingen (d. 1182), the count-palatine of Swabia, hanged several Welf ministerials in a county that he held in fief from Duke Welf VI and destroyed their castle. The chief, hardly unbiased source, the *History of the Welfs*, reported that some unnamed individuals thought that the ministerials' condemnation had been unjust. Otto of St. Blasien, writing in the early thirteenth century, provided a possible explanation of why the ministerials' execution was criticized. Hugo had captured three "robbers" and, in an act of partisan justice, had executed one of them, a Welf retainer, but had spared the other two, who were his own men. Welf VI complained to Hugo, who responded submissively to avoid a feud without offering appropriate satisfaction to the duke. Welf refrained from an attack but did not abandon his complaint. Since he intended to go to Italy to assert the Welf territorial claims there, he summoned his son, Welf VII, who was in Italy, to return home and take charge. Welf VII renewed his father's accusations and pressed Hugo repeatedly for compensation. The count-palatine, trusting in the assistance of Frederick of Rothenburg, who envied Welf VI's good reputation and who urged Hugo not to yield, rejected Welf VII's demands. As a result, all of Swabia was plunged, the pro-Welf chronicler wrote, into "abominable misfortune and unfortunate devastation."[37]

There has been some skepticism whether the execution of one or more ministerials/robbers could have been the cause of such a fray, and Karl Schmid proposed, therefore, that the participants were really fighting over the inheritance of Count Rudolf of Bregenz (d. c. 1150). (Bregenz is on the eastern end of Lake Constance in modern Austria.) Rudolf's heirs were his daughter Elizabeth, Hugo's wife, and the son of Rudolf's sister, Count

Rudolf of Pfullendorf (Barbarossa's companion on the Second Crusade), who fought on the Welf side. Elizabeth's mother Wulfhild, Rudolf's wife, was another sister of Welf VI and Barbarossa's aunt; and the conflict may have been, thus, about Wulfhild's dowry. However, there is not the slightest hint in the sources that the Bregenz inheritance was an issue; but clearly the feud pitted Welf VI and Welf VII against the husband of their niece/cousin. For his part, Barbarossa became embroiled not only in this dispute among his maternal relatives but also in a conflict, seemingly about injured honor, between his Staufer and Welf first cousins. Since the emperor supported the Welfs, the feud cannot be characterized as another round in the alleged rivalry between the two lineages; but Frederick of Rothenburg appears to have revived his father's enmity with Welf VI, whom the duke supposedly envied.[38]

Welf VII appealed to his "friends, kinsmen, and retainers" for aid. Among those who responded were the bishops of Augsburg, Speyer, and Worms, Duke Berthold IV of Zähringen, Margrave Berthold II of Vohburg, and Margrave Hermann IV of Baden. A total of 2,200 or more armed men camped on the evening of Saturday, 5 September 1164, near the castle of Tübingen, and planned to rest on the Sabbath. A small number of the Welf party, not thinking about the possible consequences, left the camp on Sunday morning and encountered the enemy near the castle. The brawl soon became a general melee, and the completely disorganized Welf forces suffered an ignominious defeat. Only one man was killed—the chronicler indicated that it was easier to capture than to kill them because they were so well armored—but the count-palatine's men took 900 prisoners and much booty. Welf VII managed to escape with only three companions. At this point both Barbarossa and Welf VI returned from Italy, and at an imperial court held in Ulm in early November 1164, Welf VI procured the captives' release and a year-long truce.[39]

After the expiration of the truce and during the winter of 1165–66, the Welfs devastated the count-palatine's domains, destroyed two of his castles, and captured forty of his men. Hugo, disheartened, appealed to his protector, Duke Frederick, for assistance; and he called, in turn, upon the Staufer's cousin, Duke Frederick of Bohemia, the son of Vladislav II. The Bohemians, "a horrible people, hateful to both God and men," plundered and burned all of Germany between Bohemia and Lake Geneva from Epiphany, 6 January 1166, until Candlemas, 2 February. Finally, Barbarossa arranged for Hugo's submission at an assembly held in Ulm on 13 or 15 March. According to Otto of St. Blasien, the emperor commanded Hugo to submit unconditionally or be banished from the Reich. In the presence of Barbarossa,

Henry the Lion, Frederick of Rothenburg, and Welf VI, Hugo prostrated himself three times at the feet of Welf VII. The count-palatine was led away in chains and kept a prisoner in one of Welf VII's castles until after the latter's death on 12 September 1167. Hugo's humiliation was extreme—normally, the defeated and repentant feudist was restored to grace immediately—and Barbarossa's partisan intervention on the Welfs' behalf, perhaps motivated by his need for their military might in Italy on the fourth campaign, was unprecedented; but did Frederick of Rothenburg, who had egged Hugo on, simply watch the disgrace of his onetime ally and escape unscathed?[40]

The answer is no. Italian narrative sources like the Morenas routinely referred to Frederick as the duke of Rothenburg after his main paternal inheritance rather than as the duke of Swabia; the former title was another way to indicate that he was the late king's son. In contrast, there is no certain evidence that the imperial chancery used that designation before 1164. However, on 1 November 1164, in the original charter issued at the assembly in Ulm where Hugo agreed to the release of the 900 prisoners, Frederick was identified as the duke of Stauf. Thereafter, the chancery called him the duke of Stauf, the duke of Rothenburg, or simply, once more, Duke Frederick, the son of King Conrad. He was never again styled the duke of Swabia. It appears that Barbarossa may have deprived his cousin of the duchy of Swabia and left him, like the Zähringer, as the duke of a titular duchy composed of the Staufer domains around Stauf and Rothenburg. The charter of 1 November also contains the first documentary reference to Barbarossa's eldest son, the future, short-lived Duke Frederick V of Swabia, who was born in Pavia in July 1164. No chronicler mentioned Frederick of Rothenburg's loss of Swabia, but it looks as if Barbarossa took advantage of his cousin's alienation of the Swabian magnates in the first phase of the Tübingen Feud to acquire the duchy for his own descendants.[41] Barbarossa's treatment of his Staufer cousin is the first sign of how the emperor's relations with the princes changed after he became a father.

The question arises whether there was any connection between the Tübingen Feud and the attack by Frederick's brother Conrad on Rainald of Dassel in the spring of 1164, another conflict in which Frederick of Rothenburg, according to later sources, was also involved. Were these unrelated territorial fights or did both Staufer princes resent that their brother/cousin heeded the archbishop of Cologne and the Welfs more than them—the *History of the Welfs* mentioned Frederick of Rothenburg's envy of Welf VI as a motive for his actions—and did the empress's pregnancy increase their fear of being further marginalized in the emperor's counsels? Certainly, Frederick's relations with his two Staufer kinsmen reached their low point in the mid-1160s. Unlike Conrad, Frederick of Rothenburg, angry, perhaps, about the loss of his duchy, refused to swear at Würzburg in May 1165, in an open defiance of the emperor, that he would never recognize Alexander III as pope. Yet in 1166 Frederick of Rothenburg wed Gertrude, at that time Henry the Lion's only child. It is tempting to speculate that Barbarossa arranged this marriage to reconcile his cousin with the Welfs, though none of the sources that deal with the Tübingen Feud mentions the marriage, and/or to compensate his cousin for the loss of Swabia with the hope of acquiring one or both of his father-in-law's duchies. We will never know because Frederick of Rothenburg, seemingly once again on good terms with the cousin who had obtained the crown in his place, died on 19 August 1167, during Frederick's fourth Italian campaign.[42]

The anonymous continuer of the Morenas' chronicle commented that upon the news of Frederick of Rothenburg's death, "immeasurable grief and sorrow filled nearly all of Italy because he had been extraordinary and a man of great virtue and charm." After the duke's death, Barbarossa conferred upon his cousin the honorifics he had denied him in life. He now was the emperor's "beloved," even his "most beloved cousin," the duke of Rothenburg. The chronicler who recorded the turmoil in the archdiocese of Salzburg during the schism had a more sober assessment. Conrad III's son had been, because of his power and might, a threat to the emperor.[43]

Beatrice of Burgundy

Frederick may have met Beatrice when he stayed in Besançon in February 1153. She was the only child of the late count-palatine of Burgundy, Rainald III (d. 1148), and Agatha, the daughter of Duke Simon I of Upper Lorraine and the sister of Duke Matthew. Since Beatrice's paternal uncle and guardian, Count William IV of Mâcon, was in actual possession of her county and since it was unclear whether he and his sons would surrender Burgundy voluntarily, Frederick may not even have contemplated a Burgundian marriage in 1153; and he dispatched in September an embassy to Constantinople in the hopes of procuring a Greek bride and continuing Conrad III's alliance with Byzantium. Anselm of Havelberg, who had gone to Constantinople a second time in 1154 to continue the negotiations, returned without a Byzantine princess in the spring of 1155; but Frederick sent Wibald from Ancona on the same mission yet again in August 1155. William of Mâcon's death in September 1155 altered the situation, and

Duke Matthew may have reminded his brother-in-law the emperor of his niece's availability—Matthew met with Frederick in Strasbourg in January 1156.[44] Archbishop Hillin of Trier anointed Beatrice as queen in Worms on Saturday, 9 June 1156. Frederick married her sometime between 10 and 17 June in Würzburg at an assembly attended, Otto said, by many princes. She was around twelve years of age; Frederick was thirty-three. The great disparity in their ages and her numerous pregnancies between 1164 and 1179 may explain why, unlike Empress Richenza or her contemporary, Eleanor of Aquitaine, Beatrice only rarely played an active role in politics.[45]

Part of Beatrice's attraction in 1156 may have been strategic and military. In conjunction with his report of Frederick's marriage to Beatrice, Otto provided a mini-history of Burgundy, starting with how Beatrice's father and Conrad of Zähringen had fought to rule it from 1127 "almost to the present." Otto said nothing about Frederick's unimplemented 1152 agreement with Berthold IV, but the bishop indicated that the emperor granted Berthold three cities situated between the Jura mountains and the Great St. Bernard Pass in modern Switzerland, namely, Lausanne, Geneva, and Sion. Everything else had been left to the empress. Her province extended, Otto wrote, from the castle of Montbéliard, west of Basel and northeast of Besançon, as far south as the Isère river, a tributary of the Rhone. Burgundy was connected to Provence, which stretched, Otto said, from the Isère to the mouth of the Rhone. Otto concluded with the misleading statement that after his marriage, Frederick "began in his wife's name to hold personally ... not only Burgundy but also Provence, long alienated from his empire."[46] In reality, Beatrice had no inherited right to all of Upper Burgundy, as Otto defined it, and none to Provence; but Otto's comment may simply reflect the court's ignorance of Burgundian realities.

However, the county of Burgundy itself was easily accessible, via the Belfort Gap, from Frederick's own domains in Alsace, and provided him with an alternative to the Brenner Pass, which the Veronese had blocked in 1155, and with the means to attack Milan from the west as well as the north and east. The Burgundian route from Germany to Italy led, via the Doubs, which flows by Besançon, to the Saône and Rhone valleys, and then via the Isère to the Mont Cenis Pass and the upper Po valley, west of Turin. Frederick left Italy via the Mont Cenis Pass in 1162 and again in 1168, and he entered Italy via that crossing on his fifth campaign in the autumn of 1174. Moreover, Burchard of Ursberg reported around 1230 that not only had Beatrice inherited all of her father's domains, but also, it was said, 5,000 knights as her dowry. That figure is, no doubt, a gross exaggeration;

but Beatrice brought badly needed additional troops to her husband in July 1159 during the siege of Crema. The manpower at her disposal may have been her chief attraction for Frederick upon his return from Italy in September 1155.[47]

We have no information about what lands or income, if any, Frederick assigned to Beatrice as her widow's dower; but recipients of imperial favors or individuals who were restored to Frederick's grace were required to give her as well as him "gifts." As we have already seen, Boleslav IV of Poland promised in September 1157, at the end of Frederick's first Silesian campaign, to give him 2,000 marks of gold and 20 to Beatrice. She was assigned an unspecified share of the 9,000 marks Milan agreed to pay after it submitted to Frederick in 1158. Following Milan's second capitulation in 1162, its ally, Piacenza, agreed to give 6,000 marks of pure silver to the emperor, empress, and the courtiers; there is no indication how the sum was to be divided among the recipients. Later that year, Frederick enfeoffed Count Ramón Berengar III with the counties of Provence and Forcalquier and the city of Arles. He owed the emperor 12,000 marks, the empress 2,000 marks, and the members of the court 1,000 marks. Finally, Frederick and Count Baldwin V of Hainaut reached an agreement in May 1184 about turning Namur into a margraviate. After the accord had been implemented, Baldwin was required to pay Frederick, his son Henry, and the court 80 marks of silver and the empress 5 marks of gold.[48] It is impossible to tell how common such payments were.

After their marriage Frederick needed to compensate Beatrice's cousins, the sons of Count William IV of Mâcon, for their rights to the Burgundian palatinate. The elder son, Stephen II, who attended Beatrice's wedding, obtained the county of Auxonne on the east bank of the Saône. His younger brother Gerard held the counties of Mâcon, on the west bank of the Saône in France, and Vienne, on the east bank of the Rhone in the Empire, in fief from Stephen. Both men were loyal supporters of Frederick. Stephen's marriage to Duke Matthew's daughter, Judith of Lorraine, who bore the name of Frederick's mother and who was both his niece and Beatrice's cousin, strengthened the bond between the three lineages. The house of Lorraine figured in another dynastic connection. Around 1172, as part of the resolution of the Polish–Silesian succession dispute, Judith's brother Frederick married Ludmila, daughter of Mieszko III, the younger brother of Boleslaw IV and his successor as Polish grand duke.

Another familial connection proved more significant. The half-brother of Beatrice's maternal grandfather, Duke Simon I of Lorraine, was the count of Flanders, Thierry of Alsace (r. 1128–68). His son, Count Philip of

Flanders (r. 1168–91), a vassal of the king of France but an active participant in imperial politics, was thus the first cousin of Beatrice's mother. Just as Frederick was related through the Babenbergs to many of the major rulers on the eastern border of the Reich, so he was linked through his sister Bertha, the duchess of Upper Lorraine, and through Beatrice to several powerful princes along the border with France.[49]

Acerbus Morena described Beatrice in 1162, when she would have been about twenty, as being

> of medium height, with shining, golden hair, a most beautiful face, and white, well-shaped teeth; her posture was upright, her mouth small, her countenance modest, and her eyes sparkled; she was bashful when charming and flattering words were addressed to her; she had most beautiful hands and a slender figure; she was completely submissive to her husband, feared him as her lord, and loved him in every way as her husband; she was literate and devoted to God; and just as she was named *Beatrix*, so she was in fact happy ("beata").

The unnamed poet who sang Frederick's deeds in Lombardy exalted her "as surpassing Venus in beauty, Minerva in intelligence, and Juno in power. Never was there another like her except for Mary, the mother of the Lord Jesus, to whom Queen Beatrice was happy to give precedence." It is impossible to tell how many of these words are true or simply courtly topoi.[50]

In conjunction with Beatrice's coronation as queen of Burgundy in Vienne on 8 September 1178 the Anglo-Norman chronicler Ralph of Diceto wrote that "although Frederick was always most constant in adversity, he was, nevertheless reputed by many to be uxorious, seeking in all things how he might please his wife." We may read Ralph's words, from the perspective of a modern companionate marriage, as complimentary; but, surely, they were not intended as such. There is no way to know whether Ralph was repeating unfounded gossip about the imperial couple's private lives or whether Frederick was dotingly submissive to her even in public. Or, conceivably, Frederick and Beatrice engaged, in Ralph's opinion, in too frequent intercourse, another possible connotation of the Latin word *uxorius*. For what it is worth, there is no evidence that Frederick was ever unfaithful. Perhaps they were happily married.[51]

In the late 1160s the poet Gautier d'Arras dedicated his epic romance, *Ille et Galeron*, to Beatrice, who unlike her husband could read Latin. The dedication raises the question whether she was involved in the transmission of French courtly culture and literature to the imperial court. However,

Gautier, perhaps disheartened by a lack of support, rededicated his epic to Count Thibaut V of Blois after her death in 1184. The evidence for Beatrice's literary patronage is, thus, meager; and it is unrealistic to suppose that a girl who entered in her early teens her husband's German-speaking world would have had much exposure in her homeland prior to her marriage to the latest French poetry or would have acquired much familiarity with it at his court.[52]

Beatrice must have had considerable stamina to cross the Alps eight times on horseback and to survive eleven pregnancies. The couple's three daughters died young as did three sons: Duke Frederick V, who was born in Pavia in 1164, and Rainald and William, who were named after the empress's father and paternal uncle in the expectation, in all probability, that one of them would inherit the Burgundian palatinate. (Alternatively, William might have been named after Frederick's uncle by marriage and the emperor's chief Italian ally, William of Montferrat.) Five of the couple's sons reached maturity: Emperor Henry VI (d. 1197); Duke Frederick VI of Swabia (d. 1191), who was originally named Conrad and renamed after Frederick V's death; Otto (d. 1200), the count-palatine of Burgundy; Duke Conrad of Swabia-Rothenburg (d. 1196); and King Philip of Swabia (d. 1208). The last, who bore a name hitherto unknown in the imperial genealogy, may have been named after Beatrice's kinsman, Count Philip of Flanders; or he may have been named after the influential Archbishop Philip of Cologne, because as the couple's youngest son the boy was intended for an ecclesiastical career. In either case, the name of an Apostle would have been especially appropriate for a future archbishop.[53]

As Otto of Freising noted, Frederick governed the palatinate on behalf of his young wife. Already at their wedding, Frederick confirmed the privileges and donations her father Rainald III had made to various Burgundian monasteries without bothering to indicate that he was acting at Beatrice's behest. In 1157 the emperor said, at least, that he was giving a meadow to a Cistercian monastery with the consent and at the request of his most beloved wife; and in 1178 he conferred on a Carthusian house various properties and rights that Burgundian nobles had turned over to him and Beatrice at the couple's instigation.[54] In 1166, as the co-rulers of Burgundy, in recognition of his devoted service they conferred jointly on Beatrice's most illustrious kinsman Odo I of Champlitte, viscount of Dijon and son of Count Hugh of Troyes and Beatrice's paternal aunt, several places that her father Rainald had formerly possessed. Odo's heirs were to have no right to these properties, which were to revert on his death to the emperor and empress and their heirs.[55]

Beatrice interceded occasionally for a non-Burgundian religious foundation: for example, the house of Augustinian canons that Bishop Conrad I of Eichstätt had founded in his diocese in Rebdorf or the Benedictine abbey of Saint-Ghislain in the county of Hainaut. (There may have been a familial reason for the latter intervention, because Count Baldwin V of Hainaut was married to Beatrice's cousin, the sister of Philip of Flanders.) In 1174, at the intercession of "the companion of our bed" and their children, Frederick settled a dispute between his kinsman, Otto of Andechs, the provost of St. Mary's in Aachen, who subsequently became the bishop of Bamberg, and the canons about the selection of the bailiffs of two manors.[56] Sometime between their marriage and her death in 1184, the couple jointly confirmed the establishment of a confraternity of clerics and lay persons that had been organized in Goslar more than thirty years earlier to provide for poor and sick townspeople and for their burial and remembrance. The guild members were presumably expected to pray for their imperial patrons.[57]

Beatrice was sometimes involved, rather perfunctorily, in Italian affairs. When the Milanese were unable to obtain an audience with the empress after their humiliating ceremonial capitulation on 6 March 1162, they appealed for her help by throwing the crosses they were carrying through the lattices in the windows of her chamber. A Genoese notary reported that she, along with the princes, subsequently persuaded Frederick to spare the lives of the Milanese. However, unlike her predecessors who entreated their husbands and sons publicly and successfully to be merciful to repentant rebels, as Empress Richenza did for Frederick's own father in 1135, Beatrice had not even been present at Milan's formal surrender earlier in the day.[58] On 5 October 1164, just before the couple left Italy at the conclusion of the third campaign, Frederick, at Beatrice's petition, enfeoffed William of Montferrat and his heirs with a long list of possessions and the attendant regalia and rights; but Frederick did not need his wife to remind him to reward his most important noble supporter in Italy, especially just after the imperial couple had entrusted their newborn son, Frederick V, who was too frail to cross the Alps, to the care of the margrave and Frederick's aunt.[59] In March 1176, at Beatrice's entreaty, Frederick made a preliminary secret agreement with Tortona about the terms for the city's restoration to imperial favor. The initiative for the negotiations appears to have come from the city, which was threatened by the Lombard League's foundation of the nearby city of Alessandria. For his part, Frederick was eager to separate Tortona from his other Lombard enemies. Under these circumstances, Beatrice's intercession was a face-saving way for Frederick to change course after he had destroyed the city in 1155. Significantly, no mention was made in the final agreement, in early 1177, of her role in the proceedings.[60] Finally, in 1178, in a puzzling transaction, Frederick and his son Henry VI purchased from Bishop Guala of Vercelli for the exorbitant sum of £2,580 the harbors and tolls along the Sesia river, a tributary of the Po that flows through Vercelli, and the Cervo, a tributary of the Sesia. They conferred these regalia in turn on Beatrice, who, to the honor and glory of the Virgin Mary and for the benefit of her own soul and the souls of Frederick and their ancestors, renounced the right to collect any payments from those who used the ports or the bridge or any other means to cross the streams. It has been suggested that Frederick wanted to strengthen his influence in Vercelli, which was a member of the Lombard League; but it is hardly self-evident why Frederick did not free the inhabitants from the charges himself.[61]

The one occasion on which Beatrice became substantially involved in a political matter was at the behest of her mother's uncle, Count Thierry, and cousin, Count Philip of Flanders. They were determined to control the bishopric of Cambrai, the westernmost episcopal see in the Empire and a suffragan of the archbishop of Reims in France. Henry V had acknowledged the Flemish lordship over Cambrai, but Conrad III had confirmed in 1145 Cambrai's privileges and freedom. Thierry had attended Frederick's first Christmas court in Trier in 1152 and, in a distinctive honor, had carried the sword in front of the king in the Christmas Day procession. Frederick and the lay princes agreed to the revocation of Conrad's privilege on 26 December, and the count swore the required oath of fealty for the receipt of Cambrai. The requisite charter had not yet been fully drafted, but since Thierry was eager to return home after the main meal, he entrusted his nephew, Duke Matthew of Lorraine, with securing the document. The scribe had been working on the charter in the archiepiscopal residence when Bishop Nicholas II, who had heard of Thierry's visit to the court and who suspected the count's intentions, arrived unexpectedly, questioned the scribe, and learned about the charter's unfavorable contents. Upon leaving the archbishop's quarters, Nicholas encountered several bishops and had procured their support. When Matthew presented the finished charter to Frederick to be sealed, Nicholas protested. The prelates supported their colleague, while the lay princes, led by Matthew, demanded in a heated confrontation—in another example of the princely conflicts that broke out behind closed doors—that Frederick approve Thierry's request to which they had already consented. Frederick summoned Thierry back and informed him in the presence of the entire court that he had no choice but to revoke his earlier decision. The king calmed the ensuing tumult and imposed, with considerable difficulty, a truce upon the parties until Pentecost, which Nicholas, fearful of the count's revenge, had requested. The furious Thierry left the court, and Frederick confirmed Conrad's charter for Cambrai on 29 December 1152.[62]

Nicholas' death on 1 July 1167 offered Thierry and Philip another chance to assert their control over Cambrai. The greater and wiser part of the clergy of Cambrai elected Peter, Thierry's youngest son, who had the support, allegedly, of both the nobles of the diocese and the burghers of the city. No doubt, his father had a hand in the outcome. Peter, whom the decidedly pro-Flemish chronicler, Lambert of Waterlos, called a "youth" and "adolescent," had not attained the canonical age for elevation to the episcopate. The minority chose the archdeacon Alard instead. The latter's envoys reached Frederick first in Pavia, where he was staying in September after his hasty departure from Rome in early August and the decimation of his army by dysentery. The archdeacon's adherents succeeded initially, with falsified letters and with a liberal distribution of gifts to members of the court, or so Lambert claimed, to win support for Alard's candidacy. Thierry and Peter's brothers, Philip and Count Matthew of Boulogne, sent their own embassy, which arrived in Pavia three days after Alard's. They also carried letters addressed to Beatrice, the counts' kinswoman, who had joined Philip at the Christmas court in Aachen in 1165, in an "indissoluble friendship" and who had pledged on that occasion to aid Philip in the future. She supported Peter's cause at the court, and the princes voided Alard's election.

Frederick consoled the clergy and vassals of Cambrai about the death of Nicholas, whom the entire Empire mourned, and expressed his regret that they had been unable to reach a unanimous decision. He was dispatching to them an embassy, which was charged with conducting a new election within six weeks of its arrival in Cambrai. If the electors were unable to choose "a person pleasing to God and the Reich," the emperor would assert, he told them, the right granted to him by the Concordat of Worms to select, in consultation with the princes, a new bishop. At the same time he wrote to Counts Thierry and Philip that, on account of his love for them and his wife, he was favorably disposed to their request to recognize Peter as the bishop; but since he did not wish to infringe upon Cambrai's electoral rights, he had sent envoys to the city to preside over a new election. The emperor also informed the cathedral canons and castellan of Cambrai that he had welcomed their letters on Peter's behalf, both because he was "a kinsman of his wife the empress" and because Frederick knew that Peter's selection would bring "great honor to the Empire and advantage to the church of Cambrai." The emperor was sending Provost Arnold of Aachen to Cambrai to secure Peter's selection. Not surprisingly, Peter was unanimously and joyously elected, according to Lambert, by the clergy and people of Cambrai.

In 1168, at Peter's request and with the backing of Archbishop Christian of Mainz and Henry the Lion, Beatrice was able to block Archbishop Philip's attempt to transfer the bishopric of Cambrai from the metropolitan province of Reims to Cologne. Peter was never ordained, but on Count Philip's advice he resigned the bishopric in 1174 in the hope that he would father a male heir because Philip was childless. Peter died in 1176, leaving behind only a daughter.[63] The disputed Cambrai episcopal election was the only substantive issue in which Beatrice intervened in a decisive way, but it is unlikely that Frederick would have risked alienating the powerful counts of Flanders during the schism and after the annihilation of his army, even if she had remained silent.

There was a subtle change in the couple's relationship after the birth of their first son (Frederick V) in July 1164, and they had truly become one flesh. Thereafter, Frederick specified in some confirmations of monastic possessions and rights that he was acting to benefit his soul and the souls of his wife and children. For example, on 1 November 1164, in the charter for the Swabian Premonstratensian abbey of Weissenau, the emperor stated that he was doing so "for the good fortune (*prosperitas*) and salvation of ourselves and of our most dear wife, Empress Beatrice, and of our most dear son, Frederick the Younger." The choice of the word *prosperitas*, which can mean not only good fortune but also good health, may indicate that the emperor was concerned about the survival of his sickly firstborn, Frederick V, who died a few years later aged six at most. Frederick had not previously evinced any interest, at least in the charters, in Beatrice's eternal well-being.[64]

Another piece of evidence that points to Beatrice's increased stature as the mother of Frederick's children is that the royal mint in Frankfurt, which began striking coins in the early 1160s, issued bracteates (thin silver discs) that depicted both Frederick and Beatrice, the first time the imperial couple appeared on Staufer coins. The mint at Gelnhausen even struck a bracteate that showed only the empress.[65] Perhaps these issues were intended to celebrate Frederick's success in assuring the continuity of his dynasty.

Intriguingly, Beatrice was identified both in the preliminary Peace of Anagni of 1176 and in the final Peace of Venice of 1177 as Frederick's fortunate wife (*felix eius uxor*). The root meaning of *felix* is "fertile" and by extension, "happy", "fortunate", or "lucky". *Felix*, thus, had pagan charismatic overtones—it was the ruler's good fortune (*felicitas*) that caused the crops to grow—and the word had been used previously only for saints or the deceased, who were described as being of happy memory. Frederick himself was never called *felix* in his charters. The designation of Beatrice in her lifetime as *felix* conveyed the idea that her bearing of numerous sons had been a source of blessing for the realm and for an emperor who had long lacked an heir.[66]

Strained Relations with Berthold IV of Zähringen

In conjunction with his marriage to Beatrice in 1156, Frederick granted Berthold IV the right to invest the bishops of Lausanne, Geneva, and Sion, which Frederick had retained in 1152, in return for the surrender of his Burgundian rectorate west and south of the Jura, where the Zähringer had competed unsuccessfully with the counts-palatine of Burgundy. This arrangement, which was similar to Frederick's grant of the bishoprics north and east of the lower Elbe to Henry the Lion, authorized Berthold to consolidate his power in a region where he had inherited extensive holdings and rights. Berthold founded the cities of Fribourg (Freiburg im Üchtland), southwest of Bern, and Bern itself, and retained control of Lausanne, on the north bank of Lake Geneva; but he was unable to dislodge the counts of Savoy from Sion on the upper Rhone, southeast of Lake Geneva and north of the Great St. Bernard Pass. Moreover, Bishop Arducius of Geneva, whom Frederick had enfeoffed in 1154 with the regalia of the church of that city, resisted his mediatization. Berthold's rectorate was thus limited effectively to the area east of the modern French–Swiss border between Lausanne and Basel, basically the valley of the Aare river and its tributaries—Bern is on the Aare and Fribourg on the Saane.[67]

Berthold suffered additional setbacks at Frederick's hand after 1156. Henry the Lion was eager to round out and expand his Saxon holdings and persuaded Frederick to exchange properties with him. Henry surrendered to his cousin the Swabian inheritance of his wife Clemence, who was Berthold's sister: the castle of Badenweiler in southern Baden along with 100 ministerials and 500 hides. In return, Frederick conferred on the duke as allods the imperial castles of Herzberg and Scharzfeld and the imperial manor at Pöhlde in the Harz mountains in southern Saxony. Only the right to hunt in the region, which Henry continued to hold in fief from the emperor, was excluded from this allodialization of the imperial domain. Since it was the emperor's duty, as Frederick's charter explained, always to increase and never to diminish the state, he had procured a princely judgment on 1 January 1158, namely that he needed to compensate the Reich for the loss of the imperial possessions he had conferred on Henry; that is, the princes distinguished, as they had in 1125, between the imperial domain and the Staufer's dynastic holdings. Frederick transferred to the crown, therefore, other properties that he had inherited from his father or that he had purchased.[68] The acquisition of Badenweiler, on the right bank of the Rhine, opposite the Staufer's holdings in Alsace, strengthened Frederick's position on the upper Rhine and the connection between Burgundy and the lineage's possessions further downstream in Rhenish Franconia. Berthold would have preferred, no doubt, that Henry the Lion, whose interests were focused on Saxony, had retained Badenweiler. The old Staufer–Zähringer territorial rivalries in Swabia were again in play.

Sometime after June 1161, when Frederick chose Conrad of Wittelsbach rather than Berthold's brother Rudolf as the archbishop of Mainz, and the autumn of 1162, Berthold wrote to Louis VII that he was prepared to serve and obey the French king in all matters. If the emperor, "a destroyer of churches and laws," should carry out his threats against Louis, then Berthold, all of his friends and vassals, and some of the greatest German princes—either because of their love for or out of their kinship with the duke or because they shared Berthold's hatred of the emperor—would advise and assist Louis as he directed. As Berthold reminded Louis, Rudolf had been canonically elected; but Frederick out of hatred of the Zähringer had rejected his candidacy. Berthold was dispatching his brother to Louis and asked that the king recommend Rudolf to Alexander III, so the pope would restore Rudolf to his rightful position—Berthold was obviously contemplating abandoning Frederick's anti-pope.[69]

Frederick's response to Berthold's potential treason was swift. On 7 September 1162, at St.-Jean-de-Losne, the princes confirmed Bishop Arducius' contested status as an imperial prince and voided Berthold's alienation of the regalia of the church of Geneva.[70] If we are to believe two thirteenth-century chroniclers, Frederick then advised Henry the Lion to divorce his wife Clemence, Berthold's sister, and provided the sworn testimony that led to the dissolution of their marriage on 23 November 1162, on the grounds of consanguinity. According to Gilbert of Mons, Frederick testified on Henry's behalf because he feared the combined strength of the dukes of Zähringen and Saxony; but Gilbert's account, written in the mid-1190s, may have been influenced by Henry's loss of his duchies in 1180. Henry, who had married Clemence in 1147 but who lacked a son, may not have needed much prompting to try his luck elsewhere.[71]

Berthold and Frederick's estrangement did not last long. The duke participated in Frederick's fourth Italian campaign in 1166–67 and was one of the fortunate survivors.[72] For his part, Frederick supported Berthold's ambitions in the Low Countries and so, incidentally, diverted Berthold's attention from Swabia. Berthold's mother Clemence was one of the three sisters and potential heirs of the childless Count Henry the Blind of Namur and Luxembourg. In 1167 Henry and Frederick arranged for the election of Rudolf of Zähringen as bishop of Liège. At Frederick's express request and with Henry of Namur's consent, Archbishop Arnold of Trier agreed in 1171 to transfer to Berthold and his son Berthold V, after the count's death, the fiefs Henry held from the church of Trier. When the Zähringer took actual possession of the fiefs, they were to pay the archbishop or his successor £350. Bishop Rudolf, who was to serve as Berthold V's guardian in the event of his father's early death, and Frederick pledged properties as surety for the fulfillment of the agreement.[73] Frederick thus succeeded in establishing the Staufer in Burgundy without permanently alienating Berthold IV of Zähringen.

The End of the Byzantine Alliance and the Rapprochement with Hungary

Frederick's marriage to Beatrice in 1156 ended the Byzantine alliance, which he had still pursued as late as August 1155 when he dispatched Wibald to Constantinople. It is generally assumed that Frederick decided to marry Beatrice after he learned about the Byzantine occupation of Apulia, aided by the letters the Greeks had allegedly acquired surreptitiously at Ancona from the imperial chancery;[74] but it is possible that he had already recognized the value, militarily, of the Burgundian connection when he decided, in September 1155 at the latest, to punish Milan. At the time of the emperor's wedding in mid-June 1156 in Würzburg, the Germans did not yet know that William of Sicily had defeated the Byzantines and the Apulian rebels at Brindisi on 28 May. Otto explained that although his nephew hated William, "Frederick was nevertheless unwilling that the frontiers of his empire—seized by Roger's tyrannical frenzy—should be taken by foreigners [the Greeks]," and he had the princes swear at Würzburg to undertake a campaign against the Byzantines in Apulia. When the news of William's victory reached Germany shortly thereafter, Frederick reversed course again. He freed the princes from their oaths, and they agreed at Fulda, on Palm Sunday, 24 March 1157, to prepare instead for a campaign against Milan and to assemble in Ulm on 7 June 1158, the eve of Pentecost. The emperor notified Otto and Wibald, who had not been in Fulda, of the decision, and summoned them to participate.[75] The really interesting thing about this change of plan is the revelation that Frederick was more offended by the Greek than the Norman presence in "his empire." This helps to explain why he could decide in the 1180s to ally with William II.

The emperor finally received in Nuremberg, in July 1156, the Greek envoys who had accompanied Wibald upon his return from Constantinople in June and who had been kept waiting in Salzburg during the wedding festivities in Würzburg. Frederick's marriage made their matrimonial proposals irrelevant, but the ambassadors also tried to arrange an immediate joint attack on Hungary to avenge the recent Hungarian defeat of a Byzantine army and the death in that battle of Manuel I's ally, Boris, a pretender to the Hungarian throne. Frederick informed the Byzantine ambassadors that there was not sufficient time to launch an expedition against Hungary by September 1156, but he did send his chaplain Stephen to learn Manuel's will. The dispatch of an otherwise unknown chaplain rather than an envoy of Anselm of Havelberg or Wibald's stature is indicative of the deterioration in relations between the two empires.[76]

Manuel made peace with the Hungarian king Géza II in September 1156, and in July 1157 Frederick dispatched Bishop Daniel of Prague to the king. Géza agreed to provide Frederick with 500 "Saracens" for the campaign against Milan—according to Rahewin, 600, presumably Christian, Hungarian archers crossed the Alps in 1158. The emperor may also have sent Daniel to Géza to intercede on behalf of the king's brother, Stephen IV. According to Rahewin, Géza suspected Stephen, who may have been falsely maligned, of seeking the throne and had proceeded against the members of his brother's household. Fearing for his life, Stephen had fled to the imperial court and had professed his innocence. Frederick, believing him, sent unnamed ambassadors—Bishop Daniel?—to Hungary to request Stephen's reinstatement. Géza's envoys arrived in January 1158 at the assembly in Regensburg—the same court where Vladislav II of Bohemia was made a king—and refuted all of Stephen's accusations. The emperor realized, Rahewin said, that the dispute could be resolved only by a division of the kingdom or by the condemnation of one of the plaintiffs. Frederick decided to postpone his decision, in effect siding with Géza. The Hungarian envoys, who had arrived with gifts worth almost a thousand pounds, returned to their king with a message of peace and with presents of comparable value. Frederick permitted Stephen, as he had requested, to travel via Venice to Constantinople, where he married a Greek bride.

Frederick sought a rapprochement with Géza because he needed Hungary as a buffer against Byzantine aggression in the Balkans.[77]

While Bishop Daniel was negotiating with Géza in August 1157, Frederick embarked on 4 August on his first Polish campaign. He ordered Wibald to go to Worms to meet and negotiate with the Greek envoys, who were expected shortly and who had been instructed to wait there for the emperor's return from Poland. At the beginning of September, Frederick informed the abbot of the apparently successful outcome of the Polish expedition and directed him to come to Würzburg by the eve of the feast of St. Michael the Archangel, 28 September, to conduct the negotiations with the ambassadors.[78]

The discussions initially went badly. According to Rahewin, the Greeks' words were arrogant, overly flowery, and smacked of royal pride. Frederick was offended, and if he had not disguised his true feelings, some members of the court might have given the envoys a too blunt, undiplomatic answer. The ambassadors finally succeeded "by their many entreaties and tears" in appeasing the emperor; and they pledged that in the future "they would bring him in their salutations only such reverence as befits a Roman prince and the ruler over the City and the world." The issue, once again, as was the case whenever relations between the two empires were tense, was the emperors' rival claims to the imperial title. The ostensible purpose of the Byzantine mission was the request of the Empress Eirene, supported by her husband Manuel, that her nephew, Frederick of Rothenburg, be girded with a sword and knighted in the diplomats' presence. In light of the Byzantine backing of the Hungarian pretender Boris, her intervention was not quite so innocuous. The ceremony was a none too subtle reminder that the young duke, who was the recipient of "many magnificent gifts" from his Greek relatives, had been denied his father's crown. No wonder Barbarossa seethed.[79]

This time the emperor did not send an unknown chaplain to Constantinople but his most experienced diplomat, Wibald. In the spring of 1158 the abbot was unable to prevent the conclusion of a peace, mediated by Pope Adrian IV, between Manuel and William I and potentially aimed against Frederick. The abbot died on his way home, in Bitolj (Monastir, now in the Republic of Macedonia), on 19 July 1158; and on Frederick's orders his bones were exhumed and returned for burial in Stavelot. Relations between the two empires were so bad that Greek envoys who arrived at the imperial court in Italy in January or February 1159 asked for a safe conduct because they feared they would be blamed for Wibald's death.[80] Nevertheless, Rahewin put the best possible gloss on imperial–Byzantine relations in his summary of Frederick's deeds. "He prevailed upon Manuel, the emperor of Constantinople, who voluntarily sought friendship and alliance with him, to term himself emperor not of Rome, but of New Rome, whereas he had been—like his predecessors—calling himself emperor of the Romans" (4.86).

After meeting with the Greek envoys in Würzburg at the end of September and the beginning of October 1157, Frederick set out for Besançon to receive the homage of his Burgundian subjects and participate in the dramatic confrontation between his new chancellor, Rainald of Dassel, and the papal chancellor, Cardinal Roland. Frederick's conviction that the cardinal had insulted him at Besançon prevented him from accepting Roland as Pope Alexander III for eighteen years.

CHAPTER EIGHT

THE HOLY EMPIRE

Rainald of Dassel

After the chancellorship had been vacant for nearly two years, Frederick selected Rainald of Dassel as the new incumbent—he was identified for the first time as the chancellor on 10 May 1156, eight months after Frederick's return from the *Romzug*.[1] Rainald's appointment has often been depicted as a decisive turning point in Frederick's reign, as can be seen in the chancery's apparent adoption, in 1157, during Rainald's tenure, of the designation *sacrum imperium*, Holy Empire, for the Reich.[2] Although, after 1156, Frederick was no longer willing to recognize the pope's exclusive sovereignty in Rome and the Patrimony, as he had in the Treaty of Constance, and was determined to bring Lombardy under his direct control to compensate for his loss of Swabia, there was, in fact, no fundamental change in imperial ideology after Rainald became chancellor.[3] The chancery's use of imperial epithets and even the title *imperator* for Conrad III, who was never crowned as emperor, and Frederick's letter notifying Pope Eugenius about his election as king, indicate that the court believed the monarch's imperial authority stemmed from his election and not from his coronation in Rome. Rainald was simply more blunt in presenting this argument, most famously in the aftermath of Besançon, because, ironically, Frederick's imperial coronation had legitimized his coup d'état and because he was in a far stronger position in Germany after his accommodation with the Babenberg party. Ultimately, Rainald was Frederick's servant.

Rainald, who was born around 1120, was the younger son of the count of Dassel, one of the many Saxon nobles who had utilized the turmoil of the Investiture Conflict to turn a complex of fiefs, allods, advocacies, and other rights into a county. The future archbishop received his initial education in the nearby episcopal see of Hildesheim and almost certainly studied in France—probably in Paris but that cannot be proven. Otto of Freising addressed Rainald, in the letter where he requested that the chancellor "interpret" *The Two Cities* for his nephew, "as a philosopher," who was familiar with Boethius and Aristotelian syllogisms. In 1149 Rainald, by then the provost of the cathedral chapter of Hildesheim, exchanged books with Wibald, including, revealingly, a treatise on military strategy, and offered to assist him, if the abbot so wished, in obtaining the archbishopric of Cologne. Rainald may even have been Wibald's protégé. As far as we know, Frederick first met Rainald sometime between the duke's return from the Second Crusade in the spring of 1149 and 10 June 1150. Rainald attended the new king for the first time in Goslar on 9 May 1152.[4]

Rahewin offered this intertwined description of Rainald and Frederick's chief lay lieutenant, Otto V of Wittelsbach, whose impetuosity nearly led to bloodshed at Besançon:

> . . . these illustrious men possessed a pleasant and imposing presence, nobility of family, an intellect strong in wisdom, unperturbed spirits; in fact, they were men to whom no task was too unfamiliar, no post too dangerous, no armed foe too terrible. They permitted themselves no misdeeds, no passions; they were eager for praise, generous with money; they wished for great glory and honorable wealth. They were youthful and remarkably eloquent; similar in manner, save that one was marked by the gentleness and pity consonant with his clerical status and rank, whereas the sternness of the sword that he bore not in vain had added dignity to the other. The one offered a refuge to the wretched, the other doom to evildoers (3.19).

Acerbus Morena said that Rainald was

> of medium height and of a compact build, with an attractive and reddish countenance, well-shaped limbs of appropriate length, his hair was thick and almost blond; he was a skillful speaker and well educated, eloquent, prudent and very shrewd, most desirous to increase the honor of the emperor—indeed so much so that the emperor heeded no one's advice more than Rainald's; he was also generous, jovial, affable, genial, willingly undertook tasks, and by his shrewdness and exertions the splendor of the Empire was greatly enhanced.

As for Otto of Wittelsbach, the Lodi magistrate wrote:

> ... he was of large stature, with finely formed and compact limbs; he was grave, wise and prudent in his counsels and most brave in battle; he had long, nearly black hair, large eyes, and a longish, almost red face; and he was exceedingly faithful to the emperor and the Empire, much loved by the emperor, and was his kinsman.[5]

It is highly revealing that Rahewin compared Rainald to a lay magnate rather than another churchman, even if he ascribed to Rainald, not very convincingly, the virtues suitable to a cleric. Previous generations of historians have depicted Rainald either as Frederick's most brilliant and loyal counselor, a staunch German patriot who abandoned the pro-curial policies of Wibald and Conrad III's other clerical advisers,[6] or as the emperor's evil puppet master, who "spoke the brutal language of a North German Junker" and who persuaded an illiterate monarch to embark on a reactionary and disastrous course.[7] Rainald differed from Frederick's other advisers, not in his conception of imperial authority, but in his intellectual interests, conduct, and temperament. The low-born Wibald repeatedly sought affirmation of his importance, Otto of Freising wrote works of historical theology, and Anselm of Havelberg disputed with Greek theologians. Rainald, the self-assured aristocrat, led men into battle and patronized the Archpoet who sang about the joys of the tavern.[8] In his inner counsels Frederick gradually replaced the pious scholar-clerics who might have pondered the implications of his actions and, like Otto after the destruction of Tortona, urged caution, with worldly warrior prelates like Rainald and Christian of Buch who were not inclined to restrain their master. Simply put, Frederick found the two archbishops personally more simpatico. He thus bears the final responsibility for the disastrous consequences of Rainald's policies, which he abandoned with the utmost reluctance only a decade after the chancellor's death in 1167. To blame Rainald is to deny Frederick's own agency.

Sacrum Imperium

The first definite appearance of *sacrum imperium* in a chancery production occurs in Frederick's letter of March 1157, nine months after Rainald became chancellor, commanding Otto to ready troops for the second Italian campaign.[9] The adjective *sacrum*, "sacred" or "holy," had been applied in late antiquity to a variety of imperial institutions such as the emperor's palace but not to the Empire itself or the person of the ruler. The monk Otloh employed the phrase, in its first known occurrence, in a letter he forged in the eleventh century in the name of Emperor Arnulf of Carinthia

(r. 887–99) on behalf of the Benedictine abbey of St. Emmeram in Regensburg. This forgery was included in the *Codex Udalrici*, a collection of formulas that the Bamberg cathedral scholastic Ulrich (*Udalricus*) dedicated in 1125 to Bishop Gebhard I of Würzburg and that Frederick's notaries utilized.[10] *Sacrum imperium* was clearly intended as a pendant to the designation of the Church as *sancta ecclesia*, that is, its use was another way to stress the equality between the two highest authorities in Christendom. (Although we translate both *sanctus* and *sacer* in English as "holy," the two words are not exact synonyms. *Sanctus* means sanctified, "rendered sacred" or established as inviolable, whereas *sacer* implies that the object has been consecrated from its inception.)[11]

However, there is some evidence that the chancery's adoption of *sacrum imperium* may pre-date Rainald's appointment and that its use may be yet another example of Wibald's continuing influence. Peter the Deacon, the librarian and archivist of Monte Cassino—Wibald had briefly served as the abbot of Monte Cassino in 1137—concocted in Wibald's name a letter addressed to Lothar, in which the abbot had allegedly referred to the emperor's "most sacred empire" ("sacratissimum vestrum imperium"). Although this letter was a stylistic exercise that was almost certainly never sent, Wibald may have acquired his knowledge of this Byzantine usage from Peter. Regardless, Wibald employed the phrases "sacratissimo imperio vestro" and "your most holy empire" ("sanctissimi imperii vestri") in letters he wrote to Manuel I in 1153. It was an easy next step to apply the same terminology to the western empire.[12] Moreover, the anonymous Tortona cleric who told the story of his city's destruction shortly after the event seems to have borrowed *sacrum imperium*, in the formulation "on account of the glory and honor of the king and of the *sacri imperii*," from a lost charter that was presumably written before Frederick's coronation as emperor in 1155. While Rainald was thus, in all probability, not responsible for the chancery's use of *sacrum imperium*, its employment, primarily for Italian recipients, largely coincided with his tenure as chancellor and arch-chancellor of Italy. The chancery abandoned almost completely *sacrum imperium* after Rainald's death in August 1167. It resurfaced, mainly for use in Italy, only in the 1180s. Altogether, s*acrum* or *sacratissimum imperium* appeared thirty-two times in Frederick's letters and charters but did not replace *imperium Romanum*, which was utilized on seventy-four occasions. The choice of terminology was almost certainly that of the individual notary and not the chancellor, let alone Frederick.[13]

The two designations for the Reich were combined by the chancery on one occasion, in a charter of 3 November 1184, written during Frederick's meeting with Pope Lucius III in Verona, as *sacrum imperium Romanum.* Starting in 1180, imperial notaries in Rome began to employ the formula, *sacrum Romanum imperium*, a construction that paralleled the description of the Church as *sancta Romana ecclesia*, Holy Roman Church. The second sequence, *sacrum Romanum imperium*, was employed after the 1180s in documents written in Italy for Italian recipients and became after 1254 the standard designation for the Reich—Holy Roman Empire. Roman notarial usage seems thus to have been the source for the name that stressed the Empire's sacrality.[14]

When Pope Adrian IV, no longer dependent on Frederick's military might after he made peace with William I of Sicily at Benevento in 1156, seemed to imply in the letter Cardinal Roland delivered to Frederick at Besançon that the ruler of the *sacrum imperium* was the pope's vassal, Frederick had to restrain Otto of Wittelsbach from manhandling the papal messenger.

The Confrontation at Besançon

In October 1157, after the seemingly successful conclusion of his first Polish campaign, Frederick headed from Würzburg to Besançon, where "Romans, Apulians, Tuscans, Venetians, Franks, English and Spaniards, awaited the emperor's arrival." Frederick "was received," Rahewin said, "with the most festive display and solemn acclaim. For the whole world recognized him as the most powerful and most merciful ruler, and undertook, with mingled love and fear, to honor him with new tokens of respect, to extol him with new praise." The purpose of the visit was to order "the affairs of the empire in the kingdom of Burgundy," which had "become insolent and disobedient" after the extinction of its native royal dynasty 125 years earlier. The emperor was so successful in pacifying the realm that he could have traveled, Rahewin averred, all the way to its capital Arles "almost without escort." Rahewin indicated that Barbarossa dealt with Burgundian matters after his meeting with the papal legates. Since Frederick issued charters in Besançon on 24 and 27 October, the best guess is that the two-day confrontation with Cardinal Roland occurred shortly before 24 October.[15]

According to Rahewin, "practically all the chief men" of Burgundy assembled in Besançon. No living person could remember the last time such men as the archbishops of Vienne and Lyons, the bishops of Valence and Avignon, or the "great and powerful prince of Clérieux" had come to court, pledged their fealty, paid homage, and received their fiefs from the emperor. (Rahewin employed the loaded word, *beneficia*, for fiefs.) In fact, Hugh of Vienne and Silvio of Clérieux, among other Burgundian magnates, had already attended the king in Worms in June 1153; but Frederick was ready to reaffirm such ties in 1157. For example, the emperor conferred the shared lordship over the city of Vienne both on Hugh's successor, Archbishop Stephen, and on the dean of the cathedral William, confirmed their possession of the regalia, and named Stephen "arch-chancellor of our sacred palace in the kingdom of Burgundy." Similarly, he invested Archbishop Heraclius of Lyons, the primate of Gaul, with the city of Lyons and with all the regalia in the archbishopric, and he appointed him "the most glorious exarch of our sacred Burgundian palace and chief prince of our council."[16] Pretentious titles were good politics.

The reality was not quite so impressive. Rahewin explained that "the archbishop of Arles and all the other archbishops, bishops, primates, and nobles would have come and done the same [attended the court], had they not been hindered by the brevity of the emperor's visit." They sent Frederick instead letters promising their "complete subjection and due fidelity to the Roman empire." Frederick did thank Archbishop Silvio of Arles for getting at least as far north as Lyons. The alleged brevity of Frederick's stay—he was still in Besançon on 25 November—was a face-saving excuse to explain the lords' absence. After all, envoys from as far away as England and Apulia had managed to come. In spite of Otto of Freising's assertion that his nephew's marriage to Beatrice allowed him to rule Provence as well as Burgundy, the count of Provence and most of the other Provençal lords thought otherwise. Their absence at Besançon revealed the limits of Frederick's authority in the Rhone valley.[17]

It is important to remember that Otto and Rahewin—the latter was the main source on the confrontation—were not personally present in Besançon and that Rahewin relied on the testimony of others and the letters and circular he inserted in the *Deeds* to construct his narrative. He left it to the reader to "choose freely the side to which he desires to lend his favor."

According to Rahewin, Frederick withdrew from the assembly and received Cardinal Roland, the papal chancellor, and Cardinal Bernard "in the secluded retreat of a certain oratory . . . with honor and kindness, claiming (as they did) to be the bearers of good tidings." In his subsequent letter of protest, Pope Adrian conceded that Frederick had "received them [Cardinals Roland and Bernard] gladly when first they came into his presence" and that he had taken umbrage only on the next day when the papal letter was read. However, even if one translates *beneficia* as "good deeds" rather than "fiefs," it is hard to see how the envoys could have characterized a papal letter of protest as good news for Frederick; and they should have conveyed the pope's concerns to the emperor in private, as was customary, to spare him public embarrassment in the presence of men from all over Christendom. The court perceived as deliberate provocations the two cardinals' violation of protocol and the dispatch, as Adrian's representative, of Roland, who had negotiated at Benevento the new papal alliance with the Normans.[18] The legates' greeting was also disturbing, though it did not elicit an immediate response: "Our most blessed father, Pope Hadrian, salutes you, and the College of Cardinals of the Holy Roman Church, he as father, they as brethren." Frederick was the pope's son in the Lord, but the description of the two cardinals as the emperor's brothers could be interpreted to mean that he, like they, received his authority in delegation from the pope.[19] If Frederick and Rainald did not hear the substance of the pope's message until the next day, it means that the chancellor did not have time to prepare a proper translation of Adrian's letter or an appropriate response.

Rainald read and translated at the public assembly the following day the pope's letter of 20 September 1157. The pope began by reminding Frederick that he had previously written to him, in a letter that does not survive, about a "dreadful and accursed deed." On his way home from the curia, Archbishop Eskil of Lund had been captured somewhere "in the German lands . . . by certain godless and infamous men," who had robbed him and his companions and who were still holding Eskil captive. The news of this outrage had spread everywhere, but instead of punishing the evildoers, Frederick had done absolutely nothing to secure Eskil's release.[20]

Eskil was very much a persona non grata in the Empire. In 1104 Pope Paschal II had elevated the bishopric of Lund, at the extreme southern tip of Sweden, which was then part of the kingdom of Denmark, to an archbishopric and had transferred the metropolitan rights of the see of Hamburg-Bremen in Scandinavia to Lund. Bremen had regained its jurisdiction over Sweden and Norway in 1123, but in 1152 the papal legate in Scandinavia, Nicholas Breakspear, the future Pope Adrian IV, had established the Norwegian ecclesiastical province of Trondheim. Adrian had recognized, on 15 January 1157, during Eskil's visit to Rome, the archbishop of Lund as the primate of Sweden as well as Denmark. Bremen had thus been deprived of its metropolitan jurisdiction over its former missionary territories in Scandinavia, but in so far as the papacy adhered to the principle that each kingdom should have its own ecclesiastical province, Adrian's measure also challenged the Empire's claim to imperial suzerainty in the Baltic. In addition, Eskil had sided with the opponents of

Frederick's companion, Sven III, whom Barbarossa had enfeoffed with the kingdom of Denmark in 1152. The capture of Eskil on his return from Rome, even if Frederick did not plan it, occurred, therefore, at a highly fortuitous moment for him. It was also a personal affront to the pope, who knew Eskil from his legation in Scandinavia.[21]

Pope Adrian probably suspected Frederick of complicity in Eskil's capture as well as laxity in procuring his release, but he did not state his suspicions in writing. However, in 1160, in an encyclical addressed among others to Archbishop Eberhard I of Salzburg and his suffragans, Alexander III, the former Cardinal Roland, charged Frederick with capturing archbishops and bishops returning from the apostolic see. Eskil was presumably the prime and perhaps only example. Eskil himself wrote to the Danish people during his imprisonment that the emperor was accusing him of injuring Frederick's realm and crown even though the archbishop was seeking only to preserve the honor of the Danish kingdom and to exalt the Danish Church.[22] So the odds are that Eskil's capture occurred with Frederick's prior knowledge and perhaps even his approval. At Besançon the emperor seemingly offered no defense of his role in the archbishop's imprisonment; and neither Frederick nor Adrian referred to the event in their subsequent attempts to sway "public" opinion. Eskil was released by his unknown captors sometime after the emperor confirmed for Archbishop Hartwig on 16 March 1158 Louis the Pious' ninth-century privilege for Hamburg. It had granted that church metropolitan authority over all the peoples of the North. Frederick did so, he said, so that Bremen might prevail in future litigation. The Danish primate was home by 18 April.[23]

Pope Adrian, feigning ignorance of the court's angry reaction to the Treaty of Benevento, was mystified, he wrote, at Frederick's indifference to Eskil's fate, because the pope was unaware that he had offended the emperor in any way. Rather, he had always loved Frederick as "our most dear and specially beloved son and most Christian prince, who, we doubt not, is by the grace of God grounded on the rock of the apostolic confession," the inference being that the pope did indeed have reason to question Barbarossa's devotion. Adrian reminded the emperor how gladly he had received Frederick two years earlier in Rome and with what pleasure the Church had satisfied all his wishes and had conferred on him the imperial dignity. The pope then made the inflammatory statement that he "would have rejoiced" if he could have bestowed upon Frederick "maiora beneficia."

Beneficium had three different meanings in the twelfth century: "good deed," as Adrian pointed out in his conciliatory letter of June 1158; "an ecclesiastical living," the modern English "benefice"; and "fief." By the mid-twelfth century *feudum* had replaced *beneficium* in France, Burgundy, and most of Italy, as the common designation for a fief; and the word was rarely used in the feudal sense in Adrian's native England. However, *beneficium* remained the preferred term for a fief in Germany, and the curia, including Roland as papal chancellor, employed *beneficium*, meaning fief, in letters and charters addressed to German recipients. For example, in 1155 the pope forbade anyone from granting in fief ("in beneficium concedere"), without the monks' consent, any of the possessions of the monasteries of Stavelot, Malmedy, and Corvey.[24] Thus, Rainald, as a German, could plausibly have translated *beneficium* as "fief," as he did, especially if he was reading Adrian's letter for the first time, without intending either to create an incident or to expose a nefarious papal stratagem, if there was one. It is worth noting that no one at Besançon tried to calm the ensuing uproar by offering the alternative translation of "good deed," but the only "German" bishop who witnessed any of Frederick's thirteen, extant Burgundian charters was Adalbert II of Trent. Eberhard of Bamberg was probably there, too; but seemingly he did not object to the translation.[25] Rahewin, perhaps repeating Otto of Freising's own views, declared it a "sufficiently faithful translation."[26] Scholars have long argued, largely along confessional lines, whether Adrian meant "fief" or "good deed"; but in light of the advocatorial clause in the Treaty of Constance, Wezel's condemnation of the curia's citation of the Donation of Constantine, and the legates' greeting of Frederick as their brother, it is more likely that the pope meant "fief" but left himself a fallback position if he was challenged.[27] However, that is hardly a proven fact.

Since Frederick was ignoring the heinous crime that had been committed, the pope continued, he feared that Frederick had been led astray "at the suggestion of an evil man." Adrian had already written to Wibald on 19 January 1157, that is, before Eskil's capture, that he should counter the advice of those who were seeking to turn Frederick against the Roman Church. It is generally assumed, in light of subsequent events, that the pope meant Rainald. While this assumption is probably correct, it was also a topos to blame a ruler's advisers rather than the ruler himself, so he could change course without a loss of prestige.[28] Adrian had dispatched, accordingly, Cardinals Roland and Bernard to Frederick to deal with the archbishop's mistreatment and with other unspecified matters. The German bishops' subsequent letter to the pope indicates that the envoys had also been authorized to discuss the Treaty of Benevento and other pacts the pope had made in Italy. The emperor was to "accept without any hesitation" the legates' words, Adrian wrote, "as though proceeding from our mouth."[29]

Rainald's reading and translation of Adrian's letter greatly angered the princes, who were irate at the sharp tone of the pope's words and by the possibilities for future misunderstandings that it contained. Above all, they were indignant at the implication that Adrian had enfeoffed Frederick with the imperial dignity and crown. The princes were ready "to accept the literal meaning of these words [*maiora beneficia*, that is, greater fiefs]," Rahewin explained, because "some Romans" had previously asserted that "our kings had possessed the imperial power over the City, and the kingdom of Italy, by gift of the popes . . ." The curialists had made such declarations "not only orally, but also in writing and in pictures."

Rahewin pointed out that there was such a picture of Emperor Lothar in the Lateran Palace with the following inscription above it:

> Coming before our gates, the king vows to safeguard the City,
> Then, liegeman to the Pope ['homo fit pape'], by him he is granted the crown.

Men loyal to the Empire had told Frederick about the existence of this painting during his earlier stay in the outskirts of Rome. Infuriated, the emperor, "after a friendly remonstrance," had obtained Adrian's assurance, presumably as part of the negotiations at Sutri, that the offending depiction and inscription "would be removed, lest so trifling a matter might afford the greatest men in the world an occasion for dispute and discord." According to the *Cologne Royal Chronicle*, Innocent II had commissioned the painting that showed Lothar bending forward, with hands clasped, and receiving the crown from the pope.[30]

In fact, the painting was still visible in the chapel of St. Nicholas in the Lateran Palace during the mid-sixteenth century when the antiquarian Onofrio Panvinio commissioned a sketch of the mural (Fig. 10). It showed three scenes in the coronation ritual. In the first, Lothar swore an oath on the Gospels before the doors of the Lateran basilica, in which, according to Rahewin's inscription, he pledged to respect the rights of the city of Rome. In the second scene, the bareheaded monarch, not yet attired in his coronation robes, leaned forward to exchange a kiss of peace with the seated pontiff, who wore a single-crown tiara. In the third, the bareheaded pontiff, standing or seated behind the altar, held a crown above the head of the standing emperor, who was now garbed in his coronation regalia with hands clasped. The mural thus showed, in chronological order, the three main events in the imperial coronation. The focus was on the central scene that depicted the pope as the highest authority on earth receiving the future emperor. While the kingship was presented as subordinate to the priesthood, only the inscription turned the second scene into a feudal act of commendation and the third into a vassal's investiture.

The inscription may have been a later addition. In the letter that Rainald drafted in January 1158 to the German bishops on Frederick's behalf, the start of the conflict with the pope was traced back to the mural:

> It [the conflict] began with a picture, the picture became an inscription, the inscription seeks to become an authoritative utterance. We shall not endure it, we shall not submit to it; we shall lay down the crown before we consent to have the imperial crown and ourself thus degraded. Let the pictures be destroyed, let the inscriptions be withdrawn, that they may not remain as eternal memorials of enmity between the empire and the papacy.

The inscription was removed, and the mural survived for centuries because it depicted the customary coronation ritual.[31]

Since the participants in Frederick's *Romzug* had not set foot in the Lateran in 1155, it is unlikely that most of the individuals who were at Besançon had seen the painting themselves, let alone recalled it when Adrian's letter was read. Rainald probably raised the matter in the letter that he drafted for Frederick in January 1158 to justify retroactively his possibly spontaneous translation of *beneficum* as "fief," and Rahewin then linked the mural in his narrative to the events that occurred at Besançon.[32]

One of the ambassadors, presumably Roland, added to the uproar caused by the pope's "insolent . . . message" by allegedly enquiring—Rahewin signaled his uncertainty by adding the parenthetical phrase, "it is said"—"From whom then does he [the emperor] have the empire, if not from our lord the pope?" On a literal level, the question was innocent enough because no one denied that the pope had the right to crown the emperor, but the inference was that the emperor derived his authority from the pope. The furious Otto of Wittelsbach threatened the legate with his sword—Rahewin inserted another parenthetical comment in his narrative to express his doubts as to whether the event actually occurred—but Frederick intervened because he had granted the envoys a safe conduct. Adrian subsequently informed the German bishops, based on the legates' own report, that the emperor had "blazed forth with such great anger that it was disgraceful to hear and would be painful to repeat the insults that he is said to have hurled at us and our legates." Frederick commanded the two cardinals to be escorted to their quarters and to leave early the next morning.

They were not to tarry in the bishops' or abbots' domains but were to take the most direct route to Rome.[33]

Before the two cardinals left Besançon, Frederick ordered his men to search the envoys' quarters. In the circular he sent after the event, he reported that they found many copies of Adrian's letter and "blank parchments with seals affixed that were still to be written on at their discretion, whereby—as has been their practice hitherto—they were endeavoring to scatter the venom of their iniquity throughout the churches of the Teutonic realm, to denude the altars, to carry off the vessels of the house of God, to strip crosses of their coverings . . ." Frederick was deliberately appealing to the bishops' dislike of papal exactions. Adrian notified the bishops, in turn, that Frederick had forbidden any German from visiting the Apostolic See and was alleged to have posted guards at the borders of the realm to detain anyone who dared to go to Rome.[34] Papal centralization of authority, as was the case in Thomas Becket's fight with Henry II, had become an additional cause of conflict.

Before Frederick left Besançon, he sent his subjects a circular in which he proclaimed the divine origins of his authority. God had entrusted Frederick, the Lord's anointed, with the governance of both the kingdom and empire and had "ordained that the peace of the churches" was "to be maintained by the imperial arms." Yet the head of the Church had become a source of dissension and evil and was threatening her unity. The circular summarized next what had happened at Besançon: the honorable reception of the legates on the first day; the "arrogant disdain" and the "execrable haughtiness" of the cardinals; Adrian's declaration that he would not have regretted bestowing upon Frederick "maiora beneficia" (greater fiefs) than the imperial crown; the emperor's and the princes' indignation—the "two wicked priests" would have been killed if Frederick's own presence had not averted it; and the discovery of the incriminating letters and blank parchments in the cardinals' baggage. Frederick then asserted that he had obtained both the kingdom and the Empire "from God alone . . . through election by the princes." Like the use of the imperial epithets by the uncrowned king, this declaration was an explicit statement that the German king exercised his imperial authority from the day of his election. Anyone who said that he "received the imperial crown 'pro beneficio' from the lord pope contradicts the divine ordinance [that the world is subject 'to dominion by the two swords'] and the doctrine of Peter ['Fear God, honor the king'] and is guilty of a lie."

Since Frederick had "striven to snatch from the hand of the Egyptians the honor and freedom of the churches, so long oppressed by the yoke of undeserved slavery," presumably a reference to prior papal intrusions into the affairs of the German Church, he appealed to the recipients' loyalty not to "permit the honor of the empire, which has stood, glorious and undiminished, from the founding of the City and the establishment of the Christian religion even down to your days, to be disparaged by so unheard-of a novelty . . ." In other words, the emperor's imperial authority antedated the beginnings of Christianity and the papacy. The supposedly moderate Eberhard of Bamberg rather than the extremist Rainald of Dassel wrote this vigorous defense of imperial autonomy. Eberhard did not discuss in the circular the correct translation of *beneficium*. It was irrelevant whether the word meant "good deed" or "fief," because the emperor obtained his authority solely from God.[35]

The French envoys who had awaited Frederick's arrival at Besançon had probably been charged with arranging a conference between Louis VII and Frederick. Meanwhile the French king had traveled as far as Dijon, due west of Besançon on the French side of the border, to meet with his German counterpart. However, the meeting did not take place, according to Rahewin, because Frederick was already on his way home. Instead, Rainald and Count Ulrich IV of Lenzburg, who as a member of Frederick's entourage had met Louis on the Second Crusade, represented the emperor; Louis' chancellor served as the king's ambassador. Ostensibly, the envoys were charged with the conduct of royal business, but the real purpose of their gathering was, as Rahewin said dismissively, "regal display." Rahewin reported that he had learned from Bishop Henry of Troyes that Louis had been so frightened by the demonstration of imperial power in Burgundy that he feared Frederick had come "not to confer . . . but to fight." The French king had assembled, in turn, so large a military force that nine bishops and their military retinues had lodged on the same night in Troyes, northwest of Dijon.[36] The real reason why the two monarchs did not meet may have been that Louis did not want to take sides, or to be perceived to be doing so, in a dispute between the two highest authorities in Christendom.

In the meantime Cardinals Roland and Bernard had returned to Rome, and, according to Rahewin, recounted what had happened in such a way as to provoke Adrian further. The Roman clergy was divided, Rahewin said, between those who favored "the emperor and blamed the thoughtlessness or inexperience" of the envoys and those who understood the pope's real wishes. Rahewin reiterated that he respected too much both the pope and the king "to make a rash judgment concerning one of them," and so left it to his readers to draw their own conclusions from the letter that the pope sent the German bishops in late 1157.

Adrian wrote with "the deepest sorrow" about an unprecedented event, namely, Frederick's reception and treatment of the papal envoys. It is worth noting that while he only inferred in the first letter that the imperial crown was a *beneficium*, he explicitly called it such in citing the passage that had aroused the emperor's ire: "we have bestowed upon you the benefice of the imperial crown ('insigne videlicet corone beneficium')." The pope's one consolation was that Frederick had acted without the advice of the bishops and princes—another indication that few German bishops had been at Besançon—and so he was confident that they could calm the monarch's wrath. Just as Frederick had reminded the bishops, in his circular, of papal exactions and interventions in the affairs of the German Church, so Adrian stressed that the bishops' interests, their own liberty, were also at stake. They were not only to lead the emperor back "to the right way," but to see that Rainald and the count-palatine, who had spewed forth "great blasphemies against" the legates and the Roman Church, apologized publicly for their outrageous words. It is noteworthy that Adrian offered neither an explication of the relationship between the pope and the emperor nor repudiated Rainald's translation. The bishops could thus conclude that the pope really thought that the Empire was a papal fief.[37]

The bishops responded to the pope's letter in January 1158 at the assembly in Regensburg, the same court where Frederick elevated Vladislav of Bohemia to royal rank in a perhaps intentional display of the emperor's preeminent place in Christendom, which had been called into doubt by Eskil's new primatial dignity. Although the bishops were confident that no storm could prevail against the Church, the letter the two cardinals had delivered at Besançon had thrown the Empire into confusion and was threatening to become "the source of great evil" between the pope and the emperor. The bishops could not "uphold or approve . . . those words . . . unfortunate ambiguity of meaning," a formulation that provided Adrian with his subsequent diplomatic out. They had advised the emperor, as the pope had commanded, and had "received from him, the following reply, worthy of a Catholic prince," which they inserted into their letter to the pope.

Adrian could hardly have been pleased with Frederick's response, which Rainald drafted, probably with Eberhard of Bamberg's assistance, and which the bishops made part of their own statement. The royal letter sharpened the argument in the circular. The Empire was governed, the emperor said, by two things: "the sacred laws of the emperors [Justinian's *Code*], and the good customs of our predecessors and our fathers." Frederick was glad to give the pope the reverence he was due, but the emperor refused to overstep the limits his predecessors had placed, in law and in custom, on the Church. Rainald rejected any suggestion that the imperial crown was a fief or even "a good deed," which could be granted or revoked at the donor's pleasure. Instead, Frederick ascribed the "free crown of empire . . . solely to the divine beneficence (*beneficium*)." The good deed was God's, not the pope's. The chancellor then outlined the procedure for selecting the king/emperor, which reduced the pope's role, explicitly, to the ceremonial function of consecrator: "We recognize first in the election the vote of the archbishop of Mainz, then those of the other princes, according to their rank; the anointing as king we recognize as the prerogative of the archbishop of Cologne; the final anointing as emperor, indeed, pertains to the supreme pontiff. 'Whatsoever is more than these cometh of evil [Matthew 5:37].'" Just as the archbishop of Cologne did not confer upon the German king his royal authority, so the pope did not bestow any power on the emperor. Rainald thus made explicit what was implicit in the use of the imperial epithets and title by the German king prior to his coronation in Rome.

Frederick continued that he had intended no disrespect to his "most beloved and reverend father and consecrator" when he ordered the cardinals to depart, but he could not permit them to disgrace the Empire "with their letters, written or blank." Contrary to what Adrian had said in his letter, Frederick had not prohibited individuals heading to Rome with their bishops' permission, either as pilgrims or on their own business, from visiting the Holy See. However, the emperor intended, in yet another successful appeal to the bishops' resentment at the centralization of papal authority, "to resist those abuses by which all the churches of our realm have been burdened and weakened, and almost all the discipline of the cloisters killed and buried." He concluded with a reversal in the relationship between the kingship and the priesthood as it had been set forth in the Donation of Constantine. God had exalted the Church in Rome, "through the power of the empire"; now the Church in Rome, beginning with the incriminating picture in the Lateran Palace and its inscription, was seeking, "not through the power of God," to destroy the Empire.

The bishops then indicated in their own concluding comments that they had learned many others things from the emperor, most notably about the Treaty of Benevento. They had been unable to talk to Otto of Wittelsbach, who had already left for Italy to prepare for Frederick's second campaign; but they had heard from those who had been present at Besançon that Rainald had been "of meek and peaceful bearing," except when he had intervened to protect the two cardinals from bodily harm. No wonder Rahewin was uncertain about what had transpired at the assembly after the chancellor translated the letter. The bishops advised the pope, "like a good shepherd," to "calm the high spirits of your son with a letter more conciliatory than that former one." The bishops' letter shifted the blame for the altercation from Frederick and Rainald to Adrian and Roland.[38]

Since Adrian was unable to procure the bishops' support and, more ominously, since Frederick had dispatched Otto of Wittelsbach and Rainald to Italy to prepare for his second Italian campaign, the pope heeded the bishops' advice and also the counsel of Henry the Lion; accordingly, he sent Cardinal Henry of Sts. Nereus and Achilles and Cardinal Hyacinth, the future Pope Celestine III (1191–98), to Germany. Rahewin, expressing the court's animosity toward Cardinals Roland and Bernard, observed that the new envoys were "men of prudence in secular matters, and much better qualified for dealing with affairs of state than those previously sent." The new cardinals "made show of humility (hitherto rare)" among members of the curia, Rahewin snarled in an aside, and went to Modena to meet with Otto and Rainald because they could not expect Frederick's envoys to travel to them. Otto and Rainald granted the legates permission to continue their journey because they came for "the cause of peace and the honor of the empire." The news of the cardinals' approach preceded them as they traveled northward. Since it was known that the emperor "was hostile to the Romans," local lords sought to extort money from the legates out of pretended devotion to Frederick. To protect the cardinals, Bishop Adalbert II of Trent—the only "German" bishop who had witnessed a charter at Besançon—accompanied them through the Adige valley. Counts Frederick and Henry of Eppan, whose castle was located between Trent and Bozen, captured, robbed, and held the cardinals and the bishop in chains until the brother of Cardinal Hyacinth gave himself as a hostage in the legates' place. God took care of the bishop, Rahewin said. Shortly thereafter, Henry the Lion, "out of love for the Holy Roman Church and to the honor of the Empire," freed the hostage and forced the counts to make restitution.[39] We can surmise that Rahewin could have told a similar tale about Eskil's capture, except that Frederick did not act in the same way as his cousin in procuring the captive's release.

In June 1158 the new cardinals arrived in Augsburg, where the imperial army was assembling for the second Italian expedition. Frederick received them graciously, and they responded "[w]ith due reverence and downcast eyes . . . The bishop of the Holy Roman Church, Your Excellency's most devoted father in Christ, salutes you as the very dear and spiritual son of St. Peter. Salutations also from our venerable brothers, your clergy, all the cardinals, to you as lord and emperor of the City and of the world." These carefully chosen words were a repudiation of the greeting that had aroused suspicions at Besançon. The cardinals were brothers, but they were Frederick's clerics, not his brothers, that is, the cardinals were Frederick's subordinates, not his equals, and consequently Frederick's filial relationship with the pope was different than theirs. The pope's letter would indicate, they said, how much the Church esteemed the Empire's "dignity and honor" and how it "had endured your anger without consciousness of guilt."[40]

In Rainald's absence, Otto of Freising read and translated the letter. Rahewin said that his master "felt a peculiar grief at the controversy between the kingship and the priesthood," which cast into doubt Otto's hope that Frederick had restored the harmony that had existed between them before the Investiture Conflict. He thus gave the papal letter a "favorable interpretation" and so mollified the emperor.

Adrian wrote that he had always been "careful to do honor to Your Magnificence in all matters, that your love of us and veneration for the apostolic see might daily increase." When the pope heard that "certain people" had aroused Frederick's feelings against him—this time, the pope avoided mentioning Rainald by name, he had dispatched "two of our best and most distinguished brothers," Cardinals Roland and Bernard, to Frederick and was astonished "that they were treated otherwise than behooved the imperial dignity." The cause of the emperor's anger was, the pope had been told, the word *beneficium*. Adrian trivialized Frederick's response in an ironic aside: "this should not have vexed the heart of even one in lowly station, to say nothing of so great a man." The pontiff then utilized the bishops' comment about the ambiguous meaning of *beneficium* to explain that he had meant "good deed," *bonum factum*, and not a "fief," because everyone recognized that placing the crown upon Frederick's head had been a good deed. It was wrong to give a feudal connotation to his use of the formula: "we have conferred upon you the imperial crown ('contulimus tibi insigni imperialis corone')." Adrian had simply meant that he had placed ("imposuimus") the crown upon Frederick's head. Whether *confero* and *impono* were really synonyms is debatable. If the report was true—another diplomatic out—that Frederick had ordered Cardinals Roland and Bernard to return to Rome, he needed to "realize how unseemly an act that was." He should have conveyed, instead, his displeasure by means of his envoys and letters. Adrian's complaint was hypocritical if the cardinals had waited until the public assembly at Besançon to inform the emperor of the contents of the pope's letter. Adrian hoped that, through the mediation of Henry the Lion, who had advised him to send the mission, all cause of discord would be removed.[41]

Henry's mediation and Otto's "favorable interpretation" of the pope's letter were successful, and Frederick became more graciously disposed. He indicated that there were other unspecified matters that disturbed him and that might become the grounds for conflict if they were not resolved. The legates gave a favorable response and promised that the pope "would do nothing derogatory to the royal dignity, but would always preserve inviolate the honor and just claims of the empire." The unspecified matters were, judging by Frederick's complaints in 1159: the pope's violation of the Treaty of Constance; the financial burdens that the cardinals on their legatine missions imposed upon the churches without the emperor's permission; and the pope's hearing of "unjust appeals."[42] For his part, Frederick guaranteed "peace and friendship" to the pontiff and the Roman clergy and sealed the concord with the kiss of peace. The cardinals, "enriched with royal gifts," returned to Rome.[43] Both Frederick and Adrian desired peace at the moment when the imperial army was about to embark on the second Italian campaign.

It is striking that the two individuals who made the greatest contribution to resolving the conflict were, as Frederick said in settling the dispute about Munich at the same assembly, his "most beloved paternal uncle," Otto of Freising, and his "most noble kinsman," Henry the Lion. In the end, it was the emperor's kinsmen, in spite of their own differences, who assumed the traditional role of mediators. It is thus unlikely that Frederick would then have turned around and treated his uncle unfairly in clarifying Otto and Henry's respective rights in Munich.

Envoys from the newly elected king of Denmark, Valdemar I, who had defeated and succeeded Sven III, also attended the assembly in Augsburg and requested that Frederick invest Valdemar with the kingdom. Frederick accepted their assurances that their master would come to the imperial court to be enfeoffed within forty days of the emperor's return from Italy. Since Archbishop Eskil had opposed Sven, Frederick's recognition of Valdemar's kingship resolved one of the issues that had led to the capture and imprisonment of the Danish primate.[44]

The Trier Stylistic Exercises

Rahewin's narrative and the letters and circular he included in his account are our chief source about the confrontation at Besançon, but sometime between 1157 and 1165, most likely 1162–64, a member of the imperial chancery composed the so-called Trier stylistic exercises, a fictitious exchange of letters between Frederick, Archbishop Hillin of Trier, and

Pope Adrian. The wide distribution of the forgeries in the twelfth century—the oldest copy had already been made in 1165—suggests they were imperial propaganda produced during the schism. Frederick and Adrian's supposed letters to Hillin, pastiches of biblical citations and mutual vituperation, state in the most extreme form the arguments the emperor and the pope had made in the aftermath of Besançon and show what the court thought retroactively had been at stake. Hillin's letter to the pope, though clearly enunciating the imperial position, is the *via media*.

The imperial letter, which utilized Frederick's circular, began with the assertion that the imperial dignity and the peace of the churches, as well as the honor of the king and the fear of God, were identical. Hence, the pope was a liar and a disturber of the peace when he declared that the emperor had received the imperial crown in fief from the pope. Frederick, whom God had chosen before the foundation of the world, owed his dignity to his election by the princes; the pope had only consecrated him. "We have not received the realm from him," Frederick declared, "but from God." The pope had seized Viterbo, which belonged to the imperial domain, and was making it his residence in place of Rome, which he had turned into a "den of thieves and the habitation of devils." Since the archbishop of Trier was the primate of Germany and since the city, which possessed the staff of St. Peter, was the second Rome, Hillin was to take the pope's place north of the Alps. Conceivably, some members of the court were proposing to establish the archbishop of Trier as an intermediary instance to hear appeals from episcopal judgments.

Adrian's supposed letter to Hillin and the two other Rhenish archbishops contains the first formulation of the curial theory of the transfer of the Roman Empire from the Greeks to the Franks, which Pope Innocent III propounded in 1202 in the decretal *Venerabilem* to justify his intervention in the disputed imperial election of 1198. The author of the exercises may have utilized as his model a lost papal letter that was written when the anti-pope, Victor IV, resided in Trier and Pope Alexander III (the former Cardinal Roland) was toying in 1162–63 with the idea of granting the imperial crown to Manuel I. The German king had been the least of all the kings, pseudo-Adrian declared, until Pope Zacharias had made Charlemagne emperor. (The forger confused Zacharias' deposition of the last Merovingian in 751 with Leo III's coronation of Charlemagne in 800.) By the same token, the pope could return the imperial dignity to the Greeks. The pope repeated and answered the rhetorical question Roland had posed at Besançon: "Whence, therefore, does he have the Empire, except from us? From the election of his princes, namely the Germans, he has the name of king and not of emperor; however, from our unction, he has the name of emperor and Augustus and Caesar. Therefore, he rules ['imperat'] through us." The papal letter was a rejoinder to the chancery's use of the imperial title for the uncrowned German king.

Hillin's letter informed Adrian how greatly his assertion that the emperor received the Empire in fief from the pope had offended Frederick and how the ensuing dissension threatened to be "the ruin of the whole world and the Empire." Like the German bishops in January 1158, Hillin did not blame Frederick for the conflict and advised the pope to make peace. The author, expressing his own views through Hillin, omitted any reference to either an autocephalous German Church or the transfer of the Empire. Instead, Hillin reminded Adrian, in a restatement of Gelasian dualism, that if the pope was Frederick's "father and lord" in spiritual matters, the emperor was not the pope's inferior because God had appointed him "father and lord" in the earthly realm. The peace of the churches depended on both of them "because, if you are the pastor of souls, he is the pastor of bodies." The attribution of such views to Hillin, who had played a prominent role in imperial affairs since Frederick's election, may be an indication that Hillin, like Otto of Freising and Henry the Lion, had acted as a mediator after Besançon. In any case, the bitter acrimony in the imperial and papal letters fits the period after Cardinal Roland's election as pope in September 1159 better than the immediate aftermath of Besançon when Frederick and Adrian sought, superficially at least, to resolve their differences. Still, Frederick had already described Roland in the circular as "inspired by the Mammon of unrighteousness, by lofty pride, by arrogant disdain, by execrable haughtiness"; and it is hardly surprising that he refused in 1159, during his second Italian expedition, to accept the election, as Pope Alexander III, of the man who had shamed him before an international audience.[45]

CHAPTER NINE

THE SECOND ITALIAN CAMPAIGN

Preliminary Preparations

THE PURPOSE OF FREDERICK'S second Italian expedition was to punish Milan for its repeated acts of defiance—the destruction of his seal, the failure to supply him with adequate provisions, its subjugation of Como and Lodi, and its support of Tortona. The emperor's goals were also to stop Milan's hegemonic aspirations in Lombardy, reassert imperial authority in Italy, and create a territorial lordship under his own control after he had turned over most of the Staufer's German domains to his brother, Conrad, and cousin, Frederick of Rothenburg. During his absence in Germany between September 1155 and June 1158, Milan had strengthened its position. It had reoccupied and partially rebuilt Tortona. Milan's ally, Brescia, had won a decisive victory in March 1156 against its long-time enemy, pro-imperial Bergamo. Under the command of Count Guido of Biandrate, a citizen of Milan, the city had defeated its rival Pavia in May 1157 and installed its own *podestà* there. Pavia had rebelled, but Milan then destroyed many Pavian castles and in September 1157 repulsed an attack by Pavia and Cremona. In April 1158 Milan had destroyed Old Lodi for the second and last time. Altogether, Milan had spent, according to the Milanese Anonymous, more than 500,000 marks on building fortifications and bridges over the Ticino and Adda to attack Pavia, Novara, and Cremona.[1] Most of the Italian communes sided with Frederick in 1158 because Milan threatened their freedom.

Frederick had learned during the *Romzug* the need for a larger army, adequate supplies, and the maintenance of proper military discipline. To achieve the first, he had secured the services of the Austrians, Bohemians, and Hungarians. Shortly after the assembly in Regensburg in January 1158, his chancellor Rainald of Dassel joined Frederick's standard-bearer, Otto of Wittelsbach, who was already in Italy, to prepare the way for the second expedition. They took the castle of Rivoli, which controlled access to the defile on the Adige river north of Verona, where the imperial forces had been ambushed on their return in 1155. The bishop and citizens of Verona received them with respect, and they as well as the townspeople of Mantua, Cremona, and Pavia swore an oath of fealty to the emperor:

> I swear that from this time forth I shall be faithful to my lord Frederick, the emperor of the Romans, against all men, as is my lawful duty to my lord and emperor, and I shall aid him to retain the crown of empire and all its prerogatives in Italy, namely and specifically the city of N. and whatsoever jurisdiction he is entitled to have in it, or in his power over the county or bishopric of N. I shall not deprive him of his royal rights ("regalia sua") here or elsewhere, and if they should be taken from him I shall in good faith aid him to recover and retain them. I shall be party to no plot or deed to cause him the loss of life or limb or honor or to be held in dire captivity. Every command of his, given me personally, or in writing, or through his representative rendering justice, I shall faithfully observe, and I shall by no evil means evade hearing or receiving or complying with it. All of these things I shall observe in good faith without deceit. So help me God and these four Holy Gospels.

The oath proclaimed Frederick's intention to rule Italy.

The envoys headed from Verona, via Mantua, to Cremona, where they held an assembly attended by the archbishops of Ravenna and Milan, fifteen of their suffragans, and many Italian magnates and representatives of the communes. Then they made their way, through the Romagna and Emilia, to Ravenna. There they learned, in spite of the Greeks' defeat at Brindisi in 1156, that Byzantine envoys were again in Ancona, ostensibly to hire mercenaries to fight William of Sicily but really to gain control of the cities on the western coast of the Adriatic. Outside Ravenna, Rainald and Otto of Wittelsbach encountered prominent members of the local elite who had conferred with the Byzantines; and the headstrong Otto seized a leading citizen of Ravenna and held him captive until Otto was finally placated. Frederick's legates assembled a considerable military force outside Ancona, summoned Manuel I's envoys, and accused them of treason. The Greeks protested their innocence, and since no evidence of their duplicity could be found, they were allowed to go home after they had given Rainald and Otto "munificent gifts." Frederick's envoys returned to Modena, where they received the papal legates who were on their way to Germany to assuage the emperor's anger after the confrontation with Cardinals Roland and Bernard at Besançon.[2]

The agreement Rainald and Otto of Wittelsbach made in June 1158 with Piacenza, Milan's erstwhile ally and its port on the Po, is indicative of the measures they took to secure additional men and supplies for Frederick. Piacenza agreed to provide the emperor with 100 knights and 100 archers for the duration of the siege of Milan and with the services of another 400 archers for a month; to grant their former enemies, the Pavians and Cremonese, who were joining the imperial forces, free passage through Placentine territory; and to establish markets where Frederick's men could procure provisions and places where they could exchange money. Piacenza was to terminate its alliance with Milan on 15 June, prohibit the Milanese from entering its territory, commence hostilities when it learned of the emperor's arrival in Italy, pay him 600 marks and the members of the court 60 marks, and not make peace with Milan as long as Frederick remained in Italy. In return, the imperial envoys assured the Placentines that any of them who joined the imperial army would enjoy the emperor's grace and that he would forgive all the citizens' prior offenses if they were willing to make amends.[3]

We have to assume that Rainald and Otto of Wittelsbach made similar agreements with the fifty-seven other cities, including Rome, that sent troops to besiege Milan.[4] It thus seems plausible that Frederick was able to muster for the siege a force of at least 15,000 German and Italian knights, as the Milanese Anonymous reported, and an uncountable number of foot soldiers and other personnel.[5] The imperial forces greatly outnumbered Milan's communal militia of approximately 3,000 knights and 9,400 foot soldiers, but the defense was favored in a siege. The Milanese militia was divided into six units, consisting of both knights and infantry and named after the city's six major gates (*portae*). The heart of Milan's army and the other communal militias was the *carroccio*, or battlewagon. Milan's had a mast, topped by a banner, which bore the image of its patron saint, Ambrose, who had become a symbol of resistance to a tyrannical ruler because of his defiance of Emperor Theodosius the Great (r. 379–95). The *carroccio* was of some tactical importance in the field because the foot soldiers could use it as a reference point in a battle, but its primary significance was symbolic.[6]

Before leaving for the mustering of the imperial army in Augsburg in June 1158, Frederick spent some days in May in the palace he had built at Kaiserslautern. He settled unspecified family matters and consulted with "religious and saintly men," most notably Bishop Hartmann of Brixen. The emperor "submitted his private affairs" to the prelate's scrutiny and judgment, and Hartmann and the other priests assured Frederick that "the reasons for the war" were "just." Pope Adrian had already ruled, after the fight between the Romans and the imperial forces at Frederick's coronation, "that a soldier fighting for his own prince and bound to obey him" was "not a murderer but an avenger."[7] Was Frederick really so concerned that his campaigns met the criteria for St. Augustine's just war, or were these passages merely Otto of Freising and Rahewin's learned and pious touches intended to convince the reader and themselves of the justice of the emperor's cause? The question is unanswerable.

The First Siege of Milan

Only some of the imperial forces assembled in Augsburg in June 1158, because of the logistical problems of crossing the Alps with a large army. After Frederick consulted with the princes, they determined that the army would follow four different routes. The Austrians, Carinthians, and Hungarians were to cross via the Val Canale, south of the modern Austrian border with Italy in Carinthia. The men from Franconia, the Rhineland and Swabia would take the Septimer Pass between the upper Rhine valley and Chiavenna and Lake Como, north of Milan. Berthold IV of Zähringen and the Lorrainers would use the Great St. Bernard Pass. Frederick, accompanied by the Bohemians, his brother Conrad, his cousin Frederick of Rothenburg, and the three Rhenish archbishops, would enter Italy via the Brenner Pass. The decision to split the army also made strategic sense. As Frederick approached Verona, whose loyalty was doubtful, from the north, the Austrian contingent was to put pressure on the city from the east before meeting up there with the emperor. In turn, Frederick's combined forces would threaten Milan from the east, the Rhinelanders and Swabians would do the same from the north, and the troops from Burgundy and Lorraine under Berthold's command would reach Milan from the west. Frederick's communal allies were to control access to Milan from the south. Barbarossa's forces would envelop Milan from all directions.[8]

Frederick, who had learned of the Bohemians' prowess on the Polish campaign in 1157, sent them ahead. They crossed the Adige on a pontoon bridge the emperor had ordered Verona to build and camped south of Lake Garda among olive groves they cut down for kindling. The Veronese suggested, according to Vincent of Prague, that, instead of devastating their territory, the Bohemians should move westward and attack Brescia, which had allied with Milan. Bergamo joined the Bohemians, for two weeks in

July, in devastating the *contado* of their old enemy Brescia. Frederick, who had advanced in the meantime as far as the Oglio, the tributary of the Po between Brescia and Bergamo, participated in the continuing destruction until the Brescians sued for peace. Burchard of Ursberg reported that the imperial forces inflicted 60,000 marks worth of damage on Brescia. The Brescians turned over sixty hostages to Frederick, gave substantial amounts of money to both the emperor and the Bohemian king, and swore to send troops to fight Milan. The Brescian campaign was a test of the tactics that Barbarossa would employ on a larger scale against Milan between 1160 and 1162.[9]

After Brescia's submission, Frederick issued regulations that were intended to maintain discipline within his camp, protect Italian noncombatants, and keep the peace between the Germans and Italians in the army. Bystanders were to employ staves rather than weapons to break up a fight among men in the encampment; women were barred from the men's quarters; severe penalties were imposed on anyone who set fire to a village or a house or robbed a church or market, on knights who insulted another knight, and on German merchants who sold merchandise in the camp for a higher price than they had paid in the city; and only Italians who spoke German were permitted in the camp.[10]

According to Rahewin, Frederick then addressed the entire army, recruited from both sides of the Alps, and men learned in the law. All were, supposedly, ignorant of the objectives of the campaign. Frederick said that Milan's rebellion "against lawful authority" was the "just cause for war." The soldiers responded enthusiastically, "each in his native tongue"; but the jurists informed Frederick that the Milanese, in spite of their wicked behavior, had either to be summoned three times or to be issued a one-time so-called "preemptory summons," lest they complain that they had been unlawfully condemned without being given a chance to respond. (It is unclear why this legal procedure was necessary if Milan had already been outlawed during the *Romzug* and the princes had agreed to launch a war against the city.) The Milanese sent envoys to the imperial court in the vain hope of getting the princes to intervene on their behalf and to appease Frederick with a large sum of money; but the emperor's honor could be satisfied only by the city's complete submission. And so Milan was formally condemned.[11]

Milan's defense hinged on its ability to hold the Adda, the river that flows from Lake Como into the Po between Piacenza and Cremona and that formed the boundary between Milan to the west and Cremona to the east. About 1,000 Milanese knights patrolled the western bank of the

Adda. Frederick arrived on 23 July 1158 on the eastern bank, between the bridge to the north, where the old Roman road from Milan to Bergamo crossed the Adda, and the bridge to the south near Cassano on the road from Milan to Brescia. Melting snow in the Alps had turned the Adda into a torrent and had destroyed or badly damaged both bridges. A third bridge, at Trezzo, north of the Milan–Bergamo road crossing, was intact; but it was defended by fortifications at the western bridgehead.

Frederick and the princes demonstrated considerable strategic sense in overcoming the Milanese defenses. Duke Henry V of Carinthia was sent to guard the eastern approaches to the bridge at Trezzo and so prevent the Milanese from crossing the Adda and attacking the imperial forces from the north. The emperor dispatched King Vladislav, who had successfully forded the Oder in 1157, and Duke Conrad of Dalmatia (the same person as Count Conrad of Dachau whom Frederick had captured and magnanimously released in 1146) southward to find an alternative place to cross the Adda. They found a seemingly shallow spot to ford the river, south of Cassano, and plunged in. Approximately sixty men died in the raging stream. Yet the main force crossed successfully, marched northward along the west bank of the Adda, and secured the Cassano bridge, whereupon the Milanese fled. Vladislav repulsed a Milanese counterattack on 24 July 1158. By 26 July the main imperial force had crossed the hastily repaired bridge, which nonetheless collapsed under the weight of the men, causing further loss of life. The castle at Trezzo was taken after a brief siege, and a German garrison installed. Milan's eastern front had been overrun.[12]

The imperial forces did not head directly west from Cassano to Milan but south to the Lambro river and camped amidst the ruins of Old Lodi. On 2 August the homeless Lodiese carrying crosses—Vincent of Prague said the delegation included the bishop, the clergy, monks and nuns, widows, and the poor—prostrated themselves before the emperor, demanded justice, and requested that he grant them a new site where they could remain "to his and the Empire's honor and service." The next day, a Sunday, "the most holy Frederick"—Otto Morena's words—and the princes visited the proposed location at Monteghezzone, a hill on the west bank of the Adda, surrounded by swamps; and Frederick immediately invested the consuls with their new home and delineated its boundaries. The speed with which Frederick acted suggests that the whole transaction had been arranged in advance. Later, on 3 December, the emperor formally placed New Lodi under his protection and the sole jurisdiction of the Empire, and granted it special privileges, including the right to build the only harbor on the Adda. Frederick made substantial contributions to the construction of New Lodi's fortifications, palace, and cathedral. The new location provided Frederick with a secure crossing of the Adda and controlled the roads linking Milan, Piacenza, and Cremona.[13]

As the imperial forces advanced on 4 and 5 August from Old Lodi west toward Milan, Milanese envoys appeared with a final offer to regain the emperor's grace. Vincent reported that many of the princes, eager to return home, recommended that the emperor accept Milan's promise of restitution and that he restore the city to his favor. No doubt, the princes found fighting in the summer heat exhausting and were alarmed at the prospect of a long siege. However, Anselm of Havelberg, the archbishop of Ravenna, warned Frederick against being deceived by the envoys' humble words and urged him to requite Milan for all the churches and cities it had destroyed. The emperor heeded Anselm's counsel not to show Milan mercy—curious advice from a bishop, who matched Rainald in bellicosity—and, in accordance with the supposed custom of ancient emperors, Frederick threw down his glove and publicly outlawed Milan. Vincent added that when Anselm died suddenly on 12 August, it was bruited about in the army that God had struck him down for advising Frederick to besiege the city. Such murmuring shows how dependent Frederick was on the princes' cooperation, even at the height of his power, and that some of them opposed his harsh treatment of Milan. Their reluctance to fight is one of the reasons Frederick had such difficulties in maintaining sufficient forces in Italy.[14]

Several chroniclers recorded, independently, an incident on 5 August that reveals how hard it was for Frederick to rein in, as Rahewin put it, the desire of the nobles "for praise and distinction" in rival feats of valor, and the emperor's determination to restrain them. Vincent commented that the Germans were motivated by jealousy of the Bohemians' exploits. Frederick sent the marshal with fifty knights to reconnoiter the fortifications and possible camping sites around Milan. More than 500 other knights, under the leadership of Count Ekbert III of Formbach-Pitten, joined them without Frederick's authorization. Most of the scouts had headed back to camp when a superior force of Milanese—nearly, 2,000 men, we are told—rushed out of the city and attacked the remaining imperial forces outside. Ekbert dismounted to aid a comrade who had been thrown from his horse, and then he fought almost alone on foot. For a long time Ekbert held the Milanese at bay, but he was struck by a lance, his armor was stripped off, and he was beheaded—Rahewin added that he had heard that Ekbert was captured alive and decapitated within the city. Several other knights were killed or captured. The furious emperor berated the returning troops for their disobedience in words Rahewin lifted nearly verbatim from the historian Josephus; but ultimately Frederick pardoned the soldiers' transgression with the warning to act more prudently. Rahewin said that Ekbert's death nevertheless intensified Frederick's determination to inflict vengeance upon his adversaries.[15] The emperor's ability to hold such heroic individualism in check was a considerable achievement.

The next day, 6 August 1158, Frederick reached Milan. The army was divided on the march, according to Vincent who was there, into seven units. The first under Frederick's brother, Count-Palatine Conrad, included Pavians and Cremonese. The second, under Duke Frederick of Rothenburg and Margrave William of Montferrat, was joined by men from Verona, Brescia, and Mantua. King Vladislav commanded the third contingent that was so large, Vincent proudly said, it did not require additional Lombard troops. Henry Jasomirgott was in charge of the fourth battalion. Frederick himself marched at the center with a force that was exceedingly terrible and so long and wide that it was most difficult to gauge its extent. Otto of Wittelsbach and his brothers led the sixth detachment consisting of Bavarians and men from other regions of Germany. Unnamed German and Lombard princes brought up the rear.[16] Upon the army's arrival, Frederick positioned his own men in front of the Porta Romana, the Roman Gate. The other units set up their camps in an arc around the eastern side of the city. On Frederick's right flank were the camps of Otto of Wittelsbach, at the farthest remove from the emperor, then those of Frederick of Rothenburg and Count-Palatine Conrad, Vladislav of Bohemia, a mixed group, and Henry Jasomirgott. The left flank consisted of the camps of the Pavians and of Archbishop Frederick II of Cologne, the arch-chancellor of Italy.[17] Frederick lacked the manpower to encircle the entire city.

Milan's walls dated to the fourth century and were in disrepair. Rahewin said that the walls rose from a flat plain, were not especially high, and had a circumference of more than 100 *stadia* (a *stadium* was approximately 607 feet), or more than 12 miles—a considerable exaggeration. There were six Roman-style double gates with flanking towers and at least three smaller gates that had been added in later centuries. In preparation for the war with Frederick, between 1156 and 1158 Milan had built a moat around the city, under the direction of the engineer Guintelemo. The earth from the excavation had been used to construct a rampart, topped by a wooden platform, with gates and bridges over the moat. The communal militia manned the rampart. Rahewin added that the Milanese relied more on the number and valor of their own and their allies' soldiers than on their fortifications. The princes concluded, in turn, he reported, that it would be impossible to take the city with towers or battering rams. It would have to be either exhausted by a long siege or perhaps defeated in a battle if the Milanese, trusting in their numbers, sallied forth from behind their walls. The Cologne chronicler observed that the imperial troops fought for fame (*gloria*), the Milanese for deliverance (*salus*).[18]

It is impossible to reconstruct the specific details or the precise chronology of the events between Frederick's arrival on 6 August and Milan's capitulation on 1 September, because the chroniclers provided few exact dates and Rahewin, Otto Morena, and Vincent focused on skirmishes involving, respectively, Germans, Italians, and Bohemians. For example, as the imperial forces were deploying on 6 August and their camps were not yet fortified, the Milanese attacked the contingent commanded by the count-palatine and Frederick of Rothenburg, either because their detachment was smaller than the others, Rahewin speculated, or because their youthful lack of experience made them an easy target (Conrad was about twenty, Frederick just thirteen). They were saved, as Vincent also noted, by the arrival of the Bohemians. The Italian sources make the Bohemians rather than the Staufer princes the object of the attack, and Otto Morena placed the event after 6 August.[19]

In another incident, Otto of Wittelsbach and his brothers, Frederick and Otto the Younger, observed that the Porta Nuova was poorly guarded. So the Wittelsbachs attacked at night, set the ramparts and the bridge over the moat on fire—a blaze that threatened to burn down the entire city—and seized the gate before returning to their camp. There were many wounded on both sides. (Was Otto of Wittelsbach, the advocate of Freising, Rahewin's source about this incident?) According to the Milanese Anonymous, unidentified enemy soldiers killed some of the defenders in the moat and in the press at the Porta Nuova; but the citizens resisted manfully and extinguished the flames. It is impossible to determine when the melee at the Porta Nuova occurred, and similar skirmishes involving Henry Jasomirgott, Count Albert II of the Tyrol, or a fight at the Porta Tosa that pitched the Milanese against Germans, Cremonese, and Lodiese.[20]

Frederick himself led patrols every day, sometimes only a few men and on other days a large cohort, in circuits around the city to detect weaknesses in the fortifications, provoke an attack, destroy Milan's agricultural base, and block access to the city from the west, where imperial forces were not encamped. He sent other men to devastate the Milanese *contado*. The raiders wreacked havoc in the fields, uprooted grape vines and olive trees, destroyed mills, and burned houses. Much of the rural population took refuge in the city. Unable as they were to pasture their animals outside, the Cologne chronicler noted that the livestock caused an awful stench within the city.

According to Vincent, the Pavians, Cremonese, and Lodiese destroyed Monza and many other castles of the Milanese and their allies; but he also acknowledged that the Bohemians burned castles and villages and seized many beautiful young women whom they brought back to the Bohemian camp—a rare admission about the reality of medieval warfare. Bishop Daniel of Prague procured the women's release through his entreaties and, more effectively, with money, returning them to Milan. Rahewin, too, stressed the courage of the Cremonese and Pavians and their hatred of the Milanese, because the two contingents had been unable to defeat the superior forces of Milan on their own. Neither side in the communal rivalries showed any mercy to their captives, whom they killed immediately and brutally.[21]

The most important event during the siege, which all the chroniclers reported, was Frederick's capture of the Arcus Romanus. This was situated 600 meters in front of the Porta Romana, where his own camp was located. This late-antique stone structure, which had been built shortly after 380, was a four-sided Roman triumphal arch, at the beginning of the road that led from Milan to Rome. Excavations indicate that it was 10.85 meters wide and 18 meters long. The pillars of the arches supported a room on top of the structure, where Rahewin said the Milanese had stationed forty men with weapons and provisions. The arch served as an observation post—whoever held it could look either into the city or at the surrounding encampment—and blocked access to the Porta Romana.

The sources differ as to how Frederick captured the arch. According to Rahewin, it was too strong to be leveled by siege engines. So the emperor surrounded it with three ranks of archers, who rained down arrows on anyone venturing out onto the battlements. If we are to believe the poetical account of Frederick's deeds, the emperor, contrary to all knightly custom, loosed arrows himself. The overwhelmed garrison surrendered and Frederick granted them a safe conduct. Rahewin added that the arch was then taken over by the imperial forces. Otto Morena reported that the Germans besieged the arch for eight days and tried to demolish the supporting pillars with hammers and axes. They so weakened the structure that the garrison, fearing the arch would collapse, surrendered and withdrew. Frederick then placed his own men on the arch and installed a petrary that hurled large stones at the gate. (The arch was, apparently, in better condition than the defenders had feared.) The Milanese retaliated by building their own petrary, which, the Milanese Anonymous noted, broke the beam of the petrary on the arch, forcing Frederick's men to abandon the arch. Milanese knights rushed out of the city and seized so many of the squires' horses that a horse then sold in Milan for only four shillings.[22]

In spite of this apparent setback, Rahewin, Vincent, and Burchard of Ursberg presented the capture of the arch, along with the impact of the devastation of the Milanese *contado*, as the decisive turning point in the conduct of the siege. Since Otto Morena indicated that the imperial forces besieged the arch for eight days, the earliest date for its surrender, assuming that Frederick recognized immediately the arch's strategic significance, was 14 August. Rahewin said that Milan, thronged with refugees from the countryside, suffered from hunger and disease—though it is hard to believe that the consuls would not have stocked the city with provisions in anticipation of the siege.

More prudent men advocated that the city sue for peace, and, according to Rahewin, Count Guido of Biandrate, a "native-born citizen of Milan" and "a trustworthy mediator," delivered a speech to that effect to his fellow citizens. While Guido's words are almost certainly imaginary, he was the ideal person to intercede on the city's behalf. Guido was, after all, one of the envoys who had represented Frederick in the negotiations that had led to the Treaty of Constance, as well as the commander of the Milanese forces that had defeated the Pavians in 1157. His presence in Milan during the siege is a reminder that great nobles were not inveterate opponents of the communes and that there was a pro-imperial faction in the city. In fact, shortly after Milan's ceremonial capitulation on 8 September, Frederick enfeoffed the count and his heirs, because of his great services, with the imperial regalia pertaining to the castle and manor of Chieri, which Bishop Charles of Turin had conferred on Guido. The communal assembly accepted Guido's advice and initiated negotiations with Frederick through intermediaries. On the imperial side, the death of Anselm of Havelberg on 12 August had removed the foremost advocate of a harsh policy toward Milan; and many of the princes must have welcomed the opportunity to end a protracted siege conducted in the August heat.[23]

Milan's First Capitulation

In suing for peace, the Milanese initially approached Patriarch Pilgrim of Aquileia, Bishops Eberhard of Bamberg and Daniel of Prague, and possibly also Archbishop Frederick of Cologne. Rainald and Otto of Wittelsbach represented Frederick at the negotiations. The emperor's kinsmen, his uncle Henry Jasomirgott and above all Vladislav of Bohemia, were the chief intermediaries. Vladislav dictated the terms of the agreement to Vincent of Prague. Rahewin included the actual text, which is dated 1 September 1158, in the *Deeds*. It must have taken several days after the capture of the Arcus Romanus to hammer out the details of an accord that punished Milan for its repeated insults to Frederick's honor while preserving some of the city's autonomy.

The Milanese recognized the independence of Lodi and Como, a demand Frederick had already made in 1154, and agreed not to hinder the reconstruction of the two cities or to impose any new obligations upon their former subjects. In a crucial concession, Frederick permitted Milan to retain its other communal alliances. All Milanese between the ages of fourteen and seventy, regardless of rank, were required to swear fealty to the emperor. Milan committed itself to erecting a palace for the emperor and keeping it in good repair and to paying the emperor, empress, and the courtiers, in three installments, a total of 9,000 marks in gold, silver, or coins. Three hundred hostages were the surety that Milan would abide by its commitments—Vincent indicated that they included 150 nobles and 150 commoners, and the Milanese Anonymous added that they were between the ages of twelve and twenty. Vladislav and the other princes insisted that fifty of the hostages could be taken to Germany if the emperor so desired. All the hostages were to be released by Christmas 1159.

The consuls who were currently in office were to retain their positions until 1 February 1159 and were to swear an oath of fealty to the emperor. The people were to elect their successors, subject to confirmation by Frederick. Half of the new consuls were to present themselves to the emperor as long as he remained in Lombardy. If Frederick was elsewhere, only two of them needed to attend him and take the oath of allegiance to the emperor on behalf of themselves and their colleagues. The other consuls were to swear the oath in the presence of their fellow citizens; the same procedures were to be followed if the emperor sent a legate to Italy. Legates who visited Milan were authorized to reside in Frederick's palace and to hear cases there "for the honor of the empire." The conflict would revive in January 1159 when Frederick failed to observe these procedures for selecting the new consuls and the Milanese mistreated his legates.

All the captives Milan had taken during the preceding communal wars were to be entrusted to Vladislav before the imperial forces departed. The king was to turn the prisoners over to the emperor when Frederick made peace between Milan and its allies—Tortona, Crema, and Isola Comacina in Lake Como—"and the people of Cremona, Pavia, Novara, Como, Lodi, and Vercelli." If the emperor failed to do so, the prisoners would be returned to Milan; and he would not hold the city and its allies accountable for the unsuccessful negotiations. Milan was required to surrender to the emperor such imperial regalia as "the coinage, market tolls, transit tolls, gate tolls, and counties." If someone asserted a legal right to the regalia but refused to have his claims adjudicated before the emperor or his representative, the Milanese were to exact retribution on his person and possessions and were to restore the regalia to the emperor. This stipulation implemented the program for recuperating alienated regalia that Rainald and Otto of Wittelsbach had enunciated earlier in the year in the oath of fealty they had demanded from the communes. The Milanese were obligated to observe the terms of the peace accord in good faith, unless they were impeded for a legitimate reason, or Frederick, his representative, or successor agreed to a revision of the conditions.

In return, the emperor agreed to restore the people of Milan and Crema—after the latter had paid a penalty of 120 marks—to his favor; to revoke, at a major assembly, the ban that had been imposed upon the Milanese and their allies; to turn over to Vladislav all the prisoners he had taken, in the past or recently; to terminate the siege two or three days after Milan had handed over its hostages and captives; and to deal graciously with Milan and its allies. The Milanese could continue to impose dues on their customary allies, except for Como, Lodi, and the inhabitants of the county of Seprio, northwest of Milan, which had recently sworn fealty to the emperor. No additional demands were to be made upon Milan for its misdeeds. Rainald as chancellor formally verified the convention on behalf of the arch-chancellor of Italy, Archbishop Frederick of Cologne.[24]

Milan's ceremonial capitulation and restoration to Frederick's grace occurred on 8 September, the feast of the Nativity of the Virgin. Vincent, who offered the most detailed account, indicated that the staging had been the subject of considerable negotiations, since it was the visible display of the extent of Milan's submission to the emperor. Frederick pitched his magnificent tent, which he had received as a gift from King Henry II of England—a fact Vincent duly noted—outside the Porta Romana, near the arch, thus linking himself to his imperial predecessors who had built the Arcus Romanus. So many imperial soldiers were present that the Milanese wended their way with difficulty from the gate to the tent through the throng. Archbishop Obert of Milan, escorted by Bishops Eberhard of Bamberg and Daniel of Prague, who had helped mediate the settlement, headed the procession. The clergy, carrying crosses, missals, and censers, followed two by two. After them came, in accordance with their rank, the canons, monks, and abbots, garbed in their vestments. Frederick, who was seated on his throne, received Obert with a kiss of peace; and Obert took his place among the other archbishops after he had been assured that the emperor would deal mercifully with "the most ancient imperial city."

Twelve of Milan's consuls, who had been selected to perform the ritual act of collective contrition and humiliation, approached the emperor "in disheveled garb, barefoot, bearing drawn swords upon their necks." The swords signified that they merited execution. They had offered the emperor a great deal of money, Vincent said, to be allowed to wear shoes; but the request had been denied. However, the consuls were not required to prostrate themselves at Frederick's feet, the final step in the finely calibrated ceremony of submission. One of the consuls, Obertus ab Orto, whom Vincent, an eyewitness, identified as a learned man fluent in both Lombard and Latin, then addressed the emperor: "We have sinned, we have acted unjustly, we beg for forgiveness. Our necks, which we bow to your lordship and sword, are those of all Milanese; and with these swords, all our weapons are subject to your imperial power." The selection of Obertus as Milan's spokesman can hardly have been accidental. He had served as Frederick's legal adviser at Roncaglia in 1154 and had then guided the imperial army on its fateful journey through the Milanese *contado*, seemingly escaping blame. Presumably, Obertus, like Count Guido, was a member of the pro-imperial party in the city. Frederick took each consul's sword, handed it to his servants, and received them in his grace.

Archbishop Obert concluded the solemnities in the tent with the Mass for the Virgin's Nativity. He employed the Ambrosian liturgy, a symbol of Milan's proud ecclesiastical autonomy and communal heritage. Both Frederick and Vladislav wore their crowns during the Mass. The Milanese released their captives, more than 1,000 Pavians and citizens of other communes, some of whom had been prisoners, Vincent added, for more than a decade. As a sign of the emperor's triumph the imperial banner was hoisted on the spire of the cathedral—the Milanese Anonymous could not resist adding proudly that it was the tallest structure in Lombardy. Milan's capitulation was a great victory for Frederick but not a total defeat for Milan. It had been forced to acknowledge the emperor's lordship, to recognize Como and Lodi's independence, and to surrender the regalia; but its walls were intact, some of its allies remained loyal, and it retained the right to elect its own consuls, albeit subject to the emperor's confirmation. The consuls had approached the emperor shoeless, but, as we have seen, they had not been obliged to prostrate themselves at his feet. The distinction was significant.[25]

In the second half of September the emperor headed northeastward from Milan to Monza, "the seat of his Italian realm," even though it had been burned by the Pavians in the recent fighting; and he wore the crown there, "in accordance with the custom of former emperors." (In fact, the only king who is known to have been crowned at Monza, and then only as an anti-king in 1128, was Frederick's uncle, Conrad III.) Barbarossa ordered the church to be rebuilt at his expense. Afterwards, Frederick dismissed much of his army. King Vladislav, Henry Jasomirgott, the Hungarians, Archbishop Arnold of Mainz, and Duke Berthold IV of Zähringen went home. Vincent explained that Vladislav was ill, but one wonders whether these princes had been the ones who had wished already in early August to negotiate with Milan rather than to besiege the city. In any case, Frederick thanked Vladislav by bestowing on him gifts and 1,000 of the marks the emperor had received from Milan. Vladislav reluctantly agreed to let Bishop Daniel of Prague, who was useful to Frederick because he spoke Italian fluently, remain behind. Frederick dispatched Daniel to secure oaths of fealty and hostages from several Italian cities, including even the emperor's most loyal allies, Cremona and Pavia. Otto of Wittelsbach went on a similar mission to Ferrara, where he arrived unexpectedly and took forty hostages. Rahewin commented that Frederick's imposition of order in Italy caused "great terror and fear" so that no one dared to rebel, "though secretly many had malice in their hearts."[26]

Frederick set out for Verona in October to deal with Turisendus, whom Rahewin called a citizen of Verona, but who was also the nephew of the late bishop of Verona, Theobald. His uncle had probably granted Turisendus the castle of Garda on Lake Garda, northwest of Verona, which Frederick claimed as a royal castle. Frederick had ordered the Veronese to restore Garda to the Empire, but they had refused, and he had declared them to be enemies. To inspire the Veronese with fear, Frederick's men devastated the area around the city. Then he headed south, across the Po, to administer the Matildine Lands, an act that risked a confrontation with the papacy. He also expelled the large number of prostitutes and camp followers who had attached themselves to his army. Most important of all, he summoned the Italian nobles, the consuls of the communes, and the four experts on Roman law, whom he had met in Bologna in 1155, to attend a great assembly in Roncaglia on 11 November 1158. Its purpose was, Rahewin said, to "proclaim the laws of peace" and to "discuss, with the very necessary collaboration of the experts, the rights of the realm, which had for a very long time been forgotten and neglected by them [the Italians], and to elucidate what had long been ignored."[27]

The Roncaglia Assembly of 1158

The concept of regalian or royal rights had originated during the Investiture Conflict, after publicists and canonists grasped the distinction between the bishops' spiritual and secular authority. The contrast was between those temporalities that a bishop held from the king and those earthly rights and church properties the prelates had acquired from other sources or that were allodial possessions. Pope Paschal II had agreed in February 1111 that the German bishops were to return to Henry V all the regalia that had pertained to the kingdom since the days of Charlemagne, Louis the Pious, Henry I, and all the king's predecessors. The pope defined the regalia as: "cities, duchies, marks, counties, mints, tolls, markets, advocacies, hundred courts, manors that manifestly belonged to the kingdom, with their appurtenances, vassalages, and royal castles." In twelfth-century Germany *regalia* continued to refer, exclusively, to the lands and rights of government that the ecclesiastical princes held by feudal tenure from the king.[28]

Notaries rarely employed the word *regalia* in Italy prior to Frederick's accession, but, when they did, they expanded the term to include the rights that nobles and communes as well as churches had obtained from the crown. For example, in 1140 Conrad III granted Count Guido of Biandrate the entire royal regalia (*tota regalia illa regis*) that the men of Castano and Lonate held, namely, mills they had built along the banks of the Ticino river.[29] Prior to 1158, Conrad's chancery and Frederick's notaries had occasionally included in charters for Italian and Burgundian recipients a clause, "saving our rights in all things," that protected the crown's unspecified residual rights.[30] As we have already seen, a princely court in Germany had abolished in 1155 all tolls that were being levied along the Main river without written royal authorization. In the spring of 1158, Rainald and Otto of Wittelsbach had required the communes to swear to assist the emperor in recovering and retaining the crown's alienated rights ("regalia sua"); and in September Milan had been compelled to surrender the rights it had appropriated.[31] The purpose of the Roncaglia assembly in November 1158 was to define the regalia precisely and to implement the program of recuperation throughout Italy, using the procedure that had been devised in the case of the tolls along the Main.

Rahewin had traveled to Roncaglia to inform Frederick of the death of his uncle, Otto of Freising, and to obtain his permission to continue the *Deeds*. He reported that the emperor pitched his camp, with the remaining forces he had brought from Germany, on the plain of Roncaglia, on the south bank of the Po, near Piacenza, while the Italians were on the opposite side of the river. Within two days of Frederick's arrival on 11 November, a bridge had been built across the Po to link the two camps. The army was still organized, Rahewin said, according to "the ancient custom of the Roman soldiery," which he then conveniently described in words taken from Josephus' *The Jewish War* (4.1–2). Is this description merely one more example of Rahewin's pedantry or did medieval commanders like Frederick, advised by learned bishops, emulate Roman practices?

Rahewin said that after Frederick's arrival at Roncaglia the emperor spent three days in deliberations with the bishops and "a very few princes who were secretly cognizant of his plan"—Rainald, Otto of Wittelsbach, and Daniel of Prague?—to devise a program "for a sound administration of affairs in Italy, that they might rejoice at the peace and tranquility of the Church of God, and that the royal power and glory of the empire might be advanced with due honor." It is plausible that the four Bolognese jurists, whose presence at Roncaglia was noted by Otto Morena, also participated in these discussions. On the fourth day Frederick addressed the assembly through an interpreter. The speech, which contains numerous quotations from Sallust and Gratian's codification of canon law, was Rahewin's concoction; yet it indicates, if Rahewin's eyewitness testimony is in any way reliable, that Frederick did not intend to promulgate laws simply on his own authority but planned to revive forgotten customs with the Italians' assistance. In another of Rahewin's fictional addresses, Archbishop Obert of Milan responded on behalf of everyone that Italy rejoiced "after many centuries [that] . . . the renowned victor, the peaceful conqueror" would rule them not as a tyrant but would treat the Italians "as kinsmen and brothers." Although Frederick's will was law, in accordance with the statement in Justinian's *Institutes*, "What pleases the prince has the force of law," the emperor was "pleased to consult" with them "about the laws and justice and the honor of the empire." The meeting on the fourth day lasted until the evening.[32]

Frederick, advised by the four doctors and other communal jurists, spent the next few days from morning until night hearing numerous cases. The plaintiffs appeared, in accordance with Italian custom, Rahewin observed, carrying crosses. Frederick supposedly remarked "that he marveled at the wisdom of the Latins, who gloried much in their knowledge of law, yet were so often found to be transgressors." To deal with the backlog, the emperor appointed judges to hear cases in each diocese; but to ensure impartiality he did not let them serve in their own city. Frederick issued at least eight charters at Roncaglia between 17 and 26 November.[33]

Rahewin singled out cases involving Piacenza and Milan for special mention. While the Cremonese had been traveling to the assembly, the Placentines had sallied forth from Piacenza and had challenged their ancient enemies to a tournament. Men from both cities had been wounded, taken prisoner, and killed. The Cremonese claimed that the attack had been an affront to the emperor—the Placentines had sworn in the agreement they had reached with the imperial legates prior to Frederick's arrival in Italy that the Cremonese on their way to the emperor would have safe passage through Placentine territory. The Placentines countered that they had not attacked the emperor but their old enemies who had been devastating their territory and were now pretending to have suffered injuries. Frederick, unconvinced by the Placentines' denials, ruled in favor of Cremona because Piacenza's treachery had been detected on many previous occasions. Piacenza was restored to royal favor after it paid a considerable fine—Rahewin did not provide a specific amount—and after the citizens agreed to fill in the moat they had recently built, so they could not rebel against the emperor in the future, and to tear down their towers. Rahewin and Otto Morena disagree whether Piacenza complied. The communal, anti-Milanese coalition that Frederick had forged between bitter enemies was very fragile. The emperor himself brought charges against Milan over its possession of Monza, and the court, which was hardly impartial, ruled in his favor. This decision was another cause of Milan's subsequent rebellion in January 1159.[34]

On 23 November 1158 the emperor assigned to the four Bolognese jurists the task of determining, in all truthfulness, all the regalian rights that pertained to him in Lombardy and that ought to belong to him by right of the Empire. They responded that they did not wish to do so without the advice of the judges of the other Lombard cities—no doubt, to lend greater credibility to their determination. Frederick selected two judges from each of fourteen Lombard cities, twenty-eight in all, to assist the four master jurists. In accordance with the oath of fealty they had sworn to him, he charged them to investigate diligently all the royal rights and to announce them publicly. It is highly likely that Otto Morena, our source on these proceedings, was one of the communal judges. The legal experts conferred among themselves, returned to the emperor, and gave him—in the presence of all the princes—a written statement listing all the regalia.[35]

It is noteworthy that Rahewin, who normally included the text of key laws and letters in his narrative, merely summarized the decisions of the Roncaglia assembly because, in all probability, Frederick never promulgated them in writing. The extant texts of the four laws he issued at Roncaglia—the complete texts of the laws on palaces and taxation were discovered only in the 1960s—were, in fact, brief summaries of the decisions that were produced later for the benefit of chancery and communal notaries; they usually cited the relevant portions of the laws from memory and adapted the underlying legal principles to specific situations. In accordance with Germanic legal procedures, the jurists "found" existing laws that had been forgotten or neglected; they did not proclaim new laws. For that reason, in spite of his reliance on the civilian jurists, Frederick did not order their inclusion (unlike the *Authentica Habita*) in Justinian's *Code*.[36]

The first law on the regalia was a list of the regalian rights, in no particular order, which pertained to the king: *arimanni* (free, allodial landholders); public roads; navigable rivers and those that joined to become navigable streams; harbors; riverbanks; tolls; mints; land without an owner; the goods of those who had contracted incestuous unions or who had been outlawed for crimes mentioned in the *Novels* of Justinian; the right to demand the conveyance of goods on main and side roads and to commandeer ships for the emperor's service; the right to levy an extraordinary tax for an imperial expedition; the power to appoint magistrates to administer justice; silver mines; palaces in the customary cities; the income from fisheries and salt works; the property of traitors; and half of the treasure found in places belonging to the emperor or to a church and all of the treasure if the emperor assisted in its discovery. Rahewin's list of the regalia, presumably based on what he remembered from the proceedings, included, in addition to some of the same tolls, duchies, marks, counties, the *fodrum*, mills, bridges, and the payment of an annual property and head tax. Charters issued shortly thereafter indicated that among the other regalia granted to the emperor at Roncaglia were the holding of courts, the right to hospitality, ovens, forests, and the use of measurements and weights for the sale of wine, grain, and other measurable commodities. In short, the demand for the restoration of the regalia was a program not only to recuperate the crown's alleged lost rights of governance but also to tap the wealth of Italy for the emperor's profit.[37]

The second law, *Omnis jurisdictio*, asserted: "All jurisdiction and all coercive power (*districtus*) pertain to the prince and all judges should receive their administrative authority from the prince and swear the oath that is established by law." The use of the word *princeps* rather than *imperator* for the monarch was taken from Roman law, and the claim to imperial sovereignty was derived from one of Justinian's *Novels*; but the terms *jurisdictio* and *districtus* were medieval in origin. For example, the peace ordinance that Frederick issued at Roncaglia specifically forbade the sale of the *districtus* and *jurisdictio* that belonged to the Reich and that were held in fief from the emperor along with the allod to which the rights of governance were attached. Judges (*iudices*) referred not only to the presiding magistrates at a court but to all holders of public authority.[38]

In the third law, *Palacia et pretoria*, the jurists ruled: "The prince ought to have palaces and official residences (*pretoria*) in those places that are pleasing to him." The Bolognese jurists took the phrase "palacia et pretoria" from a law in Justinian's *Code* that prohibited a provincial governor from demanding a private dwelling in cities where palaces and *pretoria* were at the governor's disposal; but they turned that provision into an imperial right to demand the construction of palaces, as Frederick did in Milan, Monza, and Lodi. Intriguingly, the communal jurists subsequently succeeded in limiting the general applicability of the law on palaces by inserting the phrase, "in the customary cities," in the law on the regalia. The king's right to have palaces in the Italian cities had been an issue since the Pavians had destroyed the palace in Pavia after the death of Emperor Henry II in 1024. His angry successor, Conrad II, had asserted that their action had been an offense against the Reich, because the palace belonged to the kingdom rather than to the king personally.[39]

The fourth law, *Tributum dabatur*, was not a law that mandated specific actions, but a brief in which the Bolognese doctors identified—on the basis of Justinian's *Code*, supplemented by Jesus' words in Matthew 22:21 about rendering unto Caesar the things that are Caesar's—the taxes ancient Roman emperors had levied, namely, a head tax and a tax on fields, and explained how and when these assorted taxes had been collected. The "law" did not authorize Frederick to impose such a system of direct taxation throughout Italy, but it points to an unrealized intention to do so at a later date. Imperial officials did collect each year a hearth tax and a tax on draught animals in areas that were under direct imperial administration. But whether these taxes were the same as the *fodrum*, or simply the taxes the communes had imposed in their *contadi* and that had been returned to the crown, is a highly disputed topic. Rahewin included, it should be noted, in his list of the regalia, "the payment of an annual tax, not only on the land, but also on their [the Italians'] own persons."[40] Even if Frederick did not attempt to impose an annual direct tax throughout the peninsula, his program for the restoration of lost imperial rights was breathtaking in its sweep.

After the doctors and the communal jurists had announced their determination, "the emperor spoke earnestly," Rahewin said, "about the justice of the realm and the regalia which, for a long time past, had been lost to the empire, either by reason of the impudence of usurpers or through royal neglect." Since the Italians had no legal basis for possessing the regalia, the bishops, nobles, and communes, led by Archbishop Obert of Milan and the Milanese consuls, resigned all the regalia to the emperor. He then graciously returned the regalia to their former holders, who could document that they had possessed the rights by a royal grant. The crown retained the remaining regalia that had been appropriated illegally and that provided, according to Rahewin, an annual income of approximately £30,000. The Roncaglia assembly thus established the principle that all rights of lordship in Italy were held in fief from the Reich, but the decision favored ecclesiastical and noble vassals, who were more likely than the communes to have obtained privileges from the crown documenting their rights.[41]

In addition the assembly ruled, Rahewin said, that it was the emperor's right to "select, with the consent of the people, the *podestàs*, consuls, and all other magistrates, who (being both loyal and wise) would know how to maintain both the emperor's honor and due justice for the citizens and their native state." This determination infringed upon the right of the Milanese, guaranteed by the accord of 1 September, to elect their own consuls, subject to confirmation by the emperor. The attempt by Frederick's legates to introduce this procedure in Milan in January 1159 precipitated the city's revolt. To ensure the observance of the agreements that had been made, all the cities bound themselves with an oath and agreed, if Frederick wished, to supply hostages to guarantee their compliance. Milan, Cremona, Pavia, and Piacenza gave the emperor numerous hostages; but Otto Morena added that Milan and Cremona kept the peace for less than seven months and had attacked Lodi even earlier, for no good reason.[42]

Additionally, Frederick issued at Roncaglia a revised version of his 1154 law on fiefs, which was applicable in both Germany and Italy. Burchard of Ursberg noted, in accordance with the custom of the German princes, that the emperor also issued a *Landfriede*, or peace ordinance. Unlike the so-called Roncaglia laws, Rahewin included the texts of both acts in the *Deeds*. Both constitutions also survive, apart from his narrative, in Italian but not in German sources, and in the compilation of Lombard feudal laws, the *Libri feudorum*. How much practical validity these enactments thus had in Germany is in doubt, but it is noteworthy that Frederick was treating the Empire, in this instance, as a single entity.[43]

Besides requiring vassals in both kingdoms to participate in all imperial campaigns and not just the *Romzug*, the 1158 law on fiefs forbade the division of duchies, marks, and counties, as was beginning to occur in Germany. Other fiefs could be divided, but each vassal had to swear an oath of fealty to the lord. The son of a vassal or a sub-feudatory who offended the vassal's lord was barred from inheriting or retaining the fief if he failed to make amends. A lord was authorized to settle a dispute between his vassals; a vassal's peers were to judge a dispute between him and his lord. The emperor was to be expressly excluded in all oaths of fealty to lesser lords. In theory, at least, all vassals thus owed their liege homage to the emperor; the reality was another matter.[44]

In the peace ordinance Frederick commanded all individuals, throughout the Empire, who were directly subject to his authority to keep the peace in perpetuity. "Dukes, margraves, counts, captains, vavassours [sub-feudatories], and the rulers of all places, with all their inhabitants, great and small, between the ages of 18 and 70" were to swear every five years that they would maintain the peace and assist the rulers in doing so or they would have their property confiscated and their houses destroyed.[45] Besides requiring crimes to be punished by the proper authorities in accordance with the law, Frederick prohibited the imposition of illegal exactions, in particular upon churches, a long-standing abuse in cities and fortified places, and invalidated all contractual obligations that had been extorted by force or intimidation. Judges and all other magistrates who had obtained their office from the emperor were liable for all damages if they failed to punish violations of the peace. If they were higher magistrates, they were to pay in addition a fine of ten pounds of gold to the "sacred treasury." The fines for violating the peace were stiff: a city (*civitas*), that is in Italy an episcopal see, owed the imperial treasury £100 of gold; a town (*oppidum*), £20; dukes, margraves, and counts, £50; captains and the greater vavassours, £20; and lesser sub-feudatories and all other breakers of the peace were fined six pounds of gold and were required to make restitution in accordance with the law. Frederick ordered the bishops to impose ecclesiastical censures upon violators of the peace until they repented. Burchard of Ursberg, who supplied a slightly different scale of fines—according to him, a margrave owed only £40 and lesser peace-breakers fines that ranged between three and ten pounds—indicated that the emperor installed judges in the Italian cities to collect the tariffs and to enforce the law. The judges received, Burchard said, a twentieth or less of the fine. He added that the Lombards soon murmured against the emperor's measures because it was not their custom to pay fines but rather to seek vengeance.[46]

One other provision angered the Lombards. Frederick expressly prohibited all associations (*conventicula*) and sworn brotherhoods (*coniurationes*), even ones based on kinship, within or outside a city, between cities, individuals, or a city and an individual. He abolished all existing arrangements of this type and fined each member of a brotherhood a pound of gold. This decree superseded, in Frederick's view, the agreement he had made on 1 September with Milan, which had permitted the city to retain its communal alliances. It is hardly surprising that Milan responded to this further blow to its hegemony, to the additional restrictions on its right to choose its own consuls, and to the adverse ruling over Monza, by rebelling in January 1159.[47]

Renewal of the Conflict with Milan

Frederick's first attempt after the Roncaglia assembly to implement his lordship over the Italian communes involved Genoa and Pisa rather than Milan. He dispatched Bishop Conrad of Eichstätt and Count Emicho of Leiningen to assert imperial jurisdiction over the islands of Corsica and Sardinia. Both cities refused the envoys the necessary armed escort to reach Sardinia because of the profits, Rahewin speculated, they derived from there. Frederick ignored Pisa's disobedience, perhaps because it had supplied troops for his siege of Milan, whereas Genoa had allied with Milan and Tortona. The emperor advanced as far as Bosco in Genoese territory. Yet neither Frederick, who had dismissed most of his forces after Milan's capitulation, nor Genoa, whose walls were unfinished, desired an armed confrontation. Genoa agreed to return the regalia to the emperor and to give him a one-time payment of 1,200 marks of silver. Frederick placed both Savona and Ventimiglia, on the Mediterranean coast west of Genoa, directly under the Reich. Not surprisingly, the archbishop and city sided with Pope Alexander III after the outbreak of the schism.[48]

Frederick spent the winter of 1158–59 in northwestern Italy and sent envoys to all of Tuscany, the Adriatic coast, and the Campania to collect the *fodrum*. He dispatched several princes to various communes—Vincent of Prague singled out Cremona, Pavia, Piacenza, Milan, and New Lodi by name—to install consuls and *podestàs* chosen from among each city's citizens. (Confusingly, chroniclers employed *consules* and *potestates* as synonyms, that is, a *podestà* could be a consul as well as the sole governor of the city.) The princes were accompanied by scribes, who recorded the amount of money that was paid to the treasury from the regalia that had been returned to the crown at Roncaglia—the notaries' accounts may have been the basis for Rahewin's statement that the regalia Frederick recouped were worth annually £30,000. Imperial agents secured the revenue from the Matildine Lands that Frederick had assigned to Welf VI in 1152 but that his uncle, who had remained in Germany, had not been able to collect. Upon Welf's arrival in Italy in late September 1159, Frederick handed over this income, which had been considerably augmented in the interim. Rahewin added that anyone who had traveled along the Po was "aware of the great extent of these estates and the abundant wealth of the land."

However, the implementation of the Roncaglia laws did not go as smoothly as anticipated. Frederick ordered the fortress of Crema, which had been identified as Milan's ally in the September peace agreement, to destroy its walls and moat by 2 February 1159. The Milanese Anonymous commented that it was rumored Cremona had paid the emperor 15,000 marks of silver to issue the directive. The inhabitants of Crema attacked and tried to kill the imperial messengers who brought the mandate, but the latter managed to escape and reported to Frederick what had occurred. He was annoyed but, Otto Morena said, took the news calmly. Crema's defiance was the legal grounds for its total destruction the following January. Milan opposed the installation of Lodiese as *podestàs*, really consuls in this context, in Lodi. In contrast, the emperor rewarded Cremona for its loyalty. On 22 February 1159 he freed, for example, the city's trade from most tolls and exactions on the Po and its tributaries.[49]

Milan quickly re-emerged as the center of opposition to Frederick. Shortly before Milan's new consuls were to take office on 1 February 1159, Frederick sent several of his key lieutenants to the city to oversee the magistrates' selection: Rainald of Dassel (Frederick had just ordered his election as archbishop of Cologne);[50] Bishop Daniel of Prague; Otto of Wittelsbach; the Milanese citizen Count Guido of Biandrate, who had initiated Milan's peace negotiations with Frederick in August; and Count Goswin III of Heinsberg, whom the emperor had invested in September as the count of Martesana and Seprio, territory that had formerly been part of Milan's *contado*.[51] (Goswin's brother Philip succeeded Rainald as chancellor and archbishop of Cologne.) Frederick had agreed the preceding September to confirm the election of the consuls whom the Milanese had chosen after the consuls-elect had sworn an oath of fealty to him, but at Roncaglia the emperor had insisted on his right to select the consuls with some vaguely defined popular participation. According to Vincent of Prague, who was present and who pointed out in this context that he had drafted the September accord, the envoys insisted that the election could occur only under their supervision, a demand the Milanese saw as an infringement of their electoral rights.

The crowd responded, Vincent said, with shouts of "throw them out and kill them," and even, Otto Morena noted, stole some of the envoys' horses. The legates took refuge in the church of St. Mary's, and the mob threw rocks through the windows. The consuls rushed to the scene, quieted the populace, assured the envoys that the people had acted without the consuls' prior knowledge, requested that the legates not inform the emperor about what had happened, and promised the envoys a large sum of money as compensation for the injuries they had suffered. The nobles led by Count Guido desired peace but could not stop the commoners. Even some of the nobles, Rahewin noted, found "pleasure in sheer disorder and rebellion." Rainald and Daniel stayed behind while the other envoys slipped out of Milan during the night. The Milanese Anonymous, admittedly a highly partisan source, indicated that early the next morning an amazingly large number of knights gathered in the garden of the monks of S. Ambrogio and promised to obey the emperor's commands. The Milanese author added that the mendacious Rainald gave a deceptively positive response to the knights, but sought from that day the city's destruction. The envoys rushed to Frederick in Occimiano, near Montferrat, with the news of their hostile reception. The Milanese had, as Rahewin pointed out, grossly violated the law of nations on the treatment of ambassadors, which even barbarians observed, and had thus grievously insulted the emperor's honor. However, Frederick had reneged, from the Milanese perspective, on the agreement he had made with them in September. The result was a three-year war.[52]

At the Candlemas court in Occimiano, Frederick complained to the princes about the Milanese insult to his and the Reich's honor. According to Rahewin, who was almost certainly present, Frederick reminded them that he was the head of the Empire and they the members; and the princes pledged their support. The assembly summoned the Milanese to come to the imperial estate at Marengo, where Frederick stayed between 7 and 22 February 1159. Vincent, who was also present, related that the Milanese were prepared to compensate Frederick as he deemed appropriate for the mistreatment of his envoys; but the fundamental issue, Frederick's insistence that the Roncaglia laws superseded his September agreement with Milan, could not be resolved. After Archbishop Obert had withdrawn on the grounds of "an actual or a pretended illness," Rahewin placed in the mouths of the remaining Milanese envoys the casuistical reply: "We did, indeed, swear but we did not promise to keep our oaths!" The negotiations failed, and Frederick ordered the empress, Henry the Lion, and other unnamed bishops and nobles to bring additional troops to Italy in the spring.[53]

While Frederick waited for the legal process to play itself out and for the German reinforcements to arrive, he prepared for the resumption of hostilities. Most of the imperial forces camped out after Ash Wednesday (25 February) in the vicinity of Bologna, but the emperor with some of his men reconnoitered the terrain in the Po valley and built several fortifications—it is unclear whether these were situated in the Piedmont and/or in Milan's former *contado*. At the beginning of March, Barbarossa headed north to Como, at the southern terminus of the passes that led from the upper Rhine valley toward Milan. He allied with Como, summoned home the citizens whom Milan had exiled, and built a castle above the city, where he installed a German garrison to protect Como against a Milanese attack. During his stay in Como, Frederick made peace between it and the inhabitants of Isola Comacina, who lived on an island on Lake Como and who had still been allied with Milan in September. Frederick set sail with a few men and warned the islanders that they could receive him as an enemy or a friend. When he landed they acclaimed the emperor, swore oaths of fealty, and presented him with gifts. Rahewin noted that the islanders had been since then "quite faithful to us."

En route to Cremona, Frederick learned that the Milanese were planning an attack on Lodi to destroy its half-built walls and to kill or capture its citizens. Joined by men from Cremona, Pavia, and Novara, Frederick hastened to Lodi's assistance and on 23 March issued a charter there for Como. In recognition of Como's loyalty to his predecessors and the dangers it had endured on his behalf, the emperor placed Como under his protection and confirmed the citizens' right to dispose freely of fiefs they had bought on the condition that the purchasers swore fealty to the lords of the fiefs. He also commanded that all the captains and sub-feudatories in the city and bishopric of Como, aged fifteen to seventy, swear an oath of allegiance to him by 19 April. Anyone who refused was to be placed under the imperial ban. Frederick thus put into effect in Como the feudal law and peace ordinance of 1158 and consolidated his power there.[54]

The loyalty of Milan's erstwhile ally, Piacenza, was very much in doubt. It had not carried out his orders to demolish its fortifications. Moreover, Placentine robbers had ambushed and robbed the imperial agents who were bringing Frederick some of the money, approximately £500, that Genoa was paying him. The emperor demonstrated his power by celebrating Palm Sunday (5 April) in Piacenza, and he yielded to the citizens' entreaties to take back the stolen money, that is, not to turn the theft into a *casus belli*. By late summer Frederick had declared Piacenza an enemy of the Reich because it was secretly supplying Milan with grain and other necessities and because it was sending men to assist Crema, which he was besieging.[55]

On his way along the Via Emilia to rejoin his troops in Bologna, Frederick spent Easter (12 April) in Modena; and on the following Tuesday he watched the younger princes and knights joust. He learned during the tournament that on 11 April Milan had attacked the castle of Trezzo on the Adda river, northeast of Milan, where he had left a German garrison after crossing the river in July 1158. The Germans had collected the *fodrum* and, according to the Milanese Anonymous, had oppressed the inhabitants along the Adda. Before Frederick could come to the garrison's assistance, he was apprised in Lodi that the Milanese had captured and destroyed the castle on 13 April with heavy loss of life. The Milanese had seized a considerable amount of money that Frederick had left there, had freed their fellow citizens who had been held hostage in Trezzo, and had taken eighty Germans, including the commander, as prisoners to Milan. (Otto Morena put the number at more than 200.) Frederick was back in Bolognese territory on 16 April, the third or fourth date that had been fixed for the Milanese to respond to the charges that had been leveled against them. The judges and jurists of Bologna, whom the emperor had consulted, ruled that the Milanese were "contumacious rebels and traitors." All the Italian cities were notified about the impending siege of Milan, and plans were initiated to raise a large army of Germans and Italians.[56]

At the beginning of May, Frederick held another court in Roncaglia, which devised the military strategy the emperor pursued until Milan's surrender in 1162. After his experiences during the first siege of Milan in 1158, when he had not been able to surround the entire city, he decided not to begin a siege until the city would be compelled by starvation to seek peace or would be so weakened by hunger that it could be taken more readily. To that end, as Frederick had already done during August 1158, he devastated the countryside between the Adda in the east, the Ticino in the west, and the Po in the south, and blocked the shipment of grain and other supplies into Milan. Occasionally, for example on 18 May, Frederick and his men approached the walls of the city in hopes of provoking an attack. After forty days of such fighting, the imperial forces had captured all but two of Milan's castles and fortified towns. For their part, 500 Milanese knights violated the sanctity of Whitsunday, 31 May, by stealing Lodi's cattle, and were duly punished for their sacrilege. According to Rahewin, a force of Germans under the command of the bishop of Mantua and Margrave Werner of Ancona put the Milanese to flight—apparently they were terrified at the sound of a few German voices—killed others, and captured sixteen prominent men. Otto Morena credited his fellow citizens with this success as well as the capture of fifteen horses and added that Lodi turned the prisoners over to Frederick, who publicly praised and thanked the city for its heroism.[57]

Brescia, which had been forced in July 1158 to submit to Frederick, reverted to its alliance with Milan in June 1159. The Brescians invaded and ravaged the territory of Cremona, but the Cremonese, forewarned, ambushed the invaders, who fled after a short fight. The Cremonese recovered the booty that the Brescians had stolen, and they killed or captured sixty-seven Brescian knights and about 300 foot soldiers. On 11 June the Milanese planned a surprise attack on Lodi, while the city was preoccupied with fending off Crema's assault on a bridge that Lodi was constructing across the Adda to link it to Cremona. The Lodiese detected the Milanese and fought courageously on both fronts, and by noon Milan and Crema had withdrawn their forces. Milan may have been testing Lodi's defenses. At the end of June, Frederick dismissed his Italian soldiers in Lodi because he was expecting at any moment the arrival of the German troops led by Empress Beatrice and Henry the Lion.[58]

Increasingly desperate, the Milanese tried to assassinate Frederick, or that is what the Germans, caught up in the bewildering communal enmities, suspected at the time. The Milanese found, according to Rahewin, a giant of a man who feigned madness and thus managed to gain entry into Frederick's camp outside Lodi. When Frederick awoke at daybreak and left his tent to perform his morning devotions, the madman seized the emperor and tried to drag him to the precipice above the Adda. The two became entangled during the fight in the ropes of the tent, and Frederick's guards, roused by his shouts, came to his rescue and cast the would-be assassin into the river. Rahewin added that he subsequently learned that the man was really mad and thus innocent by reason of insanity. The Milanese then hired eight of their citizens to burn Lodi. One of them was caught during the night trying to do so and was hanged in the morning on a gallows facing Milan. The same fate awaited another spy who was disguised as a monk.

Subsequently, Frederick received a letter from a "divinely inspired seer" that a monstrously ugly old man, a Spaniard or an Arab Muslim, had come to Italy with twenty of his disciples intending to gain great glory by killing the emperor—a reference, perhaps, to a member of the Ismaili sect of Islam known as the Assassins. The man was a master poisoner and also carried a dagger if the poison failed. Frederick ordered his men to be alert for the villain's arrival, and the "magician" was arrested. In spite of promises that he would not be punished if he revealed who had instigated his crimes, and threats of torture if he did not, the assassin remained silent and was crucified.[59]

The Siege of Crema

If Lodi served as Frederick's headquarters during his second Italian campaign, nearby Crema on the Serio river, east of the Adda, became from

July 1159 to 26 January 1160 the focal point of his confrontation with Milan. Even by medieval standards, both sides acted with incredible brutality. Crema's conduct can be excused, at least, as the desperate acts of a city fighting for its survival. Technically, Crema was not a city (*civitas*) but only a small fortified settlement (*castrum*) because, anomalously for an Italian city, it was not an episcopal see. The community had been founded in the late eleventh century on highly productive, cleared swamp land in the diocese of Cremona; and the drainage ditches added to its defenses. Crema was strategically located on the roads that led from Brescia via Lodi to Pavia and from Milan to Cremona. Margravine Matilda of Tuscany had granted the comital rights in the area around Crema in 1098 to the bishop and commune of Cremona. Crema resisted Cremona's attempts to enforce its jurisdiction by allying with Milan.

Crema had been included among Milan's allies in the emperor's convention with Milan in September 1158. At the prompting of Cremona, which had allegedly paid him 15,000 marks of silver, in January 1159 Frederick ordered Crema to destroy its walls and moats immediately. The Cremans' attack, in conjunction with Milan, on Lodi on 11 June may have been the final provocation. It was declared an enemy of the Reich after the Cremans repeatedly refused to respond to summonses to appear at the imperial court. At a meeting in the tent of Henry the Lion on 18 September 1159, Frederick announced that with the princes' consent he had outlawed the Cremans as well as the Milanese, Brescians, and all others who were within Crema. The rebels' fiefs and allods had been confiscated, and the emperor reserved the allods of all free men for his own disposition. According to Rahewin, the Cremonese promised to pay Frederick £11,000 to destroy Crema. (It is unclear whether this is the same bribe as the 15,000 marks mentioned by the Milanese Anonymous or whether the first sum pertained only to the destruction of Crema's fortifications.)[60]

The Cremonese started the siege of Crema on 2 July, while Frederick with his German troops again ravaged the Milanese *contado*. Milan sent 400 foot soldiers and some knights to bolster Crema's garrison. Frederick joined the siege on 9 July, but on the night of 13 July he left Crema with more than 300 German knights and headed for Lodi intent on ambushing the Milanese. The next day Frederick, Berthold of Zähringen, and men from Lodi and Pavia, headed in the direction of Landriano, west of Lodi, where they planned to ambush the Milanese in the nearby forest of Cavagnera. A force of 100 Pavian knights was sent toward Milan to steal cattle and so lure the pursuing Milanese into the trap set by Frederick. However, the Milanese caught up with the Pavians, who were slowed down by the cattle and consequently had taken a different road, and they wounded and captured many of them. When Frederick realized what had happened, he sent the Pavians who were with him on one road to Milan, while he took another in search of the Milanese. The second group of Pavians caught up with the Milanese at Siziano, northwest of Lodi and south of Milan. The Milanese were winning the battle until Frederick arrived. Hearing German, the Milanese realized it was the emperor and fled. According to Otto Morena's eyewitness report, the imperial forces captured more than 300 knights, 250 foot soldiers, and more than 500 horses. In a letter to Bishop Albert of Freising, Frederick boasted that he had captured 600 of the boldest men and killed another 250. It was not possible to count the number who had drowned or been wounded.[61]

Beatrice, Henry the Lion, and Bishop Conrad of Augsburg arrived on 20 July with additional troops, including 1,200 knights; Welf VI followed in late September with 300 knights. Intriguingly, while Frederick had relied the preceding summer on his Babenberg paternal kinsmen—Henry Jasomirgott and Vladislav of Bohemia—he turned to his maternal relatives in 1159. Did he judge it advisable to keep them apart? After Beatrice left the camp outside Crema, all the people of Lodi—knights and foot soldiers, men, women, and children—went out to greet her and escorted her with great joy into their city. Such receptions, the later *joyeuse entrée*, were customary—as had been the case in Pavia in 1155. The empress then took up residence in the nearby castle of San Bassano, where Frederick visited her.[62]

The arrival of the reinforcements made it possible for the emperor to tighten the siege of Crema, which, unlike Milan the previous summer, was completely surrounded. It was the responsibility of the princes and Cremona to build siege equipment. Cremona employed an engineer who had worked in the Holy Land to construct a six-storey, mobile wooden siege tower, which was mounted either on wheeled axles or logs and whose sides were protected by bundles of faggots. Men could be stationed on each floor. The first level was at the height of the city walls with a drawbridge that could be lowered onto the battlements. Crema tried to stop the construction of the tower and catapults with repeated raids that were repulsed. The Germans were until this point unfamiliar with the more advanced siege technology that had been developed in the Mediterranean.

There was little activity between July and October because Frederick was waiting for additional troops and hoped that the blockade would weaken Crema. In August the emperor resumed his devastation of Milanese territory but had to stop due to a lack of fodder. Rainald went to Germany to assume the archbishopric of Cologne and returned with more men in October, while Otto of Wittelsbach was in Rome in August and September. The start of the schism on 7 September, with or without Otto's connivance, put Frederick under additional pressure to end the siege as quickly as possible, so he could turn his full attention to the disputed papal election. As it was, he had to postpone the synod of Pavia, which was originally scheduled to convene on 13 January 1160. Terror became a weapon of war. Frederick hanged prisoners who, in accordance with Roman law, were judged to be rebels. Crema retaliated by doing the same and so further insulted the emperor's honor by claiming, in effect, equality with him. It is impossible to date most events precisely, but a long period of preparation preceded several weeks of intense fighting in January.

The original plan was to cross the moat and to breach the wall with two battering rams, with archers on the tower following behind and providing cover for the men below. Two thousand wagons brought dirt to fill in the moat, and the battering rams crossed over it; but when the tower got within range of projectiles, it was attacked by stones hurled by five mangonels and a number of petraries. To stop the assault, Frederick ordered hostages attached to the upper floors and even had lit candles placed in their hands at night in the expectation that the defenders would not kill their own people; but the desperate Cremans continued even though some of the hostages were severely wounded or killed. Frederick had the tower withdrawn, perhaps because of his lack of success or because, maybe, even he was repelled by the barbarity. In response, Crema executed imperial prisoners. The human shield was replaced by double-braided bundles of faggots, hides, and bales of wool (wool does not burn readily); and the tower was able to continue its advance toward the wall.

In the meantime, the battering ram had managed by the end of December to create a gap of allegedly 20 ells in the wall, but Crema prevented entry via the breach by building new fortifications of wood and earth. Frederick's archers were limited to shooting arrows from the tower onto the defenders below. As a countermeasure, the Cremans dug a tunnel to the edge of the moat, next to the battering ram; and a commando group tried to set the ram on fire. A hail of arrows from the tower forced the commandos to flee back into the city. On 6 January 1160, Cremans sought to set fire to the ram by pouring, through a shoot in the wall, an incendiary substance that set fire to the roof covering the ram, which burned for several hours. The emperor was suddenly in great danger because he was supervising the action inside the shed housing the ram.

In various places the princes used the battering rams they had built in the hope of filling in the moat and breaching the walls at different spots. Perhaps in a diversionary move to reduce the pressure on Crema, the Milanese invaded the Martesana, the region around Lake Como, and besieged Erba, south of the lake. Count Goswin III of Heinsberg, to whom Frederick had granted the Martesana, avoided a direct fight but stayed close to the invaders to hinder them from achieving their objectives. Frederick sent Goswin 500 knights, and the Milanese, fearing they would be cut off from Milan, abandoned the siege of Erba. However, there was an increasing risk that Milan would take the offensive elsewhere if the imperial forces continued to be tied down at Crema. At the beginning of January 1160, Frederick was forced to postpone the opening of the Council of Pavia from 13 January to 2 February.

At this point Crema's engineer, Marchesius, who knew the weaknesses in the town's defenses, fled to Frederick. It is not known whether he had been held against his will in Crema or was bribed to desert. Marchesius recommended that Frederick attack again in the area where the wall had originally been breached, and he constructed a second tower so that the walls could be assailed simultaneously in two places. This second tower was of a different design to the first—Otto Morena referred to the first as a *castellum* and to the second as a *machina*. It was not intended to serve as a platform for archers but as a device to storm a city. The second tower had a seesaw-like bridge that could be adjusted to fit walls of different heights. Both towers were moved up to the walls of Crema.

The imperial forces attacked on 21 January. Frederick's brother Conrad led the forces in the first tower. Protected by the archers, the count-palatine's men were able to set foot on the walls but were unable to unite with the troops in Marchesius' "machine," who may have encountered greater resistance. Conrad's standard-bearer, Bertolf of Urach, was able to break out of the bridgehead but was isolated and killed. One of the defenders scalped Bertolf and after carefully combing his hair, attached the scalp to his own helmet, or so, Rahewin reported, it was said. He also duly noted Otto of Wittelsbach's courage. The Cremans lobbed rocks continuously from their mangonels at both towers and partially destroyed the bridge of the first one. Conrad was wounded and, fearful that his men would be cut off, ordered a retreat; the men in the other tower did the same. The assault had failed, but both structures were kept close to the walls and the bridge was quickly repaired in anticipation of another assault.

The Cremans realized that their situation was hopeless and initiated negotiations, via Patriarch Pilgrim of Aquileia, with Frederick, who was eager to end the siege so he could devote all his attention to the schism. They capitulated on 26 January 1160. Frederick spared the Cremans' lives, and Rahewin reported that 20,000 men, women, and children, each taking with them what they could carry on their backs, left the city on 27 January. The Milanese and Brescians who had come to Crema's aid were also allowed to leave, but had to surrender their weapons and all their possessions. The Germans and Italians stormed into the abandoned city to plunder it. When the knights claimed the exclusive right to loot, the resentful sergeants, fearing they would not get their proper share, set fires that engulfed most of Crema. The Cremonese were especially eager to destroy the city, including the churches; but Otto Morena conceded that his fellow citizens joined with the Cremonese in filling in the moat and leveling the walls. The destruction lasted five days. All the siege equipment, which had cost more than 2,000 marks of silver to build, was burned. Frederick and his army returned to Lodi, and he gave the Lodiese more than 300 suits of armor. On 2 February the emperor was joyously welcomed on his arrival in Pavia by the entire population of the city, which had been "adorned like a temple." Before going to the palace, Rahewin said, he went to the cathedral to thank God "for the triumph he had been vouchsafed."[63]

The council that had been summoned to settle the disputed papal election convened in Pavia on 5 February 1160. For the next seventeen years Frederick's fight with Milan would be inextricably linked to his refusal to accept Cardinal Roland as Pope Alexander III.

CHAPTER TEN

THE SCHISM

Deteriorating Relations with Adrian IV

FREDERICK AND ADRIAN'S REPRESENTATIVES had smoothed over at Augsburg, in June 1158, the confrontation that had occurred over the pope's use of the word *beneficium* in the letter Cardinal Roland had delivered at Besançon; but the fundamental question about the proper relationship between the emperor and the pope remained unresolved. Other issues were in dispute as well: the ownership of the Matildine Lands; legatine exactions and papal jurisdiction over the Church in the Empire; Frederick's assertion that all regalian rights in Italy, including in the Patrimony and Rome itself, were derived from the crown; and Adrian's alliance in 1156 with the Normans.

The choice of a new archbishop of Ravenna after the death of Anselm of Havelberg on 12 August 1158 revived the conflict between Frederick and the pope. Sometime in the late autumn the clergy of Ravenna elected Guido, son of the emperor's supporter, Count Guido of Biandrate, and nephew of William of Montferrat, in the presence of the imperial and papal legates, Bishop Hermann of Verden and Cardinal Hyacinth, who had represented Adrian at Augsburg. Since Adrian had already accepted the young Guido, at Frederick's request, as a member of the Roman Church and ordained him as a sub-deacon, the emperor sent Bishop Uguccio of Vercelli to the pope to obtain his permission to transfer Guido from Rome to Ravenna, because, as Frederick explained when he repeated his petition for a second time in January 1159: "it is most fitting that the Holy Roman Church, as the mother of all churches, should gather her sons . . . and should scatter those thus assembled in other houses and families to the embellishment of the house of God." Adrian, who had no desire to strengthen further the imperial position in what Frederick called in his letter to the pope the greatest Church in the world save Rome itself, had not acted on Frederick's initial request.[1]

It is difficult to reconstruct what happened between Frederick's first and second requests that Adrian transfer Guido to Ravenna. This is because Rahewin, the primary source on the deterioration in papal–imperial relations during the winter and spring of 1159, obtained much of his information from the letters that he included in his chronicle but whose chronology and content he misconstrued in constructing his own narrative. According to Rahewin, unnamed individuals—Cardinal Roland?—persuaded Adrian to disrupt the peace that had prevailed since Augsburg. While Frederick was in his winter quarters, the pope complained about an unspecified insult to his envoys, the insolence of the imperial officials who had been sent to levy the *fodrum* (presumably in the Patrimony), and the mistreatment of unidentified papal castellans. Adrian accused Frederick of being ungrateful for the *beneficia* he had shown him—surely a loaded word, in light of the confrontation at Besançon, if the pope really used the word *beneficia* in the message Rahewin summarized. In addition, since Adrian was trying to provoke Frederick, he criticized the emperor, Rahewin said, for requiring bishops and abbots as well as the cities and nobles to surrender their regalia. Rahewin indicated that while Adrian's letter at first hearing appeared to be "quite mild," it was really "full of sharp criticism." Perhaps it was; but Rahewin borrowed this description from a letter Bishop Eberhard of Bamberg wrote about a papal legation to Frederick the following June. Rahewin continued that a "certain unworthy messenger—a low fellow—presented it and disappeared before it was read."[2]

Bishop Eberhard provided more specific information about this "unworthy messenger" in his letter to Cardinal Henry of Sts. Nereus and Achilles, written sometime after 25 February and mid-March. According to Eberhard, Adrian had ordered Frederick "in strong terms," in January 1159, not to intervene in a dispute between Brescia and Bergamo over several castles. The papal mandate had been delivered, in a calculated insult that violated all the conventions of courtly etiquette, by "a certain beggarly fellow, a kind of enemy and spy," who had "thrust [it] scornfully upon the lord emperor, and was seen no more."[3]

After the messenger disappeared, Frederick decided to retaliate in kind. In writing to the pope, he ordered his notaries to place the emperor's name before the pontiff's and to address the pope in the informal singular—in epistolary practice the name of the superior was placed first. Rahewin explained that this ordering of the correspondents' names had been the customary procedure in antiquity but had been altered "out of a certain reverence and respect for the persons addressed." The emperor is alleged to have said "that either the pope ought to observe the custom of his predecessors in writing to an imperial personage, or he himself should follow in his letters the style of the emperors of old."[4]

To shame the pope further, Frederick replied to the papal affront "through an honorable rather than through a lowly envoy." He dispatched Bishop Hermann of Verden to the curia in January 1159 with the second letter seeking Guido's transfer to Ravenna, in which Frederick put his name first but addressed the pope in the formal plural. Presumably, Hermann, who was actively engaged in implementing the Roncaglia laws, was also charged with discussing the pope's other complaints. Frederick and his advisers could hardly have expected a favorable response to a petition that flouted diplomatic protocol, and Adrian rejected it on the specious grounds that it was more suitable for a man of Guido's lineage, character, and learning to remain in Rome and eventually procure a "loftier status" than as archbishop of Ravenna. Rahewin added that this exchange of insulting letters created such enmity that the pope is said to have sent letters to Milan and to other cities urging them to rebel. Both the pope and the emperor had violated their sworn commitment in the Treaty of Constance of 1153 to respect each other's personal and transpersonal honor. As for Guido, Frederick invested him as the schismatic archbishop of Ravenna the following year, in April 1160.[5]

Eberhard of Bamberg, Cardinal Henry of Sts. Nereus and Achilles, the other legate who had represented Adrian at Augsburg, and the future antipopes, Cardinals Octavian and Guido of Crema, tried vainly in the following months of 1159 to mediate between the emperor and the pope. Sometime before 25 February, Henry implored Eberhard to use his influence in Frederick's counsels to guide him "along a course of peace and justice." The emperor was being led astray by unnamed princes (Rainald of Dassel and/or Otto of Wittelsbach?), "however noble they may be," who were ignorant of canon law and not aware of "matters which were long ago settled and ordained by the fathers." By heeding such erroneous advice, Frederick was endangering the peace that Eberhard and Henry had re-established.

Eberhard responded by mid-March that he had been unaware of Frederick's insulting letter to the pope seeking Guido's appointment to Ravenna until he had received Cardinal Henry's letter. The members of Frederick's court were searching ancient records and finding in them the format for imperial letters that had suited an earlier age—an allusion, in all probability, to Rainald's antiquarian interests. The delivery of the pope's letter about Brescia's dispute with Bergamo had reignited the conflict. Each side was waiting for the other to initiate negotiations. Eberhard confided to Henry that he had thought of going himself to the curia, but had decided against doing so because the emperor was too opposed. So the bishop counseled that Adrian should not wait for an invitation but should send envoys with a message of peace and with "letters . . . written in the customary manner." Eberhard concluded with his own very revealing assessment of Frederick's character: "You know the kind of man he is. He loves them that love him, and is estranged from others, because he has not yet completely learned to love even his enemies." Forgiving one's enemies was not a common noble virtue, even if the emperor's predecessors had imitated Christ by pardoning rebels.

At the same time Eberhard sent a deferential letter to Adrian warning him against turning a war of words into an open conflict. He advised the pope to write to Frederick "with paternal affection" and to avoid any words whose meaning could be misinterpreted. It was the same tactic that had eased the crisis caused by the pope's use of the term *beneficium*. Yet neither side was now willing to compromise because the issue was no longer about words or diplomatic niceties but about the exercise of imperial authority in Italy and Rome, which threatened the independence from imperial control that the papacy had gained during the Investiture Conflict.[6]

Around 16 April 1159, when Frederick declared the Milanese to be rebels, Cardinals Henry and Guido of Crema arrived in the imperial camp near Bologna. The emperor's reception of the papal legates indicates that Adrian must have heeded Eberhard's advice to write to the monarch in a more conciliatory fashion, but the substance of their discussions is unknown.[7]

In June or July both Frederick and Eberhard wrote to Archbishop Eberhard I of Salzburg about the emperor's negotiations with Cardinals Octavian and William of St. Peter in Chains conducted while he had been devastating the Milanese *contado* in June.[8] It was Octavian and William's message that Eberhard of Bamberg described as having "a mild beginning and an apparently peaceful introduction," but that contained "the most severe demands." Adrian was demanding that Frederick adhere to the terms of the Treaty of Constance that had recognized the pope's exclusive lordship in Rome. Frederick insisted in his letter to the archbishop that he "had in fact kept that peace inviolate until now," but that he was not obligated to do so in the future because the pope had violated their convention first by making an agreement with the "Sicilian" without Frederick's consent. Technically, the pope had been under no such constraint, but it was reasonable for the emperor to assume that he would be consulted if the pope negotiated with their common enemy, William I. Of course, the emperor for his part had not honored his commitment to restore papal rule in Rome and to expel the Normans and Byzantines from southern Italy. Besides, Adrian might well not have believed that the Byzantine envoys had stolen sealed blank pieces of parchment and had forged the letters in which Frederick had allegedly authorized the Greeks in 1155 to occupy the Adriatic coastline and Apulia.

The bishop of Bamberg summarized for the archbishop the pope's "severe demands." The emperor was not to send envoys to Rome without the pope's prior knowledge; all the magistrates and all the regalia in the city were to be solely under the jurisdiction of St. Peter; the *fodrum* could be collected from the pope's domains only in conjunction with the emperor's coronation; the emperor could require from the Italian bishops only an oath of fealty but not homage; and imperial envoys were not to be housed in episcopal palaces. As part of the pope's program for recuperating the lost properties and rights of the papacy in the Patrimony, Adrian also demanded the return of an extensive list of possessions, including Tivoli, Ferrara, and all the lands located between Acquapendente, about 90 miles north of Rome, and Rome. In addition, the pontiff claimed the domains Frederick had granted Welf VI in 1152: the Matildine Lands, the duchy of Spoleto, Sardinia, and Corsica as well. In short, the pope was barring the emperor from exercising any secular jurisdiction in Rome and claiming lordship over the islands in the Tyrrhenian Sea.

If we are to believe another one of Rahewin's set speeches, Frederick mocked the pope in his reply to the demands the cardinals had delivered. The words are probably Rahewin's invention—the emperor is not likely to have cited Gratian's *Decretum* or Justinian's *Digest*. Yet they almost certainly stated the court's position, which had been enunciated at Roncaglia, that the bishops, including the pope, possessed their rights of lordship in delegation from the Empire. Frederick was more than willing to forego the Italian bishops' homage, if they preferred not to hold any regalia. He concurred that imperial envoys were not to stay in episcopal palaces, provided, of course, that the structures stood on the bishops' own land; but if they had been built on crown land, then the palaces belonged to the Reich, and it would be unjust for the envoys not to use them. The pope's claim to exclusive sovereignty in Rome required "more serious and mature consideration" because it challenged the essence of the imperial dignity. Frederick is alleged to have said: "For since, by divine ordinance, I am emperor of Rome and am so styled, I have merely the appearance of ruling and bear an utterly empty name, lacking in meaning, if authority over the city of Rome should be torn from my grasp." Rahewin's words may in this instance echo Frederick's own thoughts as a pragmatic politician.[9] Conversely, however, if the Petrine regalia were an appurtenance of the Empire, then the emperor had a right to deny the regalia to the pontiff and to intervene in a disputed papal election in a city that was subject to imperial jurisdiction. Both sides could deduce the implications of the other's stance.

Eberhard of Bamberg informed the archbishop that Frederick had countered with his own demands to limit legatine and papal authority in the Empire—as Henry II of England did a few years later in his dispute with Thomas Becket. The emperor objected to cardinals traveling about the realm without his permission, staying in the bishops' palaces, burdening the churches by hearing appeals from lower courts in cases that did not fall under the purview of the curia, and many other matters that Eberhard for brevity's sake could not relate. As had been true at Besançon, Frederick was seeking to gain the support of the bishops by voicing their displeasure at the centralization of papal authority.

Frederick proposed, initially, to submit the disputed issues to trial and judgment, "whether in accordance with human or divine law"; or, if such a procedure was "too stern," to allow "the princes and men of religion, out of love for God and the Church," to devise a peaceful accommodation. However, the Gregorian reformers had insisted that the pope was subject to no earthly authority, and so the cardinals rejected the first proposal out of hand. It was decided, instead, to obtain Adrian's approval to empanel arbiters, namely six cardinals representing the pope and six bishops—"pious, wise, and God-fearing"—on the emperor's behalf. In his own letter, Frederick asked Archbishop Eberhard, one of the most respected members of the German hierarchy, to come immediately if he was summoned, presumably to serve as one of the six episcopal arbiters on his side. Arbitration was not incompatible with the pope's status and was employed, in fact, in the peace negotiations that culminated in the Treaty of Venice of 1177; but Adrian insisted that the Treaty of Constance, which in his reading had recognized the pope's allodial rights of lordship in Rome, was the only basis for peace and he refused the offer. The papacy had opted for a confrontation.[10]

While Frederick was negotiating with Cardinals Octavian and William in June 1159, a delegation of Roman citizens, "desiring conditions of peace," appeared at the court. Frederick's imperial coronation on 18 June 1155 had ended in a bloodbath and with the pope's departure from Rome. Adrian had returned to the city in November 1156, after the Treaty of Benevento, with the de facto support of the Normans. William I of Sicily was a more immediate threat to Roman communal independence than Frederick in Germany, and several Roman senators and aristocrats, including Cardinal Octavian's nephew Otto, had already engaged in unspecified negotiations with Rainald of Dassel and Otto of Wittelsbach in May 1158. A Roman contingent under the leadership of the papal prefect of Rome, Peter Di Vico, another of the cardinal's nephews, and his senatorial supporters had then participated in Frederick's siege of Milan in August 1158. Their presence outside Milan indicated a desire for a rapprochement with the emperor and that the commune had been reconciled with the nobles, whom it had expelled from the city in the 1140s. Frederick received the Romans in June 1159 in a friendly fashion—precisely, Rahewin added, "because he had dealt very severely with them on his former expedition"—and Frederick reported to Archbishop Eberhard that they "were amazed and indignant" at the papal demands. He sent them home with gifts. Frederick's friendly reception of the Roman envoys was a public rejection of Adrian's demand that the emperor abide by the terms of the Treaty of Constance, which prohibited such separate negotiations.[11]

During Cardinal Octavian's stay at the court in June 1159, the emperor rewarded him and his brothers, the counts of Monticelli, his "most beloved vassals and friends" and very distant kinsmen, by enfeoffing them with the city and county of Terni, northeast of Rome; and with all the pertinent regalia, within and outside the county's carefully delineated boundaries, excepting only the jurisdiction and honor of the Empire. Octavian's support was more valuable in the College of Cardinals than in Rome itself. Probably at the same time, Frederick placed the canons of St. Peter's and all their possessions under imperial protection and granted them a hundred years to reclaim alienated properties and rights. Some of the canons subsequently became ardent supporters of the anti-pope Victor IV, even though their role, legally, in the choice of a new pope was minimal at best.[12]

After Adrian rejected Frederick's offer of arbitration, Barbarossa sent to Rome, at the cardinals' request, Otto of Wittelsbach, Count Guido of Biandrate, and Provost Heribert of Aachen—who subsequently became the archbishop of Besançon—to make peace with Adrian; if that failed, they were to come to terms with the senate and the Roman people. The choice of Otto, who had had to be restrained from attacking Cardinal Roland at Besançon, and of Guido, who had been unable to procure the archbishopric of Ravenna for his son, was hardly designed to allay the pope's fears about Frederick's intentions. In the case of Rome, Frederick was ready to legalize the senate's existence in return for the Romans' acceptance of the prefect—in accordance with the Roncaglia laws—as the emperor's chief magistrate in the city, in effect as the imperial *podestà* rather than as the pope's representative. The ambassadors failed to achieve either objective. It is hard to believe that these three close associates of Frederick, who would attend Adrian's funeral on 4 September, were not in contact with Cardinal Octavian and the canons of St. Peter's prior to the double papal election—of Alexander III and Victor IV—three days later. On the other hand, it is worth noting that Pope Alexander's biographer, Cardinal Boso, did not accuse Otto and Guido of being directly implicated in the events of 7 September. The envoys must thus have made Frederick's preferences about Adrian's successor known and assured Octavian of the emperor's support if he was elected. Yet they must also have left the management of the affair to the pro-imperial faction among the cardinals and the Romans, so that the emperor could plausibly deny involvement in the outcome.[13]

While Frederick was negotiating with the cardinals in June, Pope Adrian, the pro-Sicilian cardinals, and William I's other adherents left Rome and went to Anagni. There, according to Victor IV's supporters, this group of cardinals, who were also in contact with Milan and its allies, swore in the pope's presence to excommunicate the emperor, to "oppose his honor and will to the death," and after Adrian's death to elect as pope only one of their number. The pro-Alexandrine account by the Milanese Anonymous of events in the summer of 1159 corroborates these accusations about an anti-imperial conspiracy. He reported that after Frederick began the siege of Crema in July, the Milanese allied with the Brescians and Placentines and sent envoys to Adrian in Anagni. They and the Cremans swore that they would not make peace or any agreement with Frederick without Adrian's permission or that of his legitimate successor. For his part, the pope agreed, but did not swear, that he would excommunicate the emperor within the next forty days, but he died on 1 September 1159 before he could act.[14] A split in the College of Cardinals was thus almost preordained with or without Frederick's connivance.

The Papal Election of 7 September 1159

Rahewin warned his reader not to determine what occurred on 7 September and in the following months "from what we say or write," but to reach his personal conclusion on the basis of the parties' own accounts that he included in his narrative (4.59 and 4.75). Although most of this material originated, understandably, in the imperial camp, Rahewin's inclusion of the letters of Pope Alexander (formerly Chancellor Roland) and the twenty-three cardinals who eventually adhered to him—written, respectively, shortly before and after Cardinal Octavian's consecration as Victor IV on 4 October—suggests that Rahewin may have been signaling his personal doubts about the legitimacy of Victor IV's election. Indeed, he may have stopped writing the *Deeds* precisely because he found his own position increasingly irreconcilable with his imperial commission.[15] Jürgen Petersohn, echoing Rahewin's perplexity, has described the election as one of the major events of the twelfth century whose course has not yet been satisfactorily elucidated.[16]

Adrian died at Anagni, southeast of Rome, on 1 September; and the body was brought back for burial in St. Peter's on 4 September. Before leaving Anagni, the cardinals had agreed, according to the report which the canons of St. Peter's sent to the Council of Pavia, that if they could not find a cardinal who was acceptable to everyone, they would select someone from outside the college who was. After two days of haggling about the site of the election, the cardinals assembled on 5 September behind the altar of St. Peter's to begin their deliberations. When they could not reach a unanimous decision, "those who desired peace and concord in the Church" proposed that the others leave the choice to them. These cardinals then polled their colleagues in private, but were unable to identify a consensus candidate, the pro-Victorine cardinals said, "on account of the conspiracy of the opposing party." Since it was a common procedure in medieval elections to empower a subset of electors to find a compromise nominee to avoid embarrassing any of the participants in public, it is quite plausible that the cardinals sought in this way to reach a consensus, even though only the pro-Victorine sources mention the Anagni agreement and the behind-the-scenes negotiations. Finally, on 7 September, after three days of deliberations, Alexander reported, "everyone present except three . . . agreed harmoniously and with one accord upon our person . . ."[17]

While all the sources agree that the majority of the cardinals voted for Cardinal Roland, as Pope Alexander he misrepresented the truth when he declared that Octavian had received only three votes. Five cardinals informed Christendom, shortly after Victor's consecration, that they were among the nine cardinals who had not taken the "accursed oath" to select only one of their number as pope and who had elected Octavian; but they conceded that fourteen of their brethren had preferred Roland (4.62). Eberhard of Bamberg likewise wrote to his namesake in Salzburg in February 1160 that nine cardinals had voted initially for Victor but hinted that some "afterward withdrew" (4.81). In any case, by October 1159 at least twenty-three cardinals were in Alexander's camp (4.63). As Cardinal Roland he had received, in all probability, two-thirds of the votes, if not on 7 September then shortly thereafter, as some of the cardinals who had initially backed Octavian shifted their obedience and the cardinals who had been absent committed themselves to Roland. We can infer this because the Third Lateran Council of 1179, in all likelihood in a retroactive legitimization of Alexander's election, stipulated that the rightful pontiff required two-thirds of the votes.[18] (The total number of cardinals in 1159 is unknown.) Although Octavian's supporters were in the minority, they claimed that they were the wiser party and cited the example of Innocent II; he had been chosen in 1130 by only sixteen cardinals, whereas the anti-pope, Anacletus II, had received twenty-seven votes.[19]

Alexander and Boso provided almost identical, dramatic eyewitness accounts of what happened next in St. Peter's on 7 September. Cardinal-Deacon Odo placed around Roland's neck, in spite of his pro-forma protests of unworthiness, the red papal mantle, the symbol of the nominee's acceptance of his election. Octavian, "like a maniac," reacted by tearing the mantle off. In the ensuing uproar, one of the senators "had snatched the mantle from the madman's hand." The frenzied Octavian then signaled his chaplain to bring another mantle he had "craftily" prepared for just such an eventuality. The chaplain, another of Octavian's clerics, and the cardinal himself garbed Octavian's body with the substitute mantle because none of the other cardinals was willing to assist him. God immediately revealed the hollowness of Octavian's aspirations because, as Boso put it, "that part of the mantle which should have fallen over the front of his body covered his back—which all saw and laughed at—and the more he tried to correct the cause of so much mockery, the more he, beside himself at not being able to find the cowl, got the hem of the garment twisted around his neck." "And so," Alexander added, "his mantle was put on crooked and awry, in token of his damnation." At that moment the doors of St. Peter's were opened, and armed men whom Octavian had hired rushed in and surrounded him. Alexander and his followers were forced to seek refuge within the church for the next nine days.[20]

Needless to say, Victor IV's supporters told a very different story. The five cardinals who backed him conceded that Chancellor Roland had received fourteen votes to Octavian's nine, but the determination of Roland's party to invest him with the mantle violated the earlier agreement the cardinals had made that their choice had to be unanimous. The nine forbade Roland, accordingly, from accepting the mantle. Although he ignored the cardinals' command and sought to obtain the mantle, he was not invested because they, "in response to a petition of the Roman people, upon election by all the clergy, and with the assent of almost the entire senate and of all the captains, barons, and nobles," had invested and enthroned Octavian. They had then led him "with all due honor to St. Peter's palace, all the people shouting their acclaim, the clergy chanting a hymn" (4.62).

Cardinal Roland was consecrated and crowned as Pope Alexander III by six cardinal-bishops at Ninfa, not far from Rome, on 20 September. The Victorine sources are reticent on the topic of Octavian's consecration as Victor IV on 4 October at Farfa, northeast of Rome, where his family's power was concentrated, because Imar of Tusculum was the only cardinal-bishop who participated in the ceremony.[21] The month-long delay between Victor's election and his consecration by only a few bishops indicates that he was the candidate of only a small fraction of the Roman nobility and clergy, and that he probably counted on the support Frederick had promised him via Otto of Wittelsbach and his colleagues if he managed to arrange his election.[22]

Beyond their disagreements about the basic facts, the supporters of Roland and Octavian differed about the proper procedure for selecting the pope. Alexander's party emphasized that he had been elected, in accordance with the papal election decree of 1059, by the majority of the cardinals, including six of the seven cardinal bishops, with the consent of the clergy and people of Rome. To compensate for Victor's lack of support in the College of Cardinals, his adherents stressed that he had been chosen, like any other twelfth-century bishop, by the clergy and people of his diocese. The glaring weakness in this Victorine argument was that the pope's cathedral as the bishop of Rome was St. John Lateran, not St. Peter's; and the canons of the former rather than the latter should have participated in the election. The fundamental issue was whether the pope was merely the bishop of the most prestigious church in the Empire, subject ultimately to the emperor's authority, or the supreme pontiff of the universal Church, who was beholden to no one on earth.[23]

Frederick's Professed Neutrality

If either candidate formally notified Frederick of his election and requested his recognition, the announcement has not survived. However, on 16 September 1159, that is, before either pope had been consecrated, Frederick informed Archbishop Eberhard of Salzburg, from the camp at Crema, about Pope Adrian's death, the divisions in Rome, and the measures he had already taken. Barbarossa wanted a pontiff who would provide the Church with peace and treat the Reich and its subjects honorably. At the request of Louis VII, Frederick had sent Bishop Peter of Pavia to make peace between France and England, because the emperor desired the three kingdoms of France, England, and the Empire to be in concord. Peter was to urge the two western monarchs to favor only the person who was acceptable to the three of them—in essence, what had occurred after the double election of 1130 when Louis VI, Henry I, and Lothar had opted for Innocent II rather than Anacletus, but implicitly also a united rejection of Roland's election. Frederick had already sent similar directives to Germany, Burgundy, and Aquitaine, asking the now unknown recipients not to make a hasty decision; and the emperor urged Archbishop Eberhard and his suffragans to act only in consultation with him, because Frederick would accept as pope only someone who would respect the honor of the Empire and provide the Church with tranquility and unity.[24]

Frederick was so eager for Eberhard's approbation because the elderly Benedictine monk was, as Rahewin explained, a man "of remarkable faith and unusual piety ... kindliness and affection ...," who taught by the "perfect doctrine" of both his words and actions. Eberhard's approval was crucial for Victor's acceptance, even in Germany.[25]

Frederick's criteria for determining the rightful pope excluded from the start Alexander III, the chief proponent of the papacy's pro-Sicilian policy. Cardinal Roland had never regained the emperor's grace after Besançon. The depth of Frederick's rancor was common knowledge in Europe. For example, an anonymous English eyewitness of the emperor's reconciliation with Alexander in Venice in 1177 attributed Frederick's hatred of the pope, in an otherwise unreliable account, to the former papal chancellor's failure to show Frederick the deference he was due in public.[26]

The emperor ignored in early October 1159 the complaints of the pro-Alexandrine cardinals that Otto of Wittelsbach was persecuting Alexander in support of "Octavian's presumption," and that the Bavarian count-palatine and the anti-pope had invaded the Campania and the Patrimony and were trying "by every means to subject that land" to their control. According to Boso, Otto and Count Guido of Biandrate knew that the emperor and Octavian were very good friends and "[s]o they made great display to Octavian of their favor ..." It is inconceivable that the emperor's confidants were continuing his policy of asserting imperial prerogatives in the Patrimony, which had already angered Adrian, and were associating with Victor IV without Frederick's knowledge and approval. His public neutrality was a pretense.[27] In his missive of 28 October to the German princes and the members of the imperial household, Victor, perhaps familiar with the content of Frederick's letter to Archbishop Eberhard, emphasized how much he had always "esteemed . . . the honor of the Roman empire" and requested that the recipients exhort the emperor, as the Church's "divinely appointed guardian and defender," to come to her aid (4.60).

After both claimants had been consecrated and had mutually excommunicated each other, Frederick met before 23 October, during the siege of Crema, with twenty-two German and Italian bishops and, he informed Bishop Hartmann of Brixen, "all the other princes and devout men zealous for God and the Church." The participants determined "that the controversy could be ended only by a judgment of the Church itself." An examination of the "decretals of the Roman pontiffs and statutes of the Church," and the example of such former emperors as Constantine, Theodosius the Great, Justinian, Charlemagne, and Otto the Great, indicated that Frederick had the authority to convene an assembly to end the schism. Accordingly, on 23 October he summoned his confessor, Hartmann of Brixen, to attend "a solemn court ['curiam sollempnem'] and general assembly ['generalem conventum'] of all churchmen" in Pavia on 13 January 1160. Similar summonses were sent to "the two who call themselves pontiffs of Rome," all the bishops in the Empire, in France, England, Spain, Hungary, and Denmark, and Henry II of England.[28]

The "devout men" whom Frederick consulted included the archbishop of Tarentaise in the kingdom of Burgundy, and the abbots of Cîteaux, Morimond, and Clairvaux. He also consulted ten other abbots who, the emperor wrote to Eberhard of Salzburg, had appeared at Crema "as though sent by God" and in hopes of making peace between himself and Milan. At the end of October they conveyed Frederick's terms to the Milanese, but the latter insisted that they had sworn to the pope and the cardinals not to be reconciled with the emperor without the curia's consent. When the mediators pointed out that Adrian's death had freed the Milanese from this obligation, the townspeople insisted that they were still bound by their oath to the cardinals. Frederick added that his agents had "intercepted on the highways many proofs" that the pope had conspired with Milan in this fashion.[29]

Although the assembly at Pavia has traditionally been called a "council" (*concilium*) or "synod" (*synodus*), Frederick did not employ these words in his summonses. Instead, he used the standard term for a secular assembly, "court" (*curia*). However, a "general assembly (*conventus*) of all churchmen" was synonymous with a *concilium*. Admittedly, in his opening remarks to the assembly at Pavia on 5 February 1160, Frederick allegedly insisted "by virtue of my office and the dignity of the empire" that he had "the authority to convoke councils [*concilia*]," and he cited his Roman and German predecessors as precedents. However, the choice of Latin words in the summary of the emperor's speech was Rahewin's and not Frederick's. During the siege of Crema in October 1159 the bishops and abbots may thus have made their consent to the summoning of the assembly contingent upon Frederick's curtailment of his more extreme theocratic claims. Unlike Constantine at Nicaea in 325, Frederick did not preside at Pavia.[30]

To some extent such caution was a diplomatic necessity if Frederick hoped to obtain foreign recognition of Victor IV. The emperor employed identical language in his letters of 23 and 28 October to Hartmann of Brixen and Henry II, respectively, in describing the origins of the schism, the consultations at Crema, and the need to defer a decision until the council at Pavia met; but in his letter to Henry, Frederick spoke merely of the need to preserve the unity of the Roman Church and the English king's duty as one of her chief members to do everything to achieve that end. Presumably, the summonses Frederick sent to other rulers and bishops outside the Empire were equally discreet. In contrast, Frederick wrote to Hartmann that "at the time of His passion Christ was content to have two swords [Luke 22:38] . . . the Roman Church and the Roman Empire, since by these two institutions the whole world is directed in both divine and human matters." This was hardly a formulation of the Empire's position in Christendom that would have pleased Henry II.[31]

For his part, Pope Alexander dispatched envoys to Frederick at the beginning of November 1159, during the siege of Crema. At first, the emperor refused to accept the letters they carried and even threatened, according to Boso, to hang the papal messengers. Welf VI and Henry the Lion, who favored a more conciliatory policy toward the papacy (Henry had helped resolve the Besançon crisis), persuaded their kinsman to forego such a rash act. Frederick finally heeded the advice of the princes and received the papal emissaries but did not deign to reply to the pope. This strange incident, if true, is further evidence of how much Cardinal Roland had offended Frederick's honor at Besançon. Only the princes' intervention made it possible for the papal envoys even to gain access to the monarch.[32]

The court held at Crema had advised the emperor to send Bishops Hermann of Verden and Daniel of Prague, Otto of Wittelsbach, and Provost Heribert of Aachen to Cardinals Roland and Octavian to summon them to attend the council at Pavia. It is hard to imagine that Frederick could have selected a more partisan group of envoys, unless he had included

Rainald of Dassel in the delegation. All of them were implicated in the formulation and implementation of Frederick's regalia policy and/or the events preceding and following the double papal election. Moreover, Heribert drafted the emperor's letter of late October to Alexander, which addressed him as Chancellor Roland. Since Frederick had been chosen by God as emperor with a special responsibility to defend the Church of Rome, "the seat of our empire"— that is, where he exercised temporal authority—he was grieving over the dissension, and on the advice of "men of religion" he was convening "a general court and council" where churchmen alone would resolve the dispute. The two bishops and the Bavarian count-palatine, Frederick's "kinsman," would guarantee the safe passage of the papal chancellor and his cardinals. If Roland was "unwilling to accept God's justice and that of the Church in so solemn a council, may God see it and judge."

Boso reported that the legates failed to show Alexander III the proper obeisance at their meeting in Anagni in November 1159, but such deference would have prejudged the case in the pope's favor. In contrast, Boso added, Frederick had addressed Octavian as the pontiff in his summons, which the envoys delivered to Victor IV at Segni southeast of Rome in late November but which does not survive. This canard became part of Alexandrine propaganda, which John of Salisbury repeated, for example, in the summer of 1160; but Master Heribert and Frederick's other clerical advisers would hardly have been foolish enough to make such a diplomatic blunder and so publicly reveal the emperor's true stance. It was crucial that Frederick appear to be neutral, but it is hard to believe that the imperial envoys did not treat Victor with greater respect than Alexander.

Alexander acknowledged, with a dig, in his response to Frederick's invitation, that the emperor's office made him "the protector and particular guardian of the holy Roman Church," and for that reason the pope honored him more than "every other prince of the world, even when it is not strictly his due." The pontiff was surprised that for his part Frederick had failed to show the pope, therefore, the "sincere affection" he was due as Peter's "lowly successor" and had "overstepped the bounds of his office" by calling a council, the pope's exclusive prerogative. Frederick had insulted "his Mother," the Church, by writing to her "as if she were one of his subjects." Alexander concluded that he was "not allowed by either canonical tradition or the revered authority of the holy Fathers to attend this council or to accept a decision in this matter." The pontiff was defending a fundamental principle of papal ecclesiology. Frederick and Alexander's conceptions of the authority of their respective offices were irreconcilable.[33]

The Council of Pavia

Frederick opened the assembly in Pavia on 5 February 1160, after a time of fasting and prayer, with an address in which he reaffirmed his right as emperor to convene councils but in which he also acknowledged that he did not have the authority as a layman to judge matters that pertained to God. Since judgment in such instances was the exclusive prerogative of the clergy, he withdrew from the deliberations. Patriarch Pilgrim of Aquileia presided, being the highest-ranking member of the clergy present and, unlike the cardinals, not a party to the dispute. Archbishops Arnold of Mainz, Wichmann of Magdeburg, and Hartwig of Bremen, and the archbishop-elect of Cologne, Rainald of Dassel, assisted Pilgrim. Bishop Eberhard of Bamberg wrote to his absent archiepiscopal namesake in Salzburg that most of the fifty bishops who had assembled initially favored a postponement until they were better informed and until a "more general council" could consider the disputed papal election—an admission that the gathering was hardly representative of Christendom. However, the behavior of Alexander III's party—"the conspiracy against the empire" before the election and the alliance with the Reich's Sicilian and Lombard enemies; the fact that Victor IV, like Innocent II in 1130, had been invested first with the papal mantle; and the refusal of Cardinal Roland and his supporters to attend or send representatives, even though they had been assured of their safety—had left the attendees with no other alternative but to proceed.[34]

The synod deliberated until 11 February, and Eberhard stressed to his colleague in Salzburg that the council had investigated thoroughly "the time and order of the election." The canons of St. Peter's and the Roman clergy had testified in writing and under oath, through their envoys, about what had transpired in Rome. The attendees had also questioned prominent members of the Roman nobility, including the prefect of the city. Otto of Wittelsbach, Guido of Biandrate, Provost Heribert, and the unnamed bishops who had accompanied Frederick's legates to Rome (Hermann of Verden and Daniel of Prague?) had reported on "what they had discovered concerning the lord chancellor [Roland] and his followers." Rahewin included both the canons' memorandum and a summary of the oral testimony of the Roman clergy and nobles in the *Deeds*.[35]

Provost Henry of Berchtesgaden, who represented Eberhard of Salzburg at Pavia, informed the archbishop that Frederick's adherents had intercepted sealed letters that Alexander and his cardinals had sent to the Lombard bishops and communes. Henry added that these missives, which revealed "the machinations and plots of these people against the empire," had been publicly read. It is quite possible that the fragmentary account of Adrian IV and Chancellor Roland's dealings with King William I of Sicily and with Milan, which portrayed the papal chancellor as the chief instigator of these hostile policies, was also presented in evidence. In any case, the final version of the encyclical that summarized the synod's findings accused Roland of conspiring with Sicily and Milan. The council concluded, Henry said, that any further postponement of action threatened both the Church and the Empire.[36]

In spite of all the evidence that had been presented against Pope Alexander in five days of deliberations, the council was reluctant to condemn him. On 11 February, in an open consistory, the case against him was reviewed again; and the canons of St. Peter's and the rectors of the Roman clergy swore on the Gospels that the facts they had presented about the election were true. Vincent of Prague reported that most of the Lombard bishops wished to postpone Alexander's condemnation until he had been summoned again three times. Bishop Peter of Pavia, whom Frederick had sent to France to persuade Louis VII and Henry II not to act hastily, and Bishop Hugh of Piacenza refused altogether, according to John of Salisbury, to recognize Victor IV. However, the German bishops pressed for a decision, Vincent said, because it was far more difficult for them to cross the Alps and to reassemble in Italy for another council. Pilgrim of Aquileia, Arnold of Mainz, and Rainald of Dassel insisted that the council proceed, because Roland had scorned the emperor's summons and the judgment of the Church, whereas Octavian had humbled himself and submitted to the synod's jurisdiction.

According to the final encyclical, which was issued in the name of these three prelates, the council confirmed "the election of Lord Victor, who had come like a gentle and innocent lamb, humbly to accept the judgment of the Church." Then, after all the bishops and all the clergy had approved, "the most Christian emperor . . . last of all—upon the advice and request of the council—accepted and approved the election of Lord Victor." Finally, all the princes and people who were present were asked three times whether they concurred; and they "joyfully replied in a loud voice: 'We are content.'" Support for the synod's determination was more lukewarm than the encyclical indicated, because Henry of Berchtesgaden informed Archbishop Eberhard that Pilgrim, Eberhard of Bamberg, and the bishops of Passau and Regensburg had only given "their assent because of the exigencies of the empire . . . [and] subject to a later judgment by the Catholic Church." As Eberhard of Bamberg wrote to his colleague in Salzburg, "As these bad beginnings gave promise of a worse ending, namely, perpetual discord and division between the empire and papacy . . . we accepted Lord Victor in the hope of peace and concord between the empire and the papacy."[37] Even pro-imperial bishops, who were angered by the papal chancellor's hostility toward the Empire, had their doubts about the validity of Octavian's election; but their loyalty to Frederick prevailed.

The next day, 12 February, Patriarch Pilgrim and the archbishops escorted Victor, who had been staying outside the city in the monastery of S. Salvatore, to the cathedral at Pavia. Frederick grasped the bridle of the pope's white palfrey when the pontiff approached the church and held the stirrup as Victor dismounted, that is, the emperor performed the marshal and squire's services he had initially refused Pope Adrian at Sutri. Then, Frederick and Pilgrim led Victor by the hand, the emperor on the right side and the patriarch on the left, to the altar; and after the pontiff had been enthroned, everyone—Pilgrim, the archbishops, bishops, abbots, princes, and the emperor—kissed his feet. On Saturday, 13 February, Victor IV and the council solemnly anathematized "Chancellor Roland, the schismatic, and his principal followers . . ."[38]

At Anagni on Maundy Thursday, 24 March 1160, Pope Alexander III reciprocated. He excommunicated Frederick "as the chief persecutor of the Church of God," freed his subjects from their oaths of fealty, and renewed the excommunication of Octavian and his followers. (Alexander, unlike Gregory VII in his confrontation with Henry IV, never threatened to depose Frederick.) In a letter to Eberhard of Salzburg on 4 April, Alexander listed many of Frederick's misdeeds: his capture and imprisonment of archbishops and bishops returning from the Holy See (who else besides Eskil?); his well-known mistreatment of the future pope (Cardinal Roland) and his colleague (Cardinal Bernard) at Besançon; and his invasion of the Patrimony during Adrian IV's lifetime with the intention, it was rumored, of making Octavian pope if the opportunity presented itself. Frederick and his envoys who were in Rome had enabled Octavian to intrude into the papal office after Alexander's "canonical and unanimous election"; and Frederick had convoked a council in Pavia contrary to the sacred canons. Strikingly, Alexander singled out by name among the emperor's excommunicated principal associates only Otto of Wittelsbach, whom Alexander probably suspected of complicity in the events of 7 September, and not Rainald of Dassel, who is commonly seen as the chief architect of Frederick's anti-papal policy after 1157 but who had not been in Rome in September 1159.[39]

A careful reading of the final version of the encyclical about the proceedings of the council, which was sent out in the names of the patriarch and the German archbishops, reveals how limited was the support for Octavian's elevation to the chair of St. Peter. According to Eberhard of Bamberg, Rahewin, and Henry of Berchtesgaden, about fifty archbishops and bishops from both sides of the Alps attended the council; and forty-seven or forty-eight prelates appended their names to the encyclical. The encyclical concluded with the statement that altogether 153 archbishops and bishops had been present or had expressed their concurrence in writing; that an uncountable number of abbots, archpriests, and provosts who had come to Pavia from many kingdoms had given their consent; and that Henry the Lion, Welf VI, Berthold IV of Zähringen, Frederick of Rothenburg, the counts-palatine of the Rhine, Saxony, and Bavaria, and an unknown number of margraves and counts had been present.

The encyclical exaggerated the degree of episcopal support for Victor. The absent archbishops of Trier and Salzburg were included among the signatories because their envoys had supposedly given their consent and the archbishops themselves had allegedly assented in writing. While Archbishop Hillin of Trier did subsequently concur with the decision, Eberhard of Salzburg never did. According to Eberhard of Bamberg, the archbishops of Arles, Vienne, Lyons, and Besançon approved "by letters and agent"; but the last two are missing in the final list of subscribers. Above all, the number of signatories does not add up to 153, even if one includes all the suffragans of the patriarch of Aquileia and the archbishops of Mainz, Cologne, Magdeburg, and Bremen who are said to have consented along with their metropolitans. The bishops who were actually present included three Burgundians, twenty-seven Italians, seventeen Germans, and the Danish bishop of Ripen, who probably represented his king. Since at least seven of the German attendees were already in Italy with Frederick when he summoned the council to meet, ten German bishops, at most, had heeded his command to cross the Alps. The council was hardly representative of all of Christendom. The poor attendance revealed to Europe that Frederick's assertion of his right as emperor and as the defender of the Roman Church to summon a council in Pavia was a hollow pretense. John of Salisbury famously mocked: "Who has subjected the universal Church to the judgment of one church in particular? Who has appointed the Germans to be judges of the nations?"[40]

Frederick's Claim to World Dominion

Frederick's futile efforts to gain international recognition for Victor as the rightful pope are linked to the bigger question of how he and his advisers and other rulers perceived the Empire's status within Christendom. Answering this question depends in part on how much weight one assigns to literary texts written in the early 1160s. These include *The Play of Antichrist*, in which the king of France submits to the emperor, and the "Emperor Hymn," which the Archpoet composed at Rainald of Dassel's court after the defeat of Milan:

> God save the lord of the world,
> Hail our Caesar!
> whose yoke is light to all good men;
> Whoever kicks against it,
> thinking it heavy,
> is hard of heart
> and of a crooked neck.
>
> Emperor Frederick,
> Prince of all princes of the world,
> Whose trumpet causes
> all hostile castles to fall:
> We bow our heads to you,
> as do tigers and ants,
> along with the cedars of Lebanon,
> brambles and tamarisks
>
> . . .
>
> May the understanding of Christ
> fill the Christian mind,
> so that I might sing with worthy praise
> about the Lord's anointed ("christo domini"),
> who powerfully bearing
> an earthly burden
> restores the Roman Empire to its former state.

The problem is that the illiterate Frederick was most likely unaware of the content of these works, and, moreover, the Archpoet hailed Rainald as the real architect of the victory.[41]

Anti-Staufer papal propaganda, which charged Frederick with seeking world dominion, must likewise be read with some skepticism. In the same letter in which John of Salisbury asked who had appointed "the Germans to be judges of the nations," he declared that Frederick, in his very first embassy to Pope Eugenius after the king's election in 1152, had "revealed the shamelessness of his vast and audacious scheme . . . [to] reshape the governance of the whole globe and . . . [to] make the world subject to the City." In reality, Abbot Wibald had quoted in the election announcement the Gelasian formula which Eugenius had himself employed, to assure the pope of Frederick's desire for harmony between them on the basis of equality.[42]

The imperial chancery tailored its arguments to the specific audience. As we have seen, Frederick invited Henry II to participate in the Council of Pavia, because it was his duty as one of the chief members of the Church to preserve her unity; but Frederick informed Hartmann of Brixen in his invitation that Christ had established two institutions at His passion, the Roman Empire and the Roman Church, to direct the world "in both divine and human matters," and that there was "one God, one pope, [and] one emperor."[43] Frederick's relations with the western monarchies were different from his dealings with Denmark, Bohemia, and Hungary, which had been traditionally in the German orbit. He could hardly have gained Louis VII and Henry II's acceptance of Victor by stressing his own superiority to them.

Frederick had initiated diplomatic contacts with Henry II, in all probability in May 1157. On 6 May Frederick, whom Wibald styled grandiloquently, "august emperor, great and pacific and crowned by God," wrote to "his most beloved brother and intimate and special friend Henry, the illustrious king of the English and duke of the Normans and the Aquitanians," to whom he was connected by "the most firm bond of fraternal love and indissoluble friendship." The greeting was addressed to an equal, though Frederick placed his name first as a token of his higher secular dignity; but, conversely, he was honoring Henry by initiating the correspondence. It was incumbent upon "imperial majesty," Wibald averred, to aid churches and monasteries, so that they could intercede with God on Frederick and his people's behalf. Abbot Gerald of Solignac, whose monastery was situated in the diocese of Limoges and, Frederick stressed, in Henry's principality, had come to Aachen to procure a letter from the emperor with the assistance of "the most faithful and most dear Wibald." Frederick requested that Henry, as befitted "royal clemency," take Gerald and Solignac under his protection and defend the abbey from the attacks of evil men.[44]

In late September 1157 an English embassy led by Master Herbert of Bosham, Thomas Becket's future biographer, arrived at Würzburg, where

Frederick was celebrating the apparently successful conclusion of the recent imperial campaign against Duke Boleslaw IV of Poland. Henry II's ambassadors joined envoys from the Byzantine emperor Manuel I, who requested that the nephew/brother of Manuel's wife, Frederick of Rothenburg, be knighted by Barbarossa. Additionally, representatives from Denmark, Hungary, Italy, and Burgundy vied with each other, Rahewin said, in bringing gifts and petitions to Frederick. Such a scene of jostling envoys bearing presents was a classical literary topos intended to demonstrate that the entire world acknowledged the exalted rank of the ruler. Master Herbert brought a letter from King Henry that Becket, as the king's chancellor, may have drafted with Frederick's May letter in mind. Henry's letter, which outdoes Frederick's epistle in its effusive flattery, was the centerpiece of Rahewin's panegyric description of the Würzburg assembly. The letter is the proof text in modern scholarly arguments about the Staufer's assertion of imperial ascendancy over the other European kingdoms and of the other monarchs' apparent recognition of the emperor's superior dignity.

Henry addressed Frederick, whose name he placed first, as "the friend dear to his heart," "invincible emperor of the Romans," "Your Excellency," "best of rulers," "Your Magnificence," and "Your Serenity." He thanked the emperor for deigning to send him first ambassadors, letters, and gifts—a reference to the May embassy or another mission?—and above all for his desire "to enter into treaties of peace and love with us." The king rejoiced that Frederick was willing to help Henry in setting in order the affairs of his realm—no one has been able to ascertain to what internal difficulties Henry was alluding. In a rhetorical crescendo, the Angevin king assured Frederick, "with sincere and heartfelt affection, that we are prepared to bring to pass according to our ability whatever we know tends toward your glorification. We lay before you our kingdom and whatever is anywhere subject to our sway, and entrust it to your power, that all things may be administered in accordance with your nod, and that in all respects your imperial will may be done." Henry desired, "therefore, between us and our peoples an undivided unity of affection and peace, safe commercial intercourse, yet so that to you who excel us in worth, may fall the right to command; while we shall not lack the will to obey."

In the hope that Frederick would remember him, Henry was sending the emperor "the most beautiful things we could find, and what was most likely to please you." According to the English Pipe Rolls, the Exchequer expended £12 6s 8d during the third year of Henry's reign—that is, between 19 December 1156 and 18 December 1157—for four falcons that were given to the "emperor of Germany"; and the treasury spent £25 3s on presents for the German envoys. Rahewin singled out among the royal gifts a very large tent of the finest materials and unmatched workmanship that required special machinery to pitch and that Frederick subsequently employed during his second Italian campaign. In his concluding chapter about Frederick's appearance, character, and accomplishments, Rahewin turned Henry's letter into a grossly exaggerated summary of his hero's diplomatic relations with all of his fellow monarchs: "Although the kings of Spain, England, France, Denmark, Bohemia, and Hungary always mistrusted his power, Frederick so bound them to himself through friendship and alliance that as often as they sent him letters or ambassadors, they proclaimed that they accorded him the right to command, while they did not lack the will to obey"—language derived ultimately from Einhard's *Life of Charlemagne*.[45]

In plain Latin, Henry's seemingly obsequious letter was a put-down. In an apparent aside at the end of the letter, the king got to the crux of the diplomatic mission: his envoys would respond orally to the emperor "regarding the hand of the blessed James." Frederick's great-grandfather, Emperor Henry IV, had obtained this apostolic relic for the imperial chapel in 1072; but it was among the treasures that Empress Matilda, Henry II's mother, had taken with her to England after Emperor Henry V's death in 1125. Shortly before the death in 1135 of Matilda's father, Henry I, the king had given the relic to the monastery of Reading, where he was then buried. Bishop Henry of Winchester, the brother of Stephen, Matilda's rival for the English throne, had taken possession of the hand, which Henry II had returned to Reading after he became king. For both Henry II and Frederick the hand was not only an exceedingly precious relic but also a symbol of dynastic restoration. Henry's "honeyed speech," as Rahewin phrased it, and valuable gifts were a polite denial of the emperor's request for the relic's return to him that undercut all of the king's deferential "graceful language."[46] The gap between imperial pretensions and political reality was immense.

The English envoys accompanied Frederick from Würzburg to the court he held in Besançon in October 1157. Along with the other men from all over Europe, they witnessed the confrontation with Cardinal Roland. Rahewin, harping on his theme of imperial grandeur, commented: "For the whole world recognized him [Frederick] as the most powerful and most merciful ruler, and undertook, with mingled love and fear, to honor him with new tokens of respect, to extol him with new praises." This time, it was Louis VII who rebuffed Frederick by refusing to meet with him after the court at Besançon, as had originally been planned, probably because he did not wish to be seen as siding with the emperor against Pope Adrian.[47]

While Frederick was dealing in January and February 1159 with Milan's rejection of the Roncaglia laws, the envoys of Louis VII and Henry II appeared in close succession at the imperial court and sought to gain with flattery and gifts the emperor's support for their respective masters. Rahewin recorded rather cryptically that there had been "incessant enmities and dissensions" between them since Louis had divorced Eleanor of Aquitaine and Henry had married her in 1152, "whether on account of the delimitation of their respective territories or because of some other less evident cause." In fact, Henry was claiming Toulouse as part of Eleanor's inheritance, and Louis was aiding his brother-in-law, Count Raymond V of Toulouse. Open hostilities broke out in March 1159, but Henry lifted his siege of Toulouse in September 1159 because Louis, his feudal lord, had taken up residence in the city. As we have already seen, Frederick informed Archbishop Eberhard of Salzburg on 16 September that he had dispatched Bishop Peter of Pavia, at Louis' request, to make peace between the two kings and to urge them to recognize only a pope who was acceptable to the three monarchs. Since neither ruler wished to alienate Frederick while they were at odds with each other, they could not immediately reject Victor, even though the French and English bishops favored Alexander. Hence the kings prevaricated initially about adhering to the decisions of the Council of Pavia.[48]

After the close of the council, Frederick sent Rainald of Dassel to France, Hermann of Verden to Spain, Daniel of Prague to Hungary, and embassies to Denmark and Bohemia. Alexander countered, after he had excommunicated Frederick on Maundy Thursday 1160, with his own legations. The imperial ambassadors accomplished little.[49]

Archbishop Theobald of Canterbury cautioned Henry II in early 1160 against a premature recognition of either papal candidate. Yet by May or June the archbishop informed the king that the French Church had opted for Alexander, who was known by all to be "more virtuous, more prudent, more learned, and more eloquent than his rival," and who was preferred by "[a]lmost the whole Church of Rome." Theobald warned Henry not to listen to Frederick's overtures on Octavian's behalf, because in the numerous schisms that had plagued the Church since the selection of the anti-pope, Clement III, in 1080, the pontiff backed by the French Church had always prevailed against the man "whom Teutonic impetuosity had thrust into the papal chair." In May 1160 Louis and Henry settled their dispute over Toulouse and agreed on a common course in regard to the schism. The

French and English Churches formally recognized Alexander as the rightful pope in July at councils held in Beauvais and in London.[50]

Frederick's attempt to gain Hungarian recognition of Victor was intermeshed with his relations with Byzantium, because the Magyar kingdom was a buffer state between the two empires. Bishop Daniel of Prague met in vain on 27 March 1160 with Archbishop Lucas of Esztergom, an ecclesiastical reformer who soon recognized Alexander; but the Hungarian king, Géza II, remained non-committal. To pressure Géza, Alexander, and William I of Sicily, in April Frederick dispatched Duke Henry V of Carinthia, the proto-notary, Henry of Würzburg, and the son of the Venetian doge to meet with Manuel I. The emperor offered him territorial concessions along the Italian Adriatic coast and, Rahewin said, "certain more secret enquiries regarding opposition to William." Frederick must have been desperate even to contemplate the restoration of a Greek presence in southern Italy, and no one seems to have taken the possibility seriously. Manuel was negotiating with Alexander by December 1160, and Archbishop Lucas persuaded Géza in the second half of 1161 also to adhere to Alexander.

After Géza's death on 31 May 1162 his brothers, Ladislas II (r. 1162–63) and Stephen IV (r. 1163), who were the successive Byzantine candidates for the Hungarian throne, sought to replace their nephew, the minor Stephen III (r. 1162–72), for whom Archbishop Lucas was serving as regent. Both Stephens vied for Frederick's recognition. The emperor wrote to Archbishop Eberhard of Salzburg in 1163 or 1164 that the pretenders and many of the Hungarian barons "freely desired to place themselves under the yoke of our lordship." Stephen III prevailed with the assistance of Frederick's surrogates and kinsmen: Vladislav of Bohemia, Henry Jasomirgott, whose daughter Agnes later married Stephen III, and Ottokar III of Styria. Stephen's younger brother, the future Béla III (r. 1172–96), grew up at the Byzantine court as the fiancé of Manuel's daughter and received, as the Hungarian and Greek heir presumptive, Dalmatia and Croatia as an appanage. Frederick's assertion of his feudal lordship over Hungary took precedence, seemingly, over procuring recognition of the anti-pope Victor, because Stephen III remained loyal to Alexander. Manuel's installation of Béla III as the Hungarian monarch in 1172 ended the kingdom's dependency upon the western empire.[51]

Until Bishop Daniel of Prague died in 1167 on Frederick's fourth Italian expedition, Bohemia adhered to the anti-popes, Victor IV and Paschal III. Frederick sent Christian of Buch, the future archbishop of Mainz, to Denmark at the end of 1159 to obtain Valdemar I's adherence to Victor.

The bishop of Ripen probably represented Valdemar at the Council of Pavia, and the king duly recognized the anti-pope because he needed to be formally enfeoffed by Frederick and, more importantly, he required Henry the Lion's support in fighting their common Slavic enemies in the Baltic. Valdemar I and Vladislav of Bohemia attended or were represented in September 1162 at Frederick's failed attempt at St. Jean-de-Losne to resolve the schism in Octavian's favor, but by 1163 or at the latest by 1164 the Danish king was in contact with Alexander.[52] Foreign recognition of Victor was thus limited to the two realms, Bohemia and Denmark, which were most closely linked to the Empire; and even in Germany some bishops, most notably, Archbishop Eberhard of Salzburg, were steadfast in their opposition to Victor. Staufer hegemony was a literary fantasy.

Oddly, although Frederick's assertion of imperial sovereignty in Rome had been a major cause of the deterioration in imperial–papal relations, he made no effort after the outbreak of the schism to consolidate his position in the city, where he spent a total of only twenty-one days in a thirty-eight-year reign. For all its glory, Rome was always peripheral in his plans. Victor IV, too, left the city two weeks after his elevation, without taking possession of the Lateran Palace; and his itinerary largely matched Frederick's after February 1160. Alexander resided in Anagni, near the border between the Patrimony and the Norman kingdom; but he was able to return briefly to Rome on 6 June 1161, because most of Octavian's Roman supporters were attending the Council of Lodi, which Frederick had called to reconfirm Victor's selection. However, Alexander's situation in Rome and the Patrimony was insecure, and by 30 September he had reached the western coast of Italy. William provided the papal party with Sicilian ships, and the pope arrived in Genoa on 21 January 1162. Milan's second capitulation on 1 March made Alexander's continued stay in Italy dangerous, so he fled Genoa on 25 March and landed at Maguelone on the French coast on 11 April 1162.[53] Frederick's victory in Italy did not resolve the schism in Victor's favor.

CHAPTER ELEVEN

THE DEFEAT OF MILAN

A War of Attrition

ALTHOUGH FREDERICK'S HOPES OF gaining international recognition for Victor as pope were linked to his defeat of Milan, he disbanded his army after the Council of Pavia. Henry the Lion, Berthold IV of Zähringen, and most of the bishops went home. Until fresh troops arrived from Germany in 1161, the emperor was largely dependent upon his Italian noble and communal supporters.[1] Since he lacked the men to besiege Milan, a difficult undertaking under the best of circumstances, Frederick resorted to a war of attrition: a blockade of the roads supplying Milan, the devastation of its countryside, and chance, indecisive skirmishes. The city was surrounded by hostile forces. New Lodi, to the southeast, impeded Milan's access to Piacenza. Frederick had enfeoffed Count Goswin III of Heinsberg in September 1158 with two counties that had belonged to Milan: Seprio, located northwest of the city and to the east of the Ticino river, and Martesana, which extended northeast of Milan from south of Lake Como to the upper Adda. Frederick's communal allies, Novara and Vercelli, controlled the Ticino valley, west of Milan. Pavia, south of Milan, completed the encirclement of the city and its *contado*.[2]

The year 1160 was filled with indecisive fighting. On 22 March the Milanese attacked Lodi, but the Lodiese beat off the attackers in a battle outside the city. Frederick arrived in Lodi a few days later, thanked the citizens for their heroism in the Empire's defense, but warned them against being lured in the future into a fight outside the walls, lest they be ambushed and the city taken. In April, German, Lodiese, and Cremonese forces seized two Milanese castles located east of the Adda and tightened the blockade of Milan; but Frederick prohibited his troops from attacking the Milanese who had appeared on the opposite bank of the river because he suspected a trap. Frederick spent May, along with contingents from Cremona and Pavia, devastating the western portion of the Milanese *contado*. On 2 June the Milanese and 200 Placentine knights, supported by 100 wagons that served as mobile field fortifications and platforms for the infantry and archers, confronted the imperial army. Frederick could not risk losing his greatly reduced forces in a battle and withdrew to Pavia, where he furloughed the Italian knights. The emperor had saved his small army, but Milan had halted the destruction of its food supply.[3]

While Frederick was in Pavia, the Milanese attacked Lodi on 9 June. Most of the Milanese stayed a short distance from Lodi, while more than forty knights were sent to lure the Lodiese into an ambush. Not heeding Frederick's earlier warning, the Lodiese pursued the Milanese. In the ensuing melee, both sides took prisoners. There was a repeat performance the next day, but this time the Lodiese saw the advancing main Milanese force, hurried back to Lodi, and the opposing forces faced off outside the walls. Neither dared to attack, and the Milanese withdrew. After this fiasco, the Milanese decided to attack on 18 June with men from all six quarters in the city. The Milanese had a good chance of success because Lodi's walls had not yet been completed and its defenses consisted mainly of earthen ramparts and two moats. By the afternoon the city was largely surrounded, but the Milanese were unable to advance with a sufficient number of men through the swamps to complete the encirclement of Lodi. Placentine reinforcements arrived in the evening to assist the Milanese, but Lodi retained control of the bridge over the Adda and sent to Cremona and Pavia for aid. At dawn on 19 June the besiegers spotted the Cremonese on the opposite bank of the Adda and dismantled their tents after a siege that had lasted only a day and a half. On 3 August work began on Lodi's new walls. Milan's attempt to destroy New Lodi had failed.[4]

In July the area east of the Adda, between Bergamo and Brescia, was the scene of military activity. Frederick advanced eastward from Bergamo into Brescian territory, forced the Brescians to lift the siege of a castle, and destroyed a bridge on a road that linked Milan to Brescia. On 28 July he took Iseo, on the southern tip of Lake Iseo, the headwaters of the Oglio, the stream that separated Brescian and Bergamese territory. The main highway that linked Milan to Brescia crossed the Adda at Cassano, and in early August a combined Lodiese and Cremonese force destroyed the bridge there. However, the Brescians had been able to join the Milanese campaign in the Martesana.[5]

At the end of July knights and infantry from three of Milan's six quarters had headed northward to begin the siege of Carcano, which is situated between the two branches of Lake Como: the western branch, Lake Como proper, with Como at its southern end, and the eastern branch, known as Lake Lecco, from which the Adda exits Lake Como. The Milanese offensive threatened to break the imperial blockade in the north and to cut the route that led via Como and the eastern Swiss passes to Germany. Frederick broke off his Brescian campaign to relieve the imperial garrison in Carcano. He hoped to trap the besieging Milanese, as he explained shortly after the battle in a letter to Patriarch Pilgrim of Aquileia, because his own army would be situated between them and Milan. What Frederick did not know until he arrived at Carcano on 8 August was that the Milanese forces had been reinforced with troops from the city's three other quarters and greatly outnumbered his own. His army consisted of contingents from Como, Novara, and Vercelli; the knights of the Seprio and the Martesana, presumably under the command of Count Goswin III of Heinsberg; and the Italian magnates William of Montferrat, Guido of Biandrate, and Guido of Lomello. There were also a few Germans: Berthold IV of Zähringen, who was hoping to procure Frederick's consent to the election of his brother Rudolf as archbishop of Mainz and who had arrived with only his bodyguard; Vladislav's exiled cousin, Duke Oldřich of Bohemia; and the Thuringian, Count Conrad of Ballhausen. The imperial army had been assembled at short notice and was small.

The Germans pitched camp on 8 August on the shores of Lake Alserio, a kilometer south of Carcano. Frederick's Italian troops were camped on a ridge, two kilometers southwest of the emperor's quarters. The battle on 9 August took place in two separate encounters. Frederick's German troops routed the Milanese infantry, destroyed the Milanese *carroccio*, slaughtered the oxen that pulled the battlewagon, and seized the gold cross and the banner of St. Ambrose that adorned it. However, the Milanese knights thoroughly defeated the emperor's Italian allies. More than 2,000 of them fled, including William of Montferrat; and many men, especially the Novarese, were killed. The Milanese controlled the heights that overlooked Frederick's camp besides the lake. The emperor was left, according to the Milanese Anonymous, with a mere 200 knights who could still fight. Only the rocky terrain and a torrential downpour prevented the Milanese from attacking the Germans on the lakeshore. The emperor was able to withdraw to a castle outside Como because the Milanese feared he was merely feigning a retreat. They plundered the German camp and freed the prisoners Frederick had taken.

Two hundred Cremonese and eighty Lodiese knights, unaware of what had happened at Carcano, set out on 10 August from Lodi with the substantial provisions that Frederick had requested. The heavy load slowed them down, and on the morning of 11 August the Milanese spotted and ambushed the knights in a swamp. The Milanese captured ten Lodiese and fourteen Cremonese; the others escaped by leaving behind their armor and 200 horses. As soon as Frederick learned what had taken place, he came to the rescue of his allies and the Milanese fled. The Milanese subsequently exchanged around 200 knights from Cremona, Como, Pavia, and other pro-imperial communes for all the hostages that the emperor held.[6]

In his exculpatory letter to Pilgrim of Aquileia, Frederick expressed his desire to correct any erroneous rumors the patriarch might have heard about what had occurred at Carcano. Although the Milanese had broken through the ranks of his Lombard allies and he had suffered some losses, the Germans had killed more than thirty Milanese knights who had defended the *carroccio*; and the Milanese had needed seventy-five carts, each carrying three or four corpses, to bring their dead home. The tale of an imperial victory prevailed in Germany. According to the continuation of Otto of Freising's *Deeds*, around 500 "of the enemy were slain; of our men, only five." Perhaps, the chronicler was including only the Germans among "our men." In reality, the battle was at best a draw. The Milanese did abandon the siege of Carcano on 19 August, but the emperor had not trapped the Milanese army, and Milan had regained the upper hand in the Seprio and the Martesana. More Milanese than Germans may have died, but the city had reserves of men that Frederick lacked. Milan allowed the emperor to withdraw—perhaps as part of the prisoner exchange—and by 24 August he was in Pavia, where he spent the autumn and winter of 1160–61. The bishops of Novara, Vercelli, and Asti, William of Montferrat, Guido of Biandrate, and other Italian magnates swore shortly after 26 August to supply Frederick with knights and archers from 8 September 1160 until 16 April 1161, that is, until two weeks before he anticipated receiving German troops.[7] For the time being, the emperor was totally dependent on his Italian allies.

In his letter Frederick also corrected some other misinformation Pilgrim might have received. It was not true, he assured the patriarch, that Victor had lost support. Rather, the kingdoms of Spain, Hungary, Denmark, and Bohemia, Count Ramón Berenguer IV of Barcelona, Count Raymond V of Toulouse, and all of Provence and Burgundy obeyed him. This assertion, too, was stretching the truth. By the end of 1160, the kings of León, Castille, and probably Navarre as well had recognized Alexander. Raymond, who also held the marquisate of Provence, between the Isère and the Durance rivers, was married to Louis VII's sister Constance and depended on his brother-in-law's assistance in his fight with Henry II over Toulouse. Raymond welcomed Alexander upon his arrival in Montpellier in April 1162.

The notable exception was Ramón Berenguer, because the counts of Barcelona were also the counts of Provence and thus imperial vassals. In 1161 Ramón's nephew, Ramón Berenguer III of Provence, married Frederick's cousin Richildis, the daughter of Barbarossa's Babenberg aunt Agnes and the exiled Duke Wladyslaw of Poland and the widow of King Alfonso VII of León-Castille. In June 1162 Frederick agreed to enfeoff the two counts with the counties of Provence and Forcalquier and the city of Arles; and the counts promised in turn to recognize Victor as pope, not to permit Alexander, his cardinals, or legates to enter their domains, and to seize the pope and his agents wherever they could. Immediately after the death of the count of Barcelona on 6 August 1162, Frederick, on his way to St. Jean-de-Losne, enfeoffed Ramón III. Intriguingly, the charter recording the enfeoffment did not include the provisions about recognizing Victor or capturing Alexander, perhaps because Ramón III refused to commit himself to the anti-pope.[8] In his letter to the patriarch, Frederick either overestimated or deliberately exaggerated the extent of Victor's backing in the Iberian Peninsula and in Provence.

Frederick's real reason for dispelling the patriarch's misapprehensions was that on 25 July 1160 a princely assembly at Erfurt had sworn to undertake an imperial expedition against Milan the following year. The list of attendees is a who's who of princes not present in Italy in the summer of 1160: the archbishops of Trier, Cologne, and Magdeburg; the bishops of Bamberg, Zeitz, and Meissen; Henry the Lion, Frederick of Rothenburg, the emperor's brother Conrad, Louis II of Thuringia, Albrecht the Bear, and Otto I of Meissen. The emperor ordered Pilgrim, likewise, to appear with appropriate forces in Pavia on 30 April 1161, two weeks after Easter, because he could not spare the services of a single prince in the coming campaign. Many princes had sought, in fact, to be absolved from the duty. Archbishop Eberhard of Salzburg received a similar mandate at the same time, but it was silent about Carcano and Victor.[9]

While Frederick waited for German reinforcements, he made two failed attempts to disrupt Milan's connections with Piacenza, its port on the Po. On 24 August 1160 the emperor set out from Pavia with an army of men from Cremona, Pavia, and Lodi and with the Pavian fleet to destroy the bridge of boats across the river at Piacenza. The Placentines were able to moor their boats along the southern bank of the Po by the city and so prevented their destruction. The same thing occurred on 19 October. Milan was more successful. Archbishop Obert, who had spurred the Milanese on to fight at Carcano, was able to occupy various key positions in the Seprio. The consuls stationed 100 knights in the ruins of Crema, in a check to both Lodi and Cremona; and Milan rebuilt the bridge over the Adda at Pontirolo, which had been destroyed in the spring. From there the Milanese launched a surprise attack on Lodi on 28 October. Both sides took prisoners, Otto Morena's son Manfred among them. Milan's only serious setback in 1160 was a fire in August that destroyed between a third and a half of the city. Without sufficient German troops, Frederick was only the commander of an Italian communal army, the weaker one at that. The year 1160 had been a military failure for him.[10]

The communal skirmishes resumed in the spring of 1161. On 12 March the Placentines and Lodiese simultaneously invaded each other's territory, and the Placentines prevailed because they caught the Lodiese in the morning before they had put on their armor. There was another encounter between knights of the two cities on 4 April. The Milanese began a siege of the castle of Castiglione Olona, northwest of Milan in the Seprio, on 17 March. The garrison was soon in great distress because there was no water inside the castle, and it appealed to the emperor for help. Frederick assembled an Italian army in Lodi, reinforced by fifty knights whom Count Ramón Berenguer IV of Barcelona had brought with him to the imperial court. Upon Frederick's approach, the Milanese withdrew on 15 April after burning all their siege equipment. The emperor had regained the upper hand in the Seprio. The Milanese Anonymous noted in this context that the Milanese were spending considerable sums to procure provisions.

The German troops finally started to arrive: Frederick of Rothenburg with more than 600 well-armed knights; Rainald of Dassel with more than 500; Louis II of Thuringia with 500; and Vladislav II of Bohemia's brother Duke Theobald and the king's son Frederick with more than 300. On 29 May the emperor headed to Milan with a combined German-Italian army to devastate the countryside around the city. The Milanese sallied out of the city several times and skirmished with the Italians. On one such occasion, Frederick ordered a prominent Milanese captive hanged in sight of his fellow citizens. The Germans obeyed Frederick's strict orders that they not engage in unauthorized fights with the Milanese. Both Frederick's resort to terror and his ability to maintain discipline among his own troops are striking. In a span of ten days the imperial forces devastated the Milanese *contado* and destroyed grain, vineyards, orchards, and dwelling places for a distance of 10 to 15 miles around the city. To control the rising cost of food in the city, each parish elected two men and each of the six quarters chose three men from among these parish representatives to set the price of grain, wine, and merchandise. The Milanese Anonymous was one of the eighteen commission members.[11]

Around 7 June the emperor withdrew from Milan to the Adda. The Germans remained there, while he dismissed the Italians. In response to the French and English recognition of Pope Alexander III the preceding year, Victor IV had summoned a council to meet in Lodi. Frederick presided at the council, which opened on 19 June, and it unanimously confirmed Victor's election. The kings of Denmark, Norway, Hungary, and Bohemia, six archbishops, twenty bishops, many Cistercian abbots, and the abbots and provosts of other orders apologized for not attending but affirmed their adherence to Victor. The church fathers excommunicated the archbishop of Milan, the bishops of Piacenza and Brescia, the consuls of these cities, and their advisers. The bishop of Bologna was irrevocably deposed, and several other bishops were suspended and given until 1 August to be reinstated. The council also excommunicated the murderers of Archbishop Arnold of Mainz, and Victor enthroned Conrad of Wittelsbach, Frederick's choice, as Arnold's successor. After the close of the council, the Lodiese chased off twenty-four Milanese knights who were planning to attack a number of bishops returning to Pavia and they seized four of the knights.[12]

On 25 June the emperor captured, burned, and leveled a fortress at the confluence of the Adda and Po. He ordered the amputation of the hands of the Milanese members of the garrison and of seventeen of the other prisoners. The other captives were imprisoned in Lodi. Count Goswin of Heinsberg resumed the offensive in the Seprio in July.

The Milanese, now clearly on the defensive, made the first peace overture on 7 August. While the imperial forces were camped on the Lambro, south of Milan, the Milanese consuls contacted Frederick's brother Conrad, his brother-in-law, Louis II of Thuringia, and one of the Bohemian dukes, probably Vladislav's brother Theobald. It was customary to ask high-ranking intermediaries, preferably a ruler's kinsmen, to initiate negotiations with a deeply offended monarch. The *Cologne Royal Chronicle* indicates that, in order to appease the emperor, Milan proposed to fill in a section of its moat; to destroy a portion of the walls, 40 ells in length, so the imperial army could easily enter and leave the city; to demolish thirty houses that were comparable to towers—presumably like those that can still be seen in Italian cities such as Bologna and Verona; to hand over 300 hostages; and to pay a fine of 10,000 marks and an annual tribute levied on the city and its territory. The emperor had already rejected these terms, according to the Cologne chronicler; but the Milanese sought, nevertheless, to regain

Frederick's grace through the intervention of the landgrave and the king (sic) of Bohemia. The chronicler added that the other princes' hatred of these two men thwarted Louis and Theobald's attempt. In any case, according to either Otto or Acerbus Morena, the consuls and the princes had guaranteed each other's safe conduct to and from the negotiations; but Rainald of Dassel's knights, who allegedly knew nothing about these secret discussions, captured the consuls. Milanese knights rode to their rescue and fighting ensued.

The princes, furious about an act that called into doubt their own sworn word and honor and that sabotaged the peace negotiations, determined to kill Rainald, who was still in the imperial camp and, supposedly, knew nothing about what was happening. He hastened to Frederick and assured him of his innocence. The emperor ordered the princes to desist from their murderous intentions and summoned Frederick of Rothenburg, the imperial standard-bearer, and the other princes to fight. The angry Louis II of Thuringia and Vladislav II's brother Theobald refused to participate. Barbarossa attacked the Milanese from the south; his Swabian cousin Frederick of Rothenburg struck from the north. The Milanese retreated toward the city, but the other consuls who had remained in Milan forbade the townspeople to come to the rescue of their fellow citizens fighting outside the walls. Frederick himself pursued the Milanese as far as the bridge over the moat; his men captured, the Morenas said, eighty Milanese knights and 266 foot soldiers and killed others as well. The Milanese Anonymous put the number of captives at more than 300, and Burchard of Ursberg reported that around 1,000 naked captives were kept, in Lodi, pitifully in chains in the winter cold. In the fighting at the bridge, the emperor's horse had been repeatedly slashed and Frederick slightly wounded—one more example of his engaging in hand-to-hand combat. He wrote to Victor a few days later about his participation in the battle and put the number of dead at more than 600.

The episode on 7 August raises a number of unanswerable questions. Was Rainald really in the dark about the secret negotiations or did he deliberately, out of personal pique at the Milanese attack on him and the other imperial envoys in January 1159, sabotage them? Were the princes, as had already been the case during the first siege in August 1158, seeking a compromise to end the conflict with Milan; and was Rainald, the probable source of the information in the Cologne chronicle, more in tune with Frederick's own determination to keep on fighting? Were the other princes, especially the emperor's kinsmen, jealous of Rainald's predominant influence; and was the count-palatine's and landgrave's humiliating inability to guarantee the consuls' safety, as they had sworn, a cause of their feud with Rainald in 1164? Regardless, the incident provides a rare insight into the tension at the court.[13]

Frederick resumed his devastation of the countryside on 9 August and tightened his siege of the city. If any Milanese dared to leave the city, say, to collect firewood, he ordered the culprit's right hand cut off. The same fate awaited anyone from Piacenza or elsewhere who was caught bringing wares to Milan; there were twenty-five amputations on one day alone. Bands of knights skirmished outside the walls. Five prominent Milanese prisoners, including two captains, were blinded after one such incident; the sixth man lost his nose but only one eye, so he could lead his compatriots home. Frederick concluded he had to stop completely Milan's access to the markets in Piacenza and Brescia that were continuing to supply the city with provisions. Therefore, in the winter of 1161–62 he blocked all the roads leading to Milan. Anyone who tried to run the blockade and was caught by the Lodiese and Germans patrolling the highways day and night lost his right hand.

The Milanese made one final foray to obtain provisions. In December, while Frederick was in Cremona, more than 500 Milanese knights approached Lodi. Most hid in a nearby forest, but around 100 of them advanced to the outskirts of Lodi and took much booty. Empress Beatrice and Frederick of Rothenburg's knights sallied forth in pursuit and regained most of the loot; but then the concealed Milanese knights counterattacked, put the Germans and Lodiese to flight, and seized the contraband again. They even killed one of the empress's most warlike knights.

However, Milan was being starved into submission. Acerbus Morena reported that a measure of salt cost 12 new Milanese pennies and that the Milanese did not have sufficient stores of grain, which was selling for two shillings a measure, to last until the next harvest. The Milanese Anonymous remembered that grain had been exceptionally expensive. A bushel of grain or beans had cost 20 pennies; a quarter bushel of salt 30 shillings; and a pound of cheese eight pennies. Meat had been exceedingly dear. He had paid 21 shillings for a quarter of a dead ox. The poor, unable to obtain food, had lain in the mire from morning to night, he recalled; and many had perished. Fathers and sons, husbands and wives, and brothers had argued whether they should surrender, especially because some of the most prominent citizens were plotting to leave. Finally, the Milanese decided, Acerbus Morena wrote, that "it would be better to make peace with the emperor in accordance with his will, to atone for their misdeeds, and to implore his mercy than to remain in such distress and need."[14]

Unconditional Surrender

The negotiations about the terms of Milan's capitulation and the enactment of its unconditional surrender extended over several weeks and were designed to assuage the grievous insult to the Reich and Frederick's honor and to demonstrate the triumphant authority of the Empire. We are exceptionally well informed about these events because there are five eyewitness accounts: Frederick's own letters; the histories of Acerbus Morena, the Milanese Anonymous, and Vincent of Prague; and a detailed letter written by the imperial notary, Burchard of Cologne, to Abbot Nicholas of Siegburg, who compiled the *Cologne Royal Chronicle* until the mid-1170s.

On 21 February 1162, Ash Wednesday, the Milanese dispatched three consuls to Frederick in Lodi with two proposals: they would either submit unconditionally to him or regain his grace through a negotiated settlement. In a harsher version of the 1158 peace and the rejected overture of 1161, they offered, "for the sake of his honor," to fill in the moat completely; to destroy the wall and the towers; to let the emperor select 300 hostages, whom he could hold as prisoners for three years; to accept as their *podestà* whomever the emperor preferred, a German or an Italian; to surrender all the regalia; to pay Frederick an unspecified amount; to build at their own expense a palace, as large as he desired, inside or outside the city; never to erect in the future a moat or wall nor to ally or to make a sworn agreement with any other city or person without the emperor's permission; to exile 3,000 men; and to receive the emperor and his army in Milan for as long as he wished to stay.

Frederick sought the counsel of the German and Italian princes and his communal allies. Their dilemma was that the obligation of a Christian ruler to show mercy to the repentant was incompatible with their desire to turn Milan into an object lesson of the folly of disobedience. Some of the princes, led by Rainald, advised against acceptance of the proposed terms so that Frederick could seek revenge. Most of the participants concurred, however, with Guido of Biandrate's recommendation that Frederick should negotiate. Guido did so for the cynical reason, Burchard of Cologne explained, that the Milanese would find the latter option more palatable than unconditional surrender but that the starving inhabitants would not be able to fulfill the agreement as long as Frederick continued to blockade the supply lines to the city. Punishing the Milanese for their failure to honor their sworn word rather than for rebellion would be, Guido argued, less of a violation of the divine command to be merciful; and Frederick would be free then to deal with the city as he pleased. The Milanese understood this, too, but also knew that they could not prevail in a battle. So, after terminating their alliance with Brescia and Piacenza, they submitted unconditionally to Frederick's mercy. Strictly speaking, it was not an unconditional surrender because the citizens' lives had been spared—killing them after their surrender would have been a dishonorable act—but unlike the capitulations of Tortona, Milan in 1158, or even Crema, Frederick had made no other commitments about the fate of the people or the city. Normally, such details were worked out in advance of the formal submission and reconciliation.

The capitulation occurred in two extended, ceremonially staged phases: the personal humiliation of widening groups of Milanese citizens and the determination of Milan's future. On 1 March 1162 twenty Milanese citizens, including at least nine consuls, appeared before the emperor in his palace in Lodi—an added humiliation because of the enmity between the two cities. They carried unsheathed swords in their hands, as a sign that their lives were at his mercy, prostrated themselves before him, and swore that they and their fellow citizens would obey all his commands. Three days later, on 4 March—the second Sunday in Lent, when Burchard of Cologne noted, the introit, "Be mindful of thy mercy, O Lord" (Psalm 24:6 in the Vulgate; 25:6 in the King James), was fittingly sung—the consuls and 300 or more of the most prominent knights, including the thirty-six standard-bearers, returned. They handed over the banners to the emperor and kissed his feet. The engineer Guintelmo, who had for years designed Milan's catapults, siege equipment, and defensive works and whom Acerbus Morena described as "most inventive," surrendered the keys to the city. (Guintelmo may have been chosen for this "honor" to satisfy Pavia's desire for revenge because Milan had installed him as its *podestà* in Pavia after that city had surrendered to Milan in 1157.)[15] Everyone swore on their own and their fellow citizens' behalf that they would obey in the future, without deceit, all the emperor's commands. Frederick ordered all men who had served as consuls during the preceding three years and a portion of the infantry to be present on 6 March. He retained 286 of the Milanese knights as hostages.

Milan's ceremonial surrender reached its climax on 6 March. It was pouring with rain when the Milanese arrived, Burchard of Ursberg reported seventy years later; and the emperor made the exhausted Milanese stay outside the gates of Lodi while he finished his midday meal, so they would grasp the magnitude of their defeat. Frederick, seated on an elevated throne in front of the palace, then received them. One thousand foot soldiers, marching in their customary battle order and carrying more than one hundred flags representing their specific neighborhoods, and the remaining knights paraded for hours before him. The *carroccio*, the symbol of Milan's communal autonomy, was at the center of the procession. (According to Burchard of Ursberg, it had to be partially demolished to be brought inside Lodi.) Two trumpeters who stood on the battlewagon sounded a loud dirge, Burchard of Cologne observed, to the city's pride. When they had finished playing, they gave their instruments to the emperor. Then the great men of each of Milan's quarters surrendered, one by one, their standards to him. A mast, topped by a cross, on whose front was painted an image of St. Ambrose in benediction, stood in the center of the *carroccio*. As a final act of submission, the mast was lowered so far to the ground in front of the emperor, the Cologne notary noted, that those who stood like him beside the throne feared the whole contraption would topple over. It remained in that position until the emperor picked off the ground the fringes of the banner of St. Ambrose, lest the saint be dishonored. It is not clear whether this gesture was planned in advance as a sign that Frederick would ultimately be merciful to Ambrose's people; but the notary wrote that the *carroccio* stood before Frederick as a symbol of the city's subjection.

Then, all the knights and foot soldiers fell on their faces before the emperor and, weeping, begged for mercy. Burchard of Cologne commented that a consul then spoke in such a way as to arouse the emperor's pity. According to Vincent of Prague, another eyewitness, the consul acknowledged that the Milanese had sinned in taking up arms against the emperor, their natural lord. They were submitting their necks to his imperial majesty and were offering him the keys to the city. The consul implored the emperor to be merciful and to grant peace to his subjects "for the love of God and Saint Ambrose and of the saints who rest within the city's walls." When the consul had finished, the crowd again fell to the ground and, extending before them the crosses they carried, pleaded with great wailing for mercy in the name of the cross. All who heard these lamentations wept, but the emperor's visage remained unaltered. Guido of Biandrate acted as the third interlocutor on behalf of "his former friends." He moved everyone to tears by holding up the cross, and everyone joined him in humbly supplicating the emperor, whose "face remained fixed like stone." (Frederick's conduct on 6 March sounds remarkably similar to his behavior at his coronation when the ministerial pleaded in vain for mercy in spite of the princes' entreaties.) Rainald declared after this final act of abasement that the Milanese had formally submitted without any reservations, a point Frederick also stressed in the letters that were sent afterwards in his name. The emperor ended the ceremony with the vague assurance, according to the notary, that he would do what was appropriate and with the promise that he would show the Milanese mercy at the proper time.

Beatrice's absence at this carefully arranged ceremony is striking because in the past empresses had customarily interceded on behalf of individuals who had offended their husband or son. It is also indicative, as we have seen, of both her apparent lack of influence at this stage in her life and the general shift in emphasis from mercy to justice in the practice of kingship. Nevertheless, the desperate Milanese, after leaving the royal presence, hoped that she could help them. Since their request for an audience with her had been turned down, they threw the crosses they were carrying through the lattices in the windows of her chambers. Their appeal may not have gone totally unheeded because a Genoese notary reported that she did intercede on Milan's behalf.

The Milanese returned on 7 March. Frederick informed them that strict adherence to the law demanded that they should all forfeit their lives, but that it was also incumbent upon princes to be merciful. They had to acknowledge once again that they deserved to die before Frederick spared them and lifted the imperial ban. According to Acerbus Morena, the emperor ordered the Milanese to send another 114 knights to join the 286 he had already detained on 4 March, that is, 400 in all, from whom he would select forty as hostages. Burchard of Cologne wrote that "all the consuls, ex-consuls, great men and knights, legal experts and judges" stayed behind but that the common people who were less guilty were allowed to depart. As a collective punishment of the city and in a further denigration of its communal identity, Frederick commanded that the Milanese demolish all the gates and sections of the wall and moat adjacent to each gate, so the imperial army could march into the city in battle formation. He also dispatched twelve men, six Germans and six Italians, to supervise the destruction and to receive oaths of obedience from the remaining citizens by Saturday. (Acerbus Morena noted that, as the *podestà* of Lodi, he was one of the twelve.) The next day, Sunday, 11 March, 114 knights and an additional twenty-six men appeared before the emperor and swore to obey him. Nothing had been decided at this point, at least publicly, about the fate of Milan itself, because Burchard of Cologne, who probably wrote his letter before Frederick's departure for Pavia on 13 March, did not mention any such measure.[16]

On 13 March, Frederick, Beatrice, and the princes headed from Lodi to Pavia; and on 19 March, Barbarossa commanded the Milanese to evacuate their city by 26 March. Some, taking their possessions with them, went to neighboring Lombard cities, but most remained outside the walls in the hope that the emperor would permit them to return to their homes. The imperial party arrived in Milan on 26 March, and Frederick consulted with the princes and Milan's communal enemies. According to Vincent of Prague, the Lombards urged that Milan suffer the same fate it had meted out to others; and Vladislav's brother, Duke Theobald of Bohemia, lit the first fire. The Milanese Anonymous accused Frederick of succumbing to the Lombards' bribes. Each of the Italian allies was assigned the destruction—and plunder—of a particular quarter of the city. The Lodiese, remembering all the sorrow the Milanese had inflicted on them, demolished not only the quarter that had been consigned to them, but also a large part of another district. This work, which Burchard of Ursberg likened to the actions of wild beasts and demons, continued until 1 April. Acerbus Morena said the Lombards wrecked more buildings in five days than was initially thought possible to accomplish in two months; and he estimated that only a fortieth of the city remained standing. According to him, Frederick personally ordered the destruction of the campanile, a structure of wondrous beauty and great height and width, which crashed into the cathedral, demolishing a good portion of the church. The Milanese Anonymous indicated that there were three separate campaigns of destruction in 1162 and that nearly all the Lombards labored to fill in the moat.

The chroniclers probably exaggerated the extent of the destruction. It would have been impossible to raze a city of Milan's size in five days. The actual demolition was likely limited to structures such as the campanile and the city gates that were of symbolic significance. The wall, constructed of immense stones, with its nearly one hundred attached towers, remained largely intact. Most of the damage had been done by the fire the preceding August and the fires that were set at the end of March 1162. Such conflagrations were common occurrences in medieval cities, and towns could be quickly rebuilt because many of the stones were readily available for reuse. Milan was no exception, and it was swiftly reconstructed after 1167.

The exiled Milanese settled in four surrounding villages and work began on fortifying these on 2 May. Frederick appointed Bishop Henry of Liège as his vicar in Milan. Markward III of Grumbach, whose father had accompanied Frederick to Aachen in 1152, succeeded Henry two years later. When the emperor left Italy in August 1162, one hundred hostages, who were rotated every month, remained in imperial custody in Pavia. However, Archbishop Obert, who had encouraged Milan's resistance, and several other clerics had escaped on 18 March and joined Alexander III in Genoa. Milan's defeat did not solve the problem of the schism.[17]

While the Italian communes deserve much of the blame for the destruction of Milan, Frederick, who had become entangled in their rivalries and was largely dependent on their military support, was ultimately responsible. More importantly, the emperor, starting with his refusal to show mercy to the ministerial who pleaded for forgiveness at his coronation, displayed a vindictive streak in dispensing justice. No doubt, a twelfth-century king needed to be ruthless, and modern "civilized" men have been guilty of far greater atrocities; but there are just enough hints that some of the princes counseled Frederick on several occasions to pursue a more restrained approach in dealing with the pope and the communes.

The Triumphant Emperor

The chancery proclaimed Frederick's triumph to the world. The word *triumphus* had been employed only once, in a secular context, in the *arenga* of an authentic imperial charter prior to Frederick's reign. (The *arenga* was the formal statement of the reasons for a charter's issuance.) Two charters drafted in 1158 and 1159 had referred to the triumph(s) God had granted Frederick over his enemies. According to the second document, an in-house production, "the King of kings and Lord of lords had subjected in a marvelous triumph the enemies of His church and the Empire to our lordship." A letter of 27 January 1160, notifying Bishop Roman I of Gurk about the capture and destruction of Crema, had been dated "in triumpho Cremę."

The notaries ratcheted up such language after Milan's second capitulation. The circular announcing the victory spoke about "most glorious triumphs, such as, we believe, were not granted to any of our predecessors." Frederick's charter of 6 April 1162 for Pisa was dated "after the destruction of Milan"; and he was identified in the line where the seal was affixed as "the most invincible conqueror" (*triumphator invictissimus*). The next day, in a charter for the church of Gurk in Carinthia, the notary combined Charlemagne's title, "emperor of the Romans, great and peaceable, crowned by God," with Justinian's designation as "renowned conqueror and ever august" to style Frederick as "Romanorvm imperator á deo coronatus magnus et pacificus inclitus triumphator et semper augustus." Likewise, the words *victoria*, *victrix* (victor), or *invictus* (invincible) rarely appeared before the twelfth century in the *arengae* in reference to military successes. They were employed during Frederick's reign mainly in the context of the emperor's defeat of Milan, Crema, and the Romans in 1167. For example, Frederick wrote in the circular he sent out on 4 March 1162, or around that time, about how he had "obtained a happy and glorious victory over Milan with a total fullness of honor." Such hyperbolic language disappeared almost completely in chancery productions after the annihilation of the imperial army in 1167.[18] We do not know whether Frederick personally authorized the use of such terminology, but surely these words express his and the court's exaltation over the defeat of Milan and its allies.

The Pacification of Lombardy and Emilia-Romagna

After Milan had been plundered and burned, Frederick celebrated Palm Sunday on 1 April 1162 outside Milan at the monastery of S. Ambrogio, where he received the olive branch that was, according to Burchard of Ursberg, "the triumphant palm of victory." The court returned to Pavia for Easter. Many bishops, margraves, counts and other Italian nobles and nearly all the *podestàs* in Lombardy accompanied Beatrice and Frederick, who wore his crown, to Mass in the cathedral. Frederick had sworn three years earlier, Acerbus Morena said, not to wear his crown until Milan had been defeated. Afterwards the magnates and the consuls, including, Acerbus proudly noted, himself, sat down to a meal in the episcopal palace with the imperial couple, who wore their crowns throughout the repast. "Exceeding joy and exceeding happiness" prevailed, Acerbus commented, "on account of the good fortune God had granted the emperor."[19]

On 10 April the dinner guests reassembled in the garden of the monastery of S. Salvatore outside Pavia and swore to besiege Milan's chief ally Piacenza. (Acerbus mentioned that as the *podestà* of Lodi he joined his colleagues from Cremona, Novara, Como, Vercelli, and Parma in taking the oath.) Fearful of Frederick's wrath, Brescia surrendered on 22 April on terms similar to those that Milan had proposed unsuccessfully in 1162. The Brescian consuls and many other knights appeared with unsheathed swords and agreed to the destruction of all their fortifications; to accept whomever the emperor chose as their *podestà*; to give Frederick all the money that Milan had paid them for fighting against him and to pay him an additional £6,000; and to hand over all the castles and other fortifications in the bishopric of Brescia. In addition, all Brescians were required to swear to obey all imperial commands in regard to an expedition to Rome, Apulia, or wherever the emperor ordered them to go, as well as in all other matters.

Frederick's brother Conrad interceded on behalf of Piacenza, and its consuls capitulated on 11 May at S. Salvatore, Acerbus reported, on terms similar to Brescia's. He also indicated that Piacenza returned all the regalia to the emperor, a detail that Acerbus probably omitted inadvertently in the case of Brescia. According to the extant written text of Piacenza's capitulation, it was fined 6,000 marks, four times the £6,000 that Brescia owed. (A mark was the equivalent of four Pavian pounds. Acerbus was aware of the difference in the fines the cities paid.) Frederick was to select 500 Placentines as hostages, seventy of whom were to be in his custody for three months at a time, until the fine was paid, the moat filled in, and the walls leveled. The Placentines were to expel their pro-Alexandrine (unnamed) bishop, but Frederick gave him a safe conduct to travel to Venice, Genoa, or France, that is, the bishop was free to join Alexander in exile.[20]

The Council of Lodi had deposed Bishop Gerardo of Bologna in 1161 for recognizing Alexander. In June 1162, Frederick, accompanied by his brother Conrad and uncle Henry Jasomirgott, marched to Bologna, "which had not yet," in Acerbus' words, "submitted completely to the imperial yoke." The imperial forces occupied all the fortifications on both banks of the Reno, and the Bolognese, "aware that they had not served the emperor very faithfully" and fearful that Milan's fate awaited them, surrendered. They agreed to do whatever Frederick commanded about the moat and walls, to pay a large sum of money, and to accept the *podestà* he appointed. Imola and Faenza did the same. Acerbus concluded: "All the cities of Lombardy and of all of Italy, all the castles and fortifications were subjected that summer [1162] to the lordship of the emperor." The one exception was, he noted, the castle of Garda near Verona. Here, Turisendus, a nephew of Bishop Theobald of Verona, continued to defy Frederick until the imperial vicar, Markward III of Grumbach, commanding a force from Bergamo, Brescia, Verona, and Mantua, after a siege of nearly a year, reached an agreement with Turisendus in the summer of 1163. Frederick's victory in northern Italy seemed complete.[21]

In the spring of 1162 Frederick installed a largely German administration to govern imperial Italy: Bishop Henry of Liège in Milan; the Franconian nobleman Markward III of Grumbach as the *podestà* in the rival communes of Brescia and Bergamo; Egenolf of Urslingen and later Arnold of Dorstadt, who was usually called Arnold Barbavaria on account of his salt and pepper beard, in Piacenza; Count Gebhard of Leuchtenberg in Piedmont; Count Conrad of Ballhausen, who had been with Frederick at Carcano, in Ferrara; Azo in Parma; and Master Paganus in the county of Como. Acerbus Morena added that there were men like them in many other cities and castles but that Frederick permitted Cremona, Pavia, Lodi, and some other cities—Pisa and Genoa are examples—to be governed by native consuls like himself.[22]

The terms of Cremona's self-governance were set forth in an agreement that Frederick reached with the city on 13 June 1162, as a reward for its great services to the Reich. If Frederick was in Lombardy, his envoys would choose the consuls with the advice of the wise men of the city; and the monarch would invest the consuls with their authority. If Frederick was elsewhere, Cremona would be free to select the consuls, provided that they were men loyal to the Empire. In exchange for an annual payment of 200 marks of good silver, Frederick conceded to Cremona all the regalia in the city and bishopric of Cremona. The Cremonese did not owe this payment in years that the *fodrum* was levied, an indication that this extraordinary levy was more than 200 marks. The city was barred from allying with another commune without the emperor's permission. Finally, Frederick clarified his earlier grant of Crema to Cremona on 7 March, the day of Milan's final capitulation. He prohibited Crema's reconstruction and the building of any fortifications between the Adda and Oglio. The remainder of Crema's former territory became part of the imperial domain.[23]

In essence, Frederick recognized the commune of Cremona, like the German princes or the Italian magnates and churches, as a constituent member of the Reich, though with considerably less autonomy, in the ongoing feudalization of the imperial constitution. In that sense, Frederick's privilege for Cremona was the equivalent of the Austrian *Privilegium minus* or Würzburg's "Golden Liberty." The difference between Germany and Italy was not ethnic or that the communes were corporate entities—so were the bishoprics and the imperial abbeys—but that many of the communes were hostile and that Frederick and his agents alienated even his communal allies with his excessive exactions. In principle, the Peace of Constance of 1183 would remedy that flaw in the imperial system.

The Magi

In describing the destruction of his native city, the Milanese Anonymous singled out among the crimes of the imperial forces the profanation of altars and the theft of relics. More specifically, he wrote that in 1164, "On the eleventh day of this month [June], Rainald, chancellor and archbishop of Cologne, took the bodies of the holy martyrs Nabor and Felix and that of the holy confessor [Maternus?] . . . as it was said, and three other bodies which had been placed in a sarcophagus which was in the church of Blessed Eustorgius and which were said to be those of the three Magi, and he sent them to Cologne." The next day Rainald informed the church and people of Cologne that Frederick had given him "the bodies of the most blessed three Magi and kings" and those of the martyrs Felix and Nabor, and he commanded that Cologne prepare a suitable welcome for their saintly guests. When Rainald, carrying "the most precious gifts," entered his archiepiscopal see on 24 July 1164, he was magnificently received, according to the *Cologne Royal Chronicle*, "especially on account of the relics, which he brought to Cologne to the everlasting glory of Germany." In the late 1180s Archbishop Philip, the brother of Count Goswin III of Heinsberg, transferred the bodies to the magnificent gold, jeweled shrine which Nicholas of Verdun, the greatest twelfth-century German goldsmith, had fashioned and that still stands on the high altar in the cathedral (Fig. 11). Their presence turned Cologne into a holy city and a major pilgrimage site, and by the Late Middle Ages after their coronation in Aachen it became customary for German kings to worship at the shrine of their royal predecessors.

Rainald not only transformed the oriental magicians into kings, but the whole story of the Magi's prior presence in Milan may have been his or the Milanese clerics' pious or not so pious invention. There is no contemporary evidence for the veneration of the Wise Men in Milan before the city's sack in 1162. It was only in the thirteenth century that Italians, familiar with the cult in Cologne, appropriated the tale and lamented the theft. The account of Rainald's acquisition of the bodies does not appear in the oldest extant, late twelfth-century version of the chronicle of the Milanese Anonymous. The addition of this passage in later manuscripts may explain the chronicler's surprising uncertainty about the identity of such venerable relics. Did Rainald deliberately concoct the whole story to elevate the prestige of his Church? Could any twelfth-century archbishop, even Rainald, have been quite so cynical; or could Milanese clerics have pawned the bones off on Rainald to deflect his attention from "authentic" relics? Did Frederick, also deceived, really give Rainald the relics or did the arch-chancellor just take them? It is worth mentioning that the emperor conferred on his "most dear prince" Rainald on 9 June 1164, extensive properties and rights along the Ticino "on account of his vast and innumerable services," and that Rainald in his letter singled out the relics as the emperor's greatest gift, even though Frederick did not mention the relics in his charter. Could the real act of imperial favor have inspired the fraud, if it was such? Once again, the truth is elusive; but it is worth pondering that Rome never officially sanctioned the cult of the Holy Three Kings, in spite of their biblical significance and the popularity of their cult. Perhaps the popes did not want to confirm the actions of a schismatic, or, just maybe, the curia knew the truth.[24]

The Defiance of Archbishop Eberhard I of Salzburg

Frederick showed far greater forbearance in dealing with Archbishop Eberhard I of Salzburg, the leader of the Alexandrine party in Germany, than he did with the Italian communes because the elderly Benedictine monk was revered for his piety, learning, and the integrity of his life, and because the success of the emperor's Italian policy depended on the support of the German princes and the maintenance of peace north of the Alps. These political realities limited Frederick's ability to punish Eberhard for his repeated defiance of the emperor's commands.

Eberhard had supported Frederick's transfer of Bishop Wichmann from Naumburg to Magdeburg and the emperor's stance at Besançon. As we have seen, both Eberhard of Bamberg and Frederick, who saw the archbishop as a possible arbiter, had kept him informed in 1159 about the emperor's increasingly troubled relations with Adrian IV; and Frederick had notified the archbishop on 16 September 1159 about the double papal election and had asked him to postpone judgment.

Eberhard of Salzburg set out to attend the Council of Pavia but halted at Treviso because, he said, he had become ill. This claim may well have been a convenient excuse since, as he notified his suffragan, Roman I of Gurk, in January 1160, he had learned on the way how limited Cardinal Octavian's support was in Italy. The archbishop turned around and designated Provost Henry of Berchtesgaden as his representative at the deliberations. The provost took with him to Pavia two mule loads of fish and cheese and 30 marks as Eberhard's gift for the emperor—the same tactic Henry II had employed in sending a tent rather than the hand of St. James that Frederick had requested. The emperor thanked Eberhard for the presents but asked him, sometime after 26 January 1160, to accept whatever the synod would decide. On 15 February, after the council had formally recognized Octavian as Victor IV, Frederick repeated the request. Alexander III notified Eberhard and his suffragans, in turn, on 4 April, about Octavian and Frederick's excommunication and released the bishops from their oath of fealty to the emperor. The archbishop, Roman, and Frederick's confessor, Hartmann of Brixen, adhered from the start to Alexander. Initially their Bavarian colleagues, Albert of Freising and Frederick's uncle, Conrad of Passau, remained neutral; only Hartwig II of Regensburg, the son of Duke Engelbert of Carinthia, recognized Victor.

Both the archdiocese and the metropolitan province of Salzburg had been major centers of the Gregorian reform movement during the Investiture Conflict. Benedictine abbeys like Eberhard's own family foundation, Biburg, had accepted the Hirsau reforms; and many collegiate churches, including Berchtesgaden and the cathedral chapters of Salzburg and Gurk, had adopted the strict Augustinian Rule. Hartmann and Roman were leading proponents of the latter movement. Salzburg's opposition to Frederick's ecclesiastical policies was thus almost preordained.

After the princes agreed at Erfurt on 25 July 1160 to join the campaign against Milan, Frederick commanded Eberhard, who had been excused from participating in earlier expeditions, to appear on 30 April 1161 in Pavia with his military cohort, as his oath of fealty required. In an ominous undertone, Frederick made clear that he would consider anyone who refused to come to be unfaithful to him and the Empire. Eberhard was a no-show. Around 22 June 1161 Frederick, clearly irritated, expressed his displeasure that Eberhard, whom the emperor especially esteemed and held most dear and whose advice regarding both the Church and the Empire he especially valued, had ignored his summons as well as mandates, delivered both in writing and by messengers, to attend another assembly in Pavia in May and the Council of Lodi in June. Next, Frederick ordered Eberhard as well as Hartmann of Brixen to come to Cremona on 8 September. The archbishop acknowledged in July the receipt of the mandate, but a conflict between Henry the Lion and Hartwig of Regensburg had necessitated, he claimed, the postponement of his visit. Eberhard, who was actively working in the second half of 1161 to procure Alexander's recognition by Géza of Hungary and by Ulrich II, the new patriarch of Aquileia, wanted, presumably, to avoid a personal meeting with the excommunicate emperor.[25]

An even angrier Frederick expressed shortly after 8 September his and the princes' astonishment at Eberhard's third failure to come. It was, he wrote, the special duty of the ecclesiastical princes to provide him with advice. The church of Salzburg was especially obligated to serve the Empire because it had been more richly endowed than any other see by his predecessors—a not so subtle hint that he might deprive Eberhard of the regalia for non-compliance. The emperor reminded Eberhard of Jesus' words in Matthew 22:21 about rendering "unto Caesar the things which are Caesar's." Frederick ordered Eberhard and his troops to appear, this time, in the field outside Verona on 23 April 1162. Eberhard was to swear his compliance in the hands of Frederick's chaplain and emissary, the notary Burchard of Cologne. If Eberhard remained defiant, the emperor would consult with the princes and clerics, he warned, about taking additional measures so that "the honor of God and the faith would not be diminished and the prescribed service to the Reich would be rendered in the future."

Frederick was threatening the archbishop with deposition. At the same time he conveyed to Roman of Gurk the substance of his letter to Eberhard and asked the bishop to urge his metropolitan to comply. Otherwise, Roman, like the other princes, would have to judge Eberhard guilty of "contempt and an affront [to the emperor]."

In December 1161 Burchard met with Eberhard, whom he described to Abbot Nicholas of Siegburg, the compiler of the *Cologne Royal Chronicle*, as "a pious bishop and a mad old man," in a letter about his legation on Frederick's behalf. The archbishop had not disguised his adherence to Alexander and had equivocated about performing his military obligations. At a subsequent meeting between Eberhard and Patriarch Ulrich of Aquileia in Villach, Carinthia, which the notary had also attended, Burchard had publicly read a lost letter that Frederick had addressed to the vassals and ministerials of the church of Salzburg, in which the emperor had commanded them to secure the archbishop's obedience. The irate Eberhard had stood up on a rock, crossed himself, declared that the Holy Ghost was speaking through him, and delivered a harangue in favor of Alexander. The speech was so effective that Burchard had found it difficult to regain the listeners' allegiance to Frederick. However, Eberhard had declared his willingness to serve the Reich, Burchard reported, and had offered to redeem the military obligations he could not perform in person by paying the emperor a sum of money. The archbishop was trying to find a way to render unto both Caesar and God their due.

Eberhard wrote to Frederick in December 1161, following Burchard's mission, that he had received with proper respect the emperor's letter shortly after 8 September. While the emperor's predecessors had richly endowed the church of Salzburg, much of this wealth had been alienated, so that the church lacked the material resources to undertake a military expedition. Moreover, the frailty of his own body and his monastic profession ruled out his personal participation. However, since Eberhard desired Frederick's grace, he was sending an envoy to negotiate the monetary compensation for the military service he owed. Frederick did not reply until Burchard had returned to the court and had reported in the presence of Eberhard's envoys about his dealings with the archbishop. Burchard wrote to Abbot Nicholas that the emperor was livid and that Eberhard's removal as archbishop was a real possibility. Frederick showed more restraint in his own letter of early January 1162 to Eberhard, who was still the recipient, in the salutation, of the emperor's grace and best wishes. The emperor rejected Eberhard's offer of financial indemnification, because "it is not our custom to accept money from anyone against whom we harbor hatred in our mind"; but he was prepared to receive the archbishop and to discuss with him the problems of the Church and Reich.

Frederick had serious reasons to be angry with Eberhard: his contumacious disregard of the emperor's commands to attend him in the field and at court; his refusal to provide Frederick with the military service and, above all, the counsel he was obliged as a vassal to offer; and his recognition of Alexander and his public advocacy of the pope's cause, though, it should be noted, this point was never explicitly stated in the imperial correspondence. Eberhard's most egregious offense was, however, his refusal to meet in person with the excommunicate monarch, an intolerable affront to the emperor's honor. In modern parlance, the archbishop was publicly snubbing the emperor. That was the reason Frederick was so insistent that the archbishop had to meet with him and could not atone for his non-appearance with money. Eberhard understood the situation perfectly. In a letter to Abbot Godfrey of Admont in January 1162, the archbishop likened Frederick's letter to peals of thunder.

The archbishop asked Bishop Eberhard of Bamberg and the chancellor, Ulrich of Dürrmenz, to intercede for him—unlike the Italian communes, Eberhard of Salzburg could count on powerful friends to act on his behalf at the court. In fact, the chancellor referred in his letter to Eberhard of Salzburg to the *familiaritas*, a word that could mean acquaintanceship and/or possibly kinship, which existed between them. Eberhard of Bamberg and the chancellor Ulrich reported to him in January 1162 that they had succeeded in calming Frederick's wrath; but it was essential that Eberhard of Salzburg come in person, along with Hartmann of Brixen and Roman of Gurk. His presence, the bishop of Bamberg assured the archbishop, would extinguish any remaining sparks of Frederick's anger; and Ulrich warned Eberhard not to make any more excuses about his physical infirmities. He was to fear no compulsion, that is, no pressure to recognize Alexander, and would be free to depart after he had a "private conversation" with the emperor. The archbishop then wrote to Abbot Godfrey, whom he asked to join him, that the emperor had granted them a safe conduct.

Eberhard of Salzburg, accompanied by Hartmann, Roman, and Provost Gerhoch of Reichersberg, refused on his way to the imperial court to meet with Victor IV at Cremona. The anti-pope sent two of his cardinals ahead of Eberhard to stir up Frederick's anger against the elderly monk, but without success. The archbishop arrived in Pavia in March, after the fall of Milan, and was well received by Frederick. The two Victorine cardinals, twelve bishops, and many other princes attended Eberhard's less than private conversation with the emperor. The archbishop proclaimed, when he was sharply questioned, his allegiance to Alexander and said only a few words to the schismatic cardinals; but Frederick did not object. Eberhard's mere presence had satisfied Frederick's slighted honor. The archbishop stayed long enough at the court to participate in Frederick's celebration of Easter on 8 April. For his part, to demonstrate his renewed favor, the emperor issued charters for both Reichersberg and Gurk, an archiepiscopal proprietary bishopric. (Gurk's legal status was unique in twelfth-century Christendom.)

For the remainder of his life, Eberhard succeeded in balancing his competing loyalties. Frederick did not invite the archbishop to participate in the council at St. Jean-de-Losne, where he hoped to obtain Louis VII's recognition of Victor IV; and on 28 February 1163 Alexander named Eberhard, the only one of the six German archbishops who recognized him at the time as pope, as the papal legate in the German kingdom. In spite of his pro-Alexandrine stance, Frederick received the archbishop and Hartmann in an honorable manner at the court in Mainz at the end of March 1163 and permitted the pair to depart in peace. As the papal legate, the archbishop may have been trying to resolve the schism in Alexander's favor. Frederick overlooked the archbishop's stance in the schism and charged Eberhard, assisted by Hartmann, Roman, and possibly also Frederick's cousin, Ottokar III of Styria, in the spring of 1164, with the settlement of a dispute between the emperor's two Babenberg uncles, Henry Jasomirgott and Conrad of Passau. Somewhat earlier, the emperor, in response to the formation of the Veronese League, had summoned Eberhard to come by Pentecost, 31 May 1164, to Treviso "with as many men as you are able to bring," because the emperor required both his counsel and his aid in a campaign against the rebellious cities of Padua and Vicenza. We do not know how Frederick expected Eberhard to be simultaneously in Austria and Venetia or how the archbishop would have responded to the emperor's latest demand for military service, but death freed Eberhard from his dilemma on 22 June 1164.[26]

We can only speculate why the emperor treated Eberhard of Salzburg, in spite of his contumacy, differently than he did the Italian communes; and, even more significantly, Eberhard's successors, Archbishops Conrad II and Adalbert II, who were, after all, Frederick's uncle and cousin. Surely, their kinship with the emperor trumped Eberhard's court connections. Perhaps Frederick did respect Eberhard, whose "piety, knowledge, and character" Alexander singled out in the announcement of the archbishop's appointment as the German legate. It is also possible that the emperor saw little advantage in fighting an elderly prelate who was likely to die fairly soon in any case and/or that Frederick felt magnanimous after the defeat of Milan, especially if he also believed that the universal recognition of Victor was now a foregone conclusion. The emperor's diplomatic defeat at St. Jean-de-Losne in September 1162 destroyed that illusion, and he resorted to harsher tactics, even in Germany, in the vain hope of imposing his anti-pope on the Church. In the end Salzburg, too, burned.

A Change in Plans

Vincent of Prague reported that all of Italy trembled after the destruction of Milan and that Frederick was planning an assault on Sicily from Apulia. One of the terms of Brescia's capitulation on 22 April 1162 was that the Brescians would participate in a campaign directed toward Rome, Apulia, or wherever the emperor commanded. Pisan and Genoese naval support was essential for such an undertaking. In 1158 both cities had blocked Frederick's attempt to assert imperial jurisdiction over Sardinia and Corsica, but the emperor had ignored the disobedience of normally pro-imperial Pisa.

At the beginning of 1162 the burghers of Pisa had prevented their pro-Alexandrine archbishop from providing the pope with refuge in their city. After lengthy negotiations, on 6 April Frederick enfeoffed the consuls and envoys of Pisa with all the properties and rights it had obtained from the Reich during the preceding thirty years or would acquire in the future, both in the city of Pisa and, on the mainland and on the islands, in its *districtus* (the area where it exercised coercive power), whose boundaries were carefully delineated. Pisan merchants were freed from all tolls and other levies in the Empire and, significantly, also in Sicily, Calabria, and Apulia, whose conquest Frederick anticipated. He granted Pisa in fief the Tyrrhenian coastline from Civitavecchia, northwest of Rome, to Portovenere, north of Pisa, with port and commercial rights, as well as half of the cities of Palermo, Messina, Salerno, and Naples in the Norman kingdom, along with half of their *districti* and half of the revenue collected in these cities and their hinterlands. Frederick also assigned to the Pisans a third of William I's treasure. Not a word was said, however, about Pisa's claims to Sardinia. In exchange, the Pisans committed themselves to a war against the Sicilian king, which was to commence on 1 September 1162; and the consuls duly commissioned in the spring the building of forty galleys. Frederick promised to place under the imperial ban anyone who injured the Pisans while they were in the Empire's service and not to restore the malefactors to his grace until they had made proper satisfaction to Pisa.

Unlike Pisa, Frederick had nearly gone to war with Genoa in 1158; and the city had provided Alexander with refuge after his flight from Rome. The Genoese, realizing that they were dangerously isolated after the defeat of Milan, opened negotiations with Frederick in April 1162 and reached an agreement, similar to Pisa's, on 9 June. He enfeoffed Genoa with the coastline, adjoining Pisa's grant, between Portovenere to the southeast of Genoa and Monaco to the west, excluding the rights of the margraves and counts in the region, and with all the possessions and rights Genoa had or would hold in Italy and abroad. Frederick recognized the citizens' right to select their own consuls. He gave the Genoese the city of Syracuse on the island of Sicily, a quarter of William I's treasure, except for his jewels, and in every port city, their own street, church, bath, and warehouse. Genoese merchants in the former Norman kingdom were to enjoy extraterritoriality. The city's consuls were authorized to expel rival Provençal and French merchants from Sicily and from the coastlines of Apulia and Calabria. Nothing was said, however, about Genoa's continued adherence to Alexander. As was true in the case of Archbishop Eberhard of Salzburg, Frederick overlooked Genoa's repudiation of his anti-pope Victor IV because it was politically expedient.

It is a testimony to Frederick's overwhelming power in the spring of 1162 that he could bind the two maritime arch-rivals to a joint campaign. Within days of the conclusion of the 9 June accord, hostilities broke out between the two cities because of a Pisan attack on Genoese merchants in Constantinople and their rival claims to Sardinia and Corsica. At the beginning of July Frederick sent Rainald of Dassel to make peace, and the archbishop arranged for a hearing of the dispute at the imperial court in Turin in August. The Genoese arrived four or five days before the Pisans and were able to win the princes' backing, in part by a judicious expenditure of money. Since Frederick was hastening to his meeting with Louis VII at St. Jean-de-Losne and did not have time to settle the conflict, he postponed a decision until his return to Italy and imposed a truce in the meantime on the rivals. The Pisans felt betrayed and by October had allied with William I.

Frederick's abandonment of the Sicilian campaign in the summer of 1162 has often been blamed on the outbreak of the fighting between Genoa and Pisa, but while Brescia had agreed on 22 April to participate in the invasion of Apulia, there was no such clause in Piacenza's capitulation on 11 May. Moreover, the emperor's convention with Genoa included the proviso that the campaign against Sicily might be postponed until May 1163 or even a later year. In part, William's suppression of the latest rebellion against Hauteville rule had made an invasion of his realm more difficult, but the real explanation for the postponement of the attack on the Norman kingdom is that in May Frederick had decided not to hold a council in Rome, as he had previously planned, but rather to detach Louis VII from Alexander at a council on the imperial–French border. The emperor could hardly be in Burgundy on 29 August 1162 and in Apulia on 1 September.[27] Frederick's second Italian campaign had seemingly been a success.

CHAPTER TWELVE

IN PURSUIT OF ALEXANDER

St. Jean-de-Losne

FREDERICK LEFT ITALY IN late August 1162 confident after his victory that he would be able to persuade Louis VII at St. Jean-de-Losne, on the border between their realms in Burgundy, to recognize Victor IV as the rightful pontiff. The aborted meeting turned, instead, into a major diplomatic defeat; and Frederick spent the next five years shuttling back and forth between Germany and Italy in a fruitless pursuit of Alexander III, by both military and diplomatic means, that ended with the annihilation of his army.

We do not know for certain which monarch initiated the negotiations and the chronology of the events preceding and during the meeting at St. Jean. Helmold of Bosau and Abbot Nicholas of Siegburg's contradictory accounts in the *Slavic Chronicle* and the *Cologne Royal Chronicle*, respectively, illustrate why it is hard to reconstruct what really happened. According to Helmold, after the conquest and destruction of Milan, Frederick, "his heart raised high with pride," summoned Louis, as well as the kings of Denmark, Hungary, and Bohemia, all the archbishops, bishops, the highest potentates of his realm and the regular clergy to an assembly at St. Jean to restore the unity of the Church. Louis hesitated to come when he learned that Frederick was approaching with a large army, but the French king arrived, nevertheless, on the appointed day and stood on the bridge across the Saône between 8 a.m. and 3 p.m. Frederick did not appear, and Louis washed his hands in the river as a sign that he had honored his sworn word and left the same day for Dijon. The emperor arrived during the night and dispatched distinguished men to recall the king, but Louis, happy that he had both fulfilled his obligations and escaped Frederick's stratagem, refused to return.

Nicholas of Siegburg, probably relying on information that stems from Burchard of Cologne and ultimately Rainald of Dassel, related a very different story. Louis, wishing to re-establish the peace and unity of the Church, sent envoys, most notably Count Henry of Troyes, to the emperor requesting that he summon a general synod and bring Victor IV with him; whereas Louis swore that Pope Alexander would accompany him so that by the judgment of the Church justice would be done to both claimants. Frederick concurred, and even built a palace nearby to house his entourage. The emperor, accompanied by Victor and a great multitude of archbishops, bishops, abbots, dukes, and princes, arrived at the site on 29 August; but when Louis approached the other bank of the river, the Cistercians persuaded him to leave for Dijon. It should be obvious that these two narratives are nearly irreconcilable. To complicate matters further, the authors of the most detailed accounts, Cardinal Boso and Hugh of Poitiers, a monk of Vézelay, were both pro-Alexandrine and sought to exonerate Louis by portraying him, in Boso's words, as "a pious man but having the simplicity of a dove," who was deceived by the cunning Frederick and the duplicitous Count Henry.[1]

Boso and Hugh were trying to answer the central question posed by the incident: why was Louis, who had recognized Cardinal Roland as Pope Alexander in 1160, suddenly willing in 1162 to reopen the discussion? Shortly after Alexander left Genoa on 25 March 1162, Frederick had written to Louis' chancellor, Bishop Hugh of Soissons, that he had learned from reliable sources that Roland had sailed for France to gain adherents and to raise money to pay his debts. Frederick warned Hugh not to receive the former papal chancellor, who was an enemy of the Reich, his pseudo-cardinals, or any of his envoys, lest great, almost inextinguishable hatred arise between the Empire and France. Louis may have interpreted this admonition as a threat that Frederick would attack him in conjunction with Henry II because, Burchard of Cologne informed Nicholas of Siegburg, Henry's envoys had been at the imperial court in December 1161 to strengthen the compact between their masters, and because more important English ambassadors were expected shortly. In addition, Count Ramón Berenguer III of Provence, whose uncle Ramón Berenguer IV of Barcelona had allied with Henry II to fight Louis' brother-in-law, Count Raymond V of Toulouse, had married Frederick's cousin in 1161.[2] Louis may thus have feared that he was about to be encircled by a hostile coalition.

The French monarch sent Count Henry I of Troyes, whose sister Adèle had married Louis in 1160, to Frederick in Lombardy. Hugh of Poitiers said that Louis selected his brother-in-law for this mission because he was a distant kinsman of both the emperor and Victor and thus pro-imperial. The count had a personal interest, too, in preventing an alliance between Frederick and Henry II, because their domains surrounded the lands of his own dynasty, the house of Blois-Champagne, which had opposed the Plantagenets' accession to the English throne. (King Stephen, who had fought Henry II's mother, was the count's uncle.) While Louis initiated the negotiations with Frederick, it was the emperor's menacing letter to the French chancellor that triggered Louis' actions.

After receiving Frederick's message, Louis, heeding the emperor's warning to Hugh of Soissons, sent envoys to Alexander in Montpellier to inform him that his cardinals were not welcome at the French court. The pope treated the French ambassadors rudely, so badly in fact that the irate Louis regretted, according to Hugh of Poitiers, that he had recognized Alexander as the pontiff instead of Victor.

Louis authorized Count Henry, via Bishop Manasses of Orléans in supplementary oral and written instructions, to negotiate a formal agreement with Frederick. Since Piacenza's submission to the emperor on 11 May 1162, unlike Brescia's on 22 April, no longer included the specific obligation to participate in the Sicilian campaign in September, the tentative plan for a royal conclave north of the Alps in late summer may have been in place by mid-May. On 31 May Frederick wrote to his beloved kinsman Louis that he had received with an attentive ear his letters and envoy. He was delighted that "the brightness of genuine love" had replaced "the cloud of rancor," which had existed "between relatives and related realms," and that a "treaty of friendship" would bind them in unbreakable love. He had arranged with his "beloved kinsman" and Louis' vassal, Count Henry of Troyes, "whatever was necessary to maintain the integrity of their mutual love"; and he would see to it that their agreement was inviolably observed. Frederick did not spell out the specific terms of the accord, but presumably the count and the emperor's own envoys supplied Louis with the particulars.[3]

The terms of the agreement can be pieced together from the reports of the chroniclers and Frederick's own letters. The two monarchs agreed to meet on 29 August 1162 at St. Jean-de-Losne to resolve the schism at a general council of the Church. Both would bring their pope to the assembly and would abide by the decision of a board of arbitration, composed of ten high-ranking churchmen chosen by Louis and Frederick. If either Alexander or Victor refused to attend, the other would be recognized as the rightful pontiff. Count Henry guaranteed that his sovereign would abide by the accord by pledging to receive his French fiefs from the emperor if Louis did not comply. Hugh of Poitiers insisted that Louis did not know all the terms of the agreement until he arrived at Dijon, but it seems highly implausible that Count Henry would or could have kept his brother-in-law in the dark for nearly three months. If Henry did, Louis was not merely "simple" but downright stupid.

For his part, Frederick informed the pro-Victorine bishops of the Empire in a circular sent in May—Archbishop Eberhard of Salzburg did not receive an invitation—and his brother-in-law, Duke Matthew of Upper Lorraine, that he and his beloved kinsman, the king of France, had agreed to end the schism at a general council of the churchmen and magnates of both their realms, which was to be held on 29 August on the River Saône in the diocese of Besançon. At the council Louis, the entire French Church, and all the French princes would accept Victor as the rightful pope, as had been arranged by binding sworn guarantees. Frederick's summons hardly sounds as if he was waiting for the decision of impartial arbiters, but since Alexander had always insisted that he would not submit to the judgment of a council, the foregone conclusion was that he would not appear at St. Jean and that Victor would prevail by default. The ecclesiastical and lay princes were ordered to assemble four days earlier in Besançon, and, as a precaution, to come with their fully armed knights, and to bring their tents since housing was scarce at the appointed site. For his own accommodations, according to Hugh of Poitiers and the *Cologne Royal Chronicle*, Frederick commissioned the construction of a palace of remarkable size at Dôle on the Doubs, downstream from Besançon. In the summons sent to Archbishop Eraclius of Lyons, Frederick indicated that Count Henry had honored Victor as the rightful pope during his stay in Pavia and that the emperor would stop in Lyons on his way to the council.[4]

Since most French churchmen adhered to Alexander and since it was imperative to keep the pope in the dark as long as possible about the change in royal ecclesiastical policy, Louis apparently concealed the accord from his own entourage until July. (Did the French king, to exonerate himself, spread the story of Count Henry's deception after the agreement became known?) Louis' brother, Archbishop Henry of Reims, learned from an unnamed third party in July about Frederick's circular, which he inserted in his letter to the king, and he rebuked Louis in the strongest language for entering into such an arrangement. The source of the archbishop's information may have been Eberhard of Salzburg. The latter kept a copy of Frederick's summons in his letter collection and he had asked Archbishop Henry in June or July about the state of the Church in France and England, because rumors were circulating that the French clergy was on the verge of abandoning Alexander. Henry assured his colleague in Salzburg in July or

August that the French Church was committed unto death to Alexander and that his royal brother had averred he would rather have his head cut off than switch allegiances. Alexander was still unaware, on 10 July, of Louis' secret understanding but had learned about it, perhaps from Archbishop Henry, by 23 or 24 July, when Alexander asked Bishop Hugh of Soissons to dissuade Louis. The pope and the king met north of Clermont on 22 or 23 August. As expected, Alexander refused to accompany Louis to St. Jean because as pope he could not be judged. In a compromise, he agreed instead to send five cardinals to prove the legitimacy of his election. The pontiff then withdrew to the monastery of Déols in the diocese of Bourges and, more significantly, within Henry II's sphere of power. Louis was caught between the French Church that was adamant in its opposition to Cardinal Octavian (Victor IV) and an approaching, victorious imperial army.[5]

What actually happened at St. Jean is, given the contradictory and partisan sources, a matter of scholarly conjecture. The following is a plausible scenario, but the events could have played themselves out quite differently. Louis appeared on the bridge on 29 August 1162, without Alexander, and waited from 8 a.m. to 3 p.m. for Frederick, who arrived only late at night with Victor in tow. Why Frederick was late for his all-important rendezvous with Louis is one of the minor mysteries of the story, but as recently as 21 August the emperor had still been in Turin, on the other side of the Alps. Theoretically, Louis should have recognized Victor as pope because Alexander was absent. Frederick was desperate to salvage something from the meeting, and Louis managed to procure a three-week postponement so that he could make one more attempt to produce his pope. As surety, the king offered himself as a captive to Frederick if he did not execute his promise to bring Alexander to St. Jean. In addition, Hugh of Poitiers said, the duke of Burgundy and the counts of Flanders and Nevers served as hostages and guarantors on the king's behalf. Nevertheless, Louis was unable to persuade Alexander to come, if he tried at all; and so the penalty for the king's non-compliance went into effect: Frederick enfeoffed Henry of Troyes with the count's French fiefs. Louis was able to break his agreement with Frederick because Alexander had obtained during the three-week grace period Henry II's commitment to come to the military assistance of his feudal overlord if Frederick attacked Louis. What had started as a potential alliance between Frederick and Henry against Louis turned, thanks to the pope's skilled diplomacy, into a coalition between Henry and Louis against Frederick.

Another factor may also have been behind the collapse of the negotiations: Frederick may have been facing potentially dangerous opposition to his policies in Germany. As we have already seen, Duke Berthold IV of Zähringen, angry over Frederick's rejection, in June 1161, of the candidacy of the duke's brother for the archbishopric of Mainz, had written to Louis sometime before the meeting at St. Jean. In his letter Berthold wrote that he and other disgruntled German princes were prepared to aid Louis if the emperor, "a destroyer of churches and laws," carried out his threats against Louis—a reference to Frederick's letter of March or April to Bishop Hugh of Soissons?[6] Nothing came of Berthold's offer, but Frederick's position in Germany was less secure than it seemed.

The emperor must have sensed pretty quickly that he was losing the game. St. Jean-de-Losne was not equipped to supply food to a large gathering of princes for several weeks. According to Boso, a loaf of bread of average size cost a silver mark. It was urgent, therefore, to bring the assembly to a conclusion. Before opening the council on 7 September, that is, before the expiration of the three-week delay Frederick had granted Louis, the emperor sent Rainald to the French king. According to both Boso and Hugh of Poitiers, Rainald declared to Louis that the right to decide a disputed papal election was the exclusive prerogative of the emperor as the defender of the Church and of his bishops. Boso said that the French king responded with the mocking question: since Christ had committed His sheep to Peter and his successors, "are the Bishops of my Kingdom not of the sheep which the Son of God entrusted to Peter?" The query, whether or not Louis really posed it, revealed the central fallacy in Rainald's argument: the pope was not an imperial bishop but the head of the universal Church, while the emperor, unlike his Ottonian and Salian predecessors, no longer had either the power or the prestige to dictate the fate of the papacy in the era following the Investiture Conflict. Louis declared, Hugh added, that by his non-appearance the emperor had broken the agreement Count Henry had brokered, and the French king then rode off.[7]

Rebuffed in this dramatic fashion, Frederick and Rainald tried to salvage what they could. The anonymous and pro-Alexandrine Danish chronicler, Saxo Grammaticus (died c. 1220), the chief source for the events of 7 September 1162, indicated that Victor opened the synod by arguing that he was the legitimate pope because he had been selected in the proper fashion and that, unlike Alexander, he had submitted his case to the judgment of a general council. Then Frederick declared, in a brief speech, that he had invited "the kings of provinces" ("provinciarum reges") to attend the council, so as not to ignore their views completely. Ultimately, it was, however, the exclusive prerogative of the emperor to decide a disputed papal election because Rome was situated in the Empire; and the other kings lacked jurisdiction over a bishop in a foreign realm. Frederick's argument was the logical conclusion of his contention that the pope, like any other bishop in the Empire, held the regalia in fief from the emperor. In a curious way, Frederick's argument—assuming he made it—undercut the imperial claim to world lordship. That is, if the pope was only the bishop of Rome whose jurisdiction was limited to his Italian ecclesiastical province, and not the universal pontiff, then Frederick's authority as the advocate and defender of the Roman Church was likewise curtailed, and the emperor was reduced to the same status as the other European monarchs, "a king in his own empire."[8]

In his concluding address to the council Rainald asserted, according to the Danish historian, that it was presumptuous for the "provincial kings" to call the emperor's justice into question, because they would regard it as a grave violation of their own prerogatives if the emperor intervened in a disputed episcopal election in a see situated in their realms, as they were trying to do in the case of Rome. To make sure that all the attendees understood his words, Rainald delivered his speech first in Latin and then in French and German. Not surprisingly, Victor was once again judged to be the rightful pope and Alexander was condemned. Frederick had reverted to his original policy of imposing his pope on the Church by his own authority.[9]

It is tempting to dismiss the denigrating designation of the other European monarchs as "provincial kings" as the invention of the hostile Danish chronicler, who wrote around 1200; but the imperial notary, Burchard of Cologne, in the letter that he sent to Abbot Nicholas of Siegburg at the turn of the year 1161/62, wrote that "all the kinglets ('reguli') had dared to recognize" Cardinal Roland "as pope more out of fear and hatred of the emperor than at the prompting of justice." Such linguistic assertions of imperial superiority flourished in the circles around the archbishop-elect of Cologne. Like the "Emperor Hymn," which hailed Frederick as "Lord of the World" after the defeat of Milan, the disparaging words about the other European monarchs are often cited as evidence that the Staufer, at the zenith of Frederick's power, claimed world dominion. In light of the emperor's failure to procure Louis' recognition of Victor, the words sound like empty bluster, the temper tantrum of a spoiled child who did not get his way.[10]

Helmold of Bosau, writing a few years later, concluded his brief account of the abortive council at St. Jean-de-Losne with the words: ". . . the shrewder French secured by cleverness what seemed to be unattainable by military might. From this time on, Pope Alexander gained ever greater influence." It was a damning indictment of Frederick and Rainald's failed diplomacy.[11]

Even Frederick's one apparent success at St. Jean proved fleeting. Valdemar I, the only other monarch who attended the council, finally paid homage to Frederick for the kingdom of Denmark on 7 September, as his envoys had promised at Augsburg in June 1158. However, in 1182, after Frederick's prestige had been greatly diminished by his submission to Alexander at Venice in 1177 and by his inability to protect Henry the Lion from his princely enemies in 1180, Valdemar's son and successor, Knut VI (r. 1182–1202), refused to become Frederick's vassal. According to Saxo Grammaticus, whose chronicle was a celebration of Denmark's emancipation from imperial suzerainty, Archbishop Absalon of Lund informed Frederick's envoy that Knut had the same right to govern his own kingdom as the emperor had to rule the Roman Empire.[12] Frederick and Rainald's argument at St. Jean-de-Losne had been turned against them. The *reguli* were the emperor's equals.

After 1162 Alexander III made several overtures to Frederick. Already on 18 September the pope had invited Eberhard of Salzburg or his representative to visit him and authorized the archbishop, if he could, to call upon the emperor and to seek to recall him to the unity of the Church; Eberhard and Bishop Hartmann of Brixen may have attended the imperial assembly in Mainz in April 1163 for that purpose. At the Council of Tours on 19 May 1163, Alexander repeated the excommunication of Victor IV and his adherents but did not explicitly include Frederick in the condemnation. A papal embassy visited the imperial court in Nuremberg in August 1163 to assure him that there was no papal anti-imperial conspiracy, but Frederick refused to receive Alexander's cardinals, but he met with the other envoys. They agreed to select two neutral churchmen, who in turn would empanel a seven-member board of arbitration to resolve the schism. Nothing more came of this scheme. Frederick could not pursue such potential openings without conceding, with an immense loss of imperial and personal prestige, that the position he had staked out at Pavia in 1160, at Lodi in 1161, and at St. Jean-de-Losne in 1162 was wrong.[13]

The Punishment of Mainz

Frederick's major accomplishment during his brief stay in Germany between October 1162 and his return to Italy a year later was the punishment of Mainz for the murder of Archbishop Arnold on 24 June 1160. Frederick had elevated Arnold of Selenhofen, a Mainz ministerial who had been his first chancellor, to the chair of St. Boniface after the deposition of Archbishop Henry in 1153. Arnold's policy of regaining his see's alienated lands, as well as his humble origins and cantankerous personality, had aroused the opposition of the Rhenish nobles. Frederick had sentenced Hermann of Stahleck and Arnold, at the Christmas court in 1155, to the peculiar punishment of carrying dogs for disturbing the peace.

The cause of the conflict after 1155 was Arnold's imposition of a tax on the ministerials and the burghers of Mainz who did not participate in Frederick's second Italian campaign and their refusal to pay the levy. During the first siege of Milan in 1158, the princes ruled, in response to Arnold's suit, that the penalty for non-compliance was forfeiture of the recalcitrant vassal's fief. In Arnold's absence, the Meingote, the Selenhofer's ministerial rivals within the city, led an uprising against the archbishop, who had to fight his way into Mainz on his return. He exiled several of the rebels, who went to Italy to plead their case. Frederick ordered Arnold to restore them to his grace after they had provided him with suitable satisfaction. When Arnold refused to accept their proposed compensation, a mob desecrated the cathedral and plundered the archiepiscopal palace. On 1 November 1159 the archbishop excommunicated the leaders of the uprising and imposed the interdict on Mainz. He returned to Italy, and Frederick, who needed Arnold's support after the outbreak of the schism, received him with the greatest honors in the imperial camp outside Crema. Mainz was condemned, and Frederick ordered the burghers to make restitution for the damage they had caused.

Arnold, escorted by imperial envoys, arrived outside Mainz around 1 April 1160, and waited for the inhabitants to submit. Some did, but some of his exiled opponents returned to the city and the rebellion revived. Arnold appealed to the princes for military assistance and assembled forces from the archiepiscopal domains. The city notified Arnold that it was ready to surrender, and on 23 June the archbishop, minus most of his entourage, took up residence in the monastery of St. James on a hill overlooking the city to await Mainz's ritual submission. Negotiations broke down the next day, but Arnold, who had been assured by Abbot Godfrey of his safety, remained in the abbey. The citizens, under the leadership of the Meingote, broke into the courtyard on 24 June and set the monastery on fire. A knight discovered Arnold, who was hiding, and killed him with a blow of his sword to the temple. The body was hacked to pieces.

As emperor, Frederick was obligated to punish such an egregious violation of the peace. He stayed in Mainz from at least 31 March to 18 April 1163. The leaders of the uprising and Arnold's murderers had absconded. At the court held on 7 April the guilty were exiled in perpetuity, their property confiscated, and their houses demolished, but only one burgher was executed. Abbot Godfrey was deprived of his office and banished, and the monastic community of St. James was dissolved. The walls and towers of the city were razed and the moat was filled in. The city's privileges were voided, and Mainz was deprived of its legal status. It was a harsh punishment but less severe than the penalties imposed on Tortona, Spoleto, or Milan. Strangely, most of Arnold's clerical and ministerial opponents were quickly restored to the emperor's grace. Frederick may have concluded, in spite of his obligation to avenge the murder of an archbishop, that the troublesome Arnold had been a bad choice; and the weakening of the archbishop's secular authority permitted Frederick to expand the imperial domain at Mainz's expense.[14]

The Third Italian Campaign

At the conclusion of the Council of St. Jean-de-Losne in September 1162, Frederick had sent Rainald back to Italy to govern the peninsula in his absence. Rainald, who as the archbishop-elect of Cologne was also the arch-chancellor of Italy, visited the cities of Lombardy, the mark of Ancona, Tuscany, and the Romagna. According to Acerbus Morena, Rainald, through his extraordinary exertions, made all the cities of the mark and Tuscany love and obey the emperor; and, to honor Pope Victor, he replaced bishops who adhered to Alexander. At the end of the year, Bishop Hermann of Verden joined Rainald. Frederick charged Hermann with hearing and deciding in his place all legal cases, both original suits and appeals. The emperor borrowed from the papacy the use of such legates, and Rainald's successor, Christian of Buch, was the first to style himself the "legate of all of Italy."[15]

Frederick and Beatrice followed in October 1163. Ostensibly, the purpose of the third Italian campaign was to launch the delayed attack on the Norman kingdom, but it is hard to believe that this was ever a serious objective because the emperor brought with him only minimal forces from Germany. The imperial couple entered Lodi on 28 October. Allegedly, they were accompanied by many princes, but the only individuals Acerbus Morena named who had crossed the Alps with Frederick were the three Wittelsbach brothers and his cousin Welf VII. All the other Germans whom Acerbus mentioned were already in Italy in various administrative capacities. Victor joined Frederick in Lodi on 2 November, and on 4 November the anti-pope, the emperor, Patriarch Ulrich of Aquileia, Abbot Hugh of Cluny, and other unnamed archbishops and bishops carried the relics of St. Bassianus on their shoulders from Old to New Lodi. Frederick gave £30 and the empress £5 toward the construction of the new cathedral in Lodi.[16] The level of princely opposition to Frederick's policies may not have been as intense as Berthold of Zähringen's letter to Louis VII might suggest, but there was no enthusiasm in Germany for further Italian adventures.

The invasion of Sicily was dependent upon ships supplied by Genoa and Pisa. After the defeat of Milan, Frederick had succeeded in winning both cities for the undertaking, with promises of territorial concessions and commercial privileges in the *Regno*. Even before he had left Italy in August 1162, the plan had been endangered by Genoa and Pisa's rival claims to Sardinia. The legal status of Sardinia was, even by medieval standards, a muddle. In Late Antiquity the island had been divided into four provinces, among them Arborea, which had evolved into autonomous sub-kingdoms ruled by judges. Nominally, the pope was the feudal overlord of Sardinia, but Pisa dominated three of the "judgeships," while Genoa controlled Arborea. In 1133 Innocent II had placed the Sardinian bishoprics under the archbishop of Pisa and the three Corsican dioceses under Genoa. To complicate matters further, Frederick had granted the principality of Sardinia to his uncle Welf VI in 1152; but he had done nothing to assert imperial suzerainty.

In late February 1164 Genoese consuls met Frederick at Fano on the Adriatic coast and enquired whether he was planning to attack William of Sicily; in 1162, according to the *Genoese Annals*, they had been obligated against their will to join the campaign within a year after the emperor announced it. Frederick responded, incredibly, that he could not answer them because the German and Lombard princes were not present to advise him. It is hard to imagine that Frederick was really so dependent upon the princes' counsel. Perhaps it was a convenient way to avoid replying to an embarrassing question. He told the Genoese to attend him in mid-Lent in Parma, where he was from 13 March to 17 April; but there, too, nothing definite was decided. The Sicilian expedition was dead.

In the meantime another Genoese embassy and a Sardinian bishop arrived in Parma on behalf of the judge, Bareso of Arborea. He requested that Frederick grant him the entire island of Sardinia in fief as his kingdom in return for 4,000 marks of silver. Frederick agreed. On 3 August 1164 Frederick, wearing his own crown, invested Bareso with the kingdom and crowned him in the church of S. Siro in Pavia with a diadem that had been made in Genoa. Bishop Henry of Liège consecrated Bareso, who swore fealty to the emperor. The Pisans who were present objected to the proceedings because Bareso was, they claimed, their vassal and Sardinia belonged to Pisa. The Genoese countered that the Pisans were, in fact, Bareso's vassals and that Sardinia was theirs. Finally, Frederick asserted that Sardinia was part of the Empire and that he was entitled, in the judgment of his court, to bestow the island on Bareso. The irate Pisans departed. At Bareso's request, Frederick ordered a notary to prepare a charter about the king's enfeoffment with Sardinia—it does not survive—but Bareso was unable to pay the 4,000 marks he owed Frederick. The Genoese lent Bareso the money, and he was able to discharge his obligation; but he was then detained in Genoa as an insolvent debtor.

Yet eight months after Bareso's coronation, on 17 April 1165, while in Frankfurt and in the presence of Genoese envoys, Frederick enfeoffed a Pisan consul with Sardinia on behalf of his commune, including all the rights that pertained to it, and he revoked any prior grant to another city or to Duke Welf VI. Frederick's chancellor, Christian of Buch, had already invested Pisa with Sardinia in exchange for the enormous sum of £13,000. There are several possible explanations for Frederick's sudden reversal of policy in regard to Sardinia and the two maritime cities: the unreliability of Bareso, who had run out of funds and was clearly a Genoese puppet; the simple fact that Pisa outbid Genoa; and that Christian and Rainald, who inclined toward Pisa, were now Frederick's principal advisers, having replaced the pro-Genoese Conrad of Mainz, who had left the court after Bareso's coronation.[17]

If Frederick did have any real plans to invade Sicily in 1164, mounting resentment about imperial misrule and rebellion in the mark of Verona made it impossible to do so. The Milanese Anonymous, admittedly an extremely hostile source, paints a picture of oppression and corruption. After the surrender of Milan, its inhabitants had been resettled in four separate communities (*borghi*) under the lordship of Bishop Henry of Liège. When he left Italy with Frederick in August 1162, Henry had placed in charge of these *borghi* an otherwise unidentified Peter of Cumino, who found numerous ways to oppress the population and enrich himself. For example, Peter acquired for himself the property of every person who died without a son. Around 1 September 1163 Bishop Henry, who had heard about Peter's misconduct, removed him and installed in his place the cleric Frederick, nicknamed the Schoolmaster, but who proved to be even greedier and more unbending than Peter—or so the Milanese Anonymous said.

On 3 December 1163, while Frederick was passing through Milanese territory, the men and women of one of the *borghi* prostrated themselves before him in the mud and pouring rain and pleaded for mercy. He continued on his way, but he delegated to Rainald the hearing of the

Milanese complaints. Rainald agreed to the release of the remaining hostages and summoned twelve representatives from each of the four *borghi* to come to him. When he asked the Milanese how much they would give the emperor voluntarily, they pleaded poverty. He commanded them with threatening words to pay £880 in the new imperial coinage by 26 January 1164, and they did. (After the abolition of the Milanese mint in 1162, Frederick had introduced a new imperial penny with a greater silver content than the local issues. It became the preferred super-territorial coin in northern Italy for the remainder of the century and was generally used in payments to the crown.)[18]

After Verona had tried to block Frederick's return to Germany in 1155, a pro-imperial regime had been established there. During his passage through Veronese territory in October 1163, at the start of the third campaign, Frederick had enfeoffed Otto of Wittelsbach with the castle of Garda near Verona. Otto's exactions were, according to Acerbus Morena, the cause of the rebellion in the mark of Verona. The rebels swore, Boso reported, not to give the emperor more than his predecessors had received. The Milanese Anonymous placed the beginning of the conspiracy against imperial rule during the winter of 1163–64. The revolt may have been limited, initially, to Padua and Vicenza—Frederick mentioned only these two cities when in early 1164 he commanded Archbishop Eberhard of Salzburg to bring troops to Italy—but the emperor's privilege for Ferrara of 24 May also have included Venice and Verona among the rebel cities.

Venice, bankrolled by Constantinople, financed the uprising. A Venetian source indicated that Doge Vitale II Michiel, whom the chronicler identified as a friend of Manuel I and William I of Sicily, distributed 12,000 marks among the cities. Moreover, Venice gave refuge to Cardinal Hildebrand Crassus, who was the pope's sole representative in northern Italy in the early 1160s, and to exiled, pro-Alexandrine Lombard clerics. The formation of the Veronese League in April 1164 was thus part of a larger coalition directed against Frederick.

To contain the revolt, on 24 and 27 May the emperor granted extensive privileges to Ferrara and Mantua, which controlled access from the mark of Verona to Lombardy and the Romagna, respectively. He permitted Ferrara to elect its consuls freely. Frederick conferred on Mantua the regalia, free from any annual payment; exempted it from participation in the Sicilian campaign and the war against the Veronese League; agreed not to stay in the city or bishopric of Mantua without the commune's permission while he was fighting Verona and its allies; promised to protect Mantua and its suburbs from destruction; and committed himself to the city's defense if it became involved in the fighting In return, Mantua swore not to enter into any agreement with the members of the Veronese League during the war and to renew the oath every year at the annual election of the consuls. To retain the loyalty of Treviso, situated northeast of the rebellious cities, in May Frederick expressed his regrets at the unauthorized exactions that his officials had imposed upon the inhabitants; confirmed Treviso's right to elect its own consuls; freed the city from participation in the Sicilian campaign and from the payment, for the time being, of the *fodrum*; and absolved Treviso's merchants from levies they had sworn to pay the Empire. Once again, Frederick was relying on communal rivalries and the judicious grant of privileges to encircle his enemies and to maintain his position in northern Italy.

In May 1164 Frederick also sent envoys from his traditional communal allies—Cremona, Pavia, Novara, Lodi, and Como—to Verona to negotiate and to assure the rebellious cities that he was ready to rectify any injustices they had suffered at the hands of imperial officials. After extensive discussions, the rebels agreed to meet with the emperor in Pavia; but the negotiations broke down because the cities of the mark refused to submit to the jurisdiction of an imperial *podestà*. The next month Frederick invaded the mark with a force of Lombard knights and the few Germans at his disposal, and he destroyed many castles and settlements around Verona. In spite of these apparent successes, he soon withdrew from the mark, in fear and humiliation, according to both the hostile Cardinal Boso and the pro-imperial Acerbus Morena, due to the inadequacy of his forces and because his supposed Lombard allies sympathized with the rebels. The imperial couple left Italy in October via the eastern Swiss passes because Verona blocked the Brenner route. Disappointed at the outcome of the expedition, Frederick returned to Germany intending to raise, Acerbus said, a large army. It was an inglorious end to a failed campaign.[19]

The chief reasons for Frederick's failure were the small size of his army, itself indicative of his loss of support in Germany, and the growing resentment at imperial rule in Italy, even among his communal allies. Yet personal considerations may also have been factors in the emperor's decision to withdraw from the mark of Verona in June and from Italy in October. At the end of March illness had prevented him from making a planned visit to Pisa; and in June and July he suffered from the intermittent fevers commonly associated with malaria. (Frederick may have been infected during the Second Crusade, because Wibald of Stavelot wrote some years afterwards, in 1154, that the king was incapacitated by "quartan fever.") Beatrice gave birth on 16 July 1164 in Pavia to the couple's first known child, the sickly Frederick V who was too frail to accompany his parents home in October.[20] We do not know how involved medieval husbands, and Frederick in particular, were in their wives' deliveries; but if it was a difficult pregnancy, Frederick, who at forty-one still lacked an heir, might have been inclined to terminate the Veronese campaign so he could be close to Beatrice.

Tyrannical Rule in Italy

In spite of Frederick's expressions of regret to the members of the Veronese League and to Treviso about the excessive exactions of his officials, the imperial administration became even more oppressive and corrupt during his absence from Italy between 1164 and 1166. Boso asserted that after the formation of the League, Frederick so distrusted the Italians that he appointed only Germans as imperial administrators. Boso exaggerated, and a Cremonese or Pavian would have been even more hated than a German in Milan; but most of the individuals Acerbus Morena named—they were too many, he said, to list all of them—were Germans.

After the death of Bishop Henry of Liège on 4 September 1164, shortly before Frederick's return to Germany, the emperor placed Markwart III of Grumbach in charge in Milan. Hoping to gain Markwart's sympathies, the inhabitants of the *borghi* presented him with a silver vessel worth 14 imperial pounds—to no avail. He prohibited the citizens of Milan and some of the peasants from hunting with dogs, nets, snares, or pits. Markwart delegated the collection of the annual tax on land to five Italian subordinates. In the case of land that had been under cultivation for less than twenty years, he directed that they tax mowed meadows and cut timber. To levy this tax, the officials compiled a cadastre listing all the hides, hearths, and yokes of oxen, which became known, the Milanese Anonymous noted, as the "Book of Afflictions or Sorrows." These impositions were probably a continuation of the taxes Milan had collected from the rural population in its *contado* rather than a general imperial tax that was imposed throughout imperial Italy. Markwart's Italian subordinates demanded 500 pigs, each worth six shillings, 1,000 cartloads of wood and hay, and chickens and eggs without number. When the cut timber ran out, they commanded the peasants to deliver a load of wood from each yoke of land or to pay six imperial pennies. The peasants were also required to deliver beams and boards for the construction of houses, posts for fences, and hoops for barrels, and to transport beams and stones from the ruins of Milan to build houses in Pavia. In July 1165 Markwart gave the inhabitants eighteen days to pay another £400. Those who could not do so had either to pay double the assessed amount later or had their property confiscated. When Count Henry II of Diez, a Rhinelander, succeeded Markwart as *podestà* in 1166, he collected from the inhabitants of the *borghi* a *fodrum* of £1,500. Boso even accused Frederick's agents of permitting his men to rape the Lombards' wives and daughters "without risk of punishment—a thing that is not allowed among pagans without payment of the ultimate penalty."[21]

It would be easy to dismiss the Milanese Anonymous and Boso as especially biased sources. Yet the anonymous continuer of the Morena chronicle, possibly Otto Morena himself, who wrote, admittedly, after Lodi had joined the Lombard League, was equally critical. If imperial officials had collected only what legitimately belonged to the emperor, no one, the chronicler insisted, would have objected or been hurt. Instead, Frederick's officials extorted more than sevenfold the amount that rightfully pertained to him from everyone—bishops, magnates, consuls, and nearly all Lombards, great or small, who served the emperor whether out of love or fear. The Milanese, who had to pay so much from the produce of their lands that only "a third of a third remained," were hit particularly hard. Nobles, peasants, and burghers alike paid annually three shillings from every hearth. The owner of every mill on a navigable stream was assessed 24 pennies and on a non-navigable stream three shillings. Fishermen were required to hand over a third of their catch. If a hunter killed, without the officials' authorization, an animal or bird, he had to surrender his kill, and a penalty was imposed on his property and sometimes his person, too. The emperor did not recognize the lordship rights of owners of castles, even if their ancestors had exercised those rights for 300 years. The Lombards endured, the chronicler said, many other types of oppression, which they found intolerable because they were accustomed to live well and in freedom. Yet they took no measures to defend themselves or their property, he stressed, because they awaited the emperor's return to set things right.[22] Frederick's failure to heed their complaints caused the collapse of imperial rule in Italy.

Gertrud Deibel tried to prove in the early 1930s, by compiling all references to the money Frederick collected in Italy, that while his Italian expeditions had diverted his attention from strengthening royal authority in Germany—the standard *kleindeutsch* critique of Staufer policy—the stays had at least been profitable. Rahewin indicated, presumably based on information he received from his sources in the chancery, that Frederick obtained annually £30,000 from the regalia he had reclaimed at Roncaglia. In 1185

1. Peter of Eboli, *Liber ad honorem Augusti*: Frederick drowning in the Saleph.

2 and 3. Baptismal bowl (2) and the Cappenberg head (3): gifts from Frederick to his godfather, Provost Otto of Cappenberg.

ISAIAS·EZE
PHETA·CHIAS
REX

10. The coronation of Lothar III: a sixteenth-century sketch of a fresco in the Lateran Palace.

11. The Shrine of the Magi (front) on the altar of Cologne Cathedral.

12 and 13. The chandelier in St. Mary's, Aachen (12), and the arm reliquary of Charlemagne (13): gifts from Frederick and Beatrice of Burgundy in conjunction with Charlemagne's canonization.

14. The Great Hall in the restored Palace of Goslar.

15 and 16. *Barbarossa's Awakening* (15) and *The Proclamation of the Reich* (16): Hermann Wislicenus paintings in the Great Hall of the restored Palace of Goslar.

17. The equestrian statues of Barbarossa and Wilhelm I in front of the restored Palace of Goslar.

18. The Kyffhäuser Monument: the structure erected to celebrate the twenty-fifth anniversary of the establishment of the Second Reich.

19. *Barbarossa's Awakening* on the lower portion of the Kyffhäuser Monument.

20. The interior of the hall of the Kyffhäuser Monument during the Third Reich.

the emperor charged that by organizing the Lombard League in 1167, Cremona had deprived him of 300,000 marks, or 555,000 imperial pounds. The Norman chronicler Robert of Torigny, who was the abbot of Mont-Saint-Michel, reported that Frederick's total receipts from Lombardy in 1164 were 50,000 marks, or £84,000. If Robert's report is reliable, Frederick's Lombard income would have been second in the 1160s only to the revenue that Henry II collected from England and Normandy. However, we know almost nothing about Frederick's expenditures. Much of the money must have been spent to cover the cost of his military operations—most notably, gifts and subventions to the princes, the wages of mercenaries, and procuring provisions. There is no evidence that an appreciable amount was repatriated to Germany. So, while Frederick may have been able to finance his Italian campaigns locally, it is hard to make the case that they made much economic, let alone political sense.[23]

Paschal III

While Frederick was staying in Pavia, on 20 April 1164 Victor IV died in Lucca. Two days later Rainald arranged the election of Cardinal Guido of Crema as Paschal III, and Bishop Henry of Liège consecrated him. The other individuals who were specifically identified as being present at Paschal's election and installation were Cardinal John of St. Martin, the bishop of Lodi, several Tuscan bishops, the prefect of Rome, and many Roman nobles. The small number of participants shows how little support there was for Frederick's ecclesiastical policy.

It is not clear whether Rainald acted on his own or with the emperor's prior knowledge and approval. There is some evidence that Frederick may have hesitated after Victor's death. According to a letter from an anonymous participant, Frederick told the imperial court in Würzburg in 1165 that Rainald had arranged for Paschal's election before he received written authorization from the emperor to act, and that Conrad of Mainz had warned Frederick against continuing the schism by recognizing another anti-pope. An unknown informant wrote to Thomas Becket that after Victor's death for unspecified reasons the emperor had summoned the exiled Bishop Peter of Pavia, who had represented Pope Alexander at the failed negotiations in Nuremberg in August 1163, and that rumors were circulating that Frederick was considering returning to the unity of the Church. However, it seems unlikely that Frederick and Rainald would not have discussed in advance what they would do in the event of Victor's death or that Rainald and Henry of Liège were unaware of the emperor's wishes in such a crucial matter. In any case, Frederick did not repudiate their actions; and in June 1164 he rewarded Rainald for his enormous and countless services with extensive properties and rights in Lombardy and valuable relics, including possibly the bodies of the Magi. If Victor's death provided Frederick with a chance to change course, he did not seize the opportunity.[24]

Paschal's election increased the discomfiture of the German bishops, some of whom had postponed consecration so as not to have to choose between the rival pontiffs, whereas others had accepted Victor as pope more out of loyalty to Frederick than conviction. Conrad of Mainz, who may already have expressed his doubts to Frederick in April 1164, left the imperial court in Italy in late summer, ostensibly to go on a pilgrimage to Santiago de Compostela, where he stayed for more than half a year. On his way home, he stopped in Sens and swore obedience to Alexander. However, Conrad's complete break with Frederick did not occur until the court at Würzburg in May 1165, which he may have attended in the hope of arranging a rapprochement between the pope and the emperor.

After the death of Archbishop Eberhard of Salzburg on 22 June 1164, on 29 June the clergy and ministerials moved quickly to elect Bishop Conrad of Passau as archbishop to forestall Frederick's intervention. It was a clever choice because as a bishop Conrad did not require consecration by either of the rival popes or their partisans, and as one of Frederick's Babenberg uncles Conrad could perhaps count on his nephew's forbearance. Conrad had equivocated before 1164 about his loyalties; his electors demanded that Conrad commit himself openly to Alexander. When Conrad visited the imperial court in Pavia in September 1164 and refused to recognize Paschal, Frederick denied his uncle the regalia and so prevented Conrad from legally exercising any secular authority. Upon his return from Italy, the emperor summoned Conrad and his electors to attend in November the imperial assembly in Bamberg, where Conrad was to be tried by an episcopal court. The trial did not take place, but Frederick again refused to enfeoff Conrad with the regalia. Alexander granted Conrad a dispensation to legalize his transfer from Passau to Salzburg and sent him in March 1165 the pallium, the symbol of Conrad's assumption of his archiepiscopal office.[25] Frederick could not press Conrad of Mainz and Conrad of Salzburg too hard without running the risk of alienating their powerful brothers, Otto of Wittelsbach and Henry Jasomirgott; but Frederick's antipathy to Pope Alexander was straining the ties of kinship and the whole system of consensual lordship in Germany upon which his reign was based.

The Würzburg Assembly of 1165

Since the capitulation of Milan in March 1162, Frederick had suffered a series of setbacks: the diplomatic fiasco on the Saône; the formation of the Veronese League; the princes' lack of enthusiasm for either his Italian or papal policies; and the forging of the loose anti-Staufer alliance between Byzantium, Venice, the Lombards, Sicily, and the papacy. According to John of Salisbury, "the German tyrant," who had "intimidated the world by the greatness of his name" and had sent "embassies to offer surrender rather than alliance," complained "that his successes" had "been falling off ever since he came to Saint-Jean-de-Losne in order to separate the king of the French and the French Church from the faith . . ."[26] Frederick may have conceived of an alliance with Henry II and possibly with Louis VII, too, as a way to regain the initiative and to pressure Pope Alexander.

For his part, Henry II was embroiled in his bitter conflict with Thomas Becket, who had fled to France on 2 November 1164. It is not certain which monarch initiated contacts, but an English envoy may have attended Frederick's court in mid-November in Bamberg, and Rainald began negotiations in late 1164 or early 1165 about a marriage alliance. In any case, Rainald and Henry the Lion met with Henry II at Rouen in April 1165. They arranged for the English king's daughters, the nine-year-old Matilda and the three-year-old Eleanor, to marry, respectively, Henry the Lion (then aged about thirty) and Barbarossa's infant son and heir, Frederick V. Only the first marriage actually took place because Frederick V died a few years later. Rainald then crossed the Channel at the king's expense and was well received by the English court except by the royal justiciar. The clerics John of Oxford and Richard of Ilchester accompanied Rainald back to Germany.

Modern scholars long assumed that this marital alliance was Henry II's warning to both Alexander and Louis not to support Becket, lest Henry recognize Paschal, and Frederick's signal to Louis to desist from giving the pope refuge and from backing the pro-Alexandrine party in Burgundy and Provence. However, neither the English chroniclers nor even Becket and his partisans connected the proposed marriages to the schism; and Frederick did not mention the engagements in his account of the assembly at Würzburg, where he swore never to recognize Alexander and which Henry's envoys attended. In fact, Archbishop Rotrou of Rouen explained to Cardinal Henry of Pisa that, even though Frederick's envoys had tried in three days of negotiations at Rouen to win Henry II over to the anti-pope, there was no provision in the marriage agreements aimed against Alexander and that the archbishop and the king's mother had urged Henry to dispel immediately rumors to the contrary.

Intriguingly, Rainald wrote to Louis after his stay in England that Frederick had instructed him to visit the French king as well as Henry to discuss the state of the Church and aid for the embattled Christians in the East. Rainald apologized that the length of his negotiations with the English king and the need for his immediate return to Germany had prevented him from seeing Louis; but it was likely, Rainald assured him, that at the conclusion of the forthcoming court at Würzburg, Frederick would send Rainald or some other suitable envoy to continue the discussion of these matters. In the meantime, he requested, in light of Louis' kinship with Frederick, that the king not aid "the heretic and schismatic Roland, a public enemy of the Roman Empire." Rainald's talk about assistance to the Eastern Christians may have been only a convenient pretext for meeting, but the calling of a crusade could have provided, conceivably, in spite of the derogatory words about Roland, a face-saving cover for Frederick's reconciliation with Alexander in the guise of defending Christendom.

One piece of evidence hints that Frederick may have been contemplating taking the cross. In April 1165, while Rainald was talking to Henry II, Archbishop Wichmann of Magdeburg met with Cardinal Bernard of Porto at Compiègne. The topic of their discussion is unknown, but Wichmann, who swore the Würzburg Oath only reluctantly in May, had returned in 1164 from a pilgrimage to the Holy Land—he had been captured by Saracens on the way—and had met with Frederick in February 1165. Could the offer of a crusade have been on the table as part of an overall settlement of the schism? Whatever Frederick and his advisers may have intended during their diplomatic offensive in April, the assembly at Würzburg made it virtually impossible for Frederick ever to recognize Alexander without an enormous loss of prestige.[27]

As is so often the case in writing Frederick's biography, contradictory and biased sources make it impossible to reconstruct with complete certainty what occurred when the princes celebrated Whitsunday in Würzburg on 23 May 1165. Frederick announced the court's decision on 1 June in a circular that Rainald may have drafted and that survives in several variants, one of which was sent to Louis VII's former envoy, Count Henry of Troyes. Like other such "public" pronouncements, it depicts the assembly's determinations as unanimous. The other significant source, the anonymous so-called "Letter of a Friend to Pope Alexander," survives in a shorter version, which may have been an eyewitness summary of the acrimonious proceedings, and in a reworked longer form that may have incorporated information contained in the circular. The author was, in all likelihood, a German opponent of Rainald, conceivably Conrad of Mainz, who blamed Rainald for prolonging the schism after Frederick made tentative overtures to reach an accommodation with Alexander.

According to the letter, the princes assembled in Würzburg on the Saturday before Whitsunday to discuss making peace between Frederick and Alexander, and they resumed their talks on Monday. The return of Rainald that day with the two English envoys altered the tenor of the proceedings. Rainald pointed out to Frederick that the earlier councils he had summoned had failed to depose Alexander and that the better part of the German episcopate adhered to the pope—Rainald singled out the archbishops of Mainz and Salzburg as the most prominent examples. However, if Frederick heeded Rainald's advice, Paschal would quickly prevail because fifty or more bishops and archbishops in Henry II's domains were prepared to adhere to Paschal, as the king's ambassadors would attest. (It is highly unlikely that there were anywhere near fifty bishops in England and the Plantagenet holdings in France who would have done any such thing, because the English and French Churches were firmly committed to Alexander.) Rainald informed Frederick that Henry and his bishops were prepared to recognize Paschal if Frederick abjured Alexander and his successors; and, in the letter's longer version, Rainald then provided the assembly with the substance of the Oath of Würzburg contained in the circular. Rainald also recommended that the princes, upon their return home, should compel the clergy in their domains and their own vassals to swear the oath. The penalty for non-compliance should be, he proposed, confiscation of the non-juror's property, the loss of his fiefs and belt of knighthood, and expulsion from the Empire. Everyone else who refused to swear was to suffer corporal punishment.

Wichmann of Magdeburg and his episcopal colleagues objected that since the future was unpredictable and God's will unknown, they did not want to bind themselves irrevocably to Paschal, and that Wichmann personally preferred returning the regalia to the emperor to taking the oath. They reluctantly agreed to swear if Rainald swore first and was finally ordained as a priest and consecrated as an archbishop. Rainald declined once again. Frederick was livid and accused Rainald of having arranged for Guido's election as Pope Paschal before Rainald had received written authorization to proceed. He declared that Rainald was "a traitor and deceiver" and that he should have heeded Conrad of Mainz's "salutary counsel" not to commit himself to another anti-pope after God had freed him from his previous danger. Frederick insisted that Rainald step into the snare he had set for others and do what the princes demanded, presumably because his continued refusal to be consecrated threatened to alienate the bishops completely. Rainald was duly ordained before he left Würzburg and was consecrated in Cologne Cathedral on 2 October 1165, in the presence of the emperor and empress.

After Rainald took the oath, the English envoys swore, in Henry II's name, that the king would be firmly bound by the emperor's own commitments. John of Oxford subsequently admitted, in his own words, according to John of Salisbury, that he had "fallen into vile heresy by swearing the Emperor an impious oath, and ... [had] communicated with the schismatic 'archbishop' of Cologne ..." Frederick followed and, contrary to custom, swore in person rather than having a proxy take the oath on his behalf. At Wichmann's insistence, a further stipulation had been added to the oath: if both popes happened to die simultaneously and their respective cardinals agreed upon a common candidate, the juror would be permitted to accept their choice. Rainald undercut even this minimal concession—how likely was the stipulated eventuality?—by adding the proviso that the papal election must have occurred with the emperor's consent. Rainald and Frederick were sticking to the position they had enunciated on the Saône, namely, that the emperor had the final say in the selection of any bishop in the Empire, including the pope, who received the regalia from the crown. This stance made it virtually impossible to resolve the schism, because neither Alexander nor the other European monarchs would accept such imperial control of the Church.

Seemingly, only four of the lay princes swore the oath at Würzburg: Henry the Lion, Albrecht the Bear, Frederick's brother Conrad, and their brother-in-law, Landgrave Louis II of Thuringia. The emperor's cousin Frederick of Rothenburg, who had arrived at court with 1,500 knights, left when he heard about the prescribed oath.

The German episcopate was split. Initially, all the bishops who attended, except for Frederick's stalwart supporter, Hermann of Verden, asserted they would rather renounce the regalia than swear the oath; but they were informed that they had no such option. Besides Hermann, the only other bishops who took the oath without any reservations were Rainald and two of his suffragans, and the interloper Gero of Halberstadt, who had replaced the deposed pro-Alexandrine Ulrich of Halberstadt. Wichmann wept but swore the oath. He stipulated, however, that he would be bound by his oath only as long as he retained the regalia and if the absent bishops also complied. Eberhard of Bamberg set the same conditions for his adherence. Richard of Verdun and Albert of Freising pleaded that they could not commit themselves in the absence of their metropolitans and were given until 29 June to comply. The longer version noted that Ulrich of Aquileia, Conrad II of Salzburg, Hillin of Trier and their suffragans were absent. (The bishops of Verdun and Freising, who attended, were, in fact, suffragans of Trier and Salzburg respectively.) Archbishop Hartwig of Bremen and two of his suffragans took the oath later.[28] Support among the bishops for Frederick's ecclesiastical policies, which had always been half-hearted at best, was waning.

There was no hint of any internal dissension in Frederick's tendentious circular of 1 June. After explaining how Victor had been recognized as the rightful pope at the councils held in Pavia, Lodi, Milan, and St. Jean-de-Losne, the bishops and cardinals had chosen Paschal as Victor's successor. (In reality, only one cardinal, John of St. Martin, is known to have participated in the election besides Guido of Crema.) At the prompting of the Holy Ghost and with the advice of all who were present at the general court at Würzburg, Frederick had sworn by his own hand on the relics of the saints that he would never recognize as pope the schismatic, Roland, or any member of his party, nor would the emperor ever permit anyone else to do so. He would deny his grace to any of Alexander's adherents until they returned to the unity of the Church. Instead, the emperor would obey, honor, and revere Paschal as the rightful pope and would never depart from his obedience. Frederick promised that he would never allow any bishop who had been consecrated or would be consecrated during the pontificates of Paschal and his successors to be deprived of his office, and that he would never himself seek or accept absolution from this oath. (The fate of bishops who had been consecrated by the anti-popes and their partisans was a major obstacle in finally making peace between Alexander and Frederick.) Frederick's yet-to-be-chosen successor was to be bound by the same oath.

In a complete misrepresentation of the facts, the imperial circular declared that forty archbishops, bishops, and bishops-elect who had been present had sworn the oath upon the Gospels. (There were forty-four German bishops, including those of Basel, Cambrai, and Trent, who were directly subject to the crown. The letter indicates that many of the bishops were absent and/or had declined to take the oath.) Inspired by the Holy Ghost, everyone had concurred that all the bishops-elect, beginning with Rainald, should receive Holy Orders on 29 May. The absentees were given until 18 September to do the same thing or they would forfeit their offices. In addition, the legates of his "illustrious friend, Henry, the glorious king of the English" swore on his behalf, upon the relics of the saints in the presence of the entire court, that Henry and his entire realm would stand with Frederick and would "always be bound with us to the Lord Pope Paschal, to whom we adhere."

The emperor directed the "archbishops, bishops, abbots, clerics, dukes, margraves, counts, and all his vassals" to assemble in one place all the faithful members of the Church, namely, "the clergy, vassals and ministerials, abbots and provosts, prelates and parish priests" and to swear the oath in their presence. The recipients of the mandate were likewise to command "the archdeacons, provosts, prelates of churches, abbots and all village priests" to take the oath and to pray for Paschal by name in their Masses. If a cleric or monk disobeyed this directive, he would lose his benefice; a layman would be deprived of his allods, fiefs, and whatever he possessed. The addressees were given until 6 July to implement the mandate.[29] If the original purpose of the Würzburg assembly had been to make peace between Frederick and Alexander, Rainald's dramatic announcement of Henry II's willingness to recognize Paschal made the schism almost irresolvable because of the binding oath that the emperor had sworn personally.

The real puzzle is Henry's role in the story. The king and the royal loyalists denied that he or his envoys had made any commitment at Würzburg to recognize Paschal; and there is no indication that Henry subsequently made any effort to gain the approval of the English bishops for suddenly abandoning Alexander, whom he had recognized as the rightful pope in 1160. Becket's supporters were certainly aware of what had transpired at Würzburg, because copies of both the circular and the letter in both its variants survive in manuscripts that contain the archbishop's correspondence, but not even he accused Henry of contemplating a change in papal allegiances. Becket's first biographer, Herbert of Bosham, writing in the archbishop's name, informed Alexander that Henry's planned meeting with Frederick on 6 October had not occurred because the king had conveniently pretended that he was engaged in a war in Wales, and that Henry had not required sixty (sic) bishops to swear allegiance to Guido of Crema. Thus his treaty of friendship with Frederick had been abrogated. Of course, it was in Alexander's best interest, whatever his doubts about the veracity of such assurances, to accept them and not risk a confrontation with the king. Did Henry deceive Rainald and later Alexander about his intentions, or did Rainald misrepresent Henry's position to Frederick and the princes and in the circular?

Frederick's circular is quite explicit that the English envoys had sworn that their master would join Paschal's party, but "The Letter of a Friend to Pope Alexander" is vague about the precise nature of Henry's commitment and even John of Salisbury referred only to John of Oxford's "impious oath." One possible explanation, as was true in the case of the Treaty of Constance in 1153, is that the oral agreement Rainald had reached with Henry before the council convened was ambiguous, perhaps deliberately so, and could thus be interpreted differently by both contractors. They had negotiated an alliance of friendship that was directed against the monarchs' common enemies, but they may not have identified explicitly who those enemies were. If this interpretation is correct, then the Angevin–Staufer alliance of 1165 was not a medieval example of English perfidy or further evidence of Rainald's baneful manipulation of his naive sovereign, but a mutually beneficial misunderstanding of the other side's intentions.

Some skepticism is warranted about this attempt by Hannah Vollrath to absolve Henry of the charge of double-dealing. John of Salisbury was insistent in July 1166 that when John of Oxford was "on the point of swearing to the German tyrant in the king's name . . . aid and counsel against all men, except only the French king," Frederick had asked through his interpreter, as John of Salisbury had heard from numerous witnesses: "'Roland, the enemy of the Church and empire, is a man and mortal, and so are all his cardinals, and none of them is the French king. And so I understand, and wish it to be understood, in this alliance of myself and the English king, that none of them is excluded.'" John of Oxford responded: "'We and our lord understand it just as you do, and on this understanding we offer our oaths on behalf of our king.'" Admittedly, John of Salisbury may have been misinformed or may have misrepresented the facts. He was certainly furious that Alexander had accepted John of Oxford's denials about swearing an oath, had lifted his excommunication, and had restored the deanery of Salisbury to the royal cleric. The shrewd pope may have seen the diplomatic advantages of giving Henry a way to extricate himself from his alliance with Frederick. Whatever really happened in Würzburg, Rainald hardly emerges as a master diplomat. All he accomplished at St. Jean-de-Losne in 1162 and at Rouen, Westminster, and Würzburg in 1165 was to isolate the emperor even further internationally and to intensify German misgivings about the course Frederick had pursued since 1159.[30]

Initially, relations between Frederick and Louis were tense after the Whitsunday court of 1165, because in the circular the emperor accused the French king of siding, in spite of repeated warnings, with Roland against the Empire. Frederick even threatened war. Duke Hugh III of Burgundy had expelled his mother Mary, who had served until 1164 as regent for him; and she had appealed for assistance to Louis as her son's feudal lord.

Louis had decided to invade the duchy on her behalf. Frederick wrote to Count Henry of Troyes, the brother of the exiled duchess and Louis' brother-in-law, sometime before 24 June 1165, that he was prepared to aid his friend Hugh with the full force of the Empire. The emperor requested and commanded that Henry—out of the love he bore Frederick—dissuade Louis from his plans and that the count not assist Louis with his counsel or aid. Frederick indicated that he was prepared to mediate between Hugh and his mother. Louis, who was persuaded for his part, according to John of Salisbury, that the Germans, "if they could and dared, would gladly attack his kingdom," was angry at the canonist, Master Gerard Pucelle, who had settled at the turn of 1165–66 among the "barbarians" and "schismatics" in Cologne. Alexander's departure from France in the summer of 1165 eased the strain between the two monarchs.[31]

Frederick was determined to enforce in Germany the decisions of the Würzburg assembly. He was in Passau on 29 June, when Bishop Rupert of Passau compelled all his subjects to swear the oath, and in Vienna in July, when Bishop-Elect Eberhard of Regensburg, Albert of Freising, Henry Jasomirgott, and other unnamed princes took the oath.[32] Frederick was astonished, he wrote to Bishop Nicholas of Cambrai sometime after 4 October, that he had not required the clergy, prelates, and religious of his diocese to swear the oath and so demonstrate the honor they owed the Empire and the obedience and respect due to Paschal. He had dispatched Abbot Erlebold of Stavelot, Wibald's brother, to Cambrai, therefore, to oversee the swearing of the oaths; and Frederick ordered Nicholas to assist Erlebold. Non-jurors were to be expelled from the bishopric. Nicholas must have capitulated quickly to Frederick's demands because he witnessed an imperial charter on 29 December in Aachen, and in September 1167 Frederick indicated that the entire Reich mourned Nicholas' death.[33]

The major hold-outs were Conrad of Mainz and Conrad of Salzburg. The former left Würzburg to avoid swearing the oath and joined Alexander in France. He then accompanied the pope to Italy. In December 1165 Alexander made Conrad a cardinal-priest and shortly thereafter consecrated him as cardinal-bishop of Sabina and archbishop of Mainz. In the meantime, Frederick had replaced Conrad in September with his chancellor, Christian of Buch, who had been one of the two rival candidates for the archbishopric after the murder of Archbishop Arnold in 1160. John of Salisbury could not resist the dig: "not Christian, but Anti-Christ."[34]

The emperor's uncle Conrad of Salzburg was almost completely isolated after his suffragans and his own brother, the duke of Austria, took the oath and Frederick installed his kinsman, Otto of Andechs, as Bishop Hartmann's successor in Brixen. The clergy of the reformed houses of Augustinian canons in the archdiocese, including the cathedral chapter, and the archiepiscopal ministerials were Conrad's chief mainstay. Frederick invited the archbishop and the ministerials to attend his court in Worms in September 1165. When they did not appear, the emperor summoned his uncle three times, in six-week intervals, to be judged. After the third grace period had almost elapsed, Conrad, who had tried to appease his nephew with gifts but had also prepared his castles for war, arrived in Nuremberg on 14 February 1166. He was accused of taking possession of the archbishopric illegally, because Frederick had not invested him with the regalia and Paschal had not conferred the pallium on him. Henry the Lion, who served as Conrad's spokesman, countered that the archbishop had been canonically elected by the clergy, ministerials, and people of Salzburg and had sought investiture with the regalia on three occasions. Conrad left Nuremberg without regaining his nephew the emperor's grace.

On 29 March 1166 the princes, at an assembly held in Laufen on the Salzach river, north of Salzburg, imposed the imperial ban on the archbishopric after Conrad's brother, Henry Jasomirgott, and the other princes had been unable to persuade Conrad to yield. The church of Salzburg was deprived of all its fiefs and allods, which Barbarossa conferred immediately on his supporters. Paschal banned and excommunicated prelates and monasteries that remained loyal to Conrad. Frederick left the execution of the sentence of outlawry to the nobles who hoped to profit from Salzburg's discomfiture: the Wittelsbachs; Duke Hermann of Carinthia; Styrian ministerials; and, above all, the counts of Plain, whose domains were situated near the city of Salzburg. Frederick thanked the counts for the energetic actions they were taking against the Salzburgers and commanded the Plains to persist in conducting the war against Conrad, in which his own honor was at stake. He issued the same mandate to the duke of Austria and the bishop of Passau, though there is no evidence that the duke took up arms against his brother. The archiepiscopal ministerials led the resistance. On the night of 4 April 1167 the counts of Plain burned the city of Salzburg, including the cathedral. Conrad took refuge in the Alpine portions of his vast archdiocese and made peace with his noble enemies. He died in the monastery of Admont on 28 September 1168. Nevertheless, Frederick and Conrad had shown some restraint during their confrontation: Conrad had rejected Patriarch Ulrich of Aquileia's proposal for a military alliance against his nephew, and Frederick never deposed his uncle, as he did Conrad of Mainz. Conrad of Salzburg's successor and nephew, Adalbert of Bohemia, was less fortunate.[35]

Frederick thus succeeded in maintaining his grip on the German Church in the years immediately after the Würzburg assembly. Most of the bishops, however reluctantly and sometimes under duress, swore the prescribed oath. A study of Pope Alexander's grant or confirmation of the privileges of churches and monasteries shows how little contact German clerics had with the curia in the 1160s. At least twenty-four ecclesiastical institutions in the metropolitan province of Salzburg, the center of his support, sought such privileges during the schism; but only four of these were conferred before 1170.[36] However, the degree of the princes' commitment to Frederick's papal policy should not be exaggerated. Herbert of Bosham notified Alexander at the end of 1165 that there were reports that several princes were conspiring to elect a new emperor if Frederick did not respect the freedom of the Church. The rumors were false, but there is evidence in other sources that the individuals whom Herbert named—Hillin of Trier, Wichmann of Magdeburg, Conrad of Salzburg, some of the archbishops' suffragans, Frederick of Rothenburg, Henry Jasomirgott, Berthold IV of Zähringen, Welf VI, and Conrad of Mainz's brother, Frederick—either recognized Alexander as pope or had sworn the Würzburg Oath only reluctantly.[37] Whoever was spreading the rumors was well informed about the true feelings of the German princes.

For that reason, Frederick, in spite of the oath he had sworn, may not have closed the door completely to reaching a negotiated settlement with Alexander. In the late summer of 1166 the Augustinian canon Gerhoch of Reichersberg drafted a treatise addressed to Alexander's cardinals, in which Gerhoch sought a compromise that would respect both the honor of the Empire and the pope's insistence that he was not subject to any earthly judgment. Frederick was ready to come to an understanding, but the major obstacle to ending the schism was, as Gerhoch had learned in several private conversations with the emperor, the cardinals' conspiracy with the Reich's enemies, Milan and Sicily, to elect only one of their number as pope. The conspiracy was, Frederick believed, a clear violation of Peter's teachings: "Fear God. Honor the king" (1 Peter 2:17). The provost recommended that the cardinals send Frederick, as a first step to making peace, a humble letter repudiating the accusation. There is no evidence that the treatise was even sent, let alone that it elicited any response if it was, but maybe it was a feeler.[38]

The Canonization of Charlemagne

When Frederick confirmed on 8 January 1166 the privileges of St. Mary's and of the city of Aachen, "the head and seat of the German kingdom," he indicated that he had arranged for Charlemagne's canonization on 29 December, St. David's Day, during the Christmas court in Aachen, at the "assiduous request of our most dear friend Henry, the illustrious king of England." (Apparently, Frederick had not yet heard that his "treaty of friendship" with Henry II had been terminated.) Henry had procured in 1161 the canonization of Edward the Confessor, the great-great-uncle of his maternal grandmother, Queen Matilda. Edward and Charlemagne joined two other rulers who were raised to the altar in the middle of the twelfth century: Emperor Henry II in 1146, and in 1169 Knut Lavard, the duke of Schleswig and the father of King Valdemar I of Denmark. Gregory VII had attacked royal sanctity during the Investiture Conflict. In a letter to Bishop Hermann of Metz in 1081, the pope had observed: "Let them [monarchs] therefore consider carefully how dangerous, even awesome is the office of emperor or king, how very few find salvation therein . . . From the beginning of the world to the present day we do not find in all authentic records [seven] emperors or kings whose lives were as distinguished for virtue and piety as were those of a countless multitude of men who despised the world . . ." The canonizations of the twelfth century were a rejoinder that sanctity and kingship were compatible and that the new saints' realms and successors could rely on the divine protection of their holy predecessors. Charlemagne's elevation to the altar, in particular, was another way to assert the divine origins of imperial authority that the papacy had challenged at Besançon.

Frederick had acted at Aachen, he declared, "with the consent and by the authority of the Lord Pope Paschal and with the counsel of all the princes, both lay and ecclesiastical." Charlemagne had been a "true apostle" because he had converted the Saxons, Frisians, Westphalians, Spanish, and the Vandals with the Word and the sword; and his willingness to die every day for the furtherance of the Gospel had made him a martyr. Paschal had delegated the canonization to the newly consecrated archbishop of Cologne, Rainald of Dassel. Such papal commissions were not unusual. For example, Becket had conducted St. Anselm's canonization in 1163 at the behest of Pope Alexander III, and the same procedure was employed in the cases of Bishops Anno of Cologne in 1186 and Otto of Bamberg in 1189. Charlemagne's canonization on Paschal's orders was thus an assertion that the latter was, indeed, the rightful pontiff.

Monarchs customarily participated in the translation of a saint's relics, as Frederick did in the case of St. Bassianus in Lodi in 1163, because in the twelfth century unction was still considered to separate the ruler from the rest of the laity. The unusual aspect of Charlemagne's canonization was

Frederick's apparently solitary involvement in the proceedings. He explained in the charter of 8 January 1166 that he had "lifted with fear and reverence the most holy body . . . to the praise and glory of the name of Christ, for the strengthening of the Roman Empire, and for the salvation of our beloved wife, Empress Beatrice, and of our sons Frederick and Henry," from the tomb where it had been concealed, as the *Cologne Royal Chronicle* put it, for 352 years; this occurred in the presence of "a large gathering of princes and a great multitude of clergy and people [singing] hymns and canticles." The emperor had then placed the exhumed bones in a gold container adorned with precious jewels and carried them to the altar. (Frederick II transferred the relics to the existing reliquary on 27 July 1215, two days after his coronation in Aachen and on the first anniversary of the battle of Bouvines that had assured him the crown.)

The immediate model for Frederick's actions may have been the translation of the relics of St. Edward the Confessor after Henry II returned in 1163 from a long stay on the Continent. Hagiographers did not want to taint Edward's memory by ascribing too great a role to Henry and so stressed Becket's participation in the translation, but other sources indicate that the king had carried the reliquary on his shoulders in a procession through Westminster Abbey. Rainald may have learned how that ceremony had been conducted during his stay in England in 1165. The model for both canonizations may have been, in turn, the transfer by Louis VII, in 1144, of the relics of St. Denis from the crypt of the abbatial church to the altar of the newly built Gothic choir of the abbey. Rainald may even have witnessed this ceremony during his student days in France in the early 1140s. All three churches were associated with their respective monarchies as coronation churches, royal burial sites, and/or repositories for the royal insignia.

St. Denis and Aachen were rival sites of the Charlemagne cult, which appealed to knights who believed that the Frankish emperor had been the first crusader and was described in Frederick's charter as a propagator of the Gospel. When Emperor Henry V invaded the West Frankish Kingdom in 1124, Abbot Suger had placed the relics of St. Denis temporarily on the altar and had then conferred on Louis VI the banner of St. Denis, which was thought to be identical with the Oriflamme that Charlemagne had carried, according to *The Song of Roland*, into battle when fighting the Muslims. The monks had forged a charter in Charlemagne's name, in which the emperor, thankful that St. Denis had elevated him to the pinnacle of lordship, had decreed that the monastery was to be "the head of all churches of our kingdom" and that his successors as kings of the Franks were to be crowned only in St. Denis. The canons of St. Mary's had responded before 1147 with their own forgery, in which Charlemagne had ruled, with the consent of the pope and the magnates of the Frankish and Italian kingdoms, that Aachen was "the royal site and head of Gaul beyond the Alps" and the only place where the king could be enthroned before his coronation as emperor in Rome. Frederick confirmed this forgery, which was inserted into his charter for Aachen of 8 January. The canons may thus have provided the impetus for the canonization of Charlemagne, who was interred in their church, as the best way to counter the rival claims of St. Denis. By his translation of the relics Frederick indicated that he alone was Charlemagne's rightful successor.[39]

According to the *Cologne Royal Chronicle*, Frederick and Beatrice gave St. Mary's, in conjunction with the canonization, "royal gifts," specifically, gold vessels and silk cloths, and, in addition, an annual income of ten marks. There were even more splendid gifts. Most famously, the couple commissioned a chandelier of gilded copper, 4.2 meters in diameter (Fig. 12). It hangs on a 27-meter-long chain from the cupola of the church, approximately four meters above the floor. It is composed of eight semicircular segments. An inscription on the chandelier indicates that Frederick wanted the shape to harmonize with the octagonal structure of the church; and the ratio between the area of the chandelier and the space demarked by the walls of the octagon is, in fact, 1:4. Eight larger, three-storied towers are situated at the outermost point of each semicircular segment. Two curved, filigree bands connect the large towers to smaller, round towers at the back of each semicircle where the adjoining segments meet. The chandelier represents, the inscription says, the walls of the New Jerusalem that St. John saw descending from heaven in Revelation 21—the same structure as the lower level of the pedestal on which the Cappenberg Head stands. The bottom plates in the square towers depict personifications of the Beatitudes, with the accompanying verses from the Sermon on the Mount in scrolls. The Beatitudes, which were read during the liturgy for All Saints' (and still are), point the viewer underneath the chandelier to the path that leads to the Heavenly City above. The chandelier doubled as a monumental nimbus for the new saint, whose shrine was placed below it. Unlike the Cappenberg Head, which does not mention Frederick, the inscription on the chandelier beseeches Mary, "the star of the sea," to whom the church is dedicated, to remember the royal donors. However, just as the bust connected the Heavenly City to Rome, the chandelier linked the New Jerusalem to Aachen, "the head and seat of the German kingdom."[40]

The couple's other gift was a narrow, long reliquary, made of oak and sheathed in gilded tin (Fig. 13). It is 54.8 centimeters long, 13.5 wide, and

14 high. An inscription on the inside of the flat lid states that it contains "the arm of the most glorious emperor, Saint Charles." On the sides, twelve arcades, which are separated by gilded bronze pilasters, surround reliefs, which are identified by inscriptions. The central figure on the front side is the Virgin, the patron saint of the church, in the garb of an empress with a diadem on her head. She holds her infant son in her left arm and a scepter of lilies in her right. She is flanked by the Archangels Michael and Gabriel, who incline to her in homage. The two outer arcades show Frederick to the Virgin's right (the viewer's left) and Beatrice to the left (the viewer's right). Charlemagne's son, Louis the Pious, the first monarch who was crowned in Aachen, and Otto III, who opened Charlemagne's tomb in 1000, adorn the ends of the casket. Christ bestows His blessing in the center arcade in the rear. He is flanked on His right by Peter and Conrad III and on His left by Paul and by a figure in armor holding a lance with three attached banners, identified as "Frederick, Duke of the Swabians," that is, Barbarossa's father. The emperors are portrayed with the insignia of their office: the crown, scepter, and an orb topped with a cross. Conrad and Frederick's crowns have two crossed arches, the other rulers' crowns only one. Beatrice wears a diadem with pendicles and holds a Byzantine double cross in her hands. If the iconography of the Cappenberg Head suggested that Frederick was the new Constantine, then Beatrice with her Byzantine cross was St. Helena.

It is generally assumed that Frederick commissioned the reliquary between 1166 and 1170 to show the dynastic continuity between Charlemagne and the Staufer, who are being presented by the angels and the princes of the Apostles to Christ and His mother and to the new saint in the reliquary. Frederick indicated in the charter of 8 January that he had acted not only to procure his and Beatrice's salvation but also to benefit his young sons, Frederick V and Henry VI—the latter was born in Nijmegen in October or November 1165, just before the Christmas court in Aachen. In spite of the obvious political implication of Charlemagne's canonization, namely, the assertion of the divine origins of imperial authority, unmediated by the papacy, it was also an act of piety.[41]

The Fourth Italian Campaign

Frederick had ignored the city of Rome after the outbreak of the schism, and most of the Roman clergy, including even the canons of St. Peter, had recognized Alexander as pope by 1162. Through a judicious distribution of money, as Boso conceded, the cardinal who represented Alexander in Rome was able to secure on 1 November 1164 the election of a pro-Alexandrine senate. The Romans invited the pope to return. Alexander consulted, Boso said, the kings of France and England about accepting the Romans' invitation—Henry II would have been extraordinarily duplicitous if he was negotiating at the same time with Rainald about recognizing Paschal—and in the late summer of 1165 the pope sailed from Montpellier to Messina. William I of Sicily provided the pope with five galleys, and Alexander entered Rome in triumph on 23 November. However, the Romans welcomed him as their bishop and not as lord of their city.[42]

Manuel I tried to take advantage of Alexander's uneasy situation in Rome. According to Boso, after the death of William I on 7 May 1166 and the accession of his thirteen-year-old son, William II, the Byzantine emperor, aware of the injuries Frederick was causing Alexander, offered to reunite the Latin and Greek Churches under the leadership of the pope. In return, Manuel wanted the Apostolic See to restore to him "the crown of the Roman Empire" because, "he declared, it belonged to him by right and not to that German, Frederick." If this occurred, Manuel was prepared to supply so much silver and gold and so many men that all of Italy would submit to the Church. Since it is inconceivable that Manuel was asking, contrary to Byzantine custom, to be crowned emperor by the pope or merely desired a physical object, the most plausible explanation of what he meant by the crown is that he wished the pope to acknowledge Byzantium's lordship in Italy and Rome itself. Alexander and the cardinals took the proposal under advisement and sent an embassy to Constantinople to pursue the matter, but the curia was not ready to exchange German for Greek dominion in Rome. Nothing came of this offer or of Manuel's similar proposition after Alexander fled from Rome in July 1167.

Frederick may have responded to Manuel's diplomatic initiative by dispatching, sometime in 1166, his uncle Henry Jasomirgott, along with the duke's wife, the Byzantine princess Theodora, and Otto of Wittelsbach, to the *basileus* in Sofia. The objective was to make peace between Frederick's candidate for the Hungarian throne, Stephen III, and Manuel, and perhaps by extension between the two emperors. The mission was unsuccessful, and Stephen subsequently married Henry's daughter and Frederick's cousin, Agnes.[43]

In the meantime, the princes had agreed at the court held in Nuremberg in February 1166 to finance another expedition to Italy to install Paschal in Alexander's place and to conquer the Norman kingdom. This call to arms prompted Count Sigiboto IV of Falkenstein to commission, among other things, a survey of his properties and the renders they owed and a book of conveyances that summarized his property transactions; this was to guide his father-in-law, who was serving as his grandsons' guardian, in Sigiboto's absence. Bishop Hermann of Hildesheim mortgaged a manor to raise 400 marks so he could be excused from participating in the campaign. Such commutations of military service, which were known in England as scutage, presumably helped to pay the wages of Frederick's mercenaries, the Brabanters, many of whom hailed from the duchy of Brabant in modern Belgium and were mentioned for the first time during this campaign. Frederick's employment of the Brabanters is a sign that he could no longer rely on the princes to supply him with sufficient numbers of men. Sigiboto placed at the front of the *Codex Falkensteinensis*, the oldest European family archive, a family portrait with the inscription: "Sons, bid your father farewell and speak respectfully to your mother. Dear one who reads this, we beseech you, remember us. All may do this, but especially you, dearest son." Sigiboto, who was among the fortunate few to return, had doubts about his chances. He was quite prescient.[44]

The imperial forces assembled in Augsburg in mid-October 1166. Before their departure, Frederick and Rainald entrusted Duke Henry II of Limburg with the oversight of both the Empire's and Cologne's interests on the left bank of the Rhine. Since Verona blocked the southern terminus of the Brenner crossing, the imperial forces had to take a more difficult route that avoided the city to reach the Lombard plain. Among the princes who accompanied Frederick across the Alps were Archbishop Christian of Mainz, Bishops Daniel of Prague, Gero of Halberstadt, and Udo II of Naumburg, Abbot Hermann of Fulda, and his cousin Frederick of Rothenburg—not a particularly impressive number. (Rainald, accompanied by one hundred knights, had used the Great St. Bernard Pass and had arrived in Ivrea in northwestern Italy on 31 October; Berthold IV of Zähringen may have taken the same route.) The main army had to fight its way through the territories of traditionally hostile Brescia but also of the previously pro-imperial Bergamo to get to Lodi. The Brescians had to give Frederick sixty hostages. The unfriendly reception should have been a warning to the emperor about the depth of discontent.

The army encamped outside Lodi, while Frederick, Beatrice, and the German and Italian princes entered the city in November for a well-attended assembly, which determined that the entire imperial force would march on Rome. According to the anonymous continuer of the Morena chronicle, "bishops, margraves, counts, captains, other prominent individuals, and many ordinary Lombards," some carrying crosses, complained, with specific details, about the numerous evils they had suffered at the hands of Frederick's officials. At first, he listened sympathetically, but he decided that their complaints were greatly exaggerated and he did nothing. The Lombards were dismayed and concluded that the imperial agents had acted in accordance with the emperor's orders and that even worse might befall them in the future. The Lombards' loss of confidence in the emperor's fairness was a major factor in the subsequent revolt. In addition, the envoys of Genoa and Pisa quarreled at the court about their respective claims to Sardinia. Finally, both accepted the Genoese proposal to keep the peace for the duration of the campaign; and the emperor's current and former chancellors, Christian of Buch and Rainald of Dassel, who had defended, respectively, the positions of Pisa and Genoa at the assembly, were sent to "their" city to procure the release of the other city's hostages.

After spending several weeks in Pavia, Frederick celebrated Christmas in a camp outside Brescia and forced that city to pay a large sum of money and possibly to hand over also an additional sixty hostages to regain his grace. During this stay, he invested Christian of Buch with the archbishopric of Mainz; he appointed Philip of Heinsberg, brother of Goswin III, the count of Seprio and Martesana, as Christian's successor as chancellor. The emperor returned to Lodi in early January 1167, and Frederick and Beatrice headed south on 11 January.[45]

The imperial forces passed through the territory of Piacenza, forced both Tortona and Parma to submit, and marched to the southeast along the Via Emilia, the Roman road that linked Piacenza on the Po with Rimini on the Adriatic. By 10 February the army was near Bologna and may have devastated the Bolognese *contado*. Frederick gave the soldiers time to rest while he entered the city. He demanded a hundred hostages and £6,000. Around 16 February he was in Faenza and by the end of February in Ferrara, northeast of Bologna. Sometime in February the emperor met his uncle Welf VI, who was on a pilgrimage to the Holy Land and commended his son Welf VII to his nephew. In the meantime Frederick had summoned his cousin, the aforementioned Welf VII, who brought additional troops via the Septimer Pass to Italy. In Pavia around Easter (9 April), Frederick's envoys paid Welf VII the subsidy he had been promised for coming—a rare piece of evidence that the princes' participation was not gratis—and Welf joined his cousin outside Rome in mid-July.

Likewise in February, near Faenza in the castle of Modigliana (belonging to Count Guido Guerra) Beatrice gave birth to the couple's third son, Conrad, who was renamed Frederick (Frederick VI) after the death of the couple's like-named, first-born son. The delay occasioned by the empress's delivery may have been one factor in the army's seemingly slow progress.

After the detour to Ferrara, the troops returned to the Via Emilia; and Frederick extorted large sums of money from Imola, Faenza, and Forli. On 4 March, while the emperor was staying in Imola, Bishop Hermann of Verden ordained Christian of Buch as a priest and Guido of Ravenna and Eberhard of Regensburg as deacons. The next day Daniel of Prague and the other bishops consecrated Christian as an archbishop. The emperor split his forces in Imola in order to secure both the western and eastern coasts of Italy from a Sicilian and/or a Greek attack. He sent Rainald, Christian, and the new chancellor, Philip of Heinsberg, with 1,500 Brabanters to Tuscany and on to Rome to assist Paschal III and to raise funds. Christian went via Genoa and Rainald proceeded via Pisa, with the latter in the lead. The Pisan consuls swore to participate in the planned attack on Apulia, Sicily, and Calabria and to replace their pro-Alexandrine archbishop with a prelate who was to be ordained by Paschal on Easter Sunday. The men under the archbishops' command collected considerable booty and subjected central Italy to imperial control. Frederick himself headed towards the Adriatic and forced Ravenna, east of Imola, to submit. By 23 April Frederick was in the territory of Rimini, the eastern terminus of the Via Emilia.[46]

While the imperial forces were heading in a pincer movement toward Rome, the simmering unrest in Lombardy erupted. The origins of the Lombard League are obscure, no doubt because conspiracies leave few traces. According to Boso, the Lombard cities, led by Cremona, but including also Piacenza, Brescia, Bergamo, and the exiled Milanese, concluded already in late 1165 or early 1166 that the only way to protect their freedom was to ally with Verona. The other cities rejoiced but did not dare to disobey the emperor. Boso's report explains why Frederick had to fight his way through the territory of Brescia and Bergamo in November 1166 and why in 1185 he singled out Cremona for its disloyalty. The root causes of Cremona's disaffection were that it was equally opposed to both Milanese and imperial hegemony and felt that it had not been sufficiently rewarded, like Pavia, with a portion of Milan's territory for its exertions on the emperor's behalf. Nevertheless, the Cremonese must have dissembled about their intentions because in early 1167 Frederick, out of the love he bore the Cremonese (as he recalled in 1185), had agreed to take Cremonese knights with him to Rome at his own expense rather than require the city to pay for mercenaries—or did he take them as potential hostages because he was suspicious of Cremona's loyalty?

By March 1167 Cremona had banded together in a sworn association with Bergamo, Brescia, and Mantua to protect their liberties, saving the fealty they owed the emperor. The imperial *podestà* in Milan, Count Henry II of Diez, tried to prevent the scattered Milanese population from adhering to the alliance by sending 100 hostages to Pavia on 23 March and then demanding £500 from various former inhabitants of the city and an additional 300 hostages. He threatened to destroy the Milanese *borghi*, or settlements, if they did not comply. On 27 April, in a public act of defiance, the allies escorted the Milanese back into their city after expelling the *podestà*; and on 5 September the exiled pro-Alexandrine Archbishop Galdin returned to his see. The allies were willing to rebuild their ancient enemy because the alliance was also a peace association with mechanisms to resolve disputes among its members. After a siege of ten days, 12–23 May, and guarantees of assistance against any future Milanese aggression, Lodi, too, joined the insurgents. Piacenza followed on 27 May. Schismatic bishops were expelled from the member cities and replaced by prelates loyal to Alexander. On 10 August the allies captured and destroyed the imperial fortress of Trezzo on the Adda, whose possession had been hotly contested in earlier campaigns, after Frederick failed to come to the garrison's assistance.

Strangely, the emperor's only step to contain the revolt was seemingly to dispatch Hermann of Verden to Pavia in May 1167, and the bishop's exertions may be one reason why Pavia remained loyal to Frederick after the destruction of his army. Frederick may have expected, given his past experiences with the volatility of Italian communal alliances, that the old animosities would quickly resurface and that the League would collapse after he occupied Rome, captured Alexander, and defeated the Normans. If, however, he failed to achieve his objectives, his route northward was likely to be blocked by the hostile coalition. It was his greatest strategic miscalculation.[47]

On 27 April, the day the Milanese diaspora ended, Archbishop Rainald freed Siena from the obligation to participate in the march on Rome, in recognition of the great services the Tuscan city had performed for the Reich and its payment of 1,300 marks in addition to the *fodrum* it owed. With the assistance of eight Pisan vessels, on 18 May the archbishop captured Civitavecchia, Rome's port on the Tyrrhenian Sea. The Romans were devastating the territory of pro-imperial Tusculum, southeast of Rome; and Raino, the lord of Tusculum, appealed to the emperor for help. Rainald, with a force of Germans, Lombards, Tuscans, and mercenaries, fewer than 1,000 knights in all, reached the city on 27 May. The next day, Whitsunday, a far larger Roman army, allegedly composed of 40,000 knights and foot soldiers, surrounded Tusculum. When Archbishop

Christian of Mainz arrived on 29 May with a relief force of 500 men, including some Brabanters, the Romans attacked Christian's exhausted men as they were setting up their camp. Rainald utilized this diversion to charge down the hill from Tusculum and attack the Romans from the rear. After hard fighting, the Romans fled; and the imperial forces pursued them to the gates of Rome. Supposedly, barely 2,000 Romans managed to make it home, more than 9,000 Romans were killed (mainly by the Brabanters, according to the Lodiese Anonymous), and another 9,000 were captured. Two cardinals were among the dead, and a son of Oddo Frangipane, the leader of the pro-papal aristocratic faction in Rome, was among the captives. Boso called it the worst Roman defeat since Hannibal destroyed the Roman army at Cannae in 216 B.C.[48]

The Roman populace turned against Alexander, and on 31 May the pope abandoned the Lateran Palace and took refuge in a fortress near the Colosseum belonging to the Frangipani. Rainald demanded that the Romans surrender Alexander, his cardinals, and Oddo Frangipane if they desired peace. The pontiff managed to regain some support in the city through the distribution of money supplied by William II of Sicily, but turned down the king's offer to leave the city on a Sicilian galley. Perhaps Alexander hoped that the Lombard uprising would force Frederick to withdraw. During June and July, Rainald and Christian, assisted by Rome's hostile neighbors, had sufficient manpower to devastate the countryside around the city but not to attack Rome.

In the meantime, for nearly three weeks in May the emperor, along with the bishops of Regensburg, Prague, and Verden, and Frederick of Rothenburg, had been besieging Ancona on the Adriatic coast, south of Rimini, because Manuel I had purchased its allegiance and Greek forces had occupied the city. Barbarossa initially rejected Ancona's offer to pay him tribute and to give him fifteen hostages. After Frederick learned of the archbishops' victory at Tusculum, he was eager, however, to end the siege and asked the Pisan envoys who were in his camp to mediate between him and Ancona. The city capitulated on 31 May on terms similar to its first proposal. As he was heading toward Rome, the emperor ordered the Pisans and Genoese to bring the troops they had promised. He accepted the Pisans' offer to supply him with double the number of men that Genoa had agreed to provide if he would forego Genoa's services, because the Pisans did not wish to fight alongside their arch-rivals. For its part, Genoa made the sending of its troops contingent upon Frederick's procuring the release of the Genoese captives that the Pisans were holding. Barbarossa ignored this demand because he was assured of Pisa's support.

Sometime in June he was informed that William II was besieging a castle that was loyal to the Empire. Frederick left Beatrice and the infantry behind and, taking only the knights, hastened to the castle. William withdrew, and Frederick was able to capture some of the king's fleeing men as they were trying to cross a stream. He fortified the castle, took another, and devastated and plundered the territory along the Tronto, the stream that formed the boundary between the mark of Ancona and the Norman kingdom along the Adriatic. It was the only time Frederick ever set foot in the *Regno*. He finally responded to the repeated requests of Paschal III, who was staying in Viterbo, not to delay his coming any longer and to expel Pope Alexander from Rome. Frederick and Paschal arrived outside Rome—the sources give the date variously as 19, 22, or 24 July—and the emperor set up his camp in the traditional location on Monte Mario.

The imperial forces defeated the Romans who were defending the Porta Viridaria, one of the gates of the Leonine City; and the Romans retreated to the opposite bank of the Tiber. Frederick was unable to take the Castel S. Angelo, where Alexander's forces were ensconced; and he spent several days, from at least 24 to 29 July, besieging the heavily fortified St. Peter's. Since the emperor lacked the forces or the inclination to launch a full-scale, protracted siege of the city, he initiated, according to Boso, negotiations with the cardinals and the Romans. Conrad of Mainz, now the cardinal-bishop of Sabina, served as the intermediary. If the cardinals could persuade Alexander to resign, then Frederick said he would urge Paschal to do the same and not interfere in the subsequent new election. As expected, the cardinals rejected the proposal because the pope was not subject to any earthly judgment. It is hard to believe that Frederick was really prepared to abandon Paschal at the moment when victory seemed to be within his grasp. Barbarossa's real objective—assuming Boso's report is true—may have been to turn the Romans against Alexander, who was prepared to let them endure a siege rather than resign the papacy. At some point in late July—the chronology is uncertain—Alexander realized that his situation had become untenable. He fled the city disguised as a pilgrim and made his way to Benevento 160 miles to the south. Frederick's prey had slipped out of his grasp.

On 29 July Frederick's men set fire to the church of S. Maria in Turri, which adjoined St. Peter's, and burned, according to the continuer of the Morena chronicle, several priceless paintings: a likeness of Christ made of the purest gold and magnificently decorated, unlike any in Italy, and a very beautiful image of St. Peter in the same materials and of similar workmanship. The fire spread to the atrium and doors of St. Peter's, and the defenders surrendered. Welf VI, who was returning from his pilgrimage to the Holy Land immediately after these events, cursed his nephew and the entire army for their sacrilege—or did the author of the *History of the Welfs* ascribe, with the benefit of hindsight, this prophetic curse to the duke? Frederick enthroned Paschal III in St. Peter's on 30 July, and the pope placed a gold crown on the emperor's head. At Barbarossa's request, Paschal consecrated fifteen prelates including Archbishop Heribert of Besançon, Abbot Hermann of Fulda, and the bishops of Basel and Strasbourg. Two days later, on 1 August, the feast of St. Peter in Chains, Paschal crowned both Beatrice and Frederick. Only Alexander's escape seemed to mar the emperor's triumph.[49]

While Frederick was in possession of the Leonine City, except for the Castel S. Angelo, the heart of the ancient and medieval city, including the Lateran Palace, was located on the opposite bank of the Tiber. Barbarossa was eager to reach an agreement with the Romans so that he could install Paschal in the papal palace as visible proof that he was, indeed, the rightful pontiff, and launch the long-postponed attack on the Normans. The arrival on 2 August of a Pisan galley convinced the Romans, who had been making peace overtures since their defeat at Tusculum, to come to an understanding with Frederick. The emperor's golden bull proclaiming the terms of the accord does not survive, but a written summary of the binding oral agreement made between him and the Romans was inserted into the *Cologne Royal Chronicle*. The source was undoubtedly the chancellor, Philip of Heinsberg, who must have played a major role in negotiating the terms and subsequently succeeded Rainald as archbishop of Cologne.

The pact of 1167 was a bilateral agreement. The Romans abandoned their radical assertions about communal independence and accepted imperial sovereignty. Frederick recognized, in turn, for the first time, the Romans' right to be governed by the senate, whose members were to be installed in office by him or his legate. The senators and the entire Roman population swore fealty to the emperor. They agreed to defend the crown of the Roman Empire against all men, to aid the emperor in retaining all the regalian rights within and outside the city, and never to participate by word or deed in any hostile action against the emperor. Frederick confirmed in perpetuity, for his part, the existence of the senate, whose stature would be increased, he said, by its status as an imperially sanctioned institution rather than as a self-constituted popular assembly. He promised not to alienate to a third party, most likely the papacy, the possessions and lordship rights the commune held legally from the crown. He recognized the city's good customs and the validity of leases for three or four generations. Finally,

Frederick freed the Romans from the payment of any tolls or other exactions in the Empire, a stipulation that benefited the Roman burghers who had been the driving force behind the communal movement that had been aimed against both the Roman nobility and the papacy.

All these provisions were to be included in the golden bull that the emperor would issue and that the princes were to sign. The same type of documentation had been employed in imperial grants to the Roman Church since Charlemagne's privilege of 774, and its use in 1167 conferred on the commune, implicitly, the same rank in the hierarchy as the Church possessed. Scholars long thought that the outbreak of the epidemic on 2 August prevented the drafting of the golden bull, but Jürgen Petersohn proved that the bull served as a model for the agreement in which the senate recognized papal sovereignty in 1188. Frederick, who had accepted papal dominion in the Treaty of Constance of 1153 and then claimed that the pope received the regalian rights in Rome and the Patrimony in fief from the crown, had excluded the pope completely from the secular governance of his see and had turned Rome into an imperial city. The Romans remained loyal to Frederick when imperial rule collapsed elsewhere in Italy, because he imposed no financial exactions on them and did not force them to adhere to his anti-pope.[50]

The terms of Rome's submission had been negotiated by 3 August at the latest. The Romans gave Frederick 280 hostages, and he installed fifty senators in their office. The emperor sent his agents, including Acerbus Morena, to receive over several days oaths of fealty from individual Romans, except those nobles, most notably the Frangipani, Pierleoni, and Corsi, who possessed towers and fortified residences in the city. The Romans committed themselves to proceed against these pro-papal families, especially the Frangipani. Acerbus, who had asked several times, in vain, for permission to go home, continued at his task until he became feverish and was finally allowed to leave. He was carried in a litter from the stricken city to Siena, where he remained for more than twelve weeks until he died on 18 October.[51]

"The Hand of God"[52]

Acerbus Morena was one of the thousands of victims of the epidemic that struck the army and city of Rome after a torrential downpour in the early afternoon of 2 August 1167. It had been a beautiful but exceedingly hot morning. The sudden storm swamped the camp and tore the tents away. Within hours many men and horses began to die. The symptoms included a high fever, headaches, intense pains in the stomach and intestines, great fatigue, and an awful stench emitted by the stricken before they died. Scholars long believed that the disease was malaria, which remained a scourge in Rome until Benito Mussolini drained the swamps. However, while some men may have been infected with malaria during the army's southward advance through malaria-ridden regions and during the two-month stay of the archbishops' troops outside the city, and while malaria may have weakened their resistance, the eight-day incubation period of malaria precludes it from being the primary cause of the epidemic that began killing a large number of men within hours of the storm. Conversely, if malaria had been the culprit, there would have been a substantial number of deaths before 2 August among the men who had been exposed during the preceding months. An explanation that better fits the epidemiology of the outbreak is dysentery, which also killed Henry VI, Frederick II, and Louis IX. The flood that swept through the camp with its primitive sanitary conditions would have contaminated the water supply with feces. Frederick and Beatrice may have been spared because the emperor was descending into the valley when he saw the storm approaching and returned to their camp on top of Monte Mario, where the water was not polluted.

He remained there until 6 August, when the chancery was still functioning well enough to draft a charter on behalf of the church of St. Bartholomew on the island in the Tiber. The princes who witnessed the charter were the following: Archbishops Christian and Rainald; the bishops of Liège, Speyer, Prague, Zeitz-Naumburg, and Halberstadt; the abbot of Fulda; Frederick of Rothenburg; Duke Berthold IV of Zähringen; and Welf VII. The only survivors of the epidemic among the witnesses were Christian, Udo II of Naumburg, Gero of Halberstadt, and Berthold. Daniel of Prague died on 9 August, Alexander of Liège on 9 or 10 August, Hermann of Verden on 11 August, Rainald of Dassel on 14 August, Frederick of Rothenburg on 19 August, Eberhard of Regensburg on 24 August, Welf VII in Siena on 12 September, Conrad of Augsburg on 24 November, and Godfrey of Speyer on 28 January 1168. Other known victims of the epidemic were: Duke Theobald of Bohemia, the brother of King Vladislav II; Counts Burchard of Hallermund, Henry of Nassau, Berchtold of Pfullendorf, Berengar II of Sulzbach, Henry of Tübingen, and Markwart of Leuchtenberg; Rainald's brother, Count Ludolf I of Dassel; Burgrave Hermann of Cologne; and the nobleman, Hermann of Lippe. The chroniclers differ greatly about the total death toll. For example, the continuer of the Morena chronicle said that more than 2,000 knights had died by the time Frederick reached Lombardy in early September; whereas

Lambert of Waterlos reported in the *Annals of Cambrai* that 7,000 soldiers and 20,000 Romans perished. They agreed, however, with Boso that the annihilation of the imperial army had been an act of God. For the Lodiese Anonymous, for instance, the epidemic was "a divine miracle," while the author of the *Cologne Royal Chronicle* noted that God had cast down nearly all the dignitaries of the priestly order and had overthrown the princes in accordance with the command in Ezekiel 9:6 to slay everyone, beginning in the sanctuary.[53]

Leaving the dying behind, Frederick left Rome on 6 August or shortly thereafter and traveled northward as quickly as he could. Paschal III remained in Viterbo, and the Roman hostages were placed in his custody. By 29 August the emperor was in Lucca. On 31 August the knights and clergy of Pisa welcomed him, Beatrice, and their son, presumably Conrad (Frederick VI), who had been born in February, and escorted them to the cathedral and then to the archiepiscopal palace. Barbarossa thanked the people at their assembly for their services at Ancona and for their naval help at Civitavecchia and Rome. The inhabitants of Pontremoli, situated between Pisa and Genoa at the southern approach to the La Cisa Pass that linked the Ligurian coast and Lombardy, blocked his passage. During the fighting, even Beatrice was forced, according to Godfrey of Viterbo, to ward off arrows with a shield. The imperial party could not gain access to the pass and had to be escorted by Margrave Obizzo Malaspina on steep mountain paths through his territory. Frederick and Beatrice finally reached Pavia in the margrave's company on 12 September. In a public address on 21 September the emperor outlawed all the Lombard cities that had conspired against him, except for Cremona and Lodi, whose loyalty he vainly hoped to regain, and threw down his glove in a gesture of defiance. (Frederick had done the same thing in August 1158 when he publicly outlawed Milan.) He gave the princes who had survived the epidemic permission to return to Germany.[54]

On 25 or 26 September the emperor, with knights from Pavia, Novara, and Vercelli, and accompanied by Margraves William of Montferrat and Obizzo Malaspina and William's brother-in-law, Count Guido of Biandrate, devastated, looted, and burned the Milanese *contado*. Frederick returned to the outskirts of Pavia on the news that a Lombard army composed of men from Lodi, Bergamo, Brescia, Cremona, and Parma was approaching; but after eating a meal without dismounting from his horse, he crossed the Po and raided the territory of Piacenza. Once again, the approach of the Lombards forced him to withdraw, on 29 September or shortly thereafter. In October the Pavians and the few German knights that Frederick still had at his disposal—the Lodiese Anonymous stressed the reduction in the number of Germans—plundered and burned the castle and village of Mombrione on the Lambro. In a skirmish in Milanese territory on 11 November the emperor lost twenty-five knights and fled back to Pavia; but he no longer felt secure there after his men blinded a Pavian noble in a melee. Frederick's position became even more difficult on 1 December, when the Lombard rebels and Veronese League merged "in an alliance of cities," which became known officially in 1168 as the Lombard League (*Societas Lombardie*). The cities agreed to aid each other against anyone who attacked a member and to pay the crown no more than the communes had owed the emperor between the reign of Henry IV and Frederick's accession. Margrave Obizzo Malaspina adhered to the League on 27 December. Frederick, essentially cornered, spent the winter of 1167–68 moving about the territories of Pavia, Novara, Vercelli, Montferrat, and Asti. According to John of Salisbury, an army of allegedly 20,000 Lombard knights pursued him; and Frederick did not dare to spend more than two or three nights in the same place.[55]

John of Salisbury repeatedly referred to Frederick as an ex-emperor (*ex-Augustus*) in a bit of wishful thinking and in the mistaken belief that the Lateran Synod of 1167 had deposed Frederick in the same way that Gregory VII had removed Henry IV from office in 1080. Yet Pope Alexander had technically only released the Italians from their oaths of fealty to Frederick. In practice, it amounted to the same thing as far as Frederick's diehard opponents were concerned: Frederick had forfeited his imperial dignity, in John of Salisbury's view, when he became a schismatic. John wrote, probably already in 1165: "there is no emperor today as far as Christ is concerned, since a schismatic is striving by force and fraud . . . to cleave the indivisible unity . . . and to take the Roman imperial dignity from Christ." John also repeated the rumor that God had afflicted Frederick with gout, so that he could walk only with the aid of his servants.[56]

Desperate, Frederick was ready to negotiate with his enemies, if only to gain time so he could escape from Italy. He was open to a rumored Lombard proposal, Provost Sigiboto of Salzburg informed Archbishop Conrad II, that Conrad and his brother Henry Jasomirgott mediate between their nephew and the Lombards. John of Salisbury reported in the spring of 1168 that on the advice of a Carthusian monk, almost certainly Frederick's presumptive natural son, Dietrich of Silve-Bénite, the emperor had summoned to his court the prior of the Grande Chartreuse, the abbot of Cîteaux, and the exiled Bishop Peter of Pavia about ending the schism if they could procure Frederick's release from the Würzburg Oath. Nothing came of these efforts because, as John pointed out, Margrave William of

Montferrat procured permission from his nephew, Count Humbert III of Savoy and Maurienne, who had been blocking Frederick's escape, to allow Frederick, in exchange for "mountains of gold," to pass through the count's domains. The real price for the count's consent may have been the county of Turin, which Frederick conferred on Humbert. Around 9 March the emperor reached Susa, west of Turin in the Po valley at the eastern approach to the Mont Cenis Pass, which led to the Rhone valley in Burgundy. The townspeople forced Frederick, John wrote, to release the remaining Italian hostages he had with him before they would let him proceed. According to Otto of St. Blasien, the emperor was warned that the citizens were plotting to murder him. In a device invented by Berthold IV of Zähringen, the knight and imperial chamberlain, Hartmann of Siebenich, took the emperor's place in bed; and Frederick disguised as a servant, accompanied by only two other men (the number of men varies in the sources from one to five), crossed over the Alps. It was an ignominious end to the fourth Italian campaign. Upon his return to Italy in 1174, Frederick would level Susa. According to Godfrey of Viterbo, Beatrice, who had stayed behind in the hostile city in 1168, rejoiced at its destruction.[57]

How did Frederick react to the Roman catastrophe? After Rainald of Dassel's death on 14 August, a still-triumphant Frederick wrote to the advocate of Cologne, who was charged with collecting the revenue from the archiepiscopal domains, that on account of Rome's submission, "we have excelled all our predecessors in glory and honor." In the hour of victory, "Rainald, the most beloved archbishop of Cologne," had died, to Frederick's immense sorrow. "It had always been his [Rainald's] chief wish and the purpose of his steadfast will," the emperor said, "to place the honor of the Empire and the increase of the state above his personal interests and to advance ardently whatever seemed to him to be advantageous to our glory." The advocate and his colleagues were to secure the election of the chancellor, Philip of Heinsberg, the only person in the Empire worthy to succeed Rainald as archbishop.[58] Frederick's words were most certainly not a repudiation of Rainald's policies, but the letter to the Cologne officials was neither the moment nor the occasion to do so (anymore than when the President of the United States accepts with regret the resignation of a member of the cabinet for unspecified family reasons). None of Frederick's subsequent advisers was as influential as Rainald of Dassel.

Frederick's tone was very different in a general circular he "sent throughout the entire extent of his kingdom"—probably in conjunction with the outlawing of the Lombard cities on 21 September—in which he announced "the destruction of his men and the rebellion of the Italians." In the extant copy

Bishop Albert of Freising received, the emperor proclaimed that "the heavens were astonished and the whole world trembled" at the news that "certain cities of Lombardy, namely, Milan, Piacenza, Cremona, Bergamo, Brescia, Mantua, and the mark of Verona" had rebelled "against our majesty, against the honor of the Empire without cause . . ." (Was he really that clueless about the causes of the rebellion?) The revolt was aimed not only against Frederick's own person, he said, but also against the empire of the Germans, "which has been bought and preserved till now with great exertion and much expense and with the blood of many princes and illustrious men." (This letter was the only occasion on which Frederick's chancery used the term *Teutonicorum imperium.*) The Italians no longer wished to be ruled by him or to be subject to the lordship of the Germans. Frederick preferred to die fighting the enemy than to allow the destruction of the Reich.[59] At the very moment when Frederick had become almost completely dependent on soldiers supplied by the few Italian communes and magnates who remained loyal to him, he chose to emphasize the German character of his realm, a curious admission that critics like John of Salisbury were right: he was not the temporal head of Christendom but only one king among many. Surely that was a repudiation of Rainald of Dassel's denigration of other European monarchs as mere provincial kings, perhaps an unwitting one in a moment of crisis when Frederick was appealing to some sense of German ethnic identity and pride.

Perhaps we should not make too much of this isolated use of *Teutonicorum imperium*, but, as we have already seen, after 1167 Frederick was no longer described as triumphant or victorious, and *sacrum imperium* virtually disappeared from chancery productions until the 1180s. Likewise, the use of the words *honor* and *gloria* in the *arengae* of imperial charters is concentrated in the period between 1158 and 1167, when Rainald's voice was the dominant one at court and Frederick was at the height of his power. The emperor continued to be concerned after 1167, according to the *arengae*, about the honor and glory of the Empire; but the terms were no longer employed by the notaries in reference to the princes' obligation to serve the realm. The catastrophic epidemic of August 1167, in which so many princes paid with their lives, ended their alliance with the emperor; and he became, like them, a paterfamilias whose primary concern was the well-being of his sons and dynasty.[60] When Frederick left Italy on 9 March 1168, he had been king for exactly sixteen years. The remaining twenty-two years of his reign are in some ways only a coda. If Frederick had died outside Rome, it is doubtful that he would have been remembered as Germany's greatest medieval ruler.

CHAPTER THIRTEEN

A BITTER HOMECOMING

The Nadir of Frederick's Fortunes

FREDERICK ARRIVED IN BASEL on 15 March 1168; and he returned to Italy via Basel in September 1174. This was to be his longest continuous stay in Germany during his reign. We know less about these six and a half years than any other period after his accession in 1152, and we have less information, in general, about the last twenty-two years of his reign than the first fifteen. The diminution of his influence and the decline of interest in his activities are evident in the *Regesta Imperii*, the chronological ordering of all references to Frederick in narrative sources, letters, and charters. The largest number of entries (201) occurs, not surprisingly, in 1189, when he went on the Third Crusade. The four other peak years with more than 150 notices each concern the outbreak of the schism, the destruction of Milan, his third Italian expedition, and the annihilation of his army: 1159 (154), 1162 (173), 1164 (151), and 1167 (155). Seven of the eight years with fewer than 50 entries, three of them in the period between 1168 and 1174, are after 1167: 1169 (the nadir with 36), 1171 (42), 1173 (42), 1175 (46), 1180 (50), 1182 (39), and the year of his death 1190 (a half year with 46). Not a single letter or charter survives for between 10 January and 28 June 1168, an indication that the chancery may have ceased to function.[1] Yet it was during this stay in Germany that Frederick initiated the policies he pursued for the remainder of his reign.

John of Salisbury wrote, probably in May 1168, that the "ex-emperor, driven out in disgrace and shame, is a fugitive and an exile from Lombardy, has thrown his own Burgundy into confusion as he passed through and has found all Germany in uproar. Now the fall he has earned seems to be at hand."[2] A comparison of Frederick's itinerary during the first year of his reign, when he had traversed his entire realm north of the Alps, with the little that is known about his travels in the year after his return on 15 March 1168, shows the magnitude of his defeat. On 5 May he was in Würzburg; on 1 June, in Frankfurt; from 28 June to 10 July, back in Würzburg; on 29 September, in Schwäbisch-Gmünd, south of Würzburg; on 26 November, in Worms; at Christmas in Alsace (Haguenau?); on 20 January 1169, in Heiligenstadt, near Erfurt; and in February in Wallhausen, a palace in northern Thuringia. He finished the circuit in Nuremberg. Except for his foray in early 1169 into Thuringia, where his sister was the landgravine, his journeys had been confined to the Staufer heartland on the Middle Rhine between Haguenau and Worms and to the Main valley.

If the purpose of such royal peregrinations was to see and to be seen, Frederick had lost contact with the princes. Indeed, in May 1168 the Saxon princes, who were fighting Henry the Lion, ignored, according to a monk in Pöhlde, two summonses by Frederick to attend his court. Even more revealing is the witness list in Frederick's most important act in 1168: the "Golden Liberty" in which on 10 July he granted the bishop of Würzburg total jurisdiction in the bishopric and duchy of Würzburg. Numerous counts, nobles, and even ministerials witnessed the charter; but the names of only seven laymen of princely rank, brothers at that, were appended to the document: Frederick's own brother Conrad; Margrave Otto of Meissen and his brothers Margrave Dietrich of Lusatia and Count Henry I of Wettin; the stalwart Otto of Wittelsbach and his brother Frederick; and the emperor's former brother-in-law, Margrave Berthold II of Vohburg. Except for the emperor's immediate relatives, the princes rarely appeared at court during the last two decades of his reign. After his return from Italy, Frederick had to compel newly elected bishops, who were reluctant to be consecrated by a schismatic, to be ordained by Archbishop Christian of Mainz; and Albo of Passau, who refused, was deposed. The kingdom was in disarray.[3]

After the death of Paschal III in Rome on 20 September 1168, and the election of Abbot John of Struma, whom Frederick did not know personally, as Calixtus III (resigned 29 August 1178), Frederick made tentative overtures to reach an accommodation with Pope Alexander. If Boso is to be believed, Frederick "was inwardly deeply grieved" at Calixtus' selection. The emperor dispatched Henry the Lion, who had married Matilda of England on 1 February 1168, and Archbishops Christian of Mainz and Philip of Cologne, to mediate between the English and French kings in hopes of using their good offices in his own dealings with Alexander. They met with Henry II in Rouen, sometime after 14 October; and Archbishop Philip then went by himself to talk to Louis. The two Western monarchs did make peace in January 1169.[4]

Encouraged perhaps by the favorable outcome of this diplomatic initiative, Frederick invited Alexander of Cologne, who was the abbot of Cîteaux, and Abbot Pons of Clairvaux to his court to negotiate on his behalf with Alexander III. They met with the emperor on Ash Wednesday (5 March 1169), and they asked that Bishop Eberhard of Bamberg accompany them to Rome. The Lombards subsequently detained Eberhard, who had resumed his role as a mediator after Rainald's death; but the two abbots met with Pope Alexander in Benevento. According to a letter written by John of Salisbury at the end of August, "the German tyrant" was asking the pope to accept as "emperor" his second son, Henry, who had been elected as king (Henry VI) in June, and to have Catholic bishops consecrate his son "as a person ready to obey the Holy See, so long as Frederick himself is not compelled on his account (unless he so wishes) to accept any pope save Peter himself and the other popes in Heaven." Alexander would have accepted the offer, John wrote, if Frederick had "not inserted a condition that clergy ordained and consecrated by schismatic heresiarchs remain in the orders and dignities they had received." John was optimistic, nevertheless, that peace might be made. Securing papal acceptance of Henry's succession had been linked to Frederick's effort to terminate the schism.[5]

The Election of Henry VI

The death of so many princes on the fourth Italian campaign and the frail health of his eldest son, Frederick V—if he was still alive—may have convinced Frederick of the need to secure his son Henry's selection as king. Henry was elected as king, in the presence of the anti-pope's cardinal-legates, at the Whitsunday court that met in Bamberg between 8 and 24 June 1169; the exact date is unknown. Archbishop Christian placed the child's name in nomination on Frederick's behalf. We know nothing about the conduct of the actual proceedings. There does not seem to have been any opposition to Henry's elevation to the throne, because Frederick had been confident enough about the outcome to entrust the Cistercian abbots and Bishop Eberhard already on 6 April, at a prior court in Bamberg, with obtaining Alexander's consent. Archbishop Philip of Cologne crowned the infant, in the absence of his father, in Aachen on 15 August.

John of Salisbury's report about the abbots' negotiations with Pope Alexander is puzzling in several ways. Theoretically, Frederick had bound his yet-to-be-chosen successor at Würzburg in 1165 not to recognize Cardinal Roland as pope. The emperor was apparently ready to abandon that commitment for his son but not for himself. Since Frederick never questioned the pope's right to crown the king of the Romans as emperor, it is not likely that he would have offered to have his son consecrated as emperor by Catholic bishops. Such a proposed violation of papal prerogatives would have been a non-starter. The best explanation may be that Frederick was ready to have Henry crowned as king by non-schismatic bishops and was asking Alexander in turn to accept Henry as a co-emperor. Alexander demanded, presumably, in spite of what John wrote, his recognition as pope. Frederick may have waited for two months after Henry's election for Alexander's response before having the schismatic archbishop of Cologne crown his son.[6]

John's letter is the chief piece of evidence that Henry was Frederick's second son, but in the charter Barbarossa issued for St. Mary's in Aachen on 8 January 1166, he had listed his son Frederick ahead of Henry, another sign that Frederick V was the older brother. Barbarossa had referred on 29 September 1168 to "his most beloved son, Duke Frederick of Swabia"; but we do not know whether the young duke was Frederick V or Henry VI's younger brother Frederick VI, who had originally been named Conrad but was renamed after his oldest brother's death. If Frederick V was still alive in June 1169, then the choice of Barbarossa's second son as king may have been a subtle recognition of the elective rather than the hereditary nature of the German monarchy, which had been reaffirmed at Besançon in 1157. Some scholars have rejected this constitutional explanation for Henry's election because there is no evidence of any princely opposition to the choice of Henry that would have necessitated such a concession, but perhaps things went so smoothly precisely because Henry was not the firstborn. Alternatively, Frederick V may have been too sickly to be considered a candidate for the crown in June 1169 and died shortly thereafter. Politically, it would have been far easier for Barbarossa to arrange for the selection of another of his sons as duke of Swabia than as king.[7] In either case, Frederick had provided for two of his sons.

Diplomatic Initiatives

Henry VI's election had diplomatic ramifications, because Frederick V had been engaged in 1165 to Eleanor, the daughter of the English king Henry II. In 1170 she married instead Alfonso VIII of Castile. We do not know whether the engagement was broken off because Frederick V was no longer the heir to the imperial throne or because he had died. Regardless, Alfonso joined Henry II and King Alfonso II of Aragon, who in 1167 had become the margrave of Provence, in a coalition directed against Louis VII's brother-in-law, Count Raymond V of Toulouse, who also claimed Provence. Raymond appeared at Frederick's court in Burgundy in the autumn of 1170, and Frederick turned for an ally to the French king, whom he had almost fought in 1165.

They met on 4 February 1171, near Vaucouleurs on the French–imperial border in Lorraine, to discuss "the restoration of the unity and peace of the Church," the marriage of Louis' daughter to Henry VI, and an alliance of friendship. Frederick and Louis agreed to fight the Brabanters in the region between the Rhine, Alps, and Paris, and not to employ them in the future. Only those mercenaries who had married a woman living in the lordship of a baron in the region or had been hired before the date of the agreement were excluded from the prohibition. Duke Matthew of Upper Lorraine and Count Henry of Troyes swore that their respective brothers-in-law would uphold the convention. Alexander appealed successfully to Louis' brother, Archbishop Henry of Reims, to block the marriage negotiations; but Vaucouleurs was the first step in the formation of an informal Capetian–Staufer alliance.[8]

In the meantime in 1170 Frederick had renewed the discussions with Alexander that had been broken off in the summer of 1169 over the pope's refusal to accept schismatic ordinations. The emperor gave Bishop Eberhard of Bamberg, whom Boso described as "ever a good Catholic at heart," full power to negotiate in accordance with the instructions he had received but to do so only in private meetings with the pope. Alexander insisted that the Lombards, who were not mentioned in Eberhard's mandate and who suspected Frederick's intentions, be included in the deliberations. Since the Normans prohibited Eberhard from entering their territory, the pope moved from Benevento to Veroli in the Campania and finally met with the bishop alone on 19 March 1170. Frederick was prepared to desist from any further hostile measures against the pope and to accept the validity of his ordinances and to enforce them, but he was unwilling to show Alexander in public the reverence that was due to the successor of St. Peter. Alexander rebuked and dismissed Eberhard for presenting such terms, and after the bishop reported on the failure of his mission, Frederick declared at the court held in Fulda on 7 June that he would never recognize Cardinal Roland as pope. The seemingly insurmountable obstacles to ending the schism were thus Frederick's refusal to submit in person to his enemy and so atone for his insults to the pope's honor, Alexander's demand that the Lombards be included in any settlement, and the fate of clerics, including Archbishops Christian and Philip, who had been ordained by schismatics.[9]

Frederick benefited, however, from the tensions between Venice, Byzantium, and the Normans, who had supported the formation of the Veronese and Lombard Leagues. Paradoxically, the annihilation of Frederick's army in 1167 had removed the threat he had posed to them and thus ended their need for unity. Venetian control of the Adriatic was threatened by the Greek occupation, in 1167, of Dalmatia, the coastal region of modern Croatia, and by Byzantium's alliance with Ancona on the opposite shore; and Venice ordered its citizens to leave the Byzantine Empire. Manuel I countered by renewing Byzantium's commercial treaties with Genoa and Pisa in 1169 and 1170, and on 12 March 1171 he imprisoned all Venetians residing in the eastern empire. Venice prepared a fleet to attack the Greeks, and Manuel engaged his daughter Maria to William II of Sicily, who could block the Venetians' passage from the Adriatic to the Mediterranean. An epidemic decimated the Venetian forces in March 1172. Manuel, no longer needing Norman support, left William, greatly insulted, waiting for his bride.

Maria was a pawn in another of her father's diplomatic schemes. Archbishop Christian, who knew Greek, had gone to Constantinople in 1170; but the purpose of his mission is unknown. However, in June 1171 a Byzantine embassy arrived in Cologne proposing a marriage between Frederick's unnamed son and Manuel's unnamed daughter, most likely, Henry VI and Maria. Frederick's failure to procure a Capetian bride for Henry earlier in the year may have tempted the emperor to respond favorably to Manuel's offer. Frederick dispatched Master Hugo of Honau, a theologian, to Constantinople. After Manuel broke off his daughter's engagement to William in 1172, Frederick's emissary, Bishop-Elect Conrad II of Worms, and Henry the Lion, who was passing through Constantinople on his way to and from Palestine on a pilgrimage, may have reopened the marital negotiations. Greek envoys were still pursuing the possibility at Frederick's court in Regensburg in June 1174.

Sometime after 12 October 1171, Frederick had sent Archbishop Christian to Italy as his legate to make peace between Genoa and Pisa, to strengthen imperial authority in central Italy, and to prepare for Frederick's fifth Italian campaign, which was formally announced at Worms on 26 March 1172. Christian, assisted by a Venetian fleet of forty ships, began the siege of Ancona, the center of Byzantine influence in Italy, on 1 April 1173; but he abandoned the undertaking in mid-October. During the siege

Christian proposed that William II marry Frederick's daughter Beatrice, but the Sicilian king rejected the offer because he was unwilling to antagonize Alexander. Earlier in 1173 the pope had blocked, once again through the agency of Archbishop Henry of Reims, a proposal that Beatrice marry Louis VII's son, Philip Augustus.

As part of his anti-Byzantine maneuvers, in 1172 Christian sent Genoese envoys to Saladin's court in Cairo with an offer of friendship. According to a letter Saladin wrote, probably in April 1173, the sultan was uncertain whether the proposal came from Frederick or only from his arch-chancellor. To find out, Saladin's envoy stopped in Genoa on his way to Frederick's court. He arrived in Germany in October 1173, bringing rare and valuable gifts, and stayed until June 1174, when he returned home with great honor and appropriate tokens of imperial munificence. The author of the *Cologne Royal Chronicle* recorded the rumors that Saladin had proposed to marry his son to Frederick's daughter, that Saladin and his realm were prepared to convert to Christianity, and that he would release Christian prisoners. In 1175 Frederick sent the cleric Burchard of Strasbourg to Saladin. His mission must have been successful since Frederick felt obligated in 1188, after he took the cross, to abrogate the alliance formally because he could no longer be Saladin's friend.

Frederick and Christian, who seems to have been directing imperial affairs, were largely responding in the early 1170s to events, most notably the deterioration in Byzantium's relations with Venice and William II, rather than adhering to a preconceived foreign-policy agenda. Nevertheless, Christian succeeded in detaching Venice from the Lombards; and it became the site of Frederick's reconciliation with Alexander in 1177. William rejected Christian's proposal that he marry a Staufer princess, but the offer was the first indication that the imperial court was prepared to treat the Hautevilles as equals. The political constellation in the Mediterranean had subtly shifted by the mid 1170s to Frederick's advantage, but his excommunication made it impossible for his children to marry their royal peers.[10]

Archbishop Adalbert II of Salzburg

Within Germany, Salzburg continued to be the major center of opposition to Frederick during the schism. After the death of Archbishop Conrad II in 1168, the clergy and ministerials tried to demonstrate again that allegiance to Alexander was compatible with loyalty to the emperor by electing his cousin, the twenty-three-year-old Adalbert, son of Frederick's

Babenberg aunt, Gertrude, and King Vladislav II of Bohemia. Although Frederick had outlawed Conrad, he had never actually deposed his uncle, who had managed to keep his lay opponents at bay. Adalbert (1168–77) lacked the maturity and diplomatic finesse to balance his competing obligations—he was far more successful during his second tenure as archbishop (1183–1200)—and Frederick, after his loss of prestige in Italy, was no longer willing to tolerate Salzburg's defiance. Adalbert postponed asking his cousin for investiture with the regalia, but acted as if he was already in possession of his secular authority. In violation of the Concordat of Worms, Patriarch Ulrich II of Aquileia nevertheless consecrated Adalbert on 15 March 1169, even though Pope Alexander had not yet recognized Adalbert's election. The pope concealed his displeasure, but Frederick refused to receive Adalbert when he appeared in June in Bamberg, even if the emperor risked snubbing Vladislav, who had accompanied his son. Frederick arrived at the beginning of August in Salzburghofen, today Freilassing, just outside the city of Salzburg, and threatened to destroy all the monasteries and churches in the archdiocese if Adalbert did not submit. On the advice of the princes, most notably his maternal uncle, Henry Jasomirgott, Adalbert surrendered all the earthly possessions, rights, income, and ministerials of the church of Salzburg to Frederick without regaining his grace; and the emperor assumed the direct governance of the ecclesiastical principality. Adalbert's act was unprecedented, but it is worth recalling that at Würzburg, in 1165, the bishops, led by Wichmann of Magdeburg, had offered to return the regalia if they would not be required to swear allegiance to Paschal III. Frederick did not permit Adalbert to remain in his see but did not depose him either.

Frederick returned to the archdiocese in 1170. He was in February in Salzburg itself, where the most prominent archiepiscopal ministerials waited for him, and in March in the major centers of the archbishops' secular lordship in the Alps: Friesach in Carinthia and Leibnitz in Styria. To gain the loyalty of the Salzburg clergy, he issued charters for the Augustinian canons of St. Zeno in Bad Reichenhall in Bavaria and for the Benedictines of St. Lambrecht in Styria and St. Paul in the Lavant valley in Carinthia. Frederick was especially generous to the archiepiscopal proprietary bishopric of Gurk, which received all the existing and yet-to-be-developed mines and salt works located in its Carinthian domains, because Bishop Henry I was serving as Adalbert's vicar in his absence. However, most of the Salzburg clergy refused to abandon either Alexander or Adalbert, but urged the archbishop to procure peace for the Church.

In 1171 Vladislav asked Archbishop Wichmann to mediate between his son and Frederick, and Wichmann procured permission for Adalbert to attend Frederick's court in Goslar in November. He did not come, but the Bohemian king made major concessions in writing on his son's behalf, which were kept secret. Frederick held a court in Salzburg on 20 February 1172. Adalbert again failed to attend, and Frederick gave the clerics the option of electing a new archbishop or accepting his choice. He then ordered the reading of his sealed agreement with Vladislav to the astonished clergy. Adalbert had promised, it said, to pay Frederick an enormous sum of money, to burn in the emperor's presence the pallium that Alexander had sent him, and to join the imperial side. At this critical juncture Adalbert suddenly appeared and denied agreeing to any such terms. He was given the choice of accepting the princes' immediate judgment, postponing the decision to a later court, or submitting to the emperor's grace with the prospect of receiving honorable compensation for the loss of the archbishopric. Adalbert asked for time to consider, but the next morning it was discovered that he had absconded during the night. The incensed emperor demanded an immediate new election, but finally agreed to give the clergy until 24 June to decide upon a candidate. Nothing happened.

Adalbert alienated many of his remaining supporters, and after his father's abdication in 1173 he was forced to flee from the Bohemian court and take refuge with his Austrian uncle, Henry Jasomirgott. Both appeared at Frederick's court in Regensburg on 26 May 1174, which was attended by all of Adalbert's suffragans, except the bishop of Freising. The princes, except for the duke of Austria, agreed to Adalbert's deposition; and the clergy and ministerials elected Provost Henry of Berchtesgaden, who had represented Archbishop Eberhard at the Council of Pavia in 1160. Frederick invested the new archbishop with the regalia, and Henry granted the princes and nobles, led by Henry the Lion, their archiepiscopal fiefs. Since the emperor no longer demanded that Archbishop Henry and the Salzburg clergy explicitly repudiate Alexander, there was some reason to hope that the court's decision would gain general acceptance. In September 1174 Frederick went to Italy.

Nevertheless, Adalbert still had some backers in the archdiocese; and he appealed to Alexander, who invalidated Henry of Berchtesgaden's election and ordered the suffragan bishops and prelates of Salzburg to obey Adalbert. The result was a schism within a schism. The papal legate, Cardinal Conrad of Sabina, the former archbishop of Mainz, who had a very low opinion of Adalbert, did not assist him and instead complained about his conduct to the pope. Alexander delegated, therefore, to Cardinal

Walter of Albano the examination of the case; and on 1 August 1176, at Györ in Hungary, the legate ruled against Henry, who had ignored the summons, and in favor of Adalbert on account of his steadfast loyalty to the pope and the persecution he had endured. The dispute was finally resolved in Venice in August 1177.[11]

Frederick's Interventions in Bohemia

The striking aspect of Frederick's confrontation with Adalbert is how little support the archbishop received from his father Vladislav II. The king was even prepared in 1171 to make secret concessions to the emperor, which were unacceptable to Adalbert. Vladislav's real objective was to secure the succession of his eldest son, Duke Frederick, as king of Bohemia. In theory, the Bohemian freemen, that is, the free landowning warriors, were entitled to select any Přemyslid as duke but with a preference for seniority. For example, in 1140, the freemen had elected Vladislav II, the son of Duke Vladislav I (r. 1109–25), rather than his young cousin Vladislav, the son of the deceased regnant duke, Soběslav I (r. 1125–40). The winner could seek investiture from the emperor, who was not otherwise involved in the internal affairs of Bohemia; but such imperial confirmation was not mandatory or binding. Often it was the losing candidate in a disputed election or a duke dealing with a revolt who appealed to the German king for assistance. The losers, if they did not die in battle, were exiled, imprisoned, or blinded. Soběslav's son, Oldřich (Ulrich), spent many years at the imperial court; and his brother, Soběslav II, was imprisoned by Vladislav II from 1161 to 1173. Vladislav may have hoped to circumvent the electoral rights of the freemen by procuring a crown from the emperor in 1158 and turning Bohemia into a hereditary monarchy, but they had objected to this infringement of their prerogatives.

Old and sick, Vladislav abdicated in 1173 (he died two years later) in favor of his son Duke Frederick, without seeking either the freemen or the emperor's consent. Vladislav's cousin Oldřich utilized the king's political blunder and his own influence at the imperial court to seek the release of his imprisoned brother Soběslav II. Barbarossa ordered Soběslav freed and brought to Prague. Soběslav, afraid that he would be blinded, fled to the emperor; and Duke Frederick followed. In September 1173, the German princes ruled that the duchy—Bohemia was no longer called a kingdom—was to be conferred on Oldřich; but he asked that the emperor enfeoff instead his older brother Soběslav II (r. 1174–78, d. 1180). Soběslav and Oldřich, who became the duke of Olomouc in Moravia, promised to supply Barbarossa with men for his fifth Italian campaign. Oldřich, who had previously accompanied the emperor to Italy, subsequently commanded the Bohemian forces that participated in Frederick's siege of Alessandria.[12]

Soběslav did not enjoy the emperor's favor for long. In the winter of 1174–75 Barbarossa rebuked the duke for preventing the emperor's kinsman, Bishop Frederick of Prague, from visiting the imperial court, and for depriving another of Barbarossa's kinsmen, Jerome, of the chapel that King Vladislav had granted him. (The letter made the titular distinction between Soběslav and Vladislav.) The emperor was ready to forgive the duke's offenses if Soběslav gave the provostry of Mělník, at the confluence of the Vltava and Elbe rivers, to Jerome—the unspoken cause of Barbarossa's displeasure was that Soběslav had conferred the provostry on Adalbert. The emperor also asked for a written report about Archbishop Wichmann's embassy to King Béla III of Hungary—another piece of evidence that more use was made of writing than the extant record suggests—and that Soběslav urge the knights he had sent to Italy to fulfill their obligations. The real kicker in the letter was Frederick's not very veiled warning that he had hoped for greater things ("maiora") from Soběslav on account of the "beneficiis" (kindnesses or fiefs?) the emperor had granted him.[13] Did the chancery deliberately utilize language that was eerily reminiscent of Pope Adrian's at Besançon in 1157?

The duke did not take the hint. Soběslav invaded and devastated the duchy of Austria north of the Danube in 1176 and 1177, and he ignored Barbarossa's summonses to come to his court. The emperor therefore reinstated Duke Frederick—who had spent the intervening four years as an exile in Hungary and at the imperial court—as the ruler of Bohemia (r. 1178–89), though Duke Frederick still had to fight his way to the throne. In 1179 Barbarossa settled at a court in Eger, with the advice of the princes, the dispute between his kinsmen, his first cousins, Duke Leopold V of Austria and Duke Frederick of Bohemia, about the boundary between their duchies. The Austrian border was extended considerably into what had been Bohemian-Moravian territory, one of the rare instances when a medieval emperor delineated a specific frontier. For a long time scholars interpreted Barbarossa's interventions in Bohemian affairs in 1173 and 1178 from the perspective of the German-Czech antagonism of the nineteenth and twentieth centuries, but the emperor's involvement was no different in this instance than in his other adjudications of his relatives' quarrels.[14]

The Přemyslids continued to call upon the emperor in the 1180s to settle their internecine feuds. The first quarrel, in 1182, involved the relationship between Bohemia and Moravia. Duke Břetislav I (r. 1037–55) had assigned to his younger sons domains in Moravia, and their descendants ruled over the vice-duchies of Brno, Znojmo, and Olomouc. The Bohemians rebelled in 1182 against the hated Duke Frederick and elected Conrad Otto, who held the duchies of Znojmo and Brno, in his place. Duke Frederick fled to his imperial cousin, who summoned Conrad Otto and his supporters to his court. At Regensburg, in September 1182, the emperor ended the dispute with a show of force. According to the Premonstratensian abbot, Gerlach of Milevsko:

> [t]he nobles were presented to the emperor alone. Wishing to terrify them, he ordered a large number of pick-axes brought, as if he wanted to have them beheaded. When they threw themselves at his feet, they sought forgiveness and, necessity having changed into will, they accepted Frederick as their lord and duke. They returned with him to Prague, considering themselves and Conrad very rich, because they were not punished for the crime of treason. Thus the wise emperor wisely repressed the plot of the rebels; he returned Bohemia to one man, and ordered the other to be content with Moravia.

Historians long thought that Barbarossa made Conrad Otto the ruler of a new imperial principality, Moravia, directly subject to the German crown (the first such new entity after the establishment of the estate of the imperial princes in 1180); but Moravia remained, in fact, part of Bohemia, though it retained a distinct identity as a secundogeniture for Přemyslid princes.[15]

The second quarrel occurred in 1187 and involved Bishop Henry of Prague, Vladislav II's nephew and Duke Frederick's cousin. Most bishops of Prague were the duke's creatures, but as a member of the regnant dynasty, Henry's position was different. The specific cause of the tension between the cousins is not totally clear, but the bishop objected to violations of the Church's privileges by ducal officials. He took his case to the imperial court, where he witnessed a charter on 11 November 1186. Barbarossa was favorably disposed to Henry—according to Gerlach, the emperor assumed the cost of maintaining the bishop's entourage, invited him to meals, and allowed him, with the permission of the ordinaries, to consecrate chapels in German dioceses—but Henry had to wait until a court in Regensburg in March 1187 for a resolution of his suit. The duke's representative argued that Henry, like all his predecessors, was merely a ducal chaplain and thus lacked standing to file charges against his lord at the imperial court. The princes, especially the bishops, were incensed and determined "that the bishop of Prague, according to the custom of German bishops, ought to be entirely free from any subjection to the duke and ought to be subject and obliged to the emperor alone, of whose empire he is a prince, whose court he is to visit, and from whom he receives the scepter and investiture." The judgment was recorded in a lost imperial privilege sealed with a golden bull. The princes' decision is understandable because the bishop of Prague was a suffragan of the archbishop of Mainz; but even Bishop Daniel, whose conduct most resembled that of an imperial bishop, never forgot his subordination to Vladislav. Gerlach, our source, added that the privilege "obtained fully in the days of that bishop, but later not at all." It became a dead letter when Bishop Henry doubled as the duke of Bohemia (r. 1193–97).[16]

When Barbarossa reinstated Duke Frederick in 1182, the latter may have ceded to the emperor the western Bohemian province of Sedlec (Zettlitz), just east of Eger (today Cheb). Bohemia regained the lordship in the 1190s, perhaps in conjunction with Bishop Henry's installation as duke in 1193.[17] Frederick had acquired or reacquired the Egerland itself, which may have been the dowry of his first wife Adela of Vohburg, upon the death of his cousin Frederick of Rothenburg in Italy in 1167. The emperor probably visited Eger for the first time in 1179, when he settled there the boundary dispute between Duke Frederick of Bohemia and Leopold V of Austria.

Territorial Acquisitions

Ironically, the death of so many princes and nobles on Frederick's fourth Italian campaign enabled him to enlarge the Reich's and the Staufer's dynastic holdings in Germany and so to accept eventually the thwarting of his Italian territorial ambitions, which he had pursued after ceding Swabia to his cousin, Frederick of Rothenburg. The emperor turned defeat into victory, but it placed him, hitherto a largely absentee monarch, in direct competition with the German princes, most notably his cousin Henry the Lion. Barbarossa ceased to be the impartial arbiter of their disputes, if he ever really was; and he became simply the first among equals in the scramble for land and power.

Swabia

In a famous passage, Otto of St. Blasien commented that upon Frederick's return from Italy in 1168, he "obtained by hereditary succession all the land

and the entire fortune of Duke Frederick of Rothenburg, the son of his father's brother, a prince exceedingly well endowed with properties and afterwards he brought under his control the possessions of many barons." Frederick of Rothenburg's inheritance consisted of the duchy of Swabia, as it had been constituted north of the Danube in 1098, and the lands in Franconia that had been assigned to Conrad III after the death of Duke Frederick I.

Otto and the canon of Steingaden, who continued the *History of the Welfs*, explained in some detail how Barbarossa obtained the domains of two of the "barons," his maternal uncle Duke Welf VI and Count Rudolf of Pfullendorf. If we are to believe the canon, after 1167 Welf VI consoled himself over the death of his only son and heir, Welf VII, with riotous living. The duke repudiated his pious wife and found comfort in the arms of other women, hunting, drinking, lavish feasts, and extravagant largesse. To finance his lifestyle, he sold to Frederick for gold and silver in 1173 or 1174 the principality of Sardinia, the duchy of Spoleto, the mark of Tuscany, and the manor of Elisina, which was said to have been the "house" of Margravine Matilda—lordships to which Welf had never paid much attention and which Frederick had long treated as his own. The canon insisted that Welf gave a large part of the proceeds to various monasteries, most notably Steingaden, the Premonstratensian abbey he had founded; but the canon admitted that after the sale Welf had also staged an elaborate tournament near Augsburg at Pentecost in 1175.

The duke's really valuable holdings were the Welf domains in Swabia, around Ravensburg, north of Lake Constance, and in western Bavaria. Welf agreed to convey these possessions to his nephew, Henry the Lion; but Henry postponed making the actual payment, Otto of St. Blasien said, in the mistaken belief that his elderly uncle would soon die and that as the son of Welf's brother, he had the better claim than his Staufer cousin, the son of Welf's sister, to the duke's domains. In contrast, Frederick was ready at Worms in January 1179 to satisfy his maternal uncle's immediate need for cash. Frederick retained some of the Welf lands, but enfeoffed his uncle with the remainder and also with some of the Staufer's holdings. In doing so, Frederick may have reinstated Welf as an imperial prince after he had alienated the Italian domains that were the legal basis for Welf's princely rank. Henry and Frederick's competition for their avuncular inheritance was one factor that contributed to their alienation in the 1170s.[18]

Frederick's other major Swabian acquisition that Otto of St. Blasien singled out for special mention was the domains of his long-time companion, Count Rudolf of Pfullendorf, whose only son had been another victim of the emperor's fourth Italian campaign. However, Rudolf had a daughter, Ita, who was married to Count Albrecht III of Habsburg. While the emperor might have had some claim to Rudolf's fiefs, his allods clearly belonged to Ita. Nevertheless, Otto said Rudolf "conferred all his allods on the emperor in place of his heir." Pfullendorf, north of Lake Constance, was situated on the road that linked Ulm on the Danube, which belonged to the Staufer, via Überlingen on Lake Constance, another of Rudolf's possessions, to the city of Constance. In addition, Rudolf owned a castle at Rheineck, where the Rhine flows out of the Alps into Lake Constance; the advocacy of the Benedictine monastery of Saint Gall, located south of Lake Constance; and the advocacy of the bishopric of Chur, on the uppermost stretch of the Rhine, which controlled access to the Swiss passes that led to Lake Como, north of Milan. Since Frederick announced on 15 May 1170 that Bishop Egino of Chur had enfeoffed his son, Duke Frederick VI of Swabia, with the advocacy of Chur that had previously belonged to Count Rudolf, the terms for the Staufer's acquisition of the Pfullendorf inheritance must have been worked out by that date—even though Rudolf disappears from the historical record only in 1180, when he left for the Holy Land. Rudolf's holdings thus secured the most direct route between the Staufer lands north of the Danube and Lombardy.

In compensation, Albrecht of Habsburg received the county of Zürich, the advocacy of the Benedictine nunnery of Säckingen, and Biederthal in Upper Alsace. The previous owner of the first two had been Count Ulrich IV of Lenzburg, who, like Rudolf of Pfullendorf, had accompanied Frederick on the Second Crusade and had still witnessed in 1170 Duke Frederick's enfeoffment with the advocacy of Chur. Barbarossa was in Lenzburg on 20 February 1173, presumably to take possession of the castle after Ulrich's death; and Frederick probably conferred Ulrich's former possessions on Albrecht on this occasion. These holdings rounded out the Habsburgs' own domains in northwestern Switzerland with the now ruined castle of Habsburg. (Ita of Pfullendorf was the great-grandmother of the future king, Rudolf of Habsburg.)[19]

After Frederick's acquisition of Welf VI's and Rudolf of Pfullendorf's holdings, the heart of the Staufer duchy of Swabia shifted, therefore, from north of the Danube to the region around Lake Constance, with major centers at Pfullendorf and at Ravensburg, Welf's chief castle. Otto of St. Blasien, writing in the early thirteenth century, distinguished in his narrative between these acquisitions and the duchy: Barbarossa had enfeoffed his son Frederick, Otto explained, with the duchy of Swabia, which had been assigned to Frederick of Rothenburg in 1152, and "with the inheritance of Welf and the allods of Count Rudolf of Pfullendorf." Thereafter, the duchy of Swabia referred to the Staufer's expanded territorial lordship in southwestern Germany, composed of both the Staufer's own dynastic holdings and crown lands.[20]

Frederick obtained the lands of other Swabian magnates as well. Otto wrote: "Besides the properties of many nobles, who lacked heirs, he acquired, as a gift or by paying money, the holdings of the following: Schwabeck, Warthausen, Biberach, Herlingen, Schweinhausen, Biederthal [which he granted to Albrecht of Habsburg], Lenzburg, and Donauwörth, and also of many others in other regions, who are unknown to us. These are all the things he procured in Swabia alone." Otto concluded that Frederick "took actual possession of all the fiefs that the above named men and others as well held by homage from ecclesiastical princes, both bishops and abbots—their allods were under the jurisdiction of Caesar—by having the fiefs assigned to his sons." In addition to the advocacy of Chur, Frederick VI obtained the advocacy of the bishopric of Augsburg, which had belonged to Adelgoz III of Schwabeck, another of Barbarossa's companions on the Second Crusade. As for Frederick's other sons, Otto pointed out that Henry was the heir to the throne; Conrad received the non-Swabian dignities, fiefs, and allods of Frederick of Rothenburg; Otto was assigned the "arch-throne" of Arles and Burgundy, along with the Burgundian Palatinate that had belonged to his maternal grandfather Rainald; and that Philip, the future king, was still a child.[21]

The Sulzbach Domains

Like Otto of St. Blasien, we know less about Frederick's non-Swabian acquisitions. Barbarossa arranged for his sons to obtain, after the death of Count Gebhard II of Sulzbach in 1188, the fiefs that Gebhard held from the church of Bamberg. Frederick had made a preliminary agreement with either Bishop Eberhard (d. 17 July 1172) or his successor Hermann II (1172–77), sometime after Gebhard's only son, Berengar II, succumbed on his way back from Rome in 1167. (Berengar II's mother Matilda was Frederick's maternal aunt.) The terms were revised in June 1174 at the court in Regensburg, which chose Provost Henry of Berchtesgaden as the new archbishop of Salzburg. Initially, if Gebhard consented, the bishop agreed to confer the count's fiefs after his death on Frederick's sons. In return, the bishop would receive 1,000 marks of silver, the cathedral chapter a property with a yearly income of £10, and the bishop's "friends," that is, his kinsmen, £20. Until these payments were actually made after Gebhard's demise, the bishop would hold in pledge the portion of Gebhard's fief located between Amberg and Bamberg, the canons would have a lien of £15 on the revenue from a toll, and the friends would get annually ten cartloads of wine (*carrada* or *Fuder*, 800 to 1,800 liters per cartload depending on the region.) These fiefs in the Bavarian Nordgau, essentially the county of Sulzbach, situated between Bamberg and Regensburg, connected the imperial domains around Nuremberg, west of Sulzbach, to the Egerland, northeast of Bamberg. The acquisition of the Sulzbachs' Bamberg fiefs rounded out the Staufer holdings in what is today the Upper Palatinate.

In addition, Frederick also procured a few of the Sulzbachs' extensive Bavarian holdings south of the Danube, specifically, Bad Aibling on the Mangfall, a western tributary of the Inn, and the castle of Ebbs in the Tyrol, on the east bank of the Inn, upstream from its confluence with the Mangfall. Bad Aibling and Ebbs were located on the route that led from Augsburg to the Brenner Pass and were thus, like Pfullendorf and Chur, of great strategic importance in securing Frederick's communications with Italy. The bishop agreed to confer the fiefs on the emperor's sons even if Gebhard did not consent but died without a son (Gebhard had daughters who inherited his allods) or if Frederick predeceased the count.

Beatrice joined her husband in revising, in June 1174, the earlier agreement he had made with the bishop. If the emperor died before the count, the empress would assume the obligation to pay the purchase price of the fiefs, which was raised from 1,000 to 1,200 marks. The inclusion of Beatrice in the contract indicates that the acquisition of the Bamberg fiefs, which were assigned to Frederick VI and Otto rather than the young king, was a dynastic rather than a crown matter. On 13 July 1174, in an addendum to the accord, Frederick purchased for 122 marks, payable within a year, the Bamberg fiefs that had been specifically excluded in the preliminary accord: the count's judicial rights in the Lungau, the southeastern section of the modern Austrian province of Salzburg; and fiefs in the Danube valley in Lower Bavaria and Upper Austria. Frederick also acquired the immediate use of Bad Aibling and Ebbs. The emperor may have learned the strategic value of the Lungau, which straddles the Tauern mountain range, in 1170, when he traveled through the region on the way from Salzburg to Friesach in Carinthia. The Lungau provided access from Bavaria to the Drava valley, the Balkans, and northeastern Italy. Once Frederick's conflict with Archbishop Adalbert was resolved, the remote Lungau lost its significance to the Staufer; and King Frederick II conferred all the lordship rights of the Empire in the Lungau on the church of Salzburg in 1213.[22]

The Pleissenland and the Vogtland

Frederick laid the foundation for the establishment of two imperial rather than dynastic domains situated between the Saale river and the Upper Elbe, north of the Egerland and the modern Czech–German border in the former East Germany. German settlers, protected by imperial ministerials, were engaged in extensive land clearance in this region that was inhabited by the Slavic Sorbs. Altenburg (Old Castle), which is located south of Leipzig, just west of the Pleisse river, on the route that led from Goslar to Prague via Chemnitz, was built in the tenth century. Both Lothar III and Conrad III had stayed in the castle, and Frederick, while heading for Rome in the spring of 1155 for his coronation, asked his brother-in-law, Landgrave Louis II of Thuringia, to look after the affairs of his vassal, Burgrave Henry of Altenburg. In 1158 Frederick exchanged various imperial holdings in the Harz mountains for the possessions in Swabia that had belonged to the dowry of Henry the Lion's wife, Clemence of Zähringen. The emperor compensated the Reich by conferring on it allods he had inherited from his father as well as allods he had purchased "for not a little money," the charter said, from Count Rapoto of Abenberg, the advocate of Bamberg; according to Arnold of Lübeck, Frederick had paid 500 marks. Among these allods, which were located around Altenburg, were several castles including the fief of Burgrave Henry, a market, and the fief of the ministerial Thimo of Colditz (another of the castles), and his children. Altogether, there were allods and fiefs in twenty villages. This complex on the Pleisse was soon known as the Pleissenland ("terra Plyssne")—Arnold of Lübeck said that Altenburg was also called Pleisse—and in 1172 an imperial ministerial, Hugo of Wartha, was identified for the first time as the imperial judge in the Pleissenland. Frederick was in Altenburg six times between 1165 and 1188, and in 1181 he founded and endowed a hospital there—his favorite type of pious donation and an indication that a town was forming around the castle. He took the hospital and its possessions under his protection in 1183.

There was another imperial domain, the Vogtland (Advocate Land), southwest of Altenburg, on the upper reaches of the Elster, a tributary of the Saale. (The Pleisse is a tributary of the Elster.) The territory's odd name was derived from the imperial ministerials who served as the *Vögte* (advocates) of the castles of Gera, Weida, and Plauen on the Elster, upstream from its confluence with the Pleisse. Although the advocate, Henry of Weida, was mentioned for the first time in an extant document only in 1209, the scholarly consensus is that the development of the Vogtland began during Barbarossa's reign. Frederick thus promoted colonization along the eastern frontier of the German kingdom.[23]

Thuringia

Along with the crown, Frederick acquired an extensive royal domain, west of the Saale river, in northern Thuringia: the palace complexes at Allstedt, Wallhausen, Tilleda, Nordhausen, and Mühlhausen. Numerous ministerials manned the palaces and castles. The two other major princely players in Thuringia were Frederick's brother-in-law, Landgrave Louis II of Thuringia (after 1172, Frederick's nephew Louis III), and the archbishop of Mainz, who was the lord of Erfurt. Conrad III had taken a major step in 1147 to secure the imperial position in Thuringia by placing under the Reich's protection the new Cistercian monastery of Ichtershausen, situated on the road that led from Würzburg to Erfurt and founded by the nobleman Markwart II of Grumbach and his mother. (Markwart was the only nobleman of non-comital or non-ducal rank known to have accompanied Frederick, after his election in Frankfurt, to Aachen for his coronation in 1152; his son Markwart III served in the 1160s as the imperial *podestà* in Milan.) Like Count Rudolf of Pfullendorf in Swabia, both Markwarts were thus charged with guarding a route that was of strategic importance.

In 1168, while Landgrave Louis was accompanying Frederick on imperial business, his wife Jutta (Judith) began building a castle at Weissensee, north of Erfurt. Count Frederick of Beichlingen complained to the emperor that it was situated in his territory. The landgrave publicly ordered Jutta, at her brother's command, to stop, but then secretly told her to continue. Since Weissensee, on the northern continuation of the road from Würzburg, provided access to the imperial domain in northern Thuringia, where Frederick built a major fortress on the Kyffhäuser, above the palace of Tilleda, Louis and Jutta may have acted in connivance with the emperor. The chronicler who recorded this incident also reported that Frederick spent several days in 1172, after his second Polish campaign, with his sister Jutta (Judith) and nephew Landgrave Louis III of Thuringia because he loved them.[24] Familial and personal ties mattered.

Frederick's relations with the other key Thuringian territorial lord, the archbishopric of Mainz, were contradictory. On the one hand, the archbishops, most notably Christian of Buch, were crucial in the implementation of imperial policy; on the other, a weak archbishop or one who was preoccupied elsewhere made it easier for Frederick to consolidate his power in Thuringia and the Wetterau. Paradoxically, Christian's military and diplomatic service on Frederick's behalf in Italy severely strained the archbishopric's finances and so enabled the emperor to expand at Mainz's expense. An anonymous Cistercian abbot, styling himself a "zealous emulator of God," blamed Christian, who behaved more like Mars than St. Martin (the patron saint of Mainz), for the archbishopric's sorry state in the 1170s and the clergy's moral decay. Conrad of Wittelsbach, who admittedly resented that Christian was allowed to retain the archbishopric in 1177, cataloged in 1189 or 1190 the long list of properties and rights that Christian had alienated to Frederick as well as to numerous nobles and ministerials, mainly to finance his military undertakings, properties and rights that Conrad had regained after he returned to Mainz in 1183 following Christian's death. The archbishopric's total income in the first year after Conrad's reinstatement as archbishop had been a mere 45 shillings in Mainz and seven pounds in Thuringia.[25]

The Wetterau

The Wetterau, the region between two right-bank tributaries of the Rhine, the Lahn and Main, consisted of the imperial cities of Frankfurt, Gelnhausen, Friedberg, and Wetzlar, and their hinterlands. The palace complex at Frankfurt, including the collegiate church of St. Bartholomew, dated back to the Carolingian period and had been the site of Frederick's election. A royal mint began operations in Frankfurt in the 1160s, but there is no surviving evidence for the emperor's personal involvement in the city's evolution. Indeed, Frederick, who was in Frankfurt on ten occasions during his reign, ceased his visits after 1174. He stayed, instead, seven times in Gelnhausen between 1170 and 1188.

Archbishop Conrad complained in 1189 or 1190 that Archbishop Christian of Mainz had alienated half of the castle of Gelnhausen with its appurtenances, but, unlike Christian's other alienations, Mainz was never able to regain the castle. In 1170, during his first known stay in Gelnhausen, Frederick indicated that he had established a new settlement next to the castle. Scholars, using written and archaeological evidence, disagree whether this castle, or at least the site, was identical with the palace Frederick built on an island in the Kinzig, a tributary of the Main, which was navigable as far as Gelnhausen. (Merchandise coming up the Main from Frankfurt had to be unloaded in Gelnhausen for transport by land to Fulda and, from there, via the Fulda Gap, to the headwaters of the Weser.) The castle was probably located within the new settlement, which formed on the right bank of the Kinzig, rather than on the island; but work on the palace must have been sufficiently advanced by April 1180, when the court that divided Saxony between Archbishop Philip and the Ascanians, convened in Gelnhausen, in all likelihood in the palace rather than in the castle.

During his stay in Gelnhausen in 1170, Frederick took measures that enabled the inhabitants to provision such a large assembly a decade later. He freed the merchants who had settled in Gelnhausen from the payment of tolls anywhere in the Empire—the only other cities granted this valuable privilege were Aachen, Haguenau, Monza, Rome, Pisa, and Venice. In addition, the heirs of the inhabitants who were subject to his jurisdiction—the charter specified that the heirs included sons, daughters, wives, and next of kin—could freely inherit their houses and other possessions in the settlement. The inhabitants could also sell their houses and other real estate to their fellow citizens. These proto-townspeople were subject to the exclusive jurisdiction of the emperor and his bailiff ("villicus," *Schultheiss*). Frederick subsequently commanded all his subjects throughout the Empire not to impose any exactions on the merchants of Gelnhausen wherever they ventured. To remove any doubt about their exemption from such levies, he ordered a mandate to this effect to be drafted and sealed. It seems implausible that individual merchants would have carried a copy of this document with them, but, if they did, it would point to a far greater use of writing in Germany in this period than is commonly supposed.

While Frederick was in Gelnhausen in April 1180, he confirmed that his townspeople in Wetzlar on the Lahn owed their landlord, the collegiate church of St. Mary's, an annual rent of only four pennies for their lots, and were free from any additional exactions. Their heirs or anyone who purchased their property would hold the lots on the same terms after they paid a one-time fee of 12 pennies. In addition, the emperor granted the burghers the same right and liberty to conduct their commercial transactions as his men in Frankfurt enjoyed. (Frederick may thus have conferred on or confirmed for Frankfurt a now lost privilege to that effect.) The fourth city in the Wetterau, Friedberg, developed somewhat later.[26]

Frederick, who had retained only Alsace on his accession in 1152, had obtained by the end of his reign, largely after 1167, a strong territorial base of his own in Germany, stretching from Alsace and Swabia in the southwest through the Main valley to the Egerland, northern Thuringia, and the region between the Saale river and the Elbe in the east. His acquisitions demonstrated considerable strategic sense. The possessions of Rudolf of Pfullendorf and Welf VI secured the direct route between the Staufer lands north of the Danube and Milan. The Sulzbachs' Bamberg fiefs, once Frederick and his sons took actual possession of them, linked the imperial domains around Nuremberg with the Egerland, the Pleissenland, and the Vogtland, controlled the route that led from Augsburg to the Brenner Pass, and provided access to Carinthia and Styria. The development of the Wetterau, most notably Gelnhausen, opened the way between the middle Rhine valley and Thuringia and Saxony. Frederick had turned the decimation of his army in 1167–68 to the crown's and the Staufer's advantage.

Frederick's Promotion of Economic Development

Frederick was not very interested, seemingly, in economic matters north of the Alps prior to his visit in 1165 to the lower Rhine valley, the most economically developed region in Germany, maybe because he had been until then a largely absentee monarch. As we have already seen, upon his return from Italy in 1155 he had eliminated unauthorized tolls on the Main, except for the imperial toll at Frankfurt and the four pennies that were levied on every new ship at both Neustadt and Aschaffenburg seven days before and after the Assumption of the Virgin (15 August). Merchants traveling upstream either by water or the royal road along the banks were to be free from all charges.[27]

One other act prior to 1165 had economic implications: Frederick's confirmation on 6 April 1157 of a lost privilege that his great-grandfather Henry IV had granted around 1090 to the Jews of Worms. It placed all the Jews' property, real or personal, land or people, which they possessed by hereditary right, under the king's protection, and granted them the right to trade throughout the realm without paying tolls or any other public or private exaction. They could serve as moneychangers throughout the city of Worms, except in front of the mint and the places where the moneyers exchanged money. The Jews could not own Christian slaves, but could employ Christians as maids and wet-nurses. They could not be compelled to contribute to the king's or the bishop's campaigns, nor could anyone be quartered in their homes against their will. The forced baptism of Jewish children was prohibited, but if they converted voluntarily, they would lose their paternal inheritance just as they had relinquished the laws of their fathers. Jews were to be judged by their own laws, even in cases involving Christians. It is hard to tell whether Frederick was merely confirming his great-grandfather's privilege, even if it had been superseded by other practices, or whether the charter provides an accurate picture of the Jews' relatively favorable situation in Germany in the mid-twelfth century.[28]

However, although Frederick declared that the Jews pertained to the imperial chamber, he was merely asserting that all rights of lordship, including the right to protect the Jews and the payments they owed for their defense, were regalian rights. The charter said nothing about the personal legal status of the Jews, that is, whether they were free or servile; and the emperor's assertion should not be equated with the institution of Jewish chamber serfdom that appears for the first time in a 1236 privilege of Emperor Frederick II.[29]

Barbarossa, more attune perhaps to the importance of commercial transactions after three stays in Italy, became far more proactive in the autumn of 1165. On 24 September he confirmed the rights of the moneyers of Worms. A consortium of ministerials was in charge of the mint. A new member was required to give half an uncia of gold, that is, 14.61 grams, to the bishop and a gold penny or 60 silver pennies to the master of the mint and the episcopal chamberlain. The profits from the mint belonged to the bishop, but he had to pay the master three shillings for his work and six pennies to the laborer. Only the moneyers, except for the Jews, could exchange money in the city. (This provision suggests that Frederick's 1157 privilege for the Jews was not a dead letter.) When the emperor or the king of the Romans came to Worms, he could deliver to the moneyers as much silver bullion as he wished to be struck into coins; and the minters could not retain any of the silver or coins for their own profit. During such visits, if the bishop did not have sufficient ministerials of his own to look after the court, he could employ the moneyers as the marshal, seneschal, butler, or chamberlain because, the charter said, the mint was part of the imperial chamber; but the minters could not be compelled to serve against their will in a lesser household or municipal office.[30]

Although minting coins was a royal prerogative, the right to issue coins had devolved, either through royal grants or usurpation, to ecclesiastical and lay lords. There were only about two dozen active mints in Germany in the first half of the twelfth century, and the major mints, like the one at Worms, were in the hands of the bishops, who were the lords of the most important cities in the kingdom. During the reigns of Lothar III and Conrad III the only royal mints that still functioned were those in Goslar and Nuremberg. By 1197, when Henry VI died, there were 215 mints: sixty-one belonged to bishops, forty-five to monasteries, eighty-one to lay lords, and twenty-eight to the king. Twelve of the royal mints, including the ones in Aachen, Donauwörth, Ulm, Haguenau, Duisburg, Kaiserswerth, Frankfurt, Gelnhausen, and Dortmund, were started during Frederick's reign. The proliferation of mints testifies to the enormous economic growth that occurred during Frederick's reign, but it is impossible to tell how much he was personally responsible for this development.[31]

In November 1165, at the request of the bishop of Utrecht and the counts of Holland, Guelders, and Cleves, who were concerned about the flooding of the Rhine, during a stay in Utrecht Frederick authorized the construction of a canal between the river in the territory of Neuda, near Utrecht, and the North Sea. He also ordered the removal of a dike the count of Holland had built without permission, so that no obstacles would impede the flow of the Rhine.[32]

After work began on the construction of the new palace at Kaiserswerth (perhaps in 1158), the imperial court no longer halted in its travels at the former Carolingian manor at Duisburg, situated at the confluence of the Ruhr and the Rhine, downstream from Cologne; but the settlement at Duisburg prospered from its location at the western terminus of the *Hellweg*, the road that linked the Rhine to the Weser, and from the growing trade between the Rhine valley and England. At the Christmas court of 1165 in Aachen that canonized Charlemagne, Frederick freed the burghers of Duisburg from the duties that Bishop Godfrey of Utrecht had illegally imposed on them, except for the penny they owed for the use of the episcopal measures. Conceivably, merchants from Duisburg had complained to the emperor about this abuse while he was in Utrecht in November.

Another attendee at the Aachen court, Philip of Flanders, had come to pay homage to Frederick and be enfeoffed by him with Cambrai. As a descendant of Charles the Bald's daughter Judith, Philip may also have had a dynastic interest in the canonization of Charlemagne. During Philip's stay Frederick granted Flemish merchants the right to travel freely throughout the Empire, because Cologne had been preventing the merchants of Ghent from transporting merchandise upstream on the Rhine beyond Cologne.[33]

Although Frederick's charter of 8 January 1166 is our chief source on Charlemagne's canonization, it was not a formal announcement, per se, of the emperor's elevation to the altar but a confirmation of the privileges of the coronation church of St. Mary's and of the city of Aachen. The settlement that had formed around the palace complex was not located along a major river, but in an extensive forested royal domain where the kings liked to hunt. Potentially, however, Aachen was in a position to profit from trade passing overland between Flanders with its burgeoning cloth industry, the Meuse valley, just to the west, with its metallurgy, and the Rhine valley to the east. Frederick placed the city, along with the burghers, both great and small, under imperial protection; confirmed all the rights and privileges that the "most holy Charles" and his successors had conferred on them; freed the city's merchants from all tolls and other exactions in the Roman Empire; manumitted the inhabitants who were legally serfs; and prohibited future monarchs from enfeoffing any person with any of the appurtenances that pertained to Aachen. In fact, there was nothing especially new about Frederick's grant because in a charter of 1145 Conrad III had already referred to the merchants' freedom to trade.

The next day, 9 January 1166, Frederick took more concrete measures to promote the economic development of Aachen and the lower Rhine region as a whole. In words borrowed from Charlemagne's forged charter for St. Mary's, Frederick indicated he was following his predecessor's example and protecting Aachen, which "excelled all other provinces and cities" in dignity and honor, with privileges and rights in the same way as it would be "with a wall and towers." (In 1171 he authorized the construction of real walls.) With the princes' consent, he was establishing two annual fairs in Aachen. The first was to commence on the first Sunday of Lent and to last fifteen days; the second was to start eight days before the feast of the Archangel Michael (29 September) and to run another eight days thereafter. Frederick had consulted merchants from neighboring cities because he wished the two fairs to benefit everyone. Altogether, there were ten or eleven such annual markets in the region, distributed throughout the year; and he did not want them to compete with one another. Merchants could buy and sell goods at the two fairs and throughout the year in Aachen, free from any levies. No merchant or any other person would be liable for a debt or any other obligation incurred before the fairs, but would be responsible for business undertaken at them. Frederick re-established the mint in Aachen and determined that its coins were to have the same silver content as the Cologne penny, but merchants would not be required to use the new local currency. He even stipulated that Charlemagne's image was to appear on one side of the penny and his own on the other.[34]

At the request of Philip of Flanders, Frederick revised these arrangements in 1173, perhaps because they had not proven to be as effective as he had hoped. To attract Flemish merchants, he granted them the exclusive right to sell their cloth at four annual markets, each lasting fourteen days: in Duisburg, for merchants traveling by water, starting on the fourth Sunday in Lent and on St. Bartholomew's Day (24 August), and in Aachen, for merchants coming overland, beginning on Ash Wednesday and on the feast of the Archangel Michael. Non-Flemish merchants were permitted to sell their cloth and other wares during the remainder of the year. No fees were imposed on merchandise sold in Aachen, but merchants doing business in Duisburg were charged the same duties as were levied in Cologne. To facilitate commerce, the emperor established a new mint in Duisburg to strike pennies that were slightly heavier than the Cologne penny; and he charged the mint in Aachen with issuing lighter-weight obols. Both coins were, with Philip's permission, to circulate freely in Flanders to spare Flemish merchants the extra expense of changing money. While these measures were designed to promote commercial activity in Aachen and Duisburg, the new coins were unable to compete with the Cologne coinage.[35]

Some scholars have seen Frederick's actions at the Christmas court in Aachen in 1165 as the first steps in a plan to counter the territorial expansion of the archbishops of Cologne on the lower Rhine, a precursor to his conflict in the 1180s with Rainald's successor, Archbishop Philip. The emperor's promotion of Aachen and Duisburg is even said to have been the opening salvo in a "trade war" with Cologne, which was trying to dominate commerce between the North Sea and Germany; this was because Duisburg, north of Cologne, provided an alternative terminus for merchants traveling between Flanders and Westphalia, while merchants passing overland through Aachen could reach the Rhine south of Cologne. Since 1164 the emperor had backed the archbishop of Cologne, Rainald of Dassel, in his dispute with Frederick's own brother, Conrad, over the castle of Rheineck, and since Frederick conferred on the archbishop on 1 August 1167 the imperial manor at Andernach, upstream from Cologne, along with the mint and toll located there, it seems unlikely that Frederick was already thinking in such anti-Cologne geopolitical terms in 1165. Rather, as had been true previously in the emperor's dealings with his cousin Henry the Lion and uncle Henry Jasomirgott, or with Pisa and Genoa, he was simply seeking to balance the competing claims of the count of Flanders against those of the archbishop and burghers of Cologne.[36]

Frederick's Urban Policy in Germany

There is no explicit indication in Frederick's privileges for Aachen, Gelnhausen, and Wetzlar that he acknowledged the inhabitants' participation in the governance of the new settlements. Indeed, in 1161 he had reaffirmed his earlier prohibition of a commune or conspiratorial co-swearing in Trier ("communio . . . civium Treuerensium, quę coniuratio dicitur"); and he had severely punished the inhabitants of Mainz in 1163 for the murder of Archbishop Arnold. Yet in his charter for Haguenau in 1164, the emperor had referred, approvingly, to the "association of citizens" ("consortio civium") and to the judgments made "by the sworn members of the city" (*coniurati civitatis*).[37] In the case of Gelnhausen, Frederick clearly recognized that it was a separate legal entity. It is hard to believe that the inhabitants of Gelnhausen, like the citizens of Haguenau, did not participate as jurors in the proceedings of the bailiff's court, or, for that matter, in the construction of the new settlement's walls, or in the enforcement of their trading privileges.

The real, unanswerable question is how much Frederick was personally involved in the formulation of policies that promoted the economic development of older, proto-urban, royal palace complexes like Aachen or Frankfurt; or in the decision to establish new communities such as Gelnhausen or Wetzlar on the imperial and Staufer domains and to further their growth. Did he grasp that the German kingdom was being transformed economically and socially or were his unnamed clerical advisers responsible for the issuance of such privileges? The detailed provisions of the charter for Haguenau may be based on Frederick's own knowledge of his father's favorite residence, where the future emperor may well have spent much of his childhood; but the privileges for Gelnhausen and Wetzlar are perfunctory in comparison. Frederick's cognizance of the content of the privileges that were issued in his name is even more problematic in the case of episcopal sees, the most important cities in twelfth-century Germany. Did the initiative for the grant of royal charters to these cities come from the crown, the bishops, or even the townspeople? To put it another way, was there a general imperial urban policy, whether or not it originated with Frederick himself, or was each charter a response to specific local circumstances and so *sui generis*?

Cambrai

In the case of Cambrai, situated on the Schelde (today in northern France), Frederick reacted to conflicting pressures. Already at the Christmas court in 1152 he had recognized the lordship of Count Thierry of Flanders over Cambrai, only to reverse course when Bishop Nicholas mobilized the support of his colleagues. Thierry succeeded in installing his young son Peter as the bishop after Nicholas' death in 1167 by obtaining the support of his great-niece, Empress Beatrice. Peter, who was never ordained, resigned in 1174 and married. Frederick took advantage of the situation and ordered the city to send him money to finance his fifth Italian campaign. The chronicler, a canon of St. Géry in Cambrai, asserted that neither Frederick nor any other ruler before or after him had done anything like that. The demand implied that the emperor was recognizing, at least tacitly, the existence of a communal entity that could levy taxes.

Bishop Roger complained at the imperial court in Mainz in 1182 that the townspeople of Cambrai had infringed upon the liberties of the clergy by establishing a commune; and Frederick declared that the burghers' actions violated the privileges he and his predecessors had granted the bishops of Cambrai. The commune was abrogated, and the bishop's lordship over the city was reinstated. Bishop Roger was authorized to settle disputes among the burghers himself or to delegate the responsibility to a provost, to local legal experts and fact-finders (*scabini*, *Schöffen*, or *échevins*), or to men of good repute of his own choice. This judgment did not resolve for long the dispute about the governance of the city and its customs and legal status. In 1184 the burghers, who were supplied with ample funds, the chronicler said, sued the bishop at the imperial court in Gelnhausen for abusing his authority. Frederick issued no fewer than five charters concerning Cambrai on this occasion. In the chief privilege, which was sealed with a golden bull, the emperor recognized the de facto existence of the commune, except that instead of using the offensive word *communio*, which was "hateful to all who loved the liberty of the church," it was called the *peace* (*pax*). (The Cambrai canon was quite explicit that the change in terminology was deliberate but added that the "peace" was not peaceful.) Frederick's charter referred, for example, to "the jurors of the peace" ("iurati pacis") who heard cases. The specific stipulations were taken, nearly verbatim, however, from a privilege that Count Philip of Flanders had granted St. Omer in 1168 and that the burghers had presumably brought with them to Gelnhausen. In this case Frederick was ratifying an agreement that the litigants had worked out themselves.[38]

Cologne

The emperor was probably, again, reinstating a previous agreement when he announced on 18 August 1180 the resolution of a dispute between Archbishop Philip and the burghers of Cologne. In defiance of the archbishop's prohibition, the citizens had incorporated three suburban settlements within the city by enlarging the circuit of Cologne's walls and moat, the final ring of fortifications that survived until the nineteenth century. The townspeople had also erected buildings, without Philip's permission, on the path along the bank of the Rhine, around the market, and on other public spaces, that is, on land that belonged to the church of Cologne. The case may have been brought to Frederick's attention at the court he held in

Gelnhausen in April 1180, but the report by the Cologne chronicler is far from clear on that point. Frederick ruled in August, with the advice of the princes, that the townspeople were to pay Philip a fine of 2,000 marks but could finish the fortifications. The builders of the illicit structures were allowed to retain them by hereditary right in return for an annual rent of two Cologne pennies for a small lot and four pennies for a large one. Other stipulations dealt with the building code: for example, no one could enlarge or add an additional storey to a building so that it blocked a neighbor's light. Frederick confirmed "all the rights of the citizens and of the city and all its good and reasonable customs" and ordered Philip and his successors to observe them inviolably, saving only the jurisdiction of the Empire and of the church of Cologne. On the face of it, the privilege was a victory for the burghers, which occurred at the archbishop's expense. However, the imperial charter is a nearly verbatim copy of an agreement that Philip had reached with the citizens on 27 July. Frederick's only substantive addition was a mandate that the market not be moved from its existing site. The charter is hardly evidence that the emperor was implementing some carefully conceived policy in regard to episcopal sees or was engaged in a trade war with Archbishop Philip. At most, Frederick may have mediated at Gelnhausen between the archbishop and the burghers, and then placed his imprimatur on their agreement as part of his commitment to maintaining the peace in the German kingdom.[39]

Trent

Frederick may have been more directly involved in the attempt in 1182 to shore up episcopal authority in Trent and to prevent the establishment of a Lombard-style commune in this strategically important city on the German–Italian border. An imperial army had crossed the Brenner Pass for the last time in the autumn of 1166, and without the emperor's occasional presence in Trent the bishop's control of his see may have weakened. Frederick forbade the establishment of a consular form of government and declared that the city was to be governed by its bishop, as was the case in all other cities in the "German kingdom"—one of the rare instances that the latter term was used by the chancery to differentiate Germany from the rest of the Empire. The citizens were barred from fixing their own weights and measures for bread and wine; from levying any taxes within or outside the city; from issuing any ordinance about the bridge, shipping on the Adige, or the mint; from giving refuge to anyone who was fleeing from another lordship; and from subjecting the inhabitants of villages and castles in the surrounding countryside to their authority—that is, Frederick was blocking the formation of a *contado* subject to urban jurisdiction. The charter had little effect, maybe because the emperor's acceptance of Lombard communal self-government the following year in the Peace of Constance (1183) rendered the prohibitions outdated.[40]

The intriguing thing about Frederick's charter for the bishopric of Trent is that it asserted that there was a general policy concerning the governance of episcopal sees in Germany. The charters he issued about the same time for Cologne and Cambrai belie that proposition. The burghers of Cologne paid a large fine for building massive fortifications without the archbishop's permission, but, crucially, were allowed to continue. They could have done neither thing if they had not had their own municipal magistrates, whether or not they were called *consuls*, with the power to levy taxes and various imposts and to direct the work. (By 1180 Cologne was governed by the college of *scabini* [*Schöffenkollegium*] and the *Richerzeche*, literally "the guild of the rich.") Frederick recognized, likewise, the de facto existence of an organ of burgher self-government in Cambrai, except that it was called the *pax* rather than a commune. As was the case with the emperor's enforcement of the four laws he issued at Roncaglia in 1158, he was prepared to adapt general principles, in this instance the prohibition of communal autonomy in German episcopal sees, to the facts on the ground.

Frederick returned from Italy in 1168 as a king who had lost his divine sanction. His travels were curtailed and the princes avoided him. As long as he was excommunicate, he could not arrange marriages between his children and those of other monarchs. Nevertheless, there were some successes. He strengthened the Staufer's territorial base in Germany. The anti-imperial alliance of Venice, Byzantium, and Sicily that had been arrayed against him in the 1160s broke up due to its own internal conflicts. Frederick interfered to an unprecedented extent in the internal affairs of Bohemia. The emperor's acceptance of Henry of Berchtesgaden in 1174 as the new archbishop of Salzburg, even though the provost had not formally renounced his allegiance to Alexander, indicated that Frederick was ready to compromise in regard to schism if he had to; but he made one last, half-hearted effort during his fifth Italian campaign to impose his will on the Lombards and the papacy. He failed.

CHAPTER FOURTEEN

THE FIFTH ITALIAN CAMPAIGN

The Failed Siege of Alessandria

IT IS HARD TO see what Frederick really hoped to accomplish during his fifth Italian campaign, which he undertook, according to Cardinal Boso, at the instigation of Margrave William of Montferrat and Pavia. Possibly, as Archbishop Romuald of Salerno thought, the emperor hoped to avenge the injuries that the Lombards had caused him.[1] He had failed to obtain any lasting international recognition of his anti-popes; there was at most perfunctory support in Germany for Calixtus III, whom Frederick did not know personally; and he had signaled his willingness to accept Alexander III as the head of the Church if he did not have to acknowledge him publicly as pope. However, Alexander insisted that Frederick honor him as he had Victor IV. More fundamentally, Frederick had to abandon any pretense that he could as emperor call a church council or decide a disputed papal election. He could hardly have hoped to alter these realities by force of arms. Moreover, did Frederick really think, after his earlier losses, that he could defeat the Lombard League with an army of mercenaries; or was he counting upon the revival of the latent conflicts among the Italians, most notably between Milan and Cremona?

On 9 June 1174 the emperor met with representatives of the Italian princes at Avenches in western Switzerland to discuss his journey across the Alps and the services they would perform. Accompanied by Beatrice and his young children, the emperor crossed the Mont Cenis Pass from Burgundy to Italy in September with, supposedly, 8,000 fighters (*pugnatores* rather than, say, *milites*, knights). The army consisted, according to Romuald of Salerno, of "a great multitude of Brabanters and other hirelings." Boso described them as "a great army of barbarian people, men accustomed to the practice of war, men most evil, rapacious desperadoes, whom he had gathered together from Flanders and the regions that lie thereabout, and whom, since they have love for no man, none loves." Frederick had to rely on mercenaries because few German princes joined the expedition. Between his arrival in Italy in September and the lifting of the siege of Alessandria in April 1175, Frederick issued five charters. Several ecclesiastical princes served as witnesses: Archbishops Philip of Cologne and Arnold of Trier, and the bishops of Bamberg, Regensburg, Verden, Augsburg, Halberstadt, and Naumburg-Zeitz. (Archbishop Christian of Mainz besieged and captured a Bolognese castle in March.) The only lay princes who were named were Frederick's brother Conrad, Otto of Wittelsbach, and Duke Oldřich of Bohemia, whose older brother had just been installed as the regnant duke in exchange for a promise of Bohemian military aid in Italy.[2] Frederick's dependence, militarily, on the bishops explains why he had to negotiate with Alexander when they insisted that he end the schism.

Frederick burned Susa, except for the house of Count Humbert III of Savoy, in retribution for its mistreatment of the imperial couple on their flight from Italy in 1168. Turin and Asti submitted, and Frederick advanced on Alessandria. Inhabitants from eight rural settlements in the valley of the Tanaro, a tributary of the Po, had combined, with the backing of Milan and its allies, to form a new city, which they named after the pope as a deliberate insult to Frederick. It was mentioned for the first time on 3 May 1168, when it was already a member of the Lombard League. Alessandria was located in the territory of Margrave William of Montferrat at the junction of the Via Emilia and the road that led from Milan to Genoa. An army proceeding down the Po valley, to the north of Alessandria, could easily have bypassed a city defended only by ditches and the Tanaro and that was called derisively by the Germans "Straw City" or "Chaff City" (*Palea*), either because its houses had only thatched roofs, as Romuald wrote, or metaphorically because its defenses were like chaff.

Frederick indicated on two later occasions that the destruction of Alessandria had been from the start the primary objective of the fifth Italian campaign. He recalled in 1180 that he had been in Tilleda, at the foot of the Kyffhäuser, in February 1174, when he was about to set out "on the campaign against Alessandria." Five years later he declared that the construction of Alessandria, now renamed Caesarea, had been an affront to his and the Empire's honor, and that to avenge this injury he had ordered the expedition and had besieged the city. If that really was his motive, personal pique had overridden his political and strategic sense.

The citizens were prepared to surrender immediately, according to Godfrey of Viterbo, an eyewitness; but Margrave William of Montferrat advised against accepting their offer, because Alessandria's continued existence would be a perpetual threat. Was Godfrey trying to exonerate Frederick by blaming William—after relations between Frederick and the Montferrats had deteriorated following the Peace of Venice in 1177—for the decision to undertake the unsuccessful siege of Alessandria? In any case, William and Pavia provided the majority of the allegedly 20,000 men who besieged the city from 29 October 1174 to 13 April 1175. As had been true at Constance in 1153 and at Tortona in 1155, Frederick's Italian allies had succeeded in playing on his aggrieved sense of honor.[3]

The emperor and his allies grossly underestimated the difficulty of taking Alessandria, even though its fortifications were unfinished and only 150 Placentine foot soldiers had come to its aid. The ditches and river proved to be formidable barriers. Incessant rains turned the imperial camp into a quagmire. The winter was unseasonably cold. Provisions were scarce. The Bohemians deserted. Finally, Frederick resorted to duplicity. On Maundy Thursday, 10 April, he offered the townspeople a truce until Monday morning. During the night between Good Friday and Holy Saturday, 200 of his best men tried to enter the city through tunnels while Frederick and the rest of the army waited in front of the gates for a chance to attack. The invaders were spotted and killed as they tried to exit the tunnels; the others perished when the tunnels collapsed. The defenders sallied out and set on fire a wooden tower, manned by Genoese, that Frederick had moved up to the fortifications. The occupants died in the flames. On the morning of Easter Sunday, 13 April, the emperor burned and abandoned his camp and marched northeast in the direction of Pavia and an approaching Lombard army that was coming to relieve Alessandria. God had punished Frederick's sacrilegious violation of a truce during the holiest days of the Christian year. Romuald of Salerno commented that "Straw City" had proven to be made of iron.[4]

The Aborted Peace of Montebello

The Lombards, unaware of what had transpired at Alessandria, armed; but both sides avoided a battle. According to the *Cologne Royal Chronicle*, the Lombards feared the Germans' martial capabilities; and their standard-bearer (perhaps Margrave Obizzo Malaspina) informed his son, who was fighting under the imperial banner (an intriguing example of perhaps calculated, divided familial loyalties), that the Lombards were ready to negotiate. They met with Archbishop Philip and the other princes and persuaded them that the Lombards preferred peace to war. On Easter Monday, 14 April, in Boso's version of events, certain nobles who were viewed favorably by both sides (the standard-bearer and his son?) spoke first to the emperor in a humble manner and then to the Lombards about the folly of either a lord or his servants seeking to procure by violence what rightfully belonged to the other. (Romuald described the intermediaries as "certain religious persons and wise men.") After many entreaties, presumably by Archbishop Philip, Frederick reluctantly agreed, according to Boso, to submit the conflict to arbitration if the rights of the Empire were maintained. The Lombards likewise concurred on condition that the liberties of the Church, as well as their own for which they were fighting, were preserved. Both parties prepared written briefs listing their demands, which were to provide the basis for the arbitration award. Only the Lombard memorandum survives. Six arbiters, including Archbishop Philip on the imperial side, met on 16 April in the territory of Pavia, on the field by the castle of Montebello belonging to Margrave William, to establish the mechanism for settling the specific issues that were in dispute, to arrange the Lombards' formal submission to the emperor the next day and their restoration to his grace.[5]

In its brief the Lombard League, representing twenty-four cities in Lombardy, the mark of Verona, Venetia, and the Romagna, Margrave Obizzo Malaspina, and other communities and persons who lived in harmony with the Church and the League, expressed its desire for peace with the emperor on the precondition that he was reconciled with the Church and Pope Alexander. When peace was finally made, the members of the League were prepared to grant the emperor whatever services their ancestors had performed freely since the death of Henry V, that is, when imperial authority had been at its weakest in Italy. If a specific city or lord's obligations to the crown were in dispute, the consuls of that city or the individual lord who belonged to the League were to swear under oath what they owed the crown; and Frederick was to be satisfied with their testimony. The cities and the other members were to possess all other rights they had exercised since 1125, in particular the right, in the case of the cities, to their consular form of government. Frederick was to leave to all League members their customary rights of pasturage, fishing, milling, baking, changing money, trading, selling meat, and the building of houses on public ways, that is, the lesser, purely economic regalia. The Lombards were proposing, essentially, to substitute their restrictive definition of the regalia for the expansive list that Frederick had put forth at Roncaglia in 1158.

The Lombards also demanded the restoration of all the possessions and rights that Frederick had seized from them; permission to retain or to rebuild all their existing castles, except Crema; recognition of the permanent existence of Alessandria, which was identified as a constituent member of the League; and the abolition of appeals from judgments made by the communal consuls and the rectors of the League to the emperor. In return, they would pay him the *fodrum* and the other customary payments on the *Romzug*, permit him peaceful transit through their territories and provide him with suitable markets to procure provisions if he did not delay his progress with specious excuses, and allow imperial vassals and the townspeople to swear the customary oaths of fealty. If any disputes arose about any of the articles in the brief, the consuls of the city, the lord, or the rural community that was involved were to adjudicate the case in accordance with local customs such that the rights of both the emperor and the other party were respected—it is hard to see how this could occur if one of the parties was a judge in its own case. The Lombards were demanding, in effect, a legalization of minimal, absentee imperial lordship in Italy.[6]

The six arbiters met on 16 April at Montebello, between the opposing armies, to set up the procedure for reconciling the Lombard claims for virtual autonomy from imperial rule with Frederick's assertions of his prerogatives. Regrettably, in the absence of the imperial brief, we do not know how much Frederick still adhered to the maximal position he had enunciated at Roncaglia. The six determined that both Frederick and the League were to select three arbiters, who were to base their award on the briefs both parties had submitted; but the arbiters, after swearing that they would be impartial, were free to make the necessary emendations to secure lasting peace and harmony. They had until the middle of May to reach their decision. If they were unable to do so—a likely possibility since no provision was made for a neutral seventh umpire to resolve an impasse—the consuls of Cremona were to settle collectively the remaining issues within an additional fifteen days. As surety that he would adhere to the peace immediately, the emperor was to give the kiss of peace to the cities and their League. In return, ten men chosen by the emperor from each city were to swear oaths of fealty—the vassals as vassals, the citizens as citizens—to the emperor and his son King Henry. Count Humbert III of Savoy, the nephew of William of Montferrat, and the other princes who adhered to the accord assured the League that the peace would be binding on the Lombards only if all members of the League, that is, Alessandria, too, were included.

The next day, 17 April, a consul of Pavia came to Frederick and swore on behalf of himself and all his colleagues that Pavia would observe until the middle of June a truce with Alessandria, which, the notary who summarized the agreement indicated, was called by its enemies "Straw City." Margrave William swore the same thing on behalf of himself and his sons. Otto of Wittelsbach, the imperial chancellor, Godfrey of Spitzenberg-Helfenstein, Margrave Henry Guercio of Savona, and Count Humbert committed Frederick, by handshakes and kisses, to keeping the truce. If the emperor broke the truce, the two Italians would place themselves in the custody of the Lombards in Vercelli; the two Germans were not bound in this fashion. Although Alessandria as a League member had been included in the preliminary peace, Frederick suddenly insisted, perhaps at the prompting of Margrave William and Pavia, that its fate be treated as a separate issue. The emperor may have argued that Alessandria could not be restored to his grace, like the other cities, because it had never enjoyed his favor. The notary stated that the arbiters, or, if they were unable to do so, the consuls of Cremona, were to deal separately with the business of Alessandria. It proved to be an irresolvable problem in 1175, and this may explain why its destruction came to be seen, with hindsight, as the primary objective of Frederick's fifth Italian campaign. However, the emperor granted the kiss of peace to Ezzelino I da Romano and Anselm da Dovara, the rectors of the League, on behalf of all the other members.

The notary said nothing about the Lombards' ceremonial submission to the emperor on 17 April. Such rituals were arranged orally, and, besides, the Lombards hardly wished to have a written record of their public humiliation. It was precisely such ceremonies rather than the specific terms of an accord that attracted the attention of chroniclers. The author of the *Cologne Royal Chronicle*, Nicholas of Siegburg, who probably obtained his information from Archbishop Philip, indicated that the Lombards, presumably all the individuals who were required to swear fealty to the emperor, came to Frederick's camp and sought peace and mercy. They carried unsheathed swords around their necks and surrendered the standards of their cities to him. Some kissed the emperor's cloak, others his feet, and yet others his tent. They confirmed their fealty with oaths. According to another chronicler, they handed their unsheathed swords to the emperor with the blade pointed at them. Such acts were gestures performed by the defeated party, but Frederick was hardly the victor at Alessandria and Montebello. Rather, the Lombards' symbolic contrition was designed to preserve the emperor's honor and thus allow him to submit to the arbitration of his differences with repentant subjects whom he had graciously forgiven. In reality, he had recognized the existence of the Lombard League by agreeing to negotiate with it and by bestowing the kiss of peace upon its rectors.[7]

It seems rather odd that the consuls of Cremona, who had been the driving force behind the creation of the League, should have been chosen as the referees if the arbiters were unable to reach a decision. The answer to this puzzle may be that the rebuilding of Milan in 1167 had revived the tensions between the two rivals and that Cremona was by 1175 only nominally a member of the League. No Cremonese contingent participated in the army that had been sent to Alessandria's relief, according to Boso, because of Cremona's traditional friendship with Pavia; and no representative of Cremona was named in the notarial statement among the men who were singled out as swearing fealty to Frederick. On the other hand, the League had its supporters in Cremona, too. The rector of the League, Anselm da Dovara, came from a powerful Cremonese family. Boso said that the Cremonese were so furious that peace had been made without their participation that the townspeople razed the palaces and houses of the consuls, seized their possessions, and installed other consuls in their place.[8] So Cremona could be seen by both sides as sympathetic to their cause, but the factional volatility of communal politics further complicated all attempts at peacemaking.

Frederick was apparently confident that the peace would hold. He returned with Beatrice and some of their children to Pavia, where they were welcomed in a festive way. The emperor dismissed most of his troops, perhaps because he could not afford the mercenaries' wages; but the more powerful men, the Cologne chronicler noted, stayed. The peace proved to be, in the words of the Milanese Anonymous, false.[9]

Since the Lombards had made Frederick's reconciliation with the Church and Alexander a precondition for concluding peace with him, he invited the pope to send legates to him. Three cardinals arrived in Pavia at the beginning of May 1175. After they had seated themselves on folding stools in front of him, Frederick took off his cap and greeted them in German with the help of an interpreter. Cardinal-Bishop Humbald of Ostia expressed his regrets that they could not greet Frederick in the customary manner because he was excommunicate. In the following weeks, the cardinals negotiated sometimes with Frederick alone or with the emperor and his advisers about including the Lombards, William II of Sicily, and Manuel I in the final settlement; but it was decided that discussions about making a permanent peace with the Lombards were more likely to be successful if the cardinals spoke, not directly with Frederick, but with his representatives: Chancellor Godfrey, Archbishops Christian and

Philip, and the imperial proto-notary Wortwin. At the same time, separate discussions were conducted in various places with the rectors of the Lombard League. Archbishop Philip, who was one of the arbiters charged with resolving Frederick's remaining differences with the League, may have been the linchpin between the two sets of discussions.

The parallel negotiations broke down because, Boso said, Frederick demanded from the Church "in spiritual matters what can nowhere be discovered to have been granted to a layman; and from the Lombards, more than that with which the Emperors Charles [Charlemagne], Louis [the Pious], and Otto [I] had been content." It is uncertain what Boso meant by "spiritual matters" (*spiritualia*), but it may have been a recognition of Frederick's right, like his imperial predecessors, to summon a church council or to intervene in a disputed papal election. Such a council would have provided him with a face-saving cover for acknowledging Alexander as the rightful pope. Frederick's demand that Alessandria be destroyed made peace with the Lombards likewise impossible, because they insisted upon the city's inclusion in the final settlement. Alexander indicated that the negotiations had failed when he recognized Alessandria's legal status as a city by making it a bishopric—an episcopal see was by definition a *civitas*—and by assigning to it a portion of the diocese of Pavia, which was deprived of its archiepiscopal rank. Finally, no agreement could be reached about including the Normans and the Byzantines in a general peace.[10]

The consuls of Cremona did make an award, but since Frederick had not been reconciled with the pope and refused to include Alessandria in the peace, it was only a non-binding attempt at mediation between the emperor and the Lombards. Among other things, the consuls proposed that six arbiters, three chosen by each side, were to decide disputes between the emperor and members of the League rather than to leave the determination solely to the League member in its own cause. The Lombards were allowed to retain their consuls and *podestàs*, but the emperor or his representative was to invest them with their offices. The communal officials were to collect the *fodrum* and the poll tax (*colta*), but their assessments could be appealed to the emperor. He was not to levy taxes in the cities or their outskirts. The members of the League, as well as the emperor, were to return the possessions and rights they had seized. Both parties were to retain the right of self-help if the other broke the agreement. The Lombards could continue to adhere to Alexander. Frederick was to permit the inhabitants of Alessandria to return with all their dependants and possessions to their original communities, that is, the new city was to be abandoned.[11] If the Cremonese proposal was in any way an attempt to strike a balance between the demands contained in the Lombard and imperial briefs, then Frederick must already have been prepared to grant the communes considerable autonomy if they acknowledged his lordship.

Chiavenna

After the collapse of the negotiations with Alexander and the Lombards at the end of May 1175, Frederick found himself in Pavia with only minimal forces and more dependent than ever on his Italian allies. The only German princes who witnessed the three extant charters Frederick issued during the summer and autumn of 1175 were the three Rhenish archbishops and the bishop of Verden. In November, Frederick resumed hostilities in Lombardy. The chief target was Alessandria, which enjoyed the energetic support of the other communes. Sometime after 20 November, Frederick sent Archbishop Philip back to Germany to raise a new army. The bishops seem to have provided most of the reinforcements. Very late in the year the emperor ordered the cathedral chapter of Würzburg to put church property at the disposal of the bishop-elect, Reinhard (1171–86), so he could borrow 350 marks and join the other princes he had summoned to Italy to fight the rebellious Lombards and their Greek and Sicilian allies. (Reinhard is an example of a bishop who was avoiding consecration during the schism.) Similarly, in 1176 Frederick assigned to Liège all the imperial property situated west of the Meuse, except for the collegiate church of St. Servatius in Maastricht and the abbey of Nivelles, because Bishop Rudolf had mortgaged church property for 1,000 marks to finance his participation in the fifth Italian campaign.[12]

In January or February 1176, at Chiavenna, north of Lake Como, Henry the Lion is alleged to have denied his cousin the emperor the military assistance he so desperately needed, even after Frederick prostrated himself at the duke's feet; and Henry's refusal is commonly seen as a major cause of his subsequent downfall. The problem is that no contemporary source mentions the incident. All the accounts we have were written after Henry the Lion's death in 1195, that is, long after he had been deprived of Bavaria and Saxony in 1180, and (except for Gilbert of Mons' chronicle) during or after the fight for the crown from 1198 to 1208 between Philip of Swabia and Otto IV. The incident, if it occurred, thus acquired far greater significance with the benefit of hindsight. For instance, Gilbert, writing in 1195–96, attributed Henry's loss of his duchies in 1180 to his refusal to assist Frederick even after the emperor had humbled himself in 1176. The impact of the later battle for the throne is clear in the tale, recounted by Burchard of Ursberg around 1230, that Henry's seneschal, Jordan of Blankenburg, told his master, after Frederick had knelt at the duke's feet: "Lord, let the crown roll to your feet; it will yet rise to your head." The long-dominant paradigm of Staufer–Welf antagonism between 1125 and 1235, in which Chiavenna was a crucial milestone, influenced, in turn, modern scholarly interpretations of the incident.

It is generally accepted today that the cousins did meet, that Frederick begged for help (five chroniclers reported the emperor's prostration), and that Henry rejected the request. Chiavenna was a likely meeting place because it is situated at the southern terminus of the most direct route between Swabia and Lombardy. What is less certain is why Henry declined the emperor's request. Henry was, it should be stressed, under no legal obligation to aid Frederick. After all, none of the other German lay princes, except for the counts-palatine of the Rhine and Bavaria, had accompanied Frederick to Italy in 1174. According to Provost Frederick of St. Thomas in Strasbourg, Henry VI's chaplain and the author of the *Marbach Annals*, Henry the Lion demanded, as compensation for all the knights he had lost at the earlier sieges of Crema and Milan, to be enfeoffed with the town of Goslar in Saxony—Frederick had reclaimed in 1167 the advocacy of Goslar, which he had granted earlier to Henry. Otto of St. Blasien related that Frederick declined the request because he considered his cousin's demand demeaning. So, Otto commented, Henry, who alone had the power and wealth to assist Frederick, had left him in danger. It is likely that the status of Goslar was an issue, because Provost Eckhard of the collegiate church of Sts. Simon and Jude in Goslar was at Frederick's court on 20 November 1175. Since the emperor customarily rewarded the princes for their services, Henry had every reason to believe that he deserved similar consideration. Frederick probably refused to return the advocacy to Henry because Goslar was the last major royal domain in Saxony. No chronicler connected Henry's refusal to the cousins' competing claims to the domains of Welf VI, his paternal uncle.

Joachim Ehlers suggested in 2008 that the real reason for Henry the Lion's reluctance to go to Italy may have been dynastic and personal. His oldest son was not yet three years old, and Henry may have remembered what had happened when he had become a duke as a small child in 1139 and how many lords had perished in 1167. He may have been unwilling to tempt fate.

Frederick's prostration at Henry's feet, which has perturbed modern German historians, was not, in fact, unprecedented. Emperor Henry II had done so in 1007 in Frankfurt to obtain the bishops' consent to the founding of the bishopric of Bamberg, and Conrad II had employed the same tactic in 1035 to force his son, the future Henry III, to agree to the deposition of Duke Adalbero of Carinthia. To refuse such an entreaty, a monarch's ultimate form of persuasion, was, however, an unforgivable insult. The pro-Welf Arnold of Lübeck, who wrote around 1210, tried to soften the magnitude of Henry the Lion's affront by having him at least help Frederick get up. Two mid-thirteenth-century chroniclers assigned that role, instead, to Beatrice.

Henry's folly in refusing Frederick's entreaties was that he forgot he owed his preeminent position in Germany to the emperor. According to Arnold's invented dialogue, Frederick reminded his cousin how he had exalted Henry and had aided him against all his enemies. After Chiavenna, the emperor was no longer as inclined to come to his cousin's rescue, even if he could have, when Henry's princely adversaries determined to bring him down. Beyond that, Henry, unlike his opponents, was not in Italy to protect his own interests in the negotiations that culminated in the Peace of Venice of 1177. (Count Bernard of Anhalt, who obtained the duchy of Saxony in 1180, was at the imperial court by the winter of 1176.) Chiavenna proved to be a disaster for both men.[13]

Legnano

After the botched meeting at Chiavenna, Frederick returned in February 1176 to Pavia, where contingents from Cremona and Como joined his forces. He wrote to the German magnates and enjoined them to come to Italy. Archbishop Philip, who had returned to Germany, secured the commitment of some of the Saxon and Rhenish princes to the campaign and mortgaged two manors for 400 marks to finance his own participation. By making substantial concessions to Tortona, which was threatened by the foundation of Alessandria just to the west, Frederick won to his side in March 1176 the city he had leveled in 1155. Likewise in March, Archbishop Christian, who had asserted imperial control over Bologna in October 1175, invaded the Norman kingdom and defeated the Sicilian forces; but he withdrew after Frederick's defeat at Legnano on 29 May 1176. It was the emperor's last attempt to impose his will on the Hautevilles by force.[14]

In May 1176 Frederick headed from Pavia to Como to meet the 2,000 knights who were coming from Saxony and the lower Rhineland, via the Lukmanier Pass. They were under the leadership of Archbishops Philip of Cologne and Wichmann of Magdeburg, Bishop-Elect Conrad II of Worms (he, too, had been postponing his consecration since his election in

1171), and Count Philip of Flanders. Other German magnates who were at Frederick's court by the summer at the latest were: the bishops of Münster, Osnabrück (both were suffragans of Cologne), Würzburg, Hildesheim, and Brandenburg; Frederick's nephew, Landgrave Louis III of Thuringia; and Count Florence of Holland.

After their rendezvous the Germans, strengthened by a contingent from Como, started back toward Pavia, through Milanese territory, which they devastated on their way. According to Boso, the Pavians were supposed to strike Milan from the south. The Milanese did not wait for reinforcements from all members of the Lombard League. Instead, with men from Piacenza, Verona, Brescia, Novara, and Vercelli, on 29 May they intercepted the vanguard of the imperial forces, including 1,000 German knights, at Legnano, northwest of Milan. Otto of St. Blasien numbered the Lombard army at 100,000 fighters; other pro-imperial writers gave a figure of 12,000. A modern estimate is that each of the opposing forces comprised between 3,000 and 4,000 knights.

The Lombard knights and infantry gathered around the Milanese *carroccio*. The use of the Milanese battlewagon as a common rallying point was another sign that the League was becoming, after the de facto withdrawal of Cremona and Pavia, an alliance between Milan and those communes where it was installing its own citizens as *podestàs*. The fighting raged for six hours. A lance transfixed the imperial standard-bearer, who was trampled by the horses' feet. Frederick stood out in his armor in the fray, but when he fell from the saddle and disappeared from sight, the Germans fled, Boso said, a distance of eight miles. Some were cut down, some drowned in the Ticino, and some were captured. The captives included Count Berthold IV of Andechs, Count Philip of Flanders, and Archbishop Philip's brother, Count Goswin III of Heinsberg. Only the men of Como remained on the battlefield, and they were killed or captured. The Milanese seized many weapons and horses and inestimable wealth, including the shield, standard, cross, and lance of the emperor—or so they wrote to the Bolognese. Frederick's whereabouts were unknown for several days. Beatrice was already mourning her husband's death when he reappeared in Pavia, supposedly, Romuald of Salerno said, under the cover of night. The surviving Germans also trickled in. Wilhelm von Giesebrecht concluded his account of the battle with the comment that Frederick had "suffered a very severe setback, which made his situation in Lombardy more difficult. But his position could hardly have been considered desperate." Militarily, Giesebrecht may have been correct, because the emperor's Italian allies remained loyal to him; but after the annihilation of Frederick's army in 1167, his failure to take Alessandria, and his losses at Legnano, he had lost the war in Italy politically and psychologically.[15]

Cremona's Second Mediation Award

In June and July 1176, that is, immediately after the battle of Legnano, the consuls of Cremona sought a diplomatic solution to the conflict. They issued a revised mediation award, which is an almost verbatim repetition of the consuls' first proposal. The major, highly significant revision was that the consuls proposed that Alessandria be allowed to retain its status as a city. The sheet of parchment that contains the second award also has a copy of Frederick's declaration, drafted by the imperial chancery and addressed to all the consuls and people of the Lombard cities, that the consuls of Cremona and a great multitude of its people and knights had entreated him to finish the peacemaking he had begun at Montebello and his envoys had pursued in subsequent negotiations. Although some of the terms the consuls proposed were hard for the emperor to accept, he had decided, upon taking counsel with the princes and his Lombard vassals, to confirm the accord for the sake of peace and to be bound by it. In another attempt to preserve the emperor's honor, the declaration made it look as if the initiative for making peace had come not from Frederick after his defeat at Legnano but from Cremona.

Even though Frederick was now ready to accept the permanent existence of Alessandria, one of the two major issues that had derailed the negotiations between the Lombards and the emperor in the spring of 1175, the Lombards rejected the consuls' revised award. According to Romuald of Salerno, a Milanese judge, Gerardo Cagapisto, asserted on the League's behalf during the negotiations in Venice in 1177 that the allies would have accepted the proposed settlement if Frederick had not sought, as part of the deal, to detach them from the Roman Church and to persuade them to abjure Pope Alexander.[16]

As for Cremona, it feared the resurgence of Milan's power to the west. To reward the city for its attempt at mediation and to induce it to abandon its nominal Lombard allies, on 29 July 1176 Frederick confirmed all the customary rights that the commune and its citizens exercised within and outside the city, in the diocese of Cremona, and in all areas subject to the commune's jurisdiction; all the benefits and income that the commune derived from those rights; and all the privileges Cremona had previously received. The emperor recognized the commune's consular form of government and the citizens' right to travel freely on the Po, to build and to possess bridges over the river, and to levy excise taxes. Frederick conferred on Cremona all the imperial rights in Crema to the northwest and between the Adda and Oglio, that is, the district around Crema he had refused Cremona in 1160, and the emperor promised not to authorize a third party to build fortifications in that region. Most valuable of all, he gave Cremona one-third of the communes of Luzzara and Guastalla, which are situated south of the Po, downstream from Cremona, and which had been part of the Matildine Lands. The toll stations at the two communes were crucial for controlling trade on the river.[17]

The Preliminary Peace of Anagni

Boso indicated that some time after the battle of Legnano, perhaps after the failure of Cremona's second attempt at mediation, all the princes, ecclesiastical and lay, informed Frederick that they would no longer follow or aid him if he did not make peace with the Church. The emperor initially employed the same backchannels he had used in the late 1160s to contact the curia: the Cistercians and the Carthusian lay brother Dietrich of Silve-Bénite, who may have been his natural son. We have only minimal information about these secret feelers. In August 1176 the emperor wrote to the Cistercian abbot Hugh of Bonnevaux that he had gladly received Hugh's advice on how to restore peace within the Church. Frederick had discussed Hugh's proposal with his closest advisers in Dietrich's presence, and he was dispatching the Carthusian to Hugh to convey Frederick's own thoughts and to continue the dialogue. The emperor notified Hugh in another letter the same month that the negotiations about ending the schism were going well, and he invited the abbot to come to Lombardy on 29 September, the feast day of the Archangel Michael, to participate in the discussions.

We do not know the contents of Hugh's proposal, how involved Dietrich had been in its formulation, or what role either man played in the negotiations that led to the Peace of Anagni in early November. However, after peace between the pope and the emperor was finally concluded in Venice in July 1177, both Alexander and Frederick, in letters to the Cistercians, praised Hugh, Dietrich, and Bishop Pons of Clermont (who as the abbot of Clairvaux had already negotiated with the pope in 1169 on Frederick's behalf) for their role in re-establishing concord between the two highest authorities in Christendom.[18]

At the assembly in late September 1176 Frederick may have invited all the ecclesiastical princes in the Empire, including "Pope Calixtus and him whom his followers call Alexander," to attend a council in Pavia in

November. At the end of October his uncle Welf VI, who had heard about the summons, expressed his astonishment to Cardinal Hyacinth, the future Pope Celestine III, because, in Welf's view, Alexander was the rightful pontiff. It is hard to imagine that Frederick still clung at this late date, and after his experiences at Pavia in 1160 and at St. Jean-de-Losne in 1162, to the illusion that he had the authority as emperor to convene a synod that would decide a disputed papal election. Alexander's supporter, Patriarch Ulrich II of Aquileia, who had learned that Bishop Roman II of Gurk and other prelates of the church of Salzburg had received such an invitation, wrote to Provost Otto of Raitenbuch, Welf's representative at the curia, that he had no intention to attend. The council never convened, ostensibly, the emperor informed Ulrich in November, because there had not been sufficient time for prelates from remote regions to come.[19]

Frederick had decided, instead, to initiate negotiations with Alexander. The patriarch indicated in his letter to Provost Otto that the emperor had sent to the pope Archbishop Wichmann of Magdeburg, who had only reluctantly acknowledged Paschal III as pope at Würzburg, Bishop-Elect Conrad II of Worms, and the proto notary Wortwin. The original purpose of their mission may have been simply to persuade the pope to attend the council in Pavia. Yet Frederick, who was ill, perhaps with a recurrence of the malaria he had contracted on the Second Crusade—and so conceivably concerned about his salvation—had sworn, according to the patriarch, to abide by Wichmann and Conrad's advice in matters that concerned the Church.

Boso, presumably one of the cardinals who met at Anagni with the imperial envoys, is our chief source for the conduct of the actual negotiations. Two cardinals conducted the three envoys to Anagni, where Alexander was staying south of Rome. Archbishop Christian, who had dismissed his army after destroying Fermo on the Adriatic on 21 September, joined them on 21 October. (Boso ignored Christian's participation in the proceedings, but the patriarch and several chroniclers focused on the archbishop's role.) The envoys notified Alexander that Frederick had granted them plenary power to resume the negotiations between the emperor and the pope that Frederick had broken off in May 1175. The pope rejoiced at the news, but insisted that William II, the Lombards, and Manuel I be included in the overall settlement. Alexander refused, in other words, to make a separate peace with the emperor as Frederick clearly hoped. The discussions took place in secret, Boso said, because there were individuals on both sides who opposed peace, and they lasted more than a fortnight because of the complexity of the issues. The negotiators consulted during their deliberations, Boso noted, patristic authorities, imperial privileges, ancient customs, "and a thousand other matters." In fact, the third and seventh paragraphs of the preliminary peace contain formulations borrowed, respectively, from the Concordat of Worms (1122) and the Treaty of Constance (1153).[20]

The preliminary Peace of Anagni, many of whose terms were adopted verbatim in the Peace of Venice, settled in the Church's favor most of the central Italian territorial matters that had been in dispute between Frederick and the papacy since 1155, and set up a mechanism for resolving the remaining points of contention. The parties exchanged sealed texts of the agreement and sworn promises in which each side elucidated the meaning of the specific provisions. The only documents that survive are a later copy of the text that the imperial envoys gave the pope and their commentary on it, in which they swore that Frederick would observe the terms of the peace. The envoys' acceptance of such unfavorable terms indicates how eager they were to end the schism and how dire Frederick's situation must have been after the failed siege of Alessandria and the battle of Legnano.

The emperor, empress, their son Henry, and all the princes agreed, in the first paragraph, to recognize Alexander as the universal pontiff and to show him the same reverence that their Catholic predecessors had paid previous popes. In an echo of the Treaty of Constance, both pope and emperor promised to respect the other's honor and rights and to aid each other as befit a kind father and the vicar of St. Peter and a devoted, most dear son and a most Christian emperor. Nothing was said about how Frederick would demonstrate publicly his acceptance of Alexander's authority, but it must have been understood that the emperor would have to honor the pope in the same way he had Victor IV in Pavia in February 1160.

Frederick was to grant "true peace" to Alexander, all his successors, and the whole Roman Church, and was to restore all the regalia and possessions of St. Peter, which he or others had seized and which the Church had possessed during the pontificate of Innocent II (1130–43), that is, before the establishment of the Roman commune and senate. In effect, Frederick was repudiating his recognition of the senate in 1167. Likewise, he was to return the prefecture of Rome to the pope; but the papacy was prepared to consider, after its return, any evidence that proved it belonged to the Empire. The provision concerning the prefecture appears to have been a compromise that recognized the pope's de facto sovereignty in Rome without totally excluding the Empire's theoretical rights. All the papal vassals who had entered imperial service during the schism were to serve the pope again. The papacy was to possess the Matildine Lands as it had owned them at the time of Lothar III, Conrad III, and at the beginning of Frederick's own reign. The emperor was also obligated to return to all other churches whatever had been taken from them during the schism.[21]

Frederick was also to make a lasting peace with the Lombards in accordance with the decision of mediators chosen by the pope, emperor, and the Lombards. If they were unable to reach a final agreement, an equal number of arbiters chosen by the pope and the emperor would decide by majority vote, after Alexander and Frederick had been reconciled, the remaining issues that were in contention between the emperor and the Lombard League. Unlike the failed negotiations that had followed the preliminary Peace of Montebello, the Lombards were not treated at Anagni as an equal partner of the pope and emperor. Neither Alexander nor Frederick was willing to let the Lombards prevent the resolution of their own differences and were prepared, therefore, to impose a settlement upon them. The imperial envoys, in a major victory for Frederick, had succeeded in driving a wedge between the pope and his communal allies. The way was thus opened up for excluding the Lombards at Venice from the final peace.

The king of Sicily, William II, the emperor of Constantinople, Manuel I, and all others who had aided the pope were to be included in the peace; and Frederick was to bear them no ill will. Mediators selected by the pope and the emperor were to decide the disputes that had occurred either between the pope and emperor before Adrian IV's pontificate or between the emperor and the king of Sicily. Until the mediators made their determination, the parties were to observe a truce.

Alexander agreed to recognize Christian and Philip, respectively, as the rightful archbishops of Mainz and Cologne. In compensation for his loss of Mainz, Conrad of Wittelsbach was to be assigned the first archbishopric that became vacant in the German kingdom and which Conrad deemed suitable. In the meantime, the pope and emperor would see to it that the cardinal-bishop of Sabina was honorably provided for. Alexander was prepared in this instance to sacrifice a loyal supporter for the higher good of peace and to allow the two schismatic archbishops who were Frederick's chief clerical lieutenants to retain their offices. This papal concession was not, however, a total victory for the emperor. In effect, Christian and Philip now had a very personal stake in the successful outcome of the negotiations: the retention of their archiepiscopal rank. Their interests and Frederick's were no longer necessarily identical.

At the Synod of Tours in 1163, Alexander had invalidated all ordinations performed by schismatic bishops. This condemnation would have applied, for example, to Christian, who had been installed in his office in 1167 by Bishop Daniel of Prague, an avowed partisan of the antipopes. However, a council held in Piacenza in 1095 had recognized the validity of ordinations undertaken by schismatic bishops who had themselves been consecrated by a bishop in communion with Rome. For the sake of peace, Alexander was willing to accept this canon in the case of German clerics like Christian and Philip. The cases of Bishops Rudolf II of Strasbourg and Louis of Basel, ordained by Paschal III, were deferred to the judgment of eight or ten bishops who were to determine whether they could retain their offices without danger to the souls of the emperor and pope. They, along with Frederick's nephew, Thierry of Metz, the son of Duke Matthew, were deposed in 1179. The pope was to decide the fate of the schismatic bishops in the non-German portions of the Empire, but Frederick was allowed to make the legal case for the validity of the ordinations of as many as ten or twelve of the Italian bishops. Calixtus III was to be given an abbey, and his so-called cardinals were to return to the offices they had held before the schism. Alexander was willing to accommodate Frederick in personnel matters that were of particular interest to the emperor.

Archbishop Wichmann of Magdeburg used his stay in Anagni to weaken the position of the absent Henry the Lion in Saxony. In 1160 Frederick had willingly agreed to the deposition of Bishop Ulrich of Halberstadt, who had incurred the emperor's displeasure by not participating in the *Romzug* and who had adhered to Alexander, and to Ulrich's replacement by the cathedral provost, Gero. The new bishop was Henry's creature, and he had enfeoffed the duke with many of Halberstadt's possessions to the detriment of both Magdeburg and the Ascanians, the family of Albrecht the Bear. Ulrich was to be restored to his office, and all of Gero's alienations of church property were to be nullified by the joint authority of the emperor and pope.

A similar fate seemed to await Archbishop Baldwin of Bremen. After the death, in 1168, of Archbishop Hartwig, Henry the Lion's long-time opponent, there had been a double election. One of the candidates had been Siegfried, another son of Duke Henry's enemy, Albrecht the Bear, margrave of Brandenburg. In June 1169 Frederick had voided the election of both men and had designated Baldwin, Henry's choice, as the new archbishop. The negotiators agreed to an examination of the canonicity of Siegfried's election, and, if it had been canonical, Siegfried was to be transferred to Bremen from Brandenburg, where he had been serving since 1173 as one of Magdeburg's suffragan bishops. The church of Bremen was to regain all its possessions that Baldwin had alienated to Henry. However, Baldwin ended up dying in office on 18 June 1178; and he was succeeded not by Siegfried but by a Cologne cleric, Berthold (also known as Bertram), who was acceptable to both Henry and Frederick. In the end, Wichmann and Henry's other opponents prevailed. The Third Lateran Council deposed Berthold in 1179, and Frederick enfeoffed Siegfried with the regalia of the church of Bremen in April 1180 at the court in Gelnhausen, where he also conferred the duchy of Saxony on Siegfried's brother, Bernard. The removal of Gero and Baldwin served the ecclesiastical and territorial interests of Wichmann and the Ascanians rather than the emperor's desire for revenge after his humiliation at Chiavenna.

The church of Salzburg was also to regain all its alienated possessions. The agreement was silent about the fate of Archbishop Adalbert and Frederick's appointee, Provost Henry of Berchtesgaden. The resolution of the Salzburg schism was a bigger problem because both men were avowed supporters of Alexander, and a final decision was postponed at Anagni.

Alexander and all the cardinals were required to recognize Frederick, Beatrice, and Henry as the rightful rulers and were to grant them their peace. Beatrice was to be crowned as empress by the pope or a legate. Her coronation by Paschal III in St. Peter's was thus, by inference, voided because it had been performed by an anti-pope. (She was never re-crowned.) All those who had aided Frederick were included in the peace, except those whose cases were being assigned to the judgment of the pope and the Roman Church or who had seized the property of St. Peter. The pope was to call as soon as possible a council to excommunicate all those who broke the agreement; subsequently an ecumenical council was to do the same. The emperor and the princes were to swear to keep the peace and to confirm the agreement in writing. The pope and the cardinals were also to issue a sealed charter, and the nobles of Rome and the Campania were to confirm it by their oaths. While the peace negotiations continued, Frederick was not to attack the lands of the pope or those territories that the king of Sicily held in fief from the papacy. If the negotiations failed, the truce was to last another three months. Wichmann, Christian, Conrad of Worms, and the imperial proto-notary Wortwin signed the preliminary peace.

In their separate explanatory declaration, the envoys swore that they would make sure Frederick observed the terms of the preliminary peace agreement. They assured the pope, the cardinals, other clerics, and their servants that they would be able to travel safely to and from Venice, Ravenna, or any other place where the ongoing peace discussions would be held, whether or not the negotiations were successful. The envoys and the emperor would order that anyone traveling through the Empire on business with the curia could do so freely.

The most difficult matters remained unsettled at Anagni: the form of the public enactment of Frederick's recognition of Alexander; the emperor's relations with the Lombard League, Sicily, and Byzantium; and the schism within the church of Salzburg. The final terms were settled in eight months of hard bargaining.[22]

Lombard Recalcitrance

Two of the curious features of the preliminary Peace of Anagni are that the Lombards, unlike the Normans, were not included in the truce while the final details were worked out; and that the arbiters chosen by the pope and emperor were authorized to impose a settlement upon the Lombards without their representation if direct negotiations between them and the emperor failed, so that they could not block the conclusion of the final peace. Around 1 December 1176 the pope assured the Lombards, who had started a new campaign against Como and Pavia, that, contrary to the rumors Frederick was spreading, Alexander had not made a separate peace with him and would not do so without their participation, and that he intended to come to Lombardy as soon as the League's rectors and consuls had arranged for his safety. This visit never occurred. Alexander spent Christmas and Epiphany (6 January 1177) in Benevento, south of Rome. From there he headed for the coast of the Adriatic, and, after being delayed by storms, he reached Venice on 24 March. The pope seemingly never allayed the Lombards' suspicions, because the Milanese Anonymous merely noted in his chronicle that Frederick had sent envoys to the pope and that they had concluded a secret agreement at Anagni.[23]

In the meantime the emperor headed from Pavia, where he had stayed during the negotiations in Anagni, to Cremona, which feared that it would be politically and militarily isolated if Alexander succeeded in mediating a peace between Frederick and the Lombard League. We have two highly tendentious accounts of what transpired in December during Frederick's stay in Cremona. Each presents the very different perspectives and interests of the Cremonese consuls and emperor at the time when the respective narratives were written.

The first is a summary statement, penned by a Cremonese notary, about the agreement that the city made with Frederick on 12 December 1176 in the monastery of St. Agatha in Cremona. The people had received Frederick with love and honor as their father and lord. Count Conrad of Ballhausen had sworn on the Gospels that Frederick would protect Cremona's property, would provide the city with military assistance in consultation with the consuls, and would not leave Italy until Cremona had been reconciled with the Lombards or arrangements had been made for its defense in the emperor's absence. If hostilities resumed after Frederick's departure, the emperor would return to Italy with 1,000 German knights no later than six months after the consuls had requested his aid. The agreement also laid out the alternative arrangements if he could not do so in the allotted time. If peace had not been concluded by 1 June 1177, or if the Lombards remained at war with Cremona, Frederick would assign 1,000 German knights to its defense. His son Henry VI and the princes were also bound to the agreement's terms.

In 1185, after Frederick had allied with Milan against Cremona, he blamed Cremona for all the misfortunes he had suffered in Italy since the 1150s. Among the city's many misdeeds, the Cremonese had invited him in 1176 to come to their city, on the pretext of conducting him to the Matildine Lands, and had promised to receive him "with the greatest honor." In fact, the emperor could not recall that they had given him as much as a loaf of bread to eat during his stay at St. Agatha. At a meeting in the refectory, they had pressured him so intensely to grant them Luzzara and Guastalla in their entirety that he had feared he would not escape with his life. Through God's grace, he had managed to leave without issuing a charter to that effect, even though the large number of clerical and lay princes who were present had implored him to yield to the Cremonese demands so they could depart unharmed. Whatever occurred in St. Agatha on 12 December, Cremona remained loyal to Frederick in the following years; but the city had made the conclusion of a final peace with the Lombards contingent upon its inclusion in that peace. However, Frederick did not forget Cremona's role in the formation of the Lombard League and in the rebuilding of Milan, or the humiliating terms the Cremonese had tried to impose on him in St. Agatha.[24]

Frederick's envoys had guaranteed on his behalf at Anagni that the pope and the cardinals could travel safely to and from Venice or Ravenna or anywhere else where the peace would be finalized, but it took months to arrange such a meeting because the Lombards refused to accept an imposed peace. The emperor ordered Patriarch Ulrich of Aquileia, sometime in November 1176, to attend the council that was scheduled to convene in Ravenna on 25 January 1177; but the rectors of the mark of Verona forbade the clergy and laity of the mark, especially the bishops, from participating until the League had made peace with the emperor. Sometime after 13 December the emperor received two cardinal-legates with great honor in Modena and swore to observe the safe conduct his envoys had granted the pope. According to Archbishop Romuald, the legates and Frederick decided, in the presence of the Lombards, to hold the council in Bologna. Yet sometime in late December or early January the emperor once again commanded Ulrich to travel to Ravenna, where the council was now scheduled to meet on 2 February. Frederick himself was in Ravenna in late January, and on 24 February he enfeoffed his cousin Leopold V with the duchy of Austria in Pesaro, which is situated on the Adriatic coast between Ravenna and Ancona.[25]

While Frederick was staying in Cesena, south of Ravenna, he learned of Alexander's arrival in Venice on 24 March. He sent Wichmann, Conrad of Worms, and Wortwin, the proto-notary, to Venice to assure the pope that he was eager to conclude the negotiations they had undertaken on his behalf in Anagni but that Bologna was an unacceptable meeting place. Frederick feared for the safety of his own person and that of Christian of Mainz, they explained, because the archbishop had defeated the Bolognese in October 1175 and caused them much injustice and many injuries. Accordingly, the emperor requested that the council meet in either Ravenna or Venice. Alexander replied that since Frederick had agreed during the negotiations in Modena that the council should assemble in Bologna, the pope could not grant the emperor's request without the consent of the Lombards and the cardinals. The pontiff ordered the cardinals, other prelates, and the Lombard *podestàs*, rectors, and consuls who were awaiting his arrival in Bologna to join him in Ferrara on Passion Sunday, 10 April, the fifth Sunday in Lent. Surely, Frederick knew about Bologna's hostility before late March, so one wonders whether Frederick had ever agreed to meet there. His presence in Ravenna in late January would suggest otherwise.

On 11 April the pope and the Lombards, along with Archbishop Romuald and Count Roger of Andria, who represented the king of Sicily, met to discuss Frederick's request for a change of venue. Romuald is the sole source for the meeting. He included in his chronicle the speeches that Alexander and the unnamed representatives of the Lombards allegedly delivered. The pope expressed his eagerness, after eighteen terrible years of schism, to take advantage of Frederick's change of heart; but he had refused, Alexander said, the emperor's offer at Anagni to make a separate peace with him and the king of Sicily but without the Lombards. In their reply, the Lombards reminded the pope how much they had endured and suffered to protect the freedom of Italy and the liberty of the Church, and how they had rejected Frederick's offers to conclude a separate peace with them. It was contrary to reason, therefore, for the pope even to listen to the emperor's proposals, let alone to reach an agreement with him that excluded them. They would be glad to make peace, they insisted, if the honor of Italy and the liberties they had inherited from their fathers, grandfathers, and ancestors were preserved. What those liberties were was, of course, the heart of the dispute. If the Lombards' alleged words bear any resemblance to what they actually said, then they were objecting to any peace plan that allowed the emperor and pope to define their relationship to the crown without their participation. A dictated delineation of the Lombards' rights was no more acceptable at Venice in 1177 than at Roncaglia in 1158.

The imperial embassy arrived in Ferrara on 13 April 1177 and consisted of the archbishops of Mainz, Cologne, Magdeburg, and Trier, Conrad of Worms, Chancellor Godfrey, and the imperial notary Wortwin. In accordance with the arbitration mechanism that had been set up at Anagni, the pope selected seven cardinals and the Lombards chose four bishops, judges from Milan and Verona (these two cities were the leaders of the Lombard and Veronese sections of the League), and a burgher of Brescia to represent them. Alexander ordered Romuald and Count Roger to participate in the negotiations on William II of Sicily's behalf.

Before these deliberations could commence, the question of the meeting place had finally to be resolved. Bologna was unacceptable to the imperial envoys, and they proposed Pavia, Ravenna, or Venice as possible alternatives. The Lombards countered with Bologna or, alternatively, Piacenza, Ferrara, or Padua. They were initially opposed to Venice, because it had provided Christian with naval assistance during the siege of Ancona and had received imperial envoys, in violation of its obligations as a member of the Lombard League; but Alexander and the Sicilian envoys favored the *Serenissima.* The Lombards finally agreed to meet in Venice after Doge Sebastiano Ziani and the Venetians swore that they would not let Frederick enter the city without the pope's permission and had guaranteed the safety of everyone traveling to and from the city. At the end of April both Alexander and Frederick invited all the prelates and princes in Christendom to come to Venice. The haggling about the site of the council had been a tactic to ensure that the Lombards would be treated as equals in the deliberations.[26]

The Peace of Venice

Alexander returned to Venice on 10 May 1177. Romuald, the Sicilian representative at the negotiations, is the main source for the discussions that were held over many days in the chapel of the palace of the patriarch of Grado-Venice. The pope instructed the negotiators to make peace first between the emperor and the Lombards; this would require more protracted deliberations than would be necessary to reconcile Frederick with the Church and William II, whose interests were, Alexander said, identical. In essence, both Alexander and Frederick had become hostages of their respective Lombard allies. After much debate, Christian, who had replaced Wichmann as the chief imperial negotiator, presumably because he was an expert on Italian affairs, proposed that the Lombards act justly in regard to the regalia: they should either implement the judgment of the Bolognese doctors of law at Roncaglia or grant the emperor those things their ancestors had owed the elder Henry, that is, Henry IV.

The Milanese judge Gerardo Cagapisto responded on the Lombards' behalf. While they were prepared to acknowledge the emperor's rights, the rights in question pertained not to one man or city but to many. They required, therefore, a postponement to discuss Christian's proposal and to give a collective reply at a suitable time and place to their common judge. However, Gerardo rejected the Roncaglia laws out of hand, because they had been imposed on the Lombards while many of them had been absent—not, he stressed, out of contumacy—and were thus not legally binding. As far as Henry IV was concerned (r. 1056–1106), no one was alive, on either side, who could remember what they had owed him. Besides, Henry had not been a just ruler but a tyrant, who had taken Pope Paschal II prisoner in St. Peter's in 1111; his actions could not therefore serve as precedents. (In reality, it had been Henry V who had captured the pope. Gerardo's [or Romuald's] error proved his point that no one could really remember what had occurred during Henry IV's reign.) The Lombards were prepared, however, to give to Frederick what their ancestors had rendered to the younger Henry, that is, Henry V, Lothar III, Conrad III, and Frederick himself. If this proposal was or seemed to be too restrictive to the emperor, the Lombards were ready to observe the written peace terms the Cremonese had presented after Montebello. (Gerardo was referring, presumably, to Cremona's second proposal that recognized the continued existence of Alessandria.) The Lombards would have accepted the terms then, Gerardo said, if Frederick had not demanded that they also repudiate Alexander.

When the text of the second Cremonese arbitration award was read, Romuald indicated that the Germans challenged some of the provisions, twisted the meaning of others to their own advantage, or rejected some of the terms altogether. The Lombards countered with their own arguments and called upon the Cremonese, even though they were the Lombards' enemies, to repudiate the Germans' interpretations. The parrying went on for days. The status of Alessandria was, presumably, the major issue in contention. If Frederick was no longer willing to accept Alessandria's continued existence, as he had done, however reluctantly, after Legnano, it may be because his military situation had improved substantially. After all, the German princes who were coming to attend the council brought troops with them. For example, Duke Leopold V of Austria, whom Frederick had enfeoffed in February, and Duke Hermann of Carinthia, who had accompanied Leopold, are said to have commanded at Venice, respectively, 160 and 125 men. For their part, the Lombards were no doubt confident after Legnano that they could repulse an imperial attack.

The impasse was finally brought to the attention of Alexander, who realized that the question of the emperor's precise rights in Lombardy could not be resolved quickly. The pope proposed, therefore, a compromise that separated the ending of the schism from making peace between Frederick and the Lombards, and that broke the diplomatic logjam. The emperor was to grant the Lombards a six-year truce in the hope that additional time would make it easier to arrange a permanent peace. Further, he was to conclude with the Sicilian king either a permanent peace or one that lasted at least fifteen years. Christian replied that the envoys needed to obtain Frederick's consent, because they were not authorized to agree to a truce in place of a final peace.[27]

Frederick was livid when he heard the proposed terms and accused his envoys of being more concerned "about the honor and advantage of Pope Alexander than the dignity of the Empire." He ordered them to inform the pope that while he would gladly make peace with Alexander and the Church, he would not agree to a truce with either the Lombards or the king of Sicily. Was Frederick really angry because a truce denied him the opportunity to require the Lombards to submit to him, as they had at Montebello, and so counterbalance to a degree his own pending, humiliating submission to the pope? Or did he feign anger in the hope of extracting more concessions from the pope? There is no way to read the emperor's mind. Or did Romuald invent the story to explain why Frederick obtained more favorable terms from the pope in Venice than the imperial envoys had procured at Anagni?[28]

What happened next is the most inexplicable part of Romuald's story. Unbeknown to Christian and his colleagues, after their departure Frederick sent Chancellor Godfrey, Bishop Pons of Clermont, and Abbot Hugh of Bonnevaux on a secret mission to Alexander in Venice. They were to inform the pope, personally and confidentially, that out of the emperor's love for him, Frederick was prepared to agree to a fifteen-year peace with William of Sicily and a six-year truce with the Lombards if the pope granted Frederick's request without knowing what it was. The envoys were to convey the request, instead, to two cardinals whom Alexander would select; and the pope would be obliged to grant it if the cardinals advised him to do so. The pope, suspecting German trickery, declared that it did not behoove "the apostolic authority" to accept a request whose content was unknown to him. If Frederick was really asking for something that was not "contrary to the honor of God" and that did not cause harm to the Church, he would gladly consent. Godfrey left angrily, but Pons and Hugh reluctantly revealed the request to the pope—perhaps because, unlike the chancellor, they were not acting in an "official capacity."

Instead of returning the Matildine Lands to the pope immediately, as the imperial envoys had promised at Anagni, Frederick now wished to obtain the income from the margravine's disputed inheritance for fifteen years, that is, for the duration of the truce with William of Sicily. After the expiration of the truce, Frederick was to retain the domains until he was able to prove that the lands pertained legally to the Empire. Alexander countered that to ensure William's inclusion in the peace, he would let Frederick keep the income for fifteen years on condition that the lands would be restored to the Church at the termination of the truce. Frederick could then prove his legal title to the domains. The emperor did not like Alexander's counteroffer, when Pons and Hugh relayed it to him, because the pope was merely delaying the return of the Matildine Lands to the papacy for fifteen years; and so the issue remained, Romuald said, unresolved.

However, the clause on returning the Matildine Lands was dropped in the final agreement. Moreover, the provisions in the preliminary Peace of Anagni that had required Frederick to restore to Alexander "the prefecture of the city" as well as "all the regalia and other possessions of St. Peter . . . which the Roman Church had owned from the time of Innocent II" were likewise deleted at Venice. They were replaced by a vaguer stipulation that employed terminology usually referring to private property. It committed Frederick to restore "[e]very possession and holding ('tenementum')" of the Roman Church, including the prefecture but not the regalia, that the emperor and others had seized, "saving all the rights of the empire." Mediators chosen by the pope and emperor were to decide what these possessions were. On account of these revisions in Frederick's favor, the Peace of Venice was long considered to have been a diplomatic triumph for him; but the pope did not abandon his claims to earthly dominion, and he expected to return to Rome, with imperial support, as the city's ruler. The potential for further conflict was built into the settlement, because it left the precise rights of the papacy and crown in Rome and the Patrimony undefined.[29] Beyond that, the lasting image of the Peace of Venice was Frederick's prostration before the pope.

When Christian and his colleagues learned that Frederick had been negotiating behind their backs, they were upset and told Alexander, according to Romuald, that unnamed individuals envious of the envoys were spreading false reports about them to the emperor, so endangering the successful conclusion of the negotiations. They recommended that Frederick be allowed to come closer to Venice, so that embassies could be exchanged more quickly and give less time for opposition to develop. Alexander consulted with the Sicilian ambassadors and the Lombards and agreed that Frederick, accompanied by only a small entourage, could come to Chioggia, about fifteen miles from Venice, on the condition that he move closer to Venice only at the pope's command and with his permission. Christian provided the sworn assurances. Archbishop Philip, who was joined in Ravenna by the doge's son and many nobles, escorted Frederick from Cesena to Chioggia.

It is hard to believe that Frederick would have tried, as Romuald reported, to negotiate with the pope without the knowledge of the German archbishops. They were his principal advisers and, more to the point, they provided a substantial portion of the imperial forces. Archbishop Philip supposedly had 400 men with him in Venice, Christian and Wichmann 300 each, while Arnold of Trier had 50. In fact, Frederick wrote to Ulrich of Aquileia at the beginning of June 1177 that he had learned from his beloved princes Christian and Philip, who had just returned from the peace negotiations, about the patriarch's efforts on his behalf—Ulrich had been charged with borrowing money in Venice on Frederick's behalf—and that they would apprise Ulrich of the emperor's intentions. This letter hardly sounds as if Frederick was at odds with his envoys. In Romuald's story of Frederick's duplicitous treatment of his own envoys we may be dealing with a medieval version of the "good cop/bad cop" routine. Officially, Christian told Alexander that Frederick would not agree to a truce with the Lombards and William of Sicily; unofficially, Pons and Hugh said the emperor would agree, if he got something in return for the pope's failure to persuade the Lombards to make peace on terms acceptable to Frederick. The temporary acquisition of the Matildine Lands would compensate the emperor for the lack of the Lombards' formal submission to his authority, as had occurred at Montebello, and so partially make up for his own loss of honor in submitting to the pope.

Intriguingly, the Venetian chronicler, who indicated that 8,420 onlookers from all over Europe (5,856 of whom he identified by name) witnessed Frederick's formal reconciliation with Alexander in front of St. Mark's on 24 July 1177, began his long list with the names of Bishop Pons and Abbot Hugh; the chronicler said that they had been sent by the kings of France and England as mediators. If this report is true, Pons and Hugh were speaking for Louis VII and Henry II as well as for Frederick in the negotiations; and their intervention would help to explain why the Treaty of Anagni was modified in Frederick's favor in Venice. The pope could not disregard the wishes of the Western monarchs.[30]

In spite of the pressure from the German bishops and possibly also from the Western monarchs to yield, Frederick still resisted the inevitable at Chioggia, where he arrived on 6 July. Once again, Romuald is the chief source. He may have told the tale because it ascribed to him a crucial role at the last minute in the successful outcome of the negotiations. Some unidentified Venetian commoners approached Frederick and advised him that if he came to the city without the pope's permission, they would help him conclude a peace with the Church and the Lombards on his own terms. He was tempted by their offer and told them to turn their words into deeds by winning over the rest of the people to their proposition. In the meantime, Alexander sent five cardinals and the German negotiators to Frederick. If he allowed the German princes to swear on the emperor's soul, in the presence of the Sicilian envoys and representatives of the Lombards, that he would keep the various accords, then Alexander would allow Frederick to come to Venice and would grant him his blessing and grace. Since Frederick was awaiting a response from the Venetians, he stalled, to the growing unease of the cardinals, by pretending that the proposed peace terms were new to him and that he required additional time to deliberate.

At an assembly in St. Mark's most of the people turned against Doge Sebastiano Ziani, who reminded them that they had sworn not to permit Frederick to come to Venice without the pope's authorization. They countered that the emperor had done so already by setting foot in Chioggia, which was situated in Venetian territory. The Lombards who were in Venice feared Frederick's arrival and fled to the territory of Treviso. The Sicilian envoys assured Alexander of their support—four galleys were at his disposal if he needed to leave—and warned the Venetians of the consequences for their commerce and for their citizens in the *Regno* if they broke their oath. Venetian popular opinion turned against the instigators of the conspiracy, and the doge asked Alexander for forgiveness. Sicilian support at a critical juncture had saved the negotiations, if we are to believe Romuald.

When Frederick realized that he could not count on the Venetians, he began to address the cardinals in a friendlier fashion. Christian and the other ecclesiastical princes reminded the emperor that they had gone at his behest to Anagni, but under the influence of evil men he was ignoring their advice. They were prepared to obey him in temporal matters because they held their regalia from him, but he was not the lord of their souls. Hence they would acknowledge Alexander from that moment forward as the rightful pope. As Otto of St. Blasien put it thirty years later, it was the German bishops who forced Frederick to make peace. His willingness even to contemplate joining a popular insurrection against the doge shows how personally distasteful was the prospect of publicly acknowledging his enemy as the supreme pontiff.

Confronted with the threat of total isolation, Frederick capitulated on 21 July. He assured the princes that he intended to adhere to the terms of the peace they had negotiated. The next day Count Dedo V of Groitzsch, a son of Margrave Conrad of Meissen, Frederick's cousin Margrave Conrad of Montferrat, and the imperial ministerial and chamberlain Sigiboto gave their oaths in Venice that the emperor would swear his adherence to the various agreements. Alexander summoned the Lombard representatives back to Venice, freed the doge and the Venetian people from their oath not to let Frederick enter the city, and ordered them to conduct the emperor in an honorable fashion to Venice.[31]

On 22 July in Chioggia the cardinals and princes signed the final draft of the Peace of Venice. Most of the text was taken verbatim from the preliminary accord, but it included the significant revisions about the Matildine Lands and the regalia that had been made during the negotiations conducted between May and July. Beatrice and her son Henry VI, as well as Frederick, were required to accept Alexander "as the catholic and universal pope"; and the young king was to swear the same oath as his father. Frederick agreed to a fifteen-year peace with William of Sicily and a six-year truce with the Lombards, which was to commence on 1 August. His Lombard allies were to swear to observe the truce, and if any of them refused, the emperor was to command his other supporters by the fealty they owed him not to aid them. He was not to revoke this mandate for the duration of the truce. The four archbishops (Christian of Mainz, Philip of Cologne, Wichmann of Magdeburg, Arnold of Trier) and the proto-notary (Wortwin), who had been the chief negotiators, signed the copy of the peace that was handed to the pope. It is the only copy that survives.[32]

The more specific terms of Frederick's truce with the Lombards were worked out in the next few days. The names of the League members and Frederick's allies who adhered to the truce are indicative of the volatility of northern Italian politics. Venice, not Milan or Verona, headed the list of League members, which also included Como and Lodi, on whose behalf Frederick had intervened in 1154, as well as Alessandria. On the imperial side, the first four places were assigned to Cremona, Pavia, Genoa, and Tortona, which Frederick had destroyed in 1155. To monitor the observance of the truce, these cities and the territory of Margrave William of Montferrat were to select two truce keepers each. A violation of the truce by an individual member would not end the truce if the other parties condemned the action and paid appropriate compensation. Both sides were prohibited from intervening in the internal disputes of the other. The emperor was not to compel any clerical or lay member of the League to swear an oath of fealty to him during the truce, nor was he to judge them. The Lombards accepted the truce only reluctantly. In his account of the peace, the Milanese Anonymous accused Alexander of abandoning his promise of good faith to the Lombards, of violating his pledge not to make peace without the Milanese, of reinstating bishops who had been removed from their offices, and of appointing bishops of his own choice. Alexander and the German bishops had clearly exerted a great deal of pressure on the Lombards and Frederick even to agree to a truce—and, in Frederick's case, to accept Alexander as the pope.[33]

Frederick's Public Humiliation in Venice

Nothing was said in the final draft of the peace agreement about the public enactment of Frederick's reconciliation with Alexander, but the cardinals and the imperial envoys must have choreographed that ceremony carefully in advance. While Romuald is the sole source for much of what we know about the negotiations that preceded Frederick's restoration to communion on 24 July 1177, dozens of chroniclers mentioned, if only briefly in passing, the events that took place in Venice. Besides Boso's *Life of Alexander III* and Romuald's *Annals*, which highlighted his own role in the negotiations, there are three other eyewitness accounts: a letter that Alexander wrote only two days later, on 26 July, to Archbishop Roger of York and Bishop Hugh of Durham; the less partisan *Pisan Annals* of Bernardo Maragone (d. 1188/90), who relied on information supplied by the two Pisan envoys in Venice; and a bystander's account by an English monk, perhaps Master Nicholas of Dunstable from the abbey of Bury St. Edmunds. The chronicler who composed *The History of the Venetian Doges* between 1239 and 1247 may have utilized Venetian records on the housing and provisioning of the participants to compile his list of 8,420 attendees—a number that does not include the members of the emperor and the pope's own immediate entourages and the Venetians themselves. Venice has rightly been called the site of the first international peace conference. In contrast, there is no extant eyewitness account by a pro-imperial participant. In the more than twenty extant letters and charters that were drafted in Frederick's name during his stay in Venice, the emperor himself made only one passing allusion to the specific terms of his agreement with the pope. The imperial silence speaks volumes about how he assessed what had happened and who he thought had "won" at Venice.[34]

As instructed by Alexander, on the evening of 23 July 1177 the doge and the people of Venice escorted Frederick on six festively decorated galleys from Chioggia to the monastery of St. Nicholas on the Lido, two miles from the city. Early on the morning of Sunday, 24 July, seven cardinals sent by the pope brought Frederick from his quarters to the abbatial church. They released him from excommunication after he had renounced the three anti-popes he had served and promised obedience to Pope Alexander and his successors. Archbishop Christian, as the arch-chancellor of Germany, swore the same thing on the Gospels. The other princes who were present followed their example and were, likewise, restored to communion. Frederick had to be formally reconciled with the Church before he arrived in Venice, because the pope could not meet with an excommunicate. The emperor then boarded the doge's galley and seated between the doge and the patriarch of Grado-Venice; he disembarked at St. Mark's Square around the third hour of the day. Two poles, with banners of St. Mark that touched the ground, stood on the embankment. A procession of cardinals and the bishops in Frederick's entourage, headed by the clergy and people of Venice carrying banners and crosses, led the emperor, who walked between the doge and the patriarch, from the dock to the papal throne that had been erected on a wooden tribunal in front of St. Mark's. The patriarchs of Grado-Venice and Aquileia were at Alexander's right and left, while other archbishops, bishops, and cardinals were arrayed around him in a setting modeled after the pope's reception of the emperor in Rome.

Frederick and Alexander then played out the most dramatic and famous/infamous scene in their meeting: the public enactment of Frederick's reconciliation with the Church that had already happened in the church of St. Nicholas. Frederick removed his red mantle and other imperial insignia to indicate that he was acting as an individual sinner rather than as an emperor.

In accordance with the ritual for restoring an excommunicate to the community of the faithful, he then prostrated himself with outstretched arms in front of the pope. As was customary in a meeting between the emperor and the pope, Frederick then kissed Alexander's feet and knees as a gesture of respect and recognition of the pope's spiritual authority, and so showed Alexander the reverence he had promised in the peace treaty. Alexander himself wrote that Frederick "in the presence of an innumerable multitude of men and women" had shown him "humbly and reverently obedience and reverence as the supreme pontiff." However, Frederick's act also invoked the image of Mary Magdalene, whose sins were forgiven as she wept at Jesus' feet and kissed and anointed them. Alexander, who was crying, rose slightly, helped Frederick rise, took the emperor's head in his hands, gave him the kiss of peace, and offered him a seat at his side. The anonymous English observer alone added that Alexander said "It is good that you came, son of the Church." The Germans then either started or joined in the singing of the *Te Deum laudamus*, "We Praise, You, Oh God." It was a very different scene from the one that had been staged at Besançon.

The ceremony in front of St. Mark's thus combined elements of the liturgy for the reconciliation of an excommunicate with the ritual for a meeting between the two highest authorities in Christendom. It was not intended as such to humiliate the emperor but to demonstrate the pope and emperor's mutual recognition of each other's authority. Nevertheless, the silence of the German sources about the events in Venice suggests that some Germans, including perhaps Frederick, thought otherwise. A thirteenth-century Augustinian canon in the archdiocese of Magdeburg, who assigned to Archbishop Wichmann the principal role in brokering peace, told the probably apocryphal tale that Margrave Dietrich of Lusatia (the brother of Count Dedo, who had sworn on Frederick's behalf on 22 July) protested that the imperial dignity had been injured when Frederick prostrated himself. When the margrave's words were translated for Alexander, he hastened to lift Frederick up and to kiss him.[35]

Frederick, following the protocol for an imperial–papal meeting, then took the pope by the right hand into St. Mark's—in the ceremony of reconciliation it was the bishop who took the right hand of the repentant sinner—and led Alexander to the high altar, where with bowed head Frederick received a papal blessing. They left together. Frederick and his entourage went to the doge's palace, while Alexander, the cardinals, and the Sicilian envoys headed by ship to the papal quarters in the patriarch's residence. The anonymous English witness reported that Alexander sent

Frederick a variety of dishes in gold and silver vessels and a fattened calf along with a citation from the parable of the prodigal son: "let us eat and make merry; for this my son was dead, and is alive again; he was lost, and is found" (Luke 15:23–24). (Romuald wrote that Alexander cited the same verses on 1 August.) That evening Frederick requested that Alexander celebrate the next day, the feast of St. James, with a festive Mass in St. Mark's in the Apostle's honor; and the pope agreed. The events that occurred on 25 July may thus not have been preplanned.

St. James had been transformed in medieval hagiography into a warrior who fought the Spanish Moors and was the patron saint of knights. There is circumstantial evidence that Frederick may have been especially devoted to the Apostle. In the 1090s the emperor's paternal ancestors had founded the Alsatian abbey of St. Foy, which was affiliated with the French monastery of the same name situated on the pilgrimage route leading to Santiago de Compostela; and in 1157 Frederick had asked the English king Henry II to return the hand of St. James that the king's mother had brought back with her to England. Perhaps it was just a coincidence that 25 July happened to be the Apostle's feast day, but maybe Frederick's request to celebrate St. James at a festive Mass was another way to demonstrate that he was a Christian knight and a defender of the faith. It may even have foreshadowed his taking of the cross in 1188.[36]

Around the first hour of the day on 25 July the emperor awaited the pope and the cardinals outside St. Mark's and walked forward to meet Alexander. They entered the church together, with the emperor on the pope's right side. Alexander and the cardinals put on their liturgical vestments, while Frederick, as a token of his humility and penitence, once again took off his mantle. Then, with the aid of a staff, Frederick cleared the way to the altar for the papal procession and expelled the laity from the choir. Romuald likened Frederick's actions to those of the doorkeeper—we might compare him to the sergeant-at-arms at a State of the Union address. Frederick remained in the choir with the clergy during the papal Mass—a sign that he was not an ordinary layman. After the reading of the Gospel, Alexander ascended the pulpit and Frederick moved closer, Romuald said, to listen attentively to the pope's homily. Alexander noticed Frederick's "pious bearing" and, presumably, his difficulty in understanding the Latin, and he asked Ulrich of Aquileia to translate. After the recitation of the Creed, Frederick once again kissed the pope's feet, offered gold at his feet, and received the sacrament. (The Pisan chronicler reported that Frederick gave the pope a pound of gold.) The two left the church together. Frederick held the stirrup of Alexander's white palfrey as he mounted. Romuald said the emperor led the horse by the bridle a few paces, but Boso reported that the pope "accepted . . . the intention for the deed" and declined the honor. Alexander simply wrote that Frederick had shown him the same honor and respect his predecessors had granted previous popes. In this instance the marshal and squire's service, which the emperor or king usually performed on the pope's arrival, was turned into a ceremony of departure. Both then went to their separate quarters.[37]

On 26 July, at about the ninth hour and accompanied by only a small entourage, Frederick paid Alexander a visit. They met in the pope's private chamber and, in the presence of the bishops and cardinals, engaged in both small pleasantries and weightier discussions. Cardinal Boso, who alone mentioned this meeting, was likely present. The English monk (Master Nicholas of Dunstable?) noted, without giving particular details, that Frederick stayed in Venice for two months and spoke with the pope both publicly and in private with the aid of interpreters.

Romuald is the chief source, on the other hand, for Frederick's formal swearing of the peace with the Church and William II and of the truce with the Lombards, which occurred on 1 August in the great hall of the patriarch's palace. Alexander was seated on a folding stool at an elevated place. Frederick and Romuald, as the representative of the Sicilian king, were also seated on folding stools, respectively, at the pope's right and left. The cardinals stood in front of them, as was the case at a papal consistory. Alexander rose and delivered a speech, in which, according to Romuald, he likened Frederick's reconciliation with the Church to the return of the prodigal son and hailed the restoration of unity and peace. Then Frederick got up and for the third time removed his mantle. Perhaps this was to indicate his sorrow that his high rank, as he allegedly said in his address, had not prevented him from listening to evil men and from falling into error, and his joy that he had been restored to communion. The large assembly acclaimed the emperor's words, which Archbishop Christian had translated from German into Latin. Afterwards the Gospels, relics, and a wooden cross were placed in the middle of the hall; and Count Henry II of Diez, who had served as the imperial *podestà* in Milan, swore on the emperor's soul that he would abide by the terms of the peace and truce, without any deception, as they had been negotiated and written down, and that Henry VI would do the same.

Romuald said that twelve unnamed, clerical and lay princes of the Empire then took a similar oath with their hands on the Gospels, in recognition of the fact that the emperor and the princes jointly constituted the Reich—a chaplain of Archbishop Philip had sworn on 22 July that the princes would endorse the peace in this fashion. Sometime between

14 August and 18 September twelve Germans confirmed for Alexander in a charter they all sealed that Frederick would abide by his commitments. Presumably they were the same men who had sworn on 1 August. Not surprisingly, seven of them were the men who had negotiated the peace. Two of the other jurors were Count Dedo V of Groitzsch, who had sworn on Frederick's behalf on 22 July, and Count Henry II of Diez, who had done the same on 1 August. Although many lay princes such as Leopold V of Austria were in Venice, the only one who swore an oath was Dedo's brother, Margrave Dietrich of Lusatia, he who is alleged to have objected to Frederick's prostration before the pope. The absence of the lay princes at such a crucial moment is symptomatic of their withdrawal from imperial affairs during the last two decades of Frederick's reign.

Archbishop Romuald and Count Roger of Andria then swore that after the emperor had sent his envoys to Sicily, William would within a space of two months have one of his princes swear on the king's soul that he would keep the fifteen-year truce and would have ten of his other princes take the same oath. Thirteen representatives of the Lombard League swore that they would observe the truce. Gerardo Cagapisto, who had argued the Lombard case during the negotiations, headed that list.[38] Stefan Weinfurter has observed that whereas in January 1077 Henry IV had stood abject and virtually alone in the snow outside the castle of Canossa for three days, Frederick's ritualized humiliation before an international audience in Venice lasted three weeks.[39]

Settling Other Business

Alexander and Frederick presided for fourteen days over a council that was attended by dignitaries from all over Christendom, including, allegedly, 514 bishops. The council implemented the provisions of the Peace of Venice that dealt with the ordinations performed by the anti-popes and schismatic bishops, and with disputed elections and appointments in various dioceses.

The biggest remaining problem was the archdiocese of Salzburg, because both Archbishop Adalbert and Provost Henry of Berchtesgaden had adhered to Alexander. Adalbert defended himself in person, through intermediaries, and in a lengthy brief against the charges that he had procured his election through violence, had been consecrated by Patriarch Ulrich of Aquileia before the pope had confirmed his election, and had alienated church property. In the end, Adalbert had to accept the political reality that the pope and emperor needed to find a vacant archbishopric for Conrad of

Wittelsbach, who had only reluctantly resigned Mainz in favor of Archbishop Christian. On 9 August 1177 Alexander and Frederick wrote to the clergy and ministerials of the church of Salzburg and the laity in Carinthia and Styria. They said that, in order to restore peace, after lengthy discussions and with the consent of the princes, Archbishops Adalbert and Henry of Berchtesgaden had both resigned. The Salzburg clergy who were in Venice would have preferred to postpone a new election until their return to Salzburg, but at the pope's command and upon the advice of Frederick and the princes, they had elected the emperor's kinsman, Conrad of Wittelsbach. Frederick had invested Conrad with all the regalia that the church of Salzburg had possessed in the days of Archbishop Eberhard I (1147–64), because all the enfeoffments and alienations of properties that had occurred while the archiepiscopal temporalities had been in Frederick's possession were void. The emperor assured the letter's recipients of his grace, even though they had gravely and repeatedly provoked and injured him. Henry of Berchtesgaden received the bishopric of Brixen in 1179. Adalbert was promised a vacant archbishopric or bishopric sometime in the future. The ending of the Salzburg schism is a good example of how difficult it could be to balance competing political, ecclesiastical, and familial claims.[40]

Sometime between 2 and 13 August the Sicilian envoys paid a courtesy call upon Frederick in the doge's palace. As a special sign of his favor, the emperor permitted Romuald to deliver his flowery address while seated on a folding stool rather than standing, as he recorded in his chronicle. William II had sent Frederick, "his dearest friend and brother," his greetings and indicated his desire to live in unity and peace with all Christian princes, because he wished to fight only "the enemies of the cross of Christ" on land and sea. Since William was so completely committed to the service of God, Frederick, "as the special son and defender of the Church of God," had to love William, Romuald said, more than any other prince in the world. There was no reason for hostility between the two monarchs. In fact, William could not recall an instance when Frederick had injured him or he had harmed Frederick. If we are to believe Romuald, Chancellor Godfrey replied in kind on Frederick's behalf. Although "popular opinion" believed that the monarchs were enemies, Frederick had never attacked William or his kingdom, and the king had never caused the emperor any offense. Technically, the speeches were not total fabrications—there had been only minor border incursions in 1167 and 1176—but both Romuald and Godfrey, if they really said the things that Romuald reported, were stretching the truth.

Romuald did not rely solely on rhetoric, but asked that Frederick issue a charter, sealed with a golden bull, that set forth the terms of the fifteen-year peace between the Empire and the Normans. Interestingly, the charter's style indicates that it was probably drafted by a member of the Sicilian rather than the imperial chancery. Count Henry of Diez again swore on the emperor's soul that Frederick would keep the peace, and the nine other oath-takers were the same men who had sworn on the emperor's behalf on 1 August. A suitable person was to procure Henry VI's commitment by the middle of September. For even greater security, the envoys asked Alexander and the cardinals to confirm the imperial charter, which was inserted in the papal privilege.

On the orders of the pope and emperor, Cardinal Huguccio, accompanied by a member of the imperial chancery, Romuald's notary, and Count Roger's chaplain, went to the castle of *Gayue*, most likely Gavi near Pavia, to obtain Henry VI's assent. In the presence of Beatrice, Conrad of Montferrat, and some of the rectors of the Lombard League, Bishop Hugo of Verden swore the prescribed oath on Henry's soul. It is worth noting that there is no evidence that the empress and Henry had accompanied Frederick to Venice, possibly because Beatrice was pregnant with the couple's youngest son Philip or recovering from his birth. Frederick promised to dispatch Archbishop Christian to the Sicilian court to receive William II's oath, but Christian never went. A lower-level imperial embassy finally arrived in Palermo in February or March 1178 and received a charter acknowledging William's adherence to the peace.[41]

On 14 August, Alexander and Frederick, seated next to each other on thrones in St. Mark's, presided at the closing session of the council. It was attended by the doge, the Sicilian envoys, German and Italian clerics, and a multitude of lay persons. After prayers, the recitation of the customary litany used at synods, and a sermon about peace, the pope ordered that burning candles be distributed to the emperor and everyone else. Alexander solemnly excommunicated anyone who broke the peace or truce. The candles were thrown to the ground and extinguished, and Frederick shouted in a loud voice with the rest: "Let it be so. Let it be so." The pope and emperor gave Romuald and Count Roger permission to leave, and they sailed on 16 August to report to William of Sicily on their mission.[42]

Frederick remained in Venice for another four weeks. He rewarded the Venetians on 17 August for hosting the peace congress by renewing his predecessors' treaty with the *Serenissima* with one crucial addition: like the merchants of Haguenau, Aachen, Gelnhausen, Rome, Monza, and Pisa, the Venetians were freed from the payment of all tolls and imposts throughout the Empire. In September an imperial representative swore on Frederick's behalf a binding peace with the doge and his successors—in late

July, Venice had still been listed first among the members of the Lombard League—and Frederick granted the Venetians and their goods secure transit throughout the Empire.[43]

Frederick was soon testing the limits of his truce with the Lombards. After most of the participants in the peace conference had left Venice, some nobles of Treviso approached the emperor and engaged in secret negotiations and an exchange of oaths with him. There was uproar when their dealings were discovered and, fearing for their lives, they were forced to reveal to the Lombard League officials the content of their talks and oaths. The rectors punished them severely, and thereafter the League was on its guard against any additional treachery by its "cunning enemy." At the insistence of Alexander and the cardinals, Frederick declared in September that he would not punish any of his vassals in Lombardy, the mark of Verona, or the Romagna who failed to perform their feudal obligations during the truce because they belonged to the League, nor would he deprive them of their fiefs after the expiration of the truce.[44]

Before leaving Venice for Ravenna on 18 September, Frederick visited Alexander to secure his permission to depart. In the presence of the bishops, cardinals, and the princes, Alexander requested that Frederick return the regalia of St. Peter and the possessions of the Roman Church, as had been agreed upon at Anagni—specific reference to the regalia had been omitted in the final version of the peace. Frederick responded that he would do so immediately except for the Matildine Lands and the county of Bertinoro—which the recently deceased, childless Count Cavalcante had bequeathed to the Holy See—because he believed both rightly belonged to the Empire. Frederick proposed that the pope should select three of the princes, while he would choose three of the cardinals, to reach a mutually acceptable settlement that would be irrevocably binding on both sides. Although Alexander felt that the peace had assigned the Matildine Lands to the papacy, even if they were no longer specifically mentioned in the Treaty of Venice, he reluctantly acceded to Frederick's request, Boso said, for the sake of peace. In reality, the communes and nobles had long since usurped most of the Matildine Lands, so that the papal concession did not entail a substantial loss to the papacy. In return, Frederick charged Archbishop Christian with restoring to the pope, within three months, the regalia of St. Peter and all the other alienated possessions of the Roman Church. (Christian's preoccupation with this task explains why he did not go to Sicily to procure William's sworn adherence to the fifteen-year peace.) At the end of their meeting, Frederick knelt before the pope and kissed his feet—he did not prostrate himself as he had outside St. Mark's because he was not there as a penitent—and received the kiss of peace from the pontiff and all the cardinals.

Frederick marched in October from Cesena to Bertinoro, which was situated off the Via Emilia about halfway between Bologna and Rimini on the Adriatic, and demanded that the papal envoys who had taken possession of the castle on the pope's behalf surrender it immediately. When the envoys declared that they lacked the authority to do so, the emperor seized Bertinoro. Alexander urged Frederick to restore the castle to the Holy See, but he refused. To preserve the peace, the pope reluctantly accepted this fait accompli as well. Alexander was willing to overlook Frederick's high-handed behavior because he needed imperial forces to regain control of Rome and the Patrimony.[45]

Frederick spent the next nine months traversing those portions of imperial Italy that remained under his nominal control after the Peace of Venice. Godfrey of Viterbo lauded the emperor for traveling through Tuscany with only a few soldiers so as not to burden the population needlessly; he was presenting Frederick's lack of a sizeable entourage in the best possible light. Judging by the witness lists in his charters, the only German princes who accompanied Frederick, even briefly, were Christian, Bishop Conrad of Worms, and in January 1178, Bishop-Elect Otto II of Bamberg (Otto of Andechs, previously provost of St. Mary's, Aachen, and bishop of Brixen). The other Germans were: the proto-notary Wortwin; a few counts such as Rupert of Walldürn, one of Frederick's oath-takers in Venice; those who had been granted an Italian fief, such as Conrad of Urslingen, the count of Assisi; and imperial ministerials. The other witnesses were Italian magnates. There clearly was little interest in Germany in continuing Frederick's Italian policy, and the princes were keeping their distance from the emperor.

In mid-February 1178 the emperor was reunited in Genoa with Beatrice, who had been staying in Gavi. The couple had been apart since at least early July, when Frederick left for Chioggia. Since no pressing business seemingly required the emperor's presence in Umbria and Tuscany between October 1177 and February 1178, it does seem odd that Frederick made no attempt, to our knowledge, to visit his wife, who may have been recovering from a difficult pregnancy, and his youngest son Philip. Beatrice was delivered of her last child, Agnes, at the beginning of 1179.[46]

"Ruler of the Greeks"

Although in the final treaty the negotiators retained the clause in the preliminary Peace of Anagni that required Frederick to conclude "a true peace with the emperor of Constantinople and all helpers of the Roman Church," there is no indication that after November 1176 the Greeks participated in the peace negotiations. Already around 1 December, when Alexander assured the rectors of the mark of Verona that he would not make peace without them, the king of Sicily, and other helpers of the Church, he no longer specifically included the Byzantine emperor among the interested parties. By then, the news of the Seljuk Turks' defeat of Manuel I at Myriokephalon on 17 September 1176 may have reached the West. In fact, Boso interrupted his account of Alexander's actions after Anagni with a description of the battle, in which the Greeks were butchered and robbed, and Manuel was captured and then released by the God-fearing sultan.

An embassy from Sultan Kilic Arslan II of Iconium arrived at Frederick's court at the beginning of 1177 and informed him of the Turkish victory. Shortly thereafter, Frederick received valuable gifts and a letter from Manuel, written in gold ink, telling him that the sultan had surrendered to Manuel, had pleaded for mercy, and had promised to provide the *basileus* with military service against everyone. Frederick, who knew the truth, was not amused. According to the thirteenth-century chronicler Albert of Stade, who incorporated Manuel and Frederick's correspondence in his history, Frederick was especially incensed that Manuel had placed his own name ahead of Frederick's, thus signifying his superiority. He was also angry that Manuel had styled himself "Romanorum moderator," that is, ruler or governor of the Romans, and had addressed Frederick as "the king of Germany and emperor."

According to Godfrey of Viterbo, at Venice Alexander urged Frederick to make peace with the Greeks, but he refused. The pope did not press the emperor on the issue, in all probability because, after Myriokephalon, it was no longer worth insisting on Manuel's inclusion; such pressure would alienate both William II, who had not forgotten that he had been left waiting at the altar by his Byzantine bride, and the Venetians, who remembered that Manuel had imprisoned their fellow citizens. The Byzantine emperor had ceased to be a significant player in Mediterranean politics.

Frederick eventually responded to Manuel in a letter, whose authenticity was long in doubt and whose date is uncertain. In a calculated riposte, Frederick styled himself emperor of the Romans and "Graecorum moderator," "ruler of the Greeks," and Manuel as "king of the Greeks and emperor." Barbarossa's imperial predecessors had transmitted to him "the monarchy of the city of Rome," to which the kingdom of the Greeks was also subject. Just as the King of kings had established the Roman Empire as the head of the whole world, so, too, had He constituted the Roman Church as the mother and teacher of all Churches. Frederick admonished Manuel, therefore, to show him and his Empire the honor that was their due and to pay the supreme pontiff the requisite obedience and honor. He offered to mediate Manuel's dispute with Patriarch Michael III of Constantinople and congratulated Manuel on his victory over the sultan, whom Frederick pointedly called his friend and with whom he had been conducting unspecified negotiations. Finally, Frederick expressed his astonishment that the *basileus* had tried through his envoys and bribes to subvert the loyalty of Frederick's subjects. Manuel was wasting his efforts. However, if he was willing to love Frederick and his empire, Frederick was ready to reciprocate. After the Peace of Venice, it was Frederick who was the defender of the Church and Manuel who was the schismatic.[47]

Coronation in Arles

Frederick, Beatrice, and their sons Henry and Philip set out for Provence in mid-July 1178 via the Mont Cenis Pass, which the emperor had used in September 1174 at the beginning of the fifth Italian campaign. On Sunday, 30 July, Frederick was crowned as king of Burgundy in Arles, which Rahewin had called in the 1150s the "capital of the kingdom of Burgundy." Barbarossa was the first German monarch to be honored in this fashion since Conrad II had added Burgundy to the Empire in 1033, and the last until Charles IV copied Frederick's example in 1365. The imperial insignia were carried in front of Frederick in a festive procession, he was seated on a specially erected throne, a hundred organs (wind instruments) played, and there was a feast afterwards. Henry VI wore his crown, but there is no indication that Beatrice was crowned along with her husband. Instead, Frederick, who according to the English chronicler Ralph of Diceto was "uxorious . . . and seeking how to please her in all things," had her crowned on 15 August, the feast of the Virgin's Assumption, in Vienne (Burgundy), upstream on the Rhone from Arles. He, too, would have worn the crown on this occasion. Frederick spent the middle of September in Besançon, and by 11 October he was in Haguenau.

Clearly, the two ceremonies were intended to demonstrate that Frederick was the ruler of Burgundy, an area where imperial authority had always been weak. As Ralph of Diceto explained, Frederick was crowned in Arles to counter the negative impression caused by his defeat in Italy and because he was the ruler of four peoples: the Lombards, Bavarians, Austrasians (Lorrainers), and Burgundians. While Frederick had visited Beatrice's domains on several occasions, no German monarch had ever set foot in Provence. Yet the double coronations in Arles and Vienne underscored that Upper Burgundy and Provence were separate entities.

Frederick may have had a diplomatic reason for his display of imperial authority in Provence. In 1167 the boy-king of Aragon and count of Barcelona, Alfonso II, had been installed as the margrave of Provence; and his younger brother Peter became the count of Provence under the name Ramón Berenguer IV. As part of his policy of forging an anti-Staufer alliance in the Mediterranean, Manuel I had engaged his niece, probably in 1176, to Alfonso's brother. However, when the bride arrived in Provence in 1178, the Provençals were too afraid of Frederick to allow the marriage to proceed; and she married instead William VIII of Montpellier. Manuel and Frederick engaged in an endless game of diplomatic chess.

It is harder to explain Beatrice's separate coronation in Vienne, which only Ralph of Diceto mentioned. The Peace of Venice had nullified her coronation as empress in 1167 because it had been performed by an antipope, but there is no indication that the ceremony was repeated. Perhaps she was crowned in Vienne in compensation or to signal her new role as the resident countess-palatine of Burgundy.[48]

Beatrice may not have accompanied Frederick to Germany in October 1178. As far as we know, she was there on only three occasions during the last six years of her life: the feast of Sts. Peter and Paul on 29 June 1179, and the Pentecost courts of 1182 and 1184. She had issued only one extant charter on her own before 1181, but nine, one of dubious authenticity, survive from the period between 1181 and her death on 19 November 1184. All dealt with Burgundian affairs. We can only speculate about the reasons for her apparent separation from Frederick. She may very well have been exhausted from her life in the saddle and from her numerous pregnancies. One of her charters was witnessed by her physician. Her death at about forty suggests that she did have serious medical problems. Perhaps awareness of her mortality made Beatrice turn her attention to her own county, which was always intended to be the inheritance of one of her younger sons. In fact, Conrad and his teacher witnessed several of the charters, though in the end his brother Otto obtained Burgundy. Did Beatrice, like Eleanor of Aquitaine, retreat to her own domains because her marriage had gone sour, perhaps already during her lengthy separation from Frederick in 1177? It has been suggested that one possible cause of their estrangement may have been the question of her imperial title, because she was called in her own charters the *imperatrix*—but not after 1177 in chancery productions.[49]

Frederick was in Italy when she died and was interred in the crypt of the cathedral of Speyer. One clue that the couple may have grown apart is that he did not make, seemingly, substantial provisions for her remembrance. In 1187 he gave the Benedictine monks of St. Ulrich and St. Afra in Augsburg three manors to commemorate his own anniversary as well as his wife's. In April 1189, just before he left on the Third Crusade, Frederick and his son Otto conferred on the canons of St. Stephen's in Besançon a village, with all its appurtenances, to benefit the souls of the emperor's beloved wife and of her comital predecessors. She had established in St. Stephen's an altar dedicated to St. George and had installed two priests to pray for the remission of her father's and her ancestors' sins. Each year £16 were to be paid from the village's income for the maintenance of the two priests. (Beatrice was not identified in either charter as the empress.)[50] It may well be that Frederick made additional arrangements that have not survived in the extant documentation. Yet these gifts appear to be fairly modest donations to ensure the eternal well-being of an empress, especially if Otto, as the count of Burgundy, rather than Frederick was the real benefactor of St. Stephen's. Frederick did the "right thing," but his donations are not those of a husband who was disconsolate at the loss of his beloved wife and who founded, say, an abbey in her memory.

There is no indication that Frederick contemplated remarriage. Admittedly, he had waited more than three years between his divorce from Adela and his marriage to Beatrice, when the need to father an heir must have been a pressing concern; and he could easily enough satisfy his sexual desires, if he was so inclined, outside marriage. Was he a grieving husband or, mindful of his own, occasionally strained relations with his younger half-brother, Conrad, did he not want, as the father of five living sons, to cause dissension within his own family by siring another boy? We will never know.

The Temporary Return of the Papacy to Rome

After the conclusion of the negotiations in Venice, Frederick charged Archbishop Christian of Mainz with the restoration of papal rule in Rome and the Patrimony. If Alexander and Frederick really believed that this could be accomplished within three months, they grossly underestimated the difficulty of the task. The Romans had remained loyal to Frederick after the annihilation of the imperial forces in August 1167 and had adopted a policy of neutrality in regard to the schism. The anti-pope Calixtus III had resided after 1170 in Viterbo, while Alexander had settled in 1173 in Anagni. The reality was that the Roman nobility, whether they were nominally loyal to the emperor or the pope, pursued their own local factional interests and desired as much independence as possible from both. Alexander was thus dependent after July 1177 on Frederick's good will if he wished to regain control of Rome.

Alexander returned to Anagni in December 1177 and, backed by Christian's armed might, the pope finally entered the Eternal City on 12 March 1178, more than a decade after his flight at the approach of Frederick's army. Calixtus took refuge in a castle near Albano, southeast of Rome; and Frederick threatened him with outlawry if he did not submit. At the end of May, Christian succeeded in winning the townspeople of Viterbo to Alexander's side; but the local nobles refused to yield and besieged Christian in Viterbo. The Romans, led by the prefect and Margrave Conrad of Montferrat, who had turned against his imperial cousin out of opposition to Frederick's truce with the Lombards, joined the rebellious nobles. Their siege of Viterbo failed, and Conrad of Montferrat, who was captured, paid a ransom of 12,000 gold pieces to regain his freedom and swore fealty to Frederick and Christian. Deprived of any support, Calixtus prostrated himself before Alexander on 29 August 1178. Alexander presided in March 1179 over the Third Lateran Council that retroactively legitimized his election, but he left Rome for good in July and died two years later on 30 August 1181.

In the meantime, at the end of 1178, Manuel I had dispatched a mercenary army to the mark of Ancona and the Patrimony. Conrad of Montferrat allied with Manuel and captured Christian in late September 1179. Conrad went immediately to Constantinople to report on his success. Christian was finally released at the end of 1180 or in early 1181 after he agreed to the return of Conrad's ransom and the destruction of Alessandria, which had been included in the six-year truce with the Lombards. Christian died in Tusculum on 25 August 1183, without re-establishing effective papal lordship in Rome and the Patrimony. The situation of Alexander's successor, Lucius III (1181–85), became even more precarious after Christian's death.[51]

The Peace of Constance

One piece of unfinished business remained in Italy: the pending expiration of the six-year truce with the Lombards. While many communes included the Peace of Constance of 25 June 1183 in their collections of laws, because it was the official recognition of their autonomy, contemporary chroniclers like Godfrey of Viterbo or the author of the *Cologne Royal Chronicle* ignored it completely. In addition to the text of the actual peace agreement, the Lombard League's response to Frederick's lost initial proposal "on the question of the regalia" and the preliminary Peace of Piacenza of 30 April, which formed the basis for the final accord, also survive. It is thus possible to determine the compromises both sides made in the course of the negotiations. Yet without a narrative source like Boso or Romuald, we do not know for certain who initiated the discussions and when, where, and why they started. It is also impossible to tell whether the chroniclers were silent because they thought that the peace was a local affair that merely settled the unfinished business remaining after Frederick and the League had agreed to a truce in 1177; or whether they believed it was best to ignore a peace that had been a defeat for the emperor, who was compelled to abandon his policy of asserting direct imperial control over the communes, even if the final terms were better than the ones he had been ready to accept after the defeat at Legnano in 1176. Burchard of Ursberg's retrospective assessment around 1230 was negative. He commented that Frederick had made peace because the Italian campaigns had exhausted him and that the Lombards refused to perform any services for the crown that were not contained in the written text of the peace.[52]

Neither Frederick nor the Lombards were in as strong a position in 1183 as they had been six years earlier in Venice. The emperor could not count on the German princes to support another Italian campaign, and the removal of the imperial threat and the restoration of peace between the Empire and the Church allowed all the tensions among the League members to resurface. The biggest symbolic obstacle remained Alessandria, whose very name was an affront to Frederick, even though he had been reluctantly prepared to recognize its existence after Legnano and had accepted its inclusion in the truce.

Alessandria was eliminated as a problem on 14 March 1183 at the court held in Nuremberg. Frederick set forth the conditions under which he was restoring to his grace the men of Caesarea, who lived on the banks of the Tanaro, that is, in Alessandria. All the inhabitants were required to leave the city and remain outside until an imperial legate led them back in and conferred on them the city Frederick had founded and named Caesarea, "emperor city." He retained for the crown all the rights and possessions the Montferrats had previously exercised in Alessandria and its environs, that is, Frederick was punishing the margraves for Conrad's capture and imprisonment of Archbishop Christian. Frederick thus broke with his principal Italian ally just as he had abandoned his other cousin, Henry the

Lion, three years earlier in a reshuffling of communal and familial alliances. Two envoys from Caesarea swore fidelity to Frederick and his son Henry VI in Nuremberg, while the imperial chamberlain Rudolf swore on the souls of both the emperor and the king that they would observe the agreement as long as Caesarea remained faithful to the monarchs. The only prince who witnessed the accord was Frederick's son, Duke Frederick VI of Swabia; but more significantly, nine Italian burghers served as witnesses, including representatives from two cities that belonged to the League, Milan and Brescia. Caesarea was listed in the Peace of Constance in June among the communes that were on the imperial side.[53]

This remarkable piece of diplomacy, which finessed the Alessandria problem by pretending that a city by that name did not exist, must have been the product of lengthy negotiations; but it is precisely here that the narrative sources leave us in the dark. Had the terms been worked out in Italy? In that case the agreement must have been reached already in 1182 or very early 1183 to allow time for the communal representatives to cross the Alps in winter. Did Frederick, satisfied that his honor had been preserved by this diplomatic stratagem, then authorize his envoys to negotiate a final settlement with the Lombards on the basis of the initial imperial proposal on the regalia and the Lombard counteroffer? Or did the Italians travel to Nuremberg—and if so, on their own volition or at the emperor's summons—to devise the agreement about Alessandria there and only then take up the issue of the League itself? On balance the first alternative seems the more plausible one.

Regardless, sometime in March 1183 the emperor authorized three experts on Italian affairs to negotiate a peace between him and the Lombard "rebels": Bishop William of Asti, who had represented the communes in the negotiations in Venice and who ended his career as the archbishop of Ravenna; Margrave Henry Guercio of Savona, who had participated in Frederick's third, fourth, and fifth Italian campaigns and who had accompanied him on his progress through imperial Italy after the Peace of Venice; and the Carthusian, Dietrich of Silve-Bénite, whose putative kinship with the emperor might have given him special authority to cut a deal. It is likely that these men had represented the emperor in the discussions with Alessandria, when and wherever the settlement was negotiated. Frederick committed himself to accepting any terms the envoys procured, but the envoys must have known how much leeway they had in concluding an acceptable agreement. The imperial ministerial and chamberlain Rudolf of Siebenich, who had just sworn on Frederick's behalf in Nuremberg, joined them. (According to Otto of St. Blasien, Rudolf's brother Hartmann had taken Frederick's place in Susa and so had enabled the emperor to escape from Italy in 1168.) The striking thing is that Frederick did not rely upon a single German prince in such an important piece of imperial business.[54]

In the preliminary Peace of Piacenza of 30 April 1183, Frederick and Henry VI granted all the members of the Lombard League, outright, numerous regalia. In the case of those regalia that were not included in this broad grant, impartial men of good repute from each city and diocese, including the bishop, were to determine which regalia pertained to the emperor. If the Lombards did not want to conduct such an inquest, Frederick was prepared to accept instead an annual payment of 2,000 marks for abandoning the regalia in dispute; it would have been possible to purchase for 2,000 marks in Genoa 1,300 slaves or 33 substantial houses. However, this provision was dropped in the Peace of Constance, so Frederick may not have received any compensation for surrendering these rights. The emperor recognized the validity of all the privileges he or his predecessors had conferred on the Lombards before the outbreak of hostilities and voided all measures that he had taken against them. Cases that involved amounts exceeding £25 could be appealed to the emperor. They were to be heard within two months, not in Germany, but by the emperor's representative in the city or diocese where the appeal had originated in accordance with the laws and customs of that city. The imperial negotiators succeeded at Piacenza in expanding the emperor's appellate jurisdiction in this instance, because the Lombards had originally proposed that such appeals be limited to cases involving more than £100. The consuls were to be invested with their offices by the emperor or his legate, and all citizens of the communes between the ages of sixteen and seventy were required to swear fealty to the emperor. A few articles dealt with issues that were of concern to individual nobles or communes. For example, Frederick acknowledged Milan's jurisdiction in the counties of Seprio and Martesana, which he had taken from Milan in 1158. He pardoned all the injuries the Lombards had caused him or his adherents and agreed to return all properties that they had possessed legally and that had been taken from them.

Frederick recognized the League's existence and the Lombards' right to renew their association. In a clause that was added at Piacenza, he would not interfere in the League's internal affairs by hearing complaints that arose about agreements the members had concluded among themselves without resorting to violence. In return, the members of the League were obligated to assist the emperor in maintaining his possessions and rights, and if they were lost, to help him regain them. If a city refused to observe the terms of the peace, the other members were to compel it to fulfill its obligations. When the emperor entered Lombardy, he was to receive the *fodrum* and to enjoy his other customary rights; and the Lombards were required to repair the roads and bridges and to provide him and his forces with markets sufficient for their needs. For his part, the emperor was not to stay too long in a city or diocese to its detriment. Disputes between the emperor and another party about a fief were to be settled by the vassal's peers in the city or bishopric where the controversy arose, in accordance with the customs of the locality. However, in another provision that was added at Piacenza, if the emperor was in Lombardy, the case could be brought before him if he wished.[55]

A separate document, written sometime in March or April 1183, dealt with the implementation of the agreement. At a court that was to be held by 12 June, Frederick and his sons, Henry VI and Frederick VI, were to swear, or have someone swear on their behalf, that they would keep the peace. The representatives of the League, numerous German princes who were specifically identified, and the knights, consuls, and *podestàs* of the cities were to take a similar oath. The princes and knights who were not present at the June court had until 1 September to do so. The consuls of the cities were given three months to comply after the return of the League envoys from the court in Germany. The League was to outlaw any member who refused to take the oath within two months of being ordered to do so.

Another provision in this supplementary notarial instrument is of much greater interest. It specified that the £15,000 the League owed the emperor and the £1,000 due to Frederick's envoys and the provost of S. Antonino, where the Peace of Piacenza was sworn, were to be paid to them in Milan in installments. To raise this large sum, each League member had been assigned a specific allocation. The imperial envoys and the rectors and the consuls of the League had agreed that if a city did not pay its share within two months after it was commanded to do so, the emperor was to outlaw it; and the city was not to be released from the imperial ban until it had paid double its allocation. The other members were not liable for its debts, but were obligated to aid in forcing the recalcitrant member to comply. The sum of £15,000 was an enormous amount; it would have been possible to purchase 6,400 slaves or 170 houses of better quality in Genoa for this sum. The money was meant, no doubt, to compensate Frederick for his loss of honor in agreeing to the peace and for foregoing the League's ceremonial public submission to his authority, as had occurred at Montebello. The Lombards paid the £16,000 promptly, because the imperial chamberlain Rudolf acknowledged on 22

November 1183 that Piacenza had paid its share: £711 and nine and a half shillings. Rudolf's own cut was 14 pennies per pound or 5.8 percent of the total.[56] Frederick and the envoys' personal financial gain, his price for making peace, was not included in the formal agreement.

On Sunday, 30 April 1183, after the Mass of the Holy Ghost was said in the church of S. Antonino in Piacenza, Frederick's mandate to his envoys was read out. They and the representatives of the League swore to uphold the peace in the presence of numerous witnesses. Dietrich of Silve-Bénite, as a Carthusian monk, did not swear but promised the same on behalf of his order.[57]

Rudolf swore the oath on Frederick and Henry VI's souls in Constance on 20 June. Otto of St. Blasien, writing at least a quarter of a century later, reported that the envoys of the Italian cities gave the emperor the insignia of their cities and gold keys as tokens of their submission. Frederick forgave them—he may have returned the keys as a sign of their restoration to his grace—and they went joyfully back to their homeland. This ceremony, if it really occurred, was a far cry from Milan's capitulation in 1158, let alone in 1162, or the Lombards' submission at Montebello in 1175.

However, the written format of the Peace of Constance preserved Frederick's honor. Since the emperor could make a treaty only with an equal and not with his subjects, the peace took the form of a privilege that Frederick and Henry granted on 25 June to rebels who had greatly offended them but who had been magnanimously restored to the monarchs' grace. The text of the preliminary Peace of Piacenza was inserted verbatim into the charter, except for the requirement that the Lombards were to pay the emperor annually 2,000 marks for the regalia. The privilege listed the names of the cities that were included or excluded from the peace and the names of the men who swore the peace on behalf of the emperor and the communes. Intriguingly, the list of "the princes and nobles of the court" who swore to keep the peace in Constance bears little resemblance to the long list of lay princes from throughout Germany who had been identified in Piacenza as the future oath-takers. The only princes who seemingly attended the court that dealt with a matter of such importance as the termination of the Empire's long conflict with the Lombards were the heads of the southern German princely dynasties: the Staufer, Wittelsbachs, Zähringer, and Andechses. The German monarchy's withdrawal from north of the Main had begun.[58] If the deposition of his cousin as the duke of Bavaria and Saxony in 1180 was Frederick's greatest political triumph, as many German scholars long believed, why did so few of the princes attend his court in Constance in June 1183?

CHAPTER FIFTEEN

THE DOWNFALL OF HENRY THE LION

Frederick and Henry the Lion's Princely Opponents

UNTIL RECENTLY GERMAN HISTORIANS cast Henry the Lion, who was already suspected in the Middle Ages of conspiring with Manuel I and the Lombards against Frederick,[1] as the arch-villain of Frederick's reign. Henry's deposition as the duke of Bavaria and Saxony in 1180 could be depicted, therefore, as Frederick's greatest triumph and as the dramatic high point in the long and disastrous rivalry between the Staufer and Welfs, which had started with Lothar III's election in 1125 and ended only with the establishment of the Welf duchy of Brunswick in 1235. Karl Hampe, the author of what was for decades the standard general history of the Salian and Staufer emperors, wrote for example:

> For Frederick himself, however, the sudden and total defeat of a widely feared adversary was an important success, even if he shared his victory with the princes; his prestige grew fast both inside and outside the Empire. The brilliant courts of the next few years radiate an air of secure peace and confident power, particularly the Whitsunday feast of 1184 at Mainz, renowned of the poets.[2]

In reality, Frederick owed his crown largely to the Welfs; and he had rewarded his cousin by conferring on him a vice-regal position north and east of the lower Elbe and by returning the duchy of Bavaria. Henry's fatal miscalculation was that he forgot he was ultimately dependent on Frederick's good graces and support. It was the princes who took advantage of the cousins' alienation in the 1170s and Frederick's defeat in Italy to destroy Henry. The princes were the real winners in 1180.[3]

Henry's position was not as secure as it appeared. Thanks to his paternal and maternal inheritances, he possessed numerous counties, allods, fiefs, advocacies, castles, and ministerials, which were concentrated around Brunswick and Lüneburg, in the Harz mountains, and in southern Saxony. He was the advocate of some fifty churches including the bishoprics of Bremen, Osnabrück, and Verden, the imperial abbey of Corvey, and such dynastic foundations as St. Blasien in Brunswick. Approximately 400 lineages of Welf ministerials served the duke. He was trying to mold this complex of disparate rights and domains and his conquests in the Slavic lands beyond the Elbe into a territorial lordship. As the duke of Saxony, Henry exercised few rights per se; but what so alarmed the other Saxon princes and counts was that he was trying to insert himself between them and the emperor by reformulating his relationship with the Saxon lords in feudal terms, just as Frederick had done in the *Privilegium minus* for the duke of Austria or in the "Golden Liberty" for the bishop of Würzburg. If the magnates held their counties in fief from the duke rather than as allodial lordships or royal fiefs, then Henry could limit the inheritance rights of women and collateral relatives to the counties and claim the counties of men who had died without a son as vacant fiefs.

Ironically, Henry possessed in Bavaria the lordship rights he lacked in Saxony: he was the feudal lord of many of the counts, summoned provincial assemblies, adjudicated disputes among the magnates, and preserved the peace. However, except for some ducal holdings around Regensburg, which were attached to the duchy, Henry's Bavarian allods, which he shared with his uncle Welf VI, were limited to the fringes of the duchy in the valley of the Lech and in the Tyrol. The great Bavarian lineages, most notably the Wittelsbachs and Andechses, possessed far more extensive and compact domains in the heart of the duchy. The establishment of the separate duchy of Austria in 1156 blocked further Bavarian expansion under ducal auspices down the Danube valley, while the Staufer were competing with the Sulzbachs and Vohburgs for control of the Bavarian Nordmark, the region between Regensburg, Nuremberg, and Bohemia. It is not certain that Henry, who grew up in Saxony, even understood the Bavarian dialect. While Henry did make some important acquisitions in Bavaria, the duchy was always peripheral to his interests. Until 1174, when he spent six months in Bavaria, he had visited his second duchy only in 1157 and on his marches to and from Italy in 1159, 1161, and 1162. Revealingly, only 15 percent of Henry's extant charters concern Bavaria. The events of 1179–81 played themselves out in Saxony and attracted little attention in Henry's second duchy.[4]

Frederick was forced repeatedly to come to his cousin's assistance. Already during Henry's absence in Italy in 1154–55, Archbishop Hartwig I of Bremen plotted against Henry; the archbishop was the first victim of the young duke's aggressive pursuit of power when Henry or, more likely, his guardians had seized the county of Stade after the death of Hartwig's brother in 1144. Hartwig was aided in his plotting by, among others, Archbishop Wichmann of Magdeburg, Bishop Ulrich of Halberstadt, and Albrecht the Bear, whose son eventually replaced Henry as the duke of Saxony in 1180.[5] At the court in Nuremberg in August 1163, Frederick was able to persuade Vladislav of Bohemia, Henry Jasomirgott, Margrave Ottokar III of Styria (whose mother was Henry and Frederick's aunt), and even Welf VI not to conspire against Henry with Albrecht, Adalbert of Sommerschenburg, who was the count-palatine of Saxony, and Landgrave Louis II of Thuringia.[6]

A far more serious threat to Henry's rule developed in 1166. Helmold of Bosau provided the following introduction to his history of the Saxon War (1166–68): "On account of his enormous wealth, his resounding victories, and his double ducal dignity in Bavaria and Saxony, Henry was so exalted in his renown that all the princes and nobles of Saxony deemed the situation intolerable. Yet fear of the emperor stayed the hands of the princes." Frederick's departure on his fourth Italian campaign in October 1166 unleashed the conflict. The usual suspects, who were bound to each other by ties of kinship, were involved: Wichmann, Louis II of Thuringia, Albrecht the Bear, his sons and son-in-law Margrave Otto of Meissen, the latter's brothers, and Adalbert of Sommerschenburg. It was a strictly Saxon feud; no Bavarian chronicler thought the conflict significant enough to mention. The allies failed to take Henry's castle at Haldensleben, which was situated only 19 miles northwest of Magdeburg and which played a central role again in the fighting after the princes returned from Venice; but to free up his forces, Henry had been forced to recall the exiled Obodrite prince, Pribislav, and to abandon his plan to create a territory directly subject to his rule east of the Elbe. Pribislav was the ancestor of the later dukes of Mecklenburg.

The conflict expanded on 12 July 1167, when the representatives of Rainald of Dassel, who was in Italy, joined the coalition against Henry. Conrad III had recognized the archbishops of Cologne in 1151 as the rulers of a Lotharingian duchy on the left bank of the Rhine. Rainald, in direct competition with Henry, was seeking to create a similar territorial duchy, east of the Rhine, in the Wesphalian portion of the archdiocese and in the diocese of Paderborn. Rainald's death on 4 August 1167 ended the immediate threat to Henry; but Archbishop Philip was even more determined than Rainald to turn Cologne's Westphalian network of vassals into a territorial lordship. In the autumn of 1167 Frederick sent Christian of Mainz and Berthold IV of Zähringen to arrange a truce and to procure the troops that the emperor desperately needed in Lombardy after the annihilation of the imperial army. The Saxons ignored the appeal and did not attend the court that Frederick summoned to meet in Würzburg on 5 May 1168, after his return from Italy; but he succeeded in ending the hostilities temporarily on 1 June in Frankfurt.

The selection of a new archbishop of Bremen after Hartwig's death on 11 October was thus of crucial importance to both Henry and his opponents. Frederick rejected both candidates who had been chosen in the ensuing double election, one of whom was Albrecht the Bear's son Siegfried. Instead, in June 1170 the emperor installed as the new archbishop Provost Baldwin of Halberstadt, Henry's choice. Henry attacked Archbishop Wichmann of Magdeburg, who had given refuge to Siegfried. The emperor was able to impose an uneasy peace upon the parties, and the death of Albrecht in November removed another of Henry's most determined enemies. Henry's check, with Frederick's assistance, of the formidable coalition of north German princes that had been arrayed against him between 1166 and 1170 may have convinced the duke in 1180 that he could overcome them again.[7]

The difference in 1180 was that the cousins had grown apart in the 1170s as they competed to provide for the material well-being of their young sons. Both had tried to obtain the domains of their childless uncle, Welf VI; and Henry had probably denied Frederick at Chiavenna the men he so desperately needed in early 1176 because Frederick refused to give Henry the town of Goslar, which figured in each of their territorial plans. Frederick, who blamed Henry, in all likelihood, for his defeat at Legnano in May of that year, was either unable and/or unwilling to stop Archbishop Wichmann, during the peace negotiations in Anagni, from proceeding against Henry's chief clerical supporters in Saxony, Archbishop Baldwin of Bremen and Bishop Gero of Halberstadt, who had deposed the pro-Alexandrine Bishop Ulrich in 1160. Ulrich's demand that he be reinstated as the rightful bishop of Halberstadt, in accordance with the peace agreement, triggered the sequence of events that led to Henry's ouster.[8]

The Gelnhausen Charter of 1180

While Frederick remained in Italy and Burgundy for fifteen months after the conclusion of the Peace of Venice (1177), Henry the Lion's opponents acted. Bishop Ulrich of Halberstadt returned to Saxony in the autumn of 1177 and demanded that Henry surrender the ecclesiastical fiefs the schismatic interloper Gero had granted him. Archbishop Philip, who was related through his mother and sisters to prominent members of the Saxon high aristocracy and who sought Cologne's territorial aggrandizement in Westphalia, came to Bishop Ulrich's assistance in June 1178 on the grounds that Henry had nearly destroyed the church of Halberstadt. The archbishop attacked Henry, who was caught by surprise; and the Cologne forces were able to advance as far as Hameln on the Weser. Wichmann arranged a brief truce, but fighting soon erupted around the Hopelberg, south of Halberstadt, where Bishop Ulrich's men were building a new castle under the protection of Albrecht the Bear's son, Count Bernard of Anhalt, the future duke of Saxony, and Albrecht's son-in-law, Margrave Otto of Meissen. On his return to Germany in October 1178, Frederick ordered work on the castle to cease. Once again, as had been true since his accession, the emperor was being forced to choose between his cousin and the other princes.[9]

Both Henry the Lion and Archbishop Philip appeared before Frederick in Speyer in November 1178 and accused each other of disturbing the peace. The emperor postponed making a decision and ordered them to attend his court in Worms in January 1179. It was at Worms that Frederick's agreement with his uncle Welf VI, concerning the Staufer's acquisition of the Welfs' south German allods, was publicly announced. Henry could only have interpreted his disinheritance as a hostile act, and he thus had more than one reason to show his displeasure by not coming to Worms. His nonappearance triggered the legal proceedings against him.[10]

Frederick ordered Henry to appear in June in Magdeburg, but for the second time the duke was a no-show. The pro-Welf Arnold of Lübeck related, around 1210, that one of the Wettin brothers, Margrave Dietrich of Landsberg, accused Henry at that assembly of treason and challenged the duke to a duel, but that he did not respond to the provocation. Conceivably, Dietrich charged Henry with plotting with several Swabian counts against Frederick after their meeting at Chiavenna, an allegation that Burchard of Ursberg recorded half a century later. In any case, through intermediaries Henry sought a meeting with Frederick, who left Magdeburg and went to the nearby castle of Haldensleben, which had been the scene of fighting between the duke and his enemies in 1166 and where Henry was staying. Normally, the emperor did not negotiate in person with individuals who had lost his grace, but he had more flexibility in dealing with a kinsman than with rebellious townspeople. Henry tried to placate his cousin, but Frederick demanded 5,000 marks as his price for mediating between Henry and the princes. Henry rejected the demand as exorbitant and left.

It was not unusual for Frederick to seek such payments—the Lombard League gave him £15,000 in 1183 to regain his grace. While 5,000 marks was certainly a large amount, the Jewish communities in the Rhineland paid Frederick, in August 1179, a fine of 500 marks and Archbishop Philip 4,200 marks, because the Jews of Boppard had allegedly killed a Christian woman. Surely, the duke of Saxony and Bavaria could have raised a similar amount if he had wanted to do so; so the unanswerable question is why Henry did not accept his cousin's offer—stinginess, pride, and/or an erroneous assessment of his situation? The story, assuming it is true, indicates that Frederick did not desire Henry's complete destruction but wished to escape from the trap the princes were setting for the emperor. It was at Magdeburg, at least according to the *Cologne Royal Chronicle*, that the princes were finally able to persuade Frederick, angered perhaps by his cousin's rebuff of his proposal, of Henry's criminal treachery; and he was outlawed in Magdeburg on 29 June 1179.[11]

Henry did not appear in July at a court in Naumburg, but he sent his men to meet Philip's forces, who had invaded Saxony. They defeated the archiepiscopal army near Osnabrück on 1 August. Around 17 August the emperor presided at a court in Kayna, south of Naumburg, where he charged Henry with scorning his summons three times. The princes proscribed Henry, deprived him of his duchy and all his fiefs, and declared that another man was to be appointed in his place. Frederick confirmed the princely judgment, and all the princes committed themselves to fighting Henry.

Frederick stayed until early September in Saxony. Archbishop Philip joined the Saxon princes' siege of Haldensleben Castle, but it had to be lifted because of conflicts among the princes. On 23 September Henry's men captured Halberstadt, burned the city and cathedral, and captured Bishop Ulrich. Henry had also occupied the castle of Sommerschenburg, which was situated southwest of Haldensleben and which Henry had claimed as a vacant fief after the death of Philip's maternal uncle, the Saxon count-palatine, Adalbert. Philip, who had assembled a force of 4,000 mercenaries, along with Archbishop Wichmann (who had purchased Sommerschenburg from Adalbert's sister), Otto of Meissen, and Frederick's nephew, Louis III of Thuringia, all resumed the fighting over Haldensleben. However, they were again unable to take the castle and blamed each other for the outcome. Henry's allies advanced as far as Magdeburg, and the imprisoned Bishop

Ulrich lifted Henry's excommunication and restored the Halberstadt fiefs to him. The year 1179 ended with Henry victorious.[12]

During the second week of January 1180, princes from Swabia, Franconia, and Saxony, including Welf VI—but, strikingly, no princes from Bavaria—assembled in Würzburg. The chief source on what happened there and on the legal proceedings against Henry is the Gelnhausen Charter, one of the most important but obscure and convoluted documents in medieval German constitutional history, which Frederick issued on 13 April 1180. The *narratio*, the historical summary of the facts of the case, provided the following rationale for depriving Henry of his imperial fiefs:

> Wherefore let the generality of the present as well as the future subjects of our empire know, that Henry the former duke of Bavaria and Westphalia, for the reason that he gravely oppressed the liberty of the churches of God and of the nobles of the empire, occupying their possessions and diminishing their rights,—on account of the urgent complaints of the princes and of very many nobles, inasmuch as being summoned he scorned to present himself before our majesty: did, both for his contumacy and for scorning the Swabian princes of his rank, incur the sentence of our proscription. Then, as he did not desist from raging against the churches of God and the rights and liberties of the princes and nobles, being cited by a lawful triple edict, according to feudal law ("sub feodali iure"), before our presence, as well to answer for the injury to the princes as for the repeated contempt shown to us, and, chiefly, for the evident crime of high treason:—for the reason that he absented himself and sent no one to respond for him he was judged contumacious; and, for the future, as well the duchy of Bavaria as that of Westphalia and Angaria, and also all the benefices ("beneficia") which he has held from the empire were, in the solemn court held at Würzburg, by unanimous sentence of the princes declared forfeited by him and adjudged to our jurisdiction and power.[13]

All of this is a single Latin sentence!

Much ink has been spilled to reconcile this statement with what is known about the actual sequence of events; to explain the use of both territorial or customary law (*Landrecht*), because Henry had disturbed the peace, and feudal law, because Henry had ignored Frederick's summonses; and to explain the relationship between the two legal systems in the proceedings. (Henry was subject to Swabian rather than Bavarian or Saxon customary law, because the Welfs hailed from Swabia and he was born there.) In the heyday of German liberal constitutionalism, when it was assumed that Staufer like Wilhelmine Germany had been a *Rechtsstaat*, a state that adhered to the rule of law, scholars focused on the jurisprudence as if Frederick and the princes were following the procedures outlined in a medieval textbook of imperial constitutional law—rather than conducting a political trial, in which the legal justifications for depriving Henry of his duchies were devised after the fact.

The consensus today is that that there were not separate territorial and feudal legal proceedings, which followed each other in strict chronological order, but that Henry's enemies invoked feudal law to circumvent the procedural delays of territorial law. The charge of contumacy was leveled against Henry because it enabled his opponents to move more quickly against him and so reduced the possibility that Frederick might forgive and pardon his cousin; an individual who had been outlawed for disturbing the peace had a year and a day to be reconciled with the community. (Since Henry was outlawed on 29 June 1179, Frederick would have been required by territorial law to wait until late June 1180, six months longer than he did, to deprive Henry of his fiefs.) If Frederick had stayed, according to Helmold of Bosau, the princes' hands before 1167, it was they who forced his hand after his return to Germany[14]

At Würzburg, Henry was deprived of his duchies and all his imperial fiefs, and probably his allods as well, by the unanimous judgment of the princes. They accused him of violating the liberties of the churches and nobles and seizing their possessions, and committing high treason by contumaciously scorning three times the emperor's summons to respond to the accusations. The vacant fiefs escheated to the emperor. The charge of contumacy was unprecedented because it turned Henry's offense into a criminal breach of the peace and precluded an arbitrated settlement, which Frederick had pursued at Haldensleben.[15]

At Gelnhausen in April the princes agreed to the division of Saxony into its constituent parts, Westphalia and Angaria (Engern in German). (In the Carolingian period Engern had referred to the portion of Saxony situated along the Weser between Westphalia and Eastphalia.) Frederick granted the Westphalian section of the diocese of Cologne and the entire diocese of Paderborn to Archbishop Philip as a second duchy. However, the new duchy was not considered to be part of the regalia of the church of Cologne but a separate secular entity. Accordingly, Frederick enfeoffed Philip with a banner, as was the case with a principality bestowed on a lay prince, and not with the scepter, as was the case with a principality conferred on a prince-bishop. Frederick granted the other half of Saxony, situated east of the Weser, to Albrecht the Bear's youngest son, Count Bernard of Anhalt. His brother, Bishop Siegfried of Brandenburg, became the new archbishop of Bremen. Nothing was said about Bavaria's fate.[16]

The Execution of the Judgment

It was one thing to declare Henry the Lion's fiefs forfeited, quite another to enforce the sentence. Instead of proceeding immediately against the former duke, the Saxon princes agreed after the Würzburg court to a truce with Henry that was to last until 27 April 1180, the Sunday after Easter. They may simply have decided against fighting in the winter or realized that Henry was a more formidable opponent than they had imagined. They may also have had second thoughts about the use of feudal law in the proceedings because, as the disputes over the Stade and Sommerschenburg inheritances had shown, treating counties as fiefs rather than allods limited the inheritance rights of collateral relatives such as Archbishop Hartwig and women like Archbishop Philip's aunt. Finally, the Saxon princes may have had their doubts about how committed Frederick really was to stripping his cousin of his fiefs, because the emperor indicated in November 1181, when Henry finally submitted, that he had sworn an oath (at some unspecified time) not to restore the duke to his former rank without the princes' consent. The princes may have exacted this oath from Frederick, as the price of their military assistance, to ensure that Frederick would not try to reach an understanding with Henry, as he had attempted at Haldensleben in June 1179.

Before the truce expired, Frederick, at Philip's request, ordered his nephew Louis III of Thuringia, who had replaced the deceased Adalbert of Sommerschenburg as the count-palatine of Saxony, to attack Henry. The emperor also commanded all the princes to assemble on 25 July 1180 for a campaign against his cousin. Henry the Lion struck first. He devastated the silverworks around Goslar, which Louis had occupied on his uncle's behalf; burned Nordhausen in early May; captured the landgrave, his brother, and several hundred Thuringian knights; forced Duke Bernard, who had come to Louis' aid, to flee; and destroyed Mühlhausen before he returned in triumph to Brunswick with his captives and much booty. If the princes had compelled Frederick to prosecute Henry, it was equally clear that they could not defeat him on their own. Perhaps the emperor was not quite as cornered as recent scholarship has come to believe.[17]

Frederick, with an army largely supplied by the Saxon princes, started the campaign against Henry shortly after 25 July; and it was successful immediately. Many Welf ministerials abandoned Henry and surrendered their castles to the emperor. He took other castles by force. Philip brought his own army that included such prominent participants as Duke Godfrey III of Brabant. The important castle of Lichtenberg, situated between Goslar and Brunswick, capitulated on 7 August after a siege of only a few days. At a court held in Werla, between Goslar and Lichtenberg, on 15 August, Henry's supporters were given three dates to join the imperial side or lose their possessions: 8 September, the Nativity of the Virgin; 29 September, the feast of St. Michael the Archangel; and 11 November, the feast of St. Martin. In an act that symbolized the restoration of imperial rule in Saxony, Frederick occupied and refortified the Harzburg, the castle near Goslar that the Saxons had destroyed in 1074 when they had rebelled against his great-grandfather, Henry IV. After the destruction of Henry's last major East Saxon castle, Blankenburg, Frederick disbanded his army on 8 September, the first date that had been fixed for the surrender of his cousin's men, and indicated that he would return to Saxony on 11 November. Many of Henry's remaining adherents submitted to Frederick by the end of the year. The duke's power was confined, except for Brunswick and Haldensleben, to the area north of the Elbe. The emperor celebrated Christmas in Erfurt and called for his forces to reassemble at Pentecost, 24 May 1181.[18]

Frederick finally reordered affairs in Bavaria at a court held on 16 September 1180 in Altenburg, south of Leipzig, that is, outside Bavaria. Henry had been deprived of the duchy of Bavaria as well as Saxony the preceding January, but no Bavarians had attended the court in Würzburg, and the only Bavarian magnate who witnessed the Gelnhausen Charter in April had been Archbishop Conrad III of Salzburg. Although no one took up arms in Bavaria on Henry's behalf, it would have been possible, conceivably, to challenge his deposition as the duke of Bavaria because it had occurred without the Bavarians' consent. However, at a well-attended assembly in Regensburg at the end of June, that is, after Henry had been outlawed for a year and a day, the Bavarians had consented to Henry's loss of his duchy, allods, and fiefs; but the Bavarian magnates had been unable to agree on his successor. In Altenburg, Frederick finally installed his long-time companion, Otto of Wittelsbach, as the new duke of Bavaria; and Otto's brother, who was also named Otto, replaced him as the Bavarian count-palatine. The three most important offices in Bavaria were thus, until Archbishop Conrad's transfer to Mainz in 1183, in the hands of the Wittelsbachs, who were destined to rule Bavaria until the end of World War I.

Yet many of the counts and nobles refused to pay homage to Duke Otto, their former peer. To placate them, Frederick freed the two leading Bavarian magnates from the duke's lordship. Styria, like Austria in 1156, was separated from Bavaria in 1180 and elevated from a mark (Steiermark) into a duchy. Since the new duke of Styria, Ottokar IV, was a childless leper, in 1186 he named his distant kinsman, Duke Leopold V of Austria, as his heir. The Babenberg succession in Styria may already have been planned in 1180 to gain Leopold's assent to the new arrangements in Bavaria. In a similar fashion Frederick accommodated the Wittelsbachs' other major rival, the counts of Andechs, who had extensive holdings in the Alpine forelands and in the Tyrol. He made Berthold IV of Andechs the titular duke of Meranien, the region around Fiume (today Rijeka in Croatia) adjacent to the Istrian Peninsula. (Berthold was initially called the duke of Dalmatia and Croatia.) The new Wittelsbach duchy was thus considerably smaller than the pre-1180 duchy, but the Wittelsbachs' extensive domains and rights in the Bavarian heartland around Munich gave it a stronger territorial base. We have a hint about Frederick's personal feelings for Otto of Wittelsbach, because there is circumstantial evidence that the emperor may have attended Otto's burial around 20 July 1183, in the Wittelsbach dynastic monastery of Scheyern—two of Frederick's sons were certainly there.[19]

In the meantime, Henry remained defiant in Saxony. One of the few Saxons who was still loyal to him, the Westphalian nobleman Bernard of the Lippe, was ensconced in the winter of 1180–81 in Haldensleben and used it as a base for raiding the area around Magdeburg. On 1 or 2 February 1181 Archbishop Wichmann began a siege of the castle and town. Since the archbishop could not storm it or starve it into submission, he dammed the Ohre river and flooded Haldensleben, which capitulated on 3 May.[20]

Henry II of England sought to lessen the pressure on his son-in-law and daughter, Henry the Lion and Matilda, by trying to persuade the young French king, Philip II Augustus, and Philip of Flanders to attack Frederick. However, Count Henry of Troyes, before his death on 16 March 1181, had convinced his nephew Philip II that such a move was inadvisable because Frederick had done neither Philip nor his late father, Louis VII, any harm. Envoys from the two Philips arrived in Sinzig, north of Koblenz, in May 1181 to assure Frederick that they had never intended to come to Henry the Lion's aid; and the emperor dismissed them in honor and peace. In late July or early August the English king allegedly dispatched an envoy directly to Frederick, offering him much silver and gold if he desisted from his campaign against Henry the Lion; but the emperor, for once, scorned the bribe.[21]

On 25 May 1181, a day after the campaign against Henry had been scheduled to resume, Frederick was still in Stauf, the only time he is known to have stayed in his ancestral castle. Accompanied this time by sizeable contingents from Swabia and Bavaria, the latter under the command of Duke Otto, Frederick arrived in Saxony in June. The Saxon princes awaited him near the castle of Hornburg, situated between Goslar and Brunswick. He besieged Brunswick in July, but since the townspeople refused to surrender, he left the siege to Archbishop Philip and several other princes. Frederick headed toward Lüneburg, which was directly south of the lower Elbe, in pursuit of his retreating cousin. Duke Bernard and his brother, Margrave Otto I of Brandenburg, remained behind at the end of July or at the beginning of August in Bardowick, located on the Ilmenau river between Lüneburg and its confluence with the Elbe. Frederick allowed Henry's wife Matilda, who had taken refuge in Lüneburg, to retain the city, which had been assigned to her as her widow's dower. Barbarossa may have decided not to anger her father, the English king, needlessly. Henry the Lion escaped downstream to Stade, near the mouth of the Elbe. As for Frederick, accompanied by Wichmann, Bishop Otto II of Bamberg (whose nephew Berthold IV of Andechs had just been made duke of Meranien), Margrave Otto of Meissen, and perhaps also Duke Otto of Bavaria, he crossed the Elbe at Artlenburg, just north of Lüneburg. The emperor arrived in August outside the walls of Lübeck on the Baltic coast.[22]

Other lords joined Frederick outside Lübeck: the Pomeranian prince, Bogislav I of Szczecin (Stettin in German), who had submitted to Henry the Lion in the 1160s; Niklot of Werle, the nephew of the Obodrite prince, Pribislav, who had become Henry's vassal in 1168; and Count Adolf III of Schauenburg and Holstein, whose father Adolf II had founded Lübeck. The emperor enfeoffed Bogislav and Niklot with their lordships. More importantly, Frederick won over King Valdemar I of Denmark—even though his son Knut VI was married to the daughter of Henry the Lion and Clemence of Zähringen—by engaging his son Frederick VI to Valdemar's unnamed daughter. The first installment of her dowry of 4,000 marks was payable upon her arrival in Germany; the balance was due in six years when she was old enough to marry. Valdemar arrived at the mouth of the Trave (Travemünde) with a large fleet. Lübeck was surrounded by land and sea.[23]

The townspeople of Lübeck realized that their situation was unsustainable. They sent their bishop, Henry I, to Frederick to obtain his permission to dispatch a delegation of citizens to Stade, where their lord Henry the Lion was holed up. The delegation was to seek the duke's consent to their surrender. Although Frederick was angered by the arrogance of the burghers' words, which the bishop had conveyed to him, he agreed to their request; and the citizens returned a few days later from Stade with the duke's authorization. The townspeople made their capitulation contingent upon Frederick's confirmation of the privileges that Henry had granted them. He did, and he also confirmed for the cathedral canons of Lübeck and Ratzeburg the income from the tolls in Lübeck that Henry had assigned to them. Frederick enfeoffed Count Adolf III of Schauenburg with half of the income from the tolls, mills, and money-changing booths in the city, in recognition of the count's services and of his claims to the lordship of the city his father had founded. Frederick entered Lübeck in August 1181 to the cheers of the clergy and people. Lübeck had become an imperial city.[24]

Henry the Lion, who remained in Stade, had heavily fortified the city and initiated negotiations about his own submission to the emperor. He asked for permission to come to Frederick. A large number of Frederick's knights escorted the duke on the last stretch from Bardowick to the emperor's camp outside Lüneburg. Henry is alleged to have said, according to Arnold of Lübeck: "I am not accustomed to receive an escort from another in these parts but rather to give it." He sought through intermediaries to mollify his cousin. To that end Henry released two of Frederick's nephews who had been the duke's prisoners since May 1180, namely Landgrave Louis III of Thuringia and his brother Henry Raspe III, so that they, too, might intercede on Henry's behalf with their uncle. Their entreaties were, likewise, of no avail.

Archbishop Wichmann escorted Henry to Erfurt, where, in accordance with the princes' judgment in Würzburg in January 1180, he submitted completely to the emperor's grace on 11 November 1181. The former duke prostrated himself at his cousin's feet. Frederick lifted Henry up and, crying because their dispute had lasted so long and because Henry was the cause of his own undoing, kissed him. Arnold of Lübeck, our main source on these events, thought the emperor's tears were feigned because he made no attempt to restore Henry to his former state; but Arnold conceded that Frederick had sworn "by the throne of his kingdom," at the princes' insistence, to return Henry to his old rank only with the approval of all the princes, precisely because Frederick was personally inclined, in all probability, to be lenient to his cousin. Henry was allowed to retain his Saxon allods, specifically, another chronicler said, Brunswick and Lüneburg. Yet he was required to leave Germany with his wife and children for three years, commencing on 25 July 1182, the feast of St. James, and not to return to his homeland without the emperor's permission. Since immediately upon his arrival in Henry II's continental domains Henry undertook a pilgrimage to the shrine of St. James in Santiago de Compostela, it is possible that he was required to go to Spain as a condition for lifting the excommunication he had incurred in conjunction with his outlawing for violating the liberties of the churches. The imposition of this penance would explain why 25 July 1181 was fixed as the date for his departure.

There are reports that Henry the Lion was exiled initially for seven years or even for life. These reports may contain a kernel of truth, because Henry II would have had little reason in late 1184 to request Pope Lucius III's assistance in procuring Frederick's permission for Henry's return if his exile was going to end in 1185 in any case. So there may have been some hard bargaining in Erfurt about Henry's fate, which is echoed in the conflicting reports about the length of his exile. Odilo Engels proposed, therefore, that as part of the deal that Frederick struck with the princes, the restoration of Henry's fiefs was made contingent upon the princes' consent and that the length of his exile was left open-ended. In return, Henry was allowed to retain some of his Saxon allods. With the benefit of hindsight, the chroniclers assumed that he had been exiled for three years in Erfurt, because he came home in 1185. Henry and his family spent his exile in the Angevin Empire at his father-in-law's considerable expense.

At Erfurt, at the request of Archbishop Siegfried and the cathedral canons, Frederick also conferred on the church of Bremen the castle and town of Stade with all its appurtenances, including the ministerials, which Henry and his men had seized in the 1140s. The emperor gave the Saxon palatinate to his nephew Henry Raspe III after Louis III had renounced his rights in favor of his younger brother. Finally, Barbarossa returned to Count Bernard of Ratzeburg and Count Adolf III of Schauenburg the castles and domains that Henry the Lion had taken from them. Henry's Slavic colonial lordship north and east of the lower Elbe had disintegrated.[25]

The Consequences of Henry's Downfall

Archbishop Philip, Bernard of Anhalt, and Otto of Wittelsbach were the chief beneficiaries of Henry's downfall; but other princes also benefited. The Ludowings of Thuringia obtained a second principality, the Saxon palatinate; the Andechses acquired a titular duchy in Croatia; and the Babenbergs became in 1192 the rulers of the new duchy of Styria. Knut VI, who succeeded his father as the king of Denmark in 1182, refused to repeat

Valdemar I's homage to Frederick; forced the Obodrite princes in Mecklenburg and Bogislav of Pomerania-Szczecin to become his vassals; and in 1187 declined to pay the balance of the dowry of his sister, who had been engaged in 1181 to the emperor's son Frederick VI. Knut clearly attached little importance to the diminished prestige of the Staufer connection. Barbarossa retaliated by sending the princess and her trousseau back to Denmark, and Louis III of Thuringia, who had just married Knut's widowed mother, did the same. Knut was able to snub Frederick because the Danish king had replaced the duke of Saxony as the dominant power in the Baltic.[26]

German historians long regretted that Frederick was unable to add Bavaria and Saxony to the royal domain in 1180. If he had, it was argued, Germany might have been united in the Middle Ages, just as Philip Augustus' acquisition of Normandy, Anjou, Maine, Touraine, and Poitou after the defeat of King John in 1204 and 1214 paved the way for the spectacular growth of the French monarchy; but the German crown's annexation of the two duchies was never a politically feasible alternative. The princes had not removed Henry as a double duke so as to replace him with a more powerful emperor.[27] Knut Görich has suggested that the story of Chiavenna was invented not to explain the origins of the conflict between the cousins but why Frederick was unable to help Henry.[28] Frederick's tears at Erfurt were genuine. He was mourning not only the pathos of Henry's situation but his own weakness.

Still, Henry's downfall was not a total defeat for Frederick. Henry would almost certainly have challenged the Staufer's acquisition of Welf VI's Swabian domains. Frederick was also able to establish an imperial presence in the Baltic by subjecting Lübeck directly to the Reich. He intervened in 1188, for example, on the side of the burghers in their disputes with their comital neighbors, Bernard of Ratzeburg and Adolf III of Schauenburg; but Frederick's successors were very distant overlords.[29]

Frederick's failure to secure greater gains for the Reich was long blamed on the *Leihezwang*, compulsory re-enfeoffment, which supposedly required a vacant princely fief to be re-granted within a year and a day; but he was under no such legal constraint. It was the events of 1180 that provided the precedent for such an interpretation of the German "constitution" by medieval legal experts like Eike von Repgow and by modern professors of law like Heinrich Mitteis.[30] Frederick could not retain Saxony and/or Bavaria for the crown because he was dependent, politically and militarily, on the princes and not because he was legally prohibited from doing so.

The *Leihezwang* is closely linked to two other constitutional constructs that allegedly also originated in 1180. The first was the *Reichsfürstenstand*, the estate of the imperial princes who were the tenants-in-chief of the crown and possessed a duke-like position, even if they were called margraves, landgraves, or counts-palatine, because they had other lords, most notably counts, as their own vassals. Gilbert of Mons, who in 1184 drafted the agreement about Baldwin of Hainaut's elevation to princely rank, defined in 1195–96 a lay imperial prince as someone who "could not give homage to anyone who had not been consecrated. It was permitted for them to give homage to kings only and to bishops and abbots who are called royal." Eike von Repgow, in his codification of Saxon law around 1220, defined a prince as the holder of a banner fief who "shall have no layperson as lord except the king." The other related constitutional innovation was the *Heerschildordnung*, the military order of precedence, which defined the six or seven strata of the feudal hierarchy. According to Eike, "Within this hierarchy, the king belongs to the first order, the bishops, abbots, and abbesses to the second, the lay princes to the third since they became vassals to the bishops; the free lords [including counts] belong to the fourth; the *Schöffen* class and the vassals of the free lords to the fifth; and their vassals to the sixth order."[31] The servile ministerials made up the seventh rank. However, in 1180 Frederick promulgated no imperial constitution that defined the prerogatives and membership of the second and third orders, that is, respectively, the ecclesiastical and lay princes who held their principalities in fief from the emperor.

Rather, the relationship between the emperor and the magnates had been gradually reformulated in feudal terms in the course of the twelfth century; most notably, in the Concordat of Worms, which declared that the bishops and the abbots and abbesses of imperial abbeys held the estates they had received from the crown, and their secular juridical rights, that is, the regalia, in fief from the monarch. Other milestones in the creation of a closed estate of princes were: the grant of the Burgundian rectorate to Conrad of Zähringen in 1127; the establishment of the landgraviate of Thuringia in 1131; the revival of Cologne's supposed Lotharingian duchy in 1151; the Austrian *Privilegium minus* of 1156; and Frederick's bestowal of total jurisdiction "in the bishopric and duchy of Würzburg and in all the counties situated in the same bishopric and duchy" on the bishop of Würzburg in the "Golden Liberty" of 1168. The destruction of the two remaining so-called tribal or stem duchies in 1180 increased the number of territorial principalities—Cologne's Westphalian duchy, Styria, and Meranien—and transformed the portions of Saxony and

Bavaria that remained under Ascanian and Wittelsbach control into similar entities.

The princes may have agreed informally in 1180 that each princely lineage was entitled to a maximum of two principalities: Andechses (Istria and Meranien), Ascanians (Brandenburg and Saxony), Ludowings (the Saxon palatinate and Thuringia), Wettins (Lusatia and Meissen), Wittelsbachs (Bavaria and the Bavarian palatinate), and Zähringer (Baden and Zähringen). This understanding may explain why the Wettins, who already possessed two imperial principalities, Lusatia and Meissen, did not benefit directly from Henry the Lion's removal. It may also explain why the Babenbergs, who were only distantly related to the Ottokare, were able to obtain Styria a few years later.

Thereafter, it took a formal imperial act to elevate a lesser lord to the rank of the princes. Thus, already in 1184, at the great Pentecost court in Mainz, Frederick indicated that after Count Baldwin V of Hainaut acquired the allods of his maternal uncle, Count Henry the Blind of Namur and Luxembourg, he would turn the allods and Henry's imperial fiefs into the margraviate of Namur, which Baldwin would then hold in fief from the crown as a "prince of the Empire and liege vassal" ("princeps imperii et ligius homo"); and that the new margrave "would enjoy the privilege of the princes of the Empire" ("principium imperii gaudebit privilegio"). The losers in the formation of the new closed princely estate were those counts directly subject to the crown but no longer classified as princes because they did not have their own comital vassals. The emperor and the princes together comprised the Reich; and among the princes' chief privileges was their right to consent to the monarch's actions.[32]

In reality, the princes made little use of that right in the 1180s, because many of them no longer visited the court on a regular basis; this continued the trend that had begun with the annihilation of Frederick's army in 1167 during the fourth Italian campaign. At Barbarossa's death in 1190, there were twenty-two lay princes who belonged to fifteen interrelated lineages. (There were also ninety-two ecclesiastical princes or princesses: forty-seven archbishops and bishops, twenty-eight abbots, and seventeen abbesses.) Altogether, in the 1180s the lay princes stayed a combined 114 times at the fifty-five courts that Frederick held in Germany, mainly south of the Main. More than half of the attendees were either his immediate relatives, namely, his sons and younger brother Conrad, or other close relatives like his first cousin, Leopold V of Austria, or his nephew, Louis III of Thuringia. Conversely, Duke Hermann of Carinthia and his son Ulrich II never came to court; and even Frederick's nephew Duke Simon II of Upper

Lorraine, attended only once in the 1180s. In some cases, there were extenuating circumstances for the princes' absence: for example, Ottokar IV of Styria was a leper, and Louis I was ten in 1183 when he inherited Bavaria from his father, Otto of Wittelsbach.

Episcopal attendance was likewise sporadic. In the 1150s a third of the bishops had visited the court on average once a year; in the 1180s only a tenth of them attended that frequently. Only three bishops came more often, two of whom, Conrad of Wittelsbach, the archbishop of Salzburg and Mainz, and Otto II of Andechs, the bishop of Bamberg, had dynastic reasons for doing so. The bishops of Augsburg, Basel, Chur, Constance, and Strasbourg stopped attending court after 1167, because the emperor's acquisition of the duchy of Swabia after the death of Duke Frederick IV put him in direct territorial competition in Alsace and Swabia with their churches and with the dynastic interests of the bishops' own families; and because Frederick was not inclined to award the prelates and their sees at the expense of the Staufer. By the 1180s not a single abbot of an imperial monastery attended even once every year. In the last decade of his reign, Frederick's itinerary, which was confined largely to the region south of the Main, and the composition of his court resembled more Rudolf of Habsburg's a century later than his own in the 1150s. Like his late-medieval successors, Frederick's power by the 1180s rested largely on his *Hausmacht*, his dynastic holdings; and he was concerned primarily with the advancement of his own lineage.

Counts, lesser nobles, and imperial ministerials took the place of the absent princes in the imperial entourage; but there were distinct regional variations in their attendance. The nobles of the lower Rhine valley followed the lead of their feudal lord, Archbishop Philip, and did not come to court. In contrast, their Alsatian, Swabian, and Franconian peers, many of whom were the Staufer's vassals, were more frequent attendees. Some non-princely magnates came so as to demonstrate that they were directly subject to the emperor and not to some princely intermediary. While ministerials had witnessed 33 percent of Lothar III's charters, 35 percent of Conrad III's, and only 20 percent of Frederick's in the 1150s, their presence ballooned after 1167, reaching its peak in the 1190s under Henry VI, when they appeared in 83 percent of Henry's charters. Only one ministerial, the chamberlain Anselm, had witnessed the Treaty of Constance in 1153; five princes, three counts, and four ministerials witnessed the Peace of Constance in 1183. No German prince was involved in 1183 in the negotiations with the Lombards; the Germans among Frederick's four envoys were his putative son Dietrich of Silve-Bénite and the chamberlain and imperial ministerial, Rudolf of Siebenich. Acerbus Morena did not include a single ministerial in 1162 in his list of Frederick's chief advisers, but four out of Henry VI's five main counselors in the 1190s were ministerials. At the end of Frederick's reign his court was a very different place from what it had been at his accession.[33]

The Mainz Court of 1184

The disappearance of the princes from regular meetings of the imperial court sheds a very different light upon the famous Whitsunday court of 1184, which historians like Karl Hampe saw as the glorious climax of Frederick's reign and of the full flowering of German knighthood and courtly culture. Indeed, Bernhard von Simson, in his continuation of Wilhelm von Giesebrecht's monumental history of the medieval emperors, declared: "The Pentecost festival in Mainz in 1184 marked not only a high-point in the life of Emperor Frederick the Red Beard, but also in the history of the German imperial epoch, indeed of the Middle Ages altogether. Here a power and a splendor were displayed as one had not yet seen at a German imperial diet (*Reichstag*) and one believed would never again be seen in the future." Such celebrations had in fact occurred at other major events in Frederick's reign: the destruction of Tortona in 1155, the knighting of Frederick IV in 1157, the defeat of Milan in 1162, the canonization of Charlemagne in 1165, and Frederick's coronation as king of Burgundy in Arles in 1168. Princes, like Welf VI who invited many guests to a lavish festival outside Augsburg at Pentecost in 1175, could also stage such celebrations, which were known in German as *hôchgezît* or *hôchzît*, literally a high time. (*Hochzeit* acquired its modern meaning of "wedding" only later.) Such festive gatherings might include the wearing of their crowns by the emperor and empress, processions, Masses, tournaments, banquets, dancing, singing, and lavish gift-giving.[34]

However, contemporaries already recognized that the festivities at Mainz, between 20 (Whitsunday) and 22 May 1184, were of a different magnitude. They accompanied the knighting of Barbarossa's two eldest sons, Henry VI and Frederick VI, in celebration of the princes' formal coming of age. The most detailed account is in Gilbert of Mons' *Chronicle of Hainaut*, because in his narrative the court served as the elaborate backdrop for the planned elevation of his master, Baldwin V, to the rank of imperial prince; but other chroniclers were similarly impressed. The author of the *Cologne Royal Chronicle* declared that no assembly of Frederick's predecessors could compare to Frederick's court in Mainz, which was renowned and famous throughout the entire Roman world. Guests had come not only from the Empire but also from other kingdoms, and Frederick had provided lavishly for them over three days. Otto of St. Blasien noted that all the princes of the Empire—"Franks, Germans, Slavs, Italians who dwelled between Illyria and Spain"—as well as magnates from neighboring realms, "an incredible multitude of men from different regions and of diverse tongues," had been present. Arnold of Lübeck resorted to the superlative. "Every dignity of power and rulership, sublimity of archbishops and bishops, glory of kings, joyfulness of princes, and multiplicity of nobles" had heeded Frederick's summons to attend "the most famous and most celebrated court." The poet Heinrich von Veldeke proclaimed in his epic, the *Eneit*, that no festival could compare to Aeneas' wedding to Lavinia save for Frederick's Pentecost court, which Heinrich had attended. "[G]oods worth many thousands of marks were consumed and given away . . . Emperor Frederick won there such renown that one could keep telling wondrous things of it until Judgment Day, without lying. More than a hundred years from now people will still be speaking and writing about it." The Mainz celebration was the exemplar by which all others were judged.

To handle the expected crowd, Frederick erected temporary accommodations outside the city: a wooden palace, with a large hall, for the emperor and his entourage; and a spacious church. The sumptuous houses of the princes, as befitted their rank, encircled the imperial quarters. A sea of tents of different colors filled the fluvial plain, as if one had built an exceedingly large city. "Nothing was lacking in provisions, in the variety of attire, in the ornate equipage of the horses, and in the pleasure of the entertainments," Otto of St. Blasien commented critically, "to display the fame of excess to the misery of the world." Arnold of Lübeck likened the "abundance, indeed the superabundance of provisions, which had been brought from every land," and the great quantities of wine that had been shipped to Mainz from up and down the Rhine valley, to Ahasuerus' banquet in the Book of Esther. The attendees were especially impressed by two large chicken coops housing all the poultry that fed the guests and could not believe, Arnold said, that there were so many fowl in the whole world. The princes also spent lavishly. Baldwin, who was especially eager to show that he had the wealth to match his princely aspirations, dressed in embroidered silk garments, brought much silver tableware, and outfitted his men elegantly. He had "many more beautiful tents," Gilbert assured the reader, than anyone else.

According to Gilbert, 70,000 people from north of the Alps, "excepting clerks and men of lesser status," assembled in Mainz. Duke Frederick of

Bohemia arrived with 2,000 knights, Leopold V with 500, Bernard of Saxony with 700, Frederick's brother Conrad and his nephew Louis III with more than 1,000 each, Archbishop Conrad of Mainz with 1,000, Archbishop Philip with 1,700, Archbishop Wichmann with 600, and Abbot Conrad II of Fulda with 500. Other attendees included the archbishops of Trier and Besançon; the bishops of Regensburg, Cambrai, Liège, Metz, Toul, Verdun, Utrecht, Worms, Speyer, Strasbourg, Basel, Constance, Chur, Würzburg, Bamberg, Münster, and Hildesheim; the abbots of Lorsch and Prüm; Welf VI, Berthold IV of Zähringen, Simon II of Upper Lorraine, Otto II of Brandenburg, and Otto of Meissen. Altogether, the *Annals of Marbach* reported, more than seventy princes attended. If one excludes the seventeen imperial abbesses, then more than 71 percent of the ninety-seven male clerical and lay princes witnessed the dubbing of Frederick's sons, the public recognition that they were adults and were taking their designated places in the Staufer dynasty.

On Whitsunday, 20 May 1184, the emperor, Beatrice at her last known public appearance before her death in November, and Henry VI wore their crowns. Frederick's brother Conrad, nephew Louis, first cousins, the dukes of Bohemia and Austria, and his second cousin, Duke Bernard of Saxony, vied to carry the sword before the imperial family; but Frederick entrusted the task to Baldwin. Did the emperor select the count of Hainaut to honor him, as Gilbert of Mons said, or to avoid having to choose from among his kinsmen? Only kings, dukes, and margraves, Arnold noted, performed the four ceremonial court offices during the festivities. In all likelihood, the count-palatine of the Rhine, the duke of Saxony, the margrave of Brandenburg, and the duke of Bohemia served, respectively, in Mainz as the imperial steward, marshal, chamberlain, and butler, as Eike von Repgow indicated in 1220 was their right. The day was marred, however, by a dispute between Archbishop Philip and Abbot Conrad of Fulda about which of them was entitled to sit at Frederick's left.

The celebrations began on Monday morning with a Mass. Afterwards Frederick girded Henry VI and Frederick VI with their swords. The new knights, the princes, and other knights gave horses, precious garments, and gold and silver to poor knights, captives, crusaders, and male and female jugglers and jesters. They did so, Gilbert said, "not only for their lords' honor, namely the emperor and his sons, but also for spreading the reputation of their own name." Twenty thousand knights then participated in a knightly game, the *gyrus* or buhurt, which did not involve the use of weapons. Instead, the buhurt was a display of equestrian skills. "The knights delighted," Gilbert declared, "in carrying shields, spears and banners and in racing the horses without blows." Frederick himself, "although he was not greater or more becoming in body than the others," led the sport. Baldwin carried his lance. The games continued on Tuesday, but in the evening a blast of wind destroyed the wooden church, some of the princes' dwellings, and many tents. Arnold said fifteen men died. The author of the *Cologne Royal Chronicle* called the storm a divine judgment, and Otto of St. Blasien pronounced "that the children of the world misuse in their lifetimes 'the wisdom that is foolishness with God' [I Corinthians 3:19]." A French-style tournament with actual combat, which was scheduled to occur in nearby Ingelheim on 28 May, the octave of Pentecost, was canceled.[35]

It is easy to see how Frederick became associated in the scholarly as well as the popular imagination with knighthood and the new courtly literature that glorified the exploits of knights. His father Duke Frederick II and paternal uncle Conrad had staged in 1127 the first known tournament in Germany. Frederick had been trained, according to Otto of Freising, "in military sports"; he knighted his sons at a legendary feast; and he led the buhurt in person at Mainz. There is no evidence, however, that the emperor, like Henry the Lion or his own sons, patronized epic or lyric poets. Heinrich von Veldeke may have sung Frederick's praise, but he worked for Louis III of Thuringia and his wife. It was the Welfs, Ludowings, and the Babenbergs who embraced the new literary styles.

More fundamentally, was Frederick's identification with knighthood an assertion of his triumphant authority or one more sign of the diminution in his status? The words *miles* and *Ritter* had acquired by the time of Frederick's reign a multiplicity of meanings: a heavily armed cavalryman, a noble vassal, a soldier of Christ (metaphorically in the case of a monk, literally in the case of a crusader), a euphemistic designation for a ministerial, and the servile retainer of a ministerial. Frederick was functionally, as a professional warrior, a knight; but as such he was merely one of the thousands of men who assembled in Mainz. Did an emperor who had once claimed that he had, as the successor of Constantine and Charlemagne, the right to call a church council and to decide a disputed papal election really gain in status by participating in knightly games, by becoming, in effect, one of the boys? Every prince could celebrate his son's coming of age in the same fashion and many did; only the emperor wore a crown that depicted Christ and the holy kings of Israel. The Mainz court was a direct consequence of the scene that had played itself out in front of St. Mark's: another admission that the imperial dignity had been secularized and that the emperor was no different in kind than any other king or prince.[36]

The Margraviate of Namur

The major item of business in Mainz in 1184 was the creation of the margraviate of Namur. In 1163 the childless Count Henry the Blind of Namur and Luxembourg had chosen his sister Alix, her husband, and their son Baldwin V of Hainaut as the joint heirs of his allods; and in the winter of 1182–83 Count Henry had probably added his fiefs to the bequest. In response to an invitation from Frederick, Baldwin, bearing a letter of support from his maternal uncle, had visited the emperor in Haguenau on 11 March 1184, where he had been well received by Frederick, Henry VI, and Frederick VI. They had agreed that Baldwin would attend the emperor in Mainz to finalize the matter.

Gilbert of Mons drafted in Mainz the agreement that outlined the terms for Baldwin's elevation to princely rank as the margrave of Namur. Baldwin was to arrange that either he or his uncle would confer on the Reich all of his uncle's allods, including his proprietary monasteries and churches and all other appurtenances. When that had occurred, Frederick would enfeoff Baldwin with his uncle's former allods and the fiefs the older count had held from the Empire, and would raise Baldwin to princely rank. If a margrave did not have a son, his brother would inherit the fief; and in the absence of a brother, the margrave's daughter would be the heiress. (Collateral relatives and women did not have an automatic right to inherit a fief. For example, when Margrave Dietrich of Landsberg died in 1185, Frederick treated Dietrich's mark, Lower Lusatia, as an escheated fief; and his brother, Count Dedo V of Groitzsch, had to pay the emperor 4,000 marks to obtain the fief.) After the emperor had enfeoffed Baldwin, the count was to give the emperor, Henry VI, and the court 800 marks of silver, and the empress five marks of gold. When all the conditions had been implemented, the emperor would grant Baldwin a privilege conferring the margraviate on him. Although two bishops and the chancellor witnessed the agreement, not a single lay prince gave his de facto assent to the accord by doing so.[37]

The opposition to the establishment of a new principality in the northwestern corner of the Empire, which may have been designed to counter Cologne's predominance in Lower Lorraine, soon manifested itself. Baldwin had expected to have the support of his brother-in-law, Philip of Flanders; but Philip's envoys worked secretly against Baldwin in Mainz, according to Gilbert of Mons, because the Flemish count had been told, allegedly falsely, that Baldwin had allied with his son-in-law, Philip Augustus of France, against Philip of Flanders. Archbishop Philip, Henry VI, who was related through his mother to the Flemish count, and many unnamed "others" sided with Philip of Flanders against Baldwin and the French king.[38]

There was one other major player in the Namur game: Henry II of England, the first cousin of Philip of Flanders. (Philip's mother Sibylle was the sister of Henry's father, Count Geoffrey of Anjou.) There are cryptic reports that Henry the Lion, protected by Archbishop Conrad of Mainz, came to Mainz but was unable to gain Frederick's grace. Neither Gilbert nor Arnold of Lübeck, our chief sources on the Pentecost court, mentions his presence there; but the Norman exchequer paid for Henry the Lion's visit to "Saxony" in 1184. It would have been foolhardy, if not downright dangerous, for the exiled former duke to attend the emperor's court without his permission. Odilo Engels proposed, therefore, that the English king sent his son-in-law, Henry the Lion, to Frederick with the offer of an Angevin–Staufer, anti-Capetian alliance in return for the Lion's partial restoration to his former dignities. In any case, Archbishop Philip and Philip of Flanders arrived in England in September 1184, ostensibly on a pilgrimage to Canterbury, but really to arrange a marriage between Richard the Lionheart and Frederick's young daughter Agnes. (Agnes died before a final agreement could be reached.) Henry II agreed to the proposal on the condition that the archbishop was reconciled with Henry the Lion. Archbishop Philip reluctantly agreed, but balked at interceding personally with Frederick on Henry the Lion's behalf. Instead, the archbishop advised Henry II to ask Pope Lucius III to serve as an intermediary. The pontiff did, in fact, talk to Frederick about Henry the Lion when they met in Verona at the end of the year.

On the face of it, it is hard to see why Archbishop Philip would ever have consented to Henry the Lion's restoration in Saxony, even a partial one, because such an act would have threatened Cologne's right to its new Westphalian duchy. Conceivably, Philip perceived the proposed margraviate as a greater and more immediate threat to his territorial ambitions than Henry's return to Saxony; and the archbishop certainly had an interest in protecting Cologne's lucrative commercial ties with England. Frederick, who had never desired his cousin's total destruction, may, for his part, have welcomed the archbishop's reconciliation with Henry the Lion, because it removed the major obstacle to ending Henry's exile and because it enabled Frederick to employ Henry, once again, as a counterweight to the other Saxon princes. There is one piece of evidence that Frederick may have been thinking along these lines. On 19 October 1184, after he had arrived in Italy on his sixth and last campaign, Frederick enfeoffed Margrave Obizo of Este with the marks of Genoa and Milan and all the other fiefs Margrave Azzo II of Este, the father of Welf IV, had held from the Reich. Obizo would be allowed to retain his fiefs even if Henry the Lion or his children regained their other domains. Henry was back in Brunswick in the autumn of 1185,[39] but Frederick was soon entangled in interconnected disputes in Germany and Italy about, among other things, the fate of Henry of Namur's allods and fiefs.

Frederick extricated himself from these entanglements by taking the cross at "the court of Jesus Christ" in Mainz on 27 March 1188, and so redeemed his reputation. However, the defense of Christendom was no longer the special responsibility of the emperor but was a duty, undertaken at the pope's behest, incumbent on every *miles Christi*. Like his participation in the buhurt, Frederick's response to the fall of Jerusalem was a perhaps unintended acknowledgment of his diminished status.

CHAPTER SIXTEEN

NEW ENTANGLEMENTS

The Council of Verona

AT THE BEGINNING OF July 1183, immediately after he had sworn his adherence to the Peace of Constance, Frederick wrote to Pope Lucius III, his "most dear father," that he had discussed with the two papal legates who had been in Constance how the remaining differences between the Church and Empire could be settled. The chief problem was the dispute over the possessions and rights both claimed in central Italy. The issue could be resolved if each party adhered to the terms that had been written down at Chioggia and confirmed in Venice in 1177. However, since both of them were apt to insist upon their rights, the attempt to determine by legal means the rightful owner was more likely, Frederick's advisers felt, to be a cause of dissension than harmony. The emperor was therefore dispatching Archbishop Conrad III of Salzburg, soon to be again Conrad of Mainz, with two proposals on how to end the dispute.

The first was that the pope and his successors would renounce their claims to the Matildine Lands and receive in return a tenth of the income that the Empire had or would collect in the future from its domains in Italy; the cardinals would obtain a ninth. There would be appropriate safeguards to ensure that the agreement would be observed by both parties in perpetuity. The obvious drawback to this plan was that it made the papacy financially dependent on imperial goodwill and thus threatened the papacy's hard-won independence. The other proposal was for the Church to possess certain properties "quietly and freely," except for the payment of the *fodrum* due the crown. In those instances, where the title was uncertain, prudent and mature men from the vicinity were to determine the rightful owner. The pope and the emperor could then exchange properties that had been assigned to one of them when it was mutually advantageous to do so.

The legates and Frederick had agreed that he would meet with Lucius on Lake Garda, northwest of Verona, on 29 June 1184, the feast of Sts. Peter and Paul; but any place where Frederick and his men would be safe was acceptable to him. The pope was to head to Verona, Brescia, or Mantua. Lucius, whose situation had become increasingly precarious after the death of Archbishop Christian on 25 August 1183, left the Patrimony and arrived on 22 July 1184 in Verona, where he spent the rest of his pontificate.[1]

Since the only source that reported Frederick's actual departure from Germany on 1 September 1184 was written in Regensburg, scholars long assumed that Frederick reached Italy via the Brenner Pass on his sixth Italian campaign; but it is hard to see how he could have arrived in Milan on 19 September, if he took that route, without first stopping in Verona. It is more likely that he went directly from Swabia to Milan via the Lukmanier Pass. Frederick's nephew Louis III of Thuringia is the only German prince whom a chronicler singled out by name as accompanying the emperor across the Alps; but Archbishop Conrad of Mainz, who had arranged the forthcoming meeting between the emperor and the pope, five other German bishops, and two abbots of imperial monasteries witnessed one of Frederick's charters in Milan on 22 September. It was hardly an impressive retinue for such an important occasion, but the emperor did not need a German army because his erstwhile enemies, Milan and Sicily, were now his allies. Frederick issued his first charter in Verona only on 19 October.[2]

However, most of the Bavarian princes had joined Frederick in Pavia by 1 October to deal with an issue that was of particular concern to the Bavarian Church: the status of the bishopric of Gurk. Archbishop Gebhard of Salzburg had obtained the unique right in 1072, when he founded Gurk, to name, invest, and consecrate its bishop. The Gurk ordinaries had utilized the chaos in the archdiocese during the schism to claim a status comparable to that of the archbishop's other suffragans who were directly subject to the crown. Both Frederick and Alexander had reaffirmed the archbishop's rights in 1178 and 1179, respectively. The case was re-examined at Verona during their council in late 1184, and the emperor and the pope confirmed Salzburg's proprietary rights. The Bavarian princes, except for Leopold V of Austria, returned home immediately thereafter.[3]

Archbishop Adalbert notified the cathedral provost and burgrave of Salzburg in early November that the pope and emperor had upheld Salzburg's rights. His letter is a major source on the first session of the council, which ended on 4 November. There is no hint of any conflict between Frederick and Lucius in the letter. The pope and the council had excommunicated the Cathars, and Frederick had outlawed them. An anonymous Lyonese chronicler recorded that Frederick had thrown his glove to the ground and promulgated a law depriving of all their rights various sects of heretics who were infesting Lombardy. Adalbert also reported that the patriarch of Jerusalem, several bishops from the Holy Land, and the Templars and Hospitalers had described to the council the great threat that Saladin posed to the Lord's sepulcher, and had requested that the pope and emperor launch an expedition against the "pagans." Frederick had declared that he and the princes would undertake such a campaign the year after he returned to Germany, that is, in 1186. On 24 November 1184 the emperor took all the possessions of the Templars, whose incessant battle "against the enemies of the cross of Christ" he lauded, under his protection and freed them from all exactions in the Reich. He granted the Hospitalers a similar privilege. Adalbert's letter is the first indication that Frederick was seriously contemplating going on another crusade.[4]

Four and a half years passed before Frederick honored that commitment, at least in part because his relations with Lucius suddenly deteriorated. The difficulties arose during Frederick's second stay in Verona in mid-December 1184. Lucius had initially been inclined to show clemency, as Frederick had requested, to the numerous German clerics who had been ordained by schismatic bishops and had come to Verona to receive dispensations; but, Arnold of Lübeck reported, the pope insisted unexpectedly that they present their petitions in writing and that their cases be handled on an individual basis. Later Lucius decided that in accordance with the decisions made in Venice, the clerics' cases would have to be considered at a general council and promised that he would summon such an assembly to meet in Lyons. Likewise, no agreement could be reached about the Matildine Lands, the original purpose for Frederick's meeting with Lucius in Verona. Each side presented privileges in support of their position, Arnold said, but was unable to convince the other of the justice of their case. After much discussion and on the advice of the princes and cardinals, Lucius also rejected Frederick's request that he crown his son Henry VI as emperor because there could not be two emperors simultaneously.

In fact, Pope John XIII had crowned Otto II as Otto I's co-emperor on Christmas Day, 967; but the council may have been unaware of that historical precedent. Regardless, during his stay in Faenza on 28 and 29 June 1184, while on his way to Verona, Lucius had indicated that he was prepared to crown Henry. Peter Csendes has even suggested that Henry announced his engagement to Constance of Sicily on 29 October 1184, in Augsburg, the traditional starting point for imperial expeditions to Italy, because he intended to march south as soon as Lucius gave his expected consent to Henry's coronation as emperor.[5]

Henry's engagement has often been seen as the cause of the breakdown in imperial–papal relations at Verona, because the potential union of the Empire and Sicily under a single monarch threatened the independence of the papacy; but this explanation presupposes there was a serious reason to believe in 1184 that Constance's nephew, William II of Sicily, would remain childless and that she would inherit the Sicilian crown. Otto of St. Blasien and the author of the *Cologne Royal Chronicle* reported that Frederick initiated the marriage negotiations with Sicily because, the Cologne chronicler said, he was "troubled by the kingdom of the Greeks." Although both chroniclers' facts are otherwise quite garbled, it is plausible that Frederick sought such a tie to the Hautevilles because Archbishop Christian had already proposed in 1173, during his siege of Ancona, that William marry Frederick's daughter Beatrice. For his part, William, who had turned his attention toward the Byzantine Empire, which was in chaos after Manuel I's death in 1180, would have found a Staufer–Hauteville match attractive for two reasons: he needed peace in Italy to pursue his crusading agenda in the eastern Mediterranean, and his aunt's marriage to the future emperor legitimated his upstart dynasty. Unless contemporaries knew something about William's virility that we do not, there was no reason to assume he would not father an heir. Admittedly, Joan of England, whom he had married in 1177, had not yet borne him a child; but she was only twenty in 1184, approximately the same age as Beatrice when she delivered her first child after eight years of marriage to Frederick. William did require his barons to swear to accept Constance and her husband as his heirs if he died without issue, but that was a formality in making a marriage alliance and is not evidence per se that he expected this eventuality to occur. It was the Staufer who ran the greater risk to the continuity of their dynasty because the previously never-married Constance was already thirty, whereas Henry VI was only nineteen; but there had been a similar difference in ages between Eleanor of Aquitaine and Henry II, and that marriage had proven quite fruitful. The primary reason for the engagement was that both monarchs, Frederick and William II of Sicily, wished to make permanent the fifteen-year truce they had concluded in 1177, and Lucius had no reason in principle to oppose that.[6]

However, the marriage and Frederick's insistent requests, starting in 1184, to have his son Henry crowned as emperor may have been linked. As

Constance's husband, Henry could claim the *Regno* by hereditary right if William died without an heir; but the king of Sicily was also the pope's vassal. As emperor, Henry could assert that the entire peninsula was part of the Empire and thus subject to his authority, independent of any papal claims of feudal lordship over the Norman kingdom. Likewise he could refute any Byzantine argument that as Constance's husband Henry was merely, like her Norman predecessors, a usurper of territory belonging to the Eastern Roman Empire. If Frederick was so determined to have Henry crowned as emperor in order to obtain a non-hereditary basis for his son's succession in Sicily, he may have known something, after all, about William's ability to procreate; but Frederick's primary motive was, no doubt, to ensure that Henry succeeded him without incident.[7]

Neither Arnold of Lübeck nor the anonymous author of the *Deeds of the Archbishops of Trier*, the chief sources on the Council of Verona, even mentioned Henry VI's engagement. Both attributed, instead, the sudden deterioration in imperial-papal relations in December 1184 to Henry's rash intervention in the disputed archiepiscopal election in Trier. Shortly after the death of Archbishop Arnold on 25 May 1183, the cathedral canons had split their votes between Folmar, the archdeacon of Metz, and Rudolf of Wied, the cathedral provost. Folmar had prevailed initially in Trier, but Frederick had invoked at Constance in June 1183 his right to intervene in a disputed election. Rudolf had been re-elected in Frederick's presence and invested with the regalia. Folmar had appealed to the pope, and Lucius had summoned both candidates to Verona. According to Arnold, Frederick had even supplied Rudolf with two canon and two civil lawyers to plead his case at the curia. The council learned, while it was meeting, that Henry had ordered his men to ransack the homes of Folmar's clerical supporters in Trier and Koblenz and that Folmar's own house had been leveled. "This deed," the Trier chronicler explained, "was the beginning and the cause of the great evil and discord between the kingship and the priesthood." Pope Lucius wept at the news and demanded the return of the property that had been seized from the clergy. Frederick initially defended his son's conduct because Folmar's supporters had violated the crown's rights, but he then conceded that if Henry had acted without a princely judgment, he was ready to compensate the clerics for their losses. Lucius was so disturbed, according to Arnold, that he wanted to recognize Folmar immediately as the rightful archbishop; but Frederick warned the pope that if he did, it would end their harmonious relations. He threatened Lucius with even worse consequences that the imperial envoys deemed best not to relay to the pope. Arnold concluded that "relations between the pope and emperor had been so disrupted that all their plans were turned to naught," including, understandably, Henry's imperial coronation. All of the issues in contention were still unresolved when Pope Lucius died in November 1185.[8]

Frederick's Alliance with Milan

The change in Frederick's relations with his erstwhile Lombard enemies was on display in early 1185, in what was essentially an imperial progress through the previously hostile communes of northern Italy. Upon his arrival in Bergamo in January 1185, the clergy escorted him in a festive procession to the cathedral. In mid-January some inhabitants of Crema, which the emperor had besieged and destroyed in 1159–60, appealed to him near Lodi. They threw their crosses on the ground before him and complained how Cremona was oppressing them. Frederick then witnessed how the Cremonese with drawn swords drove the Cremans back, beat them, and severely wounded several of them. Even more astonishingly, Frederick attended in Piacenza on 21–22 January a meeting of the rectors of the Lombard League.[9]

The new-found harmony between the emperor and his once rebellious Lombard subjects culminated in his agreement with Milan on 11 February. On behalf of himself and his son Henry VI, Frederick conceded to the city, in return for a yearly payment of £300, all the regalia the Empire possessed in the archbishopric of Milan and in any places east of the Adda that the Milanese would regain from Cremona, the unnamed target of the alliance. The Milanese were obliged, however, to provision Frederick's son and his successors when they came to Milan or Monza for their coronations as the kings of Italy and to quarter the imperial forces in Monza. Frederick committed himself to defend Milan's possessions and rights against everyone. If a dispute arose between Milan and Pavia, he would use his good offices to settle it; and if that failed, he would come to Milan's aid. (This eventuality did not arise, but the provision reveals that he was ready to back Milan even against his hitherto most loyal communal ally.) Frederick would not ally with any other commune or person without the consent of the Milanese consuls or the majority of them. In another provision that was clearly also aimed against Cremona, Frederick committed himself to the rebuilding of Crema at a date which the consuls of Milan would fix; and, revealingly, the consuls of Crema were among the witnesses on 11 February. For their part, the Milanese swore to help Frederick and Henry preserve all the rights of the Empire in Italy, "especially over the land of the late

Countess Matilda." The imperial chamberlain Rudolf of Siebenich swore on Frederick's behalf that he would adhere to the terms of the agreement; Bishop William of Asti was the first witness; and Brother Dietrich of Silve-Bénite was the last clerical witness. It is an educated guess that these three men who had negotiated the Peace of Constance were also instrumental in arranging the terms of Frederick's alliance with Milan. While the emperor was clearly allying with Milan against Cremona, the accord was also a warning to Pope Lucius that Frederick would make no concessions on the Matildine Lands.[10]

On 7 May the emperor, accompanied by 100 Milanese knights, Milanese foot soldiers who guarded the *carroccio*, 200 Placentine knights, and smaller contingents from other communes, led the Cremans to the site of their former city and authorized its reconstruction. He stayed for a month in Crema as work commenced on its rebuilding.[11]

Frederick justified his alliance with Milan against Cremona in an indictment that was prepared sometime between the meeting of the Lombard League in Piacenza on 21 January and the outlawing of Cremona around 10 July. It rewrote history. In exchange for Cremona's assistance against Milan in 1158, Frederick had agreed not to leave Italy until Crema had been destroyed. He had spent thirty or more weeks besieging Crema at great expense and danger to his own person, and he had lost many nobles, vassals, ministerials, and soldiers who could not easily be replaced before Crema had been taken and destroyed. At the Pentecost court in Würzburg in May 1165 the emperor had freed Cremona from the obligation to pay him annually 200 marks for the use of the regalia in the bishopric of Cremona, because he was confident that it would never oppose him. During the fourth Italian campaign, on account of the love he bore the city, Frederick had employed at his own expense Cremonese knights rather than mercenaries.

Cremona had repaid him by betraying him. To the detriment of his and the Empire's honor, it had helped the exiled Milanese to return to their city, an act that was the source of all the evil that had befallen him in 1167/68. Out of fear of Cremona, Lodi, which Frederick had founded, had turned against him; and Parma sent back to Bologna the hostages he had entrusted to its custody. On his retreat from Rome, Cremona had blocked the road that would have taken him directly from Tuscany to Lombardy; and he had been compelled to take a difficult route through the territory of Margrave Obizzo Malaspina. He, his army, wife, and sons had incurred great danger; and he had lost the imperial regalia in Lombardy on account of Cremona's treachery.

Then the Cremonese had participated in the founding of Alessandria sometime in 1167–68. Wazo of Cremona, who was a member of the Lombard League army that had marched to the relief of Alessandria in April 1175, had plotted to assassinate the emperor. While Frederick was staying in Cremona in December 1176, the Cremonese had been inhospitable and had pressured him to surrender Luzzara and Guastalla in their entirety to them. More recently, in January 1185, they had attacked the Cremans in his presence and had broken into the houses of the Cremans, burned them, and stolen their contents while he was in Piacenza. Altogether, Frederick calculated that Cremona had caused him over the years 300,000 marks in damages. Since the Cremonese refused to submit to his justice, he outlawed them around 10 July 1185.[12]

Frederick headed south at the beginning of July to welcome his future daughter-in-law. Constance, who had been promised a dowry of 40,000 marks, brought with her 150 mules laden with gold, silver, jewels, and expensive garments. He met her at Foligno, southeast of Perugia, where he was on 31 August. Constance may then have gone directly from Foligno to Milan, the site of her wedding.[13]

In the meantime, the groom was again causing his father problems in Germany. As we have already seen, Henry VI had sided with his kinsman, Philip of Flanders, and Archbishop Philip of Cologne against Baldwin of Hainaut and his son-in-law, Philip II Augustus of France, after Frederick had authorized the creation of the margraviate of Namur at Mainz in May 1184. Fighting had broken out in the autumn. Sometime in 1185 Philip of Flanders, who had already appealed to Frederick for aid, went to Germany to seek Henry's assistance—they probably met in Speyer on 28 August 1185, at Beatrice's entombment. Henry was astonished, Gilbert of Mons reported, that the count had not waited for his help against Philip Augustus and Baldwin before agreeing to yet another truce. On the advice of Philip of Flanders and the archbishop, Henry summoned Baldwin to meet with him in Liège in September 1185. Henry commanded Baldwin, after his arrival, to aid the count of Flanders, who was Baldwin's brother-in-law, against Philip Augustus, to put his castles at Henry's disposal, and to allow the imperial forces free transit across Hainaut to attack the Capetian domains. Baldwin responded that the passage of the imperial forces would devastate his territory and that as the ruler of a county situated on the border between the Empire and France it was his responsibility "to guard his land during their wars." Besides, as a vassal of the bishop of Liège (he held Hainaut from the bishop), he was not directly subject to the emperor. Baldwin left Liège fearing Henry's wrath. Frederick, who throughout his reign had avoided being drawn militarily into the conflicts on his western border, commanded his son not to help the count of Flanders against the French king and so saved Baldwin from an attack. The emperor did authorize Henry, however, to assist Philip of Flanders if the king violated the count's rights.[14] For Frederick, leaving his twenty-year-old son in Germany as the de facto regent had its drawbacks.

Urban III

Lucius III died on 25 November 1185; and Frederick's already badly strained relations with the papacy deteriorated even further. The cardinals elected unanimously on the same day the archbishop of Milan, Cardinal Uberto Crivelli, as Urban III. During Frederick's wars with Milan, he had held some of Uberto's kinsmen prisoner, some of whom had been outlawed and others mutilated at the emperor's command. Uberto was filled, therefore, with great hatred for Frederick, the Trier chronicler wrote, and sought as pope only "how he might humiliate the dignity and excellence of the emperor." Uberto's elevation to the chair of St. Peter's was a clear signal that the cardinals were opposed to any accommodation with Frederick.[15]

Negotiations between Urban and the emperor proved futile. They could find no common ground on the Matildine Lands, the disputed election in Trier, or Henry VI's coronation. According to Arnold of Lübeck, Urban raised two other issues: Frederick's appropriation of the income of vacant bishoprics, the so-called right of spoils; and his removal of many abbesses from their offices under the pretext of reforming their convents and then retaining the income from the nunneries for himself. Frederick did, in fact, on 22 February 1186, void all the alienations of property by the deposed abbess of a convent in Pavia.[16]

Henry VI and Philip of Flanders traveled together to Pavia, where they celebrated Christmas 1185 with Frederick. Although princes from north and south of the Alps, including the *Regno*, are said to have attended Henry's wedding to Constance in the monastery of S. Ambrogio in Milan on 27 January 1186, Philip is the only guest whose name survives. Two cardinals represented Urban. Archbishop Robert of Vienne crowned Frederick as part of the festive crown-wearing; a German bishop, in all likelihood Conrad of Mainz who was in Milan, crowned Constance as queen of the Romans; and Patriarch Godfrey of Aquileia crowned Henry as king of Italy without altering his title or position as a co-king subordinate to his imperial father. These events affirmed that the kings of Italy were to be crowned in Milan rather than Pavia, in accordance with

Frederick's privilege of 11 February 1185, and highlighted the city's central role in Frederick's post-1183 Italian policy.

Andrew of Marchiennes commented that there were many reasons for the enmity between Urban III and Frederick, but the principal one was that the patriarch of Aquileia, assisted by other bishops, had crowned Henry without the pope's consent. Pope Urban had suspended, therefore, all of the officiants from their offices. Urban, who had retained the archbishopric of Milan after his election as pope, presumably viewed Godfrey's actions as a violation of his archiepiscopal prerogatives. Something even more disturbing had occurred in Milan. Several chroniclers, most notably Radulf of Diceto, who provided the most extensive account of the events in the city, reported that Frederick had elevated Henry to the rank of Caesar.

In antiquity the title of "Caesar" had been bestowed on the adopted son and designated successor of the emperor, and "Caesar" became part of the complete imperial title. The name was employed in this fashion in Byzantium, too; but the title could be granted in the twelfth century in Constantinople to other members of the imperial family as well. On occasion, some of Frederick's charters written outside the chancery, before or after he became emperor, used "Caesar," that is, *Kaiser* in German, as a synonym for *imperator*. Henry's elevation to Caesar was thus intended to be a substitute for the denied imperial coronation. Frederick's effrontery further infuriated Urban. Still, we should not attach too much significance to Frederick's act. Henry was never called Caesar in an extant imperial charter, and there was no extension of his authority. Most important of all, Frederick renewed his efforts to procure his son's imperial coronation after Urban's death, presumably because the title of "Caesar" was not really a substitute for consecration by the pope in St. Peter's.[17]

The Capitulation of Cremona

With a largely Milanese army as well as contingents provided by the Italian bishops and other Lombard communes, Frederick devastated the *contado* of Cremona in the spring of 1186 and besieged the recently built Cremonese fortification of Castel Manfredi, today Castelleone, about 18 miles northwest of Cremona. On 8 June, during the siege of Castel Manfredi, the consuls of Cremona agreed to the terms for the commune's restoration to the emperor's grace. Cremona had to surrender Guastalla and Luzzara with all their appurtenances and the rights that Margravine Matilda had exercised there; but the church of Cremona and private individuals who had owned property from old in these places could retain these possessions on condition that they paid the required services to the imperial court and Reich. Cremona was also obliged to return to the emperor Crema, the area between the Adda and the Oglio, and the imperial privileges that had granted these places to Cremona. Finally, the Cremonese had to turn over Castel Manfredi to the emperor, who could destroy it if he so pleased. Frederick's envoy was to enter the castle with the imperial standard, and all the members of the garrison were to leave, taking with them only what they could carry. Two charters issued the next day were dated "at the destruction of Castel Manfredi." The consuls and various named burghers had to swear to keep the peace with Crema, Milan, and Piacenza. In return, Frederick and Henry VI forgave all the offenses of the Cremonese.

The next day, 10 June, motivated "by the largesse of imperial munificence," the emperor conferred on Milan all the places situated between the Adda and Oglio it had formerly owned, as he had promised the city on 11 February 1185; and he revoked all privileges to the contrary that he or his predecessors had given to others. As was the case in other restorations to imperial favor, in the text of the notarial instrument that outlined the terms of Cremona's capitulation no mention was made of the monetary arrangements that had procured Frederick's grace. According to a separate instrument, the city was required to pay Frederick £1,500 in two installments and another £300, within two weeks, to the imperial court. (The entire amount was paid on 29 June.) Cremona thus lost the territorial gains it had made as Frederick's ally, but compared to his treatment of Milan or Tortona, it was a relatively mild punishment because the consuls and citizens were spared a degrading public submission and the destruction of their city. Perhaps Frederick was inclined to be merciful in light of the commune's previous service and/or because the Cremonese were smart enough to yield quickly to the overwhelming power of their communal enemies who were fighting under the emperor's banner.[18]

Frederick's campaign against Cremona became another cause of conflict between him and Urban III. The pope, professing a desire for peace between the papacy and the Empire, responded on 18 June 1186 to a lost letter that Frederick had sent him before Cremona's surrender, in which the emperor had complained about the measures Urban had taken to aid Cremona. The pope denied having done any such thing. Instead, he had refused the repeated requests of the Cremonese, who had beseeched him to take their city under papal protection, and had ordered Bishop Sicard of Cremona to try to make peace. Urban had not forbidden the bishops and cities of Lombardy from participating in the imperial campaign against Cremona, as Frederick charged, although he could have done so in the case of the bishops because the emperor was imposing new burdens on their churches in violation of their privileges. The pope had enjoined some of the Lombards, however, to spare during the fighting properties that belonged to the church of Cremona. If Frederick had any papal writings that appeared to say anything to the contrary about the pope's actions, Urban requested that Frederick forward them to him for scrutiny.[19]

The pope also countered with complaints of his own. Imperial ministerials in the dioceses of Turin and Ivrea were levying unauthorized exactions on the clergy, but Urban focused in particular on the actions in Tuscany and the Patrimony of Henry VI, Berthold of Hohkönigsburg, who was the imperial legate in Italy, and Duke Conrad of Spoleto. They were enforcing a policy which Frederick had enunciated already on 1 August 1185, while he was staying in Florence. He had deprived all the cities in Tuscany, except for Pisa and Pistoia, of their jurisdiction over the counties in which they were situated. In essence, the emperor was applying in Tuscany the policy of regaining alienated regalia that had failed in Lombardy. On 30 May 1186 his son had begun a siege of Siena, which several weeks later surrendered the county of Siena and all the properties and rights that had belonged to Margravine Matilda. Siena's capitulation may have prompted the pope's complaint. By 24 June Henry had reached Orvieto, between Siena and Viterbo in the northeastern corner of the Patrimony. He took Orvieto after a siege of two weeks.

Frederick had informed Urban before Cremona's submission that he had entrusted Henry with the task of subjecting the Patrimony to the pope's authority—Urban never set foot in the Patrimony during his pontificate. Urban complained on 18 June that Henry, instead of executing his mission, had turned into the oppressor of the cities and places that were under the pope's jurisdiction. Henry spent the early summer of 1186 asserting imperial control over the Campania with the aid of some of the same Roman aristocrats or their kinsmen, most notably the Frangipani, who had opposed his father in the 1150s; but unlike Frederick in that decade, Henry's efforts did not extend to Rome itself. After Frederick left Italy in late June 1186, Henry headed northward. The young king remained in northern Italy, representing his father, until the middle of November 1187. He probably celebrated that Christmas with Frederick in Trier.[20]

Trier

Although Urban III did not mention Trier in his letter of 18 June 1186, this was the other major source of contention between him and the emperor.

Urban had assured Frederick's envoys, Bishop Hermann II of Münster, Bishop William of Asti, the chief architect of the emperor's new Italian policy, and the Milanese judge, Otto Cendadarius, that he would not consecrate Folmar, the archdeacon of Metz, as archbishop of Trier. Nevertheless on 17 May 1186, that is, while Frederick was proceeding against Cremona, Urban had the briefs that the candidates had submitted to the curia read to the cardinals and decided to act immediately. He ignored the advice of some of the cardinals that it might be wiser to void the election and hold a new one or at least defer a decision to a more opportune time. Rudolf of Wied, the provost of Trier Cathedral, was not even granted a day's delay. His candidacy was rejected because he had been invested, in accordance with the Concordat of Worms, by the emperor before his consecration. Urban confirmed Folmar's election and consecrated him as archbishop of Trier on 1 June. Rudolf, who as the archbishop-elect of Trier witnessed Frederick's charters in Castel Manfredi on 8 and 9 June, may have brought the news of the pope's actions in person to the emperor. Arnold of Lübeck reported that Frederick was livid and added that from that day onward there was great enmity between him and the pope. The emperor was accustomed, according to the Trier chronicler, to disguise his true feelings and so concealed his anger with a smile. He ordered his son Henry to avenge the injury Urban had caused the Reich, and the young king accordingly occupied or devastated the Campania and blocked access to the Apostolic See. Since Urban was in Verona and not in Rome, it is hard to see why Henry would have taken the last measure; but Frederick, after his return to Germany in July 1186, did close the Alpine passes, according to Arnold, to stop traffic between the curia and northern Europe. Urban was a virtual prisoner in Verona until nearly the end of his pontificate.

Clad in servile garb, Folmar fled Verona at night, evaded the sentries who guarded the passes, and reached Upper Lorraine. Bishop Peter of Toul, "out of fear and reverence of the emperor," refused Folmar entry into his episcopal see; but another of Folmar's suffragans, Bishop Bertram of Metz, welcomed him. Since imperial ministerials controlled Trier, Folmar took up his residence in the abbey of Petersberg, in the territory of Count Thibaut I of Bar. Folmar suspended immediately, without due legal process, his clerical opponents from their offices and prebends, and excommunicated other clerics and laymen. Rudolf's supporters guarded the roads leading to Trier and brought men and women who adhered to Folmar in chains to the emperor. Among the prisoners was a Cistercian monk, who was alleged to be Folmar's emissary and was held captive in the archiepiscopal palace until Frederick could determine his fate. Philip Augustus eventually procured the monk's release on condition that the king would not permit any of Folmar's agents or letters to be sent from France to Trier. So the situation in the archdiocese deteriorated rapidly.[21]

Frederick remained in Italy until the end of June 1186. He then traveled through Switzerland via Chur, where he was in July, and reached Mulhouse in Alsace, where he presided over a court on 26 August. Sometime in November, Frederick expounded to the princes in Kaiserslautern the injuries Urban had caused him and the outrages Folmar had committed. Upon the princes' advice, he gave the cathedral canons of Trier, whom he had summoned to his palace, two options: either they could accept Rudolf, who was in Kaiserslautern, as their archbishop or they could elect another man. They decided that the first alternative was the lesser of two evils because electing a new archbishop would further antagonize Urban. So Rudolf accompanied the canons back to Trier, where he was received with the honors due to an archbishop-elect. Frederick was especially angry at Bishop Bertram, because the emperor had installed him in Metz after the Third Lateran Council had invalidated Bertram's election as archbishop of Bremen in 1179. The emperor thus viewed Bertram's reception of Folmar as a betrayal. To regain Frederick's grace, Bertram swore that he had not known of the emperor's displeasure at Folmar's consecration by the pope when Bertram had welcomed him in Metz.[22]

As Frederick had done after the assembly in Besançon in 1157, he rallied the German Church behind him in his dispute with the pope. All the German archbishops, except for Rudolf of Trier, attended Frederick's court in Gelnhausen on 28 November 1186. According to the words that Arnold of Lübeck put into Frederick's mouth, he was dismayed by the pope's baseless hostility toward him. Urban declared, Frederick told the princes, that it was unjust for the laity to possess tithes intended for the priests' maintenance, but the emperor countered that the laymen had been enfeoffed with the tithes so that they could defend the churches from their enemies. Likewise, the pope complained that laymen had improperly acquired advocacies over the properties and dependants of the churches, but Frederick pointed out that this was an ancient practice. It is hard to believe that the emperor could have expected much sympathy from the ecclesiastical princes with such arguments, because many bishops and reform-minded clerics were trying to regain alienated tithes and to curb the power and abuses of their advocates. Arnold said that after Frederick finished speaking, Conrad of Mainz proposed that the bishops, who were bound to serve both the pope and the emperor, write letters to Urban so that he would know what to do to have peace with the emperor.

Shortly thereafter, Wichmann of Magdeburg and Adalbert of Salzburg, along with their suffragans, wrote similar letters of protest addressed, respectively, to Urban and to the cardinals. After expressing their desire for concord between the pope and the emperor, the archbishops gave their nearly identical versions of what had transpired at Gelnhausen and set out what must have been the collective position of most of the German bishops. Frederick had repeated many of the same accusations he had levied against the pope before the fall of Cremona and that Urban had refuted in his response of 18 June. The emperor had complained at the court about the pope's hostility toward his beloved son, Henry, to whom Frederick had assigned the dangerous task of defending the liberty of the Church, that is, papal rights in the Patrimony. Although Urban had denied that he had urged the cities and bishops of Italy not to participate in Frederick's campaign against Cremona and had challenged Frederick to produce the incriminating letters, the bishops declared that they had seen and read such papal missives.

The disputed election in Trier was of particular concern to Frederick and the archbishops. By ordaining Folmar before he had been invested with the regalia by Frederick, the pope had violated, in an unprecedented way, the customs of the German kingdom, and the specific assurances he had made to Bishop Hermann of Münster, Bishop William of Asti, and Otto Cendadarius, as Hermann had testified at Gelnhausen. By retaining for himself the archbishopric of Milan, Urban had deprived the Empire of the income from the vacant see and had not given Frederick the opportunity to install a suitable person in a key Italian bishopric. Finally, the bishops complained, as they had after Besançon, that German churches and monasteries that barely had sufficient bread to sustain themselves were compelled to pay large sums of money to Rome and to provide the pope's agents with hospitality. Archbishops Wichmann and Adalbert urged the pope to be more conciliatory and indicated that Frederick desired a resolution of the conflict either by a mutually acceptable agreement or through arbitration. To achieve that end, the archbishops and their suffragans were dispatching to the pope and cardinals three learned, prudent, and discreet men.[23]

According to the *Annals of Pegau*, Frederick sent his own envoys to Urban after the pope had cited him for interfering in spiritual matters, but they returned without having achieved anything. In response to the archbishops' letters, on 19 February 1187 the pope wrote to Wichmann that he had repeatedly urged the emperor, as a precondition for peace between the Church and the Empire, to return the possessions of the Roman Church, but that he had not received a satisfactory response. The pope requested that Wichmann, if he had the opportunity to meet with the emperor personally, counsel him to adopt a more favorable attitude toward the Church. If Frederick did not heed the archbishop's advice, then the blame for the continuing dissension would lie with him. The letter may have reached Wichmann while he was attending a court in Regensburg in March 1187. He may have persuaded Frederick on that occasion to send his former chancellor, Bishop Godfrey of Würzburg, along with Bishop Otto II of Bamberg and Abbot Siegfried of Hersfeld, on another embassy to Pope Urban.

The sources disagree whether the envoys were successful or not. According to the *Annals of Magdeburg*, in September 1187 they reported to Frederick in Kaiserslautern that they had been able to arrange a tentative peace with the pope; and in early October the emperor sent Otto and Siegfried back to finalize the accord. Gervase of Canterbury indicated, likewise, that peace was restored between the pope and emperor and that Urban was finally able to leave Verona and go to Ferrara, where he died on 20 October. On the other hand, the *Marbach Annals* stated that it was impossible to make peace between the pope and emperor, because Urban was contemplating the excommunication of both Frederick and Henry VI. Arnold of Lübeck wrote that only the protests of the Veronese, who feared the consequences of the emperor's wrath if Urban took such a step in their city, prevented the pope from banning the monarchs before his death. The most plausible explanation is that Urban went to Ferrara, which was hostile to the Staufer, with the intention of excommunicating Frederick and his son. The imperial envoys only arrived in Ferrara after Urban's death and quickly came to terms with the newly elected Gregory VIII (21 October–17 December 1187); the new pope was eager for peace after news reached the curia that Saladin had captured Jerusalem on 2 October. Northern European chroniclers could easily have been confused about the identity of the pope with whom the envoys had negotiated.[24]

Conflict with Archbishop Philip of Cologne

Episcopal support for Frederick in his fight with Urban had not been unanimous. The Pegau chronicler reported that in 1186 some of the bishops conspired against the emperor, but that Frederick was able to win them over—except for Philip of Cologne and a few others. The removal of Henry the Lion had left the archbishop as the most powerful prince in northern Germany, if not the whole kingdom. Some scholars have traced the origins of the conflict between the emperor and the archbishop to Frederick's promotion of Aachen and Duisburg at the expense of Cologne's commerce before Philip had even succeeded Rainald of Dassel as archbishop in 1167. Other experts think that Frederick had slighted Philip, or so he felt, by assigning to the abbot of Fulda the place of honor at the Pentecost court in Mainz in 1184; and the archbishop had opposed in turn the creation, at the same assembly, of the margraviate of Namur that had the potential to check Cologne's further expansion in Lower Lorraine. For his part, Frederick may never have forgiven Philip for orchestrating the proceedings against his cousin, Henry the Lion. Nevertheless, Frederick still had enough confidence in the archbishop to send Philip to England in September 1184 to negotiate a Staufer–Angevin marriage alliance. A combination of accumulated personal grievances and divergent territorial interests led Philip to side with Urban and Folmar in 1186.[25]

Philip was identified for the first time in June or July 1186 as the papal legate in the metropolitan province of Cologne. Arnold of Lübeck reported that Frederick began to suspect Philip's loyalty in the summer of 1186 and that the archbishop strengthened the fortifications of Cologne. Prior to the assembly in Gelnhausen in November, Frederick allegedly discussed with Philip his strained relations with Urban; but Philip made his support of Frederick contingent upon the emperor's renunciation of his right to the possessions of deceased bishops, that is, the right of spoils, the same thing Urban was demanding. Frederick refused to concede any of the traditional prerogatives of the crown and persuaded Philip not to attend the court at Gelnhausen. Since Philip was in fact there, it is impossible to tell whether any part of Arnold's report is true.[26]

Several months after Philip became the papal legate in Cologne, the pope, at Folmar's request, assigned the same role to Folmar in the metropolitan province of Trier. Folmar summoned a provincial synod to meet on 15 February 1187, in Mouzon, a castle that belonged to the archbishop of Reims, located just over the boundary between the ecclesiastical provinces of Trier and Reims. Numerous French clerics, including several bishops, participated. Frederick prohibited Folmar's suffragans from attending. Bishop Peter of Toul, who had refused to welcome Folmar the previous year, and Bishop Henry of Verdun obeyed the emperor; but Bishop Bertram of Metz, despite the oath he had sworn in November 1186, went to the synod. Folmar proceeded against those prelates who had heeded the emperor's orders. He excommunicated Peter of Toul, while Henry of Verdun resigned his bishopric. Frederick expelled Bertram from Metz and confiscated the episcopal properties. Bertram took refuge for nearly three years with Philip in Cologne.[27]

When Richard the Lionheart attacked Philip Augustus, the French king sent envoys to Frederick to arrange a treaty of friendship between them. The embassy was most welcome because Folmar was dependent on French support—the archbishop of Reims was the king's maternal uncle, William of Champagne. Frederick reached an agreement with the French envoys in Toul at Pentecost, 17 May 1187. The text does not survive; but, according to the Trier chronicler, it committed Philip Augustus to Folmar's expulsion from France. Folmar was forced to leave Mouzon, but Archbishop William gave him refuge in Reims. Baldwin of Hainaut also sent a delegation to Frederick in Toul. Baldwin's septuagenarian uncle, Henry of Namur, who had "married" Agnes of Guelders in 1168, had finally consummated his marriage in 1185. He had then engaged their infant daughter Ermesinde, now the heiress presumptive of Namur, to Count Henry II of Champagne, who was both the nephew and cousin of Philip Augustus. Frederick assured Baldwin's envoys that he would abide by the promise he had made in Mainz in 1184 to grant Henry of Namur's fiefs to Baldwin, because he "would not permit anyone in the kingdom of France to succeed to the count of Namur's allods."[28]

Frederick ordered the construction of a bridge across the Mosel. The rumor spread in Cologne that the emperor was planning to march through the archbishop's territory to aid Philip Augustus in his fight with Richard the Lionheart. Out of fear of the imperial army's transit through the archbishop's domains, the citizens strengthened the city's fortifications. Archbishop Philip forbade the imperial army from crossing his territory and, according to a later report, commanded the destruction of the bridge over the Mosel. It is unlikely that Frederick had any intention of intervening militarily in the conflict between the Angevins and Capetians, something that he had avoided throughout his reign. Conceivably, he was planning to attack Henry of Namur. On 25 July 1187 the emperor imposed an embargo on Cologne.[29]

At a court in Worms on 15 August, the feast of the Virgin's Assumption, Frederick began formal proceedings against the absent Philip. The emperor charged that the archbishop had prevented the transit of imperial forces through his territory and had denigrated him. The other bishops, including Conrad of Mainz, who had been accused of joining Urban's conspiracy with Philip against the Reich, were allowed to clear themselves with an oath. Frederick commanded Philip to attend the next court in Strasbourg.[30]

Philip did not come, but by the time the court convened in Strasbourg around 1 December 1187, the international situation had changed completely to the archbishop's detriment. Saladin had captured Jerusalem on 2 October, and Urban had died on 20 October. On 27 October the new pope, Gregory VIII, had notified the German clergy of his election and had instructed them to win the emperor, princes, and the people of the German kingdom over to the cause of the Holy Land. Cardinal Henry of Albano had written to Frederick before 11 November that he had been appointed to preach the crusade, and around 23 November the emperor had the letters of entreaty that the princes in the Crusader States had sent him and which the pope read out publicly. Cardinal Henry informed the Strasbourg assembly about conditions in the Levant, but when no one responded to his call to arms, Bishop Henry of Strasbourg added his voice to that of the papal legate. A comital ministerial was the first to volunteer, and many princes and around 500 knights allegedly followed the ministerial's example. Frederick declared that he, too, wanted to take the cross immediately but that his conflict with Archbishop Philip prevented him from doing so. He subsequently sent envoys to Philip Augustus to persuade him to join the crusade. A Jewish source reported that Frederick imposed a tax on the Jews, but not a substantial amount, ordered the clergy not to preach against the Jews, and placed them under his protection.[31]

Frederick and Philip Augustus met before 25 December 1187, between Yvois-Carignan and Mouzon on the German–French border in the Meuse valley. They were joined by Cardinal Henry of Albano and the archbishop of Tyre. Both monarchs had invited Baldwin of Hainaut to attend even though, Gilbert of Mons insisted, the count owed homage to neither. Baldwin served as the emperor's trusted adviser at the meeting and also, presumably, as a mediator between his imperial overlord and his son-in-law Philip. Frederick urged the French king to participate in the crusade and promised his assistance, but Philip insisted that he could not commit himself to the undertaking because he was at war with Henry II of England. This problem was temporarily resolved when both western monarchs met at Gisors in January 1188 and took the cross.

Archbishop William of Reims and his brother Count Thibaut V of Blois tried to get Philip to back the claims to Namur of their nephew, Count Henry II of Champagne, Ermesinde's "husband"; but Philip opted for Baldwin rather than his own nephew and cousin, presumably because the king wanted Frederick's friendship and did not desire a further increase in the power of the house of Champagne-Blois, whose lands surrounded the royal domain. Frederick refused, however, to renew his 1184 agreement with Baldwin until Henry VI was present. Baldwin was to await Henry's return from Italy, and Frederick promised that he would intercede with his son on the count's behalf. After Henry VI had been on the verge of attacking Baldwin in September 1185, Frederick may have deemed it wisest to make sure that Baldwin's acquisition of Namur and Luxembourg was really acceptable to his son. Philip again agreed, as he had in Toul at Pentecost, not to grant Folmar refuge in his kingdom. Folmar fled to Tours, where the English Henry II provided him with his daily maintenance and where he later died.[32]

At the Christmas court in Trier shortly after his meeting with Philip Augustus, Frederick complained that at his advanced age—he had probably just celebrated his sixty-fifth birthday—he was compelled, against his will, to devastate imperial territory on account of his conflict with Archbishop Philip. The counts and nobles of Lorraine, especially those who lived in the archdiocese of Cologne, refused to join Henry VI in a campaign against their feudal lord Philip. They insisted that they owed their primary allegiance to their prince and not the emperor or king. Nevertheless, without papal support and with the growing European determination to retake Jerusalem, Philip's position had become untenable. After ignoring several prior summonses, the archbishop appeared at the Candlemas court in Nuremberg (2 February 1188). A final decision was postponed to 27 March, significantly the third Sunday before Easter, *Laetere Jerusalem*, the day in the liturgical calendar when Frederick had been crowned as king of the Romans. The text of the introit to the Mass, which is taken from Isaiah 66:10, "Rejoice with Jerusalem, and be glad for her, all you who love her; rejoice with her in joy, all you who mourn over her," fit perfectly the purpose of the assembly, which became known by Frederick's own designation as the "Court of Christ."

The papal cardinal-legate, Bishop Henry of Albano, made peace between the emperor and the archbishop. Philip had to swear a triple oath to clear himself, twice for his failure to obey the summonses to attend the emperor in Worms and Strasbourg, and the third time for imposing a levy on the Jews in defiance of the emperor's command. He had to pay Frederick 2,000 marks and the court 200 marks. In addition, one of the gates of the city of Cologne was to be destroyed and the moat filled in at four places for a length of 400 feet; but these measures, which were presumably designed to demonstrate the archbishop's submission to the emperor, were rescinded the next day. The citizens of Cologne had to demolish their newly built wall in four places.

Frederick did not preside at the court in Mainz, because Christ was the Lord of lords. After a letter was read out publicly about what had happened the previous year in the Holy Land and Bishop Godfrey of Würzburg had preached a crusade sermon, Frederick enquired whether he should go to the aid of the Holy Land. He took the cross, at the urging of the assembly, from the hands of Cardinal Henry. Duke Frederick VI of Swabia and many bishops, princes, nobles, and a very large number of knights followed his example. Besides his son, all the other lay princes who reportedly took the cross at Mainz were the emperor's kinsmen: his cousins Frederick of Bohemia and Leopold V of Austria, and his nephew Louis III of Thuringia. Even at this crucial moment in the history of Christendom, Frederick's support among the lay princes was limited.

Frederick, on orders from the pope and with the advice of all the princes, proclaimed a "general expedition against the pagans." Preparations were to take place between 17 April 1188 and the next celebration of Easter on 9 April 1189. The crusaders were to assemble in Regensburg on 23 April 1189, the feast of St. George, the patron saint of knights. The poorest participants were to have at least three marks, the minimum necessary to support themselves for two years; and wealthier individuals were to be provided for in accordance with their means. Frederick wanted to ensure that the crusade did not degenerate into a poverty-stricken mob. He summoned another general assembly to meet in Goslar in August, which Henry the Lion was also ordered to attend.[33]

Unlike the pogroms that accompanied the First and Second Crusades in Germany and the preaching of the Third Crusade in England, Frederick protected the Jews from violence during the court session in Mainz. After a mob had invaded the Jewish quarter in Mainz on Friday, 29 January 1188, most members of the community had fled to the nearby castle of Münzenberg in the Wetterau, where they remained until the end of April. Their choice of Münzenberg as a refuge was hardly coincidental. Its lord was the prominent imperial ministerial, Cuno I of Münzenberg, one of the individuals who had sworn the Peace of Constance on the emperor's behalf in 1183. More to the point, Cuno was probably also responsible for collecting the taxes that the Jews owed the emperor. He had even issued in the 1170s his own bracteates, which depicted Cuno on a seat with a small figure wearing a Jewish hat at his side and identified in Hebrew as "David the Priest."

Rabbi Eleazar Ben Judah wrote a brief memoir about what befell the Jews between the autumn of 1187 and their return to Mainz at the end of April 1188. He included in his account a letter that his brother-in-law,

Rabbi Moses, who had remained in the city, had written to the refugees in Münzenberg. There had been a series of incidents, which began when the first attendees arrived in Mainz on 9 March 1188, and culminated on 26 March, the Sabbath, when thousands of crusaders—indeed, tens of thousands, the rabbi wrote—gathered in the marketplace to invade the Jewish quarter. The imperial marshal, Henry of Kalden-Pappenheim, dispersed the mob. On 29 March, according to Rabbi Moses, the emperor himself proclaimed that "Anyone who attacks a Jew and wounds him shall have his hand cut off. Anyone who kills a Jew will be killed." The wealthy Jew, Rabbi Moses ha-Cohen, who had negotiated with the emperor, rode with Frederick through the streets to assure the remaining Jews of their safety, and he wrote a letter to his co-religionists notifying them that the king had conferred upon them his peace. It is not clear whether Frederick's edict, which was almost certainly committed to writing but which does not survive, applied only to the Jews of Mainz or placed all Jews in the realm under the emperor's protection. In any case, the emperor prevented a repetition of the attacks on the Jews that had accompanied the preaching of the Second Crusade in 1147.[34]

Preparing for the Third Crusade

Before he left for the Holy Land in May 1189, Frederick settled, tentatively at least, some of the problems he faced in the 1180s—whether he could have if Saladin had not captured Jerusalem on 2 October 1187 is far from certain. At his meeting with Philip Augustus in December 1187, Frederick had refused to renew his 1184 agreement with Baldwin V of Hainaut until Henry VI could give his consent. Accordingly, when Baldwin learned around Easter 1188 that the young king had returned from Italy, he called upon Henry at the palace of Ingelheim and obtained his favor. At Seligenstadt on 16 May 1188 both Frederick and Henry, in separate charters, confirmed that Baldwin would inherit the allods and fiefs of his uncle, Henry of Namur. Gilbert of Mons noted that Queen Constance interceded on her kinsman's behalf—Constance's mother was Baldwin's first cousin.

Since the combined forces of Henry of Namur, his future son-in-law, Count Henry II of Champagne, and Duke Godfrey of Brabant were mustering to attack Baldwin, his envoys appealed to Frederick and his son for help at Erfurt on 8 November 1188. Bishop Peter of Toul, who was also in Erfurt, offered Frederick and Henry VI each 5,000 marks, Constance 1,000, the court 1,000, and other royal advisers around 1,700 marks, if they would support the claims of Henry of Champagne to Namur and

Luxembourg. However, Baldwin's envoys, Gilbert of Mons among them, prevailed, even though they promised only 1,550 marks. It was agreed that Baldwin would surrender to Henry VI all the allods and fiefs of his uncle, Henry of Namur, both those that were already in Baldwin's possession and those that his uncle had retained, and receive back the margraviate of Namur as a fief held directly from the Empire. This transaction occurred at Worms on 23 December 1188, when Henry VI enfeoffed Baldwin with all of Henry of Namur's allods in the counties of Namur, Laroche and Durbuy, as well as his uncle's imperial fiefs. Since Luxembourg was not included in the enfeoffment, Baldwin's real price for obtaining the emperor's support had not been 1,550 marks but the surrender of Luxembourg to the Staufer. The new mark was to be inseparable from the county of Hainaut. Frederick stipulated that the enfeoffment was to remain secret until either Henry of Namur died or he accepted that his nephew Baldwin rather than his young daughter Ermesinde was his heir.

Henry VI established the new imperial principality of Namur, officially, only after Frederick's death, at the imperial court held in Schwäbisch-Hall on 23 September 1190; but the whole arrangement was, in fact, stillborn. When Baldwin inherited Flanders in 1191 from his brother-in-law Philip, Namur became only of secondary importance. He bequeathed Namur in 1195 to Philip, his second son. Philip held the mark in fief from his older brother, Baldwin VI, the count of Flanders and Hainaut, in direct contravention of the terms that had been worked out at Mainz in 1184 and at Erfurt and Worms in 1188.[35]

On 30 November 1187, several weeks after he became pope, Gregory VIII reminded Archbishop Folmar that Solomon said there is a time to speak and a time to be silent (Ecclesiastes 3:7), and that the Church needed Frederick and his son. Accordingly, the pope enjoined Folmar from excommunicating or deposing anyone in the archbishopric of Trier without apostolic permission. Clement III, who succeeded Gregory VIII on 20 December 1187, dispatched two cardinals to Germany in June 1188 to resolve the Trier schism. The pope and the legates summoned Folmar three times to appear in Rome and warned him that if he did not present himself by 12 February 1189, Clement would proceed against him. Folmar ignored the summonses. Around 10 April, Frederick and Henry VI received from the cardinals a written memorandum outlining the terms of the proposed settlement, and they appended golden bulls to a transcription of the agreement. Clement removed Folmar from office, voided his and Rudolf's actions during the schism, restored to their former status the clerics whom Folmar had deposed, and authorized the cathedral canons to hold a free election. At the suggestion and request of Henry, who was in Trier in the autumn of 1189, the clergy of Trier chose Frederick's last chancellor, John, as their new archbishop. The exiled Bertram of Metz was allowed to return to his see.[36]

Frederick held a court in Goslar between 25 July and 8 August 1188 to settle various disputes, chief among them, according to Arnold of Lübeck, the rival claims of Henry the Lion and his successor Bernard to the duchy of Saxony. The emperor allegedly presented his cousin with three options: Henry could be satisfied with a partial restoration to his old position; he could participate in the crusade at the emperor's expense and upon his return regain everything he had lost; or he and his like-named son, Henry of Brunswick, could go into exile for three years. Henry chose the last because, Arnold said, "he did not want to go where he did not wish or to have his former honor diminished." It is highly unlikely that Frederick could have proposed to restore his cousin to his lost dignities without antagonizing the other princes, but Henry did leave for England around Easter 1189.[37]

Upon his return from his fifth Italian campaign, Frederick had renewed on 18 February 1179, in Wissembourg in Alsace, a two-year peace for Rhenish Franconia. This was at the request of the princes and nobles of the land, but also of the ministerials and the other inhabitants of the region. Charlemagne had allegedly instituted the peace, but in fact it had originated in the late eleventh century. The last provision, supposedly a rediscovered long-forgotten law, deprived anyone who committed arson at night, and who did not deny the crime, of his allods and fiefs.[38]

Arson was the subject of a separate peace ordinance that Frederick promulgated in Nuremberg on 29 or 30 December, probably in 1188. Like the 1179 peace (but unlike that of 1152, when Frederick had relied exclusively on the princes' counsel), this peace ordinance was issued with the advice and consent not only of the princes but also of the emperor's other faithful subjects, both free men and ministerials—as Frederick expanded his circle of advisers during the last two decades of his reign. In keeping with the decentralization of royal authority that Frederick had promoted during his reign, the enforcement of the law was explicitly assigned to the magnates in whose lordship the arson had occurred; but only the emperor could absolve the criminal with the agreement of the judge, after the incendiary had made proper restitution. An arsonist was to be outlawed after his conviction. If the culprit refused to make proper satisfaction, the bishop of the diocese where the arson had occurred was to excommunicate him. After the perpetrator had abjured his crimes, the bishop, in a provision borrowed from the legislation of Popes Innocent II and Eugenius III, was to impose upon him as a penance a pilgrimage to either Jerusalem or Compostela. Anyone who was outlawed and remained excommunicate for more than a year was deprived of all his rights, including the right to possess a fief ever again. Frederick may have learned of the papal legislation against arsonists during his negotiations with Pope Alexander in Venice in 1177. According to the chronicle of the monastery of St. Michael in Lüneburg, the pope and emperor had established that arsonists and the destroyers of vineyards and orchards could be released from excommunication only on the pope's authority. The final provision of the 1188 law stipulated that individuals who cut down vines and apple trees were subject to the same penalties of outlawry and excommunication as arsonists.

A tangential provision of the 1188 law (expanding on the attempt in the 1152 peace ordinance to delineate the boundary between knights and the rest of society) forbade the girding of the sons of priests, deacons, and peasants. Men who had been improperly knighted were to be excluded by the judges from the ranks of knighthood. A lord who continued to employ them in this way was to pay the judge a fine of £10, and the "serf" was to be deprived of all the rights of knighthood. The provision was a dead letter at a time when the majority of knights, that is, the ministerials, were legally serfs. Frederick specified that the law against arsonists, like the *Authentica Habita* of 1155, was to be added to Justinian's *Codex*; but there is no evidence that it ever was.[39]

Gregory VIII and Clement III were willing to accommodate the emperor's wishes in Trier, because they desired Frederick's participation in the crusade. However, the disputes over the rival papal and imperial claims to the Matildine Lands and in the Patrimony, and over Frederick's request that the pope crown Henry VI as emperor, were harder to resolve. During his brief pontificate, Gregory took the first conciliatory steps. He is alleged to have promised, according to the *Roman Annals*, to surrender to Henry all the rights that pertained to the Empire, because it was not the duty of the pope and cardinals to bear arms but rather to sing Christ's praise in poverty. In response, Henry offered to escort the pope and curia safely wherever they wished to go within the Roman Empire. It is doubtful that Gregory had really embraced Arnold of Brescia's radical call for the papacy's renunciation of its earthly wealth and power, but the report suggests that Gregory was ready to make concessions. In a letter of 29 November 1187 he did address Henry, in fact, as the "emperor-elect of the Romans," as he called upon the king to persevere in his good intentions toward the Roman Church. As far as we know, this was the first time the papacy employed this title, which became the customary designation for the emperors after they ceased to be crowned by the pope in the early modern period. On one level, Gregory was merely acknowledging that every king of the Romans had the right, if he was acceptable to the pope, to be crowned as emperor; but in the context of the refusal of Popes Lucius and Urban to do so, the salutation was a signal that Gregory was prepared to grant Frederick's request.[40]

The pro-imperial Roman aristocrat Leo de Monumento, who had been enfeoffed by Henry VI with the city, bishopric, and county of Sutri on 27 November 1186, and who had secured Clement's election, helped the pope, a native Roman, to return to Rome from Pisa. On 31 May 1188 Clement reached an agreement with the senate, modeled after Frederick's pact of 1167. The senators recognized the pope's lordship over the city and returned the papal regalia, income, churches, and mint they had seized. In return, Clement acknowledged the senate's existence, made extensive financial concessions to the Romans, and continued the customary papal gifts to the senators and other Roman officials. Papal lordship over Rome, which Henry VI had not challenged during his 1186 campaign, was thus reaffirmed; but Frederick's supporters controlled the city.

Frederick sent Provost Frederick of the collegiate church of St. Thomas in Strasbourg and the proto-notary, Master Henry, the scholastic of Utrecht Cathedral, to Rome to negotiate an agreement with Clement. In Strasbourg on 3 April 1189, shortly before Frederick's departure for the Holy Land, Henry VI restored to Clement the papal possessions in the Patrimony, including Orvieto and Viterbo. The papacy had held these during the pontificate of Lucius III, and Henry had seized them in 1186. Henry now freed the men of these places from the oaths of fealty they had sworn to him and his father. He excluded from this restoration only "the rights of the empire, the *proprietas* as well as the *possessio*." The notary who drafted this agreement was here making a distinction, unknown in Germany but derived from Roman law and so familiar to the curia, between the current ownership and use of a property (*possessio*) and ultimate dominion (*proprietas*). At Venice in 1177, Frederick and Alexander, while reserving the rights of their respective institutions, had committed themselves only to the return of each other's alienated *possessiones*. While Henry was abandoning the more extreme claims his father had made in the late 1150s, he was asserting that the Patrimony and Rome itself, where the prefect was an imperial official, were part of the Empire and thus subject to the emperor's lordship. However, nothing was said on 3 April about the Matildine Lands, and the potential for conflict about the legal status of individual holdings remained.

Frederick, writing from Haguenau to Clement on 10 April 1189, told the pope that he had learned both from the pope's letters and from his envoys that Clement was prepared to crown the emperor's son and daughter-in-law, Henry and Constance. Two papal legates and Leo de Monumento had confirmed the report. Frederick was therefore sending the proto-notary, Leo, and Gerlach of Isenburg to Rome to explain why the couple's departure would be delayed—presumably, Frederick deemed it best for Henry to remain in Germany while he was on crusade. The emperor requested that the imperial coronation take place, when it occurred, in the customary fashion. Henry sent a similar letter on 18 April, but he was not crowned until after his father's death.[41]

Frederick provided for his younger sons' future as well. An imperial envoy was at the court of King Alfonso VIII of Castile in May 1187 to arrange a marriage between the king's older daughter Berenguela, the heiress presumptive to the throne, and Frederick's third surviving son, Conrad. A Castilian embassy arrived in Seligenstadt in April 1188 to confirm the arrangements; a member of the Spanish delegation drafted the marriage contract, which is dated 23 April. The contract dealt with every conceivable eventuality if the princess succeeded her father and was designed to prevent Conrad from asserting any claim to the throne of Castile in his own right. Conrad went to Spain, and Alfonso girded his future, twenty-one-year-old son-in-law at a splendid court that was held at Carrión in July 1188 and engaged him to Berenguela—since she was only eight, she could not give her consent to a legally binding marriage. Conrad did not remain long in Spain; he was with his father and brothers in Haguenau on 14 April 1189. The marriage never materialized because Alfonso had a son in 1189, and a papal legate dissolved the union in the winter of 1191–92 because a potential Staufer succession in Castile as well as Sicily was unacceptable to the papacy. Conrad died unmarried on 15 August 1196, when he was caught and killed in Durlach for raping a woman.

In the contract, Frederick assigned to Conrad and Berenguela as their marriage dower all the allods the emperor possessed or that had belonged to his late cousin, Frederick of Rothenburg, in the diocese of Würzburg, eastern Franconia, Swabia, and between the Rhine and Swabia—a detailed list of castles and allods was included in the agreement. Conrad, who was originally designated as his mother's successor in Burgundy, was identified for the first time as Conrad of Rothenburg in the contract; and Frederick's fourth son, Otto, became the Burgundian count-palatine. The youngest son Philip was intended for the Church. It is noteworthy that Frederick no longer considered the daughters of the German princes as suitable brides for his sons but engaged them instead to foreign princesses—Frederick VI was betrothed first to the daughter of the Danish king and then to a Hungarian princess. The choice of spouses was another sign of the growing distance between the Staufer and their former peers.[42]

At Strasbourg in early December 1187 Frederick rejected the proposal of his former chancellor, Bishop Godfrey of Würzburg, that the crusaders take the "easier, if longer" sea route "than the difficult expedition by land." Since it was not possible to sail between November and March, the drawback of the sea route was that crusaders risked being aboard a ship in very close quarters in hot weather; and transporting men, horses, and their equipment on ships was even more expensive than going by land. It required a stern warning from Clement III to put a stop to Godfrey's proposal that had been inspired by the Devil, in the view of Ansbert, the alleged author of the chief account of Frederick's crusade, *The History of the Expedition of the Emperor Frederick*. Nevertheless, numerous crusaders arrived in the *Regno*, but, at Frederick's request, according to the *Cologne Royal Chronicle*, William of Sicily prohibited them from sailing; they could not be assured of adequate supplies in Outremer, and a small band of knights would be no match for Saladin until the arrival of the emperor and the English and French kings. Frederick and Clement may thus have feared that Saladin would capture all the ports along the eastern Mediterranean before the crusaders arrived and would prevent early arrivals from landing. Taking the land route through Anatolia instead would, in such an eventuality, allow the crusaders to attack Syria and Palestine from Antioch.[43]

Frederick, who had traveled through the Balkans and Anatolia in 1147, could have had no illusions, however, about the difficulties the land route posed: provisioning a large force on a long march across mountains and deserts, potential Byzantine treachery, and attacks by the Seljuk Turks. To deal with the enormous logistical problems, and shortly after he took the cross in Mainz on 27 March 1188, the emperor sent Archbishop Conrad of Mainz to Béla III of Hungary, the knight Godfrey of Wiesenbach to Kilic Arslan II, the sultan of Iconium (today Konya in modern Turkey), and unnamed envoys to Isaac II Angelos, the Byzantine emperor, to make the necessary preparations. Frederick probably also entered into negotiations with Leo II, the Rupenid prince of Little Armenia (Cilicia in southeastern Turkey). Count Henry II of Diez, the *podestà* of Milan in the 1160s, left on 26 May 1188 on a separate mission to Saladin. He was instructed to terminate Frederick's long friendship with the sultan unless the latter withdrew immediately from the Holy Land, returned the True Cross to the Church of the Holy Sepulcher, and gave appropriate satisfaction for the Christians whom he had killed. The emperor was observing the chivalric niceties of defying an enemy before an attack.[44]

Frederick celebrated his last Christmas in Germany in Eger (now Cheb in the Czech Republic). A few days later at a court in Nuremberg he received envoys from King Béla, Isaac II, Kilic Arslan, Stephen Nemanja, who was the zupan (the great count or great ruler) of Serbia, and perhaps also from Saladin; the emperor probably also promulgated his law against arsonists. The Hungarians and Turks promised to supply the crusaders with provisions and to give them safe conduct. The Hungarians agreed, for example, to provide for a mark four high-quality oxen or fodder for 100 horses. The Seljuk delegation supposedly consisted of 1,000 men and 500 horses, but the chroniclers noted that the Seljuks' assurances proved false. The Serb envoys indicated that the zupan awaited Frederick's arrival with great joy and would receive him in Niš, the chief city of the zupan's realm. Frederick gave the customary rich gifts to all the ambassadors.

John Dukas Kamateros, the Logothete of the Drome or "foreign minister," headed the Byzantine delegation. Isaac II was deeply suspicious of the crusaders' motives, according to "Ansbert." The Byzantine monarch feared that the new expedition was a cover for an imperial–French attack on the Greek Empire and he threatened to block the crusaders' passage through the Bulgarian Gates, the passes between Sofia and the Maritsa valley. To calm Isaac's fears, Bishop Godfrey of Würzburg, Frederick VI, and Leopold V of Austria swore that the crusaders would come in peace. The Greeks swore, in turn, "true and firm friendship" and promised to provide the crusaders with "a good road, the best possible market preparations," and free transit across the sea. The author of *The History of the Pilgrims* indicated, more specifically, that the Greeks agreed to allow the crusaders "to take fruit from the trees, vegetables from the gardens, wood to make fires provided houses were not damaged, and fodder and straw for the needs of their horses." To prepare the way for the crusading army, Frederick sent on ahead Bishop Hermann of Münster, Count Rupert III of Nassau, Henry of Diez's son, Henry III, and the imperial chamberlain and ministerial, Markwart of Neuenburg, accompanied by an entourage of knights (the sources give the figures variously as 100, at least 200, and 500 knights).[45]

The sources say little about how Frederick financed the crusade. It is estimated that he would have required approximately 80,000 to 90,000 marks to purchase essential supplies for an army of 12,000 to 15,000 men, including 3,000 knights; and he and the princes would have needed considerably more money to maintain themselves and their entourages in a manner commensurate with their rank. There is no indication that Saladin's tithe was levied in Germany, as it was in England and France. Conceivably, Frederick hoped to use Berenguela's dowry of 42,000 gold pieces to underwrite the cost of the undertaking, but she and her dowry never arrived in Germany. As was the case with his Italian campaigns, bishops and abbots may have been required to make monetary contributions in lieu of participating. For example, the abbot of Murbach gave Frederick a property whose income was sufficient to equip 250 knights. However, most of the funds must have come from the Staufer's own extensive domains. Frederick brought with him, as befitted an emperor, chests full of silver. Several parcels of silver that were buried after his death were discovered in Anatolia between 1982 and 1985. This so-called Barbarossa Hoard consisted of about eight kilograms of silver: around 7,700 complete coins or fragments from dozens of German mints; silver ingots; and Seljuk silver jewelry. (Two-fifths of the coins were Cologne pennies, the most widely used coinage in Germany; and the majority of these were struck during Philip's archiepiscopate.) Individual participants had to raise their own funds. Frederick's crusade was the most meticulously planned and organized crusade of the twelfth century.[46]

Frederick displayed during the mid-1180s considerable diplomatic finesse in his dealings with Milan and Philip Augustus, and in retaining the loyalty of most of the German bishops in his confrontations with Urban III and Archbishop Philip. Whether Frederick could have made peace so quickly with Urban's successors and Philip if Saladin had not captured Jerusalem is another matter. The impetuous Henry VI, who had caused trouble in Trier and Hainaut, might quickly have become Frederick's biggest problem, especially after Constance inherited the Sicilian throne.

On 15 April 1189 Frederick received, according to Gilbert of Mons, the scrip and staff of a pilgrim. He then set out from Haguenau, the place where he may have been born and may have spent much of his childhood and adolescence, on the pilgrimage that would lead to his watery death.[47]

CHAPTER SEVENTEEN

THE THIRD CRUSADE

FREDERICK'S TAKING OF THE cross attracted the attention of Christendom. The three major contemporary accounts are based on eyewitness reports. "Ansbert," the alleged compiler of *The History of the Expedition of the Emperor Frederick*, relied on the diary of Tageno (d. 1190), the dean of the cathedral of Passau, and a letter that Frederick wrote to his son Henry VI in November 1189. The Augustinian canon and chronicler Magnus of Reichersberg (d. 1195) used the same diary and a letter that Bishop Diepold of Passau (d. 1190) sent to Duke Leopold of Austria, Frederick's first cousin. The emperor's former chancellor, Bishop Godfrey of Würzburg, may have been the author of a newsletter that described the crusade's passage through Anatolia and Frederick's death. At the beginning of the thirteenth century, Otto of St. Blasien and Arnold of Lübeck supplied additional details about the expedition. Frederick's death, ironically the most recorded event in his life, turned the persecutor of the Church into a defender of the faith.[1]

The Political Situation in Southeastern Europe

The political situation that awaited Frederick in southeastern Europe in 1189 was extremely complicated and was, potentially, a threat to the success of the crusade. After Manuel I's death in 1180, his widow Maria of Antioch had assumed the regency for their twelve-year-old son Alexius II. She was perceived as pro-Latin and in 1182 Manuel's cousin, Andronicus Komnenos, who had spent much of Manuel's reign in exile, had utilized the discontent and marched on Constantinople. At his approach a mob in the capital had massacred the Latins, in particular the Genoese and Pisans, who were eager

Map 4. The Third Crusade.

for revenge. Andronicus had Maria strangled and became the co-emperor. Shortly thereafter, in 1183, he had Alexius secretly murdered.

During his reign Manuel had suppressed repeated Serbian revolts. In battles with the Hungarians he had reasserted Byzantine control over southern Dalmatia and Bosnia as far north as the Sava, which enters the Danube at Belgrade. In 1180 the Serbian zupan, or great count, Stephen Nemanja, had again repudiated Byzantine suzerainty and begun a policy of Serbian expansion. By 1189 he ruled the southern portion of the Dalmatian coastline, northern Macedonia, Kosovo, and the territory between Niš and modern Sofia in Bulgaria. Not surprisingly, Frederick's negotiations in Nuremberg with Stephen's envoys in late December 1188 had aroused Constantinople's suspicions about Barbarossa's intentions, which were not allayed by his subsequent meeting with Stephen in Niš in July 1189.

Frederick's dynastic ties to the Hautevilles were another cause of concern in Constantinople. Following in the footsteps of his Norman ancestors, William II of Sicily had seized Durrazo (the modern Durrës on the Adriatic coast in Albania) in 1185 and sacked Thessalonica (Salonika). When the Normans had advanced on Constantinople after taking Thessalonica, the population rebelled against Andronicus and in late 1185 placed Isaac II Angelos on the Greek throne. The Normans had been defeated and expelled, but the march of Barbarossa, the father-in-law of the heiress presumptive to the Sicilian throne, through Byzantine territory added to Isaac's mistrust of Frederick's intentions.

Upon ascending the throne in 1185, Isaac had married Margaret, the young daughter of Béla III of Hungary. While the Hungarians and Byzantines were united by their opposition to Serbian expansion, Margaret's marriage to Isaac placed Béla in the potentially awkward position of having to choose between his Greek son-in-law and his obligations as a Latin Christian to support the crusade.

Fear of the Turks, as well as the Latins, made both Andronicus and Isaac eager for an alliance with Saladin. The Seljuk victory at Myriokephalon in 1176, which had ended any Byzantine hopes of re-establishing Greek rule in eastern Anatolia, was a threat to both Byzantine control of western Asia Minor and to Saladin's hold on northern Syria. When the Normans occupied Thessalonica in 1185, Andronicus, who had befriended Saladin's predecessor Nur-ed-Din during his exile in Damascus and Baghdad, had sent an embassy to Saladin. By the time the sultan replied, Isaac had deposed Andronicus; but Isaac, who had found refuge at Saladin's court during Andronicus' reign, had continued the Byzantine alliance with the sultan. After the fall of Jerusalem in October 1187, Saladin and Isaac had exchanged lavish gifts in a series of embassies. As Frederick was setting out for the Holy Land in April 1189, at Saladin's request Isaac was permitting public prayers to be said in the mosque in Constantinople in the name of the Abbasid caliph. The Byzantine dealings with Saladin were well known in the West—how accurate the specific reports were is in dispute—and the crusaders readily attributed Isaac's failure to honor the commitments his envoys had made before Frederick at Nuremberg in 1188 to his alliance with the infidels.

Finally, the Vlachs, who lived south of the Danube in modern Bulgaria and spoke a Romance dialect related to modern Romanian, had rebelled in 1186 under the leadership of the brothers Peter (Kalopeter) and Asen against Byzantine rule. The Vlachs had joined the Bulgarians and the Cumans—a nomadic Turkish-speaking people inhabiting what is now modern Romania, north of the lower Danube—in a loose confederation under Peter, who had assumed the title of emperor. Isaac had conducted a series of campaigns against the Vlachs but had been unable to defeat them decisively. Like Stephen Nemanja, Peter viewed Frederick as a potential ally.

When the crusaders traversed the Balkans, they thus found themselves in a region in political turmoil and devastated by years of fighting. Understandably, they blamed Isaac's treachery for the lack of supplies and the constant attacks they endured from the local population; but, in reality, the harassment was a sign of the Byzantines' loss of effective control rather than of Isaac's perfidy. In this atmosphere of mutual misunderstandings and fears, it is hardly surprising that Frederick seriously contemplated attacking Constantinople. His refusal, ultimately, to do so or to accede to Stephen and Peter's overtures is indicative of Frederick's commitment to the liberation of Jerusalem. At sixty-seven he was more concerned about his eternal salvation than with extending Western imperial suzerainty in the Balkans; but Frederick's conflict with Isaac revealed Byzantium's weakness and would prepare the way for the capture of Constantinople by leaders of the Fourth Crusade in 1204.[2]

Departure

On 16 April 1189, the day after Frederick set out from Haguenau on his pilgrimage to the Holy Land, he established with the consent of his son Frederick VI a hospital in Haguenau for the benefit of his soul and those of their ancestors. While journeying to Regensburg, where the emperor had ordered the crusaders to assemble on 23 April, and then in the Bavarian "capital," where he arrived sometime between 7 and 10 May, Frederick issued privileges for various churches, monasteries, and nobles. The most important actions he took in Regensburg were the enfeoffment of Conrad Otto of Moravia as the duke of Bohemia, after the death of the emperor's cousin Duke Frederick, and the appointment of Henry VI as regent.[3]

The crusaders had started to assemble in Regensburg around 1 May. Frederick was initially disheartened, according to Arnold of Lübeck, by the small size of the force that awaited him and thought about terminating the undertaking. After taking counsel, he learned that many of the crusaders had joined "a large crowd from all nations" and were awaiting him near the Austro-Hungarian border. He decided to proceed. However, contrary to his hope of leading an army of adequately funded and properly equipped knights, many of these unexpected additional participants were, besides the usual hucksters, religiously inspired non-combatants who were on foot and whose defense and feeding posed an ongoing problem.

The composition of the army reflected the changes in Frederick's entourage after 1167. The only lay princes joining him besides his son, Duke Frederick VI, who proved to be a very able second-in-command, were: Duke Berthold IV of Andechs, who had participated in Frederick's sixth Italian campaign; Margrave Berthold III of Vohburg, the nephew of the emperor's first wife, Adela; and Margrave Hermann IV of Zähringen-Baden. Frederick's nephew, Landgrave Louis III of Thuringia, sailed from Italy to the Holy Land; and the emperor's cousin, Duke Leopold of Austria, took the same maritime route later. In contrast, his uncle, Conrad III, had been accompanied by Frederick, Welf VI, Otto of Wittelsbach, the dukes of Bavaria and Bohemia, and the margrave of Styria. No German archbishop went with Frederick in 1189, though Archbishop Hartwig II of Bremen participated in the naval expedition that captured Silves in Portugal. The episcopate was represented by the bishops of Basel, Liège, Meissen, Münster, Osnabrück, Passau, Regensburg, and Würzburg. Bishop Godfrey of Würzburg was Frederick's chief clerical adviser. The only abbot who is known to have gone on the crusade is Isenrich of Admont. Twenty-six counts and "the fearsome and well-disciplined force of ministerials," who could not be named individually, "Ansbert" said, provided the backbone of the imperial forces. The four ministerial court office-holders accompanied Frederick: the marshal, Henry of Kalden; the chamberlain, Markwart of Neuenburg; the seneschal, Markwart of Annweiler; and the butler, Conrad of Waldhausen. Altogether, "Ansbert" named seventy such participants.

It is hard to ascertain the total size of the crusading army. German chroniclers provided figures ranging from 13,000 to 100,000, whereas

Arab sources placed the number at 200,000, 260,000, or even 300,000 warriors. The best estimate is between 12,000 and 15,000 men, including 2,000 to 3,000 knights. However, Hungarians joined the crusade; and Archbishop Aimo of Tarentaise and Bishop Peter of Toul led reinforcements from Burgundy and Lorraine, respectively, to assist Frederick in the Balkans. The total size of the emperor's force, before malnutrition, disease, and fighting reduced it, may thus have been somewhat larger than when he left Germany.[4]

The army marched, on average, 12 miles a day. Frederick traveled more quickly by ship along the Danube as far as Braničevo, downstream from Belgrade; while the bulk of his men who went by land had to catch up with him at the frequent stops along the way: Vienna, Bratislava, Esztergom, Belgrade, and Braničevo. From there, the crusaders used for the most part the old Roman roads in the Balkans and Asia Minor, which were in various stages of disrepair. The pace slowed to between just seven and nine miles a day in the Serbian "Bulgarian Forest," northern Macedonia, and in Bulgaria. They covered more than 12 miles a day in Anatolia, in spite of Turkish attacks and insufficient food and water; and after the army had rested and been freshly provisioned in Iconium (today Konya), its pace quickened to more than 19 miles a day. During the last three days before Frederick's death on 10 June 1190, when the crusaders were faced with nearly Alpine terrain, they were still averaging around 12 miles a day.[5]

Frederick sailed from Regensburg on 11 May 1189, but the greater part of the army had preceded him by land. Bishop Dietpold of Passau and many of his cathedral canons joined the crusade on 16 May. Frederick burned the village of Mauthausen, downstream from Passau, because the inhabitants had dared to levy a toll on the crusaders (*Maut* means "toll"). Leopold V welcomed his cousin with appropriate pomp in Vienna and provided the crusaders with an ample market to purchase provisions. During his stay there, the emperor expelled from the army 500 men, who were, according to Arnold of Lübeck, "fornicators and thieves and other useless men," presumably some of the unwanted non-combatants who had joined the crusade. Leopold, who did not go on the crusade because of a border conflict with King Béla of Hungary, accompanied Frederick as far as the present-day capital of Slovakia, Bratislava, along with Bishops Otto II of Bamberg and Otto II of Freising; the emperor stayed in Bratislava for four days and celebrated Pentecost on 28 May.

Frederick mustered his army in the camp he pitched opposite Bratislava—"Ansbert" listed the participants at this point in his narrative. As Frederick had done at the beginning of his second Italian campaign, and on the advice of all the princes, he issued an ordinance to preserve discipline and peace in the army. The original compiler of *The History of the Expedition of the Emperor Frederick* inserted the text of this "law against malefactors"—as the author of the *Cologne Royal Chronicle* called it—at this point in his history of the crusade; but all later copyists of "Ansbert's" chronicle omitted the complete text. The compiler insisted such "peace, concord and the utmost tranquility prevailed in this army of Christ and the Holy Cross" that on many occasions lost or mislaid purses full of coins, or horses that had broken loose, were returned to their owners. "Pilgrims" who wounded others had their hands cut off immediately, in accordance with the ordinance; and violators of the market regulations were beheaded. Many years of commanding soldiers had taught Frederick the need for maintaining strict discipline.[6]

Hungary

Béla's envoys awaited Frederick in Bratislava. On 4 June the king, accompanied by 1,000 knights, welcomed the emperor at Esztergom, the seat of the Hungarian metropolitan; he stayed for four days. Queen Margaret, the older half-sister of Philip Augustus of France, gave Frederick a beautiful large tent that was divided into four rooms. It was lined with red linens, embroidered carpets covered the floor, and it was furnished with a bed and an ivory throne. It took three wagons to transport the tent—perhaps not the most suitable equipment for a journey through difficult terrain. (Tents seem to have been the royal gift par excellence among monarchs.) In return, Margaret asked that the emperor intercede with Béla to release his brother, whom he had imprisoned for fifteen years. Béla responded favorably to Frederick's entreaties. The king opened two storehouses in Esztergom, one filled with flour and the other with oats, to feed the poor pilgrims. (Arnold of Lübeck said that it was Frederick's decision to give the flour to the poor and added that in the ensuing tumult three pilgrims suffocated in it.) Béla provided the imperial army with boats and wagons laden with bread, wine, and barley for the horses, "as well as oxen and sheep sufficient for many days," and even three camels. After Frederick left Esztergom, Béla entertained him for two days on an island in the Danube, probably situated south of Budapest, where the two monarchs went hunting—inappropriate behavior for a man on a pilgrimage. To seal their friendship, Béla engaged his daughter Constance to the emperor's son Frederick VI. The marriage was to take place after the groom's return from the crusade.

However, things did not go quite so smoothly. Frederick was unable to settle the conflict between Béla and Duke Leopold (preventing the latter from joining the crusade) about the boundary between Hungary and the duchy of Styria, which Ottokar IV was bequeathing to the Babenbergs. (Leopold acquired Styria in 1192.) The Hungarians cheated the Germans, "Ansbert" said, by using in their market transactions exchange rates that were unfavorable to the crusaders. Moreover, he added ominously, they did not yet know how suspiciously Béla would act during Frederick's confrontation with Isaac II Angelos.

Béla accompanied Frederick as he proceeded down the Danube toward the nominal Hungarian border with the Byzantine Empire at Belgrade. Several men and horses were swept away by the swift current when the crusaders crossed the Drava. Three knights drowned at the fording of the Tisza. After this passage, Béla again supplied the crusaders with an abundance of provisions. After 24 June the imperial army passed the ruins of the once famous Roman city of Sirmium on the south bank of the Danube, and on 28 June it crossed without incident the Sava at its confluence with the Danube at Belgrade, which had been left half-ruined in the fighting between the Hungarians and Byzantines. The feast of the Apostles Peter and Paul the next day was celebrated, on Frederick's orders, with knightly games. The emperor knighted sixty squires on this occasion. A census of Frederick's forces indicated, according to Arnold of Lübeck, that he commanded, improbably, 50,000 knights and a total of 100,000 men under arms. The emperor presided in Belgrade over a court that sentenced two Alsatian nobles and two merchants to be beheaded for violating his peace ordinance; four serfs lost their hands for the same reason. Around this time, Frederick wrote to Isaac that he had entered Byzantine territory.[7]

The Balkans

The crusaders set out from Belgrade on 1 July and crossed the Serbian Morava, a river that flows into the Danube from the south. They arrived the next day at Braničevo, which had replaced Belgrade as the center of what remained of the Byzantine administrative structure in the area. They stayed there until 11 July. The duke, the chief Byzantine official in Braničevo, received them seemingly well, but "Ansbert" added "that he was deceitful and most wicked just like the other Greeks." Archbishop Aimo of Tarentaise, the Burgundians under his command, and burghers from Metz joined Frederick at Braničevo, while Béla returned home to Hungary. The king gave Frederick numerous wagons filled with flour, each pulled by two oxen, and four camels laden with gifts at an estimated value of 5,000 marks. Since the crusaders were traveling from this point onward by land (the impassable Iron Gates of the Danube between Romania and Bulgaria were situated downstream), all the supplies they had brought by boat had to be loaded onto wagons. Frederick conferred the boats, "constructed by the carpenters with extraordinary skill," on Béla to recompense him for his hospitality. The treacherous Byzantine duke of Braničevo, allegedly on Isaac's orders, deliberately directed the crusaders away from the main Roman road; but the Hungarians who had joined them and set out ahead of the main force were able to find the proper route. Arnold of Lübeck likewise accused the duke of conspiring with Isaac to thwart the crusaders, but Arnold also reported that the duke gave Frederick a golden vessel and enough provisions to last the imperial army for eight days.

The army marched southward, through the "Bulgarian Forest" (today the Serbian Forest), either along the banks of the Morava or somewhat to the east of the river. They were following the so-called highway of Trajan that led from Belgrade to Constantinople. "Greeklings," Bulgarians, Serbians, and "semi-barbarous Vlachs" ambushed stragglers and foragers. These bandits killed some of the foragers and were "endlessly stealing horses and plundering any carts traveling without an armed escort." Many of those who died were pilgrims who were on foot or the poor who had exhausted their supplies of food. The crusaders captured some of the robbers, who confessed before they were hanged that they were acting on the orders of the duke of Braničevo and ultimately Isaac. Whether this was really true is another matter.

At Ćuprija on 25 July a Hungarian envoy informed Frederick that Isaac was besieging a rebel in Philadelphia (modern Alaşehir in Asia Minor), so it was not surprising that Frederick had not heard anything from the Greek emperor. In addition, the envoy reported, more German crusaders—presumably the men from Lorraine under the command of Bishop Peter of Toul—had entered Hungary and were on their way to Frederick. A messenger from the Greek chancellor, John Dukas, also arrived. Isaac was astonished, the chancellor wrote, that Frederick had not informed the *basileus* of his arrival, so that the Greeks could have provided the crusaders with a "hospitable welcome" and "a good market." Nevertheless, Isaac was sending men to await Frederick in Sofia. The emperor responded that he had in fact sent envoys to Isaac: Bishop Hermann of Münster, Count Rupert of Nassau, and the imperial chamberlain, Markwart of Neuenburg. In the meantime Frederick had received a letter from them, notifying him of their arrival in Constantinople after a difficult journey and indicating that they were awaiting Isaac's return from Philadelphia. So far the basic problem in German-Greek relations seems to have been missed communications, aggravated by mutual suspicion of each other's intentions.[8]

Around the same time, messengers from Stephen Nemanja and his brother Count Casimir notified Frederick that their masters would meet him in Niš, east of the Morava, in modern Serbia, and promised him their services and obedience. The brothers welcomed the emperor on 27 July "with great ceremony" in Niš. The city had been partially destroyed in the fighting between Béla and Andronicus and recently occupied by the Serbs, who had expanded their lordship as far east as Sofia. The grand zupan supplied the crusaders with copious amounts of food and wine and gave Frederick six seals, a tame boar, and three tame deer. Stephen and his two brothers sought to be enfeoffed by the emperor of the Romans with the lands they had conquered. Frederick demurred on the grounds that he did not wish to be distracted from his "pilgrimage against the oppressors of the land of Jerusalem" or to harm any other Christian ruler, including the king of Greece, if the latter honored his commitment to provide "trustworthy guides and good markets." He did give his consent, however, to the proposed marriage of the daughter of Berthold IV of Andechs, who was the duke of Dalmatia, to Stephen's nephew, whose father was the ruler of the Serbian provinces adjacent to Dalmatia. Peter, the ruler of the Vlach–Bulgarian confederation, likewise sent his greetings via letters and messengers to Frederick and promised to assist him against his enemies. Barbarossa may not have harbored any designs of imperial world dominion; yet his very meeting with the Serbian zupan, who had ended Byzantium's lordship in the western Balkans and occupied Greek territory, was, in the eyes of Constantinople, a hostile act.

Isaac's cousin Alexius also arrived in Niš with assurances from the *basileus* that Frederick would be provided with proper guidance and markets throughout Greece if he came in peace. The duke of Braničevo had disobeyed Isaac's orders, Alexius claimed, by not giving the crusaders correct directions and the services they required. A Greek army under Alexius' command was assembling in Sofia to fight the Serbs, but Frederick was not to harbor any suspicions about Byzantine intentions. All Alexius' words were, "Ansbert" said, lies.

Frederick continued to be concerned about maintaining discipline in the crusading army. The servants and boys, under the pretext of gathering fodder and supplies and in connivance with their knightly masters, were stealing from the local population and so violating the peace ordinance. On the advice of the princes, Bishop Godfrey of Würzburg preached a sermon in which he reminded the assembled host how God had denied the Israelites victory because Achan, in violation of Yahweh's command, had stolen a precious garment, silver, and gold from the ruins of Jericho. Godfrey's words had the desired effect, and the servants' conduct improved.

Since the crusaders were going to enter potentially hostile Greek territory, the emperor divided his army into four squadrons. His son Duke Frederick headed the vanguard. Berthold of Vohburg and Hermann of Baden went with him. The Bohemians and Hungarians, each with their own standard-bearer, formed the second division. (Duke Frederick of Bohemia, who had taken the cross, had died; but his men were keeping their crusading vows.). Berthold IV of Andechs led the third unit. Bishop Godfrey accompanied him. The emperor was in charge of the remaining forces. Among the individuals who were under Frederick's direct command were the archbishop of Tarentaise, the bishop of Meissen, the count of Holland, and sixteen other counts. Although Count Rupert of Nassau was one of the envoys whom Frederick had sent to Constantinople, he was granted the coveted honor of being the standard-bearer of the fourth contingent. Later at Philippopolis (today Plovdiv, Bulgaria), Frederick organized a separate division composed of the infantry and the stronger servants.[9]

The crusaders left Niš and their "friends," the Serbian counts, on 30 July. The old Roman road from Niš in the Morava valley to Sofia, toward the southeast, ran through mountainous, heavily forested terrain. The two passes along the way had been blocked with felled trees covered with rocks. The inhabitants of the region, who were variously identified as Greeks, Vlachs, and Bulgarians, repeatedly ambushed the crusaders, shot poisoned arrows at them, stole their goods, and killed many foragers. Many of the men suffered from malaria and dysentery. The leaders of the army finally realized that it was necessary to protect the supply train with archers and knights. The vanguard of Swabians and Bavarians under Duke Frederick and the third division under Duke Berthold and Bishop Diepold of Passau beat off numerous attacks and captured many bandits, who were summarily hanged. Some of the attackers were more than peasants and shepherds irate at the foragers' theft of a chicken or lamb. Two sons of a local count with at least 100 men attacked Berthold and Diepold, who had only a dozen knights at their disposal. Fighting with swords and spears, the Germans put the attackers to flight and hanged twenty-four of them by their feet like wolves. On 13 August the crusaders finally reached Sofia, which had been abandoned by most of its inhabitants, who had taken their foodstuffs with them. Diepold wrote to Duke Leopold that the army suffered greatly from a shortage of wine. Neither the chancellor John Dukas nor Isaac's cousin Alexius was there. "Ansbert" thought Isaac was responsible for the crusaders' hostile reception east of Niš; Diepold assigned the blame specifically to the duke of Braničevo.[10]

Bishop Peter of Toul and the Lorrainers caught up with Frederick the day after he left Sofia, 14 August. A Greek force of 500 men had occupied the last and highest pass through the Balkan mountains, the so-called Trajan's Gates, on the road from Sofia to Philippopolis in the Maritsa valley in southern Bulgaria. "Ansbert" said that Frederick himself took some of the knights and after a brief fight put the Greeks to flight, whereas Bishop Diepold reported that the Greeks fled without a fight at the sight of the scouts of Duke Frederick's vanguard. In any case, the crusaders arrived on 20 August at Pazardzhik in the Maritsa valley, west of Philippopolis, where they found abundant supplies.[11]

Conflict with Isaac II Angelos

A Hungarian count, Lectoforus, whom Frederick had sent, perhaps already from Čuprija, to Constantinople, met the emperor in Pazardzhik and may have informed him about the hostile reception of his envoys in the Byzantine capital. The crusaders arrived outside Philippopolis on 24 August and a nearby Greek army fled at their approach. A Byzantine envoy, James of Pisa, delivered a letter from Isaac the next day; Frederick learned that his ambassadors had been shamefully mistreated in Constantinople. The bishop of Münster, the count of Nassau, and the chamberlain had been robbed of their possessions, mocked in the presence of Saladin's envoys whose favor Isaac was currying, and imprisoned under squalid conditions. On 26 August the crusaders entered Philippopolis, which had been abandoned and was filled with provisions. According to "Ansbert," thereafter they freely plundered the Greeks' property and destroyed what they could not steal.

Bishop Diepold, who had presumably either read Isaac's letter himself or had been present when it was read to Frederick, wrote to Duke Leopold that the Greek king had arrogantly styled himself the emperor of the Romans—titles were always a source of tension between the two empires—"an angel of God and the source of our faith." Isaac, who addressed Frederick as "the king of Germany," had learned from the kings of France and England and the duke of Braničevo that the emperor was planning to put his son, Duke Frederick, on the Byzantine throne in Isaac's place. Moreover,

Isaac deemed Frederick's "treaty of friendship" with Stephen Nemanja a hostile act. He would implement, therefore, the agreement his envoys had negotiated with Frederick at Nuremberg, namely, to provision his army and to allow the crusaders to cross the Dardanelles—but only after Frederick sent him hostages. According to *The History of the Pilgrims*, which supplemented the information contained in "Ansbert's" account, Isaac demanded that Duke Frederick, six bishops, and other princes join the three imprisoned envoys as hostages. Finally, the *basileus* wanted half of the land that the crusaders would conquer from the Saracens. Diepold indicated that the "emperor and the princes were extremely annoyed," but deemed it wiser and more diplomatic to reply to the Byzantine envoy that they would consider a favorable response to Isaac's requests when Frederick's envoys had been released. "Ansbert" said Frederick received the letter "with his customary mildness, opposing his complete humility to the unbridled pride of that man (Isaac)"; but he did not send a formal reply until later.[12] (Since the Trier chronicler also reported that Frederick had concealed his anger with a smile when he learned that Urban III had consecrated Folmar as archbishop of Trier in 1186,[13] the emperor may have learned, as he matured, the wisdom of controlling his temper.)

The crusaders' further transit through the Byzantine Empire was blocked because they could not cross the Dardanelles straits without naval support. They would stay in Philippopolis until 5 November 1189, treating the lodgings in the town and the surrounding vineyards and crops as their own. Meanwhile, Frederick contacted the nearby Byzantine commander, Isaac's nephew Manuel Kamytzes, and indicated that the crusaders wanted only to travel quickly and unhindered through Greek territory. Since the commander did not respond, Duke Frederick attacked the Greeks before dawn on 29 August and killed fifty of them while the others fled. On either 30 August or 6 September, Duke Frederick and Berthold of Andechs captured, without a fight, the city of Berrhoë (today Stara Zagora, Bulgaria), northeast of Philippopolis, and returned with abundant provisions. The imperial marshal Henry of Kalden seized and garrisoned a castle called Scribention. Bishop Diepold and Duke Berthold joined the marshal in taking two other towns and ten castles. "Ansbert" indicated that Frederick could have occupied all of Macedonia if he had not been constrained by his desire to liberate the Holy Land. In return for being allowed to live in peace, the Armenians and some of the Bulgarians who lived in the surrounding villages swore fealty to Frederick and agreed to supply the market in Philippopolis for the duration of the crusaders' stay. When some adolescents in the army plundered the market, Frederick ordered those who were apprehended to be beheaded; the Armenians were subsequently even more willing to take care of the crusaders' needs.

To exert greater disciplinary control over the army, Frederick divided the knights into fifty-man units under the command of pentarchs, who were responsible for both military matters and the settlement of disputes under the overall jurisdiction of the imperial marshal. "He also chose," "Ansbert" said, "sixty of the best and wisest men from the army, by whose advice and direction all the affairs of the army might be ordered." Later, for the sake of efficiency, their number was reduced to sixteen.[14]

Frederick, who had so far ignored Isaac's "vainglorious and quite unworthy embassy," now sought to procure the release of his three envoys. He sent to Constantinople a canon of St. Victor's in Mainz, Werner, and the knight Godfrey of Wiesenbach, whom he had previously dispatched to the sultan of Iconium. They were to reassure Isaac that Frederick had not enfeoffed Stephen Nemanja with Greek territory and had not conspired with any other ruler against Byzantium. They were also to remind the *basileus* of the agreement his chancellor, John Dukas, had made in Nuremberg and that the imprisonment of the imperial ambassadors was an unprecedented crime that brought Isaac into disrepute. Isaac detained Werner and Godfrey, too. The *basileus* finally yielded, perhaps, because as Bishop Diepold wrote to Duke Leopold on 11 November, all of Macedonia as far as the walls of Constantinople was under Frederick's control, the Vlachs were his allies, and the Armenians his loyal subjects. On 28 October Bishop Hermann of Münster, Count Rupert of Nassau, his kinsman Count Walram, Count Henry III of Diez, the chamberlain Markwart of Neuenburg, Werner, and Godfrey arrived, to great rejoicing, in Philippopolis. "Ansbert" said that Frederick wept with joy. Diepold reported that more than 3,000 fully armed knights rode out at least six miles to greet the envoys, many crusaders shouted "*Hiute here din tach*" ("Today, Lord, is Your day"), and that Frederick, weeping, embraced the bishop and Count Rupert.

The next day, 29 October, the three envoys provided Frederick and the assembled crusaders with a detailed account of their mistreatment. To add to their injuries, Isaac had given the Germans' best horses to Saladin's envoys. The Saracens had then ridden the horses in circles around Frederick's representatives and had made mocking, insulting gestures. Even worse, the patriarch of Constantinople, John Dositheus, had preached on feast days that the pilgrims were "dogs" and that any Greek who killed 100 crusaders, even a Greek who had murdered ten other men, would be absolved from all his sins. Frederick wrote to his son Henry VI in mid-

November that the envoys had been returned to him "like goods well used" and that Isaac had pocketed more than 2,000 marks belonging to them.

The chancellor, John Dukas, and four other Greek nobles had accompanied the envoys to Philippopolis; and Frederick received them after he had heard his ambassadors' report. They handed him a letter from Isaac. Once again, Isaac offered, in the words Frederick wrote to Henry: "safe transit [across the Hellespont], an abundance of ships, good markets and the customary exchange [rate]." After all that had transpired, Frederick did not trust Isaac's promises, whose tricks had been revealed, "Ansbert" said, by the envoys and by Armenians loyal to Barbarossa. Frederick informed Henry: "as the popular saying goes, 'he who has been burned fears the fire.'" He demanded that Isaac back up his promises, Diepold wrote, by giving "as hostages his son, brother and uncle." "Ansbert" accused "the crafty Greek emperor" of having deliberately postponed the crusaders' crossing of the Hellespont until winter. Isaac was planning, with the assistance of the Turks and Cumans, to attack the pilgrims when they were on both sides of the Dardanelles, while Isaac's and his allies' galleys would surround the ships transporting other crusaders across the strait and kill them. Was "Ansbert" imagining such a scheme or had the Armenians, say, betrayed such a plan to Frederick? We cannot know how much the Germans and the Greeks were by this point simply ascribing the worst intentions to each other.

Both "Ansbert" and Diepold reported that Frederick took particular offense at Isaac's salutation of him as "king of the Germans." Their accounts of the emperor's angry response are so similar that they may either be transcribing some semblance of his actual words (or, more likely, the words that a learned cleric addressed to the Greeks on his behalf) or some sort of borrowing occurred between the two narratives. There was only one Roman emperor, Frederick declared, just as there was only "one universal father" of the Church. The imperial dignity had been transferred from Constantinople back to Rome under Charlemagne. The pope had consecrated Frederick as emperor, and he had ruled the Empire, without challenge, for more than thirty years (Diepold said "for almost thirty-eight years"). Even Manuel I, when the two rulers had been enemies, had not denied Frederick his rightful title, Diepold noted. Isaac had betrayed, according to "Ansbert," their "fraternal love" by his non-brotherly treatment of Frederick's envoys. (Diepold wrote that Isaac's actions mocked his self-designation as "holy.") Frederick insisted that he would have no further dealings with Isaac until he greeted him with proper respect and had compensated the envoys for their losses. The Greek envoys, citing Frederick's speech as a pretext, had no other choice but to withdraw. "Ansbert" observed that the emperor's words were not without effect, because in his next letter Isaac greeted Frederick as "Emperor of Germany" and thereafter as "'the most noble Emperor of ancient Rome.'"[15]

After John Dukas and his colleagues had left Philippopolis, a messenger arrived with a letter from King Béla of Hungary, who had learned of the dissension between his son-in-law Isaac and Frederick. Since the crusaders were not making progress on their pilgrimage, the king requested that the Hungarians be allowed to withdraw. Frederick, who was preparing to leave Philippopolis and feared that the Hungarians' departure would weaken his forces, did not respond immediately. On 5 November he and the main body of crusaders proceeded down the Maritsa towards Adrianople (today Edirne, Turkey), 130 miles northwest of Constantinople; but the archbishop of Tarentaise and the bishops of Liège, Passau, Münster, and Toul remained behind, because Frederick did not want the Greeks to reoccupy Philoppopolis. The crusaders reached Blisimos (Čirpan?) on 7 November and stayed there until 14 November. Frederick himself returned to Philippopolis for secret discussions with the bishops, and on 19 November he gave the Hungarians permission to go home. Three Hungarian counts or barons stayed with him, while six counts and the bishop of Rába left. Frederick sent two envoys with them: one to Béla to explain in detail Isaac's deceptions and lies, the other to Henry VI.

Frederick's letter to his son was written between 16 and 19 November and recounted what had occurred after the crusaders entered the Byzantine Empire. ("Ansbert" inserted the letter into his narrative and made extensive use of its content.) The emperor had decided to winter at Philippopolis, while Duke Frederick would stay with a substantial portion of the army at Berrhoë, about ten miles away. Since it would be impossible to cross the Dardanelles until he had received "men of great distinction and importance" as hostages for Isaac's good behavior and until he had subjected the Byzantine Empire to his authority, Frederick requested that Henry procure galleys and other ships "in Genoa, Venice, Ancona, Pisa and other places" to meet him in mid-March at Constantinople. The Italians were to attack the city from the sea while he did so from the land. (Did Frederick discuss with the bishops the plan to attack Constantinople during their secret negotiations in Philippopolis?) Henry was to collect the money that Frederick was owed in various places, with the assistance of the chancellor, the proto-notary, the imperial ministerial Werner II of Bolanden, and the notary Richolf, and was to dispatch the funds to his father's agent in Venice for transmission to Tyre. It was necessary to raise these additional sums because of the unexpected delay caused by Isaac's intransigence and because Frederick had not received the money he was owed by Ancona, Metz, Bremen, and the count of *Honau* (Baldwin V of Hainaut?).

Although he had "a host of chosen knights in the army of the life-giving Cross," what the emperor really required was intercessory prayers. He requested that Henry make every effort to ensure that Frederick received them and that Henry "act with burning zeal against evildoers." Frederick directed his son to write to Clement III, asking him to preach a crusade "against the enemies of the Cross, and especially against the Greeks," because the patriarch of Constantinople had publicly announced in St. Sophia, in the presence of Frederick's envoys, that he would grant an indulgence to any Greek who killed 100 pilgrims. Parenthetically, Frederick instructed his son to complete and guard the palaces at Kaiserswerth and Nijmegen. More than 100 crusaders had died so far, Frederick reported, and many horses had been lost. Isaac had imprisoned many pilgrims, especially those from Provence and Soest near Cologne, who had planned to meet Frederick in Constantinople. The Greeks had abandoned every town and castle between Philippopolis and Constantinople. At the same time, Frederick wrote a similar letter to his first cousin Leopold of Austria, but indicated he was planning to winter in both Philippopolis and Adrianople before proceeding against Constantinople. He asked for the duke's prayers on behalf of himself and the crusaders and that Leopold forward the letter Frederick had written to Clement, which presumably also called for the summoning of a crusade against the Greeks. The tragic events of 1204 could easily have occurred in 1190.[16]

The emperor and the main force of the crusaders arrived on 22 November in Adrianople, where they wintered. From there, the way led due east to Constantinople or south to the Dardanelles. They harried the countryside. Bishop Conrad III of Regensburg, with the aid of a burgher of Regensburg who was familiar with the area and spoke Greek, took a city northeast of Adrianople. On 24 November Duke Frederick captured Didymōtichon, south of Adrianople, which Cumans and Greeks had bravely defended, and killed everyone except the women and children; only three German knights died. The seneschal, Markwart of Annweiler, and the butler, Conrad of Waldhausen, seized a castle to the east of Adrianople. On 7 December the emperor dispatched Duke Berthold IV of Andechs, the count of Holland, and the advocate of Passau, Frederick of Berg, to Philippopolis to escort the garrison he had left there to Adrianople. "Ansbert" said they had 1,200 armed men under their command; according to *The History of the Pilgrims*, they had 300 knights at their disposal. On their way, the commanders learned that the Greeks had ambushed and killed fourteen men in the retinue of the bishop of Passau. The crusaders spotted the band and in the ensuing battle killed more than 300 Greeks—it is impossible to verify the accuracy of any of these figures. Frederick of Berg, followed by the bishop of Passau and Berthold, ravaged the area between Philippopolis and Thessalonica to the southwest and seized an abundance of supplies. When they discovered in the churches depictions of the Greeks sitting on the necks of the pilgrims, they burned the churches.

Frederick also charged Duke Berthold and the others to meet with Stephen Nemanja at the Bulgarian passes to procure Serb assistance for the planned assault on Constantinople. The meeting did not occur. But around Christmas 1189, Peter, the lord of the Vlachs, offered to send Frederick 40,000 Vlach and Cuman archers in the spring for the coming campaign, in exchange for the crown of the Byzantine Empire. Frederick sent a friendly response but did not commit himself.

However, negotiations continued for a peaceful resolution of the conflict with Isaac. As "Ansbert" noted, Frederick's goal was "to fight against the invaders of the holy city of Jerusalem and he greatly regretted the unprofitable prolongation of our exile in Greece, especially since he inwardly detested the shedding of Christian blood," which was being spilled in their encounters. Accordingly, the emperor indicated, both through letters and envoys, that he was prepared to leave the area as soon as concord had been restored between the two realms, and he had been guaranteed a safe passage across the strait and access to markets. Since Isaac had mistreated his previous envoys, Frederick was insistent, however, that the *basileus* give him hostages. Finally, on the day before Christmas a high-ranking Byzantine official, Eumathios Philokales, and James of Pisa, who had conveyed Isaac's message to Frederick on 25 August, appeared to accept the crusaders' terms only then to object to previously sworn clauses. The irate crusaders declared war on the Greeks.[17]

At the end of December and in early January 1190, Duke Frederick went on raids throughout Macedonia and procured so many provisions that some called him in jest the "steward of the army." On one such raid, he got as far as Enez at the mouth of the Maritsa river on the Aegean Sea. Upon his return to Adrianople, he ranged through the forests and mountains surrounding the city, where the crusaders had been repeatedly ambushed, and recovered the weapons that had been taken from them. To stop the duke's sorties, the inhabitants promised to supply the market in

Adrianople, and as a token of their good faith returned eighteen horses they had stolen. However, they then set upon and killed the men whom the emperor had sent to arrange the holding of the market.

Nevertheless, the opportunity to obtain booty and the enforced idleness were so great, "Ansbert" reported, that there was a serious breakdown in discipline among the crusaders in both Adrianople and Philippopolis. Drunkenness and fornication were rampant. Those who were zealous for the Lord's cause stripped the clothes from fornicators, both men and women, whom they caught, paraded them naked "around the city by a rope tied to their genitals," and on some occasions even dunked them in the icy river. The author of *The History of the Pilgrims* likened Frederick's punishment of sexual transgressors to the actions of Phineas, the grandson of Aaron, who slew an Israelite and the Midianite woman he had brought back to his tent. On Frederick's orders, the crusaders who had remained in Philippopolis abandoned the city on 15 January 1190 and burned it.

Both Isaac and Frederick thus had ample reasons—the devastation of Byzantine territory and the breakdown in morale among the crusaders—to make peace. On 21 January Eumathios Philokales and James of Pisa, who had visited Frederick on Christmas Eve, returned with another peace offer. The emperor sent the nobleman Berthold of Hohkönigsburg, who had been the imperial legate in Tuscany during the sixth Italian campaign, and the imperial ministerials, Markwart of Annweiler and Markwart of Neuenburg, back to Constantinople with the Byzantine emissaries to negotiate a peace agreement. Duke Berthold IV of Andechs also arrived from Philippopolis on 21 January along with an embassy from Stephen Nemanja, who was eager for discussions. Berthold had been unable to execute his earlier mission to meet with the Serbian zupan at the Bulgarian passes and volunteered to do so now. He set off on 22 January.

Around the same time, the cleric Eberhard, whom Frederick had dispatched to Béla on 19 November 1189, came back with letters from the Hungarian king to Isaac, criticizing his son-in-law for his hostile reception of the crusaders. Béla was also angry at the crusaders on account of Duke Frederick's destruction of Didymōtichon. In addition, Eberhard brought Frederick the latest news from the West: the deaths of Henry II of England on 6 July 1189 and of William II of Sicily on 18 November; Henry VI's claim to the Sicilian crown on Constance's behalf; and the pending departures of Philip Augustus of France and the new English king, Richard the Lionheart, on the crusade. Finally, the cleric horrified the crusaders with the report that the Bulgarians had disinterred the bodies of the pilgrims who had been buried along the road.

The resumption of peace negotiations did not stop the raids. Duke Frederick took the deserted city of Arcadiopolis (today Lüleburgaz between Adrianople and Constantinople) on 1 February 1190. The next day, in the duke's absence, there was an encounter between his men and a Byzantine mercenary army of Vlachs and Cumans. Afterwards the two sides exchanged prisoners and horses. The Bohemians took and plundered with great success an unnamed coastal town. A contingent comprising the men of Bishop Godfrey of Würzburg and of the counts of Salm, Wied, and Sponheim devastated territory belonging to the Vlachs, captured two abandoned towns and slaughtered, allegedly, 5,000 people in a third town. Another force, led by Count Frederick of Abenberg and Frederick of Berg, the advocate of Passau, fought "the enemies of the army of the Holy Cross," who lived south of Adrianople, killed many of them, and seized much booty.

In the meantime, the crusaders who had left and burned Philippopolis on 15 January had detoured and also burned Berrhoë after plundering it, and had reached Constantia (today Harmanli on the Maritsa, upstream from Adrianople). Duke Berthold of Andechs had been unable to meet Stephen Nemanja, but, after making contact through a messenger with the zupan, had joined the crusaders in Constantia. On 5 or 6 February they arrived in Adrianople and for first time since 5 November 1189, the entire army was assembled in the same place.[18]

On St. Valentine's Day 1190, Berthold of Hohkönigsburg and the two Markwarts, accompanied by Eumathios Philokales and James of Pisa, returned from Constantinople to Adrianople with a written peace accord. The "Emperor of Constantinople" renounced any claims for compensation for the losses the Byzantine Empire had suffered, promised to pardon all his subjects—Greeks, Armenians, and Latins—who had aided the "Emperor of the Romans," and pledged to release all the men of the Roman Empire, both pilgrims and merchants, whom he had imprisoned since the outbreak of hostilities. Isaac agreed to provide 220 ships to transport the crusaders' horses across the strait and fifteen fully equipped galleys, so that Frederick could guard his army while it crossed either at Gallipoli (today Gelibolu), where the Sea of Marmara enters the Dardanelles, or further to the southwest, close to where the Dardanelles reaches the Aegean Sea. Isaac was to grant the crusaders two coastal towns on the Asian side, where the army could rest afterwards; but they were not to harm the towns or their inhabitants. The Byzantines were required to establish markets along the crusaders' route and to charge them the same prices Isaac paid. If his subjects failed to provision the crusaders, the crusaders could deal with the inhabitants as they saw fit, except that the crusaders could not alienate the Byzantines' land to unbelievers, presumably the Turks in Asia Minor. The Greek army was to stay a four-day march "from the army of Christ and the Emperor of the Romans" during its transit through the Byzantine Empire. Isaac agreed to compensate the imperial envoys, with Frederick's advice, for their losses during their captivity. "[F]ive hundred of the better men of the city and the empire" were to swear in St. Sophia, in the presence of the patriarch, that Isaac and his subjects would observe the terms of the peace; and the patriarch was to sign the agreement as proof of his adherence. As security, Isaac was to give Frederick "twenty-two carefully selected hostages of the royal kin and ducal rank," who were specifically identified and were to accompany Frederick as far as Philadelphia. (Other sources, including "Ansbert" elsewhere, give different numbers of hostages.)

For their part, Frederick and the crusaders were to leave Adrianople for the Hellespont within twenty days. They were not to harm or burn the settlements along the way and were to "refrain from the unnecessary seizure of animals and clothing," but could requisition grain and wine. Five hundred knights swore in Constantinople on 22 February 1190 that the crusaders would observe the accord. The Greek hostages arrived in Adrianople on 27 February.

"Ansbert" indicated that the whole army had favored an attack on Constantinople if Isaac had not yielded. Frederick had already sent letters and envoys, according to the chronicler, to Italy, Apulia, and other maritime regions to procure galleys; an army of 60,000 Serbs and Vlachs was, allegedly, at Frederick's disposal for such an assault. With hindsight, it is easy to say that Isaac was foolish not to hasten the crusading army through his domains as quickly and as far from Constantinople as possible; but he sat uneasily on the Greek throne, and he had every reason to be suspicious of Frederick's ties to Genoa, Pisa, the Normans, the Serbs, the Vlachs, and the Turks. Beyond that, no one in Constantinople had forgotten that relations between Manuel I and Frederick had often been strained. Fortunately for Byzantium, Frederick was probably sincere in his determination to reach the Holy Land; and so we will never know whether he could have captured Constantinople in 1190.[19]

The Seljuk Turks

On 15 February, the day after Frederick had received the written text of the accord with Isaac, Tokili, an envoy of Sultan Kilic Arslan II, and Godfrey of Wiesenbach whom Frederick had sent to Iconium, also arrived in

Adrianople. Isaac had imprisoned them for eight weeks and stolen their property, including the present that the sultan had sent Frederick. (Isaac promised reparations.) Kilic Arslan styled himself in his letter to the emperor as the "'great lord and ruler' of the Turks, Armenians and Syrians," and promised Frederick, whom he greeted affectionately, his assistance and markets throughout his realm. Three days later the sultan's son, Qutb al-Dīn Malikshāh, whom "Ansbert" called *Malik*, king of the Arabs, sent a letter with similar assurances. "Ansbert" was quick to point out, with the benefit of hindsight, that their promises were false; but what neither he nor Frederick understood was that the Seljuk rulers had little control over the nomadic Turcomans in central Anatolia, and that while Kilic Arslan had retained the title of sultan and his nominal overlordship, he had surrendered effective authority to his nine sons, a brother, and a nephew. Qutb al-Dīn had established himself, with the help of the Turcomans, as the dominant figure in Iconium. He was less inclined than his father to cooperate with the crusaders, and was in contact with Saladin, who recognized the danger of the approaching German army to the Muslim position in Syria. In fact, "Ansbert" reported the rumor that the crusaders found in Iconium the dowry "the evil Saladin had given him [Malik] along with his daughter."[20]

Before his departure from Adrianople, and on the advice of the princes, Frederick required all the knights to swear to obey him alone until six weeks after they had left Antioch. (It is striking that the knights did not automatically owe fealty to the emperor.) He ordered the pentarchs to make lists of all the knights under their command and their places of origin, and the emperor then relieved the pentarchs of their duties because they were unpopular with the men. Isaac's unnamed great steward requested that Frederick join a large Byzantine army in attacking the Vlachs; and Peter, whom the Vlachs called the "Emperor of Greece," likewise sought Frederick's assistance. He turned both of them down.

The vanguard of Swabians and Bavarians under Duke Frederick left Adrianople in the direction of the Dardanelles on 1 March, and Frederick followed the next day. No paved Roman road led from Adrianople to Gallipoli, so the crusaders suffered greatly during Holy Week because the incessant rain had turned the land into a quagmire. After Palm Sunday (18 March), they abandoned their wagons and loaded most of their supplies onto pack animals. Frederick had sent Berthold of Hohkönigsburg and Markwart of Neuenburg ahead to reconnoiter, and they must have decided that it was better to cross the Dardanelles at Gallipoli than closer to the Aegean. (A lesser nobleman and a ministerial thus assumed a role that lay princes and warrior archbishops had played earlier in Frederick's reign.) The two envoys had ordered Venetian ships that were transporting grain and other provisions to Constantinople to remain in Gallipoli to supply the crusaders. The Venetians had disobeyed and had set sail, but a contrary wind had blown them back to port, and they were soon relieved of their cargo. Pisans, who had received the emperor's summons to send ships to besiege Constantinople, also docked and were eager to aid him.

Duke Frederick was the first to cross the Dardanelles on Maundy Thursday (22 March), and the remainder of the Swabians and Bavarians followed on Good Friday and Holy Saturday. A downpour prevented the rest of the army from sailing on Easter Sunday (25 March), so they celebrated the Resurrection on land. The emperor, escorted by five galleys filled with warriors and other ships, was the last to leave Gallipoli on 28 March. Eighteen Greek hostages accompanied him (not the twenty-two he was originally promised), and he released thirteen of them immediately. The other five stayed with the army until Philadelphia. Frederick sent a last letter to Henry VI from the banks of the Dardanelles, informing him about the resolution of the quarrel with his "brother Isaac, the emperor of *Romania*." (The letter says the Greeks provided eighteen hostages and breaks off abruptly with his beloved son, Duke Frederick, on the verge of crossing the strait. Frederick indicated that he had returned all the cities and castles he had occupied, but not that the crusaders as well as the Greeks had sworn in Constantinople to keep the peace.) The crusaders got rid of their remaining wagons, and on 29 March they set out once again for the Holy Land. "Ansbert" commented that the one fortunate thing about the long delay in Adrianople was that the crusaders were spared marching across Anatolia in the winter cold. The heat of late spring was to prove equally deadly.[21]

The crusaders did not follow the easier but longer coastal route. Instead, they headed due east, south of the Sea of Marmara, for three days, and then turned south to Philadelphia (today Alaşehir). Much of the terrain was hilly, forested, and depopulated from decades of Turkish raids and border fighting. Supplies were hard to procure. Dean Tageno of Passau recorded in his diary on 7 April that when they met the road that came from Constantinople, the crusaders furnished themselves with sufficient provisions for seven days because they were going to travel through an uninhabited region. The Greeks continued to rob and kill stragglers. On one occasion, Frederick of Berg, the advocate of the church of Passau, caught a band of marauders and killed more than sixty of them. "Ansbert" was quick to ascribe such attacks to the Greeks' "customary treachery," but in reality

Isaac's authority was minimal; his siege of the usurper in Philadelphia the preceding summer had, for example, been unsuccessful.

Not surprisingly, the crusaders were disappointed on 21 April by their reception in Philadelphia, the last major Byzantine outpost in the interior of Asia Minor. The governor and citizens had not prepared the substantial market Isaac had promised and greeted those who ventured into the city with insults. In the ensuing melee, some of the crusaders were arrested and held as prisoners overnight; and their goods were seized. When Frederick demanded an explanation the following morning, the governor and the leading citizens swore an oath of purgation, blamed young hotheads for the trouble, and compensated the emperor and the crusaders. They also reminded the crusaders, according to "Ansbert," that Philadelphia was a frontier bastion in the defense of the Christian faith and that its destruction would thus be a far greater sin than the burning of Philippopolis. The Bohemians and the knights of Bishop Conrad III of Regensburg had already launched an attack on one of the gates of the city and had struck and wounded with their arrows some of the defenders on the walls. Frederick, satisfied with the governor's explanation, called them off. In spite of these provocations, the emperor graciously released the remaining five Greek hostages. Italian archers, apparently mercenaries who had entered the Byzantine Empire for a variety of reasons, joined the crusaders in Philadelphia and subsequently fought valiantly against the Turks.

When the army left Philadelphia on 22 April, some citizens attacked the rearguard but were quickly dispersed. There may have been more to this encounter than "Ansbert" chose to say, because the author of *The History of the Pilgrims* reported that 500 cavalrymen assaulted the rearguard with a considerable loss of life among the Greeks. The next day the vanguard made contact with the Turks for the first time, and more than fifty Turks died. The crusaders marched towards Laodicea (today Laodikeia) in the Maeander valley (today the Menderes), southeast of Philadelphia. Most of their horses were weak from a lack of fodder, and the men had consumed most of their supplies, except for their bread. They passed two ruined Greek cities and entered Turkish territory. The valley was fertile, and they camped on 26 April on the plain outside Laodicea. Tageno noted that the Turks "received them cheerfully and with all humanity, and provided as best they could a market for the army." The sultan's envoys awaited them.[22]

"Ansbert," relying on Tageno's diary, declared that between 28 April and 18 May, when the crusaders occupied Iconium, "we were beset by evils unheard of in past ages." For three weeks they crossed the high arid steppes and rugged terrain of central Anatolia. Much of the time they lacked water and sufficient food for themselves and adequate pasture for their horses. Most of the Greek population had fled, so little land was under cultivation. Turcoman nomads, over whom the sultan exercised little control, shot arrows, almost continuously, from a safe distance at the crusaders and prevented them from foraging. "Ansbert" stated explicitly that "[i]n this desperate situation all our men, insofar as they had arms, marched in their armor . . ."

East of Laodicea, on 27 April, the crusaders passed by a salt lake, in a region that Tageno insisted was "incapable of supporting crops or human life." They found, however, large flocks of animals, including even camels, about 5,000 in all; but the nomads had fled at the army's approach. Yet, oddly, the crusaders could not find forage for their horses that night. They refrained from taking anything because they trusted the assurances of goodwill they had received three times in a span of less than two years from Kilic Arslan. Early on the morning of 30 April nomads entered the crusaders' campsite after the main force had departed, in the hope of stealing the property they had left behind and of capturing the men who were too exhausted to continue. Frederick, cleverly, had a smoky fire lit; and the crusaders were able to kill nearly 300 Turks blinded by the smoke. The surviving nomads trailed the crusaders, and on 2 May there was another encounter with a similar outcome.

The crusaders were warned on Ascension Day, 3 May, that more than 30,000 Turks, allegedly, were waiting for them at the same narrow pass where the Seljuks had destroyed Manuel's army. A Turkish prisoner showed them an alternative route, "accessible only to the mountain goats." The Turks rained arrows and rocks at the crusaders from above, and Duke Frederick was wounded—he is said to have lost one or two teeth. Some of the crusaders scrambled up the mountainside and killed more than sixty Turks. Many of the horses and pack animals perished on the precipitous descent to a fertile valley, where, unknown to Frederick, the crusaders slaughtered Turks, including "their wives and little children." Food was in very short supply.

Both Magnus of Reichersberg and "Ansbert" reported in nearly identical words taken from Tageno an incident when, either on 4 or 5 May, "we knew for certain that the friendship and the gold of the sultan 'was [sic] turned into dross.'" The sultan's envoys, who had accompanied the crusaders since Adrianople (really Laodicea?) as both hostages and spies, fled on a pretext and took Godfrey of Wiesenbach as a prisoner with them. Both chroniclers explained that Kilic Arslan had reached an agreement with the

Greeks, "since they could not resist us in battle, they would destroy us with treachery." From this point onward, the crusaders were dealing not only with nomadic raids but also with resistance organized by Malik, probably not in collaboration with Isaac as Tageno thought, but rather, like Isaac, in collusion with Saladin.

On the way to Philomelium (today Akşehir), which the crusaders reached on 7 May, the Turks again assaulted the rearguard. To everyone's great sorrow, the noted *Minnesänger*, Frederick of Hausen, who had served as one of Frederick's envoys to Baldwin V of Hainaut, fell from his horse in pursuit of the Turks and died. On that evening the Turks attacked the crusaders' camp outside Philomelium. Under the leadership of Frederick VI and Berthold of Andechs, the Christians beat off the Seljuks. The crusaders learned later that they had killed 4,174 Turks—the figure is too precise to be true—and that another 600 were unaccounted for.

By this point, many of the men were starving. An ox or a cow sold for five or even nine marks, and a small loaf of bread for one mark. Horse or mule flesh was deemed a delicacy. Some of the people on foot were so exhausted by the long marches and lack of food that they crossed themselves, said the "Our Father," and, waiting for death, lay down on the ground in the shape of the cross. The Turks who followed the army beheaded them and made them instantaneous martyrs. A few people were so desperate that they converted to Islam.

The Turks attacked daily. On 14 May the crusaders were confronted by, allegedly, 300,000 horsemen under the command of the sultan's sons—the author of the letter about Frederick's death said there were a mere 40,000 Turks but only 600 mounted crusaders. Frederick ordered the first line of crusaders, led by Henry of Kalden, the imperial marshal, to charge; and the Seljuks fled. Louis of Helfenstein, the brother of Bishop Godfrey of Würzburg, saw a man on a white horse and clad in white raiment, who was believed to have been St. George, striking down the Turks. The emperor then led a force up a mountain held by two of the sultan's sons. The Turks retreated, and Duke Frederick pursued them. Malik himself was knocked off his horse.

After a day of "great heat and hardship," the army found itself at sunset on 14 May in a waterless desert. Many of the horses died, and the men were reduced to drinking their own urine and the blood of their horses. Some even chewed horse dung to extract some moisture. They finally reached a bog on 15 May, but could find no fuel to cook their horse meat. So they burned their saddles, tents, and clothes. The next day the Turks killed sixty boys who lacked armor. On 16 May Malik's envoy offered Frederick safe passage through the sultanate and the opening of a market three days later, in exchange for 300 *centenarii* (hundredweights) of gold and the crusaders' acquiescence to the Turks' annexation of the neighboring realm of the Armenians. Frederick turned down the offer as unbecoming to an emperor or a knight in Christ's army. The envoy responded that the Turks would fight the crusaders the next day. The crusaders were disheartened, but the bishops entreated them to call upon God and St. George, who had been seen already on several occasions—perhaps not quite so miraculously by the brother of Bishop Godfrey. Tageno noted in his diary that even Frederick was apprehensive but kept his fears to himself.

On the morning of 17 May the crusaders attended Mass and received the sacrament. A large number of Turks surrounded them, but while the Muslims yelled and attacked the crusaders as they proceeded toward Iconium, the Seljuks lost sixty of their own men without inflicting any deaths on the Christians. The crusaders spent the night outside the city in the sultan's park, which had abundant vegetation and water; but thunderstorms disturbed their sleep. According to the letter-writer, the crusaders destroyed two of the sultan's palaces located in the park.[23]

On 18 May, at dawn, Frederick divided the army between himself and his son. The clergy, knights who no longer had their own weapons (according to the letter-writer, there were scarcely 500 knights who still had horses), the common people, and the pack animals marched between the two units. The emperor prohibited any plundering, if the army was victorious, until the Turks had capitulated. While these preparations were being made, the sultan and Malik sent an envoy with a final peace offer. Frederick made further negotiations contingent upon the release of Godfrey of Wiesenbach, but then decided that the overtures were a ruse designed to delay an attack. Frederick ordered his son to advance. When the duke reached the gate of Iconium, the sultan released Godfrey who assured them that God would place the city into the crusaders' hands. Kilic Arslan, with 600 knights, ventured out of the city; but at the sight of Duke Frederick's forces, he and his men took refuge in the citadel. Most of the inhabitants, carrying their valuables and plentiful provisions, followed them. The duke captured the city, which the letter-writer said was about the size of Germany's largest city Cologne; and his men slaughtered everyone, including women and children, whom they caught. The knights would have stormed the citadel that night, Tageno noted, except that two weeks without adequate nourishment had greatly weakened them.

In the meantime, the emperor and his men who were in the gardens surrounding Iconium were unaware of what was going on inside the city.

"A vast horde of Turks"—the letter-writer placed their number at a highly improbable 200,000—surrounded them. The bishops and priests put on their vestments and said Mass in preparation for martyrdom. Tageno, who presumably was with the other clerics, likened the knights who defended the clergy to the Theban legion; under the leadership of St. Maurice they had been martyred by Emperor Maximian (r. 286–305), because the soldiers had refused to sacrifice to the pagan gods. "In their midst," Tageno wrote, "was that glorious Emperor of the Romans Frederick, to whom no equal could be found in the whole world." Although he had conquered "Tuscany, Lombardy, Apulia and Burgundy," Tageno continued, Frederick cried and said that he was prepared to die if through his death "the Christian army" was able to reach Antioch. He concluded by shouting the words of acclamation for medieval rulers: "May Christ rule [us], Christ be victorious, Christ command [us]." Then, although he was tired from his exertions, Frederick led the charge and scattered the enemy. About 3,000 Turks died. It is impossible to tell how much of this story is really true—Barbarossa may well have played the role that was expected of him. In the eyes of most of Christendom, Iconium was the moment of Frederick's rehabilitation.

Duke Frederick welcomed his father in the city, and the vast stores of food they discovered in Iconium satisfied the men's hunger. They also found "gold, silver, jewels and purple cloth" with an estimated value of 100,000 marks.

The next day the crusaders celebrated their victory with a Mass. The sultan and his sons sued for peace, and Frederick, eager to continue on the road to Jerusalem, was content with the terms of his original agreement with Kilic Arslan: safe conduct for the crusaders and the provision of good markets. Ten emirs and ten barons served as hostages for the accord's implementation. The crusaders, overcome by the stench of decaying bodies, left Iconium on 23 May and camped again in the sultan's park. There Kilic Arslan had set up a market where the crusaders were able, at a steep price, Tageno observed, to purchase more than 6,000 horses and mules, as well as asses, and ample provisions.[24]

The crusaders left Iconium on 26 May and continued their trek across the steppes to the southeast. They passed through a well-watered region, but the Turks continued to harass them. Frederick warned the hostages that they would be killed if the attacks did not cease. After that threat, the Turks no longer bothered the army. (The immediate cessation of the attacks raises the question how much Malik had orchestrated the earlier difficulties.) Kilic Arslan adhered to his agreement with Frederick and provided the crusaders with a good market on 28 May. Late on 30 May the army reached Laranda (today Karaman) at the eastern end of the Anatolian steppes, within sight of the Taurus mountains, and at the limits of the sultan's control. On the night between 1 and 2 June the crusaders were awakened by the noise of an earthquake, which they mistook initially, the letter-writer said, for the sound of the Turks charging them but which they subsequently realized was an omen of Frederick's approaching death.[25]

Death

The crusaders were overjoyed when they left Laranda and saw crosses planted in the ground in an Armenian village. Tageno wrote in his diary: "We had neither seen nor heard for a long time anything of those who belonged to the glorious Christian religion." The Turkish hostages demanded they be released, but Frederick, on the princes' advice, placed them under stricter guard because the crusaders did not trust the Turks' intentions. The army had to cross the first range of the Taurus mountains to reach the valley of the Saleph (today the Göksu), which flows into the Mediterranean at Seleucia (today Silifke). The fortress of the Armenian prince, Oşin of Sibilia (today Mavga Kalesi), guarded the border and the high pass. He welcomed the crusaders and provided them with a market. They reached the Saleph valley on 7 June and camped besides a lake, where there was good grazing and where they rested for two days; but even the princes had little to eat except horse-meat.

Envoys of the Armenian ruler, Leo II, welcomed Frederick on 7 June and promised him Leo's assistance. There is circumstantial later evidence that Frederick, in his role as Roman emperor, agreed to Leo's elevation to the Armenian kingship but that Frederick's death prevented the coronation. (Archbishop Conrad of Mainz crowned Leo in Tarsus in 1198.) For Leo, the distant Western emperor was a natural ally against the neighboring Byzantines, Turks, and Saladin. Since the Saleph valley passed through a narrow defile, the Armenians advised the emperor about the route the army should follow. Frederick, not wanting to frighten his men and confident that they would find a good market and rest in Seleucia, did not inform them of the difficulty of the route. To escape the daytime heat, the greater part of the army (without the emperor) started to traverse a high mountain during the night of 9–10 June. The customary military formation broke down as each man scrambled by himself along the rocky path. Some bishops and princes even dismounted, while others too sick to walk had to be carried over the mountain in litters. The darkness increased the danger, but on 10 June the vanguard reached the plain below, five miles from Seleucia. Tageno's diary ends at this point.

Frederick himself wanted to avoid, "Ansbert" wrote, "the dreadful heat and . . . the mountain peaks" and opted on the Armenians' advice to follow an equally difficult shortcut along the river. At this point the most contemporary accounts diverge. Magnus of Reichersberg said nothing specifically about the circumstances surrounding Frederick's death. According to "Ansbert," the emperor, against everyone's advice, chose to swim "across the fast-flowing river" and was swept away by the current. The author of the *Letter Concerning the Death of the Emperor Frederick* indicated that Frederick crossed the river safely and ate a meal on the opposite bank. The letter-writer continued: "after the many and terrible exertions that he had undergone in the previous month and more, he decided to bathe in that same river, for he wanted to cool down with a swim. But by the secret judgment of God there was an unexpected and lamentable death and he drowned."

If the letter-writer was in fact Bishop Godfrey of Würzburg, Frederick's former chancellor, he probably witnessed the emperor's death. We know that Frederick, who went bathing with Otto of Wittelsbach in the Adriatic, liked to swim, so the letter-writer's report is the most plausible account of what happened. Did Frederick have a heart attack? No doubt, after decades in the saddle he was in excellent physical condition, and he presumably had sufficient food and water on the trek across Anatolia; but it was very hot, he was exhausted from weeks of marching in armor over difficult terrain, the Saleph was an icy mountain torrent, and he was sixty-seven. (In 1971 the German embassy in Ankara placed a marker at the probable site of Frederick's death.)[26]

The body was brought to Seleucia and embalmed. The crusaders mourned for four days. The intestines were removed and the body was caked in salt. It was then transported 56 miles eastwards on the old Roman coastal road, to Tarsus, the home of the Apostle Paul, where the crusaders arrived around 17 June. The intestines were interred in the cathedral. Some of the crusaders opted to sail for Tripoli, which remained in Christian hands, or to Antioch, where they landed on 19 June. Duke Frederick, who had succeeded his father as leader of the crusade, took the remainder of the army and possibly his father's body overland and reached Antioch in early July. There, the flesh was boiled from the bones of Frederick Barbarossa and buried in a sarcophagus to the left of the altar in the cathedral of St. Peter. According to the necrology of the Austrian monastery of Melk in the diocese of Passau, where much of our information about the crusade originated, the interment had already occurred on 24 June. If this report is true, then Frederick's body must have been shipped by sea and not have been brought by his son to Antioch. Since Frederick would probably have wished to be buried in the church of the Holy Sepulcher in Jerusalem, in all likelihood Duke Frederick took the bones with him from Antioch. He may have interred his father's remains in Tyre or taken them, as some chroniclers reported, as far as Acre, where the duke died on 20 January 1191. If Frederick Barbarossa had died in Germany, he would almost certainly have found his final resting place beside his wife Beatrice and his Salian ancestors in the crypt of Speyer Cathedral; but he would never have become the embodiment of German yearning for national unity.[27]

CONCLUSION

If Henry (VI) had not died in 1150, Frederick Barbarossa would be no better known today than his brother Conrad, the count-palatine of the Rhine. In that scenario, experts in medieval German history might remember Frederick as an Alsatian magnate and as the ruler of the duchy of Swabia as it had been constituted in 1098; but he would not have succeeded, probably, in expanding his power south of the Danube, because his Swabian peers would not have died on his disastrous fourth Italian campaign.

The death of his cousin, Henry (VI), and the failure of his uncle Conrad III to arrange the election of his younger son allowed Frederick, with the backing of his Welf kinsmen, to obtain the crown in a coup aimed against the predominant influence of the late queen Gertrude of Sulzbach's relatives and the Babenbergs. As an accidental king, Frederick had not been prepared for kingship. Unlike his English and French counterparts, Henry II and Louis VII, and his own sons, Frederick was illiterate. This raises the ultimately unanswerable question of how familiar he was with the content of the charters that were written in his name, especially the rationales for their issuance contained in the *arengae*—let alone how well he comprehended Otto of Freising's historical theology or Rainald of Dassel's assertions of imperial world dominion. Their views were not necessarily his.

However, Frederick was not a cipher. He was a man of enormous physical stamina who spent his life in the saddle, went on two crusades, and crossed the Alps six times. He was a courageous, tough warrior, who at the age of fifty-three was in the midst of the fighting at Legnano. After the disastrous outcome of the Second Crusade and the logistical difficulties of the *Romzug*, he learned the need for careful preparation, securing adequate supplies, and maintaining military discipline. The German component of the Third Crusade was the best-organized crusade of the twelfth century, and, to his credit, Frederick prevented the anti-Jewish violence that had marred the First and Second Crusades in Germany and that occurred in England before the Third Crusade. It is impossible to tell how much he was personally responsible for devising the strategy of attrition that led to Milan's defeat in 1158 and 1162, because he had to rely on the forces and the collective judgment of the princes.

Frederick had the ability to secure the cooperation of proud, often cantankerous men. His courts during the first fifteen years of his reign were the gatherings of an extended family, in which the emperor, who was related to most of the key princely players, adjudicated their differences. He was able to gain the lifelong loyalty, indeed friendship, of such men as Otto of Wittelsbach and his companions on the Second Crusade, Rudolf of Pfullendorf and Ulrich of Lenzburg. It is noteworthy that Frederick, unlike his predecessors, never faced a rebellion in Germany. Ironically, the downfall of Henry the Lion, which was long viewed as Frederick's greatest triumph, was his worst political failure because he was unable to protect his cousin from his princely enemies or to secure any great advantage for the crown.

Frederick could be incredibly brutal, for example, when he suspended the prisoners from the siege tower at Crema or amputated the limbs of the Milanese captives. He rarely tempered justice with mercy, as his destruction of Tortona, Spoleto, Crema, Milan, and Susa amply illustrates. Imperial rule in Italy was oppressive but no worse than Norman governance in England or Sicily—or many a modern colonial regime. High medieval society was built on conquest and the exercise of brute force. There is no evidence that Frederick ever heeded Otto of Freising's warning about the dangers of being drawn into Italian internecine conflicts or Eberhard of Bamberg's reminder about the Christian obligation to forgive one's enemies, if the bishop ever offered such counsel. However, as revealed by the emperor's smiling reaction to the news of Urban III's consecration of Folmar as archbishop of Trier, the more mature and aging Frederick may have learned—unlike Henry II and his rash words that led to Becket's murder—the wisdom of controlling his immediate violent impulses.

His favor could be readily bought and often was, but not, as the Milanese and Archbishop Eberhard discovered, when the emperor's honor was at stake. The need to preserve his and the realm's honor was central to Frederick's thinking and conduct. He was so reluctant to accept Alexander as the rightful pope precisely because Chancellor Roland had publicly shamed him at Besançon, and that made Frederick's submission at Venice before thousands of onlookers all the more humiliating. Manly pride did not preclude his crying in public anymore than it did Charlemagne in *The Song of Roland*. Frederick's piety, like his concern for his reputation, was conventional. However, he was attracted to the new religious currents of the twelfth century represented by his godfather, Otto of Cappenberg, and his spiritual counselor, Hartmann of Brixen; and Frederick may have founded hospitals because he had been genuinely impressed by the work of the Hospitalers in Jerusalem. In short, he was a typical German prince of his era, whose primary concerns were the preservation of his honor and the enrichment and continuation of his dynasty

Yet Frederick had to surrender the duchy of Swabia to his young cousin, Frederick of Rothenburg, to secure the crown, and the Staufer's lands along the middle Rhine to his brother Conrad. Without a strong territorial base of his own in Germany and without an heir, the emperor could be the fairly impartial arbiter of the princes' disputes. He turned his attention, instead, to Italy, and was soon caught up in the quarrels of his noble and communal allies and their bewildering shifts of allegiance. It is totally anachronistic to judge that decision by the nationalistic criteria of Wilhelmine Germany or Risorgimento Italy. Frederick was proud of his German ethnicity, as revealed by the circular he issued after the annihilation of his army in 1167; but his other identities, namely, as a Christian, a noble, a knight, and a Swabian, were more important in defining his being. Territories were essentially interchangeable. His Italian wars were not a proto-democratic clash between the agrarian, aristocratic rural north and the commercial, bourgeois urban south, as nineteenth-century liberal historians imagined. Frederick, who promoted the economic development of Aachen, Duisburg, Gelnhausen, and Haguenau, was not oblivious to the power of money. Indeed, the policy of recuperating the crown's alienated regalian rights, many economic in nature, was first applied on the Main in response to the proliferation of illegal tolls that hampered commerce and was subsequently implemented in Italy as well. Frederick failed to establish lasting control in Italy, unlike William the Conqueror in England, because he never had sufficient forces of his own but had to rely on the German princes, the Italian magnates and communes, and mercenaries.

The decimation of Frederick's army in his seeming moment of victory in 1167, which he must have perceived like everyone else as a divine judgment, was the decisive turning point of his reign. The triumphal language disappeared from his charters, and for a decade there was no more talk about a holy empire. He had to abandon the antiquated pretense that as the emperor he could, like Constantine, summon a church council, or like his own ancestor Henry III decide a disputed papal election. Frederick's diminished stature was on display, in a paradoxical way, when he entered the lists at the celebrated Whitsunday court at Mainz in 1184, the supposed apex of German chivalric culture. There were thousands of knights in Europe who could joust, but only one monarch who wore a crown that depicted the Pantocrator and the holy kings of Israel. His death on the Third Crusade redeemed Frederick's reputation, but he went because the pope had summoned the kings and knights of Europe and not because it was the emperor's special responsibility to defend Christendom.

The death of so many princes and nobles on the fourth Italian campaign allowed Frederick to obtain for the first time since his accession in 1152 a major territorial base of his own in Germany and to abandon eventually, however reluctantly, his ambitions in Italy—provisionally at Venice in 1177 and conclusively at Constance in 1183. He became, in effect, one of the German princes, albeit the one with the most prestigious title, who competed for power and land for their sons. The princes ceased to attend his court on a regular basis, and his own itinerary was increasingly confined to the area south of the Main, where most of the Staufer domains were situated. By the 1180s Frederick's exercise of royal authority resembled more the style of governance of Rudolf of Habsburg, the quintessential example of a monarch concerned with the advancement of his own dynasty, than his own form of governance at his accession. Frederick legalized the princes' authority in the *Privilegium minus* and the "Golden Liberty" and so continued the redefinition, in feudal terms, of the relationship between the crown and princes, which had started at Worms in 1122. While no imperial constitution established in 1180 the estate of the imperial princes, who were the tenants-in-chief of the crown and the monarch's chief counselors, no emperor could ever assert, like Louis XIV, that he was the state. The emperor was, henceforth, the head of the imperial polity, and the princes the members. Frederick became in the nineteenth century the embodiment of the German yearning for national unity. In reality, Frederick furthered the decentralization of authority that characterized the Holy Roman Empire—a designation that was first used only in passing during his reign—until the end of its existence in 1806. Perhaps that makes him, after all, an appropriate hero for the German Federal Republic.

EPILOGUE

The Reaction to Frederick's Death

THE INITIAL REACTION TO the news of Frederick's death was mixed. It was the drowning that was inexplicable. Frederick had not died in a battle against the infidel or in the Holy Land, but while swimming or taking a bath. Worst of all, he had died without confessing his sins or receiving the viaticum. The author of the *Cologne Royal Chronicle* expressed the disbelief and grief but also the doubts. "However, in this place and in this sad narrative, our pen fails and our mouth is silent, unable to describe the fear and sorrow that gripped the army of pilgrims in their moment of greatest danger." Yet the chronicler marveled that others had been able to ford without difficulty the stream that had not been especially high, whereas Frederick had drowned. He concluded that "God, whose power no one can withstand . . . had acted as it pleased Him, justly, of course, in accordance with the unchanging and inalterable determination of His will, but yet, if one is permitted to say it, without mercy . . ." Gerald of Wales (c. 1146–c. 1223) wondered why a man who had set out to serve Christ had perished so ignominiously with much of his army. Perhaps, Gerald speculated, God had punished Frederick because he had ascribed the fame he hoped to attain to his own strength rather than to God; or, more likely, God had smitten Frederick on account of the twenty-year schism during which so many clerics and laymen had been mutilated or killed on their way to Rome and St. Peter's had been burned. Since Frederick may not have been truly contrite, God had struck him and his army because the people are often punished for the sins of their prince.

To allay such misgivings about his salvation, some chroniclers changed the story of Frederick's drowning so the dying emperor had a chance to repent. According to Gilbert of Mons, writing in the mid-1190s, Frederick, against the advice of his entourage, had insisted on fording the Saleph on horseback rather than taking a boat. He had nearly drowned in the powerful current, but with the help of God and his men he had made it to the opposite shore. On account of the season, he had been very hot; and he had caught a mortal illness in the icy water and died eight days later. Almost all of Christendom had lamented Frederick's death. Gilbert was certain that if Frederick had lived, he would have been a great help to the Holy Land, "because he seemed more powerful, energetic and courageous than other kings and princes . . . and he had with him all the most virtuous men of his Empire with a great abundance of gold and silver." Gilbert did not say so explicitly, but Frederick presumably had sufficient time to be assured of his eternal well-being during the eight days he lingered on the banks of the Saleph. Nearly a century later, the Franciscan, Salimbene, had no doubts that Frederick had died shriven. After Frederick struck a rock in the river, two knights had pulled the emperor half-alive out of the water; and he was given the sacrament before he died. Albert of Stade, in the 1240s, even turned Frederick into a martyr. The drowning monarch had cried out: "Blessed is the crucified Son of God, who receives me with the water that gave me new life and that makes me a martyr after it made me a Christian!" By the mid-thirteenth century there no longer was any question that the former persecutor of the Church had been granted a good death.[1]

The Conflation of Frederick and his Grandson

If Frederick had died in Germany or if his mortal remains had been interred in Jerusalem or laid besides Beatrice's in the crypt of Speyer Cathedral, his ghost would not have haunted later German history. However, in the Later Middle Ages it was his grandson, Frederick II, who was the subject of apocalyptic imaginings about a returning last emperor ready to punish and/or purify a corrupt Church. The younger man was the subject, from the start of his reign, of eschatological expectations, based on the Book of Revelation and Sibylline prophecies. Frederick II was identified as the Last Emperor who would liberate the Holy Sepulcher in preparation for the Second Coming of Christ. Conversely, adherents of the Calabrian abbot, Joachim of Fiore (1145–1202), thought that the excommunicated emperor fit the description of the Beast of the Apocalypse or the seventh head of the Dragon, if not the Antichrist. When Frederick II died in his bed on 13 December 1250, ten years too soon to fulfill the Joachite prophecies about the beginning of the Third Age of the Holy Ghost, stories spread in

Germany that this Frederick, who had been an absentee monarch, was merely sleeping and would return or that a third Frederick would arise. Several such pseudo-Fredericks appeared in Germany in the following decades. Most famously, the Franciscan friar John of Winterthur reported in 1348, the year of the Black Death, the spread of alarming, popular expectations in southern Germany about Frederick's return. "As soon as he has risen from the dead and stands once more at the height of his power, he will marry poor women and maidens to rich men, and *vice versa* . . . He will see to it that everything that has been stolen from minors and orphans and widows is returned to them, and that full justice is done to everyone." Even worse, "he will persecute the clergy so fiercely that if they have no other means of hiding their tonsures they will cover them with cow-dung . . ."[2]

However, as the centuries passed, it became increasingly difficult to keep the two like-named emperors separate. The conflation of the two Fredericks is apparent in the lengthy title of the so-called *Folk Book of the Emperor Frederick Barbarossa* by an anonymous Bavarian author, which was printed in 1519, after Martin Luther's posting of the Ninety-Five Theses had plunged Germany into turmoil: *A True History of the Emperor Frederick, the First of His Name, with a Long Red Beard, Whom the Italians Call Barbarossa, the Same Won Jerusalem, and through Pope Alexander III was Betrayed to King Soldan [Saladin], Who Held Him Captive Some Time, and How the Bundschuh Arose in Bavaria*. The tale is a curious mixture of misremembered history, legends, and contemporary events. Contrary to the title, Clement III was the pope during the Third Crusade; and it was Frederick II, not Barbarossa, who captured Jerusalem, in spite of the opposition of Pope Gregory IX (1227–41). The jealous Alexander III is alleged to have betrayed Barbarossa to the sultan, who released Frederick after he perceived the nobility of his captive's character. After his release Barbarossa supposedly attacked and defeated Venice, where the pope had taken refuge, and ordered the quadriga to be placed above the portal of St. Mark's, where the four bronze horses stand (and still do today), the unknown author averred, as a symbol of Barbarossa's victory. (There was no such attack on Venice, and the Venetians stole the quadriga from the hippodrome in Constantinople during the Fourth Crusade in 1204.) For the sake of his soul, Frederick made peace with the pope, who out of boundless pride placed his foot on the emperor's neck—this is the first time this calumny about the pope's arrogance appeared in Germany. During the subsequent Third Crusade, Barbarossa was not permanently lost in the Saleph, according to the *Folk Book*, but was alive, peasants said, in a hollow mountain. He would return to punish the clergy and to hang his shield on a withered tree—a metaphor, perhaps, for the cross. The emperor's supposed banner, a *Bundschuh*, a clog that a Bavarian peasant had affixed to a spear, was a symbol of late medieval peasant uprisings. Barbarossa had replaced his Italian-born and absentee grandson in this historically mixed-up version of the legend of the returning emperor.[3]

Barbarossa was alleged to be sleeping in a number of different places, including the Untersberg near Hitler's retreat at Berchtesgaden. However, as early as 1416 the Kyffhäuser in Thuringia, near two other places that resonate in German history, Wittenberg and Weimar, was identified as Barbarossa's hideout. Henry IV (r. 1056–1106) had built on top of the mountain a castle, which Frederick rebuilt and visited at least once (1174), but which had been abandoned by the beginning of the fifteenth century. Rebellious peasants inspired by Luther's teaching of Christian freedom assembled under the leadership of Thomas Münzer at the foot of the Kyffhäuser and were soundly defeated on 15 May 1525. In February 1546 the rumor spread that Frederick Red Beard had risen from the dead and had been seen wandering about the castle ruins. More than three hundred local inhabitants rushed to the site and found a man with a long black beard, who was quickly placed in protective custody for the remainder of his life. In the early modern period Barbarossa's resting place shifted, as he was increasingly mythologized, from the castle to the inside of the mountain.[4]

Frederick's reign lent itself to different confessional interpretations. Luther thought that his protector, the Elector Frederick the Wise of Saxony (r. 1486–1525), a direct descendant of Barbarossa, had fulfilled the prophecy of the returning emperor by freeing the Holy Sepulcher—in Luther's exegesis, the Holy Scriptures—from their imprisonment by the papists. The emperor's capture by the sultan at Alexander's instigation and the pope's treading on Frederick's neck in Venice were proof of the papacy's malignancy. Barbarossa was, in this Protestant narrative, God's protagonist and the defender of the true Church; whereas Alexander was the agent of the Antichrist and of the false Church that sought, in violation of the Gospels, power and lordship on earth. Catholics glorified, for their part, the papal triumph over the emperor at Venice in 1177. During the Enlightenment, when Frederick was of little political relevance, the tale of the sleeping emperor was ridiculed and dismissed as a silly fable.[5]

The Romantic Rediscovery of Frederick

The Romantics rediscovered the Staufer in the second half of the eighteenth century, but their attention focused, initially, on members of the dynasty who were more likely subjects for opera libretti and tragic drama: Frederick's niece Agnes, the count-palatine's sole heir, who had eloped in 1194 with Henry of Brunswick, the son of Barbarossa's arch-enemy and cousin, Henry the Lion; and the last Staufer, the grandson of Frederick II, Conradin, who had died at sixteen on the scaffold in Naples, a victim of the evil Frenchman Charles of Anjou and a treacherous French pope. The Prussian court composer Gasparo Spontini wrote, for example, an opera, *Agnes von Hohenstaufen*, which had its premier in 1829 in Berlin at the wedding of the future Wilhelm I. It did not enter the repertory. There are more than one hundred known plays or fragments of plays about Conradin. Even the young Friedrich Schiller pondered in 1783 writing a tragedy about the last scion of the dynasty.[6]

Barbarossa came into his own only in the bitter aftermath of the War of Liberation (1813–15), when the Congress of Vienna dashed patriotic dreams of a united Germany. In 1816 the brothers Jacob and Wilhelm Grimm, in their *German Folk Tales*, brought the Thuringian legend "Frederick Red Beard on the Kyffhäuser" to the attention of the educated elite. Their emperor is a timeless figure, disconnected from either the Staufer past or the present, whom peasants and shepherds occasionally encountered on the mountain. The Grimms were unfamiliar with the *Folk Book*, and neither the words "Germany" nor "Barbarossa" appeared in their synopsis of the tale.[7]

Friedrich von Raumer, a professor at the University of Berlin, published between 1823 and 1825 the first scholarly history of the Staufer, which provided the raw material for several playwrights. For example, Ernst Raupach wrote sixteen plays about the Staufer, including four about Barbarossa, as well as the libretto for Spontini's *Agnes von Hohenstaufen*. Christian Dietrich Grabbe in his 1829 play about Frederick did not allude to the Kyffhäuser legend, but Grabbe was apparently the first to portray the Hohenzollern as the successors of the Staufer. These widely performed dramas shaped the popular image of Frederick, just as Shakespeare did in the case of Henry V or Richard III. Yet the Revolution of 1848 ended, thankfully, Richard Wagner's plan to write an opera, mixing Germanic and medieval elements, about Barbarossa; the composer called him a second Siegfried who sat in the Kyffhäuser surrounded by the treasures of the Nibelungs.[8]

It was, however, Friedrich Rückert's 1817 poem "Barbarossa" that fixed the Kyffhäuser legend in the German imagination. The poem began:

The ancient Barbarossa,
Friedrich, the Kaiser great,

Within the castle-cavern
Sits in enchanted state.

He did not die; but ever
Waits in the chamber deep,
Where hidden under the castle
He sat himself to sleep
The splendor of the Empire
He took with him away,
And back to earth will bring it
When dawns the promised day.

Frederick is seated, the poem continues, on an ivory chair; and his beard, not flaxen but glowing like fire, has grown through the marble table where he props his head. Half-nodding, he beckons his page to see whether ravens still circle the mountain. If they do, he must sleep "enchanted for many a hundred years."[9]

To hasten the emperor's arrival during the Revolution of 1848, a group of patriots, after obtaining the local prince's permission, climbed up the Kyffhäuser on 31 March, planted the national black-red-gold flag among the castle ruins, and declaimed an anonymous poem, "Barbarossa's Awakening." (The topic was a popular poetic theme.) In this poem the singing arouses the emperor, and he urges the singers to act.[10] Rückert's verses, more than any other, expressed, however, the deepest yearnings of Germans for national unity; and the poem became as familiar to generations of German schoolchildren as Henry Longfellow's "Paul Revere's Ride" was to their American counterparts—the poems are of comparable literary merit. Indeed, after 1871 Rückert's poem was a mandatory part of the school curriculum.[11]

Not everyone shared this enthusiasm for a slumbering emperor. The republican poet Heinrich Heine mocked in 1844:

It would be best, you stayed at home
Here in the old Kyffhäuser—
If I consider the matter precisely,
We do not need a Kaiser.[12]

The Wilhelmine Appropriation of Barbarossa

The south German princes, who had backed Austria against Prussia in 1866 and lost, used the Kyffhäuser legend to signal Berlin that they expected to share in the governance of the new Second Reich as their ancestors had done during Barbarossa's reign. In the spring of 1871, in conjunction with the return of victorious German troops from the Franco-Prussian War, theatricals were staged, among other places, in the court theaters of Stuttgart and Karlsruhe, the capitals, respectively, of the kingdom of Württemberg and the grand duchy of Baden. The Karlsruhe production, *Emperor Red Beard*, by the director of the theater, Otto Devrient, began with the recitation of Rückert's poem. The dreaming Frederick was seated in the Kyffhäuser, his life's work long destroyed by the internal feud with the Welfs and external wars with the French. French assassins had murdered Conradin and his loyal companion, Margrave Frederick of Baden—a not so subtle reminder that Zähringer blood had been shed long ago for the Reich. There were a series of historical tableaus in which the Habsburgs and the French were the villains. God had sent Luther to provide spiritual consolation to the powerless Germans, but the Protestants had not won the Thirty Years War. The Germans had defeated Napoleon during the War of Liberation, but the victory had been followed by a bad peace. So, the ravens had continued to circle. Then, in 1866, Barbarossa had heard the distant tones of the "Watch on the Rhine," had placed the imperial crown on his head, and had shouted "Hallelujah, the hour is here, the hour of salvation!" The ravens had vanished. He had fought in the air above the Prussians in a strategic rewriting of Baden's actual role in the war. The second act showed major battle scenes of the Franco-Prussian War, enacted by real soldiers, whom the enthusiastic audience hailed at the end of the performance. In the grand finale Barbarossa removed the imperial crown from his head and placed it on a giant bust of Wilhelm I.[13]

Before 1871 the Protestant Hohenzollern dynasty and most Prussian historians did not share this Barbarossa mania.[14] Unlike most of their princely peers—the Wittelsbachs of Bavaria, the Wettins of Saxony, or the Zähringer of Baden—the Hohenzollern's ancestors, the counts of Zollern, had not been of princely rank in the twelfth century. The counts had merely been called upon to witness charters that concerned the Staufer duchy of Swabia; Barbarossa did not consult with the Zollern in matters of greater concern.[15] More importantly, the Catholic Holy Roman Empire was identified with the Prussian king's rivals, the Austrian Habsburgs, who had held the imperial dignity for centuries.

Johann Gustav Droysen was a notable exception to this Prussian rejection of the Old Reich. As a delegate to the Frankfurt national assembly in 1848, he had called for the unification of Germany under Prussian leadership because the Hohenzollern deserved to fill the place that had been vacated by the demise of the Staufer. Seven years later Droysen published the first volume of his massive *History of Prussian Politics* (*Geschichte der preussischen Politik*; 1855–86). In the introduction he declared that just as the Staufer—who had begun their rise following their enfeoffment with the duchy of Swabia in 1079—had restored the Empire to its former greatness after the Investiture Conflict, so the Hohenzollern—who had started their ascendency with the acquisition of Brandenburg in 1417—were destined to end Germany's long night. The new state would have an anti-ultramontane or, as Droysen called it, a Ghibelline mission to resist papal pretensions—as Barbarossa had once done.[16]

More typical of the Prussian position prior to 1871 was the stance of the pro-Prussian Heinrich von Sybel, in his famous debate between 1859 and 1862 with the Austrian Julius Ficker about the role of the Holy Roman Empire in German history. The publication of the first two volumes of Wilhelm von Giesebrecht's massive *Geschichte der deutschen Kaiserzeit* (1855–88) triggered the dispute. Giesebrecht declared in his introduction that "the imperial epoch was the period, in which our folk, strong in its unity, attained the highest development of its power, when it had not only disposed freely of its own destiny, but had also commanded other peoples, when the German man counted the most in the world, and when the German name resounded most fully." On 28 November 1859, eighteen days after Austria had been forced to surrender Lombardy to Sardinia at the conclusion of the Italian War of 1859, Sybel, an expert on revolutionary France and the founder of the *Historische Zeitschrift*, attacked Giesebrecht's interpretation in a formal lecture: "About Newer Presentations of the German Imperial Epoch." Otto I's decisions to intervene in Italy in 951 and to assume the imperial crown in 962 had been major mistakes. "The vital energies of the nation, which had formerly been applied with unerring instinct to the colonization of the eastern lands, were from now on," Sybel asserted, "squandered because of a seductive and deceptive chimera of power . . . the German nation followed its rulers on their murderous journeys to Rome against its own will . . ." Even worse, the emperors became embroiled in deadly battles with the papacy, "a fight which was conducted on every ground except that of German national interest," so that after the Investiture Conflict, the German monarchy of the Staufer had been "an incorporeal phantom."

Ficker, a professor at the University of Innsbruck, whose editions of texts and monographs about the medieval German constitution and imperial rule in Italy remain of scholarly value, responded that "the German kingdom displayed an ideal combination of centralized power and local autonomy" and that its political structure "was better suited than any other in history for a sublime, dual task: it could do justice to the national destiny of a people as well as to the ancient Western heritage of universalism," that is, sub voce, just like the Habsburg Monarchy of Franz Joseph I. The Empire's collapse, which Ficker attributed to the battle for the throne that followed the death of Henry VI in 1197 and to the absentee rule of Frederick II, "left a gap in Europe that has never been more clearly felt than in our own time." The real issue in the Sybel–Ficker debate was whether Germany would be united under Prussian leadership, minus Austria, the so-called little German (*kleindeutsch*) solution, or whether the Habsburgs' non-German lands would be included in a central European, great German (*grossdeutsch*) empire. After 1871, Ficker's interpretation of the medieval empire, albeit modified by Droysen's Ghibelline slant, prevailed. In 1893 the Prussian government granted Ficker its highest civilian decoration, and he became a corresponding member of the Prussian Academy of Sciences.[17]

Crown Prince Friedrich, the son of Wilhelm I and the future Emperor Friedrich III (1888), who was familiar with Sybel's arguments and who initially opposed his father's acceptance of the imperial title, quickly recognized its symbolic value, the added prestige it would give to Germany in a world of empires, and its appeal to the other German princes who preferred to be the subordinates of an emperor rather than a fellow king. Inspired perhaps by the example of his English mother-in-law, Queen Victoria, who addressed Parliament from a throne in the House of Lords, Friedrich chose to link the Second Reich to the First. He arranged for Wilhelm to deliver his opening address, on 21 March 1871, to the Reichstag of the newly united Germany from the bronze throne that had been made for Henry IV around 1075 and that had stood for centuries in the imperial palace at Goslar.[18] The crown prince was even favorably disposed to a proposal to crown Wilhelm, using the insignia of the Holy Roman Empire, which were still in Franz Joseph's possession, either in Aachen, where medieval German kings had been crowned, or in Frankfurt, where the ceremony had occurred in later centuries. The scheme was rejected because Chancellor Bismarck saw no reason needlessly to antagonize Franz Joseph, Germany's most likely potential ally, by asking for the surrender of the insignia.[19]

The linkage between the Old Reich and the New, but in a way that suggested Barbarossa was the precursor rather than the equal of Wilhelm, was acted out even more dramatically in the festivities that surrounded the return of the Prussian army from France in June 1871. On 16 June, 42,000 troops, led by Wilhelm, paraded through Berlin. When they reached Unter den Linden, the city's main ceremonial avenue, Berlin's magistrates greeted Wilhelm with the words: "The great work is now completed: Hohenstaufer's glorious scepter now rests in Hohenzollern's strong hand." On Sunday, 18 June, all of Germany joined in a service of thanksgiving. Although this day was the anniversary of Barbarossa's imperial coronation in 1155 and the Anglo-Prussian victory at Waterloo, the date was chosen, inexplicably, to commemorate the Great Elector's defeat of Sweden at Fehrbellin in 1675, even though that battle had been fought on 28 June.

On 17 June Wilhelm hosted a banquet for the German princes at the now demolished city palace in Berlin and a gala performance at the opera. He ordered that the production, a mixture of occasional music and historical tableaus, was to show three major historical epochs: the Seven Years War when the Prussian king Frederick the Great had defeated Austria and France; the beginning of the War of Liberation; and rather vaguely, "'the new time' Kyffhäuser." The play that was originally selected to be performed, by an officer on the staff of Field Marshal Helmuth von Moltke, was rejected as too Prussian, as too militaristic for a celebration of peace, and as an inadequate response to the implied message of the Stuttgart and Karlsruhe theatricals. The actual performance was a hastily improvised concoction, parts of which were borrowed from both the rejected and the Karlsruhe spectacles. The play opened with Barbarossa, surrounded by ravens and subterranean spirits, seated at the table inside the Kyffhäuser. He recalls the past, specifically in the first scene, the Third Crusade and his apparent death in the Saleph, when the spirits had snatched him away to the Kyffhäuser, where he was to remain until he was saved by a divinely sent knight—Wilhelm, of course. Then Frederick dreams, prophetically, about future events and the rebirth of the German Reich: among other things, the Great Elector's capture of the island of Rügen in 1678, Frederick the Great's defeat of Austria at Torgau in 1760, the battle of Leipzig in 1813, and an allegorical representation of the victory of 1870. At the end of the performance, the orchestra played the *Emperor Wilhelm March*, which had been composed for the occasion; the curtain lifted, revealing an equestrian statue of Wilhelm; and pandemonium broke out in the audience. In short, Barbarossa had been integrated into Prussian history.[20]

Bismarck, who had scoffed at the nationalistic exuberance of the Barbarossa cult, quickly recognized its value for inculcating loyalty to the new Reich.[21] In 1872, rather inexplicably at the height of the *Kulturkampf*, the chancellor's fight with the Catholic Church, an extreme ultramontanist,

Johannes Nepemuk Sepp, convinced Bismarck that Barbarossa's bones had been brought from Asia Minor to Tyre and interred in the cathedral, which he had located. Bismarck agreed in 1873 to purchase the site and to finance excavations conducted by Sepp and Hans Prutz, a lecturer at the University of Berlin who had just written the first scholarly biography of Barbarossa. The recovered remains were to be reinterred in Germany's foremost Catholic shrine, Cologne's unfinished Gothic cathedral. In spite of its opposition to Rome, the Prussian government was underwriting the completion of the church to symbolize Germany's new national unity. Fortunately, the bones were never found or they might have rested in proximity to the possibly equally fraudulent Magi on the high altar.[22]

The Wilhelmine appropriation of Barbarossa culminated in two extraordinary monuments: the reconstructed palace at Goslar and the Wilhelm I monument on the Kyffhäuser. Henry II had initiated the enlargement of the modest royal manor at Goslar in 1017, and the new palace became a favorite residence of Frederick's Salian ancestors, Conrad II and Henry III. By the mid-nineteenth century the palace, the oldest extant building in Germany that had been used for secular purposes, was in ruins. After Prussia annexed the kingdom of Hanover in 1866, the government began the restoration of the structure. Wilhelm took a personal interest in the project, and in 1875 he and the crown prince visited the palace. In 1876 the ministry of culture asked for proposals to decorate the main hall, a room 42.2 meters long, 15.19 wide, and 5.84 high (Fig. 14). The announcement specified that the proclamation of the Second Reich was to be depicted in a vaulted space at the center of the west wall. This painting was to serve as the backdrop for the throne from which Wilhelm had addressed the Reichstag in 1871. Hermann Wislicenus, a professor at the Düsseldorf Academy of Fine Arts and a well-known painter of historical frescoes, won the competition; and he and his assistants spent nearly two decades painting fifty-three pictures.

There were seven large windows on the east wall and doors in the middle of the shorter south and north walls. The story of Sleeping Beauty, that is, Germania, was depicted on the south wall next to the windows. Above the door on the opposite north wall, Wislicenus portrayed Wilhelm, on his visit to Goslar, as the prince who awakens the princess. *Barbarossa's Awakening* (Fig. 15) appears on the north wall, next to the windows and opposite *Sleeping Beauty*. The emperor, wearing the imperial crown, is already standing with an unsheathed sword in his hand. He looks toward the allegorical representation of the founding of the Second Reich at the center of the west wall. Beneath Barbarossa the artist showed, in a predella, the bier of Queen Luise, who had vainly pleaded with Napoleon, after Prussia's defeat in 1806, for leniency and whom Prussian hagiography had turned into the inspiration for the War of Liberation. Her husband Friedrich Wilhelm III and her sons, Friedrich Wilhelm IV and Wilhelm I, kneel beside the casket. Field Marshal Blücher, who led the Prussian forces at Waterloo, and others kneel nearby, while the volunteers of 1813 leave to fight the French in the War of Liberation.

Wislicenus embedded the *Proclamation of the Reich* in a historical cycle that begins in the southwest corner, next to the door in that wall, with Charlemagne's destruction in 772 of the Irminsul, the idol of the pagan Saxons. Below it, the artist showed the baptism of their leader, Widukind. The cycle ends on the opposite wall with Luther at the Diet of Worms in 1521 and with the Protestant princes and their wives receiving, below the larger painting, the sacrament in both kinds. In other words, this was a Ghibelline interpretation of medieval German history that starts with the Catholic universal empire of Charlemagne and ends with a Protestant but divided Germany, in which the pope and the princes are presented as the villains. Three large paintings flank, on either side, the *Proclamation of the Reich*, at the center of the west wall. The three paintings to the left depict the imperial coronation of Henry II, the builder of Goslar, by Benedict VIII; Henry III crossing the Alps in 1047 after he had removed three rival popes, with a snarling Hildebrand, the future Gregory VII, accompanying the caged, deposed Gregory VI; and Henry IV in Mainz after his son had deposed him in 1105. The last painting replaced Wislicenus' original proposal to show Henry IV's humiliation at Canossa, which the ministry of culture rejected—at the height of the *Kulturkampf*—as inappropriate.

In the first large painting to the right of the *Proclamation of the Reich*, Barbarossa kneels in 1176 before his cousin Henry the Lion, begging in vain at Chiavenna for military assistance against the Lombards. In the two smaller paintings beneath this scene, Barbarossa, as a precursor of Luther, rejects at Besançon in 1157 Adrian IV's insinuation that the Empire was a papal fief and receives at Erfurt in 1181, in a reversal of fortune, his defeated cousin. The middle painting shows the victorious Frederick at the battle of Iconium during the Third Crusade. Below it, Wislicenus presented Frederick's meeting after the battle with his son Duke Frederick VI of Swabia and the removal of the emperor's body from the Saleph. Barbarossa was the subject of three additional smaller pictures: Henry the Lion's enfeoffment with Bavaria (1156), the capitulation of Milan (1162), and the great court in Mainz where Barbarossa's two oldest sons were knighted (1184).

In the *Proclamation of the Reich* (Fig. 16), Wislicenus chose not to show the actual scene in the Hall of Mirrors at Versailles but an allegorical representation. The painting, befitting the public enactment of the Barbarossa–Wilhelm linkage, is a combination of a medieval triptych and a theatrical stage with columns separating the side panels or loges from the central panel. The German princes are in the left box, and King Ludwig II of Bavaria offers Wilhelm, in a completely imaginary scene, the crown—there was no crown and Ludwig was not at Versailles. In the right box, Empress Augusta and Crown Princess Victoria hold palms of victory, and the future Wilhelm II stands at his mother's knee. Wilhelm's Prussian predecessors, with the Great Elector and Frederick the Great in the most prominent positions, decorate the proscenium arch. Wilhelm and, behind him, the crown prince are on horseback at the center of the main panel or stage. Two standing women, the personifications of Alsace and Lorraine, which had been restored to the Reich, are to the men's right; while to the emperor's front and left, Bismarck swings a hammer on the cornerstone of the Second Reich on which Germany will be built. Field Marshals Moltke and Roon, the architects of Prussia's military victories, accompany the chancellor. Queen Luise, garbed as Germania, holds the crown of the medieval empire over her son's head; while Barbarossa, like God the Father at the baptism of Jesus, points in approbation to the scene below. Lest the viewer failed to see the connection between Frederick and Wilhelm, equestrian statues of Barbarossa and Barbablanca, or White Beard, as Wilhelm came to be known in an analogy with Frederick, were erected between 1899 and 1902 outside the entry to the palace (Fig. 17).

Oddly, no member of the imperial family attended the dedication of the great hall on 29 March 1897; and Wislicenus received only a minor decoration as a reward for the two decades he had devoted to the project. Wilhelm II objected to the depiction of the founding of the Reich as the culmination of German rather than Prussian history and to the suggestion that Bismarck and the princes had played anything but subordinate roles in its establishment. The Second Reich was, in his view, the sole creation of his grandfather, Wilhelm the Great; and Wilhelm II was thus, implicitly, the divinely ordained ruler of the new polity. The young Kaiser closely monitored the program of the Kyffhäuser Monument to ensure that it conveyed this outdated ideology.[23]

Wilhelm I died on 9 March 1888. On 22 March, Alfred Westphal, the executive director of the national veterans' organization, proposed that it finance and construct a monument to the emperor on the plateau on top of the Kyffhäuser (Fig. 18). The biggest remnant of the ruined castle, which was first mentioned in 1118 and which had stretched for over 600 meters on the western end of the ridge, was the keep or so-called Barbarossa Tower. The architect Bruno Schmitz designed a monument 81 meters high and 130 meters wide, carved partially into the mountainside and rising above the eastern end of the plateau. Like Mount Rushmore, it can be seen from miles around. The equestrian statue of Wilhelm, in uniform, at the top of the mountain, is 9.7 meters high; and two allegorical figures are seated at his feet: a Germanic warrior, the embodiment of War, and History who holds in her left hand an oak wreath, a symbol of victory, and whose right hand rests on a tablet with the words "Sedan-Paris-1870." A tower 57 meters in height, capped by the heraldic crown of the Second Reich (no such object existed), rises behind the statue. Schmitz had proposed that the statue face the keep at the other end of the plateau, but Wilhelm, at his grandson's insistence, turns his back to the castle. The completed monument dwarfs the 25-meter-high Barbarossa Tower. The connection between the Old Reich and the New was thus symbolically severed.

The much smaller statue of Barbarossa was carved into the mountainside below the tower and the equestrian statue on top of the plateau (Fig. 19). It is situated at the back of a 25-square-meter courtyard, which is surrounded by a heavyset, neo-Romanesque arcade. The sculptor Nikolaus Geiger used Michelangelo's *Moses* as a model. For financial reasons not all the boulders were removed, so the work looks unfinished. Unlike at Goslar, where Barbarossa is already on his feet with a sword in his hand, Geiger depicted Frederick at the very moment of his awakening. His arms still rest on the back of his throne, and he appears to be reaching with his right hand for his sword while his left moves toward his beard. The overall impression is one of decay and, like medieval representations of the Church and the Synagogue, of supersession.

The veterans had proposed that cannon and military standards be added to the complex, but Wilhelm II vetoed the proposal because their inclusion would have suggested that the Reich had also been the creation of the folk in arms rather than his grandfather's sole accomplishment. He also rejected in 1897, for a similar reason, a recommendation that statues or busts of the princes, generals, and statesmen who had played a role in the foundation of the Reich, and who had been depicted in Goslar, be placed in the large hall at the base of the tower. The Kaiser dedicated the monument on 18 June 1896, the twenty-fifth anniversary of the victory celebration in Berlin. At the insistence of the local regnant prince, Bismarck was invited to the ceremony; but he declined to attend. Wilhelm II did not mention Barbarossa in his dedicatory speech, though he did name one of the five battleships in the emperor class, the *Barbarossa.* A tower was subsequently erected in Bismarck's honor next to the keep. Symbolically, Barbarossa and Bismarck had been exiled to the western end of the Kyffhäuser in the Kaiser's glorification of the Hohenzollern.[24]

Operation Barbarossa

After the fall of the monarchy in 1918, the monument acquired a new symbolism. Field Marshal Paul von Hindenburg, the supreme commander of the German forces in World War I and the honorary president of the veterans' organization, spoke of the Kyffhäuser spirit (*Kyffhäusergeist*), the faith and determination to rebuild the fatherland, at the ceremonies that commemorated in 1921 the twenty-fifth anniversary of the monument's dedication. In the 1920s the veterans proposed that a monument to the war dead, comparable to the memorials in London, Paris, and Washington, be erected on the Kyffhäuser; but these proposals were never implemented. During the Third Reich a plaque honoring the two million fallen soldiers of World War I, the dead of the *Freikorps* (the right-wing paramilitary groups that had suppressed leftist uprisings in Germany after the country's capitulation and that had fought the Bolsheviks and Poles), and the martyrs of the Nazi movement was placed in the hall at the base of the tower. The hall was also decorated with battle flags and urns containing soil from the territories Germany had ceded at Versailles. Most important of all, it was decorated with busts of Gerhard von Scharnhorst, who had rebuilt the Prussian army after 1806, Bismarck, Field Marshals Moltke and Roon, Crown Prince Friedrich, and, of course, Hitler. Barbarossa had been linked visually to the Führer and German hopes of regaining the country's lost eastern lands (Fig. 20).[25]

However, naming the attack on the Soviet Union in June 1941 after Barbarossa was not quite as inevitable as the Nazi iconography of the Kyffhäuser Monument might suggest. Hitler rarely visited the monument, which was too closely associated with Prussia's aristocratic traditions and whose style did not fit with his own architectural preferences.[26] Besides, Barbarossa had focused his military efforts on Italy, not the East, a delicate topic because Mussolini was Germany's main ally. Revealingly, drawings of historical battles, which were prepared in 1940 for a proposed set of tapestries that were to be hung in the new chancery, excluded the Staufer and their Italian campaigns.[27]

Moreover, some German historians, most notably Georg von Below, had revived in the 1920s Sybel's critique of the medieval emperors' foreign policy. Von Below declared: "One thing is certain: the true area for German expansion and activity was to the north or the east." Henry the Lion, who had conquered the lands north and east of the lower Elbe, was an example of what might have been.[28] While the duke could be depicted, as was the case in the Goslar frescoes, as the most brazen example of princely particularism, his ruthless expansion in the Baltic made him a hero for many Nazis, including Heinrich Himmler, who financed Karl Jordan's edition of the duke's charters. The Lutheran church of St. Blasien in Brunswick, which Henry had built and where he and his wife were buried, was deconsecrated and turned into a national shrine. After the flight of Hitler's deputy, Rudolf Hess, to Scotland in May 1941—just as Henry had once sought refuge in England—Hitler dismissed Henry as a peasant "smallholder" (*Kleinsiedler*). The name "Operation Barbarossa," which appeared for the first time on 18 December 1940 in Directive No. 21, as the German general staff was planning the invasion, was, apparently, Hitler's personal choice—perhaps because an emperor, not a rebellious duke, was the proper inspiration for the Führer.[29] Whatever Hitler's motives, the name was the culmination of the nationalistic appropriation of Frederick that had started after the War of Liberation.

Since 1945

After the war Friedrich Heer, Austria's leading postwar public intellectual and cultural critic, likened Frederick's Italian policies to Hitler's in occupied Europe. In *The Tragedy of the Holy Reich* (1952), Heer depicted Frederick's chancellor, Rainald of Dassel, as guiding "the 'reactionary' policies of Frederick I to world historical excess" between 1157 and 1167. The "Germans" imposed on the Italian cities a "lordship of horror" that utilized "fear and terror." After Rainald's death, Barbarossa abandoned his adviser's attempt to restore the old sacral-political organization of society that had existed before the Investiture Conflict and returned to the more realistic views of his youth. The result was that Germany experienced between 1170 and 1220 the first of its three great flowerings of culture (the other two were the Age of Dürer and the Age of Goethe). The collapse of Rainald's policies left the Reich, however, politically and socially divided. Perhaps Heer hoped that the latest catastrophe in German history would have similar cultural consequences and, even, that the Vienna of the film *The Third Man* would resume its traditional role as a bastion of Western civilization; he declared that the palaces Frederick built were the precursors of Austria's great Baroque abbeys, the symbols of the triumph of the Counter-Reformation and of the Habsburgs' defeat of the Turks.[30]

The Cold War and the future of a divided Germany influenced the postwar scholarly debate about Frederick's policies. In 1959 Hans Joachim Kirfel denied that Barbarossa and Rainald had sought world dominion and had perceived other monarchs, like Heer thought, as dependent rulers or "shadow kings" (*reguli*). While poets, legists, and canonists found such ideas in classical literary and legal texts and repeated them in their own writings, Frederick's relations with the kings of England and France were based on a policy of friendship and alliance with equals.[31] East German historians like Gottfried Koch propounded an odd mixture of *kleindeutsch* nationalism and historical materialism. They retorted that their Western colleagues, in the service of German imperialists and in a policy of "national nihilism," were invoking the chimera of a common European or Western identity, an utterly reactionary concept, and were denying the aggressive nature of the medieval Empire. Contrary to what Kirfel had argued, the Empire had not promoted the development of individual nations.[32]

The Kyffhäuser Monument, which was located in the German Democratic Republic, posed a perplexing problem for the regime. East German Communists desired its removal—or at the very least the removal of the statues of Wilhelm, War, and History, and the crown on the top—because the monument was a symbol of German militarism; but the Soviet occupation authorities favored its retention as a token of their commitment to German reunification. In 1951, Prime Minister Otto Grotewohl decided that the monument should be kept for the time being; and it was depicted in 1990 on one of the last East German stamps to celebrate the end of Germany's postwar division.[33] The delicious irony is that in 1888 the architect Bruno Schmitz designed the chief landmark of downtown Indianapolis, the Soldiers' and Sailors' Monument, a symbol, presumably, of the triumph of American democracy during the Civil War; and that the work of Henry Hobson Richardson, which Schmitz saw in Boston, inspired the supposedly quintessentially German, neo-Romanesque style of the Kyffhäuser *Denkmal*.[34]

Barbarossa's awakening could also be invoked, however, on behalf of the "other" Germany, the good Germany of Bach and Beethoven, even if Frederick had shown no interest in the efflorescence of German literature that occurred at the end of his reign.[35] Frederick had already been connected in Weimar to German high culture at the laying of the cornerstone of the statue to Goethe's patron, Grand Duke Karl August of Saxony-Weimar-Eisenach, on 3 September 1857, the hundredth anniversary of the grand duke's birth; and the next day at the dedication of the monument to Goethe and Schiller in front of the court theater. On the evening of 3 September the director of the theater, Franz Dingelstedt, staged a play of his own devising, *The Harvest Wreath* (*Der Aerntekranz*). The play opens with Barbarossa sleeping in the Kyffhäuser, surrounded by the customary accoutrements required by Rückert's poem about him. The moment of his awakening is the duke's birthday. In a Thuringian village, in an idyllic image of social harmony, the people—peasants, the schoolmaster, invalids—celebrate the duke and the two poets, Goethe and Schiller. The scene ends with a parade, the playing of marches, the singing of Luther's "A Mighty Fortress is Our God," and the waving of the grand duchy's and other German flags. In the finale, Barbarossa declaims:

> Hail you, pantheon of the Germans! Hail you, Weimar, Ilm-Athens!
> Eternally may your princes, your poets enjoy fame!
> . . .
> If the power that you possessed, as my scepter led you,
> Remains denied to you, although it is an inheritance that rightly belongs
>   only to you,
> So conquer, so preserve in art and knowledge
> Your spirit's inner unity, your free strength of ruling!
> In the course of days, the day, even after a long night, will come
> In which you and your princes will be reinstated in their old power;
> And on this harvest day, this feast of jubilee filled with joy,
> Your Emperor Frederick returns
> And with him returns your Karl August![36]

As the example of Karl August shows, it was the princes in 1800 as well as 1200 who patronized German artists. The disastrous experience of a unified Germany inspired in the postwar Federal Republic a new appreciation for a more decentralized political structure and for the princes who had promoted Germany's economic, social, and cultural development during the High Middle Ages—even if there is little continuity between the medieval princely territories and the modern German states, which are largely creations of the nineteenth and twentieth centuries.[37] In 1977, to celebrate the twenty-fifth anniversary of the establishment of the state of Baden-Württemberg and to overcome the lingering tensions between the two former states, the government staged in Stuttgart the exhibition *Die Zeit der Staufer* (*The Epoch of the Staufer*)—because the Staufer duchy of Swabia was the heart of the new postwar state. It should be stressed that the date had no particular significance in the dynasty's history.

In the preface to the exhibition catalog Hans Filbinger, the prime minister of Baden-Württemberg, indicated that the Staufer era was unique in German history because it was the only time when great cultural and intellectual achievements coincided with the growth of the state and the economy. Germans have more difficulties with history than other nations, he said, because they inherited great moments like that of the Staufer and terrible ones like that of the recent past. Under the circumstances it was tempting to forget history, but no folk could escape the past. The highest goal of the great Staufer rulers had been a humane one. They had not wanted to establish a tyrannical state but rather a universal order of law and peace. The Staufer wished to protect the individual from arbitrary power, and even, in the context of their times, to advance human freedom. Filbinger conceded that no one would be so foolish as to equate the medieval concept of freedom with that of the present-day democratic, egalitarian, and constitutional state; but the modern understanding of freedom originated in the age of the Staufer.[38] Perhaps it is cynical to note that in the course of furthering law and peace, Barbarossa destroyed the cities of Tortona, Spoleto, Crema, Milan, and Susa, that he would have dearly loved to add Alessandria to the list, and that Filbinger was forced to resign in 1978 over revelations of his actions as a lawyer in the navy during the war.[39]

The Cappenberg Head appeared on both the posters advertising the exhibition and on the cover of the five-volume exhibition catalog, which is approximately 2,586 pages. The exhibition was an astonishing success. Instead of the anticipated 300,000 visitors, 671,000 viewers saw the exhibition in a span of seventy-two days. The initial run of 20,000 catalogs sold out immediately; in the end visitors purchased 153,000 sets and 13,000 copies of the Cappenberg Head poster.[40] Barbarossa had retained his grip on the German imagination.

In 2010 another Staufer exhibition was held in Mannheim, the second-largest city in Baden-Württemberg: *Transformations of the Staufer Realm: Three Innovative Regions in High-Medieval Europe.* Baden-Württemberg and the states of Rhineland-Palatinate and Hesse sponsored the exhibition about the regions that comprised the heartland of the Staufer Empire: the Rhine–Main–Neckar area, northern Italy, and the kingdom of Sicily. The editors of the scholarly volume that was published in advance of the exhibition explained that while the 1977 show had concentrated on Germany, both scholars and the public were more interested at the beginning of the twenty-first century in the European connections among the Continent's historic regions with which they identified.[41] The emphasis in the articles, unlike in 1977, was on Frederick II, in part because Sicily, which Barbarossa never ruled, was one of the three regions that were highlighted, but also because the Italian-born son of a Sicilian Norman princess was much more European than his German grandfather. In short, the exhibition was an example of what I once facetiously called "Common Market History."[42] It remains to be seen whether the current German disillusionment with the European Union will cause yet another reassessment of Barbarossa's place in history.

For nearly two centuries every German regime has invoked Frederick Barbarossa. Rarely has a historical figure been more misrepresented and his public persona more shaped by legends and momentary political needs. In 2002, to commemorate the fiftieth anniversary of the establishment of the state of Baden-Württemberg, an eight-sided stele was erected on top of the Hohenstaufen. The inscription, in both German and Italian, reads:

Hohenstaufen
A Mountain
A Castle
A Dynasty
An Epoch
A Myth.[43]

ABBREVIATIONS

AQ	Ausgewählte Quellen zur deutschen Geschichte des Mittelalters: Freiherr-vom Stein Gedächtnisausgabe
CEH	*Central European History*
Constitutiones	MGH: *Constitvtiones et acta pvblica imperatorvm et regvm*
DA	*Deutsches Archiv für Geschichte des Mittelalters*; since 1937, *Deutsches Archiv für Erforschung des Mittelalters*
DFI	MGH: *Die Urkunden Friedrichs I.* (*Friderici I. diplomata*)
DKIII	MGH: *Die Urkunden Konrads III. und seines Sohnes Heinrich* (*Conradi III. et filii eius Heinrici diplomata*)
DLIII	MGH: *Die Urkunden Lothars III. und der Kaiserin Richenza* (*Lothari III. diplomata nec non et Richenzae imperatricis placita*)
EHR	*English Historical Review*
FKPM	Forschungen zur Kaiser- und Papstgeschichte des Mittelalters: Beihefte zu J. F. Böhmer, Regesta Imperii
FMG	Forschungen zur mittelalterlichen Geschichte
FS	*Frühmittelalterliche Studien*
HF	Historische Forschungen
HS	Historische Studien
HZ	*Historische Zeitschrift*
Marbach Annals	*Annales Marbacenses*. Available in Latin and German editions.

MF	Mittelalter Forschungen
MGH BdK	Monumenta Germaniae historica: Die Briefe der deutschen Kaiserzeit
MGH SS	Monumenta Germaniae historica: Scriptores
MGH SSrG	Monumenta Germaniae historica: Scriptores rerum Germanicarum in usum Scholarum
MGH UdKK	Monumenta Germaniae historica: Die Urkunden der deutschen Könige und Kaiser
MGM	Monographien zur Geschichte des Mittelalters
MGSL	*Mitteilungen der Gesellschaft für Salzburger Landeskunde*
Milanese Anonymous	*Narratio de Longobardie obpressione et subiectione*
MIÖG	*Mitteilungen des Instituts für österreichische Geschichtsforschung*
NA	*Neues Archiv der Gesellschaft für ältere deutsche Geschichtskunde*
NF	Neue Folge
Otto of Freising, *Chronicle*	*Chronica sive historia de duabus civitatibus.* Available in Latin, English, and German editions.
Otto of Freising, *Deeds*	*Ottonis et Raewini gesta Friderici I. imperatoris.* Available in Latin, English, and German editions.
Otto of St. Blasien, *Chronicle*	*Ottonis de Sancto Blasio Chronica.* Available in Latin and German editions.
QEbG	Quellen und Erörterungen zur bayerischen Geschichte
RI	J. F. Böhmer, *Regesta Imperii*
UB	Urkundenbuch
VF	Vorträge und Forschungen herausgegeben vom Konstanzer Arbeitskreis für mittelalterliche Geschichte
VMPIG	Veröffentlichungen des Max-Planck-Instituts für Geschichte
WF	Wege der Forschung
ZbLG	*Zeitschrift für bayerische Landesgeschichte*
ZGORh	*Zeitschrift für die Geschichte des Oberrheins*
ZRG GA	*Zeitschrift der Savigny-Stiftung für Rechtsgeschichte: Germanistische Abteilung*

NOTES

Introduction

1. Thomas Brune and Bodo Baumunk, "Wege der Popularisierung," *Die Zeit der Staufer: Geschichte—Kunst—Kultur: Katalog der Ausstellung*, 5 vols (Stuttgart, 1977), 3:331. The choice of names proved to be unfortunate because Allied propaganda soon pointed out that Frederick had died on the Third Crusade. Werner Hechberger, "Bewundert—instrumentalisiert—angefeindet: Staufer und Welfen im Urteil der Nachwelt," in Werner Hechberger and Florian Schuler, eds, *Staufer & Welfen: Zwei rivalisierende Dynastien im Hochmittelalter* (Regensburg, 2009), pp. 234–35.
2. Klaus Schreiner, "Friedrich Barbarossa—Herr der Welt, Zeuge der Wahrheit, die Verkörperung nationaler Macht und Herrlichkeit," *Die Zeit der Staufer* 5:521–79. For a general overview of German historiography, see Stefan Berger et al., *Writing National Histories* (London and New York, 1999).
3. Excerpted and translated by Robert Edwin Herzstein, *The Holy Roman Empire in the Middle Ages: Universal State or German Catastrophe?* (Boston, 1966), p. 19.
4. Paul Kirn, "Die Verdienste der staufischen Kaiser um das Deutsche Reich," *HZ* 164 (1941): 263–64.
5. Hermann Heimpel, "Kaiser Friedrich Barbarossa und die Wende der staufischen Zeit," *Strassburger Universitätsreden* 3 (1942): 4–32. When the article was republished in a collection of important articles about the emperor, Gunther Wolf, ed., *Friedrich Barbarossa* (Darmstadt, 1975), pp. 1–25, the offensive introductory words were eliminated.
6. Arno Borst, "Barbarossas Erwachen—Zur Geschichte der deutschen Identität," in Odo Marquard and Karlheinz Stierle, eds, *Identität* (Munich, 1979), p. 20; and Knut Görich, *Friedrich Barbarossa: Eine Biographie* (Munich, 2011), p. 348. Rahewin, in Otto of Freising and Rahewin, *Deeds* 4.86, said Frederick's hair was blond (Schmale edition, p. 708, line 14); and Otto and Acerbus Morena, *Libellus de rebus a Frederico imperatore gestis*, p. 186, described him as ruddy with almost blond hair. In the poetical account of Frederick's deeds, the *Carmen de gestis Frederici I. imperatoris in Lombardia*, written perhaps already in the 1160s, p. 69, lines 2086–87, he is depicted as the "ruddy [red-haired?] king, the leader of the German rage ('rex ruffe, furoris Teutonici ductor')." See below, n. 21, n. 49, and n. 50 for the editions.
7. This presentation of Frederick as a prince draws heavily upon Karl J. Leyser's "Frederick Barbarossa and the Hohenstaufen Polity," *Viator* 19 (1988): 153–76.
8. Herbert Grundmann, "Litteratus—illiteratus: Der Wandel einer Bildungsnorm vom Altertum zum Mittelalter," in *Herbert Grundmann: Ausgewählte Aufsätze*, vol. 3: *Bildung und Sprache* (Stuttgart, 1978), pp. 11–15.
9. It is customary to refer to men who were elected as king in their father's lifetime but who did not actually succeed to the throne with their numerical designation in parentheses. It was Barbarossa's son who became Henry VI.

10. Bernd Schneidmüller, "Konsensuale Herrschaft: Ein Essay über Formen und Konzepte politischer Ordnung im Mittelalter," in Paul-Joachim Heinig et al., eds, *Reich, Regionen und Europa in Mittelalter und Neuzeit: Festschrift für Peter Moraw* (Berlin, 2000), pp. 53–87.
11. On the importance of siblings, see Jonathan R. Lyon, *Princely Brothers and Sisters: The Sibling Bond in German Politics, 1100–1250* (Ithaca, N.Y., and London, 2013), particularly pp. 89–119.
12. On Frederick's German economic policy, see Johannes Fried, "Die Wirtschaftspolitik Friedrich Barbarossas in Deutschland," *Blätter für deutsche Landesgeschichte* 120 (1984): 195–239.
13. The Latin text of the play is in Karl Young, ed., *The Drama of the Medieval Church* (Oxford, 1933), pp. 371–87. For an English translation, see *The Play of Antichrist*, trans. John Wright (Toronto, 1967). For the Latin text with a facing German translation, see Gisela Vollmann-Profe, ed. and trans., *Ludus de Antichristo*, 2 vols (Lauterberg, 1981). Peter Munz, *Frederick Barbarossa: A Study in Medieval Politics* (Ithaca, N.Y., and London, 1969), pp. 377 and 384–85, thought that the play was indicative of Frederick's own thinking.
14. Knut Görich, *Die Ehre Friedrich Barbarossas: Kommunikation, Konflikt und politisches Handeln im 12. Jahrhundert* (Darmstadt, 2001), pp. 1–57.
15. Stefan Weinfurter, "Venedig 1177—Wende der Barbarossa-Zeit? Zur Einführung," in Weinfurter, ed., *Stauferreich im Wandel: Ordnungsvorstellungen und Politik in der Zeit Friedrich Barbarossa* (Stuttgart, 2002), pp. 9–25; and in the same collection: Wolfgang Georgi, "Wichmann, Christian, Philipp und Konrad: Die 'Friedensmacher' von Venedig?" pp. 41–84; and Johannes Laudage, "Gewinner und Verlierer des Friedens von Venedig," pp. 107–30.
16. Theo Kölzer, "Der Hof Friedrich Barbarossas und die Reichsfürsten," in Weinfurter, ed., *Stauferreich im Wandel*, pp. 220–36.
17. Franz Böhm, *Das Bild Friedrich Barbarossas und seines Kaisertums in den ausländischen Quellen seiner Zeit* (Berlin, 1936), pp. 105–31.
18. For Otto's biography, see Hans-Werner Goetz, *Das Geschichtsbild Ottos von Freising: Ein Beitrag zur historischen Vorstellungswelt und zur Geschichte des 12. Jahrhunderts* (Cologne and Vienna, 1984), pp. 25–49; and Joachim Ehlers, *Otto von Freising: Ein Intellektueller im Mittelalter: Eine Biographie* (Munich, 2013). On his episcopal career, see Josef Mass, *Das Bistum Freising im Mittelalter*, 2nd ed. (Munich, 1988), pp. 157–75.
19. Goetz, *Das Geschichtsbild Ottos von Freising*, pp. 137–61 and 181–219. The standard edition of the *Chronicle* is Adolf Hofmeister, ed., *Ottonis Episcopi Frisingensis Chronica sive Historia de duabus Civitatibus*, 2nd edn., MGH SSrG (Hanover, 1912). The Hofmeister text was republished with only minor revisions, with a facing German translation by Adolf Schmidt, in Walther Lammers, ed., *Chronik oder Die Geschichte der zwei Staaten*, in AQ 16 (Darmstadt, 1960). Charles Christopher Mierow provided an English translation: *The Two Cities: A Chronicle of Universal History to the Year 1146 A.D.* (New York, 2002). This edition of the Mierow translation, which was published originally in 1928, contains a foreword and an updated bibliography by Karl F. Morrison, and includes a biography of Otto. English translations will be taken from the Mierow translation. However, since readers are likely to have access to different Latin, German, and English editions, I will normally simply cite Otto of Freising, *Chronicle*, with the book and chapter citation. To avoid the endless repetition of footnotes, I will cite the book and chapter reference, where appropriate, in the text itself.
20. Goetz, *Das Geschichtsbild Ottos von Freising*, pp. 110–39 and 258–75; and Ehlers, *Otto von Freising*, pp. 166–213. On such apocalyptic speculation in twelfth-century historical writing, see Peter Classen, "*Res gestae*, Universal History, Apocalypse: Visions of Past and Future," in Robert L. Benson and Giles Constable, eds, *Renaissance and Renewal in the Twelfth Century* (Cambridge, MA, 1982), pp. 387–417, esp. 400–03.
21. Frederick's letter to Otto serves as a prologue to Otto of Freising's *The Deeds of Frederick Barbarossa*, translated by Charles Christopher Mierow (New York, 1953; paperback edition, New York, 1966). The Mierow translation is based upon the edition by Georg Waitz and Bernhard von Simson, *Ottonis et Rahewini Gesta Friderici I. Imperatoris*, in MGH SSrG (Hanover, 1912). Franz-Josef Schmale published the Latin text, with a facing German translation by Adolf Schmidt, in *Die Taten Friedrichs oder richtiger Cronica*, in AQ 17 (Darmstadt, 1965). No autograph copy of the *Deeds* by either Otto or his secretary Rahewin survives. The Waitz-Simson text is a composite of three separate manuscript traditions, based upon

18 texts that were known in 1912 (by 1999 that number had increased to 26), and thus does not replicate a specific text that ever existed. In contrast, the Schmale text is based on a late twelfth-century manuscript, which appears to be a copy of the text that Rahewin presented to Frederick and that was kept in the library in the royal palace in Haguenau. Schmale's text was by the fifteenth century, at the latest, in the Alsatian monastery of Marbach and is now in the Bibliothèque Nationale in Paris. The Schmale edition is considered to be better than the Waitz-Simson one, but not the definitive critical edition because it does not consider the variants provided by the two other manuscript traditions, which were derived from the copy that Rahewin retained in Freising. The chapter numbers in the Waitz-Simson and Schmale editions are not always identical. On all of this, see Roman Deutinger, *Rahewin von Freising: Ein Gelehrter des 12. Jahrhunderts* (Hanover, 1999), pp. 27–72. Since anglophone readers are most likely to use the Mierow translation, I will use its chapter numbers and will cite them, where appropriate, in the text to cut down on an excessive number of footnotes. On account of the multiple editions in different languages, I will refer to the text as Otto of Freising, *Deeds*, and add Rahewin's name in those sections where he was the author.

22. DFI, no. 534 (6 August 1167). See Gerald Schwedler, "Kaisertradition und Innovation: Die Bezugnahme Barbarossas auf andere Kaiser," in Stefan Burkhardt et al., eds, *Staufisches Kaisertum im 12. Jahrhundert: Konzepte—Netzwerke—Politische Praxis* (Regensburg, 2010), pp. 231–34.
23. Otto of Freising, *Chronicle*, Dedicatory letter to Frederick; and idem, *Deeds*, Prologue to Book I. On Frederick as the *rex justus* in the *Deeds*, see Sverre Bagge, "Ideas and Narrative in Otto of Freising's *Gesta Frederici*," *Journal of Medieval History* 22/4 (1996): 356–66.
24. Otto of Freising, *Chronicle*, Dedicatory letter to Frederick.
25. Walther Lammers, "Weltgeschichte und Zeitgeschichte bei Otto von Freising," *Die Zeit der Staufer* 5:77–90, ascribed the difference to the change in genres. Karl F. Morrison, "Otto of Freising's Quest for the Hermeneutic Circle," *Speculum* 55 (1980): 235–36, argued that Otto shifted from an "eschatological mode" of exposition in the *Chronicle* to a "philosophical one" in the *Deeds*. Ehlers, *Otto von Freising*, pp. 214–60, contended that there was in fact no fundamental change in Otto's pessimistic interpretation of history in the *Deeds*. Otto was forced to present Frederick's reign in a favorable fashion because the mortally ill Otto was fearful about the future of the church of Freising after his death, for Otto V of Wittelsbach, Freising's hostile advocate, and Henry the Lion, the new duke of Bavaria who had just destroyed Freising's bridge and market in Föhring, were Frederick's favorites. It is no longer certain, however, that Henry destroyed the bridge and market in 1158. See below, pp. 166–68.
26. Goetz, *Das Geschichtsbild Ottos von Freising*, pp. 275–99; and Bagge, "Ideas and Narrative," pp. 348–56.
27. Otto of Freising, *Deeds*, Prologue to Book I.
28. Otto of Freising, *Deeds,* Letter of the August Emperor, Frederick, to Otto, Bishop of Freising. See Goetz, *Das Geschichtsbild Ottos von Freising*, p. 24; and Schmale edition of the *Deeds*, pp. 22–23. Ehlers, *Otto of Freising*, pp. 222–23, provides a table of concordance between Frederick's list of his accomplishments and the chapters in Book II of the *Deeds*.
29. On this passage, see Alphons Lhotsky, "Die Historiographie Ottos von Freising," in idem, *Aufsätze und Vorträge*, ed. Hans Wagner, 5 vols (Vienna, 1970–76), 1:49–63; and idem, "Fuga und Electio," 1:83–91.
30. Otto's letter to Rainald is published as a prologue to the various editions of the *Chronicle*. Lars Hageneier, "Die frühen Staufer bei Otto von Freising oder Wie sind die *Gesta Friderici* entstanden?" in Hubertus Seibert and Jürgen Dendorfer, eds, *Grafen, Herzöge, Könige: Der Aufstieg der frühen Staufer und das Reich (1079–1152)* (Ostfildern, 2005), pp. 363–96; and Goetz, *Das Geschichtsbild Ottos von Freising*, pp. 276–77. Bagge, "Ideas and Narrative," makes the case for the internal coherence between the first two books of the *Deeds* that Otto wrote. Book I describes the crisis in the Church and Empire and Book II how Frederick overcame it (p. 345).
31. Otto of Freising, *Chronicle*, Dedicatory letter to Frederick.
32. Rahewin, *Deeds*, Prologue to Book III.

33. On the ministerials, see Benjamin Arnold, *German Knighthood, 1050–1300* (Oxford, 1985); and John B. Freed, *Noble Bondsmen: Ministerial Marriages in the Archdiocese of Salzburg, 1100–1343* (Ithaca, N.Y., and London, 1995).
34. Deutinger, *Rahewin von Freising*, pp. 7–26.
35. Ibid., pp. 17–19, 25–26, and 88–96; and the Schmale edition of the *Deeds*, pp. 42–48. On Henry of Würzburg, see Friedrich Hausmann, *Reichskanzlei und Hofkapelle unter Heinrich V. und Konrad III.* (Stuttgart, 1956), pp. 138–67; and Wolfram Ziegler, *König Konrad III. (1138–1152): Hof, Urkunden und Politik* (Vienna, Cologne, and Weimar, 2008), pp. 335–38. Hausmann's identification of Henry of Würzburg as Henry of Wiesenbach is no longer accepted. See Heinrich Appelt, "Einleitung," *Die Urkunden Friedrichs I.* 5:20–22.
36. Deutinger, *Rahewin von Freising*, pp. 96–123.
37. Rahewin, *Deeds*, Prologue to Book III; and Deutinger, *Rahewin von Freising*, pp. 75–77 and 123–26. Robert Holtzmann, "Das Carmen de Frederico I. imperatore aus Bergamo und die Anfänge einer staufischen Hofhistoriographie," *NA* 44 (1922): 252–313, proposed that Rainald of Dassel promoted the development of a court historiography that glorified Barbarossa. German scholars did not totally abandon Holtzmann's thesis until the 1970s. For a recent treatment of this topic, see Roman Deutinger, "Imperiale Konzepte in der hofnahen Historiographie der Barbarossazeit," in Burkhardt et al., eds, *Staufisches Kaisertum im 12. Jahrhundert*, pp. 25–39, esp. pp. 25–26.
38. J. R. Gillingham, "Why Did Rahewin Stop Writing the Gesta Frederici?" *EHR* 83 (1968): 294–303. Peter Munz responded in "Why Did Rahewin Stop Writing the Gesta Frederici? A Further Consideration," *EHR* 84 (1969): 771–79, that Rahewin was serious about not writing more than four books because it was never Otto's or his intention to write an ongoing chronicle of Frederick's *Deeds*. The purpose, which Munz spelled out in greater detail in his biography of Frederick, was rather to cover up the fact that in 1156 the emperor had abandoned his alliance with the papacy and Byzantium. The Council of Pavia was an appropriate high note on which to end a commissioned work of court historiography. Munz's thesis about why Otto wrote the *Deeds* has gained little acceptance. See Goez, *Das Geschichtsbild Ottos von Freising*, pp. 298–99; and Deutinger, *Rahewin von Freising*, p. 124.
39. Deutinger, *Rahewin von Freising*, pp. 18–25 and 89–92. Rahewin composed for his students' benefit a verse version of Peter Lombard's *Sentences*, which Deutinger published on pp. 233–304. Deutinger, pp. 211–19, discussed the authorship of the so-called appendix to the *Deeds*, which Simson included in his critical edition and Mierow translated on pp. 335–39. Deutinger believed that Rahewin could have been the author of the short version of this text that appears in a manuscript from Tegernsee.
40. Wilhelm Bernhardi, *Lothar von Supplinburg* (Leipzig, 1879), pp. 790–803. For a positive assessment of Lothar and a negative assessment of Frederick, see Franz-Josef Schmale, "Lothar III. und Friedrich I. als Könige und Kaiser," in Theodor Mayer, ed., *Probleme des 12. Jahrhunderts: Reichenau-Vorträge 1965–1967* (Constance, 1968), pp. 33–52.
41. Wilhelm Bernhardi, *Konrad III.* (1883; reprint, Berlin, 1975), pp. 927–31.
42. Henry Simonsfeld, *Jahrbücher des Deutschen Reiches unter Friedrich I.* (1908; reprint, 1967), 1:1.
43. Bernhardi, *Lothar von Supplinburg*, p. 123.
44. Werner Hechberger, *Staufer und Welfen 1125–1190: Zur Verwendung von Theorien in der Geschichtswissenschaft* (Cologne, 1996), pp. 18–38 and 98–104.
45. Otto of Freising, *Deeds*, Prologue to Book I. On this passage, see Lammers, "Weltgeschichte und Zeitgeschichte," pp. 78–81.
46. For the text, see Gunther der Dichter, *Ligurinus*, ed. Erwin Assmann, MGH SSrG 63 (Hanover, 1987).
47. For the text, see *Gotifredi Viterbiensis Gesta Friderici I. et Heinrici VI.*, ed. Georg Heinrich Pertz, in MGH SSrG 30 (Hanover, 1870; reprint, Hanover, 1993).
48. For the texts of both the *Marbach Annals* and Otto of St. Blasien's *Chronicle*, with facing German translations, see Franz-Josef Schmale, ed., *Die Chronik Ottos von St. Blasien und die Marbacher Annalen*, in AQ 18a (Darmstadt, 1998).
49. Vincent of Prague, *Annales*, ed. Wilhelm Wattenbach, in MGH SS 17 (Hanover, 1861), pp. 658–83. Franz-Josef Schmale published the text of the Morenas' *Libellus de rebus a*

Frederico imperatore gestis and the Milanese Anonymous' *Narratio de Longobardie obpressione et subiectione*, with facing German translations, in *Italienische Quellen über die Taten Kaiser Friedrichs I. in Italien und der Brief über den Kreuzzug Kaiser Friedrichs I.*, in AQ 17a (Darmstadt, 1986).

50. *Carmen de gestis Frederici I. imperatoris in Lombardia*, ed. Irene Schmale-Ott, in MGH SSrG 62 (Hanover, 1965).
51. Matthias Becher published the text of Provost Burchard of Ursberg's *Chronicon* and the *History of the Welfs*, with facing German translations, in *Quellen zur Geschichte der Welfen und die Chronik Burchards von Ursberg*, in AQ 18b (Darmstadt, 2007). For further information on all these sources and their use of Otto of Freising and Rahewin, see Deutinger, *Rahewin von Freising*, pp. 19, 75–77, 89–90 and 149–78; Heinz Krieg, *Herrscherdarstellungen in der Stauferzeit: Friedrich Barbarossa im Spiegel seiner Urkunden und der staufischen Geschichtsschreibung* (Ostfildern, 2003), pp. 19–43; and Holger Berwinkel, *Verwüsten und Belagern: Friedrich Barbarossas Krieg gegen Mailand (1158–1162)* (Tübingen, 2007), pp. 10–19.
52. *Chronica regia Coloniensis (Annales maximi Colonienses)*, ed. Georg Waitz, in MGH SSrG 18 (Hanover, 1880; reprint, Hanover, 2003); Arnold of Lübeck, *Chronica Slavorum*, ed. Johann Martin Lappenberg, in MGH SS 21 (Hanover, 1869), pp. 101–250; and Gilbert of Mons, *Chronicle of Hainaut*, trans. Laura Napran (Woodbridge, Suffolk, 2005). On the authorship of the Cologne chronicle, see Weinfurter, "Venedig 1177," p. 20.
53. *Die Urkunden Lothars III. und der Kaiserin Richenza*, ed. Emil von Ottenthal and Hans Hirsch, in MGH: Die Urkunden der deutschen Könige und Kaiser (UdKK) 8 (Berlin, 1927; reprint, Munich, 1993), pp. vii–xiv (cited as DLIII); *Die Urkunden Konrads III. und seines Sohnes Heinrich*, ed. Friedrich Hausmann, in UdKK 9 (Vienna, 1969; reprint, Munich, 1987), pp. vii–xiv (cited as DKIII); and *Die Urkunden Friedrichs I.*, ed. Heinrich Appelt, 5 vols, in UdKK 10 (Hanover, 1975–90), 10/1: vii–xiv (cited as DFI). The *Monumenta* is the learned society that for nearly two centuries has been publishing the sources relevant to the history of medieval Germany, broadly conceived. For its history, see David Knowles, *Great Historical Enterprises* (London, 1962), pp. 63–97.
54. Hausmann, *Reichskanzlei und Hofkapelle*, pp. 167–257, esp. p. 177; Ziegler, *König Konrad III.*, pp. 295–313; and Franz-Josef Jakobi, *Wibald von Stablo und Corvey (1098–1158): Benediktinischer Abt in der frühen Stauferzeit* (Münster, 1979). Philipp Jaffé published the letters in the *Monumenta Corbeiensia*, in his Bibliotheca rerum Germanicarum 1 (Berlin, 1864). Timothy Reuter was working at his death on a new edition for the Monumenta Germaniae Historica. This edition is now available: *Das Briefbuch Abt Wibalds von Stablo und Corvey*, 3 vols, ed. Martina Hartmann, MGH BdK 9 (Hanover, 2012). Since the letters are numbered differently in the Jaffé and Hartmann editions, I will also give the Jaffé numbers. See Hartmann's introduction to the edition: *Studien zu den Briefen Abt Wibalds von Stablo und Corvey sowie zur Briefliteratur in der frühen Stauferzeit* (Hanover, 2011). Hartmann's account of Reuter's work on the edition, "Timothy Reuter and the Edition of Wibald of Stavelot's Letter Collection for the MGH," is in Patricia Skinner, ed., *Challenging the Boundaries of Medieval History: The Legacy of Timothy Reuter* (Turnhout, 2009), pp. 185–91.
55. *Die Admonter Briefsammlung nebst ergänzden Briefen*, ed. Günther Hödl and Peter Classen, in MGH BdK 6 (Munich, 1983); and *Die Tegernseer Briefsammlung des 12. Jahrhunderts*, ed. Helmut Plechl, in MGH BdK 8 (Hanover, 2002).
56. *Die Regesten des Kaiserreiches unter Friedrich I. 1152 (1122)–1190*, 4 vols, ed. Ferdinand Opll, in J. F. Böhmer, Regesta Imperii IV/2 (Vienna, 1980–2011). Opll is working on an index that will be published in the fifth volume. For an overview of the project, see RI IV2/4:vii–xviii. (In this citation, IV stands for the series on the Ältere Staufer; 2 for the section on Frederick; and 4 for the fourth volume or *Lieferung*.) *Die Regesten des Kaiserreichs unter Lothar III. und Konrad III.* are section 4/1 of the Regesta Imperii and appeared in two parts: on Lothar, edited by Wolfgang Petke (1994), and on Conrad III, edited by Jan Paul Niederkorn (2008). The two volumes on Henry VI, *Die Regesten des Kaiserreiches unter Heinrich VI. 1165 (1190)–1197*, section 4/3, edited by Katrin and Gebhard Baaken, appeared in 1972 and 1979 respectively.
57. Simonsfeld, *Jahrbücher des Deutschen Reiches unter Friedrich I.* 1:v–ix.

58. Wilhelm von Giesebrecht and Bernhard von Simson, *Geschichte der deutschen Kaiserzeit*, vol. 5 in two parts and vol. 6 (Leipzig, 1880–95). Since the book was long out of print, Wilhelm Schild published a revised version minus the footnotes (Meersburg, 1929–30). Schild pointed out at the end, p. 278 in volume 6, that he had made minor revisions to Giesebrecht's text but had completely reworked Simson's text without indicating the specific places he had altered. Schild's edition must thus be used with extreme caution. A good indication of the popular character of Giesebrecht's history and how it was used to inculcate patriotism is that my copies of volumes 5 and 6 in the first edition were originally located in libraries in a normal school in Kiel, in a gymnasium in Baden, and in a district military library in Mainz. I could find no evidence that Giesebrecht's history was reprinted after World War II. For a discussion of the Sybel–Ficker dispute about the medieval Empire, see pp. 525–26.
59. The book relied greatly on the articles Barraclough edited in *Mediaeval Germany 911–1250*, Vol. 2: *Essays by German Historians* (Oxford, 1938). The earliest one was published in 1895.
60. Marcel Pacaut, *Frédéric Barberousse* (Paris, 1967); and idem, *Frederick Barbarossa,* trans. A. J. Pomerans (New York, 1970), pp. 10 and 30. It has some amazing mistakes. For example, Pacaut did not realize that Otto of Freising did not accompany Frederick to Italy in 1154.
61. On Munz, see Russell Price, "Obituary," *The Guardian*, 12 March 2007.
62. Munz, *Frederick Barbarossa*, pp. 92–145; the quotation is on p. 104. Munz did not devise the term. Pacaut, *Frédéric Barberousse*, p. 88, wrote in 1967 about Frederick's "grands desseins et d'étonnantes entreprises." In the English edition, p. 51, it is the "grand design." Munz, p. 401, cited Pacaut's book as one of the major works on Frederick. Geoffrey Barraclough in "What Is to Be Done about Medieval History?" *New York Review of Books* 14/11 (4 June 1970): 51–57, stated in passing: "I can only express total disbelief in Mr. Munz's strident and wearisomely reiterated assertion that Frederick Barbarossa was a 'statesman' with a 'Great Design' " (p. 54). In an exchange with Munz, on 5 November 1970, 15/8: 45–46, Barraclough rejected "speculations about the motives and alleged designs of rulers such as Frederick Barbarossa" (p. 46). German scholars reject any notion that Frederick had a "Great Design." See, for example, Knut Görich, "Konflikt und Kompromiss: Friedrich Barbarossa in Italien," in Hechberger and Schuler, eds, *Staufer & Welfen*, pp. 79–80.
63. Ferdinand Opll, *Das Itinerar Kaiser Friedrich Barbarossas (1152–1190)* (Vienna, Cologne, and Graz, 1978); and idem, *Stadt und Reich im 12. Jahrhundert (1125–1190)* (Vienna, Cologne, and Graz, 1986).
64. Ferdinand Opll, *Friedrich Barbarossa* (Darmstadt, 1990).
65. Johannes Laudage, *Friedrich Barbarossa (1152–1190): Eine Biographie*, ed. by Lars Hageneier and Matthias Schrör (Regensburg, 2009). Laudage's earlier book is *Alexander III. und Friedrich Barbarossa* (Cologne, Weimar, and Vienna, 1997). Görich, *Friedrich Barbarossa: Eine Biographie*, esp. pp. 18–21. Görich's *Habilitationsschrift* is his *Die Ehre Friedrich Barbarossas*.
66. On the exercise of power in the twelfth century, see Thomas Bisson, *The Crisis of the Twelfth Century: Power, Lordship, and the Origins of European Government* (Princeton, N.J., 2009).
67. Peter Cornelius Claussen, "Stauferbilder—Bildnisse der Staufer," in Bernd Schneidmüller et al., eds, *Verwandlungen des Stauferreichs: Drei Innovationsregionen im mittelalterlichen Europa* (Darmstadt, 2010), pp. 352–54 and Plate XIX.

Chapter 1 "Two Renowned Families"

1. Otto of Freising, *Chronicle* 6.20 and 6.28; and DFI, no. 417 (25 October–13 November 1163). Otto obtained his knowledge of the Salians' ancestry from Wipo's *The Deeds of Conrad II*, trans. Theodor E. Mommsen and Karl F. Morrison, in *Imperial Lives and Letters of the Eleventh Century* (New York and London, 1962), pp. 61–62, ch. 2, and p. 69, ch. 4. On Otto's description of the "two renowned families," see Odilo Engels, "Beiträge zur Geschichte der Staufer im 12. Jahrhundert (I)," *DA* 27 (1971): 437–38; Karl Schmid, "'De regia stirpe Waiblingensium': Bemerkungen zum Selbstverständnis der Staufer," *ZGORh* 124 (NF 85) (1976): 63–73, esp. 63–70; Hechberger, *Staufer und Welfen*, pp. 135–50; Tobias Weller, *Die Heiratspolitik des deutschen Hochadels im 12. Jahrhundert* (Cologne, Weimar, and Vienna,

2004), pp. 192–95; and Hubertus Seibert, "Die frühen 'Staufer': Forschungsstand und offene Fragen," in Seibert and Dendorfer, eds. *Grafen, Herzöge, Könige*, pp. 3–5.

2. Karl Schmid, "Zur Problematik von Familie, Sippe und Geschlecht, Haus und Dynastie beim mittelalterlichen Adel: Vorfragen zum Thema 'Adel und Herrschaft im Mittelalter,'" *ZGORh* (NF 66) (1957): 33–34. Many of Schmid's articles about the familial structure of the nobility are reprinted in his *Gebetsgedenken und adliges Selbstverständnis im Mittelalter: Ausgewählte Beiträge: Festgabe zu seinem sechzigsten Geburtstag* (Sigmaringen, 1983).
3. The family of Queen Victoria's mother and husband, the house of Saxe-Coburg-Gotha, descends from the marriage of Emperor Frederick II's daughter Margaret (d. 1270) to Margrave Albrecht of Meissen and Thuringia. See Armin Wolf, "Staufisch–sizilische Tochterstämme in Europa und die Herrschaft über Italien," in Sönke Lorenz and Ulriche Schmidt, eds, *Von Schwaben bis Jerusalem: Facetten staufischer Geschichte* (Sigmaringen, 1995), pp. 117 and 133.
4. Heide Dienst, "Werden und Entwicklung der babenbergischen Mark," in Anna Drabek, ed., *Österreich im Hochmittelalter (907 bis 1246)* (Vienna, 1991), pp. 65 and 67. For a historiographical summary of the debate about the structural transformation of the nobility, see Werner Hechberger, *Adel im fränkisch-deutschen Mittelalter: Zur Anatomie eines Forschungsproblems* (Sigmaringen, 2005), pp. 303–46. Some key items on the debate in English are: Karl J. Leyser, "The German Aristocracy from the Ninth to the Early Twelfth Century: A Historical and Cultural Sketch," *Past and Present* 41 (1968): 25–53; John B. Freed, *The Counts of Falkenstein: Noble Self-Consciousness in Twelfth-Century Germany* (Philadelphia, P.A., 1984), pp. 1–13; and Constance Brittain Bouchard, *"Those of My Blood": Constructing Noble Families in Medieval Francia* (Philadelphia, P.A., 2001).
5. DFI, no. 45 (27 January 1153). This charter is a verbatim confirmation of the foundation charter of the monastery of St. Foy in Sélestat, which had been founded by Frederick's kinsmen, among whom Frederick included both the duke and his brothers. Conrad III, too, never mentioned his father in a charter.
6. DFI, no. 128 (27 November 1155), p. 215, line 8. See Rudolf Schieffer, "Friedrich Barbarossa und seine Verwandten," in Theo Kölzer et al., eds, *De litteris, manuscriptis, inscriptionibus . . . Festschrift zum 65. Geburtstag von Walter Koch* (Vienna, 2007), pp. 578–80.
7. Wibald of Stavelot, *Briefbuch* 3:812–13, no. 385 (Jaffé, no. 408).
8. The most detailed Staufer genealogy is Hansmartin Decker-Hauff's "Das Staufische Haus," *Die Zeit der Staufer* 3: 339–74; and now Eduard Hlawitschka, *Die Ahnen der hochmittelalterlichen deutschen Könige, Kaiser und ihrer Gehmahlinnen: Ein kommentiertes Tafelwerk*, 3 vols (Hanover and Wiesbaden, 2006–13), vol. 2, pp. 1–52. For a critique of Decker-Hauff's reconstruction of the early "Staufer" genealogy, see Weller, *Die Heiratspolitik des deutschen Hochadels*, pp. 196–226; and idem, "Auf dem Weg zum 'staufischen Haus': Zu Abstammung, Verwandschaft und Konnubium der frühen Staufer," in Seibert and Dendorfer, eds, *Grafen, Herzöge, Könige*, pp. 56–64. For a map showing the location of Wäschenbeuren, see Heinz Krieg, "Adel in Schwaben: Die Staufer und die Zähringer," in Seibert and Dendorfer, eds, *Grafen, Herzöge, Könige,* p. 87. Frederick I's ancestors are presented in this fashion in Opll, *Friedrich Barbarossa*, pp. 19–20; and Odilo Engels, *Die Staufer*, 8th edn. (Stuttgart, 2005), p. 9, and the genealogy following p. 244. On the "Staufer" counts-palatine of Swabia, see Sönke Lorenz, "Die Pfalzgrafen in Schwaben vom 9. bis zum frühen 12. Jahrhundert," in Andreas Bihrer et al., eds, *Adel und Königtum im mittelalterlichen Schwaben: Festschrift für Thomas Zotz zum 65. Geburtstag* (Stuttgart, 2009), pp. 214–18 and 223–25.
9. Daniel Ziemann, "Die Staufer—Ein elsässisches Adelsgeschlecht?" in Seibert and Dendorfer, eds, *Grafen, Herzöge, Könige*, pp. 117–24. It is generally assumed that the Staufer inherited the property in Sélestat from Hildegard. The identification of Hildegard's natal family depends, therefore, on the reconstruction of the proprietary history of Sélestat. She is thus often identified as a member of the comital house of Mousson-Mömpelgard. See, for example, Opll and Engels (n. 8 above). However, the most recent scholarship is inclined to make her the daughter of Count Gebhard III of Dagsburg-Egisheim (d. 1038) and Bertha, a niece of the Welf king of Burgundy, Rudolf III (d. 1032). See Weller, *Die Heiratspolitik des deutschen Hochadels*, pp. 12–13; and Hlawitschka, *Die Ahnen der hochmittelalterlichen deutschen Könige*, vol. 2, pp. 22–23 and 28–34. Ziemann, esp. pp. 131–33, contended that Alsace, which

was often linked to Swabia, may have been the original home of the "Staufer," i.e., that Sélestat was part of Frederick of Büren's rather than Hildegard's inheritance and that the "Staufer" moved from Alsace to Swabia. Ziemann's thesis caused a popular uproar. In January 2008 the *Stuttgarter Zeitung* ran an article: "Die Staufer müssen Schwaben bleiben," cited in Hechberger, "Bewundert—instrumentalisiert—angefeindet," p. 238. On the stained-glass window, see *Die Zeit der Staufer, Katalog* 1.276. Barbarossa's confirmation charter is DFI, no. 45 (27 January 1153).

10. On dynastic monasteries, see Karl Schmid, "Adel und Reform in Schwaben," in Josef Fleckenstein, ed., *Investiturstreit und Reichsverfassung* (Sigmaringen, 1973), pp. 295–319; and Christine Sauer, *Fundatio und Memoria: Stifter und Klostergründer im Bild 1100 bis 1350* (Göttingen, 1993).
11. *Wirtembergisches Urkundenbuch* 1, edited. by the Royal State Archives in Stuttgart (Stuttgart, 1849), pp. 334–35, no. 264 (1102; forged foundation charter), and pp. 383–84, no. 303 (1136); and DKIII, no. 38 (December 1139). Otto of Freising, *Deeds* 1.9, merely said that Frederick "was buried in the monastery at Lorch, erected on his own land." Archeologists have not been able to locate a residential complex at the site of the monastery above the Rems but have discovered a fortified manorial complex in the valley. See Seibert, "Die frühen 'Staufer,'" pp. 32–33.
12. DFI, no. 77 (3–17 May 1154). On the foundation of Lorch, see Ziemann, "Die Staufer," pp. 109–16; and Gerhard Lubich, "Territorien-, Kloster- und Bistumspolitik in einer Gesellschaft im Wandel: Zur politischen Komponente des Herrschaftsaufbaus der Staufer vor 1138," in Seibert and Dendorfer, eds, *Grafen, Herzöge, Könige*, pp. 196–201. Frederick's statement about the advocacy of Lorch is a corrective to Hechberger's contention that the Staufer lacked any sense of agnatic identity.
13. Otto of Freising, *Deeds* 1.70 (Conrad III's burial). See Caspar Ehlers, *Metropolis Germaniae: Studien zur Bedeutung Speyers für das Königtum (751–1250)* (Göttingen, 1996), pp. 73–183, esp. pp. 175–83; Klaus Graf, "Staufer-Überlieferungen aus Kloster Lorch," in Lorenz and Schmidt, eds, *Von Schwaben bis Jerusalem*, pp. 209–40; Olaf Rader, "Die Grablegen der Staufer als Erinnerungsorte," in Schneidmüller et al., eds, *Verwandlungen des Stauferreichs*, pp. 20–33; and Werner Hechberger, "Konrad III.—Königliche Politik und 'staufische Familieninteressen'?" in Seibert and Dendorfer, eds, *Grafen, Herzöge, Könige*, pp. 327–31.
14. See Engels, *Die Staufer*, pp. 9–10.
15. Ibid.; and Lubich, "Territorien-, Kloster- und Bistumspolitik," p. 185.
16. Odo of Deuil, *De profectione Ludovici VII in orientem: The Journey of Louis VII to the East*, edited with an English translation by Virginia Gingerick Berry (New York, 1948), pp. 102–03. Berry, like everyone else, identified *Estufin* as the Staufer castle of Hohkönigsburg, southwest of Sélestat, where St. Denis also had extensive holdings, even though Königsburg appears in Frederick's charters as *Kungisbergh* (see DFI, no. 898 [5 March 1185], line 22). Ziemann, "Die Staufer," p. 129, found it intriguing that Odo should have called Hohkönigsburg *Staufen*, but the more plausible explanation is that Odo meant Stauf, located east of Esslingen, which he also claimed. Knut Görich, "Wahrung des *honor*: Ein Grundsatz im politischen Handeln König Konrads III.," in Seibert and Dendorfer, eds, *Grafen, Herzöge, Könige*, pp. 278–80, doubted that the incident occurred. It would have been provocative for Louis VII to raise the issue in public after Conrad had declined his request in private. Görich suggested that Odo may have been trying to impress his abbot, the famous Suger, the recipient of Odo's ongoing accounts of the crusade, with his zeal for the interests of St. Denis.
17. Opll, *Das Itinerar Kaiser Friedrich Barbarossas*, p. 134.
18. Engels, "Beiträge zur Geschichte der Staufer im 12. Jahrhundert," pp. 446–47; Hechberger, *Staufer und Welfen*, pp. 110–12; and Seibert, "Die frühen 'Staufer,'" pp. 6–7.
19. Burchard of Ursberg, *Chronicon*, pp. 146–47.
20. Ibid., pp. 106–07. See Engels, "Beiträge zur Geschichte der Staufer," pp. 446–47; Schmid, "'De regia stirpe Waiblingensium,'" pp. 63–73; Hechberger, *Staufer und Welfen*, pp. 140–46; and Lubich, Territorien-, Kloster- und Bistumspolitik, pp. 186–87.
21. Otto of Freising, *Deeds* 1.8. See Ziemann, "Die Staufer," pp. 99–102.
22. Otto of Freising, *Deeds* 1.8. See Engels, *Die Staufer*, pp. 15–16; Helmut Maurer, "Das Herzogtum Schwaben in staufischer Zeit," in *Die Zeit der Staufer* 5.91–105; idem, *Der*

Herzog von Schwaben: Grundlagen, Wirkungen und Wesen seiner Herrschaft in ottonischer, salischer und staufischer Zeit (Sigmaringen, 1978), esp. pp. 57–75 (on Zürich) and pp. 218–300 (on the Staufer period); and Weller, *Die Heiratspolitik des deutschen Hochadels*, pp. 13–21 and 396–401 and Tafel 4. For a discussion of these events in English, see I. S. Robinson, *Henry IV of Germany 1056–1106* (Cambridge, 1999), pp. 171–210 and 298–99.

23. Gerd Althoff, "Die Zähringerherrschaft im Urteil Ottos von Freising," in Karl Schmid, ed., *Die Zähringer: Eine Tradition und ihre Erforschung*, in Veröffentlichungen zur Zähringer-Ausstellung I (Sigmaringen, 1986), pp. 43–58; Thomas Zotz, "Dux de Zaringen—dux Zaringiae: Zum zeitgenössischen Verständnis eines neuen Herzogtums im 12. Jahrhundert," *ZGORh* 139 (NF 100) (1991): 1–44; and Krieg, "Adel in Schwaben," pp. 65–97. For a more detailed genealogy, see the second volume in the Zähringer exhibition catalog: Hans Schadek, ed., *Die Zähringer: Anstoss und Wirkung*, especially pp. 12–13; and Hlawitschka, *Die Ahnen der hochmittelalterlichen deutschen Könige* 2:150–54 and 158–74. For a dated article on the Zähringer in English, see Theodor Mayer, "The State of the Dukes of Zähringen," in Barraclough, ed., *Mediaeval Germany 911–1250* 2:175–202.
24. Otto of Freising, *Deeds* 1.10 and 1.14. Otto, 1.14, described Frederick II as "tam fidus principi miles." Mierow translated *miles* as *knight,* but Schmidt in the Schmale edition used *vassal.*
25. *Constitutiones et acta publica imperatorum et regum* 1, in MGH Legum Sectio IV, ed. Ludwig Weiland (Hanover, 1893; reprint, Hanover, 2003), pp. 137–39, nos. 83 and 85. See Jürgen Dendorfer, "*Fidi milites?*: Die Staufer und Kaiser Heinrich V.," in Seibert and Dendorfer, eds, *Grafen, Herzöge. Könige*, pp. 213–39; and Uta-Renate Blumenthal, "*Patrimonia* and *Regalia* in 1111," in Kenneth Pennington, ed., *Law, Church, and Society: Essays in Honor of Stephan Kuttner* (Philadelphia, P.A.,1977), pp. 9–20.
26. Otto of Freising, *Deeds* 1.12. See Hansmartin Schwarzmaier, "*Pater imperatoris*: Herzog Friedrich II. von Schwaben, der gescheiterte König," in Jürgen Petersohn, ed., *Mediaevalia Augiensia: Forschungen zur Geschichte des Mittelalters* (Stuttgart, 2001), pp. 256–58.
27. DKIII, no. 91 (10 July 1143); DFI, no. 447 (15 June 1164); and DFI, no. 995 (16 April 1189). See Opll, *Das Itinerar Kaiser Friedrich Barbarossas*, p. 133; idem, *Stadt und Reich im 12. Jahrhundert*, pp. 83–89; and Fred Schwind, "Friedrich Barbarossa und die Städte im Regnum Teutonicum," in Haverkamp, ed., *Friedrich Barbarossa*, pp. 488–89.
28. DKIII, no. 246 (c. 8 April 1151); and DFI, no. 270 (6 May 1159). Schwarzmaier, "*Pater imperatoris*," p. 275, raised the question whether Judith was also buried in St. Walbourg; but surely Frederick would have remembered his mother as well as his father.
29. DFI, no. 136 (February 1156); and DFI, no. 206 (27 February 1158). See Schwarzmaier, "*Pater imperatoris*," pp. 274–76; Ziemann, "Die Staufer," pp. 124–29; and Knut Schulz, "Die Zisterzienser in der Reichspolitik während der Stauferzeit," in Kaspar Elm, ed., *Die Zisterzienser: Ordensleben zwischen Ideal und Wirklichkeit* (Cologne, 1982), pp. 168–69.
30. Heinrich Büttner, "Erzbischof Adalbert von Mainz, die Kurie und das Reich in den Jahren 1118 bis 1122," in Fleckenstein, ed., *Investiturstreit und Reichsverfassung*, pp. 395–410; Dendorfer, "*Fidi milites?*" pp. 250–58; and Lubich, "Territorien-, Kloster- und Bistumspolitik," pp. 205–07. The text of the 1121 agreement is *Constitutiones* 1:158, no. 106.
31. *Constitutiones* 1.159–61, nos. 107 and 108. For an English translation, minus the list of subscribers, see Brian Tierney, *The Crisis of Church & State* (Englewood Cliffs, N.J., 1964), pp. 91–92, no. 44. For accounts in English of these events, see Uta-Renate Blumenthal, *The Investiture Controversy: Church and Monarchy from the Ninth to the Twelfth Century* (Philadelphia, P.A., 1988), pp. 167–73; and Mary Stroll, *Calixtus II (1119–1124): A Pope Born to Rule* (Leiden and Boston, 2004), pp. 357–422, esp. pp. 383–400.
32. Peter Classen, "Das Wormser Konkordat in der deutschen Verfassungsgeschichte," in Fleckenstein, ed., *Investiturstreit und Reichsverfassung*, pp. 411–60; and Gerd Althoff, "Staatsdiener oder Häupter des Staates: Fürstenverantwortung zwischen Reichsinteresse und Eigennutz," in idem, *Spielregeln der Politik im Mittelalter: Kommunikation in Frieden und Fehde* (Darmstadt, 1997), pp. 136–40.
33. *Narratio de electione Lotharii Saxoniae ducis in regem Romanorum*, ed. Wilhelm Wattenbach, in MGH SS 12 (Hanover, 1856), p. 510, line 37: "Porro dux Fridericus ambicione cecatus . . ." See Dendorfer, "*Fidi milites?*" pp. 235–37 and 258–65, esp. p. 264 on *ambitio*; and Schwarzmaier, "*Pater imperatoris*," pp. 254–55. Henry V's illegitimate daughter Bertha

married Count Ptolemy II of Tusculum (d. 1153). See Peter Partner, *The Lands of St. Peter: The Papal State in the Middle Ages and the Early Renaissance* (Berkeley and Los Angeles, 1972), p. 153; and Jürgen Petersohn, *Kaisertum und Rom in spätsalischer und staufischer Zeit: Romidee und Rompolitik von Heinrich V. bis Friedrich II.* (Hanover, 2010), pp. 24–25.

34. Otto of Freising, *Deeds* 1.14; and Weller, *Die Heiratspolitik des deutschen Hochadels*, pp. 21–26, 239–41, and 402–03.
35. Karl Schmid, "Welfisches Selbstverständnis," in Josef Fleckenstein, ed., *Adel und Kirche: Gerd Tellenbach zum 65. Geburtstag* (Freiburg, 1968), pp. 389–416; Bernd Schneidmüller, *Die Welfen: Herrschaft und Erinnerung* (Stuttgart, 2000), pp. 7–129; Hechberger, *Staufer und Welfen*, pp. 115–34; Joachim Ehlers, *Heinrich der Löwe: Eine Biographie* (Munich, 2008), pp. 21–31; Matthias Becher, "Von 'Eticho' zu 'Welf': Gedanken zur frühen welfischen Hausüberlieferung," in Bihrer et al., eds, *Adel und Königtum im mittelalterlichen Schwaben*, pp. 235–47; and Hlawitschka, *Die Ahnen der hochmittelalterlichen deutschen Könige* 2:91–134.
36. Weller, *Die Heiratspolitik des deutschen Hochadels*, pp. 38–40 and 167–80.
37. Ibid., pp. 230–37; Ehlers, *Heinrich der Löwe*, pp. 31–36; Schneidmüller, *Die Welfen*, pp. 130–62; and Manfred Weitlauff, "Das 'welfische Jahrhundert' in Bayern und sein kirchengeschichtlicher Hintergrund," in Hechberger, *Staufer und Welfen*, pp. 11–23.
38. DFI, no. 803 (1 March 1181). See Schieffer, "Friedrich Barbarossa und seine Verwandten," pp. 583–84.
39. Wibald of Stavelot, *Briefbuch* 3:709–13, no. 339 (Jaffé, no. 375; also *Constitutiones* 1.192–93, no. 138); and RI IV2/1:3, no. 1. See also Herbert Grundmann, *Der Cappenberger Barbarossakopf und die Anfänge des Stiftes Cappenberg* (Cologne, 1959), pp. 27–30; and Ferdinand Opll, "Die Winterquatember im Leben Friedrich Barbarossas," *MIÖG* 85 (1977): 332–41. Opll's argument for dating Frederick's birth in December hinges on Frederick's arranging for prayers to be said on his behalf until he died on the ember days in winter, that is, on the Wednesday, Friday, and Saturday of the third week of Advent. See DFI, no. 957 (17 April 1187). Opll pointed out that Duke Frederick did not attend Henry V's courts in Speyer at Christmas 1122 or in Strasbourg in January 1123. Since Haguenau lies between these two episcopal sees, it is conceivable that the court stopped there in conjunction with the birth of the emperor's great-nephew and that the infant was baptized on this occasion. Frederick's godfather, Otto of Cappenberg, was, according to Opll, in the vicinity of Frankfurt around Christmas and could, presumably, have reached Haguenau fairly quickly before or after 25 December. There is one other clue that Haguenau was of special significance to Frederick. He granted the citizens of only seven places exemption from the payment of all tolls in the Reich. Three were "capital" cities: Aachen, Monza, and Rome. Two, Pisa and Venice, were of naval and/or diplomatic importance to him. The other two were the settlements around his new palaces at Gelnhausen and Haguenau. See Petersohn, *Kaisertum und Rom in spätsalischer und staufischer Zeit*, p. 239.

Chapter 2 Baptismal Hopes

1. DFI, no. 333 (June 1161); and DFI, no. 963 (21 August 1187). See also *Chronica regia Coloniensis*, p. 89.
2. *Die Zeit der Staufer, Katalog*, 1.394–96, no. 536; 2, Abbildung 323; Alfried Wieczorek, Bernd Schneidmüller, and Stefan Weinfurter, eds, *Die Staufer und Italien: Drei Innovationsregionen im mittelalterlichen Europa*, 2 vols (Darmstadt, 2010), 2.33; Görich, *Friedrich Barbarossa*, pp. 29–31; and Caroline Horch, *"Nach dem Bild des Kaisers": Funktionen und Bedeutungen des Cappenberger Barbarossakopfes* (Cologne, Weimar, and Vienna, 2013), pp. 23–27. The Latin text of Otto's will is in Horch, p. 20, n. 43 (a German translation is in the text).
3. Freed, *Noble Bondsmen*, p. 87. On the social and political significance of sponsorship in the early Middle Ages, see Joseph H. Lynch, *Godparents and Kinship in Early Medieval Europe* (Princeton, N.J., 1986); and Bernhard Jussen, *Spiritual Kinship as Social Practice: Godparenthood and Adoption in the Early Middle Ages*, revised and expanded English edition translated by Pamela Selwyn (Newark, DE, 2000).
4. See the genealogy in Grundmann, *Der Cappenberger Barbarossakopf*, p. 15, n. 11. The vita of Godfrey of Cappenberg stressed the kinship. See *Die Viten Gottfrieds von Cappenberg*, ed.

Gerlinde Niemeyer and Ingrid Ehlers-Kisseler with Veronika Lukas, in MGH SSrG 74 (Hanover, 2005), p. 159, ch. 54.

5. *Chronica regia Coloniensis*, pp. 59–60 (it ascribes the primary responsibility for Münster's destruction to the Cappenbergs); and *Die Viten Gottfrieds von Cappenberg*, introduction, pp. 29–62; and *Vita I*, esp. pp. 119–20, ch. 12; pp. 132–34, ch. 28 (Utrecht); and pp. 139–40, ch. 34 (Worms). See Grundmann, *Der Cappenberger Barbarossakopf*, pp. 12–34; and idem, "Gottfried von Cappenberg," *Westfälische Lebensbilder* 8 (1959): 1–16; Wolfgang Bockhorst, "Die Grafen von Cappenberg und die Anfänge des Stifts Cappenberg," in Irene Crusius, ed., *Studien zum Prämonstratenserorden* (Göttingen, 2003), pp. 57–74; and Horch, *"Nach dem Bild des Kaisers,"* pp. 58–76. On Norbert, see Kaspar Elm, ed., *Norbert von Xanten: Adliger, Ordensstifter, Kirchenfürst* (Cologne, 1984); and Stefan Weinfurter, "Norbert von Xanten und die Entstehung des Prämonstratenserordens," in idem, *Gelebte Ordnung—Gedachte Ordnung: Ausgewählte Beiträge zu König, Kirche und Reich* (Ostfildern, 2005), pp. 65–92.
6. *Die Viten Gottfrieds von Cappenberg*, pp. 159–61, ch. 54. On the date of the vitae, see *Die Viten*, pp. 4–9. See Horch, *"Nach dem Bild des Kaisers,"* pp. 20 (text of Otto's will), 54–57, 76–94, 241–56, and 277–78 (text of Johannes Gamans' life of Godfrey in the *Acta Sanctorum* in 1643).
7. *Die Viten Gottfrieds von Cappenberg*, pp. 139–40, ch. 34 (Worms); p. 144, ch. 37 (latrine), and pp. 147–48, ch. 43 (critique of Norbert). See Horch, *"Nach dem Bild des Kaisers,"* pp. 75–76 and 87–88.
8. DKIII, no. 104 (May 1144); and DFI, no. 404 (3 August 1163). Barbarossa ignored the role of Count Dietrich of Hüneburg in the foundation of Münsterdreisen. See Sabine Penth, *Prämonstratenser und Staufer: Zur Rolle des Reformordens in der staufischen Reichs- und Territorialpolitik* (Husum, 2003), pp. 52–55.
9. DKIII, no. 113 (July/September 1144); DFI, no. 127 (29 October 1155); and Penth, *Prämonstratenser und Staufer*, pp. 56–57.
10. DFI, no. 82 (23 June 1154).
11. DFI, no. 811 (25 May 1181); *Wirtembergisches UB* 2, ed. Royal State Archives, Stuttgart (Stuttgart, 1858), pp. 217–19, no. 429; pp. 237–38, no. 441; and pp. 263–64, no. 459; and Penth, *Prämonstratenser und Staufer*, pp. 57–61.
12. See Penth, *Prämonstratenser und Staufer*, pp. 74–92, esp. p. 85, and pp. 114–23; and Weinfurter, "Norbert von Xanten und die Entstehung des Prämonstratenserordens," pp. 87–90.
13. DFI, no. 470 (1 November 1164). See Penth, *Prämonstratenser und Staufer*, p. 163.
14. *Die Urkunden Friedrichs II. 1212–1217*, ed. Walter Koch, in MGH UdKK 14/2 (Hanover, 2007), pp. 312–14, no. 329. See Penth, *Prämonstratenser und Staufer*, pp. 43–47 and 106–09. The Welfs and Babenbergs also placed reformed canons, though not Premonstratensians, in the centers of their lordships. See Weinfurter, "Norbert von Xanten und die Entstehung des Prämonstratenserordens," pp. 88–90.
15. *Die Viten Gottfrieds von Cappenberg*, pp. 159–61, ch. 54; Horch, *"Nach dem Bild des Kaisers,"* p. 20, n. 43 (text of Otto's will); *Die Zeit der Staufer, Katalog* 1:393–94, no. 535; 2, Abbildungen 324–325; and Wieczorek et al., eds, *Die Staufer und Italien* 2.32–33. See Wolfgang Christian Schneider, "Die Kaiserapotheose Friedrich Barbarossas im 'Cappenberger Kopf': Ein Zeugnis staufischer Antikenerneuerung," *Castrum Peregrini* 217/18 (1995): 8–12; Willibald Sauerländer, "Dynastisches Mäzenatentum der Staufer und Welfen," in Hechberger and Schuler, eds, *Staufen & Welfen*, p. 126, and Horch, pp. 22 and 47–54. Claussen, "Stauferbilder," p. 354, called the head an idol. Görich, *Friedrich Barbarossa*, pp. 642–48, questioned whether the Cappenberg Head is in fact the head made in the likeness of the emperor, because a gilded bronze cannot be described as a silver head. Moreover, if Frederick had given the head to Otto, presumably so that he and the canons would intercede on the emperor's behalf in prayer, that fact would have been stated in the inscription. The bust is thus not a likeness of Frederick. (If it isn't, then what is it? It is hardly the standard representation of a saint.) If Görich is right, we are left, however, with two heads: the Cappenberg Head and a presumably lost silver head in the likeness of an emperor that Otto did give to Cappenberg. Ironically, the Cappenberg Head appears on the cover of Görich's biography.

16. Horch, *"Nach dem Bild des Kaisers,"* pp. 34–37, 117–23, 183–89, and 206–07. The Alexander reliquary is plate 33 and the Augustus cameo is plate 39. On the Alexander reliquary, see *Die Zeit der Staufer, Katalog* 1:404–06, no. 542; 2, Abbildung 333.
17. The texts are in Horch, *"Nach dem Bild des Kaisers,"* p. 38.
18. Morena, *Libellus de rebus a Frederico imperatore gestis*, pp. 186–87; and Grundmann, *Der Cappenberger Barbarossakopf*, pp. 35–67.
19. Claussen, "Stauferbilder," p. 357. Sauerländer, "Dynastisches Mäzenatentum," pp. 126–27, said that it is naive to think that the bust really resembled Frederick, but that it was unprecedented to represent a medieval monarch as an ancient Roman emperor.
20. Schneider, "Die Kaiserapotheose Friedrich Barbarossas," pp. 9–10 and 31–32; Lieselotte E. Saurma-Jeltsch, "Aachen und Rom in der staufischen Reichsimagination," in Schneidmüller et al., eds, *Verwandlungen des Stauferreichs*, pp. 274–81; Ursula Nilgen, "Staufische Bildpropaganda: Legitimation und Selbstverständnis im Wandel," in Wieczorek et al., eds, *Die Staufer und Italien* 1:86–90; and Horch, *"Nach dem Bild des Kaisers,"* pp. 22–25 and 111–17.
21. Schneider, "Die Kaiserapotheose Friedrich Barbarossas," pp. 7–12, 14–23, and 32–33; and Horch, *"Nach dem Bild des Kaisers,"* pp. 37–40.
22. Schneider, "Die Kaiserapotheose Friedrich Barbarossas," pp. 12–16; and Horch, *"Nach dem Bild des Kaisers,"* pp. 37–46. Sauerländer, "Dynastisches Mäzenatentum," p. 126, insisted that the base was a later addition. On the chandelier, see p. 333; and on the imperial crown, which I believe Wibald of Stavelot may have designed, see pp. 58–59.
23. Saurma-Jeltsch, "Aachen und Rom," pp. 268–74 and 276; Claussen, "Stauferbilder," p. 357; and Wieczorek et al., eds, *Die Staufer und Italien*, 2.32. On the golden bull, see *Die Zeit der Staufer, Katalog*, 1.22, no. 31; 3.II, Abbildung 2 and 3.V, Abbildung 5; and Wieczorek et al., eds, *Die Staufer und Italien*, 2.24.
24. Horch, *"Nach dem Bild des Kaisers,"* pp. 145–54, esp. p. 153.
25. Claussen, "Stauferbilder," pp. 358–59.
26. *Codex Falkensteinensis: Die Rechtsaufzeichnungen der Grafen von Falkenstein*, ed. Elisabeth Noichl (Munich, 1978), Plate 1. See John B. Freed, "Artistic and Literary Representations of Family Consciousness," in Gerd Althoff, ed., *Medieval Conceptions of the Past: Ritual, Memory, Historiography* (Washington, D.C., 2002), pp. 233–45.
27. Grundmann, *Der Cappenberger Barbarossakopf*, pp. 43–44; and Opll, *Das Itinerar Kaiser Friedrich Barbarossas*, p. 142. For Wibald as the designer of the bust, see Horch, *"Nach dem Bild des Kaisers,"* pp. 198–215. I had reached the same conclusion several years before Horch's book was published in 2013. See Wibald of Stavelot, *Briefbuch* 1:167–70, nos. 96 and 97 (Jaffé, nos. 119–20; correspondence with the goldsmith; a German translation is in Horch, pp. 150–51); 2:731–32 (Jaffé, no. 350; seal and bull); 3:733–36, no. 351 (Jaffé, no. 377; seal and bull); and 3:891–92, no. 429 (Jaffé, no. 456; Beatrice's seal). On Rupert of Deutz, see John H. Van Engen, *Rupert of Deutz* (Berkeley, 1983), pp. 275–82.

Horch, pp. 215–30, argued that the head was originally intended for St. Mary's in Aachen as a representation of the divine origins of Frederick's lordship. When that message was deemed to be too provocative in Frederick's dealing with the papacy, the head became a potential embarrassment; and it was sent to Cappenberg, where its original function was quickly forgotten after it was transformed into a reliquary. Horch conceded that there is no evidence that the head ever was in Aachen. However, there are additional problems with Horch's thesis. She never indicated when, prior to Otto's death in 1171, the head was deemed so provocative that it had to be consigned to a dignified oblivion. (The schism did not end until 1177.) Presumably, Frederick, who proclaimed in 1162 that he had the right as the emperor to decide a disputed papal election and who committed himself and the German Church in 1165 never to recognize Alexander III as the rightful pope, would not have found such a message objectionable during the 1160s. Finally, the section in Godfrey's vita that indicates that Otto placed the relics of St. John into a gilded head (ch. 54) could have been written by 1158, that is, shortly after Frederick's visit in April 1156 to Münster. See *Die Viten Gottfrieds von Cappenberg*, p. 9.

Horch, pp. 213–14, also argued that Wibald left on his first mission to Constantinople immediately after the imperial coronation on 18 June 1155, and could thus have commissioned the head only after his return in the spring of 1156, that is, too late for Frederick to have given it to Otto of Cappenberg in April (she does not mention Frederick's stay in Münster), and before his departure for his second mission to Constantinople in October 1157. However, Wibald witnessed an imperial charter after 7 July 1155 (DFI, no. 116), so he would have had at least a few weeks prior to his departure to arrange for the making of the head.

28. Horch, *"Nach dem Bild des Kaisers,"* pp. 222–56, esp. pp. 237–41 and 255–56.

Chapter 3 A Fortunate Youth

1. DKIII, no 8 (1/23 April 1138).
2. German scholars have devoted considerable attention to the development of the kingdom's elective monarchy, which has been seen as a major cause for Germany's failure to achieve national unity before the nineteenth century. See Ulrich Schmidt, *Königswahl und Thronfolge im 12. Jahrhundert* (Cologne and Vienna, 1987), pp. 1–33 (historiographical summary) and 261–65 (conclusion). The legal historian Heinrich Mitteis was the chief proponent of the view that blood descent continued to be important. See his *Die deutsche Königswahl: Ihre Rechtsgrundlagen bis zur Goldenen Bulle*, 2nd expanded edn. (Brno, Munich, and Vienna, 1944; reprint, Darmstadt, 1965); and his modified stance in "Die Krise des deutschen Königswahlrechts," in Eduard Hlawitschka, ed., *Königswahl und Thronfolge in ottonisch-frühdeutscher Zeit* (Darmstadt, 1971), pp. 216–302. Mitteis' chief opponent was Fritz Rörig, who argued for a strictly free election in "Geblütsrecht und freie Wahl in ihrer Auswirkung auf die deutsche Geschichte," in Hlawitschka, ed., *Königswahl und Thronfolge*, pp. 71–147. On the development of the electoral proceedings, specifically of the *Kur*, the formal casting of votes, see Ulrich Reuling, *Die Kur in Deutschland und Frankreich: Untersuchungen zur Entwicklung des rechtsförmlichen Wahlaktes bei der Königserhebung im 11. und 12. Jahrhundert* (Göttingen, 1979).
3. Bernd Kannowski, "The Impact of Lineage and Family Connections on Succession in Medieval Germany's Elective Kingdom," in Frédérique Lachaud and Michael Penman, eds, *Making and Breaking the Rules: Succession in Medieval Europe, c. 1000–c. 1600* (Turnhout, 2008), pp. 13–22; and Björn Weiler, "Suitability and Right: Imperial Succession and the Norms of Politics in Early Staufen Germany," in Lachaud and Penman, eds, *Making and Breaking the Rules*, pp. 71–86.
4. Hanna Vollrath, "Politische Ordnungsvorstellungen und politisches Handeln im Vergleich: Philipp II. August von Frankreich und Friedrich Barbarossa im Konflikt mit ihren mächtigsten Fürsten," in Joseph Canning and Otto Gerhard Oexle, eds, *Political Thought and the Realities of Power in the Middle Ages* (Göttingen, 1998), pp. 47–48, explained why Otto was proud that the German monarchy was elective.
5. Otto of Freising, *Chronicle* 7.17. Mierow translation, p. 424, n. 84, said that there is no evidence that Charles was considered a possible candidate, but see RI IV1/1:50–51, no. 89; and Matthias Becher, "Karl der Gute als Thronkandidat im Jahr 1125: Gedanken zur norddeutschen Opposition gegen Heinrich V.," in Gerhard Lubich, ed., *Heinrich V. in seiner Zeit: Herrschen in einem europäischen Reich des Hochmittelalters* (Vienna, Cologne, and Weimar, 2013), pp. 137–50.
6. On Henry the Black's motives, see Hechberger, *Staufer und Welfen*, p. 18, n. 2; Bernd Schneidmüller, "1125—Unruhe als politische Kraft im mittelalterlichen Reich," in Hechberger and Schuler, eds, *Staufer & Welfen*, pp. 41–42; Schmidt, *Königswahl und Thronfolge im 12. Jahrhundert*, pp. 70–71; and Ehlers, *Heinrich der Löwe*, p. 36.
7. *Narratio de electione Lotharii Saxoniae ducis in regem Romanorum*, pp. 509–12. All the relevant texts about the election of 1125 are presented in RI IV1/1:52–61, no. 92. On the election, see Heinz Stoob, "Zur Königswahl Lothars von Sachsen im Jahre 1125," in Helmut Beumann, ed., *Historische Forschungen für Walter Schlesinger* (Cologne and Vienna, 1974), pp. 438–61; Schmidt, *Königswahl und Thronfolge im 12. Jahrhundert*, pp. 34–59; and Schwarzmaier, "*Pater imperatoris*," pp. 262–65.
8. RI IV1/1:64–76, nos. 98, 101, 106, and 115.

9. Otto of Freising, *Deeds* 1.18; *Historia Welforum*, pp. 57–59, ch. 17; and RI IV1/1:99–180, nos. 155, 173, 202, 208, 211–12, and 281. See Engels, *Die Staufer*, pp. 28–31.
10. Hechberger, "Konrad III.—Königliche Politik und 'staufische Familieninteressen'?" p. 337.
11. Otto of Freising, *Deeds* 1.22.
12. Ibid., 1.23 and 1.41. On the political and territorial implications of Frederick II's second marriage, and of the marriage of his only full sister Gertrude to Count Hermann of Stahleck, whom Conrad III enfeoffed with the Rhenish Palatinate in 1142, see Odilo Engels, "Grundlinien der rheinischen Verfassungsgeschichte im 12. Jahrhundert," in idem, *Stauferstudien: Beiträge zur Geschichte der Staufer im 12. Jahrhundert: Festgabe zu seinem sechzigsten Geburtstag*, ed. Erich Meuthen and Stefan Weinfurter (Sigmaringen, 1988), pp. 137–41; Weller, *Die Heiratspolitik des deutschen Hochadels*, pp. 26–29 and 34–37; idem, "Auf dem Weg zum 'staufischen Haus,'" pp. 48–51; and Ziegler, *König Konrad III.*, pp. 68–78 and 460–66.
13. Otto of Freising, *Chronicle* 7.17–18; idem, *Deeds* 1.17–19; and RI IV1/1:92–162, nos. 141, 145, 149–50, 164, 166–67, 169–70, and 263.
14. See Schmidt, *Königswahl und Thronfolge im 12. Jahrhundert*, pp. 60–68; Seibert, "Die frühen 'Staufer,'" p. 18; Schwarzmaier, "*Pater imperatoris*," pp. 248–51 and 268–73; and Lyon, *Princely Brothers and Sisters*, pp. 9–11.
15. Bernhardi, *Lothar von Supplinburg*, p. 555, n. 26.
16. *Historia Welforum*, pp. 62–65, chs. 20–21; Otto of Freising, *Chronicle* 7.19; and RI IV1/1:152–293, nos. 248, 325, 411–15, 417, 429, and 456–57. See Weller, *Die Heiratspolitik des deutschen Hochadels*, pp. 255–59; Ziegler, *König Konrad III.*, pp. 56–69; and Seibert, "Die frühen 'Staufer,'" pp. 25–26.
17. RI IV1/1:320–404, nos. 494, 534, 580–81, 598–99, 602, 635, and 651; and Helmold of Bosau, *Slawenchronik*, ed. and trans. Heinz Stoob, AQ 19, 7th edn. (Darmstadt, 2008), pp. 168–70, ch. 41.
18. Otto of Freising, *Chronicle* 7.22–23; idem, *Deeds* 1.23; Balderich, *A Warrior Bishop of the Twelfth Century: The Deeds of Albero of Trier, by Balderich*, trans. Brian A. Pavlac (Toronto, 2008), pp. 52–56, ch. 20; and RI IV1/2:25–43, nos. 67, 79, 80–87, 96, 100, and 102–04. See Engels, "Beiträge zur Geschichte der Staufer im 12. Jahrhundert," pp. 38–44; Schmidt, *Königswahl und Thronfolge im 12. Jahrhundert*, pp. 69–108; Seibert, "Die frühen 'Staufer,'" p. 19; Jan Keupp, "Interaktion als Investition: Überlegungen zum Sozialkapital König Konrads III.," in Seibert and Dendorfer, eds, *Grafen, Herzöge, Könige*, pp. 309–10; and Ziegler, *König Konrad III.*, pp. 40–49.
19. Grundmann, "Litteratus—illiteratus," pp. 3–15; and Alfred Wendehorst, "Who Could Read and Write in the Middle Ages?" in Alfred Haverkamp and Hanna Vollrath, eds, *England and Germany in the High Middle Ages* (Oxford, 1996), pp. 61–70. Schwarzmaier, "*Pater imperatoris*," pp. 251–52, 268–69, 278, and 281–93, discussed whether the Staufer brothers had agreed that Barbarossa would succeed Conrad as king, because only Frederick II had a son in 1127. The election of Conrad's son Henry (VI) in 1147 would have violated that understanding. The failure to prepare Barbarossa for such a role argues, in my mind, against any such agreement.
20. RI IV1/2:51–52, no. 122. On the education of Frederick's sons, see Otto of St. Blasien, *Chronicle*, pp. 64–65, ch. 21. It is highly unlikely that either man would have made such a self-deprecating comment.
21. Wibald of Stavelot, *Briefbuch* 2:709–13, no. 339 (Jaffé, no. 375; also *Constitutiones* 1.192–93, no. 138).
22. Otto of Freising and Rahewin, *Deeds* 3.10; and Romuald of Salerno, *Chronicle* (a facing edition of Romuald's eyewitness account of the Peace of Venice with the Latin text and a German translation), in Schmale, trans., *Italienische Quellen*, pp. 348–49. A complete text of the chronicle is in MGH SS 19 (Hanover, 1866): Romuald of Salerno, *Romoaldi II. archiepiscopi Salernitani Annales*, ed. Wilhelm Arndt, pp. 387–461. On this chronicle, see D. J. A. Matthew, "The Chronicle of Romuald of Salerno," in R. H. C. Davis, ed., *The Writing of History in the Middle Ages: Essays Presented to Richard William Southern* (Oxford, 1981), pp. 239–74.

23. DFI, no. 376 (24 July 1162).
24. *Codex Falkensteinensis*, p. 29*, n. 2; and no. 183. See Freed, "Artistic and Literary Representations of Family Consciousness," in Althoff et al., eds, *Medieval Conceptions of the Past*, pp. 234–36; and Patrick Geary and John B. Freed, "Literacy and Violence in Twelfth-Century Bavaria: The 'Murder Letter' of Count Sigiboto IV," *Viator* 25 (1994): 115–29. On Frederick's command of Latin, see Görich, *Friedrich Barbarossa*, pp. 206–08. On the creation of the archive, see John B. Freed, "The Creation of the *Codex Falkensteinensis* (1166): Self-Representation and Reality," in Björn Weiler and Simon MacLean, eds, *Representations of Power in Medieval Germany* (Turnhout, 2006), pp. 189–210.
25. DFI, no. 1014 (1155–86). On Frederick's intellectual interests, see Peter Ganz, "Friedrich Barbarossa: Hof und Kultur," in Haverkamp, ed., *Friedrich Barbarossa*, pp. 623–50; and a more positive assessment in Peter Johanek, "Kultur und Bildung im Umkreis Friedrich Barbarossas," in Haverkamp, ed., *Friedrich Barbarossa*, pp. 651–77.
26. Ganz, "Friedrich Barbarossa: Hof und Kultur," pp. 636–39.
27. *Historia Welforum*, pp. 50–53, ch. 14; and Gilbert of Mons, *Chronicle of Hainaut*, pp. 126–27, ch. 150. For a general discussion of childhood in medieval Germany, based on literary and narrative texts, see James A. Schultz, *The Knowledge of Childhood in the German Middle Ages, 1100–1350* (Philadelphia, P.A., 1995).
28. RI IV2/1:4, no. 9; and Otto of Freising, *Deeds* 2.5. See Odilo Engels, "Friedrich Barbarossa und Dänemark," in Haverkamp, ed., *Friedrich Barbarossa*, pp. 370–72; and Ziegler, *König Konrad III.*, pp. 765–68.
29. Boso, *Les vies des papes rédigée par le Cardinal Boson et insérées dans le Liber Censum*, ed. Louis Duchesne, in *Le Liber Pontificalis: Texte, Introduction et Commentaire*, 2 vols (Paris, 1892), vol. 2, pp. 388–446, esp. p. 433. For an English translation, see *Boso's Life of Alexander III*, trans. G. M. Ellis with an introduction by Peter Munz (Oxford, 1973), p. 97.
30. DFI, no. 522 (27 January 1167). On hunting "as a symbol of imperial ideology, political legitimacy, and divine favor," see Eric J. Goldberg, "Louis the Pious and the Hunt," *Speculum* 88 (2013): 613–43, esp. 623–25. For information on the organization of such a royal park 150 years later, see Sharon Farmer, "Aristocratic Power and the 'Natural' Landscape: The Garden Park at Hesdin, ca. 1291–1302," *Speculum* 88 (2013): 644–80.
31. Otto of Freising and Rahewin, *Deeds* 4.43 and 4.86. The Schmale edition of the *Deeds*, pp. 709–11, is better than Mierow's edition at identifying the passages that Rahewin took from Apollinaris Sidonius and Einhard's *Life of Charlemagne*, and at explaining what Rahewin probably meant when he said that Frederick was "blessed by the holy relics" after the Mass.
32. Morena, *Libellus de rebus a Frederico imperatore gestis*, pp. 188–89.
33. Ferdinand Opll, "Amator ecclesiarum: Studien zur religiösen Haltung Friedrich Barbarossas," *MIÖG* 88 (1980): 77, n. 35.
34. DFI, no. 34 (20 October 1152).
35. DFI, no. 834 (7 October 1182); and no. 957 (17 April 1187); *Annales SS. Udalrici et Afrae Augustenses a. 1106–1334*, ed. Philipp Jaffé, in MGH SS 17 (Hanover, 1861), p. 430; and RI IV2/4:186–87, nos. 3067–69. On DFI, no. 957, see Opll, "Die Winterquatember im Leben Friedrich Barbarossas," pp. 332–34.
36. DFI, no. 152 (17 September 1156); and no. 228 (25 October 1158).
37. Opll, "Amator ecclesiarum," pp. 74–75; and DFI, no. 647 (January 1167; Hospitalers in Lombardy); nos. 820 and 836 (13 December 1181 and 25 January 1183; Altenburg); and no. 995 (16 April 1189; Haguenau); RI IV2/4:42, no. 2683 (1182; Reichardsroth); and *Die Urkunden Friedrichs II.*, pp. 312–14, no. 329 (Kaiserslautern).
38. Opll, "Amator ecclesiarum," p. 81; *The Letters of Hildegard of Bingen*, trans. Joseph L. Baird and Radd K. Ehrman, vol. 1 (New York, 1994), Introduction, pp. 11–12; 3 (2004), pp. 112–16, nos. 312–16; and DFI, no. 398 (18 April 1163). Frederick's only known stay in Ingelheim was in 1163. See Opll, *Das Itinerar Kaiser Friedrich Barbarossas*, pp. 134–35.
39. *Vita beati Hartmanni Episcopi Brixinensis (1140–1164)*, ed. Anselm Sparber (Innsbruck, 1940), pp. 58–60. I suspect that the author may have had a copy of Otto and Rahewin's *Deeds* at his disposal when he wrote these words that echo both 3.15a and 4.86. He, too, insisted that the nearly thirty-year-old Frederick was a youth at his election (p. 58).

40. Opll, "Amator ecclesiarum," pp. 76 and 80–81; Stefan Weinfurter, *Salzburger Bistumsreform und Bischofspolitik im 12. Jahrhundert: Der Erzbischof Konrad I. von Salzburg (1106–1147) und die Regularkanoniker* (Cologne, 1975), esp. pp. 26–37, 51–54, 80–81, 92–94, and 208–20; Anselm Sparber, *Die Brixner Fürstbischöfe im Mittelalter: Ihr Leben und Wirken* (Bolzano, 1968), pp. 56–66; and DFI, no. 284 (23 October 1159); no. 307 (15 February 1160); no. 327 (shortly after 21 May 1161); no. 355 (4 April 1162); no. 358 (7 April 1162); no. 398 (18 April 1163); and no. 449 (22 March–22 June 1164). Relations between Henry Jasomirgott and his two churchmen brothers, Otto of Freising and Conrad of Passau, were strained at times. See Lyon, *Princely Brothers and Sisters*, pp. 82–86.
41. Georges Duby, "Youth in Aristocratic Society: Northwestern France in the Twelfth Century," in idem, *The Chivalrous Society*, trans. Cynthia Postan (Berkeley and Los Angeles, 1977), pp. 112–22.
42. DKIII, no. 8 (17/23 April 1138); and nos. 56–58, 72, 95, 98, 113 (father and son appear as the co-advocates of Lorch), 128, 130 (May 1145), and 278 (a forgery). Conrad, identified as Frederick's brother, witnessed his first charter on 12 January 1152, just before his brother's election as king (DKIII, no. 269). For a critique of Duby's model, with special reference to Barbarossa, see Jonathan R. Lyon, "Fathers and Sons: Preparing Noble Youths to be Lords in Twelfth-Century Germany," *Journal of Medieval History* 34/3 (September 2008): 291–310.
43. Hechberger, *Staufer und Welfen*, esp. pp. 160–83 and 216–18; and idem, "Konrad III.," esp. pp. 332–36.
44. Weller, "Auf dem Weg zum 'staufischen Haus,'" p. 56: "unsicheren Kantonisten."
45. Otto of Freising, *Chronicle* 7.23–25; idem, *Deeds* 1.23; *Historia Welforum*, chs. 24 and 25; Helmold of Bosau, *Slawenchronik*, pp. 201–11, chs. 54 and 56; and RI IV1/2:43–68, nos. 105–09, 113, 116, 124–26, 131, 151, 156, and 160. See Schneidmüller, *Die Welfen*, pp. 175–79; Ziegler, *König Konrad III.*, pp. 355–69 and 388–91; Görich, "Wahrung des *honor*," pp. 290–94, and Steffen Patzold, "Konflikte im Stauferreich nördlich des Alpen: Methodische Überlegungen zur Messbarkeit eines Wandels der Konfliktführung im 12. Jahrhundert," in Schneidmüller and Wieczorek, eds, *Verwandlungen des Stauferreichs*, pp. 150–55. Ehlers, *Heinrich der Löwe*, pp. 34 and 47–48, argued that Henry was born in 1133/35 rather than 1130 as maintained by Karl Jordan, *Henry the Lion: A Biography*, trans. P. S. Falla (Oxford, 1986), p. 22. Jordan, who edited Henry's charters, was the foremost authority on the duke in the mid-twentieth century. I use Ehlers' rather than Jordan's biography because the former incorporates more recent scholarship.
46. Otto of Freising, *Chronicle* 7.23–26; *Historia Welforum*, pp. 68–75, chs. 24–25; and RI IV1/2:50–113, nos. 116, 128, 161, 185, 193–99, 221–22, 240, and 265. See Ziegler, *König Konrad III.*, pp. 350–51, 370–75, 396–400, and 444–52.
47. *Chronica regia Coloniensis*, p. 79. Otto of Freising, *Chronicle* 7.26, placed Welf's claim after Leopold's enfeoffment in 1143, whereas the *Historia Welforum*, ch. 25, mentioned the claim in conjunction with the fighting around Valley and Weinsberg in 1140. See Hechberger, *Staufer und Welfen*, pp. 18–32 and 201–16. Most recently, Opll in RI IV1/2:93, no. 222, has argued for the later date.
48. Otto of Freising, *Chronicle* 7.26; *Historia Welforum*, pp. 72–75, ch. 25; and RI IV1/2:115–16, nos. 271 and 272.
49. Hechberger, *Staufer und Welfen*, pp. 32–35 and 216–18. On these events, see Jürgen Dendorfer, "Von den Babenberger zu den Welfen: Herzog und Adel in Bayern um die Mitte des 12. Jahrhunderts," in Hubertus Seibert and Alois Schmid, eds, *München, Bayern und das Reich im 12. und 13. Jahrhundert: Lokale Befunde und überregionale Perspektiven* (Munich, 2008), esp. pp. 232–35 and 240–41.
50. Freed, *Noble Bondsmen*, pp. 104–13.
51. DKIIII, no. 104 (May 1144).
52. DKIII, no. 130 (May 1145); and no. 164 (4 January 1147). On identifying the Duke Frederick in no. 164 as Barbarossa, see RI IV2/1:5, no. 20.
53. DKIII, no. 147 (13 March/3 April 1146; Aachen); no. 149 (14 May 1146; Nuremberg); no. 155 (21 July 1146; Ulm); and no. 156 (2 August 1146; Fulda).
54. Otto of Freising and Rahewin, *Deeds* 1.26 and 4.17. Conrad of Dachau appeared as "dux Meranus" in DFI, no. 14 (end of June to the beginning of July 1152). *Meranien* referred to

the coastal area of Croatia along the Adriatic. In no. 173 (4 July 1157) he was styled "Cunradus dux et comes Dachowe."

55. Jürgen Dendorfer, *Adelige Gruppenbildung und Königsherrschaft: Die Grafen von Sulzbach und ihr Beziehungsgeflecht im 12. Jahrhundert* (Munich, 2004), pp. 69–71; Weller, *Die Heiratspolitik des deutschen Hochadels*, pp. 248–51; and Ziegler, *König Konrad III.*, pp. 157–71. A good genealogy of the counts of Wolfratshausen is in *Die Andechs-Meranier in Franken: Europäisches Fürstentum im Mittelalter* (Mainz, 1998), p. 387. On Frederick's continuing animosity, see Görich, *Friedrich Barbarossa*, p. 212.
56. Otto of Freising, *Deeds* 1.27. See Görich, *Friedrich Barbarossa*, pp. 67–71.
57. DKIII, no. 175 ("Fridericus dux iunior;" 2 March 1147); no. 176 (13 March 1147); no. 177 (15 March 1147); and no. 178 (23 March 1147). On Frederick II's death date, see RI IV2/1:6, no. 26.
58. Knut Görich, *Ein Kartäuser im Dienst Friedrich Barbarossas: Dietrich von Silve-Bénite (c. 1145–1205)* (Salzburg, 1987), esp. pp. 24–34. See DFI, no. *1148 (1167 or earlier). The Carthusian historian Nicholas Molina (1563–1638) copied a notice in which Frederick referred allegedly to "Terricum carissimum et fidelem nostrum de progenie nostra oriundum" (p. 19); and Dietrich styled himself in 1170 in a charter that survives in a copy as "Ego Terricus . . . de domo et progenie magni Friderici" (p. 23). The question is whether Dietrich was the son of Frederick or another member of the lineage. For a critical assessment of Görich's argument, see RI IV2/2:298, no. 1762. Görich, *Friedrich Barbarossa*, pp. 420–21, backed off his earlier identification of Dietrich as Frederick's son.

    Laudage, *Friedrich Barbarossa*, p. 107, said that we do not know when the other seven sons and daughters Frederick is reputed to have fathered, in addition to his eleven legitimate children, were born. Laudage then observed that these seven children may merely be "scholarly inventions." He provided no footnotes. Decker-Hauff, in his detailed genealogy, "Das Staufische Haus," p. 357, listed only one possible illegitimate offspring—with a question mark—Ulrich (c. 1140/45–after 1205–06), who was assigned property near Stauf. Weller, *Die Heiratspolitik des deutschen Hochadels*, p. 224, doubted Ulrich's existence.
59. Jonathan Phillips, *The Second Crusade: Extending the Frontiers of Christendom* (New Haven and London, 2007), pp. 93–94 and p. 302, n. 93. Phillips' source is a letter that Welf VI sent to Louis VII in early 1147. Otto of Freising, *Deeds* 1.42, stated that Welf took the cross on Christmas Eve, perhaps in a formal ceremony, on his own estate located in Peiting, southwest of Munich. On this problem, see RI IV1/2:178, no. 421. The *Historia Welforum*, pp. 74–77, ch. 27, a source that Phillips did not list in his bibliography, says, certainly wrongly, that Welf VI decided to leave only after the king and Barbarossa had determined to set out. On Welf's brother Conrad, see *Historia Welforum*, pp. 52–57, ch. 15; and Ehlers, *Otto von Freising*, pp. 15–19, esp. p. 17.
60. Otto of Freising, *Deeds* 1.40; and RI IV1/2:178–79, no. 422. See Phillips, *The Second Crusade*, pp. 80–98, esp. pp. 95–96.
61. Otto of Freising, *Deeds* 1.45; and RI IV1/2:189–91, no. 446. On Henry (VI)'s election, see Schmidt, *Königswahl und Thronfolge im 12. Jahrhundert*, pp. 109–22.
62. *Die Traditionen des Klosters Wessobrunn*, ed. Reinhard Höppl (Munich, 1984), pp. 45–47, no. 30.
63. Morena, *Libellus de rebus a Frederico imperatore gestis*, pp. 190–91. (Rudolf of Lindau is the same person as Rudolf of Pfullendorf.) See Karl Schmid, *Graf Rudolf von Pfullendorf und Kaiser Friedrich I.* (Freiburg im Breisgau, 1954), pp. 58–63; and Christian Uebach, *Die Ratgeber Friedrich Barbarossas (1152–1167)* (Marburg, 2008), pp. 87–91 and 209–10 (Ulrich IV of Lenzburg) and pp. 210–14 (Rudolf of Pfullendorf). On their court appearances, see Alheydis Plassmann, *Die Struktur des Hofes unter Friedrich I. Barbarossa nach den deutschen Zeugen seiner Urkunden* (Hanover, 1998), pp. 140–47.
64. Otto of Freising, *Chronicle* 6.20; idem, *Deeds* 1.69; Morena, *Libellus de rebus a Frederico imperatore gestis*, pp. 190–91; and RI IV1/2:302–20, nos. 704 and 747. Wulfhild and Otto III's mothers were half-sisters. See Weller, *Die Heiratspolitik des deutschen Hochadels*, p. 759 and Plate 11. I am adopting Weller's numbering of the Wittelsbachs. Frederick mentioned his kinship with Otto V and his brother, Archbishop Conrad of Mainz and Salzburg. See Schieffer, "Friedrich Barbarossa und seine Verwandten," pp. 585–86.

65. Otto of St. Blasien, *Chronicle*, ch. 10; and Burchard of Ursberg, *Chronicon*, pp. 148–49. For a complete listing, see RI IV2/1:47–48, no. 167.
66. DFI, no. 73 (11 April 1154). Berthold was identified as the margrave of Cham in DFI, no. 70 (3 February 1154), and as the margrave of Vohburg in DFI, no. 158 (5 February 1157).
67. Dendorfer, *Adelige Gruppenbildung und Königsherrschaft*, pp. 325–58 and 393–406; Weller, *Die Heiratspolitik des deutschen Hochadels*, pp. 248–51, 786–96, and Plate 13; Ziegler, *König Konrad III.*, pp. 495–502; Eduard Hlawitschka, "Weshalb war die Auflösung der Ehe Friedrich Barbarossas und Adelas von Vohburg möglich?" *DA* 61 (2005): 525–36; and idem, *Die Ahnen der hochmittelalterlichen deutschen Könige* 2, Plate XXXVII and pp. 135–94, esp. 139–41 and 144–48; and Tobias Küss, *Die älteren Diepoldinger als Markgrafen in Bayern (1077–1204): Adlige Herrschaftsbildung im Hochmittelalter* (Munich, 2013), pp. 180–219 and 238–43. On the Bavarian revolt, see Stefan Weinfurter, "Reformidee und Königtum im spätsalischen Reich: Überlegungen zu einer Neubewertung Kaiser Heinrichs V.," in idem, *Gelebte Ordnung—Gedachte Ordnung*, pp. 289–333.
68. DKIII, no. 150 ("marchio Gebehardus": 22 May 1146); no. 153 (10 July 1146); no. 204 ("Gebehardus marchio de Solzbach": 1 June 1149); but DFI, no. 70 ("Pertolfus marchio de Cambe" and "Gebhardus comes de Sulzbach": 3 February 1154). Jan Paul Niederkorn, "Der Übergang des Egerlandes an die Staufer: Die Heirat Friedrich Barbarossas mit Adela von Vohburg," *ZbLG* 54/3 (1991): 620–22, argued that Conrad III confiscated the Nordmark after Diepold's death. Ziegler, *König Konrad III.*, pp. 501–02, accepted Niederkorn's argument and in an appendix, pp. 755–65, explained the disputed Polish succession. Weller, *Die Heiratspolitik des deutschen Hochadels*, pp. 84–86, saw no evidence that Diepold had opposed Conrad's Polish policy. Dendorfer, *Adelige Gruppenbildung und Königsherrschaft*, pp. 408–09, argued that Gebhard II served as the guardian of Diepold's heirs between 1146 and 1149. I am inclined to accept Dendorfer's argument because when Conrad took Waldsassen under royal protection, the king referred to the late Diepold as the "vir illustrissimus marchio Theobaldus," hardly the designation for a man whose fief had been confiscated after his death. See DKIII, no. 175 (2 March 1147).
69. *Fundatio monasterii Waldsassensis*, ed. Oswald Holder-Egger, in MGH SS 15/2 (Hanover, 1888), p. 1092.
70. DKIII, no. 175 (2 March 1147).
71. Küss, *Die älteren Diepoldinger*, pp. 86–87, n. 120, argued that Conrad treated the Egerland as an excheated fief and that Gebhard of Sulzbach, as the king's brother-in-law, the stepfather of Diepold V, and the guardian of Diepold's heirs, persuaded them to accept this arrangement. Since Küss, pp. 50–51, also insisted that Diepold V had attained his majority by 1146, it is unclear why he would have required a guardian and why Gebhard would have taken his place as the margrave of the Nordmark, especially since Küss rejected the thesis that Diepold III had opposed Conrad's Polish policy (pp. 218–19).
72. See Hans Patze, "Kaiser Friedrich Barbarossa und der Osten," in Theodor Mayer, ed., *Probleme des 12. Jahrhunderts: Reichenau Vorträge 1965–1967* (Constance and Stuttgart, 1968), pp. 381–85.
73. *Der Codex Eberhardi des Klosters Fulda*, ed. Heinrich Meyer zu Ermgassen, 3 vols (Marburg, 1995–2007), 2:300; and Küss, *Die älteren Diepoldinger*, pp. 121 and 133.
74. In addition to Diepold III and Berengar's joint appearances at court and Gebhard II's probable guardianship of Diepold's heirs, Berengar and Diepold's mother had been the co-founders around 1100 of the Benedictine abbey of Kastl, which subsequently served as the Sulzbachs' burial church. Such a joint foundation was often the work of kinsmen, but we do not know the nature of the genealogical connection. They seem to have been united, instead, by their common commitment to the Gregorian reform movement. See Dendorfer, *Adelige Gruppenbildung und Königsherrschaft*, pp. 121–32; and Küss, *Die älteren Diepoldinger*, pp. 143–45.
75. Dendorfer, *Adelige Gruppenbildung und Königsherrschaft*, pp. 95–102; Weller, *Die Heiratspolitik des deutschen Hochadels*, pp. 38–43, 57–84, 481–85, 540–47, 550–57, 591–97, and Plates 5, 7/1, and 8; and Hlawitschka, *Die Ahnen der hochmittelalterlichen deutschen Könige*, 1/2:649–52 (Lothar and Simon as half-brothers), and 2, Plate 34 and pp. 53–76 (Sulzbach genealogy).

In a letter of April 16/20, 1150 (DKIII, no. 229), Conrad addressed Eirene with "paternal love." They were bound to each other both "by the ties of kinship and by the love of adoption." On Frederick's preference for his relatives in Thuringia, see Schieffer, "Friedrich Barbarossa und seine Verwandten," pp. 581–82. Frederick's ties to Louis III duplicated his own relationship with Welf VI.

76. DKIII, no. 196 (mid-April 1148); and RI IV1/2:226–32, nos. 531 and 546. See Dendorfer, *Adelige Gruppenbildung und Königsherrschaft*, pp. 407–12.
77. DKIII, no. 204 (1 June 1149). See Dendorfer, *Adelige Gruppenbildung und Königsherrschaft*, pp. 412–18.
78. Wibald of Stavelot, *Briefbuch* 2:731–32, no. 350 (Jaffé, no. 376); 3:733–36, no. 351 (Jaffé, no. 377); and 3:891–93, no. 429 (Jaffé, no. 456).
79. Ibid., 3:812–13, no. 385 (Jaffé, no. 408). Wibald's table of consanguinity is reproduced on p. 3.
80. Hlawitschka, "Weshalb war die Auflösung der Ehe Friedrich Barbarossas und Adelas von Vohburg möglich?" pp. 509–36.
81. RI IV2/1:47–48, no. 167. Otto of St. Blasien, *Chronicle*, pp. 32–33, ch. 10, writing in 1209, referred to Adela's numerous adulteries. A canon of St. Peter's on the Lauterberg in the diocese of Merseburg, writing in the 1220s, said that Frederick repudiated her "on account of the infamy of adultery." *Chronicon Montis Sereni*, ed. Ernst Ehrenfeuchter, MGH SS 23 (Hanover, 1874), p. 149. Erwin Rundnagel, "Die Ehescheidung Friedrich Barbarossas," in Walter Möllenberg, ed., *Kritische Beiträge zur Geschichte des Mittelalters: Festschrift für Robert Holtzmann zum sechzigsten Geburtstag* (Berlin, 1933), pp. 145–59, argued that Adela was guilty of adultery.
82. Burchard of Ursberg, *Chronicon*, pp. 148–49. On Dietho of Ravensburg and Adela's ministerial descendants, see Karl Bosl, *Die Reichsministerialität der Salier und Staufer: Ein Beitrag zur Geschichte des hochmittelalterlichen deutschen Volkes, Staates und Reiches*, 2 vols (Stuttgart, 1950–51), 2:413–15. See Hlawitschka, "Weshalb war die Auflösung der Ehe Friedrich Barbarossas und Adelas von Vohburg möglich?" p. 516.
83. See Leah Otis-Cour, "*De jure novo:* Dealing with Adultery in Fifteenth-Century Toulousain," *Speculum* 84 (2009): 349–50.
84. John W. Baldwin, *The Government of Philip Augustus: Foundations of French Royal Power in the Middle Ages*, (Berkeley and Los Angeles, 1991), pp. 82–87; and Constance M. Rousseau, "Neither Bewitched nor Beguiled: Philip Augustus's Alleged Impotence and Innocent III's Response," *Speculum* 89 (2014): 410–36.
85. Eike von Repgow, *The Saxon Mirror: A* Sachsenspiegel *of the Fourteenth Century*," trans. Maria Dobozy (Philadelphia, P.A., 1999), p. 135, 3.74. John of Salisbury indicated that when the marriage of Count Ralph of Vermandois was dissolved on the ground of consanguinity at the Council of Reims in 1148, he was required to return his wife's dowry. John of Salisbury, *The* Historia Pontificalis *of John of Salisbury*, ed. Marjorie Chibnall (Oxford, 1956; slightly revised reprint, Oxford, 1986), pp. 12–13, ch. 6.
86. Weller, *Die Heiratspolitik des deutschen Hochadels*, pp. 424–28 and 792–96; and Küss, *Die älteren Diepoldinger*, pp. 220–30.
87. RI IV2/1:7, nos. 33 and 34. See Phillips, *The Second Crusade*, pp. 171–73.
88. Odo of Deuil, *De profectione Ludovici VII in orientem*, pp. 48–51 and 88–97, esp. p. 93; and RI IV1/2:216–21, nos. 500–01, 503–12, and 514–18. See Phillips, *The Second Crusade*, pp. 173–84.
89. Odo of Deuil, *De profectione Ludovici VII in orientem*, pp. 97–109; Otto of Freising, *Deeds* 1.62–64; John of Salisbury, *Historia Pontificalis*, pp. 58–59, ch. 26; Gilbert of Mons, *Chronicle of Hainaut*, pp. 53–54, ch. 53; and RI IV1/2:221–43, nos. 519, 521–26, 529–30, 534–35, 538–40, 544–47, 552, 554–55, 558–65, and 569–71. See Phillips, *The Second Crusade*, pp. 212–27.
90. RI IV1/2:244–45, no. 575. See Weller, *Die Heiratspolitik des deutschen Hochadels*, pp. 357–62.
91. Otto of Freising, *Deeds* 1.64; RI IV1/2:246–53, nos. 580–97; and RI IV2/1:9, no. 45.
92. For an overview of Barbarossa's Norman policy, see Hubert Houben, "Barbarossa und die Normannen: Traditionelle Züge und neue Perspektiven imperialer Süditalienpolitik," in Haverkamp, ed., *Friedrich Barbarossa*, pp. 109–28.

93. DKIII, no. 224 (after 8 February 1150) and no. 229 (16/20 April 1150); Wibald of Stavelot, *Briefbuch* 2:406–08, no. 192 (Jaffé, no. 198); 2:430–32, no. 204 (Jaffé, no. 232); 2:476–79, no. 223 (Jaffé, no. 252); 2:539–41, no. 253 (Jaffé, no. 273); 3:814–16, no. 386 (Jaffé, no. 410); and 3:816–18, no. 387 (Jaffé, no. 411); RI IV1/2:246–328, nos. 580, 622, 629, 641, 654, 670, 674, 683, 692, and 764; and RI IV2/1:60, no. 197. See Weller, *Die Heiratspolitik des deutschen Hochadels*, pp. 63–76.
94. Otto of Freising, *Deeds* 1.25. For the Latin text of Conrad's letter, see DKIII, no. 69 (12 February 1142). For the Latin text of John II's letter, see the Schmale edition of the *Deeds*, pp. 174–76. Once Conrad reached Constantinople during the Second Crusade, the chancery began to style Manuel as the emperor of the Greeks. See DKIII, no. 195 (end of February 1148); no. 219 (January 1150); no. 397 (after 8 February 1150); no 229 (16/20 April 1150); and no. 261 (after 17 February 1151). On this usage, see Peter Schreiner, "Byzanz und der Westen: Die gegenseitige Betrachtungsweise in der Literatur des 12. Jahrhunderts," in Haverkamp, ed., *Friedrich Barbarossa*, pp. 567–68.
95. Gottfried Koch, *Auf dem Wege zum Sacrum Imperium: Studien zur ideologischen Herrschaftsbegründung der deutschen Zentralgewalt im 11. und 12. Jahrhundert* (Vienna, Cologne, and Graz, 1972), pp. 12–18, 21, and 111–13; Eckhard Müller-Mertens, *Regnum Teutonicum: Aufkommen und Verbreitung der deutschen Reichs- und Königsauffassung im frühen Mittelalter* (Vienna, Cologne, and Graz, 1970), esp. pp. 145–81 and 375–83; and Jörg Schwarz, *Herrscher- und Reichstitel bei Kaisertum und Papsttum im 12. und 13. Jahrhundert* (Cologne, Weimar, and Vienna, 2003), pp. 11–53.
96. DKIII, no. 1 (14 July 1129); no. 33 (July/August 1139); no. 36 (October 1139); no. 37 (October 1139); no. 184 (19/c. 23 March 1147); and no. 185 (19/c. 23 March 1147). See Schwarz, *Herrscher- und Reichstitel*, pp. 81–85 and 111–23.
97. DKIII, no. 69 (12 February 1142); and Schwarz, *Herrscher- und Reichstitel*, pp. 82–83. On the chaplain Albert, see Hausmann, *Reichskanzlei und Hofkapelle*, pp. 279–92.
98. Engels, "Beiträge zur Geschichte der Staufer," pp. 34–58. See the list of emperors that Otto included as an appendix to the *Chronicle*, pp. 450–51. It does not include the east Frankish king Conrad I but does list Lothar of Italy.
99. *Historia Welforum*, pp. 74–75, ch. 26. See Harald Zimmermann, "Die deutsch-ungarischen Beziehungen in der Mitte des 12. Jahrhunderts und die Berufung der Siebenbürger Sachsen," in Lorenz and Schmidt, eds, *Von Schwaben bis Jerusalem*, pp. 155–57.
100. *Historia Welforum*, pp. 74–77, ch. 27; Otto of Freising, *Deeds* 1.64; DKIII, no. 229 (16/20 April 1150); and RI IV1/2.237–38, no. 558. See Schneidmüller, *Die Welfen*, pp. 184–85.
101. We know about Roger's letters to the German princes and his negotiations with the pope from a missive that Wibald included in his letter collection in the spring of 1150 (*Briefbuch* 2:497–99, no. 233 [Jaffé, no. 147]). See John of Salisbury, *Historia Pontificalis*, pp. 59–61, chs. 27 and 28; RI IV1/2:245–46, no. 579; RI IV2/1:9, no. 42; Hechberger, *Staufer und Welfen*, pp. 34–35; Hubert Houben, *Roger II. von Sizilien: Herrscher zwischen Orient und Okzident*, 2nd rev. edn. (Darmstadt, 2010), pp. 89–91 and 93–99; and Petersohn, *Kaisertum und Rom in spätsalischer und staufischer Zeit*, p. 98, n. 100. Timothy Reuter, who began the new edition of Wibald's letters, was skeptical about the reliability of the letter. See Reuter, "Vom Parvenü zum Bündnispartner: Das Königreich Sizilien in der abendländischen Politik des 12. Jahrhunderts," in Theo Kölzer, ed., *Die Staufer im Süden: Sizilien und das Reich* (Sigmaringen, 1996), pp. 45–47.
102. *Historia Welforum*, pp. 76–77, ch. 28; DKIII, no. 224 (after 8 February 1150), no. 229 (16/20 April 1150), no. 268 (7 January 1152); DH(VI) in DKIII, nos. 10 and 11 (16/20 April 1150); Wibald of Stavelot, *Briefbuch* 2:441–44, no. 209 (Jaffé, no. 234); and RI IV1/2:277–333, nos. 651–54, 660, 670, 698, and 777. See Schneidmüller, *Die Welfen*, pp. 184–86; and Hechberger, *Staufer und Welfen*, pp. 216–18.
103. Schneidmüller, *Die Welfen*, pp. 186–87; and Ehlers, *Heinrich der Löwe*, pp. 77–78.
104. For a positive reassessment of Conrad's reign, see Friedrich Hausmann, "Die Anfänge des staufischen Zeitalters unter Konrad III.," in Mayer, ed., *Probleme des 12. Jahrhunderts*, pp. 53–78. Hechberger, "Konrad III.," pp. 336–40, addressed the question why Conrad III's reign was ultimately a failure. He was not merely unlucky, for example, the untimely deaths of Gertrude of Saxony after she had married Henry Jasomirgott and of Henry (VI). Conrad also relied too

much on the Babenbergs, who were too weak to fight the Welfs on their own; whereas Frederick, with a different set of relatives, turned to his powerful maternal kinsmen for support.

105. RI IV1/2:322–27, nos. 754 and 761; and Bernhardi, *Konrad III.*, p. 887.
106. See, for example, Reinhart Staats, *Theologie der Reichskrone: Ottonische "Renovatio imperii" im Spiegel einer Insignie* (Stuttgart, 1976), pp. 19–24; and idem, *Die Reichskrone: Geschichte und Bedeutung eines europäischen Symbols* (Göttingen, 1991), pp. 13–24.
107. Sebastian Scholz, "Die Wiener Reichskrone: Eine Krone aus der Zeit Konrads III.?" in Seibert and Dendorfer, eds, *Grafen, Herzöge, Könige*, pp. 341–62.
108. DKIII, no. 69 (12 February 1142).
109. DKIII, no. 222 (February 1150); no. 224 (after 8 February 1150); no. 229 (16/20 April 1150); Wibald of Stavelot, *Briefbuch* 2:396–98, no. 187 (Jaffé, no. 205); and RI IV1/2:264, no. 622.
110. Staats, *Theologie der Reichskrone*, pp. 43–46; and idem, *Die Reichskrone,* pp. 57–61, interpreted the Isaiah text as a reminder to every monarch that his days were numbered. Herwig Wolfram, *Conrad II, 990–1039: Emperor of Three Kingdoms*, trans. Denise A. Kaiser (University Park, PA, 2006), pp. 146–53, argued that Otto II commissioned the crown and that the Hezekiah plaque refers to Otto I's recovery from a serious illness. Oddly, Scholz, "Die Wiener Reichskrone," did not explain the selection of the Isaiah text, which I think clinches his argument that Conrad commissioned the crown. Since Wibald addressed Conrad as "glorioso Romanorum imperatori augusto" (*Briefbuch* 2:396–98, no. 187 [Jaffé, no. 205]), and, above all, since Wibald was charged with procuring both Frederick and Beatrice's seals and probably with the creation of the Cappenberg Head, I wonder whether Wibald may not have been responsible also for the design and making of the crown.

Chapter 4 King of the Romans

1. DFI, nos. 1–4 (9–12 March 1152). On Markwart of Grumbach, see Plassmann, *Die Struktur des Hofes unter Friedrich I. Barbarossa*, pp. 168–70; and Uebach, *Die Ratgeber Friedrich Barbarossas*, pp. 109–11 (Markwart II) and 229–31 (Markwart III). Before 1167, Markwart and/or his like-named son witnessed 35 percent of Frederick's German charters.
2. Gilbert of Mons, *Chronicle of Hainaut,* pp. 54–55, ch. 54; and RI IV2/1:12–13, no. 64. Engels, "Beiträge zur Geschichte der Staufer im 12. Jahrhundert," pp. 399–432, took Gilbert's account seriously and argued that Henry the Lion as Lothar's grandson was a serious contender for the crown. Engels' argument has been largely rejected. See Schmidt, *Königswahl und Thronfolge im 12. Jahrhundert*, pp. 123–34; Werner Goez, "Von Bamberg nach Frankfurt und Aachen: Barbarossas Weg zur Königskrone," in Jürgen Schneider, ed., *Festschrift Alfred Wendehorst zum 65. Geburtstag*, in *Jahrbuch für fränkische Landesgeschichte* 52 (1992): 61–64; and Jan Paul Niederkorn, "Friedrich von Rothenburg und die Königswahl von 1152," in Lorenz and Schmidt eds, *Von Schwaben bis Jerusalem*, pp. 51–52 and 57–58. For a critical assessment of Otto's tendentious narrative, see Stefanie Dick, "Die Königserhebung Friedrich Barbarossas im Spiegel der Quellen: Kritische Anmerkungen zu den 'Gesta Friderici' Ottos von Freising," *ZRG GA* 121 (2004): 200–37, esp. 205–26. Niederkorn, in "Zu glatt und daher verdächtig? Zur Glaubwürdigkeit der Schilderung der Wahl Friedrich Barbarossas (1152) durch Otto von Freising," *MIÖG* 115 (2007): 1–9, argued that Otto's account is trustworthy. Conrad recommended his nephew's selection because he realized that his young son could not deal with Henry the Lion's demands nor continue Conrad's Italian policy.
3. Niederkorn, "Friedrich von Rothenburg," pp. 58–59; and Gerd Althoff, "Friedrich von Rothenburg: Überlegungen zu einem übergangen Königssohn," in Karl Rudolf Schnith and Roland Pauler, eds., *Festschrift für Eduard Hlawitschka zum 65. Geburtstag* (Kallmünz, Upper Palatinate, 1993), p. 307. The regnal numbers of sons who did not succeed their fathers as kings are given in parentheses.
4. Ziegler, *König Konrad III.*, pp. 78–83.
5. *Chronica regia Coloniensis*, p. 88.
6. Wibald of Stavelot, *Briefbuch* 3:814–16, no. 386 (Jaffé, no. 410): "patruus noster, inclitus triumphator, sanctissimus videlicet imperator Conradus moriens, cum nos declarasset imperii sui successores . . ."

7. DFI, no. 5 (March–April 1152); and Wibald of Stavelot, *Briefbuch* 2:709–13, no. 339 (Jaffé, no. 375).
8. On this point, see Kannowski, "The Impact of Lineage and Family Connections on Succession," pp. 13–14.
9. *Chronica regia Coloniensis*, p. 89 (this appears in the thirteenth-century second recension of the chronicle); and RI IV2/1:52–53, no. 178. See Schmidt, *Königswahl und Thronfolge im 12. Jahrhundert*, p. 137; and Dick, "Die Königserhebung Friedrich Barbarossas," pp. 204–05 and 233–35.
10. DKIII, no. 267 (1–6 January 1152, Basel), no. 268 (7 January 1152, Constance), and no. 269 (12 January 1152, Freiburg). On Conrad of Zähringen's death, see Bernhardi, *Konrad III.*, p. 915. Opll, RI IV2/1:11, no. 59, dated the Memmingen meeting as occurring on a 1 February between 1143 and 1152; but Görich, *Friedrich Barbarossa*, p. 90, placed it in 1152.
11. Wibald of Stavelot, *Briefbuch* 2:676–83, nos. 319–22 (Jaffé, nos. 364–67), and pp. 709–13, no. 339 (Jaffé, no. 375); and RI IV2/1:12, no. 62.
12. RI IV2/1:11–12, no. 61: "colloquium . . . de reformando et componendo regni statu."
13. DFI, no. 38 (15 February–12 December 1152). The composition and dating of this charter, which is crucial in proving that Frederick and Henry the Lion met before the election, pose considerable problems that are discussed in the head note. The chief article is Heinrich Appelt, "Heinrich der Löwe und die Wahl Friedrich Barbarossas," in idem, *Kaisertum, Königtum, Landesherrschaft: Gesammelte Studien zur mittelalterlichen Verfassungsgeschichte*, ed. Othmar Hageneder (Vienna, 1988), pp. 97–108. Both Frederick and Henry were identified in no. 38 simply as "dux" without any territorial or ethnic addition. Laudage, *Friedrich Barbarossa*, pp. 39–42, maintained that the Duke Henry in this charter was Henry Jasomirgott and that Henry the Lion was thus a possible alternative candidate for the throne. That interpretation ignores Frederick's close ties to the Welfs before and after the election and his strained relations with his Babenberg uncle. It was, after all, Henry the Lion, not Henry Jasomirgott, who accompanied Frederick to Aachen.
14. Goez, "Von Bamberg nach Frankfurt und Aachen," p. 61.
15. Goez, "Von Bamberg nach Frankfurt und Aachen," pp. 61–71, was the first to point out the incredible speed with which Barbarossa was elevated to the throne; but Goez thought that Conrad was planning Barbarossa's election prior to his planned departure for Italy. Niederkorn, "Friedrich von Rothenburg und die Königswahl von 1152," pp. 51–59, argued that Conrad was planning his son's accession. Thomas Zotz, "Friedrich Barbarossa und Herzog Friedrich (IV.) von Schwaben: Staufisches Königtum und schwäbisches Herzogtum um die Mitte des 12. Jahrhunderts," in Petersohn, ed., *Mediaevalia Augiensia*, pp. 285–90, accepted Niederkorn's argument. Zotz said that the two men exchanged roles in 1152. On the decision not to bury Conrad in Lorch, see Dick, "Die Königserhebung Friedrich Barbarossas," pp. 228–29.
16. Wipo, *The Deeds of Conrad II*, pp. 70–71, ch. 5, and pp. 67–68, ch. 3.
17. Otto of Freising, *Chronicle* 6.28.
18. Scholz, "Die Wiener Reichskrone," p. 349.
19. Otto of Freising, *Chronicle* 7.17; and idem, *Deeds* 1.17.
20. On this scene and the shift from mercy to justice, see Gerd Althoff, "Konfliktverhalten und Rechtsbewusstsein: Die Welfen im 12. Jahrhundert," in idem, *Spielregeln der Politik im Mittelalter*, pp. 57–84, esp. pp. 63–65 and p. 65, n. 25; Klaus Richter, *Friedrich Barbarossa hält Gericht: Zum Konfliktbewältigung im 12. Jahrhundert* (Cologne, Weimar, and Vienna, 1999), pp. 19–22 and 149–50; and Weiler, "Suitability and Right," pp. 82–83. On the staging of such scenes, see Althoff, "Demonstration und Inszenierung: Spielregeln der Kommunikation in mittelalterlicher Öffentlichkeit," in idem, *Spielregeln*, pp. 229–57. Althoff, "Demonstration," p. 243, n. 43, commented that Barbarossa did not forgive the ministerial because the forgiveness had not been negotiated in advance, but that misses, I think, the point of the contrived playlet that Frederick would not be swayed by personal considerations from dispensing impartial justice.
21. Otto of Freising, *Deeds* 2.4; and Wibald of Stavelot, *Briefbuch* 2:709–13, no. 339 (Jaffé, no. 375). See Petersohn, *Kaisertum und Rom in spätsalischer und staufischer Zeit*, pp. 130–31.

22. Otto of Freising, *Deeds* 2.6. On such consultations, see Gerd Althoff, "Colloquium familiare – colloquium secretum – colloquium publicum: Beratung im politischen Leben des früheren Mittelalters," in idem, *Spielregeln der Politik im Mittelalter*, pp. 157–84. There is no scholarly agreement on the princes' reasons for opposing the Hungarian campaign. See Hechberger, *Staufer und Welfen*, pp. 261–63.
23. Otto of Freising, *Deeds* 1.67–69 and 2.4; DKIII, no. 244 (late March 1151); RI IV1/2:302–21, nos. 703, 717, 721, 723, 725, 737 and 749; and RI IV2/1:17–18, nos. 74 and 77. On the Utrecht dispute, see Richter, *Friedrich Barbarossa hält Gericht*, pp. 23–27 and 144–46.
24. DKIII, no. 184 (19–23 March 1147; also in *Constitutiones* 1:179, no. 124). On this point, see Friedrich Kempf, "Der 'favor apostolicus' bei der Wahl Friedrich Barbarossas und im deutschen Thronstreit (1198–1208)," in Wolf, ed., *Friedrich Barbarossa*, pp. 104–20, esp. p. 106.
25. Koch, *Auf dem Wege zum Sacrum Imperium*, pp. 21–22 and 62–63. For an English translation of Gelasius' letter, see Tierney, *The Crisis of Church and State*, pp. 13–14, no. 3.
26. Wibald of Stavelot, *Briefbuch* 3:748–50, no. 357 (Jaffé, no. 362). On Wibald's use of the Gelasian formula, see Rainer Maria Herkenrath, "Regnum und Imperium in den Diplomen der ersten Regierungsjahre Friedrichs I.," in Wolf, ed., *Friedrich Barbarossa*, pp. 323–59, esp. pp. 326–28.
27. DFI, no. 5 (March–April 1152; also in *Constitutiones* 1:191–92, no. 137). Scholars have argued about Wibald and Eberhard's specific contributions to the composition of the letter, because a somewhat annoyed Wibald indicated he had been instructed to send his draft to Eberhard and Henry of Würzburg for possible emendations and because he advised Eberhard, though the bishop had the authority to make changes, not to alter the text. See Wibald of Stavelot, *Briefbuch* 2:707–09, no. 338 (Jaffé, no. 374) and 3:733–36, no. 351 (Jaffé, no. 377). Since only Wibald's draft survives, it is not known whether any alterations were made in the final version which the envoys delivered to the pope. The consensus today is that the letter was Wibald's handiwork, that the draft he sent to Eberhard already contained the bishop and the proto-notary's input, and that no significant additional revisions were made in the final letter. Besides, as the leader of the embassy, Eberhard would have had leeway in presenting Frederick's views to Eugenius. See Herkenrath, "Regnum und Imperium," pp. 323–31; head note to DFI, no. 5; and Uebach, *Die Ratgeber Friedrich Barbarossas*, pp. 54–73, esp. pp. 58–61.
28. Wibald of Stavelot, *Briefbuch* 2:709–13, no. 339 (Jaffé, no. 375). Wibald referred to a letter the bishops were sending the pope, but it has not survived. In the past, Wibald has been accused of "perfidy" in recommending, contrary to the letter he drafted for Frederick, that the pope confirm the king's election. The head note to DFI, no. 5, sees this as one place where Bishop Eberhard overruled Wibald's preferences. However, Hausmann, *Reichskanzlei und Hofkapelle*, pp. 233–34, argued that Wibald did not advise the pope to confirm the election. Hausmann translated *declarare* as "verkünden." It is worth noting that in the letter Wibald drafted for Frederick informing Manuel of Barbarossa's election (*Briefbuch* 3:814–16, no. 386 [Jaffé, no. 410]), the abbot likewise used *declarare* to indicate that Conrad had recommended or declared that Frederick should succeed him as king (see above, n. 6). Wibald did not employ *declarare* as a synonym for *confirmare*.
29. John of Salisbury, *The Letters of John of Salisbury*, ed. William James Millor and Harold Edgeworth Butler, revised by C. N. L. Brooke, 2 vols (London, 1959; and Oxford, 1979; reprint Oxford, 1979–86), vol. 1, pp. 204–15, esp. p. 207. See Petersohn, *Kaisertum und Rom in spätsalischer und staufischer Zeit*, pp. 132–35.
30. Wibald of Stavelot, *Briefbuch* 3:784–86, no. 374 (Jaffé, no. 382). For an exposition of what Eugenius meant by the phrase, "benigno favore sedis apostoliçe approbamus," which was long interpreted as the pope's confirmation of Frederick's election, see Kempf, "Der 'favor apostolicus' bei der Wahl Friedrich Barbarossas," esp. pp. 104–10. See also Ulrich Schmidt, "A quo ergo habet, si a domno papa non habet imperium?: Zu den Anfängen der 'staufischen Kaiserwahlen,'" in Lorenz and Schmidt, eds, *Von Schwaben bis Jerusalem*, esp. pp. 61–65, 74–76, and 81–82. For a very negative account of Octavian's mission to Germany, written during the schism, see John of Salisbury, *Historia Pontificalis*, pp. 75–77, ch. 38. For an English translation of *Venerabilem*, see Tierney, *The Crisis of Church and State*, pp. 133–34, no. 75.

31. See, for example, the head note to DFI, no. 5; Jakobi, *Wibald von Stablo*, pp. 164–65; and Laudage, *Friedrich Barbarossa*, pp. 56–57. On Wibald's displeasure, see *Briefbuch* 2:707–09, no. 338 (Jaffé, no. 374) and 3:733–36, no. 351 (Jaffé, no. 377).
32. Wibald of Stavelot, *Briefbuch* 2:731–32, no. 350 (Jaffé, no. 376), 3:733–36, no. 351 (Jaffé, no. 377), and 3:812–13, no. 385 (Jaffé, no. 408). See Hausmann, *Reichskanzlei und Hofkapelle*, pp. 230–57; and Jakobi, *Wibald von Stablo*, pp. 164–88.
33. DFI, no. 1 (9 March 1152). See Hausmann, *Reichskanzlei und Hofkapelle*, p. 230; and Jakobi, *Wibald von Stablo*, p. 164.
34. See above, p. 57.
35. Otto of Freising, *Deeds*, "Letter of the August Emperor, Frederick, to Otto, Bishop of Freising," pp. 17–18; and 2.6, 2.8, and 2.10; *Chronicon Montis Sereni*, p. 149; and Dietrich Claude, *Geschichte des Erzbistums Magdeburg bis in das 12. Jahrhunderts*, 2 vols (Cologne and Vienna, 1972–75), vol. 2, pp. 71–175, esp. pp. 71–84.
36. Bernhard Töpfer, "Kaiser Friedrich I. Barbarossa und der deutsche Reichsepiskopat," in Haverkamp, ed., *Friedrich Barbarossa*, pp. 389–422, esp. 402 and 413–14.
37. DFI, no. 3 (12 March 1152). There was opposition to the alienation of Niederaltaich. See no. 70 (3 February 1154) and no. 306 (14 February 1160). On Eberhard II, see Uebach, *Die Ratgeber Friedrich Barbarossas*, pp. 45–49 and 161–68.
38. Joachim Ehlers, "Heinrich der Löwe und der sächsische Episkopat," in Haverkamp, ed., *Friedrich Barbarossa*, pp. 435–36; and Ehlers, *Heinrich der Löwe*, pp. 115–41. On the Welf ministerialage, see Claus-Peter Hasse, *Die welfischen Hofämter und die welfische Ministerialität in Sachsen: Studien zur Sozialgeschichte des 12. und 13. Jahrhunderts* (Husum, 1995).
39. Ehlers, *Heinrich der Löwe*, pp. 65–70; and Hans Patze, "Kaiser Friedrich Barbarossa und der Osten," in Mayer, ed., *Probleme des 12. Jahrhunderts*, pp. 342–45.
40. Ehlers, *Heinrich der Löwe*, pp. 75–77; and idem, "Heinrich der Löwe und der sächsische Episkopat," pp. 442–43.
41. DFI, no. 80 (end of May–beginning of June 1154). See Ehlers, "Heinrich der Löwe und der sächsische Episkopat," pp. 444–48; and idem, *Heinrich der Löwe*, pp. 149–62.
42. RI IV2/1:21–22, no. 88, and pp. 35–36, no. 135; Ehlers, "Heinrich der Löwe und der sächsische Episkopat," p. 438; idem, *Heinrich der Löwe*, pp. 65–66 and 84–85; and Patze, "Kaiser Friedrich Barbarossa und der Osten," pp. 348–49.
43. Patze, "Kaiser Friedrich Barbarossa und der Osten," pp. 355–57; Opll, *Stadt und Reich im 12. Jahrhundert*, pp. 77–83; and Ehlers, *Heinrich der Löwe*, p. 83.
44. Plassmann, *Die Struktur des Hofes unter Friedrich I. Barbarossa*, pp. 20–21.
45. Helmold von Bosau, *Slawenchronik*, pp. 272–77, ch. 80; and RI IV2/1:22–23, nos. 91 and 92. See Ehlers, *Heinrich der Löwe*, p. 92; Jiří Kejř, "Böhmen und das Reich unter Friedrich I.," in Haverkamp, ed., *Friedrich Barbarossa*, pp. 248–49; Kejř, "Böhmen zur Zeit Friedrich Barbarossas," in Evamaria Engel and Bernhard Töpfer, eds, *Kaiser Friedrich Barbarossa: Landesaufbau-Aspekte seiner Politik-Wirkung* (Weimar, 1994), pp. 107–08; and Michael Lindner, "Friedrich Barbarossa, Heinrich der Löwe und die ostsächsischen Fürsten auf dem Merseburger Pfingsthoftag des Jahres 1152," *Zeitschrift für Geschichtswissenschaft* 43 (1995): 204–05.
46. Ehlers, "Heinrich der Löwe und der sächsische Episkopat," p. 439.
47. Helmold von Bosau, *Slawenchronik*, pp. 201–03, ch. 54.
48. *Die Urkunden Heinrichs des Löwen Herzogs von Sachsen und Bayern*, ed. Karl Jordan, in MGH: Laienfürsten- und Dynastenurkunden der Kaiserzeit 1 (Leipzig, 1941), pp. 26–27, no. 8.
49. DFI, no. 13 (5 July 1150 [!]), no. 14 (end of June–beginning of July 1152), and nos. 58–62 (11–14 June 1153); and Otto of Freising, *Deeds* 2.7, 2.9 and 2.11.
50. Otto of Freising, *Deeds* 2.11. On Frederick's preliminary efforts to resolve the dispute between his cousin and uncle, see Heinrich Appelt, *Privilegium minus: Das staufische Kaisertum und die Babenberger in Österreich* (Vienna, 1973), pp. 32–37; idem, "Das Herzogtum Österreich," in Drabek, ed., *Österreich im Hochmittelalter*, pp. 277–78; and Richter, *Friedrich Barbarossa hält Gericht*, pp. 30–35 and 185–86.
51. On the avoidance of a direct confrontation with a ruler, see Gerd Althoff, "Ungeschriebene Gesetze: Wie funktioniert Herrschaft ohne schriftlich fixierte Normen?" in idem, *Spielregeln der Politik im Mittelalter*, p. 294; and Görich, *Die Ehre Friedrich Barbarossas*, pp. 32–33. On the resolution of the conflict, see below, pp. 162–66.

52. *Historia Welforum*, pp. 76–77, ch. 28; and DFI, no. 4 (9–14 March 1152), no. 6 (20 April 1152), no. 9 (8 May 1152), no. 10 (9 May 1152), and no. 14 (end of June–beginning of July 1152). See Schneidmüller, *Die Welfen*, pp. 185–86.
53. Werner Goez, "Über die Mathildischen Schenkungen an die Römische Kirche," *FS* 31 (1997): 158: "Zankapfel"; and David J. Hay, *The Military Leadership of Matilda of Tuscany 1046–1115* (Manchester, 2008), p. 180: "a veritable scholarly snakepit."
54. *Die Urkunden und Briefe der Markgräfin Mathilde von Tuszien*, ed. Elke Goez and Werner Goez, in MGH: Laienfürsten- und Dynastenurkunden der Kaiserzeit 2 (Hanover, 1998), pp. 213–17, no. 73 (also *Constitutiones* 1:653–55, no. 444); Goez, "Über die Mathildischen Schenkungen," pp. 158–96; and Hay, *The Military Leadership of Matilda of Tuscany*, pp. 179–81. For a reconstruction of Matilda's possessions, see Alfred Overmann, *Gräfin Mathilde von Tuscien: Ihre Besitzungen: Geschichte ihres Gutes von 1115–1230 und ihre Regesten* (Innsbruck, 1895; reprint, Frankfurt, 1965). The foldout map at the back is especially useful.
55. RI IV1/2:14, no. 32; and RI IV1/1:219–21, no. 353.
56. *Wirtembergishes UB*, edited by the Royal State Archives in Stuttgart, 4 (Stuttgart, 1883), "Nachtrag zum zweiten Bande," pp. 363–64, no. 63 (1140 or 1160?). Hansmartin Schwarzmaier, "Dominus totius domus comitisse Mathildis: Die Welfen und Italien im 12. Jahrhundert," in Schnith, and Pauler, eds *Festschrift für Eduard Hlawitschka*, pp. 283–305; and idem, "Die monastische Welt der Staufer und Welfen im 12. Jahrhundert," in Lorenz and Schmidt, eds, *Von Schwaben bis Jerusalem*, pp. 249–51. See the map of the Po Basin in Hay, *The Military Leadership of Matilda of Tuscany*, p. xv. The 1140 document is a copy of a lost document and is dated 1140. Because of Welf's titles, the editors dated it circa 1160, that is, after Frederick Barbarossa granted the titles to his uncle in 1152; but they conceded that some of the witnesses appear in an 1140 charter for the Cistercians of Salem. Schwarzmaier argued for the 1140 date.
57. *Die Urkunden Heinrichs des Löwen*, pp. 42–44, no. 30; RI IV2/2:63, no. 798; Simonsfeld, *Jahrbücher des Deutschen Reiches unter Friedrich I.*, 1:246; and Schwarzmaier, "Dominus totius domus comitisse Mathildis," p. 295.
58. Otto of Freising and Rahewin, *Deeds* 4.13.
59. Otto of Freising, *Deeds* 1.26; DKIII, no. 270 (2–15 February 1152); and DFI, no. 14 (end of June or beginning of July 1152). See above, p. 42.
60. Otto of Freising, *Deeds* 2.48; DFI, no. 12 (before 1 June 1152; also Wibald of Stavelot, *Briefbuch* 3:736–39, no. 352 [Jaffé, no. 383]; and *Constitutiones* 1:199, no. 141). See Heinrich Büttner, "Friedrich Barbarossa und Burgund: Studien zur Politik der Staufer während des 12. Jahrhunderts," in Mayer, ed., *Probleme des 12. Jahrhunderts*, pp. 79–89; Hartmut Heinemann, "Die Zähringer und Burgund," in Schmid, *Die Zähringer* 1:59–63; and René Locatelli, "Frédéric Ier et le royaume de Bourgogne," in Haverkamp, ed., *Friedrich Barbarossa*, pp. 169–76.
61. DFI, no. 46 (30 January 1153), no. 47 (4 February 1153), nos. 48 and 49 (15 February 1153); and RI IV2/1:46, no. 163.
62. DFI, nos. 40 and 42 (28 December 1152), no. 43 (29 December 1153), and no. 44 (10 January 1153); RI IV2/1:41, no. 148; and Weller, *Die Heiratspolitik des deutschen Hochadels*, Plate 7/1.
63. DFI, nos. 58 and 60–64 (June 1153); and Wibald of Stavelot, *Briefbuch* 3:834–35, no. 398 (Jaffé, no. 428). See also DFI, no. 69 (17 January 1154), and Zotz, "Dux de Zaringen—dux Zaringiae," pp. 24–26.
64. DFI, no. 97 (13 January 1155). Welf VI did not go on Frederick's first Italian expedition. See Simonsfeld, *Jahrbücher des Deutschen Reiches unter Friedrich I.* 1:252. Boleslav of Poland was the son of Frederick's Babenberg aunt, Agnes; Ottokar III was the son of Frederick's Welf aunt, Sophia. See Weller, *Die Heiratspolitik des deutschen Hochadels*, Plates 2, 3, and 12.
65. Otto of Freising, *Deeds* 1.70; and Burchard of Ursberg, *Chronicon*, pp. 140–41.
66. DFI, no. 61 (June 1153, drafted by Wibald), no. 62 (June 1153), no. 69 (17 January 1154), and no. 77 (3–17 May 1154).
67. DFI, no. 173 (4 July 1157), and no. 174 (5 July 1157). Zotz, "Friedrich Barbarossa und Herzog Friedrich (IV.) von Schwaben," pp. 294–95, argued that Frederick was listed first among the dukes in the second charter because his maternal uncle, Count Gebhard II of Sulzbach, was present and protected his nephew's interests. However, Gebhard had presumably also been present on the preceding day.

68. DFI, no. 153 (October 1156), no. 157 (2 February 1157), and no. 160 (16 March 1157); and RI IV2/1:132, no. 427. See Zotz, "Friedrich Barbarossa und Herzog Friedrich (IV.) von Schwaben," pp. 291–98. On the division of the children of ministerials, see Freed, *Noble Bondsmen*, esp. pp. 73–81.
69. Otto of Freising and Rahewin, *Deeds* 3.6. Althoff, "Friedrich von Rothenburg," pp. 307–16, pointed out the potential for conflict in the cousins' ambiguous relationship. On Frederick's subsequent dealings with his cousin, see below, pp. 178–82.
70. DFI, no. 25 (end of July–beginning of August 1152; also in *Constitutiones* 1:194–98, no. 140). See Simonsfeld, *Jahrbücher des Deutschen Reiches unter Friedrich I.*, 1:59–68. For an English translation, see Ernest F. Henderson, *Select Historical Documents of the Middle Ages* (New York, 1965), pp. 211–15.
71. Hanna Vollrath, "Ideal and Reality in Twelfth-Century Germany," in Haverkamp and Vollrath, eds, *England and Germany in the High Middle Ages*, pp. 93–104. For the text of Henry IV's peace, see *Constitutiones* 1:125–26, no. 74.
72. For more information on twelfth-century German counts and the administration of justice, see Benjamin Arnold, *Princes and Territories in Medieval Germany* (Cambridge, 1991), esp. pp. 112–20 and 186–210; and Björn Weiler, "The King as Judge: Henry II and Frederick Barbarossa as Seen by their Contemporaries," in Skinner, ed., *Challenging the Boundaries of Medieval History*, pp. 115–35. For the study of specific comital dynasties, see Benjamin Arnold, *Count and Bishop in Medieval Germany: A Study of Regional Power, 1100–1350* (Philadelphia, P.A., 1991); and Freed, *The Counts of Falkenstein*.

Chapter 5 Itinerant Kingship

1. Wolfram, *Conrad II*, p. 4; and Theo Kölzer, "Der Hof Kaiser Barbarossas und die Reichsfürsten," in Peter Moraw, ed., *Deutscher Königshof, Hoftag und Reichstag im späteren Mittelalter* (Stuttgart, 2002), p. 7. The article was republished with the slightly different title, "Der Hof Friedrich Barbarossas und die Reichsfürsten," minus the footnotes, in Weinfurter, ed., *Stauferreich im Wandel.*
2. Ehlers, *Heinrich der Löwe*, p. 80; and Carlrichard Brühl, *Fodrum, gistum, servitium regis: Studien zu den wirtschaftlichen Grundlagen des Königtums im Frankenreich und in den fränkischen Nachfolgerstaaten Deutschland, Frankreich und Italien vom 6. bis zur Mitte des 14. Jahrhunderts*, 2 vols (Cologne and Graz, 1968), vol. 1, pp. 162–63.
3. The standard monograph outlining Frederick's itinerary is Opll, *Das Itinerar Kaiser Friedrich Barbarossas* (for the first year, pp. 8–11). Opll drew the map that charted all the places where Barbarossa stayed in *Die Zeit der Staufer*, vol. 4, Map III: "Kaiser Friedrich I.: Karte der Aufenhaltsorte 1152–1189." Maps showing Barbarossa's itinerary in Germany in the periods 1152–74 and 1178–89 are in Kölzer, "Der Hof Kaiser Barbarossas," pp. 45 and 46. Hans Patze, "Friedrich Barbarossa und die deutschen Fürsten," *Die Zeit der Staufer* 5:35–75, included maps, drawn by Herbert Reyer, showing Barbarossa's itinerary for the years 1152 through 1157 (the map for 1152 is on p. 43). See also Brühl, *Fodrum, gistum, servitium regis*, vol. 1, pp. 116–219; and vol. 2, maps in an attached packet showing the itineraries of various German and French monarchs between Charlemagne and Frederick II and Louis IX. For an introduction in English to itinerant kingship, see John W. Bernhardt, *Itinerant Kingship and Royal Monasteries in Early Medieval Germany c. 936–1075* (Cambridge, and New York, 1993).
4. DFI, no. 502 (8 January 1166). See Patze's comments in "Friedrich Barbarossa und die deutschen Fürsten," p. 56; and Brühl, *Fodrum, gistum, servitium regis*, vol. 1, pp. 149–54.
5. Otto of Freising, *Deeds* 1.12 and 2.46.
6. Kölzer, "Der Hof Kaiser Barbarossas," pp. 6–9; and Brühl, *Fodrum, gistum, servitium regis*, vol. 1, pp. 160–61. On the definition of a palace, see Brühl, *Fodrum, gistum, servitium regis*, vol. 1, pp. 770–73; and Mathias Hensch, "Baukonzeption, Wohnkultur und Herrschaftsrepräsentation im Burgenbau des 11./12. Jahrhunderts in Nordbayern—neue Erkenntnisse der Archäologie," in Seibert and Dendorfer, eds, *Grafen, Herzöge, Könige*, p. 164. For a list of the times Frederick stayed in different places in Germany, see Opll, *Das Itinerar Kaiser Friedrich Barbarossas*, pp. 122–57. The extent of Frederick's withdrawal from

Lower Lorraine after 1174 should not be overstated. While he visited Liège only twice (1156 and 1171), Henry VI was there three times in the 1180s. See Jean-Louis Kupper, "Friedrich Barbarossa im Maasgebiet," in Haverkamp, ed., *Friedrich Barbarossa*, p. 227.

7. In addition to Kölzer's and Opll's work cited in n. 3, see Fritz Arens, "Die staufischen Königspfalzen," in *Die Zeit der Staufer* 3:129–42. Opll, *Stadt und Reich im 12. Jahrhundert*, discussed the following imperial castle-palace complexes that developed into cities: Altenburg, pp. 30–32; Gelnhausen, pp. 73–77; Goslar, pp. 77–83; Haguenau, pp. 83–89; Kaiserswerth, pp. 92–94; and Nuremberg, pp. 125–28. For a report on the excavations at Ingelheim, see Holger Grewe, "Visualisierung von Herrschaft in der Architektur: Die Pfalz Ingelheim als Bedeutungsträger im 12. und 13. Jahrhundert," in Burkhardt et al., eds, *Staufisches Kaisertum im 12. und 13. Jahrhundert*, pp. 383–403. On visits to lay magnates, see Werner Goez, "Möglichkeiten und Grenzen des Herrschens aus der Ferne in Deutschland und Reichsitaliens (1152–1220)," in Kölzer, ed., *Die Staufer im Süden*, p. 98.
8. Otto of Freising and Rahewin, *Deeds* 3.7 and 4.43. The queen of Hungary gave Frederick an elaborate tent on the Third Crusade. For a description of that tent, see below, p. 489.
9. Brühl, *Fodrum, gistum, servitium regis*, vol. 1, pp. 168–70; and Wolfgang Metz, *Das servitium regis: Zur Erforschung der wirtschaftlichen Grundlagen des hochmittelalterlichen deutschen Königtums* (Darmstadt, 1978), pp. 61–62.
10. Eike von Repgow, *The Saxon Mirror* 3.57; and DFI, no. 419 (27 November 1163), no. 447 (15 June 1164), and no. 477 (17 April 1165). See Brühl, *Fodrum, gistum, servitium regis*, vol. 1, pp. 165–67; Bosl, *Die Reichsministerialität der Salier und Staufer* 2:483–88 and 614–15, and idem, "Die Reichsministerialität als Element der mittelalterlichen deutschen Staatsverfassung im Zeitalter der Salier und Staufer," in idem, *Frühformen der Gesellschaft im mittelalterlichen Europa: Ausgewählte Beiträge zu einer Strukturanalyse der mittelalterlichen Welt* (Munich and Vienna, 1964), pp. 350–52; and Jan Ulrich Keupp, *Dienst und Verdienst: Die Ministerialen Friedrich Barbarossas und Heinrichs VI.* (Stuttgart, 2002), pp. 99–299 and 348–60.
11. Eike von Repgow, *The Saxon Mirror* 3.62; and Werner Rösener, "Die Hoftage Kaiser Friedrichs I. Barbarossa im Regnum Teutonicum," in Moraw, ed., *Deutscher Königshof, Hoftag und Reichstag im späteren Mittelalter*, pp. 359–86. Rösener provided a list of all the sites where assemblies met (p. 368), a table of the number of such meetings per decade (p. 369), and a map showing the location of all the assemblies (p. 381). Opll, *Stadt und Reich*, pp. 542–46, listed all the places where assemblies met and the monarchs celebrated Easter, Pentecost, and Christmas between 1125 and 1190. German scholars today employ the terms *Hof* for the daily court or *curia* and *Hoftag* for major assemblies. They no longer employ *Reichstag*, which first appeared in the sources only in 1495 and which was employed by scholars in the nineteenth century to link the medieval assemblies to the new Wilhelmine *Reichstag*. For that reason, I will not use *Diet*, the customary English translation for *Reichstag*, to describe, for example, the courts that were held at Besançon in 1157 or at Roncaglia in 1158.
12. Eike von Repgow, *The Saxon Mirror* 3.64; Otto of Freising, *Deeds* 2.44; Kölzer, "Der Hof Kaiser Barbarossas," pp. 11–12; and Rösener, "Die Hoftage Kaiser Friedrichs I. Barbarossa," pp. 369–71. On the case of Bishop Hartwig, see Richter, *Friedrich Barbarossa hält Gericht*, pp. 36–39.
13. DFI, no. 21 (July 1152), no. 66 (September–October 1153), no. 126 (September 1155), and no. 162 (24–31 March 1157). See Karl-Heinz Spiess, "Der Hof Kaiser Barbarossas und die politische Landschaft am Mittelrhein," in Moraw, ed., *Deutscher Königshof, Hoftag und Reichstag im späteren Mittelalter*, p. 60.
14. Gilbert of Mons, *Chronicle of Hainaut*, pp. 86–90, ch. 109.
15. Balderich, *The Deeds of Albero of Trier*, ch. 32.
16. *Vita Arnoldi archiepiscopi Moguntini*, in Philipp Jaffé, ed., *Bibliotheca rerum Germanicarum*. vol. 3: *Monumenta Moguntina* (Berlin, 1866; reprint, Aalen, 1964), pp. 635–40; and RI IV2/2:59, no. 779. See Hausmann, *Reichskanzlei und Hofkapelle*, pp. 129–34; Spiess, "Der Hof Kaiser Barbarossas," pp. 63–64; and Opll, *Stadt und Reich im 12. Jahrhundert*, pp. 118–20. On the *Vita Arnoldi*, see Stefan Weinfurter, "Wer war der Verfasser der Vita Erzbischof Arnolds von Mainz (1153–1160)?" in Schnith and Pauler, eds, *Festschrift für Eduard Hlawitschka*, pp. 317–39.

17. Arnold of Lübeck, *Chronica Slavorum*, pp. 151–53. See Spiess, "Der Hof Kaiser Barbarossas," pp. 64–65; Keupp, *Dienst und Verdienst*, pp. 381–83; and Heinrich Fichtenau, *Living in the Tenth Century: Mentalities and Social Orders*, trans. Patrick J. Geary (Chicago and London, 1991), pp. 16–29, esp. pp. 16–17.
18. Otto of Freising and Rahewin, *Deeds* 3.33; DFI, no. 173 (4 July 1157), and no. 174 (5 July 1157); and *Codex Falkensteinenis*, pp. 39*–43*. See Kölzer, "Der Hof Kaiser Barbarossas," pp. 12–13; Plassmann, *Die Struktur des Hofes unter Friedrich I. Barbarossa*, pp. 1–19; Spiess, "Der Hof Kaiser Barbarossas," pp. 50–59; and Uebach, *Die Ratgeber Friedrich Barbarossas*, pp. 20–26.
19. Johannes Fried, "Die Wirtschaftspolitik Friedrich Barbarossas in Deutschland," *Blätter für deutsche Landesgeschichte* 120 (1984): 208–12; and Caroline Göldel, *Servitium regis und Tafelgüterverzeichnis: Untersuchungen zur Wirtschafts- und Verfassungsgeschichte des deutschen Königtums im 12. Jahrhundert* (Sigmaringen, 1997), pp. 26–27, 64–65, and 113–14. Other imperial abbeys that Frederick gave to episcopal sees were: Niedernburg in the city of Passau, although Frederick retained the advocacy and the bishop of Passau was required to pay £40 to the imperial fisc each year at Epiphany (DFI, no. 322; 29 January 1161); Nienburg, except for the advocacy, in a property exchange with Archbishop Wichmann of Magdeburg (no. 506; 8 March 1166); shortly thereafter, Frederick gave Magdeburg the advocacy, which Albrecht the Bear had held until then from the king (no. 516; 20 August 1166); and the Benedictine nunnery of Herford and the Benedictine monastery of Werden in a property exchange with Archbishop Philip of Cologne (no. *1243; 1168–89). On Wibald, see Uebach, *Die Ratgeber Friedrich Barbarossas*, p. 56.
20. Morena, *Libellus de rebus a Frederico imperatore gestis*, pp. 186–93. See Schmid, *Graf Rudolf von Pfullendorf*, pp. 64–88 and 213–17; Plassmann, *Die Struktur des Hofes unter Friedrich I. Barbarossa*, pp. 28–29, 41–42, 126, and 141–57; Kölzer, "Der Hof Kaiser Barbarossas," pp. 18–25 and 30–39; and Uebach, *Die Ratgeber Friedrich Barbarossas*, pp. 168–78 (Hermann of Verden) and 242–63.
21. Wibald of Stavelot, *Briefbuch* 2:544–46, no. 255 (Jaffé, no. 282; c. 15 August 1150).
22. Brühl, *Fodrum, gistum, servitium regis*, vol. 1, p. 182.
23. The standard edition of the *Tafelgüterverzeichnis* is Carlrichard Brühl and Theo Kölzer, *Das Tafelgüterverzeichnis des römischen Königs (Ms. Bonn S. 1559)* (Cologne and Vienna, 1979). On the heading, see p. 53. Kölzer, p. 2, dated the codex itself between 23 May 1174 and c. 1192; but Brühl, p. 12, dated the inclusion of the register in the codex to the period c. 1177–86, when Frederick's chancellor, Godfrey of Spitzberg-Helfenstein, was the provost. More recently, Thomas Zotz, "Zur Grundherrschaft des Königs im Deutschen Reich vom 10. bis zum frühen 13. Jahrhundert," in Werner Rösener, ed., *Grundherrschaft und bäuerliche Gesellschaft im Hochmittelalter* (Göttingen, 1995), pp. 109–10, and Göldel, *Servitium regis und Tafelgüterverzeichnis*, pp. 162–65, have accepted for paleographical reasons the date 1165–74 for the list's inclusion in the codex. The text of the *Tafelgüterverzeichnis* can also be found in *Constitutiones* 1:646–49, no. 440, but the editor, Ludwig Weiland, dated it 1064/65.
24. Brühl, *Fodrum, gistum, servitium regis*, vol. 1, pp. 181–95, and the map of German manors, Beilage I, following p. 192, and Italian ones, Beilage II, after p. 624; and Brühl and Kölzer, *Das Tafelgüterverzeichnis des römischen Königs*, pp. 13–32. On the Falkenstein register, see John B. Freed, "Bavarian Wine and Woolless Sheep: The *Urbar* of Count Sigiboto IV of Falkenstein (1126–ca. 1198)," *Viator* 35 (2004), esp. pp. 91–92. The register is in the *Codex Falkensteinensis*, pp. 10–66, nos. 5–102.
25. Besides Brühl's work on the register, see the following evaluations of its content: Wolfgang Metz, *Staufische Güterverzeichnisse: Untersuchungen zur Verfassungs- und Wirtschaftsgeschichte des 12. und 13. Jahrhunderts* (Berlin, 1964), pp. 6–51; idem, *Das servitium regis*, pp. 21–63; Zotz, "Zur Grundherrschaft des Königs im Deutschen Reich," pp. 100–11; and Göldel, *Servitium regis und Tafelgüterverzeichnis*, pp. 128–58.
26. Freed, "Bavarian Wine and Woolless Sheep," pp. 93, 101–02, 105–06, and 109–110. Fried, "Die Wirtschaftspolitik Friedrich Barbarossas in Deutschland," pp. 218–20, believed that the payments in kind listed in the *Tafelgüterverzeichnis* were being converted into cash payments. Göldel, *Servitium regis und Tafelgüterverzeichnis*, pp. 146–54, insisted that the list

does not provide evidence for the persistence of a natural economy in Germany; but I find her argument, pp. 165–84, that the properties were intended to serve as the endowment of a royal canonry in Aachen after the canonization of Charlemagne in 1165, totally unconvincing. It is inconceivable that at a moment when Alexander III was challenging Frederick's position as emperor, anyone associated with the chancery or the royal chapel in Aachen would have given him the title king of the Romans. There is a long German and Italian historiographical tradition, based perhaps on the nineteenth-century linkage of urbanization and capitalism with the development of constitutional government, which stresses the contrast between urban and commercial Italy and rural and feudal Germany. Barbarossa is said not to have comprehended the totally different Italian situation and to have pursued a reactionary policy of trying to assert outdated rights with great brutality to the detriment of both the Italians and himself. See Alfred Haverkamp, *Herrschaftsformen der Frühstaufer in Reichsitalien*, 2 vols (Stuttgart, 1970–71), vol. 1, pp. 57–61.

27. DLIII, no. 119 (23 September 1137); DKIII, no. 87 (May/June 1143) and no. 167 (30 January 1147); and DFI, no. 3 (12 March 1152). See Metz, *Das servitium regis*, pp. 74–86; and Göldel, *Servitium regis und Tafelgüterverzeichnis*, pp. 69–75. Göldel, pp. 109–12, argued that Lothar's charter for Stavelot, the oldest such commutation of an abbey's obligation to provide the king with hospitality into a cash payment, is a forgery.
28. DFI, no. 128 (27 November 1155); *Mainzer Urkundenbuch*. Vol. 2: *Die Urkunden seit dem Tode Erzbischof Adalberts I. (1137) bis zum Tode Erzbischof Konrads (1200)*, ed. Peter Acht (Darmstadt, 1971), pp. 876–85, esp. p. 881, no. 531. See Metz, *Das servitium regis*, pp. 87–115, esp. pp. 114–15; and Göldel, *Servitium regis und Tafelgüterverzeichnis*, pp. 75–78. On Hermann of Constance, see Uebach, *Die Ratgeber Friedrich Barbarossas*, pp. 49–54.
29. *Codex Falkensteinensis*, pp. 7–9, no. 3, and pp. 97–99, no. 131. The count-palatine and the duke were the same person. On the Falkenstein *Hantgemal*, see Freed, *The Counts of Falkenstein*, pp. 36–40. On Waiblingen as the Salian-Staufer *Hantgemal*, see Schmid, "'De regia stirpe Waiblingensium,'" p. 457.
30. Gilbert of Mons, *Chronicle of Hainaut*, pp. 110–11, ch. 136; and RI IV2/4:205, no. 3127.
31. *Codex Falkensteinensis*, pp. 4–7, no. 2, and pp. 149–50, no. 170. On Frederick's acquisition of Gebhard of Sulzbach's Bamberg fiefs, see DFI, no. 624 (August 1167–13 July 1174) and no. 625 (13 July 1174); and Dendorfer, *Adelige Gruppenbildung*, pp. 293–95 and 419–20. On the place and date of Sigiboto's enfeoffment, see Hensch, "Baukonzeption, Wohnkultur und Herrschaftsrepräsentation," pp. 164–65. Opll, RI IV2/4:259, no. 3262, was seemingly unfamiliar with Hensch's article and thought that Sigiboto's enfeoffment occurred around 10 May 1189, in Gebhard's house in Regensburg; but Sigiboto's insistence that the meeting had occurred in a heated room fits January better than May. In addition to this meeting, Count Sigiboto of Neuburg had witnessed earlier in Regensburg Frederick's charter for the bishop of Freising (DFI, no. 798; 13 July 1180). Neuburg is wrongly identified in the index (p. 431) as being situated near Passau in Lower Bavaria; it was located on the Mangfall, west of Rosenheim, in Upper Bavaria. The two men would almost certainly have met on the Second Crusade and Frederick's fourth Italian expedition.
32. Gilbert of Mons, *Chronicle of Hainaut*, pp. 115–17, chs. 140 and 141. As Weiler, "The King as Judge," p. 117, n. 8, pointed out, in the absence of any administrative records, a book, like Richter's *Friedrich Barbarossa hält Gericht*, relied exclusively on Otto and Rahewin's narrative.
33. DFI, no. 2 (10 March 1152), and no. 8 (end of April–beginning of May 1152). See Karl J. Leyser, "Frederick Barbarossa: Court and Country," in idem, *Communications and Power in Medieval Europe: The Gregorian Revolution and Beyond*, ed. Timothy Reuter (London and Rio Grande, OH, 1994), pp. 143–55, esp. pp. 148–49.
34. DFI, nos. 21–23 (July 1152); and Wibald of Stavelot, *Briefbuch* 3:753–55, no. 359 (Jaffé, no. 384), and 3:772–74, no. 369 (Jaffé, no. 391). See Hausmann, *Reichskanzlei und Hofkapelle*, p. 235; and Spiess, "Der Hof Kaiser Barbarossas," p. 67.
35. DFI, no. 108 (May–June 1155), no. 168 (April–May 1157), and no. 169 (April–May 1167); and Otto of Freising and Rahewin, *Deeds* 4.32. See Leyser, "Frederick Barbarossa: Court and Country," pp. 150–51; Keupp, *Dienst und Verdienst*, pp. 360–71; and Spiess, "Der Hof Kaiser Barbarossas," pp. 65–67.

36. DFI, no. 59 (14 June 1153; also *Constitutiones* 1:204–06, no. 146). See Rösener, "Die Hoftage Kaiser Friedrichs I. Barbarossa," pp. 374–75.
37. DFI, no. 866 (22 September 1184; also *Constitutiones* 1:425, no. 300).
38. Heinrich Appelt, "Kaiserurkunde und Fürstensentenz unter Friedrich Barbarossa," in idem, *Kaisertum, Königtum, Landesherrschaft*, pp. 81–96.
39. DKIII, no. 145 (6 January 1146); and DFI, no. 63 (June 1153) and no. 64 (June 1153). See Heinrich Appelt, "Die Reichsarchive in den frühstaufischen Burgunderdiplomen," in idem, Appelt, *Kaisertum, Königtum, Landesherrschaft*, pp. 151–61.
40. Leyser, "Frederick Barbarossa: Court and Country," p. 155. See also Rösner, "Die Hoftage Kaiser Friedrichs I. Barbarossa," pp. 375–76; Goez, "Möglichkeiten und Grenzen des Herrschens aus der Ferne," pp. 93–111; and Weiler, "The King as Judge," pp. 115–35. For a list of the circulars Frederick sent, see Krieg, *Herrscherdarstellung in der Stauferzeit*, p. 47, n. 21.
41. Hausmann, *Reichskanzlei und Hofkapelle*, pp. 93–97; and Appelt, "Einleitung," in DFI 5:12–16 and 100–01. On Lothar's chancellery, see Wolfgang Petke, *Kanzlei, Kapelle und königliche Kurie unter Lothar III. (1125–1137)* (Cologne and Vienna, 1985).
42. Hausmann, *Reichskanzlei und Hofkapelle*, pp. 122–34; Ziegler, *König Konrad III.*, pp. 342–43; Appelt, "Einleitung," in DFI 5:16–19; and Uebach, *Die Ratgeber Friedrich Barbarossas*, pp. 101–04 and 156–59 (Arnold).
43. Hausmann, *Reichskanzlei und Hofkapelle*, pp. 138–67; Ziegler, *König Konrad III.*, pp. 335–38; Appelt, "Einleitung," in DFI 5:20–24; and Uebach, *Die Ratgeber Friedrich Barbarossas*, pp. 105–06 and 226–26 (Henry of Würzburg). For the career of the proto-notary and bishop of Worms, Henry, under Henry VI, see Peter Csendes, *Heinrich VI* (Darmstadt, 1993), passim.
44. Appelt, "Einleitung," in DFI 5:24–80, esp. pp. 38–39 and 76. See also Walter Koch, "Zu Sprache, Stil und Arbeitstechnik in den Diplomen Friedrich Barbarossas," *MIÖG* 88 (1980): 36–69; Töpfer, "Kaiser Friedrich I. Barbarossa und der deutsche Reichsepiskopat," pp. 414–15; and Krieg, *Herrscherdarstellung in der Stauferzeit*, pp. 43–50.
45. DFI, no. 6 (20 April 1152). For a favorable assessment of Godfrey and his proximity to Frederick and Henry VI, see Gerhard Baaken, "Zur Beurteilung Gottfrieds von Viterbo," in idem, *Imperium und Papsttum: Zur Geschichte des 12. und 13. Jahrhunderts: Festschrift zum 70. Geburtstag*, ed. Karl-Augustin Frech and Ulrich Schmidt (Cologne, Weimar, and Vienna, 1997), pp. 159–80; and Friedrich Hausmann, "Gottfried von Viterbo: Kapellan und Notar, Magister, Geschichtsschreiber und Dichter," in Haverkamp, ed., *Friedrich Barbarossa*, pp. 603–21 (there are no footnotes). Loren J. Weber, "The Historical Importance of Godfrey of Viterbo," *Viator* 25 (1994): 153–95, questioned whether Godfrey really held a high position in the chancery, was closely associated with the Staufer rulers, and whether he really was a court propagandist (p. 153). The translated quotation appears on p. 175.
46. DFI, no. 555 (October 1169), no. 727 (25 January 1178, as a canon of Lucca), and no. 728 (30 January 1178, as a canon of Pisa). On Godfrey as a cathedral canon in Speyer and Mainz and provost of St. Bartholomew's, see Hausmann, "Gottfried von Viterbo," pp. 613–14.
47. Wendehorst, "Who Could Read and Write in the Middle Ages?" p. 62; and Appelt, "Einleitung," in DFI 5:86–87.
48. Krieg, *Herrscherdarstellungen in der Stauferzeit*, pp. 43–44, thought it inconceivable, given the importance of the charters, that they could have been drafted without Frederick's knowledge of their content.
49. DFI, no. 52 (23 March 1155) and no. 98 (January 1155).

Chapter 6 The *Romzug*

1. Otto of Freising, *Deeds* 2.7; and RI IV2/1:35–36, no. 135. On Guido of Biandrate, see DFI, nos. 31 and 32 (17 October 1152), no. 33 (18 October 1152), and no. 36 (October 1152); and Uebach, *Die Ratgeber Friedrich Barbarossas*, pp. 217–21.
2. Otto of Freising, *Chronicle* 7.31; idem, *Deeds* 2.28; and John of Salisbury, *Historia Pontificalis*, pp. 59–60, ch. 27, and pp. 62–65, ch. 31. See Partner, *The Lands of St. Peter*, pp. 178–83; Petersohn, *Kaisertum und Rom in spätsalischer und staufischer Zeit*, pp. 82–96; and George William Greenaway, *Arnold of Brescia* (Cambridge, 1931).

3. Carrie E. Beneš, "Whose SPQR? Sovereignty and Semiotics in Medieval Rome," *Speculum* 84 (2009): 874–81.
4. Otto of Freising, *Deeds* 1.29 (wrongly recorded by Otto under the events of 1146); and Wibald of Stavelot, *Briefbuch* 2:414–18, no. 197 (Jaffé, no. 214). See Koch, *Auf dem Wege zum Sacrum Imperium*, pp. 200–04; Robert L. Benson, "Political *Renovatio*: Two Models from Roman Antiquity," in Benson and Constable, eds, *Renaissance and Renewal in the Twelfth Century*, pp. 340–47 and 355–59; Matthias Thumser, "Die frühe römische Kommune und die staufischen Herrscher in der Briefsammlung Wibalds von Stablo," *DA* 57 (2001): 116–27; and Petersohn, *Kaisertum und Rom in spätsalischer und staufischer Zeit*, pp. 96–104.
5. Wibald of Stavelot, *Briefbuch* 2:420–22, no. 199 (Jaffé, no. 216); and Thumser, "Die frühe römische Kommune," pp. 128–29.
6. DKIII, no. 262 (after 17 September 1151; also Wibald of Stavelot, *Briefbuch* 2:713–15, no. 340 [Jaffé, no. 345]; and *Constitutiones* 1:187–88, no. 132); and Wibald of Stavelot, *Briefbuch* 3:748–50, no. 357 (Jaffé, no. 362), and 3:784–86, no. 374 (Jaffé, no. 382). See Petersohn, *Kaisertum und Rom in spätsalischer und staufischer Zeit*, pp. 110–30.
7. John of Salisbury, *Historia Pontificalis*, pp. 65–69, chs. 32–34. See Houben, *Roger II. von Sizilien*, pp. 102–03.
8. Wibald of Stavelot, *Briefbuch* 3:803–09, no. 383 (Jaffé, no. 404). See Koch, *Auf dem Wege zum Sacrum Imperium*, pp. 204–05; Benson, "Political *Renovatio*," pp. 348–50 and 357–59; Thumser, "Die frühe römische Kommune," pp. 133–47; and Petersohn, *Kaisertum und Rom in spätsalischer und staufischer Zeit*, pp. 135–37.
9. On when Wezel's letter reached Frederick, see Petersohn, *Kaisertum und Rom in spätsalischer und staufischer Zeit*, p. 135, n. 17.
10. Wibald of Stavelot, *Briefbuch* 3:800–03, no. 382 (Jaffé, no. 403). See Benson, "Political *Renovatio*," pp. 349–50; Thumser, "Die frühe römische Kommune," pp. 145–46; and Petersohn, *Kaisertum und Rom in spätsalischer und staufischer Zeit*, pp. 137–38.
11. Penth, *Prämonstratenser und Staufer*, pp. 142–43, and Uebach, *Die Ratgeber Friedrich Barbarossas*, pp. 39–45 and 159–60.
12. Ziegler, *König Konrad III.*, pp. 176–77.
13. Otto of Freising, *Deeds* 2.35.
14. Peter Rassow, *Honor Imperii: Die neue Politik Friedrich Barbarossas 1152–59* (Munich and Berlin, 1940; reprint, Darmstadt, 1961), p. 47.
15. DFI, no. 52 (23 March 1153; also *Constitutiones* 1:202–03, no. 145). See Odilo Engels, "Zum Konstanzer Vertrag von 1153," in Ernst-Dieter Hehl et al., eds, *Deus qui mvtat tempora: Menschen und Institutionen im Wandel des Mittelalters: Festschrift für Alfons Becker zu seinem fünfundsechzigsten Geburtstag* (Sigmaringen, 1987), pp. 235–44. On the oath, see Keupp, *Dienst und Verdienst*, p. 372. The best summary of recent scholarship about the treaty is Laudage, *Alexander III. und Friedrich Barbarossa*, pp. 33–62.
16. DFI, no. 51 (also *Constitutiones* 1:202–03, no. 144; and Wibald of Stavelot, *Briefbuch* 3:809–13 [Jaffé, no. 407]).
17. Herkenrath, "Regnum und Imperium in den Diplomen der ersten Regierungsjahre Friedrichs I.," pp. 331–35; and DFI, head note to no. 52.
18. Herkenrath, "Regnum und Imperium," pp. 331–32.
19. DFI, head note to no. 52; Baaken, "Zur Beurteilung Gottfrieds von Viterbo," pp. 375–76 and 382–86; and Hausmann, "Gottfried von Viterbo," pp. 609–13.
20. DFI, no. 52. On the format of the treaty, see Rassow, *Honor Imperii*, pp. 47–65. On Anselm, see Keupp, *Dienst und Verdienst*, pp. 289–91.
21. Rassow, *Honor Imperii*, pp. 55–56; and Jürgen Petersohn, "Das Präskriptionsrecht der Römischen Kirche und der Konstanzer Vertrag," in Klaus Herbers, Hans Henning Kortüm, and Carlo Servatius, eds, *Ex ipsis rerum documentis: Beiträge zur Mediävistik: Festschrift für Harald Zimmermann zum 65. Geburtstag* (Sigmaringen, 1991), pp. 307–15; and Petersohn, *Kaisertum und Rom in spätsalischer und staufischer Zeit*, pp. 138–48. Unlike other Churches, the statute of limitations for papal claims to property and rights was one hundred years. See Petersohn, "Kaiser, Papst und römisches Recht im Hochmittelalter: Friedrich Barbarossa und Innocenz III. beim Umgang mit dem Rechtsinstitut der langfristigen Verjährung," in

idem, *Mediaevalia Augiensia*, pp. 307–10 and 312. The 1155 confirmation is DFI, no. 98 (January 1155; also *Constitutiones* 1:213–14, no. 151).

22. John of Salisbury, *Historia Pontificalis*, foreword to 1986 edition, pp. vii and xix–xxiv, and pp. 68–69, ch. 34. An English translation of the Donation is in Henderson, *Selected Historical Documents of the Middle Ages*, pp. 319–29, esp. p. 328. See Laudage, *Alexander III.*, pp. 43–50; and idem, *Friedrich Barbarossa*, pp. 43–45 and 67–69; and Jürgen Petersohn, "Friedrich Barbarossa und Rom," in Haverkamp, ed., *Friedrich Barbarossa*, pp. 131–32; and idem, *Kaisertum und Rom in spätsalischer und staufischer Zeit*, pp. 144 and 325–26.
23. Laudage, *Alexander III.*, pp. 50–58 and 63–64; and Ulrich Schludi, "*Advocatus sanctae Romanae ecclesiae* und *specialis filius beati Petri*: Der römische Kaiser aus päpstlicher Sicht," in Burkhardt et al., eds, *Staufisches Kaisertum im 12. Jahrhundert*, pp. 41–47. For Lothar's oath, see *Constitutiones* 1:168, no. 115.
24. Rassow, *Honor Imperii*, pp. 56–57 and 61–62.
25. Otto of Freising, *Deeds* 2.11 and 2.27; John of Salisbury, *Historia Pontificalis*, pp. 61–62, ch. 29; and Wibald of Stavelot, *Briefbuch* 3:814–16, no. 386 (Jaffé, no. 410), pp. 816–18, no. 387 (Jaffé, no. 411), pp. 857–58, no. 411 (Jaffé, no. 424), and pp. 858–59, no. 412 (Jaffé, no. 432). See Engels, "Zum Konstanzer Vertrag," pp. 255–58; Wolfgang Georgi, *Friedrich Barbarossa und die auswärtigen Mächte: Studien zur Aussenpolitik 1159–1180* (Frankfurt, Bern, and New York, 1990), pp. 12–13; and Weller, *Die Heiratspolitik des deutschen Hochadels*, pp. 74–78.
26. Schludi, "*Advocatus sanctae Romanae ecclesiae*," pp. 48–73.
27. Rassow, *Honor Imperii*, esp. pp. 45–65. Herbert Grundmann, in an otherwise favorable review of the book in *HZ* 164 (1941): 577–82, criticized Rassow for his too narrow definition of *honor*.
28. Gunther Wolf, "Der 'Honor Imperii' als Spannungsfeld von lex und sacramentum im Hochmittelalter," in idem, *Friedrich Barbarossa*, pp. 297–322, esp. pp. 315–18; Görich, *Die Ehre Friedrich Barbarossas*, pp. 1–36; and Krieg, *Herrscherdarstellung in der Stauferzeit*, pp. 139–298.
29. Rassow, *Honor Imperii*, pp. 58–62, denied vehemently that the provision was aimed against ordinary criminals in Germany and Italy; the major targets were Roger and the communes. In contrast, Engels, *Die Staufer*, pp. 64–65, insisted that the provision was not aimed at Roger; rather it was insurance against potential princely opposition in Germany, since it was unclear in 1152/53 whether Frederick could reach a settlement with Henry the Lion. However, Engels' argument is in line with his questionable contention that Henry was a serious contender for the crown in 1152. See above, p. 560 n. 2.
30. Otto of Freising, *Deeds* 2.9; and RI IV2/1:52–53, no. 178. See Stefan Weinfurter, "Friedrich Barbarossa und Eichstätt: Zur Absetzung Bischof Burchards 1153," in Schneider and Rechter, eds, *Festschrift Alfred Wendehorst*, pp. 73–84.
31. Morena, *Libellus de rebus a Frederico imperatore gestis*, pp. 34–45; the quotation is on p. 34. On the problematic aspects of the story, see above, pp. 128–29 and 131–33. See Görich, *Die Ehre Friedrich Barbarossas*, pp. 36–48, 186–87, 214–17, and 350–59; idem, *Friedrich Barbarossa*, pp. 169–75; Opll, *Stadt und Reich im 12. Jahrhundert*, pp. 294–308; and idem, "Friedrich Barbarossa und die Stadt Lodi: Stadtentwicklung im Spannungsfeld zwischen Reich und Städtebündnis," in Helmut Maurer, ed., *Kommunale Bündnisse Oberitaliens und Oberdeutschlands im Vergleich* (Sigmaringen, 1987), pp. 63–74.
32. Otto of Freising and Rahewin, *Deeds* 2.11 and 3.26; and Vincent of Prague, *Annales*, p. 668. See Brühl, *Fodrum, gistum, servitium regis* 1:459–60 and 586; Josef Riedmann, "Die Bedeutung des Tiroler Raumes für die Italienpolitik Kaiser Friedrich Barbarossas," in Engel and Töpfer, eds, *Kaiser Friedrich Barbarossa*, pp. 81–92; and Berwinkel, *Verwüsten und Belagern*, pp. 69–70. On the absence of cattle in Bavaria and the Alps—cheese was made from sheep's rather than cow's milk, see Freed, "Bavarian Wine and Woolless Sheep," pp. 104–06.
33. Otto of Freising, *Deeds*, "Letter of the August Emperor, Frederick, to Otto, Bishop of Freising," p. 20; and *Narratio de Longobardie obpressione*, pp. 259–59 (the size of Frederick's forces in 1158).
34. On the size of Frederick's forces, see Brühl, *Fodrum, gistum, servitium regis* 1:526–31; Berwinkel, *Verwüsten und Belagern*, pp. 34–57, esp. p. 41; and Timothy Reuter, "*Episcopi cum*

sua militia: The Prelate as Warrior in the Early Staufer Era," in Reuter, ed., *Warriors and Churchmen in the High Middle Ages: Essays Presented to Karl Leyser* (London and Ronceverte, West VA, 1992), pp. 82–84.

35. Gina Fasoli, "Federico Barbarossa e le città lombarde," in Mayer, ed., *Probleme des 12. Jahrhunderts*, pp. 127–28; trans. Katharina Arndt as "Friedrich Barbarossa und die lombardischen Städte," in Wolf, ed., *Friedrich Barbarossa*, pp. 159–60.
36. Brühl, *Fodrum, gistum, servitium regis* 1:453–57 and pp. 580–84.
37. Ibid., 1:587–90, 593–95, 599, and 605–15; and 2, Itinerarkarte VI. See also Opll, *Das Itinerar Kaiser Friedrich Barbarossas*, pp. 110–22 and p. 257, map showing the itinerary south of the Alps; and *Die Zeit der Staufer* 4, Map III.
38. Mass, *Das Bistum Freising im Mittelalter*, pp. 173–74.
39. Otto of Freising, *Deeds* 2.15 and 2.35. On the *fodrum*, see Brühl, *Fodrum, gistum, servitium regis* 1:534–77 and pp. 659–745; and Haverkamp, *Herrschaftsformen der Frühstaufer in Reichsitalien* 2:669–91. Brühl and Haverkamp got into a bitter argument over whether Barbarossa tried to turn the *fodrum* into a regular annual tax in central Italy (Brühl) or whether such levies were limited to areas directly under imperial control (Haverkamp). The debate got personal and nasty. For example, Brühl, in "Die Finanzpolitik Friedrich Barbarossas in Italien," *HZ* 213 (1971): 25 and 25, n. 59, referred to Haverkamp as "a young hothead," whose "strong suit was clearly not prudence of judgment."
40. Otto of Freising, *Deeds* 2.15. Mierow translated *bubus* as cattle, but I think the context suggests the oxen needed for plowing. The German translation in the Schmale edition uses *Rinder*.
41. Otto of Freising, *Deeds*, "Letter of the August Emperor, Frederick, to Otto, Bishop of Freising," p. 18.
42. Morena, *Libellus de rebus a Frederico imperatore gestis*, pp. 44–49; and RI IV2/1:73–76, nos. 244–52.
43. Otto of Freising, *Deeds* 2.12 and 2.16. For a list of the princes who participated in each of Frederick's campaigns, see Jan-Peter Stöckel, "Reichsbischöfe und Reichsheerfahrt unter Friedrich I. Barbarossa," in Engel and Töpfer, eds, *Kaiser Friedrich Barbarossa*, pp. 64–72, esp. p. 64.
44. Reuter, "*Episcopi cum sua militia*," pp. 79–86; and Stöckel, "Reichsbischöfe und Reichsheerfahrt," pp. 63 and 72. For similar views, see Benjamin Arnold, "German Bishops and their Military Retinues in the Medieval Empire," *German History* 7/2 (1989): 161–83; and Berwinkel, *Verwüsten und Belagern*, p. 44.
45. Stöckel, "Reichsbischöfe und Reichsheerfahrt," pp. 63–79; and Töpfer, "Kaiser Friedrich I. Barbarossa und der deutsche Reichsepiskopat," pp. 421–31.
46. DFI, no. 91 (5 December 1154; also *Constitutiones* 1:207–08, no. 148). Lothar's constitution is DLIII, no. 105 (6 November 1136; also *Constitutiones* 1:175–76, no. 120).
47. Jürgen Dendorfer, "Roncaglia: Der Beginn eines lehnrechtlichen Umbaus des Reiches?" in Burkhardt et al., eds, *Staufisches Kaisertum im 12. Jahrhundert*," pp. 122–25.
48. DFI, no. 242 (November 1158; also *Constitutiones* 1:247–49, no. 177; and Otto of Freising and Rahewin, *Deeds* 4.10). See Haverkamp, *Herrschaftsformen der Frühstaufer in Reichsitalien* 2:363–73 and 522.
49. Eike von Repgow, *The Saxon Mirror* 4.4.
50. Karl-Friedrich Krieger, "Obligatory Military Service and the Use of Mercenaries in Imperial Military Campaigns under the Hohenstaufen Emperors," in Haverkamp and Vollrath, eds, *England and Germany in the High Middle Ages*, pp. 151–61.
51. Otto of Freising, *Deeds* 2.16. On the capture of Almeria and Tortosa, see Phillips, *The Second Crusade*, pp. 244–68. On Margrave William, see Ueber, *Die Ratsgeber Friedrich Barbarossas*, pp. 91–95 and 214–17; Alfred Haverkamp, "Friedrich I. und der hohe italienische Adel," in Raoul Manselli, Paolo Lamma, and Alfred Haverkamp, eds, *Beiträge zur Geschichte Italiens im 12. Jahrhunderts* (Sigmaringen, 1971), pp. 81–89; and Hlawitschka, *Die Ahnen der hochmittelalterlichen deutschen Könige* 3:274–79, 289–92, and 346–48. Besides being Frederick's uncle by marriage, William was the maternal uncle of Louis VII of France (Otto of Freising and Rahewin, *Deeds* 1:46 and 4:14) and the nephew of Pope Calixtus II.
52. Otto of Freising, *Deeds* 2.16; and Adolf Hofmeister, "Eine neue Quelle zur Geschichte Friedrich Barbarossas: De Ruina civitatis Terdonae: Untersuchungen zum 1. Römerzug

Friedrichs I.," *NA* 43 (1922): 97–98, 126–27, and 144, ch. 1 (on Oberto de Orto). See Laudage, *Friedrich Barbarossa*, p. 52.

53. Otto of Freising, *Deeds*, "Letter of the August Emperor, Frederick, to Otto, Bishop of Freising," p. 18, and 2.16; and *Narratio de Longobardie obpressione*, pp. 240–41. Opll, "Friedrich Barbarossa und die Stadt Lodi," pp. 70–74; and Görich, *Die Ehre Friedrich Barbarossas*," pp. 214–17. Görich, "Konflikt und Kompromiss," pp. 82–83, traced the origins of the conflict with Milan to the complaint by the two citizens of Lodi at Constance; whereas Laudage, *Friedrich Barbarossa*, pp. 45–49, was much more skeptical—rightly—about Otto Morena's account.
54. Otto of Freising, *Deeds*, "Letter of the August Emperor, Frederick, to Otto, Bishop of Freising," p. 18, and 2.17; *Carmen de gestis Frederici I. imperatoris in Lombardia* (on the coronation in Monza), pp. 8–10, verses 208–81; Morena, *Libellus de rebus a Frederico imperatore gestis*, pp. 50–51; and *Narratio de Longobardie obpressione*, pp. 240–43. The anonymous Tortona cleric also reported that Frederick received a favorable reception in the Milanese *contado*. See Hofmeister, "Eine neue Quelle zur Geschichte Friedrich Barbarossas," p. 145, ch. 1. In fact, Hofmeister, pp. 98–101, esp. p. 100, thought that the Milanese author might have used the Tortona cleric's account. Berwinkel, *Verwüsten und Belagern*, pp. 58–59, pointed out that armies faced considerable logistical problems in traversing devastated areas.
55. Otto of Freising, *Deeds*, "Letter of the August Emperor, Frederick, to Otto, Bishop of Freising," p. 18, and 2.18; Morena, *Libellus de rebus a Frederico imperatore gestis*, pp. 50–53; and *Narratio de Longobardie obpressione*, pp. 242–43. Görich, *Die Ehre Friedrich Barbarossas*, pp. 217–31, and idem, *Friedrich Barbarossa*, pp. 231–35, stressed the role of the insults to Frederick's honor in these events.
56. Otto of Freising, *Deeds*, "Letter of the August Emperor, Frederick, to Otto, Bishop of Freising," p. 18, and 2.18. See also Morena, *Libellus de rebus a Frederico imperatore gestis*, pp. 52–53; Hofmeister, "Eine neue Quelle zur Geschichte Friedrich Barbarossas," pp. 145–46, ch. 2; and *Narratio de Longobardie obpressione*, pp. 242–43. On the chronology of these events, see RI IV2/1:78–80, nos. 257–64.
57. Before leaving Italy in September 1155, the princes, at Frederick's behest, formally outlawed Milan and stripped the commune of its regalian rights. In the charters announcing that he had granted Milan's mint to Cremona, the king briefly summarized Milan's crimes and indicated that it had repeatedly ignored his summonses to respond to the accusations. DFI, nos. 120 and 121 (beginning of September 1155). Heinrich Appelt, "Friedrich Barbarossa und die italienischen Kommunen," in Wolf, ed., *Friedrich Barbarossa*, pp. 83–103, argued on the basis of the September 1155 charters that the ban may have been imposed for the first time after Milan failed to supply Frederick with provisions (pp. 89–92). Appelt overlooked a piece of evidence that supports his conclusion. According to Otto of Freising, *Deeds* 2.20, Frederick proscribed Tortona in February 1155 "as guilty of treason and numbered [it] among the enemies of the empire," because it had allied with Milan. Milan must thus have been outlawed sometime before February 1155.
58. Otto of Freising, *Deeds*, "Letter of the August Emperor, Frederick, to Otto, Bishop of Freising," p. 18, and 2.19; and Morena, *Libellus de rebus a Frederico imperatore gestis*, pp. 52–53. See Haverkamp, *Herrschaftsformen der Frühstaufer in Reichsitalien* 1:381–94; Opll, *Stadt und Reich im 12. Jahrhundert*, pp. 196–204; and Richter, *Friedrich Barbarossa hält Gericht*, pp. 70–71.
59. Otto of Freising, *Deeds* 2.20; Morena, *Libellus de rebus a Frederico imperatore gestis*, pp. 52–55; and Hofmeister, "Eine neue Quelle zur Geschichte Friedrich Barbarossas," pp. 146–49, chs. 3–4. See Richter, *Friedrich Barbarossa hält Gericht*, pp. 71–72; Görich, *Die Ehre Friedrich Barbarossas*, pp. 187–90; and Laudage, *Friedrich Barbarossa*, pp. 60–61. On Otto of Freising's treatment of the siege and destruction of Tortona, see Bagge, "Ideas and Narrative in Otto of Freising's *Gesta Frederici*," pp. 360–62.
60. On Obizzo Malaspina, see Haverkamp, "Friedrich I. und der hohe italienische Adel," pp. 63–65 and 77–81; and idem, *Herrschaftsformen der Frühstaufer in Reichsitalien* 1:409–18.
61. Otto of Freising, *Deeds*, "Letter of the August Emperor, Frederick, to Otto, Bishop of Freising," p. 18, and 2.20–23; Hofmeister, "Eine neue Quelle zur Geschichte Friedrich Barbarossas," pp. 146–47, ch. 3, and pp. 149–53, chs. 5–7; Morena, *Libellus de rebus a Frederico imperatore gestis*, pp. 54–57; and *Narratio de Longobardie obpressione*, pp. 242–43.

62. Otto of Freising, *Deeds* 2.24–26; and Hofmeister, “Eine neue Quelle zur Geschichte Friedrich Barbarossas,” pp. 153–55, ch. 8. For a detailed analysis, see Görich, *Die Ehre Friedrich Barbarossas*, pp. 190–95 and 200–14; and Krieg, *Herrscherdarstellung in der Stauferzeit*, pp. 208–12. The Tortona cleric wrote between 1155 and 1157 (Görich, p. 472, n. 32). Görich, *Friedrich Barbarossa*, p. 240, suggested that Otto might have written this passage mindful of Frederick’s support of Henry the Lion in Otto’s dispute with the duke over the tolls in Munich. See above, pp. 166–68.
63. Otto of Freising, *Deeds* 2.26; Morena, *Libellus de rebus a Frederico imperatore gestis*, pp. 54–57; and *Narratio de Longobardie obpressione*, pp. 242–43. On Bruno, see DFI, no. 51.
64. Hofmeister, “Eine neue Quelle zur Geschichte Friedrich Barbarossas,” pp. 155–56, chs. 9 and 10. See Görich, *Die Ehre Friedrich Barbarossas*, pp. 190–95.
65. Otto of Freising, *Deeds* 2.21 and 2.25. See Görich, *Die Ehre Friedrich Barbarossas*, pp. 195–200, for a discussion of these events. Görich, p. 200, suggested that the speech Otto had Tortona deliver is proof that Frederick was forced by pressure from Pavia to break “the rules of the game” for previously negotiated submissions. On Milan’s reconstruction of Tortona, see Hofmeister, “Eine neue Quelle zur Geschichte Friedrich Barbarossas,” pp. 156–57, ch. 11; Morena, *Libellus de rebus a Frederico imperatore gestis*, pp. 56–61; and *Narratio de Longobardie obpressione*, pp. 244–51. On the papal embassy, see Godfrey of Viterbo, *Gesta Friderici*, p. 5, lines 130–35.
66. DFI, no. 108 (May–June 1155).
67. Otto of Freising, *Deeds* 2.27; and Gunther der Dichter, *Ligurinus* 3:240–43, vs. 174–230. See Görich, *Friedrich Barbarossa*, pp. 148–49. On the date of Frederick’s coronation in Pavia, see, RI IV2/1:86, no. 286.
68. Otto of Freising, *Deeds*, “Letter of the August Emperor, Frederick, to Otto, Bishop of Freising,” pp. 18–19, and 2.27–28; Morena, *Libellus de rebus a Frederico imperatore gestis*, pp. 60–63; and *Narratio de Longobardie obpressione*, pp. 242–43.
69. *Carmen de gestis Frederici I. imperatoris in Lombardia*, ll. 456–502; and DFI, no. 243 (May 1155; November 1158). On the dating of the *Carmen*, see pp. xviii–xx. The 1158 date appears in fifteenth-century printed editions of the *Authentica Habita*, and Appelt, head note to DFI, no. 243, weighed the possibility that the 1155 version of the law was revised at Roncaglia in 1158 just as Frederick’s feudal law of 1154 was amended in 1158. The accepted date today is 1155. See RI IV2/1:90, no. 300; and Winfried Stelzer, “Zum Scholarenprivileg Friedrich Barbarossas (Authentica ‘Habita’),” *DA* 34 (1978): 146–53.
70. Otto of Freising and Rahewin, *Deeds* 4.6. On Irnerius and on Henry V’s and his successors’ relations with him and Bologna, see Koch, *Auf dem Wege zum Sacrum Imperium*, pp. 37–38, 59, and 118–22; Hastings Rashdall, *The Universities of Europe in the Middle Ages*, ed. F. M. Powicke and A. B. Emden, 3 vols (London, 1895; new edn. 1936), 1:87–125; and Johannes Fried, *Die Entstehung des Juristenstandes im 12. Jahrhundert: Zur sozialen Stellung und politischen Bedeutung gelehrter Juristen in Bologna und Modena* (Cologne and Vienna, 1974), pp. 46–61. Benson, “Political *Renovatio*,” pp. 363–64, said that the professors themselves wrote the privilege.
71. H. Koeppler, “Frederick Barbarossa and the Schools of Bologna: Some Remarks on the ‘Authentica Habita,’” *EHR* 54 (October 1939): 588–607, esp. 588–89; and Rashdall, *The Universities of Europe* 1:142–45.
72. DFI, no. 243; and Stelzer, “Zum Scholarenprivileg Friedrich Barbarossas,” pp. 153–62. The oldest extant text of the *Authentica Habita*, which Stelzer, p. 165, published as an appendix, begins, unlike the text in the Appelt edition, with “Imperator Federicus universis sui regni fidelibus.”
73. Otto of Freising, *Deeds*, Letter of the August Emperor, Frederick, to Otto, Bishop of Freising, p. 19.
74. Boso, *Les vies des papes rédigées par le Cardinal Boson et insérées dans le Liber Censuum*, in *Le Liber Pontificalis: Texte, Introduction et Commentaire*, vol. 2, ed. Louis Duchesne (Paris, 1892), pp. 390–92. Boso’s *Life of Adrian IV* is available in an English translation in a facing edition with the Duchesne text in Brenda Bolton and Anne J. Duggan, eds, *Adrian IV, The English Pope (1154–1159): Studies and Texts* (Aldershot, and Burlington, VT, 2003), pp. 214–33, esp. 218–33. See Simonsfeld, *Jahrbücher des Deutschen Reiches unter Friedrich I.* 1:324–31; and

Görich, *Die Ehre Friedrich Barbarossas*, pp. 94–95. Simonsfeld found it difficult to explain why Adrian might have feared Frederick's approach. He concluded it might have been due to the personality of the pope, who generally mistrusted Germans and who suffered from a certain weakness of character that made him change his mind (pp. 324–25). In reality, Frederick's destruction of Tortona probably aroused the curia's suspicions of the king's motives; and the curia had certainly not forgotten how Frederick's great-uncle, Henry V, had taken Pope Paschal II and the cardinals into protective custody in February 1111. Anne J. Duggan makes this point in "*Totius christianitatis caput*: The Pope and the Princes," in Bolton and Duggan, eds, *Adrian IV*, pp. 123–25. On Boso, see Peter Munz, Introduction to *Boso's Life of Alexander III*, trans. G. M. Ellis (Oxford, 1973), pp. 5–6. Munz identified Boso as English and as Adrian's nephew, but he was a Tuscan. See Odilo Engels, "Kardinal Boso als Geschichtsschreiber," in idem, *Stauferstudien*, p. 204. On Arnold, see Greenaway, *Arnold of Brescia*, esp. pp. 150–54.

75. Helmold von Bosau, *Slawenchronik*, pp. 276–80, 1.81. For a discussion of Helmold's account, see Achim Thomas Hack, *Das Empfangszeremoniell bei mittelalterlichen Papst-Kaiser-Treffen* (Cologne, Weimar, and Vienna,1999), pp. 525–27. I am following here Roman Deutinger's argument in "Sutri 1155: Missverständnisse um ein Missverständnis," *DA* 60 (2004): 97–133, that the issue was how Frederick performed the ceremony.
76. On the feudal interpretation of the incident, see Robert Holtzmann, *Der Kaiser als Marschall des Papstes: Eine Untersuchung zur Geschichte der Beziehungen zwischen Kaiser und Papst im Mittelalter* (Heidelberg, 1928), and the exchange between Eduard Eichmann, "Das Officium Stratoris et Strepae," *HZ* 142 (1930): 16–40; and Robert Holtzmann, "Zum Strator- und Marschalldienst," *HZ* 145 (1931): 301–50.
77. Hack, *Das Empfangszeremoniell*, pp. 504–40 and 586–88.
78. Görich, *Die Ehre Friedrich Barbarossas*, pp. 93–106, and idem, *Friedrich Barbarossa*, pp. 241–46.
79. Deutinger, "Sutri 1155," pp. 97–133; and Sebastian Scholz, "Symbolik und Zeremoniell bei den Päpsten in der zweiten Hälfte des 12. Jahrhunderts," in Weinfurter, ed., *Stauferreich im Wandel*, pp. 131–48.
80. Otto of Freising, *Deeds* 2.28; Boso, *Les vies des papes* 2:389–90 (*Boso's Life of Adrian IV*, pp. 218–19); *Carmen de gestis Frederici I. imperatoris in Lombardia*, vs. 760–860; and Gunther der Dichter, *Ligurinus* 3:246–50, vs. 262–348. See Greenaway, *Arnold of Brescia*, pp. 150–53 and 157–59; and Petersohn, *Kaisertum und Rom in spätsalischer und staufischer Zeit*, pp. 148–50.
81. Otto of Freising, *Deeds*, "Letter of the August Emperor, Frederick, to Otto, Bishop of Freising," p. 19; and Petersohn, *Kaisertum und Rom in spätsalischer und staufischer Zeit*, pp. 151–54.
82. Petersohn, "Friedrich Barbarossa und Rom," pp. 131–33; and idem, *Kaisertum und Rom in spätsalischer und staufischer Zeit*, pp. 154–56.
83. Otto of Freising, *Deeds* 2.29–30. For a discussion of what Frederick/Otto meant when they said that Rome's institutions had been transferred to the Germans, see Bagge, "Ideas and Narrative in Otto of Freising's *Gesta Frederici*," pp. 357–60; and idem, "German Historiography and the Twelfth-Century Renaissance," in Weiler and MacLean, eds, *Representations of Power in Medieval Germany*, pp. 180–83. See also Benson, "Political *Renovatio*," pp. 350–51; and Koch, *Auf dem Wege zum Sacrum Imperium*, pp. 200–15. On Wezel's letter, see above, pp. 114–16. Mierow translated Frederick's words, "tria quoque a nobis iuramenta exquisierunt," as "and also three guarantees upon oath," which makes little sense in English. I translated it as "three sworn guarantees."
84. Otto of Freising, *Deeds*, "Letter of the August Emperor, Frederick, to Otto, Bishop of Freising," p. 19, and 2.32; and Boso, *Les vies des papes* 2:392 (*Boso's Life of Adrian IV*, pp. 222–23). For a reconstruction of these events, see Simonsfeld, *Jahrbücher des Deutschen Reiches unter Friedrich I.* 1:333–38.
85. Otto of Freising, *Deeds*, "Letter of the August Emperor, Frederick, to Otto, Bishop of Freising," p. 19, and 2.32–34; and Boso, *Les vies des papes* 2:392 (*Boso's Life of Adrian IV*, pp. 222–25). Sources that mention or stress Henry the Lion's role are: *Carmen de gestis Frederici I. imperatoris in Lombardia*, vs. 672–759, esp. 707–11 (on the pope procuring the captives' release, vs. 747–51);

Vincent of Prague, *Annales*, p. 665 (Vincent also singled out Frederick of Rothenburg's participation in the fighting, but he would have been too young in 1155); and Helmold of Bosau, *Slawenchronik*, pp. 276–81, ch. 81. For a list of all the sources that deal with the coronation and the subsequent fighting, see RI IV2/1:95–96, no. 319. For a detailed analysis of the fight with the Romans, see Simonsfeld, *Jahrbücher des Deutschen Reiches unter Friedrich I.*, "Excurs V: Der Kampf mit den Römern," pp. 689–98. On the topography of medieval Rome, see Richard Krautheimer, *Rome: Profile of a City, 312–1308* (Princeton, N.J., 1980), esp. maps, pp. 245–47.

86. Otto of Freising, *Deeds*, "Letter of the August Emperor, Frederick, to Otto, Bishop of Freising," pp. 19–20, and 2.34; Boso, *Les vies des papes* 2:392–93 (*Boso's Life of Adrian IV*, pp. 224–27); DFI, no. 113 (29 June 1155; also in Boso's *Les vies des papes*, p. 393; and *Constitutiones* 1:215, no. 152); and RI IV2/1:96–98, nos. 321–27. On Frederick's relations with Farfa, see Haverkamp, *Herrschaftsformen der Frühstaufer in Reichsitalien* 1:236–38; and on Tivoli, idem, pp. 334–35; and Brenda Bolton, "*Nova familia beati Petri*: Adrian IV and the Patrimony," in Bolton and Duggan, eds, *Adrian IV, The English Pope*, pp. 164–65 and 172–73. For a general discussion of the rival claims to jurisdiction, see Laudage, *Alexander III.*, pp. 62–83; and Petersohn, *Kaisertum und Rom in spätsalischer und staufischer Zeit*, pp. 158–61.
87. Otto of Freising, *Deeds* 2.34; and DFI, no. 114 (1 July? 1155; on the Tiber near Monte Soratte); no. 115 (falsified charter, 7 July 1155; in the territory of Tusculum); and no. 116 (after 7 July 1155; in the territory of Tivoli).
88. Otto of Freising, *Deeds*, "Letter of the August Emperor, Frederick, to Otto, Bishop of Freising," p. 20, and 2.35–37; and Morena, *Libellus de rebus a Frederico imperatore gestis*, pp. 62–65. Otto Morena offered no motive for the fight. According to him, Frederick had done Spoleto no harm when the inhabitants suddenly attacked him while he was eating a meal, or so, Morena said, he was told. For the date, see RI IV2/1:101, nos. 337–38. On the incident in Spoleto, see Richter, *Friedrich Barbarossa hält Gericht*, pp. 84–86.
89. Otto of Freising, *Deeds*, "Letter of the August Emperor, Frederick, to Otto, Bishop of Freising," p. 20, and 2.36–37; *Carmen de gestis Frederici I. imperatoris in Lombardia*, vs. 1030–42 (the poet listed the presents Frederick received in a direct quotation from Virgil's *Aeneid*); Otto of St. Blaisen, *Chronicle*, pp. 26–31, ch. 7, esp. pp. 28–29; and RI IV2/1:102. On the swimming, see Hans Sudendorf, ed., *Registrum oder merkwürdige Urkunden für die deutsche Geschichte*, 3 vols (Jena and Berlin, 1849–54), vol. 2, pp. 131–33. Rainald of Dassel referred in the letter to Frederick, published by Sudendorf, about the spot in the Adriatic where he and Otto had bathed (p. 132).
90. Otto of Freising, *Deeds* 2.38.
91. Otto of Freising, *Deeds* 2.49; Boso, *Les vies des papes* 2:393–95 (*Boso's Life of Adrian IV*, pp. 226–29); and Romuald of Salerno, *Romoaldi II. archiepiscopi Salernitani Annales*, p. 428. On the rebellion in the Norman kingdom, see Ferdinand Chalandon, *Histoire de la domination normande en Italie et en Sicile*, 2 vols (Paris, 1907; reprint, New York, 1960–69), vol. 2, pp. 185–234; and Duggan, "*Totius christianitatis caput*," pp. 113–17.
92. On the whole episode of the purloined letters, see Georgi, *Friedrich Barbarossa und die auswärtigen Mächte*, pp. 12–27; and Weller, *Die Heiratspolitik des deutschen Hochadels*, pp. 77–84. On Benevento, see Romuald of Salerno, *Romoaldi II. archiepiscopi Salernitani Annales*, p. 429; and Duggan, "*Totius christianitatis caput*," pp. 117–20. The text of the treaty is in *Constitutiones* 1:588–91, nos. 413–14. For a recent assessment of the benefits the pope and William derived from the Treaty of Benevento, see Laudage, *Alexander III.*, pp. 83–88.
93. Otto of Freising, *Deeds* 2.39; DFI, nos. 120 and 121 (beginning of September 1155); and RI IV2/1:103–05, nos. 344–52. By 7 September, Frederick was already in Trent (DFI, no. 122). On the grant of the mint to Cremona, see Görich, *Die Ehre Friedrich Barbarossas*, pp. 222–23. The *Carmen des gestis Frederici I. imperatoris in Lombardia*, vs. 1567–69, indicated that Frederick authorized both Cremona and Bergamo to strike their own coins. Frederick had probably already outlawed Milan in December 1154 after it failed to provide him with provisions. See above, n. 57.
94. DKIII, no. 15 (December 1138); and DFI, no. 119 (25 August 1155). See Haverkamp, *Herrschaftsformen der Frühstaufer in Reichsitalien* 2:561–89.
95. Morena, *Libellus de rebus a Frederico imperatore gestis*, pp. 64–65; and DFI, no. 122 (shortly before 7 September 1155). Simonsfeld, *Jahrbücher des Deutschen Reiches unter Friedrich I.*

1:375–80; and "Excurs VI: Der Durchzug durch die Veroneser Klause," pp. 699–708, dealt in great detail with all the sources that discussed the events in Verona and gave little credence to Otto Morena's account of a pitched battle between the imperial and Veronese forces (p. 705). Opll, RI IV2/1:105–06, nos. 355–56, adhered to Simonsfeld's reconstruction of events; but Richter, *Friedrich Barbarossa hält Gericht*, pp. 87–95, esp. p. 93, suggested that Morena may have been describing what happened after the imperial army crossed the bridge.

96. Otto of Freising, *Deeds*, "Letter of the August Emperor, Frederick, to Otto, Bishop of Freising," p. 20, and 2.40. See the account of the passage through the gorge in Berwinkel, *Verwüsten und Belagern*, pp. 61–62. Bagge, "Ideas and Narrative in Otto of Freising's *Gesta Frederici*," pp. 362–63, argued that the account of how Frederick spared the French knight was intended to counter the image of Frederick as a merciless judge.
97. Otto of Freising, *Deeds* 2.41–42 and 2.45; and DFI, no. 123 (Trent, 7 September 1155). By 20 September, Frederick was in Peiting, south of Augsburg (DFI, no. 125).

Chapter 7 New Arrangements

1. Otto of Freising, *Deeds* 2.42–43. See Appelt, *Privilegium minus*, pp. 36–37.
2. Otto of Freising, *Deeds* 2.46; *Vita Arnoldi archiepiscopi Moguntini*, pp. 610–16; Wibald of Stavelot, *Briefbuch* 3:909–11, no. 439 (Jaffé, no. 436); and *Annales Sancti Disibodi a. 891–1200*, ed. Georg Waitz, in MGH SS 17 (Hanover, 1861), p. 29. See Simonsfeld, *Jahrbücher des Deutschen Reiches unter Friedrich I.*, 1:367, 386–88, and 400–03; and Richter, *Friedrich Barbarossa hält Gericht*, pp. 40–45. On the local context of the dispute, see Engels, "Grundlinien der rheinischen Verfassungsgeschichte im 12. Jahrhundert," pp. 155–56, n. 129. Klaus Schreiner, "'Gerechtigkeit und Frieden haben sich geküsst' (Ps. 84, 11): Friedensstiftung durch symbolisches Handeln," in Johannes Fried, ed., *Träger und Instrumentarien des Friedens im hohen und späten Mittelalter* (Sigmaringen, 1996), pp. 67–68, n. 105, emphasized the incompatibility between the two accounts. The passage in Arnold's *Life* about chastising the people of Mainz with whips and scorpions is taken from I Kings 12:11. The editor, Philipp Jaffé, did not catch the reference.
3. DFI, no. 141 (17 June 1156); no. 151 (17 September 1156); and no. 165 (6 April 1157). See Bernd Schwenk, "Das Hundetragen: Ein Rechtsbrauch im Mittelalter," *Historisches Jahrbuch* 110 (1990): 289–308.
4. Otto of Freising, *Deeds* 2.40 and 2.46. See Richter, *Friedrich Barbarossa hält Gericht*, pp. 45–46.
5. Otto of Freising, *Deeds* 2.47 and 2.55; and RI IV2/1:118, no. 396. See Appelt, *Privilegium minus*, pp. 40–51.
6. Otto of Freising, *Deeds* 2.56. For the magnates who were present in Regensburg, see the witness lists of the *Privilegium minus* (DFI, no. 151) and a privilege that Frederick issued the same day for the Knights of St. John at the request of the new duke of Austria (DFI, no. 152).
7. DFI, no. 151 (17 September 1156; also *Constitutiones* 1:220–23, no. 159; and Appelt, *Privilegium minus*, pp. 96–99). For an English translation, see Henderson, *Select Historical Documents of the Middle Ages*, pp. 215–17. On the history of the privilege, see Appelt, *Privilegium minus*, pp. 9–31.
8. On the changing meaning of the names *Österreich* and *Austria*, see John B. Freed, "Das zweite österreichische Millennium—Berufung auf das Mittelalter zur Schaffung eines österreichischen Nationalbewusstseins," *MGSL* 137 (1997): 279–94, esp. 281. The possibly falsified charter is DKIII, no. 173 (25 February 1147). *Austria* was also employed in the charter issued for the Knights of St. John on 17 September 1156 (DFI, no. 152) and in an original charter for the Augustinian canons of Neustift in the Tyrol on 5 July 1157 (no. 174).
9. Appelt, *Privilegium minus*, pp. 51–62, esp. pp. 52–53; and idem, "Die libertas affectandi des Privilegium minus," in idem, *Kaisertum, Königtum, Landesherrschaft*, pp. 174–79.
10. Appelt, *Privilegium minus*, pp. 76–80.
11. Ibid., pp. 62–76. The "Golden Liberty" is DFI, no. 546 (10 July 1168). For a discussion of both the Austrian and Würzburg charters and the translation of the latter, see Arnold, *Princes and Territories in Medieval Germany*, pp. 104–05. On Otto's feud with his brother, see Otto of Freising and Rahewin, *Deeds* 3.14; and Lyon, *Princely Brothers and Sisters*, pp. 82–83. On

the territorial implementation of the *Privilegium minus*, see Karl Lechner, *Die Babenberger: Markgrafen und Herzoge von Österreich 976–1246* (Vienna, Cologne, and Graz, 1976; reprint, Darmstadt, 1985), pp. 155–91; and Folker Reichert, *Landesherrschaft, Adel und Vogtei: Zur Vorgeschichte des spätmittelalterlichen Ständestaates im Herzogtum Österreich* (Cologne and Vienna, 1985).

12. Dendorfer, "Roncaglia: Der Beginn eines lehnrechtlichen Umbaus des Reiches?" p. 126.
13. DFI, no. 165. The ruling occurred in 1155, but the charter is dated 6 April 1157. See RI IV2/1:109–11, nos. 367 and 376; and p. 139, no. 447.
14. DKIII, no. 46 (3 May 1140); DFI, no. 218 (14 June 1158) and no. 798 (13 July 1180); and Otto of Freising and Rahewin, *Deeds* 4.14. For a traditional account of the dispute, see Rudolf Schieffer, "Heinrich der Löwe, Otto von Freising und Friedrich Barbarossa am Beginn der Geschichte Münchens," in Hechberger and Schuler, eds, *Staufer & Welfen*, pp. 67–77; and Dendorfer, "Von den Babenberger zu den Welfen," pp. 244–47. Freimut Scholz called this version of events into doubt in "Die Anfänge Münchens in neuer Sicht," *ZbLG* 70 (2007): 719–80; and idem, "Eine separate Ausfertigung für Erzbischof Konrad III. von Salzburg? Das Regensburger Urteil Friedrichs I. vom 13. Juli 1180 in neuer Sicht," *MGSL* 153 (2013): 39–63, on which I am relying. On Frederick's intervention in Höxter, see DFI, nos. 21–23 (July 1152). Frederick had ordered Otto in March 1157 to participate in the second Italian expedition (DFI, no. 163); Otto set out instead for the Cistercian general chapter and died in Morimond.
15. Otto of Freising and Rahewin, *Deeds* 3.1–5 and 3.13; DFI, no. 181 (September 1157; also in Wibald of Stavelot, *Briefbuch* 3:930–32, no. 451 [Jaffé, no. 470]); Vincent of Prague, *Annales*, pp. 666–67 (on the Bohemian role); RI IV1/2:164, no. 378; *Cosmae chronica Boemorum: Canonicorum Pragensium continuationes a. 1140–1195*, ed. Rudolf Köpke, in MGH SS 9 (Hanover, 1851), p. 164, at 1158 (the promise to supply 300 knights); and RI IV2/1:149–51, nos. 477–78 and 480–83. See Simonsfeld, *Jahrbücher des Deutschen Reiches unter Friedrich I.*, 1:544–49; Richter, *Friedrich Barbarossa hält Gericht*, pp. 49–52; Jerzy Wyrozumski, "Poland in the Eleventh and Twelfth Centuries," in David Luscombe and Jonathan Riley Smith, eds, *The New Cambridge Medieval History* 4/2 (Cambridge, 2004), pp. 284–86; and Ziegler, *König Konrad III.*, "Exkurs Nr. 1: Die polnischen Erbfolgestreitigkeiten," pp. 755–65.
16. RI IV2/2:169, no. 1226; and RI IV2/3:68, no. 1995. See Patze, "Kaiser Friedrich Barbarossa und der Osten," p. 378; and Richter, *Friedrich Barbarossa hält Gericht*, p. 52. Landgrave Louis' mother was Frederick's sister and Louis' paternal aunt was Vladislav's second wife. See Weller, *Die Heiratspolitik des deutschen Hochadels*, Plate 8.
17. Simonsfeld, *Jahrbücher des Deutschen Reiches unter Friedrich I.*, pp. 550–51, cited and discussed Ranke's comment.
18. Otto of Freising, *Deeds* 2.42; Vincent of Prague, *Annales*, pp. 665–66; and RI IV2/1:22–23, nos. 91–92. See Kejř, "Böhmen und das Reich unter Friedrich I.," pp. 248–51; idem, "Böhmen zur Zeit Friedrich Barbarossas," pp. 107–08; and Lisa Wolverton, *Hastening toward Prague: Power and Society in the Medieval Czech Lands* (Philadelphia, P.A., 2001), pp. 236–37, 247–54, and for a genealogy of the male Přemyslids in the eleventh and twelfth centuries, see pp. 104–05. On Bishop Daniel, see Uebach, *Die Ratgeber Friedrich Barbarossas*, pp. 178–84.
19. Otto of Freising and Rahewin, *Deeds* 3.14; and Vincent of Prague, *Annales*, pp. 667–68. See Kejř, "Böhmen und das Reich unter Friedrich I.," pp. 251–57. Mierow mistranslated Rahewin's phrase: "Suscepto itaque privilegio de usu diadematis aliisque regni insignibus," as "after being privileged to use a crown and other royal insignia." Rahewin was referring to the specific privilege that Frederick granted Vladislav on 18 January. The English word *crown* obscures the distinction that Vincent, Rahewin, and Frederick's privilege made between Frederick's crown and Vladislav's diadem or headband.
20. DFI, no. 201 (18 January 1158; also *Constitutiones* 1:236–37, no. 170); and no. 221 (10 July 1158). On the use of the ducal title in the 1158 charter, see Heinrich Appelt, "Böhmische Königswürde und staufisches Kaisertum," in idem, *Kaisertum, Königtum, Landesherrschaft*, pp. 40–60; and Kejř, "Böhmen und das Reich," p. 255.
21. DFI, no. 130 (18 December 1155); and no. 153 (October 1156). See Bernd Brinken, *Die Politik Konrads von Staufen in der Tradition der Rheinischen Pfalzgrafschaft: Der Widerstand gegen die Verdrängung der Pfalzgrafschaft aus dem Rheinland in der zweiten Hälfte des 12. Jahrhunderts* (Bonn, 1974), pp. 37–42.

22. Otto of Freising, *Deeds* 1.22, 1.41, and 2.20; Morena, *Libellus de rebus a Frederico imperatore gestis*, pp. 188–89; DKIII, no. 269 (12 January 1152; first reference to Conrad); and Conrad as Frederick's brother (DFI, nos. 65, 73, 77, 133, 138, 151 [*Privilegium minus*], and 152); and Conrad as duke and Frederick's brother (DFI, nos. 128–29, 134, and 142). Conrad was called the duke of Swabia in no. 136 (February 1156), but this document survives only in an eighteenth-century copy, so the designation is dubious.
23. Otto of Freising and Rahewin, *Deeds* 3.26 and 4.84–85; Morena, *Libellus de rebus a Frederico imperatore gestis*, pp. 100–05, 114–20, 130–31, and 158–61; and DFI, no. 308 (15 February 1160) and no. 326 (3 June 1161).
24. Brinken, *Die Politik Konrads von Staufen*, pp. 231–32.
25. Ibid., pp. 43–52.
26. DFI, no. 338 (1 September 1161); and Brinken, *Die Politik Konrads von Staufen*, pp. 53–166, esp. pp. 109–23 (on the Trier commune) and pp. 156–66 (summary). Conrad's letter to the burghers of Trier is published on p. 110, n. 3, of Brinken's book.
27. Weller, *Die Heiratspolitik des deutschen Hochadels*, pp. 43–46. As the advocate of Lorsch and of the bishopric of Worms, Conrad was more successful in pursuing a policy of territorial expansion on the right bank of the Rhine than he was on the left bank at the expense of Cologne and Trier. See Stefan Weinfurter, "Der Untergang des alten Lorsch in spätstaufischer Zeit. Das Kloster an der Bergstrasse im Spannungsfeld zwischen Papsttum, Erzstift Mainz und Pfalzgrafschaft," in idem, *Gelebte Ordnung—Gedachte Ordnung*, pp. 159–85, esp. pp. 162–71.
28. *Auctarium Affligemense*, ed. Ludwig Conrad Bethmann, in MGH SS 6 (Hanover, 1844), p. 404. Schmidt, *Königswahl und Thronfolge im 12. Jahrhundert*, pp. 167–69, was very skeptical about the accuracy of the monk's report; but Schmidt was also trying to prove the elective character of the German monarchy in the twelfth century. His alternative explanation of the text has not gained general scholarly acceptance. Althoff, "Friedrich von Rothenburg," p. 312, and Zotz, "Friedrich Barbarossa und Herzog Friedrich (IV.) von Schwaben," pp. 295–96, thought that Barbarossa did designate Frederick of Rothenburg as his successor.
29. Morena, *Libellus de rebus a Frederico imperatore gestis*, pp. 166–71; and DFI, no. 382 (18 August 1162; charter witnessed by Conrad). Görich, *Die Ehre Friedrich Barbarossas*, pp. 244–47, traced Conrad's hostility toward Rainald to the events of 7 August 1161. On those events, see above, pp. 282–84.
30. DFI, no. 398 (18 April 1163), no. 404 (3 August 1163), and no. 480 (1 June 1165). Conrad allegedly witnessed in Frankfurt on 17 April 1165 Frederick's charter for Pisa (DFI, no. 477), but the authenticity of the charter is in doubt.
31. *Chronica regia Coloniensis*, pp. 115–16; and DFI, no. 480 (1 June 1165), no. 481 (2 June 1165), no. 483 (beginning of June 1165), and no. 532 (1 August 1167). See Brinken, *Die Politik Konrads von Staufen*, pp. 167–74 and 195–207. Brinken, pp. 174–82, was skeptical that the desire to revenge the 1161 insult was a motive for Conrad and Louis' involvement in the Rheineck feud.
32. *Annales Egmundani*, ed. Georg Heinrich Pertz, in MGH SS 16 (Hanover, 1859), p. 463; and Otto of Freising and Rahewin, *Deeds*, Mierow edition, Appendix, pp. 336–37. On Conrad's relations with Frederick, see Brinken, *Die Politik Konrads von Staufen*, pp. 188–95.
33. Plassmann, *Die Struktur des Hofes unter Friedrich I. Barbarossa*, pp. 217–21.
34. See, for example, DFI, no. 221 (10 July 1158; Frederick, duke of Swabia); and no. 326 (3 June 1161; Frederick, duke of the Swabians, the son of King Conrad). Chroniclers referred to Frederick as both the duke of Swabia or of Rothenburg and as Conrad's son. See, for example, Otto of Freising and Rahewin, *Deeds* 3:26; and Morena, *Libellus de rebus a Frederico imperatore gestis*, pp. 100–03, 130–31, 158–61, 176–77, 190–91, 218–19, and 228–29. On Frederick of Rothenburg's knighting, see above, pp. 84–85.
35. Otto of Freising and Rahewin, *Deeds* 3.26 and 3.38. See Berwinkel, *Verwüsten und Belagern*, pp. 100–04; and p. 274, Abbildung 5: "Belagerung von Mailand, August 1158."
36. Morena, *Libellus de rebus a Frederico imperatore gestis*, pp. 100–03, 190–91, and 218–19. On the identity of the Lodi Anonymous, see Schmale, *Italienische Quellen*, "Einleitung," pp. 10–11.
37. *Historia Welforum*, pp. 80–83, ch. 30; and Otto of St. Blasien, *Chronicle*, pp. 48–53, ch. 18.

38. Schmid, *Graf Rudolf von Pfullendorf*, pp. 18–19 (genealogy) and 136–68. Althoff, "Konfliktverhalten und Rechtsbewusstsein," pp. 62–65, rejected Schmid's argument and insisted that obtaining satisfaction for a slight was a crucial part of maintaining a noble's honor.
39. *Historia Welforum*, pp. 80–85, chs. 30–31; Otto of St. Blasien, *Chronicle*, pp. 48–53, ch. 18; and Burchard of Ursberg, *Chronicon*, pp. 184–87. Otto and Burchard relied on the *Historia Welforum* for their information. All three are vague about the chronology and do not indicate where and when Welf VI procured the prisoners' release or Barbarossa's role in these events. However, Barbarossa issued a charter in Ulm on 1 November 1164 (DFI, no. 470). Among the individuals who witnessed the charter were the following participants in the feud: the bishops of Augsburg and Speyer, Frederick of Rothenburg, Welf VI and his son, and Berthold IV of Zähringen.
40. *Historia Welforum,* pp. 84–85, ch. 31; Otto of St. Blasien, *Chronicle,* pp. 52–53, ch. 19; and Burchard of Ursberg, *Chronicon,* pp. 186–87. For an analysis of the resolution of the conflict, see Althoff, "Konfliktverhalten und Rechtsbewusstsein," pp. 69–73.
41. Duke of Stauf (DFI, nos. 470 [1 November 1164], nos. 506–07, 513, and 516); duke of Rothenburg (DFI, nos. 478, 509, and 529); and Duke Frederick, son of King Conrad (DFI, nos. 523, 532, and 534). See Zotz, "Friedrich Barbarossa und Herzog Friedrich (IV.) von Schwaben," pp. 296–98.
42. Weller, *Die Heiratspolitik des deutschen Hochadels*, pp. 53–57.
43. Morena, *Libellus de rebus a Frederico imperatore gestis*, pp. 228–29; DFI, no. 559 (26 January 1170), and no. 588 (19 April 1172); and *Historia calamitatum ecclesiae Salzburgensis*, in Jacques Paul Migne, ed., *Patrologia Latina* 196 (Paris, 1855), col. 1549. See Zotz, "Friedrich Barbarossa und Herzog Friedrich (IV.) von Schwaben," pp. 303–05.
44. Otto of Freising, *Deeds* 2.11 and 2.36; *Carmen de gestis Frederici I. imperatoris in Lombardia*, vs. 1030–42; and DFI, no. 133 (25 January 1156). In his 1152 agreement with Berthold IV (DFI, no. 12), Frederick referred explicitly to the lands that William held on behalf of his niece.
45. Otto of Freising and Rahewin, *Deeds* 2.48. On the anointing, see the *Annales Sancti Iacobi Leodiensis*, ed. Georg Heinrich Pertz, in MGH SS 16 (Hanover, 1859), p. 641 (at 1158). On Beatrice's age and ancestry, see Hlawitschka, *Die Ahnen der hochmittelalterlichen deutschen Könige* 2, Plate XXXVIII and pp. 195–247. The witness lists of the charters issued at Würzburg in June 1156, DFI, nos. 141–46, confirm Otto's statement that many princes attended the festivities. On the marriage, see Weller, *Die Heiratspolitik des deutschen Hochadels*, pp. 91–99; and Ursula Vones-Liebenstein, "*Vir uxorius*?: Barbarossas Verhältnis zur *Comitissa Burgundiae* im Umkreis des Friedens von Venedig," in Weinfurter, ed., *Stauferreich im Wandel*, pp. 191–93.
46. Otto of Freising, *Deeds* 2.48. On Frederick's never implemented agreement, see above, pp. 80–81.
47. Otto of Freising and Rahewin, *Deeds* 4.28 and 4.46; Morena, *Libellus de rebus a Frederico imperatore gestis*, pp. 102–03; and Burchard of Ursberg, *Chronicon*, pp. 148–49. On the county's strategic location, see Locatelli, "Frédéric Ier et le royaume de Bourgogne," p. 172; and Dietrich Lohrmann, "Das Papsttum und die Grafschaft Burgund im 11.–12. Jahrhundert," in Ernst-Dieter Hehl, Ingrid Heike Ringel, and Hubertus Seibert, eds, *Das Papsttum in der Welt des 12. Jahrhunderts* (Stuttgart, 2002), pp. 61–62.
48. Otto of Freising and Rahewin, *Deeds* 3.5 (Poland) and 3.47 (Milan); and DFI, no. 362 (11 September 1162, Piacenza); no. 378 (before 1 August 1162, Provence); no. 382 (18 August 1162, Provence); and no. 857 (c. 20 May 1184, Hainaut).
49. Weller, *Die Heiratspolitik des deutschen Hochadels*, pp. 94–95 and 555–63, and Plates 7/1 and 7/2: "Châtenois-Oberlothringen"; Locatelli, "Frédéric Ier et le royaume de Bourgogne," pp. 180–81; Vones-Liebenstein, "*Vir uxorius*?" pp. 193–95; and Wyrozumski, "Poland in the Eleventh and Twelfth Centuries," pp. 286–87.
50. Morena, *Libellus de rebus a Frederico imperatore gestis*, pp. 188–89; and *Carmen de gestis Frederici I. imperatoris in Lombardia*, vs. 1110–14.
51. *Ex Radulfi de Diceto operibus historicis: Ex Ymaginibus historiarum*, ed. Felix Liebermann and Reinhold Pauli, in MGH SS 27 (Hanover, 1885), pp. 270–71. On the description of Frederick as "uxorious," see Johannes Fried, "Friedrich Barbarossas Krönung in Arles," *Historisches Jahrbuch* 103 (1983): 350–51; and Vones-Liebenstein, "*Vir uxorius?*" pp. 189–91. John of Salisbury, *Historia Pontificalis*, pp. 14–15, ch. 7, employed the word *uxorius* to

describe Count Ralph of Vermandois. While the count was recovering from a serious illness, his physician "warned him, as he valued his life, to abstain from intercourse with his wife; but he disregarded the warning, for he was very uxorious," and died. So it is possible that Ralph, another Anglo-Norman author, used the word in the same sense.

52. Joachim Bumke, *Courtly Culture: Literature and Society in the High Middle Ages*, trans. Thomas Dunlap (Berkeley and Los Angeles, 1991), p. 76, made the case for Beatrice's patronage. Johanek, "Kultur und Bildung im Umkreis Friedrich Barbarossas," pp. 662–63, argued the contrary.
53. On the couple's children, see Gerhard Baaken, "Die Altersfolge der Söhne Friedrich Barbarossas und die Königserhebung Heinrichs VI.," in idem, *Imperium und Papsttum*, pp. 1–29; and Weller, *Die Heiratspolitik des deutschen Hochadels*, pp. 99–180 and Plate 1. Vones-Liebenstein, "*Vir uxorius?*" p. 205, suggested that Philip was named after Philip of Flanders. Peter Csendes, *Philipp von Schwaben: Ein Staufer im Kampf um die Macht* (Darmstadt, 2003), p. 21, identified Archbishop Philip as the godfather of the Staufer prince.
54. DFI, nos. 143 and 145 (June 1156); no. 194 (c. 18 November 1157); and no. 753 (18 July–15 August 1178). See also no. 191 (14 November 1157) and no. 291 (mid-October–December 1159).
55. DFI, no. 515 (26 July 1166). On Odo of Champagne's identity, see Theodore Evergates, *The Aristocracy in the County of Champagne, 1100–1300* (Philadelphia, P.A., 2007), pp. 220 and 248: "The Counts of Champagne, 1021–1285"; and Vones-Liebenstein, "*Vir uxorius?*" pp. 196–97. Frederick along with Beatrice authorized the archbishop of Besançon in 1180/84 to reclaim fiefs which his predecessors had illegally alienated without imperial permission. See DFI, no. *1187. Heinrich Appelt, "Kaiserin Beatrix und das Erbe der Grafen von Burgund," in idem, *Kaisertum, Königtum, Landesherrschaft*, pp. 109–20, stressed that Beatrice's political involvement was limited to Burgundy.
56. DFI, no. 279 (1 August 1159); no. 614 (24 March 1174); and no. 621 (23 May 1174).
57. DFI, no. 1013 (June 1156–15 November 1184).
58. *Chronica regia Coloniensis*, p. 101. See Görich, *Die Ehre Friedrich Barbarossas*, pp. 253–54 and p. 507, n. 437 (notary's comment). On the role of queens and empresses in the resolution of conflicts, see Gerd Althoff, "Königsherrschaft und Konfliktbewältigung im 10. und 11. Jahrhundert," in idem, *Spielregeln der Politik im Mittelalter*, pp. 21–56. On Richenza's intervention, see above, p. 32, and on Beatrice's absence, see above, p. 288.
59. DFI, no. 467 (5 October 1164); and *Recueil des historiens des Gaules et de la France*, vol. 16, ed. Michel-Jean-Joseph Brial (Paris, 1814), rev. edn., ed. Léopold Delisle (Paris, 1878), pp. 143–44, no. 433 (1168; letter of William to his nephew Louis VII informing the king about his close ties to the emperor). See Baaken, "Die Altersfolge der Söhne Friedrich Barbarossas," pp. 16–21. Vones-Liebenstein, "*Vir uxorius?*" pp. 198–99, attributed the close ties between Frederick and the margrave to Beatrice's influence, but William had already been firmly on Frederick's side during the first expedition.
60. DFI, no. 648 (6? March 1176); and no. 665 (January or February 1177). See Opll, *Stadt und Reich im 12. Jahrhundert*, pp. 441–43.
61. DFI, no. 735 (23 June 1178). On the purchase of the regalia in Vercelli, see Haverkamp, *Herrschaftsformen der Frühstaufer in Reichsitalien* 2:668. Haverkamp said that the reasons for the transaction were "hard to grasp."
62. DKIII, no. 143 (30 December 1145); DFI, no. 43 (29 December 1152); and *Annales Cameracenses auctore Lamberto Waterlos a. 1099–1170*, ed. Georg Heinrich Pertz, MGH SS 16 (Hanover, 1859), pp. 523–25. See Simonsfeld, *Jahrbücher des Deutschen Reiches unter Friedrich I.*, 1:145–48; Opll, *Stadt und Reich im 12. Jahrhundert*, pp. 56–58; and Görich, *Friedrich Barbarossa*, pp. 184–91.
63. *Annales Cameracenses*, pp. 538, 540–44, and 546; DFI, nos. 539–41 (September 1167); and Gilbert of Mons, *Chronicle of Hainaut*, pp. 46–47, ch. 47. See Töpfer, "Kaiser Friedrich I. Barbarossa und der deutsche Reichsepiskopat," p. 391; and Opll, *Stadt und Reich im 12. Jahrhundert*, pp. 58–60.
64. DFI, no. 470 (1 November 1164). Other references to Beatrice's and the children's salvation and remembrance appear in charters for St. Mary's in Aachen (no. 502, 8 January 1166: Beatrice, Frederick V, and Henry VI); the Styrian Benedictine abbey of St. Lambrecht (no. 562, 3 March

1170: Barbarossa, Beatrice, and their children); the bishopric and cathedral chapter of Gurk in Carinthia (no. 563, 10 March 1170: Barbarossa, Beatrice, and their sons); and the Hospitalers in Lombardy (no. 647, January 1176: Barbarossa, his ancestors, Beatrice, and their sons).

65. *Die Zeit der Staufer: Katalog der Ausstellung* 1:130 and 2, Abbildung 98, nos. 12, 13, and 19. See Norbert Kamp, *Moneta regis: Königliche Münzstätten und königliche Münzpolitik in der Stauferzeit* (Hanover, 2006), pp. 286–94.
66. DFI, no. 658, p. 164, line 36, and p. 165, line 20; and no. 687, p. 205, lines 7 and 38–39. See Krieg, *Herrscherdarstellung in der Stauferzeit*, pp. 299–320, esp. pp. 319–20.
67. DFI, no. 69 (17 January, 1154). See Heinrich Büttner, "Vom Bodensee und Genfer See zum Gotthardpass," in Theodor Mayer, ed., *Die Alpen in der europäischen Geschichte des Mittelalters: Reichenau-Vorträge* (Sigmaringen, 1965), pp. 98–106; Büttner, "Barbarossa und Burgund," pp. 88–89 and 99–100; and Heinemann, "Die Zähringer und Burgund," pp. 63–71.
68. DFI, no. 199 (1 January 1158). See Patze, "Kaiser Friedrich Barbarossa und der Osten," pp. 359–60.
69. The text of Berthold's letter with a German translation is in Schmid and Shadek, eds, *Die Zähringer* 2:453, no. 9. On the date, see RI IV2/2:151–52, no. 1153.
70. DFI, nos. 388 and 389 (7 September 1162).
71. *Chronicon Montis Sereni*, p. 152, at 1163 (Frederick testified about the consanguinity); Burchard of Ursberg, *Chronicon*, pp. 182–85 (Frederick advised Henry to divorce Clemence); Gilbert of Mons, *Chronicle of Hainaut*, pp. 37–39, ch. 33; and RI IV2/2:155, no. 1170. See Ehlers, *Heinrich der Löwe*, pp. 183–84; Weller, *Die Heiratspolitik des deutschen Hochadels*, pp. 424–28; and Hlawitschka, *Die Ahnen der hochmittelalterlichen deutschen Könige* 3:26–29.
72. DFI, no. 523 (28 January 1167) and no. 537 (29 August 1167).
73. DFI, no. 581 (perhaps September 1171); and Gilbert of Mons, pp. 37–39, ch. 33, and the genealogy of the counts of Namur, p. xx. See Kupper, "Friedrich Barbarossa im Maasgebiet," pp. 232–34.
74. See Georgi, *Friedrich Barbarossa und die auswärtigen Mächte*, pp. 24–25; and Weller, *Die Heiratspolitik des deutschen Hochadels im 12. Jahrhundert*, pp. 52–53.
75. Otto of Freising, *Deeds* 2.49–50 (also DFI, no. 163 [24–31 March 1157] and *Constitutiones* 1:224, no. 161); and Wibald of Stavelot, *Briefbuch* 3:891–93, no. 429 (24–31 March 1157; also Jaffé, no. 456 and *Constitutiones* 1:223–24, no. 160).
76. Otto of Freising, *Deeds* 2.53. See Nora Berend, "Hungary in the Eleventh and Twelfth Centuries," in Luscombe, ed., *The New Cambridge Medieval History*, 4/2:310–13. *Die Taten Friedrichs oder richtiger Cronica,* ed. Franz-Josef Schmale (Darmstadt, 1965), p. 389, n. 49, indicates that the chaplain Stephen is otherwise unknown; this is the German facing edition of Otto of Freising's *Deeds*.
77. Otto of Freising and Rahewin, *Deeds* 3.13 and 3.26; Vincent of Prague, *Annales*, p. 667; and RI IV2/1:147, no. 471. See Berend, "Hungary in the Eleventh and Twelfth Centuries," p. 314; Georgi, *Friedrich Barbarossa und die auswärtigen Mächte*, pp. 25–26; and Günther Hödl, "Ungarn in der Aussenpolitik Friedrich Barbarossas," in Engel and Töpfer, eds, *Kaiser Friedrich Barbarossa*, pp. 131–32.
78. DFI, no. 179 (shortly after 4 August 1157; also Wibald of Stavelot, *Briefbuch* 3:923–24, no. 446 [Jaffé, no. 465]); and no. 181 (early September 1157; also Wibald of Stavelot, *Briefbuch* 3:930–32, no. 451 [Jaffé, no. 470]).
79. Otto of Freising and Rahewin, *Deeds* 3.6.
80. Ibid., 4.24; and RI IV2/2:35, no. 678. Rahewin did not indicate that Frederick sent Wibald to Constantinople, only that he died in Greece (4.24). However, Frederick's order that Wibald attend the court in Würzburg (DFI, no. 181) is the last entry in the abbot's letter collection; and he witnessed his last charter in Würzburg on 6 October 1157 (DFI, no. 182). On his death, see Hausmann, *Reichskanzlei und Hofkapelle*, pp. 247–48. On the peace between Manuel and William I, see Chalandon, *Histoire de la domination normande en Italie et en Sicilie* 2:252–58.

Chapter 8 The Holy Empire

1. DFI, no. 138 (10 May 1156).
2. See, e.g., Munz, *Frederick Barbarossa*, pp. 126–27 and p. 259, n. 1.

3. Some examples of scholars who argued that Rainald continued Wibald's policies are: Koch, *Auf dem Wege zum Sacrum Imperium*, pp. 161–62; Walter Heinemeyer, "'beneficium—non feudum sed bonum factum': Der Streit auf dem Reichstag zu Besançon 1157," *Archiv für Diplomatik, Siegel- und Wappenkunde* 15 (1969): 220–36; and Werner Grebe, "Studien zur geistigen Welt Rainalds von Dassel," in Wolf, ed., *Friedrich Barbarossa*, pp. 245–96, esp. pp. 274–75.
4. Otto of Freising, *Chronicle*, Letter to Rainald, pp. 89–91; Wibald of Stavelot, *Briefbuch* 2:401–04, nos. 189–90 (c. November/December 1149; Jaffé, nos. 207–08), and 2:411–14, nos. 195–96 (before 25 December 1149; Jaffé, nos. 212–13); DKIII, no. 235 (before 10 June 1150); and DFI, no. 10 (9 May 1152). On Rainald's life, see Rainer Maria Herkenrath, "Reinald von Dassel: Reichskanzler und Erzbischof von Köln," unpublished dissertation (Graz, 1962), pp. 8–37; and Grebe, "Studien zur geistigen Welt Rainalds von Dassel," pp. 245–56. For a biographical sketch of Rainald in English, see Peter Godman, *The Silent Masters: Latin Literature and its Censors in the High Middle Ages* (Princeton, N.J., 2000), pp. 191–202. Scholars who thought that Rainald's appointment as chancellor was a decisive break with Conrad's policies believed that Rainald was toying with the vain abbot when he offered to help him procure the archbishopric of Cologne; but Herkenrath, "Reinald von Dassel," pp. 42 and 85, stressed that Rainald was close to Wibald. Herkenrath, pp. 416–20, argued that "Reinald" is the preferred spelling; but I have retained "Rainald" because that has become the customary English spelling.
5. Morena, *Libellus de rebus a Frederico imperatore gestis*, pp. 188–91.
6. See, e.g., Albert Hauck, *Kirchengeschichte Deutschlands* (Leipzig, 1903) 4:207–09; and Walther Föhl, "Studien zu Rainald von Dassel," *Jahrbuch des kölnischen Geschichtsvereins* 17 (1935): 234–59; and 20 (1938): 238–60, esp. pp. 253–54.
7. See, e.g., Friedrich Heer, *Die Tragödie des Heiligen Reiches* (Vienna and Zürich, 1952), pp. 57–63 (quotation is on p. 62) and p. 269. On Heer and the book see the "Epilogue," esp. n. 30.
8. For a general discussion of the Archpoet, see Godman, *The Silent Masters*, pp. 202–27. On Rainald's patronage of the Archpoet, see Helmuth Kluger, "Friedrich Barbarossa und sein Ratgeber Rainald von Dassel," in Weinfurter, ed., *Stauferreich im Wandel*, pp. 32–33. See Josef Eberle, trans., *Die Gedichte des Archipoeta: Lateinisch und deutsch* (Frankfurt am Main, 1966), for the text of the poems.
9. DFI, no. 163 (24–31 March 1157).
10. On the *Codex Udalrici*, see Appelt, "Einleitung," DFI 5:118–21; and Walter Koch, "Zu Sprache, Stil und Arbeitstechnik in den Diplomen Friedrich Barbarossas," pp. 51–53.
11. Stefan Weinfurter, "Wie das Reich heilig wurde," in idem, *Gelebte Ordnung—Gedachte Ordnung*, p. 373; and Charlton T. Lewis and Charles Short, *A Latin Dictionary* (Oxford, 1879), p. 1,625.
12. Wibald of Stavelot, Jaffé edition, no. 11 (Peter's forgery). Hartmann, *Studien zu den Briefen Abt Wibalds von Stablo und Corvey*, pp. 14–18, explained why the letter is a forgery and was not included in her edition of Wibald's correspondence. Wibald's letters to Manuel are *Briefbuch* 3:816–18, no. 387 (September 1153; Jaffé, no. 411); and 3:858–59, no. 412 (December 1153–January 1154; Jaffé, no. 432). See Appelt, "Die Kaiseridee Friedrich Barbarossas," in Wolf, ed., *Friedrich Barbarossa*, pp. 218–23; Schwarz, *Herrscher- und Reichstitel bei Kaisertum und Papsttum*, pp. 86–96; Petersohn, *Kaisertum und Rom in spätsalischer und staufischer Zeit*, pp. 46–79, esp. pp. 63–65; p. 129; and pp. 338–39; and Weinfurter, "Wie das Reich heilig wurde," pp. 361–83, esp. pp. 374–77.
13. Hofmeister, "Eine neue Quelle zur Geschichte Friedrich Barbarossas," p. 155. See Schwarz, *Herrscher- und Reichstitel bei Kaisertum und Papsttum*, pp. 86–96, esp. p. 86, n. 299, on the use of *sacrum imperium* in the account of Tortona's destruction; and Petersohn, *Kaisertum und Rom in spätsalischer und staufischer Zeit*, pp. 336–43.
14. DFI, no. 881, p. 122, line 28 (3 November 1184). See Jürgen Petersohn, "Rom und der Reichstitel 'Sacrum Romanum Imperium.'" *Sitzungsberichte der Wissenschaftlichen Gesellschaft an der Johann Wolfgang-Goethe Universität Frankfurt am Main* 32/4 (Stuttgart, 1994), pp. 67–101; idem, *Kaisertum und Rom in spätsalischer und staufischer Zeit*, pp. 254–56; Kai-Michael Sprenger, "Die Heiligkeit von Kaiser und Reich aus italienischer Sicht," in

Burkhardt et al., *Staufisches Kaisertum im 12. Jahrhundert*, pp. 182–204; and Schwarz, *Herrscher- und Reichstitel bei Kaisertum und Papsttum*, pp. 101–03.

15. Otto of Freising and Rahewin, *Deeds* 3.8 and 3.12; and DFI, no. 183 (24 October 1157) and no. 184 (27 October 1157). Opll, RI IV2/1:154–55, no. 491, simply said the court met in October.
16. Otto of Freising and Rahewin, *Deeds* 3.8 and 3.12; and DFI, nos. 61–64 (June 1153; Silvio of Clérieux, Archbishop Hugh of Vienne, Dean William of Vienne, and Raymond of Arles); no. 184 (27 October 1157; Stephen of Vienne and Dean William); and no. 192 (18 November 1157; Heraclius of Lyons). On the use of the ancient titles, see Walter Koch, "Zu Sprache, Stil und Arbeitstechnik in den Diplomen Friedrich Barbarossas," pp. 58–59.
17. Otto of Freising and Rahewin, *Deeds* 2.48 and 3.8 and 3.12; and DFI, nos. 187–88 (October 1157; Silvio of Arles) and no. 197 (25 November 1157). See Büttner, "Friedrich Barbarossa und Burgund," pp. 94–96.
18. Boso, *Les vies des papes*, p. 395 (*Boso's Life of Adrian IV*, pp. 229–31).
19. Otto of Freising and Rahewin, *Deeds* 3.8 and 3.16. On the greeting, see Heinemeyer, "'beneficium—non feudum sed bonum factum,'" pp. 165–74; and Görich, *Die Ehre Friedrich Barbarossas*, pp. 106–07.
20. The text of the letter is in Otto of Freising and Rahewin, *Deeds* 3.9. The Latin text is in the Schmale edition of the *Deeds* and also in *Constitutiones* 1:229–30, no. 164. Simonsfeld, *Jahrbücher des Deutschen Reiches unter Friedrich I.*, 1:497, and other scholars, said that Eskil was captured in Burgundy. The basis for this is Otto of St. Blasien, *Chronicle*, pp. 30–33, ch. 8, who wrongly placed the assembly in 1156. However, Pope Adrian explicitly stated that Eskil was captured "in Teutonicis partibus."
21. Engels, "Friedrich Barbarossa und Dänemark," pp. 353–65 and 371–75.
22. *Die Admonter Briefsammlung*, pp. 103–06, no. 53 (Adrian's letter). The text of Eskil's letter is in Engels, "Friedrich Barbarossa und Dänemark," p. 355, n. 13.
23. DFI, no. 209 (16 March 1158). See Heinemeyer, "'beneficium—non feudum sed bonum factum,'" pp. 164–65; and Engels, "Friedrich Barbarossa und Dänemark," pp. 372–75.
24. Otto of Freising and Rahewin, *Deeds* 3.23 (also in *Constitutiones* 1:234–35, no. 168). See Heinemeyer, "'beneficium—non feudum sed bonum factum,'" pp. 160 and 214–16. He listed on p. 215, n. 194, papal documents for German recipients that employed *beneficium* in the sense of *fief*. The relevant portion of Adrian's letter to Wibald is published there. On the English usage of *beneficium*, see R. E. Latham and David R. Howlett, eds, *Dictionary of Medieval Latin from British Sources* (London, 1975), p. 192. Count Sigiboto of Falkenstein prepared in the summer of 1166 a list of the fiefs he held from other lords. It was headed: "Summa prediorum atque beneficiorum domini comitis Sibotonis." *Codex Falkensteinensis*, pp. 5–7, no. 3.
25. DFI, nos. 183–85 and 189–98. Adalbert of Trent witnessed nos. 184 and 189–90. Eberhard was the likely author of the circular Frederick sent after the confrontation (DFI, headnote to no. 186 [October 1157]). On the whole vexing question about what the pope intended and why no one dared to correct Rainald's translation, see Franz J. Felten, "Kaisertum und Papsttum im 12. Jahrhundert," in Hehl et al., eds, *Das Papsttum in der Welt des 12. Jahrhunderts*, pp. 116–17.
26. Otto of Freising and Rahewin, *Deeds* 3.10. Mierow missed the qualifying force of the word "satis" in his translation of "fida satis interpretatio" as "in a faithful interpretation." Adolf Schmidt in his German translation in the Schmale edition caught the nuance: "in ziemlich genauer Übersetzung." A later copyist removed the doubt by replacing "satis" with "nimis," i.e., "in an exceedingly faithful translation." On all of this, see Schmale, p. 415, n. 45; and Heinemeyer, "'beneficium—non feudum sed bonum factum,'" pp. 179–83.
27. For a nationalistic, anti-papal account of the events at Besançon by a Lutheran clergyman, see Hauck's monumental *Kirchengeschichte Deutschlands* 4:209–18, esp. p. 211, n. 1. For a Catholic account that absolves Adrian of duplicity and accuses Rainald of a deliberate mistranslation—the book has an imprimatur—see Marshall W. Baldwin, *Alexander III and the Twelfth Century* (Glen Rock, N.J., 1968), pp. 34–39. Duggan, "*Totius christianitatis caput*," pp. 127–34, assigned all the blame to Frederick and Rainald. Adrian's letter was "a mild rebuke" (p. 127) and "a pained reproof" (p. 130), and she concluded: "If ever there was a manufactured dispute, this was it" (p. 131). For a historiographical overview of the

older literature, see Heinemeyer, "'beneficium—non feudum sed bonum factum,'" pp. 155–60.

28. Wibald of Stavelot, *Briefbuch* 3:916–17, no. 442 (19 January 1157; Jaffé, no. 454). Henry IV reproached himself in a letter to Gregory VII in 1073 for heeding "the seductive counsels of my advisers"; and the pope warned the king in 1074 to select "such advisers," who "will promote your welfare, not their own profit." See Ephraim Emerton, trans., *The Correspondence of Pope Gregory VII: Selected Letters from the Registrum* (New York, 1932), pp. 19 and 55.
29. Otto of Freising and Rahewin, *Deeds* 3.9 and 3.17. See Heinemeyer, "'beneficium—non feudum sed bonum factum,'" pp. 176–77.
30. Otto of Freising and Rahewin, *Deeds* 3.10; and *Chronica regia Coloniensis*, pp. 93–94.
31. Frederick's letter was inserted into the bishops' response to Adrian IV in Otto of Freising and Rahewin, *Deeds* 3.17 (also *Constitutiones* 1:233–34, no. 167). On the date, see RI IV2/1:165, no. 522; and on the authorship of the letter, see Heinemeyer, "'beneficium—non feudum sed bonum factum,'" p. 209. On the painting, see Gerhart Burian Ladner, "I mosaici e gli affreschi ecclesiastico-politici nell'antico palazzo Lateranense," reprinted in idem, *Images and Ideas in the Middle Ages: Selected Studies in History and Art*, vol. 1 (Rome, 1983), esp. pp. 356–66 and fig. 9; Heinemeyer, "'beneficium—non feudum sed bonum factum,'" pp. 183–97; and Laudage, *Alexander III.*, pp. 51–54 and 90–92.
32. Heinemeyer, "'beneficium—non feudum sed bonum factum,'" p. 180.
33. Otto of Freising and Rahewin, *Deeds* 3.10 and 3.16. See Schmidt, "A quo ergo habet, si a domno papa non habet imperium?" pp. 61–62. Peter D. Clarke, "Introduction," in Clarke and Anne J. Duggan, eds, *Pope Alexander III (1159–81): The Art of Survival* (Farnham, 2012), p. 8, asserted that Duggan showed that Roland cannot be identified as the legate who had asked the infamous question. However, Duggan, in the same collection, "*Alexander ille meus:* The Papacy of Alexander III," p. 18, n. 20, offered no evidence for such an assertion, but simply repeated her view that Besançon was a *coup de théâtre* staged by Frederick and Rainald. Moreover, John Doran, "'At last we have reached the port of salvation': The Roman Context of the Schism of 1159," p. 55, in the same collection, pointed out that the other cardinal, Bernard of Porto, continued to enjoy good relations with Frederick after Besançon. The same cannot be said of Roland.
34. Otto of Freising and Rahewin, *Deeds* 3.11 and 3.16.
35. Ibid., 3.11 (also *Constitutiones* 1:230–31, no. 165; and DFI, no. 186). For Eberhard's authorship of the circular, see the headnote to no. 186. See also Heinemeyer, "'beneficium—non feudum sed bonum factum,'" pp. 204–06.
36. Otto of Freising and Rahewin, *Deeds* 3.12. See Georgi, *Friedrich Barbarossa und die auswärtigen Mächte*, pp. 39–40.
37. Otto of Freising and Rahewin, *Deeds* 3.16. See Heinemeyer, "'beneficium—non feudum sed bonum factum,'" pp. 206–07.
38. Otto of Freising and Rahewin, *Deeds* 3.17. See Heinemeyer, "'beneficium—non feudum sed bonum factum,'" pp. 207–12; and Schmidt, *Königswahl und Thronfolge im 12. Jahrhundert*," pp. 154–58.
39. Otto of Freising and Rahewin, *Deeds* 3.18, 3.21, and 3.23.
40. Ibid., 3.22. See Heinemeyer, "'beneficium—non feudum sed bonum factum,'" pp. 172–74.
41. Otto of Freising and Rahewin, *Deeds* 3.22–23. See Heinemeyer, "'beneficum—non feudum sed bonum factum,'" pp. 213–20.
42. Otto of Freising and Rahewin, *Deeds* 4.34.
43. Ibid., 3.24. See Heinemeyer, "'beneficium—non feudum sed bonum factum,'" pp. 213–20.
44. Otto of Freising and Rahewin, *Deeds* 3.25. See Engels, "Friedrich Barbarossa und Dänemark," pp. 372–75.
45. Otto of Freising and Rahewin, *Deeds* 3.11. On the Trier stylistic exercises, see Norbert Höing, "Die 'Trierer Stilübungen': Ein Denkmal der Frühzeit Kaiser Friedrich Barbarossas," *Archiv für Diplomatik, Schriftgeschichte, Siegel- und Wappenkunde* 1 (1955): 257–329; and 2 (1956): 125–249, esp. pp. 194–249. The text of the letters is 1:318–29. Höing argued that the letters were written by Bishop Eberhard II of Bamberg in the spring of 1158. On the later date, see Werner Goez, *Translatio Imperii: Ein Beitrag zur Geschichte des Geschichtsdenken und der politischen Theorien im Mittelalter und in der frühen Neuzeit* (Tübingen, 1958), pp. 137–56, esp.

pp. 142–56. See also Schmidt, *Königswahl und Thronfolge im 12. Jahrhundert*, pp. 158–61. Anne H. Latowsky, *Emperor of the World: Charlemagne and the Construction of Imperial Authority, 800–1229* (Ithaca, N,Y, and London, 2013), pp. 160–71, contended that the forgeries were the work of a single author, either Rainald or a member of the chancery working for him (p. 161). Identifying Zachary rather than Leo III as the pope who crowned Charlemagne was not an innocent mistake (p. 164) but was intended to make Adrian appear "blustering and ignorant as he makes his justifications for papal primacy over the empire" (p. 167).

Chapter 9 The Second Italian Campaign

1. Morena, *Libellus de rebus a Frederico imperatore gestis*, pp. 64–79; Hofmeister, "Eine neue Quelle zur Geschichte Friedrich Barbarossas," pp. 156–57, ch. 11; and *Narratio de Longobardie obpressione*, pp. 244–57, esp. 256–57. See Berwinkel, *Verwüsten und Belagern*, pp. 71–73.
2. Otto of Freising and Rahewin, *Deeds* 3.20; and *Chronica regia Coloniensis*, pp. 95–97. Both of these accounts are based on a letter that Rainald and Otto of Wittelsbach wrote to Frederick before 11 May 1158 (Suchendorf, *Registrum oder merkwürdige Urkunden*, 2:131–33, no. 54). On Rainald and Otto of Wittelsbach's mission, see Herkenrath, "Reinald von Dassel," pp. 108–22.
3. *Constitutiones* 1:238–39, no. 172.
4. Vincent of Prague, *Annales*, p. 673; and RI IV2/1:174, no. 576. See Laudage, *Friedrich Barbarossa*, p. 116.
5. *Narratio de Longobardie obpressione*, pp. 258–59. Rahewin, *Deeds* 3.36, said that Frederick's army numbered 100,000 or more men, a greatly inflated figure. See Berwinkel, *Verwüsten umd Belagern*, pp. 73–75.
6. Berwinkel, *Verwüsten und Belagern*, pp. 48–57, esp. p. 53; and Gianluca Raccagni, *The Lombard League, 1167–1225* (Oxford, 2010), pp. 88–89.
7. Otto of Freising and Rahewin, *Deeds* 2.34 and 3.15.
8. Ibid., 3.26; and Vincent of Prague, *Annales*, p. 668. See Berwinkel, *Verwüsten und Belagern*, pp. 75–80; and p. 270, Abbildung 2: "Der Einmarsch in die Lombardei, Juli bis August 1158."
9. Otto of Freising and Rahewin, *Deeds* 3.27; Vincent of Prague, *Annales*, p. 669; Morena, *Libellus de rebus a Frederico imperatore gestis*, pp. 78–79; *Carmen de gestis Frederici I. imperatoris in Lombardia*, pp. 66–67, vs. 2005–39; Burchard of Ursberg, *Chronicon*, pp. 152–53; and RI IV2/2:4, no. 563. See Berwinkel, *Verwüsten und Belagern*, pp. 80–82.
10. Otto of Freising and Rahewin, *Deeds* 3.28 (also DFI, no. 222; and *Constitutiones* 1:239–41, no. 173).
11. Otto of Freising and Rahewin, *Deeds* 3.29–30. See Richter, *Friedrich Barbarossa hält Gericht*, pp. 97–99; and Görich, *Die Ehre Friedrich Barbarossas*, pp. 225 and 350–59.
12. Otto of Freising and Rahewin, *Deeds* 3.31–32; Vincent of Prague, *Annales*, pp. 669–70; Morena, *Libellus de rebus a Frederico imperatore gestis*, pp. 78–83; and RI IV2/2:5–6, nos. 567–69. See Berwinkel, *Verwüsten und Belagern*, pp. 83–89 and 270–72, Abbildungen 2 and 3.
13. Morena, *Libellus de rebus a Frederico imperatore gestis*, pp. 82–85, esp. p. 82; Vincent of Prague, *Annales*, p. 671; Otto of Freising and Rahewin, *Deeds* 3.53, 4.29 and 4.86; and DFI, no. 246 (3 December 1158). See Berwinkel, *Verwüsten und Belagern*, pp. 289–91; and Opll, "Friedrich Barbarossa und die Stadt Lodi," pp. 275–78.
14. Vincent of Prague, *Annales*, pp. 671 and 674. See Görich, *Die Ehre Friedrich Barbarossas*, pp. 225–26, 230–31, and p. 488, n. 237; and Berwinkel, *Verwüsten und Belagern*, p. 91.
15. Otto of Freising and Rahewin, *Deeds* 3.34–35; Vincent of Prague, *Annales*, pp. 671–72; and *Chronica regia Coloniensis*, pp. 98–99. The author of the *Narratio de Longobardie obpressione*, pp. 256–57, mentioned a melee in which a Count Adelbert, presumably Ekbert, was killed. See Berwinkel, *Verwüsten und Belagern*, pp. 91–93; and Görich, *Die Ehre Friedrich Barbarossas*, pp. 226–29.
16. Otto of Freising and Rahewin, *Deeds* 3.35; and Vincent of Prague, *Annales*, p. 672. Vincent provided a detailed list of all the participants on p. 673.

17. Vincent of Prague, *Annales*, p. 672; Otto of Freising and Rahewin, *Deeds* 3.38; Morena, *Libellus de rebus a Frederico imperatore gestis*, pp. 84–85; and *Narratio de Longobardie obpressione*, pp. 258–59. See Berwinkel, *Verwüsten und Belagern*, pp. 274–75, Abbildung 5: "Belagerung von Mailand, August 1158."
18. Otto of Freising and Rahewin, *Deeds* 3.37–38; and *Chronica regia Coloniensis*, p. 99. See Berwinkel, *Verwüsten und Belagern*, pp. 95–99.
19. Otto of Freising and Rahewin, *Deeds* 3.38; Vincent of Prague, *Annales*, pp. 672–73; *Narratio de Longobardie obpressione*, pp. 258–59; and Morena, *Libellus de rebus a Frederico imperatore gestis*, pp. 86–87. See Berwinkel, *Verwüsten und Belagern*, pp. 102–03.
20. Otto of Freising and Rahewin, *Deeds* 3.39–40 (Henry Jasomirgott) and 3.41 (Albert of Tyrol); *Narratio de Longobardie obpressione*, pp. 260–61; and Morena, *Libellus de rebus a Frederico imperatore gestis*, pp. 86–87 (*Porta Tosa*). See Berwinkel, *Verwüsten und Belagern*, pp. 103–04 and 108–09.
21. Otto of Freising and Rahewin, *Deeds* 3.42 and 3.44; Vincent of Prague, *Annales*, p. 674; Morena, *Libellus de rebus a Frederico imperatore gestis*, pp. 88–89; and *Chronica regia Coloniensis*, p. 99. See Berwinkel, *Verwüsten und Belagern*, pp. 108–10.
22. Otto of Freising and Rahewin, *Deeds* 3.43; Morena, *Libellus de rebus a Frederico imperatore gestis*, pp. 84–87; *Narratio de Longobardie obpressione*, pp. 258–59; Vincent of Prague, *Annales*, pp. 673–74; *Carmen de gestis Frederici I. imperatoris in Lombardia*, pp. 80–81, vs. 2399–2441; and Burchard of Ursberg, *Chronicon*, pp. 154–55. See Berwinkel, *Verwüsten und Belagern*, pp. 104–08. Otto Morena's chronicle supports the Milanese Anonymous' account that Frederick's forces had to abandon the arch. After relating how Frederick captured the arch, Otto indicated that the Milanese built two petraries that hurled boulders at or beyond the tower. He then told how on another day the Milanese rushed out of the gate and underneath the arch. In the ensuing fight with the Germans and Lodiese, many Lodiese, some of whom Otto Morena named, were killed. It is hard to see how the Milanese could have done this if Frederick's men were still installed on top of the arch.
23. Otto of Freising and Rahewin, *Deeds* 3.43–47; Vincent of Prague, *Annales*, pp. 673–74; and Burchard of Ursberg, *Chronicon*, pp. 154–55; and DFI, no. 226 (after 8 September 1158; charter for Guido). See Berwinkel, *Verwüsten und Belagern*, pp. 110–14; Görich, *Die Ehre Friedrich Barbarossas*, p. 229; Haverkamp, *Herrschaftsformen der Frühstaufer in Reichsitalien* 1:44–49; and idem, "Friedrich I. und der hohe italienische Adel," pp. 71–75.
24. Otto of Freising and Rahewin, *Deeds* 3.47; Vincent of Prague, *Annales*, pp. 674–76; Burchard of Ursberg, *Chronicon*, pp. 154–56; and *Narratio de Longobardie obpressione*, pp. 260–61. The text of the agreement that is published in the edition of Frederick's charters, DFI, no. 224 (1 September 1154), and in *Constitutiones* 1:241–43, no. 174, is also based on the copy of the agreement that was made around 1200. Only the later copy contains the provisions that no additional demands would be made on Milan and that the hostages would be released by Christmas 1159 and Rainald's verification of the convention. On the relationship between the various versions of the agreement and Vincent's own summary of its content, see Josef Riedmann, *Die Beurkundung der Verträge Friedrich Barbarossas mit italienischen Städte: Studien zur diplomatischen Form von Vertragsurkunden im 12. Jahrhundert* (Vienna, 1973), pp. 63–72. See also Berwinkel, *Verwüsten und Belagern*, p. 114.
25. Vincent of Prague, *Annales*, pp. 674–75; Otto of Freising and Rahewin, *Deeds* 3.48–49; *Narratio de Longobardie obpressione*, pp. 260–61; Otto of St. Blasien, *Chronicle*, pp. 34–37; and Burchard of Ursberg, *Chronicon*, pp. 156–57. Rahewin said that the clerics, too, were barefoot "and in lowly attire"; but Vincent, who, unlike Rahewin, was there, said nothing about the clerics being barefoot and stressed that they wore their ecclesiastical vestments. According to Burchard, the consuls prostrated themselves before the emperor, but the earlier authors, Vincent, Rahewin, and the Milanese Anonymous, did not mention such an act of submission. Otto of St. Blasien stressed how reluctant Frederick was to forgive the Milanese—they had to pay him and the empress large sums of money and the princes had to intercede on their behalf—and thus implicitly criticized, perhaps with the benefit of hindsight, Frederick's severity. See Görich, *Die Ehre Friedrich Barbarossas*, pp. 229–33; and Krieg, *Herrscherdarstellung in der Stauferzeit*, pp. 211–15.

26. Otto of Freising and Rahewin, *Deeds* 3.50 and 3.52; Vincent of Prague, *Annales*, p. 675; and RI IV2/2:11–13, nos. 586–90. On the erroneous description of Monza as the seat of the Italian kingdom, see Brühl, *Fodrum, gistum, servitium regis* 1:498–501 and 617–24.
27. Otto of Freising and Rahewin, *Deeds* 3.51–53; Morena, *Libellus de rebus a Frederico imperatore gestis*, pp. 88–89; and RI IV2/2:13–16, nos. 591–604. I have modified Mierow's translation of Frederick's summons of the Italians to Roncaglia in 3.53. On Turisendus, see Haverkamp, "Friedrich I. und der hohe italienische Adel," pp. 59–61.
28. *Constitutiones* 1:138–39, no. 85. For a discussion of this in English, see Blumenthal, *The Investiture Controversy*, pp. 164–73; and idem, "*Patrimonia* and *Regalia* in 1111," pp. 9–20.
29. DKIII, no. 51 (October 1140). See Haverkamp, *Herrschaftsformen der Frühstaufer in Reichsitalien* 1:85–102.
30. DKIII, no. 67 (January/February 1142: "salvo per omnia et in omnibus iure regni ac nostro"); and DFI, no. 20 (1 August 1152: "salvo per omnia jure regni"). See Heinrich Appelt, "Der Vorbehalt kaiserliche Rechte in den Diplomen Friedrich Barbarossas," in Wolf, *Friedrich Barbarossa*, pp. 33–57; and Appelt, "Friedrich Barbarossa und das römische Recht," in Wolf, ed., *Friedrich Barbarossa*, pp. 58–82, esp. pp. 61–62. Appelt thought, as the title of his article indicates, that the reservation clause originated under Barbarossa; but in a 1974 addendum to the reprint in the Wolf edition, p. 57, he acknowledged that Haverkamp, *Herrschaftsformen der Frühstaufer in Reichsitalien* 1:102–57, esp. pp. 102–24, had demonstrated the isolated appearance of the clause in Conrad's charters.
31. DFI, no. 165 (6 April 1157); and Otto of Freising and Rahewin, *Deeds* 3.20 and 3.47. See above, p. 167
32. Otto of Freising and Rahewin, *Deeds* 4.3–5; and Morena, *Libellus de rebus a Frederico imperatore gestis*," pp. 88–91. On Frederick's speech, see Fasoli, "Friedrich Barbarossa und die lombardischen Städte," pp. 162–63.
33. Otto of Freising and Rahewin, *Deeds* 4.6; and DFI, nos. 229–36 (17–26 November 1158).
34. Otto of Freising and Rahewin, *Deeds* 4.11; Morena, *Libellus de rebus a Frederico imperatore gestis*, pp. 92–93; and RI IV2/2:28–29, no. 653. The legates' earlier agreement with Piacenza is *Constitutiones* 1:238–39, no. 172.
35. Morena, *Libellus de rebus a Frederico imperatore gestis*, pp. 88–91. See Opll, *Stadt und Reich im 12. Jahrhundert*, pp. 328 and 379–80.
36. Paul Willem Finsterwalder, "Die Gesetze des Reichstags von Roncaglia vom 11. November 1158," *ZRG GA* 51 (1931): 1–69; Vittore Colorni, *Die drei verschollenen Gesetze des Reichstages bei Roncaglia wieder aufgefunden in einer Pariser Handschrift (Bibl. Nat. Cod. Lat. 4677)*, trans. Gero Dolezalek (Aalen, 1969); Appelt, "Friedrich Barbarossa und das römische Recht," pp. 62–68; and Brühl, *Fodrum, gistum, servitium regis*, "Anhang," 1:776–78. On the Germanic nature of the Roncaglia laws, see, besides Appelt, Haverkamp, *Herrschaftsformen der Frühstaufer in Reichsitalien* 1:85–102; and Laudage, *Alexander III. und Friedrich Barbarossa*, pp. 94–102. Benson, "Political *Renovatio*," pp. 364–69, stressed the Romanistic features of the laws, such as the designation of the emperor as the *princeps*.
37. DFI, no. 237 (22 or 23 November 1158; also *Constitutiones* 1:244–45, no. 175); no. 257 (7 February 1159; this charter for Count Guido of Biandrate specifically references the court at Roncaglia, p. 58, ll. 31–32); and no. 259 (for the city of Asti, 15 February 1159, p. 65, ll. 24–28); and Otto of Freising and Rahewin, *Deeds* 4.7. See Colorni, *Die drei verschollenen Gesetze des Reichstages bei Roncaglia*, pp. 6–8; and Haverkamp, *Herrschaftsformen der Frühstaufer in Reichsitalien* 2:623–68.
38. DFI, no. 238 and head note to no. 238. The peace ordinance is DFI, no. 241, p. 34, ll. 18–19. See Colorni, *Die drei verschollenen Gesetze des Reichstages bei Roncaglia*, pp. 28–33.
39. DFI, no. 239, and head note to no. 239. See Colorni, *Die drei verschollenen Gesetze des Reichstages bei Roncaglia*, pp. 33–35; and Brühl, *Fodrum, gistum, servitium regis* 1:605–15, and "Anhang," pp. 776–78. Colorni thought that the issue was the communes' refusal to permit the construction of palaces within the cities, a point that Brühl rejected. On the destruction of the palace in Pavia, see Wipo, *The Deeds of Conrad II*, Chapter 7.
40. DFI, no. 240; and Otto of Freising and Rahewin, *Deeds* 4.7. See Colorni, *Die drei verschollenen Gesetze des Reichstages bei Roncaglia*, pp. 35–47. On the controversy about Frederick's

tax policies, see Haverkamp, *Herrschaftsformen der Frühstaufer in Reichsitalien* 2:669–92; and Brühl, *Fodrum, gistum, servitium regis* 1:776–78; and idem, "Die Finanzpolitik Friedrich Barbarossas in Italien," pp. 22–27.

41. Otto of Freising and Rahewin, *Deeds* 4.7–8; and Morena, *Libellus de rebus a Frederico imperatore gestis*, pp. 90–91. See Haverkamp, *Herrschaftsformen der Frühstaufer in Reichsitalien* 1:85–157.
42. Otto of Freising and Rahewin, *Deeds* 4.9; and Morena, *Libellus de rebus a Frederico imperatore gestis*, pp. 90–93.
43. Otto of Freising and Rahewin, *Deeds* 4.10; and Burchard of Ursberg, *Chronicon*, pp. 156–59. The text of the *Landfriede* is DFI, no. 241 (November 1158; also *Constitutiones* 1:245–47, no. 176); the text of the feudal law is DFI, no. 242 (November 1158; also *Constitutiones* 1:247–49, no. 177). On the *Libri feudorum* and the feudal law, see Susan Reynolds, *Fiefs and Vassals: The Medieval Evidence Reinterpreted* (Oxford, 1996), pp. 215–30, esp. p. 227 and pp. 447–48. Archbishop Eberhard I of Salzburg referred in 1160 to the *Landfriede*. See *Salzburger Urkundenbuch*, 4 vols, ed. Willibald Hauthaler and Franz Martin (Salzburg, 1910–33), 2:486–89, no. 349.
44. DFI, no. 242. See Haverkamp, *Herrschaftsformen der Frühstaufer in Reichsitalien* 2:342–48 and 363–73; and above, pp. 129–30, on the feudal law of 1154. On the partition of principalities in Germany, see Arnold, *Princes and Territories in Medieval Germany*, pp. 239–47.
45. Haverkamp, *Herrschaftsformen der Frühstaufer in Reichsitalien* 1:329–42, insisted that only people directly subject to the emperor's authority, including the citizens of communes that were the emperor's corporate vassals, were obligated to swear such an oath.
46. DFI, no. 241; and Burchard of Ursberg, *Chronicon*, pp. 156–59.
47. See Berwinkel, *Verwüsten und Belagern*, p. 120.
48. Otto of Freising and Rahewin, *Deeds* 4.12; and DFI, no. 247 (privilege for Savona, end of 1158). See Opll, *Stadt und Reich im 12. Jahrhundert*, pp. 279–80 and 389–90; and Berwinkel, *Verwüsten und Belagern*, pp. 121–23.
49. Otto of Freising and Rahewin, *Deeds* 4.8, 4.13, 4.23, and 4.46; Vincent of Prague, *Annales*, pp. 675–76; Morena, *Libellus de rebus a Frederico imperatore gestis*, pp. 92–93; and *Narratio de Longobardie obpressione*, pp. 260–63. See Opll, *Stadt und Reich im 12. Jahrhundert*, pp. 244–45, 254–55, 300, 371, and 379–80. For the use of *consules* and *potestates* as synonyms, see, for example, Vincent of Prague, *Annales*, p. 676. Cremona's toll privilege is DFI, no. 261 (22 February 1159). For a discussion of this privilege, see Haverkamp, *Herrschaftsformen der Frühstaufer in Reichsitalien* 2:623–24.
50. Otto of Freising and Rahewin, *Deeds* 4.16; *Chronica regia Coloniensis*, p. 101; and DFI, no. *1104 (end of 1158 or beginning of 1159). Archbishop Frederick II of Cologne died in Pavia on 15 December 1158.
51. Otto of Freising and Rahewin, *Deeds* 4.58; Morena, *Libellus de rebus a Frederico imperatore gestis*, pp. 88–89; *Narratio de Longobardie obpressione*, pp. 260–61; and RI IV2/2:12, no. 588.
52. I have relied largely on Vincent of Prague's account in the *Annales*, pp. 675–76, because he was an eyewitness. The other authors provide, with some variations, the same basic account; for example, Otto Morena, *Libellus a Frederico imperatore gestis*, pp. 92–95, said that the envoys took refuge in the palace. See also Otto of Freising and Rahewin, *Deeds* 4.23; *Narratio de Longobardie obpressione*, pp. 262–63; and RI IV2/2:30, no. 660. See Opll, *Stadt und Reich im 12. Jahrhundert*, pp. 328–30; Richter, *Friedrich Barbarossa hält Gericht*, pp. 105–14; and Görich, *Die Ehre Friedrich Barbarossas*, pp. 233–37.
53. Otto of Freising and Rahewin, *Deeds* 4.25–28; and Vincent of Prague, *Annales*, p. 376. See Görich, *Die Ehre Friedrich Barbarossas*, pp. 235–36. The charters, DFI, nos. 257–62, were issued between 7 and 22 February in Marengo.
54. Otto of Freising and Rahewin, *Deeds* 4.29–31; Burchard of Ursberg, *Chronicon*, pp. 158–61; DFI, no. 264 (23 March 1159) and no. 265 (March 1159); and RI IV2/2:35–38, nos. 677, 679–80, and 688–92. See Opll, *Stadt und Reich im 12. Jahrhundert*, pp. 237–38; and Berwinkel, *Verwüsten und Belagern*, p. 124.
55. Otto of Freising and Rahewin, *Deeds* 4.31 and 4.59. See Opll, *Stadt und Reich im 12. Jahrhundert*, p. 380; and Berwinkel, *Verwüsten und Belagern*, p. 129. Rahewin contradicted in

4.31 his statement in 4.11 that the Placentines had obeyed Frederick's command to destroy its moat and towers.

56. Otto of Freising and Rahewin, *Deeds* 3.32, 4.32–33, and 4.37; Vincent of Prague, *Annales*, pp. 676–77; Morena, *Libellus de rebus a Frederico imperatore gestis*, pp. 94–95; *Narratio de Longobardie obpressione*, pp. 260–63; and RI IV2/2:39–40, nos. 698 and 700. See Berwinkel, *Verwüsten und Belagern*, pp. 124–26; Richter, *Friedrich Barbarossa hält Gericht*, pp. 160–65; and Görich, *Die Ehre Friedrich Barbarossas*, pp. 235–37.
57. Otto of Freising and Rahewin, *Deeds* 4.38–41; Vincent of Prague, *Annales*, p. 677; Morena, *Libellus de rebus a Frederico imperatore gestis*, pp. 94–97; and RI IV2/2:41–43, nos. 706–07, 711, and 714. See Berwinkel, *Verwüsten und Belagern*, pp. 127–28.
58. Otto of Freising and Rahewin, *Deeds* 4.42; Morena, *Libellus de rebus a Frederico imperatore gestis*, pp. 96–97; *Narratio de Longobardie obpressione*, pp. 266–67; and RI IV2/2:47, no. 727.
59. Otto of Freising and Rahewin, *Deeds* 4.43–45.
60. Ibid., 4.47–48; Morena, *Libellus de rebus a Frederico imperatore gestis*, pp. 92–93 and 96–97. Frederick's proscription of Crema is DFI, no. 282 (18 September 1159; also *Constitutiones* 1:270–71, no. 191). See Opll, *Stadt und Reich im 12. Jahrhundert*, pp. 242–45; Görich, *Die Ehre Friedrich Barbarossas,* pp. 239–41; Krieg, *Herrscherdarstellung in der Stauferzeit,* pp. 220–23; and Berwinkel, *Verwüsten und Belagern*, pp. 129–32.
61. Otto of Freising and Rahewin, *Deeds* 4.48 and 51 (the letter is DFI, no. 277; after 15 July 1159); Morena, *Libellus de rebus a Frederico imperatore gestis*, pp. 98–101; *Narratio de Longobardie obpressione*, pp. 262–65; and Vincent of Prague, *Annales*, p. 677. See Berwinkel, *Verwüsten und Belagern*, pp. 132–35 and 276–79, Abbildungen 6 and 7.
62. Otto of Freising and Rahewin, *Deeds* 4.46 and 4.54; Morena, *Libellus de rebus a Frederico imperatore gestis*, pp. 102–03; and Burchard of Ursberg, *Chronicon*, pp. 182–83.
63. The chief sources on the siege of Crema are: Otto of Freising and Rahewin, *Deeds*, 4.47–51, 4.53–59, and 4.67–72; Morena, *Libellus de rebus a Frederico imperatore gestis*, pp. 100–25; Vincent of Prague, *Annales*, pp. 677–78; and *Chronica regia Coloniensis*, pp. 101–02. Frederick sent a circular informing the Empire of his victory (Rahewin, 4.73; also DFI, no. 295, and *Constitutiones* 1:271–72, no. 192; after 26 January 1160). He also notified Archbishop Eberhard I of Salzburg and Bishop Roman I of Gurk about his victory (DFI, no. 296; also *Die Admonter Briefsammlung*, pp. 94–95, no. 46; and DFI, no. 297; also *Constitutiones* 1:272, no. 193, and *Die Admonter Briefsammlung*, pp. 95–96, no. 48). These letters provide no specific information. I have relied on Berwinkel's reconstruction of the siege in *Verwüsten und Belagern*, pp. 235–63. The precise date of Frederick's arrival in Pavia is unclear. Opll, in RI IV2/2:68, nos. 817 and 818, dated his arrival as 2 or 3 February; but Heinz Wolter, "Friedrich Barbarossa und die Synode zu Pavia," in Hanna Vollrath and Stefan Weinfurter, eds, *Köln: Stadt und Bistum in Kirche und Reich des Mittelalters: Festschrift für Odilo Engels zum 65. Geburtstag* (Cologne, Weimar, and Vienna, 1993), pp. 430–31, argued that Frederick must have arrived before 3 February to allow time for the customary three days of fasting and prayer before the opening of the council.

Chapter 10 The Schism

1. Otto of Freising and Rahewin, *Deeds* 4.18–19. On the chronology, see RI IV2/2:9–27, nos. 577–78, 628, and 645. On Frederick's relations with Ravenna, see Opll, *Stadt und Reich im 12. Jahrhundert*, pp. 405–12.
2. Otto of Freising and Rahewin, *Deeds* 4.18. Eberhard's letter is in 4.34. On the date, see RI IV2/2:45–47, nos. 723 and 739. Frederick's first letter does not survive.
3. Otto of Freising and Rahewin, *Deeds* 4.22. Opll, RI IV2/2:34, no. 675, thought that Adrian sent the letter about the dispute between Brescia and Bergamo in February; but since Opll dated Frederick's response to the pope's letter in January (p. 27, no. 645), the pope's letter must have been sent already in January. See Schmale edition of the *Deeds*, pp. 550–51, n. 22; Opll, *Stadt und Reich im 12. Jahrhundert*, pp. 205–07 and 223–24; Laudage, *Alexander III. und Friedrich Barbarossa*, pp. 95–99; and Görich, *Die Ehre Friedrich Barbarossas*, pp. 118–20.
4. Otto of Freising and Rahewin, *Deeds* 4.21. Rahewin presented this directive as Frederick's response to Adrian's second rejection of the emperor's request that Guido be transferred to

Ravenna, but Frederick's petition already contained the new style for addressing the pope. Beyond that, Bishop Eberhard informed Cardinal Henry that Frederick had issued this directive in response to the insulting delivery of the letter about Brescia's dispute with Bergamo (4.22). On this, see the Schmale edition of the *Deeds*, pp. 556–58, n. 30; and RI IV2/2:26, no. 644.

5. Otto of Freising and Rahewin, *Deeds* 4.18–21; and DFI, no. 315 (16 April 1160). On Hermann's enforcement of the Roncaglia laws, see Vincent of Prague, *Annales*, p. 675; and RI IV2/2:30, no. 659 (28 January 1159).
6. Otto of Freising and Rahewin, *Deeds* 4.22; and RI IV2/2:35–37, nos. 676 and 686–87. See Görich, *Die Ehre Friedrich Barbarossas*, pp. 120–22.
7. Otto of Freising and Rahewin, *Deeds* 4.34, and RI IV2/2:40, no. 701.
8. Otto of Freising and Rahewin, *Deeds* 4.34 and 4.36. Rahewin connected the two letters to the mission of Cardinals Henry and Guido in April, but they were probably written after the June mission. On the dating problem, see RI IV2/2:40–49, nos. 701, 723, and 738–39. Frederick's letter to Archbishop Eberhard is also printed in *Constitutiones* 1:251, no. 180; and DFI, no. 269; both of these editions date the letter in April.
9. Otto of Freising and Rahewin, *Deeds* 4.34 (Bishop Eberhard's letter to Archbishop Eberhard) and 4.35 (Frederick's speech). See Petersohn, *Kaisertum und Rom in spätsalischer und staufischer Zeit*, p. 178 and pp. 320–36, esp. pp. 328–30; and Bolton, "*Nova familia beati Petri*," pp. 157–79. On episcopal palaces, see Maureen C. Miller, *The Bishop's Palace: Architecture and Authority in Medieval Italy* (Ithaca, N.Y., 2000).
10. Otto of Freising and Rahewin, *Deeds* 4.34–36. See Laudage, *Alexander III. und Friedrich Barbarossa*, pp. 96–102; Görich, *Die Ehre Friedrich Barbarossas*, pp. 122–26; and Petersohn, *Kaisertum und Rom in spätsalischer und staufischer Zeit*, pp. 177–78.
11. Otto of Freising and Rahewin, *Deeds* 4.34, 4.36, and 4.49; Vincent of Prague, *Annales*, p. 673; and RI IV2/1:174, no. 546. Rahewin's confused account suggests that there may have been more than one Roman embassy to the emperor, but there probably was only one. See RI IV2/2:45–46, no. 723. See Petersohn, *Kaisertum und Rom in spätsalischer und staufischer Zeit*, pp. 172–75.
12. DFI, no. 274 (18 May–June 1159, probably early June); and no. 275 (June 1159). On the Monticelli, see Petersohn, *Kaisertum und Rom in spätsalischer und staufischer Zeit*, pp. 168–70 and 190–91. The precise nature of Octavian's kinship to Frederick is unknown. Jochen Johrendt, "Barbarossa, das Kaisertum und Rom," in Burkhardt et al., eds, *Staufisches Kaisertum im 12. Jahrhundert*, pp. 92–97, challenged the conventional view that Frederick granted both privileges as part of a deliberate policy of building up support in Rome.
13. Otto of Freising and Rahewin, *Deeds* 4.34, 4.49–50, 4.52, and 4.76; and Boso, *Les vies des papes*, p. 400 (*Boso's Life of Alexander III*, p. 47). Rahewin said that the imperial envoys were in Rome for Adrian's funeral (4.52), but the canons of St. Peter were less certain, in a nearly contemporary report, whether they were still in Rome, let alone in the basilica, on 7 September: "Since, we believe, they [the envoys] were present in the City when the Roman clergy assembled at the church of St. Peter . . ." (4.76). The Milanese Anonymous, pp. 266–67, reported that it was alleged that Otto of Wittelsbach and Guido of Biandrate had been involved in Octavian's mantling in St. Peter's on 7 September; but if they had been, it is likely Boso would have mentioned this as part of his case against the anti-pope. On Frederick's negotiations with the cardinals and the Romans, see Jürgen Petersohn, "Rahewin IV 49: 'seu de recipiendo prefecto': Zur Rolle des Präfektur bei den kaiserlich-römischen Verhandlungen von 1159," in Karl Hauck and Hubert Mordek, eds, *Geschichtsschreibung und geistiges Leben im Mittelalter: Festschrift für Heinz Löwe zum 65. Geburtstag* (Cologne and Vienna, 1978), pp. 397–409; and Opll, *Stadt und Reich im 12. Jahrhundert*, pp. 422–23. On the scholarly debate about the extent of imperial involvement in the events of 7 September, see Petersohn, *Kaisertum und Rom in spätsalischer und staufischer Zeit*, pp. 185–87 and 192–94. On Heribert, see Lohrmann, "Das Papsttum und die Grafschaft Burgund im 11.–12. Jahrhundert," pp. 71–75; and Uebach, *Die Ratgeber Friedrich Barbarossas*, pp. 227–29.
14. Otto of Freising and Rahewin, *Deeds* 4.62, 4.77, 4.79, and 4.81; *Constitutiones* 1:257–60, no. 187, esp. p. 259, article 6; and pp. 265–70, no. 190, esp. p. 267, article 5; *Narratio de Longobardie obpressione*, pp. 206–07; and RI IV2/2:44, no. 718. Duggan, "*Totius christianitatis caput*," esp. pp. 134–38, in her attempt to exonerate Adrian for the deterioration in imperial-papal relations, argued that the notion of an anti-imperial, pro-Sicilian conspiracy was the

product of skillful imperial propagandists. However, the Milanese Anonymous made no effort to disguise Adrian's alliance with Milan and its allies. Petersohn, *Kaisertum und Rom in spätsalischer und staufischer Zeit*, pp. 182–83 and 193–94; and Görich, *Friedrich Barbarossa*, pp. 182–83, thought that there was a conspiracy.

15. Otto of Freising and Rahewin, *Deeds* 4.61 (Alexander's letter, "Eternal and Unchangeable Providence") and 4.63 (letter of the twenty-three cardinals). The copy of Alexander's letter that Rahewin used was addressed to the bishop, cathedral chapter, and university of Bologna; but other copies, dated between 26 September and 13 December, were sent to other recipients. Since Alexander indicated that Octavian had not yet been able to find a bishop to consecrate him and since Octavian was consecrated on 4 October, the letter must have been drafted before that date. See *Die Admonter Briefsammlung*, pp. 79–83, no. 41.
16. Petersohn, *Kaisertum und Rom in spätsalischer und staufischer Zeit*, p. 183. Morena, *Libellus de rebus a Frederico imperatore gestis*, pp. 124–31, summarized the version of events that appears in the encyclical issued by the Council of Pavia; whereas the Milanese Anonymous, *Narratio de Longobardie obpressione*, pp. 266–69, repeated the Alexandrine account.
17. Otto of Freising and Rahewin, *Deeds* 4.61–62 and 4.76; and *Constitutiones* 1:257–60, no. 187, p. 260.
18. According to the encyclical issued by the pro-Victorine Council of Pavia in February 1160, twenty-two cardinals were in Rome on 7 September. After Roland and Octavian withdrew, nine "of wiser counsel" voted for Octavian, i.e., Roland received eleven votes. See *Constitutiones* 1:265–70, no. 190, article 2. On Eberhard's ambiguous words, see the Schmale edition of the *Deeds*, pp. 698–99, n. 57. I would like to thank Anders Winroth for suggesting to me that the 1179 papal election decree might have been a retroactive legitimization of Alexander's election. For a text of the decree in English, see Tierney, *The Crisis of Church and State*, p. 113, no. 55.
19. Otto of Freising and Rahewin, *Deeds* 4.81, and Mierow edition, p. 325, n. 289; and *Constitutiones* 1:265–70, no. 190, article 5.
20. Otto of Freising and Rahewin, *Deeds* 4.61; and Boso, *Les vies des papes*, pp. 397–98 (*Boso's Life of Alexander III*, p. 44).
21. Otto of Freising and Rahewin, *Deeds* 4.60–62; and Boso, *Les vies des papes*, pp. 399–400 (*Boso's Life of Alexander III*, pp. 46–47).
22. Doran, "'At last we reached the port of salvation,'" pp. 51–74, stressed how limited Octavian's support was even among the Roman people.
23. See Laudage, *Alexander III. und Friedrich Barbarossa*, pp. 108–18; and Doran, "'At last we have reached the port of salvation,'" pp. 59–63. Johrendt, "The Empire and the Schism," p. 111, n. 64, pointed out that St. John Lateran, and not St. Peter's, was and still is the pope's cathedral as the bishop of Rome.
24. DFI, no. 281 (16 September 1159; also *Constitutiones* 1:252–53, no. 281; and *Die Admonter Briefsammlung*, pp. 76–78, no. 39). On this letter, see Laudage, *Alexander III. und Friedrich Barbarossa*, p. 118; and Wolter, "Friedrich Barbarossa und die Synode zu Pavia," pp. 417–18.
25. Otto of Freising and Rahewin, *Deeds* 4.83. On Archbishop Eberhard, see Heinz Dopsch, ed., *Geschichte Salzburgs: Stadt und Land: Vorgeschichte, Altertum, Mittelalter*, 3 vols (Salzburg, 1981), vol. 1, pp. 274–84.
26. Rodney M. Thomson, "An English Eyewitness of the Peace of Venice, 1177," *Speculum* 50 (1975): 29. See Görich, *Die Ehre Friedrich Barbarossas*, pp. 133–34. Laudage, *Alexander III. und Friedrich Barbarossa*, pp. 1–32, stressed that the two men, a prince and a minor Tuscan noble, came from very different backgrounds.
27. Otto of Freising and Rahewin, *Deeds* 4.63; and Boso, *Les vies des papes*, p. 400 (*Boso's Life of Alexander III*, p. 47). See Görich, *Die Ehre Friedrich Barbarossas*, pp. 127–28; and Wolter, "Friedrich Barbarossa und die Synode zu Pavia," pp. 417–18.
28. Otto of Freising and Rahewin, *Deeds* 4.64–66 and 4.74; DFI, no. 284 (23 October 1159; Hartmann of Brixen); no. 285 (end of October; Roland); and no. 307 (15 February 1160); and *Constitutiones* 1:254–55, no. 183 (letter to Henry II, 28 October 1159).
29. Otto of Freising and Rahewin, *Deeds* 4.79; and RI IV2/2:57, no. 772.
30. Otto of Freising and Rahewin, *Deeds* 4.74. See Wolter, "Friedrich Barbarossa und die Synode zu Pavia," pp. 418–22.

31. Otto of Freising and Rahewin, *Deeds* 4.76. The Latin texts of the two letters are nicely juxtaposed in *Constitutiones* 1:253–55, nos. 182 and 183. The letter to Henry II is not included in the edition of Frederick's charters. See Wolter, "Friedrich Barbarossa und die Synode zu Pavia," pp. 422–24.
32. Boso, *Les vies des papes*, p. 400 (*Boso's Life of Alexander III*, p. 47); and RI IV2/2:58, no. 774. See Görich, *Die Ehre Friedrich Barbarossas*, pp. 128–31.
33. Otto of Freising and Rahewin, *Deeds* 4.65 (also DFI, no. 285; letter to Roland), 4.74–75, and 4.80; Boso, *Les vies des papes*, pp. 400–02 (*Boso's Life of Alexander III*, pp. 47–50); and *The Letters of John of Salisbury* 1:204–15, no. 124, esp. p. 206. On this, see Wolter, "Friedrich Barbarossa und die Synode zu Pavia," pp. 424–29; and Laudage, *Alexander III. und Friedrich Barbarossa*, pp. 120–21. Wolter, pp. 424–25, insisted that the choice of envoys was not a deliberate provocation. Frederick selected two bishops who were known for their competence and personal prestige because he realized that it would not be easy to persuade Alexander to attend. Surely, if the emperor had been in the least bit interested in a peaceful resolution of the schism, he would have chosen envoys who were more acceptable to the pope, say, Eberhard of Bamberg and Henry the Lion, both of whom were in Italy and had helped to defuse the Besançon crisis. On Heribert's authorship of Frederick's letter to Alexander, see DFI, head note to no. 285.
34. Otto of Freising and Rahewin, *Deeds* 4.74 and 4.81; and *Constitutiones* 1:265–70, no. 190, p. 265. See Wolter, "Friedrich Barbarossa und die Synode zu Pavia," pp. 430–31 and 438; and Johrendt, "The Empire and the Schism," pp. 110–11.
35. Otto of Freising and Rahewin, *Deeds* 4.76–77 and 4.81. See Wolter, "Friederich Barbarossa und die Synode zu Pavia," pp. 439–40; and Doran, '"At last we reached the port of salvation,"' pp. 60–61.
36. Otto of Freising and Rahewin, *Deeds* 4.82 (Provost Henry's letter); and *Constitutiones* 1:257–60, no. 187 (indictment of Roland), and pp. 265–70, esp. p. 267, article 5. See Wolter, "Friedrich Barbarossa und die Synode zu Pavia," pp. 441–45.
37. Otto of Freising and Rahewin, *Deeds* 4.80–82; Vincent of Prague, *Annales*, pp. 678–79; and *The Letters of John of Salisbury*, 1:204–15, no. 124, esp. p. 213. See Wolter, "Friedrich Barbarossa und die Synode zu Pavia," pp. 446–48.
38. Otto of Freising and Rahewin, *Deeds* 4.80; Vincent of Prague, *Annales*, p. 679; and Gerhoch of Reichersberg, *Annales Reicherspergenses a. 921–1167*, ed. Wilhelm Wattenbach, in MGH SS 17 (Hanover, 1861), p. 467. See Wolter, "Friedrich Barbarossa und die Synode zu Pavia," pp. 448–49.
39. Boso, *Les vies des papes*, p. 403 (*Boso's Life of Alexander III*, pp. 51–52); and *Die Admonter Briefsammlung*, pp. 103–06, no. 53.
40. Otto of Freising and Rahewin, *Deeds* 4.74 and 4.80–82; *Constitutiones* 1:265–70, no. 190, esp. pp. 269–70; and the *Letters of John of Salisbury*, 1:204–15, no. 124, esp. p. 206. See Wolter, "Friedrich Barbarossa und die Synode zu Pavia," pp. 431–36 and 452–53. For a discussion of John's question, see Horst Fuhrmann, "*Quis Teutonicos constituit iudices nationum?* The Trouble with Henry," *Speculum* 69 (1994): 344–58.
41. Wright, *The Play of Antichrist*, pp. 70–73; and Eberle, *Die Gedichte des Archipoeta*, pp. 80–97. The translation is my own.
42. *Letters of John of Salisbury*, 1:204–15, no. 124, esp. p. 207. On the election announcement, see above, pp. 68–69.
43. Otto of Freising and Rahewin, *Deeds* 4.66; and *Constitutiones* 1:253–55, nos 182–83 (letters to Hartmann and Henry II). See Hans Joachim Kirfel, *Weltherrschaftsidee und Bündnispolitik: Untersuchungen zur auswärtigen Politik der Staufer* (Bonn, 1959), pp. 9–19 (historiographical overview); pp. 84–100 (John of Salisbury and the literary texts); pp. 110–13 (letters to Hartmann and Henry II); and pp. 120–28 (papal propaganda). Petersohn, *Kaisertum und Rom in spätsalischer und staufischer Zeit*, pp. 348–49, warned against the temptation to see imperial "spin doctors" behind the various facets of Frederick's Roman ideology.
44. Wibald of Stavelot, *Briefsammlung* 3:894–95, no. 430 (Jaffé, no. 461). See Karl J. Leyser, "Frederick Barbarossa, Henry II, and the Hand of St. James," *EHR* 90 (1975): 481–506. According to the *Annales Herbipolenses a. 1125–1158. 1202–1204. 1215*, ed. Georg Heinrich Pertz, MGH SS 16 (Hanover, 1859), p. 9, Henry II sent Frederick in June 1156, on the

occasion of the emperor's wedding to Beatrice in Würzburg, gifts befitting his "imperial magnificence," that is, it was Henry rather than Frederick who had initiated the contacts. Leyser, p. 219, n. 5, suggested that the Würzburg chronicler might have confused the courts that met in Würzburg in June 1156 and September 1157. However, Joseph P. Huffman, *The Social Politics of Medieval Diplomacy: Anglo-German Relations (1066–1307)* (Ann Arbor, MI, 2000), pp. 57–58, thought that the Angevin–Staufer exchange began with the 1156 mission, because a friendly monarch in Burgundy suited Henry's interests on the Continent.

45. Otto of Freising and Rahewin, *Deeds* 3.6–8 (the letter is 3.8) and 4.86. See Kirfel, *Weltherrschaftsidee und Bündnispolitik*, pp. 177–78; Leyser, "Frederick Barbarossa, Henry II, and the Hand of St. James," pp. 215–20 and 233–40; Georgi, *Friedrich Barbarossa und die auswärtigen Mächte*, pp. 37–38; Huffman, *The Social Politics of Medieval Diplomacy*, pp. 59–63; and Latowsky, *Emperor of the World*, pp. 5–9 and 147–49 (the "foreign embassy topos"). There is no indication in the content of Henry's letter that it was a response to Frederick's letter of May. On the basis of the entry in the Pipe Rolls, Huffman, p. 59, presented Henry's letter as a response to an embassy Frederick had sent to the king in late 1156. Since Huffman also believed that Henry had already sent Frederick gifts at his marriage in June 1156 (pp. 57–58), it is hard to see how Henry could have said in July 1157, if Huffman is right about the June 1156 embassy, that Frederick had initiated the contacts, whether in December 1156 or May 1157. If Henry did send wedding gifts, they could not have been the items whose expenditures were recorded in the Pipe Rolls for the third year of Henry's reign that began only in December 1156. Henry's reference to commercial relations between England and Germany is usually taken as a reference to two writs the king issued in 1157 authorizing the merchants of Cologne to sell their wine in London and taking them, their house, the so-called Steelyard, and their merchandise under royal protection. See Leyser, p. 220. For the text of the two writs, see Philippe Dollinger, *The German Hansa*, trans. D. S. Ault and S. H. Steinberg (Stanford, CA, 1970), pp. 380–81. However, Huffman, p. 59, n. 8, said these charters should be dated 1173–75. On Frederick's use of the tent in Italy, see above, pp. 229–30.
46. Leyser, "Frederick Barbarossa, Henry II, and the Hand of St. James," pp. 220–33; and Hans Eberhard Mayer, "Staufische Weltherrschaft? Zum Brief Heinrichs II. von England an Friedrich Barbarossa von 1157," in Wolf, ed., *Friedrich Barbarossa*, pp. 184–207.
47. Otto of Freising and Rahewin, *Deeds* 3.8 and 3.12. See Leyser, "Frederick Barbarossa, Henry II, and the Hand of St. James," pp. 234–35; Georgi, *Friedrich Barbarossa und die auswärtigen Mächte*, pp. 138–39; and above, p. 209.
48. Otto of Freising and Rahewin, *Deeds* 4.24; RI IV2/2:35, no. 678; and DFI, no. 281 (16 September 1159). See Georgi, *Friedrich Barbarossa und die auswärtigen Mächte*, pp. 139–41.
49. Otto of Freising and Rahewin, *Deeds* 4.82; and Boso, *Les vies des papes*, p. 403 (*Boso's Life of Alexander III*, pp. 51–52). See Georgi, *Friedrich Barbarossa und die auswärtigen Mächte*, pp. 47–49.
50. *The Letters of John of Salisbury*, 1:190–92, no. 116; and pp. 201–02, no. 122; and *Ex Radulfi de Diceto operibus historicis: Ymaginibus historiarum*, p. 262 (under 1160). See Georgi, *Friedrich Barbarossa und die auswärtigen Mächte*, pp. 50–51; and Huffman, *The Social Politics of Medieval Diplomacy*, pp. 66–68.
51. Otto of Freising and Rahewin, *Deeds* 4.84; DFI, no. 431 (letter to Archbishop Eberhard) and no. 432 (9 February–March 1164); also in *Die Admonter Briefsammlung*, pp. 178–81, nos. 20 and 22; *Die Admonter Briefsammlung*, pp. 202–03, no. 2 (29 May 1163; Alexander III's letter to Archbishops Eberhard and Lucas to resist Frederick's planned Hungarian campaign); and Vincent of Prague, *Annales*, pp. 681–82. See Georgi, *Friedrich Barbarossa und die auswärtigen Mächte*, pp. 54–59 and 95–112; and Hödl, "Ungarn in der Aussenpolitik Kaiser Friedrich Barbarossas," pp. 129–40. The chronology of the succession dispute, including the date of Frederick's letter to Archbishop Eberhard, is very confused.
52. Kejř, "Böhmen und das Reich unter Friedrich I.," p. 257; idem, "Böhmen zur Zeit Friedrich Barbarossas," pp. 104–05; Engels, "Friedrich Barbarossa und Dänemark," pp. 372–79; and Georgi, *Friedrich Barbarossa und die auswärtigen Mächte*, p. 48.
53. Boso, *Les vies des papes*, pp. 403–04 (*Boso's Life of Alexander III*, pp. 52–54); and *Die Admonter Briefsammlung*, pp. 106–07, no. 54 (Alexander's account of his entry into Rome). See

Petersohn, *Kaisertum und Rom in spätsalischer und staufischer Zeit*, pp. 195–202; Laudage, *Alexander III. und Friedrich Barbarossa*, pp. 126–28; Baldwin, *Alexander III and the Twelfth Century*, pp. 58–60; Johrendt, "Barbarossa, das Kaisertum und Rom," pp. 81 and 87–98; and Brenda Bolton, "The Absentee Lord? Alexander III and the Patrimony," in Clarke and Duggan, *Pope Alexander III*, pp. 158–59.

Chapter 11 The Defeat of Milan

1. Otto of Freising and Rahewin, *Deeds* 4.85; and Morena, *Libellus de rebus a Frederico imperatore gestis*, pp. 130–31. Otto Morena said that Frederick of Rothenburg and the emperor's brother Conrad stayed, but by July 1160 they, too, were in Germany. See RI IV2/2:86, no. 893. Otto of Wittelsbach remained in Italy. See DFI, no. 316 (after 18 June 1160). The latter charter was witnessed by a Count Robert, who was identified as the emperor's maternal uncle ("avunculus imperatoris"), theoretically a Welf. No known Welf, Staufer, or Babenberg bore that name in the mid-twelfth century. Since the charter survives only in a copy made around 1518, it is possible that this is a copyist's error.
2. Berwinkel, *Verwüsten und Belagern*, pp. 118–19, 124–26, and 163–64.
3. Morena, *Libellus de rebus a Frederico imperatore gestis*, pp. 130–35; *Narratio de Longobardie obpressione*, pp. 268–69; RI IV2/2:79–84, nos. 857, 859–61, 866, and 869–85. See Berwinkel, *Verwüsten und Belagern*, pp. 164–69.
4. Morena, *Libellus de rebus a Frederico imperatore gestis*, pp. 134–43. See Berwinkel, *Verwüsten und Belagern*, pp. 169–73.
5. Morena, *Libellus de rebus a Frederico imperatore gestis*, pp. 144–45; Burchard of Ursberg, *Chronicon*, pp. 174–75; *Chronica regia Coloniensis*, pp. 102–03; *Carmen de gestis Frederici I. imperatoris in Lombardia*, pp. 102–03, vs. 3162ff; and RI IV2/2:86–87, nos. 894–97. See Berwinkel, *Verwüsten und Belagern*, pp. 173–76 and 284–85, Abbildung 11: "Militärische Unternehmen im Kriegsjahr 1160."
6. Morena, *Libellus de rebus a Frederico imperatore gestis*, pp. 144–51; *Narratio de Longobardie obpressione*, pp. 268–73; Burchard of Ursberg, *Chronicon*, pp. 174–77; *Carmen de gestis Frederici I. imperatoris in Lombardia*, pp. 106ff, vs. 3233ff; and RI IV2/2:87–89, nos. 898–909. See Berwinkel, *Verwüsten und Belagern*, pp. 176–86, and pp. 286–87, Abbildung 10: "Die Schlacht bei Carcano, 9. August 1160."
7. DFI, no. 317 (letter to Pilgrim, shortly after 9 August 1160; also *Constitutiones* 1:274–75, no. 196); Otto of Freising and Rahewin, *Deeds* (Simson edition), Appendix, p. 347 (also in Mierow translation, p. 335); and Morena, *Libellus de rebus a Frederico imperatore gestis*, pp. 150–53. See Berwinkel, *Verwüsten und Belagern*, pp. 184–86; and Görich, *Die Ehre Friedrich Barbarossas*, pp. 241–43.
8. DFI, no. 317; no. 378 (agreement with the two counts, before 1 August 1162; also *Constitutiones* 1:304–05, no. 215); and no. 382 (enfeoffment of the count of Provence, 18 August 1162; also *Constitutiones* 1:305–08, no. 216). See Georgi, *Friedrich Barbarossa und die auswärtigen Mächte*, pp. 70–73 and 78–79; Fried, "Friedrich Barbarossas Krönung in Arles," pp. 351–52; Opll, *Stadt und Reich in 12. Jahrhundert*, p. 495; Myriam Soria, "Alexander III and France: Exile, Diplomacy, and the New Order," in Clarke and Duggan, eds, *Pope Alexander III*, p. 184; Damian J. Smith, "Alexander III and Spain," in Clarke and Duggan, eds, *Pope Alexander III*, pp. 204–07; and Hlawitschka, *Die Ahnen der hochmittelalterlichen deutschen Könige* 3:180–86 (on Richildis and Ramón III). The truth about Victor's lack of support in the Western Church must have been known in Germany by early 1161 because *Die Admonter Briefsammlung* contains a letter of Alexander to Archbishop Eberhard, dated 20 January 1161, notifying him of Alexander's recognition by the Catholic Church in the Holy Land, and by Henry II, Louis VII, and Ferdinand II of León. The pope included in his letter copies of their letters of recognition. See pp. 118–27, nos. 65–70.
9. DFI, nos. 317 and 318 (shortly after 9 August 1160; also in *Constitutiones* 1:273–74, no. 195; and *Die Admonter Briefsammlung*, pp. 100–03, nos. 51 and 52); and RI IV2/2:86, no. 893 (Erfurt assembly).
10. Morena, *Libellus de rebus a Frederico imperatore gestis*, pp. 150–55; and *Narratio de Longobardie obpressione*, pp. 272–73. See Berwinkel, *Verwüsten und Belagern*, pp. 186–89.

11. Morena, *Libellus de rebus a Frederico imperatore gestis*, pp. 154–63 and 170–71; Burchard of Ursberg, *Chronicon*, pp. 176–77; and *Narratio de Longobardie obpressione*, pp. 272–73. See Berwinkel, *Verwüsten und Belagern*, pp. 189–91.
12. Morena, *Libellus de rebus a Frederico imperatore gestis*, pp. 162–65; *Annales Sancti Disibodi*, p. 30; and RI IV2/2:98–102, nos. 950, 953, and 962–63. See Berwinkel, *Verwüsten und Belagern*, pp. 191–92; Laudage, *Alexander III. und Friedrich Barbarossa*, p. 128; and Görich, *Die Ehre Friedrich Barbarossas*, p. 135.
13. Morena, *Libellus de rebus a Frederico imperatore gestis*, pp. 164–69; *Narratio de Longobardie obpressione*, pp. 272–75; Burchard of Ursberg, *Chronicon*, pp. 176–77; *Chronica regia Coloniensis*, pp. 103–04; and RI IV2/2:105, no. 977 (letter to Victor; 7–14 August 1161; it is not in DFI). See Görich, *Die Ehre Friedrich Barbarossas*, pp. 244–47; Berwinkel, *Verwüsten und Belagern*, pp. 192–94; and above, pp. 176–77.
14. Morena, *Libellus de rebus a Frederico imperatore gestis*, pp. 168–73; *Narratio de Longobardie obpressione*, pp. 274–77; Vincent of Prague, *Annales*, p. 680; and RI IV2/2:109–11, nos. 991 and 999. See Berwinkel, *Verwüsten und Belagern*, pp. 194–97, and pp. 286–87, Abbildung 12: "Blockade gegen Mailand im Winter 1161–1162."
15. Görich, *Friedrich Barbarossa*, p. 343.
16. Ferdinand Güterbock, "Le lettere del notaio imperiale Burcardo intorno alla politica del Barbarossa nello scisma ed alla distruzione di Milano," *Bullettino dell'istituto storico italiano per il medio evo* 61 (1949): 1–65, esp. pp. 59–65, no. 2; Morena, *Libellus de rebus a Frederico imperatore gestis*, pp. 172–77; *Narratio de Longobardie obpressione*, pp. 276–77; Vincent of Prague, *Annales*, p. 680 (the consul's alleged speech on 6 March); Burchard of Ursberg, *Chronicon*, pp. 176–78; DFI, no. 351 (Frederick to Eberhard of Salzburg, 4 March 1162 or shortly thereafter; also in *Constitutiones* 1:279–80, no. 203); DFI, no. 352 (Frederick to Count Ivo of Soissons, 6 March 1162 or shortly thereafter; also in *Constitutiones* 1:281, no. 204); *Die Admonter Briefsammlung*, pp. 116–17, no. 63 (letter of Frederick to Bishop Roman I of Gurk, after 1 March 1162); and RI IV2/2:116–20, nos. 1020, 1025–31, and 1033–37. Burchard's letter to Nicholas of Siegburg was quoted nearly verbatim in the *Chronica regia Coloniensis*, pp. 108–11. See Görich, *Die Ehre Friedrich Barbarossas*, pp. 247–55; and Berwinkel, *Verwüsten und Belagern*, pp. 196–99 and 249–58 (on Guintelmo). Görich, p. 508, n. 443, thought that Burchard's letter might have been written between 11 and 13 March. He provided extensive quotations from the letter. On Beatrice's absence, see above, p.187.
17. Morena, *Libellus de rebus a Frederico imperatore gestis*, pp. 176–80; *Narratio de Longobardie obpressione*, pp. 276–79; Vincent of Prague, *Annales*, p. 680; Burchard of Ursberg, *Chronicon*, pp. 178–79; and RI IV2/2:121–23, nos. 1042 and 1046. See Görich, *Die Ehre Friedrich Barbarossas*, pp. 255–56; and Berwinkel, *Verwüsten und Belagern*, pp. 199–201.
18. Krieg, *Herrscherdarstellung in der Stauferzeit*, pp. 99–115. The documents that are discussed are: DFI, no. 231, p. 20, ll. 15–16 (23 November 1158); no. 253, p. 53, ll. 18–20 (26 January 1159); no. 297, p. 110, l. 5 (27 January 1160); no. 351, p. 191, ll. 18–19 and 27–28 (4 March 1162 or shortly thereafter); no. 356, p. 203, ll. 34–35 and 41 (6 April 1162); and no. 358, p. 205, ll. 16–17 (7 April 1162).
19. Morena, *Libellus de rebus a Frederico imperatore gestis*, pp. 178–81; *Narratio de Longobardie obpressione*, pp. 278–79; and Burchard of Ursberg, *Chronicon*, pp. 178–79.
20. Morena, *Libellus de rebus a Frederico imperatore gestis*, pp. 180–83; and DFI, no. 362 (11 May 1162). See Opll, *Stadt und Reich im 12. Jahrhundert*, pp. 224–25 and 379–81.
21. Morena, *Libellus de rebus a Frederico imperatore gestis*, pp. 182–85. See Opll, *Stadt und Reich im 12. Jahrhundert*, pp. 217–19. On Turisendus of Verona, see Haverkamp, "Friedrich I. und der hohe italienische Adel," pp. 59–61. The terms of Turisendus' "submission" can be inferred from Frederick's charter for him on 7 April 1164 (DFI, no. 434).
22. Morena, *Libellus de rebus a Frederico imperatore gestis*, pp. 182–83; *Narratio de Longobardie obpressione*, pp. 280–83; and RI IV2/2:129–30, no. 1076. On Arnold of Dorstadt, see DFI, no. 522 (27 January 1167). On Rainald's appointment of Germans in Tuscany and Spoleto, primarily from the ranks of counts from the lower Rhineland who had accompanied him to Italy, see Herkenrath, "Reinald von Dassel," pp. 248–57.

23. DFI, no. 353 (7 March 1162); and no. 369 (13 June 1162). See Opll, *Stadt und Reich im 12. Jahrhundert*, pp. 245–46 and 255–56.
24. *Narratio de Longobardie obpressione*, pp. 278–79 and 284–85; *Chronica regia Coloniensis*, p. 115; Giovanni Domenico Mansi, ed., *Sacrorum conciliorum nova amplissima collectio* 21 (Venice, 1776), pp. 865–66 (Rainald's letter); DFI, no. 445 (9 June 1164); and RI IV2/2:201–02, nos. 1368–69. See Patrick J. Geary, "The Magi and Milan," in idem, *Living with the Dead in the Middle Ages* (Ithaca N.Y., and London, 1994), pp. 243–56; and Kluger, "Friedrich Barbarossa und sein Ratgeber Rainald von Dassel," pp. 36–39. On the dating of the different versions of the *Narratio*, see the Schmale edition, pp. 14–17. I have adapted Geary's translation of the quotations from the Milanese Anonymous and Rainald's letter. The imperial anti-bishop, Gero of Halberstadt, obtained the relics of Saints Gervasius and Prothasius after the sack of Milan; but the circumstances are unknown. See RI IV2/2:125, no. 1057. On Nicholas of Verdun, see Hermann Fillitz, "Nicolaus von Verdun," *Die Zeit der Staufer* 5:279–90.
25. On Ulrich II of Aquileia, see Reinhard Härtl, "Friedrich I. und die Länder an der oberen Adria," in Haverkamp, ed., *Friedrich Barbarossa*, pp. 318–38. The patriarchate was considered to be part of the German rather than the Italian kingdom. Ulrich himself was a scion of the Carinthian counts of Treffen—Carinthia south of the Drava was under the patriarch's jurisdiction. Like Eberhard, Ulrich tried to be loyal to both Frederick and Alexander, but after the formation of the Lombard League in 1167, he opposed the emperor.
26. Most of the documents that deal with Frederick's dispute with Eberhard are in *Die Admonter Briefsammlung*. Hödl's edition reproduces the documents in the order they appear in that manuscript and in the separate *Salzburger Briefsammlung*, a continuation of the Admont collection, rather than in chronological order. An appendix contains nine of Alexander's letters dealing with the schism in Salzburg. The three collections are numbered separately. In this footnote, I have rearranged the citations in chronological order as they are discussed in the text; and I have given in parentheses the citations to Frederick's own letters in the MGH edition of his charters and letters. I have used Hödl's dates because he is the most recent editor.

    Die Admonter Briefsammlung, pp. 87–88, no. 43 (Eberhard to Roman; before 25 January 1160); pp. 94–95, no. 46 (Frederick to Eberhard; after 26 January 1160; also DFI, no. 296); pp. 96–98, no. 49 (Frederick to Eberhard and his suffragans; 15 February 1160; also DFI, no. 307; *Constitutiones* 1:263–65, no. 189; and Otto of Freising and Rahewin, *Deeds*, 4.79); pp. 103–06, no. 53 (Alexander to Eberhard and his suffragans; 4 April 1160); pp. 102–03, no. 52 (Frederick to Eberhard; August 1160; also DFI, no. 318; and *Constitutiones* 1:273–74, no. 195); pp. 107–08, no. 55 (Frederick to Eberhard; around 22 June 1161; also DFI, no. 327; and *Constitutiones* 1:275–76, no. 197); p. 109, no. 56 (Eberhard to Frederick; July 1161; also *Constitutiones* 1:276, no. 198); pp. 110–11, no. 57 (Frederick to Eberhard; after 8 September 1161; also DFI, no. 341; and *Constitutiones* 1:276–77, no. 199); pp. 111–12, no. 58 (Frederick to Roman; between 8 and 29 September 1161; also DFI, no. 342; *Constitutiones* 1:277–78, no. 200); p. 128, no. 71 (Eberhard to Frederick; mid-December 1161; also *Constitutiones* 1:278, no. 201); pp. 112–13, no. 59 (Frederick to Eberhard; beginning of January 1162; also DFI, no. 346; and *Constitutiones* 1:278–79, no. 202); pp. 113–14, no. 60 (Eberhard of Bamberg to Eberhard; beginning of January 1162); pp. 114–15, no. 61 (Ulirch of Dürrmenz to Eberhard; beginning of January 1162); pp. 115–16, no. 62 (Eberhard to Godfrey of Admont; January 1162); pp. 117–18, no. 64 (Eberhard to Godfrey of Admont; 31 March–7 April 1162); pp. 140–41, no. 83 (Eberhard to Hartmann of Brixen on not being invited to St. Jean-des-Losne; July–August 1162); pp. 201–02, no. 1 (Alexander to the clergy and people of Germany on Eberhard's appointment as legate; 28 February 1163); pp. 176–77, no. 18 (Frederick to Eberhard; end of 1163 to beginning of May 1164; also DFI, no. 439; and *Constitutiones* 1:311–12, no. 220); pp. 177–78, no. 19 (Frederick to Eberhard directing him to resolve the dispute between his Babenberg uncles; mid-March–June 1164; also DFI, no. 449; and *Constitutiones* 1:310–11, no. 219). See also DFI, no. 355 (privilege for Reichersberg; 4 April 1162); and no. 358 (privilege for Gurk; 7 April 1162); Güterbock, "Le lettere del notaio imperiale Burcardo," pp. 51–58, no. 1, esp. pp. 54–56 (the description of Eberhard is on p. 54), and p. 58 (Eberhard's possible deposition); and Gerhoch of Reichersberg, *Annales Reicherspergenses*, pp. 468–70. Eberhard's efforts to procure Géza II's and Patriarch Ulrich's recognition of Alexander are documented in *Die Admonter Briefsammlung*, pp. 131–38, nos. 74 and 76–80.

On the conflict, see Leopold Grill, *Erzbischof Eberhard I. von Salzburg* (Stift Rein, 1964), pp. 51–85; Dopsch, *Geschichte Salzburgs* 1/1:274–84; and Görich, *Die Ehre Friedrich Barbarossas*, pp. 58–73. On the Augustinian canons, see Weinfurter, *Salzburger Bistumsreform*; and on the Hirsau reform in Salzburg, see Helmut J. Mezler-Andelberg, "Die rechtlichen Beziehungen des Klosters Admont zum Salzburger Erzbistum während des 12. Jahrhunderts," *Zeitschrift des historischen Vereins für Steiermark*, 44 (1953): 31–46; and idem, "Admont und die Klosterreform zu Beginn des 12. Jahrhunderts," *Zeitschrift des historischen Vereins für Steiermark* 47 (1956): 28–42.

27. Vincent of Prague, *Annales*, p. 680; Morena, *Libellus de rebus a Frederico imperatore gestis*, pp. 180–81; DFI, no. 356 (Pisa, 6 April 1162; also *Constitutiones* 1:282–87, no. 205); no. 357 (Pisa, April 1162); and no. 367 (Genoa, 9 June 1162; also *Constitutiones* 1:292–97, no. 211); RI IV 2/2:124–43, nos. 1055–56, 1063, 1079, 1090–91, 1103, 1111, 1118, and 1121; and Güterbock, *Le lettere del notaio imperiale Burcardo*, pp. 57–58, no. 1 (planned council in Rome). See Chalandon, *Histoire de la domination normande en Italie et en Sicile* 2:293–97; Georgi, *Friedrich Barbarossa und die auswärtigen Mächte*, pp. 61–63; Opll, *Stadt und Reich im 12. Jahrhundert*, pp. 279–81 and 389–93; and Berwinkel, *Verwüsten und Belagern*, pp. 201–02.

Chapter 12 In Pursuit of Alexander

1. Helmold of Bosau, *Slawenchronik*, pp. 316–19; *Chronica regia Coloniensis*, pp. 112–13; Boso, *Les vies des papes*, pp. 405–07, esp. p. 405 (*Boso's Life of Alexander III*, pp. 54–58 [quotation is at p. 55]); and Hugh of Poitiers, *Liber de libertate monasterii Vizeliacensis*, ed. Georg Waitz, in MGH SS 26 (Hanover, 1882), pp. 146–49. On the source problem, see Beate Schuster, "Das Treffen von St. Jean-de-Losne im Wiederstreit der Meinungen: Zur Freiheit der Geschichtsschreibung im 12. Jahrhundert," *Zeitschrift für Geschichtswissenschaft* 43/3 (1995): 211–45, esp. p. 233.
2. RI IV2/2:123–24, no. 1051; Güterbock, "Le lettere del notaio imperiale Burcardo," pp. 51–58, no. 1, esp. p. 58. Frederick's letter was not published in the edition of his charters, but it is summarized in the *Regesta Imperii*. Laudage, *Friedrich Barbarossa*, p. 189, translated part of it. On Frederick's relations with the counts of Barcelona and Provence, see above, pp. 279–80.
3. Hugh of Poitiers, *Liber de libertate monasterii Vizeliacensis*, p. 146; and *Constitutiones* 1:289, no. 207 (Frederick's letter to Louis; it is not in the edition of his charters).
4. Hugh of Poitiers, *Liber de libertate monasterii Vizeliacensis*, pp. 146–47; Boso, *Les vies des papes*, pp. 405–06 (*Boso's Life of Alexander III*, pp. 54–56); *Chronica regia Coloniensis*, pp. 112–13; Morena, *Libellus de rebus a Frederico imperatore gestis*, pp. 184–87; and DFI, no. 363 (May 1162; general circular sent to the bishops in the Empire; also in *Constitutiones* 1:290–91, no. 208; and in *Die Admonter Briefsammlung*, pp. 145–46, no. 86); no. 364 (May 1162; summons sent to Duke Matthew; also in *Constitutiones* 1:291, no. 209); and no. 365 (May 1162; summons sent to Archbishop Eraclius of Lyons; also in *Constitutiones* 1:291–92, no. 210). Archbishop Eberhard asked Bishops Hartmann of Brixen and Roman of Gurk in July or August whether he should attend the council, to which he had not been invited. See *Die Admonter Briefsammlung*, pp. 140–41, no. 83, and pp. 143–45, no. 85.
5. Hugh of Poitiers, *Liber de libertate monasterii Vizeliacensis*, pp. 146–47; Boso, *Les vies des papes*, p. 406 (*Boso's Life of Alexander III*, p. 56); *Die Admonter Briefsammlung*, p. 139, no. 81 (June/July 1162; Eberhard to Henry of Reims); p. 140, no. 82 (July/August 1162; Henry of Reims to Eberhard); pp. 143–45, no. 85 (July/August 1162; Eberhard to Roman of Gurk informing him of Frederick's circular); and pp. 145–46, no. 86 (copy of Frederick's letter of late May or early June notifying Bishop Conrad of Augsburg about the council); and *Recueil des historiens des Gaules et de la France* 16:30–31, no. 101 (Henry of Reims to Louis); and p. 203, no. 13 (Alexander to Hugh of Soissons). On the French Church, see Soria, "Alexander III and France," pp. 181–201.
6. See above, p. 192.
7. Boso, *Les vies des papes*, p. 407 (*Boso's Life of Alexander III*, p. 58); and Hugh of Poitiers, *Liber de libertate monasterii Vizeliacensis*, p. 148.

8. Stefan Burkhardt, "Barbarossa, Frankreich, und die Weltherrschaft," in Burkhardt et al., eds, *Staufisches Kaisertum im 12. Jahrhundert*, pp. 151 and 158.
9. Boso, *Les vies des papes*, p. 407 (*Boso's Life of Alexander III*, p. 58); *Chronica regia Coloniensis*, p. 113; and Saxo Grammaticus, "Ex Saxonis Gestis Danorum," ed. Georg Waitz, in MGH SS 29 (Hanover, 1892), p. 114.
10. Güterbock, "Le lettere del notaio imperiale Burcardo," no. 1, p. 57. According to John of Salisbury, Louis VII was angry because "the schismatic of Cologne" called him, "with impudent buffoonery," a kinglet (*regulus*). *Letters* 2:224–29, no. 186, esp. pp. 228–29. Kirfel, *Weltherrschaftsidee*, pp. 20–69, tried to make the words less offensive; but see Karl Ferdinand Werner's critique of Kirfel in "Das hochmittelalterliche Imperium im politischen Bewusstsein Frankreichs (10.–12. Jahrhundert)." *HZ* 200 (1965): 37–38, n. 2. See also Grebe, "Studien zur geistigen Welt Rainalds von Dassel," pp. 278–85.
11. Helmold of Bosau, *Slawenchronik*, pp. 318–19. The chief articles on St. Jean-de-Losne, with very different reconstructions of the events, are: Walter Heinemeyer, "Die Verhandlungen an der Saône im Jahre 1162," *DA* 20 (1964): 155–89; Franz-Josef Schmale, "Friedrich I. und Ludwig VII. im Sommer des Jahres 1162," *ZbLG* 51 (1968): 315–68; Timothy Reuter, "The Papal Schism, the Empire and the West 1159–1169," unpublished dissertation (Oxford, 1975); and Georgi, *Friedrich Barbarossa und die auswärtigen Mächte*, pp. 64–70 and 73–79. I was unable to procure a copy of Reuter's dissertation. I have relied largely on Laudage's reconstruction of the events in *Alexander III. und Friedrich Barbarossa*, pp. 128–48, and, minus the documentation, in *Friedrich Barbarossa*, pp. 189–210. However, both Uebach, *Die Ratgeber Friedrich Barbarossas* pp. 146–47, and Görich, *Friedrich Barbarossa*, pp. 399–400, following Timothy Reuter's lead, placed Rainald's meeting with Louis before rather than after the synod. I have done the same because it makes inherently more sense that Rainald would have made one more attempt to win over Louis before rather than after the synod had declared that provincial kings had no voice in the choice of the bishop of Rome.
12. Otto of Freising and Rahewin, *Deeds* 3.25; and Saxo Grammaticus, "Ex Saxonis Gestis Danorum," p. 154. See Engels, "Friedrich Barbarossa und Dänemark," pp. 376–83.
13. *Die Admonter Briefsammlung*, pp. 146–48, no. 87 (18 September 1162; Alexander to Eberhard); and pp. 202–03, no. 2 (29 May 1163; Alexander to Eberhard and Hartmann); Boso, *Les vies des papes*, pp. 408–10 (*Boso's Life of Alexander III*, pp. 59–62); and RI IV2/2:163, no. 1204, and p. 169, no. 1226. See Georgi, *Friedrich Barbarossa und die auswärtigen Mächte*, p. 81; Laudage, *Alexander III. und Friedrich Barbarossa*, pp. 148–49; and Görich, *Die Ehre Friedrich Barbarossas*, pp. 141–44. On Eberhard's mission, see above, p. 299.
14. The chief source on the revolt is the *Vita Arnoldi archiepiscopi Moguntini*, pp. 624–75. See RI IV2/2:11, no. 584; p. 13, no. 591; p. 59, no. 779; p. 61, no. 789; p. 66, no. 810; p. 79, no. 854; p. 86, no. 893; and pp. 160–62, nos. 1193 and 1197–1200. Giesebrecht, *Geschichte der deutschen Kaiserzeit* 5/1:362–74, provided a detailed account of the uprising in Mainz. See Keupp, *Dienst und Verdienst*, pp. 114–32, 135, and 448–49; Uebach, *Die Ratgeber Friedrich Barbarossas*, pp. 156–59, and above, pp. 159–60, and above, pp. 159–62, on the earlier conflict with Hermann.
15. Morena, *Libellus de rebus a Frederico imperatore gestis*, pp. 186–87. For a list of Rainald and Hermann's actions during their legation, see RI IV2/2:153–72. See Herkenrath, "Reinald von Dassel," pp. 214–24 and 248–58; and Görich, *Friedrich Barbarossa*, pp. 350–51 (on the imperial legates).
16. Morena, *Libellus de rebus a Frederico imperatore gestis*, pp. 192–95.
17. The chief source on the Bareso affair is the *Annales Ianuenses* by Obertus, which are excerpted with a facing German translation in Schmale, *Italienische Quellen über die Taten Kaiser Friedrichs I. in Italien*, pp. 296–307. See also Morena, *Libellus de rebus a Frederico imperatore gestis*, pp. 196–97; DFI, no. 477 (17 April 1165); and RI IV2/2:188, no. 1311; p. 191, no. 1322; pp. 206–07, nos. 1388–90; p. 217, no. 1432; and pp. 225–26, nos. 1467–68. See Opll, *Stadt und Reich im 12. Jahrhundert*, pp. 279–83 and 391–95; and Johannes Bernwieser, "*Ex consilio principum curie*: Friedrich Barbarossa und der Konflikt zwischen Genua und Pisa um die Vorherrschaft auf Sardinien," in Burkhardt et al., eds, *Staufisches Kaisertum im 12. Jahrhundert*, pp. 205–27.

18. *Narratio de Longobardie obpressione*, pp. 278–85. See Opll, *Stadt und Reich im 12. Jahrhundert*, pp. 333–34. On the imperial penny, see Haverkamp, *Herrschaftsformen der Frühstaufer in Reichsitalien* 2:590–611.
19. Morena, *Libellus de rebus a Frederico imperatore gestis*, pp. 194–97; *Narratio de Longobardie obpressione*, pp. 284–85; *Historia ducum Veneticorum*, ed. Henry Simonsfeld, in MGH SS 14 (Hanover, 1883), p. 77; Boso, *Les vies des papes*, p. 411 (*Boso's Life of Alexander III*, p. 64; Boso wrongly placed the campaign against Verona in 1162); DFI, no. 441 (24 May 1164, Ferrara); no. 442 (27 May 1164, Mantua; also in *Constitutiones* 1:312–13, no. 221); and no. 444 (May 1164, Treviso); and *Die Admonter Briefsammlung*, pp. 176–77, no. 18 (Frederick to Eberhard, end of 1163 until the beginning of May 1164). See Opll, *Stadt und Reich im 12. Jahrhundert*, pp. 271–72, 347–48, 446, and 467–69; Härtl, "Friedrich I. und die Länder an der oberen Adria," pp. 294–318; Raccagni, *The Lombard League*, pp. 29–36; and Georgi, *Friedrich Barbarossa und die auswärtigen Mächte*, pp. 80–94.
20. RI IV2/2:192, no. 1326; and p. 205, nos. 1381–82; and Wibald of Stavelot, *Briefbuch* 3:847–51, no. 407, esp. p. 850, ll. 5–6 (Jaffé, no. 421). See Peter Herde, "Die Katastrophe vor Rom im August 1167: Eine historisch-epidemiologische Studie zum vierten Italienzug Friedrichs I. Barbarossa," *Sitzungsberichte der Wissenschaftliche Gesellschaft an der Johann-Wolfgang-Goethe-Universität Frankfurt am Main* 24/7 (Stuttgart, 1991), pp. 159–62.
21. *Narratio de Longobardie obpressione*, pp. 284–89; and Boso, *Les vies des papes*, p. 411 (*Boso's Life of Alexander III*, pp. 64–65). On taxation policy, see Haverkamp, *Herrschaftsformen der Frühstaufer in Reichsitalien* 2:669–99.
22. Morena, *Libellus de rebus a Frederico imperatore gestis*, pp. 198–203. On the continuation of the Morena chronicle, see Schmale edition, pp. 10–11.
23. Otto of Freising and Rahewin, *Deeds* 4.8; and DFI, no. 895 (17 January–July 1185; indictment of Cremona). Gertrud Deibel, "Die italienischen Einkünfte Kaiser Friedrich Barbarossas," *Neue Heidelberger Jahrbücher*, NF, 1932, pp. 21–58 (pp. 22–42 lists all the references to Frederick's income); idem, "Die finanzielle Bedeutung Reichs-Italiens für die staufischen Herrscher des zwölften Jahrhunderts," *ZRG GA* 54 (1934): 134–77; Brühl, *Fodrum, gistum, servitium regis* 2:745–57 (Brühl quotes Robert of Torigny on p. 750); idem, "Die Finanzpolitik Friedrich Barbarossas in Italien," pp. 13–37; and Haverkamp, *Herrschaftsformen der Frühstaufer in Reichsitalien* 2:699–728, esp. pp. 711–12. On Deibel's economic rationalization of Frederick's actions, see Görich, "Konflikt und Kompromiss," p. 79.
24. Morena, *Libellus de rebus a Frederico imperatore gestis*, pp. 196–97; *Narratio de Longobardie obpressione*, pp. 284–85; *Recueil des historiens des Gaules et de la France* 16:210–212, esp. p. 211 (letter notifying Thomas Becket of Octavian's death); DFI, no. 445 (9 June 1164; Frederick's charter for Rainald) and DFI, no. 480 (1 June 1165; Frederick's circular announcing the decision of the Würzburg court, which includes a list of Paschal's electors); and "Epistola amici ad Alexandrum papam," in James Craigie Robertson, *Materials for the History of Thomas Becket, Archbishop of Canterbury (Canonized by Pope Alexander III, A.D. 1173)*, 7 vols, in Rerum Britannicarum medii aevi scriptores 67 (London, 1875–85; reprint, n.p., 1965) 5:184–91, nos. 98–99. Opll, RI IV2/2:197, nos. 1350–52, lists the chronicles that mention Paschal's election. See Herkenrath, "Reinald von Dassel," pp. 238–46 (Rainald acted without consulting Frederick); Georgi, *Friedrich Barbarossa und die auswärtigen Mächte*, pp. 86–90; Görich, *Die Ehre Friedrich Barbarossas*, pp. 144–45 (stressed Frederick's hesitation); Kluger, "Friedrich Barbarossa und sein Ratgeber Rainald von Dassel," p. 35, n. 28 (rejected the view that Rainald acted on his own); Laudage, *Alexander III. und Friedrich Barbarossa*, pp. 152–54; and Johrendt, "The Empire and the Schism," pp. 113–14.
25. Dopsch, *Geschichte Salzburgs* 1/1:284–85 and 296–97. Conrad of Mainz became archbishop of Salzburg in 1177.
26. John of Salisbury, *Letters* 2:100–17, no. 169 (June 1166), esp. pp. 102–03.
27. RI IV2/2:224–26, nos. 1466 and 1470–71; and *Recueil des historiens des Gaules et de la France* 16:120–21, no. 369 (May 1165; letter of Rainald to Louis VII), and p. 238, no. 32 (Archbishop Rotrou to Cardinal Henry). On the crusading component, see Georgi, *Friedrich Barbarossa und die auswärtigen Mächte*, pp. 117–22 and 126–36; on the English chroniclers, see Hanna Vollrath, "Lüge oder Fälschung? Die Überlieferung von Barbarossas Hoftag zu Würzburg

im Jahre 1165 und der Becket-Streit," in Weinfurter, ed., *Stauferreich im Wandel*, pp. 149–60; on Wichmann, see Claude, *Geschichte des Erzbistums Magdeburg* 2:164; and on the marriage alliance, see Weller, *Die Heiratspolitik des deutschen Hochadels im 12. Jahrhundert*, pp. 101–07 and 263–64.

28. "Epistola amici ad Alexandrum papam," in Robertson, *Materials for the History of Thomas Becket* 5:184–91, no. 98 (longer version) and no. 99 (shorter version). Laudage argued in *Alexander III. und Friedrich Barbarossa*, pp. 159–66, that the longer version, the purported letter, is a falsified version of an eyewitness account contained in the shorter text. Görich, *Die Ehre Friedrich Barbarossas*, pp. 452–53, n. 267; Vollrath, "Lüge oder Fälschung?," pp. 162–65; and most recently, Johrendt, "The Empire and the Schism," p. 115, n. 91 and n. 94, rejected Laudage's argument. On Rainald's refusal to be ordained and consecrated, see Kluger, "Friedrich Barbarossa und sein Ratgeber Rainald von Dassel," pp. 31–32. On his ordination and, consecration, see *Chronica regia Coloniensis*, p. 116. On John of Oxford's oath, see John of Salisbury, *Letters* 2:100–17, no. 168, esp. pp. 112–13.

29. DFI, no. 480 (1 June 1165; circular sent to Henry of Troyes; also in *Constitutiones* 1:314–16, no. 223); no. 481 (2 June; general circular sent to all the magnates; also *Constitutiones* 1:316–18, no. 224); no. 482 (early June; sent to the clergy and ministerials of the church of Passau; also *Constitutiones* 1:318–320, no. 225); and no. 483 (early June; sent to Abbot Erlebold of Stavelot, Wibald's brother; also *Constitutiones* 1:318–20, no. 225). On Frederick's commitment to clerics who, having been ordained and consecrated by schismatic bishops, were seen as an obstacle to peace, see John of Salisbury, *Letters* 2:650–59, no. 289, esp. pp. 656–59.

30. Robertson, *Materials for the History of Thomas Becket* 5:285–86, no. 156 (Herbert of Bosham to Alexander); John of Salisbury, *Letters* 2:122–27, no. 171, esp. pp. 124–27; pp. 178–85, no. 177, esp. pp. 182–85 (Frederick's question); pp. 346–53, no. 213, esp. pp. 348–49; and pp. 352–55, no. 214 (John's anger at Alexander's absolution of John of Oxford); and RI IV2/2:239, no. 1516. Excerpts from the letters of the unknown friend may be found in Giesebrecht and Simson, *Geschichte der deutschen Kaiserzeit* 6:452–54. Giesebrecht 5/2:499–500 presented Henry as two-faced. For a conventional view of the negotiations between Henry and Frederick, see Georgi, *Friedrich Barbarossa und die auswärtigen Mächte*, pp. 117–49. Vollrath, "Lüge oder Fälschung?" pp. 161–71, argued that the marriage alliance was not directed against Alexander but that Frederick thought it was. Johrendt, "The Empire and the Schism," pp. 115–16, n. 95, accepted her interpretation.

31. DFI, no 480, p. 396, ll. 28–32; no. 484 (before 24 June 1165); and John of Salisbury, *Letters*, 2:68–71, no. 158, esp. pp. 68–69, n. 1; and pp. 590–99, no. 277 esp. pp. 592–93. See Georgi, *Friedrich Barbarossa und die auswärtigen Mächte*, pp. 140–44; Bruno Galland, "Les relations entre la France et l'Empire au XIIe siècle," in Kölzer, *Die Staufer im Süden*, p. 65; and Herkenrath, "Reinald von Dassel," pp. 361–69 (on Gerard Pucelle).

32. Gerhoch of Reichersberg, *Annales Reicherspergenses*, p. 472; and RI IV2/2:232–33, nos. 1492 and 1495. See Johrendt, "The Empire and the Schism," p. 116, n. 99.

33. DFI, no. 494 (after 4 October 1165; also *Constitutiones* 1:320–21, no. 226); no. 500 (29 December 1165); and no. 539 (September 1167; also *Constitutiones* 1:326–27, no. 231). Nicholas probably recognized Alexander as pope before his death on 1 July 1167. See John of Salisbury, *Letters* 2:590–99, no. 277 esp. pp. 594–95, n. 10.

34. John of Salisbury, *Letters* 2:50–57, no. 152, esp. pp. 54–55. See Dopsch, *Geschichte Salzburgs* 1/1:296–97; and Uebach, *Die Ratgeber Friedrich Barbarossas*, pp. 221–24.

35. Gerhoch of Reichersberg, *Annales Reicherspergenses*, pp. 470–75; DFI, no. 438 (May–August 1165; summons of Salzburg ministerials) and no. 508 (after 29 March 1166; letter to counts of Plain). See Dopsch, *Geschichte Salzburgs* 1/1:285–88.

36. Johrendt, "The Empire and the Schism," p. 114, n. 88, and pp. 124–25, esp. n. 148 and n. 149. Johrendt said that only eleven churches in the "extensive Mainz province," three of them before 1164, sought such privileges. The problem is that he did not know, seemingly, which dioceses comprised the province. He included churches situated in the dioceses of Sion (Sitten), Lausanne, and Geneva, none of which was subject to Mainz or situated in the German kingdom. The results might have been different if he had looked at the correct dioceses.

37. Robertson, *Materials for the History of Thomas Becket* 5:286, no. 156; and RI IV2/2:243–44, no. 1533. On Welf VI, see Schneidmüller, *Die Welfen*, p. 198.

38. Gerhoch of Reichersberg, *Opusculum ad cardinales*, in Odulf van den Eynde, ed., *Gerhohi praepositi Reichersbergensis opera inedita 1: Tractatus et libelli* (Rome, 1955), pp. 309–50. See Görich, *Die Ehre Friedrich Barbarossas*, pp. 147–56.
39. DFI, no. 502 (8 January 1166); *Chronica regia Coloniensis*, p. 116; *Ex Gaufridi de Bruil prioris Vosiensis Chronica*, ed. Oswald Holder-Egger, in MGH SS 26 (Hanover, 1882), p. 202 (on the reliquary); Emerton, *The Correspondence of Pope Gregory VII*, pp. 166–75, esp. p. 172 (Gregory VII to Hermann of Metz); and RI IV2/2:243–45, nos. 1530 and 1539. See Jürgen Petersohn, "Saint-Denis—Westminster—Aachen: Die Karls-Translatio von 1165 und ihre Vorbilder," in DA 31 (1975): 420–54; Michael Borgolte, "Über Typologie und Chronologie des Königskanonikats im europäischen Mittelalters," *DA* 48 (1991): 19–44; Göldel, *Servitium regis und Tafelgüterverzeichnis*, pp. 166–78; Laudage, *Alexander III. und Friedrich Barbarossa*, pp. 167–71; Schwedler, "Kaisertradition und Innovation," pp. 238–42; Horch, *"Nach dem Bild des Kaisers,"* pp. 163–71, esp. p. 169 (the date Charlemagne's privilege was forged); and Hlawitschka, *Die Ahnen der hochmittelalterlichen deutschen Könige* 1/1, Plate XXX, and 1/2:607–09 (the Confessor's place in Henry II's ancestry). Görich, *Friedrich Barbarossa*, pp. 633–36, argued that Frederick's use of the first-person plural in describing his removal of the bones from their tomb ("elevavimus") does not mean that he acted alone; but the *Cologne Royal Chronicle* depicted the princes as onlookers rather than participants in the translation of the relics. Görich also questioned whether the canonization was a response to the desacralization of royal authority during the Investiture Conflict—for example, the charter did not use the term *sacrum imperium*—but he ignored that there were several other such royal canonizations in the twelfth century and that Frederick was acting at Henry II's request. Latowsky, *Emperor of the World*, pp. 5–6, 186–88, and 215–50, contended that the canonization was not staged primarily to counter Capetian claims to Charlemagne, whose cult became important in France only in the thirteenth century, but rather to assert the autonomy of imperial leadership of the world.
40. *Chronica regia Coloniensis*, p. 116; and *Die Zeit der Staufer* 1: *Katalog*: 396–98, no. 537; 2: *Abbildungen*, Abb. 326 and 327. See Sauerländer, "Dynastisches Mäzenatentum der Staufer und Welfen," pp. 122–23; and Horch, *"Nach dem Bild des Kaisers,"* pp. 155–63 and 168–71. For the Latin text of the inscription, see Horch, p. 156, n. 691 (a German translation is in the text).
41. *Die Zeit der Staufer* 1: *Katalog*: 398–99, no. 538; 2: *Abbildungen*, Abb. 328; and RI IV2/2:239, no. 1519 (birth of Henry VI). See Horch, *"Nach dem Bild des Kaisers,"* pp. 165–68 and 178–80; and Latowsky, *Emperor of the World*, pp. 183–99.
42. Boso, *Les vies des papes*, pp. 412–13 (*Boso's Life of Alexander III*, pp. 65–67); *Romoaldi II. archiepiscopi Salernitani Annales*, p. 434; and John of Salisbury, *Letters* 2:52–55, no. 152. See Laudage, *Alexander III. und Friedrich Barbarossa*, pp. 171–80; Petersohn, *Kaisertum und Rom in spätsalischer und staufischer Zeit*, pp. 202–09; and Doran, "'At last we have reached the port of salvation,'" pp. 74–78.
43. Boso, *Les vies des papes*, pp. 415 and 419–20 (*Boso Life of Alexander III*, pp. 69–70 and 76–77); and Otto of Freising and Rahewin, *Deeds* (Simson edition), Appendix, p. 348 (Mierow translation, p. 336; Hungarian mission). See Georgi, *Friedrich Barbarossa und die auswärtigen Mächte*, pp. 163–72; Hödl, "Ungarn in der Aussenpolitik Friedrich Barbarossas," p. 137; Laudage, *Alexander III. und Friedrich Barbarossa*, pp. 175–80; and Eleni Tounta, "Byzanz als Vorbild Friedrich Barbarossas," in Burkhardt et al., eds, *Staufisches Kaisertum im 12. Jahrhundert*, pp. 163–66. It is impossible to determine with certainty the relationship, if any, between Manuel's Roman initiative and Frederick's embassy to Manuel because the dates of both are uncertain. For example, Uebach, *Die Ratgeber Friedrich Barbarossas*, pp. 208–09, placed the imperial mission to Manuel in April or May 1166; whereas Tounta, p. 165, put it in October.
44. *Chronicon Montis Sereni* (under 1165), p. 152; RI IV2/2:247, no. 1545, and p. 255, no. 1577; and *Codex Falkensteinensis*. See Freed, "Artistic and Literary Representations of Family Consciousness," pp. 233–45; and idem, "The Creation of the *Codex Falkensteinensis* (1166): Self-Representation and Reality," in Weiler and MacLean, eds, *Representations of Power in Medieval Germany*, pp. 189–210. On the use of mercenaries, see Herbert Grundmann, "Rotten und Brabanzonen: Söldner-Heere im 12. Jahrhundert," *DA* 5 (1942): 419–92, esp.

pp. 436–64; and Krieger, "Obligatory Military Service and the Use of Mercenaries," in Haverkamp and Vollrath, eds, *England and Germany in the High Middle Ages*, pp. 164–68.

45. *Chronica regia Coloniensis*, pp. 116–17 and 119; Vincent of Prague, *Annales*, pp. 682–83; Morena, *Libellus de rebus a Frederico imperatore gestis*, pp. 202–03; Boso, *Les vies des papes*, pp. 413–14 (*Boso's Life of Alexander III*, p. 68); *Narratio de Longobardie obpressione*, pp. 288–89; and RI IV2/2:257–62, nos. 1585, 1589–90, 1592–99, 1602–07, 1610, and 1612. Berthold witnessed a charter outside Rimini on 23 April 1166 (no. 531). Some other German princes who were also present were: the bishops of Verden, Liège, Speyer, Strasbourg, and Basel; the abbot of Stavelot; Margrave Dietrich of Lusatia; and Dukes Theobald and Oldřich of Bohemia.

46. Vincent of Prague, *Annales*, p. 683; Morena, *Libellus de rebus a Frederico imperatore gestis*, pp. 202–05; *Narratio de Longobardie obpressione*, pp. 288–89; Boso, *Les vies des papes*, pp. 413–14 (*Boso's Life of Alexander III*, p. 68); Otto of Freising and Rahewin, *Deeds* (Simson edition), Appendix, p. 348 (under 1168) (Mierow translation, p. 336); *Historia Welforum*, pp. 84–87, ch. 32; and RI IV2/2:263–73, nos. 1614–18, 1625–26, 1630–35, 1638–39, 1642, 1644, 1653, and 1655. See Petersohn, *Kaisertum und Rom in spätsalischer und staufischer Zeit*, pp. 211–12; and Schneidmüller, *Die Welfen*, p. 200.

47. Boso, *Les vies des papes*, pp. 412 and 414 (*Boso's Life of Alexander III*, pp. 65 and 69); Morena, *Libellus de rebus a Frederico imperatore gestis*, pp. 204–19; *Narratio de Longobardie obpressione*, pp. 288–91; Vincent of Prague, *Annales*, p. 683; DFI, no. 895 (17 January–July 1185; also *Constitutiones* 1:426–28, no. 302; indictment of Cremona); and RI IV2/2:270–86, nos. 1643, 1646–47, 1660, and 1704. See Opll, *Stadt und Reich im 12. Jahrhundert*, pp. 208–09 (Bergamo), p. 225 (Brescia), pp. 256–57 (Cremona), pp. 302–04 (Lodi), pp. 348–49 (Mantua), pp. 334–36 (Milan), and pp. 382–83 (Piacenza); idem, "Friedrich Barbarossa und die Stadt Lodi," pp. 81–85; Raccagni, *The Lombard League*, pp. 36–42; and Alfred Haverkamp, "Der Konstanzer Friede zwischen Kaiser und Lombardenbund (1183)," in Maurer, ed., *Kommunale Bündnisse*, p. 18 (on the reasons for Cremona's dissatisfaction).

48. Boso, *Les vies des papes*, pp. 415–16 (*Boso's Life of Alexander III*, pp. 70–71); Morena, *Libellus de rebus a Frederico imperatore gestis*, pp. 218–21; *Chronica regia Coloniensis*, p. 117; Vincent of Prague, *Annales*, p. 683; Otto of St. Blasien, *Chronica*, pp. 52–57; and RI IV2/2:273–76, nos. 1657, 1662, and 1664. The chroniclers give widely divergent figures for the number of Romans who were captured or killed (see no. 1664). See Petersohn, *Kaisertum und Rom in spätsalischer und staufischer Zeit*, pp. 214–16.

49. Boso, *Les vies des papes*, pp. 414 and 416–17 (*Boso's Life of Alexander III*, pp. 68 and 71–73); Morena, *Libellus de rebus a Frederico imperatore gestis*, pp. 204–05 and 222–27; Vincent of Prague, *Annales*, p. 683; *Chronica regia Coloniensis*, p. 118; *Historia Welforum*, pp. 86–87; Otto of St. Blasien, *Chronica*, pp. 58–59; Burchard of Ursberg, *Chronicon*, pp. 186–89; and RI IV2/2:274–83, nos. 1659, 1665–67, 1670–74, 1677–85, 1687–88, 1690, and 1692–94. I am following Petersohn's reconstruction of these events in *Kaisertum und Rom in spätsalischer und staufischer Zeit*, pp. 214–20.

50. *Chronica regia Coloniensis*, p. 118 (also DFI, no. 533; and *Constitutiones* 1:324–25, no. 229); Morena, *Libellus de rebus a Frederico imperatore gestis*, pp. 226–27; and Boso, *Les vies des papes*, p. 418 (*Boso's Life of Alexander III*, p. 74). See Jürgen Petersohn, "Der Vertrag des Römischen Senats mit Papst Clemens III. (1188) und das Pactum Friedrich Barbarossas mit den Römern," *MIÖG* 82 (1974): 289–337; idem, *Kaisertum und Rom in spätsalischer und staufischer Zeit*, pp. 225–42; and Tounta, "Byzanz als Vorbild Friedrich Barbarossas," pp. 161–66.

51. Morena, *Libellus de rebus a Frederico imperatore gestis*, pp. 226–31; *Chronica regia Coloniensis*, p. 117; and RI IV2/2:283, nos. 1695–96.

52. Boso, *Les vies des papes*, p. 418 (*Boso's Life of Alexander III*, p. 74).

53. Ibid.; DFI, no. 534 (6 August 1167); Morena, *Libellus de rebus a Frederico imperatore gestis*, pp. 228–31; *Chronica regia Coloniensis*, pp. 118–19; and *Annales Cameracenses*, pp. 539–40. John of Salisbury repeatedly depicted the annihilation of Frederick's army as a divine judgment. See *Letters* 2:370–79, no. 219, esp. pp. 376–77; pp. 388–95, no. 225, esp. pp. 392–95; pp. 394–97, no. 226; pp. 426–33, no. 234, esp. pp. 430–31; pp. 452–57, no. 239, esp. pp. 454–55; and pp. 456–61, no. 240, esp. pp. 458–59. Dozens of chroniclers mentioned the destruction of Frederick's army and named the dead, sometimes erroneously. For a complete listing, see RI

IV2/2:283–85, no. 1697. My account is based on Herde, *Die Katastrophe vor Rom im August 1167*.

54. Morena, *Libellus de rebus a Frederico imperatore gestis*, pp. 230–33; Boso, *Les vies des papes*, p. 418 (*Boso's Life of Alexander III*, pp. 74–75); Godfrey of Viterbo, *Gesta Friderici*, vs. 715–62; and RI IV2/2:286–92, nos. 1701–02, 1707, 1709–24, and 1730. See Opll, *Stadt und Reich im 12. Jahrhundert*, pp. 256–57 (Cremona), 304 (Lodi), and 314 (Lucca).
55. Morena, *Libellus de rebus a Frederico imperatore gestis*, pp. 232–35; *Narratio de Longobardie obpressione*, pp. 290–91; John of Salisbury, *Letters* 2:438–47, no. 236, esp. pp. 446–47; pp. 456–61, no. 240, esp. pp. 458–59; and pp. 552–71, no. 272, esp. pp. 552–55; and RI IV2/2:293–98, nos. 1732–40, 1742–49, 1752–60, and 1765. See Haverkamp, "Der Konstanzer Friede," pp. 17–18; and Raccagni, *The Lombard League*, pp. 42–45.
56. See John of Salisbury, *Letters* 2:40–41, no. 146 (quotation); pp. 438–47, no. 236, esp. pp. 446–47; pp. 452–57, no. 239, esp. pp. 454–55; pp. 456–61, no. 240, esp. pp. 458–59; pp. 472–79, no. 242, esp. pp. 472–75 and p. 474, n. 4 (John drew the parallel with Gregory VII here); pp. 552–71, no. 272, esp. pp. 552–53; pp. 570–73, no. 273; and pp. 574–79, no. 274, esp. pp. 574–75. On Frederick's gout, see 2:630–35, no. 287, esp. pp. 632–33.
57. *Die Admonter Briefsammlung*, pp. 174–75, no. 16; John of Salisbury, *Letters* 2:552–71, no. 272, esp. pp. 552–61; Otto of St. Blasien, *Chronicle*, pp. 60–63, ch. 20; Godfrey of Viterbo, *Gesta Friderici I.*, vs. 763–828 and 865–69; and RI IV2/2:298–301, nos. 1764, 1766, 1768, and 1773–75. See Görich, *Ein Kartäuser im Dienst Friedrich Barbarossas*, pp. 35–54; Opll, *Stadt und Reich im 12. Jahrhundert*, p. 452 (Turin); and Hlawitschka, *Die Ahnen der hochmittelalterlichen deutschen Könige* 3:346–48 (on the Montferrat–Savoy connection). On the Siebenichs, see Keupp, *Dienst und Verdienst*, pp. 240–45. Keupp, pp. 244–45, doubted that the knight was really Hartmann of Siebenich because his presence at the imperial court cannot be documented during the fourth expedition, although on pp. 466–67 Keupp treated the identification as if it were true. However, our knowledge of who was at court is so fragmentary that Hartmann's failure to appear in a witness list is not sufficient to invalidate Otto of St. Blasien's report.
58. DFI, no. 535 (after 14 August 1167).
59. DFI, no. 538 (autumn 1167; also *Constitutiones* 1:325–26, no. 230; and *Die Admonter Briefsammlung*, pp. 73–74, no. 37); and Otto of Freising and Rahewin, *Deeds*, Appendix (Simson edition), p. 350 (under 1168; Mierow translation, p. 338). On the letter, see Benson, "Political *Renovatio*," pp. 379–83; the translation is on p. 381. On the use of *Teutonicorum (Teutonicum) imperium*, see Schwarz, *Herrscher- und Reichstitel bei Kaisertum und Papsttum*, pp. 98–101. The term, *Teutonicum imperium*, also appears in DFI, no. 487 (23 June 1165); but see the head note, p. 406, and Schwarz's concurring explanation for this usage.
60. Schwarz, *Herrscher- und Reichstitel bei Kaisertum und Papsttum*, pp. 86–96; and Krieg, *Herrscherdarstellung in der Stauferzeit*, pp. 99–115 and 296–98. See above, pp. 199–201, on the use of *sacrum imperium* and pp. 290–91 on the use and abandonment of triumphal language.

Chapter 13 A Bitter Homecoming

1. DFI, nos. 544 (10 January 1168, Turin) and 545 (28 June 1168, Würzburg); RI IV2/4:x–xv; and Plassmann, *Die Struktur des Hofes unter Friedrich I. Barbarossa*, pp. 14–15.
2. John of Salisbury, *Letters* 2:572–73, no. 273.
3. RI IV2/3:3–17, nos. 1779–1832 (on the itinerary); DFI, no. 546 ("The Golden Liberty"); *Annales Palidenses auctore Theodoro monacho*, ed. Georg Heinrich Pertz, in MGH SS 16 (Hanover, 1859), p. 94; and Otto of Freising and Rahewin, *Deeds*, Appendix, Simson edition, pp. 350–51 (Mierow translation, pp. 338–39; forced consecrations). On Frederick's itinerary in 1152, see pp. 88–90. On the "Golden Liberty," see pp. 165–66.
4. Boso, *Les vies des papes*, p. 420 (*Boso's Life of Alexander III*, p. 78); and RI IV2/3:10–13, nos. 1801, 1810, and 1813–15. The main contemporary source on the negotiations is the *Annales Cameracenses*, p. 545, which presented the imperial envoys as mediators between the two kings. The Appendix to Otto of Freising's *Deeds* also said that Frederick was seeking to make

peace between the two Western monarchs (Simson edition, p. 350 [Mierow translation, p. 338]). In contrast, Gervase of Canterbury, writing after 1188, reported that Frederick was trying to ally with Henry against Louis and to get him to recognize the anti-pope. *E Gervasii Cantuariensis Chronica*, p. 299, and *E Gestis regum*, p. 308, ed. Felix Liebermann and Reinhold Pauli, in MGH SS 27 (Hanover, 1885). Gervase seemingly confused the events of 1165 and 1168. I have relied on Georgi's reconstruction of these events in *Friedrich Barbarossa und die auswärtigen Mächte*, pp. 248–50 and 258–69.

5. RI IV2/3:16–20, nos. 1827, 1833, 1839, and 1840; John of Salisbury, *Letters* 2:648–49, no. 288 (c. February 1169; summoning of the abbots), and pp. 656–66, no. 289 (probably late August 1169; report on the mission to the pope); and Otto of Freising and Rahewin, *Deeds*, Appendix, Simson edition, p. 351 (Mierow translation, p. 339; Eberhard of Bamberg). See Georgi, *Friedrich Barbarossa und die auswärtigen Mächte*, pp. 270–71; Laudage, *Alexander III. und Friedrich Barbarossa*, pp. 187–88; Görich, *Die Ehre Friedrich Barbarossas*, pp. 157–58; and Johrendt, "The Empire and the Schism," pp. 118–20.
6. RI IV2/3:18–22, nos. 1834, 1839, and 1847; *Chronica regia Coloniensis*, p. 120 (April court in Bamberg and coronation); Magnus of Reichersberg, *Chronicon*, ed. Wilhelm Wattenbach, in MGH SS 17 (Hanover, 1861), pp. 489–90 (election held in Bamberg around Pentecost and legates representing Calixtus were present); *Annales Pegavienses et Bosovienses*, ed. Georg Heinrich Pertz, in MGH SS 16 (Hanover, 1859), p. 260 (Christian nominated Henry at court held in Bamberg); *Annales Palidenses*, p. 94 (election occurred on 24 June in Erfurt); and *Annales Cameracenses*, p. 550 (coronation). See Schmidt, *Königswahl und Thronfolge im 12. Jahrhundert*, pp. 180–85. Csendes, *Heinrich VI.*, p. 40, suggested that the election might have occurred on 19 June, Corpus Christi; but that feast was introduced into the church calendar only in the thirteenth century.
7. DFI, no. 502 (8 January 1166); and no. 547 (29 September 1168). See Baaken, "Die Altersfolge der Söhne Friedrich Barbarossas," pp. 1–29; and Schmidt, *Königswahl und Thronfolge im 12. Jahrhundert*, pp. 173–94. Csendes, *Heinrich VI.*, pp. 36–37, argued that Henry was Frederick's oldest surviving son in 1169 because the Duke Frederick who was named in 1168 was Frederick VI, since it is not likely that the death of even a child duke would have gone completely unnoticed. However, it is equally implausible, given the high rate of child mortality, that John would have bothered to describe Henry as the second son if his older brother was already dead.
8. DFI, no. 573 (autumn 1170), and no. 575 (mid-February 1171); and RI IV2/3:38–43, nos. 1899–1904, and 1917–19. See Georgi, *Friedrich Barbarossa und die auswärtigen Mächte*, pp. 268 and 273–84; Fried, "Friedrich Barbarossas Krönung in Arles," pp. 356–61, and Weller, *Die Heiratspolitik des deutschen Hochadels im 12. Jahrhundert*, pp. 106–10.
9. Boso, *Les vies des papes*, pp. 420–22 (*Boso's Life of Alexander III*, pp. 78–80); *Chronica regia Coloniensis*, p. 120; RI IV2/3:27–34, nos. 1866, 1875, and 1883; Georgi, *Friedrich Barbarossa und die auswärtigen Mächte*, pp. 271–72; Laudage, *Alexander III. und Friedrich Barbarossa*, pp. 188–91; and Görich, *Die Ehre Friedrich Barbarossas*, pp. 158–60.
10. *Chronica regia Coloniensis*, pp. 121–25; *Historia ducum Veneticorum*, pp. 78–82; *Romoaldi II. archiepiscopi Salernitani Annales*, pp. 439 and 441; Arnold of Lübeck, *Chronica Slavorum*, pp. 117–25; and RI IV2/3:36–122, nos. 1891, 1931, 1946–47, 1957–59, 1961, 1963, 1968–74, 1981, 1983–86, 1992–94, 1999–2000, 2005–06, 2017–21, 2024, 2035, 2040, 2050, 2052, 2055, 2070–72, 2081, and 2154. I have relied on Georgi, *Friedrich Barbarossa und die auswärtigen Mächte*, pp. 180–247, and Weller, *Die Heiratspolitik des deutschen Hochadels im 12. Jahrhundert*, pp. 110–16 and 168–70, to reconstruct Frederick's diplomatic initiatives in the early 1170s. On Henry the Lion's pilgrimage, which was long perceived as directed against Frederick, see Ehlers, *Heinrich der Löwe*, pp. 197–211; and on Frederick's relations with Venice, see Härtl, "Friedrich I. und die Länder an der oberen Adria," pp. 294–301.
11. *Die Admonter Briefsammlung*, pp. 153–59, nos. 2–5; pp. 160–63, nos. 7 and 8; pp. 166–72, nos. 11–14; pp. 175–76, no. 17; pp. 187–89, nos. 28 and 29; pp. 196–97, nos. 34 and 35; and pp. 204–14, nos. 3–9; DFI, no. 560 (22 February 1170, St. Zeno); no. 562 (3 March 1170, St. Lambrecht); no. 563 (10 March 1170, Gurk); and no. 564 (19 March 1170, St. Paul); *Annales Sancti Rudberti Salisburgenses*, ed. Wilhelm Wattenbach, in MGH SS 9 (Hanover, 1851), pp. 776–77; Magnus of Reichersberg, *Chronicon*, pp. 489–90 and 497–506; *Historia*

calamitatum ecclesiae Salzburgensis, pp. 1543–44 and 1549–52; and RI IV2/3:17–133, nos. 1832, 1837, 1839, 1846, 1867–68, 1871–74, 1948, 1956, 1964–66, 2023, 2081, and 2191. I have relied largely on Dopsch, *Geschichte Salzburgs* 1/1:288–96, in relating these events. See also Görich, *Die Ehre Friedrich Barbarossas*, pp. 79–91.

12. *Continuatio Gerlaci abbatis Milovicensis a 1167–1198*, ed. Wilhelm Wattenbach, in MGH SS 17 (Hanover, 1861), pp. 685–87; and RI IV2/3:81–82, no. 2038. See Wolverton, *Hastening Toward Prague*, pp. 210–20.
13. DFI, no. 636 (end of 1174 or the beginning of 1175). Frederick's so-called blood relative, Bishop Frederick, shared a grandmother with Barbarossa's brother-in-law, Landgrave Louis II of Thuringia. Scholars have no idea how Jerome was related to the emperor. See Schieffer, "Friedrich Barbarossa und seine Verwandten," pp. 586 and 588.
14. *Continuatio Gerlaci abbatis Milovicensis*, pp. 688–690; DFI, no. 782 (1 July 1179); and RI IV2/3:236–40, nos. 2493 and 2503. See Kejř, "Böhmen und das Reich unter Friedrich I.," pp. 257–64; and Wolverton, *Hastening Toward Prague*, esp. pp. 43–44, 104–05 (Přemyslid genealogy), and pp. 186–276 (a detailed discussion of imperial–Bohemian relations). Kejř, p. 264, referred to the events of 1173 and 1178 as the low point in Bohemia's relations with the Reich; whereas Wolverton, who sees the Přemyslids as manipulating imperial authority for their advantage, has a section titled "Last Quarter of the Twelfth Century: Dark Days?" (pp. 218–24). On the delineation of the Austro-Bohemian border, see Lechner, *Die Babenberger*, pp. 168–69.
15. *Continuatio Gerlaci abbatis Milovicensis*, p. 693; and Kejř, "Böhmen und das Reich unter Friedrich I.," pp. 264–73. I have taken the translation from Wolverton, *Hastening Toward Prague*, pp. 246–47.
16. *Continuatio Gerlaci abbatis Milovicensis*, pp. 692–93; DFI, no. 953 (11 November 1186); and Kejř, "Böhmen und das Reich unter Friedrich I.," pp. 277–82. I have taken the translation from Wolverton, *Hastening Toward Prague*, pp. 257–58.
17. Kejř, "Böhmen und das Reich unter Friedrich I.," pp. 273–77.
18. Otto of St. Blasien, *Chronicle,* pp. 62–63, ch. 21; *Historia Welforum cum continuatione Steingademensi*, pp. 86–91; RI IV2/3:110, no. 2121; and pp. 230–31, no. 2477. Ehlers, *Heinrich der Löwe*, pp. 214–15 and 329–30, thought that the tension between the cousins may have originated with Welf's alienation of his Italian holdings (p. 215) and pointed out that Henry witnessed his last imperial charter on 6 July 1174 (DFI, no. 623), six years before his deposition. Hechberger, *Staufer und Welfen*, pp. 288–93, argued there is no reason to believe that Welf preferred Henry over Frederick simply because he was a brother's son and even raised the possibility that Welf might have been one of Henry's Swabian peers who condemned him in 1179–80.
19. Otto of St. Blasien, *Chronicle*, pp. 62–65, ch. 21; and DFI, no. 566 (15 May 1170) and no. 596 (20 February 1173). See Schmid, *Graf Rudolf von Pfullendorf*, pp. 89–119 and 169–93.
20. Otto of St. Blasien, *Chronicle*, pp. 64–65, ch. 21. See Maurer, *Der Herzog von Schwaben*, pp. 268–300.
21. Otto of St. Blasien, *Chronicle*, pp. 62–65, ch. 21; and DFI, no. 577 (1 May 1177; Augsburg fiefs). On the advocacy of Augsburg, see Opll, *Stadt und Reich im 12. Jahrhundert*, p. 38. For a general discussion of how Frederick provided for his sons, see Leyser, "Frederick Barbarossa and the Hohenstaufen Polity," pp. 165–73.
22. DFI, no. 624 (between August 1167 and 13 July 1174), and no. 625 (13 July 1174); RI IV2/3:98–99, nos. 2086–87; and *Salzburger Urkundenbuch* 3:160–61, no. 655 (22 March 1213; transfer of the Lungau to Salzburg). See Ernst Klebel, *Der Lungau: Historisch-politische Untersuchung* (Salzburg, 1960), pp. 12–21; and Dendorfer, *Adelige Gruppenbildung*, esp. pp. 227–29, 287–95, and 306–14. Opll, RI IV2/3:98–99, dated no. 2086 (DFI, no. 624) between August 1167 and 13 July 1174, but gave the name of the unidentified bishop as Hermann. If Hermann was involved, then the transaction must have occurred after Bishop Eberhard's death on 17 July 1172.
23. DFI, no. 108 (May–June 1155); no. 199 (1 January 1158); no. 600 (7 May 1173, reference to the Pleissenland [line 26]); no. 820 (13 December 1181); no. 836 (25 January 1183; the charter is falsified); and Arnold of Lübeck, *Chronica Slavorum*, p. 246. See Walter Schlesinger,

"Egerland, Vogtland, Pleissenland: Zur Geschichte des Reichsgutes im mitteldeutschen Osten," in idem, *Mitteldeutsche Beiträge zur deutschen Verfassungsgeschichte des Mittelalters* (Göttingen, 1961), pp. 188–211; Bosl, *Die Reichsministerialität der Salier und Staufer* 2:482–546 and Map 7 in the pocket in the rear cover; Patze, "Kaiser Friedrich Barbarossa und der Osten," pp. 359–60; and Opll, *Stadt und Reich im 12. Jahrhundert*, pp. 30–32.

24. DKIII, no. 188 (24 April 1147); *Cronica Reinhardsbrunnensis*, ed. Oswald Holder-Egger, MGH SS 30/1 (Hanover, 1896), pp. 538–39; and RI IV2/3:7, no. 1796; Bosl, *Die Reichsministerialität der Salier und Staufer* 2:546–88 and Maps 4 and 7 in the pocket in the rear cover; and Patze, "Kaiser Friedrich Barbarossa und der Osten," pp. 340–42 and 352–53.
25. *Mainzer Urkundenbuch* 2/2:640–46, no. 392 (between the summer of 1167 and July/August 1177; criticism of Christian); pp. 646–48, no. 393 (before 22 July 1177; Conrad's reluctant acceptance of Christian's retention of Mainz); and pp. 876–85, no. 531 (after May 1189 and before 18 February 1190; Archbishop Conrad's list of Mainz's alienated properties).
26. *Mainzer Urkundenbuch* 2/2:876–85, no. 531 (alienation of Gelnhausen); DFI, no. 571 (25 July 1170, Gelnhausen); no. 572 (25 July 1170 or shortly thereafter, Gelnhausen); and no. 794 (1 April 1180, Wetzlar). See Opll, *Stadt und Reich im 12. Jahrhundert*, pp. 77–83 (Gelnhausen) and pp. 170–71 (Wetzlar); Schwind, "Friedrich Barbarossa und die Städte im Regnum Teutonicum," pp. 493–95; Bosl, *Die Reichsministerialität der Salier und Staufer* 1:287–316; and Keupp, *Dienst und Verdienst*, pp. 106–76, esp. pp. 133–35. On the archaeological findings in Frankfurt and Gelnhausen, see Arens, "Die staufischen Königspfalzen," pp. 133–36.
27. DFI, no. 165 (6 April 1157; also *Constitutiones* 1:225–26, no. 162). See RI IV2/1:109, no. 367; p. 112, no. 376; and pp. 139–40, no. 446. See above, p. 167.
28. DFI, no. 166 (6 April 1157; also *Constitutiones* 1:226–29, no. 163). Guido Kisch, *The Jews in Medieval Germany: A Study of their Legal and Social Status* (Chicago, 1949; 2nd edn., New York, 1970), pp. 96, 101, 134, 138–39, and 142, discussed the privilege as Henry IV's grant. He commented on p. 142, in regard to Frederick's 1157 confirmation, that it was characteristic of the twelfth and thirteenth centuries that "the old persisted by the side of the new, and the abolition of the old was effected only in the measure in which the innovations became more and more cogent."
29. Alexander Patschovsky, "The Relationship between the Jews of Germany and the King (11th–14th Centuries): A European Comparison," in Haverkamp and Vollrath, eds, *England and Germany in the High Middle Ages*, pp. 193–218.
30. DFI, no. 491 (24 September 1165). See Elisabeth Nau, "Münzen und Geld in der Stauferzeit," *Die Zeit der Staufer* 3:98; and Opll, *Stadt und Reich im 12. Jahrhundert*, pp. 174–75.
31. Nau, "Münzen und Geld in der Stauferzeit," *Die Zeit der Staufer* 3:89 and 3:96; and Torsten Fried, "Die Münzpragung unter Friedrich I. Barbarossa in Thüringen," in Engel and Töpfer, eds, *Kaiser Friedrich Barbarossa*, pp. 141–50.
32. DFI, no. 496 (November 1165; also *Constitutiones* 1:323–24, no. 228).
33. DFI, no. 499 (28 December 1165); Andrew of Marchiennes, *Chronica: Continuatio Aquicinctina*, ed. Ludwig Conrad Bethmann, in MGH SS 6 (Hanover, 1844), p. 411 (Flemish privilege); and RI IV2/2:241–42, no. 1526. See Opll, *Stadt und Reich im 12. Jahrhundert*, pp. 65–70; Fried, "Die Wirtschaftspolitik Friedrich Barbarossas in Deutschland," pp. 224–25; and Hugo Stehkämper, "Friedrich Barbarossa und die Stadt Köln: Ein Wirtschaftskrieg am Niederrhein," in Vollrath and Weinfurter, eds, *Köln*, pp. 370–76. Andrew of Marchiennes (c. 1115/20–1202) was the likely author of the continuation of Siegebert of Gembloux's chronicle that was made in the Alsatian Benedictine monastery of Anchin. See Rolf Grosse, "Kaiser und Reich aus der Sicht Frankreichs in der zweiten Hälfte des 12. Jahrhunderts," in Weinfurter, ed., *Stauferreich im Wandel*, pp. 184–86.
34. DKIII, no. 136 (September 1145; Conrad III grants the inhabitants and merchants of Kaiserswerth the same privileges enjoyed by Aachen); and DFI, no. 502 (8 January 1166); and no. 503 (9 January 1166). See Opll, *Stadt und Reich im 12. Jahrhundert*, pp. 27–29; Fried, "Die Wirtschaftspolitik Friedrich Barbarossas in Deutschland," pp. 224–25; Schwind, "Friedrich Barbarossa und die Städte im Regnum Teutonicum," pp. 490–91; Stehkämper, "Friedrich Barbarossa und die Stadt Köln," pp. 370–76; *Die Zeit der Staufer* 1: *Katalog*, p. 114;

2: *Abbildungen*, 94.8 and 94.9 (the Aachen penny); and Kamp, *Moneta regis*, pp. 246–61. Kamp, p. 246, pointed out that only one coin of the type described in the 1166 charter survives and that it was replaced by a lighter coin in 1173. Its circulation must thus have been very limited.

35. DFI, no. 602 (29 May 1173; also *Constitutiones* 1:334–35, no. 239). See Kamp, *Moneta regis*, pp. 353–55; and Stehkämper, "Friedrich Barbarossa und die Stadt Köln," pp. 380–85.
36. DFI, no. 532 (1 August 1167; Andernach). See Odilo Engels, "Der Niederrhein und das Reich im 12. Jahrhundert," in idem, *Stauferstudien*, pp. 188–91; and Opll, *Stadt und Reich im 12. Jahrhundert*, p. 69, for the view that Frederick was seeking as early as 1165 to block Cologne's territorial expansion. Stehkämper, "Friedrich Barbarossa und die Stadt Köln: Ein Wirtschaftskrieg am Niederrhein," pp. 367–413, developed most fully the argument that Frederick and Cologne were engaged in a trade war; but this view can also be found in Opll, pp. 30 and 69; Kamp, *Moneta regis*, pp. 257–58; and Huffman, *The Social Politics of Medieval Diplomacy*, pp. 172–73. Manfred Groten, "Köln und das Reich: Zum Verhältnis von Kirche und Stadt zu den staufischen Herrschern 1151–1198," in Weinfurter, ed., *Stauferreich im Wandel*, pp. 244–45, denied that Barbarossa's measures were either part of a trade war or intended to block Cologne's territorial expansion. The best overall summaries of Barbarossa's economic policies are Fried, "Die Wirtschaftspolitik Friedrich Barbarossas in Deutschland", and Ulf Dirlmeier, "Friedrich Barbarossa—auch ein Wirtschaftspolitiker?" in Haverkamp, ed., *Friedrich Barbarossa*, pp. 501–18. On Rainald's conflict with Frederick's brother, see above, p. 177; and on Frederick's fight with Archbishop Philip, see pp. 468–72.
37. DFI, no. 338, ll. 35–36 (1 September 1161); and DFI, no. 447 (15 June 1164). On Haguenau, see above, pp. 9–10.
38. DFI, no. 43 (29 December 1152); nos 539–41 (September 1167); no. 825 (21 May 1182), and nos. 858–62 (20 June 1184; no. 859 is also in *Constitutiones* 1:424, no. 299; the chief privilege is no. 858); *Annales Cameracenses*, pp. 523–25; and *Gesta episcoporum Cameracensium. Continuatio*, ed. Ludwig Conrad Bethmann, in MGH SS 7 (Hanover, 1846), pp. 501 and 508–10. See Opll, *Stadt und Reich im 12. Jahrhundert*, pp. 58–63; and Schwind, "Friedrich Barbarossa und die Städte im Regnum Teutonicum," pp. 474–79. On Frederick's earlier dealings with Cambrai, see above, pp. 188–90.
39. DFI, no. 799 (18 August 1180; the portions taken from Philip's charter are printed in smaller type). Opll, RI IV2/3:256, no. 2544, placed Frederick's resolution of the conflict at Gelnhausen in April 1180; but all the *Chronica regia Coloniensis* (p. 131) said, after describing the court at Gelnhausen, is that the burghers of Cologne "enlarged the moat around the walls." See Opll, *Stadt und Reich im 12. Jahrhundert*, pp. 98–101; and Schwind, "Friedrich Barbarossa und die Städte im Regnum Teutonicum," pp. 485–86. Stehkämper, "Friedrich Barbarossa und die Stadt Köln," pp. 395–400, presented the privilege as one more incident in Frederick's alleged economic war on the lower Rhine against Cologne and Archbishop Philip, in which he successfully played off the burghers against the archbishop. In contrast, Paul Strait, *Cologne in the Twelfth Century* (Gainesville, FL, 1974), pp. 33–34, discussed the privilege without even naming Frederick.
40. DFI, no. 821 (9 February 1182); and Opll, *Stadt und Reich im 12. Jahrhundert*, pp. 156–60.

Chapter 14 The Fifth Italian Expedition

1. Boso, *Les vies des papes*, p. 427 (*Boso's Life of Alexander III*, p. 88); and *Romoaldi II. archiepiscopi Salernitani Annales*, p. 439.
2. *Chronica regia Coloniensis*, p. 125 (meeting at Avenches); *Narratio de Longobardie obpressione*, pp. 290–91 (8,000 men); *Roberti de Monte cronica*, ed. Ludwig Conrad Bethmann, in MGH SS 6 (Hanover, 1844), p. 524 (empress and children); *Romoaldi II. archiepiscopi Salernitani Annales*, p. 440; Boso, *Les vies des papes*, p. 427 (*Boso's Life of Alexander III*, p. 88); *Continuatio Gerlaci abbatis Milovicensis*, p. 687 (Bohemian troops); DFI, nos. 632–35 and 637 (25 October 1174–26 March 1175); and RI IV2/3:103–12, nos. 2100, 2102–04, 2109, 2111–13, 2122–23, and 2126.

3. *Narratio de Longobardie obpressione*, pp. 290–91; Boso, *Les vies des papes*, p. 427 (*Boso's Life of Alexander III*, p. 88); *Romoaldi II. archiepiscopi Salernitani Annales*, p. 440 (Straw City); Godfrey of Viterbo, *Gesta Friderici I.*, pp. 32–34, vs. 853–94, esp. vs. 880–94; DFI, no. 801 (9 October 1180), and no. 895 (17 January–July 1185); and RI IV2/3:87–107, nos. 2056, 2079, 2104, 2106–08, and 2110. See Opll, *Stadt und Reich im 12. Jahrhundert*, pp. 183–88; Görich, *Die Ehre Friedrich Barbarossas*, pp. 264–66; and Raccagni, *The Lombard League*, pp. 113–18.
4. Boso, *Les vies des papes*, pp. 427–29 (*Boso's Life of Alexander III*, pp. 88–91); *Romoaldi II. archiepiscopi Salernitani Annales*, p. 440; *Narratio de Longobardie obpressione*, pp. 290–93; *Chronica regia Coloniensis*, p. 126; *Continuatio Gerlaci abbatis Milovicensis*, pp. 687–88 (Bohemians); DFI, no. 636 (winter 1174–75; Bohemians); and RI IV2/3:106–13, nos. 2110, 2114, 2125, 2127, and 2129. See Raccagni, *The Lombard League*, pp. 85–88.
5. Boso, *Les vies des papes*, p. 429 (*Boso's Life of Alexander III*, pp. 91–92); *Romoaldi II. archiepiscopi Salernitani Annales*, p. 440; *Chronica regia Coloniensis*, p. 126; and RI IV2/3:113–16, nos. 2130–34 and 2136. The term *brevia*, briefs, appears in the oath the arbiters swore (*Constitutiones* 1:341–42, no. 243).
6. *Constitutiones* 1:342–43, no. 244. See Laudage, *Alexander III. und Friedrich Barbarossa*, pp. 195–98, for why the Lombard brief must have been on the table by 16 April 1175. On the composition of the League, see Raccagni, *The Lombard League*, pp. 55–74.
7. DFI, no. 638 (16–17 April 1175; the text of the notarial instrument is also in *Constitutiones* 1:339–41, no. 242); *Chronica regia Coloniensis*, p. 127; Godfrey of Viterbo, *Gesta Friderici I.*, pp. 36–37, vs. 956–72; Boso, *Les vies des papes*, p. 429 (*Boso's Life of Alexander III*, p. 92); *Romoaldi II. archiepiscopi Salernitani Annales*, p. 440; and RI IV2/3:116, no. 2136. On the Peace of Montebello, see Walter Heinemeyer, "Der Friede von Montebello (1175)," *DA* 11 (1954/55): 101–39; Laudage, *Alexander III. und Friedrich Barbarossa*, pp. 194–200; and Görich, *Die Ehre Friedrich Barbarossas*, pp. 266–72.
8. Boso, *Les vies des papes*, pp. 429–30 (*Boso's Life of Alexander III*, p. 92); *Narratio de Longobardie obpressione*, pp. 290–93; and DFI, no. 639, p. 136, ll. 26–28. See Opll, *Stadt und Reich im 12. Jahrhundert*, p. 257; Haverkamp, "Der Konstanzer Friede," pp. 20–22; Görich, *Die Ehre Friedrich Barbarossas*, p. 267; and Raccagni, *The Lombard League*, pp. 70–71 (on Anselm da Dovara).
9. Boso, *Les vies des papes*, p. 429 (*Boso's Life of Alexander III*, p. 92); Godfrey of Viterbo, *Gesta Friderici I.*, p. 37, vs. 973–78 (reception in Pavia); *Chronica regia Coloniensis*, p. 127; *Continuatio Gerlaci abbatis Milovicensis*, p. 688; *Narratio de Longobardie obpressione*, pp. 292–93; and RI IV2/3:117, no. 2140.
10. Boso, *Les vies des papes*, pp. 430–32 (*Boso's Life of Alexander III*, pp. 92–96); *Romoaldi II. archiepiscopi Salernitani Annales*, p. 441; *Chronica regia Coloniensis*, p. 127; *Roberti de Monte cronica*, p. 524; and RI IV2/3:118–20, nos. 2141 and 2145. See Heinemeyer, "Der Friede von Montebello," pp. 122–33, Georgi, *Friedrich Barbarossa und die auswärtigen Machte*, pp. 297–99; and Görich, *Die Ehre Friedrich Barbarossas*, pp. 160–62. The arbiters were named in *Constitutiones* 1:341–42, no. 243. Boso referred to negotiations conducted with the rectors rather than with the arbiters "now in the towns, now in the outskirts, just as seemed most convenient to them." When Frederick reluctantly accepted Cremona's second mediation award in 1176, he named various places where his envoys had negotiated with the Lombards after Montebello. DFI, no. 650 (end of July 1176?; also in *Constitutiones* 1:349, no. 248).
11. *Constitutiones* 1:344–46, no. 245; and Görich, *Die Ehre Friedrich Barbarossas*, p. 271.
12. DFI, no. 641 (27 July 1175); no. 642 (21 August 1175); no. 643 (20 November 1175); no. 645 (end of 1175; letter to Würzburg; also *Constitutiones* 1:346–47, no. 246); and no. 663 ("wohl 1176," Liège); *Romoaldi II. archiepiscopi Salernitani Annales*, p. 441; *Chronica regia Coloniensis*, p. 127; Godfrey of Viterbo, *Gesta Friderici I.*, pp. 37–38, vs. 979–80; and RI IV2/3:121–24, nos. 2150 and 2158–59.
13. Gilbert of Mons, *Chronicle of Hainaut*, p. 55; *Marbach Annals*, pp. 164–67; Otto of St. Blasien, *Chronicle*, pp. 70–71, ch. 23; Arnold of Lübeck, *Chronica Slavorum*, pp. 127–28; Albert of Stade, *Annales Stadenses*, ed. Johann Martin Lappenberg, in MGH SS 16 (Hanover, 1859), p. 348, under 1177 (mid-thirteenth century; Beatrice lifted Frederick up and said to him: "Arise, my lord, and remember who was the cause of this and may God remember, too"); Andrew of Marchiennes, *Chronica: Continuatio Aquicinctina*, p. 418, under 1180 (Frederick summoned Henry three times, and each time he refused to come personally or to send

envoys or troops); *Chronicon Montis Sereni*, p. 157, under 1180 (Frederick summoned all the Saxon princes to meet with him in Partenkirchen, Bavaria; all of them, except Henry, who had conspired with the Lombards against the emperor, quickly agreed to help him; Henry refused to lift up the prostrate emperor; therefore, Frederick hated Henry; it was up to the reader, the chronicler commented, to decide whether Frederick had judged Henry fairly or not); Burchard of Ursberg, *Chronicon*, pp. 196–97 (written 1229/30; Frederick met Henry north of Lake Como; comment by Henry's ministerial Jordan); *Annales Bremenses*, ed. Philipp Jaffé, MGH SS 17 (Hanover, 1861), p. 857, under 1177 (reported both Beatrice's and Jordan's alleged comments); RI IV2/3:126, no. 2171; and DFI, no. 643 (20 November 1175) and no. 665 (January or February 1177; Count Bernard swore on Frederick's behalf). I have relied on Hechberger, *Staufer und Welfen*, pp. 308–21, and Ehlers, *Heinrich der Löwe*, pp. 220–27, in my account of what took place in Chiavenna. On Henry as the real loser, see Stefan Weinfurter, "Papsttum, Reich und kaiserliche Autorität, im 11.–12. Jahrhundert: Von Rom 1111 bis Venedig 1177," in Hehl et al., eds, *Das Papsttum in der Welt des 12. Jahrhunderts*, pp. 97–98; and idem, "Venedig 1177," p. 19.

14. Otto of St. Blasien, *Chronicle*, pp. 70–71, ch. 23 (Frederick in Pavia); *Annales Magdeburgenses*, ed. Georg Heinrich Pertz, in MGH SS 16 (Hanover, 1859), p. 193 (letters sent to German magnates); *Annales Pegavienses*, p. 261 (letters sent to princes in Saxony and elsewhere); *Annales Ceccanenses* and *Annales Casinenses a 1000–1212*, both ed. Georg Heinrich Pertz, in MGH SS 19 (Hanover, 1866), pp. 286 and 312 (Christian's Norman campaign); DFI, no. 648 (6 [?] March 1176; agreement with Tortona); and no. 649 (summer 1176; retroactive approval of Philip's mortgaging of the manors); and RI IV2/3:126–28, nos. 2172–77. The agreement with Tortona was revised in Frederick's favor in January or February 1177 (DFI, no. 665). On the relationship between the two agreements with Tortona, see Riedmann, *Die Beurkundung der Verträge Friedrich Barbarossas*, pp. 78–84. The text in *Constitutiones* 1:390–93, no. 284, wrongly dated 4 February 1183, combined the two versions of the agreement with Tortona. On the agreement with Tortona, see Opll, *Stadt und Reich im 12. Jahrhundert*, pp. 442–43; and on the Sicilian campaign, see Georgi, *Friedrich Barbarossa und die auswärtigen Mächte*, pp. 299–300; and Houben, "Barbarossa und die Normannen," p. 119.
15. Numerous chroniclers mentioned the battle of Legnano. For a complete listing, see RI IV2:3:129–30, no. 2182, and also nos. 2178 and 2180–84. Boso, *Les vies des papes*, pp. 432–33 (*Boso's Life of Alexander III*, pp. 96–98), provides the most complete account of the battle. Other major sources are *Romoaldi II. archiepiscopi Salernitani Annales*, pp. 441–42; Otto of St. Blasien, *Chronicle*, pp. 70–73, ch. 23, esp. p. 71, n. 15 (the Milanese captured 500 men from Como and many Germans); *Chronica regia Coloniensis*, pp. 128–29; *Annales Magdeburgenses*, pp. 193–94; *Narratio de Longobardie obpressione*, pp. 292–93 (Lodi and Novara each supplied fifty knights, Vercelli 300, and Piacenza 200; 2,000 German knights crossed the Alps, but only 1,000 accompanied Frederick to Legnano); and *Ex Radulfi de Diceto operibus historicis*, pp. 268–69 (letter of Milan to Bologna about the capture of Frederick's insignia and a list of the chief prisoners). See DFI, no. 649 (summer 1176) and no. 653 (29 July 1176) for the princes who were at court. On the battle, see Görich, *Die Ehre Friedrich Barbarossas*, pp. 272–74; on the number and composition of the opposing force, see Raccagni, *The Lombard League*, pp. 90–91; and Giesebrecht, *Geschichte der deutschen Kaiserzeit* 5/2:790.
16. *Constitutiones* 1:347–49, no. 247 (June–July 1176?; second award); and p. 348, no. 248 (Frederick's declaration; also DFI, no. 650, end of July?); and *Romoaldi II. archiepiscopi Salernitani Annales*, p. 447 (also in Schmale edition, pp. 324–27). See Heinemeyer, "Der Friede von Montebello," pp. 133–36.
17. DFI, no. 653 (29 July 1176); RI IV2/3:132, no. 2190; Opll, *Stadt und Reich im 12. Jahrhundert*, p. 258; Overmann, *Gräfin Mathilde von Tuscien*, pp. 74–77; and Haverkamp, *Herrschaftsformen der Frühstaufer in Reichsitalien* 2:629–30.
18. Boso, *Les vies des papes*, p. 433 (*Boso's Life of Alexander III*, p. 98); DFI, nos. 654 and 655 (August 1176; Frederick to Abbot Hugh); and no. 690 (end of July 1177; Frederick to the Cistercians; also in *Constitutiones* 1:366, no. 263); and *Constitutiones* 1:582–83, no. 406 (Alexander to the Cistercians). See Görich, *Ein Kartäuser im Dienst Friedrich Barbarossas*, pp. 56–61.

19. DFI, no. 659 (November 1176; quotation is on p. 166, line 11; also *Constitutiones* 1:357–58, no. 253); and *Die Tegernseer Briefsammlung*, pp. 43–44, no. 29 (Welf's letter) and pp. 59–61, no. 40 (Ulrich's letter). The summons to the council is mentioned in *Annales Palidenses*, p. 94; *Annales Pegavienses*, p. 261; and *Annales Sancti Georgii in Nigra silva*, ed. Georg Heinrich Pertz, MGH SS 17 (Hanover, 1861), p. 296. On the council, see Helmut Plechl, "Studien zur Tegernseer Briefsammlung des 12. Jahrhunderts II: Briefe zur Reichspolitik aus der Zeit der Verhandlungen in Anagni und der Vorbereitungen des Venetianer Friedenskongresses (October 1176–January 1177)," *DA* 12 (1956): 74–76 and 82–85; and Görich, *Die Ehre Friedrich Barbarossas*, p. 165. Görich, *Friedrich Barbarossa*, pp. 435–36, maintained that Frederick was summoning Ulrich to decide at Ravenna in January 1177 between the rival popes, but Welf's letter to Cardinal Hyacinth makes clear that the issue was supposed to be discussed in Pavia in November.
20. *Die Tegernseer Briefsammlung*, pp. 59–61, no. 40; and Boso, *Les vies des papes*, pp. 433–35 (*Boso's Life of Alexander III*. pp. 98–100). Other narrative sources are: *Romoaldi II. archiepiscopi Salernitani Annales*, p. 442 (Christian's participation); *Annales Ceccanenses*, p. 286 (Christian arrived in Anagni on 21 October); Thomson, "An English Eyewitness of the Peace of Venice," p. 30 (Christian's military exploits before the negotiations); Andrew of Marchiennes, *Chronica: Continuatio Aquicinctina*, p. 415 (Christian was eager to make peace); and RI IV2/3:134–35, nos. 2197 and 2200. On the Peace of Anagni, see Laudage, *Alexander III. und Friedrich Barbarossa*, pp. 202–14. Görich, *Die Ehre Friedrich Barbarossas*, p. 163, highlighted the importance of Frederick's illness in motivating his decision to negotiate. On Wichmann's role in the schism and in the negotiations, see Claude, *Geschichte des Erzbistums Magdeburg bis in das 12. Jahrhundert* 2:163–70; and Georgi, "Wichmann, Christian, Philipp und Konrad," pp. 46–60 and 64–66.
21. Petersohn, *Kaisertum und Rom in spätsalischer und staufischer Zeit*, pp. 276–79.
22. The text of the Peace of Anagni is DFI, no. 658 (early November 1176; also in *Constitutiones* 1:349–53, no. 249); the envoys' sworn declaration is *Constitutiones* 1:353–54, no. 250. See also RI IV2/3:136–38, nos. 2202–03. See *Marbach Annals*, pp. 164–65, on the bishops of Basel, Metz, and Strasbourg; and Arnold of Lübeck, *Chronica Slavorum*, p. 131. On the bishoprics of Halberstadt and Bremen, see Töpfer, "Kaiser Friedrich I. Barbarossa und der deutsche Reichsepiskopat," pp. 398–99 and 412; Ehlers, "Heinrich der Löwe und der sächsische Episkopat," pp. 453–54; and Georgi, "Wichmann, Christian, Philipp und Konrad," pp. 73–77 (on Wichmann's role).
23. *Die Tegernseer Briefsammlung*, pp. 59–61, no. 40 (resumption of hostilities); *Narratio de Longobardie obpressione*, pp. 292–93; *Constitutiones* 1:580–81, no. 404 (shortly after 6 November 1176; Alexander informs legates of his plan to visit Lombardy) and pp. 581–82, no. 405 (end of November to 6 December 1176; Alexander's letter to rectors); Boso, *Les vies des papes*, pp. 434–37 (*Boso's Life of Alexander III*, pp. 100–04); *Romoaldi II. archiepiscopi Salernitani Annales*, p. 443 (Schmale edition, pp. 308–09); and RI IV2/3:138–40, nos. 2204–05 and 2211.
24. DFI, no. 660 (12 December 1176; also *Constitutiones* 1:354–56, no. 251); and no. 895 (17 January–July 1185; also *Constitutiones* 1:426–28, no. 302). See Opll, *Stadt und Reich im 12. Jahrhundert*, pp. 258–60. Görich, *Die Ehre Friedrich Barbarossas*, pp. 276–83, argued that the Cremonese consuls did not present Frederick with their undated second mediation award in June or July 1176, while he was in Pavia, as is commonly thought (see above, pp. 391–92), but only in December, when he was in Cremona, and that they were able to exert on this occasion the type of pressure that induced him both to accept the award and to agree to come to Cremona's defense. In other words, if Görich is right, Frederick did not begin his negotiations with Alexander because the Cremonese attempt at mediation between the emperor and the Lombards in June or July had failed. The problem with Görich's argument is that the Lombards said in Venice that they had rejected Cremona's second award because Frederick was still trying to get them to abandon Alexander. It is hard to see how Frederick could have pursued such a course after Anagni without totally alienating the German bishops, especially Archbishops Christian and Philip who had a very personal stake in the successful outcome of the negotiations with the pope: the retention of their archiepiscopal dignity.

25. DFI, no. 659 (November 1176; Frederick to Ulrich); no. 662 (December 1176; Frederick to Ulrich; also *Constitutiones* 1:358, no. 254; Plechl in *Tegernseer Briefsammlung*, pp. 87–88, no. 65, now dates this letter as late December 1176 or early January 1177); *Tegernseer Briefsammlung*, pp. 66–67, no. 44 (6 November to mid-November 1176; Conrad of Mainz requested that Ulrich attend the council that was scheduled to meet in Ravenna or Florence; also in *Constitutiones* 1:359, no. 256, where the sender is identified as Christian of Mainz and the letter is dated January 1177); pp. 74–75, no. 52 (beginning of December 1176; rectors prohibit attendance at the council); and pp. 75–76, no. 53 (beginning of December 1176; rectors of Lombardy to Ulrich); Boso, *Les vies des papes*, pp. 435–37 (*Boso's Life of Alexander III*, pp. 100 and 102–04); *Romoaldi II. archiepiscopi Salernitani Annales*, pp. 443–44 (Schmale edition, pp. 308–11); *Annales Pegavienses*, p. 261 (Frederick in Ravenna); and RI IV2/3:138–50, nos. 2205–06, 2208–09, 2215–16, 2224–26, 2231–33, 2236–37, and 2243. On Leopold's enfeoffment, see *Continuatio Zwetlensis altera a. 1170–1189*, p. 541, and *Continuatio Claustroneoburgensis III. a. 1142–1233*, p. 631, both edited by Wilhelm Wattenbach in MGH SS 9 (Hanover, 1851).
26. Boso, *Les vies des papes*, pp. 437–38 (*Boso's Life of Alexander III*, pp. 104–05); *Romoaldi II. archiepiscopi Salernitani Annales*, pp. 444–46 (Schmale edition, pp. 310–23); Thomson, "An English Eyewitness of the Peace of Venice, 1177," p. 30; *Historia ducum Veneticorum*, p. 82 (general invitation to attend the council in Venice); and RI IV2/3:150–51, nos. 2243–45. See Laudage, *Alexander III. und Friedrich Barbarossa*, pp. 214–16. Boso said that Frederick was also represented in Ferrara by the archbishops of Besançon and Salzburg, but that is unlikely. See Alheydis Plassmann, "Barbarossa und sein Hof beim Frieden von Venedig unter verschiedenen Wahrnehmungsperspektiven," in Weinfurter, ed., *Stauferreich im Wandel*, pp. 89–91. See Raccagni, *The Lombard League*, pp. 99–100, for why the League objected to Venice as a meeting place.
27. *Romoaldi II. archiepiscopi Salernitani Annales*, pp. 446–47 (Schmale edition, pp. 322–29); Thomson, "An English Eyewitness of the Peace of Venice, 1177," p. 30; *Historia ducum Veneticorum*, p. 87 (number of men at Leopold and Hermann's command); and RI IV2/3:151–52, no. 2246. See Laudage, *Alexander III. und Friedrich Barbarossa*, pp. 216–18.
28. *Romoaldi archiepiscopi Salernitani Annales*, p. 448 (Schmale edition, pp. 328–29). See Laudage, *Alexander III. und Friedrich Barbarossa*, p. 218 (Frederick was trying to extort additional concessions from Alexander); Görich, *Die Ehre Friedrich Barbarossas*, p. 167 (Frederick could not require the Lombards to submit to him publicly if they made a truce rather than peace); and Georgi, "Wichmann, Christian, Philipp und Konrad," pp. 78–81 (Frederick may really have been angry or Romuald may have invented the story to explain how the emperor procured more favorable terms).
29. *Romoaldi archiepiscopi Salernitani Annales*, p. 448 (Schmale edition, pp. 330–31); and RI IV2/3:156, no. 2259. DFI, no. 658 (Peace of Anagni; articles 3 and 4 in *Constitutiones* 1:350, no. 249) and no. 687 (22 July 1177; Peace of Venice; also in *Constitutiones* 1:362–65, no. 260, article 3). The translation is taken from Henderson, *Select Historical Documents of the Middle Ages*, pp. 425–30, no. IVc. The phrase, "salva omnia justa tenementa populi Romani," appears in Frederick's 1167 agreement with the Roman senate (*Chronica regia Coloniensis*, p. 118). J. F. Niermeyer and C. Van der Kieft, *Mediae Latinitatis lexicon minus*, 2nd edn. (Darmstadt, 2002), 2:1328, translated *tenementum* in this context as "territory subject to a public authority." On the revised provisions about Rome, see Petersohn, *Kaisertum und Rom in spätsalischer und staufischer Zeit*, pp. 279–82. Paul Fridolin Kehr, "Der Vertrag von Anagni im Jahre 1176," *NA* 13 (1888): 75–118, was the first to propose that Frederick revised the Treaty of Anagni in his favor at Venice. On who really won at Venice, see Laudage, *Alexander III. und Friedrich Barbarossa*, p. 220; and idem, "Gewinner und Verlierer des Friedens von Venedig," in Weinfurter, ed., *Stauferreich im Wandel*, esp. pp. 107–10 and 121–30.
30. *Romoaldi archiepiscopi Salernitani Annales*, pp. 448–49 (Schmale edition, pp. 332–33); *Historia ducum Veneticorum*, pp. 83–84 and 89; DFI, no. 673 (beginning of June 1177; Ulrich's participation in peace negotiations; also *Tegernseer Briefsammlung*, pp. 90–91, no. 67); no. 678 (February/March to 20 July 1177; borrowing money; dated beginning of May to 20 July 1177 in *Tegernseer Briefsammlung*, pp. 83–84, no. 61); and no. 679 (before 20 July 1177; borrowing money; mid-June to 20 July in *Tegernseer Briefsammlung*, pp. 86–87, no. 64); and

RI IV2/3:152–58, nos 2247, 2254, 2260 and 2263–66. On Pons and Hugh's involvement, see Georgi, *Friedrich Barbarossa und die auswärtigen Mächte*, pp. 317–20. On the number of individuals who witnessed the reconciliation, see Plassmann, "Barbarossa und sein Hof beim Frieden von Venedig," p. 88.

31. *Romoaldi archiepiscopi Salernitani Annales*, pp. 449–52 (Schmale edition, pp. 333–45); Boso, *Les vies des papes*, p. 439 (*Boso's Life of Alexander III*, pp. 106–07); Otto of St. Blasien, *Chronicle*, pp. 72–73, ch. 23; and RI IV2/3:160–61, nos. 2273–76. Romuald alone told the story of the Venetian uprising and his own role in ending it. Boso merely said, parenthetically, that Frederick "was beset and warned by those who hated peace," while the final peace terms were being worked out in Chioggia. The sources disagree about who swore on Frederick's behalf on 22 July. Boso identified them as Dedo, Conrad of Montferrat, and the chamberlain Sigiboto. Romuald named Count Henry II of Diez as the oath-taker and mentioned the Cologne chaplain who swore on behalf of the princes. Alexander wrote to Archbishop Roger of York and Bishop Hugh of Durham on 26 July that the unnamed son of Margrave Albrecht the Bear and the chamberlain swore on Frederick's behalf. The text of the letter is in *Ex gestis Henrici II. et Ricardi I.*, ed. Felix Liebermann and Reinhold Pauli, in MGH SS 27 (Hanover, 1885), pp. 97–98. See Plassmann, "Barbarossa und sein Hof beim Frieden von Venedig," pp. 91–93; and on Frederick's efforts to avoid a public submission to Alexander, see Weinfurter, "Venedig 1177," pp. 13–14.
32. DFI, no. 687 (22 July 1177; also *Constitutiones* 1:362–65, no. 260). Frederick promised Alexander on 17 September that he would observe the peace between the Empire and the Church, which had been made by his princes and the cardinals and which was contained in a written document sealed with their seals (DFI, no. 707). Thomson, "An English Eyewitness of the Peace of Venice," p. 30, provides the date.
33. DFI, no. 689 (before 1 August 1177; also in *Constitutiones* 1:360–62, no. 259); *Narratio de Longobardie obpressione*, pp. 294–95; and RI IV2/3:166–67, no. 2288. Raccagni, *The Lombard League*, pp. 98–100, related the comment by the Milanese Anonymous in the context of the negotiations in Ferrara in April, but the chronicler made the comment after indicating that Frederick had been restored to communion on 24 July.
34. Boso, *Les vies des papes*, pp. 439–43 (*Boso's Life of Alexander III*, pp. 107–13); *Romoaldi archiepiscopi Salernitani Annales*, pp. 452–58 (Schmale edition, pp. 344–71); *Ex gestis Henrici II. et Ricardi I.*," pp. 97–98 (Alexander's letter); Bernardo Maragone, *Gli Annales Pisani di Bernardo Maragone*, ed. Michele Lupo Gentile, in Ludovicus Antonius Muratorius, Rerum Italicarum Scriptores, new edn. 6/2 (Bologna, 1936), pp. 62–64 (under 1178); and Thomson, "An English Eyewitness of the Peace of Venice," pp. 31–32 (on the author, see pp. 27–28). On the sources, see Hack, *Das Empfangszeremoniell bei mittelalterlichen Papst-Kaiser-Treffen*, pp. 648–50 and 664–69; Plassmann, "Barbarossa und sein Hof beim Frieden von Venedig," pp. 85–89 and 105–06 (on the Venetian chronicler's sources); Laudage, "Gewinner und Verlierer," pp. 110–15; and Görich, *Die Ehre Friedrich Barbarossas*, pp. 173–77, esp. p. 174. For a complete list of chroniclers who mentioned the Peace of Venice, see RI IV2/3:163–65, no. 2282. In relating the events in Venice, I am relying on the reconstructions by Hack, pp. 650–63, and Laudage, pp. 115–21.
35. Boso, *Les vies des papes*, p. 439 (*Boso's Life of Alexander III*, p. 107); *Ex gestis Henrici II. et Ricardi I.*, p. 98; Thomson, "An English Eyewitness of the Peace of Venice," p. 31 (Alexander's comment); and *Chronicon Montis Sereni*, p. 156 (Margrave Dietrich). For an analysis of the scene in front of St. Mark's, see Hack, *Das Empfangszeremoniell bei mittelalterlichen Papst-Kaiser-Treffen*, pp. 540–46; Laudage, "Gewinner und Verlierer," pp. 119–21; Scholz, "Symbolik und Zeremoniell bei den Päpsten in der zweiten Hälfte des 12. Jahrhunderts," pp. 141–48; and Görich, *Die Ehre Friedrich Barbarossas*, pp. 167–77.
36. Hack, *Das Empfangszeremoniell bei mittelalterlichen Papst-Kaiser-Treffen*, p. 656, raised the question about Frederick's devotion to James.
37. Ibid., pp. 657–58. See *Romoaldi archiepiscopi Salernitani Annales*, pp. 452–53 (Schmale edition, pp. 346–49); Boso, *Les vies des papes*, p. 440 (*Boso's Life of Alexander III*, p. 108); Maragone, *Annales Pisani*, p. 62; and RI IV2/3:165, no. 2283.
38. *Romoaldi archiepiscopi Salernitani Annales*, pp. 453–54 (Schmale edition, pp. 348–55); Boso, *Les vies des papes*, p. 440 (*Boso's Life of Alexander III*, pp. 108–09); *Constitutiones* 1:372, no. 271

(14 August–18 September; oath-takers' charter); RI IV2/3:167–68, no. 2290, and p. 186, no. 2330; and Hack, *Das Empfangszeremoniell bei mittelalterlichen Papst-Kaiser-Treffen*, pp. 459–61. On the problem of the oath-takers, see Plassmann, "Barbarossa und sein Hof beim Frieden von Venedig," pp. 93–95.

39. Weinfurter, "Papsttum, Reich und kaiserliche Autorität," p. 97; and idem, "Venedig 1177," p. 12.
40. Boso, *Les vies des papes*, p. 441 (*Boso's Life of Alexander III*, p. 109); *Romoaldi archiepiscopi Salernitani Annales*, pp. 454–55 (Schmale edition, pp. 354–59); DFI, no. 693 (9 August 1177; Frederick's letter to Salzburg; also in *Constitutiones* 1:368–69, no. 267); Magnus of Reichersberg, *Chronicon*, pp. 503–06 (Adalbert's brief and Alexander and Frederick's letters to Salzburg); *Mainzer Urkundenbuch* 2/2:646–48, no. 393 (before 22 July 1177; Conrad of Mainz's reluctant resignation); and RI IV2/3:168–72, no. 2291 (council with a summary of all the participants mentioned in the *Historia ducum Veneticorum*), and pp. 173–74, no. 2297. See Dopsch, *Geschichte Salzburgs* 1/1:295–96.
41. *Romoaldi archiepiscopi Salernitani Annales*, pp. 455–58 (Schmale edition, pp. 360–67), and pp. 459–60 (imperial embassy to the Sicilian court); RI IV2/3:174–75, nos. 2298–2300 and pp. 200–01, no. 2382. The text of the Sicilian peace in the edition of Frederick's charters (DFI, no. 694; 1–13 August 1177) is taken from Romuald's *Annals*. Neither the original document nor William's charter for Frederick survives. The castle of *Gayue* where Henry was staying has usually been identified as Gavi, situated halfway between Alessandria and Genoa (see, for example, Csendes, *Heinrich VI.*, p. 42); but Opll, RI IV2/3:175, no. 2300, said that because of the spatial distance, *Gayue* could only have been Gaibana, near Rovigo, located halfway between Chioggia and Ferrara. That argument presupposes Beatrice and Henry were staying close by, but there is no evidence that they necessarily were. The fact that Henry had until mid-September to swear would suggest that they were farther rather than closer to Venice. However, Opll, RI IV2/3:194, no. 2360, placed the birth of Frederick's son Philip at the end of 1177 in Gavi, seemingly oblivious that Beatrice would probably have been in the same castle on both occasions. More recently, Csendes, *Philipp von Schwaben*, p. 20, argued that Philip was born already in February or March 1177 in Pavia or a nearby imperial castle like Gavi and spent his early days there. The imperial couple were finally reunited in Genoa in mid-February 1178 (RI IV2/3:198–99, no. 2375). According to Maragone's account in the *Annales Pisani*, Beatrice went from Gavi to Genoa (p. 65). On the whole it makes sense that the empress, especially if she was pregnant or recovering from a difficult pregnancy, and her children would have remained close to the major center of imperial power in Lombardy, that is, in the vicinity of Pavia and Montferrat.
42. *Romoaldi archiepiscopi Salernitani Annales*, p. 458 (Schmale edition, pp. 366–71); Boso, *Les vies des papes*, p. 441 (*Boso's Life of Alexander III*, pp. 109–10); RI IV2/3:175–76, no. 2301; and Hack, *Das Empfangszeremoniell bei mittelalterlichen Papst-Kaiser-Treffen*, pp. 662–63.
43. DFI, no. 695 (17 August 1177; also *Constitutiones* 1:374–77, no. 274) and no. 708 (September 1177; also *Constitutiones* 1:373, no. 273). No. 708 is an almost verbatim repetition of Frederick's charter of 22 December 1154 (DFI, no. 294; also *Constitutiones* 1:209–13, no. 150), which copied in turn Lothar's charter of 3 October 1136 (DLIII, no. 97; also *Constitutiones* 1:171–75, no. 119). In drafting Lothar's charter, the scribe had relied on the charters of Henry IV and V.
44. Boso, *Les vies des papes*, pp. 442–43 (*Boso's Life of Alexander III*, p. 112); DFI, no. 712 (September 1177; also *Constitutiones* 1:372–73, no. 272); and RI IV2/3:184–87, nos. 2324 and 2334.
45. Boso, *Les vies des papes*, pp. 441 and 443–44 (*Boso's Life of Alexander III*, pp. 110, 112–15); and RI IV2/3:185–90, nos. 2329, 2339, and 2344. See Partner, *The Lands of St. Peter*, p. 211
46. Godfrey of Viterbo, *Gesta Friderici I.*, pp. 40–41, vs. 1063–89; and Maragone, *Annales Pisani*, pp. 64–65. For Frederick's itinerary between October 1177 and July 1178 and who accompanied him, see RI IV2/3:189–207, nos. 2343–2401. On the birth of Agnes, see RI IV2/3:230, no. 2475.
47. Boso, *Les vies des papes*, pp. 435–36 (*Boso's Life of Alexander III*, pp. 100–01); Albert of Stade, *Annales Stadenses*, p. 349; Godfrey of Viterbo, *Gesta Friderici I.*, p. 40, vs. 1057–59; and RI IV2/3:143–44, nos. 2222–23, p. 172, no. 2292, and p. 182, no. 2320. Albert, who wrote in the

1240s, included excerpts from Manuel and Frederick's letters, under the year 1179, in his account of their exchange of embassies. Frederick's letter to Manuel survives in its entirety in the Tegernsee letter collection (*Tegernseer Briefsammlung*, pp. 34–36, no. 24). It was not included in the edition of Frederick's charters and letters because it was deemed to be spurious ("Wohl kaum authentisch") (DFI, vol. 4, Anhang I, p. 508, no. 15). Both Opll, RI IV2/3, no. 2320, and Plechl, in the *Tegernseer Briefsammlung*, considered it to be authentic. Opll dated it August 1177, that is, immediately after Frederick's reconciliation with Alexander; whereas Plechl dated it circa 1178, because that was the probable date of Manuel's dispute with the patriarch. Kirfel, *Weltherrschaftsidee*, pp. 117–20, down played Frederick's apparent claim to world dominion—the letter was an angry response to a breach of etiquette—and dated it 1178. Georgi, *Friedrich Barbarossa und die auswärtigen Mächte*, pp. 335–38, thought the letter was a reaction to the landing of a Greek mercenary army in the mark of Ancona at the end of 1178 and so dated the letter 1179. Georgi, pp. 311–12, also contended that it was not the defeat at Myriokephalon per se that led to Manuel's exclusion at Venice but the reluctance of the Lombards, Venetians, and Normans to include the Byzantines after their double-dealing.

48. Godfrey of Viterbo, *Gesta Friderici I.*, p. 41, vs. 1093–1107 (coronation in Arles); *Annales Pegavienses*, p. 262 (coronation in Arles); *Ex Radulfi de Diceto operibus historicis*, pp. 270–71 (has the dates of both coronations wrong); *Chronica regia Coloniensis*, p. 129 (correct date, but places the court on 15 August in Besançon rather than Vienne and does not mention the coronation); Otto of Freising and Rahewin, *Deeds* 3.12; Maragone, *Annales Pisani*, pp. 68–69 (under 1180, the marriage of Manuel's niece); and RI IV2/3:207–25, nos. 2401–58. The paucity of references to the Burgundian coronations and the clearly erroneous reports suggest that no one was paying much attention to Frederick's actions outside Burgundy. See Fried, "Friedrich Barbarossas Krönung in Arles," pp. 347–71; Georgi, *Friedrich Barbarossa und die auswärtigen Mächte*, pp. 321–24; Vones-Liebenstein, *"Vir uxorious?"* pp. 189–91 and 207–19; Michael Lindner, "Fest und Herrschaft unter Kaiser Friedrich Barbarossa," in Engel, *Kaiser Friedrich Barbarossa*, pp. 163–65; and Fredric L. Cheyette, *Ermengard of Narbonne and the World of the Troubadours* (Ithaca, N.Y., and London, 2001), p. 20 (genealogy of the house of Barcelona), pp. 253–56, 263–64, and 266–67 (on the succession to the county of Provence).
49. RI IV2/3:238–39, no. 2500 (Magdeburg; 29 June 1179); and IV2:4:29–30, no. 2655, and p. 77, no. 2762 (Beatrice in Mainz in 1182 and 1184). Beatrice's charters are published as an addendum in DFI, vol. 4, pp. 493–505. No. *1, which survives only as a summary, was issued in March 1173. Nos. 2–10 are dated between 24 July 1181 and 30 August 1183; no. 10 is dubious. No. *11, which survives as a summary, can be dated only between 1156 and 1184. Her physician, Master Appinus, appears in no. 4. Conrad and his teacher ("doctor") Master Manegauld witnessed nos. 7–10. See Vones-Liebenstein, *"Vir uxorius?"* pp. 207–19.
50. DFI, no. 957 (17 April 1187); and no. 994 (April 1189).
51. Boso, *Les vies des papes*, pp. 445–46 (*Boso's Life of Alexander III*, pp. 116–18); *Romoaldi archiepiscopi Salernitani Annales*, pp. 459–60; RI IV2/3:206–07, no. 2400 (the Lombards' complaint about the Montferrats' violation of the truce); *Mainzer Urkundenbuch* 2/2:698–702, no. 433 (terms of Christian's release). Acht in the *Mainzer Urkundenbuch* dated no. 433 to the end of September or early October 1179. Georgi, *Friedrich Barbarossa und die auswärtigen Mächte*, pp. 331–32, placed the end of Christian's imprisonment shortly before 1 October 1180. More recently, Opll, RI IV2/3:252, no. 2535, dated the archbishop's release at the end of 1180 or early 1181. In IV2/4:3, no. 2580, Opll pushed the date to after 29 December 1180. On the events in Rome and the Patrimony, see Georgi, pp. 325–33; Petersohn, "Friedrich Barbarossa und Rom," pp. 139–40; idem, *Kaisertum und Rom in spätsalischer und staufischer Zeit*, pp. 257–75 and 283–97; Partner, *The Lands of St. Peter*, pp. 208–09 and 211–15; and Doran, "'At last we reached the port of salvation,"' pp. 78–86 and 92–96.
52. DFI, no. 843 (March–30 April 1183; response of the rectors of the League to the initial imperial proposal; also *Constitutiones* 1:396–99, no. 288); DFI, no. 844 (30 April 1183; preliminary Peace of Piacenza; also *Constitutiones* 1:400–03, no. 289); and no. 848 (25 June 1183; also *Constitutiones* 1:408–18, no. 293); and Burchard of Ursberg, *Chronicon*, pp. 200–01.

On the evolution of the text of the Peace of Constance, see Heinrich Appelt, "Das Zustandekommen des Textes des Friedens von Konstanz," in idem, *Kaisertum, Königtum, Landesherrschaft*, pp. 137–50. See also Raccagni, *The Lombard League*, pp. 77–78 and 101–02; and Görich, *Die Ehre Friedrich Barbarossas*, p. 295.

53. DFI, no. 841 (14 March 1183; also *Constitutiones* 1:407–08, no. 292); and RI IV2/4:44–45, no. 2690. On conditions in Lombardy between 1177 and 1183, see Haverkamp, "Der Konstanzer Friede," pp. 28–32.
54. DFI, no. 842 (March 1183; mandate to three envoys; also *Constitutiones* 1:395–96, no. 287); and no. *1185 (before 30 April 1183; mandate to Rudolf; mentioned in *Constitutiones* 1:404–06, no. 291); RI IV2/4:46, nos. 2692–93; and Otto of St. Blasien, *Chronicle*, pp. 60–63, ch. 20 (Hartmann in Susa). On the envoys, see Görich, *Ein Kartäuser im Dienst Friedrich Barbarossas*, pp. 80–90; and Keupp, *Dienst und Verdienst*, pp. 240–45. Appelt, who was the editor-in-chief of Barbarossa's charters, declared in 1983 in "Das Zustandekommen des Textes des Friedens von Konstanz," p. 142, that it was an "open question" whether the Lombard response to the imperial proposal (DFI, no. 843) was made before the agreement of 14 March about Alessandria; and Appelt dated DFI, no. 843, in his edition as "1183 März–April 30," that is, after the agreement with Alessandria. Appelt's student, Josef Riedmann, in what was essentially a preliminary study for the publication of the charters, *Die Beurkundung der Verträge Friedrich Barbarossas*, pp. 72–73, thought that the initiative for settling the Alessandria problem came from the city, which sent its envoys to negotiate with Barbarossa in Nuremberg. The problem is that the Lombards demanded in their response to Frederick's initial proposal that Alessandria be allowed to retain its status as a city and enjoy all the privileges of a League member (article 22). It is hard to see how they could have made such a demand after it had been agreed that Alessandria was to be refounded as Caesarea. Görich, pp. 80–84, proposed in 1987, therefore, that the three envoys must have started the negotiations with the Lombards already in the second half of 1182 and that the rectors' response to the imperial peace proposal must thus represent the respective positions of the two sides at the beginning of 1183. When it became clear in March that an agreement was actually in sight, Frederick gave the envoys full power to negotiate in Piacenza the final terms of the peace and sent Rudolf to them with this mandate. This reconstruction of the events was also Görich's position in *Die Ehre Friedrich Barbarossas*, pp. 292–93. Nevertheless, Opll, in RI IV2/4:46–49, no. 2694, which was published in 2011, retained Appelt's March–April date. It strikes me as more plausible that DFI, no. 843, should be dated before March 1183. On the agreement with Alessandria, see Görich, *Die Ehre Friedrich Barbarossas*, pp. 280–86.
55. It is easy to see the changes that were made at Piacenza in the rectors' response to the original imperial proposal because the portions that remained the same are printed in smaller type (see DFI, nos 843 and 844). In addition, Opll, RI IV2/4:49–50, no. 2695, pointed out the differences. On the Piacenza agreement, see Haverkamp, "Der Konstanzer Friede," pp. 32–35, esp. p. 33, on the purchasing power of 2,000 marks. On the textual history of clause 3, the payment of the 2,000 marks, see *Constitutiones* 1:410–11, head note to no. 293; DFI, no. 844, p. 61, footnote g; and DFI, no. 848, pp. 70–71, head note.
56. *Constitutiones* 1:403–04, no. 290 (notarial agreement) and pp. 419–20, no. 295 (receipt); and RI IV2/4:50–51, no. 2696, and p. 68, no. 2737. See Haverkamp, "Der Konstanzer Friede," p. 36, on the purchasing power of £15,000; and Görich, *Die Ehre Friedrich Barbarossas*, pp. 344–45. The payments the emperor received for granting a privilege were not mentioned in a privilege. They were mentioned only in the unofficial summaries of agreements. See Riedmann, *Die Beurkundung der Verträge Friedrich Barbarossas*, p. 167.
57. *Constitutiones* 1:404–06, no. 291; and RI IV2/4:51–52, no. 2697.
58. DFI, no. 844 (Peace of Piacenza); no. 847 (20 June 1183; the back of this charter for the Cistercians of Salem has the notation that the privilege was granted in Constance on the day peace was made between the emperor and the consuls of the Italian cities); and no. 848 (25 June 1183; Peace of Constance); Otto of St. Blasien, *Chronicle*, pp. 78–79, ch. 27; and RI IV2/4:58–62, nos. 2715–16 and 2719. See Appelt, "Das Zustandekommen des Textes des Friedens von Konstanz," pp. 137–38 (on the format of the peace); and Görich, *Die Ehre Friedrich Barbarossas*, pp. 295–96 (on the symbolism of the keys).

Chapter 15 The Downfall of Henry the Lion

1. *Ex gestis Henrici II. et Ricardi I.*, p. 101 (Manuel); and *Chronicon Montis Sereni*, p. 157 under 1180 (Lombards).
2. Karl Hampe, *Germany under the Salian and Hohenstaufen Emperors*, translated with an introduction by Ralph Bennett (Totowa, N.J., 1973), p. 206. The section on the Lion's downfall was actually written by Hampe's student Friedrich Baethgen, who became after World War II the president of the Monumenta Germaniae Historica (Preface, pp. vii–viii).
3. Hechberger, *Staufer und Welfen 1125–1190*, demolished the traditional interpretative paradigm. On the princes as the driving force in 1180, see Knut Görich, "Jäger des Löwen oder Getriebener der Fürsten? Friedrich Barbarossa und die Entmachtung Heinrichs des Löwen," in Hechberger and Schuler, eds, *Staufer & Welfen*, pp. 98–117.
4. Ehlers, *Heinrich der Löwe*, pp. 96–100, 115–30, and 162–71; Schneidmüller, *Die Welfen*, p. 209; Weinfurter, "Erzbischof Philipp von Köln und der Sturz Heinrichs des Löwen," in Vollrath and Weinfurter, eds, *Köln*, pp. 459–64 (on Henry's attempted feudalization of the Saxon counts); and Hubertus Seibert, "Die entstehende 'territoriale Ordnung' am Beispiel Bayerns (1115–1198)," in Weinfurter, *Stauferreich im Wandel*, pp. 272–87.
5. See above, p. 75.
6. RI IV2/2:169, no. 1226. See Ehlers, *Heinrich der Löwe*, p. 141.
7. Helmold of Bosau, *Slawenchronik*, pp. 356–65, chs. 103–05, and pp. 368–71, ch. 107; the quotation is on pp. 356–59, ch. 103. See Ehlers, *Heinrich der Löwe*, pp. 141–49; and Claude, *Geschichte des Erzbistums Magdeburg* 2:148–52. On the Cologne duchies, see Engel, "Grundlinien der rheinischen Verfassungsgeschichte im 12. Jahrhundert," pp. 133–59; idem, "Der Niederrhein und das Reich im 12. Jahrhundert," pp. 177–99; Groten, "Köln und das Reich," pp. 237–45; and Weinfurter, "Erzbischof Philipp von Köln," pp. 471–72.
8. See above, pp. 387–89 and 396–97.
9. Ehlers, *Heinrich der Löwe*, pp. 323–29.
10. Arnold of Lübeck, *Chronica Slavorum*, pp. 132–33; *Historia Welforum cum continuatione Steingademensi*, pp. 86–89; and RI IV2/3:226–31, nos. 2461–63 and 2476–77. See Weinfurter, "Erzbischof Philipp von Köln," pp. 467–69.
11. Burchard of Ursberg, *Chronicon*, pp. 196–97; Arnold of Lübeck, *Chronica Slavorum*, p. 133; *Chronica regia Coloniensis*, p. 130; and RI IV2/3:230–43, no. 2476 (Worms court), nos. 2496–97 and 2500 (Magdeburg court), and no. 2514 (Jews' fine). See Ehlers, *Heinrich der Löwe*, pp. 330–32; and Görich, "Jäger des Löwen oder Getriebener der Fürsten?" pp. 110–17.
12. Arnold of Lübeck, *Chronica Slavorum*, pp. 133–38 (Arnold placed the Kayna court in Goslar); *Annales Pegavienses*, pp. 262–63; *Mainzer Urkundenbuch* 2/2:695–96, no. 430 (letter of Wichmann to the clergy and people of Mainz on the destruction of Halberstadt); and RI IV2/3:240–41, nos. 2507, 2513, and 2515. See Ehlers, *Heinrich der Löwe*, pp. 333–35.
13. DFI, no. 795 (13 April 1180; also *Constitutiones* 1:384–86, no. 279). The translation is in Henderson, *Select Historical Documents of the Middle Ages*, pp. 217–18, no. 8.
14. A good example of the older legal approach is Heinrich Mitteis, *Lehnrecht und Staatsgewalt: Untersuchungen zur mittelalterlichen Verfassungsgeschichte* (Weimar, 1933; reprint, Darmstadt, 1958), pp. 431–36; Mitteis was a professor of German legal history. Some examples of more recent assessments of the proceedings are: Weinfurter, "Erzbischof Philipp von Köln," pp. 456–57 and 478–81 (the use of feudal law hastened the execution of the judgment); Bernd Schneidmüller, "Heinrich der Löwe: Innovationspotentiale eines mittelalterlichen Fürsten," in Hechberger and Schuler, eds, *Staufer & Welfen*, pp. 60–61 (the procedural rules developed in the course of the conflict); and Görich, "Jäger des Löwen oder Getriebener der Fürsten?" p. 110 (it is difficult, if not impossible, to reconstruct what actually occurred, and the separation between territorial and feudal law is not very helpful).
15. On this point, see Hanna Vollrath, "Rebels and Rituals: From Demonstrations of Enmity to Criminal Justice," in Althoff et al., eds, *Medieval Concepts of the Past*, pp. 91–92 and 106–10.
16. DFI, no. 795 (Gelnhausen charter); *Annales Ottenburani Isingrimi et minores*, ed. Georg Heinrich Pertz, in MGH SS 17 (Hanover, 1861), p. 316 (composition of the Würzburg court, but this chronicler who belonged to a monastery in what is now Bavarian Swabia said nothing about Henry's loss of his duchies); and RI IV2/3:248–53, nos. 2530 and 2538. Both

Opll, nos. 2530 and 2538, and Ehlers, *Heinrich der Löwe*, pp. 335–36, stated that the duchy of Saxony was divided and granted to Philip and Bernard at Würzburg, and given to them again at Gelnhausen. Schneidmüller, *Die Welfen*, pp. 227–28, suggested, more plausibly, that Henry was deprived of his fiefs in January and that Philip and Bernard received their duchies only in April. This is the sequence of events that appears in the *Annales Pegavienses*, p. 263. The Pegau annalist indicated that Henry lost his allods as well as his fiefs.

17. *Annales Pegavienses*, p. 263; Arnold of Lübeck, *Chronica Slavorum*, pp. 136 and 142; and RI IV2/3:253, no. 2538, and p. 257, no. 2547. See Ehlers, *Heinrich der Löwe*, pp. 235–38; Weinfurter, "Erzbischof Philipp von Köln," esp. pp. 457–58, 469–70, and 474–77; and Werner Goez, *Der Leihezwang: Eine Untersuchung zur Geschichte des deutschen Lehnrechtes* (Tübingen, 1962), pp. 231–37.
18. Arnold of Lübeck, *Chronica Slavorum*, pp. 137–39; *Annales Pegavienses*, pp. 263–64; *Chronicon Montis Sereni*, p. 158; and RI IV2/3:259–64, nos. 2553–58, 2560–61, 2567–68, and 2570. See Ehlers, *Heinrich der Löwe*, pp. 338–40.
19. RI IV2/3:257–62, nos. 2550 and 2562–63 (the chroniclers who mentioned what happened in Regensburg and Altenburg); and RI IV2/4:3, no. 2581 (Berthold's ducal rank; he was identified as a duke for the first time in a document on 5 January 1181). Frederick's charter for Freising, dated 13 July 1180 (DFI, no. 798), provides a list of the magnates who had been present in all likelihood in Regensburg at the end of June. On the magnates' refusal to pay homage to Otto, see *Continuatio Zwetlensis altera*, p. 541. On the grant of the duchy to Otto, see Max Spindler, ed., *Handbuch der bayerischen Geschichte* 2: *Das Alte Bayern* (Munich, 1966), pp. 15–21; and Seibert, "Die entstehende 'territoriale Ordnung' am Beispiel Bayerns," pp. 253–87. On the creation of the Styrian duchy, see Gerhard Pferschy, ed., *Das Werden der Steiermark: Die Zeit der Traungauer: Festschrift zur 800. Wiederkehr der Erhebung zum Herzogtum* (Graz, Vienna, and Cologne, 1980). On the Andechses, see Josef Kirmeier and Evamaria Brockhoff, *Herzöge und Heilige: Das Geschlecht der Andechs-Meranier im europäischen Hochmittelalter: Katalog zur Landesausstellung im Kloster Andechs 13. Juli–24. Oktober 1993* (Munich, 1993), p. 66; and Lyon, *Princely Brothers and Sisters*, passim. On Otto's burial, see *Die Traditionen des Klosters Scheyern*, ed. Michael Stephan (Munich, 1986), pp. 56–57, no. 54; and RI IV2/4:65, no. 2729. Frederick VI and his unnamed brother, a boy, presumably Philip, witnessed a transaction made in conjunction with the burial.
20. *Annales Pegavienses*, p. 264; and Claude, *Geschichte des Erzbistums Magdeburgs* 2:158–59.
21. Andrew of Marchiennes, *Chronica: Continuatio Aquicinctina*, p. 419; and RI IV2/4:4, no. 2585, and p. 13, no. 2609. The arrival of the French and Flemish embassies in Sinzig is in *Chronica regia Coloniensis*, p. 130. Opll, RI IV2/3:257, no. 2547, dated the embassy May 1180 on account of Frederick's itinerary but conceded that the report also fits 1181. Ehlers, *Heinrich der Löwe*, pp. 340–41 and p. 421, n. 60, thought that Opll's 1180 date was erroneous. It seems likely that both chroniclers were referring to the same incident.
22. DFI, no. 811 (25 May 1181; issued in Stauf); *Die Traditionen des Kollegiatstifts St. Kastulus in Moosburg*, ed. Klaus Höflinger (Munich, 1994), pp. 149–50, no. 143 (24 May 1181; Duke Otto of Bavaria accompanied Frederick to Saxony); Arnold of Lübeck, *Chronica Slavorum*, pp. 139–40 (Bavarians crossed the Elbe); *Annales Pegavienses*, pp. 264–65; *Annales Palidenses*, pp. 95–96; and RI IV2/4:9–13, nos. 2597–99, 2603, 2605, and 2607–11. See Ehlers, *Heinrich der Löwe*, p. 341.
23. Arnold of Lübeck, *Chronica Slavorum*, pp. 140, 143, and 162; Saxo Grammaticus, *Ex Saxonis gestis Danorum*, pp. 150–51; and RI IV2/4:13–15, nos. 2612 and 2614. See Engels, "Friedrich Barbarossa und Dänemark," pp. 381–85; Weller, *Die Heiratspolitik des deutschen Hochadels im 12. Jahrhundert*, pp. 130–36; and Ehlers, *Heinrich der Löwe*, p. 342.
24. Arnold of Lübeck, *Chronica Slavorum*, pp. 140–41; and RI IV2/4:14–15, no. 2614. See Opll, *Stadt und Reich im 12. Jahrhundert*, pp. 108–09. None of these charters survives.
25. Arnold of Lübeck, *Chronica Slavorum*, pp. 141–42; *Chronica regia Coloniensis*, p. 132 (three-year exile); *Ex Rogeri de Hoveden chronica*, ed. Felix Liebermann and Reinhold Pauli, in MGH SS 27 (Hanover, 1885), p. 146 (seven-year exile); *Ex gestis Henrici II. et Ricardi I.*, p. 107 (permanent exile); *Annales Sancti Petri Erphesfurdenses*: *Continuatio a. 1164–1182*, ed. Georg Heinrich Pertz, MGH SS 16 (Hanover, 1859), p. 25 (Frederick allowed Henry to retain only Brunswick and Lüneburg); DFI, no. 814 (16 November 1181; grant of Stade to

Bremen); and RI IV2/4:16–22, nos 2623–25, 2628, and 2633–34. See Odilo Engels, "Zur Entmachtung Heinrichs des Löwen," in idem, *Stauferstudien*, pp. 119–28; and Ehlers, *Heinrich der Löwe*, pp. 342–44.

26. Engels, "Friedrich Barbarossa und Dänemark," pp. 381–85; and Weller, *Die Heiratspolitik des deutschen Hochadels*, pp. 607–09.
27. See, for example, Mitteis, *Lehnrecht und Staatsgewalt*, pp. 260–63 and esp. pp. 431–44. Vollrath, "Politische Ordnungsvorstellungen und politisches Handeln im Vergleich: Philipp II. Augustus von Frankreich und Friedrich Barbarossa," pp. 33–51, argued that the preconditions were totally different in the two realms.
28. Görich, "Jäger des Löwen oder Getriebener der Fürsten?" pp. 116–17.
29. Arnold of Lübeck, *Chronica Slavorum*, pp. 161–62; DFI, no. 981 (19 September 1188; Frederick's charter for Lübeck contains later interpolations); and RI IV2/4:229–31, nos. 3191–92. See Opll, *Stadt und Reich im 12. Jahrhundert*, pp. 109–12.
30. Eike von Repgow, *The Saxon Mirror*, p. 129, 3.53a; p. 131, 3.60; and p. 150, 4.20. Hampe, *Germany under the Salian and Hohenstaufen Emperors*, pp. 204–05; and Mitteis, *Lehnrecht und Staatsgewalt*, pp. 431–32 and 692–700, blamed Frederick's inability to acquire Henry's duchies on the *Leihezwang*. Goez, *Der Leihezwang*, esp. pp. 226–37, demonstrated that there was no such requirement of compulsory re-enfeoffment.
31. Gilbert of Mons, *Chronicle of Hainaut*, p. 137, ch. 169; and Eike von Repgow, *The Saxon Mirror*, p. 69, 1.3 (hierarchy), and p. 175, 4.78 (prince). The classic work on the *Reichsfürstenstand* is Julius Ficker's *Vom Reichsfürstenstande: Forschungen zur Geschichte der Reichsverfassung zunaechst im XII. und XIII. Jahrhunderte*, 2 vols. 1 (Innsbruck, 1861), 2, edn. Paul Puntschart. 2 parts (Innsbruck, 1911, and Graz and Leipzig, 1921–23). Since it took sixty years for Ficker's rather disorganized book to appear in print in its entirety, Fritz Walter Schönherr's synthesis of Ficker's views, *Die Lehre vom Reichsfürstenstande des Mittelalters* (Leipzig, 1914), is still of use. On the military order of precedence, see Julius Ficker, *Vom Heerschilde: Ein Beitrag zur deutschen Reichs- und Rechtsgeschichte* (Innsbruck, 1862; reprint, Aalen, 1964).
32. DFI, no. 546 (10 July 1168; the "Golden Liberty") and no. 857 (c. 20 May 1184; also *Constitutiones* 1:423–24, no. 298; Namur); and RI IV2/4:80–81, no. 2764. On the formation of the *Reichsfürstenstand*, see Karl Heinemeyer, "König und Reichsfürsten in der späten Salier- und frühen Stauferzeit," *Blätter für deutsche Landesgeschichte* 122 (1986): 1–39. On the informal agreement limiting the number of principalities a lineage could hold, see Lyon, *Princely Brothers and Sisters*, pp. 114–19.
33. Kölzer, "Der Hof Kaiser Barbarossas und die Reichsfürsten," esp. pp. 18–21 and 30–42; reprinted without the footnotes as "Der Hof Friedrich Barbarossas und die Reichsfürsten," esp. pp. 225–27 and 230–35; Keupp, *Dienst und Verdienst*, esp. pp. 29–30 and 341–42; and Plassmann, *Die Struktur des Hofes unter Friedrich I. Barbarossa*, passim.
34. *Historia Welforum cum continuatione Steingademensi*, pp. 86–89 (Welf's festival); Giesebrecht and Simson, *Geschichte der deutschen Kaiserzeit* 6:71; Lindner, "Fest und Herrschaft unter Kaiser Friedrich Barbarossa," esp. pp. 153–56; and Bumke, *Courtly Culture*, p. 207 (*Hochzeit*).
35. Gilbert of Mons, *Chronicle of Hainaut*, pp. 86–90, ch. 109; Arnold of Lübeck, *Chronica Slavorum*, pp. 151–54; Otto of St. Blasien, *Chronicle*, pp. 76–79, ch. 26; *Marbach Annals*, pp. 168–71; *Chronica regia Coloniensis*, p. 133; Eike von Repgow, *The Saxon Mirror*, pp. 130–31, 3.57; and RI IV2/4:76–79, no. 2762. See Bumke, *Courtly Culture*, pp. 203–07 (on the Mainz festival; the quotation from Heinrich von Veldeke is on p. 206) and pp. 258–60 (on the *buhurt*). Examples of articles that treat the festivities in Mainz as the high point of German courtly culture are: Josef Fleckenstein, "Friedrich Barbarossa und das Rittertum: Zur Bedeutung der grossen Mainzer Hoftage von 1184 und 1188," in Arno Borst, ed., *Das Rittertum im Mittelalter* (Darmstadt, 1976), pp. 392–418; and William Henry Jackson, "Knighthood and the Hohenstaufen Imperial Court under Frederick Barbarossa (1152–1190)," in Christopher Harper-Bill and Ruth Harvey, eds, *The Ideals and Practice of Medieval Knighthood III: Papers from the fourth (sic) Strawberry Hill Conference* (Woodbridge, Suffolk, and Rochester, N.Y., 1990), pp. 101–20. On Archbishop Philip's dispute with the abbot of Fulda, see above, pp. 95–96.
36. Otto of Freising, *Deeds* 1.18 and 26. Otto's account of his older brothers' tournament (1.18) is the first known use of the word *turnoimentum* in a German source. Frederick's

patronage of courtly literature is a disputed topic. For a negative assessment, see Ganz, "Friedrich Barbarossa: Hof und Kultur," pp. 639–42; for a more positive view, see Johanek, "Kultur und Bildung im Umkreis Friedrich Barbarossas," pp. 661–65. Bumke, *Courtly Culture*, pp. 75–82, stressed the role of the princely courts rather than the imperial court in the reception and patronage of courtly literature. On the wide range of meanings of the words *Ritter* and *miles*, see Joachim Bumke, *The Concept of Knighthood in the Middle Ages*, trans. by W. T. H. and Erika Jackson (New York, 1982). On the use of *knight* as a synonym for *ministerialis*, see Arnold, *German Knighthood*. On the designation of the ministerials' servile retainers as knights, see John B. Freed, "Nobles, Ministerials, and Knights in the Archdiocese of Salzburg," *Speculum* 62 (1987): 575–611. For a negative assessment of Frederick's identification with knighthood in Mainz, see Keupp, *Dienst und Verdienst*, pp. 388–93.

37. Gilbert of Mons, *Chronicle of Hainaut*, pp. 84–85, ch. 107; and pp. 86–90, esp. p. 89, ch. 109; DFI, no. 857 (c. 20 May 1184; also *Constitutiones* 1:423–24, no. 298); and RI IV2/4:73–81, nos. 2752, 2760, 2762, 2764, and p. 117, no. 2857 (Dietrich's enfeoffment with Lower Lusatia). See Kupper, "Friedrich Barbarossa im Maasgebiet," pp. 232–35; and Weller, *Die Heiratspolitik des deutschen Hochadels im 12. Jahrhundert*, pp. 419–21.
38. Gilbert of Mons, *Chronicle of Hainaut*, pp. 86–91, chs. 109–10.
39. Ibid., pp. 47–48, ch. 48 (Henry II's kinship with Philip of Flanders); *Annales Pegavienses*, p. 265; *Ex gestis Henrici II. et Ricardi I.*, p. 105 (Henry attended the Mainz court, but the chronicler placed the court in 1183 and said it was prompted by the death of Duke Bernard of Saxony, when it was Otto of Wittelsbach who died that year); p. 106 (visit of Archbishop Philip and Philip of Flanders to Henry II); DFI, no. 872 (19 October 1184; also *Constitutiones* 1:426, no. 301; Obizo's enfeoffment); and RI IV2/4:87, no. 2782, and p. 92, no. 2794. See Engels, "Zur Entmachtung Heinrichs des Löwen," pp. 124–25; Huffman, *The Social Politics of Medieval Diplomacy*, pp. 111–20 (a critical response to Engels' thesis); Weller, *Die Heiratspolitik des deutschen Hochadels im 12. Jahrhundert*, pp. 172–75; and Ehlers, *Heinrich der Löwe*, pp. 360–66 (relies on Engels).

Chapter 16 New Entanglements

1. *Constitutiones* 1:420–21, no. 296; and RI IV2/4:63, no. 2722. Frederick's letter was not published in DFI. On the legates' presence in Constance, see RI IV2/4:61–62, nos. 2719 and 2721. On Lucius' stay in Rome and the Patrimony, see Petersohn, *Kaisertum und Rom im spätsalischer und staufischer Zeit*, pp. 292–97.
2. *Annales Ratisbonenses*, ed. Wilhelm Wattenbach, in MGH SS 17 (Hanover, 1861), p. 589; *Ex gestis Henrici II. et Ricardi I.*, p. 589; DFI, no. 866 (22 September 1184, Milan); and no. 872 (19 October 1184, Verona); and RI IV2/4:87–113, nos. 2782–83, 2801, and 2846. Engels, "Zur Entmachtung Heinrichs des Löwen," p. 124, and Ehlers, *Heinrich der Löwe*, p. 364, assumed that Frederick left from Regensburg, used the Brenner Pass, and detoured to Milan so he could meet the envoys Henry II was sending to Verona to get the pope to persuade Frederick to allow Henry the Lion to return to Saxony. Opll, RI IV2/4:88, no. 2783, thought so, too; but he also argued, p. 87, no. 2782, that Frederick might have gone directly to Milan via the Lukmanier Pass. Since Archbishop Philip only went to England in September, Frederick could not have known on 1 September that Henry II was going to dispatch an embassy to Verona. A better guess is that Frederick, who was still in Kaiserslautern, west of the middle Rhine, on 31 July (RI IV2/4:86, no. 2779), went by the most direct route to Milan because he was now on friendly terms with his former enemy.
3. DFI, no. 732 (14 June 1178; also *Salzburger Urkundenbuch* 2:567–73, no. 415; Frederick's privilege for Gurk); no. 868 (1 October 1184, Pavia); *Salzburger Urkundenbuch* 2:577–80, no. 419 (12 April 1179; Alexander's privilege); *Die Gurker Geschichtsquellen 864–1231*, ed. August von Jaksch, in Monumenta historica ducatus Carinthiae 1 (Klagenfurt, 1896), pp. 248–49, no. 330 (November 1184; excerpts of letter from Adalbert to Salzburg notifying the cathedral clergy of the ruling in Salzburg's favor and of the receipt of both the imperial and papal privileges); *Salzburger Urkundenbuch* 2:603–05, no. 442 (3 December 1184; also *Die Gurker Geschichtsquellen* 1:249, no. 331; Lucius' privilege); and RI IV2/3:202, no. 2386

and 2/4:105–08, nos. 2823–24 and 2830. Frederick's 1184 privilege for Gurk that Adalbert mentioned in his letter does not survive. See Dopsch, *Geschichte Salzburgs* 1/1:236–38, 294, 298–99, and 301. Leopold V also witnessed DFI, no. 903 (4 May 1185) and no. 905 (17 May 1185).

4. The complete text of Adalbert's letter is in Bernhard Pez, *Thesaurus anecdotorum novissimus seu veterum monumentorum praecipue ecclesiasticorum, ex Germanicis potissimum bibliothecis adornata collectio recentissima* 6/2 (Veith, 1729), pp. 47–48, no. 69. The text in *Die Gurker Geschichtsquellen*, cited in the preceding footnote, contains only those portions of Adalbert's letter that pertain to Gurk. DFI, no. 887 (24 November 1184; Templars); and no. 923 (28 November 1185; Hospitalers); *Ex Chronico universali anonymi Laudunensis*, ed. Georg Waitz, in MGH SS 26 (Hanover, 1882), p. 450; *Marbach Annals*, pp. 170–71 (the patriarch of Jerusalem and the masters of the two military orders warned about the situation in the Holy Land); and RI IV2/4:95–108, nos. 2801, 2810–11, and 2829–30, and pp. 143–44, no. 2937. Although Frederick's charter for the Hospitalers is dated 28 November 1185, the list of witnesses is virtually identical with the list in the charter for the Templars. The transaction thus probably occurred already in November 1184 even if the charter itself was drafted and dated (misdated?) a year later. See head note to no. 923. The text of Frederick's proscription of the heretical sects that Adalbert mentioned in his letter does not survive.
5. Arnold of Lübeck, *Chronica Slavorum*, pp. 154–56; *Chronica regia Coloniensis*, p. 134; *Marbach Annals*, pp. 170–71 (announcement of engagement); Albert of Stade, *Annales Stadenses*, p. 350 (Lucius had agreed to crown Henry); and RI IV2/4:95–97, no. 2801. Arnold's source on these events was Bishop Conrad II of Lübeck (1183–85), who was in Verona. See Gerhard Baaken, "Unio regni ad imperium: Die Verhandlungen von Verona 1184 und die Eheabredung zwischen König Heinrich VI. und Konstanze von Sizilien," in idem, *Imperium und Papsttum*, pp. 86–87 (the pope's statement in Faenza), and Csendes, *Heinrich VI.*, pp. 56–57.
6. Otto of St. Blasien, *Chronicle*, pp. 78–81, ch. 28; *Chronica regia Coloniensis*, p. 134; Andrew of Marchiennes, *Continuatio Aquicinctina*, pp. 425–26; and Richard of San Germano, *Chronica*, ed. Georg Heinrich Pertz, in MGH SS 19 (Hanover, 1866), p. 324 (paraphrase of the barons' oath). Richard wrote in the 1240s and no doubt included the oath in his narrative with the benefit of hindsight about its significance.
7. Paul Scheffer-Boichorst argued in *Kaiser Friedrich I. letzter Streit mit der Kurie* (Berlin, 1866) that the news of Henry's engagement caused the breakdown in Frederick's negotiations with the curia. Simson, in his continuation of Giesebrecht's *Geschichte der deutschen Kaiserzeit* 6:97–99, conveyed this view to the educated public. Johannes Haller rejected this argument in his "Heinrich VI. und die römische Kirche," *MIÖG* 35 (1914): 412–45, and even proposed that Lucius arranged the marriage. Baaken refuted, in 1972, in "Unio regni ad imperium," Haller's argument about Lucius' role. Heinz Wolter, "Die Verlobung Heinrichs VI. mit Konstanze von Sizilien im Jahre 1184," *Historisches Jahrbuch* 105 (1985): 30–51, maintained that the initiative came from William II. He feared the ambitions of his illegitimate cousin, Count Tancred of Lecce, who indeed seized the crown in 1189 after William's death; and that Henry the Lion, as the emissary of William's father-in-law, Henry II, proposed the match to Frederick in Mainz in May 1184. My presentation is based on Houben, "Barbarossa und die Normannen," pp. 118–28; Schmidt, *Königswahl und Thronfolge im 12. Jahrhundert*, pp. 198–206; and Weller, *Die Heiratspolitik des deutschen Hochadels im 12. Jahrhundert*, pp. 110–29.
8. *Gestorum Treverorum continuatio tertia*, ed. Georg Waitz, in MGH SS 24 (Hanover, 1879), pp. 383–85; and Arnold of Lübeck, *Chronica Slavorum*, pp. 155–56. The report in the *Chronica regia Coloniensis*, p. 134, is considerably vaguer; but it, too, connected the pope's rejection of Frederick's request that he crown Henry with Henry's seizure of property that belonged to unspecified others. Haller, *Heinrich VI. und die römische Kirche*, pp. 18–24, argued that Henry's rash actions occurred only in the autumn of 1185 and could not thus have caused the rupture in imperial–papal relations at Verona. Baaken, "Unio regni ad imprium," pp. 89–94, repudiated Haller's argument.
9. RI IV2/4:113–15, nos 2845 and 2851–52. See Opll, *Stadt und Reich im 12. Jahrhundert*, p. 249.

10. DFI, no. 896 (1 February 1185; also *Constitutiones* 1:428–31, no. 303); and RI IV2/4:117–18, no. 2859. See Opll, *Stadt und Reich im 12. Jahrhundert*, pp. 259 and 339–41; and Görich, "Ein Kartäuser im Dienst Friedrich Barbarossas," pp. 94–96.
11. RI IV2/4:125–28, nos. 2880 and 2882–83. See Opll, *Stadt und Reich im 12. Jahrhundert*, p. 248.
12. DFI, no. 895 (21 January–10 July 1185; also *Constitutiones* 1:426–28); and RI IV2/4:130–31, no. 2896 (on the dating of DFI, no. 895) and no. 2897 (outlawing of Cremona). On Frederick's mistreatment in Cremona in December 1176, see above, pp. 398–99.
13. RI IV2/4:129–37, nos. 2891 and 2913–14; and Csendes, *Heinrich VI.*, p. 58.
14. Gilbert of Mons, *Chronicle of Hainaut*, pp. 91–104, chs. 112–21, esp. ch. 121; *Ex gestis Henrici II. et Ricardi I.*, pp. 106–07 (Philip of Flanders appealed to Frederick for help); *E Gervasii Cantuariensis chronica*, pp. 303–04 (Frederick prohibited Henry's march through Hainaut); RI IV2/4:89–140, nos. 2786, 2877a, and 2926; and RI IV3:7, no. 4a (Henry VI in Speyer). See Walther Kienast, *Die deutschen Fürsten im Dienste der Westmächte bis zum Tode Philipps des Schönen von Frankreich* 1 (Utrecht, 1924), pp. 112–19; idem, *Deutschland und Frankreich in der Kaiserzeit (900–1270): Weltkaiser und Einzelkönige*, 2 vols., 2nd edn. (Stuttgart, 1974), 1:229–33; Huffman, *The Social Politics of Medieval Diplomacy*, pp. 118–19; and Csendes, *Heinrich VI.*, p. 60.
15. *Gestorum Treverorum continuatio tertia*, p. 385; and Gunther Wolf, "Imperator und Caesar—zu den Anfängen des staufischen Erbreichsgedankens," in idem, ed., *Friedrich Barbarossa*, pp. 366–67.
16. Arnold of Lübeck, *Chronica Slavorum*, pp. 158–59; *Gestorum Treverorum continuatio tertia*, p. 385; DFI, no. 932 (22 February 1186; the Pavian convent); and RI IV2/4:144–52, nos. 2938 and 2962.
17. Andrew of Marchiennes, *Chronica: Continuatio Aquicinctina*, p. 423; *Ex Radulfi de Diceto operibus historicis*, p. 274; DFI, no. 76 (3–17? May 1154; "Romanorum rex in Christo semper victor cesar augustus"), no. 212 (March 1158; "anno regni domini Friderici invictissimi cesaris"), and no. 336 (18 June 1155–16 August 1161; "imperator cesar augustus"). Wolf, "Imperator und Caesar," pp. 360–74, argued that the use of the title *Caesar* was an attempt to make the imperial dignity hereditary. Schmidt, "Königswahl und Thronfolge im 12. Jahrhundert," pp. 206–24; and idem, "'A quo ergo habet, si a domno papa non habet imperium?'" pp. 84–87, rejected Wolf's argument and downplayed the significance of the title.
18. DFI, no. 941 (8 June 1186, at the siege of Castel Manfredi; also *Constitutiones* 1:433–35, no. 306; notarial instrument on the terms for Cremona's capitulation); no. 942 (8 June 1186, at the siege; also *Constitutiones* 1:435–36, no. 307; Frederick restored Cremona to his grace); no. 943 (9 June 1186, "at the destruction of Castel Manfredi"; Frederick's grant to Milan); no. 944 (9 June 1186, "at the destruction of Castel Manfredi"; Frederick rewarded Asti for its service "in the campaign against Cremona and at the destruction of Castel Manfredi," at the request of Bishop William of Asti, who witnessed the charters issued at Castel Manfredi); *Constitutiones* 1:436–37, no. 308 (8 June 1186; fine paid by Cremona), pp. 437–38, no. 309 (24 June 1186; surrender of the privileges), pp. 438–39, nos. 310–11 (29 and 30 June; payment of the £1,500), and pp. 441–44, no. 314 (18 June 1186; participation of the bishops and the other Lombard communes in the campaign [p. 442, ll. 37–40]); Andrew of Marchiennes, *Chronica: Continuatio Aquicinctina*, p. 424 (Milanese role in defeat of Cremona); and RI IV2/4:161–67, nos. 2995–99, 3004, and 3007. See Opll, *Stadt und Reich im 12. Jahrhundert*, p. 260.
19. *Constitutiones* 1:441–44, no. 314; and RI IV2/4:161–65, nos. 2994 and 3001.
20. *Constitutiones* 1:440–41, no. 313 (June 1186; terms of Siena's submission) and RI IV2/4:168, no. 3009, and p. 206, no. 3128. On Henry's itinerary in 1186 and 1187, see RI IV3:9–31, nos. 6–65. See Partner, *The Lands of St. Peter*, p. 218; Csendes, *Heinrich VI.*, pp. 63–67; and Petersohn, *Kaisertum und Rom in spätsalischer und staufischer Zeit*, pp. 298–308.
21. *Gestorum Treverorum continuatio tertia*, pp. 385–86; Arnold of Lübeck, *Chronica Slavorum*, pp. 158–59; DFI, nos. 941 and 943 (8 and 9 June 1186; charters Rudolf witnessed outside Castel Manfredi); *Constitutiones* 1:444–48, nos. 315–316 (early December 1186; envoys who

had received Urban's assurances that he would not consecrate Folmar); and RI IV2/4:159–68, nos. 2889–92 and 3011. Gervase of Canterbury, *E Gervasii Cantuariensis chronica*, p. 304, noted that Frederick prohibited anyone in the Empire or elsewhere from making an appeal to the pope and that anyone who was caught coming and going to the pope was imprisoned and/or horribly mutilated. This was true in particular at Ivrea and Turin, Gervase said, because these castles controlled the roads that led, respectively, to the St. Bernard and Mont Cenis Passes. Urban's complaint of 18 June that imperial ministerials were levying unauthorized exactions on the clergy in the dioceses of Turin and Ivrea may have referred, conceivably, to imperial control of these passes.

One other source needs to be mentioned in this context, the so-called newer Hildesheim letter collection. It was compiled around 1195, probably in the school and chancery of the cathedral chapter of Hildesheim, as a textbook on letter writing. It contains ninety-three sample letters, thirty-six of which concern imperial or territorial history (numbers 41–77), all but two of which deal with events in the period from 1184 to 1190. While none of the letters in their present form was actually sent, the compiler had contacts with the imperial chancery, the Welfs, and Cologne, and may have used actual letters as his models. The scholarly consensus is that the specific facts contained in the letters are thus accurate. *Die jüngere Hildesheimer Briefsammlung*, ed. Rolf de Kegel (Munich, 1995), pp. 14–25; and Ferdinand Opll, "Beiträge zur historischen Auswertung der jüngeren Hildesheimer Briefsammlung," *DA* 33 (1977): 473–500. In one of the letters, pp. 88–89, no. 41 (RI IV2/4:159–60, no. 2990), Urban allegedly wrote to Frederick about the closing of the passes to those traveling to see the pope and demanded their opening. See Opll, pp. 479–80.

22. *Gestorum Treverorum continuatio tertia*, pp. 386–87; Arnold of Lübeck, *Chronica Slavorum*, p. 159; and RI IV2/4:166–74, nos. 3005–06, 3010, 3013–18, and 3030. See Giesebrecht and Simson, *Geschichte der deutschen Kaiserzeit* 6:144–46. Berthold of Bremen and Bertram of Metz was the same person. See Hauck, *Kirchengeschichte Deutschlands* 4:922.
23. Arnold of Lübeck, *Chronica Slavorum*, pp. 160–61; *Gestorum Treverorum continuatio tertia*, p. 385 (Bishop Hermann's testimony at Gelnhausen about Urban's promise); *Constitutiones* 1:444–48, nos. 315–16 (after 28 November 1186, likely December; letters of Wichmann and Adalbert), and no. 317 (19 February 1187; letter of Urban to Wichmann); and RI IV2/4:177–79, nos. 3037 and 3041–42. See Giesebrecht and Simson, *Geschichte der deutschen Kaiserzeit* 6:146–50; and Claude, *Geschichte des Erzbistums Magdeburg* 2:171–73. Frederick's charter for Bremen, DFI, no. 955, issued on 28 November 1186, provides a list of the princes who attended the court in Gelnhausen; the archbishops of Mainz, Bremen, Magdeburg, and Salzburg headed the list of witnesses.
24. Arnold of Lübeck, *Chronica Slavorum*, p. 161; *Annales Pegavienses*, p. 265; *Annales Magdeburgenses*, p. 195; *E Gervasii Cantuariensis chronica*, p. 305; *Marbach Annals*, pp. 174–75; *Constitutiones* 1:448, no. 317 (19 February 1187; letter of Urban III to Wichmann), and pp. 586–87, no. 410 (29 November 1187; letter of Gregory VIII to Frederick that he had received the envoys whom the emperor had sent to Urban, namely, Bishop Otto and Abbot Siegfried); and RI IV2/4:179–202, nos. 3043, 3054, 3058, 3064 (on Wichmann's presence in Regensburg in February and March 1187), 3102, 3109, 3111, and 3115. See Giesebrecht and Simson, *Geschichte der deutschen Kaiserzeit* 6:157–59 and pp. 165–66. Simson wrongly had the canons electing a new archbishop in 1187 as part of Gregory's peace settlement, but Folmar was deposed only in 1189.
25. *Annales Pegavienses*, p. 265. See Engels, "Der Niederrhein und das Reich im 12. Jahrhundert," pp. 191–95; Stehkämper, "Friedrich Barbarossa und die Stadt Köln: Ein Wirtschaftskrieg am Niederrhein," pp. 367–413, esp. pp. 400–03; Huffman, *The Social Politics of Medieval Diplomacy*, pp. 120–27; and Groten, "Köln und das Reich," pp. 250–51. Huffman, pp. 121–22, saw Philip's close ties to the papacy as the "initial cause" of the conflict, but I am inclined, like most German scholars, to see Philip's territorial ambitions as the cause. Görich, *Friedrich Barbarossa*, pp. 534–35, suggested that it was ultimately not commercial and territorial conflicts that were the real cause of the animosity between Frederick and Philip, but that the archbishop had compelled the emperor to proceed against his cousin. It is noteworthy that such staunch supporters of Alexander III as Conrad of Mainz and Adalbert of Salzburg were not ready to back Urban. On the seating dispute, see above, p. 95–96; on the trade war

on the lower Rhine, see above, p. 374, and pp. 450–51 and 460–61 on Philip's opposition to Baldwin of Hainaut.

26. Arnold of Lübeck, *Chronica Slavorum*, pp. 156 and 159; *Annales Aquenses (1–1196)*, ed. Georg Waitz, in MGH SS 24 (Hanover, 1879), p. 39 (enmity broke out between Frederick and Philip in 1186); and RI IV2/4:160–61, no. 2993, pp. 175–76, no. 3032, and pp. 177–78, no. 3038 (on Philip's presence in Gelnhausen in November). On the date of Philip's papal legation, see Engels, "Der Niederrhein und das Reich im 12. Jahrhundert," p. 194. It should be pointed out that Philip, unlike his colleagues in Mainz, Bremen, Magdeburg, and Salzburg, did not witness in Gelnhausen on 28 November the emperor's charter for Bremen (DFI, no. 955); so perhaps he left early.
27. *Gestorum Treverorum continuatio tertia*, p. 387; *Chronica regia Coloniensis*, p. 135; and RI IV2/4:181–82, nos. 3051 and 3053. See Giesebrecht and Simson, *Geschichte der deutschen Kaiserzeit* 6:150–51 and 156–57.
28. *Gestorum Treverorum continuatio tertia*, p. 387; Gilbert of Mons, *Chronicle of Hainaut*, pp. 57–58, ch. 58; and p. 107, ch. 129; *Chronica regia Coloniensis*, pp. 135–36; and RI IV2/4:188–89, nos. 3074–75. See Kienast, *Deutschland und Frankreich in der Kaiserzeit*, pp. 236–38.
29. *Chronica regia Coloniensis*, p. 136; and RI IV2/4:190–92, nos. 3079 and 3084. See Kienast, *Deutschland und Frankreich in der Kaiserzeit*, pp. 237–38; and Engels, "Der Niederrhein und das Reich im 12. Jahrhundert," pp. 196–97 and n. 90.
30. *Chronica regia Coloniensis*, p. 136; *Annales Magdeburgenses*, p. 195 (under 1186; bishops cleared themselves with an oath and Philip was summoned to attend the court in Strasbourg); *Annales Pegavienses*, p. 265; *Marbach Annals*, pp. 174–75 (under 1186); Gilbert of Mons, *Chronicle of Hainaut*, p. 109, ch. 132; and RI IV2/4:195, no. 3096.
31. *The History of the Expedition of the Emperor Frederick*, trans. G. A. Loud, in *The Crusade of Frederick Barbarossa: The History of the Expedition of the Emperor Frederick and Related Texts* (Farnham, Surrey, U.K., 2010), pp. 37–44 (texts of Gregory and the legate's letters); *The History of the Pilgrims*, in Loud, *The Crusade of Frederick Barbarossa*, pp. 141–43; and RI IV2/4:200–03, nos. 3110–11, 3113–14, 3116, and 3118.
32. *Marbach Annals*, pp. 176–77 (the legate did not attend); Gilbert of Mons, *Chronicle of Hainaut*, pp. 110–11, ch. 136; *Gestorum Treverorum continuatio tertia*, p. 387 (on Trier); Alberic of Trois-Fontaines, *Chronicle*, ed. Paul Scheffer-Boichorst, in MGH SS 23 (Hanover, 1874), p. 861 (Henry of Albano and the archbishop of Tyre were present, and the death of Folmar in Tours); and RI IV2/4:204–07, nos. 3125–26 and 3133. On Frederick's decision to take the cross, see Rudolf Hiestand, "'precipua tocius christianismi columpna': Barbarossa und der Kreuzzug," in Haverkamp, ed., *Friedrich Barbarossa*, pp. 58–60.
33. *Chronica regia Coloniensis*, pp. 138–39 (Frederick's dealings with Archbishop Philip and Frederick's taking of the cross); *The History of the Expedition of the Emperor Frederick*, pp. 44–45 (Frederick called it the court of Christ); Magnus of Reichersberg, *Chronicon*, p. 509 (reading of the letter and Frederick announced the general expedition); *The History of the Pilgrims*, pp. 143–44; *Continuatio Zwetlensis altera*, p. 549 (Frederick did not preside; period to prepare for expedition); Otto of St. Blasien, *Chronicle*, pp. 88–89, ch. 31 (amount of money needed by participants); Arnold of Lübeck, *Chronica Slavorum*, p. 170 (Godfrey of Würzburg preached and Henry the Lion was summoned to attend the court in Goslar); and RI IV2/4:206–13, nos. 3128, 3138, and 3145 (sources and literature that deal with the Mainz court). The portion of Otto of St. Blasien's *Chronicle* dealing with the Third Crusade has been translated in Loud, *The Crusade of Frederick Barbarossa* (see p. 176 on the court held in Mainz). Görich, *Friedrich Barbarossa*, p. 534, pointed out that the description of the vacant throne in Mainz was metaphorical, so we cannot be certain that it really was vacant.
34. RI IV2/4:213, no. 3147. See Robert Chazan, "Emperor Frederick I, the Third Crusade, and the Jews," *Viator* 8 (1977): 83–93; and Keupp, *Dienst und Verdienst*, pp. 174–75 (on Cuno and the Jews).
35. Gilbert of Mons, *Chronicle of Hainaut*, pp. 113–15, ch. 139; pp. 123–25, chs. 148–49; pp. 137–39, ch. 170; and p. 182, ch. 255; *Constitutiones* 1:465, no. 326 (16 May 1188; Henry

VI's agreement with Baldwin; the text of Frederick's agreement does not survive); and RI IV2/4:219–38, nos. 3158, 3199, and 3209; and RI IV3:33–49, nos. 67, 73, and 109. See Kupper, "Friedrich Barbarossa im Maasgebiet," pp. 236–38.

36. *Gestorum Treverorum continuatio tertia*, p. 389; *Constitutiones* 1:587, no. 412 (30 November 1187; Gregory VIII to Folmar); *Chronica regia Coloniensis*, p. 143; and RI IV2/4:221, no. 3166, and p. 248, no. 3239. John was identified for the last time as the chancellor on 16 August 1189 (DFI, vol. 5, p. 19). See Giesebrecht and Simson, *Geschichte der deutschen Kaiserzeit* 6:203–04.
37. Arnold of Lübeck, *Chronica Slavorum*, p. 170; and RI IV2/4:224–25, no. 3177. The *Chronica regia Coloniensis*, p. 140, and the *Annales Stedeburgenses auctore Gerhardo praeposito*, ed. Georg Heinrich Pertz, in MGH SS 16 (Hanover, 1859), p. 221, mention only the three-year exile. See Ehlers, *Heinrich der Löwe*, pp. 377–78.
38. DFI, no. 774 (18 February 1179; also *Constitutiones* 1:380–83, no. 277); and RI IV2/3:232–33, no. 2482.
39. DFI, no. 988 (29 or 30 December 1186 or more likely 1188; also *Constitutiones* 1:449–52, dated 29 December 1186); *Chronicon S. Michaelis Luneburgensis*, ed. Ludwig Weiland, in MGH SS 23 (Hanover, 1874), p. 396; and RI IV2/4:240–241, no. 3215. The date of the law is uncertain. Copies of the law give the year of the incarnation as 1187, that is, 1186 in our calendar, but the sixth indiction, that is, 1188. Burchard of Ursberg, who included the complete text in his *Chronicon*, pp. 216–23, said that Frederick promulgated the law after he took the cross (pp. 216–17), that is, after March 1188. Since a stay in Nuremberg in late December fits Frederick's itinerary better in 1188 than in 1186, the scholarly consensus today is that he issued the law in all likelihood in preparation for his departure on the crusade. See p. 274, head note to DFI, no. 988. An English translation of the law, except for the *arenga*, can be found in Loud, *The Crusade of Frederick Barbarossa*, pp. 209–12. See Leyser, "Frederick Barbarossa: Court and Country," pp. 151–53; and Othmar Hageneder, "Der Mainzer Reichslandfriede (1235) und die *Constitutio contra incendiarios* Friedrichs I. Barbarossa," in Richard H. Helmholz et al., eds, *Grundlagen des Rechts: Festschrift für Peter Landau zum 65. Geburtstag* (Paderborn, Munich, Vienna, and Zürich, 2000), pp. 372–73.
40. *Annales Romani*, ed. Georg Heinrich Pertz, in MGH SS 5 (Hanover, 1844), p. 479; and *Constitutiones* 1:586, no. 411 (29 November 1187; Gregory to Henry). See Petersohn, *Kaisertum und Rom in spätsalischer und staufischer Zeit*, pp. 308–09; and Schmidt, "'A quo ergo habet, si a domno papa non habet imperium?'" pp. 86–87.
41. *Annales Romani*, p. 480; *Constitutiones* 1:460–63, no. 322 (3 April 1189; Henry's restoration of the Patrimony); no. 323 (10 April 1189; Frederick's letter to Clement; it is not in DFI); and no. 324 (18 April 1189; Henry's letter to Clement); Johann Friedrich Böhmer, ed., *Acta imperii selecta: Urkunden deutscher Könige und Kaiser mit einem Anhange von Reichssachen* (Innsbruck, 1870), pp. 158–59, no. 171 (enfeoffment of Leo de Monumento); *Codice diplomatico del senato Romano dal MCXLIV al MCCCXLVII*, vol. 1, ed. Franco Bartoloni (Rome, 1948), pp. 69–74, no. 42 (31 May 1188; Clement's agreement with the senate); and RI IV2/4:247–48, no. 3238 and RI IV3:19, no. 27, and pp. 37–39, nos. 83–84. See Partner, *The Lands of St. Peter*, pp. 219–22; Petersohn, "Der Vertrag des Römischen Senats mit Papst Clemens III. (1188)," pp. 289–337; and idem, *Kaisertum und Rom in spätsalischer und staufischer Zeit*, pp. 306–19.
42. DFI, no. 970 (23 April 1188; also *Constitutiones* 1:452–57, no. 319), and no. 993 (14 April 1189); RI IV2/4:189–245, nos. 3077, 3155, 3177, and 3229. Only Alfonso's copy of the agreement survives. Otto of St. Blasien, *Chronicle*, pp. 82–83, ch. 28, commented "his other son Conrad was engaged to the daughter of the king of Spain, although it remained without effect." Otto was identified for the first time as the count-palatine on 15 February 1189 (DFI, no. 990). See Weller, *Die Heiratspolitik des deutschen Hochadels im 12. Jahrhundert*, pp. 143–55; and Miriam Shadis, *Berenguela of Castile (1180–1246) and Political Women in the High Middle Ages* (New York, 2009), pp. 51–61.
43. *The History of the Expedition of the Emperor Frederick*, pp. 43–44; *Chronica regia Coloniensis*, pp. 141–42; and RI IV2/4:202, no. 3116; and p. 247, no. 3235. Ansbert is usually said to have written *The History of the Expedition of the Emperor Frederick*, but Loud, in the introduction to *The Crusade of Frederick Barbarossa*, pp. 2–3, argued against this attribution. See Hiestand,

"'precipua tocius christianismi columpna,'" pp. 74–77. Wolfram, *Conrad II.*, p. 198, explained the disadvantages of the sea route.

44. *Chronica regia Coloniensis*, pp. 139–41; *Marbach Annals*, pp. 178–79; *The History of the Pilgrims*, pp. 144–45; and RI IV2/4:214–19, nos. 3149–51 and 3160. See Hiestand, "'precipua tocius christianismi columpna,'" p. 77; and Peter Halfter, "Die Staufer und Armenien," in Lorenz, *Von Schwaben bis Jerusalem*, pp. 190–95. Frederick and Saladin supposedly exchanged letters, but these are almost certainly forgeries. See RI IV2/4:219, no. 3159, and pp. 238–39, no. 3211; and Hiestand, p. 100, n. 326.
45. *The History of the Expedition of the Emperor Frederick*, pp. 45–46; *The History of the Pilgrims*, pp. 145–46; *Chronica regia Coloniensis*, pp. 141–42 (Christmas and the composition of the Seljuk delegation and the Serb embassy); *Marbach Annals*, pp. 178–79 (Frederick was reluctant to grant the Greek demands); and RI IV2/4:239–42, nos. 3212, 3214, and 3216. Since only the *Annales Pegavienses*, p. 266, mentioned the presence of an envoy from "the king of the Arabs," that is, Saladin, the report may not be true. See Hiestand, "'precipua tocius christianismi columpna,'" p. 77.
46. RI IV2/4:250–53, nos. 3244 and 3248. See Hiestand, "'precipua tocius christianismi columpna,'" pp. 86–91; Allan V. Murray, "Finance and Logistics of the Crusade of Frederick Barbarossa," in Iris Shagrir et al., eds, *Laudem Hierosolymitani: Studies in Crusades and Medieval Culture in Honour of Benjamin Z. Kedar* (Aldershot, 2007), pp. 357–68; and Loud, *The Crusade of Frederick Barbarossa*, pp. 18–21.
47. Gilbert of Mons, *Chronicle of Hainaut*, pp. 128–29, ch. 152; and RI IV2/4:252–54, no. 3248 (a complete listing of all the citations). See M. Cecilia Gaposchkin, "From Pilgrimage to Crusade: The Liturgy of Departure, 1095–1300," *Speculum* 88 (2013): 44–91.

Chapter 17 The Third Crusade

1. Loud, *The Crusade of Frederick Barbarossa*, pp. 1–10. The chief source, *The History of the Expedition of the Emperor Frederick*, is a composite work written at the latest around 1200. One of the two earliest copies, probably made before 1221, described the text "as written by an Austrian cleric who was present on the same [expedition]," to which a late thirteenth-century scribe added "called Ansbert." Although commonly referred to as Ansbert's chronicle, "Ansbert" was, at most, the author of a stylistically different appendix that dealt with events in the Holy Land and Empire between Frederick's death in 1190 and Henry VI's return to Italy in 1196. An unnamed compiler, who employed both the first and third persons and who may have worked in the diocese of Passau, assembled the main part of the narrative that dealt with Frederick's passage through the Balkans and Anatolia. He relied greatly on the diary of Tageno, who died in Tripoli in the autumn of 1190. The compiler copied Tageno's diary nearly verbatim from 16 May until 9 June 1190, the day before Frederick's death.

   The diary does not survive, but Magnus of Reichersberg inserted a reworked version of the diary into his chronicle *Chronicon Magni presbyteri* (*The Chronicle of Magnus of Reichersberg*). Magnus and "Ansbert's" accounts of events until Frederick's crossing of the Dardanelles are independent of each other. Magnus' main source for the crusade's progress through the Balkans was a letter that Bishop Diepold of Passau wrote on 11 November 1189 to Duke Leopold V of Austria, which the original author of *The History of the Expedition of the Emperor Frederick* did not use. A third text, *The History of the Pilgrims*, survives in a single, early thirteenth-century copy from the Swabian Cistercian monastery of Salem on Lake Constance, where it may have been assembled around 1200. Its author made extensive use of *The History of the Expedition of the Emperor Frederick*, but sometimes mangled its chronology and included additional information he may have obtained from other eyewitnesses. Loud ended his translation of *The History of the Pilgrims* with Frederick's arrival in Vienna, because it overlapped with "Ansbert's" account. He indicated in the footnotes where *The History of the Pilgrims* provides different or additional information. The newsletter was sent to Europe before Duke Frederick of Swabia, who had assumed command of the crusade after his father's death, led the survivors to Antioch in July 1190.

The complete Latin text of the *Chronicon Magni presbyteri* is in MGH SS 17:476–523. The Latin texts of the three other chronicles, *Quellen zur Geschichte des Kreuzzuges Kaiser Friedrichs I.*, edited by Anton Chroust, are in the MGH SSrG, Nova Series 5 (Berlin, 1928; reprint, Munich 1989). Opll, RI IV2/4:334–39, no. 3470, listed all the sources that mention Frederick's death. Opll commented on p. 339 that it is the best-documented event in Frederick's life. The standard modern work on the crusade is still Ekkehard Eickhoff, *Friedrich Barbarossa im Orient: Kreuzzug und Tod Friedrichs I.* (Tübingen, 1977). Eickhoff discussed the sources on pp. 188–93, but Loud is more up to date. Eickhoff is especially good in reconstructing Frederick's route, particularly in Turkey. There are several supplementary, detailed foldout maps showing the latter part of Frederick's path. Hiestand's "'precipua tocius christianismi columpna'" has superseded Eickhoff on the preparations for the crusade.

2. A. A. Vasiliev, *History of the Byzantine Empire 324–1453*, 2nd English edn., 2 vols. (Madison, WI, 1964), pp. 432–44; Robert Lee Wolff, "The 'Second Bulgarian Empire': Its Origins and History to 1204," *Speculum* 24 (1949): 167–206, esp. pp. 180–85 and 198–201; Charles M. Brand, "The Byzantines and Saladin, 1185–1192: Opponents of the Third Crusade," *Speculum* 37 (1962): 167–81; Eickhoff, *Friedrich Barbarossa im Orient*, pp. 63–65; and Martin Dimnik, "Kievan Rus', the Bulgars and the Southern Slavs, c. 1020–c. 1200," in Luscombe, ed., *The New Cambridge Medieval History* 4/2:265–66 and 269–70. Assessing the precise nature of the Byzantine dealings with Saladin depends largely on the authenticity of an anonymous letter in *The Chronicle of Magnus of Reichersberg*, pp. 153–55. Brand, p. 181, argued that it was genuine and was written in the summer or autumn of 1188 in Tyre at the behest of Conrad of Montferrat, while the letter has also been rejected as a piece of anti-Byzantine propaganda. See Loud, *The Crusade of Frederick Barbarossa*, p. 153, n. 7.
3. DFI, no. 995 (16 April 1189; hospital in Haguenau); no. 996 (26 April 1189; Benedictines of All Saints in Schaffhausen); no. 997 (29 April 1189; bishopric of Brixen); no. 998 (1 May 1189; Augustinian canons of Au in the diocese of Trent); no. 999 (3 May 1189; Benedictines of Isny); no. 1000 (end of April to early May 1189; Premonstratensians of Steingaden at the request of Welf VI); no. 1001 (7 May 1189; interpolated charter for the burghers of Hamburg at the request of Count Adolf III of Schauenburg), no. 1002 (10 May 1189; Cistercians in Krauel at Count Adolf's request); and no. 1003 (10 May 1189; Cistercian nunnery of Wechterswinkel); RI IV 2/4:253–58, no. 3247 (c. 16 April 1189; Benedictines of Selz), no. 3250 (25 April 1189; Premonstratensians of Adelberg), no. 3258 (7 May 1189; Frederick was still in Neuburg on the Danube, upstream from Regensburg), and no. 3259 (c. 10 May; court in Regensburg); *Continuatio Gerlaci abbatis Milovicensis*, p. 706 (enfeoffment of Duke Conrad Otto); *Chronica regia Coloniensis*, p. 144 (the chronicler said that Frederick appointed Henry as the regent in Regensburg on 23 April, the date the crusaders were originally supposed to meet); and *The History of the Expedition of the Emperor Frederick*, p. 47 (regency).
4. *Annales Pegavienses*, p. 266 (thousands of knights awaited Frederick); Arnold of Lübeck, *Chronica Slavorum*, p. 171; *The History of the Expedition of the Emperor Frederick*, pp. 47–57 (list of participants) and p. 68 (arrival of Peter of Toul); and RI IV2/4:263–64, no. 3274 (list of participants) and p. 294, no. 3381 (2–11 July; arrival of reinforcements at Braničevo). See Hiestand, "'precipua tocius christianismi columpna,'" pp. 65–73; and Loud, *The Crusade of Frederick Barbarossa*, pp. 21–25. Loud included in his translated texts: "An Account of the Seaborne Journey of the Pilgrims Heading to Jerusalem Who Captured Silves in 1189," pp. 193–208.
5. Eickhoff, *Friedrich Barbarossa im Orient*, pp. 51–53.
6. *The History of the Expedition of the Emperor Frederick*, pp. 46–58; Arnold of Lübeck, *Chronica Slavorum*, p. 171; *Chronica regia Coloniensis*, p. 144; *The History of the Pilgrims*, p. 147; *The Chronicle of Magnus of Reichersberg*, p. 149; and RI IV2/4:260–65, nos. 3265–76. Appelt, DFI, no. *1007, suggested that Frederick's law of 28 May 1190 might have been based on his ordinance of 1158 (DFI, no. 222). See Eickhoff, *Friedrich Barbarossa im Orient*, pp. 53–57.
7. *The History of the Expedition of the Emperor Frederick*, pp. 47 and 58–59; Arnold of Lübeck, *Chronica Slavorum*, pp. 171–72 (description of the tent; release of Béla's brother; crossing of the Tisza and the abundant provisions; census of the army at Belgrade; knightly games; and the punishment of the merchants and serfs); *Chronica regia Coloniensis*, pp. 144–45 (three wagons needed to carry the tent; engagement of Frederick VI; and the beheading of the nobles); *Continuatio Zwetlensis altera*, p. 544 (engagement; Béla accompanied Frederick to

the border; and the reason Leopold could not go on the crusade); and RI IV2/4:289–93, nos. 3368–79. See Eickhoff, *Friedrich Barbarossa im Orient*, pp. 57–58; and Weller, *Die Heiratspolitik des deutschen Hochadels im 12. Jahrhundert*, pp. 135–36.

8. *The History of the Expedition of the Emperor Frederick*, pp. 59–61; *The Chronicle of Magnus of Reichersberg*, p. 149 (Bishop Diepold wrote in the letter Magnus cited that they were attacked in the forest by Bulgarians, whom the crusaders hanged if they caught them); *The Chronicle of Otto of St. Blasien*, p. 177 (Frederick hanged Bulgarians who had opposed his passage on trees on both sides of the highway); Arnold of Lübeck, *Chronica Slavorum*, p. 172 (Béla accompanied Frederick across the Morava; his lavish gifts included the camels laden with gifts worth 5,000 marks; the Greek duke provided supplies; arrival in Čuprija on 25 July); *Chronica regia Coloniensis*, pp. 144–45 (crossed the Morava and hanged 500 of the bandits); and RI IV2/4:293–95, nos. 3380–83. Loud, *The Crusade of Frederick Barbarossa*, p. 59, n. 144, wrongly identified the river that the crusaders crossed on 1 July as the Sava; it was the Morava. The castle and settlement of Braničevo no longer exist; the term refers today to a Serbian administrative district (RI IV2/4:294, no. 3381). See Eickhoff, *Friedrich Barbarossa im Orient*, pp. 59–64.
9. *The History of the Expedition of the Emperor Frederick*, pp. 61–65; *The Chronicle of Magnus of Reichersberg*, p. 149 (Frederick and Stephen had lengthy discussions and the emperor reciprocated with gifts of his own); RI IV2/4:295–97, nos. 3384–85. The story of Achan is in Joshua 7. See Eickhoff, *Friedrich Barbarossa im Orient*, pp. 64–65.
10. *The History of the Expedition of the Emperor Frederick*, pp. 65–67; *The Chronicle of Magnus of Reichersberg*, pp. 149–50 (Diepold's letter); and RI IV2/4:297, nos. 3386–88. See Eickhoff, *Friedrich Barbarossa im Orient*, pp. 65–66.
11. *The History of the Expedition of the Emperor Frederick*, p. 68; and *The Chronicle of Magnus of Reichersberg*, p. 150.
12. *The History of the Expedition of the Emperor Frederick*, pp. 68–72 and p. 75, n. 196 (the account of Isaac's letter in *The History of the Pilgrims*), and p. 79 (Isaac had called Frederick king of Germany); *The Chronicle of Magnus of Reichersberg*, pp. 150–51 (Diepold's letter); and RI IV2/4:298–300, nos. 3389–93. Loud, *The Crusade of Frederick Barbarossa*, p. 150, wrongly translated *Bracchium*, that is, the Arm of St. George, as the Bosporus; it was the Hellespont or Dardanelles. See Eickhoff, *Friedrich Barbarossa im Orient*, pp. 66–69. On Frederick's relations with the Serbs and Isaac, see Hiestand, "'precipua tocius christianismi columpna,'" pp. 93–97. Hiestand argued that Frederick had no wish to become involved in the internal affairs of the Byzantine Empire; but Hiestand thought that Frederick VI's engagement to the daughter of Béla, who had once been the heir presumptive to the Byzantine throne as the fiancé of Manuel I's daughter, was the basis of Isaac's suspicion that Barbarossa wanted to make his son the eastern emperor. Isaac wrote to Frederick, according to Diepold, that the duke of Brindisi had informed Isaac of this plan; but Loud, p. 150, n. 2, could not identify any person with such a title. Both Hiestand, p. 96, and Opll, RI IV2/4:300, no. 3393, take it to be a reference to the duke of Braničevo.
13. See above, p. 465.
14. *The History of the Expedition of the Emperor Frederick*, pp. 69–70 and 74–75; *The Chronicle of Magnus of Reichersberg*, p. 151 (Diepold's letter); *Chronica regia Coloniensis*, p. 146 (the beheading of the adolescents and the Armenians' positive response); and RI IV2/4:300–03, nos. 3394–3400. See Eickhoff, *Friedrich Barbarossa im Orient*, pp. 69–70. Eickhoff, p. 70, thought that the confessional difference between the Armenians and Greeks caused the Armenians to ally with Frederick. Perhaps the Armenians simply wanted to protect their property and saw an opportunity to make money.
15. *The History of the Expedition of the Emperor Frederick*, pp. 70–72 (Frederick's letter to Henry; also DFI, no. 1009) and pp. 75–79; *The Chronicle of Magnus of Reichersberg*, pp. 151–52 (Diepold's letter); and RI IV2/4:303–05, nos. 3402–05. See Eickhoff, *Friedrich Barbarossa im Orient*, pp. 70–71.
16. *The History of the Expedition of the Emperor Frederick*, pp. 70–72 (letter to Henry) and pp. 79–80; *The Chronicle of Magnus of Reichersberg*, pp. 152–53 and p. 156; DFI, no. 1009 (16–19 November 1189; Latin text of Frederick's letter to Henry) and no. 1010 (16–19 November 1189; letter to Leopold V); and RI IV2/4:305–09, nos. 3406–14. See Eickhoff, *Friedrich Barbarossa im Orient*, pp. 71–74.

17. *The History of the Expedition of the Emperor Frederick*, pp. 80–85; and RI IV2/4:309–12, nos. 3416–24. See Eickhoff, *Friedrich Barbarossa im Orient*, p. 74.
18. *The History of the Expedition of the Emperor Frederick*, pp. 85–90 and p. 86, n. 227 (excerpt from *The History of the Pilgrims* likening Frederick to Phineas); *The Chronicle of Magnus of Reichersberg*, p. 156 (departure from Philippopolis on 15 January); and RI IV2/4:312–14, nos. 3425–30. The story of Phineas is in Numbers 25:7–11. See Eickhoff, *Friedrich Barbarossa im Orient*, pp. 74–75.
19. *The History of the Expedition of the Emperor Frederick*, pp. 90–94 (peace terms); *The Chronicle of Magnus of Reichersberg*, p. 156; and RI IV2/4:314–18, no. 3431 (all other reports about the agreement of 14 February) and nos. 3433–35. See Eickhoff, *Friedrich Barbarossa im Orient*, pp. 74–76 and Map 1.
20. *The History of the Expedition of the Emperor Frederick*, pp. 92–93 and p. 111 (dowry); and RI IV2/4:316–17, no. 3432. See Eickhoff, *Friedrich Barbarossa im Orient*, pp. 76–77, 111–12, and 120–21.
21. *The History of the Expedition of the Emperor Frederick*, pp. 94–96; *The Chronicle of Magnus of Reichersberg*, p. 156; *A Letter Concerning the Death of the Emperor Frederick*, p. 169; and RI IV 2/4:318–21, nos. 3436–44. Frederick's letter to Henry VI of 28 or 29 March was found too late for inclusion in the edition of his charters. See Rudolf Hiestand, "Barbarossas letztes Schreiben vom Kreuzzug," in Kölzer et al., eds, *De litteris, manuscriptis, inscriptionibus*, pp. 561–76; the text is on pp. 575–76. See Eickhoff, *Friedrich Barbarossa im Orient*, pp. 78–82.
22. *The History of the Expedition of the Emperor Frederick*, pp. 96–99 and p. 99, n. 267 (excerpt from *The History of the Pilgrims*); *The Chronicle of Magnus of Reichersberg*, pp. 156–57; *Chronica regia Coloniensis*, p. 149 (sultan's envoy); and RI IV2/4:321–25, nos. 3444–54. See Eickhoff, *Friedrich Barbarossa im Orient*, pp. 83–104.
23. *The History of the Expedition of the Emperor Frederick*, pp. 100–09; *The Chronicle of Magnus of Reichersberg*, pp. 157–59; *A Letter Concerning the Death of the Emperor Frederick*, pp. 169–72; and RI IV2/4:325–27, nos. 3455–60. See Eickhoff, *Friedrich Barbarossa im Orient*, pp. 105–33.
24. *The History of the Expedition of the Emperor Frederick*, pp. 109–13; *The Chronicle of Magnus of Reichersberg*, pp. 159–62; *A Letter Concerning the Death of the Emperor Frederick*, p. 172; and RI IV2/4:328–29, no. 3461. See Eickhoff, *Friedrich Barbarossa im Orient*, pp. 133–36.
25. *The History of the Expedition of the Emperor Frederick*, pp. 113–14; *The Chronicle of Magnus of Reichersberg*, pp. 162–63; *A Letter Concerning the Death of the Emperor Frederick*, p. 172 (the earthquake); and RI IV2/4:330, no. 3462.
26. *The History of the Expedition of the Emperor Frederick*, pp. 114–16; *The Chronicle of Magnus of Reichersberg*, pp. 163–64; *A Letter Concerning the Death of the Emperor Frederick*, p. 172; and RI IV2/4:330–39, nos. 3462–70. See Eickhoff, *Friedrich Barbarossa im Orient*, pp. 137–60; and Halfter, "Die Staufer und Armenien," in Lorenz and Schmidt, eds, *Von Schwaben bis Jerusalem*, pp. 192–97. Eickhoff, pp. 158–59 and 180–83; and Opll, RI IV2/4:334, no. 3370, argued that Frederick drowned when he went for a swim after eating a meal. There is a photograph of the likely place where Frederick drowned and the marker in Eickhoff, Plates 9 and 10.
27. *The History of the Expedition of the Emperor Frederick*, pp. 116–17; *The Chronicle of Magnus of Reichersberg*, pp. 164–65; *A Letter Concerning the Death of the Emperor Frederick*, p. 172; and RI IV2/4:340–42, no. 3471. See Eickhoff, *Friedrich Barbarossa im Orient*, pp. 161–72; and Hiestand, "'precipua tocius christianismi columpna,'" pp. 105–08.

Epilogue

1. *Chronica regia Coloniensis*, p. 151; Gerald of Wales, *Ex libro de instructione principis*, ed. Felix Liebermann and Reinhold Pauli, in MGH SS 27 (Hanover, 1885), pp. 405–06; Gilbert of Mons, *Chronicle of Hainaut*, pp. 128–29, ch. 152; Salimbene di Adam of Parma, *Cronica ordinis Minorum*, ed. Oswald Holder-Egger, in MGH SS 32 (Hanover and Leipzig, 1905–13), p. 12 (dated 8 July); Albert of Stade, *Annales Stadenses*, p. 351 (under 1191); and RI IV2/4:334–39, no. 3470, note on p. 339. See Böhm, *Das Bild Friedrich Barbarossas und seines Kaisertums*, pp. 127–34; Eickhoff, *Friedrich Barbarossa im Orient*, p. 161; and Hiestand, "'precipua tocius christianismi columpna,'" pp. 105–08.

2. Norman Cohn, *The Pursuit of the Millennium: Revolutionary Messianism in Medieval and Reformation Europe and its Bearing on Modern Totalitarian Movements*, 2nd edn. (New York, 1961), pp. 99–123; the quotation is on pp. 111–12. See also Borst, "Barbarossas Erwachen," pp. 23–25; David Abulafia, *Frederick II: A Medieval Emperor* (London, 1988), pp. 428–35; Klaus Schreiner, "Die Staufer in Sage, Legende und Prophetie," *Die Zeit der Staufer* 3:249–51 and 253–55; and Camilla C. Kaul, *Friedrich Barbarossa im Kyffhäuser: Bilder eines nationalen Mythos im 19. Jahrhundert*, 2 vols. (Cologne, 2007), 1:32–39.
3. Borst, "Barbarossas Erwachen," pp. 25–27; and Schreiner, "Friedrich Barbarossa," pp. 528–30.
4. Monika Arndt, "Das Kyffhäuser-Denkmal—Ein Beitrag zur politischen Ikonographie des Zweiten Kaiserreiches," *Wallraf-Richartz-Jahrbuch: Westdeutsches Jahrbuch für Kunstgeschichte* 40 (1978): 75–76; Engels, *Die Staufer*, pp. 195–96; Kaul, *Friedrich Barbarossa im Kyffhäuser* 1:39–48; Schreiner, "Die Staufer in Sage," pp. 255 and 259–61; and Opll, *Das Itinerar Kaiser Friedrich Barbarossas*, p. 150.
5. Schreiner, "Friedrich Barbarossa," pp. 534–36; and idem, "Die Staufer in Sage," pp. 255–57 and 261.
6. Kurt Löcher, "Die Staufer in der bildenden Kunst," *Die Zeit der Staufer* 3:296; Kaul, *Friedrich Barbarossa im Kyffhäuser* 1:53–60; and Walter Migge, "Die Staufer in der deutschen Literatur seit dem 18. Jahrhundert," *Die Zeit der Staufer* 3:276–79. For a sample of some of these works, see *Katalog der Ausstellung*, "Die Staufer und die Nachwelt," *Die Zeit der Staufer* 1:705–06, 710–18, and 727–29. On Agnes' elopement, see Ehlers, *Heinrich der Löwe*, pp. 384–85; and on Conradin, see Karl Hampe, *Geschichte Konradins von Hohenstaufen* (Innsbruck, 1894).
7. Borst, "Barbarossas Erwachen," pp. 29–31; and Kaul, *Friedrich Barbarossa im Kyffhäuser* 1:47–48, 66–75, and 82–85. For a Marxist perspective on the political utilization of Barbarossa in the first half of the nineteenth century, see Walter Schmidt, "Barbarossa im Vormärz," in Engel, *Kaiser Friedrich Barbarossa*, pp. 171–204.
8. *Katalog der Austellung*, *Die Zeit der Staufer* 1:714–15 and 723–24; Borst, "Barbarossas Erwachen," pp. 31–35; Kaul, *Friedrich Barbarossa im Kyffhäuser* 1:76–82, 85–96, and 152–63; Migge, "Die Staufer in der deutschen Literatur," pp. 275–76 and 280–81; and Schreiner, "Friedrich Barbarossa," p. 539.
9. Friedrich Rückert, "Barbarossa," trans. Bayard Taylor and Lilian Bayard Taylor-Kiliani, in *The German Classics: Masterpieces of German Literature Translated into English*, 20 vols. (New York, 1913), 5:486–87.
10. Kaul, *Friedrich Barbarossa in Kyffhäuser* 1:149–50 and 1:403; and Gunther Mai, "'Für Kaiser und Reich': Das Kaiser-Wilhelm-Denkmal auf dem Kyffhäuser," in idem, *Das Kyffhäuser Denkmal 1896–1996: Ein nationales Monument im europäischen Kontext* (Cologne, Weimar, and Vienna, 1997), p. 157. Kaul published the poems that were written about Frederick in the 1830s and 1840s (1:96–106). The title and content of a poem by Wilhelm Genth (1803–44), "Barbarossas Erwachen," match the description of the poem that was recited on 31 March 1848 (Kaul, p. 174).
11. Brune and Baumunk, "Wege der Popularisierung," p. 329. For a selection of Kyffhäuser poems written after 1870, see Arndt, "Das Kyffhäuser Denkmal," pp. 125–27. On the popularity of the Rückert poem, see Kaul, *Friedrich Barbarossa im Kyffhäuser* 1:352–53, and on Barbarossa in the schools, see pp. 474–83.
12. *Katalog der Ausstellung*, *Die Zeit der Staufer* 1:721, no. 960. The translation is my own. See also Kaul, *Friedrich Barbarossa im Kyffhäuser* 1:168–75, esp. pp. 169–73.
13. Borst, "Barbarossas Erwachen," pp. 41–45; and Kaul, *Friedrich Barbarossa im Kyffhäuser* 1:320–29. For a Marxist perspective on the political utilization of Barbarossa in the Second Reich, see Gustav Seeber, "Von Barbarossa zu Barbablanca: Zu den Wandlungen des Bildes von der mittelalterlichen Kaiserpolitik im Deutschen Reich," in Engel, *Kaiser Friedrich Barbarossa*, pp. 205–20.
14. Borst, "Barbarossas Erwachen," pp. 35–38; and Heinz Gollwitzer, "Zur Auffassung der mittelalterlichen Kaiserpolitik im 19. Jahrhundert: Eine ideolgie- und wissenschafts-geschichtliche Nachlese," in Rudolf Vierhaus and Manfred Botzenhart, eds, *Dauer und Wandel der Geschichte: Aspekte europäischer Vergangenheit: Festgabe für Kurt von Raumer zum 15. Dezember 1965* (Münster, 1966), pp. 498–500.
15. Plassmann, *Die Struktur des Hofes unter Friedrich I. Barbarossa*, p. 152.

16. Monika Arndt, *Die Goslarer Kaiserpfalz als Nationaldenkmal: Eine ikonographische Untersuchung* (Hildesheim, 1976), pp. 29–31; Engels, *Die Staufer*, pp. 166–67; Gollwitzer, "Zur Auffassung der mittelalterlichen Kaiserpolitik im 19. Jahrhundert," pp. 501–02; and Kaul, *Friedrich Barbarossa im Kyffhäuser* 1:301–02.
17. It was indicative of the Third Reich's renewed interest in Germany's imperial and expansive destiny that Friedrich Schneider published the relevant lectures and pamphlets in *Universalstaat oder Nationalstaat: Die Streitschriften von Heinrich v. Sybel und Julius Ficker zur deutschen Kaiserpolitik des Mittelalters* (Innsbruck, 1941). Schneider concluded his introductory comments with this definition of the Reich: "unity, the sovereign authority of the Führer, pure statehood within, and Western mission externally" (p. xxxvi). Schneider was also the author of the equally revealingly titled: *Die neueren Anschauungen der deutschen Historiker über die deutsche Kaiserpolitik des Mittelalters und die mit ihr verbundene Ostpolitik*, 5th edn. (Weimar, 1942). For an analysis of the debate from a Marxist perspective, see Gottfried Koch, "Der Streit zwischen Sybel und Ficker und Einschätzung der mittelalterlichen Kaiserpolitik in der modernen Historiographie," in Joachim Streisand, ed. *Die deutsche Geschichtswissenschaft vom Beginn des 19. Jahrhunderts bis zur Reichsgründung von oben* (Berlin, 1963), pp. 311–36. The quotations from Giesebrecht and Sybel (my translations) are on pp. 313 and 326. The other quotations from Sybel and Ficker are taken from Herzstein's translated excerpts of their writings in *The Holy Roman Empire in the Middle Ages*, pp. 1–2 and 6. For a more recent assessment of the medieval German involvement in Italy, see Theo Kölzer, "Die Staufer im Süden—eine Bilanz aus deutscher Sicht," in idem, *Die Staufer im Süden,* pp. 239–62. For a general discussion of the negative Prussian attitude toward the medieval empire, see Kaul, *Friedrich Barbarossa im Kyffhäuser* 1:151 and 296–312, and on the triumph of the myth after 1871, pp. 450–69. Two of Ficker's books are listed in the bibliography.
18. Gollwitzer, "Zur Auffassung der mittelalterlichen Kaiserpolitik im 19. Jahrhundert," pp. 500–01; and Arndt, *Die Goslarer Kaiserpfalz*, p. 68.
19. Arndt, *Die Goslarer Kaiserpfalz*, p. 67. Friedrich III initially considered styling himself Friedrich IV, that is, the successor of the medieval Staufer and Habsburg emperors, rather than as the successor of the Prussian king, Friedrich II (Frederick the Great).
20. Borst, "Barbarossas Erwachen," pp. 45–51; and Kaul, *Friedrich Barbarossa im Kyffhäuser* 1:323–27, esp. p. 324.
21. Borst, "Barbarossas Erwachen," pp. 38–40.
22. Ronnie Ellenblum, *Crusader Castles and Modern Histories* (Cambridge, 2007), pp. 32–36; and Kaul, *Friedrich Barbarossa im Kyffhäuser* 1:461–62. Sepp added a stanza about Barbarossa's burial in Tyre to Rückert's poem (Kaul, p. 353). Hans Prutz's biography is *Kaiser Friedrich I.*, 3 vols. (Danzig, 1871–74).
23. Arndt, *Die Goslarer Kaiserpfalz*, passim; and Kaul, *Friedrich Barbarossa im Kyffhäuser* 1:586–98. Felix Dahn (1834–1912) devised the designation *Barbablanca* for Wilhelm in his 1871 Latin and German poem, "Macte senex Imperator" ("Hail, You, Old Emperor"). See Kaul, 1:348–49.
24. Arndt, "Das Kyffhäuser-Denkmal," passim; Mai, "'Für Kaiser und Reich,'" passim; and Kaul, *Friedrich Barbarossa im Kyffhäuser* 1:643–81, 698–99, and 747–52. Wilhelm II's dedicatory remarks are reprinted in Arndt, pp. 123–24. Schmitz also designed the Wilhelm I monument at the confluence of the Rhine and the Mosel, which was dedicated in 1897; but it does not have overt medieval references. See Kaul, 1:633–36.
25. Arndt, "Das Kyffhäuser-Denkmal," p. 89, n. 75; Herbert Gottwald, "Ein Kaiserdenkmal im Sozialismus: Das Kyffhäuser-Denkmal in SBZ and DDR," in Mai, ed., *Das Kyffhäuser-Denkmal*, pp. 236–40; and Stefan Goebel, *The Great War and Medieval Memory: War, Remembrance and Medievalism in Britain and Germany, 1914–1940* (Cambridge, 2007), pp. 262–67. Abbildung 29 in Mai, ed., *Das Kyffhäuser-Denkmal*, shows the hall around 1935.
26. Gottwald, "Ein Kaiserdenkmal im Sozialismus," p. 239.
27. Löcher, "Die Staufer in der bildenden Kunst," p. 301.
28. Koch, "Der Streit zwischen Sybel und Ficker," pp. 329–33. Herzstein, *The Holy Roman Empire*, pp. 46–50, includes a brief excerpt from Below's *Die Italienische Kaiserpolitik des Mittelalters* (Munich, 1927); the quotation is on p. 49. Paul Kirn's article, "Die Verdienste der

staufischen Kaiser um das Deutsche Reich," HZ 164 (1941): 261–84, was a response to Below's argument.

29. Schneidmüller, *Die Welfen*, pp. 288–300, esp. 295–98; and Hechberger, "Bewundert," pp. 233–35.
30. Friedrich Heer, *Die Tragödie des Heiligen Reiches* (Vienna and Zürich, 1952), esp. pp. 57–59, 86–87, 104–05, 128–29, and 268–69; the quotations are on pp. 57 and 129. The book is a work of enormous erudition that relies exclusively on literary and narrative rather than documentary sources (there are no footnotes in this edition). Kohlhammer in Stuttgart published a German edition in 1952 and a separate volume containing the scholarly apparatus in 1953. Herzstein, *The Holy Roman Empire in the Middle Ages*, pp. 63–71, included some excerpts from the book. Heer wrote several books about the Empire, at least one of which was translated into English: *The Holy Roman Empire*, trans. Janet Sondheimer (New York and Washington, 1968). Munz, *Frederick Barbarossa*, p. 401, listed *Die Tragödie* as one of the major works on the emperor. For a complete bibliography of Heer's work, see Adolf Gaisbauer, *Friedrich Heer (1916–1983): Eine Bibliographie* (Vienna, 1990).
31. Kirfel, *Weltherrschaftsidee und Bündnispolitik*, pp. 9–19, 48–49, 172–90, and 208–13. See Heer, *Die Trägödie des Heiligen Reiches*, pp. 240–45.
32. Koch, "Der Streit zwischen Sybel und Ficker," pp. 333–36. On East German historiography about the Middle Ages, see Andreas Dorpalen, *German History in Marxist Perspective: The East German Approach* (Detroit, 1988), pp. 63–98.
33. Gottwald, "Ein Kaiserdenkmal im Sozialismus," pp. 236 and 245–61; *Scott Stamp Catalogue*, no. 2835.
34. Arndt, "Das Kyffhäuser-Denkmal," p. 100. On the Neo-Romanesque as the quintessential German style, see Kaul, *Friedrich Barbarossa im Kyffhäuser* 1:598–99; and Michael Bringmann, "Gedanken zur Wiederaufnahme staufische Bauformen im späten 19. Jahrhundert," *Die Zeit der Staufer* 5:581–620.
35. Not a single poet indicated that he had written at Frederick's behest or dedicated a work to him. See Ganz, "Friedrich Barbarossa: Hof und Kultur," pp. 639–43.
36. Lothar Ehrlich, "Das Goethe-Schiller-Denkmal in Weimar," in Mai, ed., *Das Kyffhäuser-Denkmal*, pp. 263–77. The quotation is on p. 267; the translation is my own. The Ilm is the river that flows through Weimar. See also Kaul, *Friedrich Barbarossa im Kyffhäuser* 1:319.
37. Arnold's *Princes and Territories in Medieval Germany* provides a positive assessment of the princes' role in promoting the country's economic growth and eastward expansion between 1050 and 1300. He stressed that the princes did not usurp royal authority but that the kings, who lacked the means to govern their diverse country by themselves, left the exercise of regional authority to the princes.
38. Hans Filbinger, "Vom Sinn dieser Ausstellung," *Die Zeit der Staufer* 1:v–x. See Hechberger, "Bewundert," pp. 236–37.
39. I wish to thank my colleague Katrin Paehler for bringing the Filbinger affair to my attention.
40. Elke Gerhold-Knittel, "Bericht über die Ausstellung," *Die Zeit der Staufer* 5:621–26.
41. Schneidmüller et al., eds, *Verwandlungen des Stauferreichs*, pp. 7–8. The editors were also responsible for the exhibition catalog: *Die Staufer und Italien.*
42. John B. Freed, "Medieval German Social History: Generalizations and Particularism," *CEH* 25 (1992): 19. In preparation for the exhibition, a scholarly conference was held in Mainz in September 2009 and the proceedings were published in Stefan Burkhardt et al., eds, *Staufisches Kaisertum im 12. Jahrhundert: Konzepte—Netzwerke—Politische Praxis* (Regensburg, 2010). In the introduction, Bernd Schneidemüller, "Staufisches Kaisertum im 12. Jahrhundert: Zur Einführung," p. 17, pointed out that scholarly interest has shifted from Frederick I to his grandson because the latter, who combined "north Alpine aspirations and Mediterranean realities," was more in tune with "a period of increasing Europeanization, globalization, and transculturalism."
43. Kaul, *Friedrich Barbarossa im Kyffhäuser* 1:753–67, esp. p. 766. The translation is my own.

BIBLIOGRAPHY

N.B. All volumes of the MGH SS were reprinted by Anton Hiersemann in Stuttgart and Kraus Reprint Corporation, New York, 1963–64.

Primary Sources

Die Admonter Briefsammlung nebst ergänzden Briefen, ed. Günther Hödl and Peter Classen. MGH BdK 6. Munich, 1983.

Alberic of Trois Fontaines, *Chronicle*, ed. Paul Scheffer-Boichorst. MGH SS 23:631–950. Hanover, 1874.

Albert of Stade. *Annales Stadenses*, ed. Johann Martin Lappenberg. MGH SS 16:271–379. Hanover, 1859.

Andrew of Marchiennes. *Chronica: Continuatio Aquicinctina*, ed. Ludwig Conrad Bethmann. MGH SS 6:405–38. Hanover, 1844.

Annales Aquenses (1–1196), ed. Georg Waitz. MGH SS 24:33–39. Hanover, 1879.

Annales Bremenses, ed. Philipp Jaffé. MGH SS 17:854–58. Hanover, 1861.

Annales Cameracenses auctore Lamberto Waterlos a. 1099–1170, ed. Georg Heinrich Pertz. MGH SS 16:509–54. Hanover, 1859.

Annales Casinenses a 1000–1212, ed. Georg Heinrich Pertz. MGH SS 19:303–20. Hanover, 1866.

Annales Ceccanenses, ed. Georg Heinrich Pertz. MGH SS 19:275–302. Hanover, 1866.

Annales Egmundani a. 875–1205. 1207–1315, ed. Georg Heinrich Pertz. MGH SS 16:442–79. Hanover, 1859.

Annales Herbipolenses a. 1125–1158. 1202–1204. 1215, ed. Georg Heinrich Pertz. MGH SS 16:1–12. Hanover, 1859.

Annales Magdeburgenses, ed. Georg Heinrich Pertz. MGH SS 16:107–96. Hanover, 1859.

Annales Ottenburani Isingrimi et minores, ed. Georg Heinrich Pertz. MGH SS 17:315–18. Hanover, 1861.

Annales Palidenses auctore Theodoro monacho, ed. Georg Heinrich Pertz. MGH SS 16:48–98. Hanover, 1859.

Annales Pegavienses et Bosovienses, ed. Georg Heinrich Pertz. MGH SS 16:234–70. Hanover, 1859.

Annales Ratisbonenses, ed. Wilhelm Wattenbach. MGH SS 17:577–90. Hanover, 1861.

Annales Romani a. 1044–1187, ed. Georg Heinrich Pertz. MGH SS 5:468–80. Hanover, 1844.

Annales Sancti Disibodi a. 891–1200, ed. Georg Waitz. MGH SS 17:4–30. Hanover, 1861.

Annales Sancti Georgii in Nigra silva a. 613–1308, ed. Georg Heinrich Pertz. MGH SS 17:295–98. Hanover, 1861.

Annales Sancti Iacobi Leodiensis, ed. Georg Heinrich Pertz. MGH SS 16:632–82. Hanover, 1859.

Annales Sancti Petri Erphesfurdenses: Continuatio a. 1164–1182, ed. Georg Heinrich Pertz. MGH SS 16:23–25. Hanover, 1859.

Annales Sancti Rudberti Salisburgenses, ed. Wilhelm Wattenbach. MGH SS 9:758–810. Hanover, 1851.

Annales SS. Udalrici et Afrae Augustenses a. 1106–1334, ed. Philipp Jaffé. MGH SS 17:428–36. Hanover, 1861.

Annales Stedeburgenses auctore Gerhardo praeposito a. 1000–1195, ed. Georg Heinrich Pertz. MGH SS 16:197–231. Hanover, 1859.

Arnold of Lübeck. *Chronica Slavorum*, ed. Johann Martin Lappenberg. MGH SS 21:101–250. Hanover, 1869.

Auctarium Affligemense a. 597. 1005–1163, ed. Ludwig Conrad Bethmann. MGH SS 6:398–405. Hanover, 1844.

Balderich. *The Deeds of Albero of Trier, by Balderich*, trans. Brian A. Pavlac. In Medieval Sources in Translation 44. Toronto: Pontifical Institute of Medieval Studies, 2008.

Böhmer, Johann Friedrich, ed. *Acta imperii selecta: Urkunden deutscher Könige und Kaiser mit einem Anhange von Reichssachen*. Innsbruck: Verlag der Wagner'schen Universitäts Buchhandlung, 1870.

Boso. *Les vies des papes rédigées par le Cardinal Boson et insérées dans le Liber Censum*. In *Le Liber Pontificalis: Texte, Introduction et Commentaire* 2:388–446, ed. Louis Duchesne. In Bibliothèques des Écoles françaises d'Athènes et de Rome, 2e série. Paris: Ernest Thorin, 1892.

—. *Boso's Life of Alexander III*, trans. G. M. Ellis with an introduction by Peter Munz. Oxford: Basil Blackwell, 1973.

—. *Vita Hadriani IV* (*Life of Adrian IV*), ed. and trans. Brenda Bolton and Anne J. Duggan. In idem, *Adrian IV*, pp. 214–33.

Brühl, Carlrichard and Theo Kölzer, eds. *Das Tafelgüterverzeichnis des römischen Königs (Ms. Bonn S. 1559)*. Cologne and Vienna: Böhlau Verlag, 1979.

Burchard of Ursberg. *Chronicon*, ed. and trans. Matthias Becher. In *Quellen zur Geschichte der Welfen und die Chronik Burchards von Ursberg*. In AQ 18b:101–311. Darmstadt: Wissenschaftliche Buchgesellschaft, 2007.

Carmen de gestis Frederici I. imperatoris in Lombardia, ed. Irene Schmale-Ott. MGH SSrG 62. Hanover: Hahnsche Buchhandlung, 1965.

Chronica regia Coloniensis (Annales maximi Colonienses), ed. Georg Waitz. MGH SSrG 18. Hanover, 1880. Reprint, Hanover: Hahnsche Buchhandlung, 2003.

Chronicon Montis Sereni, ed. Ernst Ehrenfeuchter. MGH SS 23:130–226. Hanover, 1874.

Chronicon S. Michaelis Luneburgensis, ed. Ludwig Weiland. MGH SS 23:391–97. Hanover, 1874.

Der Codex Eberhardi des Klosters Fulda, ed. Heinrich Meyer zu Ermgassen. 3 vols. In Veröffentlichungen der Historischen Kommission für Hessen 58. Marburg: N. G. Elwert Verlag Marburg, 1995–2007.

Codex Falkensteinensis: Die Rechtsaufzeichnungen der Grafen von Falkenstein, ed. Elisabeth Noichl. In QEbG, NF 29. Munich: C. H. Beck'sche Verlagsbuchhandlung, 1978.

Codice diplomatico del senato Romano dal MCXLIV al MCCCXLVII. Vol. 1, ed. Franco Bartoloni. In Fonti per la storia d'Italia 87. Rome, 1948.

Colorni, Vittore. *Die drei verschollenen Gesetze des Reichstages bei Roncaglia wieder aufgefunden in einer Pariser Handschrift (Bibl. Nat. Cod. Lat. 4677)*, trans. Gero Dolezalek. In Untersuchungen zur deutschen Staats- und Rechtsgeschichte, NF 12. Aalen: Scientia Verlag, 1969.

Constitutiones et acta publica imperatorum et regum 1, ed. Ludwig Weiland. MGH Legum Sectio 4. Hanover, 1893. Reprint, Hanover: Hahnsche Buchhandlung, 2003.

Continuatio Claustroneoburgensis III. a. 1142–1233, ed. Wilhelm Wattenbach. MGH SS 9:628–37. Hanover, 1851.

Continuatio Gerlaci abbatis Milovicensis a 1167–1198, ed. Wilhelm Wattenbach. MGH SS 17:683–710. Hanover, 1861.

Continuatio Zwetlensis altera a. 1170–1189, ed. Wilhelm Wattenbach. MGH SS 9:541–44. Hanover, 1851.

Cosmae chronica Boemorum: Canonicorum Pragensium continuationes a. 1140–1195, ed. Rudolf Köpke. MGH SS 9:163–66. Hanover, 1851.

Cronica Reinhardsbrunnensis, ed. Oswald Holder-Egger. MGH SS 30/1:490–656. Hanover, 1896.

Eike von Repgow. *The Saxon Mirror: A* Sachsenspiegel *of the Fourteenth Century*, trans. Maria Dobozy. Philadelphia: University of Pennsylvania Press, 1999.

Emerton, Ephraim, translator. *The Correspondence of Pope Gregory VII: Selected Letters from the Registrum*. In Records of Civilization: Sources and Studies 14. New York: Columbia University Press, 1932.

"Epistola amici ad Alexandrum papam." In Robertson, *Materials for the History of Thomas Becket* 5:184–91.

Ex Chronico universali anonymi Laudunensis, ed. Georg Waitz. MGH SS 26:442–57. Hanover, 1882.

Ex Gaufridi de Bruil prioris Vosiensis Chronica, ed. Oswald Holder-Egger. MGH SS 26:198–203. Hanover, 1882.

Ex gestis Henrici II. et Ricardi I, ed. Felix Liebermann and Reinhold Pauli. MGH SS 27:81–132. Hanover, 1885.

Ex Radulfi de Diceto operibus historicis, ed. Felix Liebermann and Reinhold Pauli. MGH SS 27:249–93. Hanover, 1885.

Ex Rogeri de Hoveden chronica, ed. Felix Liebermann and Reinhold Pauli. MGH SS 27:133–83. Hanover, 1885.

Fundatio monasterii Waldsassensis, ed. Oswald Holder-Egger. MGH SS 15/2:1088–93. Hanover, 1888.

Die Gedichte des Archipoeta: Lateinisch und deutsch, ed. and trans. Josef Eberle. Frankfurt am Main: Insel Verlag, 1966.

Gerald of Wales. *Ex libro de instructione principis*, ed. Felix Liebermann and Reinhold Pauli. MGH SS 27:399–407. Hanover, 1885.

Gerhoch of Reichersberg. *Annales Reichersbergenses a. 921–1167*, ed. Wilhelm Wattenbach. MGH SS 17:443–76. Hanover, 1861.

—. *Opusculum ad cardinales*, ed. Odulf van den Eynde. In *Gerhohi praepositi Reichersbergensis opera inedita 1. Tractatus et libelli*, pp. 309–50. Rome, 1955.

Gervase of Canterbury. *E Gervasii Cantuariensis Chronica*, ed. Felix Liebermann and Reinhold Pauli. MGH SS 27:297–308. Hanover, 1885.

—. *E Gestis regum*, ed. Felix Liebermann and Reinhold Pauli. MGH SS 27:308–09. Hanover, 1885.

Gesta episcoporum Cameracensium. Continuatio, ed. Ludwig Conrad Bethmann. MGH SS 7:500–10. Hanover, 1846.

Gestorum Treverorum continuatio tertia, ed. Georg Waitz. MGH SS 24:380–89. Hanover, 1879

Gilbert of Mons. *Chronicle of Hainaut*, translated with an introduction and notes by Laura Napran. Woodbridge, Suffolk: The Boydell Press, 2005.

Godfrey of Viterbo. *Gotifredi Viterbiensis Gesta Friderici I. et Heinrici VI.*, ed. Georg Heinrich Pertz. In MGH SSrG 30. Hanover, 1870. Reprint, Hanover: Hahnsche Buchhandlung, 1993.

Gunther der Dichter. *Ligurinus*, ed. Erwin Assmann. In MGH SSrG 63. Hanover: Hahnsche Buchhandlung, 1987.

Die Gurker Geschichtsquellen 864–1231, ed. August v. Jaksch. In Monumenta historica ducatus Carinthiae 1. Klagenfurt: Ferdinand v. Kleinmayr, 1896.

Güterbock, Ferdinand. "Le lettere del notaio imperiale Burcardo intorno alla politica del Barbarossa nello scisma ed alla distruzione di Milano." *Bulletino dell'istituto storico italiano per il medio evo* 61 (1949): 1–65.

Helmold von Bosau. *Slawenchronik*, ed. and trans. Heinz Stoob. In AQ 19, 7th edn. Darmstadt: Wissenschaftliche Buchgesellschaft, 2008.

Henderson, Ernest F., ed. and trans. *Select Historical Documents of the Middle Ages*. New York: Biblo and Tannen, 1965.

Hiestand, Rudolf. "Barbarossas letztes Schreiben vom Kreuzzug." In Kölzer et al., eds. *De litteris, manuscriptis, inscriptionibus*, pp. 561–76.

Hildegard of Bingen. *The Letters of Hildegard of Bingen*. Vol. 1, trans. Joseph L. Baird and Radd K. Ehrman. New York and Oxford: Oxford University Press, 1994.

Historia calamitatum ecclesiae Salzburgensis, ed. Jacques Paul Migne. *Patrologia Latina* 196, cols. 1539–52. Paris, 1855.

Historia ducum Veneticorum, ed. Henry Simonsfeld. MGH SS 14:72–97. Hanover, 1883.

Historia Welforum cum continuatione Steingademensi, ed. and trans. Matthias Becher. In *Quellen zur Geschichte der Welfen und die Chronik Burchards von Ursberg*. In AQ 18b:34–91. Darmstadt: Wissenschaftliche Buchgesellschaft, 2007.

The History of the Expedition of the Emperor Frederick, trans. Loud in *The Crusade of Frederick Barbarossa*, pp. 33–134.

The History of the Pilgrims, trans. Loud in *The Crusade of Frederick Barbarossa*, pp. 135–47.

Hofmeister, Adolf. "Eine neue Quelle zur Geschichte Friedrich Barbarossas: De Ruina civitatis Terdonae: Untersuchungen zum 1. Römerzug Friedrichs I." *NA* 43 (1922): 87–157.

Hugh of Poitiers. *Liber de libertate monasterii Vizeliacensis*, ed. Georg Waitz. MGH SS 26:143–50. Hanover, 1882.

Italienische Quellen über die Taten Kaiser Friedrichs I. in Italien und der Brief über den Kreuzzug Kaiser Friedrichs I, ed. and trans. Franz-Josef Schmale. In AQ 17a. Darmstadt: Wissenschaftliche Buchgesellschaft, 1986.

John of Salisbury. *The* Historia Pontificalis *of John of Salisbury*, ed. Marjorie Chibnall. In Oxford Medieval Texts, 1956. Slightly revised reprint, Oxford: Oxford University Press, 1986.

—. *The Letters of John of Salisbury*, ed. William James Millor and Harold Edgeworth Butler, revised by C. N. L. Brooke. 2 vols. London: Thomas Nelson, 1959; Oxford: Oxford University Press, 1979. Reprinted in *Oxford Medieval Texts*. Oxford University Press, 1979–86.

Die jüngere Hildesheimer Briefsammlung, ed. Rolf de Kegel. In MGH BdK 7. Munich, 1995.

A Letter Concerning the Death of the Emperor Frederick. In Loud, *The Crusade of Frederick Barbarossa*, pp. 169–72.

Loud, G. A. *The Crusade of Frederick Barbarossa: The History of the Expedition of the Emperor Frederick and Related Texts*. In Crusade Texts in Translation 19. Farnham, Surrey, UK, and Burlington, VT: Ashgate, 2010.

Ludus de Antichristo. In Karl Young, ed. *The Drama of the Medieval Church*. Oxford: Clarendon Press, 1933, pp. 371–87.

—. Edited with a German translation by Gisela Vollmann-Profe. 2 vols. In Litterae: Göppinger Beiträge zur Textgeschichte 82/2. Lauterberg: Kummerle Verlag, 1981.

Magnus of Reichersberg. *Chronicon Magni presbyteri*, ed. Wilhelm Wattenbach. MGH SS 17:476–523. Hanover, 1861. Partial English translation, in Loud, *The Crusade of Frederick Barbarossa*, pp. 149–67.

Mainzer Urkundenbuch: Vol. 2: *Die Urkunden seit dem Tode Erzbischof Adalberts I. (1137) bis zum Tode Erzbischof Konrads (1200)*. 2 vols. Vol. 2: *1176–1200*, ed. Peter Acht. Darmstadt: Selbstverlag der Hessischen Historischen Kommission Darmstadt, 1971.

Mansi, Giovanni Domenico, ed. *Sacrorum conciliorum nova amplissima collectio*. Vol. 21. Venice, 1776.

Maragone, Bernardo. *Gli Annales Pisani di Bernardo Maragone*, ed. Michele Lupo Gentile. In Ludovicus Antonius Muratorius, Rerum Italicarum Scriptores 6/2. New edition. Bologna: Nicola Zanichelli, 1936.

Marbach Annals. Die Chronik Ottos von St. Blasien und die Marbacher Annalen, ed. and trans. Franz-Josef Schmale. In AQ 18a. Darmstadt: Wissenschaftliche Buchgesellschaft, 1986.

Morena, Otto and Acerbus. *Libellus de rebus a Frederico imperatore gestis*, ed. and trans. Franz-Josef Schmale. In *Italienische Quellen*, pp. 34–239.

Narratio de electione Lotharii Saxoniae ducis in regem Romanorum, ed. Wilhelm Wattenbach. MGH SS 12:509–12. Hanover, 1856.

Narratio de Longobardie obpressione et subiectione, ed. and trans. Franz-Josef Schmale. In *Italienische Quellen*, pp. 240–95.

Obertus. *Annales Ianuenses*, excerpted and trans. Franz-Josef Schmale. In *Italienische Quellen*, pp. 296–307.

Odo of Deuil. *De profectione Ludovici VII in orientem: The Journey of Louis VII to the East*, ed. with an English translation by Virginia Gingerick Berry. In *Records of Civilization: Sources and Studies*, paperback. New York: W. W. Norton, 1948.

Otto of Freising. *Ottonis Episcopi Frisingensis Chronica sive Historia de duabus Civitatibus.* 2nd edn., ed. Adolf Hofmeister. In MGH SSrG. Hanover, 1912. *The Two Cities: A Chronicle of Universal History to the Year 1146 A.D.*, trans. Charles Christopher Mierow and revised by Karl F. Morrison. In *Records of Western Civilization.* New York: Columbia University Press, 2002. *Chronik oder Die Geschichte der zwei Staaten*, trans. Adolf Schmidt. In AQ 16, ed. Walther Lammers. Darmstadt: Wissenschaftliche Buchgesellschaft, 1960.

—. *Ottonis et Rahewini Gesta Friderici I. Imperatoris*, ed. Georg Waitz and Bernhard von Simson. In MGH SSrG. Hanover and Leipzig: Hahnsche Buchhandlung, 1912. *The Deeds of Frederick Barbarossa*, trans. Charles Christopher Mierow. In *Records of Western Civilization.* New York: Columbia University Press, 1953; paperback edition, New York: W. W. Norton, 1966.

Otto of St. Blasien, *Chronicle.* In *Die Chronik Ottos von St. Blasien und die Marbacher Annalen*, ed. and trans. Franz-Josef Schmale. In AQ 18a. Darmstadt: Wissenschaftliche Buchgesellschaft, 1998. Partial English translation in Loud, *The Crusade of Frederick Barbarossa*, pp. 173–91.

Pez, Bernhard. *Thesaurus anecdotorum novissimus seu veterum monumentorum praecipue ecclesiasticorum, ex Germanicis potissimum bibliothecis adomata collectio recentissima* 6/2. Veith, 1729.

The Play of Antichrist, trans. John Wright. Toronto: The Pontifical Institute of Mediaeval Studies, 1967.

Quellen zur Geschichte des Kreuzzuges Kaiser Friedrichs I, ed. Anton Chroust. MGH SSrG, Nova Series 5. Berlin, 1928. Reprint, Munich, 1989.

Recueil des historiens des Gaules et de la France, vol. 16, ed. Michel-Jean-Joseph Brial. Paris, 1814. Revised edition, ed. Léopold Delisle. Paris: Victor Palmé, 1878.

Die Regesten des Kaiserreiches unter Friedrich I. 1152 (1122)–1190, ed. Ferdinand Opll. 4 vols. In J. F. Böhmer, *Regesta Imperii* IV/2. Vienna, Cologne, Graz, Weimar: Böhlau Verlag, 1980–2011.

Die Regesten des Kaiserreiches unter Heinrich VI. 1165 (1190)–1197, ed. Katrin and Gebhard Baaken. 2 vols. In J. F. Böhmer, *Regesta Imperii* IV/3. Cologne and Vienna: Böhlau Verlag, 1972–79.

Die Regesten des Kaiserreiches unter Lothar III. und Konrad III, ed. Wolfgang Petke and Paul Niederkorn. 2 vols. In J. F. Böhmer, *Regesta Imperii* IV/1. Cologne, Weimar, and Vienna: Böhlau Verlag, 1994–2008.

Richard of San Germano. *Chronica a 1189–1243*, ed. Georg Heinrich Pertz. MGH SS 19:321–84. Hanover, 1866.

Roberti de Monte cronica, ed. Ludwig Conrad Bethmann. MGH SS 6:475–535. Hanover, 1844.

Robertson, James Craigie, ed. *Materials for the History of Thomas Becket, Archbishop of Canterbury (Canonized by Pope Alexander III, A.D. 1173)*. 7 vols. In Rerum Britannicarum medii aevi scriptores 67. London: Her Majesty's Stationery Office, 1875–85; reprinted, n.p.: Kraus Reprint Ltd, 1965.

Romuald of Salerno. *Romoaldi archiepiscopi Salernitani Annales*, ed. Wilhelm Arndt. MGH SS 19:387–461. Hanover, 1866. Excerpted and trans. Franz-Josef Schmale with facing Latin text dealing with the Treaty of Venice. In *Italienische Quellen*, pp. 308–71.

Rückert, Friedrich. "Barbarossa," trans. Bayard Taylor and Lilian Bayard Taylor-Kiliani. In *The German Classics: Masterpieces of German Literature Translated into English*, 20 vols. New York: The German Publication Society, 1913, 5:486–87.

Salimbene di Adam of Parma. *Cronica ordinis Minorum*, ed. Oswald Holder-Egger. MGH SS 32. Hanover and Leipzig, 1905–13.

Salzburger Urkundenbuch, ed. Willibald Hauthaler and Franz Martin. 4 vols. Salzburg: Die Gesellschaft für Salzburger Landeskunde, 1910–33.

Saxo Grammaticus. *Ex Saxonis Gestis Danorum*, ed. Georg Waitz. MGH SS 29:37–161. Hanover, 1892.

Sudendorf, Hans, ed. *Registrum oder merkwürdige Urkunden für die deutsche Geschichte.* 3 vols. Jena and Berlin, 1849–54.

Die Taten Friedrichs oder richtiger Cronica, trans. Adolf Schmidt. In AQ 17, ed. Franz-Josef Schmale. Darmstadt: Wissenschaftliche Buchgesellschaft, 1965.

Die Tegernseer Briefsammlung des 12. Jahrhunderts, ed. Helmut Plechl. MGH BdK 8. Hanover: Hahnsche Buchhandlung, 2002.

Thomson, Rodney M. "An English Eyewitness of the Peace of Venice, 1177." *Speculum* 50 (1975): 21–32.

Tierney, Brian. *The Crisis of Church and State*. Englewood Cliffs, N.J.: Prentice Hall, 1964.

Die Traditionen des Klosters Scheyern, ed. Michael Stephan. In QEbG, NF 36/1. Munich, C. H. Beck'sche Verlagsbuchhandlung, 1986.

Die Traditionen des Klosters Wessobrunn, ed. Reinhold Höppl. In QEbG, NF 32/1. Munich: C. H. Beck'sche Verlagsbuchhandlung, 1984.

Die Traditionen des Kollegiatstifts St. Kastulus in Moosburg, ed. Klaus Höflinger. In QEbG, NF 42/1. Munich: C. H. Beck'sche Verlagsbuchhandlung, 1994.

Die Urkunden Friedrichs I., ed. Heinrich Appelt. 5 vols. MGH UdKK 10. Hanover: Hahnsche Buchhandlung, 1975–90.

Die Urkunden Friedrichs II. 1212–1217, ed. Walter Koch. MGH UdKK 14/2. Hanover: Hahnsche Buchhandlung, 2007.

Die Urkunden Heinrichs des Löwen Herzog von Sachsen und Bayern, ed. Karl Jordan. In MGH: Laienfürsten- und Dynastenurkunden der Kaiserzeit 1. Leipzig: Verlag Karl W. Hiersemann, 1941.

Die Urkunden Konrads III. und seines Sohnes Heinrich, ed. Friedrich Hausmann. MGH UdKK 9. Vienna, Cologne, and Graz: Hermann Böhlaus Nachf., 1969. Reprint, Munich, 1987.

Die Urkunden Lothars III. und der Kaiserin Richenza, ed. Emil von Ottenthal and Hans Hirsch. MGH UdKK 8. Berlin: Weidmannsche Buchhandlung, 1927. Reprint, Munich, 1993.

Die Urkunden und Briefe der Markgräfin Mathilde von Tuszien, ed. Elke Goez and Werner Goez. In MGH: Laienfürsten- und Dynastenurkunden der Kaiserzeit 2. Hanover: Hahnsche Buchhandlung, 1998.

Vincent of Prague. *Annales*, ed. Wilhelm Wattenbach. MGH SS 17:658–83. Hanover, 1861.

Vita Arnoldi archiepiscopi Moguntini, ed. Philipp Jaffé. In idem, *Bibliotheca rerum Germanicarum 3: Monumenta Moguntina*, pp. 604–75. Berlin, 1886. Reprint, Aalen: Scientia Verlag, 1964.

Vita beati Hartmanni Episcopi Brixinensis (1140–1164), ed. Anselm Sparber. In Schlern Schriften 46 (1940). Innsbruck: Universitäts-Verlag Wagner.

Die Viten Gottfrieds von Cappenberg, ed. Gerlinde Niemeyer and Ingrid Ehlers-Kisseler with Veronika Lukas. MGH SSrG 74. Hanover: Hahnsche Buchhandlung, 2005.

Wibald of Stavelot. *Das Briefbuch Abt Wibalds von Stablo und Corvey*, ed. Martina Hartmann. 3 vols. MGH BdK 9. Hanover: Hahnsche Buchhandlung, 2012.

—. *Codex Wibaldi*, ed. Philipp Jaffé. In *Monumenta Corbeiensia*. In Bibliotheca rerum Germanicarum 1. Berlin: Weidmann, 1864.

Wipo. *The Deeds of Conrad II*, trans. Theodor E. Mommsen and Karl F. Morrison. In *Imperial Lives and Letters of the Eleventh Century*, pp. 52–100. New York and London: Columbia University Press, 1962.

Wirtembergisches UB. No editor. 11 vols. Stuttgart, 1849–1913.

Secondary Sources

Abulafia, David. *Frederick II: A Medieval Emperor*. London: The Penguin Press, 1988.

Althoff, Gerd. "Colloquium familiar—colloquium secretum—colloquium publicum: Beratung im politischen Leben des früheren Mittelalters." *FS* 24 (1990): 145–67. Reprinted in idem, *Spielregeln*, pp. 157–84.

—. "Demonstration und Inszenierung: Spielregeln der Kommunikation in mittelalterlicher Öffentlichkeit." *FS* 27 (1993): 27–50. Reprinted in idem, *Spielregeln*, pp. 229–57.

—. "Friedrich von Rothenburg: Überlegungen zu einem übergangen Königssohn." In Schnith and Pauler, eds. *Festschrift für Edward Hlawitschka*, pp. 307–16.

—. "Konfliktverhalten und Rechtsbewusstsein: Die Welfen im 12. Jahrhundert." *FS* 26 (1992): 331–52. Reprinted in idem, *Spielregeln*, pp. 57–84.

—. "Königsherrschaft und Konfliktbewältigung im 10. und 11. Jahrhundert." *FS* 25 (1989): 265–90. Reprinted in idem, *Spielregeln*, pp. 21–56.

—. *Spielregeln der Politik im Mittelalter: Kommunikation in Frieden und Fehde*. Darmstadt: Wissenschaftliche Buchgesellschaft, 1997.
—. "Staatsdiener oder Häupter des Staates: Fürstenverantwortung zwischen Reichsinterresse und Eigennutz." In idem, *Spielregeln*, pp. 126–53.
—. "Ungeschriebene Gesetze: Wie funktioniert Herrschaft ohne schriftlich fixierte Normen?" In idem, *Spielregeln*, pp. 282–304.
—. "Die Zähringerherrschaft im Urteil Ottos von Freising." In Schmid, *Die Zähringer*, vol. 1, pp. 43–58.
—, Johannes Fried, and Patrick J. Geary, eds. *Medieval Concepts of the Past: Ritual, Memory, Historiography*. In Publications of the German Historical Institute, Washington, D.C. Cambridge: Cambridge University Press, 2002.
Die Andechs-Meranier in Franken: Europäisches Fürstentum im Mittelalter. Mainz: Verlag Philipp von Zabern, 1998.
Appelt, Heinrich. "Böhmische Königswürde und staufisches Kaisertum." In *Aus Reichsgeschichte und nordischer Geschichte: Karl Jordan zum 65. Geburtstag*. In *Kieler Historische Studien* 16 (1972): 161–81. Reprinted in idem, *Kaisertum*, pp. 40–60.
—. "Einleitung." *Die Urkunden Friedrich I.*, 5:1–138.
—. "Friedrich Barbarossa und die italienischen Kommunen." *MIÖG* 72 (1964): 311–25. Reprinted in Wolf, ed. *Friedrich Barbarossa*, pp. 83–103; and Appelt, *Kaisertum*, pp. 121–36.
—. "Friedrich Barbarossa und das römische Recht." *Römische Historische Mitteilungen* 5 (1961/62): 18–34. Reprinted in Wolf, *Friedrich Barbarossa*, pp. 58–82; and in Appelt, *Kaisertum*, pp. 61–80.
—. "Heinrich der Löwe und die Wahl Friedrichs Barbarossas." In *Festschrift Hermann Wiesflecker zum sechzigsten Geburtstag*, ed. Alexander Novotny and Othmar Pickl, pp. 39–48. Graz: Historisches Institut der Universität Graz, 1973. Reprinted in Appelt, *Kaisertum*, pp. 97–108.
. "Das Herzogtum Österreich." In Drabek, ed. *Österreich im Hochmittelalter*, pp. 271–330.
—. "Die Kaiseridee Friedrich Barbarossas." *Sitzungsberichte der Österreichischen Akademie der Wissenschaften*, Philosophisch-historische Klasse 252/4:3–32. Vienna, 1967. Reprinted in idem, *Kaisertum*, pp. 11–39; and Wolf, ed. *Friedrich Barbarossa*, pp. 208–44.
—. "Kaiserin Beatrix und das Erbe der Grafen von Burgund." In *Aus Kirche und Reich: Studien zur Theologie, Politik und Recht im Mittelalter: Festschrift für Friedrich Kempf zu seinem fünfundsiebzigsten Geburtstag und fünfzigjährigen Doktorjubiläum*, ed. Hubert Mordek, pp. 275–83. Sigmaringen: Jan Thorbecke Verlag, 1983. Reprinted in Appelt, *Kaisertum*, pp. 109–20.
—. *Kaisertum, Königtum, Landesherrschaft: Gesammelte Studien zur mittelalterlichen Verfassungsgeschichte*, ed. Othmar Hageneder and Herwig Weigl. In *MIÖG*, Ergänzungsband 28. Vienna, Cologne, and Graz: Böhlau Verlag, 1988.
—. "Kaiserurkunde und Fürstensentenz unter Friedrich Barbarossa." *MIÖG* 71 (1963): 33–47. Reprinted in idem, *Kaisertum*, pp. 81–96.
—. "Die libertas affectandi des Privilegium minus." *Mitteilungen des Österreichischen Staatsarchiv* 25 (1970): 135–40. Reprinted in idem, *Kaisterum*, pp. 174–79.
—. "La Pace di Constanza 1183." *Studi e testi di storia medioevale* 8 (1983): 23–34. Reprinted as "Das Zustandekommen des Textes des Friedens von Konstanz" in idem, *Kaisertum*, pp. 137–50.
—. *Privilegium minus: Das staufische Kaisertum und die Babenberger in Österreich*. Vienna, Cologne, and Graz: Hermann Böhlaus Nachf., 1973.
—. "Die Reichsarchive in den frühstaufischen Burgunderdiplomen." In *Festschrift Hans Lentze zum 60. Geburtstag*, ed. Nikolaus Grass and Werner Ogris, pp. 1–11. In *Forschungen zur Rechts- und Kulturgeschichte* 4 (1969). Reprinted in Appelt, *Kaisertum*, pp. 151–61.
—. "Der Vorbehalt kaiserliche Rechte in den Diplomen Friedrich Barbarossas." MIÖG 68 (1960): 81–97. Reprinted in Wolf, ed. *Friedrich Barbarossa*, pp. 33–57.
Arens, Fritz. "Die staufischen Königspfalzen." In *Die Zeit der Staufer* 3:129–42.
Arndt, Monika. *Die Goslarer-Kaiserpfalz als Nationaldenkmal: Eine ikonographische Untersuchung*. Hildesheim: August Lax Verlagsbuchhandlung, 1976.
—. "Das Kyffhäuser-Denkmal—Ein Beitrag zur politischen Ikonographie des Zweiten Kaiserreiches." *Wallraf-Richartz-Jahrbuch: Westdeutsches Jahrbuch für Kunstgeschichte* 40 (1978): 75–127.
Arnold, Benjamin. *Count and Bishop in Medieval Germany: A Study of Regional Power, 1100–1350*. Philadelphia: University of Pennsylvania Press, 1991.

—. "German Bishops and their Military Retinues in the Medieval Empire." *German History* 7/2 (1989): 161–83.

—. *German Knighthood, 1050–1300*. Oxford: Clarendon Press, 1985.

—. *Princes and Territories in Medieval Germany*. Cambridge: Cambridge University Press, 1991.

Baaken, Gerhard. "Die Altersfolge der Söhne Friedrich Barbarossas und die Königserhebung Heinrichs VI." DA 24 (1968): 46–78. Reprinted in idem, *Imperium und Papsttum*, pp. 46–78.

—. *Imperium und Papsttum: Zur Geschichte des 12. und 13. Jahrhunderts: Festschrift zum 70. Geburtstag*, ed. Karl-Augustin Frech and Ulrich Schmidt. Cologne, Weimar, and Vienna: Böhlau Verlag, 1997.

—. "Unio regni ad imperium: Die Verhandlungen von Verona 1184 und die Eheabredung zwischen König Heinrich VI. und Konstanze von Sizilien." *Quellen und Forschungen aus italienischen Archiven und Bibliotheken* 52 (1972): 219–97. Reprinted in idem, *Imperium und Papsttum*, pp. 81–142.

—. "Zur Beurteilung Gottfrieds von Viterbo." In *Geschichtsschreibung und geistiges Leben im Mittelalter: Festschrift für Heinz Lowe zum 65. Geburtstag*, ed. Karl Hauck und Hubert Mordek, pp. 373–96. Cologne and Vienna: Böhlau Verlag, 1978. Reprinted in idem, *Imperium und Papsttum,* pp. 159–80.

Bagge, Sverre, "German Historiography and the Twelfth-Century Renaissance." In Weiler and MacLean, eds. *Representations of Power in Medieval Germany*, pp. 165–88.

—. "Ideas and Narrative in Otto of Freising's *Gesta Frederici*." *Journal of Medieval History* 22/4 (1996): 345–77.

Baldwin, John W. *The Government of Philip Augustus: Foundations of French Royal Power in the Middle Ages*. Berkeley and Los Angeles: University of California Press, 1991.

Baldwin, Marshall W. *Alexander III and the Twelfth Century*. In The Popes through History 3. Glen Rock, N.J.: Newman Press, 1968.

Barraclough, Geoffrey. *The Origins of Modern Germany*. 2nd revised edn. New York: Capricon Books, 1963.

—. "What Is to Be Done about Medieval History?" *New York Review of Books* 14/11 (4 June 1970): 51–57.

Becher, Matthias. "Karl der Gute als Thronkandidat im Jahr 1125: Gedanken zur nord-deutschen Opposition gegen Heinrich V." In *Heinrich V. in seiner Zeit: Herrschen in einem europäischen Reich des Hochmittelalters*, ed. Gerhard Lubich, pp. 137–50. In FKPM 34. Vienna, Cologne, and Weimar: Böhlau Verlag, 2013.

—. "Von 'Eticho' zu 'Welf': Gedanken zur frühen welfischen Hausüberlieferung." In Bihrer et al., eds. *Adel und Königtum im mittelalterlichen Schwaben*, pp. 235–47.

Beneš, Carrie E. "Whose SPQR? Sovereignty and Semiotics in Medieval Rome." *Speculum* 84 (2009): 874–904.

Benson, Robert L. "Political *Renovatio*: Two Models from Roman Antiquity." In idem and Constable, eds. *Renaissance and Renewal*, pp. 339–86.

— and Giles Constable, eds. *Renaissance and Renewal in the Twelfth Century*. Cambridge, MA: Harvard University Press, 1982.

Berend, Nora. "Hungary in the Eleventh and Twelfth Centuries." In Luscombe and Smith, eds. *The New Cambridge Medieval History* 4/2:304–16.

Berger, Stefan, Mark Donovan, and Kevin Passmore. *Writing National Histories*. London and New York: Routledge, 1999.

Bernhardi, Wilhelm. *Konrad III*. In Jahrbücher der Deutschen Geschichte, 1883. Reprint, Berlin: Duncker and Humblot, 1975.

—. *Lothar von Supplinburg*. In Jahrbücher der Deutschen Geschichte. Leipzig: Duncker and Humblot, 1879.

Bernhardt, John W. *Itinerant Kingship and Royal Monasteries in Early Medieval Germany c. 936–1075*. In Cambridge Studies in Medieval Life and Thought, 4th series. Cambridge and New York: Cambridge University Press, 1993.

Bernwieser, Johannes. "*Ex consilio principum curie*: Friedrich Barbarossa und der Konflikt zwischen Genua und Pisa um die Vorherrschaft auf Sardinien." In Burkhardt et al., eds. *Staufisches Kaisertum im 12. Jahrhundert*, pp. 205–27.

Berwinkel, Holger. *Verwüsten und Belagern: Friedrich Barbarossas Krieg gegen Mailand (1158–1162).* In Bibliothek des Deutschen Historischen Instituts in Rom 114. Tübingen: Max Niemeyer Verlag, 2007.

Bihrer, Andreas, Mathias Kälble, and Heinz Krieg, eds. *Adel und Königtum im mittelalterlichen Schwaben: Festschrift für Thomas Zotz zum 65. Geburtstag.* Stuttgart: W. Kohlhammer Verlag, 2009.

Bisson, Thomas. *The Crisis of the Twelfth Century: Power, Lordship, and the Origins of European Government.* Princeton, N.J., and Oxford: Princeton University Press, 2009.

Blumenthal, Uta-Renate. *The Investiture Controversy: Church and Monarchy from the Ninth to the Twelfth Century.* Philadelphia: University of Pennsylvania Press, 1988.

—. "*Patrimonia* and *Regalia* in 1111." In *Law, Church, and Society: Essays in Honor of Stephan Kuttner*, ed. Kenneth Pennington and Robert Somerville, pp. 9–20. Philadelphia: University of Pennsylvania Press, 1977.

Bockhorst, Wolfgang. "Die Grafen von Cappenberg und die Anfänge des Stifts Cappenberg." In *Studien zum Prämonstratenserorden*, ed. Irene Crusius and Helmut Flachenecker, pp. 53–74. In VMPIG 185. Göttingen: Vandenhoeck & Ruprecht, 2003.

Böhm, Franz. *Das Bild Friedrich Barbarossas und seines Kaisertums in den ausländischen Quellen seiner Zeit.* In HS 289. Berlin: Verlag Dr. Emil Ebering, 1936.

Bolton, Brenda. "The Absentee Lord? Alexander III and the Patrimony." In Clarke and Duggan, eds. *Pope Alexander III*, pp. 153–80.

—. "*Nova familia beati Petri*: Adrian IV and the Patrimony." In idem, *Adrian IV*, pp. 157–79.

— and Anne J. Duggan, eds. *Adrian IV, The English Pope (1154–1159): Studies and Texts.* Aldershot, U.K., and Burlington, VT: Ashgate, 2003.

Borgolte, Michael. "Über Typologie und Chronologie des Königskanonikats im europäischen Mittelalters." *DA* 48 (1991): 19–44.

Borst, Arno. "Barbarossas Erwachen—Zur Geschichte der deutschen Identität." In *Identität*, ed. Odo Marquard and Karlheinz Stierle, pp. 17–60. Munich: Wilhelm Fink Verlag, 1979.

Bosl, Karl. "Die Reichsministerialität als Element der mittelalterlichen deutschen Staatsverfassung im Zeitalter der Salier und Staufer." In idem, *Frühformen der Gesellschaft im mittelalterlichen Europa: Ausgewählte Beiträge zu einer Strukturanalyse der mittelalterlichen Welt.* Munich and Vienna: R. Oldenbourg Verlag, 1964.

—. *Die Reichsministerialität der Salier und Staufer: Ein Beitrag zur Geschichte des hochmittelalterlichen deutschen Volkes, Staates und Reiches.* 2 vols. Stuttgart: Hiersemann Verlags, 1950–51.

Bouchard, Constance Brittain. *"Those of My Blood": Constructing Noble Families in Medieval Francia.* Philadelphia: University of Pennsylvania Press, 2001.

Brand, Charles M. "The Byzantines and Saladin, 1185–1192: Opponents of the Third Crusade," *Speculum* 37 (1962): 167–81.

Bringmann, Michael. "Gedanken zur Wiederaufnahme staufische Bauformen im späten 19. Jahrhundert." In *Die Zeit der Staufer* 5:581–620.

Brinken, Bernd. *Die Politik Konrads von Staufen in der Tradition der Rheinischen Pfalzgrafschaft: Der Widerstand gegen die Verdrängung der Pfalzgrafschaft aus dem Rheinland in der zweiten Hälfte des 12. Jahrhunderts.* In Rheinisches Archiv 82. Bonn: Ludwig Röhrscheid Verlag, 1974.

Brühl, Carlrichard. "Die Finanzpolitik Friedrich Barbarossas in Italien." *HZ* 213 (1971): 13–37.

—. *Fodrum, gistum, servitium regis: Studien zu den wirtschaftlichen Grundlagen des Königtums im Frankenreich und in den fränkischen Nachfolgerstaaten Deutschland, Frankreich und Italien vom 6. bis zur Mitte des 14. Jahrhunderts.* 2 vols. In Kölner historische Abhandlungen 14. Cologne and Graz: Böhlau Verlag, 1968.

Brune, Thomas and Bodo Baumunk. "Wege der Popularisierung." In *Die Zeit der Staufer* 3:327–35.

Bumke, Joachim. *Höfische Kultur: Literatur und Gesellschaft im hohen Mittelalter.* 2 vols. Munich: Taschenbuch Verlag, 1986, trans. Thomas Dunlap as *Courtly Culture: Literature and Society in the High Middle Ages.* Berkeley and Los Angeles: University of California Press, 1991.

—. *Studien zum Ritterbegriff im 12. und 13. Jahrhundert*. In Beihefte zur Euphorion: Zeitschrift für Literaturgeschichte 1. Heidelberg: C. Winter, 1964; revised edn., 1977. Translation of revised edition by W. T. H. and Erika Jackson, *The Concept of Knighthood in the Middle Ages*. In AMS Studies in the Middle Ages 2. New York: AMS Press, 1982.

Burkhardt, Stefan. "Barbarossa, Frankreich, und die Weltherrschaft." In Burkhardt et al., eds. *Staufisches Kaisertum im 12. Jahrhundert*, pp. 133–58.

—, Thomas Metz, Bernd Schneidmüller, and Stefan Weinfurter, eds. *Staufisches Kaisertum im 12. Jahrhundert: Konzepte—Netzwerke—Politische Praxis*. Regensburg: Verlag Schnell & Steiner, 2010.

Büttner, Heinrich. "Erzbischof Adalbert von Mainz, die Kurie und das Reich in den Jahren 1118 bis 1122." In Fleckenstein, ed. *Investiturstreit und Reichsverfassung*, pp. 395–410.

—. "Friedrich Barbarossa und Burgund: Studien zur Politik der Staufer während des 12. Jahrhunderts." In Mayer, ed. *Probleme des 12. Jahrhunderts*, pp. 79–119.

—. "Vom Bodensee und Genfer See zum Gotthardpass." In *Die Alpen in der europäischen Geschichte des Mittelalters*, ed. Theodor Mayer, pp. 77–110. In VF 10. Sigmaringen: Jan Thorbecke Verlag, 1965.

Canning, Joseph and Otto Gerhard Oexle, eds. *Political Thought and the Realities of Power in the Middle Ages*. In VMPIG 147. Göttingen: Vandenhoeck & Ruprecht, 1998.

Chalandon, Ferdinand. *Histoire de la domination normande en Italie et en Sicile*. 2 vols. Paris: Librairie A. Picard et fils, 1907. Reprint, New York: Burt Franklin, 1960–69.

Chazan, Robert. "Emperor Frederick I, the Third Crusade, and the Jews." *Viator* 8 (1977): 83–93.

Cheyette, Fredric L. *Ermengard of Narbonne and the World of the Troubadours*. Ithaca, N.Y., and London: Cornell University Press, 2001.

Clarke, Peter D. "Introduction." In idem, *Pope Alexander III*, pp. 1–12.

— and Anne J. Duggan, eds. *Pope Alexander III (1159–81): The Art of Survival*. In *Church, Faith and Culture in the Medieval West*. Farnham, and Burlington, VT: Ashgate, 2012.

Classen, Peter. "*Res gestae*, Universal History, Apocalypse: Visions of Past and Future." In Benson and Constable, eds. *Renaissance and Renewal in the Twelfth Century*, pp. 387–417.

—. "Das Wormser Konkordat in der deutschen Verfassungsgeschichte." In Fleckenstein, ed., *Investiturstreit und Reichsverfassung*, pp. 411–60.

Claude, Dietrich. *Geschichte des Erzbistums Magdeburg bis in das 12. Jahrhunderts*. 2 vols. In Mitteldeutsche Forschungen 67. Cologne and Vienna: Böhlau Verlag, 1972–75.

Claussen, Peter Cornelius. "Stauferbilder—Bildnisse der Staufer." In Schneidmüller et al., *Verwandlungen des Stauferreichs*, pp. 350–76.

Cohn, Norman. *The Pursuit of the Millennium: Revolutionary Messianism in Medieval and Renaissance Europe and its Bearing on Modern Totalitarian Movements*. 2nd edn. New York: Harper Torchbacks, 1961.

Csendes, Peter. *Heinrich VI*. In Gestalten des Mittelalters und der Renaissance. Darmstadt: Wissenschaftliche Buchgesellschaft, 1993.

—. *Philipp von Schwaben: Ein Staufer im Kampf um die Macht*. In Gestalten des Mittelalters und der Renaissance. Darmstadt: Wissenschaftliche Buchgesellschaft, 2003.

Decker-Hauff, Hansmartin. "Das Staufische Haus." In *Die Zeit der Staufer* 3:339–74.

Deibel, Gertrud. "Die finanzielle Bedeutung Reichs-Italiens für die staufischen Herrscher des zwölften Jahrhunderts." *ZRG GA* 54 (1934): 134–77.

—. "Die italienischen Einkünfte Kaiser Friedrich Barbarossas." *Neue Heidelberger Jahrbücher*, NF, 1932, pp. 21–58.

Dendorfer, Jürgen. *Adelige Gruppenbildung und Königsherrschaft: Die Grafen von Sulzbach und ihr Beziehungsgeflecht im 12. Jahrhundert*. In Studien zur bayerischen Verfassungs- und Sozialgeschichte 25. Munich: Kommission für bayerische Landesgeschichte, 2004.

—. "*Fidi milites*? Die Staufer und Kaiser Heinrich V." In Seibert and Dendorfer, eds. *Grafen, Herzöge, Könige*, pp. 213–65.

—. "Roncaglia: Der Beginn eines lehnrechtlichen Umbaus des Reiches?" In Burkhardt et al., eds. *Staufisches Kaisertum im 12. Jahrhundert*, pp. 111–32.

—. "Von den Babenberger zu den Welfen: Herzog und Adel in Bayern um die Mitte des 12. Jahrhunderts." In *München, Bayern und das Reich im 12. und 13. Jahrhundert: Lokale Befunde und überregionale Perspektiven*, ed. Hubertus Seibert and Alois Schmid, pp. 221–47. In *ZbLG*, Beiheft 29. Munich: Beck, 2008.

Deutinger, Roman. "Imperiale Konzepte in der hofnahen Historiographie der Barbarossazeit." In Burkhardt et al., eds. *Staufisches Kaisertum im 12. Jahrhundert*, pp. 25–39.
—. *Rahewin von Freising: Ein Gelehrter des 12. Jahrhunderts*. In MGH Schriften 47. Hanover: Hahnsche Buchhandlung, 1999.
—. "Sutri 1155: Missverständnisse um ein Missverständnis." *DA* 60 (2004): 97–133.
Dick, Stefanie. "Die Königserhebung Friedrich Barbarossas im Spiegel der Quellen: Kritische Anmerkungen zu den 'Gesta Friderici' Ottos von Freising." *ZRG GA* 121 (2004): 200–37.
Dienst, Heide. "Werden und Entwicklung der babenbergische Mark." In Drabek, ed. *Österreich im Hochmittelalter (907 bis 1246)*, pp. 63–102.
Dimnik, Martin. "Kievan Rus', the Bulgars and the Southern Slavs, c. 1020–c. 1200." In Luscombe and Smith, eds. *The New Cambridge Medieval History* 4/2:254–76.
Dirlmeier, Ulf. "Friedrich Barbarossa—auch ein Wirtschaftspolitiker?" In Haverkamp, ed. *Friedrich Barbarossa*, pp. 501–18.
Dollinger, Philippe. *The German Hansa*, trans. D. S. Ault and S. H. Steinberg. Stanford, C.A.,: Stanford University Press, 1970.
Dopsch, Heinz, ed. *Geschichte Salzburgs: Stadt und Land*. Vol. 1: *Vorgeschichte, Altertum, Mittelalter*. 3 vols. Salzburg: Universitätsverlag Anton Pustet, 1981–84.
Doran, John. "'At last we reached the port of salvation': The Roman Context of the Schism of 1159." In Clarke and Duggan, eds. *Pope Alexander III*, pp. 51–98.
Dorpalen, Andreas. *German History in Marxist Perspective: The East German Approach*. Detroit: Wayne State University Press, 1988.
Drabek, Anna, ed. *Österreich im Hochmittelalter (907 bis 1246)*. In Veröffentlichungen der Kommission für die Geschichte Österreichs 17. Vienna: Verlag der Österreichischen Akademie der Wissenschaften, 1991.
Duby, Georges. "Youth in Aristocratic Society: Northwestern France in the Twelfth Century," trans. Cynthia Postan. In Duby, *The Chivalrous Society*, pp. 112–22. Berkeley and Los Angeles: University of California Press, 1977.
Duggan, Anne J. "*Alexander ille meus:* The Papacy of Alexander III." In Clarke and Duggan, eds. *Pope Alexander III*, pp. 13–49.
—. "*Totius christianitatis caput*: The Pope and the Princes." In Bolton, ed. *Adrian IV*, pp. 105–55.
Ehlers, Caspar. *Metropolis Germaniae: Studien zur Bedeutung Speyers für das Königtum (751–1250)*. In VMPIG 125. Göttingen: Vandenhoeck & Ruprecht, 1996.
Ehlers, Joachim. *Heinrich der Löwe: Eine Biographie*. Munich: Siedler Verlag, 2008.
—. "Heinrich der Löwe und der sächsische Episkopat." In Haverkamp, ed. *Friedrich Barbarossa*, pp. 435–66.
—. *Otto von Freising: Ein Intellektueller im Mittelalter: Eine Biographie*. Munich: Verlag C. H. Beck, 2013.
Ehrlich, Lothar. "Das Goethe-Schiller-Denkmal in Weimar." In Mai, ed. *Das Kyffhäuser-Denkmal*, pp. 263–77.
Eichmann, Eduard. "Das Officium Stratoris et Strepae." *HZ* 142 (1930): 16–40.
Eickhoff, Ekkehard. *Friedrich Barbarossa im Orient: Kreuzzug und Tod Friedrichs I*. In Istanbuler Mitteilungen 17. Tübingen: Verlag Ernst Wasmuth, 1977.
Ellenblum, Ronnie. *Crusader Castles and Modern Histories*. Cambridge: Cambridge University Press, 2007.
Elm, Kaspar. *Norbert von Xanten: Adliger, Ordensstifter, Kirchenfürst*. Cologne: Wienand Verlag, 1984.
— ed. *Die Zisterzienser: Ordensleben zwischen Ideal und Wirklichkeit*. Ergänzungsband. In Schriften des Rheinischen Museumamtes 18. Cologne: Rheinland-Verlag, 1982.
Engel, Evamaria and Bernhard Töpfer, eds. *Kaiser Friedrich Barbarossa: Landesaufbau-Aspekte seiner Politik-Wirkung*. In FMG 36. Weimar: Verlag Hermann Böhlaus Nachf., 1994.
Engels, Odilo. "Beiträge zur Geschichte der Staufer im 12. Jahrhundert (I)." DA 27 (1971): 373–456. Reprinted in idem, *Stauferstudien*, pp. 32–115.
—. "Friedrich Barbarossa und Dänemark." In Haverkamp, ed. *Friedrich Barbarossa*, pp. 353–85.
—. "Grundlinien der rheinischen Verfassungsgeschichte im 12. Jahrhundert." *Rheinische Vierteljahrsblätter* 39 (1975): 1–27. Reprinted in idem, *Stauferstudien*, pp. 133–59.

—. "Kardinal Boso als Geschichtsschreiber." In *Konzil und Papst: Festgabe für Hermann Tüchle*, ed. Georg Schwaiger, pp. 147–68. Munich, Paderborn, and Vienna: Schöningh, 1975. Reprinted in Engels, *Stauferstudien*, pp. 203–24.

—. "Der Niederrhein und das Reich im 12. Jahrhundert." *Klever Archiv* 4 (1983): 79–101. Reprinted in idem, *Stauferstudien*, pp. 177–99.

—. *Die Staufer*. 8th edn. Stuttgart: Verlag W. Kohlhammer, 2005.

—. *Stauferstudien*: *Beiträge zur Geschichte der Staufer im 12. Jahrhundert: Festgabe zu seinem sechzigsten Geburtstag*, ed. Erich Meuthen and Stefan Weinfurter. Sigmaringen: Jan Thorbecke Verlag, 1988.

—. "Zum Konstanzer Vertrag von 1153." In *Deus qui mvtat tempora: Menschen und Institutionen im Wandel des Mittelalters: Festschrift für Alfons Becker zu seinem fünfundsechzigsten Geburtstag*, ed. Ernst-Dieter Hehl, Hubertus Seibert, and Franz Staab, pp. 235–58. Sigmaringen: Jan Thorbecke Verlag, 1987.

—. "Zur Entmachtung Heinrichs des Löwen." In *Festschrift für Andreas Kraus zum 60. Geburtstag*, ed. Pankraz Fried and Walter Ziegler, pp. 45–59. In Münchner Historische Studien: Abteilung Bayerische Geschichte 10. Kallmünz, 1982. Reprinted in Engels, *Stauferstudien*, pp. 116–30.

Evergates, Theodore. *The Aristocracy in the County of Champagne, 1100–1300*. Philadelphia: University of Pennsylvania Press, 2007.

Farmer, Sharon, "Aristocratic Power and the 'Natural' Landscape: The Garden Park at Hesdin, ca. 1291–1302." *Speculum* 88 (2013): 644–80.

Fasoli, Gina. "Federico Barbarossa e le città lombarde." In Mayer, ed., *Probleme des 12. Jahrhunderts*, pp. 121–42. Translated by Katharina Arndt as "Friedrich Barbarossa und die lombardischen Städte," in Wolf, ed. *Friedrich Barbarossa*, pp. 149–83.

Felten, Franz J. "Kaisertum und Papsttum im 12. Jahrhundert." In Hehl et al., eds, *Das Papsttum in der Welt des 12. Jahrhunderts*, pp. 101–25.

Fichtenau, Heinrich. *Living in the Tenth Century: Mentalities and Social Orders*, trans. Patrick J. Geary. Chicago and London: University of Chicago Press, 1991.

Ficker, Julius. *Vom Heerschilde: Ein Beitrag zur deutschen Reichs- und Rechtsgeschichte*. Innsbruck, 1862. Reprint, Aalen: Scientia Verlag, 1964.

—. *Vom Reichsfürstenstande: Forschungen zur Geschichte der Reichsverfassung zunaechst im XII. und XIII. Jahrhunderte*. 2 vols. 1. Innsbruck, 1861. 2nd edn. Paul Puntschart. Innsbruck, 1911; and Graz and Leipzig, 1921–23.

Filbinger, Hans. "Vom Sinn dieser Ausstellung." In *Die Zeit der Staufer* 1:v–x.

Fillitz, Hermann. "Nicolaus von Verdun." In *Die Zeit der Staufer* 5:279–90.

Finsterwalder, Paul Willem. "Die Gesetze des Reichstags von Roncaglia vom 11. November 1158." *ZRG GA* 51 (1931): 1–69.

Fleckenstein, Josef. "Friedrich Barbarossa und das Rittertum: Zur Bedeutung der grossen Mainzer Hoftage von 1184 und 1188." In *Festschrift für Hermann Heimpel zum 70. Geburtstag am 19. 9. 1971*. 2 vols. 2:1023–41. In VMPIG 36. Göttingen: Vandenhoeck & Ruprecht, 1972. Reprinted in Arno Borst, ed., *Das Rittertum im Mittelalter*, pp. 392–418. In WF 349. Darmstadt: Wissenschaftliche Buchgesellschaft, 1976.

—., ed., *Investiturstreit und Reichsverfassung*. In VF 17. Sigmaringen: Jan Thorbecke Verlag, 1973.

Föhl, Walther. "Studien zu Rainald von Dassel." *Jahrbuch des kölnischen Geschichtsvereins* 17 (1935): 234–59; and 20 (1938): 238–60.

Freed, John B. "Artistic and Literary Representation of Family Consciousness." In Althoff et al., eds, *Medieval Concepts of the Past*, pp. 233–52.

—. "Bavarian Wine and Woolless Sheep: The *Urbar* of Count Sigiboto IV of Falkenstein (1126–ca. 1198)." *Viator* 35 (2004): 71–112.

—. "The Counts of Falkenstein: Noble Self-Consciousness in Twelfth-Century Germany." In *Transactions of the American Philosophical Society* 74/6. Philadelphia: The American Philosophical Society, 1984.

—. "The Creation of the *Codex Falkensteinensis* (1166): Self Representation and Reality." In Weiler and MacLean, eds. *Representations of Power in Medieval Germany*, pp. 189–210.

—. "Medieval German Social History: Generalizations and Particularism." *CEH* 25 (1992): 1–26.

—. *Noble Bondsmen: Ministerial Marriages in the Archdiocese of Salzburg, 1100–1343.* Ithaca, N.Y., and London: Cornell University Press, 1995.
—. "Nobles, Ministerials, and Knights in the Archdiocese of Salzburg." *Speculum* 62 (1987): 575–611.
—. "Das zweite österreichische Millennium—Berufung auf das Mittelalter zur Schaffung eines österreichischen Nationalbewusstseins." *MGSL* 137 (1997): 279–94.
Fried, Johannes. *Die Entstehung des Juristenstandes im 12. Jahrhundert: Zur sozialen Stellung und politischen Bedeutung gelehrter Juristen in Bologna und Modena.* In Forschungen zur neueren Privatrechtgeschichte 21. Cologne and Vienna: Böhlau Verlag, 1974.
—. "Friedrich Barbarossas Krönung in Arles." *Historisches Jahrbuch* 103 (1983): 347–71.
—. "Die Wirtschaftspolitik Friedrich Barbarossas in Deutschland." *Blätter für deutsche Landesgeschichte* 120 (1984): 195–239.
Fried, Torsten. "Die Münzpragung unter Friedrich I. Barbarossa in Thüringen." In Engel and Töpfer, eds. *Kaiser Friedrich Barbarossa*, pp. 141–50.
Fuhrmann, Horst. "*Quis Teutonicos constituit iudices nationum?* The Trouble with Henry." *Speculum* 69 (1994): 344–58.
Galland, Bruno. "Les Relations entre la France et l'Empire au XIIe siècle." In Kölzer, ed. *Die Staufer im Süden*, pp. 57–82.
Ganz, Peter. "Friedrich Barbarossa: Hof und Kultur." In Haverkamp, ed. *Friedrich Barbarossa*, pp. 623–50.
Gaposchkin, M. Cecilia. "From Pilgrimage to Crusade: The Liturgy of Departure, 1095–1300." *Speculum* 88 (2013): 44–91.
Geary, Patrick J. "The Magi and Milan." In idem, *Living with the Dead in the Middle Ages*, pp. 243–56. Ithaca, N.Y., and London: Cornell University Press, 1994.
— and John B. Freed. "Literacy and Violence in Twelfth Century Bavaria: The 'Murder Letter' of Count Sigiboto IV." *Viator* 25 (1994): 115–29.
Georgi, Wolfgang. *Friedrich Barbarossa und die auswärtigen Mächte: Studien zur Aussenpolitik 1159–1180.* In Europäische Hochschulschriften 3/442. Frankfurt, Bern, New York, and Paris: Peter Lang, 1990.
—. "Wichmann, Christian, Philipp und Konrad: Die 'Friedensmacher' von Venedig?" In Weinfurter, ed. *Stauferreich im Wandel*, pp. 41–84.
Gerhold-Knittel, Elke. "Bericht über die Ausstellung." In *Die Zeit der Staufer* 5:621–26.
Giesebrecht, Wilhelm von and Bernhard von Simson. *Geschichte der deutschen Kaiserzeit.* 6 vols. Braunschweig and Leipzig: Verlag von Duncker & Humblot, 1855–1895. Revised edition by Wilhelm Schild. Meersburg: F. W. Hendel Verlag, 1929–30.
Gillingham, J. R. "Why Did Rahewin Stop Writing the Gesta Frederici?" *EHR* 83 (1968): 294–303.
Godman, Peter. *The Silent Masters: Latin Literature and its Censors in the High Middle Ages.* Princeton, N.J.: Princeton University Press, 2000.
Goebel, Stefen. *The Great War and Medieval Memory: War, Remembrance and Medievalism in Britain and Germany, 1914–1940.* In Studies in the Social and Cultural History of Modern Warfare 25. Cambridge: Cambridge University Press, 2007.
Göldel, Caroline, *Servitium regis und Tafelgüterverzeichnis: Untersuchungen zur Wirtschafts- und Verfassungsgeschichte des deutschen Königtums im 12. Jahrhundert.* In Studien zur Rechts-, Wirtschafts- und Kulturgeschichte 16. Sigmaringen: Jan Thorbecke Verlag, 1997.
Görich, Knut. *Die Ehre Friedrich Barbarossas: Kommunikation, Konflikt und politisches Handeln im 12. Jahrhundert.* Darmstadt: Wissenschaftliche Buchgesellschaft, 2001.
—. *Friedrich Barbarossa: Eine Biographie.* Munich: C. H. Beck, 2011.
—. "Jäger des Löwen oder Getriebener der Fürsten? Friedrich Barbarossa und die Entmachtung Heinrichs des Löwen." In Hechberger and Schuler, eds. *Staufer & Welfen*, pp. 98–117.
—. *Ein Kartäuser im Dienst Friedrich Barbarossas: Dietrich von Silve-Bénite (c. 1145–1205).* In Analecta Cartusiana 53. Salzburg: Institut für Anglistik und Amerikanistik, Universität Salzburg, 1987.
—. "Konflikt und Kompromiss: Friedrich Barbarossa in Italian." In Hechberger and Schuler, eds. *Staufer & Welfen*, pp. 78–97.

—. "Wahrung des *honor*: Ein Grundsatz im politischen Handeln König Konrads III." In Seibert and Dendorfer, eds. *Grafen, Herzöge, Könige*, pp. 267–97.
Goetz, Hans-Werner. *Das Geschichtsbild Ottos von Freising: Ein Beitrag zur historischen Vorstellungswelt und zur Geschichte des 12. Jahrhunderts*. In Beihefte zum Archiv für Kulturgeschichte 19. Cologne and Vienna: Böhlau Verlag, 1984.
Goez, Werner. *Der Leihezwang: Eine Untersuchung zur Geschichte des deutschen Lehnrechtes*. Tübingen: J. C. B. Mohr (Paul Siebeck), 1962.
—. "Möglichkeiten und Grenzen des Herrschens aus der Ferne in Deutschland und Reichsitaliens (1152–1220)." In Kölzer, ed. *Die Staufer im Süden*, pp. 93–111.
—. *Translatio Imperii: Ein Beitrag zur Geschichte des Geschichtsdenken und der politischen Theorien im Mittelalter und in der frühen Neuzeit*. Tübingen: Mohr, 1958.
—. "Über die Mathildischen Schenkungen an die Römische Kirche." *FS* 31 (1997): 158–96.
—. "Von Bamberg nach Frankfurt und Aachen: Barbarossas Weg zur Königskrone." In Schneider and Rechter, eds. *Festschrift Alfred Wendehorst*, pp. 61–71.
Goldberg, Eric J. "Louis the Pious and the Hunt." *Speculum* 88 (2013): 613–43.
Gollwitzer, Heinz. "Zur Auffassung der mittelalterlichen Kaiserpolitik im 19. Jahrhundert: Eine ideologie- und wissenschaftsgeschichtliche Nachlese." In *Dauer und Wandel der Geschichte: Aspekte europäischer Vergangenheit: Festgabe für Kurt von Raumer zum 15. Dezember 1965*, ed. Rudolf Vierhaus and Manfred Botzenhart, pp. 483–512. In Neue münstersche Beiträge zur Geschichtsforschung. Münster: Verlag Aschendorff, 1966.
Gottwald, Herbert. "Ein Kaiserdenkmal im Sozialismus: Das Kyffhäuser-Denkmal in SBZ und DDR." In Mai, ed. *Das Kyffhäuser-Denkmal*, pp. 235–61.
Graf, Klaus. "Staufer-Überlieferungen aus Kloster Lorch." In Lorenz and Schmidt, eds. *Von Schwaben bis Jerusalem*, pp. 209–40.
Grebe, Werner. "Studien zur geistigen Welt Rainalds von Dassel." *Annalen des historischen Vereins für den Niederrhein* 171 (1969): 5–44. Reprinted in Wolf, ed. *Friedrich Barbarossa*, pp. 245–96.
Greenaway, George William. *Arnold of Brescia*. Cambridge: Cambridge University Press, 1931.
Grewe, Holger. "Visualisierung von Herrschaft in der Architektur: Die Pfalz Ingelheim als Bedeutungsträger im 12. und 13. Jahrhundert." In Burkhardt et al., eds. *Staufisches Kaisertum im 12. Jahrhundert*, pp. 383–403.
Grill, Leopold. *Erzbischof Eberhard I. von Salzburg*. Stift Rein: n.p., 1964.
Grosse, Rolf. "Kaiser und Reich aus der Sicht Frankreichs in der zweiten Hälfte des 12. Jahrhunderts." In Weinfurter, ed. *Stauferreich im Wandel*, pp. 172–88.
Groten, Manfred. "Köln und das Reich: Zum Verhältnis von Kirche und Stadt zu den staufischen Herrschern 1151–1198." In Weinfurter, ed. *Stauferreich im Wandel*, pp. 237–52.
Grundmann, Herbert. *Ausgewählte Aufsätze*. 3 vols. In Schriften der MGH 25. Stuttgart: Anton Hiersemann, 1976–78.
—. *Der Cappenberger Barbarossakopf und die Anfänge des Stiftes Cappenberg*. In Münstersche Forschungen 12. Cologne and Graz: Böhlau Verlag, 1959.
—. "Gottfried von Cappenberg." *Westfälische Lebensbilder* 8 (1959): 1–16. Reprinted in idem, *Ausgewählte Aufsätze* 3:169–80.
—. "Litteratus—illiteratus: Der Wandel einer Bildungsnorm von Altertum zum Mittelalter." *Archiv für Kulturgeschichte* 40 (1958): 1–65. Reprinted in idem, *Ausgewählte Aufsätze* 3:1–66.
—. Review of Rassow's *Honor Imperii*. *HZ* 164 (1941): 577–82. Reprinted in Wolf, ed. *Friedrich Barbarossa*, pp. 26–32.
—. "Rotten und Brabanzonen: Söldner-Heere im 12. Jahrhundert." *DA* 5 (1942): 419–92.
Hack, Achim Thomas. *Das Empfangszeremoniell bei mittelalterlichen Papst-Kaiser-Treffen*. In FKPM 18. Cologne, Weimar, and Vienna: Böhlau Verlag, 1999.
Hageneder, Othmar. "Der Mainzer Reichslandfriede (1235) und die *Constitutio contra incendiarios* Friedrichs I. Barbarossa." In *Grundlagen des Rechts: Festschrift für Peter Landau zum 65. Geburtstag*, ed. Richard H. Helmholz, Paul Mikat, Jörg Müller, and Michael Stolleis, pp. 367–74. In Rechts- und staatswissenschaftliche Veröffentlichungen der Görres-Gesellschaft, NF 91. Paderborn, Munich, Vienna, and Zürich: Ferdinand Schöningh, 2000.
Hageneier, Lars. "Die frühen Staufer bei Otto von Freising oder Wie sind die *Gesta Friderici* entstanden?" In Seibert and Dendorfer, eds. *Grafen, Herzöge, Könige*, pp. 363–96.

Halfter, Peter. "Die Staufer und Armenien." In Lorenz and Schmidt, eds. *Von Schwaben bis Jerusalem*, pp. 187–208.

Haller, Johannes. "Heinrich VI. und die römische Kirche." *MIÖG* 35 (1914): 385–454 and 545–669. Reprint, Darmstadt: Wissenschaftliche Buchgesellschaft, 1962.

Hampe, Karl. *Germany under the Salian and Hohenstaufen Emperors*, trans. with an introduction by Ralph Bennett. Totowa, N.J.: Rowman & Littlefield, 1973.

—. *Geschichte Konradins von Hohenstaufen*. Innsbruck: Verlag der Wagnerschen Universitäts Buchhandlung, 1894.

Härtl, Reinhard. "Friedrich I. und die Länder an der oberen Adria." In Haverkamp, ed. *Friedrich Barbarossa*, pp. 291–352.

Hartmann, Martina. "Timothy Reuter and the Edition of Wibald of Stavelot's Letter Collection for the MGH." In Skinner, *Challenging the Boundaries of Medieval History*, pp. 185–91.

—. *Studien zu den Briefen Abt Wibalds von Stablo und Corvey sowie zur Briefliteratur in der frühen Stauferzeit*. MGH: Studien und Texte 52. Hanover: Hahnsche Buchhandlung, 2011.

Hasse, Claus-Peter. *Die welfischen Hofämter und die welfische Ministerialität in Sachsen: Studien zur Sozialgeschichte des 12. und 13. Jahrhunderts*. In HS 443. Husum: Matthiesen Verlag, 1995.

Hauck, Albert. *Kirchengeschichte Deutschlands*. Vol. 4. Leipzig: J. C. Hinrichs'sche Buchhandlung, 1903.

Hausmann, Friedrich. "Die Anfänge des staufischen Zeitalters unter Konrad III." In Mayer, ed. *Probleme des 12. Jahrhunderts*, pp. 53–78.

—. "Gottfried von Viterbo: Kapellan und Notar, Magister, Geschichtsschreiber und Dichter." In Haverkamp, ed. *Friedrich Barbarossa*, pp. 603–21.

—. *Reichskanzlei und Hofkapelle unter Heinrich V. und Konrad III.* In MGH Schriften 14. Stuttgart: Anton Hiersemann, 1956.

Haverkamp, Alfred, ed. *Friedrich Barbarossa: Handlungsspielräume und Wirkungsweisen des staufischen Kaisers*. In VF 40. Sigmaringen: Jan Thorbecke Verlag, 1992.

—. "Friedrich I. und der hohe italienische Adel." In *Beiträge zur Geschichte Italiens im 12. Jahrhunderts*, ed. Raoul Manselli, Paolo Lamma, and Alfred Haverkamp, pp. 53–92. In VF Sonderband 9. Sigmaringen: Jan Thorbecke Verlag, 1971.

—. *Herrschaftsformen der Frühstaufer in Reichsitalien*. 2 vols. In MGM 1. Stuttgart: Anton Hiersemann, 1970–71.

—. "Der Konstanzer Friede zwischen Kaiser und Lombardenbund (1183)." In Maurer, ed. *Kommunale Bündnisse*, pp. 11–44.

— and Hanna Vollrath, eds. *England and Germany in the High Middle Ages*. Oxford: The German Historical Institute London and Oxford University Press, 1996.

Hay, David J. *The Military Leadership of Matilda of Tuscany, 1046–1115*. Manchester and New York: Manchester University Press, 2008.

Hechberger, Werner. *Adel im fränkisch-deutschen Mittelalter: Zur Anatomie eines Forschungsproblems*. In MF 17. Sigmaringen: Jan Thorbecke Verlag, 2005.

—. "Bewundert—instrumentalisiert—angefeindet: Staufer und Welfen im Urteil der Nachwelt." In Hechberger, *Staufer und Welfen*, pp. 216–38.

—. "Konrad III.—Königliche Politik und 'staufische Familieninteressen'?" In Seibert and Dendorfer, eds. *Grafen, Herzöge, Könige*, pp. 323–40.

—. *Staufer und Welfen 1125–1190: Zur Verwendung von Theorien in der Geschichtswissenschaft*. In Passauer historische Forschungen 10. Cologne, Weimar, and Vienna: Böhlau Verlag, 1996.

— and Florian Schuler, eds. *Staufer & Welfen: Zwei rivalisierende Dynastien im Hochmittelalter*. Regensburg: Verlag Friedrich Pustet, 2009.

Heer, Friedrich. *The Holy Roman Empire*, trans. Janet Sondheimer. New York and Washington: Friedrich Praeger, 1968.

—. *Die Tragödie des heiligen Reiches*. Vienna and Zürich: Europa Verlag, 1952. Revised 2nd edn. Stuttgart: Kohlhammer, 1952–53.

Hehl, Ernst-Dieter, Ingrid Heike Ringel, and Hubertus Seibert, eds. *Das Papsttum in der Welt des 12. Jahrhunderts*. In MF 6. Stuttgart: Jan Thorbecke Verlag, 2002.

Heimpel, Hermann. "Kaiser Friedrich Barbarossa und die Wende der staufischen Zeit." *Strassburger Universitätsreden* 3 (1942): 4–32. Reprinted in Wolf, ed. *Friedrich Barbarossa*, pp. 1–25.

Heinemann, Hartmut. "Die Zähringer und Burgund." In Schmid, ed. *Die Zähringer* 1:59–74.

Heinemeyer, Karl. "König und Reichsfürsten in der späten Salier- und frühen Stauferzeit." *Blätter für deutsche Landesgeschichte* 122 (1986): 1–39.

Heinemeyer, Walter. "'beneficium—non feudum sed bonum factum': Der Streit auf dem Reichstag zu Besançon 1157." *Archiv für Diplomatik, Siegel- und Wappenkunde* 15 (1969): 155–236.

—. "Der Friede von Montebello (1175)." *DA* 11 (1954/55): 101–39.

—. "Die Verhandlungen an der Saône im Jahre 1162." *DA* 20 (1964): 155–89.

Heinig, Paul-Joachim, Sigrid Jahns, Hans-Joachim Schmidt, Rainer Christoph Schwinges, and Sabine Wefers, eds. *Reich, Regionen und Europa in Mittelalter und Neuzeit: Festschrift für Peter Moraw*. In Historische Forschungen 67. Berlin: Duncker & Humblot, 2000.

Hensch, Mathias. "Baukonzeption, Wohnkultur und Herrschaftsrepräsentation im Burgenbau des 11./12. Jahrhunderts in Nordbayern—neue Erkenntnisse der Archäologie." In Seibert and Dendorfer, eds. *Grafen, Herzöge, Könige*, pp. 135–78.

Herbers, Klaus, Hans Henning Kortüm, and Carlo Servatius, eds. *Ex ipsis rerum documentis: Beiträge zur Mediävistik: Festschrift für Harald Zimmermann zum 65. Geburtstag*. Sigmaringen: Jan Thorbecke Verlag, 1991.

Herde, Peter. "Die Katastrophe vor Rom im August 1167: Eine historisch-epidemiologische Studie zum vierten Italienzug Friedrichs I. Barbarossa." *Sitzungsberichte der Wissenschaftliche Gesellschaft an der Johann Wolfgang Goethe-Universität Frankfurt am Main* 24/7:139–66. Stuttgart: Franz Steiner Verlag, 1991.

Herkenrath, Rainer Maria. "Regnum und Imperium in den Diplomen der ersten Regierungsjahre Friedrichs I." *Sitzungsberichte der Österreichischen Akademie der Wissenschaften*, Philosophisch-historische Klasse 264/5:24–53. Vienna, 1969. Reprinted in Wolf, ed. *Friedrich Barbarossa*, pp. 323–59.

—. "Reinald von Dassel: Reichskanzler und Erzbischof von Köln." Unpublished dissertation. Graz, 1962.

Herzstein, Robert Edwin. *The Holy Roman Empire in the Middle Ages: Universal State or German Catastrophe?* Boston: D. C. Heath, 1966.

Hiestand, Rudolf. '"precipua tocius christianismi columpna': Barbarossa und der Kreuzzug." In Haverkamp, ed. *Friedrich Barbarossa*, pp. 51–108.

Hlawitschka, ed. Eduard. *Die Ahnen der hochmittelalterlichen deutschen Könige, Kaiser und ihrer Gemahlinnen: Ein kommentiertes Tafelwerk*. 3 vols. In MGH Hilfsmittel 25/1, 25/2, 26, and 29. Hanover: Hahnsche Buchhandlung, 2006–09; and Wiesbaden: Harrassowitz Verlag, 2013.

—. "Weshalb war die Auflösung der Ehe Friedrich Barbarossas und Adelas von Vohburg möglich?" *DA* 61 (2005): 509–36.

—, ed. *Königswahl und Thronfolge in ottonisch-frühdeutscher Zeit*. In WF 178. Darmstadt: Wissenschaftliche Buchgesellschaft, 1971.

Hödl, Günther. "Ungarn in der Aussenpolitik Kaiser Friedrich Barbarossas." In Engel, ed. *Kaiser Friedrich Barbarossa*, pp. 129–40.

Höing, Norbert. "Die 'Trierer Stilübungen': Ein Denkmal der Frühzeit Kaiser Friedrich Barbarossas." *Archiv für Diplomatik, Schriftgeschichte, Siegel- und Wappenkunde* 1 (1955): 257–329 and 2 (1956): 125–249.

Holtzmann, Robert. "Das Carmen de Frederico I. imperatore aus Bergamo und die Anfänge einer staufischen Hofhistoriographie." *NA* 44 (1922): 252–313.

—. *Der Kaiser als Marschall des Papstes: Eine Untersuchung zur Geschichte der Beziehungen zwischen Kaiser und Papst im Mittelalter*. In Schriften der Strassburger Wissenschaftlichen Gesellschaft in Heidelberg, NF 8 (1928).

—. "Zum Strator- und Marschalldienst." *HZ* 145 (1931): 301–50.

Horch, Caroline. *"Nach dem Bild des Kaisers:" Funktionen und Bedeutungen des Cappenberger Barbarossakopfes*. In Studien zur Kunst 15. Cologne, Weimar, and Vienna: Böhlau Verlag, 2013.

Houben, Hubert. "Barbarossa und die Normannen: Traditionelle Züge und neue Perspektiven imperialer Süditalienpolitik." In Haverkamp, ed. *Friedrich Barbarossa*, pp. 109–28.

—. *Roger II. von Sizilien: Herrscher zwischen Orient und Okzident*. In Gestalten des Mittelalters und der Renaissance. 2nd rev. edn. Darmstadt: Wissenschaftliche Buchgesellschaft, 2010.

Huffman, Joseph P. *The Social Politics of Medieval Diplomacy: Anglo-German Relations (1066–1307).* In Studies in Medieval and Early Modern Civilization. Ann Arbor: University of Michigan Press, 2000.

Jackson, William Henry. "Knighthood and the Hohenstaufen Imperial Court under Frederick Barbarossa (1152–1190)." In *The Ideals and Practice of Medieval Knighthood III. Papers from the fourth (sic) Strawberry Hill Conference*, ed. Christopher Harper-Bill and Ruth Harvey, pp. 101–20. Woodbridge, and Rochester, N.Y.: The Boydell Press, 1990.

Jakobi, Franz-Josef. *Wibald von Stablo und Corvey (1098–1158): Benediktinischer Abt in der frühen Stauferzeit.* In Abhandlungen zur Corveyer Geschichtsschreibung 5. In Veröffentlichungen der Historischen Kommission für Westfalen 10. Münster: Aschendorffsche Verlagsbuchhandlung, 1979.

Johanek, Peter. "Kultur und Bildung im Umkreis Friedrich Barbarossas." In Haverkamp, ed. *Friedrich Barbarossa*, pp. 651–77.

Johrendt, Jochen. "Barbarossa, das Kaisertum und Rom." In Burkhardt et al., eds. *Staufisches Kaisertum im 12. Jahrhundert*," pp. 75–107.

—. "The Empire and the Schism." In Clarke and Duggan, eds. *Pope Alexander III*, pp. 99–126.

Jordan, Karl. *Heinrich der Löwe: Eine Biographie.* Munich: C. H. Beck'sche Verlagsbuchhandlung, 1979. Translated by P. S. Falla as *Henry the Lion.* Oxford: Clarendon Press, 1986.

Jussen, Bernhard. *Spiritual Kinship as Social Practice: Godparenthood and Adoption in the Early Middle Ages*, revised and expanded English edition trans. Pamela Selwyn. Newark, DE: University of Delaware Press, 2000.

Kamp, Norbert. *Moneta regis: Königliche Münzstätten und königliche Münzpolitik in der Stauferzeit.* MGH: Schriften 55. Hanover: Hahnsche Buchhandlung, 2006.

Kannowski, Bernd. "The Impact of Lineage and Family Connections on Succession in Medieval Germany's Elective Kingdom." In Lachaud and Penman, eds. *Making and Breaking the Rules*, pp. 13–22.

Katalog der Ausstellung. In *Die Zeit der Staufer* 1.

Kaul, Camilla C. *Friedrich Barbarossa im Kyffhäuser: Bilder eines nationalen Mythos im 19. Jahrhundert.* 2 vols. In Atlas: Bonner Beiträge zur Kunstgeschichte, NF 4. Cologne, Weimar, and Vienna: Böhlau Verlag, 2007.

Kehr, Paul Fridolin. "Der Vertrag von Anagni im Jahre 1176." *NA* 13 (1888): 75–118.

Kejř, Jiří. "Böhmen und das Reich unter Friedrich I." In Haverkamp, ed. *Friedrich Barbarossa*, pp. 241–89.

—. "Böhmen zur Zeit Friedrich Barbarossas." In Engel and Töpfer, eds. *Kaiser Friedrich Barbarossa*, pp. 101–13.

Kempf, Friedrich. "Der 'favor apostolicus' bei der Wahl Friedrich Barbarossas und im deutschen Thronstreit (1198–1208)." In *Speculum Historiale: Geschichte im Spiegel von Geschichtsschreibung und Geschichtsdeutung: Festschrift Johannes Spörl*, pp. 469–78. Freiburg im Breisgau: Verlag Alber, 1965. Reprinted in Wolf, ed. *Friedrich Barbarossa*, pp. 323–59.

Keupp, Jan Ulrich. *Dienst und Verdienst: Die Ministerialen Friedrich Barbarossas und Heinrichs VI.* In MGM 48. Stuttgart: Anton Hiersemann, 2002.

—. "Interaktion als Investition: Überlegungen zum Sozialkapital König Konrads III." In Seibert and Dendorfer, eds. *Grafen, Herzöge, Könige*, pp. 299–321.

Kienast, Walther. *Die deutschen Fürsten im Dienste der Westmächte bis zum Tode Philipps des Schönen von Frankreich* 1. Utrecht: Instituut voor Middeleeuwsche Geschiedenis; and Leipzig and Munich: Verlag von Duncker und Humblot, 1924.

—. *Deutschland und Frankreich in der Kaiserzeit (900–1270): Weltkaiser und Einzelkönige.* 2nd edn. 2 vols. In MGM 9. Stuttgart: Anton Hiersemann, 1974.

Kirfel, Hans Joachim. *Weltherrschaftsidee und Bündnispolitik: Untersuchungen zur auswärtigen Politik der Staufer.* In Bonner historische Forschungen 12. Bonn: Ludwig Röhrscheid Verlag, 1959.

Kirmeier, Josef and Evamaria Brockhoff. *Herzöge und Heilige: Das Geschlecht der Andechs-Meranier im europäischen Hochmittelalter: Katalog zur Landesausstellung im Kloster Andechs 13. Juli–24. Oktober 1993.* In Veröffentlichungen zur Bayerischen Geschichte und Kultur 24/93. Munich: Haus der Bayerischen Geschichte, 1993.

Kirn, Paul. "Die Verdienste der staufischen Kaiser um das Deutsche Reich." *HZ* 164 (1941): 261–84.

Kisch, Guido. *The Jews in Medieval Germany: A Study of their Legal and Social Status*. Chicago: University of Chicago Press, 1949; 2nd edn. New York: Ktav Publishing House, 1970.

Klebel, Ernst. *Der Lungau: Historisch-politische Untersuchung*. Salzburg: Gesellschaft für Salzburger Landeskunde, 1960.

Kluger, Helmuth. "Friedrich Barbarossa und sein Ratgeber Rainald von Dassel." In Weinfurter, *Stauferreich im Wandel*, pp. 26–40.

Knowles, David. *Great Historical Enterprises*. London: Thomas Nelson, 1962.

Koch, Gottfried. *Auf dem Wege zum Sacrum Imperium: Studien zur ideologischen Herrschaftsbegründung der deutschen Zentralgewalt im 11. und 12. Jahrhundert*. In FMG 20. Vienna, Cologne, and Graz: Böhlaus Nachf., 1972.

—. "Der Streit zwischen Sybel und Ficker und Einschätzung der mittelalterlichen Kaiserpolitik in der modernen Historiographie." In *Die deutsche Geschichtswissenschaft vom Beginn des 19. Jahrhunderts bis zur Reichsgründung von oben*, ed. Joachim Streisand, pp. 311–36. In Deutsche Akademie der Wissenschaften zu Berlin: Schriften des Instituts für Geschichte. Reihe 1: Allgemeine und deutsche Geschichte 20. Berlin: Akademie Verlag, 1963.

Koch, Walter. "Zu Sprache, Stil und Arbeitstechnik in den Diplomen Friedrich Barbarossas." *MIÖG* 88 (1980): 36–69.

Koeppler, H. "Frederick Barbarossa and the Schools of Bologna: Some Remarks on the 'Authentica Habita.'" *EHR* 54 (October 1939): 579–607.

Kölzer, Theo. "Der Hof Friedrich Barbarossas und die Reichsfürsten." In Weinfurter, ed. *Stauferreich im Wandel*, pp. 220–36.

—. "Der Hof Kaiser Barbarossas und die Reichsfürsten." In Moraw, ed. *Deutscher Königshof*, pp. 3–47.

—. "Die Staufer im Süden—eine Bilanz aus deutscher Sicht." In idem, *Die Staufer im Süden*, pp. 239–62.

—, ed. *Die Staufer im Süden: Sizilien und das Reich*. Sigmaringen: Jan Thorbecke Verlag, 1996.

—, Franz-Albrecht Bornschlegel, Christian Friedl, and Georg Vogeler, eds. *De litteris, manuscriptis, inscriptionibus . . . Festschrift zum 65. Geburtstag von Walter Koch*. Vienna, Cologne, and Weimar: Böhlau Verlag, 2007.

Krautheimer, Richard. *Rome: Profile of a City, 312–1308*. Princeton, N.J.: Princeton University Press, 1980.

Krieg, Heinz. "Adel in Schwaben: Die Staufer und die Zähringer." In Seibert and Dendorfer, eds. *Grafen, Herzöge, Könige*, pp. 65–97.

—. *Herrscherdarstellung in der Stauferzeit: Friedrich Barbarossa im Spiegel seiner Urkunden und der staufischen Geschichtsschreibung*. In VF, Sonderband 50. Ostfildern: Jan Thorbecke Verlag, 2003.

Krieger, Karl-Friedrich. "Obligatory Military Service and the Use of Mercenaries in Imperial Military Campaigns under the Hohenstaufen Emperors." In Haverkamp and Vollrath, eds. *England and Germany in the High Middle Ages*, pp. 151–68.

Kupper, Jean-Louis. "Friedrich Barbarossa im Maasgebiet." In Haverkamp, ed. *Friedrich Barbarossa*, pp. 225–40.

Küss, Tobias. *Die älteren Diepoldinger als Markgrafen in Bayern (1077–1204): Adlige Herrschaftsbildung im Hochmittelalter*. Munich: Herbert Utz Verlag, 2013.

Lachaud, Frédérique and Michael Penman, eds. *Making and Breaking the Rules: Succession in Medieval Europe, c. 1000–c. 1600: Proceedings of the Colloquium Held on 6–7–8 April 2006, Institute of Historical Research (University of London)*. In Histoires de famille: La parenté au Moyen Âge 9. Turnhout: Brepols, 2008.

Ladner, Gerhart Burian. "I mosaici e gli affreschi ecclesiastico-politici nell'antico palazzo Lateranense." *Rivista di Archeologia Cristiana* 12 (1935): 177–92. Reprinted in idem, *Images and Ideas in the Middle Ages: Selected Studies in History and Art*, vol. 1. In Storia e letteratura 155, pp. 347–66. Rome: Edizioni di storia e letteratura, 1983.

Lammers, Walther. "Weltgeschichte und Zeitgeschichte bei Otto von Freising." In *Die Zeit der Staufer* 5:77–90. Also in *Sitzungsberichte der Wissenschaftliche Gesellschaft der Johann Wolfgang Goethe Universität Frankfurt am Main* 14/3:75–99. Wiesbaden: Franz Steiner Verlag, 1977.

Latham, R. E. and David R. Howlett, eds. *Dictionary of Medieval Latin from British Sources*. London: Oxford University Press, 1975.

Latowsky, Anne A. *Emperor of the World: Charlemagne and the Construction of Imperial Authority, 800–1229*. Ithaca, N.J. and London: Cornell University Press, 2013.

Laudage, Johannes. *Alexander III. und Friedrich Barbarossa*. In FKPM 16. Cologne, Weimar, and Vienna: Böhlau Verlag, 1997.

—. *Friedrich Barbarossa (1152–1190): Eine Biographie*, ed. Lars Hageneier and Matthias Schrör. Regensburg: Verlag Friedrich Pustet, 2009.

—. "Gewinner und Verlierer des Friedens von Venedig." In Weinfurter, ed. *Stauferreich im Wandel*, pp. 107–30.

Lechner, Karl. *Die Babenberger: Markgrafen und Herzoge von Österreich 976–1246*. In Veröffentlichungen des Instituts für österreische Geschichtsforschung 23. Vienna, Cologne, and Graz: Hermann Böhlaus Nachf., 1976. Reprint, Darmstadt: Wissenschaftliche Buchgesellschaft, 1985.

Leyser, Karl J. *Communications and Power in Medieval Europe: The Gregorian Revolution and Beyond*, ed. Timothy Reuter. London and Rio Grande, OH: The Hambledon Press, 1994.

—. "Frederick Barbarossa: Court and Country." In idem, *Communications and Power*, pp. 143–55. Published originally as "Friedrich Barbarossa—Hof und Land." In Haverkamp, ed. *Friedrich Barbarossa*, pp. 519–30.

—. "Frederick Barbarossa, Henry II, and the Hand of St. James." *EHR* 90 (1975): 481–506. Reprinted in idem, *Medieval Germany*, pp. 215–40.

—. "Frederick Barbarossa and the Hohenstaufen Polity." *Viator* 19 (1988): 153–76. Reprinted in idem, *Communications and Power*, pp. 115–42.

—. "The German Aristocracy from the Ninth to the Early Twelfth Century: A Historical and Cultural Sketch." *Past and Present* 41 (1968): 25–53. Reprinted in idem, *Medieval Germany*, pp. 161–89.

—. *Medieval Germany and its Neighbours, 900–1250*. London: The Hambledon Press, 1982.

Lhotsky, Alphons. *Aufsätze und Vorträge*. 5 vols, ed. Hans Wagner and Heinrich Koller. Vienna: Verlag für Geschichte und Kunst, 1970–76.

—. "Fuga und Electio." In idem, *Aufsätze und Vorträge*, 1:82–91.

—. "Die Historiographie Ottos von Freising," In idem, *Aufsätze und Vorträge*, 1:49–63.

Lindner, Michael. "Fest und Herrschaft unter Kaiser Friedrich Barbarossa." In Engel, ed. *Kaiser Friedrich Barbarossa*, pp. 151–70.

—. "Friedrich Barbarossa, Heinrich der Löwe und die ostsächsischen Fürsten auf dem Merseburger Pfingsthoftag des Jahres 1152: Mit der Neuedition einer Urkunde Heinrichs des Löwen nach dem wiederaufgefundenen Original sowie einem Hinweis auf ein Derpeditum Kaiser Friedrichs I." *Zeitschrift für Geschichtswissenschaft* 43 (1995): 197–209.

Locatelli, René. "Frédéric Ier et le royaume de Bourgogne." In Haverkamp, ed. *Friedrich Barbarossa*, pp. 169–97.

Löcher, Karl. "Die Staufer in der bildenden Kunst." In *Die Zeit der Staufer* 3:291–309.

Lohrmann, Dietrich. "Das Papsttum und die Grafschaft Burgund im 11.–12. Jahrhundert." In Hehl et al., eds. *Das Papsttum in der Welt des 12. Jahrhunderts*, pp. 61–75.

Lorenz, Sönke. "Die Pfalzgrafen in Schwaben vom 9. bis zur frühen 12. Jahrhundert." In Bihrer et al., eds. *Adel und Königtum im mittelalterlichen Schwaben*, pp. 205–33.

— and Ulrich Schmidt, eds. *Von Schwaben bis Jerusalem: Facetten staufischer Geschichte*. Sigmaringen: Jan Thorbecke Verlag, 1995.

Lubich, Gerhard. "Territorien-, Kloster- und Bistumspolitik in einer Gesellschaft im Wandel: Zur politischen Komponente des Herrschaftsaufbaus der Staufer vor 1138." In Seibert and Dendorfer, eds. *Grafen, Herzöge, Könige*, pp. 179–211.

Luscombe, David and Jonathan Riley Smith, eds. *The New Cambridge Medieval History* 4/2: *c. 1024–c. 1198*. Cambridge: Cambridge University Press, 2004.

Lynch, Joseph H. *Godparents and Kinship in Early Medieval Europe*. Princeton, N.J.: Princeton University Press, 1986.

Lyon, Jonathan R. "Fathers and Sons: Preparing Noble Youths to be Lords in Twelfth-Century Germany." *Journal of Medieval History* 34/3 (September 2008): 291–310.

—. *Princely Brothers and Sisters: The Sibling Bond in German Politics, 1100–1250.* Ithaca, N.Y., and London: Cornell University Press, 2013.

Mai, Gunther. "'Für Kaiser und Reich': Das Kaiser-Wilhelm-Denkmal auf dem Kyffhäuser." In idem, *Das Kyffhäuser-Denkmal*, pp. 149–77.

—,ed. *Das Kyffhäuser-Denkmal 1896–1996: Ein nationales Monument im europäischen Kontext.* Cologne, Weimar, and Vienna: Böhlau Verlag, 1997.

Mass, Josef. *Das Bistum Freising im Mittelalter.* 2nd edn. Munich: Erich Wewel Verlag, 1988.

Matthew, D. J. A. "The Chronicle of Romuald of Salerno." In *The Writing of History in the Middle Ages: Essays Presented to Richard William Southern*, ed. R. H. Carless and J. M. Wallace-Hadrill, pp. 239–74. Oxford: Clarendon Press, 1981.

Maurer, Helmut. *Der Herzog von Schwaben: Grundlagen, Wirkungen und Wesen seiner Herrschaft.* Sigmaringen: Jan Thorbecke Verlag, 1978.

—. "Das Herzogtum Schwaben in staufischer Zeit." In *Die Zeit der Staufer* 5:91–105.

—, ed. *Kommunale Bündnisse Oberitaliens und Oberdeutschlands im Vergleich.* In VF 33. Sigmaringen: Jan Thorbecke Verlag, 1987.

Mayer, Hans Eberhard. "Staufische Weltherrschaft? Zum Brief Heinrichs II. von England an Friedrich Barbarossa von 1157." In *Festschrift Pivec (Zum 60. Geburtstag).* In Innsbrucker Beiträge zur Kulturwissenschaft 12:265–78. Reprinted in Wolf, ed. *Friedrich Barbarossa*, pp. 184–207.

Mayer, Theodor, ed. *Probleme des 12. Jahrhunderts: Reichenau Vorträge 1965–1967.* In VF 12. Constance and Stuttgart: Jan Thorbecke Verlag, 1968.

—. "The State of the Dukes of Zähringen." In *Mediaeval Germany 911–1250: Essays by German Historians*, 2 vols., ed. Geoffrey Barraclough, 2:175–202. Oxford: Basil Blackwell, 1938.

Metz, Wolfgang. *Das servitium regis: Zur Erforschung der wirtschaftlichen Grundlagen des hochmittelalterlichen deutschen Königtums.* In Erträge der Forschung 89. Darmstadt: Wissenschaftliche Buchgesellschaft, 1978.

—. *Staufische Güterverzeichnisse: Untersuchungen zur Verfassungs- und Wirtschaftsgeschichte des 12. und 13. Jahrhunderts.* Berlin: Walter de Gruyter, 1964.

Metzler-Andelberg, Helmut J. "Admont und die Klosterreform zu Beginn des 12. Jahrhunderts." *Zeitschrift des historischen Vereins für Steiermark* 47 (1956): 28–42.

—. "Die rechtlichen Beziehungen des Klosters Admont zum Salzburger Erzbistum während des 12. Jahrhunderts." *Zeitschrift des historischen Vereins für Steiermark* 44 (1953): 31–46.

Migge, Walter. "Die Staufer in der deutschen Literatur seit dem 18. Jahrhundert." In *Die Zeit der Staufer* 3:275–90.

Miller, Maureen C. *The Bishop's Palace: Architecture and Authority in Medieval Italy.* Ithaca, N.Y., and London: Cornell University Press, 2000.

Mitteis, Heinrich. *Die deutsche Königswahl: Ihre Rechtsgrundlagen bis zur Goldenen Bulle.* 2nd expanded edn. Brno, Munich, and Vienna, 1944. Reprint, Darmstadt: Wissenschaftliche Buchgesellschaft, 1965.

—. "Die Krise des deutschen Königswahlrechts." *Sitzungsberichte der Bayerischen Akademie der Wissenschaften*, Phil.-hist. Kl. 8 (1950): 1–92. Reprinted in Hlawitschka, ed. *Königswahl und Thronfolge in ottonisch-frühdeutscher Zeit*, pp. 216–302.

—. *Lehnrecht und Staatsgewalt: Untersuchungen zur mittelalterlichen Verfassungsgeschichte.* Weimar, 1933. Reprint, Darmstadt: Wissenschaftliche Buchgesellschaft, 1958.

Moraw, Peter, ed. *Deutscher Königshof, Hoftag und Reichstag im späteren Mittelalter.* Stuttgart: Jan Thorbecke Verlag, 2002.

Morrison, Karl F. "Otto of Freising's Quest for the Hermeneutic Circle." *Speculum* 55 (1980): 207–36.

Müller-Mertens, Eckhard. *Regnum Teutonicum: Aufkommen und Verbreitung der deutschen Reichs- und Königsauffassung im frühen Mittelalter.* In FMG 15. Vienna, Cologne, and Graz: Hermann Böhlau Nachf., 1970.

Munz, Peter. *Frederick Barbarossa: A Study in Medieval Politics.* Ithaca, N.Y., and London: Cornell University Press, 1969.

—. "Why Did Rahewin Stop Writing the Gesta Frederici?: A Further Consideration." *EHR* 84 (1969): 771–79.

Murray, Allan. "Finance and Logistics of the Crusade of Frederick Barbarossa." In *Laudem Hierosolymitani: Studies in Crusades and Medieval Culture in Honour of Benjamin Z. Kedar*, ed. Iris Shagir, Ronnie Ellenblum, and Jonathan Riley-Smith, pp. 357–68. Aldershot and Burlington, VT: Ashgate, 2007.

Nau, Elisabeth. "Münzen und Geld in der Stauferzeit." In *Die Zeit der Staufer* 3:87–102.

Niederkorn, Jan Paul. "Friedrich von Rothenburg und die Königswahl von 1152." In Lorenz and Schmidt, eds. *Von Schwaben bis Jerusalem*, pp. 51–59.

—. "Der Übergang des Egerlandes an die Staufer: Die Heirat Friedrich Barbarossas mit Adela von Vohburg." *ZbLG* 54/3 (1991): 613–22.

—. "Zu Glatt und daher verdächtig? Zur Glaubwürdigkeit der Schilderung der Wahl Friedrich Barbarossas (1152) durch Otto von Freising." *MIÖG* 1156 (2007): 1–9.

Niermeyer, J. F. and C. Van der Kieft. *Mediae Latinitatis lexicon minus*. 2nd edn. 2 vols. Darmstadt: Wissenschaftliche Buchgesellschaft, 2002.

Nilgen, Ursula. "Staufische Bildpropaganda: Legitimation und Selbstverständnis im Wandel." In Wieczorek et al., eds. *Die Staufer und Italien*, pp. 86–96.

Opll, Ferdinand. "Amator ecclesiarum: Studien zur religiösen Haltung Friedrich Barbarossas." *MIÖG* 88 (1980): 70–93.

—. "Beiträge zur historischen Auswertung der jüngeren Hildesheimer Briefsammlung." *DA* 33 (1977): 473–500.

—. *Friedrich Barbarossa*. In Gestalten des Mittelalters und der Renaissance. Darmstadt: Wissenschaftliche Buchgesellschaft, 1990.

—. "Friedrich Barbarossa und die Stadt Lodi: Stadtentwicklung im Spannungsfeld zwischen Reich und Städtebündnis." In Maurer, ed. *Kommunale Bündnisse*, pp. 63–96.

—. *Das Itinerar Kaiser Friedrich Barbarossas (1152–1190)*. In FKPM 1. Vienna, Cologne, and Graz: Hermann Böhlaus Nachf., 1978.

—. "Kaiser Friedrich I.: Karte der Aufenhaltsorte 1152–1189." In *Die Zeit der Staufer* 4:III.

—. *Stadt und Reich im 12. Jahrhundert (1125–1190)*. In FKPM 6. Vienna, Cologne, and Graz: Hermann Böhlaus Nachf., 1986.

—. "Die Winterquatember im Leben Friedrich Barbarossas." *MIÖG* 85 (1977): 332–41.

Otis-Cour, Leah. "*De jure novo*: Dealing with Adultery in Fifteenth-Century Toulousain." *Speculum* 84 (2009): 347–92.

Overmann, Alfred. *Gräfin Mathilde von Tuscien: Ihre Besitzungen: Geschichte ihres Gutes von 1115–1230 und ihre Regesten*. Innsbruck: Verlag der Wagner'schen Universitäts-Buchhandlung, 1895. Reprint, Frankfurt: Minerva, 1965.

Pacaut, Marcel. *Frédéric Barberousse*. Paris: Fayard, 1967. Translated by A. J. Pomerans as *Frederick Barbarossa*. New York: Charles Scribner's, 1970.

Parisse, Michel. "Présence et interventions de Frédéric Barberousse en Lorraine." In Haverkamp, ed. *Friedrich Barbarossa*, pp. 201–23.

Partner, Peter. *The Lands of St. Peter: The Papal State in the Middle Ages and the Early Renaissance*. Berkeley and Los Angeles: University of California Press, 1972.

Patschovsky, Alexander. "The Relationship between the Jews of Germany and the King (11th–14th Centuries): A European Comparison." In Haverkamp and Vollrath, eds. *England and Germany in the High Middle Ages*, pp. 193–218.

Patze, Hans. "Friedrich Barbarossa und die deutschen Fürsten." In *Die Zeit der Staufer* 5:35–75.

—. "Kaiser Friedrich Barbarossa und der Osten." In Mayer, ed. *Probleme des 12. Jahrhunderts*, pp. 337–408.

Patzold, Steffen. "Konflikte im Stauferreich nördlich des Alpen: Methodische Überlegungen zur Messbarkeit eines Wandels der Konfliktführung im 12. Jahrhundert." In Schneidmüller et al., eds. *Verwandlungen des Stauferreichs*, pp. 144–78.

Penth, Sabine. *Prämonstratenser und Staufer: Zur Rolle des Reformordens in der staufischen Reichs- und Territorialpolitik*. In HS 478. Husum: Matthiesen Verlag, 2003.

Petersohn, Jürgen. "Friedrich Barbarossa und Rom." In Haverkamp, ed. *Friedrich Barbarossa*, pp. 129–46.

—. "Kaiser, Papst und römisches Recht im Hochmittelalter: Friedrich Barbarossa und Innocenz III. beim Umgang mit dem Rechtsinstitut der langfristigen Verjährung." In idem, *Mediaevalia Augiensia*, pp. 307–48.

—. *Kaisertum und Rom in spätsalischer und staufischer Zeit: Romidee und Rompolitik von Heinrich V. bis Friedrich II.* MGH Schriften 62. Hanover: Hahnsche Buchhandlung, 2010.
—. "Das Präskriptionsrecht der Römischen Kirche und der Konstanzer Vertrag." In Herbers et al., eds. *Ex ipsis rerum documentis*, pp. 307–15.
—. "Rahewin IV 49: 'seu de recipiendo prefecto': Zur Rolle des Präfektur bei den kaiserlich-römischen Verhandlungen von 1159." In *Geschichtsschreibung und geistiges Leben im Mittelalter: Festschrift Heinz Löwe zum 65. Geburtstag*, ed. Karl Hauck and Hubert Mordek, pp. 397–409. Cologne and Vienna: Böhlau Verlag, 1978.
—. "Rom und der Reichstitel 'Sacrum Romanum Imperium'." *Sitzungsberichte der Wissenschaftlichen Gesellschaft an der Johann Wolfgang-Goethe Universität Frankfurt am Main* 32/4:67–101. Stuttgart: Franz Steiner Verlag, 1994.
—. "Saint-Denis—Westminster—Aachen: Die Karls-Translatio von 1165 und ihre Vorbilder." *DA* 31 (1975): 420–54.
—. "Der Vertrag des Römischen Senats mit Papst Clemens III. (1188) und das Pactum Friedrich Barbarossas mit den Römern." *MIÖG* 82 (1974): 289–337.
—, ed. *Mediaevalia Augiensia: Forschungen zur Geschichte des Mittelalters*. In VF 54/3. Stuttgart: Jan Thorbecke Verlag, 2001.
Petke, Wolfgang. *Kanzlei, Kapelle und königliche Kurie unter Lothar III. (1125–1137)*. In FKPM 5. Cologne and Vienna: Böhlau Verlag, 1985.
Pferschy, Gerhard, ed. *Das Werden der Steiermark: Die Zeit der Traungauer: Festschrift zur 800. Wiederkehr der Erhebung zum Herzogtum*. In Veröffentlichungen des steiermärkischen Landesarchives 10. Graz, Vienna, and Cologne: Verlag Styria, 1980.
Phillips, Jonathan. *The Second Crusade: Extending the Frontiers of Christendom*. New Haven, CT, and London: Yale University Press, 2007.
Plassmann, Alheydis. "Barbarossa und sein Hof beim Frieden von Venedig unter verschiedenen Wahrnehmungsperspektiven." In Weinfurter, ed. *Stauferreich im Wandel*, pp. 85–106.
—. *Die Struktur des Hofes unter Friedrich I. Barbarossa nach den deutschen Zeugen seiner Urkunden*. In MGH: Studien und Texte 20. Hanover: Hahnsche Buchhandlung, 1998.
Plechl, Helmut. "Studien zur Tegernseer Briefsammlung des 12. Jahrhunderts II: Briefe zur Reichspolitik aus der Zeit der Verhandlungen in Anagni und der Vorbereitungen des Venetianer Friedenskongresses (Oktober 1176–Januar 1177)." *DA* 12 (1956): 73–113.
Prutz, Hans. *Kaiser Friedrich I.* 3 vols. Danzig (Gdansk): A. W. Kafemann, 1871–74.
Raccagni, Gianluca. *The Lombard League 1167–1225*. Oxford: Oxford University Press, 2010.
Rader, Olaf. "Die Grablegen der Staufer als Erinnerungsorte." In Schneidmüller et al., eds. *Verwandlungen des Stauferreichs*, pp. 20–33.
Rashdall, Hastings. *The Universities of Europe in the Middle Ages*, ed. F. M. Powicke and A. B. Emden. 3 vols. London: Oxford University Press, 1895, new edn. 1936.
Rassow, Peter. *Honor Imperii: Die neue Politik Friedrich Barbarossas 1152–59*. Munich and Berlin: R. Oldenbourg Verlag, 1940. Reprint, Darmstadt: Wissenschaftliche Buchgesellschaft, 1961.
Reichert, Folker. *Landesherrschaft, Adel und Vogtei: Zur Vorgeschichte des spätmittelalterlichen Ständestaates im Herzogtum Österreich*. In Beihefte zum Archiv für Kulturgeschichte 23. Cologne and Vienna: Böhlau Verlag, 1985.
Reuling, Ulrich. *Die Kur in Deutschland und Frankreich: Untersuchungen zur Entwicklung des rechtsförmlichen Wahlaktes bei der Königserhebung im 11. und 12. Jahrhundert*. In VMPIG 64. Göttingen: Vandenhoeck & Ruprecht, 1979.
Reuter, Timothy. "*Episcopi cum sua militia*: The Prelate as Warrior in the Early Staufer Era." In idem, *Warriors and Churchmen*, pp. 79–94.
—. "The Papal Schism, the Empire and the West 1159–1169." Unpublished dissertation. Oxford, 1975.
—. "Vom Parvenü zum Bündnispartner: Das Königreich Sizilien in der abendländischen Politik des 12. Jahrhunderts." In Kölzer, ed. *Die Staufer im Süden*, pp. 43–56.
—, ed. *Warriors and Churchmen in the High Middle Ages: Essays Presented to Karl Leyser*. London and Ronceverte, West VA: The Hambledon Press, 1992.
Reynolds, Susan. *Fiefs and Vassals: The Medieval Evidence Reinterpreted*. Oxford: Clarendon Paperback, 1996.

Richter, Klaus. *Friedrich Barbarossa hält Gericht: Zum Konfliktbewältigung im 12. Jahrhundert.* In Konflikt, Verbrechen und Sanktion in der Gesellschaft Alteuropas, Fallstudien 2. Cologne, Weimar, and Vienna: Böhlau Verlag, 1999.

Riedmann, Josef. "Die Bedeutung des Tiroler Raumes für die Italienpolitik Kaiser Friedrich Barbarossas." In Engel and Töpfer, eds. *Kaiser Friedrich Barbarossa,* pp. 81–99.

—. *Die Beurkundung der Verträge Friedrich Barbarossas mit italienischen Städte: Studien zur diplomatischen Form von Vertragsurkunden im 12. Jahrhundert.* In Österreichische Akademie der Wissenschaften, Philosophisch-historische Klasse, Sitzungsberichte 291/3. Vienna, 1973.

Robinson, I. S. *Henry IV of Germany 1056–1106.* Cambridge: Cambridge University Press, 1999.

Rörig, Fritz. "Geblütsrecht und freie Wahl in ihrer Auswirkung auf die deutsche Geschichte." *Abhandlungen der Deutschen Akademie der Wissenschaften zu Berlin,* Phil.-hist. Kl. 6 (1948): 1–51. Reprinted in Hlawitschka, ed. *Königswahl und Thronfolge in ottonisch-frühdeutscher Zeit,* pp. 71–147.

Rösener, Werner. "The Decline of the Classic Manor in Germany during the High Middle Ages." In Haverkamp and Vollrath, eds. *England and Germany in the High Middle Ages,* pp. 317–30.

—. "Die Hoftage Kaiser Friedrichs I. Barbarossa im Regnum Teutonicum." In Moraw, ed. *Deutscher Königshof,* pp. 359–86.

Rousseau, Constance M. "Neither Bewitched nor Beguiled: Philip Augustus's Alleged Impotence and Innocent III's Response." *Speculum* 89 (2014): 410–36.

Rundnagel, Erwin. "Die Ehescheidung Friedrich Barbarossas." In *Kritische Beiträge zur Geschichte des Mittelalters: Festschrift für Robert Holtzmann zum sechzigsten Geburtstag,* ed. Walter Möllenberg, pp. 145–59. In HS 238. Berlin: Verlag Dr. Emil Ebering, 1933.

Sauer, Christine. *Fundatio und Memoria: Stifter und Klostergründer im Bild 1100 bis 1350.* In VMPIG 109. Göttingen: Vandenhoeck & Ruprecht, 1993.

Sauerländer, Willibald. "Dynastisches Mäzenatentum der Staufer und Welfen." In Hechberger and Schuler, eds. *Staufer & Welfen,* pp. 118–41.

Saurma-Jeltsch, Lieselotte E. "Aachen und Rom in der staufischen Reichsimagination." In Schneidmüller et al., eds. *Verwandlungen des Stauferreichs,* pp. 268–307.

Scheffer-Boichorst, Paul. *Kaiser Friedrich I. letzter Streit mit der Kurie.* Berlin: E. S. Mittler, 1866. Reprint, Aalen: Scientia Verlag, 1969.

Schieffer, Rudolf. "Friedrich Barbarossa und seine Verwandten." In Kölzer et al., eds. *De litteris, manuscriptis, inscriptionibus,* pp. 577–89.

—. "Heinrich der Löwe, Otto von Freising und Friedrich Barbarossa am Beginn der Geschichte Münchens." In Hechberger and Schuler, eds. *Staufer & Welfen,* pp. 67–77.

Schlesinger, Walter. "Egerland, Vogtland, Pleissenland: Zur Geschichte des Reichsgutes im mitteldeutschen Osten." In *Forschungen zur Geschichte Sachsens und Böhmens,* ed. Rudolf Kötzschke, pp. 61–91. Dresden: Silhelm und Bertha v. Baensch Stiftung, 1937. Reprinted in Schlesinger, *Mitteldeutsche Beiträge zur deutschen Verfassungsgeschichte des Mittelalters,* pp. 188–211. Göttingen: Vandenhoeck & Ruprecht, 1961.

Schludi, Ulrich. "*Advocatus sanctae Romanae ecclesiae* und *specialis filius beati Petri:* Der römische Kaiser aus päpstlicher Sicht." In Burkhardt et al., eds. *Staufisches Kaisertum im 12. Jahrhundert,* pp. 41–73.

Schmale, Franz-Josef. "Friedrich I. und Ludwig VII. im Sommer des Jahres 1162." *ZbLG* 51 (1968): 315–68.

—. "Lothar III. und Friedrich I. als Könige und Kaiser." In Mayer, ed. *Probleme des 12. Jahrhunderts,* pp. 33–52. Reprinted in Wolf, ed. *Friedrich Barbarossa,* pp. 121–48.

Schmid, Karl. "Adel und Reform in Schwaben." In Fleckenstein, ed. *Investiturstreit und Reichsverfassung,* pp. 295–319. Reprinted in Schmid, *Gebetsgedenken,* pp. 337–59.

—. "'De regia stirpe Waiblingensium': Bemerkungen zum Selbstverständnis der Staufer." *ZGORh* 124 (NF 85) (1976): 63–73. Reprinted in idem, *Gebetsgedenken,* pp. 454–66.

—. *Gebetsgedenken und adliges Selbstverständnis im Mittelalter: Ausgewählte Beiträge: Festgabe zu seinem sechzigsten Geburtstag.* Sigmaringen: Jan Thorbecke Verlag, 1983.

—. *Graf Rudolf von Pfullendorf und Kaiser Friedrich I.* In Forschungen zur oberrheinischen Landesgeschichte 1. Freiburg im Breisgau: Eberhard-Albert Universitäts-Buchhandlung, 1954.

—. "Welfisches Selbstverständnis." In *Adel und Kirche: Gerd Tellenbach zum 65. Geburtstag, dargebracht von Freunden und Schülern*, ed. Josef Fleckenstein and Karl Schmid, pp. 389–416. Freiburg, Basel, and Vienna: Herder, 1968. Reprinted in Schmid, *Gebetsgedenken*, pp. 424–53.

—. "Zur Problematik von Familie, Sippe und Geschlecht, Haus und Dynastie beim mittelalterlichen Adel: Vorfragen zum Thema 'Adel und Herrschaft im Mittelalter'." *ZGORh* (NF 66) (1957): 1–62. Reprinted in idem, *Gebetsgedenken*, pp. 183–244.

—, ed. *Die Zähringer*. Vol. 1: *Eine Tradition und ihre Erforschung*. Sigmaringen: Jan Thorbecke Verlag, 1986.

— and Hans Schadek, eds. *Die Zähringer*. Vol. 2: *Anstoss und Wirkung*. Sigmaringen: Jan Thorbecke Verlag, 1986.

Schmidt, Ulrich. "A quo ergo habet, si a domno papa non habet imperium?: Zu den Anfängen der 'staufischen Kaiserwahlen.'" In Lorenz and Schmidt, eds. *Von Schwaben bis Jerusalem*, pp. 61–88.

—. *Königswahl und Thronfolge im 12. Jahrhundert*. Im FKPM 7. Cologne and Vienna: Böhlau Verlag, 1987.

Schmidt, Walter. "Barbarossa im Vormärz." In Engel and Töpfer, eds. *Kaiser Friedrich Barbarossa*, pp. 171–204.

Schneider, Friedrich. *Die neueren Anschauungen der deutschen Historiker über die deutsche Kaiserpolitik des Mittelalters und die mit ihr verbundene Ostpolitik*. 5th edn. Weimar: H. Böhlaus Nachf., 1942.

—. *Universalstaat oder Nationalstaat: Die Streitschriften von Heinrich v. Sybel und Julius Ficker zur deutschen Kaiserpolitik des Mittelalters*. Innsbruck: Universitätsverlag, 1941.

Schneider, Jürgen and Gerhard Rechter, eds. *Festschrift Alfred Wendehorst zum 65. Geburtstag gewidmet von Kollegen, Freunden, Schülern*. In Jahrbuch für fränkische Landesgeschiche 52. Neustadt (Aisch): Degener, 1992.

Schneider, Wolfgang Christian. "Die Kaiserapotheose Friedrich Barbarossas im 'Cappenberg Kopf': Ein Zeugnis staufischer Antikenerneuerung." *Castrum Peregrini* 217/18 (1995): 7–53.

Schneidmüller, Bernd. "1125—Unruhe als politische Kraft im mittelalterlichen Reich." In Hechberger and Schuler, eds. *Staufer & Welfen*, pp. 30–49.

—. "Heinrich der Löwe: Innovationspotentiale eines mittelalterlichen Fürsten." In Hechberger and Schuler, eds. *Staufer & Welfen*, pp. 51–65.

—. "Konsensuale Herrschaft: Ein Essay über Formen und Konzepte politischer Ordnung im Mittelalter." In Heinig et al., eds. *Reich, Regionen und Europa*, pp. 53–87.

—. *Die Welfen: Herrschaft und Erinnerung*. Stuttgart: W. Kohlhammer, 2000.

—, Stefan Weinfurter, and Alfried Wieczorek, eds. *Verwandlungen des Stauferreichs: Drei Innovationsregionen im mittelalterlichen Europa*. Darmstadt: Wissenschaftliche Buchgesellschaft, 2010.

Schnith, Karl Rudolf and Roland Pauler, eds. *Festschrift für Eduard Hlawitschka zum 65. Geburtstag*. In Münchner historische Studien: Abteilung Mittelalterliche Geschichte. Kallmünz, Upper Palatinate: Verlag Michael Lassleben, 1993.

Scholz, Freimut. "Die Anfänge Münchens in neuer Sicht." *ZbLG* 70 (2007): 719–80.

—. "Eine separate Ausfertigung für Erzbischof Konrad III. von Salzburg? Das Regensburger Urteil Friedrichs I. vom 13. Juli 1180 in neuer Sicht." *MGSL* 153 (2013): 39–63.

Scholz, Sebastian. "Symbolik und Zeremoniell bei den Päpsten in der zweiten Hälfte des 12. Jahrhunderts." In Weinfurter, ed. *Stauferreich im Wandel,* pp. 131–48.

—. "Die Wiener Reichskrone: Eine Krone aus der Zeit Konrads III.?" In Seibert and Dendorfer, eds. *Grafen, Herzöge, Könige*, pp. 341–62.

Schönherr, Fritz Walter. *Die Lehre vom Reichsfürstenstande des Mittelalters*. Leipzig: Koehler, 1914.

Schreiner, Klaus. "Friedrich Barbarossa—Herr der Welt, Zeuge der Wahrheit, die Verkörperung nationaler Macht und Herrlichkeit." In *Die Zeit der Staufer* 5:521–79.

—. "'Gerechtigkeit und Frieden haben sich geküsst' (Ps. 84, 11): Friedensstiftung durch symbolisches Handeln." In *Träger und Instrumentarien des Friedens im hohen und späten Mittelalters*, ed. Johannes Fried, pp. 37–86. In VF 43. Sigmaringen: Jan Thorbecke Verlag, 1996.

—. "Die Staufer in Sage, Legende und Prophetie." In *Die Zeit der Staufer* 3:249–62.

Schreiner, Peter. "Byzanz und der Westen: Die gegenseitige Betrachtungsweise in der Literatur des 12. Jahrhunderts." In Haverkamp, ed. *Friedrich Barbarossa*, pp. 551–80.

Schultz, James. *The Knowledge of Childhood in the German Middle Ages, 1100–1350*. Philadelphia: University of Pennsylvania Press, 1995.

Schulz, Knut. "Die Zisterzienser in der Reichspolitik während der Stauferzeit." In Elm, ed. *Die Zisterzienser*, pp. 165–93.

Schuster, Beate. "Das Treffen von St. Jean-de-Losne im Wiederstreit der Meinungen: Zur Freiheit der Geschichtsschreibung im 12. Jahrhundert." *Zeitschrift für Geschichtswissenschaft* 43 (1995): 211–45.

Schwarz, Jörg. *Herrscher- und Reichstitel bei Kaisertum und Papsttum im 12. und 13. Jahrhundert*. In FKPM 22. Cologne, Weimar, and Vienna: Böhlau Verlag, 2003.

Schwarzmaier, Hansmartin. "Dominus totius domus comitisse Mathildis: Die Welfen und Italian im 12. Jahrhundert." In Schnith and Pauler, eds. *Festschrift für Eduard Hlawitschka*, pp. 283–305.

—. "Die monastische Welt der Staufer und Welfen im 12. Jahrhundert." In Lorenz and Schmidt, eds. *Von Schwaben bis Jerusalem*, pp. 241–59.

—. "*Pater imperatoris*: Herzog Friedrich II. von Schwaben, der gescheiterte König." In Petersohn, ed. *Mediaevalia Augiensia*, pp. 247–84.

Schwedler, Gerald. "Kaisertradition und Innovation: Die Bezugnahme Barbarossas auf andere Kaiser." In Burkhardt et al., eds. *Staufisches Kaisertum im 12. Jahrhundert*, pp. 231–51.

Schwenk, Bernd. "Das Hundetragen: Ein Rechstbrauch im Mittelalter." *Historisches Jahrbuch* 110 (1990): 289–308.

Schwind, Fred, "Friedrich Barbarossa und die Städte im Regnum Teutonicum." In Haverkamp, ed. *Friedrich Barbarossa*, pp. 469–99.

Seeber, Gustav. "Von Barbarossa zu Barbablanca: Zu den Wandlungen des Bildes von der mittelalterlichen Kaiserpolitik im Deutschen Reich." In Engel and Töpfer, eds. *Kaiser Friedrich Barbarossa*, pp. 205–20.

Seibert, Hubertus. "Die entstehende 'territoriale Ordnung' am Beispiel Bayerns (1115–1198)." In Weinfurter, ed. *Stauferreich im Wandel*, pp. 253–87.

—. "Die frühen 'Staufer': Forschungsstand und offene Fragen." In Seibert and Dendorfer, eds. *Grafen, Herzöge, Könige*, pp. 1–39.

— and Jürgen Dendorfer, eds. *Grafen, Herzöge, Könige: Der Aufsteig der frühen Staufer und das Reich (1079–1152)*. In MF 18. Ostfildern: Jan Thorbecke Verlag, 2005.

Shadis, Miriam, *Berenguela of Castile (1180–1246) and Political Women in the High Middle Ages*. New York: Palgrave Macmillan, 2009.

Simonsfeld, Henry. *Jahrbücher des Deutschen Reiches unter Friedrich I.*, 1908. Reprint, Berlin: Duncker & Humblot, 1967.

Skinner, Patricia, ed. *Challenging the Boundaries of Medieval History: The Legacy of Timothy Reuter* In Studies in the Early Middle Ages 22. Turnhout: Brepols, 2009.

Smith, Damian J. "Alexander III and Spain." In Clarke and Duggan, eds. *Pope Alexander III*, pp. 203–42.

Soria, Myriam. "Alexander III and France: Exile, Diplomacy, and the New Order." In Clarke and Duggan, eds. *Pope Alexander III*, pp. 181–201.

Sparber, Anselm. *Die Brixner Fürstbischöfe im Mittelalter: Ihr Leben und Wirken*. Bolzano (Bozen): Athesia, 1968.

Spiess, Karl-Heinz. "Der Hof Kaiser Barbarossas und die politische Landschaft am Mittelrhein." In Moraw, ed. *Deutscher Königshof*, pp. 49–76.

Spindler, Max. *Handbuch der bayerischen Geschichte* 2: *Das Alte Bayern*. Munich: C. H. Beck'sche Verlagsbuchhandlung, 1966.

Sprenger, Kai-Michael. "Die Heiligkeit von Kaiser und Reich aus italienischer Sicht." In Burkhardt et al., eds. *Staufisches Kaisertum im 12. Jahrhundert*, pp. 175–204.

Staats, Reinhart. *Die Reichskrone: Geschichte und Bedeutung eines europäischen Symbols*. Göttingen: Vandenhoeck & Ruprecht, 1991.

—. *Theologie der Reichskrone: Ottonische "Renovatio imperii" im Spiegel einer Insignie*. In MGM 13. Stuttgart: Anton Hiersemann, 1976.

Stehkämper, Hugo. "Friedrich Barbarossa und die Stadt Köln: Ein Wirtschaftskrieg am Niederrhein." In Vollrath and Weinfurter, eds. *Köln*, pp. 367–414.

Stelzer, Winfried. "Zum Scholarenprivileg Friedrich Barbarossas (Authentica 'Habita')." *DA* 34 (1978): 123–65.

Stöckel, Jan-Peter. "Reichsbischöfe und Reichsheerfahrt unter Friedrich I. Barbarossa." In Engel and Töpfer, eds. *Kaiser Friedrich Barbarossa*, pp. 63–79.

Stoob, Heinz. "Zur Königswahl Lothars von Sachsen im Jahre 1125." In *Historische Forschungen für Walter Schlesinger*, ed. Helmut Beumann, pp. 438–61. Cologne and Vienna: Böhlau Verlag, 1974.

Strait, Paul. *Cologne in the Twelfth Century*. Gainesville: University Presses of Florida, 1974.

Stroll, Mary. *Calixtus II (1119–1124): A Pope Born to Rule*. In Studies in the History of Christian Traditions 116. Leiden and Boston: Brill, 2004.

Thumser, Matthias. "Die frühe römische Kommune und die staufischen Herrscher in der Briefsammlung Wibalds von Stablo." *DA* 57 (2001): 111–48.

Töpfer, Bernhard. "Kaiser Friedrich I. Barbarossa und der deutsche Reichsepiskopat." In Haverkamp, ed. *Friedrich Barbarossa*, pp. 389–433.

Tounta, Eleni. "Byzanz als Vorbild Friedrich Barbarossas." In Burkhardt et al., eds. *Staufisches Kaisertum im 12. Jahrhundert*, pp. 159–74.

Tyroller, Franz. *Genealogie des altbayerischen Adels im Hochmittelalter*. In Genealogische Tafeln zur mitteleuropäischen Geschichte 4. Göttingen: Reise, 1962.

Uebach, Christian. *Die Ratgeber Friedrich Barbarossas (1152–1167)*. Marburg: Tectum Verlag, 2008.

Van Engen, John H. *Rupert of Deutz*. Berkeley: University of California Press, 1983.

Vasiliev, A. A. *History of the Byzantine Empire 324–1453*. 2nd English edn. 2 vols. Madison: University of Wisconsin Press, 1964.

Vollrath, Hanna. "Ideal and Reality in Twelfth-Century Germany." In Haverkamp, ed. *England and Germany in the High Middle Ages*, pp. 93–104.

—. "Lüge oder Fälschung? Die Überlieferung von Barbarossas Hoftag zu Würzburg im Jahre 1165 und der Becket-Streit." In Weinfurter, ed. *Stauferreich im Wandel*, pp. 149–71.

—. "Politische Ordnungsvorstellungen und politisches Handeln im Vergleich: Philipp II. Augustus von Frankreich und Friedrich Barbarossa im Konflikt mit ihren mächtigsten Fürsten." In Canning and Oexle, eds. *Political Thought and the Realities of Power*, pp. 3–51.

—. "Rebels and Rituals: From Demonstrations of Enmity to Criminal Justice." In Althoff et al., eds. *Medieval Concepts of the Past*, pp. 89–110.

— and Stefan Weinfurter, eds. *Köln: Stadt und Bistum in Kirche und Reich des Mittelalters: Festschrift für Odilo Engels zum 65. Geburtstag*. Cologne, Weimar, and Vienna: Böhlau Verlag, 1993.

Vones-Liebenstein, Ursula. "*Vir uxorius?*: Barbarossas Verhältnis zur *Comitissa Burgundiae* im Umkreis des Friedens von Venedig." In Weinfurter, ed. *Stauferreich im Wandel*, pp. 189–219.

Weber, Loren J. "The Historical Importance of Godfrey of Viterbo." *Viator* 25 (1994): 153–95.

Weiler, Björn. "The King as Judge: Henry II and Frederick Barbarossa as Seen by their Contemporaries." In Skinner, ed. *Challenging the Boundaries of Medieval History*, pp. 115–40.

—. "Suitability and Right: Imperial Succession and the Norms of Politics in Early Staufen Germany." In Lachaud and Penman, eds. *Making and Breaking the Rules*, pp. 71–86.

— and Simon MacLean, eds. *Representations of Power in Medieval Germany, 800–1500*. In International Medieval Research 16. Turnhout: Brepols, 2006.

Weinfurter, Stefan. "Erzbischof Philipp von Köln und der Sturz Heinrichs des Löwen." In Vollrath and Weinfurter, eds. *Köln*, pp. 451–88. Reprinted in Weinfurter, *Gelebte Ordnung*, pp. 335–59.

—. "Friedrich Barbarossa und Eichstätt: Zur Absetzung Bischof Burchards 1153." In Schneider and Rechter, eds. *Festschrift Alfred Wendehorst*, pp. 73–84.

—. *Gelebte Ordnung—Gedachte Ordnung: Augewählte Beiträge zu König, Kirche und Reich*, ed. Helmuth Kluger, Hubertus Seibert, and Werner Bomm. Ostfildern: Jan Thorbecke Verlag, 2005.

—. "Norbert von Xanten und die Entstehung des Prämonstratenserordens." *Schriften zur staufischen Geschichte und Kunst* 10 (1989): 57–100. Reprinted in idem, *Gelebte Ordnung*, pp. 65–92.

—. "Papsttum, Reich und kaiserliche Autorität im 11.–12. Jahrhundert: Von Rom 1111 bis Venedig 1177." In Hehl et al., eds. *Das Papsttum in der Welt des 12. Jahrhunderts*, pp. 77–99.

—. "Reformidee und Königtum im spätsalischen Reich: Überlegungen zu einer Neubewertung Kaiser Heinrichs V." *Quellen und Abhandlungen zur mittelrheinischen Kirchengeschichte* 68 (1992): 1–45. Reprinted in idem, *Gelebte Ordnung*, pp. 289–333.

—. *Salzburger Bistumsreform und Bischofspolitik im 12. Jahrhundert: Der Erzbischof Konrad I. von Salzburg (1106–1147) und die Regularkanoniker*. In Kölner historische Abhandlungen 24. Cologne and Vienna: Böhlau Verlag, 1975.

—. "Der Untergang des alten Lorsch in spätstaufischer Zeit. Das Kloster an der Bergstrasse im Spannungsfeld zwischen Papsttum, Erzstift Mainz und Pfalzgrafschaft." *Archiv für mittelrheinische Kirchengeschichte* 55 (2003): 31–58. Reprinted in idem, *Gelebte Ordnung*, pp. 159–85.

—. "Venedig 1177—Wende der Barbarossa-Zeit? Zur Einführung." In idem, *Stauferreich im Wandel*, pp. 9–25.

—. "Wer war der Verfasser der Vita Erzbishof Arnolds von Mainz (1153–1160)?" In Schnith and Pauler, eds. *Festschrift für Eduard Hlawitschka*, pp. 317–39.

—. "Wie das Reich heilig wurde." In idem, *Gelebte Ordnung*, pp. 361–83.

—, ed. *Stauferreich im Wandel: Ordnungsvorstellungen und Politik in der Zeit Friedrich Barbarossas*. In MF 9. Stuttgart: Jan Thorbecke Verlag, 2002.

Weitlauf, Manfred. "Das 'welfische Jahrhundert' in Bayern und sein kirchengeschichtlicher Hintergrund." In Hechberger and Schuler, eds. *Staufer & Welfen*, pp. 11–29.

Weller, Tobias. "Auf dem Weg zum 'staufischen Haus': Zu Abstammung, Verwandschaft und Konnubium der frühen Staufer." In Seibert and Dendorfer, eds. *Grafen, Herzöge, Könige*, pp. 41–63.

—. *Die Heiratspolitik des deutschen Hochadels im 12. Jahrhundert*. In Rheinisches Archiv 149. Cologne, Weimar, and Vienna: Böhlau Verlag, 2004.

Wendehorst, Alfred. "Who Could Read and Write in the Middle Ages?" In Haverkamp, ed. *England and Germany in the High Middle Ages*, pp. 57–88.

Werner, Karl Ferdinand. "Das hochmittelalterliche Imperium im politischen Bewusstsein Frankreichs (10.–12. Jahrhundert)." *HZ* 200 (1965): 1–60. Reprinted in idem, *Structures politiques du monde franc (VIe–XIIe siècles): Etudes sur les origines de la France et de l'Allemagne*. London: Variorum Reprints, 1979.

Wieczorek, Alfried, Bernd Schneidmüller, and Stefan Weinfurter, eds. *Die Staufer und Italien: Drei Innovationsregionen im mittelalterlichen Europa: Essays und Objeckte*. 2 vols. Darmstadt: Wissenschaftliche Buchgesellschaft, 2010.

Wolf, Armin. "Staufisch-sizilische Tochterstämme in Europa und die Herrschaft über Italien." In Lorenz and Schmidt, eds. *Von Schwaben bis Jerusalem*, pp. 117–49.

—. "Der 'Honor Imperii' als Spannungsfeld von lex und sacramentum im Hochmittelalter." In *Lex und Sacramentum im Mittelalter*, ed. Paul Wilpert, pp. 189–207. In Miscellanea Mediaevalia 6. Berlin and New York: Walter de Gruyter, 1969. Reprinted in Wolf, ed. *Friedrich Barbarossa*, pp. 297–322.

Wolf, Gunther, ed. *Friedrich Barbarossa*. In WF 390. Darmstadt: Wissenschaftliche Buchgesellschaft, 1975.

—. "Imperator und Caesar—zu den Anfängen des staufischen Erbreichsgedankens." In idem, ed. *Friedrich Barbarossa*, pp. 360–74.

Wolff, Robert Lee. "The 'Second Bulgarian Empire': Its Origins and History to 1204." *Speculum* 24 (1949): 167–206.

Wolfram, Herwig. *Konrad II., 990–1039: Kaiser dreier Reiche*. Munich: C. H. Beck'sche Verlagsbuchhandlung, 2000. Translated by Denise A. Kaiser as *Conrad II, 990–1039: Emperor of Three Kingdoms*. University Park, PA: The Pennyslvania State University Press, 2006.

Wolter, Heinz. "Friedrich Barbarossa und die Synode zu Pavia im Jahre 1160." In Vollrath and Weinfurter, eds. *Köln*, pp. 415–53.

—. "Die Verlobung Heinrichs VI. mit Konstanze von Sizilien im Jahre 1184." *Historisches Jahrbuch* 105 (1985): 30–51.

Wolverton, Lisa. *Hastening Toward Prague: Power and Society in the Medieval Czech Lands*. Philadelphia: University of Pennsylvania Press, 2001.

Wyrozumski, Jerzy. "Poland in the Eleventh and Twelfth Centuries." In Luscombe, ed. *The New Cambridge Medieval History* 4/2:277–89.

Die Zeit der Staufer: Geschichte—Kunst—Kultur: Katalog der Ausstellung, 5 vols. Stuttgart: Wirtembergisches Landesmuseum, 1977.

Ziegler, Wolfram. *König Konrad III. (1138–1152): Hof, Urkunden und Politik*. In FKPM 26. Vienna, Cologne, and Weimar: Böhlau Verlag, 2008.

Ziemann, Daniel. "Die Staufer—Ein elsässisches Adelsgeschlecht?" In Seibert and Dendorfer, eds. *Grafen, Herzöge, Könige*, pp. 99–133.

Zimmermann, Harald. "Die deutsch-ungarischen Beziehungen in der Mitte des 12. Jahrhunderts und die Berufung der Siebenbürger Sachsen." In Lorenz and Schmidt, eds. *Von Schwaben bis Jerusalem*, pp. 151–65.

Zotz, Thomas. "Dux de Zaringen—dux Zaringiae: Zum zeitgenössischen Verständnis eines neuen Herzogtums im 12. Jahrhundert." *ZGORh* 139 (NF 100) (1991): 1–44.

—. "Friedrich Barbarossa und Herzog Friedrich (IV.) von Schwaben: Staufisches Königtum und schwäbisches Herzogtum um die Mitte des 12. Jahrhunderts." In Petersohn, ed. *Mediaevalia Augiensia*, pp. 285–306.

—. "Zur Grundherrschaft des Königs im Deutschen Reich vom 10. bis zum frühen 13. Jahrhundert." In Werner Rösener, ed. *Grundherrschaft und bäuerliche Gesellschaft im Hochmittelalter*, pp. 76–115. In VMPIG 115. Göttingen: Vandenhoeck & Ruprecht, 1995.

INDEX

FB stands for Frederick Barbarossa.